# THE ROUGH GUIDE TO

# Greece

written and researched by

Nick Edwards, John Fisher, Jeffrey Kennedy,
Carol Palioudakis, John Malathronas and Greg Ward

ROUGH
GUIDES

roughguides.com

# Contents

## INTRODUCTION                                                                4

| | |
|---|---|
| Where to go | 5 |
| When to go | 8 |

| | |
|---|---|
| Things not to miss | 12 |

## BASICS                                                                      24

| | |
|---|---|
| Getting there | 25 |
| Getting around | 29 |
| Accommodation | 35 |
| Food and drink | 38 |
| Health | 42 |

| | |
|---|---|
| The media | 44 |
| Festivals | 44 |
| Sports and outdoor pursuits | 47 |
| Culture and etiquette | 48 |
| Travel essentials | 49 |

## THE GUIDE                                                                   56

| | | |
|---|---|---|
| 1 | Athens and around | 56 |
| 2 | The Peloponnese | 122 |
| 3 | The central mainland | 198 |
| 4 | The northern mainland | 262 |
| 5 | The Argo-Saronic Islands | 324 |
| 6 | The Cyclades | 352 |

| | | |
|---|---|---|
| 7 | Crete | 444 |
| 8 | The Dodecanese | 508 |
| 9 | The East and North Aegean | 594 |
| 10 | The Sporades and Évvia | 668 |
| 11 | The Ionian Islands | 702 |

## CONTEXTS                                                                    758

| | |
|---|---|
| History | 759 |
| Archeology | 785 |
| Wildlife | 790 |

| | |
|---|---|
| Music | 795 |
| Books | 801 |
| Greek | 807 |

## SMALL PRINT & INDEX                                                         818

# Introduction to
# **Greece**

While its economic reputation has taken a battering, Greece remains a premier-league travel destination. Its incredible historic sites span four millennia, encompassing both the legendary and the obscure. Its convoluted coastline is punctuated by superb beaches, while its mountainous interior urges you to dust off your hiking boots and explore. Yet perhaps its greatest riches are the islands, ranging from backwaters where the boat calls twice a week to resorts as cosmopolitan as any in the Mediterranean.

For anyone with a cultural bone in their body Greece cannot fail to inspire. Minoans, Romans, Arabs, Latin Crusaders, Venetians, Slavs, Albanians and Turks have all left their mark, and almost every town or village has a link to the **past**, whether it's a delicately crumbling temple to Aphrodite, a forbidding Venetian fort or a dusty Byzantine monastery decorated with exquisite frescoes. And let's not forget the museums stuffed to bursting with Classical sculpture and archeological treasures.

But the call to cultural duty will never be too overwhelming on a Greek holiday. The **hedonistic pleasures** of languor and warmth – swimming in balmy seas at dusk, talking and drinking under the stars – are just as appealing. Bar a few upmarket and "boutique" exceptions you may struggle to find five-star comfort – orthopaedic mattresses, faultless plumbing and cordon bleu cuisine are not the country's strongpoint – but this isn't really what the Greek experience is about. Greek **food**, for example, is at its best fresh, abundant and uncomplicated, while the genuine **welcome** you receive at the simplest taverna is often enough to get you booking next year's break as soon as you have returned home.

Whatever you come here for, it's clear that Greece needs its tourists like never before. For the last few years it's been synonymous with financial calamity with a titanic **debt crisis** (see p.784) seemingly ready to engulf Europe. However, this seems to have put off few people (visits to the islands were up 30 percent in 2011). Perhaps they know what we've known since the first edition of this guide was published thirty years ago – Greece can offer surprises and a true sense of discovery to even the most demanding traveller.

**ABOVE** THE PARTHENON, ATHENS **RIGHT** WILDFLOWERS, SITHONÍA >

# Where to go

Sprawling, globalized **Athens** is an obligatory, almost unavoidable introduction to Greece: home to over a third of the population, it is on first acquaintance a nightmare for many, but also – as Greeks themselves often joke – *tó megálo horió*: the largest "village" in the country. Aside from the show-stopping Acropolis it offers a truly metropolitan range of cultural diversions, from museums to concerts; well-stocked shops; gourmet restaurants and stimulating clubs, plus an excellent transport infrastructure. **Thessaloníki**, the metropolis of the north, has emerged in its own right as a lively, sophisticated place with restaurants and nightlife to match that of Athens, Byzantine monuments compensating for a lack of "ancient" ones, and – among the inhabitants – a tremendous capacity for enjoying life.

Apart from these cities the **mainland** shows its best side in the well-preserved **Classical ruins** of Corinth, Olympia and Delphi, the frescoed Byzantine churches and monasteries at Mount Áthos, Metéora, Ósios Loukás, Kastoriá, Árta and Mystra, the massive **fortified towns** of Monemvasiá, Náfplio, Koróni and Methóni, the distinctive architecture of Zagóri and the Máni, and the long, **sandy beaches** of the **Peloponnese** and the Pelion peninsula. Perhaps more surprisingly, the mainland mountains offer some of the best and least-exploited **hiking**, rafting, canyoning and **skiing** in Europe.

Out in the Aegean or Ionian seas, you're more spoilt for choice. Perhaps the best strategy for first-time visitors is to sample assorted islands from nearby archipelagos – Crete, the Dodecanese, the Cyclades and the northeast Aegean are all reasonably well connected with

each other, while the Sporades, Argo-Saronic and Ionian groups are best visited in single trips. If time and money are short, the best place to head for is well-preserved **Ýdhra** in the **Argo-Saronic Gulf**, just a short ride from Pireás (the main port of Athens), but an utterly different place once the day-cruises have gone. Similarly, **Skýros**, remotest and most unspoilt of the Sporades, is a good choice within modest reach of Athens or Thessaloníki. Among the **Cyclades**, cataclysmically volcanic Santoríni (Thíra) and Mýkonos with its perfectly preserved harbour-town rank as must-see spectacles, but fertile, mountainous Náxos, dramatic cliff-sided Amorgós or gently rolling Sífnos have life more independent of cruise-ship tourism and seem more amenable to long stays. **Crete** could (and does) fill an entire Rough Guide to itself, but the highlights here are Knossos and the nearby archeological museum in Iráklion, the other Minoan palaces at Phaestos and Ayía Triádha, and the west in general – the proud city of Haniá, with its hinterland extending to the relatively unspoilt southwest coast, reachable via the fabled Samarian gorge. **Rhodes**, with its unique old town, is capital of the **Dodecanese**, but picturesque, Neoclassical Sými opposite, and austere, volcanic Pátmos, the island of Revelation, are far more manageable. It's easy to continue north via Híos, with its striking medieval architecture, to balmy, olive-cloaked **Lésvos**, perhaps the most traditional island in its way of life. The **Ionian islands** are often dismissed as package-holiday territory, but their Venetian-style architecture, especially evident in Corfu, and neighbouring Paxí, make them well worth seeking out, especially on a journey between Greece and Italy.

# When to go

If anything is God-given to the Greeks, it is their **climate**. Most places are far more agreeable outside the mid-July to end of August peak season, when soaring temperatures, plus crowds of foreigners and locals alike, can be overpowering. You won't miss out on **warm weather** if you come in **June or September**, excellent times almost everywhere but particularly on the islands. An exception to this, however, is the north mainland coast – notably the Halkidhikí peninsula – and the islands of Samothráki and Thássos, which only really bloom during **July and August**. In mid-**October** you will

## DIVINE INSPIRATION

A high proportion of the ancient sites still seen in Greece today were built as shrines and temples to the **gods**, primarily the twelve who lived on Mount Olympus. **Zeus**, the lord of the heavens and supreme power; **Hera**, his wife and sister, goddess of fertility; **Athena**, the goddess of wisdom, patron of crafts and fearless warrior; **Apollo**, the god of music, of prophecy and the arts; his sister **Artemis**, the virgin huntress and goddess of childbirth; **Poseidon**, the god of the sea; beautiful **Aphrodite**, goddess of love and desire; **Hermes**, the messenger who leads the souls of the dead to the underworld; **Hephaestus**, the god of craftsmen; **Ares**, the god of war; **Demeter**, the goddess of crops and female fertility; and **Dionysus** (pictured left), god of wine and intoxication. Worshipped, feared and admired, they formed the basis for the ancient Greek religion until paganism was banned by the Romans in AD 391.

almost certainly hit a stormy spell, especially in western Greece or in the mountains, but for most of that month the "little summer of Áyios Dhimítrios" (the Greek equivalent of **Indian summer**) prevails, and the southerly Dodecanese and Crete are extremely pleasant. Autumn in general is beautiful; the light is softer, the sea often balmier than the air and the colours subtler.

**December to March** are the coldest and least reliably sunny months, though even then there are many crystal-clear, fine days. The more northerly latitudes and high altitudes endure far colder and wetter conditions, with the mountains themselves under snow from November to May. The **mildest winter** climate is found on Rhodes, or in the southeastern parts of Crete. As spring slowly warms up, **April** is still uncertain, though superb for wild flowers, green landscapes and photography; by **May** the weather is more settled and predictable, and Crete, the Peloponnese, the Ionian islands and the Cyclades are perhaps at their best, even if the sea is still a little cool for swimming.

Other factors that affect timing for Greek travels have to do with the level of tourism and the amenities provided. Service standards occasionally slip under peak season pressure and room prices on the islands can rocket. If you can only visit during midsummer, it is wise to reserve a package well in advance, buy any ferry tickets beforehand or plan your itinerary off the beaten track. You might choose, for instance, to explore the less obvious parts of the Peloponnese and the northern mainland, or island-hop with an eye for the remoter places.

**Out of season on the islands** you will have to contend with reduced ferry and plane services plus fairly skeletal facilities when you arrive. You will, however, find reasonable service on main routes and at least one hotel and taverna open in the port or main town of all but the tiniest isles. On the mainland, winter travel poses no special difficulties except, of course, in mountain villages either cut off by snow or (at weekends especially) monopolized by avid Greek skiers.

# Author picks

Our authors travelled the length and breadth of Greece, teasing out the best beaches, sampling the tastiest meze and exploring countless ancient ruins. Here are their highlights:

**Must-do museum**: Not only is the Acropolis Museum a celebration of the eternal architectural archetype of the Parthenon, but it's also a stunning edifice in itself (p.71).

**Killer views**: The photogenic whitewashed houses of the Cyclades islands make for a stunning backdrop, particularly at Santoríni and Mílos (p.434 & p.372).

**City break**: A stroll by the waterfront in Thessaloníki is a reminder that the city provides an arguably more satisfying urban experience than Athens (p.266).

**Moodiest ruins**: The temple of Apollo at Bassae, high up on a mountain and difficult to reach, has the most astonishing views of any Ancient Greek site (p.176).

**Finest treks**: The mountain village of Litóhoro, gateway to Mount Olympus, is the start of numerous hiking trails (p.282).

**Alien landscape**: It's easy to visit the seemingly extraterrestrial Stéfanos crater floor on top of Níssyros's dormant volcano and imagine yourself exploring a different planet (p.554).

**Fresh seafood**: There is nothing more quintessentially Greek than the smell of the grilled catch of the day emanating from a seaside taverna (p.40).

**Spectacular drive**: The austere beauty of the mountainous Máni can only be fully appreciated via the rugged, winding road around the peninsula (p.155).

Our author recommendations don't end here. We've flagged up our favourite places – a perfectly sited hotel, an atmospheric café, a special restaurant – throughout the guide, highlighted with the ★ symbol.

**FROM TOP** MANÍ COAST, FRESH FISH, SANTORÍNI VIEW >

# 25

# things not to miss

It's not possible to see everything that Greece has to offer in one trip – and we don't suggest you try. What follows, in no particular order, is a selective taste of the region's highlights, including beautiful beaches, outstanding treks and fascinating ancient sites. All highlights have a page reference to take you straight into the Guide, where you can find out more.

1

### 1 SUNSET ON SANTORÍNI
Page 434
If there are 1000 things to do before you die, having a sundowner overlooking Santoríni's crater would near the top of the list.

### 2 SHIPWRECK BAY, ZÁKYNTHOS
Page 757
Lie back and enjoy the unforgettable scenery of one of Greece's poster beaches.

### 3 METÉORA MONASTERIES
Page 238
Rising like ecclesiastical eagles' nests, these monasteries are among the most awe-inspiring religious sites on earth.

**4**

### 4 ÝDHRA
Page 341
The bare granite cliffs of Ýdhra (aka Hydra) soon part to reveal the fabulous horseshoe of its harbour, perhaps the most scenic in Greece.

### 5 WINE TASTING
Pages 40 & 462
There's much more to Greek wine than dodgy retsina and you should visit at least one vineyard while you're here.

### 6 CLIMBING MOUNT OLYMPUS
Page 283
A trek to the home of the Greek gods is supremely atmospheric and a worthwhile challenge for hikers.

### 7 THE PELION
Page 221
Billed as the Greek Tuscany, this region has it all: lush countryside, excellent beaches, character-packed villages and superb treks.

### 8 MÝKONOS NIGHTLIFE
Page 392
Experience the most frenetic nightlife east of Ibiza at the party capital of the Greek summer.

**5**

**6**

### 9 MYSTRA
Page 167

A ghost town that provides a time capsule for the modern tourist to step through to the Byzantine age.

### 10 SAMARIÁ GORGE, CRETE
Page 499

The 16km descent of this lush and leafy gorge enclosed by towering rock faces is an unforgettable hike.

### 11 MEZÉDHES
Page 41

For a true taste of Greece, tuck into a mezédhes (meze) platter of starters and dips accompanied by a glass of ouzo.

### 12 THE PRÉSPA LAKES
Page 290

Once a contentious border area, these lakes have been left alone for decades resulting in an almost pristine haven for birdlife.

### 13 LION GATE AT MYCENAE
Page 134

The imposing relief of lions guarding the main entrance to the Citadel of Mycenae is, incredibly, thirty-odd centuries old.

### 14 THE ACROPOLIS, ATHENS
Page 65

This small rock with its spectacular ruins is a cultural icon and a symbol of the birth of Western civilization.

**KEFALONIÁ**
Page 736

Famous as the setting for *Captain Corelli's Mandolin*, Kefaloniá remains a a firm favourite despite the crowds.

 **DELPHI**
Page 204

Located in an unbeatable natural setting, this ancient site has retained its inscrutable mystique through the centuries.

 **EASTER**
Page 44

The biggest festival in Greece, Easter combines devout Orthodox belief with joyful spring celebrations.

 **WINDSURFING**
Page 47

There are very few places on the islands where you can't turn a windy day to your advantage, especially off Lefkádha in the Ionians or Náxos, Páros and Ándhros in the Cyclades.

 **RHODES**
Page 512

Once home to the ancient Colossus and the medieval Knights of St John, this is one of the most captivating islands in Greece.

**17**

**18**

**19**

ports and perfect beaches all wait to be explored, best experienced with a rental car.

**❶ Haniá** Vying for the title of the most attractive town in Greece, this is the perfect place to relax and people-watch. **See p.492**

**❷ Samariá Gorge** The most popular hike on the Greek islands and as perfect a one-day excursion as you can hope for. **See p.499**

**❸ Réthymnon** A fascinating place with the ideal town beach offering views of a skyline of Ottoman minarets and Venetian mansions. **See p.482**

**❹ Iráklion** Crete's capital is the best base for exploring the outstanding ruins at Knossos and for hiking on the Lasíthi plateau. **See p.449**

**❺ Ierápetra** Great resort town with a spotless beach, excellent choice of excursions and a very long summer season. **See p.480**

**❻ Váï beach** You'd be forgiven for thinking you'd left the Mediterranean for the tropics at this fine-sand beach lined with exotic palm trees. **See p.478**

# THE ROAD LESS TRAVELLED

Central and northern Greece barely feature on travel agent radars but you'll find perhaps the most "Greek" places here. As well as these quirkier sights be sure not to miss Mount Olympus (see p.281) and the monasteries of Metéora (see p.235).

**❶ The Pelion** Wind your way down the hairpin roads of this spectacular peninsula, discovering lovely villages, quiet beaches and enjoying a beautifully cool climate. **See p.221**

**❷ Píndhos Mountains** The Píndhos mountain range offers rafting, skiing and one of the country's best treks along the 20km Víkos Gorge. **See p.242**

**❸ Vergina** Capital of the Macedonian dynasty, Vergina was the burial place of Alexander's father and a lot of gold, the latter on show in nearby Thessaloníki. **See p.287**

**❹ Mount Áthos** One strictly for the boys, but this male-only monastic community offers a unique glimpse of the Orthodox world. **See p.304**

SPINÁLONGA, CRETE

# Basics

**25** Getting there

**29** Getting around

**35** Accommodation

**38** Food and drink

**42** Health

**44** The media

**44** Festivals

**47** Sports and outdoor pursuits

**48** Culture and etiquette

**49** Travel essentials

# Getting there

**By far the easiest way to get to Greece is to fly, and there are direct flights to a variety of Greek destinations from all major UK airports. Even if your starting point is North America, Australia, New Zealand or South Africa, the most cost-effective way to Greece may well be to get to London – or Amsterdam, Frankfurt or another Northern European hub – and pick up an onward flight from there.**

**Airfares** are highest in July, August and during Easter week. But May, June and September are also popular, and since far fewer flights operate through the winter, bargains are rare at any time.

**Overland** alternatives from the UK or Northern Europe involve at least three days of nonstop travel. If you want to take your time over the journey, then **driving** or travelling **by train** can be enjoyable, although invariably more expensive than flying. We've included only brief details of these routes here.

When **buying flights** it always pays to shop around and bear in mind that many websites don't include charter or budget airlines in their results. Be aware too that a **package deal**, with accommodation included, can sometimes be as cheap as, or even cheaper than, a flight alone: there's no rule that says you have to use your accommodation every night, or even at all.

## Flights from the UK and Ireland

Unless you book far in advance, there are few bargain **fares** to Greece. easyJet (Ⓦeasyjet.com)

## A BETTER KIND OF TRAVEL

At Rough Guides we are passionately committed to travel. We feel that travelling is the best way to understand the world we live in and the people we share it with – plus tourism has brought a great deal of benefit to developing economies around the world over the last few decades. But the growth in tourism has also damaged some places irreparably, and climate change is exacerbated by most forms of transport, especially flying. All Rough Guides' trips are carbon-offset, and every year we donate money to a variety of charities devoted to combating the effects of climate change.

can fly you direct from Gatwick, Manchester or Edinburgh to Athens for less than £50 each way, but you'll have to move very fast to find fares this cheap. Realistically their prices are little different from those of the **scheduled** operators – British Airways (Ⓦba.com) and Aegean (Ⓦaegeanair .com) have frequent flights to Athens from Heathrow, Viking Hellas (Ⓦflyviking.gr) from Manchester – and you can expect to pay £75–150 each way at most times of the year. From **Dublin**, Aer Lingus (Ⓦaerlingus.com) have three direct flights a week from April to September, with fares starting at around €100 each way, though you can easily pay twice that. Almost all airlines, including charter operators, allow you to book one-way tickets at no extra cost, so you can fly into Athens with one, leave from an island with another.

### Regional flights

If your destination is not Athens, or you are flying from a regional airport, there's a bewildering variety of options, many of them involving **charter airlines**. In practice these operate in much the same way as budget operators, albeit with clunkier booking systems and often less convenient flight times; most of them fly only in the summer months, from May to September. Regular scheduled flights include British Airways from Gatwick to Thessaloníki; easyJet from Gatwick to Thessaloníki, Corfu, Haniá (Chania, Crete), Iráklion (Heraklion, Crete), Kos, Mýkonos, Ródhos (Rhodes), Thíra (Santoríni) and Zákynthos, **from Liverpool to** Ródhos, and from Manchester and Bristol to Iráklion and Corfu; Jet2 (Ⓦjet2.com) **from Manchester to** Iráklion, Kos and Ródhos, and from East Midlands, Leeds and Newcastle to Iráklion and Ródhos; and Ryanair (Ⓦryanair.com) from Stansted to Thessaloníki, Corfu and Ródhos and Liverpool to Ródhos. In addition, charter operators go from a variety of UK regional airports to all of the above, plus **Kalamáta**, **Kavála** (for Thássos), **Vólos** (for Mount Pílio and the Sporades) and **Préveza (for Lefkádha)** on the Greek mainland, and to the islands of **Kefaloniá**, **Skiáthos**, **Sámos**, **Lésvos** and **Límnos**. See the map on p.30 for Greek regional airports. The main operators with whom you can book direct are Monarch (Ⓦmonarch.co.uk), Thomas Cook (Ⓦflythomascook.com), Thomson (Ⓦthomson.co.uk) and Torair (Ⓦflytorair.com); others may be available indirectly, through travel agencies or third-party websites.

Prices for regional flights are generally slightly higher than London to Athens; it may cost less to travel via Athens with a connecting flight.

### Indirect flights

Still more Greek airports are accessible on **connecting domestic flights** from Athens or Thessaloníki with Aegean, Olympic (W olympicair .com) or Sky Express (W skyexpress.gr). If you're travelling out of season you may have no choice but to go indirect, and it's possible that this may be the cheapest option at any time. Most commonly, from regional airports in the UK or from Ireland, this will mean flying via London (with British Airways, or BMI/Aegean). It can pay to think laterally however: one of the best routings from Dublin, for example, is on Malev Hungarian airlines (W www.malev.com) via Budapest – with good prices and convenient connections to Athens and other Greek airports.

## Flights from the US and Canada

Direct **nonstop** flights from New York to Athens – daily for much of the year – are operated by Delta (W delta.com), Hellenic Imperial (W hellenicairways .com), both from JFK, and Continental (W continental.com) from Newark. Between May and October, US Airways (W usair.com) also flies daily from Philadelphia to Athens. Code-sharing airlines can quote through fares with one of the above, or a European partner, from virtually every major US city, connecting either at New York or a European hub such as London or Frankfurt.

**Fares** vary greatly, so it's worth putting in a little time on the internet, or using a good travel agent; book as far ahead as possible to get the best price. The lowest starting point is around US$900 for a restricted, off-season round-trip flight from the east coast, rising to about $1400 for a similar deal in summer; from the west coast, expect to pay ten to twenty percent more. The lower fares are rarely on the most direct flights, so check the routing to avoid lengthy delays or stopovers. Remember too that you may be better off getting a domestic flight to New York or Philadelphia and heading directly to Athens from there, or buying a cheap flight to London (beware of changing airports) or another European city, and onward travel from there.

As with the US, airfares **from Canada** vary depending on where you start your journey, and whether you take a direct service. Air Canada (W aircanada.com) flies to Athens out of Toronto, with a stop in Montreal, from one to four times weekly depending on the time of year. Air Transat (W airtransat.com) also have seasonal weekly flights from Toronto and Montreal to Athens. Otherwise you'll have to choose among one- or two-stop itineraries on a variety of European carriers, or perhaps Delta via New York; costs run from Can$900 round-trip in low season from Toronto to more than double that from Vancouver in high season.

## Flights from Australia and New Zealand

There are **no direct flights** from Australia or New Zealand to Greece; you'll have to change planes in Southeast Asia or Europe. Tickets purchased direct from the airlines tend to be expensive; travel agents or Australia-based websites generally offer much better deals on fares and have the latest information on limited specials and stopovers. For a simple return fare, you may also have to buy an add-on internal flight to get you to the international departure point.

Fares **from Australia** start from around Aus$1800, rising to around Aus$2600 depending on season, routing, validity, number of stopovers, etc. The shortest flights and best fares are generally with airlines like Thai (W thaiair.com), Singapore (W singaporeair.com), Etihad (W etihadairways.com) and Emirates (W emirates.com) that can fly you directly to Athens from their Asian or Gulf hubs, though you'll also find offers on Swiss (W swiss .com), KLM (W klm.com) and other European carriers. **From New Zealand**, prices are significantly higher: rarely less than NZ$2200, rising to over NZ$3000 for a more flexible high-season flight.

If Greece is only one stop on a longer journey, you might consider buying a **Round-the-World** (RTW) fare, although Greece never seems to be included in any of the cheaper deals, which means you might have to stump up around Aus$3500/NZ$4000 for one of the fully flexible multi-stop fares from One World or the Star Alliance. At that price, you may be better off with a cheaper deal and a separate ticket to Greece once you get to Europe.

## Flights from South Africa

There are currently no direct flights from **South Africa** to Athens, though Hellenic Imperial plan to restart one. Alternative routes include EgyptAir (W egyptair.com) via Cairo, Emirates (W emirates .com), Etihad (W etihadairways.com) or Qatar Airways (W qatarairways.com) via the Gulf, or just about any of the major European airlines through their domestic hub. Prices start at R6500–7000 for a good low-season deal, to double that in high season or if the cheaper seats have gone.

## FLIGHT AGENTS

**Charter Flight Centre** UK ☏ 0208/714 0010, ⓦ charterflights
.co.uk. Booking for a huge range of charter flights from the UK and
Ireland.

**Flight Centre** ⓦ flightcentre.com. Low-cost air fares worldwide
from their local websites, plus rail passes and more.

**North South Travel** UK ☏ 01245/608291, ⓦ northsouthtravel
.co.uk. Friendly, competitive flight agency, offering discounted fares
worldwide. Profits are used to support projects in the developing world,
especially the promotion of sustainable tourism.

**Skyscanner** ⓦ skyscanner.net. Comprehensive flight search site that
includes charter and budget airlines.

**STA Travel** UK ☏ 0871/2300 040, US ☏ 1-800/781-4040,
Australia ☏ 134 782, New Zealand ☏ 0800/474 400,
South Africa ☏ 0861/781 781, ⓦ statravel.com. Worldwide
specialists in independent travel; also student IDs, travel insurance,
car rental, rail passes, and more. Good discounts for students and
under-26s.

**Trailfinders** UK ☏ 0845/054 6060, Ireland ☏ 021/464 8800,
Australia ☏ 1300/780 212, ⓦ trailfinders.com. One of the
best-informed and most efficient agents for independent travellers.

**Travel CUTS** Canada ☏ 1-800/667-2887, US ☏ 1-800/592-2887,
ⓦ travelcuts.com. Popular, long-established student-travel
organization, with good worldwide offers; not only for students.

## Trains

As a result of the economic crisis, all international
and some domestic **Greek rail routes** have been
**suspended**. However, that doesn't necessarily
mean that you can't travel to Greece by train; the
most practical route **from Britain** was always in
any event to cross France and Italy before
embarking on the ferry from Bari or Brindisi to
Pátra (Patras) – with connecting buses to Athens
– and that remains unaffected. The journey takes
two-and-a-half days at least and will almost
always work out more expensive than flying. It
also takes a fair bit of planning, since there's no
through train and tickets have to be bought from
several separate operators. However, you do have
the chance to stop over on the way, while with
an **InterRail** (for European residents only; ⓦ inter
railnet.com) or **Eurail** (for all others; ⓦ eurail.com)
pass you can take in Greece as part of a wider rail
trip around Europe. Booking well in advance
(essential in summer) and going for the cheapest
seats on each leg, you can theoretically buy
individual tickets for less than £150 each way, not
including the incidental expenses along the way.
Using rail passes will cost you more, but give far
more flexibility. For full details, check out the Man
in Seat 61 website (ⓦ seat61.com).

## Car and ferry

**Driving to Greece** can be a pleasant proposition if
you have plenty of time to dawdle along the way.
It's only worth considering if you do want to
explore en route, though, or are going to stay for an
extended period. The most popular **route** is again
down through France and Italy to catch one of the
Adriatic ferries (see box below); this is much the
best way to get to western and southern Greece,
the Ionian islands, and to Athens and most of the
islands except those in the northeast Aegean. The
far longer alternative through Eastern Europe
(Hungary, Romania and Bulgaria) is fraught with
visa problems, and only makes sense if you want to
explore northern Greece on the way.

## ITALY–GREECE FERRIES

Sailing from **Italy to Greece**, you've a choice of four ports; ferries run year-round, but services
are reduced December to April. The shortest routes and most frequent ferries link Bari and
Brindisi with Corfu, Igoumenítsa (the port of the western Greek mainland) and Pátra (at the
northwest tip of the Peloponnese). Ferries also sail from Ancona and Venice to Pátra via
Igoumenítsa/Corfu. These longer routes are more expensive, but the extra cost closely
matches what you'll pay in Italian motorway tolls and fuel to get further south. On most ferries
you can stop over in Corfu for no extra charge. For direct access to Athens and the Aegean
islands head for Pátra, from where you can cut across country to Pireás.

   The following companies operate ferries: schedule and booking details for all of them are
also available at ⓦ openseas.gr and ⓦ viamare.com.

**Agoudimos** ⓦ agoudimos-lines.com. Bari and Brindisi to Corfu
and Igoumenítsa.

**ANEK** ⓦ anek.gr. Ancona and Venice to Corfu, Igoumenítsa and
Pátra.

**Endeavor Lines** ⓦ endeavor-lines.com. Brindisi to Corfu,
Igoumenítsa and Pátra.

**Minoan Lines** ⓦ minoan.gr. Ancona and Venice to Corfu,
Igoumenítsa and Pátra.

**Superfast Ferries** ⓦ superfast.com. Ancona and Bari to Corfu,
Igoumenítsa and Pátra.

**Ventouris Ferries** ⓦ ventouris.gr. Bari and Brindisi to Corfu,
Igoumenítsa, Kefaloniá and Zákynthos.

# Tour operators

Every mainstream **tour operator** includes Greece in its portfolio. You'll find far more interesting alternatives, however, through the small **specialist agencies**. As well as traditional village-based accommodation and less-known islands, many also offer **walking** or **nature holidays** and other special interests such as **yoga**, **art** and above all **sailing**, with options ranging from shore-based clubs with dinghy tuition, through organized yacht flotillas to bareboat or skippered charters.

## PACKAGE OPERATORS

**Grecian Tours** Australia ☎ 03/9663 3711, ⓦ greciantours.com .au. A variety of accommodation and sightseeing tours, plus flights.

**Greek Sun Holidays** UK ☎ 01732/740317, ⓦ www.greeksun .co.uk. Good-value package holidays mainly in smaller islands of the Dodecanese, northeast Aegean and Cyclades; also tailor-made island-hopping itineraries.

**Hidden Greece** UK ☎ 020/8758 4707, ⓦ hidden-greece.co.uk. Specialist agent putting together tailor-made packages to smaller destinations at reasonable prices.

**Homeric Tours** US ☎ 1-800/223-5570, ⓦ homerictours.com. Hotel packages, individual tours, escorted group tours and fly/drive deals. Good source of inexpensive flights.

**Inntravel** UK ☎ 01653/617001, ⓦ inntravel.co.uk. High-quality packages and tailor-made itineraries and fly-drives to unspoilt areas of the mainland, Crete and smaller islands; also walking and other special-interest holidays.

**Olympic Holidays** UK ☎ 0800/093 3322, ⓦ olympicholidays .com. Huge package holiday company specializing in Greece; all standards from cheap and cheerful to five-star, and often a good source of last-minute bargains and cheap flights.

**Simply Travel** UK ☎ 0871/231 4050, ⓦ simplytravel.co.uk. Although part of the vast TUI organization, Simply still manages a personal touch, and has plenty of excellent, upmarket accommodation in Crete and the Ionian islands as well as the mainland.

**Sun Island Tours** Australia ☎ 1300/665 673, ⓦ sunislandtours.com.au. Greece specialist offering an assortment of island-hopping, fly-drives, cruises and guided land-tour options, as well as tailor-made.

**Sunvil Holidays** UK ☎ 020/8758 4758, ⓦ sunvil.co.uk/greece. High-quality outfit with a wide range of holidays to all parts of the mainland and islands.

## VILLA AND APARTMENT AGENTS

**Cachet Travel** UK ☎ 020/8847 8700, ⓦ cachet-travel.co.uk. Attractive range of villas and apartments in the more unspoilt south and west of Crete, plus Híos and remote corners of Sámos.

**CV Travel** UK ☎ 0870/606 0013, ⓦ cvtravel.co.uk, US ☎ 1-866/308-1343, ⓦ cvtravelusa.com. Quality villas and luxury resorts, principally in the Ionian islands and Crete.

**Greek Islands Club** UK ☎ 020/8232 9780, ⓦ gicthevillacollection.com. Specialist in upmarket villas with private pools, especially in the Ionian islands.

**Houses of Pelion** UK ☎ 0870/199 9191, ⓦ pelion.co.uk. Local specialist offering an excellent collection of inland cottages, houses and apartments on the Pílio (Pelion) peninsula.

**Pure Crete** UK ☎ 01444/881 402, ⓦ purecrete.com. Lovely, converted cottages and farmhouses in western Crete, plus walking, wildlife and other special-interest trips.

**Simpson Travel** UK ☎ 0845/811 6502, ⓦ simpsontravel.com. Classy villas, upmarket hotels and village hideaways in selected areas of the mainland and on Crete, the Ionians, Skópelos, Sámos and more.

**Travel à la Carte** UK ☎ 01635/33800, ⓦ travelalacarte.co.uk. Villas and apartments on Corfu, Skiáthos, Paxí, Sými and more, plus painting, photography, yoga and creative writing courses on Paxí.

## SMALL GROUP TOURS AND YOGA HOLIDAYS

**Astra** US ☎ 303/321-5403, ⓦ astragreece.com. Very personal, idiosyncratic tours, some women-only, led by veteran Hellenophile Thordis Simonsen, during spring and autumn.

**Hellenic Adventures** US ☎ 1-800/851-6349 or 612/827-0937, ⓦ hellenicadventures.com. Small-group escorted tours led by enthusiastic expert guides, as well as itineraries for independent travellers, cruises and other travel services.

**True Greece** US ☎ 1- 800/817-7098, ⓦ truegreece.com. Upmarket escorted travel and custom-made trips including special interests such as cooking.

**Free Spirit Travel** UK ☎ 01273/564230, ⓦ freespirituk.com. Yoga and meditation in western Crete, plus some walking holidays.

**Yoga Plus** UK ☎ 01273/276175, ⓦ yogaplus.co.uk. Ashtanga yoga courses in a remote part of southern Crete.

**Skyros Holidays** UK ☎ 01983/865566, ⓦ skyros.com. Holistic yoga, dance, art, music, "personal growth" and more on the island of Skýros, as well as well-regarded writers' workshops.

## WALKING AND CYCLING

**ATG Oxford** UK ☎ 01865/315678, ⓦ atg-oxford.co.uk. Somewhat pricey but high-standard guided walks on Crete, select Cyclades islands and the Máni.

**Classic Adventures** US ☎ 1-800/777-8090, ⓦ classicadventures .com. Spring or autumn rural cycling tours crossing the north Peloponnese to Zákynthos, in the Pindus mountains, and on Crete.

**Exodus** UK ☎ 0845/287 7511, ⓦ exodus.co.uk. Week-long treks exploring southern Évvia.

**Explore Worldwide** US ☎ 1-800/715-1746, Can ☎ 1-888 /216-3401, UK ☎ 01252/760 000, ⓦ exploreworldwide.com. A variety of tours, many combining hiking with sailing between the islands.

**Freewheeling Adventures** Canada & US ☎ 1-800/672-0775, ⓦ freewheeling.ca. Eight-day cycling tours of Crete.

**Jonathan's Tours** ☎ 0033/561046447, ⓦ jonathanstours.com. Family-run walking holidays on Crete, smaller islands and the Pindus mountains.

**Ramblers Holidays** UK ☎ 01707/331133, ⊛ ramblersholidays
.co.uk. Walking trips including spring hiking in Crete, Dodecanese
island-hopping and combined island and mainland treks.
**Sherpa Expeditions** UK ☎ 020/8577 2717, ⊛ www
.sherpa-walking-holidays.co.uk. Self-guided and escorted 8-day
outings on Crete or Zagóri; more challenging escorted tours of the peaks
around Mt Olympus.
**Walking Plus** UK ☎ 020/8835 8303, ⊛ walkingplus.co.uk.
Enthusiastic Gilly and Robin Cameron Cooper offer guided and
self-guided off-season walks in the Cyclades and around Athens.

### WILDLIFE HOLIDAYS

**Naturetrek** UK ☎ 01962/733051, ⊛ naturetrek.co.uk. Fairly pricey
but expertly led one- or two-week natural history tours; offerings include
butterflies of the southern mainland, springtime birds and flora on
Sámos, and wildlife of Crete.
**The Travelling Naturalist** UK ☎ 01305/267994, ⊛ www
.naturalist.co.uk. Wildlife holiday company that runs excellent
birdwatching and wild-flower-spotting trips to Crete, Lesvós and the
mainland.

### SAILING AND WATERSPORTS

**Northwest Passage** US ☎ 1-800/RECREATE, ⊛ nwpassage.com.
Excellent sea-kayaking tours in Crete and the islands, including
island-hopping by kayak; also yoga, hiking and art in Crete.
**Nautilus Yachting** UK ☎ 01732/867445, ⊛ nautilus-yachting
.co.uk. Bareboat yacht charter, flotillas and sailing courses from a wide
variety of marinas.
**Neilson** UK ☎ 0844/879 8155, ⊛ neilson.co.uk. Half a dozen
excellent beach activity clubs, plus flotillas and bareboat charter.
**Seafarer Cruising & Sailing** UK ☎ 020/8324 3118,
⊛ seafarercruises.com. Ionian and Argo-Saronic flotillas, beach club,
bareboat charter, courses and small-boat island cruises.
**Sportif** UK ☎ 01273/844919, ⊛ sportif.travel. Windsurfing
packages and instruction on Crete, Kos, Rhodes, Sámos, Lésvos and
Kárpathos.
**Sunsail** UK ☎ 0870/112 8612, ⊛ sunsail.com. Mainland beach
club, plus flotillas and bareboat mainly in the Ionians and Sporades.
**Swim Trek** US ☎ 1-877/455-SWIM, UK ☎ 01273/739 713,
⊛ swimtrek.com. Week-long tours of Náxos and the small islands
around it, swimming between the islands.
**Valef Yachts** US ☎ 1-800/223-3845, ⊛ valefyachts.com.
Small-boat cruises around the islands and luxury crewed yacht or
motor-boat charter.

# Getting around

**The standard overland public transport
in Greece is the bus. Train networks are
limited, even more so with recent
cutbacks. Buses cover most primary
routes on the mainland and provide basic
connections on the islands. The best way**

to supplement buses is to rent a scooter,
motorbike or car, especially on the
islands where – in any substantial town
or resort – you will find at least one rental
outlet. Inter-island travel means taking
ferries, catamarans or hydrofoils, which
will eventually get you to any of the sixty-
plus inhabited isles. Internal flights are
relatively expensive, but can save literally
days of travel: Athens–Rhodes is just two
hours return, versus 28 hours by boat.

## By bus

Bus services on **major routes** are efficient and
frequent, departing promptly at scheduled departure
times. On **secondary roads** they're less regular, with
long gaps, but even the remotest villages will be
connected a couple of days weekly to the provincial
capital. On islands there are usually buses to connect
the port and main town (if different) for ferry arrivals
or departures. The national network is run by a
syndicate of private operators based in each county,
known as the **KTEL** (*Kratikó Tamío Ellinikón Leoforíon*;
☎ 14505 premium call charge and no national online
timetable). In medium-sized or large towns there may
be several scattered terminals for services in different
directions, so make sure you have the right station for
your departure.

From major departure points **ticketing** is computerized, with assigned seating, and on intercity lines
such as Athens–Pátra such buses often get fully
booked at the *ekdhotíria* (ticket-issuing office). On
secondary rural/island routes, it's first-come, first-
served, with some standing allowed, and tickets
dispensed on the spot by a conductor (*ispráktoras*).
Prices are fixed according to distance and there are
no cheap advance booking fares; Athens–Pátra
costs €27.

## By train

The Greek mainland's railway network is run by **OSE**
(*Organismós Sidherodhrómon Elládhos*; ☎ 1110,
⊛ ose.gr); with a few exceptions, trains are slower
than equivalent buses. However, they can be much
cheaper – fifty percent less on non-express services
(but much the same on express), even more if you
buy a return ticket – and some lines are intrinsically
enjoyable, none more than the rack-and-pinion
service between Dhiakoftó and Kalávryta in the
Peloponnese (see p.196).

**Timetables** are available annually as small, Greek-
only booklets, but with continual austerity measure

▲ Ancona   ▲ Venice

◀ Bari

✈ International airport
✗ Domestic airport

*ADRIATIC SEA*

Tirana

**REPUBLIC OF MACEDONIA**

**ALBANIA**

Brindisi

**ITALY**
Gallipoli   Otranto

Kastoriá   Kozáni   Véria

Thessaloníki ✈

▲ Mt Olympus

Corfu Town ✗   Ioánnina ✈

Igoumenítsa

*Corfu* ✗

Lárisa

Vólos ✗

*Paxí*

Lefkádha ✈

*Lefkádha*

*Ionian Islands*

Astakós

*Ithdki*

Lamía

Áyios Konstandínos

*Kefaloniá*

Sámi

Argostóli ✗

*IONIAN SEA*

Pátra

*Gulf of Kórinthos*

Korinth

Zákynthos ✗

Kyllíni

*Zákynthos (Zante)*

Kyparissía

*Spétses*

✈ Kalamáta

Methóni

Yíthio

Neápoli

Kýthira ✗

*Andikýthira*

M E D I T E R R A N E A N   S E A

N

**GREECE FERRIES AND AIRPORTS**

Daily
At least weekly

BULGARIA

TURKEY

SEA OF MARMARA

İstanbul

Kavála
Liménas
Thássos
Alexandhroúpoli

Samothráki

*The North Aegean*

Bursa

▲ Mt Áthos

Límnos

Mýrina

Balıkesir

*AEGEAN SEA*

Áyios Efstrátios

*The Sporades*

Mólyvos
Ayvalık

TURKEY

Skiáthos
Alónissos
Skópelos

Mytilíni

Skýros

*Lésvos*

Inoússes

Kými
Halkídha

Psará

Híos
Çeşme

İzmir

Manisa

Évvia

Híos

*The East Aegean*

ATHENS
Rafina

Sámos
Vathý

Kuşadası

Peiraiás

Ándhros

Lávrio
Kéa

Égina
Póros

*The Argo-Saronic*

Ýdhra

Kýthnos
Sýros
Delos
Mýkonos

Tínos

Ikaría

Foúrni

Pátmos
Lipsí

Léros

Bodrum

Sérifos
Páros
Náxos

Dhonoússa

Kálymnos
Kos

Marmaris

Sífnos

Andíparos

*The Cyclades*

Kos
Nίssyros

Sίkinos
Íos
Folégandhros

Amorgós
Astypálea

Sými
Tílos
Hálki

Ródhos

**Kameiros**

Milos

Santoríni
(Thíra)
Anáfi

*The Dodecanese*

Líndhos

*Rhodes
(Ródhos)*

Kárpathos

Kastellórizo ►

Haniá
Kastélli

Réthymnon

Iráklion
**Knossós**

Sitía
Zákros

Kássos

Paleohóra

Hóra Sfakíon
Áyios
Nikólaos

Ierápetra

**Gortys**

*Crete*

Gávrdhos

0    150
kilometres

reductions in services, it's better to check online or at station schedule boards or information counters. If you're starting a journey at a station with computerized facilities you can (at no extra cost) **reserve a seat**; a carriage and seat number will be printed on your ticket.

There are two basic **classes**: first and second, the latter about 25 percent cheaper. An express category of train, **Intercity** (IC on timetables), exists for departures between Alexandhroúpoli, Thessaloníki, Vólos, Kalambáka and Athens; also, when the line upgrade is completed, Pátra and Kalamáta, although at the time of writing all trains on that Peloponnesian route were terminating at Kiáto, from where bus transfers complete the journey.

A second-class ticket on the IC service between Athens and Thessaloníki costs €45 in person, €35 online, with occasional super deals as low as €9. The slower overnight train costs €25 (€19 online) for a seat, €49 (€39 online) for a sleeper.

Tickets issued on board carry a fifty-percent penalty charge; by contrast, under-26s and over-60s get 25 percent **discounts** at off-peak seasons for non-express trains. **InterRail** and **Eurail pass holders** must secure reservations, and pay express supplements, like everyone else.

# By sea

There are several varieties of sea-going vessels: **ordinary ferries**, which never exceed 17 knots in velocity; the new generation of "**high-speed**" boats (*tahyplóö*) and catamarans, which usually carry cars, and are capable of attaining 27 knots; **roll-on-roll-off** short-haul barges, nicknamed *pandófles* ("slippers"), **hydrofoils**, similarly quick but which carry only passengers; and local **kaïkia**, small boats which do short hops and excursions in season.

**Ferry connections** are indicated both on the route **map** (see p.30) and in the "Arrival and Departure" sections throughout the book. Schedules are notoriously erratic, however, and must be verified seasonally; details given are for departures between late June and early September. When sailing in season from **Pireás** to the Cyclades or Dodecanese, you should have a choice of at least two, sometimes three, daily departures. **Out-of-season** departure frequencies drop sharply, with less populated islands connected only two or three times weekly.

Reliable departure information is available from the local **port police** (*limenarhío*) at all island and mainland harbours of any size; around Athens there are offices at Pireás (☎210 45 50 000), Rafína

(☎22940 28888) and Lávrio (☎22920 25249). Busier port police have automated phone-answering services with an English option for schedule information. Many companies produce annual **schedule** booklets, which may not be adhered to as the season wears on – check their **websites** (if any) for current information, or refer to ⓦgtp.gr or, even better, ⓦopenseas.gr.

## Ferries

Except for some subsidized peripheral routes where older rust-buckets are still used, the Greek **ferry fleet** is fairly contemporary. **Routes and speed** can vary enormously, however; a journey from Pireás to Santoríni, for instance, can take anything from five to ten hours.

**Tickets** are best bought a day before departure, unless you need to reserve a cabin berth or space for a car. During holiday periods – Christmas/New Year, the week before and after Easter, late July to early September – and around the dates of elections, ferries need to be booked at least ten days in advance. Ticketing for most major routes is computerized and you cannot **buy** your ticket on board. Many companies allow you to reserve places and pay online, but tickets must still be picked up at the port at least fifteen minutes before departure.

The cheapest **fare class**, which you'll automatically be sold unless you specify otherwise, is *ikonomikí thési*, which gives you the run of most boats except for the upper-class restaurant and bar. Most newer boats seem expressly designed to frustrate summertime travellers attempting to sleep on deck. For long overnight journeys, it's worth considering the few extra euros for a **cabin bunk**; second-class cabins are typically quadruple, while **first-class** double cabins with en-suite bathrooms can cost as much as a flight.

**Motorbikes and cars** get issued separate tickets; the latter have risen in price dramatically of late to as much as five times the passenger fare, depending on size. For example, Sámos–Ikaría costs around €12 per person/€40 per car, while Sámos–Pireás is about €28/€100. It's really only worth taking a car to the larger islands like Crete, Rhodes, Híos, Lésvos, Sámos, Corfu or Kefaloniá, and only if staying a week or more. Otherwise, it is cheaper to leave your car on the mainland and rent another on arrival.

### Hydrofoils, catamarans and high-speed boats

**Hydrofoils** – commonly known as *dhelfínia* or "Flying Dolphins" – are at least twice as expensive as ordinary ferries, but their network neatly fills gaps in ferry scheduling, often with more convenient departure times. Their main drawback is that they are the first vessels to get cancelled in bad weather and even in moderate seas are not for the seasick-prone. Many don't operate – or are heavily reduced in frequency – from October to June. Hydrofoils aren't allowed to carry scooters or bicycles.

**Catamarans and high-speed boats (tahýplia)** are ruthlessly air-conditioned, usually without deck seating and with Greek TV blaring at you from multiple screens – paying extra for *dhiakikriméni thési* (upper class) merely gets you a better view. Car fares are normal, though passenger **tickets** are at least double a comparable ferry journey, ie similar to hydrofoil rates. Similarly, many don't run between October and April.

### Small boats

In season, small boats known as **kaïkia** and **small ferries** sail between adjacent islands and to a few of the more obscure satellite islets. These are extremely useful and often very pleasant, but seldom cheaper than mainline services. The more consistent *kaïki* links are noted in the text, though the only firm information is to be had on the quayside. Swarms of **taxi boats** are a feature of many islands; these shuttle clients on set routes to remote beaches or ports which can only be reached arduously, if at all, overland. Costs on these can be pretty stiff, usually per person but occasionally per boat.

### By plane

Scheduled Greek **domestic flights** are operated by national carrier Olympic Airlines (including its subsidiary Olympic Aviation; ☎801 11 44 444, ⓦwww.olympicairlines.com), Aegean Airlines (☎801 11 20 000, ⓦwww.aegeanair.com) and Sky Express (☎281 02 23 500, ⓦwww.skyexpress.gr). They cover a broad network of island and mainland destinations, though most routes are to and from Athens or Thessaloníki. Aegean often undercuts Olympic fare-wise, and surpasses it service-wise, though services are less frequent; Sky Express, established 2007, is pricey and restricted to various routes between Iráklio (Crete) and nearby islands. All three airlines are geared to web and call-centre **e-ticket sales**, there being few walk-in town offices. Tickets bought through travel agencies attract a minimum €10 commission charge.

**Fares** to/between the islands cost at least double the cost of a deck-class ferry journey, but on inter-island routes poorly served by boat

(Rhodes–Sámos, for example), consider this time well bought, and indeed some subsidized peripheral routes cost less than a hydrofoil/catamaran journey. The cheapest web fares on Aegean are non-changeable and non-refundable, but with Olympic you can **change** your flight date, space permitting, without penalty up to 24 hours before your original departure.

Island flights are often full in peak season; if they're an essential part of your plans, make **reservations** at least a month in advance. Waiting lists exist and are worth signing on to, as there are almost always cancellations. Many Olympic flights use small prop planes which won't fly in strong winds or (depending on the airport) after dark; Aegean and Sky Express use more robust jets. A 15kg baggage **weight limit** can be strictly enforced; if, however, you've just arrived from overseas or purchased your ticket outside Greece, you're allowed the standard international limits (20–23kg).

## By car, motorcycle and taxi

Greece is blessed with dramatic mountain and coastal scenery, which is undoubtedly a joy to drive through. You should, however, bear in mind that it has one of the highest fatal **accident rates** in Europe. Local driving habits can be atrocious; overtaking on bends, barging out from side roads and failing to signal manoeuvres are common practices. **Drunk driving** is also a major issue, especially on Sunday afternoons, public holidays or late at night.

**Road conditions** can be very poor, from bad surfaces and inadequate signposting to unmarked railway crossings. There is a limited but growing number of **motorways** on which tolls (€2–3) are levied, adding over €30, for example on the drive from Athens to Thessaloníki. **Fuel**, whether regular unleaded (*amólyvdhi*), super or diesel, is currently over €1.65 per litre across the country, often €1.80-plus in remoter areas. Be aware that many petrol stations close after 8pm and on Sundays, meaning quite a hunt in rural areas at those times.

**Parking** in almost every mainland town, plus the biggest island centres, is uniformly a nightmare owing to oversubscription. **Pay-and-display** systems, plus residents-only schemes, are common, and it's rarely clear where you obtain tickets.

### Rules of the road

As in all of continental Europe, you **drive on the right** in Greece. Uphill drivers demand their **right of way**, as do the first to approach a one-lane bridge; **flashed headlights** usually mean the

## FIVE SCENIC DRIVES

**Kefaloniá's West Coast** The route north from Argostóli allows vistas of the Lixoúri Peninsula, Mýrtos beach and picturesque Ássos; see p.344.

**Sithonía Circuit** Making the clockwise circuit of Sithonía keeps imposing Mount Áthos in view for half the way; see p.299.

**Arcadian mountains** The Peloponnese is at its most bucolic on the drive through the Arcadian mountains west of Trípoli; see p.172.

**Píndhos mountains** The mountains and villages north of Ioánnina offer scenic splendour, even from the twisting roads; see p.242.

**Mount Psilorítis, Crete** Drive via Tÿlissos and Anóyia for sweeping views of the fertile valleys around Mount Psilorítis; see p.467.

opposite of what they do in the UK or North America, here signifying that the other driver insists on coming through or overtaking. However, this gesture rapidly repeated from someone approaching means they're warning you of a police control-point ahead.

**Seat-belt** use (and helmet wearing on scooters and motorcycles) is compulsory and children under the age of 10 are not allowed to sit in the front seats of cars; infractions of these rules are punishable by fines. It's illegal to drive away from any kind of **accident** – or to move the vehicles before the police appear – and where serious injury has resulted to the other party you can be held at a police station for up to 24 hours.

### Car rental

**Car rental** in Greece starts at around €300 a week in peak season for the smallest vehicle from a one-off outlet or local chain, including unlimited mileage, tax and insurance. At other times, at smaller local outfits, you can get terms of €30 per day, all inclusive, with even better **rates** for three days or more – or prebooked on the internet. Rates for open **jeeps** vary from €65 to €100 per day.

Rental prices in Greece almost never include **collision damage waiver** (CDW) and personal insurance. The CDW typically has a deductible charge of €400–600, which may be levied for even the tiniest scratch or missing mudguard. To avoid this, it is strongly recommended that you pay the €5–7 extra per day for full coverage. Frequent travellers should consider **annual excess insurance** through Insurance 4 Car Hire

(Ⓦ www.insurance4carhire.com), which will cover all UK- and North America-based drivers.

All agencies will require a blank **credit card** slip as a deposit (destroyed when you return the vehicle safely); minimum **age requirements** vary from 21 to 23. **Driving licences** issued by any European Economic Area state are honoured, but an **International Driving Permit** is required by all other drivers (despite claims by unscrupulous agencies). You can be arrested and charged if caught by the traffic police without an IDP if you require one.

Avance, Antena, Auto Union, Payless, Kosmos, National/Alamo, Reliable, Tomaso and Eurodollar are dependable Greek, or smaller international, chains with branches in many towns; all are cheaper than Hertz, Sixt or Avis. Specific local recommendations are given in the guide.

### Bringing your own car

If you intend to **drive your own car to and within Greece**, remember that insurance contracted in any EU state is valid in any other, but in many cases this is only third-party cover. Competition in the industry is intense, however, so many UK insurers will throw in full, pan-European cover for free or for a nominal sum, for up to sixty days. Those with proof of AA/RAC/AAA membership are given free road assistance from ELPA, the Greek equivalent, which runs **breakdown services** on several of the larger islands; in an emergency ring ☎10400.

**EU citizens** bringing their own cars are free to circulate in the country for six months, or until their home-based road tax or insurance expires, whichever happens first; keeping a car in Greece for longer entails more paperwork. **Non-EU nationals** will get a car entered in their passport; the carnet normally allows you to keep a vehicle in Greece for up to six months, exempt from road tax.

### Scooter and motorcycle rental

Small **motor scooters** with automatic transmission, known in Greek as *mihanákia* or *papákia* (little ducks), are good transport for all but the steepest terrain. They're available for rent on many islands and in a few of the popular mainland resorts for €12–18 per day. Prices can be bargained down out of peak season, or for a longer rental period. Only models of 80cc and above are powerful enough for two riders in mountainous areas, which includes most islands.

True **motorbikes** (*mihanés*) with manual transmissions and safer tyres are less common than they ought to be. With the proper licence, bikes of 125cc and up are available in many resorts for around €20 per day. **Quads** are also increasingly offered – without doubt the most stupid-looking and impractical conveyance yet devised, and very unstable on turns – make sure helmets are supplied.

Reputable establishments demand a full **motorcycle driving licence** (Class B) for any engine over 80cc (Greek law actually stipulates "over 50cc"). You will usually have to leave your passport as a deposit. Failure to carry the correct licence on your person also attracts a stiff fine, though some agencies still demand this rather than a passport as security.

Many rental outfits will offer you (an often ill-fitting) **crash helmet** (*krános*), and some will make you sign a waiver of liability if you refuse it. Helmet-wearing is required by law, with a €185 fine levied for failure to do so; on some smaller islands the rule is laxly enforced, on others random police roadblocks do a brisk commerce in citations, to foreigners and locals alike.

Before riding off, always check the **brakes** and **electrics**; dealers often keep the front brakes far too loose, with the commendable intention of preventing you going over the handlebars. Make sure also that there's a kick-start as backup to the battery, since ignition switches commonly fail. If you **break down** on a scooter or motorcycle you're often responsible for returning the machine, although the better outlets offer a free retrieval service.

### Taxis

Greek **taxis** are among the cheapest in the Mediterranean – so long as you get an honest driver who switches the meter on and doesn't use high-tech devices to doctor the reading. Use of the meter is mandatory within city or town limits, where Tariff 1 applies, while in rural areas or between midnight and 5am Tariff 2 is in effect. On certain islands, set rates apply on specific fixed routes – these might only depart when full. Otherwise, throughout Greece the meter starts at €0.85, though the minimum **fare** is €1.75; baggage in the boot is charged at €0.35 per piece. Additionally, there are surcharges of €2 for leaving or entering an airport (€3 for Athens), and €0.80 for leaving a harbour area. If you summon a taxi by phone on spec, there's a €1.50 charge; the meter starts running from the moment the driver begins heading towards you. All categories of supplemental charges must be set out on a card affixed to the dashboard. For a week or so before and after Orthodox Easter, and Christmas, a *filodhórima* or gratuity of about ten percent is levied.

## By bike

**Cycling** in Greece is not such hard going as you might imagine (except in summer), especially on one of the mountain bikes that are now the rule at rental outfits; they rarely cost more than €8 a day. You do, however, need steady nerves, as roads are generally narrow with no verges or bike lanes and Greek drivers are notoriously inconsiderate to cyclists.

If you have your own bike, consider taking it along by **train** or **plane** (it's free if within your 20–23kg international air allowance, but arrange it in writing with the airline beforehand to avoid huge charges at check-in). Once in Greece you can take a bike for free on most ferries, in the guard's van on most trains (for a small fee), and in the luggage bays of buses. Bring any small spare parts since specialist shops are rare.

# Accommodation

**There are vast numbers of tourist beds in Greece, and most of the year you can rely on simply turning up and finding something. At Easter and in July and August, however, you can run into problems unless you've booked in advance. The economic crisis and subsequent loss of domestic tourism has tended to depress prices, and what you pay may depend on how far you are willing to bargain.**

In cities and mainland towns you'll probably stay in **hotels**, but in the resorts and islands the big hotels and self-catering complexes are mostly pre-booked by package-holiday companies for the whole season. Although they may have vacancies if you just turn up, non-package visitors are far more likely to find themselves staying in smaller, simpler places which usually describe themselves simply as "**rooms**", or as apartments or studios. Standards here can vary from spartan (though invariably clean) to luxurious, but the vast majority are purpose-built blocks where every room is en suite, and where the minimal furnishings are well adapted to the local climate – at least in summer.

## Seasons

There are typically three **seasons** which affect prices: October to April (low), May, June and September (mid) and July and August (high) –

though **Easter** and the first two weeks of August may be in a higher category still. Urban hotels with a predominantly business clientele tend to charge the same rates all year. Elsewhere, places that have significant domestic tourism, such as Náfplio, the Pelion or the Argo-Saronic islands, frequently charge significantly more at weekends.

Many of the smaller places offering rooms **close from October to April**. In winter, then, you may have to stay in hotels in the main towns or ports. On smaller islands, there may be just one hotel and a single taverna that stays open year-round. Be warned also that resort or harbour hotels which do operate through the winter are likely to have a certain number of prostitutes as long-term guests; licensed prostitution is legal in Greece, and the management may consider this the most painless way to keep the bills paid.

## Hotels

The tourist police set official **categories** for hotels, starting with L (Luxury) and then from A down to the rarely encountered E class; all except the top category have to keep within set price limits. The letter system is being slowly replaced with a star grading system; L is five-star, E is no-star, etc. Ratings correspond to the facilities available (lifts, dining room, pool etc), a box-ticking exercise which doesn't always reflect the actual quality of the hotel; there are plenty of D-class hotels which are in practice smarter and more comfortable than nearby C-class outfits.

C-class hotels and below have only to provide the most rudimentary of continental breakfasts – sometimes optional for an extra charge – while B-class and above will usually offer a buffet breakfast including cheese, cold meats, eggs and cereals.

**Single rooms** are rare, and generally poor value – you'll often have to pay the full double-room price or haggle for around a third off; on the other hand, larger groups and families can almost always find triple and quadruple rooms, and fancier hotels may have **family suites** (two rooms sharing one bathroom), all of which can be very good value.

## Private rooms and apartments

Many places categorized as apartments or rooms are every bit as comfortable as hotels, and in the lower price ranges are usually more congenial and better value. At their most basic, **rooms** (*dhomátia* – but usually spotted by a "Rooms for Rent" or Zimmer Frei sign) might be literally a room in someone's house, a bare space with a bed and a hook on the back of the door, and washing facilities outside; the sparse facilities offset by the disarming hospitality you'll be offered as part of the family. However, these days almost all are purpose-built, with comfortable en-suite accommodation and balconies – at the fancier end of the scale you'll find studio and apartment complexes with marble floors, pools, bars and children's playgrounds. Many have a variety of rooms at different prices, so if possible always ask to see the room first. Places described as studios usually have a small kitchenette – a fridge, sink and a couple of hotplates in the room itself – while apartments generally have at least one bedroom and separate kitchen/living room.

Areas to **look for rooms**, along with recommendations of the best places, are included in the guide. The rooms may also find you, as owners descend on ferry or bus arrivals to fill any space they have, sometimes with photos of their premises. This can be great, but you can also be in for a nasty surprise – usually because the rooms are much further than you had been led to believe, or bear no relation to the pictures. In some places the practice has been outlawed. In the more developed island resorts, where package holiday-makers predominate, room owners may insist on a minimum stay of a few days, or even a week.

Rooms proprietors usually ask to keep your **passport**: ostensibly "for the tourist police", but in

---

### ACCOMMODATION PRICES

The price we quote is for the establishment's **cheapest double room in high season** – there may well be other rooms that cost more, and occasionally the cheapest price will mean a shared bathroom. For much of the year, however, you can expect to pay a bit less.

Prices are for the room only, except where otherwise indicated; fancier places often include breakfast in the price – we indicate this in the listing, but check when booking.

By law, **prices must be displayed** on the back of the door of your room, or over the reception desk. You should never pay more than this, and in practice it is rare to pay as much as the sign says. If you feel you're being overcharged, threaten to make a report to the tourist office or police, who will generally take your side in such cases.

## HOT WATER AND AIR CONDITIONING

When checking out a room, always ask about the status of **hot water** and **air conditioning**. Most modern rooms and apartments have air conditioning (indicted by a/c in our listings), but it's frequently an optional extra and you'll be charged an additional €5 or so a night to use it. Just occasionally you may also be asked to pay extra for hot water. A more likely problem is that there won't be enough: rooftop solar heaters are popular and effective, but shared solar-powered tanks tend to run out of hot water in the post-beach shower crunch around 6–7pm, with no more available until the next day. A heater, either as a backup or primary source, is more reliable.

reality to prevent you leaving with an unpaid bill. Some may be satisfied with just taking down the details, and they'll almost always return the documents once you get to know them, or if you need them for changing money.

If you are **stranded**, or arrive very late in a remote mountain or island village, you may well find someone with an unlicensed room prepared to earn extra money by putting you up. This should not be counted on, but things work out more often than not.

## Villas and longer-term rentals

Although one of the great dreams of Greek travel is finding an idyllic coastal villa and renting it for virtually nothing for a whole month, there's no chance at all of your dream coming true in modern Greece. All the best villas are contracted out to **agents** and let through foreign operators. Even if you do find one empty for a week or two, renting it locally usually costs far more than it would have done to arrange from home. There, specialist operators (see p.28) represent some superb places, from simple to luxurious, and costs can be very reasonable, especially if shared between a few people. Several of the companies listed will arrange stays on two islands over two weeks.

Having said the above, if you do arrive and decide you want to drop roots for a while, you can still strike lucky if you don't mind avoiding the obvious coastal tourist spots, and are happy with relatively modest accommodation. Pick an untouristed village, get yourself known and ask about; you might still pick up a wonderful deal. Out of season your chances are much better – even in touristy areas, between October and March (sometimes as late as April and May) you can bargain a very good rate, especially for stays of a month or more. Travel agents are another good source of information on what's available locally, and many rooms places have an apartment on the side or know someone with one to rent.

## Hostels and backpackers

Over the years most traditional youth **hostels** in Greece have closed down; competition from inexpensive rooms meant that in general they were simply not as cost-effective as elsewhere in Europe. However, those that survive are generally very good, and there's a new generation of youth-oriented **backpackers**, in the cities and more popular islands, where social life and a party atmosphere may take precedence over a good night's sleep. Few of them are members of any official organization – though an IYHF card or student ID may save you a few euros – and virtually none will have a curfew or any restrictive regulations. Prices for a dorm bed vary from as little as €12 in a simple, traditional hostel to as much as €25 in the fancier Athenian or island backpackers.

If you're planning to spend a few nights in hostels, **IYHF membership** is probably a worthwhile investment. By no means all Greek hostels offer discounts, but there are other membership benefits and the card may be accepted as student ID, for example. At official hostels you may be able to buy membership on the spot; otherwise visit Ⓦ hihostels.com from where you can apply via your local youth hostel association. For booking youth hostels online try either Ⓦ hihostels.com or Ⓦ hostelworld.com.

## Monasteries

Greek **monasteries** and **convents** have a tradition of putting up travellers (of the appropriate sex). On the mainland, this is still a customary – if steadily decreasing – practice, used mostly by villagers on pilgrimage; on the islands, monastic hospitality is less common, so check locally before heading out to a monastery for the night. Also, dress modestly – no shorts or short skirts – and try to arrive early in the evening, not later than 8pm or sunset (whichever is earlier). For men, the most exciting monastic experience is a visit to the "Monks' Republic" of Mount Áthos (see p.308), on the Halkidhikí peninsula, near

## SPECIAL PLACES TO STAY

**Imaret, Kavála**. Beautifully converted hammam with pool, massage spa and original Ottoman features. See p.314

**Mount Áthos monasteries** Though currently just for male visitors, staying with the monks here is an unforgettable experience. See p.308

**Mýlos tou Markétou**, Mylos A sixteenth-century windmill converted into a stylish apartment. See p.375

**Pirgos Mavromichali**, **Liméni**, **Peloponnese** Mani tower house transformed into a luxury hotel. See p.163

**O&B, Athens** Boutique hotel with comfortable rooms and knockout views of the Acropolis. See p.99

**Spirit of the Knights**, Rhodes Exquisite B&B with a lovely courtyard tucked away in Rhodes old town. See p.520

Thessaloníki. This is, however, a far from casual travel option, involving a fair amount of advance planning and the securing of a permit.

## Camping

**Officially recognized campsites** range from ramshackle compounds on the islands to highly organized and rather soulless complexes, often dominated by camper vans. Most places cost in the region of €5–7 a night per person, plus €5–6 per tent or €6–8 per camper van, though at the fanciest sites rates for two people plus a tent can almost equal the price of a basic room. You will need at least a light sleeping bag, since even summer nights can get cool and damp. The website of the official Greek camping organization (Wpanhellenic -camping-union.gr) lists all authorized campsites, with booking for many of them.

**Camping** outside an official campsite (with or without a tent) is against the law – enforced in most tourist areas and on beaches. If you do camp rough, exercise sensitivity and discretion. Police will crack down on people camping (and especially littering) if a large community of campers develops. Off the beaten track nobody is very bothered, though it is always best to ask permission in the local taverna or café, and to be aware of rising crime, even in rural areas. If you want to camp near a beach, the best strategy is to find a sympathetic taverna, which in exchange for regular patronage will probably be willing to guard small valuables and let you use their facilities.

# Food and drink

**Although many visitors get by on moussaka or kalamári almost every night, there is a huge range to Greek cuisine, not least its wonderful mezédhes, seafood and juicy, fat olives. Despite depressed wages, most Greeks still eat out with friends or family at least once a week. The atmosphere is always relaxed and informal, with pretensions rare outside of the more chichi parts of Athens and certain major resorts. Drinking is traditionally meant to accompany food, though a range of bars and clubs exists.**

## Breakfast

Greeks don't generally eat **breakfast**, more often opting for a mid-morning snack (see below). This is reflected in the abysmal quality of most hotel "continental" offerings, where waxy orange squash, stewed coffee, processed cheese and meats, plus pre-packaged butter, honey and jam (confusingly called *marmeládha*), are the rule at all but the top establishments. There might be some fresh fruit, decent yoghurt and pure honey, if you are lucky. The only egg-and-bacon kinds of places are in resorts where foreigners congregate, or where there are returned North American- or Australian-Greeks. Such outlets can often be good value (€4–7 for the works, including coffee), especially if there's competition.

## Picnics and snacks

**Picnic** ingredients are easily available at supermarkets, bakeries and greengrocers; sampling produce like cheese or olives is acceptable. Standard white **bread** is often of minimal nutritional value and inedible within a day of purchase, although rarer brown varieties such as *olikís* (wholemeal), *sikalísio* (rye bread) or *oktáspoo* (multi-grain) fare better. Olives are ubiquitous, with the Kalamáta and Ámfissa varieties usually surpassing most local picks in quality.

Honey is the ideal topping for the famous local **yoghurt**, which is widely available in bulk. Sheep-milk yoghurt (*próvio*) is richer and sweeter than the more common cow's-milk. **Feta cheese** is found everywhere, often with a dozen varieties to choose from, made from goat's, sheep's or cow's milk in varying proportions. Harder *graviéra* is the second most popular cheese.

Greece imports very little produce from abroad, aside from bananas, the odd pineapple and a few mangoes. **Fruit** is relatively expensive and available mainly by season, though in more cosmopolitan spots one can find such things as avocados for much of the year. Reliable picnic fruits include cherries (June–July); *krystália*, small, heavenly green pears (Sept–Nov); *vaniliés*, orange- or red-fleshed plums (July–Oct); and kiwi (Oct–May). Less portable, but succulent, are figs, whose main season is August and September. Salad **vegetables** are more reasonably priced; besides the famous, enormous tomatoes (June–Sept), there's a bewildering variety of cool-season greens, including rocket, dill, enormous spring onions and lettuces.

## Restaurants

Greek cuisine and **restaurants** are usually straight-forward and still largely affordable – typically €12–20 per person for a substantial meal with house wine. Even when preparation is basic, raw materials are usually wholesome and fresh. The best strategy is to **go where Greeks go**, often less obvious backstreet places that might not look much from outside but deliver the real deal. The two most common types of restaurant are the **estiatório** and the **taverna**. Distinctions are slight, though the former is more commonly found in large towns and emphasize the more complicated, oven-baked casserole dishes termed **mayireftá** (literally, "cooked").

As one might expect, the identikit tavernas at resorts dominated by foreigners tend to make less effort, bashing out speedily grilled meat with pre-cut chips and rice containing the odd pea. You

### FAST FOOD GREEK STYLE

Traditional hot **snacks** are still easy to come by, although they are being elbowed aside by Western fast food at both international and nationwide Greek chains such as *Goody's* (burgers, pasta and salad bar), *Everest*, *Grigoris* and *Theios Vanias* (baked pastries and baguette sandwiches), and various pizzerias. Still, thousands of kebab shops (*souvladzídhika*) churn out *souvlákia*, either as small shish on wooden sticks or as *yíros* – doner kebab with garnish in *pítta* bread. Other snacks include cheese pies (*tyrópites*), spinach pies (*spanokópites*) and, less commonly, minced meat pies (*kreatópites*); these are found either at the baker's or some of the aforementioned chains.

should beware of overcharging and bill-padding at such establishments too. In towns, growing numbers of pretentious "**koultouriárika**" restaurants boast fancy decor and Greek nouvelle (or fusion) cuisine with speciality wine lists, while producing little of substance.

Greeks generally eat very late in the evening, rarely venturing out until after 9pm and often arriving at midnight or later. Consequently, most restaurants operate flexible hours, varying according to the level of custom, and thus the **opening times** given throughout the listings should be viewed as approximate at best.

### Estiatória

With their long hours and tiny profit margins, **estiatória** (sometimes known as *inomayiría*, "wine-and-cook-houses") are, alas, a vanishing breed. An *estiatório* will generally feature a variety of *mayireftá* such as moussaka, macaroni pie, meat or game stews, stuffed tomatoes or peppers, the oily vegetable casseroles called *ladherá*, and oven-baked meat and fish. Usually you point at the steam trays to choose these dishes. Batches are cooked in the morning and then left to stand, which is why the food is often **lukewarm**; most such dishes are in fact enhanced by being allowed to steep in their own juice.

### Tavernas and psistariés

**Tavernas** range from the glitzy and fashionable to rough-and-ready beachside ones with seating under a reed canopy. Really primitive ones have a very limited (often unwritten) menu, but the more elaborate will offer some of the main *mayireftá* dishes mentioned above, as well as standard taverna fare: **mezédhes** (hors d'oeuvres) or **orektiká** (appetizers) and **tís óras** (meat and fish, fried or grilled to order). **Psistariés** (grill-houses) serve spit-roasted lamb, pork, goat, chicken or *kokorétsi* (grilled offal roulade). They will usually have a limited selection of mezédhes and salads (*salátes*), but no *mayireftá*. In rural areas, roadside *psistariés* are often called *exohiká kéndra*.

The most common **mezédhes** are *tzatzíki* (yoghurt, garlic and cucumber dip), *melitzanosaláta* (aubergine/eggplant dip), fried courgette/zucchini or aubergine/eggplant slices, *yígandes* (white haricot beans in hot tomato sauce), *tyropitákia* or *spanakopitákia* (small cheese or spinach pies), *revythókeftedhes* (chickpea patties similar to falafel), octopus salad and *mavromátika* (black-eyed peas).

Among **meats**, *souvláki* and chops are reliable choices; pork is usually better and cheaper than veal, especially as *pansétta* (spare ribs). The best *souvláki*, not always available, is lamb; more commonly encountered are rib chops (*païdhákia*); lamb roasted in tin foil (*exohikó*) is another favourite. *Keftédhes* (breadcrumbed meatballs), *biftékia* (pure-meat patties) and the spicy, coarse-grain sausages called *loukánika* are cheap and good. Chicken is widely available but typically battery-farmed. Other dishes worth trying are stewed goat (*gídha vrastí*) or baked goat (*katsíki stó foúrno*) – goat in general is typically free-range and organic.

## Fish and seafood

Seafood can be one of the highlights of a trip to Greece, though there are some tips to bear in mind. When ordering, the standard procedure is to go to the glass cooler and pick your specimen, then have it weighed (uncleaned) in your presence. Overcharging, especially where a printed menu is absent, is not uncommon; have weight and price confirmed clearly. Taverna owners often comply only minimally with the requirement to indicate when seafood is **frozen** – look for the abbreviation "kat", "k" or just an asterisk on the Greek-language side of the menu. If the price, almost invariably quoted by the kilo, seems too good to be true, it's almost certainly farmed. The choicest varieties, such as red mullet, *tsipoúra* (gilt-head bream), seabass or *fangrí* (common bream), will all be expensive if wild – €45–70 per kilo. Less esteemed species tend to cost €20–35 per kilo but are usually quoted at €6–9 per portion.

    Fish caught in the summer months tend to be smaller and drier, and so are served with *ladholémono* (oil and lemon) sauce. An inexpensive May–June treat is fresh, grilled or fried *bakaliáros* (hake), the classic UK fish-and-chip shop species. *Gávros* (anchovy), *atherína* (sand smelts) and *sardhélles* (sardines) are late-summer fixtures, at their best in the northeast Aegean. *Koliós* (mackerel) is excellent either grilled or baked in sauce. Especially in autumn you may find *psarósoupa* (fish soup) or *kakaviá* (bouillabaisse).

    Cheaper **seafood** (*thalassiná*) such as fried baby squid (usually frozen); *thrápsalo* (large, grillable deep-water squid) and octopus are summer staples; often mussels, cockles and small prawns will also be offered at reasonable sums (€20–30 per kilo).

## Wine

All tavernas will offer you a choice of bottled **wines**, and most have their own house variety: kept in barrels, sold in bulk (*varelísio* or *hýma*) by the quarter-, half- or full litre, and served in glass flagons or brightly coloured tin "monkey-cups". Per-litre prices depend on locale and quality, ranging from €4 (Thessaly, Skýros) to €10–11 (Santoríni, Rhodes). Non-resinated wine is almost always more than decent; some people add a dash of soda water or lemonade. Barrelled **retsina** – pine-resinated wine, often an acquired taste – is far less common than it used to be, though you will find bottled brands everywhere: Yeoryiadhi from Thessaloníki, Liokri from Ahaïa and Malamatina from central Greece are all quaffable.

    Among **bottled wines** available nationwide, Cambas Attikos, Zítsa and Rhodian CAIR products are good, inexpensive whites, while Boutari Naoussa and Kourtakis Apelia are decent,

FOOD AND DRINK **BASICS** | 41

mid-range reds. For a better but still moderately priced red, choose either Boutari or Tsantali Merlot, or Averof Katoï from Epirus.

Travelling around **wine-producing islands** such as Límnos, Lésvos, Santoríni, Kefaloniá, Náxos, Ikaría, Rhodes and Crete you will also have the chance to sample local bottlings. Curiously, island **red wines** are almost uniformly mediocre, so you are better off ordering mainland varieties from Carras on Halki-dhikí, and various spots in the Peloponnese and Thessaly. Particularly notable vintages are mentioned throughout the guide.

Other **premium microwineries** on the mainland whose products have long been fashionable, in both red and white, include the overrated Hatzimi-hali (central Greece), the outstanding Dhiaman-dakou (near Náoussa, red and white), Athanasiadhi (central Greece), Skouras (Argolid) and the two rival Lazaridhi vintners (Dhráma, east Macedonia), especially their superb Merlots. For any of these you can expect to pay €10–16 per bottle in a shop, double that at a taverna. The best available current **guide** to the emerging Greek domaines and vintners is Konstantinos Lazarakis' *The Wines of Greece*.

Finally, CAIR on Rhodes makes "**champagne**" ("naturally sparkling wine fermented en bouteille", says the label), in both brut and demi-sec versions. It's not Moët & Chandon quality by any means, but at about €6 per bottle, nobody's complaining.

# Cafés and bars

A venerable institution, under attack from the onslaught of mass global culture, is the **kafenío**, still found in every Greek town but dying out in many resorts. In greater abundance, you'll encounter **patisseries** (*zaharoplastía*), swish modern **cafeterias and trendy bars**.

### Kafenía, cafeterias and coffee

The **kafenío** (plural *kafenía*) is the traditional Greek coffee-house. Although its main business is "Greek" (Middle Eastern) **coffee** – prepared unsweetened (*skétos* or *pikrós*), medium (*métrios*) or sweet (*glykós*) – it also serves instant coffee, ouzo, brandy, beer, sage-based tea known as *tsáï vounoú*, soft drinks and juices. Some *kafenía* close at siesta time, but many remain open from early in the morning until late at night. The chief summer socializing time for a pre-prandial ouzo is 6–8pm, immediately after the afternoon nap.

Cafeterias are the province of fancier varieties of coffee and **kafés frappé**, iced instant coffee with sugar and (optionally) condensed milk – uniquely

Greek despite its French name. Like Greek coffee, it is always accompanied by a glass of water. *Freddoc-cino* is a newer, cappuccino-based alternative to the traditional cold frappé. "Nes"(café) is the generic term for all instant **coffee**, regardless of brand. Thankfully, almost all cafeterias now offer a range of foreign-style coffees – filter, dubbed *fíltros* or *gallikós* (French); cappuccino; and espresso – at overseas prices. Alcohol is also served and many establishments morph into lively bars late at night.

### Ouzería, mezedhopolía and spirits

**Ouzería** (called **tsipourádhika** in Vólos, Thessal-oníki and other major centres of the north mainland), found mainly in select neighbourhoods of larger islands and towns, specialize in ouzo and mezédhes. In some places you also find *mezed-hopolía*, a bigger, more elaborate kind of ouzerí. These places are well worth trying for the marvel-lous variety of mezédhes they serve. In effect, several plates of mezédhes plus drinks will substi-tute for a more involved meal at a taverna, though it works out more expensive if you have a healthy appetite. Faced with an often bewilderingly varied menu, you might opt for a *pikilía* (assortment) available in several sizes, the most expensive one usually emphasizing seafood.

Ouzo is served by the glass, to which you can add water from the accompanying glass or ice to taste. The next measure up is a *karafáki* – a 200ml vial, the favourite means of delivery for *tsípouro*. Once, every ouzo was automatically accompanied by a small plate of **mezédhes** on the house: cheese, cucumber, tomato, a few olives, sometimes octopus or a couple of small fish. Nowadays "*ouzomezés*" is a separate, pricier option. Often, however, this is "off-menu" but if you order a *karafáki* you will automatically be served a selection of snacks.

### Sweets and desserts

The **zaharoplastío**, a cross between café and patis-serie, serves coffee, a limited range of alcohol, yoghurt with honey and sticky cakes. The better establishments offer an amazing variety of pastries, cream-and-chocolate confections, honey-soaked Greco–Turkish sweets like *baklavás*, *kataïfi* (honey-drenched "shredded wheat"), *loukoumádhes* (deep-fried batter puffs dusted with cinnamon and dipped in syrup), *galaktoboúreko* (custard pie) and so on. For more dairy-based products, seek out a **galaktopolío**, where you'll often find *ryzógalo* (rice pudding), *kréma* (custard) and locally made *yiaoúrti* (yoghurt). Both *zaharoplastía* and *galaktopolía* are more family-oriented places than a *kafenío*.

## THE STRONG STUFF

**Ouzo** and the similar **tsípouro** (north mainland) and **tsikoudhiá** (Crete) are simple spirits of up to 48 percent alcohol, distilled from the grape-mash residue of wine-making. The former is always flavoured with anise, the latter two may be unadulterated or also have a touch of anise, cinnamon, pear essence or fennel. There are nearly thirty brands of ouzo or *tsípouro*, with the best reckoned to be from Lésvos and Sámos islands, or Zítsa and Týrnavos on the mainland. Note that ouzo has the peculiar ability to bring back its effect when you drink water the morning after, so make sure you don't plan to do anything important (not least driving) the next day.

**Traditional specialities** include "spoon sweets" or *glyká koutalioú* (syrupy preserves of quince, grape, fig, citrus fruit or cherry) .

**Ice cream**, sold principally at the parlours which have swept across Greece (Dhodhoni is the posh home-grown competition to Haägen-Dazs), can be very good and almost indistinguishable from Italian prototypes. A scoop (*baláki*) costs €1.20–1.50; you'll be asked if you want it in a cup (*kypelláki*) or a cone (*konáki*), and whether you want toppings like *santiyí* (whipped cream) or nuts.

### Bars, beer and mineral water

**Bars** (*barákia*) are ubiquitous across Greece, ranging from clones of Spanish bodegas to musical beachside bars more active by day than at night. At their most sophisticated, however, they are well-executed theme venues in ex-industrial premises or Neoclassical houses, with both Greek and international soundtracks. Most Greek bars have a half-life of about a year; the best way to find current hot spots, especially if they're more club than bar, is to look out for posters advertising bar-hosted events in the neighbourhood.

**Shots** and **cocktails** are invariably expensive at €5–8, except during well-advertised happy hours: beer in a bar will cost €4–5, up to €12 for imports in trendier parts of Athens. **Beers** are mostly foreign lagers made locally under licence at just a handful of breweries on the central mainland. **Local brands** include the palatable Fix from Athens, milder Mythos and Veryina from Komotiní. Athens also has a **microbrewery**, Craft: they produce lager in three grades (blonde, "smoked" and black), as well as a red ale, distribution of

which is on the rise. Genuinely **imported** German beers, such as Bitburger, Fisher and Warsteiner (plus a few British and Irish ones), are found in Athens and at busier resorts.

The ubiquitous Loutraki **mineral water** is not esteemed by the Greeks themselves, who prefer various brands from Crete and Epirus. In many tavernas there has been a backlash against plastic bottles, and you can now get mineral water in glass bottles. Souroti, Epsa and Sariza are the principal labels of naturally **sparkling** (*aerioúho* in Greek) water, in small bottles. Note that despite variable quality in taste **tap water** is essentially safe all over Greece though persuading a restaurant to provide it can be difficult.

# Health

**There are no required inoculations for Greece, though it's wise to ensure that you are up to date on tetanus and polio. The main health risks faced by visitors involve overexposure to the sun, overindulgence in food and drink, or bites and stings from insects and sea creatures.**

British and other EU nationals are entitled to free medical care in Greece upon presentation of a European Health Insurance Card (see box opposite). The US, Canada, Australia and New Zealand have no formal healthcare agreements with Greece (other than allowing for free emergency trauma treatment), so insurance is highly recommended.

## Doctors and hospitals

For serious medical attention you'll find English-speaking **doctors** (mainly private) in all the bigger towns and resorts: if your hotel can't help, the tourist police or your consulate should be able to come up with some names if you have any difficulty. There are also **hospitals** in all the big cities. For an ambulance, phone ☎ 166.

## Pharmacies, drugs and contraception

For minor complaints it's enough to go to the local **pharmacy** (*farmakío*). Greek pharmacists are highly trained and dispense a number of medicines which elsewhere could only be prescribed by a doctor. In the larger towns and resorts there'll usually be one who speaks good English. Pharmacies are usually closed evenings and Saturday mornings, but all

## THE EUROPEAN HEALTH INSURANCE CARD

If you have an EHIC (ⓦwww.ehic.org.uk, ⓦehic.ie) you are entitled to free consultation and treatment from doctors and dentists. At hospitals you should simply have to show your EHIC; for free treatment from a regular doctor or dentist, you should call the IKA (the Social Insurance Institute, who administer the scheme) on their national appointments hotline, ☎184. For prescriptions from pharmacies you pay a small fixed charge plus 25 percent of the cost of the medicine; if you are charged in full, get a receipt and keep the original prescription to claim it back. You can also claim back for private treatment; take the original receipts and your EHIC to the IKA within one month, and they will reimburse you up to the limit allowed for similar treatment by the IKA.

should have a schedule on their door showing the night and weekend duty pharmacists in town.

If you regularly use any form of **prescription drug**, you should bring along a copy of the prescription, together with the generic name of the drug; this will help you replace it, and avoids problems with customs officials. In this regard, you should be aware that **codeine** is banned in Greece. If you import any you might find yourself in serious trouble, so check labels carefully; it's a major ingredient of Panadeine, Veganin, Solpadeine, Codis and Nurofen Plus, to name just a few.

**Contraceptive pills** are sold over the counter at larger pharmacies, though not necessarily the brands you may be used to; a good pharmacist should come up with a close match. **Condoms** are inexpensive and ubiquitous – just ask for *profylaktiká* (less formally, *plastiká* or *kapótes*) at any pharmacy, sundries store or corner *períptero* (kiosk). Sanitary towels and **tampons** are widely sold in supermarkets.

## Common health problems

The main health problems experienced by visitors – including many blamed on the food – have to do with **overexposure to the sun**. To avoid these, cover up, wear a hat, and drink plenty of fluids to avoid any danger of **sunstroke**; remember that even hazy sun can burn. **Tap water** meets strict EU standards for safety, but high mineral content and less than perfect desalination on many islands can leave a brackish taste not suited to everyone. For that reason many people prefer to stick to bottled water (see opposite). Hayfever sufferers should be prepared for a pollen season earlier than in northern Europe, peaking in April and May.

### Hazards of the sea

To avoid hazards by the sea, goggles or a dive mask for swimming and footwear for walking over wet or rough rocks are useful. You may have the bad luck to meet an armada of **jellyfish** (*tsoúkhtres*), especially in late summer; they come in various colours and sizes ranging from purple "pizzas" to invisible, minute creatures. Various over-the-counter remedies are sold in resort pharmacies to combat the sting, and baking soda or diluted ammonia also help to lessen the effects. Less vicious but far more common are spiny sea urchins, which infest rocky shorelines year-round. If you're unlucky enough to step on or graze against one, an effective way to remove the spines is with a needle (you can crudely sterilize it with heat from a cigarette lighter) and olive oil. If you don't remove the spines, they'll fester.

### Bites and stings

Most of Greece's insects and reptiles are pretty benign, but there are a few that can give a painful bite. Much the most common are **mosquitoes**: you can buy repellent devices and sprays at any minimarket. On beaches, sandflies can also give a nasty (and potentially infection-carrying) sting. Adders (*ohiés*) and scorpions (*scorpii*) are found throughout Greece. Both creatures are shy, but take care when climbing over drystone walls where snakes like to sun themselves, and – particularly when camping – don't put hands or feet in places, like shoes, where you haven't looked first.

Finally, in addition to munching its way through a fair amount of Greece's surviving pine forests, the pine processionary **caterpillar** – which takes its name from the long, nose-to-tail convoys – sports highly irritating hairs, with a venom worse than a scorpion's. If you touch one, or even a tree-trunk they've been on recently, you'll know all about it for a week, and the welts may require antihistamine to heal.

If you snap a **wild-fig shoot** while walking, avoid contact with the highly irritant **sap**. The immediate antidote to the active alkaloid is a mild acid – lemon juice or vinegar; left unneutralized, fig "milk" raises welts which take a month to heal.

# The media

**Greeks are great devourers of newsprint – although few would propose the Greek mass media as a paradigm of objective journalism. Papers are almost uniformly sensational, while state-run TV and radio are often biased in favour of whichever party happens to be in government. Foreign news is widely available, though, in the form of locally printed newspaper editions and TV news channels.**

## Newspapers and magazines

**British newspapers** are widely available in resorts and the larger towns at a cost of €2–3 for dailies, or €4–5 for Sunday editions. Many, including the *Guardian*, *Times*, *Mail* and *Mirror*, have slimmed-down editions printed in Greece which are available the same day; others are likely to be a day old. In bigger newsagents you'll also be able to find *USA Today*, *Time* and *Newsweek* as well as the *International Herald Tribune*, which has the bonus of including an abridged English edition of the same day's *Kathimerini*, a respected Greek daily, thus allowing you to keep up with Greek news too. From time to time you'll also find various English-language magazines aimed at visitors to Greece, though none seems to survive for long.

The main local English-language newspaper, available in most resorts, is the *Athens News* (weekly every Friday, online at ⓦathensnews.gr; €2.50), in colour with good features and Balkan news, plus entertainment and arts listings.

## Radio

Greece's airwaves are cluttered with **local and regional stations**, many of which have plenty of music, often traditional. In popular areas many of them have regular news bulletins and tourist information in English. The mountainous nature of much of the country, though, means that any sort of radio reception is tricky: if you're driving around you'll find that you constantly have to retune. The two state-run networks are ER1 (a mix of news, talk and pop music) and ER2 (pop music).

The BBC World Service no longer broadcasts to Europe on short wave, though Voice of America can be picked up in places. Both of these and dozens of others are of course available as internet broadcasts, however, or via satellite TV channels.

## Television

Greece's state-funded **TV stations**, ET1, NET and ET3, nowadays lag behind private channels – Mega, Star, Alpha, Alter and Skai – in the ratings, though not necessarily in quality of offerings. Most foreign films and serials are broadcast in their original language, with Greek subtitles; there's almost always a choice of English-language movies from about 9pm onwards, although the closer you get to the end of the movie, the more adverts you'll encounter. Although hotels and rooms places frequently have TVs in the room, reception is often dire: even where they advertise satellite, the only English-language channels this usually includes are CNN and BBC World.

# Festivals

**Most of the big Greek popular festivals have a religious basis, so they're observed in accordance with the Orthodox calendar: this means that Easter, for example, can fall as much as three weeks to either side of the Western festival.**

On top of the main religious festivals, there are scores of local festivities, or **paniyíria**, celebrating the patron saint of the village church. Some of the more important are listed below; the *paramoní*, or **eve of the festival**, is often as significant as the day itself, and many of the events are actually celebrated on the night before. If you show up on the morning of the date given you may find that you have missed most of the music, dancing and drinking. With some 330-odd possible saints' days, though, you're unlikely to travel round for long without stumbling on something. Local tourist offices should be able to fill you in on events in their area.

## Easter

**Easter** is by far the most important festival of the Greek year. It is an excellent time to be in Greece, both for the beautiful and moving religious ceremonies and for the days of feasting and celebration which follow. If you make for a smallish village, you may well find yourself an honorary member for the period of the festival. This is a busy time for Greek tourists as well as international ones, however, so book ahead: for Easter dates, see opposite.

The first great ceremony takes place on **Good Friday** evening as the Descent from the Cross is lamented in church. At dusk, the *Epitáfios*, Christ's funeral bier, lavishly decorated by the women of the parish, leaves the sanctuary and is paraded solemnly through the streets. Late **Saturday** evening sees the climax in a majestic Mass to celebrate Christ's triumphant return. At the stroke of midnight all the lights in each crowded church are extinguished and the congregation plunged into the darkness until the priest lights the candles of the worshippers, intoning "*Dévte, lévete Fós*" ("Come, take the Light"). The burning candles are carried home through the streets; they are said to bring good fortune to the house if they arrive still burning.

The lighting of the flames is the signal for celebrations to start and the Lent fast to be broken. The traditional greeting, as fireworks and dynamite explode all around you in the street, is *Khristós Anésti* ("Christ is risen"), to which the response is *Alithós Anésti* ("Truly He is risen"). On **Easter Sunday** there's feasting on roast lamb.

The Greek equivalent of **Easter eggs** is hardboiled eggs (painted red on Holy Thursday), which are baked into twisted, sweet bread-loaves (*tsourékia*) or distributed on Easter Sunday. People rap their eggs against their friends' eggs, and the owner of the last uncracked egg is considered lucky.

## Name days

In Greece, everyone gets to celebrate their birthday twice. More important, in fact, than your actual birthday, is the "**Name Day**" of the saint who bears the same name. If your name isn't covered, no problem – your party is on All Saints' Day, eight weeks after Easter. If you learn that it's an acquaintance's name day, you wish them *Khrónia Pollá* (literally, "many years").

The big name day celebrations (Iannis/Ianna on January 7 or Yioryios on April 23 for example) can involve thousands of people. Any church or chapel bearing the saint's name will mark the event – some smaller chapels will open just for this one day of the year – while if an entire village is named after the saint, you can almost guarantee a festival. To check out when your name day falls, see Ⓦ sfakia -crete.com.

## Festival calendar

### JANUARY

**January 1: New Year's Day** (Protokhroniá) In Greece this is the feast day of Áyios Vassílios (St Basil). The traditional New Year greeting is "Kalí Khroniá".

**January 6: Epiphany** (Theofánia/Tón Fóton) Marks the baptism of Jesus as well as the end of the twelve days of Christmas. Baptismal fonts,

lakes, rivers and seas are blessed, especially harbours (such as Pireás), where the priest traditionally casts a crucifix into the water, with local youths competing for the privilege of recovering it.

### FEBRUARY/MARCH

**Carnival** (Apokriátika) Festivities span three weeks, climaxing during the seventh weekend before Easter. Pátra Carnival, with a chariot parade and costume parties, is one of the largest and most outrageous in the Mediterranean. Interesting, too, are the boúles or masked revels which take place around Macedonia (particularly at Náoussa), Thrace (Xánthi), and the outrageous Goat Dance on Skýros in the Sporades. The Ionian islands, especially Kefaloniá, are also good for carnival, as is Ayiássos on Lésvos, while Athenians celebrate by going around hitting each other on the head with plastic hammers.

**Clean Monday** (Katharά Dheftéra) The day after Carnival ends and the first day of Lent, 48 days before Easter, marks the start of fasting and is traditionally spent picnicking and flying kites.

**March 25: Independence Day and the feast of the Annunciation** (Evangelismós) Both a religious and a national holiday, with, on the one hand, military parades and dancing to celebrate the beginning of the revolt against Ottoman rule in 1821, and, on the other, church services to honour the news given to Mary that she was to become the Mother of Christ. There are major festivities on Tínos, Ýdhra and any locality with a monastery or church named Evangelístria or Evangelismós.

### APRIL/MAY

**Easter** (Páskha: April 15, 2012; May 5, 2013; April 20, 2014; April 12, 2015) The most important festival of the Greek year (see opposite). The island of Ýdhra, with its alleged 360 churches and monasteries, is the prime Easter resort; other famous Easter celebrations are held at Corfu, Pyrgí on Híos, Ólymbos on Kárpathos and St John's monastery on Pátmos, where on Holy Thursday the abbot washes the feet of twelve monks in the village square, in imitation of Christ doing the same for his disciples. Good Friday and Easter Monday are also public holidays.

**April 23: The feast of St George** (Áyios Yeóryios) St George, the patron of shepherds, is honoured with a big rural celebration, with much feasting and dancing at associated shrines and towns. If it falls during Lent, festivities are postponed until the Monday after Easter.

### MAY/JUNE

**May 1: May Day** (Protomayiá) The great urban holiday when townspeople traditionally make for the countryside to picnic and fly kites, returning with bunches of wild flowers. Wreaths are hung on their doorways or balconies until they are burnt in bonfires on St John's Eve (June 23). There are also large demonstrations by the Left for Labour Day.

**May 21: Feast of St Constantine and St Helen** (Áyios Konstandínos & Ayía Eléni) Constantine, as emperor, championed Christianity in the Byzantine Empire; St Helen was his mother. There are firewalking ceremonies in certain Macedonian villages; elsewhere celebrated rather more conventionally as the name day for two of the more popular Christian names in Greece.

**Whit Monday** (Áyio Pnévma) Fifty days after Easter, sees services to commemorate the descent of the Holy Spirit to the assembled disciples. Many young Greeks take advantage of the long weekend, marking the start of summer, to head for the islands.

**June 29 & 30: SS Peter and Paul** (Áyios Pétros and Áyios Pávlos) The joint feast of two of the more widely celebrated name days is on June 29. Celebrations often run together with those for the Holy Apostles (Áyii Apóstoli), the following day.

## JULY

**July 17: Feast of St Margaret** (Ayía Marína) A big event in rural areas, as she's an important protector of crops.

**July 20: Feast of the Prophet Elijah** (Profítis Ilías) Widely celebrated at the countless hilltop shrines of Profítis Ilías. The most famous is on Mount Taïyetos, near Spárti, with an overnight vigil.

**July 26: St Paraskevi** (Ayía Paraskeví) Celebrated in parishes or villages bearing that name, especially in Epirus.

## AUGUST

**August 6: Transfiguration of the Saviour** (Metamórfosis toú Sotíros) Another excuse for celebrations, particularly at Khristós Ráhon village on Ikaría, and at Plátanos on Léros. On Hálki the date is marked by messy food fights with flour, eggs and squid ink.

**August 15: Assumption of the Blessed Virgin Mary** (Apokímisis tís Panayías) This is the day when people traditionally return to their home village, and the heart of the holiday season, so in many places there will be no accommodation available on any terms. Even some Greeks will resort to sleeping in the streets at the great pilgrimage to Tínos; also major festivities at Páros, at Ayiássos on Lésvos, and at Ólympos on Kárpathos.

**August 29: Beheading of John the Baptist** (Apokefálisis toú Prodhrómou) Popular pilgrimages and celebrations at Vrykoúnda on Kárpathos.

## SEPTEMBER

**September 8: Birth of the Virgin Mary** (Yénnisis tís Panayías) Sees special services in churches dedicated to the event, and a double cause for rejoicing on Spétses where they also celebrate the anniversary of the battle of the straits of Spétses. Elsewhere, there's a pilgrimage of childless women to the monastery at Tsambíka, Rhodes.

**September 14: Exaltation of the Cross** (Ípsosis toú Stavroú) A last major summer festival, keenly observed on Hálki.

**September 24: Feast of St John the Divine** (Áyios Ioánnis Theológos) Observed on Níssyros and Pátmos, where at the saint's monastery there are solemn, beautiful liturgies the night before and early in the morning.

## OCTOBER

**October 26: Feast of St Demetrios** (Áyios Dhimítrios) Another popular name day, particularly celebrated in Thessaloníki, of which he is the patron saint. In rural areas the new wine is traditionally broached on this day, a good excuse for general inebriation.

**October 28: Óhi Day** A national holiday with parades, folk dancing and speeches to commemorate prime minister Metaxas' one-word reply to Mussolini's 1940 ultimatum: Ohi! ("No!").

## NOVEMBER

**November 8: Feast of the Archangels Michael and Gabriel** (Mihaïl and Gavriïl, or tón Taxiárhon) Marked by rites at the numerous churches named after them, particularly at the rural monastery of Taxiárhis on Sými, and the big monastery of Mandamádhos, Lésvos.

## CULTURAL FESTIVALS

Throughout the summer you'll find **festivals** of music, dance and theatre at venues across Greece, with many of the events taking place at atmospheric outdoor venues. Some, in the resorts and islands, are unashamedly aimed at drawing tourists, others more seriously artistic. The granddaddy of them all is the Athens and Epidaurus **Festival** (Ⓦgreekfestival.gr, see p.110), which has been running every summer for over fifty years, incorporating everything from open-air performances of Classical drama in ancient theatres to jazz and contemporary art. Others include:

**Dhimitría Cultural Festival, Thessaloníki** Sept–Nov
Ⓦ dimitriathess.gr
**Domus Festival, Náxos** July–early Sept Ⓦ naxos
festival.com
**Ioánnina Folk Festival** July
**Ippokrateia Festival, Kos** July
**Iráklion Festival** July–Aug
**Kalamáta Dance Festival** July Ⓦ kalamatadance
festival.gr
**Kassándhra Festival, Halkidhikí** (held jointly in Síviri and Áfytos) July–Aug Ⓦ festivalkassandras.com
**Lefkádha Arts and Folklore festivals** Aug
Ⓦ lefkasculturalcenter.gr

**Olympus Festival, Dhíon, Mt Olympus** July–Aug
Ⓦ festivalolympou.gr
**Pátra International Festival** July–Sept
**Pátra Film Festival** Oct Ⓦ independent.gr
**Philippi Festival, Thássos**
July–Aug Ⓦ philippifestival.gr
**Réthymnon Wine Festival** July Ⓦ rethymnowinefestival.gr
**Sáni Jazz Festival, Halkidhikí** July–Aug Ⓦ sanifestival.gr
**Sými Festival** July–Aug Ⓦ symifestival.com
**Thessaloníki International Film Festival** Nov
Ⓦ filmfestival.gr
**Thíra Music Festival** Aug–Sept
**Vólos Festival** Aug Ⓦ festivalvolos.gr

## DECEMBER

**December 6: Feast of St Nicholas** (Áyios Nikólaos) The patron
saint of seafarers, who has many chapels dedicated to him.

**December 25 & 26: Christmas** (Khristoúyenna) If less
all-encompassing than Greek Easter, Christmas is still an important religious
feast, one that increasingly comes with all the usual commercial trappings:
decorations, gifts and alarming outbreaks of plastic Santas on rooftops.

**December 31: New Year's Eve** (Paramoní Protohroniá) As on
the other twelve days of Christmas, a few children still go door-to-door
singing traditional carols, receiving money in return. Adults tend to sit
around playing cards, often for money. A special baked loaf, the
vassilópitta, in which a coin is concealed to bring its finder good luck
throughout the year, is cut at midnight.

# Sports and outdoor pursuits

**The Greek seashore offers endless scope
for watersports, from waterskiing and
parasailing to yachting and windsurfing.
On land, the greatest attraction lies in
hiking, through what is one of Europe's
more impressive mountain terrains.
Winter also sees possibilities for skiing at
a number of underrated centres. As for
spectator sports, the twin Greek obsessions are football (soccer) and basketball,
with volleyball a close third.**

## Watersports

**Windsurfing** is very popular around Greece: the
country's bays and coves are ideal for beginners, with
a few spectacularly windy spots for experts (see
above). Board rental rates are reasonable and instruction is generally also available. **Waterski** boats spend
most of their time towing people around on
bananas or other inflatables, though you usually can
waterski or wakeboard as well, while **parasailing**
(parapént in Greek) is also on offer at all the big
resorts. **Jet skis** can be rented in many resorts, too,
for a fifteen-minute burst of fuel-guzzling thrills.

A combination of steady winds, appealing
seascapes and numerous natural harbours has long
made Greece a tremendous place for **sailing**. All
sorts of bareboat and flotilla yacht trips are on offer
(see p.29), while dinghies, small cats and motor
boats can be rented at many resorts. For yachting,
spring and autumn are the most pleasant seasons;
meltémi winds can make for nauseous sailing in July
and August when you'll also find far higher prices

**SIX OF THE BEST
WINDSURFING SPOTS**
**Vassilikí** on Lefkádha island, p.732
**Sánta María,** Páros, p.407
**Prassoníssi,** Rhodes, p.528
**Kokkári,** Sámos, p.606
**Kouremenos,** eastern Crete, p.478
**Karathónas,** Peloponnese, p.141

and crowded moorings. The Cyclades suffer particularly badly from the meltémi, and are also relatively
short on facilities: better choices are to explore the
Sporades from Skiáthos; to set out from Athens for
the Argo-Saronic islands and north Peloponnese
coast; or to sail around Corfu and the Ionians,
though here winds can be very light.

Because of the potential for pilfering submerged
antiquities, **scuba diving** is still restricted, though
relaxation of the controls has led to a proliferation
of dive centres across the mainland, Dodecanese,
Ionians, Cyclades and Crete. There's not a huge
amount of aquatic life surviving around Greece's
over-fished shores, but you do get wonderfully
clear water, while the rocky coast offers plenty of
caves and hidden nooks to explore.

In the Peloponnese, central mainland and Epirus,
there's much potential for **rafting** and **kayaking**.

## Skiing

**Skiing** is a comparative newcomer to Greece,
beginning on Mount Parnassós in the 1950s. With
global warming, snow conditions are unpredictable
at the southernmost resorts, and runs remain
generally short. However, there are now eighteen
ski centres scattered about the mountains, and
what they may lack in professionalism is often
made up for by an easy-going, unpretentious
après-ski scene. The season generally lasts from the
beginning of January to the beginning of April, with
a few extra weeks possible at either end, depending
on snow conditions. No foreign package operators
currently feature Greece among their offerings – it's
very much a local, weekender scene.

The most developed of the resorts is Kelária-
Fterólakkas on **Parnassós**, the legendary mountain
near Delphi, though high winds often close the lifts.
Other major ski centres include **Vórras** (Mount
Kaïmaktsalán), near Édhessa; **Veloúhi** (Mount
Tymfristós), near Karpeníssi in central Greece;
**Helmós**, near Kalávryta on the Peloponnese; and
**Vérmion**, near Náoussa in Macedonia.

## Walking and cycling

If you have the time and stamina, **walking** is probably the single best way to see the remote backcountry, with plenty of options from gentle strolls to long-distance mountain paths. This guide includes some of the more accessible mountain hikes, as well as suggestions for more casual walking on the mainland and islands; there are also plenty of companies offering walking holidays (see p.28). In addition, you may want to acquire a countrywide or regional **hiking guidebook** (see p.806) and some detailed **maps** (p.52).

Cycling is less popular with Greeks, but in an increasing number of resorts you can hire **mountain bikes**, and many of the rental places lead organized rides, which again vary from easy explorations of the countryside to serious rides up proper mountains. Summer heat can be fierce, but spring and autumn offer great riding and walking conditions. Again, there are specialist companies offering cycling breaks in Greece (p.28).

## Football and basketball

**Football** (soccer) is far and away the most popular sport in Greece – both in terms of participating and watching, its status strengthened still further by Greece's unexpected emergence as Euro 2004 champions. The most important teams are Panathanaïkós (@ www.pao.gr) and AEK (@ aekfc.gr) of Athens, Olympiakós of Pireás (@ olympiacos.org) and PAOK of Thessaloníki (@ paokfc.gr). Matches – usually Wednesday nights and Sunday afternoons – take place between September and May, and tickets are generally not too hard to come by at prices far lower than in the UK.

The national **basketball** team is one of Europe's strongest, while at club level, many of the football teams maintain basketball squads – Panathanaïkós are the most consistently successful.

# Culture and etiquette

In many ways, Greece is a thoroughly integrated European country, and behaviour and social mores differ little from what you may be used to at home. Dig a little deeper, however, or travel to more remote, less touristed areas, and you'll find that traditional Greek ways survive to a gratifying degree. It's easy to accidentally give offence – but equally easy to avoid doing so by following a few simple tips, and to upgrade your status from that of tourist to xénos, a word that means both stranger and guest.

In general, Greeks are exceptionally friendly and curious, to an extent that can seem intrusive, certainly to a reserved Brit. Don't be surprised at being asked personal questions, even on short acquaintance, or having your personal space invaded. On the other hand, you're also likely to be invited to people's houses, often to meet a large extended family. Should you get such an invitation, you are not expected to be punctual – thirty minutes late is normal – and you should bring a small **gift**, usually flowers, or cakes from the local cake shop. If you're invited out to dinner, you can offer to **pay**, but it's very unlikely you'll be allowed to do so, and too much insistence could be construed as rude.

## Dress codes and cultural hints

Though **dress codes** on the beach are entirely informal, they're much less so away from the sea; most Greeks will dress up to go out, and not doing so is considered slovenly at the least. There are quite a number of **nudist** beaches in remote spots, with plenty of locals enjoying them, but on family beaches, or those close to town or near a church (of which there are many along the Greek coast), even toplessness is often frowned on. Most monasteries and to a lesser extent churches impose a fairly strict **dress code** for visitors: no shorts, with women expected to cover their arms and wear skirts (though most Greek women visitors will be in trousers); the necessary wraps are sometimes provided on the spot.

Two pieces of **body language** that can cause unintentional offence are hand gestures; don't hold your hand up, palm out, to anybody, and don't make an OK sign by forming a circle with your thumb and forefinger – both are extremely rude. Nodding and shaking your head for yes and no are also unlikely to be understood; Greeks use a slight forward inclination of the head for yes, a more vigorous backward nod for no.

## Bargaining and tipping

Most shops have fixed prices, so **bargaining** isn't a regular feature of tourist life. It is worth negotiating over rooms – especially off season – or for vehicle rental, especially for longer periods, but it's best not

# Travel essentials

to be aggressive about it; ask if they have a cheaper
room, for example, rather than demanding a lower
price. **Tipping** is not essential anywhere, though
taxi drivers generally expect it from tourists and
most service staff are very poorly paid. Restaurant
bills incorporate a service charge; if you want to tip,
rounding up the bill is usually sufficient.

**Smoking** also deserves a mention. Greeks are the
heaviest smokers in Europe, and although legally
you're not allowed to smoke indoors in restaurants,
bars or public offices, in practice the law is almost
universally disregarded. Effective no-smoking areas
are very rare indeed.

## Women and lone travellers

Thousands of **women** travel independently in
Greece without being harassed or feeling intimi-
dated. With the westernization of relationships
between unmarried Greek men and women, almost
all of the traditional Mediterranean macho impetus
for trying one's luck with foreign girls has faded.
Foreign women are more at risk of **sexual assault** at
certain notorious resorts (including Kávos in Corfu;
Laganás in Zákynthos; Faliráki in Rhodes) by
northern European men than by ill-intentioned
locals. It is sensible not to bar-crawl alone or to
accept late-night rides from strangers (**hitching** at
any time is not advisable for lone female travellers).
In more remote areas intensely traditional villagers
may wonder why women travelling alone are
unaccompanied, and may not welcome their
presence in exclusively male *kafenía*. Travelling with
a man, you're more likely to be treated as a *xéni*.

**Lone men** need to be wary of being invited into
bars in the largest mainland towns and island ports,
in particular near Sýndagma in Athens; these bars
are invariably staffed with hostesses (who may also
be prostitutes) persuading you to treat them to
drinks. At the end of the night you'll be landed with
an outrageous bill, some of which goes towards the
hostess's commission; physical threats are brought
to bear on reluctant payers.

## Costs

The **cost of living** in Greece has increased astronom-
ically since it joined the EU, particularly after the
adoption of the euro and further increases in the VAT
rate in 2011. Prices in shops and cafés now match or
exceed those of many other EU member countries
(including the UK). However, outside the chintzier
resorts, travel remains affordable, with the aggregate
cost of restaurant meals, short-term accommodation
and public transport falling somewhere in between
that of cheaper Spain or France and pricier Italy.

**Prices** depend on where and when you go.
Larger cities and the trendier tourist resorts and
small islands (such as Sými, Ýdhra, Mýkonos, Paxí
and Pátmos) are more expensive and costs everywhere increase sharply during July–August,
Christmas, New Year and Easter.

On most islands a daily per-person **budget** of
€50/£44/US$72 will get you basic accommodation
and meals, plus a short ferry or bus ride, as one of a
couple. Camping would cut costs marginally. On
€100/£88/US$144 a day you could be living quite
well, plus sharing the cost of renting a large
motorbike or small car. See p.36 for accommodation costs.

A basic taverna **meal** with bulk wine or a beer
costs around €12–20 per person. Add a better bottle
of wine, pricier fish or fancier decor and it could be
up to €20–30 a head; you'll rarely pay more than
that. Even in the most developed of resorts, with
inflated "international" menus, there is often a basic
but decent taverna where the locals eat.

## Crime and personal safety

Greece is one of Europe's safest countries, with a
low crime rate and a deserved reputation for
honesty. Most of the time if you leave a bag or
wallet at a café, you'll probably find it scrupulously
looked after, pending your return. Nonetheless
theft and muggings are becoming increasingly
common, a trend only likely to be increased by the
economic crisis. With this in mind, it's best to lock
rooms and cars securely, and to keep your
valuables hidden, especially in cities. Civil unrest,
in the form of strikes and demonstrations, is also
on the increase, but while this might inconven-
ience you, you'd be very unlucky to get caught up
in any trouble as a visitor.

Though the chances are you'll never meet a
member of the national **police force**, the Elliniki

Astynomia, Greek cops expect respect, and many have little regard for foreigners. If you do need to go to the police, always try to do so through the **Tourist Police** (❶171), who should speak English and are used to dealing with visitors. You are required to carry suitable ID on you at all times – either a passport or a driving licence.

The most common causes of a brush with the law are beach nudity, camping outside authorized sites, **public inebriation** or lewd behaviour. In 2009 a large British stag group dressed as nuns was arrested in Mália and held for several days, having managed to combine extreme drunkenness with a lack of respect for the church. Also avoid taking **photos in forbidden areas** such as airports (see p.54).

**Drug offences** are treated as major crimes, particularly since there's a mushrooming local addiction problem. The maximum penalty for "causing the use of drugs by someone under 18", for example, is life imprisonment and an astronomical fine. Foreigners caught in possession of even small amounts of marijuana get long jail sentences if there's evidence that they've been supplying the drug to others.

## Electricity

Voltage is 220 volts AC. Standard European two-pin plugs are used; adaptors should be purchased beforehand in the UK, as they can be difficult to find locally; standard 5-, 6- or 7.5-amp models permit operation of a hair dryer or travel iron. Unless they're dual voltage, North American appliances will require both a step-down transformer and a plug adaptor (the latter easy to find in Greece).

## Entrance fees

All the major **ancient sites**, like most **museums**, charge **entrance fees** ranging from €2 to €12, with an average fee of around €3. Entrance to all state-run sites and museums is **free** on Sundays and public holidays from November to March.

## Entry requirements

UK and all other EU nationals need only a valid **passport** to enter Greece. US, Australian, New Zealand, Canadian and most non-EU Europeans can stay, as tourists, for ninety days (cumulative) in any six-month period. Such nationals arriving by flight or boat from another EU state not party to the Schengen Agreement may not be stamped in routinely at minor Greek ports, so make sure this is done in order to avoid unpleasantness on exit. Your passport must be valid for three months after your arrival date.

Vsitors from **non-EU** countries are currently not, in practice, being given extensions to tourist visas. You must leave not just Greece but the entire Schengen Group and stay out until the maximum 90-days-in-180 rule, as set forth above, is satisfied. If you overstay your time and then leave under your own power – ie are not deported – you'll be hit with a huge fine upon departure, and possibly be banned from re-entering for a period of time; no excuses will be entertained except (just maybe) a doctor's certificate stating you were immobilized in hospital. It cannot be overemphasized just how exigent Greek immigration officials have become on this issue.

### Greek embassies abroad

**Australia** 9 Turrana St, Yarralumla, Canberra, ACT 2600 ❶ 02/6273 3011, ⓦ mfa.gr/sydney.
**Britain** 1A Holland Park, London W11 3TP ❶ 020/7221 6467, ⓦ mfa.gr/london
**Canada** 80 Maclaren St, Ottawa, ON K2P 0K6 ❶ 613/238-6271, ⓦ mfa.gr/ottawa
**Ireland** 1 Upper Pembroke St, Dublin 2 ❶ 01/676 7254, ⓦ mfa.gr/dublin
**New Zealand** 5–7 Willeston St, Wellington ❶ 04/473 7775, ⓦ mfa.gr/wellington
**South Africa** 1003 Church Street, 0028 Hatfield, Pretoria ❶ 012/434-7351, ⓦ mfa.gr/pretoria
**USA** 2217 Massachusetts Ave NW, Washington, DC 20008 ❶ 202/939-1300, ⓦ mfa.gr/washington

## DISCOUNTS

Full-time students are eligible for the **International Student ID Card** (ISIC; ⓦ www.isiccard.com), which entitles the bearer to cut-price transport and discounts at museums, theatres and other attractions, though often not accepted as valid proof of age. If you're not a student but aged under 26, you can qualify for the **International Youth Travel Card**, which provides similar benefits to the ISIC. Teachers qualify for the **International Teacher Identity Card** (ITIC), offering insurance benefits but limited travel discounts.

**Seniors** are entitled to a discount on bus passes in the major cities; Olympic Airways also offer discounts on full fares on domestic flights. Proof of age is necessary.

## ROUGH GUIDES TRAVEL INSURANCE

Rough Guides has teamed up with WorldNomads.com to offer great **travel insurance** deals. Policies are available to residents of over 150 countries, with cover for a wide range of adventure sports, 24hr emergency assistance, high levels of medical and evacuation cover and a stream of travel safety information. Roughguides.com users can take advantage of their policies online 24/7, from anywhere in the world – even if you're already travelling. And since plans often change when you're on the road, you can extend your policy and even claim online. Roughguides.com users who buy travel insurance with WorldNomads.com can also leave a positive footprint and donate to a community development project. For more information go to ⓦ roughguides.com/shop.

# Gay and lesbian travellers

Greece is deeply ambivalent about **homosexuality**: ghettoized as "to be expected" in the arts, theatre and music scenes but apt to be closeted elsewhere. "Out" gay Greeks are rare, and "out" local lesbians rarer still; foreign same-sex couples will be regarded in the provinces with some bemusement but accorded the standard courtesy as foreigners – as long as they refrain from public displays of affection, taboo in rural areas. There is a sizeable gay community in Athens, Thessaloníki and Pátra, plus a fairly obvious scene at resorts like Ýdhra, Rhodes and Mýkonos. Skála Eressoü on Lésvos, the birthplace of Sappho, is (appropriately) an international mecca for lesbians. Even in Athens, however, most gay nightlife is underground (often literally so in the siting of clubs), with no visible signage for nondescript premises.

# Insurance

Despite EU healthcare privileges applying in Greece (see p.43 for details), you should consider taking out an **insurance policy** before travelling to cover against theft, loss, illness or injury. Before paying for a whole new policy, however, it's worth checking whether you are already covered: some home insurance policies may cover your possessions when overseas, and many private medical schemes (such as BUPA or WPA in the UK) offer coverage extensions for abroad. **Students** will often find that their student health coverage extends during the vacations.

Make any claim as soon as possible. If you have medical treatment, keep all receipts for medicines and treatment. If you have anything stolen or lost, you must obtain an **official statement** from the police or the airline which lost your bags – with numerous claims being fraudulent, most insurers won't even consider one unless you have a police report.

# Internet

Rates at **internet cafés** tend to be about €2–4 per hour and any town or major resort will have at least one. Most hotels and an increasing number of cafés offer free wi-fi internet access to patrons.

# Laundry

**Laundries** or *Plindíria*, as they're known in Greek, are available in the main resort towns; sometimes an attended service wash is available for little or no extra charge over the basic cost of €8–10 per wash and dry. Self-catering villas will usually be furnished with a drying line and a selection of plastic wash-tubs or a bucket. Most hotels will charge for laundry services.

# Living in Greece

EU (and EEA) nationals are allowed to stay indefinitely in any EU state, but to ensure avoidance of any problems – eg, in setting up a bank account – you should, after the third month of stay, get a **certificate of registration** (*vevéosi engrafís*). Residence/work permits for **non-EU/non-EEA nationals** can only be obtained on application to a Greek embassy or consulate outside of Greece; you have a much better chance of securing one if you are married to a Greek, are of Greek background by birth or have permanent-resident status in another EU state.

As for **work**, non-EU nationals of Greek descent and EU/EEA native speakers of English (ie Brits and Irish) have a much better chance than anyone else. **Teaching English at a private language school** (*frontistírio*) is still a relatively well-paid option but almost impossible to get into these days without a bona fide TEFL certificate.

Many people find **tourism-related work**, especially on the islands most dominated by foreign visitors, April and May being the best time to look around. This is often as a rep for a package company,

## AVERAGE MONTHLY TEMPERATURES AND RAINFALL

| | Jan | Feb | Mar | Apr | May | Jun | Jul | Aug | Sept | Oct | Nov | Dec |
|---|---|---|---|---|---|---|---|---|---|---|---|---|
| **Athens** | | | | | | | | | | | | |
| Maximum (°C/°F) | 13/55 | 14/57 | 16/61 | 20/68 | 25/77 | 30/86 | 33/91 | 33/91 | 29/84 | 24/75 | 19/66 | 15/59 |
| Minimum (°C/°F) | 6/43 | 7/45 | 8/46 | 11/52 | 16/61 | 20/68 | 23/73 | 23/73 | 19/66 | 15/59 | 12/54 | 8/46 |
| Rainfall (mm) | 62 | 37 | 37 | 23 | 23 | 14 | 6 | 7 | 7 | 51 | 56 | 71 |
| **Thessaloníki** | | | | | | | | | | | | |
| Maximum (°C/°F) | 9/48 | 12/54 | 14/57 | 20/68 | 25/77 | 29/84 | 32/90 | 32/90 | 28/82 | 22/72 | 16/61 | 11/52 |
| Minimum (°C/°F) | 2/36 | 3/37 | 5/41 | 10/50 | 14/57 | 18/64 | 21/70 | 21/70 | 17/63 | 13/55 | 9/48 | 4/39 |
| Rainfall (mm) | 44 | 34 | 38 | 41 | 40 | 40 | 22 | 14 | 29 | 57 | 55 | 56 |
| **Crete (Iráklio)** | | | | | | | | | | | | |
| Maximum (°C/°F) | 16/62 | 16/62 | 17/63 | 20/68 | 23/73 | 27/81 | 29/84 | 29/84 | 27/81 | 24/75 | 21/70 | 18/64 |
| Minimum (°C/°F) | 9/48 | 9/48 | 10/50 | 12/54 | 15/59 | 19/66 | 22/72 | 22/72 | 19/66 | 17/63 | 14/57 | 11/52 |
| Rainfall (mm) | 95 | 46 | 43 | 26 | 13 | 3 | 1 | 1 | 11 | 64 | 71 | 79 |
| **Dodecanese (Rhodes)** | | | | | | | | | | | | |
| Maximum (°C/°F) | 15/59 | 16/62 | 17/63 | 21/70 | 25/77 | 30/86 | 32/90 | 33/91 | 29/84 | 25/77 | 21/70 | 17/63 |
| Minimum (°C/°F) | 7/45 | 8/46 | 9/48 | 12/54 | 15/59 | 19/66 | 21/70 | 22/72 | 19/66 | 15/59 | 12/54 | 9/48 |
| Rainfall (mm) | 201 | 101 | 92 | 23 | 21 | 1 | 1 | 0 | 15 | 75 | 114 | 205 |
| **Ionians (Corfu)** | | | | | | | | | | | | |
| Maximum (°C/°F) | 14/57 | 15/59 | 16/62 | 19/66 | 23/73 | 28/82 | 31/88 | 32/91 | 28/82 | 23/73 | 19/66 | 16/61 |
| Minimum (°C/°F) | 6/43 | 6/43 | 8/46 | 10/50 | 13/55 | 17/63 | 19/66 | 19/66 | 17/63 | 14/57 | 11/52 | 8/46 |
| Rainfall (mm) | 196 | 132 | 100 | 70 | 41 | 14 | 4 | 20 | 95 | 184 | 237 | 259 |

although they recruit the majority of staff from the home country; all you need is EU nationality and the appropriate language, though knowledge of Greek is a big plus. Jobs in bars or restaurants are a lot easier for women to come by than men. Another option if you have the requisite skills is to work for a **windsurfing** school or **scuba** operation.

## Mail

**Post offices** are open Monday to Friday from 7.30am to 2pm, though certain main branches are also open evenings and Saturday mornings. **Airmail letters** take 3–7 days to reach the rest of Europe, 5–12 days to North America, a little longer for Australia and New Zealand. Postal rates for up to 20g are a uniform €0.75 to all overseas destinations. For a modest fee (about €3) you can shave a day or two off delivery time to any destination by using the **express service** (*katepígonda*). **Registered** (*systiméno*) delivery is also available for a similar amount but is slow unless coupled with express service. Stamps (*grammatósima*) are widely available at newsagents and other tourist shops.

**Parcels** should (and often can) only be handled in the main provincial or county capitals. For non-EU/EEA destinations, always present your box open for inspection, and come prepared with tape and scissors.

Ordinary **post boxes** are bright yellow, express boxes dark red, but it's best to use those adjacent to an actual post office, since days may pass between collections at boxes elsewhere.

## Maps

The most reliable **general touring maps** of Greece are those published by Athens-based Anavasi (Wanavasi.gr), Road Editions (Wroad.gr) and newcomer Orama (Wnakas-maps.gr). Anavasi and Road Editions products are widely available in Greece at selected bookshops, as well as at petrol stations and general tourist shops countrywide. In Britain they are found at Stanfords (☎020/7836 1321, Wstanfords.co.uk) and the Hellenic Book Service (☎020/7267 9499, Whellenicbookservice .com); in the US, they're sold through Omni Resources (☎910/227-8300, Womnimap.com).

**Hiking/topographical maps** are gradually improving in quality and availability. Road Editions, in addition to their touring maps, produce 1:50,000 topographical maps for mainland mountain ranges, including Áthos, Pílio, Parnassós, Ólymbos, Taiyettos, Ágrafa and Íti, usually with rudimentary route directions in English. Anavasi publishes a series covering the mountains of central Greece (including Ólymbos and Epirus, some on the Peloponnese, the White Mountains and Psiloritis on Crete and Mt Dhýrfis on

Évvia. The map-and-guide booklets published by Marengo Publications (☎01485/532710, ⓦmarengo walks.com) in England also prove very useful for areas including Crete, Corfu, Kálymnos, Lésvos, Messinía, Párga, the Pelion, Sámos, Sými and Thássos.

# Money

Greece's currency is the **euro** (€). Up-to-date **exchange rates** can be found on ⓦxe.com. Euro notes exist in denominations of 5, 10, 20, 50, 100, 200 and 500 euros, and coins in denominations of 1, 2, 5, 10, 20 and 50 cents and 1 and 2 euros. Avoid getting stuck with **counterfeit euro notes** (€100 and €200 ones abound). The best tests are done by the naked eye: genuine notes all have a hologram strip or (if over €50) patch at one end, there's a watermark at the other, plus a security thread embedded in the middle. If you end up with a fake note, you'll have no recourse to a refund. Note that shopkeepers do not bother much with shortfalls of 10 cents or less, whether in their favour (especially) or yours.

## Banks and exchange

Greek **banks** normally open Monday to Thursday 8.30am–2.30pm and Friday 8.30am–2pm. Always take your passport with you as proof of identity and expect long queues. Large hotels and some travel agencies also provide an exchange service, though with hefty commissions. On small islands with no full-service bank, "authorized" bank agents will charge an additional fee for posting a travellers' cheque to a proper branch.

A number of authorized brokers for exchanging foreign cash have emerged in Athens and other major tourist centres. When changing small amounts, choose those bureaux that charge a flat percentage commission (usually 1 percent) rather than a high minimum. There is a small number of 24-hour automatic **foreign-note-changing machines**, but a high minimum commission tends to be deducted. There is no need to **purchase euros** beforehand unless you're arriving at some ungodly hour to one of the remoter frontier posts. **Travellers' cheques** (best in euros rather than dollars) can be cashed at most banks, though rarely elsewhere. Cashing the cheques will incur a minimum charge of €1.20–2.40 depending on the bank; for larger amounts, a set percentage will apply.

## ATMs and credit cards

**Debit cards** have become the most common means of accessing funds while travelling, by withdrawing money from the vast network of Greek

**ATMs**. Larger airports have at least one ATM in the arrivals hall and any town or island with a population larger than a few thousand (or substantial tourist traffic) also has them. Most accept Visa, MasterCard, Visa Electron, Plus and Cirrus cards; American Express holders are restricted to the ATMs of Alpha and National Bank. There is usually a charge of 2.25 percent on the sterling/dollar transaction value, plus a commission fee of a similar amount. Using **credit cards** at an ATM costs roughly the same; however, inflated interest accrues from the moment of use.

Major credit cards are not usually accepted by cheaper tavernas or hotels but they can be essential for renting cars. Major travel agents may also accept them, though a **three-percent surcharge** is often levied on the purchase of ferry tickets.

# Opening hours and public holidays

It's difficult to generalize about Greek **opening hours**, which are notoriously erratic. Most shops open 8.30/9am and close for a long break at 2/2.30pm. Most places, except banks, reopen around 5.30/6pm for three hours or so, at least on Tuesday, Thursday and Friday. Tourist areas tend to adopt a more northern European timetable, with supermarkets and travel agencies, as well as the most important archeological sites and museums, more likely to stay open throughout the day. If you find yourself needing to tackle **Greek bureaucracy**, you can't count on getting anything essential done except from Monday to Friday, between 9.30am and 1pm.

As far as possible, times are quoted in the text for **tourist sites** but these change with exasperating

---

## PUBLIC HOLIDAYS

**January 1:** New Year's Day.
**January 6:** Epiphany.
**February/March:** Clean Monday (*katharí dheftéra*), 7 weeks before Easter.
**March 25:** Independence Day.
**April/May:** Good Friday and Easter Monday (see p.45 for dates).
**May 1:** May Day.
**May/June:** Whit Monday, 7 weeks after Easter.
**August 15:** Assumption of the Virgin Mary.
**October 28:** Ohi Day (see p.46).
**December 25/26:** Christmas Day/ Boxing Day.

frequency, especially since the economic crisis. Both winter and summer hours are quoted throughout the guide but to avoid disappointment, either phone ahead or time your visit during the core hours of 9am–2pm. **Monasteries** are generally open from approximately 9am to 1pm and 5 to 8pm (3.30–6.30pm in winter) for limited visits.

## Phones

Three **mobile phone networks** operate in Greece: Vodafone-Panafon, Cosmote and Q-Telecom/WIND Hellas. **Coverage** countrywide is good, though there are a few "dead" zones in the mountains, or on really remote islets. Contract-free plans are heavily promoted in Greece, so if you're here for more than a week or so, buying a **pay-as-you-go** SIM card (for €15–20) from any of the mobile phone outlets will pay for itself very quickly. Top-up cards – starting from €8–10 – are available at all *períptera* (kiosks). Roaming charges within the EU are capped at €0.51 equivalent per minute (or €0.26 to receive calls). North American users will only be able to use tri-band phones in Greece.

Land lines and public phones are run by OTE who provide phone cards (*tilekártes*), available in denominations starting at €4, from kiosks and newsagents. If you plan on making lots of international calls, you'll want a **calling card**, all of which involve

calling a free access number from either certain phone boxes or a fixed line (not a mobile) and then entering a twelve-digit code. OTE has its own scheme, but competitors generally prove cheaper. Avoid making calls direct **from hotel rooms**, as a large surcharge will be applied, though you will not be charged to access a free calling card number.

## Photography

You can feel free to snap away pretty much anywhere in Greece, although some **churches** display "No photography" signs, and museums and archeological sites may require **permits** at least for professional photographers. The main exception is around **airports** or **military installations** (usually clearly indicated with a "No pictures" sign). The ordeal of twelve British plane-spotters who processed slowly through Greek jails and courts in 2001–2 on espionage charges should be ample incentive.

## Time

Standard Greek time is always two hours ahead of GMT. For North America, the difference is usually seven hours for Eastern Standard Time, ten hours for Pacific Standard Time. **Greek summer time** begins at 2am on the last Sunday in March, when the clocks go forward one hour, and ends at 2am

---

### PHONE CODES AND NUMBERS

All Greek phone numbers require dialling of all ten digits, including the area code. Land lines begin with 2; mobiles begin with 6. All land-line exchanges are digital, and you should have few problems reaching any number from either overseas or within Greece. Mobile phone users are well looked after, with a signal even in the Athens metro.

#### PHONING GREECE FROM ABROAD
Dial ☎0030 + the full number

#### PHONING ABROAD FROM GREECE
Dial the country code (below) + area code (minus any initial 0) + number

| | | | |
|---|---|---|---|
| Australia | ☎0061 | UK | ☎0044 |
| New Zealand | ☎0064 | Ireland | ☎00353 |
| Canada | ☎001 | USA | ☎001 |
| South Africa | ☎0027 | | |

#### GREEK PHONE PREFIXES
| | | | |
|---|---|---|---|
| Local call rate | ☎0801 | Toll-free/Freefone | ☎0800 |

#### USEFUL GREEK TELEPHONE NUMBERS
| | | | |
|---|---|---|---|
| Ambulance | ☎166 | Police/Emergency | ☎100 |
| Fire brigade, urban | ☎199 | Speaking clock | ☎141 |
| Forest fire reporting | ☎191 | Tourist police | ☎171 (Athens); |
| Operator (Domestic) | ☎132 | | ☎210 171 (elsewhere) |
| Operator (International) | ☎139 | | |

the last Sunday in October when they go back. This change is not well publicized locally, and visitors miss planes and ferries every year.

## Toilets

Public toilets are usually in parks or squares, often subterranean; otherwise try a bus station. Except in tourist areas, public toilets tend to be filthy – it's best to use those in restaurants and bars. Remember that throughout Greece, you drop paper in the adjacent wastebins, not the toilet bowl.

## Tourist information

The **National Tourist Organization of Greece** (Ellinikós Organismós Tourismoú, or EOT; Visit Greece abroad, Ⓦ visitgreece.gr) maintains offices in most European capitals, plus major cities in North America and Australia (see below). It publishes an array of free, glossy, regional pamphlets, invariably several years out of date, fine for getting a picture of where you want to go, though low on useful facts.

In Greece, you will find official **EOT offices** in many but by no means all of the larger towns and islands where, in addition to the usual leaflets, you can find weekly **schedules** for the inter-island **ferries** – rarely entirely accurate, but useful as a guideline. EOT staff may be able to advise on **bus** and **train** departures as well as current opening hours for local sites and museums and occasionally can assist with accommodation.

Where there is no EOT office, you can get information from municipally run tourist offices – these can be more highly motivated and helpful than EOT branches. In the absence of any of these, you can visit the **Tourist Police**, essentially a division (often just a single room) of the local police. They can sometimes provide you with lists of rooms to let, which they regulate, but they're really the place to go if you have a **serious complaint** about a taxi, or an accommodation or eating establishment.

### Greek national tourist offices abroad

**Australia & New Zealand** 51 Pitt St, Sydney, NSW 2000 ☏ 02/9241 1663, ✉ hto@tpg.com.au.
**UK** 4 Conduit St, London W1R 0DJ ☏ 020/7495 4300, ✉ info@ gnto.co.uk.
**USA** 305 E 47th St, New York, NY 10017 ☏ 212/421-5777, ✉ info@greektourism.com.

## Travellers with disabilities

In general the **disabled** are not especially well catered for in Greece, though, as relevant EU-wide legislation is implemented, the situation is gradually improving. In cities, wheelchair ramps and beeps for the sight-impaired are rare at pedestrian crossings, and outside Athens few buses are of the "kneeling" type. Only Athens airport, its metro and airline staff in general (who are used to handling wheelchairs) are disabled-friendly. Ancient monuments, one of the country's main attractions, are usually inaccessible or hazardous for anyone with mobility impairments.

Some advance planning will make a stress-free holiday in Greece more likely. The Greek National Tourist Office is helpful; they also publish a useful questionnaire that you might send to hotels or self-catering accommodation. Before purchasing **travel insurance**, ensure that pre-existing medical conditions are not excluded. A **medical certificate** of your fitness to travel is also extremely useful; some airlines or insurance companies may insist on it.

## Travelling with children

**Children** are worshipped and indulged in Greece, and present few problems when travelling. They are not segregated from adults at meal times, and early on in life are inducted into the typical late-night routine – kids at tavernas are expected to eat (and up to their capabilities, talk) like adults. Outside of certain all-inclusive resorts with children's programmes, however, there are very few amusements specifically for them – certainly nothing like Disney World Paris. Water parks, tourist sites and other places of interest that are particularly child-friendly are noted throughout the guide.

Luxury hotels are more likely to offer some kind of **babysitting or crèche service**. All the same basic baby products that you can find at home are available in Greece, though some may be more expensive, so it can pay to load up on nappies, powders and creams before leaving home.

Most domestic ferry-boat companies and airlines offer child **discounts**, ranging from fifty to one hundred percent depending on their age; hotels and rooms won't charge extra for infants, and levy a modest supplement for "third" beds which the child occupies by him/herself.

# Athens and around

65  The Acropolis

74  Pláka

77  Monastiráki and Psyrrí

79  Sýndagma

82  Omónia and the bazaar

83  North of the centre

86  Western Athens

89  Kolonáki and the
    museum quarter

91  Southern Athens

92  Pireás

114 Around Athens: Attica

THE PARTHENON

# 1

# Athens and around

For all too many people, ATHENS is a city that happened two-and-a-half thousand years ago. It's true that even now the past looms large – literally, in the shape of the mighty Acropolis that dominates almost every view, as well as on every visitor's itinerary. Yet the modern city is home to over four million people – more than a third of the Greek nation's population – and has undergone a transformation in the twenty-first century.

On first acquaintance, Athens is not a beautiful place – the scramble for growth in the decades after World War II, when the population grew from around 700,000 to close to its present level, was an architectural disaster. But, helped by huge investment for the 2004 Olympics, the city is starting to make the most of what it has, with new roads, rail and metro, along with extensive pedestrianization in the centre. The views for which Athens was once famous have reappeared and, despite inevitable globalization and the appearance of all the usual high-street and fast-food chains, the city retains its character to a remarkable degree. Hectic modernity is always tempered with an air of intimacy and hominess; as any Greek will tell you, Athens is merely the largest village in the country.

However often you've visited, the vestiges of the ancient Classical Greek city, most famously represented by the **Parthenon** and other remains that top the **Acropolis**, are an inevitable focus; along with the refurbished **National Archeological Museum**, the finest collection of Greek antiquities anywhere in the world, they should certainly be a priority. The majority of the several million visitors who pass through each year do little more; they never manage to escape the crowds and so see little of the Athens Athenians know. Take the time to explore some of the city's **neighbourhoods**, and you'll get far more out of it.

Above all, there's the sheer vibrancy of the city. **Cafés** are packed day and night and the streets stay lively until 3 or 4am, with some of the best **bars and clubs** in the country. **Eating out** is great, with establishments ranging from traditional tavernas to gourmet restaurants. In summer, much of the action takes place outdoors, from dining on the street or clubbing on the beach, to **open-air cinema**, **concerts** and **classical drama**. There's a diverse **shopping** scene, too, ranging from colourful bazaars and lively street markets to chic suburban malls crammed with the latest designer goods. And with good-value, extensive public transportation allied to inexpensive taxis, you'll have no difficulty getting around.

Outside Athens are more Classical sites – the **Temple of Poseidon at Soúnio**, sanctuaries at **Ramnous** and **Eleusis** (Elefsína), the burial mound from the great victory at **Marathon** – and there are also easily accessible **beaches** all around the coast. Further afield, **Delphi** (p.204) and the **islands** of the Saronic gulf (Chapter 5) are also in easy day-trip distance. Moving on is quick and easy, with scores of **ferries** and hydrofoils leaving daily from the port at **Pireás** (Piraeus) and, somewhat less frequently, from the two other Attic ferry terminals at **Rafína** and **Lávrio**.

The Athenian Golden Age p.63
The Olympic legacy p.64
A brief history of the Acropolis p.65
The Elgin Marbles p.70
A slice of old Athens: Anafiótika p.75
Roman Athens p.76
November 17: the student uprising p.83

A city with a view p.89
City beaches p.92
Ethnic eats p.101
The Athens and Epidaurus Festival p.110
Bazaars and markets p.112
Pay beaches p.116
The Mysteries of Eleusis p.120

CAFÉ LIFE, THISSÍO

# Highlights

**① The Acropolis** Rising above the city, the great rock of the Acropolis symbolizes not just Athens, but the birth of European civilization. **See p.65**

**② Pláka** Wander the narrow alleys and steep steps of this architecturally fascinating and vibrant quarter. **See p.74**

**③ Tower of the Winds** Intriguing and elegant, this ancient clock tower is well worth seeking out. **See p.76**

**④ The bazaar** Athens' raucous and colourful market area, spilling out into the streets all around the nineteenth-century covered food hall. **See p.82**

**⑤ National Archeological Museum** The world's finest collection of ancient Greek art and sculpture. **See p.84**

**⑥ Psyrrí** The heart of Athens' nightlife, packed with bars, cafés and restaurants that are buzzing till late at night. **See p.77**

**⑦ Café life** Much of Athens' life is lived outdoors; check out the buzzing cafés of Thissío as the setting sun illuminates the Parthenon. **See p.86**

**⑧ Temple of Poseidon, Cape Soúnio** Dramatic and evocative, this sanctuary to the sea god has been a shipping landmark for centuries. **See p.117**

HIGHLIGHTS ARE MARKED ON THE MAP ON P.60–61 & P.115

## TRADITIONAL MUSIC
| | |
|---|---|
| Boemissa | 3 |

## ROCK, JAZZ & LATIN
| | |
|---|---|
| After Dark | 6 |
| Cafe Alavastron | 20 |
| An Live Club | 2 |
| Gagarin 205 | 1 |
| Half-Note | 21 |
| In Vivo | 5 |
| Kookoo Live Music Bar | 17 |
| Stavros tou Notou | 22 |

## DANCE & CLASSICAL MUSIC
| | |
|---|---|
| Dora Stratou Theatre | 19 |
| Mégaro Mousikís | 8 |

## BARS & CLUBS
| | |
|---|---|
| 45° | 16 |
| Bios | 13 |
| Candy Bar | 10 |
| Frame Garden | 14 |
| Micra Asia | 12 |
| Roi Mat Rock Club | 2 |
| Socialista | 18 |
| Soho | 15 |
| Underground | 4 |

## GAY & LESBIAN VENUES
| | |
|---|---|
| Blue Train | 7 |
| Noiz | 9 |
| Sodade | 11 |

## ACCOMMODATION
| | |
|---|---|
| Hostel Aphrodite | 1 |
| Art Gallery | 11 |
| Art Hotel | 3 |
| Athens International Youth Hostel | 5 |
| Athens Studios | 10 |
| Delphi Art Hotel | 7 |
| Exarchion | 6 |
| Marble House | 13 |
| Museum | 2 |
| Orion and Dryades | 4 |
| Pagration Athens Youth Hostel | 12 |
| Periscope | 9 |
| St George Lycabettus | 8 |

## HIGHLIGHTS
1. The Acropolis
2. Pláka
3. Tower of the Winds
4. The Bazaar
5. National Archeological Museum
6. Psyrrí
7. Café Life: Thissío

## CAFÉS
| | |
|---|---|
| Café Creperie Au Grand Zinc | 7 |
| Floral Books and Cafe | 3 |

0     200
metres

# ATHENS

## ● SHOPS

| | |
|---|---|
| Crop Circle | 4/5 |
| Elena Votsi | 9 |
| Ikologi Elladas | 7 |
| Music Machine Records | 6 |
| Oino Typo | 3 |
| Solaris | 2 |
| Thallo | 8 |
| To Thymari tou Strefi | 1 |
| Tsatsos | 10 |

Pedhío tou Áreos
(Pedhío Áreos Park)

BOÚGOU

ÁREOS

Lófos tou Stréfi
(Stréfis Hill)

LEOFÓROS ALEXÁNDRAS

Panathinaïkós
Stadium

NEÁPOLI

IPPOKRÁTOUS

Lykavitós
Theatre

Lykavitós
Hill

Áyios
Nikólaos

Christ
Church

Áyios
Yeóryios

US Embassy

Mégaro
Mousikís

National
Library

Akadhimía

Funicular
Railway

Naval
Hospital

Aléxandras
Hospital

nepistímio

Academy
of Science

Áyios
Dionýsios

Museum of
Greek Costume

Friday
Market

Yennádhion
Library

Mégaro Moussikís

Aretaíaion
Hospital

Hospital

Numismatic
Museum

British
Archeological
Society

Evangelismós
Hospital

Attica

KOLONÁKI

ÍLISIA

NDAGMA

Hótel Grande
Bretagne

Benáki
Museum

British
Council

Cycladic Art
Museum

War
Museum

Evangelismós

Hilton
Hotel

Ilissía
Park

ILEOS YEORYÍOU

VASILÍSSIS SOFÍAS

National Gallery
of Art & Aléxandros
Soútzos Museum

Syndagma

Voulí
(Parliament
Building)

Evzones
Barracks

VASILÍSSIS SOFÍAS

Syndagma

Tomb of the
Unknown
Soldier

Roman
Mosaic

Byzantine &
Christian
Museum

MIHALAKOPOÚLOU

wish
seum

Botanical
Museum

Mégaro
Maximoú

Athens
Conservatory

Anglican Church

National
Gardens

Presidential
Palace

Roman
Baths

Folk
useum

Záppio

Temple of
Olympian Zeus

Záppeion
Gardens

Pangráti
Park

Panathenaic
Stadium

Ardhittós
Hill

METS

PANGRÁTI

Street
Market (Fri)

Próto Nekrotafío
(First Cemetery)

## ● RESTAURANTS

| | |
|---|---|
| Ambrosia | 25 |
| Andreas | 11 |
| Arkhaíon Yéfsis | 4 |
| Balsamakis (To Kotopoulo) | 17 |
| Barba Yannis | 6 |
| Barbara's Food Company | 8 |
| Butcher Shop | 16 |
| Chez Lucien | 20 |
| Filíppou | 13 |
| Gazohori | 14 |
| Ikio | 15 |
| Ikonomou | 21 |
| Karavitis | 19 |
| Katsourbos | 18 |
| Lefka | 2 |
| Meson el Mirador | 12 |
| Mikri Vouli | 23 |
| Mystic Pizza | 9 |
| Pinaleon | 1 |
| Rozalia | 5 |
| Spondi | 24 |
| Vyrinis | 22 |
| Yiandes | 10 |

**1**

## Brief history

Athens has been inhabited continuously for over seven thousand years. Its acropolis, commanding views of all seaward approaches and encircled by protective mountains, was a natural choice for prehistoric settlement and for the **Mycenaeans**, who established a palace-fortress on the rock. Gradually, Athens emerged as a city-state that dominated the region, ruled by kings who stood at the head of a land-owning aristocracy known as the *Eupatridae* (the "well-born"), who governed through a Council which met on the Areopagus – the Hill of Ares.

### The birth of democracy

As Athens grew wealthier, dissatisfaction with the rule of the *Eupatridae* grew, above all among a new middle class excluded from political life but forced to pay rent or taxes to the nobility. Among the reforms aimed at addressing this were new, fairer laws drawn up by **Draco** (whose "draconian" lawcode was published in 621 BC), and the appointment of **Solon** as ruler (594 BC), with a mandate to introduce sweeping economic and political reform. Although Solon's reforms laid the foundations of what eventually became Athenian democracy, they failed to stop internal unrest, and eventually **Peisistratos**, his cousin, seized power in the middle of the sixth century BC. Peisistratos is usually called a tyrant, but this simply means he seized power by force: thanks to his populist policies he was in fact a well-liked and successful ruler who greatly expanded Athens' power, wealth and influence.

His sons **Hippias and Hipparchus** were less successful: Hipparchus was assassinated in 514 BC and Hippias overthrown in 510 BC. A new leader, **Kleisthenes**, took the opportunity for more radical change: he introduced ten classes or tribes based on place of residence, each of which elected fifty members to the *Boule* or Council of State, which decided on issues to be discussed by the full Assembly. The Assembly was open to all citizens and was both a legislature and a supreme court. This system was the basis of **Athenian democracy** and remained in place, little changed, right through to Roman times.

Around 500 BC Athens sent troops to aid the Ionian Greeks of Asia Minor, who were rebelling against the Persian Empire; this in turn provoked a Persian invasion of Greece. In 490 BC the Athenians and their allies defeated a far larger Persian force at the **Battle of Marathon**. In 480 BC the Persians returned, capturing and sacking Athens, and leaving much of the city burned to the ground. That same year, however, a naval triumph at **Salamis** sealed victory over the Persians, and also secured Athens' position as Greece's leading city-state.

### The rise and fall of Classical Athens

Perhaps the most startling aspect of Classical Athens is how suddenly it emerged to the glory for which we remember it – and how short its heyday proved to be. In the middle of the **fifth century BC**, Athens was little more than a country town in its street layout and buildings – a scattered jumble of single-storey houses or wattle huts, intersected by narrow lanes. On the Acropolis, a site reserved for the city's most sacred monuments, stood only the blackened ruins of temples and sanctuaries.

There was little to suggest that the city was entering a unique phase of its history in terms of power, prestige and creativity. But following the victory over the Persians at Salamis, Athens stood unchallenged for a generation. It grew rich on the export of olive oil and silver from the mines of Attica, but above all it benefited from its control of the **Delian League**, an alliance of Greek city-states formed as insurance against Persian resurgence. The Athenians relocated the League's treasury from the island of Delos to their own acropolis, ostensibly on the grounds of safety, and with its revenues their leader **Pericles** (see p.767) was able to create the so-called **Golden Age** of the city. Great endowments were made for monumental construction, arts in all spheres were promoted, and – most significantly – it was all achieved under stable, **democratic rule**.

The Delian League's wealth enabled office-holders to be properly paid, thereby making it possible for the poor to play a part in government.

The fatal mistake of the Athenian democracy, however, was allowing itself to be drawn into the **Peloponnesian War** (see p.767). Defeated, a demoralized Athens succumbed to a brief period of oligarchy, though it later recovered sufficiently to enter a new phase of democracy, the **age of Plato**. However, in 338 BC, Athens was again called to defend the Greek city-states, this time against the incursions of **Philip of Macedon**. Demosthenes, said to be as powerful an orator as Pericles, spurred the Athenians to fight, in alliance with the Thebans, at Chaeronea. There they were routed, in large part by the cavalry commanded by Philip's son, Alexander (later to become known as Alexander the Great), and Athens fell under the control of the Macedonian empire.

The city continued to be favoured, particularly by **Alexander the Great**, a former pupil of Aristotle, who respected both Athenian culture and its democratic institutions. Following his death, however, came a more uncertain era, which saw periods of independence and Macedonian rule, until 146 BC when the **Romans** (see box, p.76)swept through southern Greece and it was incorporated into the Roman province of Macedonia.

### Christians and Turks

The emergence of **Christianity** was perhaps the most significant step in Athens' long decline from the glories of its Classical heyday. Having survived with little change through years of Roman rule, the city lost its pivotal role in the Roman–Greek world after the division of the Roman Empire into Eastern and Western halves, and the establishment of Byzantium (Constantinople, now Istanbul) as capital of the Eastern – **Byzantine** – empire. In 529 AD the city's temples, including the Parthenon, were reconsecrated as churches.

Athens rarely featured in the chronicles of the Middle Ages, passing through the hands of various foreign powers before the arrival in 1456 of **Sultan Mehmet II**, the Turkish conqueror of Constantinople. **Turkish Athens** was never much more than a garrison town, occasionally (and much to the detriment of its Classical buildings) on the front line of battles with the Venetians and other Western powers. Although the Acropolis became the home of the Turkish governor and the Parthenon was used as a mosque, life in the village-like quarters around the Acropolis drifted back to a semi-rural existence.

---

### THE ATHENIAN GOLDEN AGE

Under the democratic reforms of Pericles, a new and exalted notion of the **Athenian citizen** emerged. This was a man who could shoulder political responsibility while also playing a part in the **cultural and religious events** of the time. The latter assumed ever-increasing importance. The city's Panathenaic festival, honouring the goddess Athena, was upgraded along the lines of the Olympic Games to include drama, music and athletic contests. The next five decades were to witness a **golden age** of cultural development during which the great dramatic works of Aeschylus, Sophocles and Euripides, and the comedies of Aristophanes were written. Foreigners such as Herodotus, considered the inventor of history, and Anaxagoras, the philosopher, were drawn to live in the city. Thucydides wrote *The Peloponnesian War*, a pioneering work of documentation and analysis, while Socrates posed the problems of philosophy that were to exercise his follower Plato and to shape the discipline to the present day.

But it was the great civic **building programme** that became the most visible and powerful symbol of the age. Under the patronage of Pericles, the architects Iktinos, Mnesikles and Kallikrates, along with the sculptor Fidias, transformed the city. Their buildings included the Parthenon and Erechtheion on the Acropolis; the Hephaisteion and several *stoas* (arcades) around the Agora; a new *odeion* (theatre) on the South Slope of the Acropolis hill; and, outside the city, the temples at Soúnio and Ramnous.

1

## THE OLYMPIC LEGACY

The **2004 Olympics** can take much of the credit for getting Athens back on the map and regenerating the city's infrastructure. Successful as they were in many ways, however, the legacy of the Games is a bitter one. In the rush to be ready on time many of the works went disastrously over budget, while inadequate planning means that few of the costly stadia have found any purpose in life since the Games finished. These decaying white elephants are a potent symbol of Greece's economic crisis and of the crazed rush to spend money that, ultimately, Greece never had.

Four centuries of Ottoman occupation followed until, in 1821, the Greeks of Athens rose and joined the **rebellion sweeping the country**. They occupied the Turkish quarters of the lower town – the current Pláka – and laid siege to the Acropolis. The Turks withdrew, but five years later were back to reoccupy the Acropolis fortifications, while the Greeks evacuated to the countryside. When the Ottoman garrison finally left in 1834, and the Bavarian architects of the new German-born monarch moved in, Athens, with a population of only 5000, was at its nadir.

### Modern Athens

Athens was not the first-choice **capital** of modern Greece: that honour went instead to Náfplio in the Peloponnese. In 1834, though, the new king Otto transferred the capital and court to Athens. The reasoning was almost purely symbolic: Athens was not only insignificant in terms of population and physical extent but was then at the edge of the territories of the new Greek state. Soon, while the archeologists stripped away all the Turkish and Frankish embellishments from the Acropolis, a city began to take shape: the grand Neoclassical plan was for processional avenues radiating out from great squares, a plan that can still be made out on maps but has long ago been subverted by the realities of daily life. **Pireás**, meanwhile, grew into a significant port again.

The first mass expansion of both municipalities came suddenly, in 1923, as the result of the tragic Greek–Turkish war in **Asia Minor** (see p.778). A million and a half "Greek" Christians arrived in Greece as refugees, and over half of them settled in Athens and Pireás, changing at a stroke the whole make-up of the capital. Their integration and survival is one of the great events of the city's history.

Athens was hit hard by German occupation in World War II: during the winter of 1941–42 there were an estimated two thousand deaths from starvation each day. In late 1944, when the Germans finally left, the capital saw the first skirmishes of **civil war**, and from 1946 to 1949 Athens was a virtual island, with road approaches to the Peloponnese and the north only tenuously kept open.

During the 1950s, the city again started to expand rapidly thanks to the growth of industry and massive **immigration** from the war-torn, impoverished countryside. By the late 1960s, Greater Athens covered a continuous area from the slopes of mounts Pendéli and Párnitha down to Pireás. Much of this development is unremittingly ugly, since old buildings were demolished wholesale in the name of a quick buck, particularly during the colonels' junta of 1967–74 (see p.782). Financial incentives encouraged homeowners to demolish their houses and replace them with apartment blocks up to six storeys high; almost everyone took advantage, and as a result most central streets seem like narrow canyons between these ugly, concrete blocks. Unrestrained industrial development on the outskirts was equally rampant.

Growth in recent decades has been much slower, but it's only in the last twenty years that much effort has gone in to improving the city's environment. Although Athens still lags far behind Paris or London in terms of open space, the evidence of recent efforts is apparent. What's left of the city's architectural heritage has been extensively restored; there's clean public transportation; new building is controlled and there's some interesting, radical modern architecture.

# The Acropolis

**1**

The **rock of the Acropolis**, crowned by the dramatic ruins of the **Parthenon**, is one of the archetypal images of Western culture. The first time you see it, rising above the traffic or from a distant hill, is extraordinary: foreign, and yet utterly familiar. As in other Greek cities the Acropolis itself is simply the highest point of the city, and this steep-sided, flat-topped crag of limestone, rising abruptly 100m from its surroundings, has made it the focus of Athens during every phase of its development. Easily defensible and with plentiful water, its initial attractions are obvious. Even now, with no function apart from tourism, it is the undeniable heart of the city, around which everything else clusters, glimpsed at almost every turn.

You can walk an entire circuit of the Acropolis and ancient Agora on **pedestrianized streets**, allowing them to be appreciated from almost every angle: in particular, the pedestrianization has provided spectacular terraces for cafés to the west, in Thissío. On the other side, in Pláka, you may get a little lost among the jumble of alleys, but the rock itself is always there to guide you.

## ARRIVAL AND INFORMATION

**Tickets** A joint ticket covers the Acropolis, Ancient Agora and South Slope, plus the Roman Forum, Hadrian's Library, Kerameikos and Temple of Olympian Zeus. The smaller sites also offer individual tickets, but only the joint one is valid for the summit of the Acropolis, so if you visit any of the others first, be sure to buy the multiple ticket or you simply end up paying twice. The ticket can be used over four days.

**Getting there** To avoid the worst of the crowds come very early in the day, or late. The peak rush comes in late morning, when coach tours congregate before moving on to lunch elsewhere. The summit can be entered only from the west, where there's a big coach park at the bottom of the hill: bus #230 from Sýndagma will take you almost to the entrance. On foot, the obvious approach is from Metro

## A BRIEF HISTORY OF THE ACROPOLIS

The Acropolis was home to one of the earliest known settlements in Greece, as early as 5000 BC. In **Mycenaean** times – around 1500 BC – it was fortified with Cyclopean walls (parts of which can still be seen), enclosing a royal palace and temples to the cult of Athena. By the ninth century BC, the Acropolis had become the heart of Athens, sheltering its principal public buildings, which remained there until in 510 BC the Oracle at Delphi ordered that the Acropolis should remain the **province of the gods**, unoccupied by humans.

Following the Persian sacking of Athens in 480 BC, a grand rebuilding project under the direction of the architect and sculptor **Fidias** created almost everything you see today in an incredibly short time: the Parthenon itself took only ten years to finish. The monuments survived unaltered for close to a thousand years, until in the reign of Emperor Justinian the temples were converted to **Christian** worship. Over the following centuries the uses became secular as well as religious, and embellishments increased, gradually obscuring the Classical designs. Fifteenth-century Italian princes held court in the Propylaia, and the same quarters were later used by the **Turks** as their commander's headquarters and as a powder magazine.

The Parthenon underwent similar changes from Greek to Roman temple, from Byzantine church to Frankish cathedral, before several centuries of use as a Turkish mosque. The Erechtheion, with its graceful female figures, saw service as a harem. A Venetian diplomat described the Acropolis in 1563 as "looming beneath a swarm of glittering golden crescents", with a minaret rising from the Parthenon. For all their changes in use, however, the buildings would still have resembled – very much more than today's bare ruins – the bustling and ornate ancient Acropolis, covered in sculpture and painted in bright colours.

Sadly, such images remain only in the prints and sketches of that period: the Acropolis buildings finally fell victim to the ravages of war, blown up during successive attempts by the Venetians to oust the Turks. In 1687, laying siege to the garrison, they ignited a Turkish gunpowder magazine in the Parthenon, and in the process blasted off its roof and set a **fire** that raged for two days and nights. The process of stripping down to the bare ruins seen today was completed by souvenir hunters and the efforts of the first archeologists (see box, p.70).

**■ ACCOMMODATION**

| | | | | | |
|---|---|---|---|---|---|
| Acropolis House | 11 | Fresh Hotel | 1 | Phaedra | 13 |
| Athens Backpackers | 15 | Grande Bretagne | 6 | Phidias | 8 |
| Athens Center Square | 2 | Hermes | 9 | Student & | |
| Attalos | 3 | Herodion | 16 | Traveller's Inn | 12 |
| Ava Apartments & Suites | 14 | Metropolis | 7 | Tempi | 5 |
| Electra Palace | 10 | O&B | 4 | | |

**● CAFÉS & BARS**

| | |
|---|---|
| 7 Jokers | 21 |
| Acropolis Museum Café | 47 |
| Amouage | 7 |
| Arodou | 17 |
| Athinaion Politeia | 31 |
| Bougatsadiko tou Psyrri | 15 |
| Brettos | 43 |
| Café Pláka | 38 |
| Dhioskouri | 34 |
| Filion | 5 |
| James Joyce | 22 |
| Krinos | 6 |
| Oasis | 41 |
| Oréa Ellás | 28 |
| Pagoto Manía | 16 |
| Ta Servetia tou Psyrri | 11 |
| Yiasemi | 36 |
| Zonar's Le Café d'Athenes | 18 |

**CENTRAL ATHENS**

**TRADITIONAL MUSIC**

| | |
|---|---|
| To Baraki Tou Vassili | 2 |
| Hilios ke Dhio Nikhtes | 7 |
| Perivoli T'Ouranou | 9 |
| Stoa Athanaton | 3 |

**BARS & CLUBS**

| | |
|---|---|
| Ghost | 5 |
| Space by Avli | 8 |
| Venti | 4 |
| Zas Bar | 6 |

**DANCE & CLASSICAL MUSIC**

| | |
|---|---|
| Greek National Opera | 1 |

**RESTAURANTS**

| | |
|---|---|
| Baïraktaris | 26 |
| Brettos Ouzerí | 42 |
| Byzantino | 40 |
| Café Abysinia | 25 |
| Cibus | 45 |
| Damingos | 44 |
| Dhimokritos | 8 |
| Dhiporto | 2 |
| Elaia | 37 |
| Elihrison | 14 |
| Filistron | 35 |
| Fu-Rin-Ka-Zan | 29 |
| Godzilla | 10 |
| Il Postino | 1 |
| Indian Masala | 20 |
| Ipeiros | 4 |
| Jackson Hall | 19 |
| Klimataria | 3 |
| Kuzina | 24 |
| Nikitas | 13 |
| Noodle Bar | 30 |
| Palia Taverna tou Psarrá | 37 |
| Paradosiako | 33 |
| Platanos | 32 |
| Skholarhio | 39 |
| Strofi | 46 |
| Taverna tou Psyrri | 12 |
| Thanasis | 27 |
| To Steki tou Ilia | 23 |
| Varoulko | 9 |

**SHOPS**

| | | | |
|---|---|---|---|
| 7+7 | 13 | Elliniko Spiti | 18 |
| Amorgos | 17 | Kendro Ellinikis | |
| Aristokratikon | 12 | Paradosis | 14 |
| Ariston | 9 | To Komboloi tou Psyrri | 5 |
| Athena's Sandals | 11 | Newsstand | 19 |
| Attica | 7 | Shop | 8 |
| Compendium | 16 | Stoa tou Bibliou | 2 |
| Crop Circle | 1 | Theotokis | 10 |
| Eleftheroudhakis | 6/15 | Xylouris | 3 |
| Elixirion | 4 | | |

Akrópoli to the south, along pedestrianized Dhionysíou Areopayítou past the Acropolis Museum, Theatre of Dionysos and Herodes Atticus Theatre (or through the South Slope site). Disabled access to the Acropolis is available via a lift on the north side (by arrangement only ☏ 210 321 4172).

**Cafés, shops and cloakrooms** You can buy water and sandwiches, as well as guidebooks, postcards and so on, from a couple of stands near the main ticket office. There's

also a handy branch of *Everest* right opposite Akrópoli metro station (at the corner of Makriyiánni and Dhiakoú) and plenty of similar places around Monastiráki metro. If you want to sit down to eat, there are cafés and tavernas nearby in almost every direction: Pláka (p.102), Monastiráki (p.102), Makriyiánni (p.107) and Thissío (p.106). Backpacks and large bags are not allowed in to the site – there's a cloakroom near the main ticket office.

## The Summit of the Acropolis

Daily: April–Sept 8am–6.30pm; Oct–March 8am–4.30pm • €12

As well as the iconic Parthenon, the summit of the Acropolis is home to the Erechtheion, the Temple of Athena Nike and the Propylaia, as well as lesser remains of many other ancient structures.

### The Propylaia

Today, as throughout history, the **Propylaia** are the gateway to the Acropolis. In Classical times the Sacred Way extended along a steep ramp to this massive monumental double gatehouse; the modern path makes a more gradual, zigzagging ascent, passing first through an arched Roman entrance, the **Beule Gate**, added in the third century AD.

The Propylaia were constructed by Mnesikles from 437–432 BC, and their axis and proportions aligned to balance the recently completed Parthenon. They – the name is the plural of propylon, gateway, referring to the fact that there are two wings – were built from the same Pentelic marble (from Mount Pendéli, northeast of the city) as the temple, and in grandeur and architectural achievement are almost as impressive. In order to offset the difficulties of a sloping site, Mnesikles combined, for the first time, standard Doric columns with the taller and more delicate Ionic order. The ancient Athenians, awed by the fact that such wealth and craftsmanship should be used for a purely secular building, ranked this as their most prestigious monument.

### The Panathenaic Way

The **Panathenaic Way** was the route of the great annual procession for ancient Athens' Panathenaic Festival, in honour of the city's patron goddess Athena. The procession – depicted on the Parthenon frieze – wound right through the Classical city from the gates now in the Kerameikos site (p.88) via the Propylaia to the Parthenon and, finally, the Erechtheion. You can see traces of the ancient route just inside the Propylaia, where there are grooves cut for footholds in the rock and, to either side, niches for innumerable statues and offerings. In Classical times it ran past a 10m-high bronze statue of Athena Promachos (Athena the Champion), whose base can just about be made out. Athena's spear and helmet were said to be visible to sailors approaching from as far away as Soúnio.

Close to the Propylaia too are the scant remains of a **Sanctuary of Artemis**. Although its function remains obscure, it is known that the precinct once housed a colossal bronze representation of the Wooden Horse of Troy. More noticeable is a nearby stretch of **Mycenaean wall** (running parallel to the Propylaia) that was incorporated into the Classical design.

### The Temple of Athena Nike

Simple and elegant, the **Temple of Athena Nike** stands on a precipitous platform overlooking Pireás and the Saronic Gulf. It has only recently reappeared, having been dismantled, cleaned and reconstructed. Not for the first time either: demolished by the Turks in the seventeenth century, the temple was reconstructed from its original blocks two hundred years later.

**1**

**FORTY YEARS OF SCAFFOLDING**

If you see a photo of a pristine Parthenon standing against a clear sky, it is almost certainly an old one. For most of the twenty-first century the Acropolis buildings have been swathed in scaffolding and surrounded by cranes – at times some structures have even been removed altogether, to be cleaned and later replaced. Though originally intended to be complete in time for the 2004 Olympics, the work is now set to continue for the foreseeable future – some claim that it will be forty years before the job is complete.

In myth, it was from the platform beside the temple that King Aegeus maintained a vigil for the safe return of his son Theseus from his mission to slay the Minotaur on Crete. Theseus, flushed with success, forgot his promise to swap the boat's black sails for white on his return. Seeing the black sails, Aegeus assumed his son had perished and, racked with grief, threw himself to his death.

## The Parthenon

The **Parthenon** temple was always intended to be a spectacular landmark and a symbol of the city's imperial confidence, and it was famous throughout the ancient world. Yet even in their wildest dreams its creators could hardly have imagined that the ruins would come to symbolize the emergence of Western civilization – nor that, two-and-a-half millennia on, it would attract some two million tourists a year.

The first great building in Pericles' scheme, it was intended as a new sanctuary for Athena and a home for her cult image – a colossal wooden statue by Fidias overlaid with ivory and gold plating, with precious gems as eyes and sporting an ivory gorgon's head on her breast. Originally the columns were brightly painted and surrounded by the finest sculpture of the Classical age, foremost among them the beautiful **Parthenon frieze** and pediments. Also brightly coloured, these are generally held to have depicted the Panathenaic procession, the birth of Athena and the struggles of Greeks to overcome giants, Amazons and centaurs. The greater part of the frieze, along with the central columns, were destroyed by the Venetian bombardment in 1687. The best surviving examples are in the British Museum in London (see box p.70); the Acropolis Museum also has a few original pieces, as well as reconstructions of the whole thing.

To achieve the Parthenon's extraordinary and unequalled harmony of design, its architect, Iktinos, used every trick known to the Doric order of architecture. The building's proportions maintain a universal 9:4 ratio while all seemingly straight lines are in fact slightly curved, an optical illusion known as *entasis* (intensification). The columns (their profile bowed slightly to avoid seeming concave) are slanted inwards by 6cm, while each of the steps along the sides of the temple was made to incline just 12cm over a length of 70m.

## The Erechtheion

To the north of the Parthenon stands the **Erechtheion**, the last of the great works of Pericles to be completed. Both Athena and the city's old patron of Poseidon-Erechtheus were worshipped here, in the most revered of the ancient temples. The site, according to myth, was that on which Athena and Poseidon held a contest, judged by their fellow Olympian gods; at the touch of Athena's spear, the first ever olive tree sprang from the ground, while Poseidon summoned forth a fountain of sea water. Athena won, and became patron of the city.

Today, the sacred objects within are long gone, but the elegant Ionic porticoes survive. By far the most striking feature, however, is the **Porch of the Caryatids**, whose columns form the tunics of six tall maidens. The ones *in situ* are replacements: five of the originals are in the Acropolis Museum, while a sixth was looted by Elgin – they're replaced here by casts in a different-colour marble.

1

## THE ELGIN MARBLES

The controversy over the so-called Elgin Marbles has its origin in the activities of Western looters at the start of the nineteenth century: above all the French ambassador Fauvel, gathering antiquities for the Louvre, levering away sculptures from the Parthenon. As British Ambassador, **Lord Elgin** obtained permission from the Turks to erect scaffolding, excavate and remove stones with inscriptions. He interpreted this concession as a licence to make off with almost all of the bas-reliefs from the Parthenon's frieze, most of its pedimental structures and a caryatid from the Erechtheion – all of which he later sold to the British Museum. While there were perhaps justifications for Elgin's action at the time – not least the Turks' tendency to use Parthenon stones in their lime kilns – his pilfering was controversial even then. Byron, for one, roundly disparaged his actions.

The Greeks hoped that the long-awaited completion of the new Acropolis Museum would create the perfect opportunity for the British Museum to bow to pressure and return the Parthenon Marbles (as they are always known here). But despite a campaign begun by the late Greek actress and culture minister Melina Mercouri in the 1980s, there is so far little sign of that happening; central to the British Museum's argument is that to return them would be to set a precedent that would empty virtually every museum in the world.

## The South Slope

Daily: April–Sept 8am–6.30pm; Oct–March 8.30am–3pm • €2 or joint Acropolis ticket • Metro Akrópoli

Entrance to the **South Slope** site is either by a path tracking around the side of the Acropolis near the main ticket office, or from below, off pedestrianized Leofóros Dhionysíou Areopayítou close to Metro Akrópoli. A great deal of restoration and excavation work is ongoing here, including the opening up of a new area on the eastern edge of the rock, above Pláka where groups of statues have been gathered together.

### Theatre of Dionysos

The **Theatre of Dionysos** is one of the most evocative locations in the city. Here the masterpieces of Aeschylus, Sophocles, Euripides and Aristophanes were first performed; it was also the venue in Classical times for the annual festival of tragic drama, where each Greek citizen would take his turn as member of the chorus. Rebuilt in the fourth century BC, the theatre could hold some 17,000 spectators – considerably more than Herodes Atticus's 5000–6000 seats. Twenty of the original 64 tiers of seats survive. Most notable are the great marble thrones in the front row, each inscribed with the name of an official of the festival or of an important priest; in the middle sat the priest of Dionysos and on his right the representative of the Delphic Oracle. At the rear of the stage are reliefs of episodes in the life of Dionysos flanked by two squatting Sileni, devotees of the satyrs. Sadly, this area is roped off to protect the stage-floor **mosaic** – a magnificent diamond of multicoloured marble best seen from above.

### Herodes Atticus Theatre

The dominant structure on the south side of the Acropolis – much more immediately obvious even than the Theatre of Dionysos – is the second-century Roman **Herodes Atticus Theatre** (Odeion of Herodes Atticus). This has been extensively restored for performances of music and Classical drama during the summer festival (see p.110) but is open only for shows; at other times you'll have to be content with spying over the wall.

### Stoa of Eumenes

Between the two theatres lie the foundations of the **Stoa of Eumenes**, originally a massive colonnade of stalls erected in the second century BC. Above the stoa, high up under the walls of the Acropolis, extend the ruins of the **Asklepion**, a sanctuary devoted to the healing god Asklepios and built around a sacred spring; restoration is ongoing, and there are extensive new signs in English.

## Monument of Thrasyllos

Above the Theatre of Dionysos, you can see the entry to a huge cave, originally sacred to Artemis. It later housed choregic awards (to celebrate victory in drama contests; see Monument of Lysikratos, p.75) won by the family of **Thrasyllos**, hence the name. The entrance was closed off around 320 BC with a marble facade – this is currently being restored. The cave was later converted to Christian use and became the chapel of Virgin Mary of the Rocks, but an ancient statue of Dionysos remained inside until it was removed by Lord Elgin (it's now in the British Museum), while the Classical structure survived almost unchanged until 1827, when it was blown up in a Turkish siege.

## The Peripatos

The **Peripatos** was the ancient street that ran around the north side of the Acropolis. Access to this side has only recently been opened up so that you can now walk right around the rock within the fenced site, starting above the Theatre of Dionysos and emerging by the entry to the main Acropolis site; there's also a new entrance from Pláka, by the Kannellopoulou museum.

There are no major monuments en route, but the numerous caves and springs help explain the strategic importance of the Acropolis. In one impressive cleft in the rock was a secret stairway leading up to the temples: this provided access to spring-water in times of war, and was also used in rituals, when blindfolded initiates would be led this way. Nearby are numerous other caves and rock arches that had cult status in ancient times.

# The Acropolis Museum

Dhionysíou Areopayítou 15 • Tues–Sun 8am–8pm, last admission 7.30pm, late opening Fri till 10pm • €5 • Ⓦ theacropolismuseum.gr • Metro Akrópoli

The new **Acropolis Museum** is a magnificent building, filled with beautiful objects, with a wonderful sense of space and light and a glass top storey with a direct view up to the Parthenon itself.

The remains of ancient Athens uncovered during building work can be seen even before you enter, protected under glass flooring that continues past through the ground floor. The displays proper start with a ramp described as the **Slopes of the Acropolis**, as that is where most of the pottery and other objects displayed here were found. At the top of the ramp are sculptures from the pediment of an early temple that stood on the site of the Parthenon, the Hekatompedon. Their surviving paintwork gives a good indication of the vivid colours originally used in temple decoration.

Statues dominate the **first floor**: the *Moschophoros*, a painted marble statue of a young man carrying a sacrificial calf, dated 570 BC, is one of the earliest examples of Greek art in marble. There's also an extensive collection of *Korai*, or statues of maidens. The progression in style, from the simply contoured Doric clothing to the more elegant and voluminous Ionic designs, is fascinating; the figures' smiles also change subtly, becoming increasingly loose and natural.

On the **top floor**, a fifteen-minute video (alternately in English and Greek) offers a superb introduction to the Parthenon sculptures. The metopes and the frieze are set out around the outside of the hall, arranged as they would have been on the Parthenon itself; the pediments are displayed separately at each end of the gallery. Only a relatively small number are original (see box, p.70); the rest are represented by plaster copies which seem deliberately crude, to make a point (there are better copies in Akropoli metro station, for example).

On the way back down through the museum are **statues** from the Temple of Athena Nike and the Erechtheion, including the original Caryatids. The sculptures from the parapet of the former, all depicting Athena Nike in various guises, include a particularly graceful and fluid sculpture known as *Iy Sandalizoméni*, which depicts her adjusting her sandal. Don't forget to check out the café too (see p.107).

**1**

# The Areopagus

Immediately below the entrance to the Acropolis • Free

Metal steps as well as ancient, slippery, rock-hewn stairs ascend the low, unfenced hill of the **Areopagus**, or "Hill of Ares". This was the site of the Council of Nobles and the Judicial Court under the aristocratic rule of ancient Athens; during the Classical period the court lost its powers of government to the Assembly (held on the Pnyx) but it remained the court of criminal justice, dealing primarily with cases of homicide. In myth, it was also the site where Ares, God of War, was tried for the murder of one of Poseidon's sons; Aeschylus used the setting in *The Eumenides* for the trial of Orestes, who stood accused of murdering his mother Clytemnestra. The Persians camped here during their siege of the Acropolis in 480 BC, and in the Roman era Saint Paul preached the "Sermon on an Unknown God" on the hill, winning among his converts Dionysios "the Areopagite", who became the city's patron saint.

Today, there's little evidence of ancient grandeur beyond various steps and niches cut into the perilously slippery rock, and the hill is littered with cigarette butts and empty beer cans left by the crowds who come to rest after their exertions on the Acropolis and to enjoy the **views**. These, at least, are good – down over the Agora and towards the ancient cemetery of Kerameikos.

# The ancient Agora

Daily: summer 8am–6.30pm, winter 8.30am–3pm • €4 or joint Acropolis ticket • Metro Monastiráki

The **Agora** or market was the heart of ancient Athenian city life from as early as 3000 BC. Approached either from the Acropolis, down the path skirting the Areopagus, or through the northern entrance on Adhrianoú, it is an extensive and confusing jumble of ruins, dating from various stages of building between the sixth century BC and the fifth century AD. As well as the marketplace, this was the chief meeting place of the city, where orators held forth, business was discussed and gossip exchanged – St Paul, for example, took the opportunity to meet and talk to Athenians here. It was also the first home of the democratic assembly before that moved to the Pnyx, and continued to be its meeting place when cases of ostracism (see p.74) were discussed for most of the Classical period.

## Hephaisteion and the Áyii Apóstoli

The best overview of the Agora is from the exceptionally well-preserved **Hephaisteion**, or Temple of Hephaistos, where there's a terrace overlooking the rest of the site from the west. Here a plan shows the buildings as they were in 150 AD, and the various remains laid out in front of you make a great deal more sense with this to help (there are similar plans at the entrances). The temple itself was originally thought to be dedicated to Theseus, because his exploits are depicted on the frieze (hence *Thissíon*, which has given its name to the area); more recently it has been accepted that it actually honoured Hephaistos, patron of blacksmiths and metalworkers. It was one of the earliest buildings of Pericles' programme, but is now one of the least known – perhaps because it lacks the curvature and "lightness" of the Parthenon's design; the barrel-vaulted roof dates from a Byzantine conversion into the church of Saint George.

The other church on the site – that of **Áyii Apóstoli** (the Holy Apostles), by the south entrance – is worth a look as you wander among the extensive foundations of the other Agora buildings. Inside are fragments of fresco, exposed during restoration of the eleventh-century shrine.

## The Stoa of Attalos

Same hours as Agora but opens 11am Mon

For some background to the Agora, head for the **Stoa of Attalos**. Originally constructed around 158 BC, the Stoa was completely rebuilt between 1953 and 1956 and is, in

**1**

every respect except colour, an entirely faithful reconstruction; with or without its original bright red and blue paint, it is undeniably spectacular.

A small **museum** occupies ten of the 21 shops that formed the lower level of the building. It displays items found at the Agora site from the earliest Neolithic occupation to Roman and Byzantine times. Many of the early items come from burials, but as ever the highlights are from the Classical era, including some good red-figure pottery and a bronze Spartan shield. Look out for the *ostraka*, or pottery shards, with names written on them. At annual assemblies of the citizens, these *ostraka* would be handed in, and the individual with most votes banished, or "**ostracized**", from the city for ten years.

# Pláka

The largely pedestrianized area of **Pláka**, with its narrow lanes and stepped alleys climbing towards the Acropolis, is arguably the most attractive part of Athens, and certainly the most popular with visitors, a welcome escape from the concrete blocks that dominate the rest of the metropolis. With scores of **cafés, restaurants and shops** to fill the time between museums and important sites such as the **Roman Forum**, it's an enjoyable place to wander.

An attractive approach to Pláka is to follow **Odhós Kydhathinéon**, a pedestrian walkway that starts near the **Anglican and Russian churches** on Odhós Filellínon. It leads gently downhill, past the Museum of Greek Folk Art, through café-crowded Platía Filomoússou Eterías, to Hadrian's street, **Odhós Adhrianoú**, which runs nearly the whole length of Pláka and on into Monastiráki and Thissío. These two are the main commercial and tourist streets of the district, with Adhrianoú increasingly tacky and downmarket as it approaches Platía Monastirakíou and the Flea Market.

## The Museum of Greek Folk Art

Kydhathinéon 17 • Tues–Sun 9am–2.30pm • €2 • W melt.gr • Metro Sýndagma or Akrópoli

The **Folk Art Museum** is one of the most enjoyable in the city, even though let down somewhat by poor lighting and labelling. Its five floors are devoted to displays of weaving, pottery, regional costumes, jewellery and embroidery along with other traditional Greek arts and crafts. The highlight, though, is on the first floor: a reconstructed room from a house on the island of Lesvós with a series of murals by the primitive artist **Theofilos** (1868–1934). These naive scenes from Greek folklore and history, especially the independence struggle, are wonderful, and typical of the artist, who was barely recognized in his lifetime, spending most of his career painting tavernas and cafés in exchange for food and board. There are two other branches of the museum: a tiny but fascinating section devoted to the world of work, entitled "**Man and Tools**" at Panós 22 (Tues–Sat 9am–2.30pm; €2), and a **ceramics collection** housed inside a mosque (see p.78).

## Jewish Museum of Greece

Níkis 39 • Mon–Fri 9am–2.30pm, Sun 10am–2pm • €6 • W jewishmuseum.gr • Metro Sýndagma

The **Jewish Museum** tells the story of Jews in Greece, elegantly presented in a series of dimly lit rooms, with plenty of explanation in English. Downstairs are art and religious paraphernalia, many of the pieces centuries old. The centrepiece is the reconstructed synagogue of Pátra, dating from the 1920s, whose furnishings have been moved here *en bloc* and remounted. Upstairs, more recent history includes World War II and the German occupation, when Greece's Jewish population was reduced from almost 80,000 to less than 10,000. There are features, too, on the part played by Jews in the Greek resistance, and many stories of survival.

## A SLICE OF OLD ATHENS: ANAFIÓTIKA

The main arteries of Pláka, above all Adhrianoú, home of the Manchester United beach towel and "Sex in Ancient Greece" playing cards, can become depressingly touristy. For a break, climb up into the jumble of streets and alleys that cling to the lower slopes of the Acropolis. Here, the whitewashed, island-style houses and ancient churches of the **Anafiótika** quarter proclaim a cheerfully architect-free zone. There's still the odd shop, and taverna tables are set out wherever a bit of flat ground can be found, but there are also plenty of hidden corners redolent of a quieter era. A particularly good view of this area can be had by following the paths that track around the base of the Acropolis, above the buildings.

## Frissiras Museum

Monís Asteríou 3 and 7 • Wed–Fri 10am–5pm, Sat & Sun 11am–5pm • €6 • ⓦ frissirasmuseum.com • Metro Sýndagma or Akrópoli

The **Frissiras Museum**, housed in two beautifully renovated, Neoclassical buildings, is the only significant permanent modern art collection in Athens. The museum has over three thousand works – mostly figurative painting plus a few sculptures, as well as a regular programme of exhibitions. The space at no. 7 houses the permanent exhibition, which includes plenty of names familiar to English-speakers – David Hockney, Peter Blake and Paula Rego among them – as well as many Greek and European artists. Temporary exhibitions, along with a fine shop and an elegant café, are at no. 3 a block away.

## The Monument of Lysikratos

In the southeastern corner of Pláka, the **Monument of Lysikratos**, a graceful stone and marble structure from 335 BC, rises from a small, triangular open area overlooked by a quiet café/taverna. It's near the end of Odhós Tripódhon, a relic of the ancient **Street of the Tripods**, where winners of drama competitions erected monuments to dedicate their trophies (in the form of tripod cauldrons) to Dionysos. The last surivor of these monuments, this example sports six Corinthian columns rising up to a marble dome on which, in a flourish of acanthus-leaf carvings, the winning tripod was placed.

In the seventeenth century the monument became part of a Capuchin convent, which provided regular lodgings for European travellers – **Byron** is said to have written part of *Childe Harold* here, and the street beyond, Výronos, is named after him.

## Ayía Ekateríni

Platía Ayía Ekateríni • Mon–Fri 7.30am–12.30pm & 5–6.30pm, Sat & Sun 5–10pm • Free • Metro Akrópoli

The church of **Ayía Ekateríni** – St Catherine's – is one of the few in Pláka that's routinely open. At its heart is an eleventh-century Byzantine original, although this has been pretty well hidden by later additions. You can see it most clearly from the back of the church, while in the courtyard in front are foundations of a Roman building. Inside, the over-restored frescoes look brand new, and there are plenty of glittering icons.

## The Athens University Museum

Thólou 5 • Mon–Fri 9.30am–2.30pm, June–Sept also Mon & Wed 6–9pm • Free • ⓦ history-museum.uoa.gr • Metro Monastiráki

High up under the Acropolis, the **Athens University Museum**, site of Athens' first university, occupies a grand old mansion, one of the oldest in the city. The building itself is a large part of the attraction – in particular the scintillating views from the top-floor terrace – but there's also a great collection of old scientific and medical instruments, sadly labelled in Greek only.

**1**

# Kanellopoulou Museum

Theorías 12 • Daily 8.30am–3pm • Free • Metro Monastiráki

Head for the highest street beneath the looming Acropolis walls, and you'll eventually emerge by the eclectic **Kanellopoulou Museum**. This private collection should have fully reopened after years or refurbishment (and may no longer be free; at the time of writing, just one room was open), and is well worth a look. There's a bit of everything – gilded icons, ancient jewellery, Classical-era pottery – and almost every object is a superb example of its kind.

# The Roman Forum

Entrance on Dhioskoúron • Daily: summer 8.30am–6.30pm; winter 8.30am–3pm • €2 or joint Acropolis ticket • Metro Monastiráki

The **Roman Forum** was built during the reign of Julius Caesar and his successor Augustus as an extension of the older Agora. As today, its main entrance was on the west side, through the **Gate of Athena Archegetis**. This gate marked the end of a street leading up from the Greek Agora, and its four surviving columns give a vivid impression of the grandeur of the original portal. On the side facing the Acropolis you can still make out an engraved edict announcing the rules and taxes on the sale of oil. At the opposite end of the Forum, a second gateway is also easily made out, and between the two is the marketplace itself, surrounded by colonnades and shops, some of which have been excavated. Inside the fenced site, but just outside the market area to the east, are the foundations of public latrines dating from the first century AD.

### Tower of the Winds

The best preserved and easily the most intriguing of the ruins inside the Forum site is the graceful octagonal structure known as the **Tower of the Winds**. This predates the Forum, and stands just outside the main market area. Designed in the first century BC by Andronikos of Kyrrhos, a Syrian astronomer, it served as a compass, sundial, weather vane and water clock – the latter powered by a stream from one of the Acropolis springs. Each face of the tower is adorned with a relief of a figure floating through the air, personifying the eight winds. Beneath each of these, it is still possible to makeout the markings of eight sundials. On top of the building was a bronze weather vane in the form of the sea god Triton. In Ottoman times, dervishes used the tower as a *tekke* or ceremonial hall, terrifying their superstitious Orthodox neighbours with their chanting, music and whirling meditation.

# The Fethiye Mosque and Ottoman medresse

The oldest mosque in Athens, the **Fethiye Tzami**, built in 1458, occupies a corner of the Forum site. It was dedicated by Sultan Mehmet II, who conquered Constantinople in

---

## ROMAN ATHENS

In 146 BC, the **Romans** ousted Athens' Macedonian rulers and incorporated the city into their vast new province of Achaia, whose capital was at Corinth. The city's status as a renowned seat of learning (Cicero and Horace were educated here) and great artistic centre ensured that it was treated with respect, and Athenian artists and architects were much in demand in Rome. Athens, though, was a backwater – there were few major construction projects, and what building there was tended to follow Classical Greek patterns.

The one Roman emperor who did spend a significant amount of time in Athens, and left his mark here, was **Hadrian** (reigned 117–138 AD). Among his grandiose monuments are Hadrian's Arch, a magnificent and immense library, and (though it had been begun centuries before) the Temple of Olympian Zeus. A generation later **Herodes Atticus**, a Roman senator who owned extensive lands in Marathon, became the city's last major benefactor of ancient times.

1453 (*fethiye* means "conquest" in Turkish). There's a fine, porticoed entrance but, sadly, you can't see inside the restored building, as it's used as an archeological warehouse. Outside the Forum site at the corner of Eólou, more or less opposite the Tower of the Winds, the gateway and single dome of a **medresse**, an Islamic school, survive. During the last years of Ottoman rule and the early years of Greek independence, this building was used as a prison and was notorious for its harsh conditions; a plane tree in the courtyard was used for hangings. The prison was closed in the 1900s and the bulk of it torn down.

For more on **Ottoman Athens**, check out also the Turkish baths (see below), the nearby ceramic collection of the Museum of Greek Folk Art (p.78) and the Benáki Museum of Islamic Art (p.87).

## The Turkish baths

Kirístou 8 • Mon & Wed–Sun 9am–2.30pm • €2 • ⓦ melt.gr • Metro Monastiráki

Close to the Fethiye Mosque is another Ottoman survival, the site of the **Turkish baths**. Constructed in the 1450s, the baths were in use, with many later additions, right up to 1965. Newly restored, they now offer an insight into a part of Athens' past that is rarely glimpsed and well worth a look. Traditionally, the baths would have been used in shifts by men and women, although expansion in the nineteenth century provided the separate facilities you see today. The *tepidarium* and *caldarium*, fitted out in marble with domed roofs and rooflights, are particularly beautiful. The underfloor and wall heating systems have been exposed in places, while upstairs there are photos and pictures of old Athens. Labelling throughout is in Greek only, but an audio tour is available (€1, plus deposit).

## The Museum of Greek Popular Musical Instruments

Dhioyénous 1–3 • Tues & Thurs–Sun 10am–2pm, Wed noon–6pm • Free • Metro Monastiráki

The **Museum of Greek Popular Musical Instruments** traces the history of virtually every type of musical instrument that has ever been played in Greece. It's all attractively displayed in a fine mansion, with drums and wind instruments of all sorts (from crude bagpipes to clarinets) on the ground floor, lyras, fiddles, lutes and a profusion of stringed instruments upstairs. In the basement there are more percussion and toy instruments. Reproductions of frescoes show the Byzantine antecedents of many instruments, and headphones are provided for sampling the music made by the various exhibits.

The museum **shop** has an excellent selection of CDs for sale, concentrating, not surprisingly, on traditional Greek music.

# Monastiráki and Psyrrí

**Monastiráki**, to the north of Pláka, is substantially less touristy than its neighbour, though there are still plenty of sights and extensive opportunities for eating, drinking and shopping. The area gets its name from the little monastery church (*monastiráki*) on central **Platía Monastirakíou**. The square, with its handy metro station, marks a return to the traffic and bustle of commercial Athens; full of fruit stalls, street performers, lottery vendors and kiosks. This neighbourhood has been a marketplace since Ottoman times, and it still preserves, in places, a bazaar atmosphere. The main market (see p.82) lies straight up Athinás from here, towards Omónia, but nearer at hand you'll see signs in either direction that proclaim you're entering the famous **Athens Flea Market**.

**Psyrrí**, northwest of Platía Monastirakíou, is a former working-class district that is now home to Athens' busiest nightlife as well as some quirky shops. This is also a great place to **eat and drink**: between them, Monastiráki and Psyrrí probably have more eating places per square metre than anywhere else in Athens.

**1**

# Athens Flea Market

These days the description of the streets around Platía Monastirakíou as a flea market is a bit of a misnomer – there's plenty of shopping, but mostly of a very conventional nature. **Odhós Pandhróssou**, to the east, is almost entirely geared to tourists, an extension (though not quite literally) of Adhrianoú. West of the square the flea market has more of its old character, and among the tourist tat you'll find shops full of handmade musical instruments, or stalls selling nothing but chess and *tavlí* boards. An alley off Iféstou is jammed with record and CD stores, with a huge basement second-hand bookshop. Around Normánou and **Platía Avyssinías** shops specialize in furniture and junky antiques: from here to Adhrianoú, the relics of a real flea market survive in hopeless jumble-sale rejects, touted by a cast of eccentrics (especially on Sundays). **Odhós Adhrianoú** is at its most appealing at this end, with a couple of interesting antique shops, and some shady cafés overlooking the metro lines, Agora and Acropolis.

The stretch of **Odhós Ermoú** fringing the flea market as it heads west from Platía Monastirakíou is the southern edge of fashionable Psyrrí, and among the workaday old-fashioned furniture stores here are some interesting new designer and retro shops; in the other direction, as it heads up towards Sýndagma, the street is much more staid. In the pedestrianized upper section are familiar high-street chains and department stores.

## The Iridhanós River

Platía Monastirakíou • Metro Monastiráki

The **Iridhanós** (or Eridanos) runs across Athens from its source on Lykavitós hill, via Sýndagma and Monastiráki to Keramikós. Celebrated in Classical times, it had effectively been lost until the work on the metro expansion uncovered its underground course early this century. Part of the ancient Greek and Roman system that turned it into an underground drain can be seen at Monastiráki metro station, and through railings and glass paving from the platía above. The brick vaulting of these ancient waterworks constitutes some impressive engineering work and, in winter and spring, substantial amounts of water still course through.

## Hadrian's Library

Entry on Áreos • Daily: summer 8am–6.30pm; winter 8am–3pm • €2 or joint Acropolis ticket • Metro Monastiráki

Bordering the north end of the Forum site, and stretching right through from Eólou to Áreos, stand the surviving walls and columns of **Hadrian's Library**, an enormous building that once enclosed a cloistered courtyard of a hundred columns. Despite the name, this was much more than just a library – more a cultural centre including art galleries, lecture halls and a great public space at its centre. The site has only recently opened to the public and is still being excavated: much of it has been built over many times, and a lot of what you can see today consists of the foundations and mosaic floors of later Byzantine churches. However, the entrance has been partly reconstructed, some of the original columns survive, and above all you get an excellent sense of the sheer scale of the original building, once enclosed by walls and covering an area even larger than the current site. The **Tetraconch Church**, for example, whose remains lie at the centre of the site, was built entirely within the library's internal courtyard.

## The Museum of Greek Folk Art: Ceramics Collection

Áreos 1 • Mon & Wed–Sun 9am–2.30pm • €2 • ⓦ melt.gr • Metro Monastiráki

Squeezed between the walls of Hadrian's library and the shacks of Pandhróssou, the **Ceramics Collection** is housed in the former Mosque of Tzisdarákis. Built in 1759, the building has had a chequered life, converted to a barracks and then a jail after Greek independence, before becoming the original home of the Greek Folk Art Museum in

1918. Today, as a branch of that museum, it houses the **Kyriazópoulos collection** of ceramics – the legacy of a Thessaloníki professor. Good as it is, the collection is likely to excite you only if you have a particular interest in pottery; most will probably find the **mosque** itself, the only one in Athens open to the public, at least as big an attraction.

Though missing its minaret, and with a balcony added inside for the museum, plenty of original features remain. In the airy, domed space, look out for the striped *mihrab* (the niche indicating the direction of Mecca), a calligraphic inscription above the entrance recording the mosque's founder and date, and a series of niches used as extra *mihrabs* for occasions when worshippers could not fit into the main hall.

## Kapnikaréa

Ermoú, at Kapnikaréas • Mon, Wed & Sat 8am–1pm, Tues, Thurs & Fri 8am–12.30pm & 5–7.30pm, Sun 8–11.30am • Free • Metro Monastiráki

The pretty Byzantine church of **Kapnikaréa** marks more or less the beginning of the upmarket shopping on Ermoú, looking tiny, almost shrunken, in these high-rise, urban surroundings. Originally eleventh century, but with later additions, it has a lovely little dome and a gloomy interior in which you can just about make out the modern frescoes. The church is allegedly named after its founder, a tax collector: *kapnós* means smoke, and in the Byzantine era there was a tax on houses, known as the smoke tax.

## Platía Mitropóleos

A welcome spot of calm among the busy shopping streets that surround it, **Platía Mitropóleos** – Cathedral Square – is home to not just one but two cathedrals. The modern **Mitrópolis** is a large, clumsy nineteenth-century edifice; the "little cathedral" or **Áyios Eleftheríos** alongside it is dwarfed by comparison, but infinitely more attractive. There is said to have been a church on this site since the very earliest days of Christianity in Athens; what you see now dates from the twelfth century. It's a beautiful little structure, cobbled together with plain and carved blocks from earlier incarnations; some almost certainly from that original church.

There are several other small churches nearby: look out especially for the dusty, tiny chapel of **Ayía Dhynámis** crouching surreally beneath the concrete piers of the Ministry of Education and Religion on Odhós Mitropóleos, a short way up towards Sýndagma.

# Sýndagma

All roads lead to **Sýndagma** – you'll almost inevitably find yourself here sooner or later for the metro and bus connections. **Platía Syndágmatos**, Constitution Square, to give it its full name, lies roughly midway between the Acropolis and Lykavitós hill. With the Greek Parliament building (the Voulí) on its uphill side, and banks, offices and embassies clustered around, it's the political and geographic heart of Athens. The square's name derives from the fact that King Otto was forced by popular pressure to declare a formal constitution for the new Greek state from a palace balcony here in 1844. It's still the principal venue for mass demonstrations and political rallies.

## The Greek Parliament and Tomb of the Unknown Soldier

Platía Syndágmatos • Not open to the public • Metro Sýndagma

The **Voulí**, the Greek National Parliament, presides over Platía Syndágmatos from its uphill (east) side. A vast, ochre-and-white Neoclassical structure, it was built as the royal palace for Greece's first monarch, the Bavarian King Otto, who moved in in 1842. In front of it, goose-stepping **evzónes** in tasselled caps, kilt and woolly leggings

**1**

– a prettified version of traditional mountain costume – change their guard at regular intervals before the **Tomb of the Unknown Soldier**. On Sundays, just before 11am, a full band and the entire corps parade from the tomb to their barracks at the back of the National Gardens to the rhythm of innumerable camera shutters.

## Hotel Grande Bretagne

Vasiléos Yeoryíou 1 • Ⓦ grandebretagne.gr • Metro Sýndagma

Along with the Voulí, the vast **Hotel Grande Bretagne** – Athens' grandest – is just about the only building on Sýndagma square to have survived postwar development. Past the impressive facade and uniformed doormen, the interior is magnificently opulent, as befits a grand hotel established in the late nineteenth century. It's worth taking a look inside or having a drink at one of the bars; recent renovation included a new rooftop pool, bar and restaurant with great views across the city. The hotel has long been at the centre of Greek political intrigue: in one notorious episode, Winston Churchill narrowly avoided being blown up here on Christmas Day, 1944, when saboteurs from the Communist-led ELAS movement placed an enormous explosive charge in the drains. According to whom you believe, the bomb was either discovered in time by a kitchen employee, or removed by ELAS themselves when they realized that Churchill was one of their potential targets.

## The National Gardens

Entrances on Amalías, Vasilíssis Sofías and Iródhou Attikoú • Sunrise–sunset • Free • Metro Sýndagma

The **National Gardens**, spreading out to the south and east of the Voulí, are the most refreshing acres in the city – not so much a flower garden as a luxuriant tangle of trees, whose shade and duck ponds provide palpable relief from the heat of summer. They were originally the private palace gardens, a pet project of Queen Amalia in the 1840s; supposedly the main duty of the minuscule Greek navy in its early days was the fetching of rare plants, often the gifts of other royal houses, from remote corners of the globe. Despite a major pre-Olympic clear-out there's still something of an air of benign neglect here, with rampant undergrowth and signs that seem to take you round in circles. It's a great place for a picnic, though, or just a shady respite from the city streets. There's a children's **playground** (on the Záppio side) and a tiny **zoo** (signed *Irattikou*) with ostriches and some exotic fowl, though most of the cages these days are occupied by chickens, rabbits and domestic cats. The **Botanical Museum** occupies an elegant little pavilion nearby; closed for refurbishment at the time of writing.

## The Presidential Palace

Iródhou Attikoú, cnr Vasiléos Yeoryíou B • Metro Sýndagma

Across the road from the far side of the National Gardens is the **Presidential Palace**, the royal residence until King Constantine's exile in 1967, where more *evzónes* stand on sentry duty. Next door, the slightly more modest **Mégaro Maxímou** is the official residence of the Prime Minister.

## The Záppio

Grounds open 24hr • Free • Metro Sýndagma

On the southern side of the National Gardens are the graceful crescent-shaped grounds of the **Záppio**. Popular with evening and weekend strollers, they're more open and more formally laid out. The Záppio itself, an imposing Neoclassical edifice originally built as an exhibition hall, is not open to the public. Although it has no permanent function, the building has taken on prestigious roles such as headquarters of the Greek presidency of the European Union and of the 2004 Olympic bid.

# The Roman baths

Leóforos Amalías • Metro Akrópoli or Sýndagma

Roman Athens expanded beyond the Classical Greek city to cover much of the area around the National Gardens. The most concrete evidence of this lies in a large **Roman baths complex** that was discovered during excavations for the metro. Dating originally from the late third century AD and substantially expanded over succeeding centuries, the baths are now visible under a metal and perspex cover alongside the busy avenue, 100m or so north of Hadrian's Arch. Complete rooms have been well preserved and are now exposed to the gaze.

# Hadrian's Arch

Leóforos Amalías • Unfenced • Free • Metro Akrópoli

**Hadrian's Arch** stands in splendid isolation across from one of the busiest road junctions in Athens, the meeting of Amalías and Syngroú. With the traffic roaring by, this is not somewhere you are tempted to linger, but it's definitely worth a look on your way to the Temple of Olympian Zeus. The arch, 18m high, was erected by the emperor to mark the edge of the Classical city and the beginning of his own. On the west side its frieze – damaged and hard to make out – is inscribed "This is Athens, the ancient city of Theseus", and on the other "This is the City of Hadrian and not of Theseus". With so little that's ancient remaining around it, this doesn't make immediate sense, but you can look up, westwards, to the Acropolis and in the other direction see the columns of the great temple completed by Hadrian.

# The Temple of Olympian Zeus

Entrance on Vasilíssis Ólgas • Daily: Summer 8am–6.30pm; winter 8am–3pm • €2 or joint Acropolis ticket • Metro Akrópoli

Directly behind Hadrian's Arch, the colossal pillars of the **Temple of Olympian Zeus** – also known as the Olympieion – stand in the middle of a huge, dusty clearing with excellent views of the Acropolis and constant traffic noise. One of the largest temples in the ancient world, and according to Livy, "the only temple on earth to do justice to the god", it was dedicated by Hadrian in 131 AD, almost 700 years after Peisistratos had begun work on it. Hadrian marked the occasion by contributing a statue of Zeus and a suitably monumental one of himself, although both have since been lost.

Today, just fifteen of the temple's original 104 marble pillars remain erect. To the north of the temple enclosure, by the site entrance, are various excavated remains including another impressive Roman bath complex. The south side of the enclosure overlooks a further area of excavation (not open to the public) where both Roman and much earlier buildings have been revealed.

# The Grand Avenues

Northwest from Sýndagma, the broad and busy avenues of **Stadhíou**, **Panepistimíou** (officially called Venizélou, though the name is rarely used) and **Akadhimías** head towards Platía Omonías. Initially lined with grandiose mansions, some converted to museums, squares with open vistas and opulent arcades with chichi shopping, they move steadily downmarket as you approach Omónia. There are three museums here of rather specialist interest: the **National Historical Museum** (Stadhíou 13, Platía Kolokotróni; Tues–Sun 9am–2pm; €3, free on Sun; ⊚nhmuseum.gr), focusing on Greek history from the fall of Constantinople to the reign of King Otto, the **City of Athens Museum** (Paparigopoúlou 7, on Platía Klafthmónos; Mon & Wed–Fri 9am–4pm, Sat & Sun 10am–3pm; €3; ⊚athenscitymuseum.gr), occupying the residence of King Otto in the 1830s, and the **Numismatic Museum**

(Panepistimíou 12; Tues–Sat 8am–8pm; €3; ⓦnma.gr) with a collection of over 600,000 coins and related artefacts.

### Platía Klafthmónos

**Platía Klafthmónos** offers a wonderful view towards three grand Neoclassical buildings on Panepistimíou. Here the planners' conceptualization of the capital of newly independent Greece can for once be seen more or less as they envisaged it, blending the nation's Classical heritage with modern, Western values. As you look up you see, from the left, the sober grey marble of the **National Library**, the rather racier **Akadhimía** (University), enlivened by frescoes depicting King Otto surrounded by ancient Greek gods and heroes, and the frankly over-the-top **Academy of Science** with its pediment friezes and giant statues of Athena and Apollo. The garish decoration gives an alarming impression of what the Classical monuments might have looked like when their paintwork was intact. Behind these buildings, on Akadhimías, is a major terminus for **city buses**, from where you can get a connection to almost anywhere in the city or its suburbs.

# Omónia and the bazaar

While Pláka and Sýndagma are resolutely geared to tourists and the Athenian well-heeled, **Platía Omonías** (Omónia Square) and its surroundings represent a much more gritty city. Here the grand avenues imagined by the nineteenth-century planners have been subverted by time and the realities of Athens' status as a commercial capital. Heading up from Monastiráki, the **bazaar area** around Odhós Athinás is home to a bustling series of markets and small shops spilling into the streets and offering some of urban Athens' most compelling sights and a cosmopolitan ethnic mix. It's also a neighbourhood being increasingly recolonised by the drug addicts and prostitutes who were cleared out in time for the Olympics; a process accelerated by the economic crisis.

**Platía Omonías** itself – brutal and shadeless – has little to offer in terms of aesthetics but it is the heart of Athens for a good portion of the population: a continuous turmoil of people and cars.

## The Bazaar

The city's bazaar area is concentrated on **Athinás** and **Eólou streets**. Here the unsophisticated stores still reflect their origins in the Oriental souk system with each street specialized in selling certain goods. Hence the Monastiráki end of Athinás is dedicated to tools; food stores are gathered around the central market in the middle, especially along Evripídhou; there's glass to the west; paint and brasswork to the east; and clothes in Eólou and Ayíou Márkou. Always raucous and teeming with shoppers, *kouloúri* (bread-ring) sellers, gypsies and other vendors, the whole area is great free entertainment.

### The meat and seafood market

The lively heart of the neighbourhood is the central **meat and seafood market**, occupying almost an entire block bordered by Athinás, Evripídhou, Eólou and Sofokléous. The building itself is a grand nineteenth-century relic, with fretted iron awnings sheltering forests of carcasses and mounds of hearts, livers and ears – no place for the squeamish. In the middle section of the hall is the fish market, with all manner of bounty from the sea squirming and glistening on the marble slabs.

### The fruit and vegetable market

Across Athinás is the colourful **fruit and vegetable** bazaar, surrounded by streets where grocers pile their stalls high with sacks of pulses, salt cod, barrels of olives and wheels of

**1**

> ## NOVEMBER 17: THE STUDENT UPRISING
>
> In November 1973, students at **Athens Polytekhnío** launched a protest against the repressive regime of the colonels, occupying the building and broadcasting calls for mass resistance from a pirate radio transmitter. Large numbers came to demonstrate support. The colonels' regime was determined to smash the protest and, on the night of November 17, snipers were positioned in neighbouring houses and ordered to fire into the courtyards while a tank broke down the entrance gate and the buildings were stormed. Even today nobody knows how many of the unarmed students were killed – estimates range from twenty to three hundred. The protest arguably marked the beginning of the end for the colonels; its anniversary is still commemorated by marches and sombre remembrance ceremonies and the date is an iconic one, used for example by the November 17 terrorist group, which was active in Greece from 1975 to 2002. The Neoclassical Polytekhnío itself, alongside the National Archeological Museum, is not open for visits.

cheese. A clear sign of Athens' increasing **multi-ethnicity** is to be seen in the streets around Evripídhou just west of here, where a growing community from South Asia, predominantly Bengalis, gather around spice-rich minimarkets.

### Odhós Eólou: the flower market
Pedestrianized **Odhós Eólou** is far less frantic than parallel Athinás and benefits from café tables in the street and benches to rest on. Its gentler nature is also reflected by the goods sold here: where Athinás has power tools and raw meat, Eólou offers clothes and the **flower market**. The latter, gathered around the church of Ayía Iríni at the southern end of the street, has stalls through the week but really comes alive on Sunday morning.

Eólou itself follows the line of an ancient road, and the sight of the Acropolis as you approached Athens in ancient times must have been awe-inspiring. The views remain impressive today, with the Erechtheion's slender columns and pediment peeking over the edge of the crag at the bottom of the street.

## Platía Kótzia
At the northern end of Odhós Eólou, **Platía Kótzia** is a far more formal enclave, and one of the city's more impressive examples of Olympic refurbishment. Surrounded by the town hall and the weighty Neoclassical buildings of the National Bank, it's a rare glimpse of elegant old Athens, spoilt only by the crumbling modern blocks above the post office. In the middle of the square a large section of **ancient road** has been uncovered and can be seen in a fenced-off site – numerous tombs and small buildings lie alongside it. Also on display, by the new Stock Exchange is an ancient city gate discovered during building work; nearby more sections of the ancient road and a drainage system are visible under glass pyramids in the middle of Eólou.

# North of the centre
North of the centre there's just one sight of any note, the fabulous **National Archeological Museum**, the finest collection of ancient Greek artefacts anywhere, and one of the world's greatest museums. Otherwise it's a rewarding part of the city for a wander – restaurants, bars, cafés and bookshops abound, while **Exárhia** and neighbouring **Neápoli** are among the city's liveliest neighbourhoods. Traditionally the home of anarchists, revolutionaries, artists and students, Exárhia is pretty tame these days, but it's still the closest thing in central Athens to an "alternative" quarter. On Saturdays, locals flock to the colourful street market on Kallidhromíou from early

morning till lunchtime. Just above, the little-visited **Stréfis Hill** provides some great views and a welcome break from the densely packed streets and dull apartment blocks surrounding it.

## The National Archeological Museum

Patissíon 44 • Mon 1.30–8pm, Tues–Sun 9.30am–4pm • €7 • ⓦ namuseum.gr • Metro Viktorías or Omónia, also dozens of buses, including trolleys 2 and 5 – look for those labelled *Mousseio*

The **National Archeological Museum** is an essential stop on any visit to Athens. However high your expectations, this unrivalled treasure trove of ancient Greek art and sculpture seems to surpass them. The interior is surprisingly plain – there's nothing flashy at all about the displays – but clear and well labelled. You could easily spend an entire morning or afternoon here, but it's equally possible to scoot round the highlights in an hour or two; arriving early in the morning or late in the afternoon should mean you won't be competing with the tour groups for space.

### Mycenaean and Cycladic art

Directly ahead of you as you enter, the **Mycenaean halls** have always been the biggest crowd pullers. The gold **Mask of Agamemnon**, arguably the museum's most famous piece, is almost the first thing you see. Modern dating techniques offer convincing proof that the funerary mask actually belonged to some more ancient king, but crowds are still drawn by its correspondence with the Homeric myth and compelling expression.

Among the other highlights are a golden-horned **Bull's Head** displayed alongside a gold **Lion's Head**; gold jewellery including a diadem and a gold-foil cover for the body of an infant from Grave III (the "Grave of the Women"); the **Acropolis Treasure** of gold goblets, signet rings and jewellery; the gold **Vafio** cups, with their scenes of wild bulls and long-tressed, narrow-waisted men; and dozens of examples of the Mycenaeans' consummate art – intricate, small-scale decoration of rings, cups, seals and inlaid daggers. There's work in silver, ivory, bronze and boars' tusks as well; there are baked tablets of Linear B, the earliest Greek writing (mainly accounting records) and Cretan-style frescoes depicting chariot-borne women watching spotted hounds in pursuit of boar and bull-vaulting. It's a truly exceptional display, the gold shining as if it were in the window of a jeweller's shop.

Still earlier Greece is represented in the adjoining rooms. Room 5 covers Neolithic pottery and stone tools from Attica and elsewhere and runs through to the early Bronze Age. The pottery shows sophisticated decoration from as early as 5000 BC, and there are many figurines, probably fertility symbols judging by their phallic or pregnant nature, as well as simple gold ornaments. Room 6 is home to a large collection of **Cycladic art** from the Aegean islands. Many of these idols suggest the abstract forms of modern Cubist art – most strikingly in the much-reproduced **Man Playing a Lyre**.

### Early sculpture

**Sculpture** makes up a large part of the museum's most important exhibits, following a broadly chronological arrangement around the main halls of the museum. Early highlights include a statue of a **kore** (maiden) from Merenda (Myrrhinous) in Attica, in room 11. Her elegantly pleated, belted *chiton* (dress) bears traces of the original paint and decoration of swastikas, flowers and geometric patterns. Nearby is a wonderful grave stele of a young *doryphoros* (spear-bearer) standing against a red background. Room 13 has the **Stele of a Young Warrior**, with delicately carved beard, hair and tunic-folds, and the **Kroisus kouros** (statue of an idealized youth), who looks as if he's been working out; both are from the late sixth century BC.

## Classical art

Just a few highlights of the massive **Classical art** collection can be mentioned. Room 15 boasts a mid-fifth-century BC bronze **Statue of Poseidon**, dredged from the sea off Évvia in the 1920s. The god stands poised to throw his trident – weight on the front foot, athlete's body perfectly balanced, the model of idealized male beauty. A less dramatic, though no less important, piece in the same room is the **Eleusinian Relief**, showing the goddess of fertility, accompanied by her daughter Persephone, giving to mankind an ear of corn – symbol of the knowledge of agriculture and associated with the Mysteries of Eleusis (p.120). In Room 20 is a small marble statue of **Athena**, a copy of the great cult statue that once stood in the Parthenon: it's a scary figure; the vast original, covered in gold and ivory, must have been extraordinary. The **Little Jockey of Artemission**, a delicate bronze figure seeming too small for his galloping horse, was found in the same shipwreck as the *Poseidon*. Room 28 has some fine, fourth-century BC bronzes including the **Antikythira Youth**, thought to depict either Perseus or Paris, from yet another shipwreck, off Andikýthira, and the bronze head of a **Boxer**, burly and battered. Still more naturalistic, in room 29, is the third-century BC bronze head of a **Philosopher**, with furrowed brow and unkempt hair.

## Later sculpture

The most reproduced of the **later sculptures** is a first-century AD statue of a naked and indulgent **Aphrodite** (room 30) about to rap Pan's knuckles for getting too fresh – a far cry (a long fall, some would say) from the reverent, idealizing portrayals of the gods in Classical times. There is also an extraordinary bronze equestrian portrait statue (without the horse) of the **Emperor Augustus**.

## Minor collections

Less visited, but still extremely worthwhile, are the collections hidden away at the rear of the museum and upstairs. These include, downstairs the **Stathatos collection**, with some truly exquisite jewellery; a wonderful **Egyptian** room; and the **bronze collection**. This is an exceptional display of thousands of items: weapons, figurines, axes, cauldrons, jewellery, mirrors, kitchen implements; even bronze sandals. Perhaps the highlight is the **Antikythira Mechanism**, at the far end. Dating from around 150–100 BC, it was discovered in a shipwreck off the island of Andikýthira in 1900, but modern scanning techniques have only recently revealed its full complexity. It is believed to be an astronomical computer capable of predicting the movements of stars and planets, and its sophisticated use of differential gears is unique – technologically, it was at least 1500 years ahead of its time.

Upstairs is a collection of hundreds of **vases**, if anything still more spectacular, with a full explanation of manufacturing techniques, changing styles of decoration and the uses of the different types of vessel. As ever, the highlights are from the Classical era. Up here, too, is a display on the excavations of Akrotíri on Thíra (p.441), including some of the famous **Minoan frescoes** discovered there.

# Stréfis Hill

Just above **Exárhia** a labyrinth of paths leads to the summit of **Stréfis Hill** (Lófos toú Stréfi), from where there are wonderful views – above all of the Acropolis with the Saronic Gulf and islands behind, but also across to nearby Lykavitós. Watch out for unguarded drops near the top and stick to the main paths as you walk up, in order to avoid one of the more obvious signs of the area's alternative lifestyle, discarded hypodermics.

**1**

# Western Athens

Some of the most interesting up-and-coming areas of Athens – **Thissío**, **Gázi**, **Keramikós** and **Roúf** – lie to the west of the centre, where the recent extension of Metro line 3 has acted as a further spur to the pace of change. Nightlife and restaurants are the chief attractions here, but there's also a cluster of new museums and galleries. Here too is **Kerameikos**, site of a substantial section of the walls of ancient Athens and an important burial ground. South of Thissío, things are rather more traditional. The **hills of the Pnyx and Filopáppou** offer a pleasant, green escape from the city as well as fine views down over the Acropolis and Agora. On the west side of the hills, the residential zone of **Áno Petrálona** is a real delight, entirely untouristy, with some excellent tavernas and a great open-air cinema, though absolutely nothing in the way of sights.

## Thissío

The cafés of **Thissío**, with tables set out on huge terraces above the Agora site, offer some of the finest views of the Acropolis, especially at night. Head south from Metro Thissío and you can follow pedestrianized Apóstolou Pávlou past these terraces and right around the edge of the Ancient Agora and Acropolis sites. It's an especially rewarding walk in the early evening, when the setting sun illuminates this side of the rock and the cafés start to fill with an anticipatory buzz. As you follow the street round there are a number of small excavations at the base of the hills on your right. First, immediately below the church of Ayía Marína, is a rocky area identified as the earliest known **sanctuary of Zeus** in Attica; there's not a great deal to see through the fence, but it's clear that the rocks have been cut into terraces.

### Sanctuary of Pan

Off Apóstolou Pávlou, on the lower slopes of the Pnyx just beyond the Thission open-air cinema • View through the fence

The cult of Pan was associated with caves, and at the **Sanctuary of Pan** you can see the opening to an underground chamber cut into the rock. Inside were found reliefs of Pan, a naked nymph and a dog. There's also a mosaic floor and, nearby, remains of an ancient road and two rock-cut, Classical-era houses.

### Fountain of Pnyx

Off Apóstolou Pávlou, on the lower slopes of the Pnyx just beyond the Sanctuary of Pan • View through the fence

Under Peisistratos (see p.62) a water system was engineered, with subterranean pipes bringing water from springs to rock-cut cisterns that supplied the city. The so-called **Fountain of Pnyx** is believed to be one of those; behind a locked entrance is a chamber with a Roman mosaic floor where the water was collected. You can also see traces of the concrete used to seal the chamber during World War II, when valuable antiquities were stored inside.

## Filopáppou Hill

From around the junction of Apóstolou Pávlou and Dhionysíou Areopayítou, a network of paths leads up **Filopáppou Hill**, known in antiquity as the "Hill of the Muses". Its pine- and cypress-clad slopes provide fabulous views of the Acropolis and the city beyond, especially at sunset (although night-time muggings have occurred here, so take care). This strategic height has played an important, if generally sorry, role in the city's history: in 1687 it was from here that the shell that destroyed the roof of the Parthenon was lobbed; more recently, the colonels placed tanks on the slopes during their coup of 1967. The hill's summit is capped by a grandiose monument to a Roman senator and consul, Filopappus. To the west, paths lead across to Áno Petrálona and the Dora Stratou Theatre (see p.110) through the ancient district of **Koile**. You can clearly see remnants of rock-cut houses here, as well as the ancient Koile road, which led from the city to the port at Pireás, protected by the Long Walls; a vital strategic thoroughfare in antiquity.

### The prison of Socrates

Filopáppou Hill

On the way up Filopáppou Hill, signed off to the left, is the so-called **Prison of Socrates**, in actual fact the rear part of a house – age unknown but probably very ancient – with rooms cut into the rock. The main structure would have been in front, and you can still see holes for joists and beams, and part of a rock-cut stairway.

### Áyios Dhimítrios

Filopáppou Hill

The main path up Filopáppou Hill follows a line of truncated ancient walls past the attractive Byzantine church of **Áyios Dhimítrios**. The church is much venerated because, the story goes, its patron saint (Dhimitrios "The Bomber") protected worshippers celebrating his saint's day here in 1656. The Turks planned to bombard the church, but instead "God sent a thunderbolt, exploding the powder and destroying their cannon, killing Yusuf Aga and his men". Inside, original Byzantine frescoes have been uncovered under later ones, the eyes of the saints gouged out.

## The Hill of the Pnyx

North of Filopáppou rises the **Hill of the Pnyx**, an area used in Classical Athens as the meeting place for the democratic assembly, which gathered more than forty times a year. A convenient semicircular terrace makes a natural spot from which to address the crowd. All male citizens could vote and, at least in theory, all could voice their opinions, though the assembly was harsh on inarticulate or foolish speakers. There are some impressive remains of the original walls, which formed the theatre-like court, and of *stoas* where the assembly would have taken refreshment. This atmospheric setting provides commanding Acropolis views, while benches on the west side allow you to contemplate the vista across Pireás and out to sea.

## The Hill of the Nymphs

The **Hill of the Nymphs** (Lófos Nymfón) lies to the west of the Pnyx and Filopáppou, overlooking Áno Petrálona. Nymphs were associated with the dusty whirlwinds to which this hill is particularly prone and it is said to be the location of the fairy sequences in Shakespeare's *A Midsummer Night's Dream*. Slightly lower and quieter than its better-known neighbours, this is a peaceful place with good views across to the western suburbs of Athens and beyond, as well as pleasant shaded walks.

## Benáki Museum of Islamic Art

Áyion Asomáton 22, corner Dhípylou • Tues & Thurs–Sun 9am–3pm, Wed 9am–9pm • €5 • Ⓦ benaki.gr • Metro Thissío

Antónis Benákis, founder of the Benáki Museum (see p.90), spent much of his life in Egypt, and this museum, in a converted Neoclassical mansion, was created to house the collection he amassed there. Exhibits in the **Benáki Museum of Islamic Art** follow a chronological course up through the building, from the seventh century on the first floor to the nineteenth on the fourth. Throughout there are beautiful, intricately decorated objects in almost every type of art: ceramics (especially tiles), metalwork and wood above all, but also textiles, jewellery, glass, scientific instruments, armour and more. The highlights, perhaps, are on the third floor, from the sixteenth- and seventeenth-century Golden Age of the Ottoman Empire under Süleyman the Magnificent. Here is a reconstructed room from a Cairo mansion, complete with inlaid marble floor, sunken

1

fountains and elaborate wooden window screens, as well as silk wall hangings (not from the mansion), shot with silver and gold thread. There's a top-floor café overlooking the Kerameikos site with industrial Gázi beyond, as well as views of the Acropolis and Filopáppou, while in the basement can be seen a substantial chunk of the ancient city wall, almost 6m high, preserved during the building's restoration.

## Kerameikos

Entrance on Ermoú • Summer Tues–Sun 8am–6.30pm; winter Tues–Sun 8.30am–3pm • €2 or joint Acropolis ticket • Metro Thissío

The **Kerameikos** (or Keramikós) site, encompassing one of the principal burial grounds of ancient Athens and a hefty section of the ancient wall, provides a fascinating and quiet retreat. Little visited, it has something of an oasis feel, with the lush Iridhanós channel, speckled with water lilies, flowing across the site from east to west.

To the right of the entrance is the stream and the double line of the **city wall**. Two roads pierced the wall here, and the gates that marked their entrance to the city have been excavated: the great **Dipylon Gate** was the busiest in the ancient city, where the road from Pireás, Eleusis and the north arrived; the **Sacred Gate** was a ceremonial entrance where the Ierá Odhós or Sacred Way entered the city – it was used for the Eleusinian and Panathenaic processions.

### The Street of the Tombs

Branching off to the left from the Sacred Way is the **Street of the Tombs**, the old road to Pireás. In ancient Greece people were frequently buried alongside roads, and especially near gates, a practice at least partly related to the idea of death as a journey. This site, by the principal routes into the Classical city, was clearly a prestigious one and numerous commemorative monuments to wealthy or distinguished Athenians have been excavated, their original stones reinstated or replaced by replicas. The flat, vertical stelae were the main funerary monuments of the Classical world; the sarcophagi that you see are later, from Hellenistic or Roman times. The large tomb with the massive semicircular base to the left of the path is the *Memorial of Dexileos*, the 20-year-old son of Lysanias of Thorikos, who was killed in action at Corinth in 394 BC. The adjacent plot contains the *Monument of Dionysios of Kollytos*, in the shape of a pillar stele supporting a bull carved from Pentelic marble.

### The museum

The **site museum** is a lovely, cool, marble-floored space displaying finds from the site and related material, above all stelae and grave markers. There are also many poignant funerary offerings – toys from child burials, gold jewellery and beautiful small objects of all sorts. The ceramics are particularly fine, including lovely dishes with horses on their lids (*pyxides*) from the early eighth century BC and some stunning fifth-century BC black-and-red figure pottery.

## Gázi

**Gázi**, to the west and north of Kerameikos, is a former industrial area where the reinvention of the old gasworks as the **Tekhnópolis** cultural centre (Pireós 100, ⓦtechnopolis-athens.com; Metro Keramikós) has helped spark a rush of hip bars and restaurants, as well as other exhibition sites such as the **Benáki Museum Pireos St Annexe** (Pireós 138, ⓦbenaki.gr; Wed, Thurs & Sun 10am–6pm, Fri & Sat 10am–10pm, closed Aug; €3–6; Metro Petrálona, or many buses along Pireós including #049, #B18 and trolley #21). By day the streets tend to be deserted, and after dark, with so many derelict buildings, the surrounding area can feel threatening. In practice it seems safe enough, but late at night you may want to take a taxi down here; Gázi really comes into its own late on Friday night and over the weekend.

1

**A CITY WITH A VIEW**

Athens is a city built on hills. Most famous is the **Acropolis** itself, which forms the backdrop to all the finest views of the city and whose summit also offers wonderful vistas across the metropolis and out to Pireás and the sea. But there are dozens of other viewpoints throughout Athens. Some of the finest views are from the café terraces of **Thissío**, packed in the early evening as the setting sun picks out the ancient monuments – try *Athinaion Politeia* (p.106) or dine on the roof at *Filistron* (p.106). There are other great views from the roof bar at the *Hotel Grande Bretagne* (p.80), Lykavitós Hill (below), Odhós Eólou (p.83), *45°* (p.108) and from Filopáppou Hill (p.86).

## Athinais Cultural Complex

Kastoriás 34–36 • ⓦ athinais.com.gr • Metro Keramikos

A magnificent restoration of an early twentieth-century silk factory, the **Athinais Cultural Complex** contains a theatre, music space, movie screen, exhibition halls, a museum and a sizeable conference centre. The museum shop is full of lavish – and lavishly priced – arty gifts, while upstairs are galleries with temporary exhibitions. Details of what's on can be found on the website or in the local press.

# Kolonáki and the museum quarter

**Kolonáki** is the city's most chic central address and shopping area. Walk up from Sýndagma, past the jewellery stores on Voukourestíou, and you can almost smell the money. It's also from Kolonáki that a funicular hauls you up **Lykavitós Hill**, where some of the best views of the city can be enjoyed. The neighbourhood's lower limits are defined by the streets of Akadhimías and Vassilísis Sofías, where grand Neoclassical palaces house embassies and **museums**.

## Platía Kolonakíou

The heart of Kolonáki is a square officially called Platía Filikís Eterías, but known to all as **Platía Kolonakíou**, after the ancient "little column" that hides in the trees on the southwest side. Dotted around the square are kiosks with stocks of foreign papers and magazines, or in the library of the **British Council** on the south side of the square you can check out the British press for free. The surrounding cafés are almost invariably packed with Gucci-clad shoppers – you'll find better value if you move away from the square a little. In the dozens of small, upmarket **shops** the accent is firmly on fashion and designer gear.

## Lykavitós Hill

**Lykavitós Hill** offers tremendous views, particularly from late afternoon onwards – on a clear day you can see the mountains of the Peloponnese. After dark, the shimmering lights of Áthens spread right across the Attica basin. To get to the summit you can take the **funicular** (daily 9am–2.30am; every 30min, more frequent at busy times; €7 return) or you can walk. The funicular begins its ascent from Odhós Aristípou, near the top of Ploutárhou. To get here is in itself something of a climb – though it doesn't look far from Kolonáki Square, it's a steep ascent through the stepped residential streets. To do the journey the lazy way take bus #060 to the base of the funicular – this starts its journey at the terminus beside the National Archeological Museum and has handy stops on Akadhimías. The principal **path** up the hill begins from the western end of Aristípou above Platía Dhexamenís, rambling through woods to the top. It's not as long or as hard a walk as it looks – easily done in twenty minutes – though the top half offers little shade.

On the summit, the brilliantly white chapel of **Áyios Yióryios** dominates – a spectacular place to celebrate the saint's name-day if you're in Athens at the time. Just below it,

*Orizontes* is a very expensive restaurant with an equally expensive café, both of which enjoy spectacular views. Over to the east a second, slightly lower peak is dominated by the open-air **Lykavitós Theatre**, which is used mainly for concerts from May to October.

## The Benáki Museum

Koumbári 1 at Vassilísis Sofías • Mon, Wed, Fri & Sat 9am–5pm, Thurs 9am–midnight, Sun 9am–3pm • €6, temporary exhibitions €3–5 • Ⓦ benaki.gr • Metro Evangelismós or Sýndagma, many buses including trolleys #3, #7 & #8

The often overlooked but fascinating **Benáki Museum** houses a private collection donated to the state in the 1950s by **Antónis Benákis**, a wealthy cotton merchant. Its exhibits range from Mycenaean jewellery, Greek costumes and folk artefacts to memorabilia of Byron and the Greek War of Independence, as well as jewellery from the Hélène Stathatos collection.

Among the more unusual items are collections of early Greek Gospels, liturgical vestments and church ornaments rescued by Greek refugees from Asia Minor in 1922. There are also some dazzling embroideries and body ornaments and unique historical material on the Cretan statesman Eleftherios Venizelos, Asia Minor and the Cretan Revolution. An additional attraction, especially if you've been dodging traffic all day, is the **rooftop café**, with views over the nearby National Gardens. The museum **shop** stocks a fine selection of art books and CDs, plus some of the best posters and postcards in the city.

## The Museum of Cycladic Art

Neofýtou Dhouká 4 • Mon, Wed, Fri & Sat 10am–5pm, Thurs 10am–8pm, Sun 11am–5pm • €7 • Ⓦ cycladic.gr • Metro Evangelismós, many buses including trolleys #3, #7 & #8

The small, private **Museum of Cycladic Art** is a beautifully presented collection that includes objects from the Cycladic civilization (third millennium BC, from the islands of the Cyclades group), pre-Minoan Bronze Age (second millennium BC) and the period from the fall of Mycenae to around 700 BC, plus a selection of Archaic, Classical and Hellenistic pottery.

The **Cycladic** objects are on the first floor – above all, distinctive marble bowls and folded-arm figurines (mostly female) with sloping wedge heads whose style influenced twentieth-century artists like Moore, Picasso and Brancusi. The exact purpose of the effigies is unknown but, given their frequent discovery in grave-barrows, it's possible that they were spirit-world guides for the deceased or representations of the Earth Goddess. Their clean, white simplicity is in fact misleading, for they would originally have been painted. Look closely, and you can see that many still bear traces.

Of the ancient Greek art on the upper floors, the highlight is the superb black-figure pottery, especially a collection of painted **Classical-era** bowls, often showing two unrelated scenes on opposite sides – for example one of the star exhibits depicts revellers on one face and three men in cloaks conversing on the other. On the ground floor and basement there's a tiny children's area and a good **shop**, as well as a pleasant **café** (with vegetarian choices) in an internal courtyard. A covered walkway connects to the nineteenth-century **Stathatos House**, magnificently restored as an extension for temporary exhibitions.

## The Byzantine and Christian Museum

Vassilísis Sofías 22 • May–Oct Tues–Sun 8am–8pm; Nov–April Tues–Sun 8.30am–3pm • €4 • Ⓦ byzantinemuseum.gr • Metro Evangelismós, many buses including trolleys #3, #7 & #8

Excellently displayed in a beautiful building, the **Byzantine and Christian Museum** is far more wide-ranging than you might expect. Exhibits start with art from the very earliest days of Christianity, whose fish and dove motifs can't disguise their extremely close parallels with Classical Greek objects. There are displays on everyday Byzantine life; reconstructions of parts of early churches (mosaic floors and chunks of masonry, some even from the Christian Parthenon); a Coptic section with antique clothing such as leather shoes decorated with gold leaf; and tombs, in some of which offerings were left, again a reminder of a pagan heritage.

But the highlights are the **icons**, with the earliest being from the thirteenth and fourteenth centuries. There are dozens of lovely examples, many of them double-sided, some mounted to be carried in procession, and you can follow the development of their style from the simplicity of the earliest to the Renaissance-influenced art of the sixteenth century. Alongside the icons are some fine **frescoes**, including an entire dome reconstructed inside the museum.

## The War Museum

Rizári 2 at Vassilísis Sofías • Tues–Sat 9am–2pm, Sun 9.30am–2pm • €2 • ⓦ warmuseum.gr • Metro Evangelismós, many buses including trolleys #3, #7 & #8

The only "cultural" endowment of the 1967–74 junta, the **War Museum** becomes predictably militaristic and right-wing as it approaches modern events: the Asia Minor campaign, Greek forces in Korea, Cyprus and so on. However, the bulk of the collection consists of weaponry and uniforms, with a large collection of eighteenth- and nineteenth-century swords and handguns, and a particular concentration on the World War II era. Earlier times are also covered with displays on changing warfare from Mycenae through to the Byzantines and Turks, and an array of models of the acropolises and castles of Greece, both Classical and medieval. Outside are artillery pieces and planes, including a full-scale model of the *Daedalus*, one of the first-ever military aircraft, which dropped bombs on Turkish positions in December 1912 during the Balkan Wars.

## The National Gallery

Vassiléos Konstantínou 50 • Mon & Thurs–Sat 9am–3pm, Wed 3–9pm, Sun 10am–2pm • €6.50 • ⓦ nationalgallery.gr • Metro Evangelismós

Despite housing some 9500 paintings the **National Gallery** is a bit of a disappointment. Its core collection is of Greek art from the sixteenth century to the present, and of the artists shown here only El Greco is well known outside Greece. One of the few modern painters to stand out is Nikos Hatzikyriakos-Ghikas (Ghika), well represented on the ground floor. On the mezzanine is a small group of canvases by the primitive painter Theophilos (see p.638). Perhaps more interesting is the large temporary exhibition space, often hosting major travelling exhibitions. Near the National Gallery lie what are believed to be the fourth-century BC foundations of **Aristotle's Lyceum** – where he taught for thirteen years and to which Socrates was a frequent visitor. Surrounded by museums, this seems an appropriate place for it, but important as the discovery is for scholars, there's nothing actually to see.

# Southern Athens

South of the centre there are very few sights, but the quiet residential districts here, easily accessible, are full of character and home to excellent restaurants and cafés that see few tourists. Immediately south of the Acropolis lies upmarket **Makriyiánni**, revitalized by the presence of the new Acropolis Museum; adjacent **Koukáki** is a plainer neighbourhood with numerous hotels and good local places to eat. **Mets**, a steep hillside area on the other side of busy Syngroú avenue, and neighbouring **Pangráti** have a wealth of small, homely tavernas and *mezedhopolía*. The latter also boasts buzzing local nightlife and good shops along Imittoú avenue, and an impressive street market every Friday on Odhós Arhimídhous, off Platía Plastíra.

**1**

## The Panathenaic Stadium

Vassiléos Konstantínou • Tram Záppio, buses including trolley #2, or walk via the Záppio gardens

The old Olympic Stadium or **Panathenaic Stadium** (also dubbed Kalimármaro, "White Marble") is a nineteenth-century reconstruction on Roman foundations, slotted tightly between the pine-covered spurs of Ardhittós hill. You can't normally go inside, but you can go right up to the open end of its horseshoe shape, from where you get a very good view.

Originally marked out in the fourth century BC for the Panathenaic athletic contests, it became an arena for gladiatorial bloodsports under the reign of Emperor Hadrian. The Roman senator Herodes Atticus later refurbished the entire stadium; the white marble from the 60,000 seats was to provide the city with a convenient quarry through the ensuing seventeen centuries.

The stadium's reconstruction dates from the modern revival of the Olympic Games in 1896, paid for by another wealthy benefactor, the Alexandrian Greek Yiorgos Averoff. Its appearance and pristine whiteness must be very much as it was when first reopened under the Roman senator. Though the bends are too tight for major modern events, it's still used by local athletes, is the finishing point of the annual Athens Marathon, and marked the end of the 2004 Olympic marathon.

# Pireás

Metro Pireás • Buses #40 from Sýndagma, #49 from Omónia, #X96 from the airport • For ferries see p.95

**PIREÁS** (Piraeus) has been the port of Athens since Classical times, when the so-called Long Walls, scattered remnants of which can still be seen, were built to connect it to the city. Today it's a substantial metropolis in its own right. The port and its **island ferries** are the reason most people come here; if you're spending any time, though, the real attractions of the place are around the small-boat harbours of **Zéa Marina** and **Mikrolímano** on the opposite side of the small peninsula. Here, the upscale residential areas are alive with attractive waterfront cafés, bars and restaurants offering some of the best seafood in town, and there's an excellent archeological museum.

### Some history

The port at Pireás was founded at the beginning of the fifth century BC by **Themistocles**, who realized the potential of its three natural harbours. His work was consolidated by Pericles with the building of the **Long Walls** to protect the corridor to Athens, and the port remained active under Roman and Macedonian rulers. Subsequently, under Turkish control, the place declined to the extent that there was just one building here, a monastery, by the end of the War of Independence. From the 1830s on, though, Pireás grew by leaps and bounds. By World War I, Pireás had become the nation's predominant port, its strategic position enhanced by the opening of the Suez and Corinth canals in 1862 and 1893 respectively. Like Athens itself, the port's great period of expansion began in 1923, with the exchange of populations with Turkey. Over 100,000 Asia Minor Greeks decided to settle in Pireás, doubling the population almost overnight – and giving a boost to a pre-existing semi-underworld

---

### CITY BEACHES

People swim from the rocks or seawall almost anywhere on the coast southeast of Pireás – especially the older generation (the youth tend to head down towards the fleshpots and pay beaches of Glyfádha) – but the closest pleasant beach to the centre is **Edem**, reached by tram to the Edem or Báthis stops. A small patch of sand with cafés and tavernas, this is busy and urban but fine for a quick swim and sunbathe and, remarkably, has Blue Flag status. There are other free beaches near the Flisvós, Kalamáki and Zéfyros tram stops.

**PIREÁS**

Dodecanese — E1

Crete, Lésvos, Híos, Ikaría & Sámos — E2

E3

E4

Kentrikó Limáni (Central Port)

Cyclades

Cyclades — E7

E5
E6

Suburban Train Station

Pireás — M

E8 — Argo-Saronic

International

Cyclades & Ikaría — E10

Argo-Saronic

E9

Market

AKTI MIAOULI

FILONOS

e ★

d ★

ETHN. ANTISTASSEOS

FILONOS

FILONOS

KOLOKOTRONI

KOLOKOTRONI

**Municipal Theatre**

IROÓN POLYTEHNIOU

IROÓN POLYTEHNIOU

**Flea Market (Sunday)**

f ★

KARAÏSKOU

KARAÏSKOU

KARAÏSKOU

**Archeological Museum**

KOUNDOURIOTI

KOUNDOURIOTI

ZANI

AKTI MOUTSOPOULOU

GRIGORIOU LAMBRAKI

GRIGORIOU LAMBRAKI

g ★

*Zéa Marina*

DELYIORYI

**Naval Museum**

NEORION

NEORION

AKTI KOUNDOURIOTI

h ★

VASSILEOS PAVLOU

**Olympiakós Stadium**

i ★

VASSILEOS PAVLOU

AKTI KOUMOUNDHOUROU

*Mikrolímano*

AKTI DHILAVERI

*Faliro* — M

SEF

**Peace & Friendship Stadium**

Central Athens

Central Athens, Glyfádha & Airport

| BUS STOPS | |
|---|---|
| #X96 & #20 | a |
| X96 & #20 | b |
| #X96 | c |
| #49 & #20 | d |
| #49 | e |
| #40, #49 & #X96 | f |
| #20 | g/h/i |

| ACCOMMODATION | |
|---|---|
| Piraeus Dream | 1 |

| EATING & DRINKING | |
|---|---|
| Aktoploïko | 1 |
| Ammos | 2 |
| Jimmy and The Fish | 3 |

0 — 50 metres

culture, whose enduring legacy was rembétika (see p.796), outcasts' music played in hashish dens along the waterside.

## The Archeological Museum

Hariláou Trikoúpi 31 • Tues–Sun 8.30am–3pm • €3 • Bus #1 from Sýndagma passes close by, local buses #300 or #904

The **Archeological Museum of Pireás** boasts an excellent collection, and for Classical enthusiasts merits a special trip. The displays begin upstairs, where one of the star exhibits is a bronze *kouros* (idealized male statue) of Apollo. Dating from 530–520 BC, this is the earliest known life-size bronze, here displayed with two similar but slightly later figures of Artemis and Athena. They were all found in 1959, in a store-room, where they had supposedly been hidden in 86 BC, when the Roman general Sulla besieged Pireás.

1

Many other items in the museum were dragged from shipwrecks at the bottom of the harbour, including, in the last room on the ground floor, second-century AD stone reliefs of battles between Greeks and Amazons, apparently mass-produced for export to Rome (note the identical pieces). Other highlights include some very ancient musical instruments, and many funeral stelae and statues.

## The small boat harbours

Local trolley #20, or walk from Metro Fáliro/Tram SEF

On the opposite side of the Pireás peninsula from the mania of the port, separated by busy shopping streets, the residential districts around the **small boat harbours** have a completely different atmosphere, calm and elegant. At **Zéa Marina** (aka Pasalimáni) you can admire the monstrous gin palaces moored beneath the swish apartments. Nearby, on Aktí Themistokléous, the **Naval Museum** (Tues–Sat 9am–2pm; €4; ⌨hmm.gr) traces Greece's maritime heritage with models and actual sections of ancient triremes and modern warships. The museum is mainly of interest to specialists and small boys; anyone else might find their time better spent wandering around the harbours. The boats at **Mikrolímano** (known to many locals as Turkolímano) are more modest than those at Zéa, but the harbour itself is prettier, and there are dozens of cafés and restaurants at which to sit and enjoy it. Between the two harbours there's a small **beach** – not Athens' finest by any means, but pleasant enough if you have a few hours to kill between ferries; the #20 bus stops immediately above.

## ARRIVAL AND DEPARTURE

### BY PLANE

**Elefthérios Venizélos Airport** (☎210 353 0000, ⌨aia.gr) at Spáta, 33km southeast of the city. Modern and efficient, Athens' airport has facilities including free wi-fi (for 60min), ATMs and banks with money-changing facilities on all levels, the usual array of travel agencies and car rental places, plus luggage storage with Pacific (☎210 353 0160, ⌨pacifictravel .gr) and both national and municipal tourist offices.

Destinations Aegean (⌨aegeanair.com), Olympic (⌨olympicairlines.com) and Sky Express (⌨skyexpress.gr) operate daily flights in summer to the following domestic destinations: Alexandhroúpoli, Haniá (Crete), Híos, Ikaría, Iráklion (Crete), Ioánnina, Kalamáta, Kálimnos, Kárpathos, Kavála, Kefaloniá, Kérkyra (Corfu), Kos, Kýthira, Léros, Límnos, Mílos, Mýkonos, Mytilíni (Lésvos), Náxos, Páros, Ródhos (Rhodes), Sámos, Skiáthos, Thessaloníki and Thíra (Santoríni). There are also regular departures to Astypálea, Kastoriá, Kozáni, Sitía (Crete), Skýros, Sýros and Zákynthos.

### FROM THE AIRPORT INTO TOWN

**By metro and rail** The metro and suburban trains share a station at the airport. Metro Line 3 (every 30min, 6.35am–11.35pm) takes you straight into the heart of the city in 45min (€8 single, €14 return, discounts for multiple tickets) where you can change to the other lines at either Monastiráki or Sýndagma. The suburban train (same fares) offers direct trains to the northern suburbs and Corinth, but for Laríssis station in the centre and Pireás, you have to change at Áno Liósia.

**By bus** Buses can be slower than the metro (1hr–1hr

30min), especially at rush hours, but they're also cheaper, more frequent (at least 2–3 per hr), run all night and offer direct links to other parts of the city: the #X95 runs to Sýndagma square; #X96 to the port at Pireás via Glyfádha, and the beach suburbs; #X93 to the bus stations. Tickets cost €5 from a booth beside the stops or on board – be sure to validate your ticket on the bus. There are also regional bus services to local destinations including the ports of Rafína (hourly; 6am–9pm; €5; ticket on the bus) and Lávrio (20 daily; 6.30am–10pm; €6).

**By taxi** Taxis can take anything from 35min to 1hr 35min (at rush hour) to reach the centre; there's a fixed fare to the centre of €35, or €50 at night, and no extras should be added. The fare to Ráfina should be similar, Pireás or Lávrio €10–15 more.

### BY TRAIN

**Laríssis station** Athens' main terminus, northwest of Platía Omonías, is on metro line 2 (Stathmós Laríssis, also known as Lárissa); this is the most convenient way to get into central Athens, or to anywhere else on the metro system including the port of Pireás (though many trains continue direct to Pireás). Alternatively, the #1 trolley bus heads for Omónia, Sýndagma and on past Akrópoli metro station (close to the Acropolis) into Koukáki. And of course there are taxis. There are often huge queues for tickets so book in advance at the office at Sína 6 (off Panepistimíou), online (⌨trainose.gr) or call central reservations on ☎1110.

Destinations Suburban trains to Kórinthos (change at Áno Liósia; hourly 6am–11pm; 1hr 30min); main line to Halkídha (15 daily; 1hr 30min); Thessaloníki (8 daily, 5 intercity; 6hr,

## MIND YOUR STEP!

Athens' traffic is chaotic, but generally observant of traffic signals, so stick to official crossings when you cross the road. If anything, **pedestrian streets** are more hazardous, as while these are generally free of cars, they are by no means traffic-free – mopeds and motorbikes see them as their property too. Potholed **pavements** are an additional danger – where cars parked on them don't force you to walk in the road.

intercity 4hr 30min) via Lárissa (4hr 30min/3hr 20min); Thíva (Thebes; 10 daily; 1hr); Vólos (1 direct daily; 4hr 35min).

### BY BUS

Athens has two principal bus terminals, at Kifissoú 100 and Liossíon 260, and a smaller terminus of Mavrommatéon. International buses use a variety of stops, most commonly Kifissoú 100 or the train station.

**Kifissoú 100** Northwest of the centre, this station serves routes to northern Greece, and the Peloponnese Bus #051 runs very frequently from here to the corner of Zínonos and Menándhrou, just off Omónia square.

Destinations Árgos (hourly; 2hr); Árta (8 daily; 5hr 30min); Corfu (3 daily; 9hr 30min); Igoumenítsa (4 daily; 7hr 30min); Ioánnina (8 daily; 7hr); Kalamáta (12 daily; 4hr); Kefaloniá (3–4 daily; 7hr); Kórinthos (hourly; 1hr); Lefkádha (4 daily; 5hr 30min); Mycenae/Náfplio (hourly; 2hr 30min); Olympia (2 daily; 5hr 30min); Pátra (every 30min; 3hr); Pýlos (2 daily; 5hr 30min); Pýrgos (9 daily; 5hr); Spárti (11 daily; 4hr); Thessaloníki (12 daily; 6hr 30min); Trípoli (15 daily; 2hr 15min); Zákynthos (4 daily; 6hr).

**Liossíon 260** Slightly further out to the north of Kifissoú 100, this station generally serves routes to central Greece. Bus #024 runs right through the centre to Omónia, Sýndagma and on past metro Akrópoli.

Destinations Áyios Konstandínos (hourly; 2hr 30min); Delphi (6–8 daily; 3hr); Halkídha (every 30min; 1hr 15min); Karpeníssi (3 daily; 4hr 30min); Kými, for Skýros ferries (1 daily, connecting with ferry; 5hr); Lamía (hourly; 3hr 15min); Lárissa (7–9 daily; 4hr 30min); Thiva/Thebes (hourly; 1hr 30min); Tríkala (6 daily; 4hr 30min); Vólos (10–12 daily; 4hr 30min).

**Mavrommatéon** If you're travelling within the state of Attica – for example from the ports at Lávrio or Rafína – you'll arrive at this terminus at the southwest corner of the Pedhíon Áreos Park. This is very close to Viktorías metro, or there are dozens of buses heading down Patissíon (aka 28 Oktovríou) past the National Archeological Museum towards the centre.

Destinations Lávrio (half-hourly 5.45am–6.45pm, less frequent until 10.30pm; 1hr 30min); Marathon (every 30min; 1hr 20min); Pórto Ráfti (hourly; 1hr 30min); Rafína (every 30min; 1hr); Soúnio via the coast (hourly on the half-hour; 2hr) or inland route (via Lávrio; 1hr 45min).

### BY FERRY

The vast majority of ferries, hydrofoils and catamarans

leave from the port of Pireás, but there are also smaller ferry terminals at Rafína and Lávrio.

### PIREÁS

Hundreds of ferries leave Pireás daily, so it's perhaps not surprising that a comprehensive list is hard to find: even the tourist office simply look up individual queries online (at ⓦ openseas.gr).

**Buying tickets** There's no need to buy tickets for conventional ferries before you get here, unless you want a berth in a cabin or are taking a car on board; during Greek holidays (August and Easter especially) these can be hard to get and it's worth booking in advance – the big companies have online booking. Flying Dolphin hydrofoil reservations are also a good idea at busy times, especially Friday night/ Saturday morning out of Athens, and Sunday evening coming back. In general, though, the best plan is simply to get to Pireás early and check with some of the dozens of shipping agents around the metro station and along the quayside Platía Karaïskáki (there are plenty of agents in central Athens too). Most of these act only for particular lines, so for a full picture you will need to ask at three or four outlets.

**Departure points** Boats for different destinations leave from a variety of points around the main harbour: it can be helpful to know the gate number, though these are primarily for drivers. Free, airport-style buses run from gate E5, near the metro, as far as E1, for the big ferries to Crete, the Dodecanese and the northwest. The main gates and departure points are marked on our map, but always check with the ticket agent as on any given day a ferry may dock in an unexpected spot. They all display signs showing their destination and departure time; you can't buy tickets on the boat, but there's usually a ticket hut on the quayside nearby.

### PIREÁS TRANSPORT

The easiest way to travel between the port and central Athens is on metro line 1; the journey takes about 20min from Omónia. Alternatively, there are buses: #40 (about every 10min from 5am–midnight; hourly 1–5am) runs to and from Sýndagma, while #49 from Omónia (roughly every 15min from 5am–midnight; hourly 1–5am) will drop you slightly closer to the ferries. Both are very slow, however – allow an hour to be safe. From the airport, you can take express bus #X96 (around 1hr 20min). Taxis cost about €10 at day tariff from the centre of Athens. It can be hard to get a taxi amid the throng disgorging from a ferry.

**1**

## ATHENS TOURS

A couple of companies, City Sightseeing (☎ 210 922 0604, Ⓦ citysightseeing.gr) and Athens City Tour (☎ 210 881 5207, Ⓦ athens-citytour.com), offer very similar open-top **bus tours** of Athens, for similar prices (€18 adults, €8 children; discounts online). The tours start from Sýndagma square at least every half hour, last about 90 minutes (an extended version also takes in Pireás) and you can hop off and on at numerous stops along the way. For kids especially, the Happy Train, an hour-long trip around the centre (€6 adults, €3 children), can be a fun alternative: it leaves from Ermoú at the corner of Sýndagma square.

More enterprising alternatives include a variety of **walking tours** with Athens Walking Tours (☎ 210 884 7269, Ⓦ athenswalkingtours.gr). These are pricey (from around €36 for three hours) but highly informative – the food tours are particularly recommended. A less professional, but free, alternative is offered by Athens Free Walking Tour (Ⓦ athensfreewalkingtour.com). If you're feeling brave, Athens by Bike (Tziréon 16 at Dhionysíou Areopayítou, metro Akrópoli, ☎ 2130 423 922, Ⓦ athensbybike.gr) offers hour-long **bike** tours from just €7.50. Wackier still, you can cruise the pedestrian streets around the Acropolis or National Gardens on a **Segway** with Athens Segway Tours (Eskhínou 9, metro Akrópoli, ☎ 210 322 2500, Ⓦ athenssegwaytours.com; €49 for 90 minutes).

### RAFÍNA

The port of Rafína (see p.118), about 30km from central Athens, has fast ferries and catamarans to the Cyclades as well as to Marmári on nearby Évvia. It is connected by KTEL bus with the Mavrommatéon terminal in Athens (every 30min; 1hr) and also has direct buses to the airport (13 daily; 40min). There are ticket agents all round the port, and the bus terminal is right on the seafront, facing the open sea; get your ticket on the bus. The main destinations served (most at least twice a day) are Ándhros, Tínos, Páros, Mýkonos, Íos, Thíra and Náxos, plus at least five daily to Marmári: the vast majority of ferries leave either early morning or late afternoon.

### LÁVRIO

**Lávrio** lies close to the southern tip of Attica, some 60km from the centre of Athens. Its ferries mainly serve Kéa (at least three daily) and Kýthnos (at least one a day) but there are also services twice or more a week to the northeast Aegean – Áyios Efstrátios, Límnos and Kavála, or Psará and Híos – and to many of the Cycladic islands via Sýros. KTEL buses run between Lávrio and the airport (20 daily; 30min), as well as the Mavrommatéon terminal in Athens (hourly; 1hr 40min).

## INFORMATION AND TOURS

**Greek National Tourist Office** Dhionysíou Areopayítou 18–20, just by the entrance to the South Slope of the Acropolis (Mon–Fri 9am–7pm, Sat & Sun 10am–4pm; Ⓦ gnto.gr; Metro Akrópoli). This is a useful first stop and they have a good free map as well as information sheets on current museum and site opening hours, bus schedules and so on. If you are arriving by plane, you can save time by calling in at the airport branch.

**Athens City Tourism** Provides an infopoint at the airport and an excellent website, Ⓦ breathtakingathens.com – check out the interactive maps.

## GETTING AROUND

Athens is served by slow but ubiquitous **buses**, a fast, mostly modern **metro** system, and a **tram** service that runs from the centre to the beach suburbs. **Taxis** are also plentiful and, for short journeys in town, exceptionally cheap. **Driving** is a traffic-crazed nightmare, and parking far worse. If you do have a car, you're strongly advised to find somewhere to park it for the duration of your stay and not attempt to use it to get around the city centre.

### BY METRO

The expanded metro system is much the easiest way to get around central Athens; it's fast, quiet and user-friendly.

**Metro lines and stations** There are three lines: Line 1 (green; Pireás to Kifissiá) is the original section, with useful stops in the centre at Thissío, Monastiráki, Omónia and Viktorías; Line 2 (red; Áyios Antónios to Áyios Dhimítrios) has central stops at Omónia, Sýndagma and Akrópoli at the foot of the Acropolis; and Line 3 (blue; Egaléo to the airport) passes through Monastiráki and Sýndagma. Some of the new stations are attractions in their own right, displaying artefacts discovered in their excavation (numerous important discoveries were made) and other items of local interest – Sýndagma and Akrópoli are particularly interesting central ones.

**Metro tips** Trains run from roughly 5.30am to midnight (later on Line 1). When travelling on the metro you need to know the final stop in the direction you're heading, as that is how the platforms are identified; there are plenty of maps in the stations. Further information on Line 1 at ⓦ isap.gr, other lines at ⓦ amel.gr.

**BY BUS**

The bus network is extensive, but crowded and confusing; most buses run from around 5am to midnight, with just a few – including those to the airport – continuing all night. **Bus routes** Routes, where relevant, are detailed in the text, and at most of the major stops there are helpful information booths. Easiest to use are the trolleybuses: #1 connects the Laríssis train station with Omónia, Sýndagma and Koukáki; #2, #4, #5, #9, #11 and #15 all link Sýndagma with Omónia and the National Archeological Museum. There's excellent city bus information at ⓦ oasa.gr.

**BY TRAM**

Athens' tram network was finished in a hurry for the 2004 Olympics – sometimes you can tell as it sways over lines that don't seem entirely straight. Nonetheless it's a great way to get to coastal suburbs and the beach, running from around 5.30am to 1am, or 2.30am on Friday and Saturday. **Tram lines** The tram runs from Leofóros Amalías just off Sýndagma to the coast, where it branches. To the right it heads northwest towards Pireás, terminating at SEF (the Stádhio Eirínis ké Filías or Peace and Friendship Stadium), an interchange with metro line 1 at Fáliro and within walking distance of Pireás's leisure harbours. Left, the tram lines run southwest along the coast to Glyfádha and Voúla. There are effectively three lines – #1, from Sýndagma to SEF; #2, from Sýndagma to Voúla; and #3, from SEF to Voúla.

**Tram tips** Numbers are displayed on the front of the tram and are worth checking as the electronic boards at the

**1**

---

## BUS, METRO AND TRAM TICKETS

The easiest and least stressful way to travel is with a **pass**. A **one-day imerísio** costs €4 and can be used on buses, trolleybuses, trams, metro and the suburban railway in central Athens (everything except the airport route beyond Doukissis Plakentias and some long-distance bus lines). You validate it once, on starting your first journey, and it is good for 24 hours from then. A **weekly pass** costs €14, while **monthly** passes are €45 (less for versions that don't include the metro). A single ticket, valid for 90 minutes on all forms of transport (and transfers between them), is €1.40; a single ticket for one journey by bus or tram only is €1.20. Tickets must be validated at the start of your journey – in the machines at the top of the stairs in metro stations, on board buses, or on the platform or on board for trams.

Tickets and passes can be bought from any metro ticket office, machines at tram stations, blue-and-yellow bus ticket booths (near most major stops) and many newsstands – you can buy several at once and then validate them as necessary.

---

stations are erratic. Trams don't automatically stop at every station, so push the bell if you're on board, or wave it down if you're on the platform. Details at ⓦtramsa.gr.

### TAXIS
Athenian taxis can seem astonishingly cheap – trips around the city centre will rarely run above €5, which means for a group of three or four they cost little more than the metro. Longer trips are also reasonable value: to Pireás, for example, is €9–12 from the centre – the exact amount determined by traffic and amount of luggage. All officially licensed cars are yellow and have a red-on-white numberplate. You can wave them down on the street, pick them up at ranks in most of the major travel termini and central squares, or phone one (or get your hotel to do it).

**Taxi tips** Make sure the meter is switched on when you get in. If it's "not working", find another taxi. One legitimate way that taxi-drivers increase their income is to pick up other passengers along the way. There is no fare-sharing: each passenger (or group of passengers) pays the full fare for their journey. So if you're picked up by an already-occupied taxi, memorize the meter reading at once; you'll pay from that point on, plus the €1.16 initial tariff. When hailing an occupied taxi, call out your destination, so the driver can decide whether you suit him or not.

## ACCOMMODATION

**Hotels** and **hostels** can be packed to the gills in midsummer – August especially – but for most of the year you'll have no problem finding a bed. Having said that, many of the better hotels are busy all year round, so it makes sense to **book in advance**. In the cheaper places especially, ask to see the room before booking in – standards vary greatly even within the same building. Wherever you stay, rooms tend to be small, and noise can be a problem; you'll get slightly better value, and a greater chance of peace, away from the centre.

### WHERE TO STAY
Though pricey and commercialized, Pláka remains highly atmospheric, and many hotels here have Acropolis views from their roofs or upper storeys; they're also within easy walking distance of the main sites. A generally better-value alternative is Monastiráki, still well placed for the sights and an equally short walk from the restaurants and nightlife of Psyrrí. Platía Omonías is very much the city centre, with dozens of characterless, high-rise hotels on busy streets; south towards the bazaar are some more interesting alternatives, though the area is a little sleazy, especially at night. North of Omónia you are further out of the tourist mainstream (though close to the archeological museum), but benefit from good-value local restaurants and the proximity of cinemas, clubs and bars. Immediately south of the Acropolis, easily reached via the metro at Akrópoli, Makriyiánni is a very upmarket residential neighbourhood with a few good, if pricey, hotels and arguably the city's best

hostel. Further south it merges into more earthy Koukáki, where prices are significantly lower. Over in Pangráti there's another good hostel with a much quieter atmosphere.

### PLÁKA
#### HOTELS
★ **Acropolis House** Kódhrou 6 ☎210 322 2344, ⓦacropolishouse.gr; Metro Sýndagma; map p.66. A rambling, slightly dilapidated 150-year-old mansion much loved by its regulars – mostly students and academics, many of whom leave behind books for other guests to read. Furnishings are individual and some rooms have (sole use) baths across the hall; there's a/c and free wi-fi throughout. Variety of prices, and discounts for longer stays. Breakfast included. **€70**

**Ava Apartments & Suites** Lysikrátous 9–11 ☎210 325 9000, ⓦavahotel.gr; Metro Akrópoli; map p.66. Between the Temple of Zeus and the Acropolis, *Ava* offers very luxurious two-room suites and apartments accommodating up to five people and ideal for families. All have balconies – some very large – with sideways Acropolis views, as well as small kitchens and wi-fi. **€195**

**Electra Palace** Nikodhímou 18 ☎210 337 0000, ⓦelectrahotels.gr; Metro Sýndagma; map p.66. Five-star luxury right in the heart of Pláka with every facility including both indoor and rooftop pools, small gym and sauna. Stunning if you have an upper-floor suite, whose large balconies have great Acropolis views, but standard rooms are rather dull. **€195**

★ **Hermes** Apóllonos 19 ☎210 323 5514, ⓦhermes hotel.gr; Metro Sýndagma; map p.66. Friendly and welcoming three-star with marble bathrooms, polished wood floors and designer touches in every room, plus TV, a/c, fridge and wi-fi (small charge). Some rooms are rather small; others have big balconies. Interconnecting rooms also available. Breakfast included. **€120**

**Phaedra** Herefóndos 16, cnr Adhrianoú ☎210 323 8461, ⓦhotelphaedra.com; Metro Sýndagma; map p.66. Small, simple rooms with bare tiled floors, TV and a/c, not all en suite (but you get a private bathroom). Polite, welcoming management looks after the place well and it's quiet at night, thanks to a location at the junction of two pedestrian alleys. One of the best deals in Pláka. **€65**

**HOSTEL**

**Student & Traveller's Inn** Kydhathinéon 16 ☎210 324 4808, ⓦstudenttravellersinn.com; Metro Akrópoli/Sýndagma; map p.66. Very friendly, perennially popular travellers' meeting place, clean and well run, though not always the quietest spot. Small courtyard breakfast area/bar, free wi-fi, luggage storage, laundry and travel agency. Rooms range from eight-bed dorms to private doubles, some en suite, some shared bath; most are triple or quad. Dorm beds **€25**, rooms **€58**

## MONISTIRÁKI AND PSYRRÍ

★ **Attalos** Athinás 29 ☎210 321 2801, ⓦattalos.gr; Metro Monastiráki; map p.66. Modern from the outside but traditional within, the *Attalos* has bright, comfortable rooms, well insulated from the noisy street, all with a/c, TV and free wi-fi (also free computer terminals in the lobby). Some balcony rooms on the upper floors have great views – there's also a roof-terrace bar in the evenings – but rooms facing the internal courtyard at the back are generally larger and quieter. Some triples. Buffet breakfast available at extra cost. **€85**

**Metropolis** Mitrópoleos 46 ☎210 321 7469, ⓦhotel metropolis.gr; Metro Sýndagma/Monastiráki; map p.66. Right by the cathedral, the friendly Metropolis has simple, plainly furnished rooms with vinyl floors, each with a good-size balcony, a/c, wi-fi and TV, some with shared bathroom. Acropolis views from the upper floors. **€65**

★ **O&B** Leokoríou 7 ☎210 331 2950, ⓦoandbhotel .com; Metro Thissío; map p.66. Understated designer hotel with exceptional service and just 22 rooms, including a couple of large suites with private terrace and Acropolis views; all rooms have free wi-fi and satellite TV, as well as DVD and CD players. Friendly and comfortable as well as elegant, plus a great location on the fringes of Psyrrí. **€150**

**Tempi** Eólou 29 ☎210 321 3175, ⓦtempihotel.gr; Metro Monastiráki; map p.66. A long-time favourite with budget travellers: book exchange, free wi-fi, drinks and shared kitchen, plus handy affiliated travel agency. Rooms are simple, some are tiny and half have shared facilities, but all have a/c and the view of the flower market at Ayía Iríni across the quiet pedestrian walkway is enchanting. **€57**

## SÝNDAGMA

**Grande Bretagne** Vassiléos Yioryíou 1, Platía Sýndagma ☎210 333 0000, ⓦgrandebretagne.gr; Metro Sýndagma; map p.66. If someone else is paying, try to get them to put you up at the *Grande Bretagne*, the grandest of all Athens' hotels with the finest location in town. Refurbished for the Olympics, it really is magnificent, with every conceivable facility. The crisis has seen prices drop dramatically, with many special offers; even so, treatments in the spa cost more than a night at many hotels. **€280**

## OMÓNIA AND THE BAZAAR

**HOTELS**

**Athens Center Square** Arostogítonos 15 ☎210 321 1770, ⓦathenscentersquarehotel.gr; Metro Omónia/Monastiráki; map p.66. A budget boutique hotel directly above the fruit and vegetable market, handy for Psyrrí too. Smallish but very well-appointed rooms with a/c, flat-screen TV and free wi-fi, some with balconies; very good online deals often available. Breakfast included. **€85**

**Delphi Art Hotel** Ayíou Konstandínou 27 ☎210 524 4004, ⓦdelphiarthotel.com; Metro Omónia; map p.60. Right by the National Theatre and Áyios Konstantínos church, this 1930s mansion has been lavishly restored with Art Nouveau touches and eclectic, individual furnishings. Facilities include wi-fi throughout (for a charge), and Jacuzzi baths in some rooms. Breakfast included. **€80**

**Fresh Hotel** Sofokléous 26 ☎210 524 8511, ⓦfreshhotel.gr; Metro Omónia; map p.66. Glossy, high-end hotel in the heart of the market area. Lavish use of colour, elegant furnishings and great lighting and bathrooms, though the cutting-edge design is perhaps starting to lose its edge; some rooms are tiny. Facilities include wi-fi throughout, bike hire and an elegant rooftop pool, bar and restaurant, open to non-residents. **€110**

**1**

**HOSTEL**

**Athens International Youth Hostel** Víktoros Ougó 16 ☏ 210 523 2540, ⊕ athens-international.com; Metro Metaxouryío; map p.60. A huge affair, with 140 beds over 7 floors in 2-, 4- and 6-bed dorms, all a/c and en suite, some women-only. Recently given a fresh coat of paint, it is cheap and always busy. To be sure of a bed it's best to book in advance. Dorms from **€13**

**NORTH OF THE CENTRE**

**HOTELS**

**Art Hotel** Márni 27 ☏ 210 524 0501, ⊕ arthotelathens .gr; Metro Omónia; map p.60. Not the greatest location – on a rather noisy, scruffy street – but a very pleasant boutique hotel in a refurbished 1920s building with individually designed rooms. Thoughtful touches include Korres toiletries in the marble bathrooms, and there's a substantial buffet breakfast. **€99**

**Exarchion** Themistokléous 55, Platía Exarhíon ☏ 210 380 0731, ⊕ exarchion.com; Metro Omónia; map p.60. This big, 1960s high-rise is a great deal less fancy inside than you might imagine, despite its recent refurbishment. Still, it's good value if you want to be at the heart of Exárhia's nightlife, there's free wi-fi, and the simple rooms have TV, a/c and fridge. The upper floors are quieter, with better views. **€65**

**Museum** Bouboulínas 16 ☏ 210 380 5611, ⊕ museum -hotel.gr; Metro Viktorías/Omónia; map p.60. Very pleasant, international-style hotel (part of the Best Western chain), right behind the National Archeological Museum and the Polytekhnío. Rooms in the new wing, which has triples, quads and small suites, are more luxurious but slightly more expensive. **€75**

**Orion and Dryades** Emmanouíl Benáki 105 at Anexartisías ☏ 210 382 7362, ⊕ orion-dryades.com; Metro Viktorías/Omónia; map p.60. Quiet, well-run twin hotels across from the Stréfis hill – a steep uphill walk from almost anywhere. Reception is in the cheaper Orion, which has shared bathrooms, a kitchen, and a communal area on the roof with an amazing view of central Athens. All rooms in the Dryades are en suite with a/c and TV; there's wi-fi throughout, for a charge. Orion **€50**, Dryades **€75**

**HOSTEL**

**Hostel Aphrodite** Inárdhou 12, between Alakmenous and Mikhaïl Vódha ☏ 210 883 9249, ⊕ hostelaphrodite .com; Metro Viktorías/Lárissa; map p.60. Friendly, clean hostel with 8- and 4-bed dorms plus some private en-suite doubles and triples, in a quiet residential neighbourhood. A/c available at extra charge; other facilities include breakfast room/bar, luggage storage and free wi-fi. Dorm **€17**

**WEST OF THE CENTRE**

**Phidias** Apostólou Pávlou 39 ☏ 210 345 9511, ⊕ phidias.gr; Metro Thissío; map p.66. With an enviable position in Thissío overlooking the Acropolis, at the heart of a newly fashionable area crammed with designer cafés, the Phidias has cosy if rather dated rooms, with TV and a/c. Service with a scowl, and overdue for a makeover, but it's decent value; almost all rooms have balconies and fabulous views. Breakfast included. **€70**

**KOLONÁKI**

**Periscope** Háritos 22 ☏ 210 729 7200, ⊕ periscope.gr; map p.60. Designer minimalism on a shopping street in Kolonáki. Some rooms are on the small side (though the penthouse suite has its own rooftop hot tub) and the matt grey submarine theme can be a bit drab, but they're very comfortable, with every facility including free wi-fi, satellite TV and DVD/CD player. **€140**

**St George Lycabettus** Kleoménous 2 ☏ 210 729 0711, ⊕ sgl.gr; map p.60. A luxury hotel and an Athenian classic, with a position high on Lykavitós hill overlooking the city. Abundant marble and leather in the public areas plus a welcome rooftop pool, and bars and restaurant fashionable with wealthy young Athenians. Some of the rooms are rather small, however, and there's no point staying here if you don't pay extra for the view. **€150**

**SOUTHERN ATHENS**

**HOTELS**

**Art Gallery** Erekhthíou 5 ☏ 210 923 8376, ⊕ artgalleryhotel.gr; Metro Syngroú-Fix; map p.60. A family-owned converted apartment block, this popular, slightly old-fashioned *pension* with many repeat customers is named for the original artworks that adorn every room. Knowledgeable and helpful staff, convenient location and a bountiful breakfast (extra) served on a terrace with Acropolis views. **€70**

**Athens Studios** Veïkóu 3a ☏ 210 923 5811, ⊕ athens studios.gr; Metro Akrópoli; map p.60. Furnished apartments for up to six people, with kitchen, sitting room, TV, free wi-fi, a/c and linen provided. Managed by the people who run Athens Backpackers (see p.60), and includes use of their bar and facilities. Great value for groups. Apartments from **€90**

**Herodion** Robérto Gálli 4 ☏ 210 923 6832, ⊕ herodion .gr; Metro Akrópoli; map p.66. This lovely four-star hotel – albeit not quite as luxurious as the exterior and lobby might lead you to believe – enjoys an enviable position right behind the Acropolis. The roof terrace looks almost straight down to the south slope of the Acropolis. **€130**

**Marble House** Cul-de-sac off A. Zínni 35A ☏ 210 923 4058, ⊕ marblehouse.gr; Metro Syngroú-Fix; map p.60. The best value in Koukáki, family run and friendly. Simple rooms with and without private bath, with free wi-fi, fans and a/c (for extra charge); also two self-catering studios for longer stays. Often full, so call ahead. **€45**

## HOSTELS

⭐ **Athens Backpackers** Mákri 12 ☎210 922 4044, ⓦbackpackers.gr; Metro Akrópoli; map p.66. Very central Athenian–Australian-run hostel with few frills, but clean rooms, communal kitchen, internet access, bar, fabulous rooftop view and great atmosphere. Dorms from €22

**Pagration Athens Youth Hostel** Dhamáreos 75, Pangráti ☎210 751 9530, ⓦathens-yhostel.com; trolleys #2 and #11 from Omónia via Sýndagma, bus #203 or #204 or (15–20min walk) Metro Evangelismós; map p.60. A bit out of the way but friendly and good value, in a decent, quiet neighbourhood with plenty of local restaurants and lively nightlife. Free use of kitchen and communal area with TV; charge for washing machine and hot water. There's no sign on the door, so look for the green gate. Dorms €15

### PIREÁS

**Piraeus Dream** Fílonos 79–81 & Notára 78–80, Pireás ☎210 411 0555, ⓦpiraeusdream.gr; Metro Pireás; map p.60. It's easy to get from the centre to Pireás, but if you do have a very early departure this friendly hotel, handy for ferries, has quiet, recently refurbished rooms (with spectacular lighting), a/c and TV. Buffet breakfast included. €70

### AIRPORT

**Peri's Hotel & Apartments** Sarandapórou and Margéti, Loútsa ☎22940 83763, ⓦperishotelapt.gr. It's only about 40min by train or metro to the centre of Athens, but if you need to stay near the airport this simple modern rooms- and-apartment complex (free shuttle bus 7am–11pm) is far better value than the outrageously expensive *Sofitel* right in the airport complex; rates include a/c, wi-fi and breakfast. €80

## EATING AND DRINKING

Athens has the best and the most varied **restaurants** and **tavernas** in Greece – and many places are sources not just of good food but of a good night out too. Fast-food and takeaway places are also plentiful – the usual international chains keep a relatively low profile, and there are plenty of more authentic alternatives. Reservations are rarely necessary – indeed the simpler places probably won't have a reservation system (they can usually squeeze in an extra table if necessary) – but it is worth calling ahead at the fancier restaurants, or if you're planning a special trip across town.

### WHERE TO EAT

While Pláka's hills and narrow lanes can provide a pleasant, romantic evening setting, they also tend to be marred by high prices, aggressive touts and general tourist hype. Still in the centre, areas like Psyrrí, Monastiráki and Thissío (or Gázi a little further afield) are where the locals go for a meal out; lively and fashionable. Omónia is business territory, a great place to grab a quick (or a long) lunch. For

better value and traditional food, it's well worth striking out into the ring of neighbourhoods around, all of which have plenty of local tavernas: Exárhia, Neápoli, Áno Petrálona, Pangráti, Koukáki or the more upmarket Kolonáki are all good bets. On the coast the big attraction, not surprisingly, is fish. The pleasure harbours of Pireás, especially, are a favourite Sunday lunchtime destination.

### ETHNIC EATS

Greek people like to eat Greek food and until recently, even in the capital, it was very hard to find anything else. You'd have to say that they have a point; many of the city's ethnic restaurants are a pale imitation of the real thing. Athens' increasing multiculturalism, however, is at last being reflected in its food. These are our favourites:

**Fu-Rin-Ka-Zan** Apóllonos 2, Sýndagma ☎210 322 9170; map p.66. Busy Japanese restaurant – especially so at lunchtimes – with sushi, sashimi, yakisoba and the like at reasonable prices. Sushi and sashimi mixed plates €17–22. Mon–Fri 1–5pm & 7–11.30pm, Sat & Sun 6–11.30pm.

**Godzilla** Ríga Palamídhou 5, Psyrrí ☎210 322 1086; map p.66. Good-value sushi bar in a little street off Platía Ayíon Anaryíron. Mostly a late-night joint. Tues–Sun 8pm–1am.

**Indian Masala** Ermoú 129, Monastiráki ☎210 321 9412; map p.66. If you're craving Indian, this is the place to come, with a menu and atmosphere much like a UK curry house, plus a few Greek twists. Meat dishes

around €8, vegetable curries €6–7, house thal €10. Daily 6pm–12.30am.

**Meson el Mirador** Ayisiláou 88, cnr Salamínos, Keramikós ☎210 342 0007; map p.60. Authentic Mexican restaurant in an elegant restored mansion in Keramikós, with some tables on a lovely roof terrace. Gets enjoyably rowdy later on. Mon–Fri 7.30pm–1am, Sat & Sun 1pm–1am.

**Noodle Bar** Apóllonos 11, Pláka ☎210 331 8585; map p.66. One of a growing local chain of Asian fast-food restaurants – predominantly Thai but also with Indian, Chinese and Indonesian flavours; noodle dishes €7–8. Simple decor with plastic tables and a roaring takeaway trade. Mon–Sat all day.

1

## PLÁKA
### RESTAURANTS

**Brettos Ouzerí** Angélou Yéronda 9 on Platía Filomoússou Eterías ☎210 321 6981; map p.66. A spin-off from the famous *Brettos* (see p.66), this new ouzerí has a great people-watching position on the square. You can have anything from drinks to full meals, but the best bet is probably the own-brand ouzo with a shared meze plate – €15 for two people, €19.50 for four. 10am–1am daily.

**Byzantino** Kydhathinéon 18 on Platía Filomoússou Eterías ☎210 322 7368; map p.66. Reliable, traditional taverna that still attracts locals on this busy, touristy square. Take a look in the kitchen at the moderately priced daily specials, such as stuffed tomatoes (€7.50) or *youvétsi* (€9.90). Daily Lunch & dinner.

**Damingos (Ta Bakaliarakia)** Kydhathinéon 41 ☎210 323 5084; map p.66. Open since 1865 and tucked away in a basement, this place has dour service, but the old-fashioned style (hefty barrels in the back room filled with the family's home vintages, including a memorable retsina), and the excellent *bakaliáro skordhaliá* (deep-fried cod with garlic sauce) for which it is famed (and named) make up for it. Best in winter. Dinner only; closed mid-July to end Aug.

**Elaia/Palia Taverna tou Psarrá** Erekhthéos 16 at Erotókritou ☎210 324 9512/321 8733; map p.66. Though they appear to be separate restaurants, these two actually share a menu and kitchen; given that, the best place to sit is on the roof terrace at Elaia, with wonderful views; there are also plenty of tables below, both inside and on a tree-shaded and bougainvillea-draped pedestrian crossroads. You're best making a meal of the mezédhes (€6–9) which include humble standards as well as seafood and fish concoctions. Live Music Thurs–Sat eves, open lunchtime till late.

**Paradosiako** Voulís 44a ☎210 321 4121; map p.66. Small place on a busy street serving excellent, unpretentious, reasonably priced, fresh Greek food. Just three or four tables on the pavement, and a similar number inside. Mon–Sat lunch & dinner.

**Platanos** Dhioyénous 4 ☎210 322 0666; map p.66. Established 1932, and it feels like there's been little change to staff or menu at this taverna since, with no concessions to pretension or presentation. There's outdoor summer seating in a quiet square under the plane tree from which it takes its name, and reasonably priced traditional dishes such as roast lamb with artichokes or with spinach and potatoes (all €9.50), washed down with cloudy wine from vast barrels. Noon–4.30pm & 7.30pm–midnight.

★ **Skholarhio** Tripódhon 14 ☎210 324 7605; map p.66. Attractive, split-level ouzerí with a perennially popular summer terrace, sheltered from the street. It has a great selection of mezédhes (all €3–6) brought out on trays

so that you can point to the ones that you fancy. Especially good are the flaming sausages, *bouréki* (thin pastry filled with ham and cheese) and grilled aubergine. The house red wine is also palatable and cheap. All-inclusive deals at €14 a head. Daily 11am–2am.

### CAFÉS AND BARS

**Brettos** Kydhathinéon 41; map p.66. *Brettos* was originally a store selling the products of their own family distillery, a simple, unpretentious place with barrels along one wall and a huge range of bottles, backlit at night, along another. They still sell bottles, but now the main business is as a bar, open all day for ouzo and meze.

**Café Pláka** Tripódhon 1; map p.66. Touristy but convenient and elegantly refurbished – offers crêpes (€6.50–8), sandwiches, ice cream, free wi-fi and a roof terrace on which to enjoy them. Daily till late.

**Dhioskouri** Dhioskoúron, cnr Mitröon; map p.66. Café right on the edge of Pláka with great views over the ancient Agora. Simple food as well as the inevitable frappés and cappuccinos. Daily 9am–7pm.

**Yiasemi** Mnisikléous 23; map p.66. A café-bistro on a steep, stepped street, *Yiasemi* offers a warm interior in winter for soup and hot chocolate, or tables outside for fresh juices and inexpensive lunchtime specials (omelettes or salads €5). Daily mid-morning to midnight.

## MONASTIRÁKI AND PSYRRÍ
### RESTAURANTS

★ **Baïraktaris** Mitropóleos 88, cnr Platía Monastirakíou ☎210 321 3036; map p.66. Over a century old, this lively restaurant occupies two buildings whose walls are lined with wine barrels and photos of local celebrities. Some tables are set on the bustling pedestrian street, but for a cosier atmosphere, eat inside with the Greek regulars where there's often some impromptu live traditional music. The menu includes *souvláki*, *yíros* and oven dishes such as *soutzoukákia* (meatballs in tomato sauce); best to stick to the simple basics. Daily lunchtime to the early hours.

★ **Café Abysinia** Kynétou 7, Platía Avysinnías ☎210 321 7047, ⊛avissinia.gr; map p.66. With two floors and a delicious, modern take on traditional Greek cooking (wild boar meatballs, €15, for example, or mussel pilaf for €10.50), *Café Abysinia* is always busy, with a local alternative crowd. Though more expensive than many, it's decent value, and there's live music most weekday evenings and weekend lunchtimes. Tues–Sat 11am–1am, Sun 11am–7pm.

**Elihrison** Ayíon Anaryíron 6 ☎210 321 5156; map p.66. Huge place at the heart of Psyrrí in a tastefully restored old building with tables on several levels, including a roof garden and an internal courtyard. Pricier than most (mains around €15), but classier too, with live

Greek music most evenings and Sunday lunchtime. Mon–Fri 8pm–2am, Sat & Sun noon–2am.

**Kuzina** Adhrianoú 9 ☎ 210 324 0133; map p.66. Far more adventurous than the average Greek taverna, Kuzina's fusion cooking sets it well apart from its many neighbouring rivals. Starters vary from Greek staples like octopus to lamb spring rolls and crab cakes; mains tend to the exotic – chicken with figs and sesame seeds (€13.50), 12-hour roasted pork with lime and basil cream (€14) or Roy's black cod (€30). There's a cheaper, simpler lunch menu, with main dishes from €7.50–10. Daily Lunch & dinner.

**Nikitas** Ayíon Anaryíron 19 ☎ 210 325 2591; map p.66. A survivor from the days before Psyrrí was fashionable, and by far the least expensive option here, with excellent grilled meats and daily specials, plus great chips. Sun–Thurs 10am–7pm, Fri & Sat 11am–midnight.

★ **Taverna tou Psyrri** Eskhýlou 12 ☎ 210 321 4923; map p.66. Some of the lowest prices and tastiest food in Psyrrí, so unsurprisingly popular. Starters like stuffed aubergine at €4 and simple dishes including moussaka and meatballs for €5.50, but be sure to check out the day's specials in the kitchen, many of them traditional country dishes like rabbit stifado or an earthy goat soup (€7). Daily Lunch & dinner.

**Thanasis** Mitropóleos 69; map p.66. Reckoned to serve the best *souvláki* and *yíros* in this part of Athens, where there's plenty of competition. Inexpensive, and always packed with locals at lunchtime: there's no booking, so you'll have to fight for a table. Daily 11am to late.

### CAFÉS AND BARS

**Arodou** Miaoúli 22, cnr Protoyénous ☎ 210 321 6774; map p.66. Miaoúli, leading up from the metro into Psyrrí, is packed with bars and crowded with people every evening. *Arodou* is right at the heart – a hugely popular place with plenty of space both outside and in. Drink prices are very reasonable, and excellent, well-priced meze (€2.50–6, shared plates from €9) are also available. Daily till late.

**Bougatsadiko tou Psyrri** Platía Iróon 1; map p.66. Open 24 hours, so a good place for late-night munchies – *tirópita* and other pies, slices of pizza, drinks and ice cream, to take away or eat in. 24 hrs.

★ **James Joyce** Ástigos 12 ☎ 210 323 5055; map p.66. Every city has to have its Irish pub, but this central Athens version was a late arrival. However, it was worth waiting for – it's a really friendly place with great atmosphere, well-kept Guinness (as well as any other drink you might care to name), Sky sports and regular live acoustic music. There's also very good pub-style food – Irish breakfast (€12), sausage and mash (€9), and steak and Guinness pie (€12), as well as Irish-style meze! Daily noon–late.

**Oréa Ellás** Mitropóleos 59 or Pandhróssou 36; map p.66. Tucked away on the upper floor of the Kendro Ellinikis

Paradosis store, this consciously old-fashioned *kafenío* offers a welcome escape from the crowded Flea Market. There's also a great view of the rooftops of Pláka on the slope towards the Acropolis. Open daily 9am–6pm.

**Pagoto Manía** Aisópou 21, cnr Táki; map p.66. Dozens of flavours of superb ice cream (€1.50 a scoop) as well as cakes, coffee and tea. Daily till late.

**Ta Servetia tou Psyrri** Eskhýlou 3; map p.66. All the rage with locals for its traditional desserts and sticky cakes, washed down with tea, coffee or ouzo, according to taste. Open all day, through to the early hours.

## SÝNDAGMA
### RESTAURANT

**Cibus** Záppio Gardens ☎ 210 336 9300; ⊕ aeglizappiou.gr; map p.66. Pricey, smart restaurant with a fabulous setting, allegedly the haunt of the rich and famous and certainly patronized by politicians and diplomats. "Modern Mediterranean" food, which here means Greek with French and Italian influences – starters around €12, mains €15–30 (eg baby cockerel "Pastitsada" with nutmeg blossom and goat cheese, €18). It's part of the Aigli complex, which also houses an all-day café/bar (*Lallabai*) and a famous old open-air cinema. Daily 7.30pm–1am.

### CAFÉS AND BARS

**7 Jokers** Voulís 7; map p.66. Open all day for coffee, drinks and snacks, 7 Jokers' quirky, overstuffed decor comes into its own in the evening as it becomes a funky cocktail bar, popular with an after-work crowd. All day, through to the early hours.

**Oasis** West side of the National Gardens, opposite cnr of Amalías and Filellínon; map p.66. An unexpected shady haven just off the main avenue, offering light meals – sandwiches, pizza, pasta – ice cream and drinks. Daily 9am–sunset.

**Zonar's Le Café d'Athenes** Voukourestíou 9 at Panepistimíou; map p.66. Revival of an historic bourgeois Athenian café on the ground floor of the Attica department store. Glamorous surroundings, great people-watching and wonderful cakes and coffee at startlingly high prices. Mon–Fri 10am–9pm, Sat 10am–7pm.

## OMÓNIA AND THE BAZAAR
### RESTAURANTS

**Andreas** Themistokléous 18 ☎ 210 382 1522; map p.60. A traditional ouzerí, specializing in fish dishes such as mussels and octopus fritters, that's a venue for long weekday lunches; mezes typically around €5, and be sure to check the kitchen for what's on special. Live music Thurs–Sat. Lunch & dinner Mon–Sat, Sun lunch only.

**Arkhaion Yefsis** Kodhrátou 22, Metaxouryío ☎ 210 523 9661, ⊕ archeon.gr; map p.60. The name means

**1**

"ancient tastes" and this highly original restaurant claims to serve ancient Greek food, based on evidence from contemporary writings. It certainly makes for an enjoyable evening, in a lovely if slightly tacky setting with bare stone walls, statues, flaming torches and a courtyard. Dishes include wild boar cutlets and goat leg with mashed chickpeas and leeks, cheese, garlic and honey (at €27 for two), as well as plenty of less meaty options. Lunch & dinner Tues–Sun.

**Dhiporto** Theátrou, cnr Sokrátous, no phone; map p.66. Two brown-painted metal trapdoors in the pavement open to a steep stairway down into a basement that feels like it belongs in an Athens of fifty years ago. Simple, inexpensive Greek food – chick-pea soup, Greek salad, fried fish – washed down with retsina is enjoyed by market workers as well as tourists and office suits. Frequently as the afternoon wears on impromptu music breaks out. Mon–Sat 6am–6pm.

**Ipeiros** Southeast corner of the meat market; map p.66. A favourite for late-night resuscitation after the clubs or for a hangover cure the following morning, Ipeiros is an entirely traditional taverna. There's a wide range of excellent, inexpensive baked dishes that you can choose from the kitchen, as well as plenty of meat, but the soups are what this place is known for, above all patsa, a tripe soup that's renowned as a cure for all ills. You're sealed off behind glass from the market, so not quite as close to the action and smells as at some of the more basic neighbouring stalls. Open all day, every day, till very late.

**Klimataria** Platía Theátrou 2 ☎ 210 321 6629; map p.66. Friendly, old-fashioned taverna serving ample portions of traditional fare at reasonable prices (mains around €8). Take a look at the daily specials in the kitchen; there are usually excellent vegetable dishes plus daily roast meats. Barrels of wine are just about the only decoration, but there's open courtyard seating in summer and live music at the end of the week. Open lunchtimes plus dinner Fri & Sat.

### CAFÉS

**Amouage** Galería Koraï off Platía Koraï; map p.66. The Galería Koraï is full of cafés and fast-food places – including the likes of Starbucks, McDonald's and Costa – as well as more local places like this, serving crêpes (€3–6), sandwiches, hot dogs and juices. Mon–Sat all day till early evening.

**Krinos** Eólou 87, behind the central market; map p.66. Operating since 1922, though thanks to recent refurbishment the only signs of that are the old photos adorning the walls. Still the place for old-fashioned treats like *loukoumádhes* (doughnut-like puffs soaked in syrup) and *bougátsa* as well as *tirópittes*, sandwiches and ice creams. Mon, Wed & Sat 7.30am–3.30pm, Tues, Thurs & Fri 7.30am–8.30pm.

## NORTHERN ATHENS
### RESTAURANTS

**Barba Yannis** Emmanouíl Benáki 94 ☎ 210 330 0185; map p.60. Neighbourhood treasure with a varied menu of home-style oven food (changes daily and displayed in large pots near entrance; around €7.50) in a relaxed atmosphere, aided and abetted by barrelled wine. Tables outside on pedestrianized street in summer. Open all day until the small hours.

**Barbara's Food Company** Emmanouíl Benáki 63–65 ☎ 210 380 5004; map p.60. Colourful café-restaurant with wonderful salads (€4.50–6) and pasta dishes, plus daily specials from around the world (€6.50–9.50), from meatballs to won-tons, and good-value lunchtime menus. Daily noon–midnight.

★ **Lefka** Mavromiháli 121 ☎ 210 361 4038; map p.60. Beloved old taverna with great *fáva* (hummus-like bean purée), black-eyed beans and baked and grilled meat with barrelled retsina. Summer seating in a huge garden enclosed by barrels. Lunch & dinner Mon–Sat, lunch only Sun.

**Mystic Pizza** Emmanouíl Benáki 76 ☎ 210 383 9500; map p.60. Tiny, unpretentious place serving pasta and salads as well as excellent pizzas (mostly €8–9). The flour they use is made from hemp (cannabis) seeds, which they claim has both health and environmental benefits. Takeaway and delivery service too. Mon–Fri 1pm–1am, Sat & Sun 7pm–1am.

**Pinaleon** Mavromiháli 152 ☎ 210 644 0945; map p.60. A classic old-style taverna, serving rich mezédhes and meaty main courses (€7–10), washed down with excellent organic wine. Dinner only; closed June–Sept.

**Rozalia** Valtetsíou 58 ☎ 210 330 2933; map p.60. Ever-popular mid-range taverna, with excellent chicken and highly palatable barrelled wine. You order mezédhes from the tray as the waiters thread their way through the throng; there's also a regular menu of grilled fish and meat. Garden seating in summer. Daily lunch & dinner.

**Yiandes** Valtetsíou 44 ☎ 210 330 1369; map p.60. Modern and, for Exárhia, upmarket restaurant serving excellent food that's based on modern Greek cuisine with Asian influences and organic ingredients. Pleasant courtyard next to the Riviera open-air cinema. Daily lunch & dinner.

### CAFÉS

**Café Creperie Au Grand Zinc** Emmanouíl Benáki 88; map p.60. The cosy, quiet, wood-lined interior makes a peaceful stop for coffee and crêpes, often to the background of a little jazz. Mon–Sat 7pm–2am.

**Floral Books and Cafe** Themistokléous 80, Platía Exarhíon; map p.60. Spacious and comfortable bookstore/ café, devoting roughly equal space to each activity. Coffee, juices and snacks in the day, with more of a cocktail bar atmosphere at night, plus free wi-fi and regular live music. Daily till late.

**FROM TOP** SPONDI (P.107); CHEZ LUCIEN (P.106); TAVERNA TOU PSYRRÍ (P.103); ELIXIRION (P.102) >

## 1

## WESTERN ATHENS
### RESTAURANTS

**Butcher Shop** Persefónis 19, Gázi ☎ 210 341 3440; map p.60. As the name and the decor – a modernist take on a traditional butcher shop – suggest, this is not one for the vegetarians. Instead there's all sorts of high-quality meat, from lamb chops (€15.40) to game birds (€12) plus a huge variety of burgers (€10–12.50), exotic sausages (€7.50–9) and the fanciest *yíros* in town (with shank and pancetta of free-range pork, €11.50). Great chips too. Daily noon–1am.

**Chez Lucien** Tróön 32, Áno Petrálona ☎ 210 346 4236; map p.60. Excellent French bistro with a short menu of authentic, well-prepared dishes at reasonable prices, and a set menu for €23. You may have to wait – there are no reservations – and/or share a table. Tues–Sat from 8.30pm; closed Aug.

**Filistron** Apóstolou Pávlou 23, Thissío ☎ 210 342 2897; map p.66. Somewhat touristy, but worth it for the roof terrace with great Acropolis view. Short menu of tasty, well-presented *mezédhes* from all over Greece (small plates €5–8.50, large ones €8–13.50), which means some interesting and unusual dishes; good value given the location. Tues–Sun noon–midnight.

**Gazohori** Dhekeléon 1 & 5 ☎ 210 342 4044; map p.60. A big, busy place in two separate buildings, attracting a typically young Gazí crowd. Traditional meze served on marble-topped tables, with wine in tin jugs, at reasonable prices; large *pikilía* (meze selection) €16. Daily lunch & dinner.

★ **Ikonomou** Tróön 41, cnr Kydhantidhón, Áno Petrálona ☎ 210 346 7555; map p.60. Wonderful, traditional taverna with home-cooked food served to packed pavement tables in summer. No menu, just a dozen or so inexpensive daily specials: check out what others are eating as the waiters may not know the names of some of the dishes in English. Mon–Sat dinner only.

★ **To Steki tou Ilia** Eptahálkou 5, Thissío ☎ 210 345 8052; map p.66. Simple, inexpensive place on a pedestrianized street above the metro tracks that's so busy the owners have opened a second branch 200m further down (at Thessaloníkis 7). Renowned for some of the finest lamb chops in the city. Tables on the street in summer. Tues–Fri dinner only, Sat lunch & dinner, Sun lunch only.

**Varoulko** Pireós 80, Keramikós ☎ 210 522 8400, ⊕ varoulko.gr; map p.66. Chef Lefteris Lazarou has earned a Michelin star every year since 2002: considering that, the exquisite seafood here is neither over-elaborate nor overpriced (even so, reckon on €70 or so a head). The elegant modern setting includes a summer roof terrace with Acropolis views; expect starters like crayfish with apple-geranium ice cream, mains such as John Dory with horseradish and sour-apple cream. Booking essential; dinner only, closed Sun.

### CAFÉ

**Athinaion Politeia** Akamántos 1, cnr Apóstolou Pávlou, Thissío; map p.66. An enviable position in an old mansion, with great views from the terrace towards the Acropolis, makes this a popular meeting place and a great spot to relax over a frappé. Rather pricey light meals also served. Daily 9am–3am.

## KOLONÁKI
### RESTAURANTS

**Balsamakis (To Kotopoulo)** Platía Kolonakíou, north side ☎ 210 360 6725; map p.60. As the name indicates, this tiny hole-in-the-wall is the place for chicken – juicy, crispy, rotisserie-style; also kebabs and *yíros*. It's strictly no-frills, lit by fluorescent lights and packed with people at all hours. A few tables on the pavement too. Mon–Sat 11am–11pm.

**Dhimokritos** Dhimokrítou 23 ☎ 210 361 3588; map p.66. Old-fashioned, posh and perhaps a bit snooty – lots of suits at lunchtime – but a beautiful building and well-prepared, reasonably priced food from a vast menu, much of which is displayed in glass counters near the entrance; try for example the *tiropitákia* (€5) followed by lamb in lemon sauce (€12) or a veal chop (€15). Mon–Sat lunch & dinner, Sun lunch only; closed Aug.

**Filippou** Xenokrátous 19 ☎ 210 721 6390; map p.60. This old-time taverna has been completely refurbished. The newly elegant interior (and a no-smoking policy that's actually enforced) hasn't changed the menu much, though; you can still check out the simmering pots and casseroles in the kitchen, or find favourites like pork in lemon sauce or rabbit with wine sauce for around €8, as well as some more ambitious, modern Greek dishes. Liveliest at lunchtime. Mon–Fri lunch & dinner, Sat lunch only.

★ **Ikio** Ploútarhou 15 ☎ 210 725 9216; map p.60. The name means "homely", and that seems to be how the locals find it – a busy, reasonably priced, bourgeois neighbourhood restaurant with a slightly modern take on Greek classics and a short menu of daily specials, such as chicken meatballs with arab pie and yoghurt sauce (€10), plus pasta and salads. Mon–Sat lunch & dinner.

★ **Il Postino** Grivéon 3, in alleyway off Skoufá ☎ 210 364 1414; map p.66. Good-value modern Italian osteria, serving freshly made pasta (from €9, spaghetti vongole €14) and simple Italian dishes (home-made gnocchi with gorgonzola and prosciutto €12) in a friendly, bustling room. Daily 1pm–1am.

**Jackson Hall** Milióni 4 ☎ 210 361 6098; map p.66. A very "Kolonáki" type of place; a big, busy, expensive American-themed diner with a music bar upstairs. Burgers (€14), steaks (€23), pasta, salads and the like, plus coffees and juices in the morning, cocktails and beer at night. Daily all day till late.

## CAFÉ

**Filion** Skoufá 34; map p.66. A local institution for coffee, cakes, omelettes, salads and breakfast: busy at all times of day with a more sober crowd than the average Kolonáki café. Daily 8am–midnight.

## SOUTHERN ATHENS
### RESTAURANTS

**Ambrosia** Dhrákou 3–5, Koukáki ☎ 210 922 0281; map p.60. A friendly *psistariá* (grill house) packed with locals, especially on summer nights when the tables spill out into the pedestrian walkway. Food is inexpensive, simple and delicious – succulent grilled chicken, pork chops, kebabs and Greek salads – and service friendly and attentive. Daily lunch & dinner.

**Da Capo** Tsákalof 1; map p.60. One of the most popular of the many establishments on this pedestrianized street, just north of Kolonáki square. *Da Capo* is very chic and, unusually, self-service. Mon–Sat 7am–midnight, Sun 8.30am–midnight.

**Karavitis** Arktínou 33, cnr Pafsaníou, Pangráti ☎ 210 751 5155; map p.60. This crumbling building, a lone single-storey survivor surrounded by high-rises, looks a dump from outside, but within there's a cheery old-style taverna with barrel wine, mezédhes and clay-cooked main courses (€7.50–10). In summer there's outdoor seating in an enclosed garden. Dinner daily, plus Sunday lunch.

**Katsourbos** Amínta 2, Pangráti ☎ 210 722 2167; map p.60. Cretan food is highly fashionable in Athens, and this modern-looking place is right on trend, with tasty food created from ingredients sourced from the island. Relatively expensive (€25–30 all in), but worth it. Daily lunch & dinner.

**Mikri Vouli** Platía Varnáva 8, Pangráti ☎ 210 756 5523; map p.60. A bustling neighbourhood *mezedhopolío*, with tables out on the square in summer and excellent meze (€5–9), including some unusual varieties. There are plenty of other places around the square. Daily lunch & dinner.

**Spondi** Pýrronos 5, just off Platía Varnáva, Pangráti ☎ 210 756 4021, ⓦ spondi.gr; map p.60. Long-time contender for the title of Athens' best restaurant, *Spondi* has two Michelin stars to show for the efforts of French chef Arnaud Bignon, and serves superb French-influenced cuisine in a lovingly restored bourgeois mansion. With starters – crab in fine herb jelly with cauliflower mousse – from €30 and mains such as milk-fed lamb with candied lemon and polenta mostly around €40, it's not cheap, but for a special occasion it's worth it. Tasting menus including wine €75 and €147; booking is essential. Daily lunch & dinner.

**Strofi** Robérto Gálli 25, Makriyiánni ☎ 210 921 4130; map p.66. An old-fashioned, upmarket taverna in a completely refurbished setting, whose chief attraction is a roof terrace with great, close-up Acropolis views. Classic Greek dishes like roast lamb (€14), *biftéki* (€9.50) or veal stew (€13.50). Well worth it if you get a roof-top table. Daily noon–1am.

## CAFÉ

★ **Acropolis Museum café** Dhionysíou Areopayítou 15, in the Acropolis Museum; map p.66. It is perhaps just as well that you can only eat here if you've bought a ticket for the museum, as otherwise it would be permanently mobbed. There's a large, cool, smoke-free internal area, plus a partly shaded terrace looking up towards the Parthenon. Food is simple – salads, sandwiches, cakes and drinks – and portions aren't huge, but the quality is superb and the prices very low by Athens standards (€14 for sandwiches, €2.50 for a cappuccino). Try the delicious *píta me fakés*, a traditional lentil pie. Tues–Sun 8am–8pm, late opening Fri till 10pm.

## PIREÁS

If you're looking for food to take on board a ferry, or breakfast, you'll find numerous places around the market area and near the metro station, as well as all along the waterfront. There are plenty of bakeries and *souvláki* joints here, including a handy branch of *Everest* on the corner of Aktí Kalimassióti by the metro. Otherwise there's little good food in the port area, but some superb fish tavernas over at Mikrolímano.

### RESTAURANTS

★ **Ammos** Aktí Koumoundhoúrou 44, Mikrolímano, Pireás ☎ 210 422 4633; map p.60. In contrast to the high-luxe places around it, *Ammos* goes for an island feel, with hand-painted tables and beach scenes. Still mainly fish (drunkard's mussels €7.80, grilled prawns or fisherman's pasta €15), but also a wide variety of meze (€5–9) and slightly lower prices and a younger crowd than its neighbours. Book at weekends. Daily lunch & dinner.

**Jimmy And The Fish** Aktí Koumoundhoúrou 46, Mikrolímano ☎ 210 412 4417; map p.60. Excellent, glamorous and inevitably expensive fish-taverna occupying the prime position among the harbourside places on Mikrolímano. Fabulous lobster spaghetti and fresh fish (priced by the kilo); *linguine vongole* €17, Caesar salad with prawns €16. Booking essential at weekends. Daily midday–2am.

## CAFÉ

**Aktoploiko** Aktí Tsélegi 4; map p.60. Less manic than most around the port, with tables outside on a pedestrianized part of the waterfront just off Platía Karaïskáki, this café serves breakfast and light meals – *souvláki*, salads, pasta – throughout the day. Daily till late.

**1**

## NIGHTLIFE

In the city centre, the most vibrant nightlife is in and around **Psyrrí**, **Gázi** and **Thissío** but there are **bars** and **clubs** almost everywhere, mostly kicking off around 10pm or later. Bars listed here mostly focus on music or morph into clubs after midnight; North European-style pubs are rare – try *Brettos* (see p.66) or *James Joyce* (see p.66); there are also plenty of cafés that function as bars at night; try *7 Jokers* (see p.66) or *Arodou* (see p.66). Some central Athens air-conditioned clubs remain open year-round, but in **summer** the scene really moves out to the long stretch of coast from Fáliro to Várkiza, where huge temporary clubs operate on and around the beaches. If you head out, bear in mind that the taxi fare will be just one of several hefty bills, although admission prices usually include a free drink.

### BARS

**45° lákhou** 18, Gázi ☎ 210 347 7729; map p.60. A big, lively, rock-music-based bar-club, one of the longest-established places in Gázi. Opens relatively early and there's a rooftop terrace with Acropolis views. From 9pm; closed Mon.

**Bios** Pireós 84, Gázi ☎ 210 342 5335, ⓦ bios.gr; map p.60. Boho art-space/café/bar/club with frequent happenings of performance art, live music or experimental theatre. There's something going on here most evenings, and a basement dance-space with late-night avant-garde sounds. Open all day till late.

**Frame Garden** Dhinokrátous 1, Kolonáki ☎ 210 721 4368; map p.60. Architect-designed garden bar at the swish St George Lycabettus Hotel, a summer meeting place of Athens' wealthy young trendsters. Food served all day, but comes alive at night for cocktails and DJ sets. Open May–Oct.

**Ghost** Lepeniótou 26, Psyrrí ☎ 210 323 6431, ⓦ ghostbar.gr; map p.66. Lively bar with theme nights, karaoke, live music, coffee and cocktails. Entry fees vary. From 9pm.

**Micra Asia** Konstantinoupóleos 70, Gázi ☎ 210 346 9139; map p.60. Old house converted to a bar on several floors, including roof space. The name means Asia Minor, and there's an Ottoman theme, with chilled music to match. Occasional exhibitions, and DJs at weekends playing electro, hip-hop, R&B and house. From 10pm nightly.

**Roi Mat Rock Club** Solomoú 17–19, Exárhia ☎ 210 330 5056, ⓦ roimatrockclub.gr; map p.60. Basement rock club that frequently hosts the after-parties from neighbouring An Live Club (see p.60). Sweaty rock'n'roll atmosphere. Usually free entry. Wed–Sun late.

**Socialista** Triptolémou 33, Gázi ☎ 210 347 4733; map p.60. Big, enjoyable bar/club in the midst of the action in Gázi, with Latin sounds and occasional live music. From 9pm nightly.

**Underground** A Metaxá 25, Platía Exarhíon, Exárhia ☎ 210 382 2019; map p.60. By day a bar-café with a rock soundtrack, *Underground* transforms into a heavy metal and thrash club from around 11pm – loud and sweaty.

### CLUBS

#### DOWNTOWN

**Candy Bar** Ierá Odhós 41, Gázi ☎ 210 346 3080; map p.60. Huge club that draws a big out-of-town crowd with wild theme-nights and visiting DJs: party atmosphere; club, house and R&B on the decks. Entry from €15. Fri & Sat from 10pm.

**Soho** Voutádhon 54, Gázi ☎ 210 342 2663, ⓦ sohobar .gr; map p.60. There's a row of half a dozen bar/clubs at the top of Voutádhon, with dance music thumping out and a youthful crowd. Soho is the biggest and arguably the best of them. In the early evening there are tables outside, food is served and it's a relatively calm meeting place; later on the volume is turned up and the action moves to the DJs inside. Daily, 4pm till late.

**Space by Avli** Iraklidhón 14, Thissío ☎ 210 347 0900; map p.66. In the heart of the Thissío bar area, this daytime café-bar on three floors evolves at night into a funky club with jazz and soul music. Daily, lunchtime till late.

**Venti** Lepeniótou 20, Psyrrí ☎ 210 325 4504, ⓦ venti .gr; map p.66. Elegant, upmarket bar/club/restaurant around a courtyard with opening glass roof. Dance music after midnight. 9pm–3am.

**Zas Bar** Ayías Théklas 12, Psyrrí mobile ☎ 693 65 61 313, ⓦ myspace.com/zasbar; map p.66. Attracts a very young crowd for hot dance nights, predominantly hip-hop, dubstep and rap. Entry and hours vary.

### SUMMER BEACH CLUBS

**Ammos Beach** Loutrá Alímou, off Possidhónos ☎ 210 985 5848; tram Loutrá Alímou. On the seafront between Pireás and Glyfádha, Ammos Beach lives up to its name, with an excellent beach. At night there are parties and themed events, plus residences from Greek and international DJs, with predominantly R&B and house music. Entry from €15, including first drink. Summer only, from 11pm.

**Island** km27 on Athens–Soúnio road between Vouliagméni and Várkiza ☎ 210 965 3563, ⓦ island clubrestaurant.gr. Stunning clifftop setting attracts a chic, stylish crowd. One way to be sure of making it past the queue and the bouncers is to book into the restaurant (see p.60). Summer only, from 11pm.

**W Poolside Dreams** Dhiadókhou Pávlou B, Glyfádha Marina ☎ 697 27 00 712. Huge seaside summer club with a pool at its heart and music from R&B to house to Greek pop. Entry from €15. Summer only, Tues–Sat.

## GAY AND LESBIAN VENUES

Athens' **gay scene** is mostly very discreet, but the city has its share of bars and clubs; most, these days, are in Gázi. For further information, check the gay sections in the listings magazines or the excellent website ⓦ www.gaygreece.gr. Athens Pride takes place in the first week of June (ⓦ athenspride.eu).

**Blue Train** Konstantinoupóleos 84, Gázi ☎ 210 346 0677; map p.60. Open from early evening, this is a popular gay meeting place before going on to the clubs, with a courtyard in summer. Upstairs, *Kazarma* (same phone) is one of the better clubs you could go on to, while *El Cielo*, higher still, is a summer roof-terrace bar. 8pm–3am.

**Noiz** Konstantinoupóleos 78, Gázi ☎ 210 346 7850, ⓦ noizclub.gr; map p.60. Lesbian bar-club with good international sounds and welcoming atmosphere. 10pm–4am.

**Sodade** Triptolémou 10, Gázi ☎ 210 346 8657; map p.60. Both lesbian- and gay-friendly, with a stylish crowd and great music – one room plays Greek and mainstream, the other quality dance music. Daily 11pm–3.30am.

## ENTERTAINMENT

Live traditional **Greek music** (see p.795) is one of the capital's big attractions but you have to visit during winter to see the best acts; in summer many musicians head off to tour the islands. This winter period – from around October to May – is also when the major **classical music**, **ballet** and **drama** performances are staged, and the **sporting** calendar is at its busiest. On the other hand, summer is the **festival** season. Most significant is the June-to-September **Athens & Epidaurus Festival** of dance, music and ancient drama, but there are also annual rock, jazz and blues events, while you may see big international bands at one of the major outdoor venues.

### LIVE GREEK MUSIC

**To Baraki Tou Vassili** Dhidhótou 3, Kolonáki ☎ 210 362 3625, ⓦ tobaraki.gr; map p.66. Daily acoustic performances: a showcase for up-and-coming rebétika acts and singer-songwriters. Entry around €15, includes first drink; reasonably priced drinks once you're in. From around 10.30pm, closed Sun.

**Boemissa** Solomoú 13–15, Exárhia ☎ 210 383 8803, ⓦ boemissarebetika.gr; map p.60. Rebétika and laïká place popular with university students, who jam the dance floor and aisles, and inevitably end up writhing on the tabletops as well. Good company of musicians play music from all regions of Greece. Drinks €7: two-drink minimum; mezédhes served. Reservations recommended. Tues–Sun 11pm–4am.

**Hilios ke Dhio Nikhtes (1002 Nights)** Karaïskáki 10, Psyrrí ☎ 210 331 7293, ⓦ 1002nyxtes.gr; map p.66. Live music venue that's also a bar and restaurant with a Middle-Eastern theme. Arabic-inspired menus from €25–50, plus

traditional Greek music which explores its eastern roots – legendary Irish lyra player Ross Daly is a regular. Entry free–€10. Most nights from 10.30pm.

**Perivoli T'Ouranou** Lysikrátous 19, Pláka ☎ 210 323 5517; map p.66. Traditional rebétika club on the edge of Pláka (so used to tourists) with regular appearances by classy performer Babis Tsertsos. Entry varies, but even when free they make up for it on the food and drink – €10 for a beer, €25–30 for main-course dishes. Open Oct–June, closed Wed.

**Stoa Athanaton** Sofokléous 19, in the meat market ☎ 210 321 4362; map p.66. Fronted by *bouzoúki* veterans Hondronakos and company. Good taverna food at reasonable prices but expensive drinks. Open Sept–April Mon–Sat 3–6pm & midnight–6am; closed Sun.

### LIVE ROCK

The indigenous Greek rock scene is small but manages to support a number of local bands, while Athenian rock

**WHAT'S ON WHEN**

Sources of information on **what's on** in English are somewhat limited. There are some listings in a number of free monthly or weekly publications distributed to hotels, but these are partial and not always accurate; better are the weekly *Athens News* (published Friday; ⓦ athensnews.gr), with full movie lisitings and coverage of most major events, or the daily local edition of the *International Herald Tribune*. Much more exhaustive listings including music, clubs, restaurants and bars, but in Greek only, can be found in local weekly *Athinorama*. These can be bought at kiosks anywhere in the city: look out too for free weeklies like *Lifo* and *Athens Voice* (again, Greek only), copies of which can be picked up in galleries, record shops and the like. Specialist record shops (see p.113) are also good sources of information in themselves, frequently displaying posters and selling tickets for rock, jazz or festival concerts.

1

enthusiasts tend to be knowledgeable to the point of obsession. For rock bars, clubs and record shops, Exárhia is the place to be. Major international bands generally appear in the summer to play open-air venues.

**After Dark** Dhidhótou 31 & Ippokrátous, Exárhia ☏ 210 360 0460, ⊛ www.afterdark.gr; map p.60. Rock, blues and soul, plus the occasional live performance by Greek indie bands to a young crowd. Typically €5 weekdays, €8 weekends. From 11pm, midnight Fri & Sat, closed Mon.

**An Live Club** Solomoú 13–15, Exárhia ☏ 210 330 5056, ⊛ anclub.gr; map p.60. Basement club featuring live performances by local and lesser-known foreign rock bands. Typically €8–10 entry. From 9pm.

**Gagarin 205** Liossíon 205 ☏ 210 854 7601, ⊛ gagarin205.gr; Metro Attikís; map p.60. Some way north, but probably the finest venue for live rock in Athens, where some 2000 fans can crowd in to see the best touring indie bands as well as local talent and club nights. Entry (around €15) and hours vary.

**Kookoo Live Music Bar** Iákhou 17, Gázi ☏ 210 345 0930, ⊛ kookoo.gr; map p.60. Fun new live music venue, featuring young Greek alternative and rock musicians in an enjoyably sweaty space. Entry typically €12, including a drink. Oct–June from 12.30am.

**Stavros tou Notou** Tharípou 37, Néos Kósmos ☏ 210 922 6975, ⊛ stn.gr; Metro Syngroú-Fix; map p.60. One of the liveliest rock clubs in town, mostly featuring Greek artists, but plenty of touring foreigners too. Entry typically €15, including first drink.

### LIVE JAZZ AND LATIN
Jazz has only a small following in Greece, but there are still some good clubs that can attract touring bands of international repute. The major events take place as part of the Jazz and Blues Festival at the end of June; information and tickets are available from the Athens Festival box office (see p.60) and some record stores.

**Cafe Alavastron** Dhamaréos 78, Pangráti ☏ 210 756 0102, ⊛ cafealavastron.gr; map p.60. Excellent atmosphere and live performances of a wide variety of music, from trad jazz to African and Latin. Entry and hours vary.

**Half-Note** Trivonianoú 17, Mets ☏ 210 921 3310, ⊛ halfnote.gr; map p.60. Athens' premier jazz club, with live jazz most nights and frequent big-name touring performers. Entry €25–30 (€20 Mon), drinks €10. Oct–May nightly at 10.30pm (9pm Sun).

**In Vivo** Harilaóu Trikoúpi 79, Neápoli ☏ 210 382 2103, ⊛ invivoclub.gr; map p.60. Classy blues, jazz and rock acts at an intimate, friendly venue; entry €6–15. Oct–June, Fri & Sat from 8pm, acts at 11pm.

### DANCE AND CLASSICAL MUSIC
Unless your Greek is fluent, the contemporary Greek theatre scene is likely to be inaccessible; along with music, it is essentially a winter pursuit.

**Dora Stratou Ethnic Dance Company** Filopáppou Hill ☏ 210 324 4395, ⊛ grdance.org; Metro Petrálona or Akrópoli; map p.60. The Dora Stratou company's show in their own open-air theatre combines traditional music, fine choreography and gorgeous costumes for an experience you'd be hard put to encounter in many years' travelling around Greece. Tickets (€15) can almost always be picked up at the door. Performances late May to late September Tues–Sat 9.30pm, Sun 8.15pm.

---

## THE ATHENS AND EPIDAURUS FESTIVAL

The annual **Athens and Epidaurus Festival** encompasses a broad spectrum of cultural events: most famously ancient Greek theatre (performed, in modern Greek, at the Herodes Atticus Theatre on the South Slope of the Acropolis), but also modern theatre, traditional and contemporary dance, classical music, jazz, traditional Greek music and even a smattering of rock.

The **Herodes Atticus Theatre** (see p.70) is a memorable place to watch a performance on a warm summer's evening – although you should avoid the cheapest seats, unless you bring along a pair of binoculars and a cushion. Other festival venues include the open-air **Lykavitós Theatre** on Lykavitós Hill, and the two ancient theatres at **Epidaurus** (see p.142). For the latter, you can buy inclusive trips from Athens from the festival box office, either by coach or boat – the two-hour boat trip includes dinner on board on the way home.

Performances are scheduled from late May right through to early October, although the exact dates vary each year. If you can, it's worth **booking** in advance (credit card bookings on ☏ 210 327 2000 and at ⊛ greekfestival.gr); tickets go on sale three weeks before the event at the box office. As well as online, programmes are available from tourist offices or from the festival box office in the arcade at Panepistimíou 39 (Mon–Fri 8.30am–4pm, Sat 9am–2.30pm). There are also box offices at the Herodes Atticus Theatre (daily 9am–2pm and 5–8pm) and Epidaurus (Mon–Thurs 9am–2pm and 5–8pm, Fri & Sat 9.30am–9.30pm) for events at those venues only.

**Greek National Opera** Olympia Theatre, Akadhimías 59 **☎** 210 361 2461, **W** nationalopera.gr; Metro Panepistimíou; map p.66. Opera primarily, but also ballet and classical concerts. Season from October to July.

**Mégaro Mousikís** Leofóros Vassilísis Sofías and Kókkali, next to the US embassy **☎** 210 728 2333, **W** megaron.gr; Metro Mégaro Mousikís; map p.60. Athens' premier concert hall hosts a variety of events year-round, though the most prestigious classical performances are during the winter.

## FILM
Athens is a great place to catch a movie. In summer dozens of outdoor screens spring up in every neighbourhood for a quintessentially Greek film-going experience. There are also plenty of regular indoor cinemas, including a number in the centre, though a significant proportion of these, with no air conditioning, close from mid-May to October. Films are almost always shown in the original language with Greek subtitles. Outdoor screens tend to concentrate on art-house and alternative offerings, classics and themed

festival seasons. To attend simply for the film is to miss much of the point. You may in any case never hear the soundtrack above the din of locals cracking *passatémpo* (pumpkin seeds), drinking and chatting (sit near a speaker if you want to hear). Snack-bars serve sandwiches, popcorn, pizza, beer and wine.

**Cine Paris** Kydhathinéon 22, Pláka **☎** 210 322 2071. Outdoor screen with a rooftop setting and side view of the Acropolis, right in the heart of town.

**Thission** Apostólou Pávlou 7, Thissío **☎** 210 342 0864. Old-fashioned outdoor summer theatre with an Acropolis view.

**Village Entertainment Park** Thívon 228, halfway between the centre and Pireás **☎** 210 427 8600; bus #B18 from Omónia. Twenty-screen multiplex in a huge shopping centre is Athens' largest; the same group has smaller multi-screens in Pángrati, Fáliro and Maroúsi.

**Zefyros**, Tróön 36, Áno Petrálona **☎** 210 346 2677. Newly done up, trendy Zefyros shows art-house and foreign-language movies as well as mainstream classics. A particular favourite of Athenian thirty-somethings.

## SHOPPING

Shopping in Athens is decidedly schizophrenic. On the one hand, the **bazaar area** is an extraordinary jumble of little specialist shops and stalls, while almost every neighbourhood still hosts a weekly **street market**. On the other hand, the upmarket shopping areas of the city centre, and the **malls** and fashion emporia of the ritzier suburbs, are as glossy and expensive as any in Europe. Somewhere between the extremes, in the city centre you'll find endless *stoas*, covered arcades off the main streets full of little shops. Some have been expensively refurbished and house cafés and designer-label stores; most, though, are a little dilapidated, and many still specialize in a single product – books here, computer equipment there, spectacles in another.

## HANDICRAFTS, ANTIQUES AND GIFTS
Greek handicrafts are not particularly cheap but the standard of workmanship is usually very high. In addition to the stores listed below, several museums have excellent shops, including the National Archeological Museum, Benáki Museum and Cycladic Art Museum, which sell original designs as well as reproduction artworks.

**Amorgos** Kódhrou 3, Pláka; map p.66. A small, old-fashioned shop filled with an eclectic collection of tasteful woodcarvings, needlework, lamps, lace, shadow puppets and other handicrafts. Mon–Fri 10am–3pm & 5.30–8pm.

**Elliniko Spiti** Kekropós 14, just off Adhrianoú, Pláka; map p.66. Amazing artworks and pieces of furniture created from found materials, especially driftwood but also metal and marble. Probably too big to take home (for your wallet as well as your suitcase), but well worth a look. Mon–Fri 10am–2pm & 4–8pm.

**Kendro Ellinikis Paradosis** entrances at Mitropóleos 59 and Pandhróssou 36, Monastiráki. As the name, "Centre of Hellenic Tradition", suggests, this pleasant upstairs emporium has a wide selection of traditional arts and crafts, especially ceramics and woodcarving, all at

reasonable prices and with little of the hard sell often encountered in the nearby flea market. Even better is a selection of old Greek film posters, postcards and the like. Daily 9am–6pm.

**Theotokis** Normánou 7, Monastiráki; map p.66. One of a number of quirky antique/junk shops in this narrow street in the Flea Market. Prints, posters, postcards, old radios, typewriters, military uniforms: if you are looking for something specific it's amazing what they can find among their stock. Mon–Sat 10am–6pm.

**To Komboloi tou Psyrri** Ayíon Anaryíron 13, Psyrrí; map p.66. A lovely little shop selling worry beads (*komboloi*) in every conceivable shape and size, plus hand-made jewellery and crafts. Daily 10am–10pm.

## FASHION AND JEWELLERY
Greeks love to shop, for clothes above all. On the whole it's familiar international labels you'll find here, in the main shopping area of Ermoú below Sýndagma, and in the dozens of malls in the suburbs. For high fashion, however, there's only one place to be, and that's Kolonáki, where wandering the narrow streets around the Platía will reward you with dozens of small boutiques. For

1

## BAZAARS AND MARKETS

Even on a purely visual level, the **central bazaar** and nearby flower market (p.83) are well worth a visit, while the surrounding streets, especially Evripídhou, are full of wonderfully aromatic little shops selling herbs and nuts, and others concentrating on supplies for a peasant way of life that seems entirely at odds with modern Athens – rope, corks, bottles and preserving jars. On Sunday mornings from around 6am until 2pm, between Monastiráki and Thissío metro stations, you will find a **flea-market** of authentic Greek junk (used phone cards and the like) spread out on the pavements, especially along the metro lines towards the Thissío end of Adhrianoú.

Among the best and most central **street markets** are: Mondays, Hánsen in Patissíon (Metro Áyios Eleftheríos); Tuesdays, Lésvou in Kypséli (Metro Viktorías) and Láskou in Pangráti (trolley #2 or #11); Fridays Xenokrátous in Kolonáki, Dhragoúmi in Ilísia (Metro Evangelismós/Mégaro Mousikís), Tsámi Karatássou in Koukáki (Metro Akrópoli) and Arhimídhous in Mets, behind the Panathenaic Stadium; and on Saturdays Plakendías in Ambelókipi (Metro Ambelókipi) and Kallidhromíou in Exárhia. Usually running from 7am to 2pm, these are inexpensive and enjoyable, selling household items and dry goods, as well as fresh fruit and vegetables, dried herbs and nuts.

something a little more alternative, wander over into adjoining Exárhia.

**Athena's Sandals** Normánou 7, Monastiráki; map p.66. Stavros Melissinos, the "poet sandal-maker", was an Athens institution, numbering The Beatles, Anthony Quinn and Sophia Loren among his celebrity clients. Now retired, his daughter carries on his tradition, with interesting leatherwork of all kinds (belts, bags, slippers) alongside the sandals – while a son has a rival store nearby. Mon, Wed, Sat & Sun 10am–4pm, Tues, Thurs & Fri 10am–8pm.

**Attica** Panepistimíou 9, Sýndagma; map p.66. Athens' prime fashion department store, with the finest window displays in the city and a huge branch of upmarket café Zonar's on the ground floor. Convenient if you want to do everything under one roof, especially in the summer when it's hot, though the designer labels include little you wouldn't find at home. Mon–Fri 10am–9pm, Sat 10am–7pm.

**Crop Circle** Themistokléous 52 & 66, Exárhia; map p.66. Reasonably priced vintage clothing and ethnic jewellery. The branch higher up the hill sells new stock, the lower one vintage. Mon & Wed 10am–2pm, Tues, Thurs & Fri 10am–2pm & 5–8pm, Sat 10am–3pm.

**Elena Votsi** Xanthoú 7, Kolonáki; map p.60. An amazing little shop (not easy to find) that's home to Elena's innovative jewellery designs, which incorporate precious and semiprecious stones as well as materials such as shells. Among other things she designed the medals for the 2004 Olympics, and has worked with the likes of Gucci and Ralph Lauren. Tues, Thurs & Fri 10am–8pm, Wed & Sat 10am–3pm.

**Shop** Ermoú 112A, Psyrrí; map p.66. Largest of a number of fashionable postmodern stores at the Psyrrí end of Ermoú. Deals in a wide range of designers and fashion labels, from Vivienne Westwood to Miss Sixty, as well as gifts, books, toys and music. Tues, Thurs & Fri 10am–9pm, Wed, Sat & Sun 10am–5pm.

**Thallo** Ploútarhou 25, Kolonáki; map p.60. Small jewellery shop that's well worth a visit. Greek plants and flowers are coated in silver and gold to gorgeous effect and the prices are among the least intimidating in Kolonáki. Tues, Thurs & Fri 10am–8pm, Wed, Sat & Sun 10am–4pm.

### FOOD AND DRINK

**Aristokratikon** Servías 9, Sýndagma; map p.66. An old Athenian favourite for traditional Greek chocolates; try the chocolate-covered prunes. Also much-coveted pistachios, sugared almonds and sour cherry jam. A token from here is always welcome when visiting someone's home. Mon–Fri 8am–9pm, Sat 8am–4pm.

**Ariston** Voúlis 10, cnr Karayeóryi Servías, Sýndagma; map p.66. Part of a small chain of local zaharoplastía (cake shops), with excellent-value sweet and savoury pies, biscuits, cakes and old-fashioned fruit jelly sweets. Mon–Sat 7am–10pm.

**Elixirion** Evripídhou 41, central bazaar; map p.66. Old-fashioned store with magnificent original fittings. Herbs, dried fruit and garlic hanging from the ceiling; teas, spices, grinders, dried fruits and honey to buy. Mon–Wed & Sat 7.30am–5pm, Thurs & Fri 7.30am–3.30pm.

**Ikologi Elladas** Panepistimíou 57, Omónia; map p.60. A big health-food supermarket with alternative medicine practitioners in-store, plus a café serving freshly squeezed juices and vegetarian and organic foods to eat in or take away. Mon–Fri 10am–6pm, Sat 10am–4pm.

**Oino Typo** Hariláou Trikoúpi 98, Neápoli; map p.60. Excellent wine merchant with over 50 varieties of Greece's famous barrelled wines (you can fill your own container), as well as 1200 international bottled wines. Mon–Sat 10am–10pm.

**To Thymari tou Strefi** Kallidhromíou 51A, Neápoli; map p.60. A lovely retro pantopolío (corner store, literally a store that sells everything) selling traditional Greek preserves, honey, nuts, dried fruit, cheese, olives and olive oil among much else. Great for edible souvenirs and gifts. Mon & Wed 9am–4pm, Tues, Thurs & Fri 9am–2pm & 5–8pm, Sat 10am–6pm.

**Tsatsos** Veïkou 45, Koukáki; map p.60. Koukáki boasts some of the finest *zaharoplastía* in Athens, and Tsatsos is one of the best of them: try the traditional *kadaifi* and *baklava*. Mon–Sat 7am–2pm & 5–10pm.

## BOOKS
These are the main places to buy English-language books; studenty Exárhia is best for Greek texts.

**Compendium** Nikodhímou 5, cnr Iperídhou, Pláka; map p.66. Long-established English-language bookshop: small secondhand section, noticeboards for travellers and residents, and regular poetry readings and other events. Mon & Wed 9am–5pm, Tues, Thurs & Fri 9am–8pm, Sat 10am–3pm.

**Eleftheroudhakis** Panepistimíou 17, Sýndagma; map p.66. Seven floors of books provide space for an extensive stock, with plenty in English; there's a travel section on the top floor, and a good café on the sixth. Smaller branch at Níkis 20, Pláka. Mon–Fri 9am–9pm, Sat 9am–6pm.

**Newsstand** Athanasíou Dhiakoú 2, Makriyiánni; map p.66. A city-wide chain, but this branch of the newsagent, right by Metro Akrópoli, specializes in international press, along with plenty of books in English, maps and guides. Daily 8am–10pm.

**Solaris** Botási 6, Exárhia; map p.60. Comics old and new,

as well as graphic novels, models of characters and other paraphernalia. Mon, Wed & Sat 9am–3.30pm, Tues, Thurs & Fri 9am–2.30pm & 5–8.30pm.

**Stoa tou Bibliou** entered from Panepistimíou 49 or Pesmazogloú 5; map p.66. A quiet arcade (or *stoa*) devoted entirely to books, with seating areas and frequent exhibitions. Almost all in Greek, but still worth a look – a couple of antiquarian dealers have old maps. Individual shop hours vary.

## MUSIC
You'll find mainstream music stores in any of the main shopping areas; below are listings for places to explore Greek sounds, as well as classic vinyl (there are dozens of specialist stores, especially in Exárhia).

**7+7** Iféstou 7, Monastiráki; map p.66. A choice selection of old and new rock and Greek music on vinyl and CD. This alley in the Flea Market has several other record and secondhand bookshops. Mon–Sat 10am–6pm.

**Music Machine Records** Dhidhótou 16, Exárhia; map p.60. Fine collection of classic vinyl and posters, along with high-end hi-fi, new and secondhand. A cool place with good music. Mon & Wed 10am–4pm, Tues, Thurs & Fri 10am–2pm & 5–8pm, Sat 10am–6pm.

**Xylouris** Panepistimíou 39 in Stoa Pesmazogloú, Omónia; map p.66. Run by the widow of the late, great Cretan singer Nikos Xylouris, this old-fashioned store is one of the best places for finding Greek pop, folk and Cretan music. Mon & Wed 9am–3pm, Tues, Thurs & Fri 9am–2pm & 5–8pm, Sat 10am–4pm.

## DIRECTORY

**Banks and currency exchange** Normal banking hours are Mon–Thurs 8am–2.30pm and Fri 8am–2pm and just about all banks can exchange money during those hours; several banks with longer hours can be found around Sýndagma, plus there are numerous currency exchange places (generally with worse rates) in Pláka and around Sýndagma, and hotels will change money at a worse rate still. Almost every bank in the centre has an ATM.

**Bike, scooter and motorbike rental** For mountain bikes try Athens by Bike, Tziréon 16 at Dhionysíou Areopayítou ☎ 2130 423 922, � athensbybike.gr. For motorized wheels Motorent, Robérto Gálli 1, cnr Kavalóti ☎ 210 923 4939, ⍈ motorent.gr. Both are in Makriyiánni, near Metro Akrópoli.

**Car rental** The vast majority of downtown car rental offices are on Leofóros Syngroú, mostly in the first section close to the Temple of Olympian Zeus. They include Avance at no. 40–42 ☎ 210 920 0100, ⍈ avance.gr; Europcar no. 25 ☎ 210 921 1444; Hertz, no. 12 ☎ 210 922 0102; and Kosmos, no. 9 ☎ 210 923 4696, ⍈ kosmos-carrental.com. The local companies are generally cheaper; if you turn up in person and compare prices, you can often haggle a better rate.

**Doctors and hospitals** The largest central hospital is Evangelismós at Ipsilándhou 45, Kolonáki (☎ 210 720 1000; Metro Evangelismós). You'll find a list of hospitals, and a few adverts for English-speaking doctors, in the weekly *Athens News*; ⍈ athens.usembassy.gov has hospital addresses and a list of practitioners (under Special Consular Services). Most doctors speak at least some English, and medical care is generally very good, though nursing and after-care tend to rely on the help of family.

**Embassies and consulates** Most major embassies are in Kolonáki or Ambelókipi, on or not far from Leofóros Vassilísis Sofías. They include: Australia, Level 6, Thon Building, cnr Kifissiás & Alexandhrás, Ambelókipi ☎ 210 870 4000, ⍈ greece.embassy.gov.au (Metro Ambelókipi); Canada, Ioánnou Yennadhíou 4 ☎ 210 727 3400, ⍈ athens .gc.ca (Metro Evangelismós); Ireland, Vassiléos Konstantínou 7, in Pangráti near the Panathenaic Stadium ☎ 210 723 2771, ⍈ embassyofireland.gr; New Zealand (honorary consulate), Kifissiás 76, Maroúsi ☎ 210 692 4136 (Metro Panormóu); South Africa, Kifissiás 60, Maroúsi ☎ 210 61 06 645 (Metro Panormóu); UK, Ploutárhou 1, Kolonáki ☎ 210 727 2600, ⍈ ukingreece.fco.gov.uk (Metro

1

Evangelismós); USA, Vassilísis Sofías 91 ☎ 210 720 2419, ⓦ athens.usembassy.gov (Metro Mégaro Mousikís).

**Emergencies** European emergency number ☎ 112; Ambulance ☎ 166; Fire ☎ 199; Police ☎ 100; Tourist police ☎ 171. For details of emergency hospitals and duty doctors and pharmacies ☎ 1434.

**Internet cafés** There's free municipal wi-fi in many parts of Athens, including Sýndagma square and the port at Pireás, as well as in many hotels and cafés. Among the more central and reliable internet cafés are: Bits & Bytes, Kapnikaréas 19, off Adhrianoú, Pláka (24hr); Athens Internet, Veïkou 3a, Koukáki (24hr); and Ivis Travel, Mitropóleos 3, Sýndagma (daily 8am–10pm).

**Laundry** Most hotels will do laundry but charge a fortune. Laundromats that do service washes include National, Apóllonos 17, Pláka (Mon & Wed 7am–4pm, Tues, Thurs & Fri 7am–8pm; €6.50 per kilo, also offers dry cleaning); Athens Launderette, Veïkou 3a, Koukáki (daily 8am–10pm; €7 per load) and a nameless place at Psárron 9, just off Platía Karaïskáki, Metaxouryío (Mon–Fri 8am–8pm, Sat 8am–5pm, Sun 8am–noon; €9 load).

**Luggage storage** Best arranged with your hotel; many places will keep the bulk of your luggage for free or for a nominal amount while you head off to the islands. Otherwise Athens Internet Cafe, Veïkou 3a, Koukáki ☎ 210 923 5811 (open 24hr) charges €3 per day; Pacific Travel, Níkis 26, Sýndagma ☎ 210 324 1007 (also at the airport), charges €6 per day, €27 for a week.

**Pharmacies** There are a number of large general pharmacies (*farmakía*) around Omónia, especially on 28

Oktovríou (Patissíon) and Panepistimíou; many also sell homeopathic remedies. Standard hours are Mon & Wed 8am–2.30pm, Tues, Thurs & Fri 8am–2pm & 5.30–8.30pm. The weekly *Athens News* has listings of pharmacies open out-of-hours: a list of these is also on display at many pharmacies, or call ☎ 1434.

**Police** Dial ☎ 100 for emergency help (☎ 112 from a mobile) or ☎ 171 for the Tourist Police; for thefts, problems with hotel overcharging, etc, it's the latter you should contact.

**Post offices** (*tahydhromía*) For ordinary letters and parcels up to 2kg, the branch on Sýndagma (cnr Mitropóleos) is open Mon–Fri 7.30am–8pm, Sat 7.30am–2pm, Sun 9am–1pm. There are machines selling stamps and phonecards. To send heavier parcels, use the post office at Mitropóleos 60, near the cathedral (Mon–Fri 7.30am–8pm), or at Koumoundhoúrou 29 by the National Theatre, Omónia. There are also major branches near Omónia at Eólou 100 (the central office for poste restante) and on Platía Kótzia. Queues can be enormous, so be sure you're at the right counter – there are often separate ones (with shorter queues) for stamps and parcels.

**Travel agencies** There are dozens of travel agencies, including many budget and youth- or student-oriented ones, in the streets of Pláka just off Sýndagma, especially on and around Filellínon and Níkis. As well as ferry and plane tickets, many of these will offer island packages or tours of Greece. Among them are Magic Travel, Níkis 33 ☎ 210 323 7471, ⓦ magic.gr; Pacific, Níkis 26 ☎ 210 324 1007, ⓦ pacifictravel.gr; and student specialist Robissa, Voúlis 38 ☎ 210 321 1188, ⓦ robissa.gr.

# Around Athens: Attica

**Attica** (Attikí), the region encompassing the capital, is not much explored by tourists – only the great romantic ruin of the **Temple of Poseidon** at **Cape Soúnio** and the beaches immediately outside Athens are at all well known. The rest, if seen at all, tends to be en route to somewhere else – the airport or the Peloponnese or to the ports of **Rafína** or **Lávrio**.

At first sight the neglect is not surprising; the mountains of **Imittós**, **Pendéli** and **Párnitha**, which surround Athens on three sides, are progressively less successful in confining the urban sprawl, while the routes out of the city are unenticing to say the least. Yet a day-trip or two, or a brief circuit by car, can make a pleasant and rewarding break, with much of Greece to be seen in microcosm within an hour or two of the capital. There are rewarding archeological sites at **Eleusis** and **Ramnous** as well as Soúnio, and **beaches** almost everywhere you turn, though none remote enough to avoid the Athenian hordes. Combine a couple of these with a meal at one of the scores of seaside *psarotavérnas* (fish restaurants), always packed out on summer weekends, and you've got a more than worthwhile day out.

## The Apollo Coast

Athens' coastline is often overlooked by visitors, who are here for their Classical fix and off to the islands for beaches. For Athenians, though, it's an essential summertime

**HIGHLIGHT**
⑧ Temple of Poseidon

**AROUND ATHENS**

safety valve and they head down here in droves: not just for beaches, but for cafés, restaurants, nightlife and shopping. In an area dubbed the "**Apollo Coast**", the southern suburbs form an almost unbroken line along the coast all the way from Pireás to Vouliagméni and Várkiza, some 20km away. Buses and the tram make it easy to head down to the beach for a quick swim and be back in the centre just a couple of hours later; astonishingly, the water almost everywhere is clean and crystal clear.

Beyond Várkiza the coast road rapidly becomes much emptier, the countryside more barren. At **Saronídha**, the furthest outpost for city buses, roughly halfway from Várkiza to Soúnio, there's a large sandy beach with a gently shelving bottom, very popular with windsurfers. Neighbouring **Anávissos** has a row of *psarotavérnas* along its more sheltered southern beach. Further still, the coast starts to get rockier, the road more winding, looking out on small islands offshore, until finally you begin to catch glimpses of the Temple of Poseidon ahead.

## Glyfádha

The heart of the city's summer suburban playground – for shopping, clubbing, dining or posing on the beach – is **Glyfádha**, a bizarre mix of glitz and suburbia.

**1**

At weekends, half of Athens seems to decamp down here. The epicentre is around the crescent of Leofóros Angélou Metáxa, lined with shops and malls, with the tram running down the centre and streets of cafés and restaurants heading off on either side.

## Vouliagméni

Glyfádha merges almost indistinguishably into its neighbour **Voúla**, and then into quieter, more upmarket **Kavoúri** and **Vouliagméni**. The latter is one of the city's posher suburbs, and its beautiful cove beaches are a traditional hangout of Athens' rich and famous. Last stop for the local buses is **Várkiza**, more of a seaside resort pure and simple.

If you are prepared to walk a bit, or are driving and happy to battle the locals for parking space, then some of the best beaches can be found around the **Vouliagméni peninsula**, off the main road. Immediately after Voúla B pay beach, a road turns off to Kavoúri, past the *Divani Palace Hotel* and some packed free beaches with excellent tavernas. Further along on this Kavoúri side of the peninsula are some still better, less crowded, free beaches: the #114 bus runs a little way inland, not far from these. Carrying on round, you get to Vouliagméni itself, with beautiful little coves, a few of which remain free, and eventually rejoin the main road by Vouliagméni A Beach. Beyond Vouliagméni the road runs high above the coast en route to Várkiza; the rocky shore a steep climb below, known as **Limanákia**, is largely nudist and has a large gay attendance.

### GETTING AROUND                                             THE APOLLO COAST

**By bus and tram** Trams run as far as Glyfádha, as do city buses #A2, #B2, #A3, #B3, #E22 from the centre of Athens; #A1 or #G1 from Pireás; the #A3 and #B3 continue to Vouliagméni, the #E22 all the way to Saronídha. Local services #114 (Glyfádha–Kavoúri–Vouliagméni) and #115/6 (Glyfádha–Vouliagméni–Várkiza) are also useful.

### EATING AND DRINKING

#### GLYFÁDHA

**Chic** Zissimopoúlou 12, Glyfádha. One of a host of packed, glam, upmarket café-bars on this street just off the main shopping drag in the heart of Glyfádha; occasional live music. Open all day, till late.

**George's Steak House** Konstantinoupoléos 4, Glyfádha ☎ 210 894 6020. Despite the name this is a fairly traditional Greek grill-house, large, reasonably priced and very popular. Located on a side street crowded with restaurants close to the main Platía Katráki tram stop. Excellent lamb chops (€9) and meatballs (€6.50). Lunch & dinner daily.

**Molly Malone's** Yiannitsopoúlou 8, Glyfádha ☎ 210 894 4247. Irish-run pub offering a warm welcome, cold

---

## PAY BEACHES

Almost all of the really good beaches within easy reach of Athens demand **payment** for entry. For your money you'll get clean sand, lifeguards, somewhere to buy food and drink, a lounger (usually at extra cost) and a variety of other facilities including beach volleyball, massage, fun parks and all sorts of watersports. Some of the fanciest, in Glyfádha and Vouliagméni, charge upwards of €10 per person at weekends (the *Astir Palace* hotel charges an exorbitant €45); more basic places cost €4–7. There are plenty of places to **swim for free**, but this may mean from the rocks, or a long hike from the road. The best sandy beach with free access is at Skhiniás (p.119), but that's a long way out on the northeast Attic coast. On summer weekends, every beach – and the roads to them – will be packed.

Among the better **pay beaches** are Áyios Kósmas (summer daily 9am–8.30pm; €6, children €3), a relatively quiet choice at Ag. Kosmas 2 tram stop; Asteria (summer daily 8am–8pm; €5, €10 weekends, children half-price), a slightly glam and busy choice right in the heart of Glyfádha; Voúla A & B (summer daily 7am–9pm; €5), large twin beaches in Voúla between Glyfádha and Vouliagméni, cheap and cheerful with decent facilities; and Vouliagméni A (summer daily 8am–8pm; €6), on the main road in Vouliagméni, with few facilities but a lovely setting.

If you **drive**, be warned that parking is a nightmare, especially in Glyfádha and Vouliagméni; the pay beaches all have parking, though some charge extra.

Guinness and a distinctively Irish–Greek craic. Good food too, from sandwiches to steaks to Irish stew. Open all day, till late.

**Vincenzo** Yiannitsopoúlou 1, Platía Espéridhon, Glyfádha ☎ 210 89 41 310. Good, reasonably priced Italian fare, including excellent pizzas (€6–10) from a wood oven. Lunch & dinner daily.

### VOULIAGMÉNI

**Akti** Possidhónos 6, Vouliagméni ☎ 210 896 0448. On the main road just beyond the Vouliagméni peninsula, with waterfront tables and great views, this is a top-class fish

taverna. Fish is expensive and so is Vouliagméni; by those standards €50–60 for a fish or lobster main course is reasonable value. Waterfront tables are very heavily in demand; booking essential. Lunch & dinner daily.

★ **Island** Limanakia Vouliagménis; km27 on Athens–Soúnio road between Vouliagméni and Várkiza ☎ 210 965 3563. Beautiful bar/restaurant/club with a breathtaking clifftop setting; very chic and not as expensive as you might expect at €15–25 for a main course. Modern Mediterranean food and a sushi lounge. Booking is essential, especially at weekends. May–Oct 9.30pm–late (club from 11pm).

# Cape Soúnio

Aktí Souníou – **Cape Soúnio** – the southern tip of Attica some 70km from the city centre, is one of the most imposing spots in Greece, for centuries a landmark for boats sailing between Pireás and the islands, and an equally dramatic vantage point from which to look out over the Aegean. On its tip stands the fifth-century BC Temple of Poseidon, built in the time of Pericles as part of a major sanctuary to the sea god.

Below the promontory are several **coves** – the most sheltered a five-minute walk east from the car park and site entrance. The main Soúnio beach, a short distance to the north, is more crowded, but has a couple of tavernas at the far end.

## The Temple of Poseidon

Daily 9.30am–sunset • €4

The **Temple of Poseidon** owes much of its fame to Lord Byron, who visited in 1810, carved his name on the nearest pillar (an unfortunate and much-copied precedent, which means the temple is now roped off) and immortalized the place in verse:

*Place me on Sunium's marbled steep,*
*Where nothing, save the waves and I,*
*May hear our mutual murmurs sweep;*
*There, swan-like, let me sing and die:*
*A land of slaves shall ne'er be mine –*
*Dash down yon cup of Samian wine!*

from *Don Juan*

In summer, at least, there is little hope of silent solitude, unless you slip into the site before the tour groups arrive or after they've left. But the setting is still wonderful – on a clear day, the view takes in the islands of Kéa, Kýthnos and Sérifos to the southeast, Égina and the Peloponnese to the west – and the temple is as evocative a ruin as any in Greece. Doric in style, it was probably built by the architect of the Hephaisteion in the Athens Agora. That it is so admired and visited is in part due to its position, but also perhaps to its picturesque state of ruin.

The rest of the site is of more academic interest. There are remains of a fortification wall around the sanctuary; a **propylaion** (entrance hall) and **stoa**; and cuttings for two shipsheds. To the north are the foundations of a small **Temple of Athena**.

### GETTING AROUND

**CAPE SOÚNIO**

**By bus** Orange KTEL Attikis buses leave from the Mavrommatéon terminal (p.95). For Soúnio via the coast (€5.20, roughly 2hr) they depart every hour on the half-hour from 6.30am to 5.30pm; there's also a more central (but in summer, very busy) stop 10min later on Filellínon,

south of Sýndagma (corner of Xenofóndos). Returns are hourly from 8am to 9pm. On the less attractive but marginally cheaper inland route via Lávrio (see p.96) there are half-hourly departures from 5.45am to 6.45pm, slightly less frequently to Lávrio from then until 10.30pm (one an

1

hour continues to Soúnio). There are also direct buses between Lávrio and the airport.

**By car** Drivers can take either route described above or complete a circuit, but there's little to see in the interior, where the road takes you via the airport and the toll motorway.

### EATING AND DRINKING

**Akroyiali** Soúnio beach ☎ 22920 39107. Right down by the water, a beachside taverna with both character and history – a number of illustrious Greek guests have dined here. The food, mainly fish, is simple but cooked to perfection (as ever, the fish is priced by weight). Lunch & dinner daily.

## The east coast

Central Attica has been blighted by the new airport and its associated motorways, and though there are still villages with Byzantine churches and countryside where wine is made, there's little incentive, when heading east, to stop anywhere before you reach the coast. This is popular with weekending Athenians and the site of many of their second homes. Almost due east of Athens lies the port of **Rafína**, and to the north of here are **Marathon** and the isolated site of ancient **Ramnous**, as well as some relatively uncrowded beaches. South of Rafína the coast is less attractive, with continuous development all the way down through **Loútsa** (aka Artemis) towards **Pórto Ráfti**; it is also directly beneath the airport flight path.

### Rafína

The port of **RAFÍNA** has fast **ferries** and **catamarans** to the Cyclades, as well as to nearby Évvia. Many Athenians have summer homes overlooking the attractive, rocky coast, but the beaches are tricky to reach even with a car, so for visitors the chief attraction, ferries aside, is gastronomic. Overlooking the harbour is a line of excellent **seafood restaurants**, many with roof terraces and a ringside view of the comings and goings at the harbour. They're interspersed with cafés and fishmongers. The pedestrianized square above the harbour is also a lively place, ringed with cafés and rather cheaper eating options. A lunchtime outing is an easy operation, given the frequency of the bus service. Evenings, when it's livelier, you'll need to get a taxi back, or stay.

### Marathon

The site of the **battle of Marathon**, the most famous and arguably most important military victory in Athenian history, is not far from the village of **MARATHÓNAS**, 42km from Athens. Here, in 490 BC, a force of 9000 Athenians and 1000 of their Plataian allies defeated a 25,000-strong Persian army. After the victory a runner was sent to Athens to declare the news: having run the first marathon, he delivered his message and dropped dead. Just 192 Athenians died in the battle (compared to some 6,000 Persians), and the burial mound where they were laid, the **Týmfos Marathóna** (Tues–Sun 8.30am–3pm; €3), can still be seen, off the main road between Rafína and Marathónas. It is a quietly impressive monument, though surrounded now by one-way roads installed for the Olympic marathon race. The **Mound of the Plataians** (Tues–Sun 8.30am–3pm; €3), where the eleven Plataians (including a 10-year-old boy) who died were laid to rest, is about 5km away, near the edge of the mountain; there's also a small, modern **archeological museum** here.

### Áyios Pandelímonas

**ÁYIOS PANDELÍMONAS**, also known as Paralía Marathónas, lies straight on past the Týmfos Marathóna. The beach isn't the greatest – though there's plenty of room to spread out – but a string of waterfront fish tavernas and an open-air movie theatre ensure plenty of local visitors in summer.

# Skhiniás

The best **beach** in the region – some would say the best in the Athens area – lies north of Marathon at **SKHINIÁS**, a long, pine-backed strand with shallow water, big enough to allow some chance of escaping the crowds. Buses run along the road behind the beach, where there are a number of stops. At the southern end there's a certain amount of development and several cordoned-off pay-beach sections offering cafés, showers, loungers and watersports; perhaps the best of these is *Karavi* (⊛karavi.gr), with free entry, a decent bar and restaurant, volleyball courts, and windsurf hire and lessons. The central section of Skhiniás beach, beyond the Olympic rowing and kayaking centre, is the least developed, with numerous tracks leading through the pines from the road to the sand. At the northern end there's more low-key development, mainly in the form of cafés and scattered **tavernas** on the sand.

# Ramnous

Daily 8am–3pm • €2

The little-visited ruins of **Ramnous** occupy an isolated, atmospheric site above the sea, with magnificent views across the strait to Évvia. The site was an Athenian lookout point from the earliest times, and remains can be clearly seen continuing way below the fenced site, all the way down to the rocky shore. Within the site, the principal ruin is a Doric **Temple of Nemesis**, goddess of divine retribution. Pausanias records that the invading Persians incurred her wrath by their presumption in bringing with them a giant marble block upon which they intended to commemorate their victory. They met their nemesis, however, at the battle of Marathon, and the Athenians used the marble to create a statue instead. There are also the remains of a smaller temple dedicated to Themis, goddess of justice, and a section of ancient road.

## GETTING AROUND                                    THE EAST COAST

**By bus** KTEL buses to the east coast leave from the Mavrommatéon terminal (p.95). Main services include those to Rafína every half-hour from 6.45am to 5.15pm, and almost as frequently outside those hours from 5.30am to 10.30pm (1 hr; €4); to Pórto Ráfti and Avláki hourly from 5.45am to 7.45pm; to Marathon half-hourly from 5.30am to 10.30pm – many via the local beaches; and to Ayía Marína at least eight times a day, to connect with ferries to

Évvia (see p.697). Ramnous is not realistically accessible by public transport, though you might get a lift for the final few kilometres if you take a bus to Ayía Marína and hitch from the junction, some 5km from the site.
**By car** The main route for drivers is straight out on Messoyíon (following airport signs) onto the eastbound Leofóros Marathónos, which heads straight for Rafína and Marathon.

## ACCOMMODATION AND EATING

### RAFÍNA

**Hotel Akti** Arafinidhón Alón and Vithinías ☎22940 29370, ⊛aktihotel-rafina.gr. Recently refurbished, with some sea views, new soundproofing and a/c, the Akti is very pleasant, though some bathrooms are almost comically cramped. Good deals often available. €80
**Hotel Avra** Arafinidhón Alón 3 ☎22940 22780, ⊛hotelavra.gr. Occupying a prime position high above the harbour, across from the Akti, this business-style designer hotel has luxury rooms and suites, many with sea views. €100
**Ouzeri Limeni** Platía Plastíra 17 ☎22940 24750. The best choice on the lively pedestrianized square above the harbour, with excellent meze and Greek standards.
**Ta Kavoúria tou Asimáki** Rafína harbour ☎22940 24551. The pick of Rafína's seafood restaurants is the first as you descend towards the harbour from the square;

though it looks fancier than its neighbours, with linen tablecloths and proper wine glasses, it's no more expensive. Head for the glassed-in roof terrace, with a great view of the harbour activity.

### ÁYIOS PANDELÍMONAS

**Tria Adhelfia** Beach road 1km north of the centre ☎22940 56461. Simple seafood taverna in a stunning waterfront position, with white tables on a whitewashed terrace; packed on a sunny weekend. Try the shrimp saganaki (€10) or lobster spaghetti (€20).

### SKHINIÁS

**Glaros** Northern end of Skhiniás beach ☎22940 63384. Busy beach bar/taverna at the heart of life at this end of Skhiniás beach – good fried fish, and loungers on which to sleep it off afterwards.

# West to the Peloponnese

The route from the centre of Athens **towards Kórinthos** (Corinth) follows the ancient Ierá Odhós – the Sacred Way – as far as Elefsína, ancient Eleusis. There's nothing sacred about it these days, though: this is as ugly a road as any in Greece, traversing an industrial wasteland. For the first 30km or so you have little sense of leaving Athens, whose western suburbs merge into Elefsína and then Mégara. Offshore lies **Salamína** (ancient Salamis, see p.328), these days just another suburb. The Attikí Odhós motorway from the airport meets the road from Athens just outside Elefsína.

Beyond Elefsína, the **old road to Thebes and Delphi** heads northwest into the hills. This route is described in Chapter Three (p.200), and is highly worthwhile, with its detours to **ancient Aegosthena** and the tiny resort of **Pórto Yermenó**. Directly west, towards the **Corinth Canal** (see p.130) and the Peloponnese, there are shingle beaches along the old coastal road at Kinéta and Áyii Theódhori. This highway, with the Yeránia mountains to the north and those of the Peloponnese across the water, follows the route where Theseus slew the bandit Skiron and threw him off the cliffs to be eaten by a giant sea turtle.

## Dhafní

Daily 8.30am–3pm • Free • You may have to buzz for entry

The **Monastery of Dhafní**, a beautiful example of Byzantine architecture, was badly damaged by an earthquake in 1999, and only reopened in 2011. Still not fully restored, it is held up by scaffolding – set to be there until 2014 at least – which offers an exceptional chance to climb right up into the dome and get up close and personal with the magnificent eleventh-century mosaics, considered among the artistic masterpieces of the Middle Ages. Ascending by rickety ladders, you pass first the Life of Christ, then the Prophets, before reching the *Pandokrátor* (Christ in Majesty) in the dome itself. The restored mosaics, glistening with gold, are magnificent, and the stern Christ depicted here is a classic Orthodox image. A chamber next to the church has an excellent display on the monastery's history and restoration, along with close-up detail of the mosaics and identification of the saints and events depicted.

---

### THE MYSTERIES OF ELEUSIS

The ancient **Mysteries** had an effect on their initiates that was easily the equal of any modern cult. Established in Mycenaean times, perhaps as early as 1500 BC, the cult centred on **Demeter**, the goddess of corn, and her daughter Persephone's annual descent into and resurrection from the underworld, which came to symbolize the rebirth of the crops and the miracle of fertility. By the fifth century BC the cult had developed into a sophisticated annual festival, attracting up to 30,000 people every autumn from all over the Greek world. The ceremonies lasted nine days: the **Sacred Objects** (identity unknown) were taken to Athens, where they were stored in the Ancient Agora for four days. Various rituals took place in the city, many on the Acropolis but also mass bathing and purification in the sea at Fáliro. Finally a vast procession brought the objects back, following the Sacred Way to the sanctuary at Eleusis. Here initiates took part in the final rituals of *legomena* (things said), *dhromena* (things done) and *dheiknumena* (things shown). One theory suggests that these rituals involved drinking a fungus-infused potion, producing similar effects to those of modern **psychedelic drugs**. The Mysteries survived well into the Christian era, but eventually fell victim to the new orthodoxy.

Demeter is said to have threatened to render the land permanently barren if her worship at Eleusis ever ceased. Looking at the ecological havoc wreaked by the area's industry, it would seem that the curse has been fulfilled.

## Eleusis

Tues–Sun 8.30am–3pm • €3

The **Sanctuary of Demeter** at **Eleusis** was one of the most important in the ancient Greek world. For two millennia, the ritual ceremonies known as the Mysteries (see box) were performed here. Today, the extensive **ruins** of the sanctuary occupy a low hill on the coast right in the heart of modern Elefsína.

The best plan on arrival is to head straight for the **museum**, which features models of the sanctuary at various stages in its history: Eleusis is impressively large, with huge walls and gates, some of which date back to Mycenaean times, but the numerous eras of building can also be confusing, especially as signage is poor and mainly in Greek. Exploring outside, the most important structure of ancient Eleusis was the **Telesterion**. This windowless Hall of Initiation lay at the heart of the cult, and it was here that the priests of Demeter would exhibit the **Sacred Objects** and speak "the Unutterable Words".

## GETTING AROUND WEST TO PELOPONNESE

**By car** The main road out of Athens towards Eleusis is the busy Leofóros Athinón, though it's also possible to follow the Ierá Odhós (Sacred Way) from the centre of town, which may have less traffic and certainly seems more appropriate.

**By bus** Bus #A16 or #B16 from Platía Eleftherías (aka Platía Koumoundhoúrou) runs along the Sacred Way several times an hour, stopping at Dhafní en route to Elefsína (the #G16 goes to Dhafní but not Elefsína). In Elefsína ask the driver to set you down at the closest stop to the ruins – the terminal is slightly further away, but still only about a 10min walk back along the waterfront.

# The Peloponnese

**129** Corinth and around

**133** The Argolid

**147** The southeastern peninsula: Vátika

**150** Kýthira

**155** The Máni

**165** Spárti (Sparta) and around

**172** Arcadia

**177** Messinía

**185** Olympia and Ilía

**191** Pátra and Aháïa

ANCIENT THEATRE, EPIDAURUS

# The Peloponnese

The cultural riches and natural beauty of the Peloponnese can hardly be overstated. This southern peninsula – technically an island since the cutting of the Corinth Canal – seems to have the best of almost everything Greek. Ancient sites include the Homeric palaces of Agamemnon at MYCENAE and of Nestor at PÝLOS, the best preserved of all Greek theatres at EPIDAURUS, and the lush sanctuary of OLYMPIA, host to the Olympic Games for a millennium. The medieval remains are scarcely less rich, with the fabulous Venetian, Frankish and Turkish castles of NÁFPLIO, METHÓNI and ancient CORINTH; the strange battle towers and frescoed churches of the MÁNI; and the extraordinarily well-preserved Byzantine enclaves of MYSTRA and MONEMVASIÁ.

Beyond this incredible profusion and density of cultural monuments, the Peloponnese is also a superb place to relax and wander. Its **beaches**, especially along the west coast, are among the finest and least developed in the country, and the **landscape** inland is superb – dominated by forested mountains cut by some of the most captivating valleys and **gorges** to be imagined. Not for nothing did its heartland province of **Arcadia** become synonymous with the very concept of a Classical rural idyll.

The Peloponnese reveals its true character most clearly when you venture off the beaten track: to the old Arcadian **hill towns** like Karítena, Stemnítsa and Dhimitsána; the **Máni tower villages** such as Kítta or Váthia; at Voïdhokiliá and Elafónissos **beaches** in the south; or a trip through the Vouraikós Gorge, possibly on the old **rack-and-pinion railway**.

The region will amply repay any amount of time you spend. The **Argolid**, the area richest in ancient history, is just a couple of hours from Athens, and if pushed you could complete a circuit of the main sights here – **Corinth**, **Mycenae** and **Epidaurus** – in a couple of days, making your base by the sea in **Náfplio**. Given a week, you could add in the two large sites of **Mystra** and **Olympia** at a more leisurely pace. To get to grips with all this, however, plus the southern peninsulas of the Máni and Messinía, and the hill towns of Arcadia, you'll need at least a couple of weeks.

If you were planning a combination of Peloponnese-plus-islands, then the **Argo-Saronic** or **Ionian islands** are most convenient. Of the Ionian islands, isolated **Kýthira** is covered in this chapter since closest access is from the southern Peloponnese ports, but **Zákynthos** or **Kefaloniá** can be reached from the western port of Kyllíni, and Greece's second port city of **Pátra** is a gateway to Corfu and eastern Italy.

Corinthian saints and sinners p.131
Mycenaean murders p.134
Palamedes – cleverest of the Greeks p.138
Snakes alive: healing in ancient Greece p.143
Kangaroo island p.154
Blood feuds in the Máni p.157
Hiking the Výros Gorge p.165

A Spartan upbringing p.167
The Mystra renaissance p.169
Across the Langádha pass p.172
Hiking near Ancient Gortys p.175
Bassae's missing metopes p.176
The battle of Navarino p.182
Telemachus takes a bath p.184
The Olympic Games p.187
The Kalávryta Express p.196

OLYMPIA

# Highlights

**❶ Mycenae** The imposing palace of legend, site of priceless treasure and the majestic tomb of Agamemnon, who was murdered upon his return from the Trojan War. **See p.133**

**❷ Náfplio** With its gently fading nineteenth-century elegance, this port makes a picturesque base for exploring the Argolid. **See p.138**

**❸ Epidaurus** One of the most beautifully preserved of all ancient theatres, epitomizing the inspiring views and perfect acoustics for which the Greeks were renowned. **See p.142**

**❹ Monemvasiá** The Byzantines' impregnable stronghold is now a unique island getaway, stylish, low-key and traffic-free. **See p.147**

**❺ Mystra** A visually stunning medieval city, once boasting a population of 20,000, preserves a superb assemblage of Byzantine frescoed churches. **See p.167**

**❻ Loúsios Gorge** A vast and lushly green ravine hides river rapids and awe-inspiring hermitages clinging to cliffsides. **See p.175**

**❼ The Máni** This rugged southern peninsula has inspired many visitors with its quirky tower houses and isolated churches. **See p.155**

**❽ Olympia** 1400 years of the Olympic Games are laid bare along the verdant valley of the Alfiós, the site's museum housing some of Greece's greatest sculptures. **See p.185**

**HIGHLIGHTS ARE MARKED ON THE MAP ON P.126**

Kastélli (Crete)

Andikýthira

Cape Maléas

Limáni Yéraka
Monemvasía ④
VÁTIKA
Kyparíssi
Neápoli
Vingláfa
Arhángelos
Dhiakófti
Moláï
Pýtra
Avlémonas
Kýthira
Kapsáli
Ayía Pelayía
Hóra
Potamós
Skála
Mylopótamos
Krokeés
Yeráki

R. EVRÓTAS
LAKONÍA

Yíthio
Skoutári
Kótronas
TAÏYETOS
Langádha
Areópoli
Ítylo
Kokkála
Pýrgos Dhiroú ⑦
MÁNI
Kámbos
Kardhamýli
Stoúpa
Yeroliménas
Vátheia

Aviá
Cape Ténaro
Gulf of
Messíni

Gulf of
Lakonía

Veliká
Andílipsi
Koróni
Petalídhi
Khráni
Finikoúnda
Methóni
Sikhíza
Pýlos
Yiálova
Korýfasio
Sapiénza

M E D I T E R R A N E A N   S E A

N

HIGHLIGHTS
① Mycenae
② Náfplio
③ Epidaurus
④ Monemvasía
⑤ Mystra
⑥ Loúsios Gorge
⑦ The Máni
⑧ Olympia

0       25
kilometres

## Brief history

Anciently known as the **Moreas**, from the resemblance of its outline to the leaf of a mulberry tree (*mouriá*), the Peloponnese was home to some of the most powerful rulers in ancient Greece. During the **Mycenaean period** (around 2000–1100 BC), the peninsula hosted the semi-legendary kingdoms of Agamemnon at Mycenae, Nestor at Pýlos and Menelaus at Sparta. In the **Dorian** and **Classical** eras, the region's principal city-state was Sparta, which, with its allies, brought down Athens in the ruinous Peloponnesian War. Under **Roman** rule, Corinth was the capital of the southern Greek province.

From the decline of the Roman Empire to the Ottoman conquest, the Peloponnese pursued a more complex, individual course from the rest of Greece. A succession of **occupations and conquests**, with attendant outposts and **castles**, left an extraordinary legacy of medieval remains. It retained a nominally Roman civilization well after colonial rule had dissipated, with Corinth at the fore until it was destroyed by two major **earthquakes** in the fourth and sixth centuries.

The **Byzantines** established their courts, castles and towns from the ninth century onward; their control, however, was only partial. The **Venetians** dominated the coast, founding trading ports at Monemvasiá, Pýlos and Koróni, which endured, for the most part, into the fifteenth century. The **Franks**, fresh from the sacking of Constantinople in the Fourth Crusade, arrived in 1204 and swiftly conquered large tracts of the peninsula, dividing it into feudal baronies under a prince of the Moreas.

Towards the mid-thirteenth century, there was a remarkable **Byzantine renaissance**, which spread from the court at Mystra to reassert control over the peninsula. A last flicker of "Greek" rule, it was eventually extinguished by the **Turkish conquest** between 1458 and 1460, and was to lie dormant, save for sporadic rebellions in the perennially intransigent Máni, until the nineteenth-century **Greek War of Independence**.

### The nineteenth and twentieth centuries

The Peloponnese played a major part in the revolt against the Turks, with local heroes **Theodhoros Kolokotronis** and **Petros Mavromihalis** becoming important military leaders. At Pýlos, the international but accidental naval battle at **Navarino Bay** in 1827 decided the war, and the **first Greek parliament** was convened at Náfplio. After independence, however, power swiftly drained away from the Peloponnese to Athens, where it was to stay. The peninsula became disaffected, highlighted by the **assassination of Kapodhistrías**, the first Greek president, by Maniots in Náfplio.

Throughout the **nineteenth** and **early twentieth centuries**, the region developed important ports at Pátra, Kórinthos and Kalamáta, but its interior reverted to backwater status, starting a population decline that has continued up to the present. It was little disturbed until **World War II**, during which the area saw some of the worst German atrocities; there was much brave resistance in the mountains, but also some of the most shameful collaboration. The subsequent **civil war** left many of the towns polarized and physically in ruins; in its wake there was substantial **emigration** from both towns and countryside, to North America and Australia in particular. **Earthquakes** still cause considerable disruption, as at Kórinthos in 1981, Kalamáta in 1986, and Éyio in 1995.

Today, the southern Peloponnese has a reputation for being one of the most traditional and politically **conservative** regions of Greece. The people are held in rather poor regard by other Greeks, though to outsiders they seem unfailingly hospitable.

## ARRIVAL AND GETTING AROUND

**THE PELOPONNESE**

**By bus** Buses from Athens (hourly, 1hr) to the Peloponnese run along the highway past Elefsína and over the Corinth Canal to the Isthmós KTEL station 6km east of the modern town of Kórinthos. If you're going on to Mycenae, Árgos or Náfplio as well as to Nemea, change here rather than at Kórinthos (see opposite). Once on the peninsula bus services are fast and regular on the main routes between the seven provincial capitals, Kórinthos, Náfplio, Trípoli, Spárti, Kalamáta, Pýrgos and Pátra.

**By train** Athens' commuter train network, the Proastiakos, runs hourly to Kiató via Kórinthos (6am–11pm, 1hr 30min), so this makes a worthwhile alternative to the bus. However, on the Peloponnese itself trains have been disrupted by the financial crisis, with a planned upgrade of narrow-gauge lines suspended. At the time of writing the only routes still operating included: Pýrgos to Olympia and the rack-and-pinion line to Kalávryta (see p.196), with replacement buses operating on other routes.

**By car** Most drivers heading from Athens to the Peloponnese will take the express tollway, Néa Ethnikí Odhós, although the old road, Paleá Ethnikí Odhós, is a more scenic option. Alternatively, cross the spectacular Andíro–Rió suspension bridge. Once on the peninsula, you will need a good map. The 1:250,000 Peloponnese map published by Emvelia is the most up to date ($\varpi$ mapgreece .gr; €7) and is sold at service stations.

**By boat** Arrival for many on the Peloponnese is by hydrofoil from the Argo-Saronic islands (see p.342), linked with the ports of Ermióni and Pórto Héli (see p.144). For details and frequencies of services, which are drastically seasonal, check with Hellenic Seaways ($\varpi$ hellenicseaways .gr), the company that runs all services here and has a local agent in Ermióni (Fun in the Sun, $\textcircled{\scriptsize T}$ 27540 31514). Pátra (see p.191) is the Peloponnese port of call for arrivals by ferry from Italy, as well as from Igoumenítsa on the mainland (see p.254) and from the Ionian islands (see p.702). There are also ferries from the island of Kýthira (see p.150) to Neápoli, Yíthio and Kalamáta.

# Corinth and around

Throughout Greek history the **ISTHMUS OF CORINTH**, the mainland gateway to the Peloponnese, was strategically important, accounting for the great significance of the city of Corinth in the Classical world. In modern times, this small strip of land was further enhanced, at least economically, by the cutting, at long last, of the **Corinth Canal**. The modern city of **Kórinthos**, the capital of its eponymous province, fails to live up to the historic hype, being now little more than a minor transport hub. By contrast, the archeological site of **ancient Corinth** is one of the high points of a visit to the Peloponnese, while the sanctuary of **ancient Nemea** is also an evocative spot.

## Kórinthos

Like its ancient predecessor, **KÓRINTHOS** (modern Corinth) has been levelled on several occasions by **earthquakes** – most recently in 1981. Repaired and reconstructed, with buildings of prudent but characterless concrete, it is largely an industrial and agricultural centre, its economy bolstered by the drying and shipping of **currants**, for centuries one of Greece's few successful exports (the word "currant" itself derives from "Corinth"). The modern city has little to offer the outsider, so plan on moving on quickly if you land up here.

### ARRIVAL AND DEPARTURE                                                    KÓRINTHOS

**By bus** Most buses between Athens and the Peloponnese avoid going into Kórinthos, instead stopping at the Isthmós KTEL station. Local buses run from here into town, leaving you one block southwest of the centre, at the corner of Aratoú and Ethnikís Andístasis, the main street. Kórinthos KTEL bus station is a few blocks east of the centre, at Dimocrátias 4 ($\textcircled{\scriptsize T}$ 27410 75424). From here you can also catch buses to Athens, Ancient Corinth and Nemea.
**Destinations** Ancient Corinth (hourly; 20min); Athens (hourly; 1hr–1hr 30min); Isthmós (4 daily; 15min); Nemea

(6 daily; 1hr).
**By train** The new Proastiakos train station is located about 3km southwest of town ($\textcircled{\scriptsize T}$ 21052 72000) alongside the Néa Ethnikí Odhós expressway; special shuttles run from Kórinthos' central square 7 times a day, between about 7am and 7pm (10min). At the time of writing train services were only running as far as Kíato from where replacement buses connect to Pátra.
**Destinations** Athens (hourly; 1hr 30min); Kíato (hourly; 15min).

### INFORMATION AND GETTING AROUND

**Services** You'll find various banks along northern Ethnikís Andístasis, and the main post office on Adhimandoú, on the south side of the park. There's a tourist police post at Ermoú 51 ($\textcircled{\scriptsize T}$ 27410 23282). For car rental try Vasilopoulos

at Adhimandoú 39 ($\textcircled{\scriptsize T}$ 27410 25573; $\varpi$ cars-hire.gr), near the post office.
**Taxis** wait along the Ethnikís Andístasis side of the park.

## ACCOMMODATION AND EATING

**Anexagoras** Ayíou Nikoláou 31. In a car park west of the marina, on a street with several other dining options, this taverna has a good range of mezédhes and grilled meats, as well as catch-of-the-day and Greek standards. About €10/person. Daily lunch & dinner.

**Blue Dolphin Camping** ☎ 27410 25766, ⓦ camping -blue-dolphin.gr. About 6km west of Kórinthos, at Léheo (part of Ancient Corinth), situated on a beach, with shady

campsites, this facility offers free transfers from Kórinthos bus and train stations. Services include a market, a taverna, beach sports and wi-fi. April–Oct. From €12.50

**Korinthos** Damaskinou 26 ☎ 27410 26701, ⓦ korinthos hotel.gr. Just a few metres from the marina, this medium-sized hotel is plain, clean and very central. Rooms are en suite and have a/c and balconies, some with good views, and there's free wi-fi. Prices discounted if you book online. €50

## The Corinth Canal

As you peer over from the bridge, the 6km **Corinth Canal** appears to be a very narrow strip of water, until a huge freighter from Pireás or cruise ship to the Ionian islands assumes suddenly toy-like dimensions as it passes nearly 80m below. Today, supertankers have tended to make it something of an anachronism but it is still used by large vessels and remains a memorable sight. At the northwestern end of the canal, by the old Kórinthos–Loutráki ferry dock, there are remains of the **diolkos** (summer Mon noon–7pm, Tues–Sun 8am–7pm; winter Tues–Sun 8.30am–3pm; free), a paved way along which a wheeled platform used to carry boats across the isthmus. In use from Roman times until the twelfth century, the boats were strapped onto the platform after being relieved temporarily of their cargo.

If you are travelling by car, the old national road passes directly over the canal, and it is fairly easy to park. Keep an eye out for a cluster of tourist shops and restaurants and you'll know you're there. Many buses also stop here.

### Brief history

The idea for a canal providing a short cut and safe passage between the Aegean and Ionian seas harks back at least to Roman times, when **Emperor Nero** himself performed the initial excavations with his little silver shovel, later heavily supplemented by Jewish slave labour. It was only in the 1890s, however, that the technology finally became available for cutting right across the 6km isthmus. Opened in July 1893, the canal, along with its near-contemporary Suez, helped establish Pireás as a major Mediterranean port and shipping centre.

## Ancient Corinth

The ruins of **Ancient Corinth** (Arhéa Kórinthos) occupy an extensive site 7km southwest of the modern city and are an essential stop. The site is split into a vast, impressively excavated city with the **Temple of Apollo** at its core, and even more compelling is the stunning acropolis site of **Acrocorinth**, towering 565m above the ancient city. To explore both you need a full day, or to stay overnight at the adjacent **village**.

### Brief history

Ancient Corinth was a key centre of the Greek and Roman worlds, whose possession meant the control of trade between northern Greece and the Peloponnese. Not surprisingly, therefore, the area's ancient and medieval history was one of invasions and power struggles that, in Classical times, was dominated by Corinth's **rivalry with Athens**, against whom it sided with Sparta in the Peloponnesian War.

Having defeated the Greek city-states of the Achaean League, the Romans **razed** the city in 146 BC, before rebuilding it on a majestic scale in 44 BC under the command of Julius Caesar. Initially it was intended as a colony for veterans, later becoming the **provincial capital**. Once again Corinth grew rich on trade –

**CORINTHIAN SAINTS AND SINNERS**

Roman Corinth's reputation for wealth, fuelled by its trading access to luxury goods, was soon equalled by its appetite for **earthly pleasures** – including sex. Corinthian women were renowned for their beauty and much sought after as *hetairai* (courtesans); over a thousand sacred prostitutes served a temple to Aphrodite/Venus, on the acropolis of Acrocorinth. **St Paul** stayed in Corinth for eighteen months in 51–52 AD, though his attempts to reform the citizens' ways were met with rioting – tribulations recorded in his two **letters to the Corinthians**.

**2**

with Rome to the west, and Syria and Egypt to the east. The city endured until rocked by two major **earthquakes**, in 375 and 521, which brought down the Roman buildings and again depopulated the site until a brief Byzantine revival in the eleventh century.

### The excavations

Daily: summer 8am–7.30pm; winter 8am–5pm • €6

Entering from the north, you are in the **Roman agora**, an enormous marketplace flanked by the substantial foundations of a huge *stoa*, once a structure of several storeys, with 33 shops on the ground floor. Opposite the *stoa* is a *bema*, a marble platform used for public announcements. At the far end are remains of a **basilica**, while the area behind the *bema* is strewn with the remnants of numerous Roman administrative buildings. Back across the agora, hidden in a swirl of broken marble and shattered architecture, there's a fascinating trace of the Greek city – a grille-covered **sacred spring**, at the base of a narrow flight of steps.

More substantial is the elaborate Roman **Fountain of Peirene**, which stands below the level of the agora, to the side of a wide, excavated stretch of the marble-paved **Lechaion Way** – the main approach to the city. The fountain house was, like many of Athens' Roman public buildings, the gift of the wealthy Athenian and friend of Emperor Hadrian, Herodes Atticus. Water still flows through the underground cisterns and supplies the modern village.

The real focus of the ancient site, though, is a rare survival from the Classical Greek era, the fifth-century BC **Temple of Apollo**, whose seven austere Doric columns stand slightly above the level of the forum, flanked by foundations of another marketplace and baths. Over to the west is the site **museum** (same hours as site; included in site admission), housing a large collection of domestic pieces, some good Greek and Roman mosaics from nearby, a frieze depicting some of the labours of Hercules, and a good number of Roman statues.

A number of miscellaneous smaller excavations surround the main site. To the west, just across the road from the enclosing wire, there are outlines of two **theatres**: a Roman **odeion** (endowed by Herodes Atticus) and a larger Greek theatre, used by the Romans for gladiatorial battles. To the north are the inaccessible but visible remains of an **Asklepion** (dedicated to the god of healing).

### Acrocorinth

Summer daily 8am–7pm; winter Tues–Sun 8.30am–3pm • Free

Rising almost sheer above the lower town and the fertile plains, the medieval fortress of **Acrocorinth** is sited on an imposing mass of rock, still largely encircled by 2km of wall. Despite the long, 4km climb (nearly an hour's broiling walk) – or a ten-minute drive up from Ancient Corinth – a visit is unreservedly recommended. Looking down over the Saronic Gulf and the Gulf of Kórinthos, you get a real sense of its strategic importance. Amid the extensive remains is a jumble of chapels, mosques, houses and battlements, erected in turn by Greeks, Romans, Byzantines, Frankish crusaders, Venetians and Turks.

**2**

The Turkish remains are unusually substantial. Elsewhere in Greece evidence of the Ottoman occupation has been removed or defaced, but here, at the start of the climb to the entrance, you can see the still-used **fountain of Hatzi Mustafa**, Christianized by the addition of great carved crosses. The outer of the citadel's **triple gates** is also largely Turkish; the middle is a combination of Venetian and Frankish; the inner, Byzantine, incorporating fourth-century BC towers. Within the citadel, the first summit (to the right) is enclosed by a **Frankish keep** – as striking as they come – which last saw action in 1828 during the War of Independence. Keeping along the track to the left, you pass some interesting (if perilous) cisterns, the remains of a Turkish bathhouse, and crumbling Byzantine chapels.

In the southeast corner of the citadel, hidden away in the lower ground, is the **upper Peirene spring**. This is not easy to find: look out for a narrow, overgrown entrance, from which a flight of iron stairs leads down some 5m to a metal screen. Here, broad stone steps descend into the dark depths, where a fourth-century BC arch stands guard over a pool of (nonpotable) water that has never been known to dry up. To the north of the fountain, on the second and higher summit, is the site of the **Temple of Aphrodite**; after its days as a brothel, it saw use as a church, mosque and belvedere.

### ARRIVAL AND DEPARTURE                                    ANCIENT CORINTH

**By bus** Buses to Arhéa Kórinthos village leave from Kórinthos 5min to the hour from 8am to 9pm and return at twenty past (20 min; €1.40).

### ACCOMMODATION AND EATING

There is a scattering of **rooms** to rent in Arhéa Kórinthos village and plenty of **tavernas** along the fence that encloses the excavation.

★ **Gemelos** ☎ 27410 31361. Large taverna with terrace seating directly overlooking the excavations. Excellent meals feature the likes of grilled chicken, home-made pitta bread and fat juicy olives (mains €15). At the time of writing there were plans to open rooms (around €50), with breakfast included. Daily morning till midnight.

**Shadow** ☎&☎ 27410 31481. Comfortable if modest hotel just after the cemetery on the road in from Kórinthos. A restaurant downstairs is decorated with an extensive collection of minerals, fossils and petrified wood. Breakfast included. €45

## Nemea

Summer daily 8am–7.30pm; winter Mon noon–7pm, Tues–Sun 8.30am–3pm • €4 • Buses run from Kórinthos to modern Neméa (6 daily; 1hr) – ask to be dropped at Arhéa Neméa, the small village just 300m west of the ruins.

**Nemea** – home to the Lion of Hercules' (Herakles) first labour – is just 31km southwest of Kórinthos, off the road to Mycenae and Árgos. Like Olympia, Nemea held athletic games for the Greek world from the sixth century BC, until these were transferred to Árgos in 270 BC.

A sanctuary rather than a town, the principal remains at the **site** are of the **Temple of Nemean Zeus**, currently three slender Doric columns surrounded by other fallen and broken drums, but slowly being reassembled. Nearby are a **palaestra** with **baths** and a Christian **basilica**, built with blocks from the temple. There is also an excellent **museum** (same hours, except summer Mon noon–7pm; included in ticket price), with contextual models, displays relating to the biennial games and items from the area.

Outside the site, 500m east, is the **stadium**, which once seated 40,000 spectators. The vaulted entrance tunnel, now reconstructed, and complete with the graffiti of ancient athletes, is the oldest known. There is a guide available, written by archeologist Stephen Miller, who organized the (now quadrennial) **New Nemean Games** in 1996 as a non-commercial alternative to the Olympics; anyone can enter if they run barefoot and wear traditional tunics.

# The Argolid

The region that you enter to the south and southeast of Corinth was known as the **Argolid** (Argolídha in modern Greek), after the city of Árgos, which held sway here in Classical times. The greatest concentration of ancient sites in Greece is found in this compact peninsula, its western boundary delineated by the main road south from Kórinthos. Within less than an hour's drive of each other are Agamemnon's fortress at **Mycenae**, the great theatre of **Epidaurus**, and lesser sites at **Tiryns** and **Árgos**.

In peak season you may want to see the sites early or late in the day to realize their magic. When ruin-hopping palls, there are the resort-town pleasures of elegant **Náfplio**, and a handful of **beach resorts**.

## Mycenae

Tucked into a fold of the hills just east of the road from Kórinthos to Árgos, Agamemnon's citadel at **MYCENAE** (Mykínes) fits the legend better than any other place in Greece. It was uncovered in 1874 by the German archeologist Heinrich Schliemann (who also excavated the site of Troy), impelled by his single-minded belief that there was a factual basis to Homer's epics. Schliemann's finds of brilliantly crafted gold and sophisticated tomb architecture bore out the accuracy of Homer's epithets of "well-built Mycenae, rich in gold". And with the accompaniment of the sound of bells drifting down from goats grazing on the hillsides, a stroll around the ramparts is still evocative of earlier times.

### Brief history

The Mycenae-Árgos region is one of the longest occupied in Greece, with evidence of Neolithic settlements from around 3000 BC. But it is to the period from around 1550 to 1200 BC that the citadel of Mycenae and its associated drama belong. This period is known as **Mycenaean**, a term that covers not just the Mycenae region but a whole **Bronze Age civilization** that flourished in southern Greece at the time, referred to in Homer's epics.

## MYCENAEAN MURDERS

According to legend, the city of Mycenae was founded by Perseus, the slayer of Medusa the Gorgon, before it fell into the bloodied hands of the House of Atreus. **Atreus**, in an act of vengeance for his wife's seduction by his brother Thyestes, murdered Thyestes' sons, and fed them to their father. Not surprisingly, this incurred the wrath of the gods: Thyestes' daughter, Pelopia, subsequently bore her father a son, Aegisthus, who later murdered Atreus and restored Thyestes to the throne.

The next generation saw the gods' curse fall upon Atreus' son **Agamemnon**. On his return to Mycenae after commanding the Greek forces in the Trojan War – a role in which he had earlier consented to the sacrifice of his own daughter, Iphigeneia – he was killed in his bath by his wife Klytemnestra and her lover, Aegisthus, who had also killed his father. The tragic cycle was completed by Agamemnon's son, Orestes, who, egged on by his sister Elektra, took revenge by murdering his mother, Klytemnestra, and was pursued by the Furies until Athena finally lifted the curse on the dynasty.

The **archeological remains** of Mycenae fit remarkably easily with the tales (see box above), at least if it is taken as a poetic rendering of dynastic struggles, or, as most scholars now believe it to be, a merging of stories from various periods. The buildings unearthed by Schliemann show signs of occupation from around 1950 BC, as well as two periods of intense disruption, around 1200 BC and again in 1100 BC – at which stage the town, though still prosperous, was **abandoned**.

No coherent explanation has been put forward for these events, but it seems that war among the rival kingdoms was a major factor in the Mycenaean decline. These struggles appear to have escalated as the civilization developed in the thirteenth century BC: excavations at Troy revealed the sacking of that city, quite possibly by forces led by a king from Mycenae, in 1240 BC. The Mycenae citadel seems to have been replanned, and heavily **fortified**, during this period.

### The Citadel

Daily: summer 8am–8pm; winter 8.30am–3pm • €8

The **Citadel of Mycenae** is entered through the famous **Lion Gate**, whose huge sloping gateposts bolster walls dubbed "**Cyclopean**" by later Greeks, in bewildered attribution to the only beings deemed capable of their construction. Above them a graceful carved relief stands out in confident assertion: Mycenae at its height led a confederation of Argolid towns (Tiryns, Árgos, Assine, Hermione – present-day Ermióni), dominated the Peloponnese and exerted influence throughout the Aegean. The motif of a pillar supported by two muscular lions was probably the symbol of the Mycenaean royal house, for a seal found on the site bears a similar device.

### Royal graves

Inside the walls to the right is **Grave Circle A**, the royal cemetery excavated by Schliemann, who believed it contained the bodies of Agamemnon and his followers, murdered on their triumphant return from Troy. Opening one of the graves, he found a tightly fitting and magnificent **gold mask** that had somehow preserved the flesh of a Mycenaean noble; "I have gazed upon the face of Agamemnon," he exclaimed in an excited cable to the king of Greece. For a time it seemed that this provided irrefutable evidence of the truth of Homer's tale. In fact, the burials date from about three centuries before the Trojan War, though given Homer's possible combining of several earlier sagas, there's no reason why they should not have been connected with a Mycenaean king Agamemnon. They were certainly royal graves, for the finds (now in the National Archeological Museum in Athens) are among the richest that archeology has yet unearthed.

Royal palace

Schliemann took the extensive **South House**, beyond the grave circle, to be the Palace of Agamemnon. However, a building much grander and more likely to be the **Royal Palace** was later discovered near the summit of the acropolis. Rebuilt in the thirteenth century BC, this is an impressively elaborate and evocative building complex; although the ruins are only at ground level, the different rooms are easily discernible. Like all Mycenaean palaces, it is centred around a **great court**: on the south side, a staircase would have led via an anteroom to the big rectangular **throne room**; on the east, a double porch gave access to the **megaron**, the grand reception hall with its traditional circular hearth. The small rooms to the north are believed to have been **royal apartments**, and in one of them the remains of a **red stuccoed bath** have led to its fanciful identification as the scene of Agamemnon's murder.

The secret cistern and merchant houses

A salutary reminder of the nature of life in Mycenaean times is the **secret cistern** at the eastern end of the ramparts, created around 1225 BC. Whether it was designed to enable the citadel's occupants to withstand siege from outsiders, rival Mycenaeans or even an increasingly alienated peasantry is not known. Steps lead down to a deep underground spring; it's still possible to descend the whole way, though you'll need to have a torch and be sure-footed, since there's a drop to the water at the final turn of the twisting passageways. Nearby is the **House of Columns**, a large and stately building with the base of a stairway that once led to an upper storey.

Only the ruling Mycenaean elite could live within the citadel itself. Hence the main part of town lay outside the walls and, in fact, extensive remains of **merchants' houses** have been uncovered near to the road. Their contents included **inscribed tablets** (in Linear B, an early form of Greek) which detailed the spices used to scent oils, suggesting that the early Mycenaeans may have dabbled in the perfume trade. The discovery of the tablets has also shown that, here at least, writing was not limited to government scribes working in the royal palaces, as had previously been thought, and that around the citadel there may have been a commercial city of some size and wealth.

Tholos tombs

Alongside the merchants' houses are the remains of **Grave Circle B**, from around 1650 BC and possibly of an earlier, rival dynasty to those kings buried in Grave Circle A, and two **tholos** (circular chamber-type) tombs, identified by Schliemann as the **tombs of "Aegisthus" and "Klytemnestra"**. The former, closer to the Lion Gate, dates from around 1500 BC and has now collapsed, so is roped off; the latter dates from some two centuries later – thus corresponding with the Trojan timescale – and can still be entered.

## The Treasury of Atreus

Same hours as the Citadel • Admission included in Citadel entrance fee

Four hundred metres down the road from the Citadel site is another, far more startling, **tholos**, known as the **Treasury of Atreus** or – the currently preferred official name – **"Tomb of Agamemnon"**. This was certainly a royal burial vault at a late stage in Mycenae's history, contemporary with the "Tomb of Klytemnestra", so the attribution to Agamemnon is as good as any – if the king were indeed the historic leader of the Trojan expedition. Whoever it belonged to, this beehive-like structure, built without the use of mortar, is an impressive monument to Mycenaean building skills. Entering the tomb along a majestic 15m corridor, you arrive at the chamber doorway, above which is a great lintel formed by two immense slabs of stone – one of which, a staggering 9m long, is estimated to weigh 118 tonnes.

by the Romans, looks oddly narrow from the road, but climb up to the top and it feels immense. Estimated to have held 20,000 spectators – six thousand more than Epidaurus – it is matched on the Greek mainland only by the theatres at Megalopolis and Dodóna. Alongside are the remains of an **odeion** and **Roman baths**.

Above the site looms the ancient **acropolis**, on a conical hill capped by the largely Frankish **medieval castle** of Lárissa (same hours; free), built on sixth-century BC foundations and later augmented by the Venetians and Turks. Massively walled, cisterned and guttered, the sprawling ruins offer wonderful views – the reward for a long, steep haul up, either on indistinct trails beyond the theatre, or a very roundabout road.

**2**

## ARRIVAL AND DEPARTURE                                                                    ÁRGOS

**By bus** You may need to change buses in Árgos since some connections are better than those in Náfplio. There are local bus stops and a ticket kiosk on Kalléryi, at the southeast corner of the market square near the Dhikastikó Katástima building, for Mykínes and Nemea. Just around the corner, on Kapodhistría, is a KTEL office for buses back towards Athens, and for Trípoli, Spárti and south towards Leonídhio.

**Destinations** Athens (6 daily; 2hr); Leonídhio (3 daily Mon–Fri, 2 daily Sat & Sun; 2hr 15min); Mykínes (Mycenae, 3 daily; 30min); Náfplio (every 30min; 30min); Nemea (2 weekly; 1hr); Spárti (8 daily; 3hr); Tiryns (every 30min; 15min); Trípoli (4 daily Mon–Fri, 3 daily Sat & Sun; 1hr).
**By taxi** Taxis leave from Fidhónos towards the ancient ruins.

# Tiryns (Tírynthos)

Daily 8.30am–3pm • €3 • The site lies just east of the main Árgos–Náfplio road, and half-hourly local buses stop for passengers outside

In Mycenaean times the impressive fortress of **Tiryns** stood by the sea, commanding the coastal approaches to Árgos and Mycenae. The Aegean shore gradually receded, leaving it stranded on a low hillock, surrounded by citrus groves, and today next to a modern prison. It's not the most enchanting of settings, which in part explains why this highly accessible, substantial site is undeservedly neglected and relatively empty of visitors. After the crowds at Mycenae, however, the opportunity to wander about Homer's "wall-girt Tiryns" in near-solitude is worth taking.

## The site

The **entrance** to the site is on the far side of the fortress from the road, from where you can explore a restricted number of passages, staircases and the parts of the palace. The walls, 750m long and up to 7m thick, formed of huge Cyclopean stones, dominate the site; the Roman guidebook writer Pausanias found them "more amazing than the Pyramids" – a claim that seems a little exaggerated today. Despite this, the sophistication and defensive function of the citadel are evident as soon as you climb the **entrance ramp**. Wide enough to allow access to chariots, the ramp is angled to leave the right-hand, unshielded side of any invading force exposed for the entire ascent. The **gateways**, too, constitute a formidable barrier; the outer one would have been similar in design to Mycenae's Lion Gate.

Of the **palace** itself, only the limestone foundations survive, but the fact that they occupy a level site gives you a clearer idea of its structure than at hilly, boulder-strewn Mycenae. The walls would have been of sun-dried brick, stucco-covered and decorated with frescoes, fragments of which are now in the Náfplio museum. From the forecourt one enters a spacious **colonnaded court** with a round sacrificial altar in the middle. A typically Mycenaean double porch leads directly ahead to the **megaron** (great hall), where the base of a throne was found – it's now in the National Archeological Museum in Athens. Some time in the sixth century BC part of the palace became the site of a **temple to Hera**, a structure whose column bases now pepper the ground. **Royal apartments** lead off on either side; the women's quarters are thought to have been to the right, while to the left is the bathroom, its floor – a huge, single flat stone – still intact.

A tower further off to the left of the megaron gives access to a **secret staircase**, as at Mycenae, which winds down to an inconspicuous **postern gate**. The walled-in **lower**

**acropolis**, north of the megaron, is the site of two underground vaulted cisterns outside its far end, on the western side.

# Náfplio and around

**NÁFPLIO** (also sometimes known as Nauplia or Navplion) is a rarity among Greek towns. A lively, beautifully sited place, it exudes a grand, occasionally slightly faded elegance, inherited from the days when it was the fledgling capital of modern Greece. The town is a popular year-round weekend retreat and remains by far the most attractive base for exploring the Argolid.

There's ample pleasure to be had in just wandering around: looking around the harbourfront, walking the coastal circuit, and, when you're feeling energetic, exploring the great twin fortresses of **Palamídhi** and **Akronafplía**. Náfplio also offers some of the peninsula's best **restaurants** and shops, plus facilities, including car rental. In the town itself there are a few minor sights, mainly part of its **Turkish heritage**, and some good **museums**. **Platía Syndágmatos**, the main square of the old town, is the focus of most interest. The nearest good **beach** is at **Karathónas**, and closer to the town is the one at **Arvanitiá**.

### Brief history

The town's past certainly stretches back to prehistory, and parts of the **Akronafplía wall** bear witness to that fact, though little else remains dating to earlier than the Byzantine era. From the thirteenth century down to the early nineteenth, it, as with the rest of the region, became an object of contention among **invading forces**. Finally came the **Greek War of Independence**, and the city was named the **first capital**, from 1829 to 1834. It was also in Náfplio that the first president, Kapodhistrias, was assassinated by vengeful Maniot clansmen, and here, too, that the young Bavarian Prince Otho, put forward by the European powers to be (briefly) the first king of Greece, had his initial **royal residence** from 1833 to 1834. He is now commemorated by a locally unpopular statue.

### Palamídhi fort

Daily: summer 8am–7pm; winter 8am–6.30pm · €4

The **Palamídhi**, Náfplio's principal fort, was a key military flashpoint of the War of Independence. The Greek commander Kolokotronis – of whom there's a majestically bewhiskered statue at Platía Kapodhistría – laid siege for over a year before finally gaining control. After independence, he was imprisoned in the same fortress by the new Greek government; wary of their attempts to curtail his powers, he had kidnapped four members of the parliament.

The most direct approach to the **fortress** is by a stairway from the end of Polyzoïdhou street, beside a Venetian bastion, though there is also a circuitous road up from the southeast end of town. On foot, it's a very steep climb up 890-plus stone-hewn steps (in shade early morning) and, when you near the 216m summit, you're confronted with a bewilderingly vast complex. Within the outer walls there are three self-contained castles, all of them built by the Venetians between 1711 and 1714, which accounts for the appearance of that city's symbol – the Lion of St Mark – above the various gateways. The middle fort, San Niccolo (Miltiádhes), was the one where Kolokotronis was incarcerated; it became a notorious prison during the 1947–51 civil war.

---

### PALAMEDES – CLEVEREST OF THE GREEKS

Palamídhi fortress takes its name from Náfplio's most famous and most brilliant legendary son, **Palamedes**. According to mythology he was responsible for a range of inventions including dice, lighthouses, measuring scales, an early form of chess and military formations for soldiers. He was killed by the Greeks at Troy, on charges of treachery trumped up by Odysseus, who regarded himself as the cleverest of the Greeks.

# NÁFPLIO

**ACCOMMODATION**
| | |
|---|---|
| Amymone | 1 |
| Byron | 6 |
| Kapodistrias | 4 |
| King Othon I | 3 |
| Leto | 7 |
| Marianna | 5 |
| Park | 2 |

**RESTAURANTS**
| | |
|---|---|
| 1986 Kakanarakis | 2 |
| Antica Gelatería di Roma | 4 |
| Byzantio | 3 |
| Ta Phanária | 5 |
| To Koutoúki | 1 |

## Akronafplía fort

Always open • Free

The **Akronafplía fort**, to the west of the Palamídhi, occupies the ancient acropolis, whose walls were adapted by three successive medieval restorers – hence the name. The fortifications are today far less complete than those of the Palamídhi, and the most intact section, the lower Torrione castle, was adapted to house hotels.

## Arvanitiá beach

A fork in the access road to Akronafplía brings you down to a small beach, **Arvanitiá**, an enjoyable enough spot to cool off in the shelter of the forts. It gets very crowded in peak season and is more pleasant in the early evening with only a few swimmers. Continue along the path from just past the beach entrance for a few minutes, and you can take steps down to some small stone platforms by the sea, or take the attractive paved path around the western end of Akronafplía, to the main town harbour. A dirt road to the southeast of Arvanitiá leads to Karathónas beach (see opposite), a 45-minute walk.

## Boúrtzi fort

Daily: 8am–sunset • Return boat trip €3, from the northeastern end of Ákti Miaoúli

The town's third fort, the much-photographed **Boúrtzi**, occupies Ayíou Theodhórou islet offshore from the harbour. Built in 1473 by the Venetians to control the shipping lane to the town and to much of Árgos bay, the castle has seen various uses in modern times – from the nineteenth-century home of the town's public executioner to a luxury hotel in the early twentieth century. In her autobiography *I Was Born Greek*, the actress and politician Melina Mercouri claimed to have consummated her first marriage there.

## Ottoman remains

Near **Platía Syndágmatos**, three converted **Ottoman mosques** survive: one, the Trianón, in the southeast corner of the square, is an occasional theatre and cinema; another, the Vouleftikón, just off the southwest corner, was the modern Greek state's original **Voulí** (parliament building). A third, fronting nearby Plapoúta, was reconsecrated as the cathedral of **Áyios Yeóryios**, having started life as a Venetian Catholic church. Nearby are a pair of handsome **Turkish fountains** – one abutting the south wall of the theatre-mosque, the other on Kapodhistría, opposite the church of Áyios Spyrídhon. On the steps of the latter, president Ioannis Kapodhistrías was assassinated by two of the Mavromihalis clan from the Máni in September 1831; there is a scar left in the stone by one of the bullets. The Catholic church, which has also been a mosque, on Potamiánou, has a monument to foreigners who died in the War of Independence, including Byron.

## Archeological museum

Tues–Sun 8.30am–3pm • €2

Náfplio's **archeological museum** occupies a dignified Venetian mansion at the western end of Syndágmatos. It has some good collections, as you'd expect in a town near the Argolid sites, including a unique and more or less complete suit of **Mycenaean armour**, the Dendra cuirass from around 1400 BC, wonderful, birdlike Mycenaean **female figurines**, and reconstructed **frescoes** from Tiryns.

## Peloponnesian Folklore Foundation Museum

Vassiléos Alexándhrou 1 • Mon, Wed–Sun 9am–3pm, closed Feb • €2

The fine **Peloponnesian Folklore Foundation Museum** features gorgeous embroideries, costumes and traditional household items from all over Greece. The exotic verve of both women's and men's finery is nothing less than dazzling, and there are also entire period rooms re-created, down to the last detail.

## War Museum

Amalías 22 •Tues–Sun 9am–2pm • Free

The **War Museum** has weaponry, uniforms, illustrations and other military memorabilia from the War of Independence to the civil war, including a series of portraits of the heroes of the War of Independence, enabling you to put faces to all those familiar Greek street names.

## Karathónas beach

The closest proper beach to Náfplio is at **Karathónas**, a fishing hamlet just over the headland beyond the Palamídhi fortress, which can be reached by a short spur off the drive going up to the ramparts. A more direct dirt road, theoretically closed to traffic, around the base of the intervening cliffs, can make a pleasant 45-minute walk; however, women alone are occasionally pestered by local scooter drivers. There are four morning bus services from Náfplio in season. The narrow **sandy beach** stretches for a couple of kilometres, with a summer taverna at its far end. Karathónas attracts plenty of Greek day-trippers in season, along with windsurfing foreigners in camper vans; in summer, cafés compete to provide the loudest music.

### ARRIVAL AND DEPARTURE

NÁFPLIO

**By bus** The KTEL bus station (☎27520 27323) is at Syngroú 8, just south of the interlocking squares, Platía Trión Navárhon and Platía Kapodhistría.

Destinations Athens (hourly; 2hr 30min); Epidaurus (4 daily; 45min); Ermióni (3 daily; 2hr); Isthmós (14 daily; 1hr 20min); Karathónas beach (4 daily; 20min); Mykínes

(Mycenae, 2 daily; 1hr); Pórto Héli (3 daily; 2hr); Tiryns (every 30min; 15min); Trípoli (2 daily; 1hr 30min).

**By car** Finding a parking space near the old town is very difficult in summer – your best chance may be on the harbourfront, or if you're staying up near the Akronafplía, there are good options on top.

### INFORMATION AND GETTING AROUND

**Tourist office** 25-Martíou 2 (daily 9am–1pm & 4–8pm; ☎27520 24444), but hours are unpredictable and the information provided is not always accurate.

**Tourist police** Koundourióti ☎27520 28131. Helpful and open daily, 7.30am–9pm.

**Taxis** There's a rank on Syngroú, opposite the bus station.

### ACCOMMODATION

Accommodation in Náfplio is generally expensive, particularly in the old town, though out of season during the week most **hotels** drop their prices significantly. There are a number of **private rooms**, mostly clustered on the slope above the main squares. A few other hotels and rooms, generally the last to fill but often more reasonably priced, are located out in the modern town on the Árgos road (known locally as "stoús Argoús"). There is nowhere to **camp** in Náfplio itself, but on the stretch of coast 10–30km southeast, there are a dozen or so campsites.

**Amymone** Óthonos 39 ☎27520 99477, ⓦamymone .gr. Come here for unique designer rooms with bespoke paintings and sculpture in a restored small mansion. Buffet breakfast included. **€85**

**Byron** Plátonos 2 ☎27520 22351, ⓦbyronhotel.gr. A beautifully restored old mansion up steep steps above Áyios Spyrídhon church. Some rooms have balconies and/or views, while the least expensive rooms are without views. Breakfast included. **€90**

**Kapodistrias** Kokínou 20 ☎27520 29366, ⓦhotel kapodistrias.gr. Boutique hotel with individually decorated rooms, in a 200-year-old house just 50m from where Kapodhistrías met his end. Breakfast included. **€70**

**King Othon I** Farmakopoúlou 4 ☎27520 27585, ⓦkingothon.gr. Popular, well-placed hotel, thoughtfully refurbished with an impressive staircase. There is a second, pricier, *King Othon 2* around the corner at Spiliádhou 5. Breakfast included. April–Oct. **€120**

**Leto** Zygomála 28 ☎27520 28098, ⓦleto-hotel.com. A friendly, recently refurbished hotel, with fridges in the rooms, located all the way up next to the Akronafplía fortress. Breakfast €6. March–Oct. **€85**

★ **Marianna** Potamiánou 9 ☎27520 24256, ⓦpensionmarianna.gr. Very comfortable, restored houses up by the Akronafplía fortress walls, with some of the best views in town from the terrace, where an organic breakfast is served. New maisonettes and

**2**

apartments on a courtyard below. Parking nearby. Breakfast included. **€85**

**Park** Dhervenakíon 1 off Platía Kapodhistría ☎ 27520 27428, ☎ 27520 27045. This large, well-run hotel – a mix of 60s and a touch of contemporary design – may have space when smaller old-town places are full. Internet and breakfast included. **€70**

## EATING AND DRINKING

Waterside Bouboulínas is lined with luxurious cafés where the beautiful people meet. A cosier place to start menu-gazing in Náfplio is Staïkopoúlou, with many enjoyable if touristy tavernas. For **breakfast** or coffee, there's the *Propylaion* right beside the bus station; assorted bakeries, ice-cream parlours and juice bars around Platía Syndágmatos are also worth investigating.

**1986 Kakanarakis** Vassilísis Ólgas 18 ☎ 27520 25371. A lively, stylishly refurbished local favourite, serving a variety of mezédhes, plus dishes such as braised cockerel (*kókoras*) with noodles, and *kokkinistó* (meat simmered in tomato sauce). About €20/person. Daily, dinner only.

**Antica Gelateria di Roma** Farmakopoúlou 3 ⓦ anticagelateria.gr. Real home-made Italian ice cream pulls the crowds here and has done so since 1870. They offer a full range of other Italian sweets, as well, including soft *torrone* and almond *cantucci*, and some tempting coffee concoctions. Daily 8am–3am. Closed weekdays in Nov.

**Byzantio** Vassiléos Alexándhrou 15. This excellent taverna is on a quiet corner of a beautiful street, under a cloud of pink and purple bougainvillea. Specialities include home-made sausages, courgette balls and catch-of-the-day. About €15/person. Daily lunch & dinner.

★ **Ta Phanária** Staikopoúlo 13 ☎ 27520 27141. The place to try great seasonal cooking featuring local veg – artichoke stew or aubergine baked with tomato filling – and lots of seafood options, too (swordfish *souvláki* €8.50). Choose cosy seating indoors, or in the bougainvillea-covered courtyard. Daily lunch & dinner.

**To Koutouki** Vassilísis Ólgas 44 ☎ 27520 24477. Stylish taverna with seating on the square and wood-beamed ceilings inside. Good mezédhes and *mayireftá*, as well as grills, their speciality. Main dishes from €10. Daily lunch & dinner.

## SHOPPING

**Maasai Mara** Vas Alexandrou 17 ☎ 27520 25471, ⓦ maasaimara.gr. Of the many antiques and jewellery shops of every sort lining the streets here, this one has the most exotic selection, including one-of-a-kind African and Asian pieces.

**Market** Saturday morning, all along 25-Martiou, on the park side. Mostly food produce, but also clothes, housewares, ceramics and jewellery.

**Odyssey** Platía Syndágmatos. A good stock of English-language books, newspapers, cassettes, CDs and videos.

## DIRECTORY

**Banks** These are concentrated around Platía Syndágmatos and along Amalías; most have ATMs.

**Car rental** Avis, Bouboulínas 51 ☎ 27520 24160, ☎ 27520 24164; Safeway, Eyíou 2 ☎ 27520 22155; or Staïkos Travel, Bouboulínas 50 ☎ 27520 27950, ☎ staikostravel@naf .forthnet.gr.

**Cinema** On Kyrinéas, near the junction of 25-Martíou and the Árgos road, showing English-language films with Greek subtitles.

**Laundries** Bubbles Asklipiou 61 (Mon–Fri 8am–9pm, Sat 8am–3pm).

**Post office** The main branch (Mon–Fri 7.30am–2pm) is on the northwest corner of Platía Kapodhistría.

**Scooter and cycle rental** MotorTraffic, Sidhirás Merarhías 15; bicycles €10/day.

**Travel agent** Staïkos Travel, Bouboulínas 50 ☎ 27520 27950 ☎ staikostravel@naf.forthnet.gr. Agents for train tickets and can also book ferries and flights.

**Watersports** Náfplio Diving Center ☎ 27520 27201, ⓦ nafpliodivingcenter.gr.

# Epidaurus (Epídhavros)

Daily: summer 8am–7.30pm; winter 8am–5pm; theatre opens late for performances • €6

**EPIDAURUS** is a major Greek site visited for its stunning **ancient theatre**, built around 330–320 BC. With its extraordinary acoustics, this has become a very popular venue for the annual Athens Festival productions of **Classical drama**, which are staged on Friday and Saturday nights from June through until the last weekend in August. The works are principally those of Sophocles, Euripides and Aeschylus; given the spectacular setting, they are worth arranging your plans around, whether or not you understand the modern Greek in which they're performed.

The theatre is just one component of what was one of the most important sanctuaries in the ancient world, dedicated to **Asklepios** (god of healing) and a site of pilgrimage for half a millennium, from the sixth century BC into Roman times. In addition to its medical activities, the sanctuary hosted a quadrennial festival, which followed the Isthmian Games.

Now a World Heritage Site, restoration and reconstruction work is perpetually under way, so varying areas of the site may be temporarily closed.

## ARRIVAL AND INFORMATION                                    EPIDAURUS

**By bus** Most people take in Epidaurus as a day-trip; there are four buses daily from Náfplio (45min) to the site. They are marked "Theatre", "Asklipion" or "Epidavros" and shouldn't be confused with those to the modern villages of Néa or Arhéa (Paleá) Epídhavros, the closest beach resort. There are also special evening buses from the site to Náfplio after shows; check at Náfplio bus station.

**Theatre tickets** Tickets are available in advance online (ⓦ greekfestival.gr), in Athens (at the festival box offices 210 327 2000), or sometimes at the site (☎ 27530 22026) during the festival. Prices range from €15–50. There have been instances of overselling and ticket-holders being turned away at the gates, so turn up early. In Athens, you can buy all-inclusive tickets for performances and return bus travel. English translations of the plays are available at the site and at the *Odyssey* bookshop in Náfplio (see opposite).

## ACCOMMODATION AND EATING

It's possible to **camp** at the grass car park on performance days, though you must wait until an hour after the play's end before setting up a tent.

**Leonidas** Paleá Epídhavros ☎ 27520 22115. Great taverna with a garden out the back; you'd be wise to book ahead if your visit coincides with a performance at the ancient theatre. Actors eat here after shows, and photos on the wall feature the likes of François Mitterrand and Sir Peter Hall. Mains around €20. Daily lunch & dinner.

## The ancient theatre

Epidaurus's **ancient theatre** is the primary sight. With its backdrop of rolling hills, this 14,000-seat semicircle merges perfectly into the landscape, so well, in fact, that it was rediscovered and unearthed only in the nineteenth century. Constructed with mathematical precision, it has an extraordinary equilibrium and, as guides on the stage are forever demonstrating, near-perfect natural **acoustics** – such that you can hear coins, or even matches, dropped in the circular orchestra from the highest of the 54 tiers of seats. Constructed of white limestone (red for the dignitaries in the front rows), the tiered seats have been repaired, though the beaten-earth stage has been retained, as in ancient times.

## The museum

Summer Mon noon–7pm, Tues–Sun 8am–7pm; winter closes 5pm • Entrance fee included in site ticket price

Most of the ruins visible today are just foundations – the sanctuary was looted by the Romans in 86 BC – but a visit to the **museum** helps identify some of the former

---

### SNAKES ALIVE: HEALING IN ANCIENT GREECE

Temples to **Asklepios**, god of medicine, were once found across ancient Greece, and his symbol, the staff and serpent, is still seen today on everything from ambulances to the logo of the World Health Organization. Although quite advanced surgical instruments have been found at Epidaurus, healing methods were far from conventional. Harmless snakes are believed to have been kept in the building and released at night to bestow a divinely curative forked-tongue lick. In other cases, snakes might have been used as a primitive kind of shock therapy for the mentally ill. The afflicted would have crawled in darkness through the maze-like Tholos (see p.144) guided by a crack of light towards the middle, where they would find themselves surrounded by writhing reptiles.

buildings. The finds displayed show the progression of medical skills and cures used at the Asklepieion.

### The sanctuary of Asklepios

The **Asklepian sanctuary**, as large a site as Olympia or Delphi, holds considerable fascination, for the ruins are all of buildings with identifiable functions: hospitals for the sick, dwellings for the priest-physicians, and hotels and amusements for the fashionable visitors to the spa. The setting, a wooded valley thick with the scent of thyme and pine, is clearly that of a health farm.

The reasonably well-labelled **site** begins just past the museum, where there are remains of **Greek baths** and a huge **gymnasium** with scores of rooms leading off a great colonnaded court; in its centre the Romans built an **odeion**. To the southwest is the outline of the **stadium** used for the ancient games, while to the northeast, a small **sanctuary of Egyptian gods** suggests a strong influence on the medicine used at the site.

North of the stadium are the foundations of the **Temple of Asklepios** and beside it a rectangular building known as the **Abaton** or **Kimitirion**. Patients would sleep here to await a visitation from the healing god, commonly believed to assume the form of a serpent. The deep significance of the **serpent** at Epidaurus is elaborated in the circular **Tholos**, one of the best-preserved buildings on the site. Its inner foundation walls form a labyrinth, thought to have been used as a snakepit (see box, p.143). Another theory is that the labyrinth was used as an initiation chamber for the priests of Asklepios, who underwent a symbolic death and rebirth, a common theme in ancient religion.

## Southwest Argolid

The roads across and around the southern tip of the Argolid are sensational scenic rides, but the handful of resorts here lack character, have disappointing beaches and are generally overdeveloped. Their only real virtue is that they are the ports of call for the **Argo-Saronic islands**, so if you find yourself there, we've provided some recommendations.

### Ermióni

**ERMIÓNI** (ancient Hermione) is a small town, on a narrow, rocky peninsula, overlooking Dhokós and Ýdhra, and perhaps saved from development by lack of a sandy beach. It has separate access roads for the two sides of town – the northern entry is simpler for drivers and leads to the main waterfront, with tavernas, cafés, banks and ATMs. On Tuesdays there is a large market for local villages and islanders from Ýdhra. The wooded tip of the peninsula – an archeological area – has pleasant walks. On the southern side there are swimming places below the coastal road.

| ARRIVAL AND DEPARTURE | ERMIÍONI |
|---|---|

**By hydrofoil** Ýdhra (3 daily; 20min); Póros (2 daily; 1hr); Spétses (3 daily; 20min).

### Pórto Héli

Extensive, developed **PÓRTO HÉLI** has pretty waterfront views around a nearly circular bay, numerous accommodation options, and facilities for yachters exploring the Argo-Saronic islands.

| ARRIVAL AND INFORMATION | PÓRTO HÉLI |
|---|---|

**By bus** The route to Náfplio from Pórto Héli is covered three to four times daily by bus, which usually dovetails with ferries and hydrofoils to and from Spétses and elsewhere.
**By hydrofoil** Ýdhra (3 daily; 1hr); Póros (1 daily; 2hr); Spétses (3 daily; 10min).

**Water-taxis** Spétses according to demand (10–20min).
**Travel agent** Hellenic Vision Travel (☎27540 51543, ⊕portoheli.hellenicvision.gr). On the war memorial square, this agent books hydrofoils and can also find accommodation.

## ACCOMMODATION AND EATING

**Kavouraki** ☎ 27540 51705. Near the harbour, one of the best taverna choices, with good views, has been serving fresh fish, plus all the fresh seasonal veggies and Greek standards, since 1945. About €20/person. Daily lunch & dinner.

**Nautica Bay** ☎ 27540 51415, ⓦ www.nauticabay hotel.gr. This is a well-equipped resort with lots of extras, including a sizeable pool, wi-fi, and a variety of activities,

including tennis and miniature golf. There are nine buildings in all, and all rooms have balconies, except a few with water views. Breakfast included. March–Oct. **€80**

**Rozos** ☎ 27540 51416, ⓦ hotelrozos.com. Large, pink Best Western hotel with freshly refurbished, comfortable rooms, all with sea-view balconies. Free wi-fi. Breakfast included. **€80**

# The east coast: south to Leonídhio

The **road south** closely follows the coastline, winding through empty, mountainous terrain. Considering its proximity to Náfplio – and Athens – the whole stretch is enjoyably low-key and comparatively unexploited. More popular with Greek holiday-makers than with foreign tourists, the few resorts along here may be fully booked well in advance for the mid-June to mid-August Greek school holidays.

## Leonídhio and around

The first town of note that you come to is **LEONÍDHIO**. Gigantic ochre cliffs that wouldn't look out of place in deserts of the American Southwest or the Canary Islands provide a dramatic backdrop to red-roofed Leonídhio (Leonídhion in formal Greek), as it slopes down almost to the sea. This prosperous and traditional market town sees little need to pander to tourists, most of whom head for the coast, either Leonídhio's diminutive port, **Pláka**, or the tiny neighbouring resort of **Poúlithra**.

### Pláka

**PLÁKA**, Leonídhio's port and beach, is just 4km away. It's a delightful place consisting of a harbour and some charming **sleeping** and **eating** options. It has a fine pebble beach, which in recent years has become popular with Greek and foreign tourists, plus a sporadic influx of yachters.

### Poúlithra

Three kilometres south of Pláka is the small, attractive resort of **POÚLITHRA**. With little development to distract you, this spot makes a relaxing staging post. Accommodation is generally easy to find and there are tavernas near the narrow strip of beach. From here, the road heads inland to small, isolated, mountain villages, leading down eventually to Monemvasiá.

### Inland from Leonídhio

The route inland from **Leonídhio** is worth taking for its own sake, climbing through the huge **Dhafnón gorge**, although the views are even better if this route is covered in the reverse direction, descending through the gorge to Leonídhio.

## ARRIVAL AND DEPARTURE                                       LEONÍDHIO AND AROUND

**By bus** Buses arrive at Leonídhio from Árgos (3 daily; 2hr 30min) and Tripoli (2 daily; 2hr 30min). A twice-daily service runs to Pláka (10min) and Poúlithra (15min).

## ACCOMMODATION AND EATING

### PLÁKA

**Dionysos** ☎ 27570 23455, ☎ 27570 22496. Appealing little hotel with quirky decoration and friendly management, just steps away from the beach (opposite *Michel-Margaret*). All rooms have a/c and balconies with sea views. **€45**

★ **Michel–Margaret** ☎ 27570 22379. The Bekarou family have run the central taverna here since 1830, with great attention to quality and service. Enjoy the views from the spacious terrace while savouring the cuisine: grilled meats and fish and excellent fresh sesame bread. About €15/person. Daily lunch & dinner.

**POÚLITHRA**

**Akroyiali ☎** 27570 29106, **☎** 27570 51262. Spacious, wood-trimmed studios with balconies facing the sea and a private pebble beach. Breakfast included. **€60**

**Kyma ☎** 27570 51250. Both rooms and self-catering apartments are available here, in a garden setting 10m from the sea – relatively lush for this arid region. Facilities

include en-suite bathrooms, balconies and a/c. April–Oct. **€40**

**Mirton ☎** 27570 51339. This simple, traditional taverna serves good Greek food from a standard menu, dishes ranging €5–15. Wash it down with the local rosé, served chilled in a terracotta jug, for about €3/litre. Dine inside or out on the sea-view terrace. Daily lunch & dinner.

**2**

# The southeastern peninsula: Vátika

The isolated southeasternmost "finger" of the Peloponnese is known as **Vátika**. It comprises a dramatic and underpopulated landscape of harsh mountains and poor, dry, rocky soil. The highlight here is the extraordinarily preserved Byzantine enclave of **Monemvasiá** – an essential visit for any tour of the southern Peloponnese. The rest of this slim peninsula is little visited by tourists, except for the area around **Neápoli**, the most southerly town in mainland Greece, which offers access to the islet of **Elafónissos**, just offshore, and to the larger island of **Kýthira**, lying on the way to Crete.

## Monemvasiá

**MONEMVASIÁ**, standing impregnable on a great island-like irruption of rock, was the medieval seaport and commercial centre of the Byzantine Peloponnese. Its modern mainland service town is called **Yéfira**, from which a 1km **causeway** takes visitors out to the medieval site. Divided into the inhabited lower town and the ruined upper town, it's a fascinating mix of atmospheric heritage, careful restoration and sympathetic redevelopment.

Fortified on all approaches, it was invariably the last outpost of the Peloponnese to fall to invaders, and was only ever taken through siege. Even today, it differs deeply in character from the nearby mainland.

### Brief history

Founded by the **Byzantines** in the sixth century, Monemvasiá soon became an important port. It later served as the chief commercial port of the Despotate of Mystra and was for all practical purposes the Greek Byzantine capital, with a population of almost 60,000. Like Mystra, Monemvasiá had something of a golden age in the thirteenth century, when it was populated by a number of noble Byzantine families and reaped considerable wealth from estates inland, wine production (the Mediera-like *Malvasia*) and from their own roving corsairs who preyed on shipping heading for the East.

When the rest of the Moreas fell to the Turks in 1460, Monemvasiá was able to seal itself off, placing itself first under the control of the papacy, later under the **Venetians**. Only in 1540 did the **Turks** gain control, the Venetians having abandoned their garrison after the defeat of their navy at Préveza.

Monemvasiá was again thrust to the fore during the **War of Independence**, when, in July 1821, after a terrible siege and wholesale massacre of the Turkish inhabitants, it became the first of the major Turkish fortresses to fall. After the war, there was no longer any need for such strongholds and, with shipping moving to the Corinth Canal, the town drifted into a village existence, its buildings allowed to fall into ruin. By the time of **World War II** only eighty families remained. Today just a handful of people are in permanent residence, but much restoration work has been done to the houses, walls and many of the churches.

### The rock: medieval Monemvasiá

From mainland Yéfira nothing can be seen of the medieval town itself, which is built purely on the seaward face of the rock. Nor is anything revealed as you cross the causeway to the **Kástro**, as locals call it; but the 1km-long entrance road, used for **parking**, finally deadends at castellated walls. Once through the fortified entrance **gate**, narrow and tactically z-shaped, everything looms into view: in the **lower town**, clustered houses with tiled roofs and walled gardens, narrow stone streets, and distinctively Byzantine churches. High above, the extensive castle walls protect the **upper town** on the summit.

## The lower town

The **lower town** once numbered forty churches and over eight hundred homes, an incredible mass of building, which explains the confusing labyrinth of alleys. A single main street – up and slightly to the left from the gateway – is lined with cafés, tavernas and souvenir shops.

At the end of this street is the lower town's main square, a beautiful public space, with a cannon and a well in its centre, and the setting for the great, vaulted **cathedral**, built by the Byzantine emperor Andronikos II Komnenos when he made Monemvasiá a see in 1293. The largest medieval church in southern Greece, it is dedicated to Christ in Chains, Elkómenos Khristós. Across the square is the domed church of **Áyios Pétros**, originally a sixteenth-century mosque, which was reconverted by the Turks back into a mosque in the eighteenth century and now houses a small **museum** of local finds (officially Tues–Sun 8.30am–3pm in winter, till 8pm in summer; free). Unusually for Ottoman Greece, the Christian cathedral was allowed to function during the occupation, and did so beside this mosque.

Access by water is as limited as by land. In peaceful times, the town was supplied from the tiny external harbour, **Kourkoúla**, below the road as you approach the entrance gateway. While in town, down towards the sea, the **Portello** is a small gate in the sea wall; you can **swim** off the rocks here.

## The upper town

The climb to the **upper town** is highly worthwhile – not least for the solitude, since most day-trippers stay down below – and it is less strenuous than it initially looks (20–30min depending on fitness). To get the most from the vast site, it's a good idea to bring some food and drink (from Yéfira, since Monemvasiá has no proper supermarket), so you can explore at leisure. There are sheer drops from the rockface, and unfenced cisterns, so descend before dusk.

The fortifications, like those of the lower town, are substantially intact, with even the **entrance gate** retaining its iron slats. Within, the site is a ruin, unrestored and deserted though many structures are still recognizable, and there are information boards. The only building that is relatively complete, even though its outbuildings have long since crumbled to foundations, is the beautiful thirteenth-century **Ayía Sofía** (usually locked), a short distance up from the gateway. It was founded on the northern rim of the rock as a monastery by Andronikos II.

Beyond the church extend acres of ruins; in medieval times the population here was much greater than that of the lower town. Among the remains are the stumpy bases of Byzantine houses and public buildings, and, perhaps most striking, vast **cisterns** to ensure a water supply in time of siege. Its weak point was its food supply, which had to be entirely imported from the mainland. In the last siege, by Mavromihalis's Maniot army in the War of Independence, the Turks were reduced to eating rats and, so the propagandists claimed, Greek children.

## Yéfira

**YÉFIRA** is little more than a straggle of hotels, rooms and restaurants serving the rock's tourist trade, with a pebble beach; though for a **beach** day-trip, it's best to head 3–4km north along the coast to Porí beach, or via a separate road to the very clean, northern, Kastráki end of the beach, by the Cyclopean walls of ancient **Epidavros Limira**.

Snorkellers can see further marble remains from the site, now underwater, as well as the wreckage of a sunken German warship.

## ARRIVAL AND INFORMATION

### MONEMVASIÁ

**By bus** Buses arrive in the modern mainland village of Yéfira, from where a minibus shuttles across to the rock every 20min (8am–midnight; €0.50). Direct buses connect with Spárti although they are not timed to allow a day visit from there.

**Destinations** Athens (4 daily; 6hr); Spárti (3 daily; 2hr 30min).

**Services** Yéfira has a bank, three ATMs, a post office and a travel agent, Malvasia Travel (☎ 27320 61752, ✉ malvtrvl@ otenet.gr), which can help with rooms and scooter rental.

## ACCOMMODATION

Accommodation in Monemvasiá is expensive – in season and out – and from June to September you should book ahead. Within the walls, the choice includes some very upmarket hotels, with attractively restored and traditionally furnished rooms. For cheaper hotel options, check out Yéfira.

### MONEMVASIÁ

**Byzantino** ☎ 27320 61254, ✇ hotelbyzantino.com. This elegant, historic property features a range of rooms with period details, some with balconies and sea views. It's on the main street so noise can be a factor. All rooms with a/c; wi-fi in the lobby. They also own the *Enetiko* café, with a panoramic terrace. **€100**

**Malvasia** ☎ 27320 61160, ✇ malvasia-hotel.gr. This well-appointed complex occupies three separate locations between the main street and the sea; call first at the hotel reception, well signposted from just inside the main gateway. Traditional stone buildings, with comfortable, sleekly modern rooms, all with a/c; wi-fi in the lobby. **€85**

★ **To Monopati** ☎ 27320 61772, ✇ byzantine -escapade.com. Multilingual Isabelle and Christos are devoted to "The Rock" and to making their lodgings (follow the signs up from the main commerical lane) as comfortable and personal as possible; they also go all out with their wonderful breakfast (€6/person), best enjoyed on the panoramic terrace. Wi-fi, stereos, a/c or fan. 2–4– night minimum stay. **€85**

### YÉFIRA

**Filoxenia** ☎ 27320 61716, ✇ filoxenia-monemvasia .gr. Located just north of the causeway, this modern hotel has comfortable rooms with a/c and large balconies with views of the sea and the Rock. Breakfast included. **€60**

**Flower of Monemvasia** ☎ 27320 61395, ✇ flower-hotel.gr. Just inland of the road, this pleasant, red-tile-roofed property has rooms with kitchenette, a/c and balconies with panoramic views. Breakfast included. **€70**

**Pramataris** ☎ 27320 61833, ✇ pramatarishotel.gr. Friendly and comfortable hotel with some balconies overlooking the sea. Rooms have fridges, a/c and other amenities. Excellent buffet breakfast included. **€60**

## EATING AND DRINKING

Monemvasiá restaurants are generally excellent, with prices to match. Several good tavernas for seafood are found in Yéfira. For nightlife, try the popular *Rock Café* bar on the southern seafront.

**Matoula** Monemvasiá central lane ☎ 27320 61660, ✇ matoula.gr. This taverna offers both excellent food and a leafy garden overlooking the sea. Main courses here hover around €10. Everything, including the plump dolmádhes, is home-made. Daily lunch & dinner. Closed two weeks in winter.

**Trata** Yéfira ☎ 27320 62084. Just at the beginning of the causeway, this seafood taverna is in an inviting converted fisherman's hut. Expect to pay about €20/person, more for fresh fish. Daily lunch & dinner.

# Neápoli

**NEÁPOLI** (full name Neápoli Vión), 42km south of Monemvasiá, is a mix of old buildings and modern Greek concrete behind a grey-sand beach with views of **Kýthira** and **Elafónissos** islands – and really only of interest for its ferry connections to these islands. For such an out-of-the-way place, however, it is surprisingly developed, catering mostly to Greek holiday-makers. Neápoli **beach** extends northwest to Vingláfia village and the little harbour of **Poúnda**, some 8km west of Neápoli, which has frequent vehicle ferry crossings over the short strait to Elafónissos island, a popular day-trip.

## ARRIVAL AND INFORMATION NEÁPOLI

**By bus** The KTEL bus office is on Dhimokratías, opposite the bus park.

Destinations Athens (3 daily; 7hr); Spárti (3 daily, 3hr).

**By ferry** Kýthira (1 daily; 1hr 15min); Elafónissos (from Poúnda, 5–15 daily; 10min). Tickets are available from the

office of the Vatika Bay Shipping Agency (☎ 27340 24004, ⓦ vatikabay.gr), just west of the pier.

**Services** There are several banks with ATMs. Taxis can be ordered on ☎ 27340 22590.

## ACCOMMODATION

**Aïvali** Akti Voion 164 ☎ 27340 22287, ⓦ aivali-neapoli .gr. This clean, unpretentious hotel is right on the seafront, near the ferry for Kýthira. Rooms have balconies, all facing the water, plus a/c and wi-fi. Breakfast included. **€50**

**Vergina** ☎ 27340 23443, ⓦ verginahotel.com. This hotel is quietly situated, a block away from the harbour. It's modestly modern, with internet access, a/c, and basic rooms with balconies. Breakfast included. **€50**

# Elafónissos

Part of the mainland until 375 AD, when an earthquake separated it, **ELAFÓNISSOS** is just 19 square kilometres and gets very busy in the short summer season, when its 700-odd resident population is vastly outnumbered by visitors, mainly Greek. The island's eponymous town is largely modern, but has plenty of rooms, mostly in the narrow backstreets, plus some good fish tavernas.

One of the island's two surfaced roads leads 5km southeast to **Símos**, one of the best **beaches** in this part of Greece, a large double bay with fine pale sand heaped into dunes and views to Kýthira; a *kaiki* (boat) leaves from the town to Símos every morning in summer. To the southwest of town is the small, scattered settlement of Káto Nisí, and **Panayítsa** beach, quieter than Símos but almost as beautiful, with views to the Máni peninsula. There is a petrol station on the Panayítsa road.

## ARRIVAL AND DEPARTURE ELAFÓNISSOS

**By ferry** Ferries to the island leave from Poúnda docks 8km west of Neápoli (5–26 per day, 10min; pay on the

boat, €2; ☎ 27340 61117, ⓦ elafonisos.net/dromolo.htm).

## ACCOMMODATION AND EATING

### ELAFÓNISSOS TOWN

**Exantas** ☎ 27340 61320. This hotel is right on the sea, with balcony views and a/c, and conveniently positioned for the tavernas on the northern seafront near the ferry dock. **€70**

**Golden Star** ☎ 27340 61271, ⓦ goldenstarelafonisos .gr. Set one row back from the western seafront, this place looks kitsch at first glance, but has rather romantic rooms with partial a/c and balconies. **€70**

★ **Menti Brothers** ☎ 27340 61263. This taverna

towards the end of the harbour serves the freshest fish in the Peloponnese – catch-of-the-day chosen each morning – at affordable prices. Shrimp a speciality. Daily lunch & dinner.

### SÍMOS

**Simos Camping and Bungalows** ☎ 27340 22672, ⓦ simoscamping.gr. Well-equipped campsite, 4km from the harbour, at the western end of the beach. There are bungalows (with a/c and fridges) as well as campsites, plus a minimarket and restaurant. May–Oct. Campsites **€25,** bungalows **€80**

# Kýthira

Isolated at the foot of the Peloponnese, the island of **KÝTHIRA** traditionally belongs to the Ionian islands, and shares their history of **Venetian** and, later, British rule; under the former it was known as Cerigo. For the most part, similarities end there. The island architecture of whitewashed houses and flat roofs looks more like that of the Cyclades. The landscape is different, too: wild scrub- and gorse-covered hills, or moorland sliced by deep valleys and ravines. Though badly affected by emigration (see box, p.154) tourism has brought some prosperity but most summer visitors are Greeks. For the few foreigners who reach Kýthira, it remains something of a refuge, with its undeveloped

**beaches** a principal attraction. Some accommodation does not open until June and closes early in September.

## ARRIVAL AND DEPARTURE

KÝTHIRA

**By air** The airport is deep in the interior, 8km southeast of Potamós; the few Olympic Airways flights, from Athens

only, are met by taxis, as are most high-season boats.
**By ferry** The huge all-weather harbour at Dhiakófti is the

2

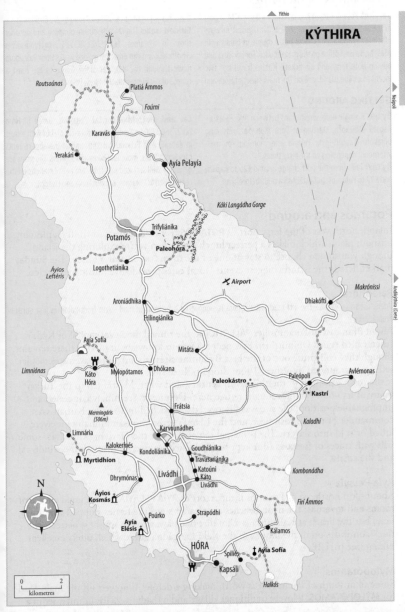

KÝTHIRA

Yíthio

Neápoli

Makrónissi

Andikýthira (Crete)

Routsoúnas

Platiá Ámmos

Foúrni

Karavás

Yerakári

Ayía Pelayía

Káki Langádha Gorge

Trifyliánika

Potamós

Paleohóra

Áyios
Leftéris

Logothetiánika

✈ Airport

Aroniádhika

Ftilingiánika

Dhiakófti

Ayía Sofía

Mitáta

Limniónas

Káto
Hóra

Mylopótamos

Dhókana

Paleópoli

Avlémonas

Mermingáris
(506m)

Frátsia

Paleokástro

Kastrí

Kaladhí

Limnária

Karvounádhes

Kalokerinés

Kondoliánika

Goudhiánika

Kombonádha

Myrtidhíon

Travasariánika

Dhrymónas

Livádhi

Katoúni
Káto

Áyios
Kosmás

Livádhi

Firí Ámmos

Poúrko

Strapódhi

Kálamos

Ayía
Elésis

HÓRA

Spiliés

† Ayía Sofía

Kapsáli

Halkós

N

0        2
kilometres

arrival point for the daily Neápoli ferries (cars €50 one-way, foot passenger €12; ⓦ kythira-kithira-kythera.com). Slightly disconcerting when arriving by sea is the sight of a container ship that went aground in 1999 on an offshore island. Dhiakófti has a sandy beach and a few places to stay, but most people move on quickly.

Destinations Andikýthira (2 weekly in season; 2hr); Kalamáta (1 daily; 4hr 30min); Kastélli (Crete, 1 daily; 3hr 40min); Neápoli (up to 4 daily; 1hr) Pireás (2 weekly in season; 6hr); Yíthio (1–5 weekly in season; 2hr 30min).

## INFORMATION AND ACTIVITIES

**Services** Potamós town has tavernas, a bank ATM, a post office and petrol stations, as well as an Olympic Airways office (☎ 27360 33362). Hóra has a couple of banks with ATMs and a post office on the main square. For booking and buying both ferry and air tickets, Kithira Travel has two locations on the island, one on the main street of Hóra and the other in Potamós (☎ 27360 31390 or 27360 31848).

**Guided walks** The Mare Nostrum camping and outdoor shop in Potamós (☎ 27360 33573, ⓔ chronisdiver @hotmail.com) can organize guided walks from Paleohóra down through the Káki Langádha Gorge to the coast a couple of kilometres south of Ayía Pelayía.

## GETTING AROUND

**By bus** A single daily service runs between Ayía Pelayía–Kapsáli–Dhiakófti, starting at 9am Mon–Sat, returning Dhiakófti–Kapsáli–Ayía Pelayía late mornings or mid-afternoon, depending on the ferry times.
**By taxi** Taxis from the port charge around €25 to Kapsáli and €17 to Potamós, but establish a price beforehand.

**Car and motorbike rental** Panayotis, based in Hóra (☎ 27360 31004, ⓦ panayotis-rent-a-car.gr) but with offices in Kapsáli, Ayía Pelayía, Dhiakófti and at the airport, rents cars, motorbikes, mountain bikes and scooters. The roads are generally well surfaced and there are petrol stations on the central road at Potamós, Kondoliánika and Livádhi.

# Potamós and around

Inland, northwest of the ferry port, is **POTAMÓS**, Kýthira's largest town. It's a pleasant, unspoilt place, which makes a perfect lunch stop when you're exploring the island, though you should choose to stay at one of the towns on or near a beach. The **Sunday market** here is the island's biggest event – local cafés provide live music to coincide.

## Paleohóra
Unenclosed site • Free • The dirt road to Paleohóra is signposted off the main road south from Potamós just north of Aroniádhika

About 3km east of Potamós lies **PALEOHÓRA**, the ruined **medieval capital** of Kýthira (then called Áyios Dhimítrios). Few people seem to know about or visit these remains, though they constitute one of the best Byzantine sites around and boast a spectacular setting, surrounded by a sheer 100m drop on three sides.

The town was built in the thirteenth century, and when Mystra fell to the Turks, many of its noble families sought refuge here. Despite its seemingly concealed and impregnable position, the site was discovered and sacked in 1537 by Barbarossa, commander of the Turkish fleet, and the island's seven thousand inhabitants were killed or sold into slavery. The principal remains are of the surviving **churches**, some still with traces of **frescoes** (but kept firmly locked, so peer in through the windows), and the **castle**.

## Ayía Pelayía
About 4km northeast of Potamós is the resort of **AYÍA PELAYÍA**, with a good choice of **rooms** and **tavernas**; the main beaches are cleaner since the ferries stopped coming here, but the beach at Kalamítsa, a 2km dirt track away to the south, is better – the track continues on to the mouth of the Káki Langádha gorge which offers excellent hiking (see p.172).

## Mylopótamos
Some 6km south of Potamós it is worth making a detour 4km west off the main road for **MYLOPÓTAMOS**, a lovely traditional village and a shady oasis in summer, set in a

wooded valley with a small stream. Follow the signs for "Katarráktis Neraïdha" to find a **waterfall**, hidden from view by lush vegetation, next to a long-closed café.

### The Ayía Sofía cave

Mid-June to mid-Sept Mon–Fri 3–8pm, Sat & Sun 11am–5pm • €3

Most visitors come to Mylopótamos to see the **cave of Ayía Sofía**, the largest and most impressive of a number of caverns on the island. A half-hour signposted walk from the village, or a short drive along a paved road off the Limniónas road. When the cave is closed, you can probably find a guide in Mylopótamos; ask at the village, giving a day's notice if possible. The cave's entrance has been used as a church and has an iconostasis carved from the rock, with important Byzantine frescoes on it. Beyond, the cave system comprises a series of chambers, which reach 250m into the mountain, although the thirty-minute guided tour (in Greek and English) only takes in the more interesting outer chambers.

---

**ACCOMMODATION AND EATING**                    **POTAMÓS AND AROUND**

#### POTAMÓS

**Panaretos** ☎ 27360 34290. Traditional taverna, dominating the central platía, with indoor seating in the main restaurant down below. Excellent home-made bread and juicy olives. Daily breakfast, lunch & dinner.

#### AYÍA PELAYÍA

★ **Kaleris** ☎ 27360 33461. The chef here specializes in inventive, original takes on a whole range of traditional dishes, such as "feta french fries". Expect about €20/person. Daily lunch & dinner.

**Moustakias** ☎ 27360 33519. A classic seafood taverna, with portside seating and very friendly service. Catch-of-the-day is always a good choice, along with whatever is in

season – green beans, artichokes or courgettes. Live music Sat eve. Daily lunch & dinner.

★ **Venardos** ☎ 27360 34100, ⌨ venardos-hotels.gr. Extensive hotel complex boasting hilltop views and located just a short walk from the beach. Facilities include a large pool, gym, sauna and spa. Rooms range from standard doubles to suites and studios. Discounts for Rough Guide readers. Breakfast included. **€80**

#### MYLOPÓTAMOS

**Platanos** ☎ 27360 33397. This shady café-taverna makes a pleasant stop for a freshly squeezed orange juice or a full meal, above the village's springs. About €12/person. Inside, there's an appealing music bar. Daily, May–Oct, noon to midnight and beyond.

---

# Kapsáli and the south

**KAPSÁLI** on the south coast is largely devoted to summer tourism – in fact, much of it closes down from September to June. Most savvy foreign visitors to Kýthira in summer stay here, and it's a popular port of call for yachts, particularly since it is sheltered from the strong north winds of summer. Set behind double coved beaches, overlooked by Hóra castle, and backed by high grey cliffs on which the tiny white monastery of Áyios Ioánnis Éngremmos perches, it is certainly memorable.

## Hóra

**HÓRA** (or Kýthira Town), the island's picturesque capital, is a steep 2km haul above Kapsáli, and is quite somnolent in comparison. It does enjoy an equally dramatic position, however, its Cycladic-style houses tiered on the ridge leading to its very own Venetian **castle**. Below the castle are both the remains of older Byzantine walls and, in Mésa Vouryó, numerous well-signed but securely locked Byzantine churches. The *Stavros* **bookshop**, on the town's main street, sells a book of **walks** (mainly around the southern half of the island).

### Hóra castle

Daily 8am–7pm • Free

Hóra's **castle** is a must mostly for the breathtaking 360-degree **panorama** it affords over the entire area – on a clear enough day you can even see Crete. Access to the

2

## KANGAROO ISLAND

Kýthira was never a rich island, but, along with Monemvasiá, it did once have a military and economic significance – which it likewise lost with Greek independence and the opening of the Corinth Canal. Since then, emigration (almost entirely to **Australia**, which islanders refer to as "Big Kýthira") has reduced the permanent population significantly. In summer many Greek Australians return to here to visit family (Greeks call it "Kangaroo Island"), which is why the English spoken on the island usually has a distinct Down Under lilt.

fortress is up a modern pathway, but, to the right of this, the original narrow tunnel entrance is still usable. Within the castle walls, most of the buildings are in ruins, except for the paired churches of Panayía Myrtidhiótissa and the smaller Panayía Orfáni (Catholic and Orthodox respectively, under the Venetian occupation). There are spectacular **views** down to Kapsáli and out to sea to the chunk of inaccessible islet known as **Avgó** (Egg), legendary **birthplace of Aphrodite**. On its cliffs grow the yellow-flowered everlasting (*sempreviva*), used locally for making small dried flower arrangements, which you see for sale in every shop, symbol of the goddess's eternal beauty.

## ACCOMMODATION AND EATING                    KAPSÁLI AND THE SOUTH

In high season, it goes without saying that you must book ahead if you want **accommodation** in Kapsáli. Finding a **hotel** in Hóra is easier, since it's well away from the beach. Both towns have plenty of good **places to eat**.

### KAPSÁLI

★ **Afrodite Apartments** ☎ 27360 31328, ⓦ hotel-afrodite.gr. This white complex stands above the town, with good views, a pleasant rear garden, and (slow) internet facilities for guests. A few really choice apartments are on the seaward side of the road, just above the beach. **€70**

**Chýtra** Named after the island offshore, the Kettle (aka the Egg), where Aphrodite is said to have been born, this appealing harbourside taverna offers all the best of Greek traditional cookery – extraordinary stewed broad green beans in season – with beachfront seating. May–Sept daily lunch & dinner.

**Hydragogio** ☎ 27360 31065. Located at the Hóra end of the beach, facing the water, this choice serves up good veggie options, such as *briam*, as well as fish (€20–70/kg). Main dishes average about €8. May–Sept daily lunch & dinner.

**Vasili Spitia** ☎ 27360 31125, ⓦ kythirabungalows vasili.gr. Located a short way up the hill amid an old olive grove, this place offers comfortable rooms and studios, all with a/c, balconies and sea views. Breakfast included. April–Oct. **€80**

### HÓRA

**Belvedere** Overlooking both the castle and the twin bays of Kapsáli, the main draw here is the impressive terrace seating. Traditional Greek dishes, plus pizzas. Daily lunch & dinner.

**Castello Apartments** ☎ 27360 31869, ⓦ castelloapts -kythera.gr. On the Kapsáli side of town, with great views all around, this cheerful structure is off the street, in a garden setting. The nine self-catering rooms, studios and apartment are simple and some have balconies and views. **€45**

★ **Margarita** ☎ 27360 31711, ⓦ hotel-margarita .com. This beautiful, immaculately maintained 1840s house is down just below the main street. There are wonderful views of the coast and the castle, and very friendly and helpful staff. Buffet breakfast €10/person. **€80**

**Zorba's** 34 on the lane that leads down from the platía ☎ 27360 31655. By far the best taverna in town, as both locals and travellers concur. Only €10–15 for a full meal, with grilled meats a speciality, served on a beautiful terrace. Tues–Sun lunch & dinner; Mon dinner only.

## Avlémonas

The prettiest destination on the east coast is Avlémonas, on a rocky bay at the top of this coast. It's a small fishing port with an end-of-the-world feel as you approach from a distance. It becomes much more attractive once reached, and has a remarkable coordination of colour schemes throughout the village. There is a small Venetian fortress and little coves with some of the clearest water around, fine for swimming.

**Maryianni** ☎ 27360 33316, ⓦ maryianni.kythera.gr. This bright, pleasantly landscaped complex is the closest one to the sea. Most rooms are fully self-catering and offer great views from private terraces. **€70**

**Sotiris** This taverna, with seating overlooking the sparkling little cove, offers a wide selection of fresh, well-prepared and reasonably priced fish dishes (around €10). Daily, lunch & dinner.

## Andikýthira

Thirteen kilometres to the south of Kýthira, the tiny, wind-blown 22-square-kilometre island of **ANDIKÝTHIRA** (ⓦ antikythira.gr) is linked to its bigger sister by a sporadic ferry service. Rocky and poor, and a site of political exile until 1964, the island only received electricity in 1984, but it has one remarkable claim to fame: the **Andikýthira Mechanism** (see p.85). Local attractions include good birdlife (a bird observatory has been built in the old school at Laziuná) and flora, but it's not the place if you want company, with only 45 residents divided among a scattering of settlements – mainly in **Potamós**, the harbour, and **Sohória**, the village. Ferries-permitting, the **festival of Áyios Mýron** is held here on August 17– an annual reunion jamboree for the Andikytheran diaspora.

Recent excavation work above Xeropótamos has revealed the site of ancient **Aigila**, a 75-acre fortress city of the Hellenistic period. At the harbour below are the remains of one of ancient Greece's best-preserved warship slipways, a *neosoikos*, carved out of the rock. Archeologist Aris Tsaravopoulos (☎ 697 30 50 204) can sometimes arrange volunteer excavation work at the sites.

**By ferry** Andikýthira has, theoretically, a twice-weekly summer connection with Kýthira (2hr) on the

Pireás–Kýthira–Kastélli (Crete) run, but landings are often impossible due to adverse weather.

**ACCOMMODATION AND EATING**

**Antikythera Rooms** Potamós ☎ 27360 33004, ⓦ antikythera.gr. The only official accommodation on the island, this set of rooms is run by the local community There

are a couple of tavernas and a village shop at Sohória, but you'd be wise to bring plenty of supplies with you. **€40**

# The Máni

The southernmost peninsula of Greece, **the MÁNI**, stretches from Yíthio in the east to Kardhamýli in the west and terminates at Cape Ténaro. It is a wild landscape, an arid Mediterranean counterpart to Cornwall or the Scottish Highlands, with a wildly idiosyncratic culture and history to match. Perhaps because of this independent spirit, the sense of hospitality is, like nearby Crete, as strong as anywhere in Greece.

The peninsula's spine, negotiated by road at just a few points, is the vast grey mass of **Mount Taïyetos** and its southern extension, **Sangiás**. The **Mésa Máni** – the part of the peninsula south of a line drawn between Ítylo and Vathý bay – is classic Máni territory, its jagged coast relieved only by the occasional cove, and its land a mass of rocks. Attractions include the coastal villages, like **Yeroliménas** on the west coast, or **Kótronas** on the east, as well as the remarkable caves at **Pýrgos Dhiroú**, but the pleasure is mainly in exploring the region's distinctive **tower-houses** and **churches**, and the solitude.

The **Éxo Máni** – the somewhat more verdant coast up from Areópoli to Kalamáta, mostly in Messinía province – sees the emphasis shift to walking and beaches. **Stoúpa** and **Kardhamýli** are both attractive resorts, developed but far from spoilt. The road itself is an experience, threading up into the foothills of Taïyetos before looping back down to the sea.

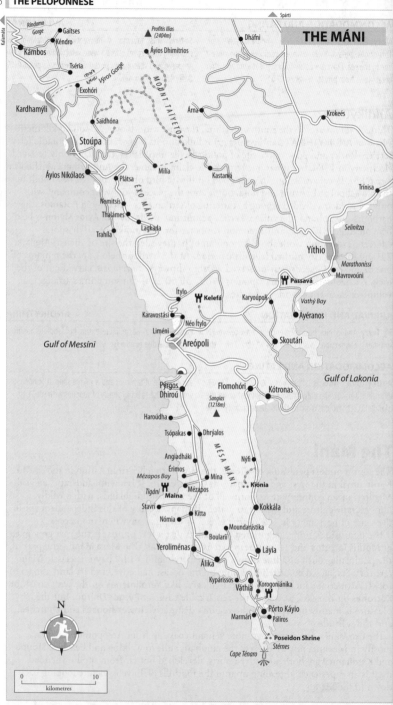

THE MÁNI

## INFORMATION                                                    THE MÁNI

You need at least three days to do the Máni justice, preferably with your own vehicle. Possible bases include Areópoli, or Yíthio, though the latter isn't typical of the region. Otherwise, pick a beach resort, such as Kardhamýli or, better yet, remote Pórto Káyio.

**Services** Opening hours of shops, tavernas, petrol stations and almost anything else can be idiosyncratic in the Mésa Máni, so it may also prove wise to bring some general supplies with you – there are banks with ATMs and well-stocked supermarkets in Areópoli, Kalamáta, Kardhamýli, Stoúpa and Yíthio, and smaller markets in Pýrgos Dhiroú and Yeroliménas.

**Books and websites** The well-illustrated website of John Chapman (w zorbas.de/maniguide) is a comprehensive information source, particularly on the history, churches and frescoes. Alternatively, try Peter Greenhalgh and Edward Eliopoulos's *Deep Into Mani* or, best of all, Patrick Leigh Fermor's classic *Mani: Travels in the Southern Peloponnese* (see p.801).

**Maps** A good, large-scale map is invaluable for navigating among the innumerable tiny settlements of the Mésa Máni: both Road Editions and Anavasi have a 1:50 000 scale map of the area, while Anavasi also produce a 1:25 000 map of the southernmost half. Recently, a number of walking routes have been signed in the area, with useful map boards at the starting points.

## GETTING AROUND

**Car and bike rental** Given sporadic public transport you really should consider renting a car or motorbike at Kalamáta, Yíthio or Stoúpa. Drivers will find the roads mostly good, and there are numerous road signs (many used for target practice).

**By bus** In the Mésa Máni, there are just two services: Areópoli–Yeroliménas–Álika–Váthia, although the Váthia section is unreliable (daily in summer; three weekly out of season), and Areópoli–Kótronas–Láyia (daily). In the Éxo Máni the Kalamáta–Ítylo bus serves the coastal towns (3–4 times daily).

**By taxi** There are a handful of taxis serving the region, generally negotiable, at Areópoli, Yeroliménas, Kótronas and Yíthio; currently, a taxi from Areópoli to Váthia would cost €30.

## Brief history

The **mountains** offer the key to Maniot history. Formidable natural barriers, they provided a refuge from, and bastion of resistance to, every occupying force of the last two millennia. **Christianity** did not take root in the interior until the ninth century (some five hundred years after the establishment of Byzantium) and the region was ruled by intense and violent internal tribalism, seen at its most extreme in the elaborate tradition of **blood feuds** (see box below).

The Turks, wisely, opted to control the Máni by granting a level of local **autonomy**, investing power in one or other clan whose leader they designated "bey" of the region. This system worked well until the nineteenth-century appointment of **Petrobey Mavromihalis**. With a power base at Liméni he united the clans in revolution in March

### BLOOD FEUDS IN THE MÁNI

**Blood feuds** were the result of an intricate feudal society that seems to have developed across the Máni in the fourteenth century. After the arrival of refugee Byzantine families the various clans developed **strongholds** in the tightly clustered villages. From these local forts, often marble-roofed towers, the clans conducted **vendettas** according to strict rules. The object was to destroy the tower and kill the male members of the opposing clan. The favoured method of attack was to smash the prestigious tower roofs; the forts consequently rose to four and five storeys.

Feuds would customarily be signalled by the ringing of **church bells**, and from this moment the adversaries would confine themselves to their towers, firing at each other with all available weaponry. The battles could last for years, even decades, with women (who were safe from attack) shuttling in food, ammunition and supplies. Truces were declared at harvest times; then, with business completed, the battle would recommence. The feuds lasted until either one side was annihilated or through **ritual surrender** whereby a whole clan would file out to kiss the hands of enemy parents who had lost children in the feud; the victors would then dictate strict terms by which the vanquished could remain in the village.

1821, and his **Maniot army** was to prove vital to the success of the **War of Independence**. Mavromihalis swiftly fell out with the first president of the nation, Kapodhistrías, and, with other members of the clan, was imprisoned by him at Náfplio – an act leading to the president's **assassination** at the hands of Petrobey's brothers. The monarchy fared little better until one of the king's German officers was sent to the Máni to enlist soldiers in a special Maniot militia.

In the twentieth century, ignored by the powerful central government in Athens, this backwater area slipped into decline, with drastic and persistent **depopulation** of the villages. In places like Váthia and Kítta, which once held populations in the hundreds, the numbers are now down to single figures. Recently, there has been an influx of money, partly due to increased tourism, partly to membership in the EU. The result has been considerable refurbishment, with many postwar concrete houses acquiring "traditional" stone facings.

## Yíthio (Gythion)

**YÍTHIO**, Sparta's ancient port, is the eastern gateway to the Máni peninsula, and one of the south's most attractive seaside towns in its own right. Its somewhat low-key harbour, with occasional ferries to Pireás and Kýthira, gives onto a graceful nineteenth-century waterside of tiled-roof houses – some of them now showing their age. There are beaches within walking distance, and rooms are relatively easy to find. In the bay, tethered by a long, narrow jetty, is the islet of **Marathoníssi**, ancient Kranae, where Paris of Troy, having abducted Helen from Menelaus's palace at Sparta, dropped anchor, and where the lovers spent their first night.

### Marathoníssi

**Marathoníssi** islet is the town's main attraction, with swimming possible off the rocks towards the lighthouse. Amid the island's trees and scrub stands the restored Tzanetákis tower-fortress, built around 1810 by the Turkish-appointed Bey of the Máni, to guard the harbour against his lawless countrymen. It now houses a **Museum of the Máni** (officially Tues–Sun 9.30am–3pm, though often closed; €2), which deals with the exploration of the Máni from Ciriaco de Pizzicoli (1447) to Henri Belle (1861), with labels in Greek and English.

### Roman theatre

Open site • Free

There are some impressive remains of a **Roman theatre** at the northeast end of the town. Follow the road past the post office for about 300m until you reach the army barracks – the site stands just to the left, inside the outer gate. With most of its stone seats intact, and 50m in diameter, the theatre illustrates perfectly how buildings in Greece take on different guises through the ages: to one side is a Byzantine church (now ruined) which, in turn, functions as an outer wall of the barracks.

## ARRIVAL AND DEPARTURE
YÍTHIO

**By bus** The bus station is close to the centre of town, with the main waterfront street, Vassiléos Pávlou, ahead of you. Destinations Athens (6 daily; 5hr); Areópoli (4 daily; 30min); Láyia (2 daily; 1hr); Mavrouvoúni ("Kamping", 4 daily; 15–20min); Monemvasiá (2 daily in high season; 2hr

30min); Pýrgos Dhiroú ("Spílea", 1 daily; 1hr); Váthia (1 daily, Mon, Wed, Fri only; 1hr 30min); Yeroliménas (3 daily; 1hr 15min).
**By ferry** Kýthira (1–5 weekly in season; 2hr 30min).

## INFORMATION

**Tourist office** There is a small EOT tourist office at Vassiléos Yeoryíou 20.
**Services** There are several banks near the bus station. The

helpful Rozaki Shipping and Travel Agency on the waterfront (☎ 27330 22650, ✉ rosakigy@otnet.gr) can provide ferry sailing times and car rental and will also change money.

**Shopping** The extensive Hasanakos bookshop at Vassiléos Pávlou 39 is worth scouring for books on the area, though prices are very high for books in English. Food supplies can be bought from the large supermarket behind the bus station.

## ACCOMMODATION

Finding accommodation shouldn't be hard, with a fair range in town – most hotels are along the waterfront, some of which suffer from late-night noise from the many bars. Numerous cheaper **rooms** are signposted up the steps behind the waterfront, or facing Marathoníssi islet. Out along Mavrovoúni beach, which begins 3km south of the town off the Areópoli road, there are numerous rooms and three **campsites**.

**Demestihas** Mavrovoúni Beach ☎27330 22775, ✆demestihas.gr. Immediately behind the beach, in a large garden, with a variety of rooms, studios and apartments, many refurbished. Good facilities for kids. €50

**Gythion** Vassiléos Pávlou 33 ☎27330 23452, ✆gythionhotel.gr. A fine old (1864) hotel with period decorated rooms, all with views of the waterfront, located above *Dodoni* ice cream parlour. Guests can use the Gythion Bay campsite's beach and private beach facilities. Breakfast included, with fresh orange juice. €65

**Leonidas** Vassiléos Pávlou 8 ☎&✆27330 22389. Friendly Petros runs this very basic, unassuming hotel, with its Deco-style entrance and very spartan rooms, which nevertheless have a/c, and most have balconies with port views. Breakfast included. €40

**Meltemi** Mavrovoúni beach, 3km from Yíthio ☎27330 23260, ✆campingmeltemi.gr. Large and nestled in a 25-acre olive grove, this pleasant spot faces a broad swathe of beach and clean sea. Facilities include a pool, minimarket, restaurant, washing machines and dryers, and free wi-fi. April–Oct. Camping €12; bungalows €45

**Saga** Tzanetáki ☎27330 23220, ✆27330 24370. Comfortable seafront *pension* run by a friendly, knowledgeable French-Greek family, with a good restaurant on the ground floor, overlooking the Marathoníssi islet. €45

## EATING AND DRINKING

**Nisaki** On Marathoníssi islet ☎27330 23830. Away from the port, on the square facing the little church, this quiet, attractive café-restaurant has both a pleasant dining room and a spacious terrace. Tzatziki €3.50, grills €5.50–12, fresh fish €50/kg. Daily breakfast, lunch & dinner.

**Poulikakos** ☎27330 22792. Located on the main square, this cosy, traditional taverna is simple but offers delicious food in large portions. Full meals run about €10–15, featuring earthy classics like giant white beans and dolmádhes, everything home-made. Fresh fish starts at €30/kg. Daily lunch & dinner.

# Yíthio to Areópoli

The road from Yíthio into the Máni begins amid a fertile and gentle wooded landscape, running slightly inland of the coast and Mavrovoúni beach, through tracts of citrus and olive groves and between hilltop towers. About 12km beyond Yíthio, the Máni suddenly asserts itself as the road enters a valley below the **castle of Passavá**. Shortly after, a turning to the left leads down to an attractive long sandy beach at **Vathý Bay** (Vathý Ayéranou), which is mostly used by German tourists.

Continuing towards Areópoli from Passavá, the landscape remains fertile until the wild, scrubby mass of Mount Kouskoúni signals the final approach to the Mésa Máni. You enter another pass, with **Kelefá castle** (see p.163) above to the north, and beyond it several southerly peaks of the Taïyetos ridge. Areópoli, as you wind down from the hills, inspires a real sense of arrival.

## Areópoli and the west coast

An initially austere-looking town, **AREÓPOLI** (Aerópoli) sets an immediate mood for the region. Until the nineteenth century it was secondary to Ítylo, 11km north and the western gateway to the Mésa Máni, but the modern road has made Areópoli, to all intents, the region's centre, and many of the stone buildings have now undergone renovation. Formerly Tsímova, its present name "Town of Ares" (the god of war) was bestowed for its efforts during the War of Independence. It was here that Mavromihalis (commemorated by a statue in the main platía) declared the uprising.

The town's sights are archetypically Maniot in their anachronisms. The **Áyii Taxiárhes** Cathedral, for example, has primitive reliefs above its doors that look twelfth century until you notice their date: 1798. Similarly, the tower-houses could readily be described as medieval, though most of them were built in the early 1800s. On its own, in a little platía, is the church of **Áyios Ioánnis**, the Mavromihalis' family church; the interior is lined with frescoes. Facing, there's a tiny but fascinating **Byzantine museum** in the Pikoulakis tower.

## The Pýrgos Dhiroú caves

Daily: June–Sept 8.30am–5.30pm; Oct–May 8.30am–3pm • €12 • The caves are 5km beyond the village of Pýrgos Dhiroú, set beside the sea and a separate beach • Taxis from Areópoli will take you to the caves, then wait and take you back

Some 8km south of Areópoli, the road forks off to the **Pýrgos Dhiroú caves** – the Máni's major tourist attraction. Often referred to simply as "Spílea", they are very much a packaged attraction but worth a visit, especially on weekday afternoons when the wait is shorter. A visit consists of a thirty-minute punt around the underground waterways of the **Glyfádha (Vlyhádha) caves**, well lit and crammed with stalactites, whose reflections are a remarkable sight in the 2–20m depth of water. You are then permitted a brief tour on foot of the **Alepótrypa caves** – huge chambers (one of them 100m by 60m) in which excavation has unearthed evidence of prehistoric occupation.

You should buy a ticket as soon as possible on arrival at the caves: this gives you a priority number for the tours. At a mid-season weekend you can wait for an hour or more, so it's best to arrive as early as possible in the day with gear to make the most of the adjacent beach. The nearby **museum** (Tues–Sun 8.30am–3pm but unreliable; €2), on a bend of the road, contains interesting Neolithic finds from the caves; the few labels are in Greek.

### ARRIVAL AND INFORMATION

### AREÓPOLI

**By bus** Buses arrive and depart from the main square, Platía Athánatos; the ticket office is two doors down from the *Europa Grill*. If you are heading north into Messinía, towards Kalamáta, you will probably need to change in Ítylo.

**Destinations** Ítylo (3 daily, no service Sun; 20min); Kalamáta (4 daily changing at Ítylo; 1hr 30min–2hr 30min); Láyia (1 daily; 40min); Pýrgos Dhiroú ("Spílea", 1 daily; 15min); Váthia (daily in season; 1hr 30min); Yeroliménas (via Liméni, 3 daily in season; 45min); Yíthio (4 daily; 30min).

**Services** On the main platía is a bank (Tues & Thurs 9am–1pm) with an ATM, and the post office. On the main road behind the square is a large supermarket for supplies (especially useful if heading on south).

### ACCOMMODATION

★ **Londas Tower** ☎ 27330 51360, 🌐 londas.com. Just steps away from the cathedral, this beautifully restructured tower-house with lots of artistic touches used to belong to the Mavromihalis family. Breakfast, a sumptuous home-made treat, is included. Minimum stay 2 nights, 4 nights in Aug; no a/c. **€85**

**Pyrgos Kapetanakou** ☎ 27330 51233. Another of the old towers, in a walled garden, has been restored as a traditional guesthouse; the two- to five-bedded rooms are austerely beautiful, decorated with local weavings, and some have balconies. Breakfast included. **€80**

**Trapela** ☎ 27330 52690, 🌐 trapela.gr. Done up in the old Maniot style, but new, this small hotel is a typical Areópoli mix of austere and cosy. A garden and their own bar are nice pluses. Breakfast included. **€70**

### EATING AND DRINKING

There are a number of **café-restaurants** around the main square, but much better gourmet **tavernas** are nearer the cathedral, behind which there's also a traditional **bakery** that produces a variety of tasty breads and sweets.

★ **Barba Petros** ☎ 27330 51205. Unassuming spot off the cobbled street towards Áyii Taxiárhes. Lots of perfectly simmered vegetable dishes and stews to choose from; mains about €10. Daily lunch & dinner.

★ **To Katoi** ☎ 27330 51201. Excellent taverna with rustic barrel-vaulted stone dining rooms, as well as atmospheric seating outside. The menu is deceptively standard, and inexpensive – the priciest item is only €9 – but the quality is extraordinary. Oven-roasted kid a speciality. Summer, daily lunch & dinner; off-season, dinner only and closed Mon.

# Yeroliménas and the south

After the journey from Areópoli, **YEROLIMÉNAS** (Yerolimín) feels like a village in limbo, but it does make a good base for exploring the southern extremities of the Máni. There are a few shops, a **post office**, a couple of **cafés** and several **hotels**. The petrol station just beyond Yeroliménas is currently the southernmost of the peninsula.

South from Yeroliménas, the scenery becomes browner, treeless and more arid; a good road (and the bus) continues to **Álika**, where it divides. One fork leads east through the mountains to Láyia (see p.162), and the other continues southwards to **Váthia** and across the **Marmári isthmus** towards **Cape Ténaro**. Between Álika and Váthia there are good coves for swimming. One of the best is **Kypárissos**, reached by following a dry riverbed about midway to Váthia. On the headland above are scattered Roman remains of ancient Kaenipolis, including (amid the walled fields) the excavated ruins of a sixth-century basilica.

## Váthia

**VÁTHIA**, a photogenic group of tower-houses set uncompromisingly on a high hillside outcrop, is one of the most dramatic villages in the Mésa Máni. It features in Colonel Leake's account of his travels, one of the best sources on Greece in the early nineteenth century. He was warned to avoid going through the village in 1805 as a feud had been running between two families for the previous forty years. Today it has the feel of a ghost town. The EOT-restored inn, occupying a dozen tower-houses, has been bankrupt and inactive for some years now, though there is a seasonal café.

## Pórto Káyio

From Váthia the road south to the cape edges around the mountain, before slowly descending to a couple of junctions. Left at the second brings you steeply down to the beach and laidback hamlet of **PÓRTO KÁYIO** ("Bay of Quails", 6km from Váthia). A pleasant short walk goes out to the Ágios Nikólaos chapel on the southeastern headland of the bay, while across the bay on the north side are the spectacular ruins of a Turkish fortress contemporary with Kelefá and the monastery of Korogoniánika.

## Marmári

Above Pórto Káyio, the right branch of the road goes south along the headland, capped by the Grigorákis tower, to the pleasant, sandy **beaches** at the double bay of **MARMÁRI**. The picturesque hamlet itself straddles a promontory between the two bays and amounts to little more than a collection of accommodation options, some of them quite luxurious for such a desolate and stony spot.

## On to Cape Ténaro

Starting from the left fork before Marmári, follow the surfaced road and signs for the fish taverna, passing a turning for Páliros and making your way along the final barren peninsula, to Stérnes (Kokkinóyia). The road ends at a knoll crowned with the squat **chapel of Asómati**, constructed largely of materials from an ancient **temple of Poseidon**.

To the left (east) as you face the chapel is the little pebbly **bay of Asómati**; on the shore is a small **cave**, another addition to the list of mythical entrances to the underworld. To the right (west) of Asómati, the marked main path continues along the edge of another cove and through the metre-high foundations of a **Roman town** that grew up around the Poseidon shrine; there is even a mosaic in one structure. From here the old trail, which existed before the road was bulldozed, reappears as a walled path, allowing 180-degree views of the sea on its 25-minute course to the lighthouse on **Cape Ténaro**.

The tip of the peninsula is so rocky and extreme that coming across any sign of civilization here is almost a shock. Yet, there are surprisingly enchanting places to stay and to eat, usually one and the same.

### YEROLIMÉNAS

**Akroyiali ☎** 27330 54204, **ⓦ** gerolimenas-hotels.com. This long-established accommodation complex has a/c in most rooms and self-catering apartments in traditional stone-built edifices. It also has its own excellent restaurant where the baked fish in lemon juice and olive oil takes some beating. Breakfast included. **€80**

**Kyrimai ☎** 27330 54288, **ⓦ** kyrimai.gr. Ensconced at the southeastern end of the bay, is this castle-like "country chic elegant" property in a restored 1870 building, with a Maniot memorabilia library, a pool and very stylish rooms. Breakfast included. **€100**

### PÓRTO KÁYIO

**★ Akrotiri ☎** 27330 52013, **ⓦ** porto-kagio.gr. This attractive taverna with rooms has an end-of-the-world feel about it, but is very welcoming. The food is simple and very good while the rooms are all different and warmly inviting, with a/c and some with sea view. Breakfast included. **€60**

### MARMÁRI

**★ Marmari Paradise ☎** 27330 52101, **ⓦ** marmari paradise.gr. A wonderful, traditional stone property with garden terraces, featuring stone rooms with sea views and its own panoramic restaurant that serves Máni recipes, most dishes ranging €7–10. Book early, as it fills up fast in high season. Breakfast included. Easter–Oct. **€70**

## The east coast

The **east coast** of the Mésa Máni is most easily approached from **Areópoli**, where there's a daily **bus** through **Kótronas** to **Láyia**. However, if you have transport, or you're prepared to walk and hitch, there's satisfaction in doing a full loop of the peninsula, crossing over to Láyia from Yeroliménas (Álika) or Pórto Káyio. The landscape of the eastern side, the "sunward coast", is different from the western "shadow coast", and it's far less developed, though it offers some of the region's most spectacular views. It works best as a **scenic drive**, rather than a place to stay. There are few **beaches** and less coastal plain, but larger, more scattered and picturesque **villages** hanging on the hillsides. Road signs are fewer than in the west.

### Láyia

From the fork at Álika (see above), it's 10km by road to **LÁYIA**, one of the highest villages (400m) in the Mésa Máni. A turning off the road, not far above Álika, takes you to **Moundanístika**, the Máni's very highest village – recommended for spectacular views. Láyia itself is a multi-towered village that perfectly exemplifies the feudal setup of the old Máni. Four families lived here, and their four independently sited settlements, each with its own church, survive. One of the taller towers, so the locals claim, was built overnight by four hundred men, hoping to gain an advantage at sunrise. Today, a council-owned café faces the main church and the village shows healthy signs of revival, with the ongoing refurbishment of a number of houses.

### Flomohóri and around

Some 30km northwards, passing views, towered hamlets and modest beaches, you reach **FLOMOHÓRI**. The land below is relatively fertile, and the village has maintained a reasonable population as well as an imposing group of tower-houses, one reckoned by some to be the Máni's highest. The way of life here survives as a bit of a time warp: the deeply traditional black dress of perpetual mourning is usual, and the locals are liable to regard you with an odd mix of amusement and bravado – as if you just stepped off a spaceship. You might feel the same.

   **Kótronas**, a few kilometres downhill, feels less harsh than the rest of the Máni. It is still a working fishing village, and there's a sandy beach here if you feel like a dip in the sea.

# The Éxo (Outer) Máni: Areópoli to Kalamáta

The 40km of road into Messinía, between Areópoli and Kalamáta, are as dramatic and beautiful as any in Greece, almost a corniche route between the **Taïyetos** ridge and the **Gulf of Messinía**. The first few settlements en route are classic Máni villages, their towers packed against the hillside. As you move north, with the road dropping to near sea level, there are several small resorts, which are appealing and popular. For walkers, there is a reasonably well-preserved *kalderími* (footpath) running parallel to (or short-cutting) much of the paved route, with superb **gorge hikes** just east of Kardhamýli, a good base for local exploration and touring.

## Liméni

At **LIMÉNI**, Areópoli's tiny traditional port, which lies 3km to the north and dramatically down, the less austere Éxo Máni begins. Liméni is a handful of houses on a curve of sparkling sea, dominated by the restored **tower-house** of Petrobey Mavromihalis, which is a newly-opened luxury **hotel**, though it resembles nothing so much as an English country parish church.

**ACCOMMODATION AND EATING**                                                          **LIMÉNI**

★ **Pirgos Mavromichali** ☎ 27330 51042, ⓦ pirgosmavromichali.gr. This newly opened luxury hotel is in the refurbished historic tower-house of the legendary clan. It's a frankly magical setting: white stone archways, secret stairways, glistening turquoise waters below, all enhanced at night by imaginative lighting. Bedrooms and suites are coolly sophisticated and perfectly appointed, and the terrace breakfast is included. **€100**

★ **Takis To Limeni** ☎ 27330 51327. A fabulously well-considered fish taverna next door to *Pirgos Mavromichali*. Perfect for a a blowout meal (fresh fish runs to €65/kg) but you can also opt for more affordable taverna dishes – Greek salads go for €7. Daily lunch & dinner; in winter, weekends only.

## Ítylo and around

The village of **ÍTYLO** (Oítylo), 8km farther along the main road after the Liméni turn-off, has been experiencing a resurgence in fortunes, with many crumbling old houses now restored. In earlier times, Ítylo was the capital of the Máni, and from the sixteenth to the eighteenth centuries it was the region's most notorious base for piracy and slave trading. The Maniots traded efficiently in slaves, selling Turks to Venetians, Venetians to Turks, and, at times of feud, the women of each other's clans to both. Irritated by the piracy and hoping to control the important pass to the north, the Turks built the sprawling **castle of Kelefá** in 1670. This is just a kilometre's walk from Ítylo across a gorge, and its walls and bastions, built for a garrison of five hundred, are substantially intact. Also worth exploring is the **monastery of Dhekoúlou**, down towards the coast; its setting is beautiful and there are some fine eighteenth-century frescoes in the chapel.

**ACCOMMODATION AND EATING**                                                            **ÍTYLO**

There are a few **rooms** to rent in Ítylo but it's best to head down to **Néo Ítylo**, just round the bay from Ítylo's port Karavostási.

**Ítylo** ☎ 27330 59222, ⓦ hotelitilo.gr. Néo Ítylo is a tiny hamlet, but as well as rooms for rent it boasts this comfortable stone hotel on the beach. There's a/c, a

restaurant and a playground for kids. Breakfast included; special offers for longer stays. **€85**

## Stoúpa

Some 20km north of Ítylo, **STOÚPA** is extremely plesant and very popular with British package holiday-makers and holiday-home owners. It has possibly the best sands along this coast, with two glorious **beaches** (Stoúpa and the smaller, deeper Kalogriá) separated by a headland, each sloping into the sea and superb for children. Submarine freshwater springs gush into the bay, keeping it unusually clean, if a bit cold. A ten-minute walk to the north of Kalogriá beach is the delightful and often deserted cove of Dhelfíni. A further 600m brings you to the pebble beach of Fonéa, wrapped around a rock outcrop and tucked into a corner of the hillside. Stoúpa was home in 1917–18 to the wandering Cretan writer, Nikos Kazantzakis, who is said to have based the title character in *Zorba the Greek* on a worker at the lignite mine in nearby Pástrova.

Out of peak season, Stoúpa is certainly recommended, though in July and August, and any summer weekend, you may find the crowds a bit overwhelming and space at a premium. A popular walking-guide booklet and large-scale map are available: ask at the efficient Doufexis Travel.

## ARRIVAL AND INFORMATION

**By bus** The Kalamáta–Ítylo bus stops at the junctions at each end of town, but does not go in, 3–4 times daily.
**By car** Driving up from the south, the main access road to town is well signed, forking off about 1km away from the centre.

**Services** Doufexis Travel (☎ 27210 77677, ✉ douftvl @hellasnet.gr) can find accommodation and organize car rental (including for the southern Peloponnese during the winter), as well as exchange money. Stoúpa taxi is on ☎ 27210 77477. On the main road there is a good bakery and two well-stocked supermarkets.

## ACCOMMODATION AND EATING

**Akroyiali** ☎ 27210 77335. This taverna at the southern end of the main beach not only has well-prepared food, including seafood, but also has views after dark of the lights of the mountain village Saïdhóna which look remarkably like an extra constellation of stars. Main dishes average €10. Daily lunch & dinner.
**Lefktron** ☎ 27210 77322, ⊛ lefktron-hotel.gr. Modern and comfortable, just to the south of town and near the

beach, rooms here have a/c, fridges and balconies, along with internet access and a pool. Breakfast included. €80
**Ta Delfinia Camping** ☎ 27210 77318, ⊛ lefktron.info /delfinia/f_camping-stoupa-kardamili.htm. Just north of town, amid an olive grove on its own quiet beach, campers rate this site among the top five on the Peloponnese. There's an on-site restaurant and market, and all basic facilities. April–Oct. From €10

## Kardhamýli

**KARDHAMÝLI**, 8km north of Stoúpa, is a major resort by Peloponnese standards and suffering from the busy main road that splits it. The **beach** is good, though not sandy – a long pebble strip north of the village, backed by olive trees. This is where the author Patrick Leigh Fermor (see p.801) chose to make his home, and it's certainly one of the greenest and loveliest of places around, an excellent base for walkers (see opposite).

Inland from the platía, it's a nice walk up to "Old Kardhamýli": a partly restored citadel of nineteenth-century houses, gathered about the church of **Áyios Spyrídhon** with its unusual multistorey bell tower. Here in the church courtyard Maniot chieftains Kolokotronis and Mourtzinos played human chess with their troops during the War of Independence. Part of the area is an interesting **museum** (Tues–Sun, 9am–2pm). Further back, on the path up to Ayía Sofía, is a pair of ancient tombs, said to be of the **Dioskoúri** (the Gemini twins).

## ARRIVAL AND INFORMATION

**By bus** The Kalamáta–Ítylo bus stops 3–4 times daily at the bookshop at the southern end of the main road, as well as at the central square at the northern end.
**By car** Driving up from the south, the main road passes through town, just 2 blocks inland.

**Taxis** Taxis are on ☎ 27210 74497, ☎ 27210 73433 or ☎ 27210 74323.
**Services** On the main road south of the platía, you'll find a bookshop and a post office (Mon–Fri). There is an ATM at the bank, next to the bridge.

## ACCOMMODATION

★ **Anniska** ☎ 27210 73600, ⊛ anniska.gr. This fresh property, the creation of an Anglo-Greek couple, enjoys a secluded spot on the hill just behind town. Self-catering

studios and apartments have sea views and easy private beach access, with facilities. Amenities include concierge service, wi-fi and PCs, a panoramic terrace coffee bar and

## HIKING THE VÝROS GORGE

The giant **Výros Gorge** plunges down from the summit ridge of Taïyetos to meet the sea just north of Kardhamýli. Tracks penetrate the gorge from various directions and are well worth a day or two's exploration. From Kardhamýli, the *kalderími* from the citadel continues to the church and village of Ayía Sofía, and then proceeds on a mixture of tracks and lanes either across the plateau up to the hamlet of **Exohóri**, or down into the gorge, where **monasteries** nestle deep at the base of dramatic cliffs. An hour or so inland along the canyon, more cobbled ways lead up to either Tséria on the north bank (there's a taverna, but no accommodation) or back towards Exohóri on the south flank, about 10km from Kardhamýli. Linking any or all of these points is a reasonable day's hiking at most; forays further upstream require full hiking gear and detailed topographical maps. One bus a day runs to Exohóri from Kardhamýli (25min), or you can take a taxi, for about €10.

### ACCOMMODATION AND EATING

**Faraggi** Exohóri ☎ 27210 73001, ✉ hotel-faraggi @gmail.com. A large stone house with breathtaking views of the gorge and six simple, very tasteful rooms. Well placed for walks, or just for enjoying the delicious food, or drinks and the mountain heights from the roof terrace bar. Breakfast included. **€60**

---

garden patio. Balconies and a/c. **€95**

**Melitsina Village** ☎ 27210 73334, ⌨ melitsina.com. This resort village, composed of charming stone studios and suites, has every sort of facility, including a safe playground, volleyball court, beach loungers, as well as spacious, self-catering accommodation with a/c and wi-fi. Located 2km north of the village. Buffet breakfast included. **€100**

★ **Notos** ☎ 27210 73730, ⌨ notoshotel.gr. Tranquil and tastefully decorated, the two-person self-catering studios here come with amenities, such as a/c and phone. The stone buildings are clustered in a hilly garden enclave, with wonderful views over the whole area. Three nights minimum for best rate. **€80**

**Skardamoula's Garden** ☎ 2721073516, ✉ skardamoula @gmail.com. An old stone mill, converted into comfortable self-catering studios and a restaurant on the ground floor. Located just off the square, 50m from the beach. **€60**

### EATING AND DRINKING

**Kiki** ☎ 27210 73148. Right on the beach, this is one of the finest of the traditional tavernas here, featuring genuine Maniot dishes created from the freshest local produce. About €10–15 per person. Daily lunch & dinner.

★ **Kyria Lela** ☎ 27210 73730. This beautifully relaxing spot near the harbour has a flowery setting and wonderful food at moderate prices, dishes averaging €9. Grilled fish is the speciality; full meals evening only. Rooms upstairs, with panoramic balcony. Daily lunch & dinner.

# Spárti (Sparta) and around

The central core of the Peloponnese is the luxuriantly spreading Mount Ménalo; but due south, in the Lakonian Evrótas valley, are **Spárti** and its Byzantine companion, **Mystra**, both overlooked and sheltered from the west by the massive and astonishing wall of the **Taïyetos** mountain ridge. Spárti had a big role in the development of ancient Greece, while Mystra, arrayed in splendour on its own hillside, is one of the country's most compelling historical sites.

## Spárti

Despite lying on the site of the ancient city-state of Sparta, modern **SPÁRTI**, capital of **Lakónia**, has few ancient ruins, and is today merely the organizational centre of a huge agricultural plain. Spárti's limited appeal is its very ordinariness – its pedestrianized side streets, café-lined squares, orange trees and evening *vólta*. The reason for coming here is basically to see **Mystra**, the Byzantine town, 5km to the west, which once controlled great swaths of the medieval world.

**2**

## Brief history

Commanding the Lakonian plain and fertile Evrótas valley from a series of low hills just west of the river, **ancient Sparta** was at the height of its power from the eighth to the fourth century BC, a period when its society was structured according to extremely harsh laws (see box opposite). The ancient "capital" occupied more or less the site of today's town, though it was in fact less a city than a grouping of villages. **Lykurgos**, architect of the warlike Spartan constitution and society, declared that "it is men not walls that make a city".

The Spartans famously defeated Athens in the **Peloponnesian War** between 431 and 421 BC and later established colonies around the Greek world. They eventually lost hegemony through defeat to Thebes. A second period of prosperity came under the Romans – for whom this was an outpost in the south of Greece, with the Máni never properly subdued. However, from the third century AD, Sparta declined, as nearby Mystra became the focus of Byzantine interest.

The annual September **Spartathlon**, a 246km run from Athens to Spárti, commemorates the messenger Pheidippides who ran the same route in 490 BC: the current course record is 20 hours and 25 minutes.

## Ancient sites

Daily 8.30am–3pm • Free

There are a few ruins to be seen to the north of the city. From the bold **Statue of Leonidas**, hero of Thermopylae, at the top of Paleológou, follow the track around and behind the modern stadium towards the old **Acropolis**, tallest of the Spartan hills. An immense **theatre** here, built into the side of the hill, can be quite clearly traced, even though today most of its masonry has gone – hurriedly adapted for fortification when the Spartans' power declined and, later still, recycled for the building of Byzantine Mystra. Above the theatre a sign marks a fragment of the **Temple of Athina Halkiakou**, while at the top of the acropolis sit the knee-high ruins of the tenth-century Byzantine church and monastery of **Ósios Níkon**.

Out on the Trípoli road (Odhós-ton-118, just past the junction with Orthias Artémidhos), a track leads to the remains of the **sanctuary of Artemis Orthia**. This was where Spartan boys underwent gruelling tests by flogging. The Roman geographer and travel writer **Pausanias** records that young men often perished under the lash, adding that the altar had to be splashed with blood before the goddess was satisfied. Being addicts of morbid blood sports, the Romans revived the custom here – the main ruins are of the spectators' grandstand they built.

## The archeological museum

Mon–Sat 8.30am–3pm, Sun 9.30am–2.30pm • €2

All moveable artefacts and mosaics have been transferred to the town's small **archeological museum** on Áyios Níkonos. Among its more interesting exhibits are a number of votive offerings found on the sanctuary site – sickles set in stone that were presented as prizes to the Spartan youths and solemnly rededicated to the goddess – and a fifth-century BC marble bust of a running Spartan hoplite, found on the acropolis and said to be Leonidas. There is a dramatic late sixth-century BC stele, with relief carvings on both sides, possibly of Menelaos with Helen and Agamemnon with Klytemnestra; the ends have carved snakes. There are fragments of Hellenistic and Roman mosaics, and numerous small lead figurines, clay masks and bronze idols from the Artemis Orthia site.

## The Museum of the Olive

Wed–Mon: summer 10am–6pm; winter 10am–5pm • €3 • Ⓦ piop.gr

At the southwest corner of town is the **Museum of the Olive and Greek Olive Oil**, at Óthonos & Amalías 129, worth a visit for its informative displays covering the primordial history, uses and production technology of the olive.

## A SPARTAN UPBRINGING

As the blood-spattered 2007 film *300* would seem to confirm, the famously tough Spartans can still stir the imagination. In part this stems from their legendary upbringing. Under a system known as the **agoge**, Spartan boys were rigorously trained by the state to develop physical toughness, loyalty and cunning. Babies judged unlikely to make the grade were left exposed on the slopes of Mount Taïyetos. Other boys were taken from their families at the age of seven to live in barracks. They were habitually underfed, so that they would learn to live off the land. At the age of twelve, they were required to form a sexual bond with a young Spartan soldier, who would act as their mentor. At eighteen, they would become provisional members of the army until the age of thirty, when it would finally be decided if they were worthy of **Spartan citizenship**. At this point they were expected to marry and produce offspring. The system was much admired in the ancient world, and boys from other city-states were sometimes sent here for their education.

2

### ARRIVAL AND INFORMATION

### SPÁRTI AND AROUND

**By bus** The main bus terminal is on the eastern edge of town at the far end of Lykoúrgou, though to reach the centre, the locals alight earlier on Lykoúrgou, near the archeological museum.

Destinations: Athens (8 daily; 3hr 15min); Kalamáta (changing at Artemisia, 2 daily; 1hr); Monemvasiá (3 daily, 2 on Sun, changing at Moláï; 2hr 30min–3hr); Mystra (11 daily, 4 on Sun; 15–30min); Neápoli (6 daily; 3hr); Pýrgos

Dhiroú (1 daily; 2hr 30min); Trípoli (4 daily; 1hr); Yeroliménas (2 daily; 3hr); Yíthio (6 daily; 1hr).

**By car** Parking tickets need to be bought for certain times in the central area.

**Information** Most of the banks are on Paleológou. There is a good bookshop and map stockist near the corner of Paleológou and Lykoúrgou.

### ACCOMMODATION

There are usually enough **hotels** to go around, many of them on the main avenue, Paleológou, where noise can be a problem. A better idea is to plan on staying at more tranquil **Néos Mystrás**, a stone's throw from the Byzantine ruins. There's also a campsite nearby.

**Maniatis** Paleológou 72–76 ☎ 27310 22665, ⊕ maniatishotel.gr. Across the street from the museum, this modern hotel – all glass and metal with blond wood trim – has good facilities: four lounge areas, a bar and two restaurants. Rooms have spotless decor, a/c and some have views of the countryside. Buffet breakfast included. **€100**

**Sparta Inn** Thermopýlon 105 ☎ 27310 21021, ⊕ spartainn.gr. This property is huge and modern, with a bar, a restaurant, a roof garden and two swimming pools. All rooms have a/c and balconies, some with views of distant hills. Substantial reductions for online bookings. **€70**

### EATING AND DRINKING

Most **restaurants** and **tavernas** are also concentrated on Paleológou. The most consistently popular **music bars** are *Ministry* opposite the *Maniatis* hotel, or *Enellax* along the side street behind *Ministry*.

**Diethnes** Paleológou 105 ☎ 27310 28636. Long-established and reliably good, with an extensive menu of traditional dishes; the interior lacks atmosphere, but a delightful garden behind with orange and lemon trees compensates. €10–15/person. Daily 8am–midnight.

**Dionysos Garden** ☎ 27310 81201. Located 1500m out on the road towards Mystra, serves up slightly more expensive dishes with style (expect about €20/person), with tables outdoors in summer. Try their signature baked chicken. Closed Sun & Mon dinner.

# Mystra

Daily: summer 8am–8pm; winter 8am–2pm • €5, good for entrance the following day, too

MYSTRA is one of the most exciting and dramatic historic sites that the Peloponnese can offer – a glorious, airy place, hugging a very steep, 280m foothill of Taïyetos. Winding up the lushly vegetated hillside is a remarkably intact Byzantine town that once sheltered a population of some 20,000, and through which you can now wander. Winding alleys lead through monumental gates, past medieval houses and palaces and above all into the churches, several of which yield superb if faded frescoes. The overall effect is of straying into a massive unearthing of architecture, painting and sculpture – and into a different age with a dramatically different mentality.

## ARRIVAL AND INFORMATION
MYSTRA

**By bus** Buses run from Spárti to the lower Mystra site entrance, (10 daily; 30min) and usually go up to the top, as well, saving a considerable climb; buses stop en route at the modern village of Néos Mystrás, 500m from the lower entrance.

**Orientation** The site of the Byzantine city comprises three main parts: the Káto Hóra (lower town), with the city's most important churches; the Áno Hóra (upper town), grouped around the vast shell of a royal palace; and the Kástro (castle). There are two entrances to the site, at the

base of the lower town and up near the Kástro; once inside the site is well signposted. A road loops up from the modern village of Néos Mystrás to Trýpi, passing near both upper and lower entrances.

**Accommodation and eating** There are no facilities at the site itself, so it's best to base yourself at nearby Néos Mystrás (see p.170). It's a good idea to stock up on refreshments before setting out: there's a mobile snack-bar at the lower gate, serving freshly pressed orange or lemon juices, but nothing in the site itself.

## Brief history

In 1249, Guillaume II de Villehardouin, fourth **Frankish** prince of the Moreas, built a castle here – one of a trio of fortresses (the others at Monemvasiá and the Máni) designed to garrison his domain. The Franks, however, were driven out of Mystra by the **Byzantines** in 1262, and by the mid-fourteenth century this isolated triangle of land in the southeastern Peloponnese, encompassing the old Spartan territories, became the **Despotate of Mystra**. This was the last province of the Greek Byzantine empire and, with Constantinople in terminal decay, its virtual capital.

During the next two centuries, Mystra was the focus of a defiant rebirth of Byzantine power before eventual subjugation by the Turks in 1460, seven years after the fall of Constantinople. Mystra remained in Turkish hands until 1687 when it was captured,

## THE MYSTRA RENAISSANCE

Throughout the fourteenth century and the first decades of the fifteenth Mystra was the principal cultural and intellectual centre of the Byzantine world, attracting the finest Byzantine scholars and theologians and sponsoring a **renaissance** in the arts. Most notable of the court scholars was the humanist philosopher **Gemisthus Plethon**, who revived and reinterpreted Plato's ideas, using them to support his own brand of revolutionary teachings, which included the assertions that land should be redistributed among labourers and that reason should be placed on a par with religion. Although his beliefs had limited impact in Mystra itself – whose monks excommunicated him – his followers, who taught in Italy after the fall of Mystra, exercised wide influence in Renaissance Florence and Rome.

More tangibly, Mystra also was home to the final flourish of **Byzantine architecture**, with the building of a magnificent palace for the despots and a perfect sequence of churches, multi-domed and brilliantly frescoed.

briefly, by the **Venetians**. Decline set in with a second stage of Turkish control, from 1715 onwards, culminating in the destruction that accompanied the **War of Independence**, the site being evacuated after fires in 1770 and 1825. **Restoration** begun in the first decades of the twentieth century was interrupted by the civil war – during which it was, for a while, a battle site – and renewed in earnest in the 1950s when the last inhabitants were relocated.

### The Upper Town and Kástro

The **Kástro**, reached by a path direct from the upper gate, maintains the Frankish design of its original thirteenth-century construction. There is a walkway around most of the keep, with views of an intricate panorama of the town below. The castle itself was the court of Guillaume II de Villehardouin but in later years was used primarily as a citadel.

#### Ayía Sofía

Following a course downhill from the Kástro, the first identifiable building you come to is the church of **Ayía Sofía** (1350). The chapel's finest feature is its floor, made from polychrome marble. Its frescoes, notably a *Pandokrátor* (Christ in Majesty) and *Nativity of the Virgin*, have survived reasonably well, protected until recent years by coatings of whitewash applied by the Turks, who adapted the building as a mosque.

#### Palatáki and the Despot's Palace

Heading down from Ayía Sofía, you have a choice of routes. The right fork winds past ruins of a Byzantine mansion, one of the oldest houses on the site, the **Palatáki** ("Small Palace"; 1250–1300), and **Áyios Nikólaos**, a large seventeenth-century building decorated with unsophisticated paintings. The left fork is more interesting, passing the fortified **Náfplio Gate**, which was the principal entrance to the upper town, and the vast, multistoreyed, Gothic-looking complex of the **Despots' Palace** (1249–1400; closed at the time of writing, undergoing extensive rebuilding and restoration). Most prominent among its numerous rooms is a great vaulted audience hall, built at right angles to the line of the building; its ostentatious windows regally dominate the skyline, and it was once heated by eight great fireplaces. Flanking one side of a square, used by the Turks as a marketplace, are the remains of a **mosque**.

### The Lower Town

At the **Monemvasiá Gate**, which links the upper and lower towns, there is a further choice of routes: right to the Pandánassa and Perivléptos monasteries or left to the Vrondohión monastery and cathedral, all very clearly signed. If time is running out, it is easier to head right first, then double back down to the Vrondohión.

2

### Pandánassa convent

When excavations were resumed in 1952, the last thirty or so families who still lived in the lower town were moved out to Néos Mystrás. Only the nuns of the **Pandánassa** ("Queen of the World") **convent** have remained; they have a reception room where they sell their own handicrafts and sometimes offer a cooling *vyssinádha* (cherryade) to visitors. The convent's church, built in 1428, is perhaps the finest surviving in Mystra, perfectly proportioned in its blend of Byzantine and Gothic. The **frescoes** date from various centuries, with some superb fifteenth-century work, including one in the gallery that depicts scenes from the life of Christ. Other frescoes were painted between 1687 and 1715, when Mystra was held by the Venetians.

### Perivléptos monastery

The diminutive **Perivléptos monastery** (1310), a single-domed church, partially carved out of the rock, contains Mystra's most complete cycle of frescoes, almost all of which date from the fourteenth century. They are in some ways finer than those of the Pandánassa, blending an easy humanism with the spirituality of the Byzantine icon traditions. The position of each figure depended upon its sanctity, and so upon the dome the image of heaven is the *Pandokrátor* (the all-powerful Christ in glory after the Ascension); on the apse is the Virgin; and the higher expanses of wall portray scenes from the life of Christ. Prophets and saints could only appear on the lower walls, decreasing in importance according to their distance from the sanctuary.

### Laskaris House

Along the path leading from Perivléptos to the lower gate are a couple of minor, much-restored churches, and, just above them, the **Laskaris House**, a mansion thought to have belonged to relatives of the emperors. Like the House of Frangopoulos, it is balconied; its ground floor probably served as stables. Close by, beside the path, is the old Marmara Turkish Fountain.

### Mitrópolis

The **Mitrópolis** or cathedral, immediately beyond the gateway, is the oldest of Mystra's churches, built between 1270 and 1292. A marble slab set in its floor is carved with the double-headed eagle of Byzantium, commemorating the 1448 coronation of Constantine XI Paleologos, the last Eastern emperor; he was soon to perish, with his empire, in the Turkish sacking of Constantinople in 1453. A stone with red stains is said to mark where Bishop Ananias Lambadheris was murdered in 1760. Of the church's frescoes, the earliest, in the northeast aisle, depict the torture and burial of Áyios Dhimítrios, the saint to whom the church is dedicated. Opposite are frescoes illustrating the miracles of Christ and the life of the Virgin; more intimate and lighter of touch, they date from the last great years before Mystra's fall. Adjacent to the cathedral, a small **museum** (included in main admission charge) contains various fragments of sculpture and pottery.

### Vrondohión monastery

The **Vrondohión monastery**, a short way uphill, was the centre of cultural and intellectual life in the fifteenth-century town – the cells of the monastery can still be discerned – and was also the burial place of the despots. Of the two attached churches, the further one, **Odhiyítria** (Afendikó; 1310), has been beautifully restored, revealing startlingly bold, fourteenth-century frescoes similar to those of Perivléptos.

## Néos Mystrás

This pleasant roadside community has a small square with several tavernas, crowded with tour buses by day but low-key at night, except at the end of August when the place buzzes with live music during the week-long annual *paniyíri* (fête).

2

**ACROSS THE LANGÁDHA PASS**

The remote and wild **Langádha pass**, the 60km road over the **Taïyetos** mountain range from Spárti to Kalamáta, is a worthwhile scenic drive. With long uninhabited sections, it unveils a constant drama of peaks and precipitous drops, magnificent at all times but startling at sunrise; the pine forests suffered extensive damage in recent fires, but are showing signs of a comeback. This route was taken by Telemachus in the *Odyssey* on his way from Nestor's palace near Pýlos to that of Menelaus at Sparta, taking him a day by chariot. The road climbs steeply into the mountains and enters the **Gorge of Langádha**, a wild sequence of hairpins. The rock of Keádhas, high above the southern side of the road a short distance from the village, is where the Spartans used to leave their sick or puny babies to die. Above Keádhas is a **climbing park** with marked routes for rock-climbers. At the **pass**, tracks and paths head north and south along the mountain ridge – peaks up to 1900m are accessible in a day's outing. On the Kalamáta side you enter the **Nédhondas Gorge** for the final zigzagging descent. **Buses** take four hours to cross the pass, including the connection at Artemísia.

---

**ACCOMMODATION AND EATING**                                    **NÉOS MYSTRÁS**

In general, it's worth paying a bit extra to stay in Néos Mystrás, rather than Spárti, just for the setting, relative quiet, and easy access to the site – though you will need to book ahead, or arrive early in the day, to find a place.

**Byzantion** ☎27310 83309, ✉byzanhtl@otenet.gr. This modern hotel has been recently refurbished and is very pleasant, with wi-fi, a garden and pool, and friendly staff. Rooms are fairly large and have balconies, some with wonderful views of the ancient site. Breakfast included. April–Oct. **€50**

**O Ellinas** ☎27310 82666. A pleasant taverna just off the main square, with a leafy terrace on the side. The food is standard fare, but reliably good; for something a bit different, try the pasta with beef (€8) or the cod fillet with garlic sauce (€12), both house specialities. Daily lunch & dinner.

# Arcadia

**ARCADIA** (Arkadhía), the heartland province of the Peloponnese, contains some of the most beautiful landscapes in Greece. Dramatic hills are crowned by a string of medieval towns, and the occasional Classical antiquity. Beautiful **Karítena** is a picture-postcard hill town, but the best area of all is around **Stemnítsa** and **Dhimitsána**, where walkers are rewarded with the luxuriant **Loúsios Gorge**. Another hill town, **Andhrítsena**, attracts archeology buffs with the nearby **Temple of Bassae**, still spectacular though tented for restoration. En route, if approaching from **Trípoli**, you may also pass through **Megalópoli**, both mainly transport hubs. Drivers should be aware that Arcadia's highways, some of the broadest and emptiest in the Peloponnese, are shared with sheep- and goat-herds moving their flocks. **Wild fires** in 2000 and 2007 severely damaged the area's oak and fir woodland, though recovery is evident and the legendary beauty still holds, especially in spring, when the slopes are bright yellow with masses of broom plants.

## Trípoli

**TRÍPOLI** is a major crossroads of the Peloponnese. Set in a huge upland plain, and surrounded by spectacular mountains, the Arcadian capital doesn't live up to expectations: it's a large, modern town, and home to one of the country's biggest army barracks. It doesn't pander to tourism and has few obvious attractions, although the **Panarcadic Archeological Museum**, Evangelistriás 6 (Tues–Sun 8.30am–3pm; €2), signposted off Vassiléos Yeoryíou (which leads off the central square, Platía Kolokotróni) and housed in a Neoclassical building with a beautiful rose garden, makes a pleasant diversion; the collection includes finds from much of Arcadia, from Neolithic to Roman.

The town's altitude of 665m means an often markedly cooler summer climate and harsh winters. Traffic can be chaotic and you may wish to escape to the quiet greenery of **Platía Áreos**. Medieval Tripolitsa was destroyed by retreating Turkish forces during the War of Independence, when the Greek forces, led by Kolokotronis in one of their worst atrocities, had earlier massacred the town's Turkish population.

## ARRIVAL AND DEPARTURE

**TRÍPOLI**

**By bus** The main bus terminal, serving all destinations in the northern Peloponnese, is 1.25km southeast from the centre on the Akhladókambos road. Services to Messinía, Kalamáta, Pýlos, the Máni and Spárti leave from the corner café on Lagopáti, directly opposite the train station. For Spárti it's best to take a direct bus (7–9 daily from Athens to Spárti, via Árgos and/or Trípoli).
**Destinations:** Andhrítsena (2 daily; 1hr 30min); Athens (13 daily; 2hr 30min); Dhimitsána (2 daily; 1hr 30min); Kalávryta (1 daily; 2hr 30min); Karítena (2 daily; 1hr);

Leonídhio (2 daily; 2hr 30min); Megalópoli (7 daily; 40min); Neápoli (2 daily; 5hr 30min); Olymbía (2 daily Mon–Fri, 1–3 Sat & Sun; 3hr); Pýlos (3 daily; 3hr); Stemnítsa (1 daily; 1hr); Vytína (6 daily Mon–Fri, 4 Sat & Sun; 1hr 15min); Yíthio (3 daily; 2hr 30min).
**By train** The train station is 1.5km southeast of the centre. At the time of writing all services were suspended due to the financial crisis. Should they resume, they will run from Kórinthos to Kalamáta, with stops here.

## ACCOMMODATION AND EATING

**Alex** Vassiléos Yeoryíou 26 ☎ 27102 23465, ✉ st-alex .gr. This modern hotel is fairly fresh and very central, with decent, rather large rooms with balconies and a/c. Free parking and wi-fi. Breakfast included in their own café. **€80**
**Anactoricon** Ethnikís Andístasis 48 ☎ 27102 22545, ⓦ anaktorikon.gr. Newly refurbished, maintaining the Neoclassical style, this is a comfortable hotel near all the

most popular bars in town. Rooms are fairly simple, but include internet and a/c. **€100**
**Klimataria Piterou** Kalavrýton 11 ☎ 27102 22058. Located beyond the *Aello* cinema and about 100m past the far end of Platía Áreos, this taverna is one of several along here. The menu is standard fare, including rabbit and lamb, and full meals go for €10–15. **Daily lunch & dinner.**

# Megalópoli

Modern **MEGALÓPOLI** is an important road junction and hub for buses, and your first thoughts on arrival may be directed towards getting out. It's a rather characterless place, with a military presence and a monstrous power station nearby that consumes lignite from vast open-cast mines. The adoption of its ancient name, "Great City", was an altogether empty joke. Still, just outside the city to the northwest is what remains of one of the most ambitious building projects of the Classical age: **Ancient Megalopolis** (site closed), which once boasted Greece's largest **theatre**, now almost entirely covered over by earth and vegetation and with the power station's twin **smokestacks**, Arcadia's sole eyesore, for a neighbour.

## ARRIVAL AND INFORMATION

**MEGALÓPOLI**

**By bus** Megalópoli has regular bus connections with Trípoli (and on to Árgos and Athens) and Kalamáta. Moving north or west into Arcadia is slightly trickier, with just two buses daily to Karítena and one then on to Andhrítsena. However, hitching is viable along this route, as local drivers are aware of the paucity of transport, and it's also possible

to negotiate a taxi to Karítena.
**Destinations** Andhrítsena (1 daily; 1hr 15min); Pýrgos (2 daily; 4hr); Karítena (2 daily; 45min); Trípoli (7 daily; 40min).
**Services** Facilities such as banks and a post office are around the central Platía Gortynías.

# Arcadian hill towns

North of Megalópoli, the best of Arcadia lies before you: minor roads that curl through a series of lush valleys and below the area's most exquisite **medieval hill towns**. The obvious first stop is lofty **Karítena**. Then the route to the northwest winds farther up around the edge of the Ménalo mountains to the delightful towns of **Stemnítsa** and

**Dhimitsána**, from either of which you can explore the **Loúsios Gorge**, including the remote site of **ancient Gortys** and the stunning eleventh-century **Ayíou Ioánnou Prodhrómou Monastery** (commonly abbreviated to Prodhrómou), as well as additional ancient monasteries on up the gorge. To the west there's the hill town of **Andhrítsena** and nearby the ancient **Temple of Bassae**. Having your own transport is pretty essential here, though there are limited **buses** from Trípoli (see p.172) and Megalópoli (p.173). The hill towns also offer plenty of great **places to stay** (see p.176).

## Karítena

Most picturesquely set, watching over the strategic Megalópoli–Andhrítsena road, **KARÍTENA** provides one of the signature Arcadian images. Like many of the hill towns hereabouts, its history has Frankish, Byzantine and Turkish contributions. It was founded by the Byzantines in the seventh century and had attained a population of some 20,000 when the Franks took it in 1209. Under their century-long rule, Karítena was the capital of a large barony under Geoffroy de Bruyères, the paragon of chivalry in the medieval ballad *The Chronicle of the Morea*, and probably the only well-liked Frankish overlord.

These days the village has a population of just a couple of hundred, but as recently as the beginning of the nineteenth century there were at least ten times that figure.

### The castle
Open site • Free

Up steps off the platía is the **Froúrio**, the castle built in 1245 by the Franks, with added Turkish towers. It was repaired by Theodhoros Kolokotronis and it was here that he held out against Ibrahim Pasha in 1826 and turned the tide of the War of Independence.

### Medieval bridge and river

Don't miss Karítena's **medieval bridge** over the River Alfiós (Alpheus). To find it, stop on the south side of the modern bridge and follow a short track down, almost underneath the new span. The old structure is missing the central section, but is an intriguing sight nonetheless, with a small Byzantine chapel built into one of the central pillars. **River rafting** is organized by the *Alpin Club* (walpinclub.gr), near the bridge.

## Stemnítsa and around

**STEMNÍTSA** (Ypsoús on many maps), 16km north of Karítena, is a winter resort at an altitude of 1050m. For centuries this was one of the premier goldworking centres of the Balkans. Although much depopulated, it remains a fascinating town, with a small **folklore museum**, an artisan school and several quietly magnificent medieval churches. Across the way from the folklore museum, the seventeenth-century **basilica of Tríon Ierarhón** is the most accessible of the town's Byzantine churches; its caretaker lives in the low white house west of the main door.

The town is divided by ravines into three distinct quarters: the Kástro (the ancient acropolis hill, worth the walk up for the views), Ayía Paraskeví (east of the stream) and Áyios Ioánnis (west of the stream).

### Folklore museum
July 1–Sept 30: Mon 10am–1pm, Wed & Thurs 10am–1pm & 5–8pm, Fri 5–8pm, Sat 10am–1pm & 5–8pm, Sun 10am–1pm; winter hours much shorter • Free

The **folklore museum** is just off the main road in the Ayía Paraskeví quarter. The ground floor is devoted to mock-ups of the workshops of indigenous crafts such as candle-making, bell-casting, shoe-making and jewellery. The next floor up features re-creations of the salon of a well-to-do family and a humbler cottage. The top storey is taken up by the rather random collections of the Savopoulos family: plates by Avramides (a refugee

## HIKING NEAR ANCIENT GORTYS

The farmland surrounding ancient Gortys belongs to the monks of the nearby **Prodhrómou Monastery**, who have carved a path along the **Gorge of the Loúsios** between Áyios Andhréas and the monastery. It's about a 40min walk up a well-graded trail following the stream. The monastery, stuck on to the cliff like a swallow's nest, is plainly visible a couple of hundred metres above the path. There are no more than five monks here, and one of them will show visitors the tiny frescoed *katholikón* (closed 2–5pm). Strict dress rules apply, with blanket-like clothing provided if necessary. The monastery is also accessible by an asphalt road that makes a circuitous 7km descent from the Stemnítsa–Dhimitsána road to a parking lot and newish chapel, and then it's a further descent on foot along a steep path.

Beyond Prodhrómou the path continues clearly to the outlying, well-signed monasteries of **Paleá** and then **Néa Filosófou** on the opposite side of the valley. The older (Paleá), dating from the tenth century, is merely a ruin and blends into the cliff against which it is flattened. The newer monastery (Néa, seventeenth century) has been restored and recently expanded considerably, but retains frescoes from 1663 inside; there is a permanent caretaker monk. From here, paths follow the west then east banks of the river, to reach Dhimitsána via Paleohóri in under two hours.

from Asia Minor and ceramics master), textiles and costumes from all over Greece, weapons, copperware and eighteenth- and nineteenth-century icons.

### Ancient Gortys

**Ancient Gortys**, 8km southeast of Stemnítsa, is a charming site, set beside the rushing river known in ancient times as the Gortynios. The remains are widely strewn over the hillside on the west bank of the stream, but the main attraction, below contemporary ground level and not at all obvious until well to the west of the little Byzantine chapel of Áyios Andhréas (by the old bridge), is the huge excavation containing the remains of a **temple to Asklepios** and an adjoining **bath**, both dating from the fourth century BC. The most curious feature of the site is a circular **portico** enclosing round-backed seats, which most certainly would have been part of the therapeutic centre.

## Dhimitsána

Like Stemnítsa, 11km to the south, **DHIMITSÁNA** has an immediately seductive appearance, its cobbled streets and tottering houses straddling a twin hillside overlooking the Loúsios River. Views from the village are stunning, and though quite a small resort, there is an excellent **accommodation** selection, making Dhimitsána a prime base for exploring the centre of the Peloponnese.

In the town, a half-dozen churches with tall, squarish belfries recall the extended Frankish, and especially Norman, tenure in this part of the Moreas during the thirteenth century. Yet no one should dispute the deep-dyed Greekness of Dhimitsána. It was the birthplace of **Archbishop Yermanos**, who first raised the flag of rebellion at Kalávryta in 1821, and of the hapless patriarch, **Grigoris V**, hanged in Constantinople upon the sultan's receiving news of the insurrection.

### Open-Air Water-Power Museum

Summer daily 10am–6pm; winter Wed–Mon 8.30am–3pm • €3 • Ⓦ piop.gr

About 2km south of Dhimitsána, the excellent **Open-Air Water-Power Museum** has a reconstructed watermill, tannery and gunpowder mill, with exhibitions on the processes involved.

## Andhrítsena and around

**ANDHRÍTSENA**, 28km west of Karítena along a beautiful route, is a traditional hill town and the base from which to visit the **Temple of Apollo** at **Bassae** (Apollo Epikourios) up in the mountains to the south. Though very much a roadside settlement today, it was a

**2**

## BASSAE'S MISSING METOPES

Many of the Bassae temple's stunning **metopes**, the marble frieze sculptures, as well as other fine pieces, were removed and installed in London's **British Museum** in 1814–15. Reportedly, an English archeologist bribed the local Ottoman pasha, who evidently did not consider preservation of the works of any importance. The metopes powerfully depict the battles of the Amazons, Lapiths and Centaurs, and they are on display in a special room with the controversial **Elgin Marbles** (see p.70), which, under similar circumstances, were boxed up and shipped to Britain in 1812.

major hill town through the years of Turkish occupation and the first century of independent Greece. It remains quite untouched, with wooden houses spilling down to a stream, whose clear ice-cold headwaters are channelled into a fountain set within a plane tree in the central platía.

### The Temple of Apollo Epikourios

Summer daily 8am–7.30pm • €3 • To get there, take the Kréstena road out of town and then, almost immediately, turn off to the left to begin the climb up

Some 14km into the mountains south of Andhrítsena stands a **World Heritage Site**, the fifth-century BC **Temple of Apollo** at **BASSAE** (Vásses), occupying one of the remotest, highest (1131m) and arguably most spectacular **sites** in Greece. In addition, it is one of the best-preserved Classical monuments in the country and is considered to have been designed by Iktinos, architect of the Parthenon and the Hephaisteion in Athens.

There's just one problem: nowadays to protect it from the elements during its complicated **restoration**, the magnificent temple is swathed in a gigantic grey marquee suspended from metal girders; and what's left of its entablature and frieze lies dissected in neat rows on the ground to one side. Panels make clear that the work is badly needed to keep the whole thing from simply tumbling, stone by stone, into the valley it overlooks – and the marquee is quite a sight in itself – but visitors are likely to feel a bit disappointed, at least until you enter the tent and are awe-struck by the sheer scale and majesty of the thing, even more so as you walk all around it.

## ACCOMMODATION

ARCADIAN HILL TOWNS

### KARÍTENA

**Vrenthi** ☎27910 31650. Good value and located on the right just before the main square: ask about their rooms to rent at their homely café/taverna on the left just beyond. Breakfast included. **€50**

### STEMNÍTSA

★ **Mpelleiko** ☎&☎27950 81286, ☒mpelleiko.gr. High above the town, overlooking the whole mountainous scene, stands this marvellous stone mansion, beautifully converted into a unique guesthouse. The rooms are all different and very cosy, with amenities such as wi-fi and CD players. Hearty buffet breakfast included. **€95**

**Trikolonion** ☎27950 29500, ☒countryclub.gr. Out of town to the east is this very comfortable luxury resort in a converted nineteenth-century building. Rooms have every amenity including fast internet and quality beauty products, and there's a gym/spa and free parking. Breakfast included. **€150**

### DHIMITSÁNA

★ **Amanites** ☎27950 31090, ☒amanites.gr. This beautiful stone building stands prominently just above the main road and offers very comfortable rooms with spectacular views over the town and valley. The lovely owners are always ready to help, and the breakfast, included, features home-made treats. **€60**

**Dimitsana** ☎27950 31518, ☒dimitsanahotel.gr. This refurbished, woodsy-luxurious and popular hotel, 1km out on the road to Stemnítsa, is easiest for parking. The cosy rooms, some with oriental rugs, have balconies with gorge views, and wi-fi. Breakfast, with fresh-squeezed orange juice, included. **€70**

★ **Xenonas Kazakoy** ☎27950 31660, ☒xenonas kazakou.gr. Up from the main road and winding around past the old church, this magnificent property beats them all, for spacious comfort, friendliness, and especially the fantastic breakfast (included and cooked to order by one of the charming, knowledgeable owners). Good wi-fi. Rates are higher in winter. **€70**

## EATING

### STEMNÍTSA

**I Stemnitsa ☎ 27950 81371.** The town's eponymous taverna turns out dishes in keeping with the wild mountain setting, plenty of fresh produce, as well as game. About €15/person. Daily lunch & dinner.

### DHIMITSÁNA

**Kioúpi ☎ 27950 31232.** This very central and amiable option has some tables with views down the valley, and an extensive menu, featuring both mountain game (wild rabbit €11, wild boar or venison €20) and vegetarian specialities, such as vegetable pie (€4.50) or their own pea soup (€6). Daily lunch & dinner.

**★ O Drymonas ☎ 27950 31116.** Set on the road at the southern entrance to town, this elegantly rustic spot has a large variety of mezédhes and local dishes, including fresh game, all of it gourmet quality. Very friendly service; menu in Greek only. About €10–15/person. Daily lunch & dinner.

# Messinía

The province of **Messinía** stretches from the western flank of the Taïyetos ridge across the plain of **Kalamáta** to include the hilly southwesternmost "finger" of the Peloponnese. Green, fertile and luxuriant for the most part, it is ringed with a series of well-preserved castles overlooking some of the area's most expansive beaches. The towns of **Koróni, Methóni** and **Finikoúnda** and their beaches draw the crowds, but the pale curve of fine sand at the bay of **Voïdhokiliá**, near Pýlos, sandwiched between sea, rock and lagoon, is one of the most beautiful beaches in Greece. Messinía's notable archeological sites, such as **ancient Messene** west of Kalamáta and **Nestor's Palace** north of Pýlos, rarely see visitors in the quantity of the Argolid sites.

## Kalamáta and around

**KALAMÁTA** is by far the largest city in the southern Peloponnese, spreading for some 4km back from the sea, and into the hills. It's quite a metropolitan shock after the small-town life of the rest of the region. Few visitors linger here, but if you are travelling for a while it's a worthwhile stop, boasting plenty of big-town facilities, decent tavernas and a pleasant historic centre. Kalamáta is synonymous with **olives** (and to a lesser extent figs), grown nearby on the Messinian plain.

### Brief history

The town flourished as a commercial centre during the Turkish period and became one of the first independent Greek towns in 1821; the first newspaper to be printed on Greek soil was produced here the same year. In 1986 Kalamáta was near the epicentre of a severe **earthquake** that killed twenty people and left 12,000 families homeless. But for the fact that the quake struck in the early evening, when many people were outside, the death toll would have been much higher. As it was, large numbers of buildings were levelled throughout the town.

### The Kalamáta old town

The **old town** is attractive in certain places, especially along pedestrianized promenades lined with palms. Much rebuilt due to **earthquakes**, the last major one in 1986, little remains of note. The typical **Kástro** (Mon–Fri 8am–2pm, Sat & Sun 9am–3pm; free) has survived, more or less, and makes for a green morning stroll among evocative ruins. The **archeological museum** (Mon 1.30–8pm, Tues–Sun 8am–8pm; €2), freshly reopened, has very modest collections, though everything is informatively labelled and panelled in world-class style. It shares a building with the new "tourist support office", and just in front of them, adorning Platía Agión Apostolón, is the diminutive and delightful **Byzantine church** for which the square is named, the oldest part dating from at least the twelfth century. Heading straight down towards the port, you'll soon walk along a pleasant city park, actually an **open-air railway museum**, with retired locomotives and train cars lined up to admire.

Not far outside of town, slightly toward the northwest, lie the extensive ruins of **ancient Messene**, good for a pastoral promenade.

## Ancient Messene

Open site • Free • Museum hours, Tues–Sun 8am–3pm • €2 • Local bus to Mavromáti from Kalamáta twice daily

Located just 22km northwest of Kalamáta, the substantial remains of **ancient Messene** are spread out just below the village of Mavromáti. This former Messinian capital was founded in 371 BC, following the liberation of the area from Spartan hegemony. The area was originally girded by 9km of Cyclopean **ramparts**, and there are remnants of massive gates. Count on three hours for a complete walkabout. Besides the walls, sights include the agora, a restored theatre, a stadium with its columned entrance, a partial colonnade of the gymnasium, various temple bases and a large Asklepion. There's also a small **museum**, housing a few very good pieces of statuary found here, including one of **Artemis Orthia**. Apart from some olive groves, most of the area is shadeless, and there are no services, so fill up bottles at the charming old **fountain** in the village before setting off.

## ARRIVAL AND DEPARTURE
### KALAMÁTA AND AROUND

**By air** The airport (☎ 27210 69442) is 10km west of Kalamáta on the highway to Messíni, Pýlos and Koróni, and buses to these destinations pass the entrance. In season there are four charters a week from the UK, all on Sundays. The airport has an automatic exchange machine, an ATM and a helpful tourist office, open when flights are due, that will book accommodation.
Destinations Athens (Aegean, 1 daily; 50min); Iráklion (Sky Express, 2 weekly; 1hr); Thessaloníki (Aegean, 3 weekly; 1hr 10min, 50min); Zákynthos (Transavia, 1 weekly; 45min).
**By bus** The bus station (☎ 27320 23145) is nearly 1km north of the centre along Nédhondos. Frequent services run north to Megalópoli, Trípoli and Athens, and west to Messíni, Koróni or Pýlos; the magnificent route over the Taïyetos ridge to Spárti also runs from here. Trípoli/Náfplio/Árgos buses leave from outside the Arkadia bus office 200m down the road.

Destinations Athens (28 daily; 4hr 30min); Exohóri (2 daily; 1hr 30min); Finikoúnda (3 daily; 1hr 45min); Kardhamýli (2 daily Mon–Fri only; 1hr); Kórinthos (7 daily; 3hr 15min–4hr); Koróni (7 daily; 1hr 30min); Mavromáti (for ancient Messene, Mon–Fri 2 daily; 1hr); Megalópoli (13 daily; 1hr); Methóni (6 daily; 1hr 30min); Pátra (2 daily; 4hr); Pýlos (5 daily; 1hr 20min); Spárti (2 daily, changing at Artemisia; 2hr–2hr 30min); Stoúpa (2 daily; 1hr–1hr 30min); Trípoli (13 daily; 1hr 30min).
**By car** Driving through Kalamáta between the Máni and Arcadia or the west, you should follow the signed southern route through the city, along Kritís, Lykourgoú and Artémidhos, and then on the western bypass (which partly follows the train line); drivers to or from Spárti must brave the narrower crowded streets of the northern part of town.
**By ferry** Services run by Lane Lines (ⓦ ferries.gr/lane).
Destinations Kastélli, Crete (1 weekly in season; 8hr 30min); Kýthira (1 daily in season; 4hr 30min).

## GETTING AROUND AND INFORMATION

**By bus** The local #1 bus (buy tickets on the bus) starts from Platía 23-Martíou, about a 600m walk from the bus station, and heads south through the centre to run the length of the Navarínou seafront and beach as far as the *Filoxenia Beach Hotel*.

**Tourist office** Try the branch at the airport (see above) or the municipal office at Platía Agíon Apostolón, in the same building as the archeological museum (☎ 27210 90413; weekdays 9.30am–8.30pm, weekends 9.30am–1.30pm).

## ACCOMMODATION

In the city centre, there are very few mid-range **hotels**, with cheaper places down by the waterfront, where there are many more hotels, most of them subject to street noise, as the traffic along there is nonstop.

**Flisvos** Navarínou 135 ☎ 27210 82177, ⓦ hotel-flisvos .gr. Quiet enough and comfortable, if a bit spartan. The rooms have balconies and a/c, and it's right on the waterfront strip next to the church of Ayía Anástasi, where

there is parking. Breakfast included. **€70**
**Haïkos** Navarínou 115 ☎ 27210 88902, ⓦ haikos.gr. Another trim, modern hotel with rather plush rooms but basic bathrooms. All rooms have balconies and a/c and

there's internet access. Rooms on the beach side can be noisy. **€85**

★ **Rex** Aristoménous 26 ☎ 27210 94440, ⊕ rexhotel .gr. Convenient and historic hotel situated in the old town. Rooms are on the small side, but fresh and well appointed, some with balconies, in a fine Neoclassical building, facing the palm-lined promenade. There's also a restaurant and a café, the former using all local ingredients, including real Kalamáta olives. Breakfast included. **€100**

## EATING AND DRINKING

In general, the best restaurants in the summer months are down by the western harbour, which has been set up as a yacht marina – accessed through a somewhat insalubrious area. There are a couple of well-priced cafés directly opposite the bus station, and a plethora of cafés, bars, ice-cream parlours and eating places along the waterfront avenue Navarínou.

**Kanna** On the marina ☎ 27210 91596. Facing the water with seating on a pretty terrace, this restaurant has good fish and many dishes are Italian-inspired. Main dishes €8–13, while fresh fish goes for €45–65/kg. Daily lunch & dinner.

**Pyrofani** Spetson/Posidhonos. At a corner on the waterfront with views of the marina and the lights of the eastern villages. There's a large selection of meat and vegetarian dishes and good local wine (mains €10). Daily lunch & dinner.

★ **Routsis** Navarínou 127 ☎ 27210 80830. Old-fashioned taverna offering fresh local olives, home-made feta, steamed greens, catch of the day or fish soup (mains aorund €12). Seating along the strip, or in a garden terrace on the beach side. Daily lunch & dinner.

## DIRECTORY

**Banks and ATMs** Most are on Aristoménous or adjacent Platía Konstandínou Dhiadhókhnou and Sidhiroú Stathmoú.

**Bike and scooter rental** Bastakos, Fáron 190 (☎ 27210 26638).

**Car rental** Agni Travel, Kessári 2 (☎ 27210 20352, ☎ 27210 22428); Maniatis, Iatropoúlou 1 (☎ 27210 27694, ✉ maniatis@kal.forthnet.gr); Stavrianos, Nédhondos 89 (☎ 27210 23041, ✉ 27210 25370).

**Cinemas** There are several cinemas near Platía Konstandínou Dhiadhókhnou; English-language films are shown with Greek subtitles.

**Market** The Wed and Sat produce market, one of the region's most colourful, is across the bridge from the bus station, below the castle.

**Post office** Near the customs house beyond the park at the seaward end of Aristoménous.

**Taxis** Ranks on Aristoménous, Nédhondos and Navarínou.

**Tourist police** Miaouli, near the harbour (☎ 27210 95555).

# Koróni

**KORÓNI**, 40km southwest of Kalamáta, has one of the more picturesque locations in Greece, stacked against a fortified bluff and commanding grand views across the Messenian gulf. It's a place to relax on the beach, drink wine and amble about a countryside lush with vineyards and olive groves. The town is rustically beautiful with tiled and pastel-washed houses arrayed in a maze of stair-and-ramp streets that can have changed little since the medieval **Venetian occupation** (1206–1500). Koróni, along with its sister fortress of **Methóni**, were the Venetians' oldest and longest-held possessions in the Peloponnese.

## The citadel

Open site • Free

Koróni's **citadel** is one of the least militaristic-looking in Greece, crowning the town more like a large, pleasantly dilapidated garden. Part of the interior is given over to private houses and garden plots, but the greater part is occupied by the nunnery of **Timíou Prodhrómou**, whose chapels, outbuildings and flower-strewn gardens occupy nearly every bastion.

## The beaches

Downhill from the citadel, you reach **Zánga beach**, which runs into **Mémi beach**, making a 2km stretch of sand with preternaturally clear water. The beach is about the only place to go during the afternoon, when Koróni strictly observes siesta.

## ARRIVAL AND INFORMATION

**By bus** Buses terminate in the square below the main church one row back from the waterfront.
Destinations Athens (1 daily; 7hr); Kalamáta (7 daily; 1hr 30min); Pýlos (5 daily; 1hr 20min).

**Services** Koróni has two banks and ATMs, and a post office. Mountain bikes are available from the Makrisa shop on the main street.

## ACCOMMODATION

If you're looking for private rooms on arrival, try the places to the right of the fishing port as you face the water; there are also cheaper, quieter rooms in the Panórama district, up behind Zánga beach.

**Auberge de la Plage** ☎ 27250 22401, ⊛ delaplage.gr. This large, rather basic hotel occupies a fine position, out on the road towards Mémi beach, with a large restaurant veranda overlooking the sea. The surrounding gardens are a plus. Rooms have a/c and views. Mid-April to Oct. **€60**

★ **Diana** ☎ 27250 22312, ⊛ dianahotel-koroni.gr. Located on a side street just as you arrive at the port, this

boutique property has simple, fresh rooms with a/c and other amenities, most with sea views. Mid-April to Oct. **€50**

**Koroni Camping** ☎ 27250 22884, ⊛ koronicamping .com. Located 200m north of town, just 60m up from a sandy beach, with beach facilities, this campsite also has a pool, a bar, a restaurant, a minimarket, washing machines and wi-fi. April–Oct. **€12**

## EATING AND DRINKING

There is a reasonable selection of restaurants on the waterfront, and some authentic tavernas (barrel-wine and oven-food places) along the main shopping street. Many people make wine or *raki* in their basement, and the heady local tipple figures prominently in the nightlife. The main venues are the sprawling *Astra Club* out towards Mémi beach and the *Zanza Club*.

**Bogris #2** ☎ 27250 22664. This port-side taverna boasts a romantic garden courtyard. Check the day's offerings on the menu: it always includes dozens of grills and an impressive wine list. Mains €5–10. Daily breakfast, lunch & dinner.
**Parthenon** ☎ 27250 22146, ⊛ magicmessinia.gr /parthenon_en.html. This taverna, on the seafront corner

below the square, also has rooms with a/c and sea views upstairs (€60). The restaurant serves up a classic mix of Greek and Italian dishes, notably seafood, and besides the main dining room there are tables right on the harbour. Breakfast included. Mid-April to Oct.

# Finikoúnda

**FINIKOÚNDA**, 18km west of Koróni and on the Kalamáta–Pýlos bus route, is a small fishing village with a superb cove-beach, another to the east, and a gigantic strand to the west. Over recent years it has gained a reputation as a **windsurfers' resort**, with half the summer intake staying at campsites on either side of the village, the others housed in a variety of rooms and a newish hotel or two, including some block-booked by British package companies.

## ACCOMMODATION

**Ammos Camping** ☎ 27230 71262, ☏ 27230 71124. Located 3km west of the village, surrounded by nature, this shady campsite is situated near sandy dunes along a beautiful beach. Facilities include a shop, a bar-restaurant, and good sanitation services. May–Oct. **€12**
**Finikounda** ☎ 27230 71208, ☏ karhotel@otenet.gr. This very central hotel complex could use some sprucing up, but it's friendly and serviceable. Rooms all have balconies and a/c. Breakfast included in the adjacent family taverna, with sea views. April–Oct. **€60**
**Golden Sun** ☎ 27230 71358, ⊛ goldensuhotel.gr. This large beachfront hotel has a lot going for it: rooms with balconies, a large pool, terraces and gardens, private parking, and a restaurant. The main problem is that it was

done on the cheap and could do with renovation. Still, it's an acceptable option, with its own restaurant and watersports on offer. Breakfast included. April–Oct. No credit cards. **€65**
**Korakakis Beach** ☎ 27230 71221, ☏ korakaki @otenet.gr. Medium-sized, quirkily decorated hotel right on the beach, which also has bungalows at similar prices. Choose top-floor front rooms for maximum panoramic effect. Bar-restaurant on premises. **€65**
**Loutsa Camping** ☎ 27230 71169, ⊛ finikounda.at /camping-loutsa. Located just about 1km to the east of town, this campsite offers ample shade and a garden setting, just steps from a 20m-wide sandy beach, with umbrellas and a shower. Sites are a bit small. There's a restaurant nearby, and washing machines are available on-site. June–Sept. **€10**

## EATING AND DRINKING

★ **Elena** ☎ 27230 71235. This taverna is renowned for its stuffed grilled sardines and its superb harbour view. It's located at the end of the pier, just above the beach. Mains from €8. They feature live music several times a week. Daily lunch & dinner.

**Oinoussés** ☎ 27230 71446. To the east on the beach, this unassuming taverna offers everything Greek and well prepared: stuffed tomatoes, various seafood options, including salads and grills. Main dishes average €8. April–Oct.

# Methóni

**2**

METHÓNI is geared more conspicuously to tourism than Koróni and gets very crowded in season. The huge Venetian fortress here is as imposing as they come – massively bastioned, washed on three sides by the sea, and cut off from the land by a great moat. The modern town, stretching inland for 1km northward, is full of charming back alleys and it meets the sea at a small, pleasant **beach** just on the east side of the gargantuan citadel.

## The fortress

Daily 8am–3pm • Free

Once used to garrison knights on their way to the Crusades, Methóni's vast **fortress** is entered across the moat along a stone bridge. Inside are very extensive remains: a Venetian cathedral (the Venetians' Lion of St Mark emblem is ubiquitous), a Turkish bath, the foundations of dozens of houses, a strange pyramid-roofed stone structure, and some awesome, but mostly cordoned-off, underground passages. Walk around the walls, and a sea gate at the southern end leads out across a causeway to explore the **Boúrtzi**, a small fortified island that served as a prison and place of execution. The octagonal tower was built by the Turks in the sixteenth century to replace an earlier Venetian fortification.

## ARRIVAL AND INFORMATION

**METHÓNI**

**By bus** The bus from Pýlos stops at the first forked junction in town, but if planning a day-trip check return times with the driver.
Destinations Finikoúnda (1–2 daily; 15min); Kalamáta

(6 daily; 1hr 30min); Koróni (only by connections in Finikoúnda, which may not match up); Pýlos (6 daily; 15min).
**Information** There's a bank and ATM near the bus stop.

## ACCOMMODATION AND EATING

**Aris** Platía Syngroú ☎ 27230 31125, ☎ 27230 31336. This friendly hotel is near the beach but without sea views. Rooms are simple and clean, with a/c and balconies. Breakfast included. April–Oct. **€50**
★ **Castello** ☎ 27230 31300, ⓦ castello.gr. Cosy hotel near the entrance to the fortress, with beautiful gardens, clean, simple rooms, with balconies and stunning views. Breakfast on the garden terrace is included. May–Oct. **€60**
★ **Klimataria** Situated in a courtyard garden opposite

and just down from the fortress, this taverna serves fresh, well-prepared dishes (including good, classically Greek veggie options) which you can pick out from the day's offerings; mains run €6–13. May–Oct; daily lunch & dinner.
**Methoni Beach** ☎ 27230 28720, ⓦ methonibeachhotel .gr. This traditional stone hotel has very comfortable rooms and its own good restaurant, where you have your buffet breakfast overlooking the sea. **€60**

# Pýlos and around

PÝLOS is a compact but surprisingly stylish town for rural Messinía; guarded by a pair of medieval castles, it occupies a superb position on one of the finest natural harbours in Greece, the almost landlocked **Navarino Bay**. The main pleasures of Pýlos are exploring the hillside alleys, waterside streets and fortress. Given the town's associations with the **Battle of Navarino**, and, more anciently, with Homer's "sandy Pýlos", the domain of wise **King Nestor** whose palace (see p.184) has been identified 16km to the north, it makes a good base for exploring this part of the Peloponnese, particularly if equipped with a car. Relying on public transport, you'll find that long afternoon gaps in services make complex day-trips impractical.

## Pýlos town centre

Shaded by a large plane tree and several of its offspring, **Platía Trión Navárhon** is a beautiful public space, encircled by cafés and colonnaded shops. At its head is a **war memorial** commemorating the admirals Codrington, de Rigny and von Heyden, who commanded the British, French and Russian forces in the Battle of Navarino (see box below). Nearby, just uphill on the Methóni road, the little **Antonopouleion Museum** (Tues–Sun 8.30am–3pm; €2) boasts remains from the battle, along with archeological finds from the region.

## Néo Kástro

Tues–Sun 8.30am–3pm • €3

The principal sight in town is the **Néo Kástro**, up the Methóni road from Antonopouleion museum. The huge "new castle" was built by the Turks in 1572, and you can walk around much of the 1.5km of arcaded battlements. For most of the eighteenth and nineteenth centuries, it served as a prison and its inner courtyard was divided into a warren of narrow yards separated by high walls. The design was intended to keep Máni clansmen, the bulk of the prison population, from continuing their murderous vendettas inside. The pens and walls have been pulled down as part of an ongoing programme to restore and convert the castle into a **museum** for underwater archeology. So far, the only attraction is René Puaux's extensive collection of historical pictures and cartoons.

## Island of Sfaktiría

Memories of the Battle of Navarino can be evoked by a visit to the **island of Sfaktiría**, across the bay, where there are various tombs of Philhellenes, a chapel and a memorial to Russian sailors. You can also hire a **boat** from the port and snorkel to see the remains of the Turkish fleet lying on the sea bed; ask at the harbour office or cafés by the port. The island was also the site of a battle between a small group of Spartans under siege by the Athenians during the Peloponnesian War – one of the few times that Spartans are known to have surrendered.

## Yiálova

**YIÁLOVA**, 6km north out of Pýlos and linked by regular buses, has tamarisk trees shading its sandy beach, and makes a delightful base for walkers, beach-lovers or naturalists drawn by **Voïdhokiliá beach and nature reserve**.

### Kástro Navarínou

Pýlos's northern castle and ancient acropolis, **Kástro Navarínou** (Paleó Kástro), stands on a hill ridge almost touching the island of Sfaktiría, at the end of the bay 5km west

---

### THE BATTLE OF NAVARINO

In 1827 during the Greek War of Independence, the Great Powers of Britain, France and Russia were attempting to force an armistice on the Turks, having established diplomatic relations with the Greek insurgents. To this end they sent a fleet of 27 warships to **Navarino Bay** below the town of Pýlos, where Ottoman leader Ibrahim Pasha had gathered his forces – 16,000 men in 89 ships. The declared intention was to coerce Ibrahim into leaving Messinía, which he had been raiding ruthlessly.

On the night of October 20, an Egyptian frigate, part of the Turks' supporting force, fired its cannons, and full-scale battle broke out. Without intending to take up arms for the Greeks, the "allies" responded to the attack and, extraordinarily, sank and destroyed 53 of the Turkish fleet without a single loss. There was considerable international embarrassment when news filtered through to the "victors", but the action had nevertheless effectively ended Turkish control of Greek waters and within a year **Greek independence** was secured and recognized.

of Yiálova. It has substantial walls and identifiable courtyards, a mix of Frankish and Venetian designs, set upon ancient foundations. The castle overlooks one of the finest beaches in the Peloponnese.

## Voïdhokiliá beach

The Pýlos–Hóra bus will take you to the turn-off to the beach from where a dirt road ends below the castle hill

**Voïdhokiliá beach** is a spectacular crescent of white sand and turquoise waters 12km north of Pýlos. The **lagoon** behind the beach is an important bird conservation area, and vehicles are not allowed on the earth road around its eastern rim. Turtles still breed at Voïdhokiliá (and at the beaches of Romanoú and Máti, further north), and there's a tiny population – the only one in mainland Europe – of **chameleons** among the dune shrubs.

A path from the southern Voïdhokiliá dunes ascends to the **Spílio toú Nestóros** (Nestor's Cave), and then (head right, up steep rocky steps) to the castle. This impressive bat cave with a hole in the roof is fancifully identified as the grotto in which, according to the *Odyssey*, Nestor and Neleus kept their cows, and in which Hermes hid Apollo's cattle.

## ARRIVAL AND INFORMATION

### PÝLOS AND AROUND

**By bus** The bus station is on Niléos (☎ 27230 22230). Getting your bearings is easy as the town is not large, and the main square facing the port is very much its heart.
**Destinations** Athens (2 daily; 5hr); Finikoúnda (3 daily, none on Sun; 45min); Hóra (2–6 daily; 35min); Kalamáta (8 daily; 1hr 45min); Methóni (5 daily; 20min); Yiálova (4 daily; 15min).

**Services** The National Bank is on the central platía. The post office is on Niléos, just west of the bus station. Car rental (also at Kalamáta airport) is available through AutoUnion (☎ 27230 22393, ✉ autounionkalamata @mailbox.gr) on the Kalamáta road, and from the *Miramare* hotel.

## ACCOMMODATION

Pýlos has somewhat limited accommodation; in the summer months you should phone ahead. A more bucolic alternative is the beachfront part of Yiálova.

### PÝLOS

**Karalis** Kalamátas 26 ☎ 27230 22960, ✉ hotel _karalis@yahoo.gr. Located up from town centre, on the main road to the north, this is an attractive port-view hotel with comfortable modern rooms with balcony. Breakfast included. Easter to end Oct. **€60**

⭐ **Karalis Beach** On the beach below the castle ☎ 27230 23021, ✉ hotel_karalis@yahoo.gr. This is the Karalis family's new luxury property right on the sea, featuring a comfortable mix of minimalist design and traditional decor. Buffet breakfast included. Easter to end Oct. **€80**

**Miramare** Myrtidhiotíssis 35 ☎ 27230 22751, ⊕ miramarepylos.gr. This well-appointed establishment faces the port. Models of ancient ships decorate the lobby and the simple rooms have balconies with views. The reception can also provide info about various lagoon wildlife tours. Breakfast included. April–Sept. **€70**

**Nilefs** René Pyot 4 ☎ 27230 22518, ☎ 27230 22575. Just down from the castle, this very simple choice is

unpretentious, clean and pleasant, with balconies overlooking the square. April–Sept. **€45**

### YIÁVOLA

**Erodios** ☎ 27230 28240, ⊕ erodioss.gr. This is a fine campsite with studios just 500m west of town, just off its own sandy beach. It offers private parking, wi-fi and recreational equipment. Also here are a restaurant, bar, minimarket, barbecue and playground, plus washing machines. March–Oct. Camping from **€15**; studios **€55**

**Helonaki** ☎ 27230 23080, ✉ helonaki@vodafone.net .gr. Here you'll find a variety of satisfactory rooms and apartments. The ground-floor taverna is very good and also serves as the breakfast spot (included). **€50**

**Zoe** ☎ 27230 22025, ⊕ hotelzoe.gr. A pleasant resort complex of fresh hotel rooms and apartments surrounded by greenery but right on the beach. Be sure to score a room with a front balcony. The taverna on the premises is fine for lunch or dinner. The affable owner has an interest in the wildlife that inhabits the local lagoons and can suggest walks. **€60**

## EATING AND DRINKING

### PÝLOS

⭐ **Faro** Paraliakí Road ☎ 27230 22739. This is where

the locals go for wonderful, hearty meals, either in the, homely interior or at the seaside tables. Fresh fish a speciality, with prices for shrimp starting at just €12. Daily lunch & dinner.

★ **Grigoris** ☎ 27230 22621. This warmly welcoming, bustling place one block up from the port has appealing home-made dishes that change every day, and there's inviting garden seating out back. €10–15/person for a full meal. Daily, lunch & dinner.

**YIÁVOLA**

**To Spitiko** ☎ 27230 22138. This pleasant taverna is situated on the water and has excellent home cooking, Cypriot style, using many ingredients from that island, including cheeses; about €15/person for a full meal. Daily lunch & dinner.

## Nestor's Palace

Summer Tues–Fri 8am–7.30pm, Sat & Sun 8.30am–3pm; winter daily 8.30am–3pm • €3 • The site is a 30min drive from modern Pýlos. Buses run from Pýlos to Hóra (3–6 daily), 4km east of the site, where the site museum is located

**Nestor's Palace**, 17km from Pýlos, is the best preserved of all the Mycenaean royal palaces. Flanked by deep, fertile valleys, the palace site looks out towards Navarino Bay – a location perfectly suiting the wise and peaceful king described in Homer's *Odyssey*, though now sheltering rather prosaically beneath a giant metal roof.

The site was discovered in 1939, but left virtually undisturbed until after World War II; thus its **excavation** – unlike most of the other major Greek sites – was conducted in accordance with modern archeological principles and techniques. The most important find was a group of several hundred **tablets** inscribed in **Linear B**, which, given their similarity to tablets discovered in Knossos (see p.457), proved conclusively a link between the Mycenaean and Minoan civilizations. The tablets were baked hard in the fire that destroyed the palace at the time of the Dorian invasion around 1200 BC, perhaps as little as one generation after the fall of Troy. The site guide by excavators Carl Blegen and Marion Rawson is an excellent buy.

### The site

The remains of Nestor's massive complex are in three principal groups: the **main palace** in the middle, on the left an earlier and **smaller palace**, and on the right either **guardhouses** or **workshops**. The basic design will be familiar if you've been to Mycenae or Tiryns: an internal court, guarded by a sentry box, gives access to the main sections of the principal palace. This contained some 45 rooms and halls. The **megaron** (throne room), with its characteristic open hearth, lies directly ahead of the entrance, through a double porch. The finest of the frescoes was discovered here, depicting a griffin (perhaps the royal emblem) standing guard over the throne; that work is now in the museum in Hóra. Arranged around are domestic quarters and **storerooms**, which yielded thousands of pots and cups during excavations; the rooms may have served as a distribution centre for the produce of the palace workshops. Further back, the famous **bathroom**, with its painted terracotta tub *in situ*, adjoins a smaller complex of rooms, centred on another, smaller, megaron, identified as the **queen's quarters**. Finally, on the other side of the car park there is a **tholos tomb**, a smaller version of the famous ones at Mycenae.

---

**TELEMACHUS TAKES A BATH**

King Nestor rates several mentions in Homer's poems, but the scene from Homer's epic that is set here is the visit of **Telemachus**, son of Odysseus, who had journeyed from Ithaca to seek news of his father from the king. As Telemachus arrives at the beach, accompanied by the disguised goddess Pallas Athena, he comes upon Nestor with his sons and court sacrificing to Poseidon. The visitors are welcomed and feasted, "sitting on downy fleeces on the sand", and although the king has no news of Odysseus, he promises Telemachus a chariot so he can enquire from Menelaus at Sparta. First, however, the guests are taken back to the palace, where Telemachus is given a bath by Nestor's "youngest grown daughter, beautiful Polycaste", and emerges, anointed with oil, "with the body of an immortal". By some harmonious twist of fate, an actual **bathtub** was unearthed here, rendering the palace ruins as a whole potent ground for Homeric imaginings.

The museum at Hóra

Officially Tues–Sun 8.30am–3pm, but can be erratic • €2

At **Hóra** (Hóra Trifylías), actually a sizeable town despite the name, which means "village", the **museum** on Marinátou, signed above the main square (with Friday-morning produce market), adds significantly to a visit to the site. If you've no transport, it might be better to take a bus here first, to the central bus station stop, and then walk the 45 minutes to the site after viewing the exhibits. In hot weather, or if pressed for time, you might be able to hitch, or get a taxi.

Pride of place in the display goes to the **palace frescoes**, one of which, bearing out Homer's descriptions, shows a warrior in a boar-tusk helmet. Lesser finds include much pottery, some beautiful **gold cups** and other objects gathered both from the site and from various Mycenaean tombs in the region.

# Olympia and Ilía

Dominated by the monumental archeological site of **Olympia**, gracing the fertile Alfíos valley, the sizeable province of **Ilía** comprises for the most part flat coastal plains with a series of undistinguished market towns, bordered on the west by long, fine, often underused **beaches**; the resort to head for here is **Arkoúdhi**.

## Olympia

The historic associations and resonance of **OLYMPIA**, which for over a millennium hosted the most important **Panhellenic games**, are rivalled only by Delphi or Mycenae. It is one of the largest ancient sites in Greece, spread beside the twin rivers of Alfíos (Alpheus) – the largest in the Peloponnese – and Kládhios, and overlooked by the Hill of Krónos. The site itself is picturesque, but the sheer quantity of ruined structures can give a confusing impression of their ancient grandeur and function; despite the crowds, tour buses, souvenir shops and other trappings of mass tourism, it deserves a visit with at least an overnight stay at the modern village of Olympía (see p.189).

### The site

May–Oct daily 8am–7pm; Nov–April Mon–Fri 8am–5pm, Sat & Sun 8.30am–3pm • €6, or €9 for combined site and archeological museum

From its beginnings the **site** was a sanctuary, with a permanent population limited to the temple priests. At first the games took place within the sacred precinct, the walled, rectangular **Altis**, but as events became more sophisticated a new **stadium** was built to adjoin it.

#### The gymnasium and official buildings

The **entrance** to the site, located just 200m from the village, leads along the west side of the Altis wall, past a group of public and official buildings. On the left, beyond some Roman baths, is the **Prytaneion**, the administrators' residence, where athletes stayed and feasted at official expense. On the right are the ruins of a **gymnasium** and a **palaestra** (wrestling school), used by the competitors during their obligatory month of pre-games training.

Beyond these stood the Priests' House, the **Theokoleion**, a substantial colonnaded building in whose southeast corner is a structure adapted as a Byzantine church. This was originally the **studio of Fidias**, the fifth-century BC sculptor responsible for the great gold and ivory cult statue in Olympia's Temple of Zeus. It was identified by following a description by Pausanias, and through the discovery of tools, moulds for the statue and a cup engraved with the sculptor's name.

To the south of the studio lie further administrative buildings, including the
**Leonidaion**, a large and doubtless luxurious hostel endowed for the most important of
the festival guests. It was the first building visitors would reach along the original
approach road to the site.

### The Temple of Zeus

The main focus of the **Altis precinct** is provided by the great Doric **Temple of Zeus**. Built
between 470 and 456 BC, it was as large as the Parthenon, a fact quietly substantiated
by the vast column drums littering the ground. The temple's decoration, too, rivalled the
finest in Athens; partially recovered, its sculptures of Pelops in a chariot race, of Lapiths
and Centaurs, and the Labours of Hercules, are now in the museum. In the *cella* was
exhibited the (lost) cult statue of Zeus by Fidias, one of the seven wonders of the ancient
world. Here, too, the **Olympian flame** was kept alight, from the time of the games until
the following spring – a tradition continued at an altar for the modern games.

### The Temple of Hera

The smaller **Temple of Hera**, behind, was the first built in the Altis; prior to its
completion in the seventh century BC, the sanctuary had only open-air altars,
dedicated to Zeus and a variety of other cult gods. The temple, rebuilt in the Doric
style in the sixth century BC, is the most complete building on the site, with some
thirty of its columns surviving in part, along with a section of the inner wall. The levels
above this wall were composed only of sun-baked brick, and the lightness of this
building material must have helped to preserve the sculptures that nineteenth-century
excavation uncovered – most notably the *Hermes of Praxiteles*.

West of the Temple of Hera, and bordering the wall of the Altis, are remains of the
circular **Philippeion**, the first monument in the sanctuary to be built to secular

2

## THE OLYMPIC GAMES

The origins of the games at Olympia are rooted in **legends** – often relating to the god Pelops, Zeus, or to Hercules (Herakles). Historically, the contests probably began around the eleventh century BC, growing over the next two centuries from a local festival to the **quadrennial** celebration attended by states from throughout the Greek world. These great gatherings extended the games' importance and purpose well beyond the winning of olive wreaths; assembled under a strict **truce**, nobles and ambassadors negotiated treaties, while merchants did business and sculptors and poets sought commissions.

### THE EVENTS

From the beginning, the main Olympic **events** were athletic. The earliest was a race over the course of the stadium – roughly 200m. Later came the introduction of two-lap (400m) and 24-lap (5000m) races, along with the most revered of the Olympiad events, the **pentathlon**. This encompassed running, jumping, discus and javelin events, the competitors gradually reduced to a final pair for a wrestling-and-boxing combat. It was, like much of these early Olympiads, a fairly brutal contest. One of the most prestigious events was the *pancratium* where contestants fought each other, naked and unarmed, using any means except biting or gouging. Similarly, the chariot races were extreme tests of strength and control, only one team in twenty completing the 7km course.

### RULES AND AWARDS

In the early Olympiads, the **rules** of competition were strict. Only free-born male Greeks could take part, and the **rewards** of victory were entirely honorary: a palm, given to the victor immediately after the contest, and an olive branch, presented in a ceremony closing the games. As the games developed, however, the rules were loosened to allow participation by athletes from all parts of the Greek and Roman world. By the fourth century BC, when the games were at their peak, the athletes were virtually all **professionals**, heavily sponsored by their home states and, if they won at Olympia, commanding huge appearance money at games elsewhere. Under the Romans, commercialization accelerated and new events were introduced. In 67 AD Emperor Nero advanced the games by two years just so that he could compete in (and win) special singing and lyre-playing events.

### DECLINE AND FALL

Notwithstanding Roman abuses, the Olympian tradition was popular enough to be maintained for another three centuries, and the games' eventual **closure** happened as a result of religious dogma rather than lack of support. In 393 AD Emperor Theodosius, recently converted to **Christianity**, suspended the games as part of a general crackdown on public pagan festivities. This suspension proved final, for Theodosius's successor ordered the destruction of the temples, a process completed by barbarian invasion, earthquakes and, lastly, by the Alfiós River changing its course to cover the sanctuary site. There it remained, covered by 7m of silt and sand, until the first excavation by German archeologists in the 1870s.

glory. It was begun by Philip II to commemorate his victory at the Battle of Chaeronea (see p.213), which gave him control over the Greek mainland; the building may have been completed by his son, Alexander the Great. To the east of the Hera temple is a small, second-century AD **fountain house**, the gift of the ubiquitous Herodes Atticus. Beyond, lining a terrace at the base of the Hill of Krónos, are the **state treasuries**, storage chambers for sacrificial items and sporting equipment used in the games. They are built in the form of temples, as at Delphi; the oldest and grandest, at the east end, belonged to Gela in Sicily. In front of the treasuries are the foundations of the **Metroön**, a fourth-century BC Doric temple dedicated to the mother of the gods.

## The Pelopeion

Between the temples of Hera and Zeus is a grove described by Pausanias, and identified as the **Pelopeion**. In addition to a cult altar to the Olympian hero, this enclosed a small mound formed by sacrificial ashes, among which excavations unearthed many of the terracotta finds in the museum. The sanctuary's principal altar, dedicated to Zeus, probably stood just to the east.

## The Bouleuterion

The ancient ceremonial entrance to the Altis was on the south side, below a long **stoa** taking up almost the entire east side of the precinct. At the corner was a house built by the Roman emperor Nero for his stay during the games. He also had the entrance remodelled as a triumphal arch, fit for his anticipated victories. Through the arch, just outside the precinct, stood the **Bouleuterion** or council chamber, where before a great statue of Zeus the competitors took their oaths to observe the Olympian rules. These were not to be taken lightly: lining the way were bronze statues paid for with the fines exacted for foul play, bearing the name of the disgraced athlete, his father and city.

## The stadium

The natural focus of the Olympic site is the 200m track of the **stadium** itself, entered by way of a long arched tunnel. The starting and finishing lines are still there, with the judges' thrones in the middle and seating ridges banked to either side. Originally unstructured, the stadium developed with the games' popularity, forming a model for others throughout the Greek and Roman world. The tiers here eventually accommodated up to 20,000 spectators, with a smaller number on the southern slope overlooking the **hippodrome** where the chariot races were held. Even so, the seats were reserved for the wealthier strata of society. The ordinary populace – along with slaves and all women spectators – watched the events from the Hill of Krónos to the north, then a natural, treeless grandstand. The stadium was unearthed only in World War II, during a second phase of German excavations between 1941 and 1944, allegedly on the direct orders of Hitler.

## The museum

May–Oct Mon noon–7.30pm, Tues–Sun 8am–7.30pm; Nov–April Mon 10.30am–5pm, Tues–Sun 8.30am–5pm • €6

Olympia's site **museum** lies a couple of hundred metres north of the sanctuary. It contains some of the finest Classical and Roman sculptures in the country, all superbly displayed.

The most famous of the individual sculptures are the **head of Hera** and the **Hermes of Praxiteles**, both dating from the fourth century BC and discovered in the Temple of Hera. The Hermes is one of the best preserved of all Classical sculptures, and remarkable in the easy informality of its pose; it retains traces of its original paint. On a grander scale is the **Nike of Paionios**, which was originally 10m high. Though no longer complete, it hints at how the sanctuary must once have appeared, crowded with statuary.

In the main hall of the museum is the centrepiece of the Olympia finds: statuary and sculpture reassembled from the **Temple of Zeus**. These include a delicately moulded frieze of the **Twelve Labours of Hercules**. Another from the east pediment depicts Zeus presiding over a famous **chariot race** between Pelops and King Oinamaos – the prize the hand of the king's daughter. The king (on the left of the frieze) was eventually defeated by Pelops (on the right), after – depending on the version – assistance from Zeus (depicted at the centre), magic steeds from Poseidon or, most un-Olympian, bribing Oinamaos's charioteer to tamper with the wheels.

The west pediment illustrates the **Battle of the Lapiths and Centaurs** at the wedding of King Peirithous of the Lapiths. This time, Apollo presides over the scene while Theseus helps the Lapiths defeat the drunken centaurs, depicted attacking the women and boy guests. Many of the metope fragments are today in the Louvre in Paris, and some of what you see here are plaster-cast copies.

The last rooms of the museum contain a collection of objects relating to the games – including *halteres* (jumping weights), discuses, weightlifters' stones and other sporting bits and pieces. Also displayed are a number of **funerary inscriptions**, including that of a boxer, Camelos of Alexandria, who died in the stadium after praying to Zeus for victory or death.

## Olymbía village

Modern **OLYMBÍA** is a village that has grown up simply to serve the excavations and tourist trade. It's essentially one long main avenue, **Praxitéles Kondhýli**, lined with shops, and with a few short side streets. Nevertheless, it is quite a pleasant place to stay and is preferable by far to Pýrgos, offering the prospect of good countryside walks along the Alfiós River and around the Hill of Krónos.

With time on your hands, there are three somewhat dutiful minor museums. The **Museum of the Modern Olympic Games** (Mon–Sat 8am–3.30pm, Sun 9am–4.30pm; €2), on the street above the *Hotel Phedias*, has commemorative postage stamps and the odd memento from the modern games, including the box that conveyed the heart of Pierre de Coubertin (reviver of the modern games) from Paris to its burial at Olympia. The **Museum of the History of the Olympic Games in Antiquity** and the **Museum of the History of Excavations in Olympia** (both: summer daily 8am–7.30pm, winter Tues–Sat 8.30am–3pm; free) lie above the coach park at the eastern end of the village, en route to the main site.

## ARRIVAL AND INFORMATION                                            OLYMPIA

Both the bus stop and the train station are within a block or two of the village centre and the sights.

**By bus** Athens to Olympía (only through connections in Pýrgos, 4 daily; 5hr 30min); Pýrgos (hourly; 30min); Trípoli (via Langádhia, 2 daily; 3hr).
**By train** The train link from Pýrgos to Olympía makes five daily runs (30min).

**Tourist office** (Mon–Sat: May–Oct 9am–3pm; Nov–April 11am–5pm; ☎ 26240 23100), on the right of Praxitéles Kondhýli, as you come into town from Pýrgos.
**Services** Olymbía has three banks on the main avenue, and a post office just uphill.

## ACCOMMODATION

**Accommodation** is fairly easy to come by, with a swift turnaround of clientele and a range of **hotels** and private **rooms**. Many of the smaller and cheaper places close outside June–Sept; it's best to check in advance. The centre of Olymbía village can get very noisy at night. Given the bucolic surroundings, **camping** is also an attractive option.

**Diana Camping** ☎ 26240 22314, ⓦ campingdiana.gr. Located just 200m west of the town and 800m from the archeological site, this campsite is set amid a pine forest and has a pool, a restaurant and good facilities, including wi-fi. March–Nov. From **€14**

**Europa** Dhroúva 1 ☎ 26240 22650, ⓦ hoteleuropa.gr. Well-run and comfortable resort hotel, part of the *Best Western* chain, situated near the top of the hill to the southwest. Amenities include wi-fi and a large pool. Ample parking. Breakfast included. **€110**

**2**

**Hercules** Tsoúreka 2 ☎ 26240 22696, ⓦ hotelhercules
.gr. A congenial small hotel by the church and school on a
side street off Praxitéles Kondhýli. Wi-fi and parking free.
Breakfast included. March–Oct. **€50**

**Kronio** Tsoúreka 1 ☎ 26240 22188, ⓦ hotelkronio.gr. A
comfortable hotel, with wi-fi access in rooms. Breakfast
included. March–Oct. **€56**

★ **Pelops** Varélas 2 ☎ 26240 22543, ⓦ hotelpelops.gr
Run by a Greek-Australian couple and recently extensively
refurbished, this pleasant hotel is situated on a square by the
church. They offer delicious evening meals, for just €15.80, a
well as a range of courses that include cooking, art and
creative writing. Breakfast included. March–Oct. **€60**

## EATING AND DRINKING

Olymbía's main avenue is loaded with **tavernas** but, besides the *Hotel Pelops*, our favourites are across from each other or
the village's only diagonal side street.

**Aegeon** Georgiou Douma ☎ 26240 22540. Highly
recommended by locals, this unassuming place offers
everything from grilled lamb or roasted chicken to pizza.
Full meals €10–15. Daily lunch & dinner.

★ **Gefsis Melathron** Georgiou Douma 3 ☎ 26240

22916. Excellent home-made dishes featuring fresh local
produce. Greek salads and *souvláki* go for €5.50, *briam*
(traditional vegetable casserole) for €5, and most mains for
only a euro or two more. Daily lunch & dinner.

# Pýrgos

**PÝRGOS** is a large, modern town and the capital of Ilía province. It's pleasant enough in
parts, though serious diversions are nonexistent for the tourist. Still, it is a public
transport hub and it's handy if you have errands to run. The town has a grim history.
When the Germans withdrew at the end of World War II, it remained under the
control of Greek Nazi collaborators. They negotiated a surrender with the Greek
Resistance, who were met by gunfire as they entered the town. Full-scale battle erupted
and for five days the town burned.

## ARRIVAL AND DEPARTURE

**By bus** The bus station is to the west of town.
Destinations Andhrítsena (2 daily; 2hr); Athens (8 daily;
5hr); Kyllíni (2 daily; 1hr); Olymbía (hourly, but none
12.30–3.30pm; 30min); Pátra (9 daily; 2hr).

**By train** The train station is on Ypsilándou, a 15min walk
downhill from the bus station. At the time of writing
services were only running to Olymbía (5 daily; 30min).

## ACCOMMODATION

**Olympos** Patron & Karkavitsa 2 ☎ 26210 33650,
ⓦ hotelolympos.gr. This modern high-rise hotel has
handsome rooms and is located right in the city centre, not

far from parks and shopping. Amenities include a/c and
internet. Bathrooms are small, but some have
hydromassage tubs. Breakfast included. **€90**

# Arkoúdhi and Cape Tripití

About 25km to the north of Pýrgos, near the point where this most westerly coast of
the Peloponnese forms Cape Tripití, is **ARKOÚDHI**, a compact village resort that has
something of an island feel to it, and a fine sandy bay enclosed by a rocky promontory.

## ACCOMMODATION AND EATING

★ **Elia** ☎ 26230 96493, ⓦ elia-arkoudi.com. Located
on a hill up from the beach, this colourful, very friendly
family-run place offers both self-catering apartments and
a restaurant, with meals (€10–15) based on recipes
handed down to chef Miranda from her grandmother.
May–Oct. **€35**

**R.Q.D.** ☎ 26230 96167, ⓦ rqd.gr. Located right down on
the beach, this restaurant-bar is mostly the latter. The food
is nevertheless gourmet and sometimes a bit pricey (pasta
dishes go for as much as €14) but the atmosphere is very
young and crackling with summer energy. Daily morning
to midnight.

## Kástro

Using Arkoúdhi as a base, it's worth taking time to hitch or walk to the village of **Kástro**, at the centre of the cape. Looming above the village and visible from many kilometres around is the Frankish **castle of Khlemoútsi** (Castel Tornese; summer daily 8am–7pm; winter Tues–Sun 8.30am–3pm; €3), a vast hexagonal structure built in 1220 by Geoffrey de Villehardouin. Its function was principally to control the province of Ahaïa, though it served also as a strategic fortress on the Adriatic. Haze permitting, there are sweeping views across the straits to Zákynthos, and even to Kefaloniá and Itháki, from the well-preserved and restored ramparts.

## Kyllíni

Heading north, you'll pass a rather clinical spa resort, **Loutra Kyllínis**, on the way to the northern tip of the cape. Here, the cheerless little port of **KYLLÍNI** has little more to offer than its **ferry connections** to Zákynthos and Kefaloniá.

**By bus** Buses arrive daily from Athens carrying passengers with through tickets for the ferries. Pre-booked buses also meet the ferries here. Otherwise there are no buses from Kyllíni except to Pýrgos (1–4 daily; 1hr).

**By ferry** Operators are ⓦionianferries.gr to all destinations and Strintzis (ⓦstrintzisferries.gr) for Póros.

**Destinations** Zákynthos (4–7 daily; 1hr); Kefaloniá Póros (5 daily summer, 2–3 daily winter; 1hr 15min–2hr 15min), Kefaloniá Lixoúri–Argostóli (1 daily summer; 2hr–2hr 30min).

# Pátra and Ahaïa

Capital of the large northern province of **Ahaïa**, **Pátra** is a major port and transport hub though offers little else to visitors. To the south are high mountains while along the narrow, densely populated coastal strip are a few decent beaches, the best at **Kalogriá**. From the drab town of **Dhiakoftó** on the Gulf of Kórinthos, you can opt for an outing on one of Greece's first railway lines, which follows the dramatic **Vouraikós Gorge**, up to **Kalávryta**.

## Pátra

**PÁTRA** (Patras) is the largest city in the Peloponnese and, after Pireás and Igoumenítsa, a major port of Greece; from here you can catch ferries to Italy as well as to certain Ionian islands. The city is also a hub of the Greek-mainland transport network (see p.193).

Unless you arrive late in the day from Italy, you won't need, or want, to spend more than a few hours here. There are no beaches and no truly essential sights. Traffic noise goes on well into the night and starts earlier than you'd want to get up. Add to that the gangs of unemployed men, who hang around the port, and it's preferable to move on quickly. That said, if you find yourself here for some time, there are a few reasonable attractions: the **Kástro**, the new **archeological museum**, and the massive **church** of Áyios Andhréas. Swimming near Pátra isn't advisable – the sea is polluted for some kilometres to the southwest. Locals head to the **beaches** around Río (7km northeast; bus #6) or to Kalogriá (see p.195).

## The Kástro

Mon–Fri 8am–7pm, Sat & Sun 8am–5pm • Free

The **Kástro**, a mainly Frankish-Byzantine and partly restored citadel fifteen minutes' walk up from the water, is not particularly exciting, but it is up away from the city bustle, surrounded by a small park and with woodland beyond. Nearby, at Boukaoúri 29, is the **hammam** (Turkish baths, ☎26102 74267; €5), still good for a steam after six hundred years.

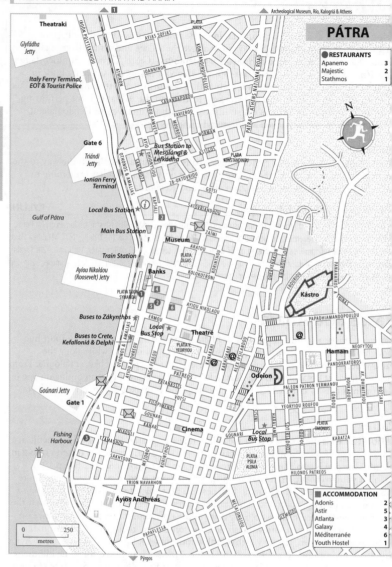

## The archeological museum

Corner Amerikis Street & New Patras-Athens National Road • ☎ 26104 20645 • Tues–Sun 8.30am–3pm • Free

Located about 3km from the centre, at the north end of the city, the new, crisply contemporary **archeological museum** is now second only in size to the new Acropolis Museum in Athens. Themed exhibits include a vast quantity of everyday objects from Ahaïa dating from the Mycenaean to the Roman eras, most of which have been in storage for the past thirty years. Though it houses one of Greece's biggest Roman mosaic collections, there's no single item of great import, and the whole approach can be a little too didactic for most.

# Church of Áyios Andhréas

Daily 8–11am, 4.30–7pm

This huge neo-Byzantine confection lies at the southwest end of the waterfront on the spot where St Andrew is said to have been martyred in 69 AD, and where an ancient temple to Demeter once stood. The saint's relics are housed within, including his skull.

## ARRIVAL AND DEPARTURE                                    PÁTRA

**By air** Patra/Araxos Airport (w araxos-airport.com), 40km south of Pátra, is mostly served by charter flights from Germany and Belgium (May–Sept only). Check w jetairfly .com and w tuifly.com.

**By bus** Buses for the Peloponnese, Athens, Ioánnina, Thessaloníki and Vólos depart from the main bus station (t 26106 23 886), a short distance northeast of the train station. Buses for Zákynthos go from Óthonos & Amalías 47 (t 26102 20993); for Lamía, Tríkala, Kefaloniá and Crete from Óthonos & Amalías 58 (t 2610 274 938); and for Mesolóngi, Agrínio, Náfpaktos and Delphi from Nórman 5 (t 26104 21205).

Destinations Athens (every 20min daily, 2.30am–9.45pm; 3hr); Agrinio (8 daily; 1hr 45min); Árgos (1 Fridays; 4hr); Éyio (12–16 daily; 1hr); Itéa (for Delphi, 2 daily, Mon–Sat; 3–4hr); Ioánnina (2 daily; 4hr 30min); Itháki (1 daily, via Kefaloniá; 6hr); Kalamáta (2 daily; 4hr); Kalávryta (2–4 daily; 2hr 15min); Kalogriá (3–5 daily in season; 1hr 15min); Kefaloniá (3 daily; 4hr); Lápas/Metóhi (for Kalogriá; 6–10 daily; 50min–1hr); Lefkádha (2 weekly; 3hr); Mesolóngi (8–10 daily; 1hr); Náfpaktos (1–7 daily; 1hr); Pýrgos (6–10 daily; 2hr); Thessaloníki (4 daily; 7hr); Trípoli (1–2 daily, via Lámbia; 3–4hr); Vólos (1 daily, except Sat; 5hr); Zákynthos (4 daily; 2hr 30min including ferry from Kyllíni).

**By train** The train station is on Óthonos & Amalías. At the time of writing all rail services were suspended. Rail replacement buses run to Kiáto from where you can connect to trains running to Athens/Pireás.

**By ferry** Ferries leave from or near the Triándi Jetty (Gate 6), at the end of Norman Street; ticket agencies are also located along here, on the waterfront street. Italy-bound ferries (see box, p.27) leave from early afternoon to midnight. You must check in with the agent's embarkation booth at least 2hrs before departure. Though services are frequent, all Italy-bound ferries stop for around 2hrs in Igoumenítsa, adding significantly to the total sailing time. Free stopovers on Corfu are not allowed. You can take the domestic ferry to Corfu and pick up Italy sailings from there, though fares will be the same as from Pátra.

International destinations Ancona (2–3 daily; 19hr 30min/20hr 30min); Bari (1–2 daily; 14hr 30min/16hr); Brindisi (1 daily; 14hr 30min); Venice (1 daily; 1day 7hr/1day 7hr 30min).

Domestic destinations Corfu (1–2 daily; 6hr 15min/6hr 45min); Igoumenítsa (3–5 daily; 4hr 45min–7hr); Kefaloniá and Itháki (1–2 daily; 3hr 20min/3hr 45min).

**By car** Pátra is linked to the mainland by the suspension bridge across the gulf from Andírio to Río (5 min; €12 car toll). The old ferry services are now used only for vehicles not permitted on the bridge. If going beyond Pátra, then there is a fast bypass to the east. From Pátra you can reach Kórinthos in 2hrs along the national highway; the onward journey to Athens takes another 90min.

## INFORMATION

**Tourist office** Info Center Patras at Óthonos & Amalías 6 (daily 8am–10pm; t 26104 61740, w infocenterpatras.gr) offer free internet (30min) and free bike rental (3hr; passport/ID necessary). They also have a kiosk on Platía Trión Symáhon (daily 9am–1pm & 5–8pm), with wi-fi access. EOT (Mon–Fri 7am–9pm; t 26104 30915) are located at the western end of Nórman, near the Triándi Jetty, Gate 6, from which ferries to Italy depart.

## GETTING AROUND

**By bus** Local buses go from Óthonos & Amalías north of the main bus station; tickets are available from kiosks, and are cheaper than when bought from the driver.

**By car** If you are driving in or through Pátra, you will find the traffic and one-way system no less frustrating than in Athens; a map showing the direction of traffic, if not vital, will at least save time and probably maintain sanity.

## ACCOMMODATION

Most of Pátra's **hotels** are on Ayíou Andhréou, one block back from Óthonos & Amalías, or on Ayíou Nikoláou, which runs back from the sea, near the train station and Platía Trión Symáhon.

**Adonis** Kapsáli 9, cnr Záïmi t 2610 224 213, e hotela lonis@pat.forthnet.gr. This large high-rise hotel is well furnished and maintained. Most rooms have balconies overlooking the harbour, though bathrooms are small. Free wi-fi throughout. **€60**

**Astir** Ayíou Andhréou 16 t 2610 277 502, w hotel

astirpatras.gr. Rather posh Art Deco styling in the public spaces, handsome rooms, plus a rooftop terrace restaurant with a pool make this a good choice. Extras include wi-fi in the lobby, parking and a sauna. Breakfast included. **€100**
**Atlanta** Zaïmi 10 ☎2610 220 098, ✉atlanta@pat .forthnet.gr. Modern, plain and central hotel, just across from the bus station, good enough for an overnighter but not especially good value. Rooms are en suite but small. **€70**
**Galaxy** Ayíou Nikoláou 9 ☎2610 275 981, ⓦgalaxy hotel.com.gr. This is a well-placed hotel, newly refurbished, with a sleekly modern lobby and decent rooms that include

wi-fi and flat-screen TVs. Good buffet breakfast included. **€8**
**Méditerranée** Ayíou Nikoláou 18 ☎26102 79602 ⓦmediterranee.gr. This hotel is modern, modest an adequate, with helpful staff. Rooms are a bit garishl decorated but have a/c. Breakfast included. **€65**
**Youth Hostel** Iróön Polytekhníou 62 ☎2610 427 278 ⓦpatrasrooms.gr/hostel.htm. A handsome ston mansion (used as Nazi headquarters in World War II) set i a garden opposite the marina, but a 1.5km walk from th centre. No curfew. Dorm beds **€10**

## EATING AND DRINKING

Pátra's restaurant choices are dominated by fast-food places around Platía Trión Symáhon, and along Ayíou Andhréou an Ayíou Nikoláou. But even here there are some reliable restaurants with character.

**Apanemo** Óthonos & Amalías 107. Seafood taverna opposite the fishing harbour, with good fresh fish and noted for its *galaktoboúreko* (custard pudding). Fresh fish priced by the kilo, otherwise expect about €15/person. Daily lunch & dinner.
**Majestic** Ayíou Nikoláou 2–4 ☎2610 272 243. This is an old-style taverna where you can choose from the day's tasty hot dishes, such as fried *saganáki*, cheese with a

squeeze of fresh lemon, or maybe seafood with spic tomato sauce. About €15/person. Daily lunch & dinner.
**Stathmos** Platía Trión Symáhon ☎2610 622 550. A lively bar/café/restaurant where you can wait befor boarding a ferry. They serve giant portions of mezédhes *souvláki* and *spanokópites*, along with grills and fresh fish Less than €15/person. Daily morning till midnight.

## ENTERTAINMENT

**Carnival** Pátra's three-week carnival (ⓦcarnivalpatras .gr), one of Greece's largest, ends on the Sunday before Lent

Monday (Katharí Dheftéra) with a grand parade throug the city centre.

## DIRECTORY

**Banks and exchange** National Bank of Greece, Platía Trión Symáhon (normal banking hours plus 6–8pm); several banks in the area have ATMs.
**Books and newspapers** Book's Corner, Ayíou Nikoláou 32, stocks useful maps and English-language newspapers; the latter are also available from kiosks on the waterfront; Lexis, Mézonos 38 Patréos 90, stocks maps and a selection of books in English; the Ermis bookshop at Zaïmi stocks Road's map of Ahaïa.
**Car rental** Alamo/National, Ayíou Andhréou 1 ☎2610 273 667, ☏2610 277 864; AutoUnion/Thrifty, Ayíou Dhionysíou 2 ☎2610 623 200, ☏2610 622 201; Avis,

28-Oktovríou 16 ☎2610 275 547; Delta, Óthonos & Amalías 44 ☎2610 272 764; Eurodollar, Albatros Travel Óthonos & Amalías 48 ☎2610 220 993; Hertz, 28-Oktovríou 2 ☎2610 220 990; InterRent-EuropCar, Ayíou Andhréou ☎2610 621 360; Sixt, Ayíou Andhréou 10 ☎2610 275 677
**Consulate** Britain, Vótsi 2 ☎2610 277 079, ☏2610 22 334.
**Post office** Cnr Mézonos Zaïmi (Mon–Fri 7.30am–8pm) also near cnr Gounári Ayíou Andhréou (Mon–F 7.30am–2pm).
**Tourist police** (daily 7am–11pm; ☎2610 452 512).

# The north coast

The resorts and villages lining the **north coast** are modest, but at least not overdeveloped. Generally you find little more than a narrow strip of beach, a campsite, a few rooms for rent and a couple of seasonal tavernas. West of Pátra is **Kalogriá**, the best beach hereabouts. To the east is **Dhiakoftó** from where you can stop for the old **Kalávryta railway** ride up into the picturesque **Vouraïkós gorge** via quaint **Zakhloroú**. After Dhiakoftó, if you're unhurried, it's worth taking the old **coast road** along the Gulf of Kórinthos; this runs below the national highway, often right by the sea.

# Kalogriá

**KALOGRIÁ** (locally Kalógria) is the best **beach** near Pátra: a 7km strand, partly naturist, bordered by a swathe of umbrella pine forests. A fair proportion of Pátra, including the gay community, descends here at the weekend. The whole area is protected as part of the **Strofyliá Forest-Kotýkhi Wetland National Park**, which covers beach dunes, the forest, and lagoons with their rare birdlife, and permanent development remains low-key. Kalogriá is not actually a village – the nearest bona fide town is Metóhi – but rather a small cluster of tavernas and stores. Behind the hotels, the 200m outcrop Mávra Voúna has a number of organized climbing routes (w geocities.com/patrasclimbing).

## ARRIVAL AND INFORMATION · KALOGRIÁ

**By bus** Regular buses run from Pátra (3–5 daily in season; 1hr 15min).

**Tourist office** There is an enthusiastic information and environmental monitoring centre (Mon–Fri, 8am–2pm; ☏ 26930 31651, e ciks@otenet.gr) for the park at nearby Láppa, in a building opposite the train station.

## ACCOMMODATION

**Amalia** ☏ 26930 31100, w amaliahotel.gr. For a quieter stay there are these simple studios, near the beach but hidden in a large garden behind their own good taverna. **€50**

**Kalogria Beach** ☏ 26930 31276, w peloponnesetravel .gr. Extensive and pleasantly modern, with colourful decor, this resort has every sort of facility: restaurants, café and bar, beach sunbeds and umbrellas, a large pool, a smaller play-pool for kids, and a full range of sports options. Buffet breakfast included. April–Oct. **€90**

# Río and Éyio

**RÍO** (Ríon), connected by local bus #6 to Pátra in thirty minutes, signals the beginning of swimmable water east of Pátra, though most travellers pass through for the **suspension bridge** across the gulf to Andírio (5min; €12.90 car toll). At the time of writing, ferries across the gulf from Río and **Éyio** (Aigio), further east, had been suspended.

# Dhiakoftó

From **DHIAKOFTÓ** (officially Dhiakoptó) an old **rack-and-pinion railway** (see box, p.196) heads south up into the **Vouraïkós gorge**, final stop **Kalávryta**. Dhiakoftó itself is typically drab, but there's a narrow pebble beach along the eastern side, and if you have to spend the night, there is at least one good option.

## ARRIVAL AND INFORMATION · DHIAKOFTÓ

**By bus** With trains suspended along the north coast Dhiakoftó is poorly served by public transport. Athens–Pátra buses stop at Éyio about 10km west, from where local buses connect to Dhiakoftó (4 daily; 30min).

## ACCOMMODATION AND EATING

**Panorama** ☏ 26910 41614, w greecepanorama.gr. Friendly and well-located hotel on its own small beach with sea-view terrace seating and a good taverna. Simple, comfortable rooms with balcony. Wi-fi available in the lobby; a/c. Breakfast €7/person. **€75**

# Zakhloroú

**ZAKHLOROÚ** is as perfect a train stop as could be imagined: a tiny hamlet echoing with the sound of the **Vouraïkós River**, which splits it into two neighbourhoods. It's a lovely, peaceful place with an old hotel.

## Méga Spiléou

Open roughly 8am–1pm, 5–7pm; museum €1 · ☏ 26920 23130 · 45min walk from the village, up a rough donkey track along the hillside · Usual monastery dress code applies

The eight-storey **Monastery of Méga Spiléou** ("Great Cave") near Zakhlouroú is the oldest monastery in Greece and spectacularly sited under a 120m cliff. The view of the gorge

**2**

## THE KALÁVRYTA EXPRESS

The 22km **rack-and-pinion railway** from **Dhiakoftó** to **Kalávryta** is a crazy feat of Italian engineering, rising at gradients of up to one in seven as it cuts inland through the Vouraïkós gorge. The journey can be hot, crowded and uncomfortable, but the route is a toy-train fantasy of tunnels, bridges and precipitous overhangs and well worth experiencing.

The railway was built between 1889 and 1896 to bring minerals from the mountains to the sea. Its 1896 steam locomotives were replaced some years ago – one (O Moutzouris) remains by the line at Dhiakoftó station (☎ 26910 43206) with other relics, and another at Kalávryta – but the track itself retains all the charm of its period. The tunnels, for example, have delicately carved window openings, and the narrow bridges zigzagging across the Vouraïkós seem engineered for sheer virtuosity.

It takes around 45 minutes to get from Dhiakoftó to **Zakhloroú** (listed on timetables as **Méga Spiléo**), and about another twenty minutes from there to Kalávryta. In peak season the ride is very popular (there are just three to six trains a day, depending on the season), so plan to buy tickets in advance of your preferred departure (return €19; one way €9.50). Despite the short distance covered, trains on this line can be subject to the same lengthy delays (or cancellations) as their grown-up counterparts on the main lines.

valley from the monastery is for many the principal attraction – sadly the monastery itself has been burned and rebuilt so many times it now resembles nothing so much as a 1970s hotel – however, its treasury, arranged as a small **museum**, is outstanding. In the main church, among its icons is a charred black wax and mastic image of the Virgin, one of three in Greece said to be by the hand of St Luke (but probably from the tenth century); a smaller chapel houses a remarkable collection of body parts from various saints, all encased in precious materials. The monastery was founded by Saints Theodhoros and Simeon, after a vision by the shepherdess Euphrosyne in 362 AD led to the discovery of the icon in the cave (Ayíazma) behind the site of the later church.

### ACCOMMODATION AND EATING                                    ZAKHLOROÚ

**Romantzo** ☎ 26920 22758, ✉ hotel-romantzo @yahoo.gr. Traditional stone and wood, this hotel has en-suite rooms and pretty well lives up to its name, in a rustic sort of way. Since this is also something of a ski resort, there's a taverna here, too. Breakfast included. €40

## Kalávryta

Despite its beautiful position amid gorgeous greenery at the end of the little train line, with Mount Helmós as a backdrop, **KALÁVRYTA** retains an air of both melancholy and poignancy due to its tragic history during World War II. On December 13, 1943, the town's German occupiers shot the entire male population over the age of twelve and set fire to the town, killing around 700 in reprisal for partisan activity. By the end of the war, the local death toll had risen to around 1200.

Greeks come here out of a sense of patriotic pilgrimage – it's crowded with school parties during the week and with families at weekends – and the attitude to foreigners is business-like rather than overtly friendly. Still, the town tries hard to generate a resort feel, everything's well turned out, with lots of souvenir shops and cafés and restaurants, and from here there's a winding scenic road of 10km north to Méga Spiléou and on to the coast, as well as a road deep into Arcadia in the other direction.

### Remembrance sights and shrines

The first and last sight you're likely to encounter is a mural, opposite the train station, that reads: "Kalávryta, founding member of the Union of Martyred Towns, appeals to all to fight for world peace." The left clocktower on the central church stands fixed at 2.34pm – the hour of the massacre. In the old primary school is the **Museum of the**

**Sacrifice of the People of Kalávryta** (daily 9am–4pm; free), while outside of town is a shrine to those massacred, with the single word "Peace" (*Iríni*), as well as the historically significant **Ayías Lávras monastery**.

Ayías Lávras Monastery

The tenth-century **monastery of Ayías Lávras** (open roughly 8am–1pm, 4–6pm), 6km southwest of Kalávryta, was the site where Yermanos, Archbishop of Pátra, raised the flag to signal the **War of Independence**. Destroyed in World War II, it has been rebuilt and features a small historical museum.

**2**

## ARRIVAL AND DEPARTURE                                    KALÁVRYTA

**By bus** Athens (1–2 daily; 3hr 30min); Pátra (4 daily; 2hr).   3.50pm, but confirm that upon arrival).
**By train** Last train back to the coast (currently leaves at

## ACCOMMODATION AND EATING

f you miss the last train out, there are several hotels here, open all year since the town is something of a ski resort. There are several adequate restaurants around the square as well as on the main pedestrian drag.

**Filoxenia** Ethnikís Andístasis 20 **☎** 26920 22422, 🌐 hotelfiloxenia.gr. This is a rather chalet-like hotel and a bit luxurious, with good amenities, including wi-fi and winter pluses such as a hammam, sauna and Jacuzzi. Breakfast included. **€60**

**Stani ☎** 26920 23000. Located off the main platía, this taverna has a quieter, less touristy atmosphere than most and good, mostly grilled, main dishes, along with all the fresh produce from the countryside to your table. About €15–20/person. Daily lunch & dinner.

# The central mainland

**200** Delphi and Stereá Elládha

**221** The Pelion peninsula

**232** Lárissa and around

**235** The Metéora

**242** The Píndhos Mountains

**254** The west coast

THE METÉORA

# The central mainland

The central mainland of Greece has long been thought of as the Greek heartland, the zone first liberated from the Turks. In fact, its most central province Stereá Elládha means literally "Greek Continent". For the visitor its most stellar attractions are the site of the ancient oracle at DELPHI, and, further north, the other-worldly rock-pinnacle monasteries of METÉORA. Close to Delphi is Ósios Loukás monastery – containing the finest Byzantine mosaics in the country – and, to the south, the pleasant port resorts of Galaxídhi and Náfpaktos along the north shore of the Gulf of Kórinthos.

North of Delphi is the vast agricultural plain of **Thessaly**, dotted with mostly drab market and industrial towns, but also boasting the mountainous **Pelion peninsula**, with its enticing villages, beaches and hiking options. On the east side of Thessaly lie the remote monasteries of the Metéora and the imposing **Píndhos Mountains** which once formed the barrier with the eastern province of **Epirus**, the last region to shake off Turkish rule. The Píndhos range makes for scenic hiking opportunities and features the dramatic **Víkos Gorge**, reputedly Europe's deepest. The Epirot capital, lakeside **Ioánnina**, still evokes an exotic past. Nearby lies ancient **Dodóna**, the majestic site of Greece's first oracle, presided over by Zeus. Finally, the **west coast** is sprinkled with some good beaches and resorts along the Ionian Sea, as well as with more historic sites from every epoch. With your own transport (highly recommended) and careful planning, you can take in the central mainland's main sights and pleasures in a couple of weeks.

# Delphi and Stereá Elládha

The inevitable magnet of the central province of **Stereá Elládha** is **Delphi**, 175km northwest of Athens. If you have your own transport, there are ample rewards in approaching it along the old road to **Thebes**, and you could also easily include the Byzantine monastery of **Ósios Loukás**. Legendary **Mount Parnassós** above Delphi offers skiing and walking opportunities depending on the season, while to the south, on the **Gulf of Kórinthos**, the port towns of **Galaxídhi** and **Náfpaktos** are good for a seaside sojourn. Further east, **Áyios Konstandínos** provides access to the island of Évvia, while heading inland brings you to Lamía and the mountainous **Karpeníssi Valley**.

## The Oedipus Road to Thebes (Thíva)

The ancient road from Athens to Delphi began at the Parthenon as the **Sacred Way to Eleusis**, climbing northwest from there towards Thebes. You can follow this route, almost

| | |
|---|---|
| The myth of Oedipus p.204 | Metéora activities p.237 |
| The world's soothsayer p.205 | The Katára pass p.242 |
| Hiking to the Corycian Cave p.208 | The Vlachs p.243 |
| Skiing on Parnassós p.212 | Ali Pasha – the Lion of Ioánnina p.246 |
| The Battle of Lepanto p.215 | Sweet treats in Ioánnina p.247 |
| Climbing Mount Kaliakoúdha p.221 | The oak tree oracle p.249 |
| Pelion legends and food p.226 | Hiking the Víkos Gorge p.251 |
| The Pelion trenáki p.229 | Byron in Mesolóngi p.260 |

DELPHI

# Highlights

**❶ Delphi** Once home to the famous oracle, these spectacularly set ruins were believed in ancient times to be the centre of the earth. **See p.204**

**❷ Ósios Loukás** A splendidly positioned Byzantine monastery with vivid eleventh-century mosaics. **See p.211**

**❸ Galaxídhi** The best-preserved settlement on the Gulf of Kórinthos, one of Greece's major ports in the nineteenth century. **See p.213**

**❹ Náfpaktos** A bustling resort with a stage-set old harbour and swooping castle walls. **See p.215**

**❺ The Pelion** The mythical home of the centaurs offers hiking trails linking mansion-filled villages clinging to wooded hillsides, as well as fine beaches. **See p.221**

**❻ The Metéora** Meaning "rocks in the air"; mind-boggling scenery and exquisite Byzantine monasteries. **See p.235**

**❼ Ioánnina** The Ottoman citadel, lakefront and island associated with locally infamous hero/villain Ali Pasha. **See p.244**

**❽ Víkos Gorge** One of the longest and deepest in Europe and a worthy rival to its Cretan counterpart. **See p.250**

**HIGHLIGHTS ARE MARKED ON THE MAP ON P.202**

# THE CENTRAL MAINLAND

ALBANIA

MACEDONIA

*Kastoriá*

*Mt Grámmos (2520m)*

Plikáti

Siátista

Samarína

*Mt Smólikas (2637m)*

Kerásovo

Dhístrato

**Vassilítsa**

Grevená

*River Aliákmonas*

Kónitsa

*Aóös River*

**PÍNDHOS**

Vovoússa

Pápingo

*Mt Gamíla (2497m)*

Tsepélovo

**VÁLIA KÁLDA**

**Vikos Gorge** ⑧

Monodhéndri

Kípi

Miliotádhes

*Katára Pass*

⑥

**ZAGÓRI**

*Mt Mitsikéli*

† **Metéora**

Kastráki

Kalambáka

Zítsa

Pérama

Lynkiádhes

Métsovo

Dholianá

Dhiává

Konispol

**PÍNDHOS MOUNTAINS**

Ravení

*Pamvótidha*

Matsoúki

Halíki

Kraniá

† **Timíou Stavroú**

Kokkinolithári

Ioánnina

⑦

*Mt Kóziakas*

Pertoúli

Tr

Filiátes

Syrráko

Kallarítes

**Brindisi, Bari, Ancona & Venice**

*Corfu*

Igoumenítsa

Melissourgí

**TRIA POTÁMIA**

Eláti

Pláka

Stournaréika

*Corfu*

Plataria

**EPIRUS**

**Dodona** ∴

Paramythiá

Prámanda

*Arakhthos River*

Ágnanda

Mesahóra

Pýli

† **Pórta Panayia**

Lefkími

*Karavostási*

**SOÚLI**

*Mt Tzoumérka (2393m)*

*Loúros River*

Pláka

*Sarakiniko*

Anthoússa

**† Ayiá**

**Párga**

Glykí

*Ahérondas River*

**AGRAFA MOUNTAINS**

*Lýkhnos*

**Nekromanteion of Acheron**

Trikastro

*Axelóös River*

*Paxí*

*Gáios*

Ammoudhiá

Mesopótamos

**† Pylés Adhi**

Kanalláki

Vráhou

Filipiádha

**Kassope** ∴

Árta

Koronissía

*Kremastón Dam*

**Rodhía Wetland Centre**

Kanáli

**Nikopolis** ∴

Menídhi

Kréndis

Fourn

*Mt Tymfristós (2312m)*

Mýtikas

Préveza

*Amvrakikós Gulf*

Frangísta

*Mt Helidhóna (1973m)*

Karp

Áktio

**IONIAN SEA**

Vónitsa

*Kremastón Reservoir*

Mikró Horió

Korysh

Gávros

Áyios Nikólaos

*Mt Kau (2098*

Lefkádha

Páleros

Amfilohía

*Áyios Vlássios*

**Proussoú †**

Proussós

**PANETOLIKÓ**

*Lefkádha*

Néa Playiá

**ÉTOLO-AKARNANÍA**

Nydhrí

Mýtikas

Kallithéa

Vassilikí

*Kálamos*

Hóra

*Lake Ozerós*

Ágrinio

*Lake Trihonídha*

Thérmo

**Thermon**

*Ithákì*

Fiskárdho

Fríkes

Astakós

*Lake Trihonídha*

Évinos

*River*

*Áxelóös River*

Ássos

Vathý

**Oeniadae** ∴

Katohí

Etolikó

**Pleuron** ∴

Háni

Baniás

Náfpakto

*Kefaloniá*

**Kalydon** ∴

④

Mesolóngi

Tourlídha

**SUSPENSION BRIDGE**

Andírio

Sámi

Río

Argostóli

**Pátra**

**PELOPONN**

N

0 — 25 kilometres

**HIGHLIGHTS**
1. Delphi
2. Ósios Loukás
3. Galaxídhi
4. Náfpaktos
5. The Pelion
6. The Metéora
7. Ioánnina
8. Víkos Gorge

Flórina
Thessaloníki
Katerini
Pláka Litohórou
Mt Olympus (2917m)
Litóhoro
Platamónas
Hasan Baba Tekkés
Kástro tís Oreás
Stómio
Karytsa
VALE OF TÉMBI
Ambelákia
Kókkino Neró
Mt Óssa (1978m)
Melívia
Velika
Lárissa
Polydhéndhri
Véneto

AEGEAN SEA

THESSALY
Fársala
Tekkés Farsálon
Sesklo
Dimíni
Néa Anhíalos
Almyrós
Zagorá
Vólos
Mt Pelion (Pílio) (1651m)
Tsangarádha
Miliés
Argalastí
PELION PENINSULA
Pagasitic Gulf
Platanías
Trikeri
Koukounariés
Skiáthos
Skiáthos
Glóssa
Skópelos
Hóra

Loutrá Ipátis
Ipáti
Lianokládhi
Ayía Marína
Stylídha
Paralía Rahón
Glyfá
Gorgopótamos
Lámia
Loutrá Thermopylíon
Karavómylos
Áyiókambos
Loutrá Edhipsoú
Límni
Mt Íti (2152m)
Pávliani
Thermopylae
Áyios Yeóryios
Arkítsa
Évvia

Iardhoússsa (2495m)
Mt Gióna (2454m)
Graviá
Lílea
Amfíklia
Káto Tithoréa
Áno Tithoréa
Kaména Voúrla
Áyios Konstandínos
Gulf of Évvia
STEREÁ ELLÁDHA
Lidhoríki
Eptálofos
Delphi
Mt Parnassós (2457m)
Herónia
Orchomenos
Glas
Kástro
Halkídha
Ámfissa
Dhelfí
Aráhova
Chaeronea
Orhomenós
Lake Ylíki
Lake Paralímni
Mornos
Khrissó
Dhístomo
Stíri
Livadhiá
Itéa
Galaxídhi
Kambláki
Ósios Loukás
Áyios Nikólaos
Ayíi Pándes
Eratiní
Thíva (Thebes)
Gulf of Kórinthos
Athens
Pórto Yermenó
Eleutherai
Psátha
Aegosthena
Athens

## THE MYTH OF OEDIPUS

Pausanias identified the fateful Triodos crossroads as the site of Oedipus's murder of his father, King Laius of Thebes. As the tale recounts, Oedipus was returning on foot from Delphi while Laius and his entourage were speeding towards him from the opposite direction on a chariot. Neither would give way, and in the ensuing altercation Oedipus killed them, ignorant of who they were. It was, in Pausanias's supreme understatement, "the beginning of his troubles". Continuing on to Thebes, Oedipus solved the riddle of the Sphinx – which had been ravaging the area – and took widowed Queen Jocasta as his wife – unaware that he was marrying his own mother.

unchanged since Oedipus supposedly trod it, by taking the minor road, signposted for "Mándhra", north off the motorway at modern Elefsína, leaving that polluted, chaotic port behind. Matters quickly improve, as the road winds up through an evocative landscape of pines and stony hills, becoming ever more striking as Mount Parnassós and its outriders loom overhead. After 22km, about halfway to Delphi, you reach the vicinity of the **Triodos** (Triple Way) or **Oedipus junction**, intersection of the ancient roads from Delphi, Daulis (today Dhávlia), Thebes (Thíva) and Ambrossos (modern Dhístomo).

# Delphi (Dhelfí)

Daily: summer 8am–8pm; winter 8.30am–3pm • €9 joint ticket Sacred Precinct and museum

It's easy to understand why the ancients considered **DELPHI** the centre of the earth, especially given their penchant for awe-inspiring sacred spots. Framed on all sides by the soaring crags of Parnassós, the site truly captures the imagination, especially in spring, when wildflowers cloak the precipitous valley. But more than a stunning setting was needed to confirm the divine presence. Sanctity, according to Plutarch, was confirmed through the discovery of a rock chasm that exuded strange vapours and reduced supplicants to incoherent – and undoubtedly **prophetic** – mutterings.

## ARRIVAL AND DEPARTURE
DELPHI

**By bus** There are 6 buses daily from Athens to Delphi, so it is conceivable to visit Delphi as a day-trip, although it makes for a very long day of at least 5–6 hours on the road. Also, you need to be sure to buy a return ticket, as the number of Athens-bound seats allocated to be sold at the Dhelfí ticket booth is limited and they sell out quickly.

**By car** As with buses, doing Delphi as a day-trip by car from Athens means spending hours on the road so on the whole it's best to spend a night in the vicinity.

Moving on from Delphi, the E75/N1 motorway barrels north towards the Pelion, skirting the coast part of the way, with Évvia visible just across the gulf. Another road leads southwest along the scenic Gulf of Kórinthos through Galaxídhi and Náfpaktos, with an optional link to the Peloponnese over the Andírio–Río bridge. A third, more remote, route leads west to mountainous Karpeníssi and then across the southernmost extensions of the Píndhos Mountains.

## INFORMATION

**Site layout** Delphi is divided by the Aráhova road into three adjacent sites: the Sacred Precinct, the Castalian spring and the Marmaria. There's also a well-lit and helpfully labelled museum. The museum and the sites are a pleasant stroll from the modern village. The attractions are best seen in two stages, covering the sanctuary ideally at the beginning or end of the day, or (in winter) at lunchtime,

to escape the coached-in crowds.

**Practicalities** At the main site itself, lots of clambering up rough stone steps and paths means you should wear sturdy shoes and bring a water bottle. There are cafés at the museum and the Castalian spring, the latter with terrace seating and panoramic views.

## Brief history

The **first oracle** established here was dedicated to Gaia ("Mother Earth") and Poseidon ("Earth Shaker"). The serpent Python, son of Gaia, dwelt in a nearby chasm, and communicated through the Pythian priestess. Python was later slain by young Apollo,

**DELPHI: THE SITES**

who supposedly arrived in the form of a dolphin – hence the name Delphi. Thereafter, the **Pythian Games** were held periodically in commemoration, and perhaps also to placate the deposed deities. Delphi subsequently became one of the major sanctuaries of Greece, its oracle widely regarded as the most truthful in the known world.

The **influence** of the oracle spread during the Classical age of colonization and its patronage grew, peaking during the sixth century BC, with benefactors such as King Amasis of Egypt and the hapless King Croesus of Lydia. Delphi's wealth, however, made it vulnerable to Greek rivalries; by the mid-fifth century BC, the oracle became the object of a struggle between Athens, Phokia and Sparta, prompting a series of **Sacred Wars**. These culminated in Philip of Macedon invading southern Greece, crushing the city-states in 338 BC at the **Battle of Chaeronea** (see p.213). Delphi's political intriguing was effectively over.

Under **Macedonian** and later **Roman** rule, the oracle's role became increasingly domestic, dispensing advice on marriages, loans, voyages and the like. The Romans thought little of its utterances, rather more of its treasure: Sulla plundered the sanctuary in 86 BC, and Nero, outraged when the oracle denounced him for murdering his mother, carted away five hundred bronze statues. Upon the proscription of paganism by Theodosius in 391 AD, the oracle ceased.

## THE WORLD'S SOOTHSAYER

For over a millennium, a steady stream of pilgrims converged on Delphi to seek divine direction in matters of war, worship, love or business. On arrival they would pay a set fee (the *pelanos*), sacrifice a goat, boar or even a bull, and – depending on the omens – wait to submit questions inscribed on lead tablets. The Pythian priestess, a village woman over fifty years of age, would chant her prophecies from a tripod positioned over the oracular chasm. An attendant priest would then "interpret" her utterings in hexameter verse.

Many **oracular answers** were pointedly ambiguous: Croesus, for example, was told that if he commenced war against Persia he would destroy a mighty empire; he did – his own. But the oracle would hardly have retained its popularity for so long without offering predominantly sound advice, largely because the Delphic priests were better informed than any others of the time. They were able to amass a wealth of political, economic and social information and, from the seventh century BC onwards, had their own network of agents throughout the Greek world.

The sanctuary site was rediscovered towards the end of the seventeenth century and explored haphazardly from 1838 onwards; systematic **excavation** began only in 1892 when the French School of Archeology leased the land. There was initially little to be seen other than the outline of a stadium and theatre, but the inhabitants of Kastrí village, set amid the ruins, were evicted to a new town 1km west (now modern Dhelfí), and digging commenced. By 1903, most of the excavations and reconstruction visible today had been completed.

## The Sacred Precinct

The **Sacred Precinct**, or Temenos (Sanctuary) of Apollo, is entered – as in ancient times – by way of a small **agora** enclosed by ruins of Roman porticoes and shops selling votive offerings. The paved **Sacred Way** begins after a few stairs, zigzagging uphill between the foundations of memorials and treasuries to the Temple of Apollo. Along each edge is a jumble of statue bases where gold, bronze and painted-marble figures once stood; Pliny counted more than three thousand on his visit, and that was after Nero's infamous raid.

The style and positioning of these **memorials** were dictated by more than religious zeal; many were used as a deliberate show of strength or as a direct insult against a rival Greek state. For instance, the Spartans celebrated their victory over Athens by erecting their **Monument of the Admirals** – a large recessed structure, which once held 37 bronze statues of gods and generals – directly opposite the Athenians' **Offering of Marathon**.

Further up the path, past the Doric remains of the **Sikyonian Treasury** on the left, lie the foundations of the **Siphnian Treasury**, a grandiose Ionic temple erected in 525 BC. Ancient Siphnos (Sífnos) had rich gold mines and intended the building to be an unrivalled show of opulence. Above this is the **Treasury of the Athenians**, built, like the city's "offering", after Marathon (490 BC). It was reconstructed in 1904–1906 by matching the inscriptions – including a hymn to Apollo with musical notation – that completely cover its blocks.

Next to the Treasury are the foundations of the **Bouleuterion**, or council house, a reminder that Delphi needed administrators, and above stretches the remarkable **Polygonal Wall** whose irregular interlocking blocks have withstood, intact, all earthquakes. It, too, is covered with inscriptions, mostly referring to the emancipation of slaves; Delphi was one of the few places where such freedom could be made official by an inscribed register. An incongruous outcrop of rock between the wall and the treasuries marks the original **Sanctuary of Gaia**.

Finally, the Sacred Way leads past the **Athenian Stoa** (which housed trophies from an Athenian naval victory of 506 BC) to the temple terrace where you are confronted with a large altar, erected by the island of Chios (Híos). The **Temple of Apollo** now visible dates from the mid-fourth century BC, two previous versions having succumbed to fire and earthquake. The French excavators found only foundations, but re-erected six of the Doric columns to illustrate the temple's dominance over the sanctuary. In the innermost part of the temple was the *adyton*, a subterranean cell at the mouth of the oracular chasm where the Pythian priestess officiated. No trace of cave or chasm has been found, nor any trance-inducing vapours, but it's conceivable that such a chasm did exist and was closed by later earthquakes. On the architrave of the temple were inscribed the maxims "Know Thyself" and "Moderation in All Things".

The theatre and stadium used for the main events of the Pythian Festival occupy terraces above the temple. The **theatre**, built during the fourth century BC with a capacity of five thousand (the seats sadly roped off), was associated with Dionysos, the god of ecstasy, the arts and wine, who ruled Delphi during the winter when the oracle was silent. A path leads up through cool pine groves to the **stadium** (its seats also off-limits), artificially levelled in the fifth century BC to a length of

178m, though it was banked with stone seats (giving a capacity of seven thousand) only in Roman times – the gift, like so many other public buildings in Greece, of Herodes Atticus.

## The Castalian spring

Following the road east of the sanctuary, towards Aráhova, you reach a sharp bend. Just to the left, marked by niches for votive offerings and by the remains of an Archaic

DELPHI: THE SACRED PRECINCT

Temenos of Dionysos

Theatre

Stage

Temenos of Poseidon

Sacred Way

Altar of Apollo

Temple of Apollo

Sacred Way

Terrace

Polygonal Wall

Sanctuary of Gaia

Athenian Stoa

Bouleuterion

Sacred Way

Treasury of the Athenians

Monument of the Admirals

Theban Treasury

Siphnian Treasury

Sacred Way

Main Entrance

Sikyonian Treasury

Offering of the Arcadians

Offering of Marathon

0 20 metres

fountain-house, the celebrated **Castalian spring** still flows from a cleft – the legendary lair of Python.

Visitors to Delphi were obliged to **purify** themselves in its waters, usually by washing their hair, though murderers had to take the full plunge. **Lord Byron**, impressed by the legend that the waters nurtured poetic inspiration, also jumped in. This is no longer possible, since the spring is fenced off owing to sporadic rock falls from the cliffs.

### The Marmaria
Same opening time as main sanctuary, but visits allowed until sunset • Free

Across and below the road from the spring is the **Marmaria** (*marmariá* means "marble quarry", after the medieval practice of filching the ancient blocks for private use).

The most conspicuous building in the precinct, easily visible from the road, is the **Tholos**, a fourth-century BC rotunda. Three of its dome-columns and their entablature have been rebuilt, but while these amply demonstrate the original beauty of the building (which is *the* postcard image of Delphi), its purpose remains a mystery.

**3**

## HIKING TO THE CORYCIAN CAVE

The **Corycian Cave** (Korýkio Ándro) plays a significant part in Delphi mythology, since it was sacred to Pan and the nymphs, and they were the presiding deities of the oracle during winter, when Apollo abandoned the spot.

Allow a full day for this outing (4hr for ascent to cave, 3hr 30min back to Dhelfí – consult *The Mountains of Greece*; see "Books" p.806), and take ample food. To reach the **trailhead** follow signposting up through Dhelfí village to the *Museum of Delphic Festivals*. Continue climbing from here to the highest point of the fence enclosing the sanctuary ruins. Where the track ends at a gate, take a trail on your left, initially marked by a black-and-yellow rectangle on a white background; these, repeated regularly, indicate the trail is part of the **E4 European long-distance route**.

Initially steep, the way soon flattens out on a grassy knoll overlooking the stadium, and continues along a ridge. Soon after, you join an ancient cobbled trail coming from inside the fenced precinct, the **Kakí Skála**, which zigzags up the slope above you in broad arcs. The path ends an hour-plus above the village, at the top of the **Phaedriades** cliffs. From one of several nearby rock pinnacles those guilty of sacrilege in ancient times were thrown to their deaths – a custom perhaps giving rise to the name Kakí Skála or "Evil Stairway".

E4 markers remain visible in the valley ahead of you as the principal route becomes a gravel track bearing northeast; ignore this and follow instead a metal sign pointing toward the cave, taking the right fork near the **Krokí spring** and watering troughs, with a complex of summer cottages on your right. This track, now intermittently paved, passes a picnic ground and a chapel of Ayía Paraskeví within fifteen minutes. Continue for some forty minutes beyond the chapel, heading gently downhill and passing another sign for the cave, until you emerge from the fir woods (2hr 40min from Dhelfí) with a view east and ahead to the rounded mass of the Yerondóvrahos peak (2367m) of the Parnassós massif.

Another fifteen minutes bring you to a second chapel (of Ayía Triádha) on the left, with a spring and picnic ground. To the left rises a steep ridge, site of the ancient **Corycian cave**. Persevere along the road for five more minutes to where a white bilingual sign indicates a newer path, marked by orange paint splodges and red-triangle signs. After forty minutes' climb on this, you meet another dirt road; turn left and follow it five minutes more to the end, just below the conspicuous cave mouth at an altitude of 1370m.

In ancient times, the cave was the site of orgiastic rites in November, when women, acting as nymphs, made the long hike up from Delphi on the Kakí Skála by torchlight. If you look carefully with a torch you can find **ancient inscriptions** near the entrance; without artificial light you can't see more than 100m into the chilly, forbidding cavern. By the entrance you'll also notice a rock with a man-made circular indentation – possibly an ancient altar for libations.

At the entrance to the precinct stood the original **Temple of Athena Pronaia** ("Fore-Temple", in relation to the Apollo shrine), destroyed by the Persians and reconstructed during the fourth century BC beyond the Tholos; foundations of both structures can be traced. Outside the precinct on the northwest side (above the Marmaria) is a **gymnasium**, again built in the fourth century BC, but later enlarged by the Romans; prominent among the ruins is a circular plunge-bath for athletes' refreshment after their exertions.

## The museum

Delphi's **museum** contains a rare and exquisite collection of sculpture spanning the Archaic to the Roman eras, matched only by finds on Athens' Acropolis. It also features pottery, bronze articles and friezes from the various treasuries and temple pediments, which give a good picture of the sanctuary's riches.

The most famous exhibit, with a room to itself at the south end of the galleries, is the **Charioteer**, one of the few surviving bronzes of the fifth century BC, unearthed in 1896 as part of the "Offering of Polyzalos", toppled during the earthquake of 373 BC. The charioteer's eyes, made of onyx and set slightly askew, lend it a startling realism. Other major pieces include two huge **kouroi** from the sixth century BC, betraying clear Asiatic/Egyptian stylistic traits; a life-size, sixth-century BC votive **bull** fashioned from hammered silver and copper sheeting; and the elegant Ionic winged **Sphinx of the Naxians**, dating from 565 BC. In the same gallery, the **Siphnian frieze** depicts Zeus and other gods looking on as the Homeric heroes fight over the body of Patroclus. Another portion of this frieze shows a battle between gods and giants, including a lion graphically mauling a warrior.

The **Athenian Treasury** is represented by fragments of the **metopes** (friezes) depicting the labours of Hercules, the adventures of Theseus and a battle with Amazons. A group of three colossal if badly damaged **dancing women**, carved from Pentelic marble around an acanthus-topped column – probably a tripod-stand – dates from the fourth century BC and is thought to represent the daughters of Kekrops. Among later works is an exquisite second-century AD figure of **Antinoös**, favourite of Roman emperor Hadrian.

## Modern Dhelfí

**Modern Dhelfí**, 500m to the west of the site, is as inconsequential as its ancient namesake is impressive. Entirely geared to mass tourism (including Greek skiers), Dhelfí's only real attraction – besides proximity to the ruins and access to Mount Parnassós (see p.212) – is its cliffside setting.

### Museum of Delphic Festivals

Thu–Mon 9am–2.30pm • €2

The stone house where the poet **Angelos Sikelianos** once lived exhibits artefacts and paraphernalia relating to the events he and Eva Palmer organized in 1927–30. Their idea was to set up a "University of the World" and make Delphi a cultural centre. The project eventually failed, though it inspired an annual **Delphic Festival**, held now in July of each year, with performances of contemporary drama and music in the ancient theatre.

---

**ARRIVAL AND INFORMATION** **DHELFÍ**

**By bus** There's a single KTEL bus terminal at the Itéa (west) end of town, where the upper and lower commercial streets link up. Westbound buses go to Ámfissa (for onward connections north), Itéa and (usually with a change) on to Náfpaktos, while eastbound services go to Aráhova and on to Athens. The main problem, since all coaches originate elsewhere, is that seats allocated for the Dhelfí ticket booth are limited and sell out quickly.

Destinations Athens (6 daily; 3hr); Ámfissa (6 daily; 30min); Arahóva (6 daily; 20min); Galaxídhi (3 daily;

3

45min); Itéa (3 daily; 30min); Lamía (2 daily; 2hr); Náfpaktos (4 daily; 3hr); Pátra (1 daily; 4hr; also connections via Itéa).
**Tourist office** In the town hall on lower main thoroughfare Vassiléos Pavloú kéh Fridheríkis (Mon–Fri

7.30am–2.30pm, Sat 8am–2pm; ☎ 22650 82900).
**Services** Vassiléos Pavloú kéh Fridheríkis has several bank ATMs, a post office and a number of bar-cafés, at least one of which will be offering internet access.

## ACCOMMODATION

Staying in the modern town is not particularly enticing, but given the quick visitor turnover and over twenty **hotels** and **pensions**, finding a vacancy should present few problems. To take advantage of the town's position, ask for a room with a view. Most hotels here, as throughout Greece, now have wi-fi. As an alternative to overly touristy Dhelfí or Aráhova, Galaxídhi, just down on the sea (see p. 000), is highly recommended, if you have your own transport. There are two notable **campsites** in the immediate area, both of them just west of Dhelfí.

### HOTELS AND GUESTHOUSES

**Acropole** Filellínon 13 ☎ 22650 82675, ⓦ delphi.com .gr. On the quietest, lowest street of the village, with unbeatable views out back over the Plistós Gorge, this hotel's rooms feature marble dresser tops, and there are three attic rooms with fireplace. The small bathrooms are a weak point; it's also a good idea to book a triple as a double. Good buffet breakfast. **€65**

**Athina** Pávlou ké Fredheríkis 55 ☎ 22650 82239, ⓕ 22650 82239. Near the bus station at the west end of town, this hotel has wood decor, well-kept if smallish rooms, mostly en suite, and views of the gulf from rear rooms. Closed Nov–Christmas and weekdays Christmas– end March. Breakfast included. **€40**

**Orfeas** Ifiyenías Syngroú 35 ☎ 22650 82077, ⓔ zdroserou@hol.gr. Rooms are spacious and well maintained, the top floor recently redone, with superb views and a/c. Better-than-average parking, with other amenities such as a garden, free wi-fi and a/c; discount to Rough Guide readers. Breakfast included. **€40**

**Pan** Pávlou ké Fredheríkis 53 ☎ 22650 82294, ⓦ panartemis.gr. All rooms, including attic quads, are well appointed, with a/c and bathrooms with tubs; balconies have fine views to the gulf. Immediately opposite is the annexe, the *Artemis*, with rooms of equal standard, but you sacrifice views. Breakfast included. **€65**

**Sibylla** Pávlou ké Fredheríkis 9 ☎ 22650 82335,

ⓦ sibylla-hotel.gr. Come here for clean, bright, recently refurbished furnishings in small-to-medium-sized en-suite rooms; there are fans rather than a/c, but some balconies overlook the gorge, all the way down to the gulf. Breakfast included. **€40**

★ **Varonos** Vasileos Pavlou 25 ☎ 22650 82345, ⓦ hotel-delphi.com. Family run and very friendly, many consider this the best option in town. Comfort and cosiness are the emphasis, with rooms done in honey tones. Views down to the sea are spectacular from the balconies of some of the 18 rooms. Free wi-fi. Substantial buffet breakfast included. **€60**

### CAMPSITES

**Apollon Camping** 1.5km west along the road to Itéa ☎ 22650 82762, ⓦ apolloncamping.gr. This beautifully positioned site, with breathtaking views, has a pool, restaurant and a minimarket, free transfers to Delphi, wi-fi, playground, and it's open all year. Self-catering bungalows **€50**

**Delphi Camping** 4km west of town on the Dhelfí/Itéa road ☎ 22650 82209, ⓦ delphicamping.com. This woodsy facility with mountain and sea views offers an on-site taverna, bar, minimarket, pool, tennis court, hot showers, a playground and wi-fi. Credit cards accepted. April–Sept. **€30**

## EATING AND DRINKING

Restaurants are not a Dhelfí strong point, despite being packed with skiers in winter. Still, most visitors are likely to have at least one meal here, so go for the places with views.

**Epikouros** Pávlou ké Fredheríkis 33 ☎ 22650 83250, ⓦ epikouros.net. Unparalleled views down to the gulf, and classic, adequately prepared Greek dishes elegantly presented make a meal here a pleasure. Appetizers and salads €4–7, main dishes €10–12. Very welcoming place, with an adjacent balcony bar for breakfast or just coffee. Daily lunch & dinner.

**Skala** Isaia 11 ☎ 22650 82762. Take the steps (*skala*) up

from nearby hotel *Sibylla*, for cheap and honest family taverna food: tsatziki, dolmades, grills and stews; main dishes €7–10. Daily lunch & dinner.

**Vakhos** Apollonos 31 ☎ 22650 83186. This typical family-run, atmospheric taverna specializes in local dishes, including some fish, and Greek wines; main dishes €7–10. Free wi-fi. Daily lunch & dinner.

# Ósios Loukás monastery

Daily: May 3–Sept 15 8am–6pm; rest of year 8am–5pm • €3

Some 6km east of Dhístomo (which by bus is 35min east of Delphi), the **monastery of Ósios Loukás** was a precursor of the final flourish of **Byzantine art** found in the great churches at Mystra in the Peloponnese (see p.167). From an architectural or decorative standpoint it ranks as one of the great buildings of medieval Greece; the remote setting is exquisite as well, especially in February when the many local almond trees bloom. Approaching along the last stretch of road, Ósios Loukás suddenly appears on its shady terrace, overlooking the highest summits of the Elikónas range and a beautiful broad valley. The complex comprises two domed churches, the larger **katholikón** of Ósios Loukás (a local beatified hermit, Luke of Stiri, not the Evangelist) and the adjacent chapel of **Theotókos**. A few monks still live in the cells around the courtyard, but the monastery is essentially a museum, with a souvenir shop on the grounds.

## ARRIVAL AND INFORMATION                                                   ÓSIOS LOUKÁS

**By bus** There are hourly daily buses from Dhelfí to Dhístomo (it's on the Livadhiá – Athens line; 35min), but nothing on to Stíri, the village 3.5km west of the monastery (the last 2.5km on a spur road), so you might have to walk, take a taxi or hitch.

**Monastery Shop** Besides selling souvenirs, this shop offers sandwiches and dozens of varieties of typically Greek sesame-based snacks. There are tables and chairs on the beautiful terrace, so you can take in the sweeping view while you refresh yourself.

## The katholikón

The design of the **katholikón**, built around 1040 to a cross-in-square plan, strongly influenced later churches at Dhafní and at Mystra. Externally it is unassuming, with rough brick-and-stone walls topped by a well-proportioned octagonal dome. The interior, however, is rich, with multicoloured-marble walls contrasting with gold-background mosaics on the high ceiling. Light filtering through alabaster windows reflects from the curved mosaic surfaces onto the marble walls and back, bringing out subtle shading.

The **mosaics** were damaged by an earthquake in 1659, replaced at many points by unremarkable frescoes, but surviving examples testify to their glory. On the right as you enter the narthex are a majestic *Resurrection* and *Thomas Probing Christ's Wound*. The mosaic of the *Niptir* (*Washing of the Apostles' Feet*) on the far left (north side) of the narthex is one of the finest here, the expressions of the Apostles ranging between diffidence and surprise. This humanized approach is again illustrated by the *Baptism*, up in the northwest squinch (curved surface supporting the dome). Here Jesus reaches for the cross amid a swirling mass of water, an illusion of depth created by the curvature of the wall. On other squinches, the Christ Child reaches out to the High Priest Simeon in *The Presentation*, while in *The Nativity*, angels predominate rather than the usual shepherds. The church's original **frescoes** are confined to vaulted chambers at the corners of the cross plan and, though less imposing than the mosaics, employ subtle colours, notably in *Christ Walking towards the Baptism*.

## The Theotókos chapel

The chapel of **Theotókos** ("God-Bearing", ie the Virgin Mary), built shortly after Luke's death, is nearly a century older than the *katholikón*. From outside it overshadows the main church with **elaborate brick decoration** culminating in a marble-panelled drum, but the interior seems mean by comparison, enlivened only by a couple of fine Corinthian capitals and the original floor mosaic, its colours now faint.

## The crypt

Finally, do not miss the vivid **frescoes** in the **crypt** of the *katholikón*, entered on the lower south side of the building. Bring a torch, since illumination is limited to three spotlights to preserve the colours of the post-Byzantine frescoes.

## Mount Parnassós and around

For a taste of the Greek mountains, **Parnassós**, rising imperiously above Delphi, is probably the most convenient peak, though its heights no longer rank as unspoilt wilderness, having been disfigured by the ski-station above **Aráhova** and its accompanying trappings. The best route for walkers is the one up from Dhelfí to the **Corycian cave** (practicable April–Nov, but not in midsummer without a dawn start; see box p.208). For further explorations, Road Editions' 1:50,000 **map** no. 42, or Anavasi Editions' 1:55,000 map no. 1, both entitled *Parnassos*, are wise investments, though neither is infallible.

### Aráhova

Arriving at **ARÁHOVA**, just 11km east of Delphi, you are well into Parnassós country. The peaks rise in tiers, sullied somewhat by the wide asphalt road built to reach the ski resort – the winter-weekend haunt of well-heeled Athenians. The town centre tends to trendy, chic and pricey, rather like a Greek Aspen, with its comprehensive après-ski boutique commercialization. A small number of houses in Aráhova retain their vernacular architecture or have been restored in varying taste, flanking narrow, often stepped, lanes twisting north up the slope or poised to the south on the edge of the olive-tree-choked Plistós Gorge. The area is renowned for its strong purplish wines, *tsípouro*, honey, candied fruits and nuts, cheese (especially cylindrical *formaélla*), the egg-rich noodles called *hilopíttes*, and woollen weavings, now mostly imported from elsewhere and/or machine-loomed.

### ARRIVAL AND INFORMATION
ARÁHOVA

**By bus** Buses pull in at a stop on the platía at the west end of town.
**Destinations** Athens (4 daily; about 3hr 30min); Dhelfí (4 daily; 20min).
**Tourist office** The municipal tourist office (Greek-signed

as DETPA; 9am–9pm; ☎ 22670 31630, ⓦ arachova.tripod .com) is close to the bus station.
**Services** The post office is a few paces from the bus stop. There are several bank ATMs, and wi-fi is available throughout the village.

### ACCOMMODATION

In the summer, most people just stop for a meal and to souvenir shop, so finding accommodation is easy, even though several establishments close down. In winter, particularly at weekends, rooms are at a premium in all senses, with prices more or less doubling.

**Apollon Inn** ☎ 22670 31057, ⓦ apollon-inn-arachova .gr. At the Delphi end of town, the last street to the right, stands this handsome though simple option whose pine and white-tiled en-suite rooms are rather spartan but spacious. **€35**

★ **Lykoreia** ☎ 22670 31180, ⓦ likoria.gr. Huge standard balconied doubles, plus a few suites, with designer baths and wi-fi. Other amenities include a terrace garden, pool, gym/ sauna and buffet breakfast served in the cosy salon; easy parking (it's 250m west from the main square). **€75**

---

### SKIING ON PARNASSÓS

There are two main **skiing** areas developed on the northwest flank of Mount Paranassós: **Keláría** (23km from Aráhova) and **Fterólakka** (29km). The top point for each is about 2200m, descending to 1600–1700m when conditions permit; the twenty or so runs are predominantly red-rated, making this a good intermediate resort, and served by fourteen lifts, of which about half are bubble-chair type. Most **facilities** (and the biggest car park) are at Keláría, but Fterólakka has longer, more challenging runs.

**Equipment** is rented on a daily basis at the resort, or for longer term in Aráhova (which teems with seasonal sports equipment shops). The main problem is high winds, which often close the lifts, so check the forecast before setting off. The skiing season is generally from mid-December to April, rarely into May.

**Maria Paradhosiakos Xenonas** ☎22670 31803, ⓦmariarooms.com. One of Aráhova's better restoration inns, occupying a pair of lovely old buildings in the village centre with an array of rustic mountain decor doubles, triples and quads. Breakfast not included. **€50**

**Pension Petrino** ☎22670 31384, ⓔpetrino @webtourists.com. Small stone-clad inn south of the through road with a basement breakfast salon; upstairs galleried rooms (sleeping four) are more exciting than the conventional ground-floor doubles. Breakfast included. **€45**

## EATING AND DRINKING

During summer, about half of Aráhova's restaurants and cafés shut, as do most of the bars, music clubs and sweet shops pitched at trendy local youth as well as visiting Athenians. More traditional *kafenío* and ouzerí tables on the main fountain-square attract an older crowd all year until late.

★ **Panayiota** ☎22670 32735. About 260 steps up behind Áyios Yeóryios church, you'll find comfy chairs and tables are set out under poplar and plane trees to take advantage of an unbeatable setting. The traditional cuisine is decent and well priced (€5–12 for main dishes). Service is good and there's usually a sweet offered on the house, in the Greek tradition. Daily lunch

& dinner; weekends only in summer.
**To Kalderimi** ☎22670 31418, ⓦtokalderimi.gr. Down from the main road, this atmospheric stone taverna is known for its traditional meaty stews, pies and assortment of local starters. Main dishes €6–10. Daily lunch & dinner; closed mid-July to mid-Aug.

## Chaeronea

Retracing the way back from Delphi and onto the Lamía road heading north, you come to **Chaeronea**, site of one of the most decisive **ancient Greek battles**. Here, in 338 BC, Philip of Macedon won a resounding victory over an alliance of Athenians, Peloponnesians and Thebans. This ended the era of city-states, from whom control passed forever into foreign hands: first Macedonian, later Roman. Beside the road, at modern **Herónia**, stands a 6m -high **stone lion**, said to have been erected by Alexander the Great to honour the **Theban Sacred Band**, composed entirely of **warrior couples**, who fought to the last man.

# Galaxídhi and around

**GALAXÍDHI** is a charming port town appearing mirage-like out of an otherwise lifeless shore along the Gulf of Kórinthos, just 35km from Delphi. With your own transport, it makes an ideal base for visiting both **Delphi** and **Ósios Loukás**, and it's also worth at least two days in its own right. Amazingly, given its size, Galaxídhi was once one of Greece's major harbours, with a fleet of over four hundred two- and three-masted *kaïkia* and schooners, trading as far afield as the UK. But shipowners failed to convert to steam power after 1890, and the town's prosperity vanished. Clusters of nineteenth-century shipowners' mansions, reminders of those heady days, reflect borrowings from Venice, testament to the sea captains' far-flung travels, and to their wealth. Despite some starts at gentrification, the town retains its authenticity, with an animated commercial high street (Nikólaou Máma) and a good range of places to eat and drink.

## The old town

The old town stands on a raised headland, crowned by the eighteenth-century church of Ayía Paraskeví (the old basilica, not the more obvious belfried Áyios Nikólaos, patron saint of sailors). With its protected double harbour, the location proved irresistible to early settlers, which explains stretches of walls – all that's left of **ancient Chaleion** and its successor **Oianthe** – between the two churches and the water on the headland dividing the two anchorages. What you see dates from 1830–70, as the town was largely destroyed during the War of Independence.

## Nautical and Historical Museum

Daily: June–Sept 10.10am–1.30pm & 5.30–8.30pm; Oct–May 10.10am–4.15pm • €5

Just uphill from the main harbour is the **Nautical and Historical Museum**, whose galleries do a well-labelled, clockwise gallop round this citadel-settlement in all eras. Ancient Chaleion is represented by painted pottery and a bronze folding mirror, then it's on to the chronicles of Galaxídhi – the place's name from Byzantine times onwards – and its half-dozen shipyards, mostly alongside the northwesterly Hirólakkas anchorage. The local two- and three-masters are followed from their birth – primitive, fascinating tools for ship building and sail-making – to their all-too-frequent sudden violent death. Along the way are propeller-operated logs, wooden rattles to signal the change of watches, a *bouroú* or large shell used as a foghorn and – best of all – superb polychrome figureheads.

## Beaches

Strolling or driving around the pine-covered headland flanking the southeastern harbour leads to tiny pebbly **coves** where most people swim. The closest "real" beaches are at the end of this road, or at **Kalafátis** just north of town, though neither is brilliant – harsh shingle underfoot and occasionally turbid water. With transport, head for better beaches at Ágios Vassílis (4km west) or Áyii Pándes (11km west).

### ARRIVAL AND INFORMATION                                            GALAXÍDHI

**By bus** Buses call at the landscaped, central Platía Iróon. **Destinations** Athens (4 daily; 4hr, with connection likely in Ámfissa or Itéa); Itéa (5 daily Mon–Fri, 4 Sat–Sun; 30min); Náfpaktos (4 daily; 1hr 15min); Pátra (1 daily; 2hr).

Services Galaxídhi is large enough to support a post office and bank ATMs. The farmers' market takes place on Thursdays from 7–10am. The nearest filling station is about 2km away, on the main road heading east.

### ACCOMMODATION

Accommodation is on the pricey side and can be scarce in summer, or at weekends year-round, though most of it is en suite, air-conditioned, and with wi-fi. The best accommodation options are converted seafarers' mansions in and near Hirólakkas, which is the area overlooking the town's second harbour, located around the bend from the marina.

★ **Arhondiko** ☎ 22650 42292 or 697 25 55 488, ⓦ archontikoarthotel.gr. Built in 2000 in traditional style, this family-run eight-room hotel occupies a secluded spot beyond Hirólakkas. Features include easy parking, sea views, themed rooms (including one with a mirrored ceiling) and self-catering facilities; breakfast is served in the ground-floor salon or out in the rock-garden courtyard. The same family also runs the *Pension Votsalo* and an appealing shop, *Avra*, on the marina, featuring local products. Breakfast included. **€50**

**Galaxa** ☎ 22650 41620, ☎ 22650 42053. Somewhat old-fashioned hillside hotel above the northwest shore of Hirólakkas with private parking; most of the rooms have some sort of water view (the best in town), all have blue-and-white decor, fridges, phones and small bathrooms. Manolis, your genial host, presides over the popular garden terrace-bar where breakfast (included) is served. **€60**

★ **Ganimede** Nikólaou Gourgoúri 20 (southwest market street) ☎ 22650 41328, ⓦ ganimede.gr. Pleasant hotel under the energetic management of the Papalexis family since 2004. There are four doubles in the finely restored old house (best is no. 1), with fridges and satellite TV, and a family suite (€150 for 4) with loft and fireplace across the courtyard-garden. Free wi-fi access, and longer-term apartments out back. In season, music and cocktails are offered in the garden every evening from 7–10pm. Breakfast included. **€75**

**Hirolakas** Platía Hirolaka ☎ 22650 41170 or 693 69 99 327. A mix of standard doubles, studios and family suites, with fridge, a/c and TV, at this cosy, relaxed spot set just back from the water. Breakfast included. **€60**

**Pension Votsalo** Platía Hirolaka ☎ 22650 41788 or 697 79 94 227, ⓦ archontikoarthotel.gr. Just three en-suite, rather basic and old-fashioned rooms with a/c, on the east shore of Hirólakkas, in a refurbished 1861 house; simple breakfast included. **€40**

### EATING AND DRINKING

Tavernas, mostly on the southeasterly quay (lánthi), are all adequate, though an obvious cluster at the head of the port is generally worth avoiding. For those with a sweet tooth, there is a string of shops purveying local pastries on Nikólaou Máma, between Platía Iróon and lánthi.

**Albatross** Satha ☎ 22650 42233. Inland and upwards on the street between the two churches, this thoroughly authentic choice (only Greek spoken) offers well-executed *mayireftá* from a short daily menu, which might stretch to octopus, spinach/cheese pie, rabbit stew, pale *taramosaláta* and the house speciality *samári* (pancetta in savoury sauce). Full meals about €10. Daily lunch & dinner.

**Barko Maritsa** Iánthi 71 ☎ 22650 41059. Cool white decor outside, warm and traditional maritime style inside,

this excellent taverna features savoury, non-greasy *píttes* and an approximation of seafood risotto. Greek salad for two costs €8, while deliciously fresh fish soup goes for €10. Daily lunch & dinner; weekends only in winter.

★ **To Maïstrali** Sygrou 32A. Located one block inland from the water, this very lively and welcoming taverna is a good, inexpensive seafood ouzerí with all the usual (fried) standards. A full meal need run to no more than €10. Daily lunch & dinner.

## NIGHTLIFE

There are a dozen quayside cafés and bars catering to sophisticated Athenian forty- and fifty-somethings. Beyond the ancient walls at the lighthouse is a late-night music club, while the *Oianthe* bar nestles below the pines across the harbour. The only establishment at Hirólakkas is *Paleo Liovtrivi*, ideal for a snack, a home-made dessert or a nightcap at the water's edge.

**3**

# Monastiráki

West from Galaxídhi, the first pleasant spot is **MONASTIRÁKI**, some 12km before you get to Náfpaktos. Monastiráki retains plenty of old stone houses, along a serpentine, tree-studded quay; there are no short-term places to stay but there is a handful of **seafood tavernas**. For a pre- or post-prandial swim, there's a pebble **beach** adjacent to *Iliopoulos* taverna, or much larger, less windy but shadeless **Parathálasso** west of the main port, backed by a lagoon and a few seasonal beach-bars. There's a sandier, 1.3km beach – exposed and not always clean – 3km further west at **Hiliadhoú**, with showers, beach-bars, accommodation and tavernas.

### EATING AND DRINKING                                    MONASTIRÁKI

**Iliopoulos** ☎ 26340 52111. This popular seafood taverna spreads out along the beach around the easterly headland. There's a good selection of wild-caught fish, cheaper

seafood appetizers, good bulk wine and home-made *píttes* – but expect brusque service at busy times. Daily lunch & dinner.

# Náfpaktos and around

**NÁFPAKTOS** (medieval Lepanto) is a lively port town and resort some two hours' drive from Delphi, or an hour by road from Pátra. It is the largest settlement on the north shore of the Gulf of Korínthos and the jumping-off point for the bridge to the Peloponnese. The town spreads out along a plane-tree-shaded seafront, below a sprawling Venetian castle. The planes are nurtured by numerous running springs, which attest to water-rich **mountains** just inland. Also inland is the ancient sacred site of **Thermon**, dedicated to the twin gods Apollo and his sister Artemis.

### The kástro

The rambling, pine-tufted **kástro** provides an impressive backdrop; most of it dates from the Venetians' fifteenth-century tenure. A complete tour is only possible by

> ## THE BATTLE OF LEPANTO
> The **Battle of Lepanto** was fought just off Náfpaktos on October 7, 1571. An allied Christian armada commanded by John of Austria devastated an Ottoman fleet – the first European naval victory over the Turks since the death of the dreaded pirate-admiral Barbarossa. Cervantes, author of *Don Quixote*, lost his left arm to a cannonball during the conflict; a Spanish-erected statue honours him at the old harbour. But Western naval supremacy proved fleeting, since the Ottomans quickly replaced their ships and had already wrested Cyprus from the Venetians that same year.

driving the well-marked 2.5km to the car park at the highest citadel, passing en route a clutch of nice cafés taking advantage of the view. At the summit are the remains of Byzantine baths and an Ottoman mosque, both converted into chapels. The curtain walls plunge down to the sea, enclosing the higher neighbourhoods and oval-shaped old harbour in crab-claw fashion (you can climb each rampart for free), with the original westerly gate giving access to Psáni beach.

## Beaches

Most of the town centre faces long, developed beaches. The more popular and less shaded west beach is **Psáni**, with its frontage road, Navmahías, lined with tavernas and hotels. To the east is **Grímbovo**, more tranquil and lined with trees (and with easier parking), where aqueducts bring mountain streams into gurgling fountains.

## Thermon

About 16km northwest of Náfpaktos, following signs for "Thérmo 46", you come to the valley of the **Évinos River** and the small village of **Háni Baniás**. A farther 10km northwest you reach **THÉRMO**, a small town with a pleasant plane-shaded square, a filling station, bank ATMs, shops and tavernas. Of potentially more interest is **ancient Thermon** (Tues–Sun 8.30am–3pm; free, photography forbidden), well signposted 1.5km southeast of the centre. This modest site, still under excavation, was the walled political capital and main religious sanctuary of the Aetolians. The main temple, c.1000 BC, orientated north-to-south rather than the usual west-to-east, was dedicated to Apollo Thermios; just east lies an even older, smaller shrine to Apollo Lyseios, while to the northwest are foundations of an Artemis temple. South of the main temple the sacred spring still flows, still potable and, in season, full of frogs. Beyond the spring extend two long *stoas* (with the occasional *exedra*), terminating at a *bouleuterion*. The keeper will unlock the small, one-room museum, crammed with unlabelled.

### ARRIVAL AND DEPARTURE                                    NÁFPAKTOS AND AROUND

**By bus** Náfpaktos has two bus stations: the KTEL Etoloakarnanías at the corner of Manássi and Bótsari, handling services to Pátra, and the KTEL Fokídhas on Asklipíou, corner Kefalóvrysou, for eastward departures. Local blue-and-white city bus #5 goes west frequently (6am–9pm) to Andírio from where there are fast buses to Athens.
Destinations Agrínio (2 daily Mon–Fri; 1hr 30min); Athens (via Dhelfí & Thíva, 4 daily, 5hr; via Andírio-Río, 2 daily,

3hr); Dhelfí (4 daily; 3hr); Galaxídhi (4 daily; 1hr 15min); Háni Baniás (2 daily; 30min); Lamía (2 daily; 3hr 30min); Mesolóngi (3 daily Mon–Fri; 50min); Pátra (8 daily Mon–Fri; 30min).
**By car** A bypass road is theoretically in the works to siphon off some of the heavy through traffic that dents the town's considerable charm.

### INFORMATION AND ACTIVITIES

**Services** The post office is on Tzavéla just east of the harbour; bank ATMs cluster further east on the same boulevard. Market day is Sat (7–11am).
**Rafting House Outdoor Activities** Háni Baniás

☎ 26340 26435, ⓦraftinghouse.gr. Offers 2hr rafting trips on the Évinos River (primarily March–May; from €55/person). Also runs climbing, horse riding and hiking trips year-round.

### ACCOMMODATION

Despite ten hotels and nearly as many rooms/apartments, accommodation can be scarce in summer, and noisy at mid-town.

★ **Akti** ☎ 26340 28464, ⓦakti.gr. To the east of the centre, in the Grímbovo area, with gulf views from about half the rooms, this pleasant place has an antique-crammed lobby and an airy, cheerful breakfast salon. Standard doubles were refurbished with butler sinks, marble dresser tables and the like in 2008, while three

palatial rooftop suites are worth the splurge. €70
**Ilion** Daliáni 7 ☎ 26340 21222. About 250m inland, in Botsaréíka at the base of the kástro, this hotel has the best views in town from its rooms – redone in 2006 with mock-antique furniture and wood floors – and from the terrace bar, where a bacon-and-egg breakfast can be had, though

it's a fair climb up with no easy parking nearby. **€60**
**Plaza** Navmahías 37 ☎ 26340 22226, ⓦ plaza-hotel.gr.
In the Psáni area, this large hotel was renovated (especially

the bathrooms) in 2007, and rooms have a/c and wi-fi. There's a pool and beach amenities provided, as well. Breakfast included. **€50**

## EATING AND DRINKING

Most of Náfpaktos's tavernas line the beaches and are all fairly comparable in quality. Otherwise, the medieval harbour and the Stenopázaro lane just inland are lined by *frappádhika* and bars, which constitute the town's nightlife.

⭐ **Papoulis** This very atmospheric spot on the pedestrian zone near the Fetiye mosque (missing its

minaret) actually comprises two adjacent premises – an ouzerí and a taverna, with large-portioned, well-executed food and good service at both, local wine and seating both indoors and out, including a balcony out back overlooking the gulf. About €15/person. Daily lunch & dinner.

# Áyios Konstandínos and around

**ÁYIOS KONSTANDÍNOS** is the closest port to Athens for the Sporades islands, with daily catamaran or car-ferry departures to Skiáthos, Skópelos and Alónissos. It lies on the coastal **Athens–Lamía motorway** which offers spectacular views of the surrounding mountains and access to the famous site of **Thermopylae** and its hot springs. En route there are various links with the island of **Évvia** (see p.693): first at Halkídha (where there's a causeway), then by ferry at **Arkítsa**. There's no reason to **stay** in **Áyios Konstandínos**.

## ARRIVAL AND DEPARTURE

ÁYIOS KONSTANDÍNOS

**By bus** The bus station is located about 200m south of the ferry landing, next to a supermarket.
Destinations Athens (hourly; 2hr 30min); Lamía (hourly; 2hr 30min); Pátra (1 daily; 3hr 30min).
**By ferry** For current information consult central agencies Bilalis (☎ 22350 31614, ⓦ bta.gr), for Saos Ferries and some Hellenic Seaways departures, or Alkyon (☎ 22350 32444, ⓦ alkyontravel.com), handling other Hellenic Seaways sailings, GA boats plus a link to Áyios Yeóryios (Évvia). Ferries also run from nearby Arkítsa to Loutrá

Edhipsoú and Évvia.
Destinations Alónissos (3 daily late June to early September; 3hr–3hr 55min); Évvia (from Arkítsa at least hourly July–Sept 15, every 2hr mid-April to late June and early Sept to end Oct, last sailing at 11pm/10pm; 45min); Skiáthos (4 daily late June to early Sept; 1hr 35min–2hr 45min); Skópelos, both ports (3 daily late June to early Sept; 2hr 10min–2hr 25min), all of the above on either Hellenic Seaways or Nel Lines.

## Thermopylae

Some 30km northwest of Áyios Konstandínos, just off the main motorway, you come to the **Pass of Thermopylae** (Thermopýles), where a majestic **monument** commemorates Spartan King **Leonidas** and his entourage, who made their stand against Xerxes' thirty-thousand-strong Persian army in August 480 BC. The Spartans' bravery is described by Herodotus (and more recently, comic-book style, by Zack Snyder's film *300*): Leonidas held the pass, the only approach an army could take to enter Attica from Thessaly, for two days with a mixed force of 7000 Spartans, Phokians, Thebans and helots. By night, however, Xerxes – tipped off by the traitor Ephialtes – sent an advance party along a little-used mountain trail and skirted the pass to attack the Greeks from behind. Leonidas ordered a retreat of the main army, but remained in place with a rearguard of about 2300, including 300 Spartans (thus the film's title), to delay the Persians' progress. All but two of them fought to their deaths on the third day.

## Loutrá Thermopylíon

**Loutrá Thermopylíon**, across the road from the gloriously heroic statue of Leonidas and midway through the pass, are thermal springs exploited since antiquity. Here you can bathe undisturbed in open-air hot cascades, while off to the side 500m away lies the grave mound of the fallen rearguard.

# Lamía and around

**LAMÍA** (population approx. 50,000) is a busy transport hub that inspires few overnight visitors. From here, most travellers head north toward Metéora, west to the mountainous Karpeníssi Valley, or east and then north to Vólos and the Pelion. To the southwest stands 2150m **Mount Íti**, one of the country's most beautiful mountains, and its national park, offering spectacular views of surrounding peaks, including Parnassós.

If you choose to stay in this city – or have to – you'll find Lamía's sprawling foothills setting attractive enough, and its main squares full of life and local colour, not to mention tavernas offering local cuisine.

## ARRIVAL AND DEPARTURE
LAMÍA

**By train** The main-line train station is at Lianokládhi, 16km west of Lamía, but there's an in-town OSE (Greek railway office) at Avérof 28, southwest of the main square, Platía Párkou.

Destinations Athens (15 daily; 2hr 30min–3hr 30min); Lárissa (11 daily; 1hr); Thessaloníki (15 daily; 2hr 30min–3hr 30min); Vólos (1 daily; 2hr 20min).

Up to 6 scheduled buses per day from Lamía serve the train station (add 20min extra & check connections; see below).

**By bus** Buses arrive at several scattered terminals, though none is much further than a 10min walk from the main square, Platía Párkou. Services for Karpeníssi and western Fthiotídha in general call at a terminal at Márkou Bótsari 3, near the little-used, in-town train station on the Stylídha–Lianokládhi spur line; buses for Dhelfí and Tríkala stop out on Thermopýlon near the corner of Nikopóleos, past the train tracks; those for Vólos use a central stop at the corner of Kapodhistríou and Rozáki-Ángeli; while buses for Athens and Thessaloníki go from the corner of Papakyriazí and Satovriándou, near the Karpeníssi station.

Destinations Karpeníssi (5 daily; 1hr 30min); Tríkala (7–8 daily; 2hr 30min); Vólos (2 daily; 2hr).

## ACCOMMODATION AND EATING

Lamia is an almost inevitable connection if using public transport to see the region, so in case you have to spend the night, there are acceptable options.

**Athina** Rozakis Angelis 41 ☎ 22310 20700, ⓦ hotelsline .gr/athina. About 2km from the main bus station and 3km from the motorway, this large, modern facility has been recently refurbished. Public rooms are rather bland, but guestrooms are large, clean and well appointed, with free wi-fi. Private parking extra. Breakfast included. **€65**

**Fitilis** Platía Laou 6 ☎ 22310 26761. One of many on this main square, this restaurant specializes in the region's grilled meats, including goat and lamb, but also offers the usual non-meat plates and *mayireftá*. Expect about €15–20/person. Daily lunch & dinner.

## Mount Íti

To the southwest of Lamía, **Mount Íti** boasts one of the most beautiful of Greek national parks – along its green northeast slopes – which is also unusually accessible by Greek standards. The classic **full traverse** of the range from Ypáti to Pávliani, taking in the summit, takes about eleven hours, best spread over two days (described in reverse in *The Mountains of Greece*; see "Books" p.806). The flat-topped peak of Pyrá ("the pyre") is where in legend Hercules immolated himself to escape the agony of the poisoned tunic which his wife Deinaneira had given him.

A rewarding **one-day outing** through Íti's sheer rock ramparts and lush meadows involves two overnights in Ypáti. The way uphill, starting from the square, is patchily marked with red paint splodges or square placards; the actual path from the top of the village leads in around four hours to an EOS refuge at **Trápeza** (usually locked, but with a spring nearby). From there you could return on a different path via Zapandólakka to Ypáti for a circular hike.

## ARRIVAL AND INFORMATION
MOUNT ÍTI

**By bus and train** Almost hourly buses cover the 22km from Lamía to Ypáti, the usual trailhead; if you arrive by train, these can be picked up en route at the main Lianokládhi station. Be sure not to get off the bus at Loutrá Ypátis spa, 5km before Ypáti proper.

**Maps** Two topographic maps of Mount Íti are available,

published by Road Editions (no. 43, 1:50,000, with route summaries in English) and Anavasi (no. 10, 1:50,000), also with a useful booklet in bilingual text.

## ACCOMMODATION AND EATING

**Arhondiko Ziaka** Ypáti ☎ 22310 98080, ⓦ xani.gr. A comfortable, modern option, built adjacent to a waterfall, with ten rooms, all with a/c, balconies and views. Breakfast included. They also have a rustic restaurant, featuring home-made country dishes, €10–15/person. **€50**

**Panorama** Ypáti ☎ 22310 98222. Just above the square, this welcoming place offers seven simple rooms, clean, if slightly dated. It also has its own restaurant, café and wine bar, open daily, lunch & dinner, €10–15/person. April–Oct. **€35**

# Karpeníssi Valley

West of Mount Íti, the **KARPENÍSSI VALLEY** is surrounded by dark fir forest and snow-fringed (Dec–May) mountains, a region promoted (with some justice) as "the Greek Switzerland". Skiing on **Mount Tymfristós (Veloúhi)** and springtime rafting or summer canyoning along local rivers are the main outdoor activities. Seasonal tourism, mostly domestic, is well established, such that accommodation prices in the region area are also authentically Swiss, boosted by a clientele of wealthy Athenians and Thessalonians, although reality has finally bitten, with arrival numbers stagnant and rates frozen. Budget travellers don't really get a look-in unless they're part of an organized adventure group. Many local businesses close weekdays in low season; we've listed more reliably open ones.

## Karpeníssi

The main road in from Lamía, after scaling a spur of Mount Tymfristós, drops down to **KARPENÍSSI**; a 1400m tunnel below the snow line guarantees year-round access and spares drivers at least twice that distance of curvy road over the pass. Karpeníssi's site is spectacular – huddled at the base of the peak and head of the valley, which extends south all the way to wall-like Mount Panetolikó – but the town itself is entirely nondescript, having been destroyed in World War II by the Germans and again in the civil war. Snow conditions at the downhill **ski centre**, 11km above town, are variable as the twelve runs and four chair lifts have a top point of only 2040m.

## ARRIVAL AND DEPARTURE KARPENÍSS

**By bus** Arriving by bus is inconvenient, since the KTEL bus station is 1.5km out on the bypass road, though shuttles occasionally do a run into town, along main drag Zinopoúlou, to the leafy, café-table-crowded platía.
Destinations Agrínio (1 at 9am Mon–Sat, 1pm Sun; 3hr 30min); Athens (3 daily; 4hr 30min); Megálo/Mikró Horió ( daily; 15min); Proussós (Mon & Fri at 5.30am & 1pm; 1hr).
**By car** Parking in the centre is difficult and heavily controlled, so we've indicated lodging where this i easier.

## INFORMATION AND ACTIVITIES

**Tourist office** basement office on the main platía (Mon–Sat 9am–2pm & 5–8pm, Sun 10am–2pm; ☎ 22370 21016, ⓦ karpenissi.gr).

**Ev Zein** Zinopoúlou 61 ☎ 22370 80150, ⓦ www.fzein evryt.gr. Rafting trips April to early May, at the Dhipótam site and on the Távropos River.

## ACCOMMODATION

Except on summer weekends or during skiing season, rooms are easily found, if not all that inspiring; many of the eigh hotels are noisy or overpriced, though bargaining at midweek is productive.

**Anesis** Zinopoúlou 50, Karpeníssi ☎ 22370 80700. A chalet-style spot, mainly worth it if you get one of the rooms with stunning valley views. Located on the edge of town, a 10min walk to the centre, parking is easy. Very substantial breakfast included. **€45**

**Elvetia** Zinopoúlou 17, Karpeníssi ☎ 22370 22465,

ⓦ elvetiahotel.gr. Not much to look at from the outside but attractive communal areas (including an arcade stone-and-wood bar and a sky-lit dining area), attention t detail and helpful management make up for somewha small rooms. Breakfast included. **€60**

**Galini** Ríga Feréou 3, Karpeníssi ☎ 22370 22914. Thi

## CLIMBING MOUNT KALIAKOÚDHA

The eight-hour **hike** up and down **Mount Kaliakoúdha** (2098m) is one of the most popular outings in the Karpeníssi Valley. There's a good, waymarked path much of the way to the top, but the final ascent conquers a pretty sharp grade and requires scrambling skills. The route and its features are shown reasonably accurately on Anavasi Editions 1:50,000 map no. 13, *Karpenisi Prousos*. With an early start, you'll polish off most of the 1250m altitude difference before the sun catches you.

From Megálo's square with its bars and cafés, head southeast, following painted red or yellow waymarks on walls until a proper path leaves the village. This passes one water source and climbs steadily through fir forest where many trees are dead or dying due to climate change, but the survivors provide welcome shade. About two hours above the village, and frequent crossing of the dirt track, the path ends temporarily just below the tree line at **Malakássa**, near the only other reliable **spring** this side of the mountain. You're forced onto the track for about another hour (unless you use some trail short cuts) to a saddle at the northeast flank of the peak. The track continues down and south towards Stournára and Pandavréhi (see below); for Kaliakoúdha, head west and relentlessly up, following red-paint waymarks. The trail is poor to nonexistent, often strewn with scree, but there's little danger of getting lost and on a fine day you'll have company. Just under an hour (roughly 4hr from the village) should see you on the **summit** with its trig point; staggering **views** over central Greece are your reward. Vardhoússia and Íti loom to the east; the Ágrafa region unfolds beyond Mount Tymfristós to the north-northeast; while Mount Panetolikó approximates the provincial border south-southwest.

Due south lies Stournára village in the Krikellopótamos Valley, poised just above **Pandavréhi**, the other big local attraction, where waterfalls pour year-round from the walls of a narrow gorge of the Krikellopótamos. As there are no reliable facilities in Stournára, most people visit Pandavréhi by car; from the sign posted junction just below Megálo Horió, it's 23km there along the track system.

---

hotel is plain and rooms small, but some have balconies with mountain views. It's down from the main thoroughfare, 250m southeast of the *Panorama* restaurant (see below); on-street parking is feasible. Breakfast included. **€3**

## EATING AND DRINKING

Eating options are surprisingly limited amid a plethora of fast-food outlets, cafés and après-ski bars. It's good to head for the following full-service tavernas downtown.

**En Elladhi** Koutsímbou 4 ☎ 22370 22235. Off the main square, this reliable family-run taverna features home-made soups, pastas and substantial casserole fare, along with tasty regional specialities. Expect about €10–15/ person. Daily lunch & dinner.

**Panorama** Ríga Feréou 18 Karpeníssi ☎ 22370 25976. This taverna has terrace garden seating with views, and offers well-executed *mayireftá* and mountain grills among a wide range of menu choices. Expect about €10–15/ person. Daily lunch & dinner.

# The Pelion peninsula

The hilly **PELION PENINSULA** confounds every stereotypical image of Greece, with its abundant fruit trees and dense forests and water gurgling up from fountains or aqueducts. Summer temperatures here can be a good 5°C cooler than on the baking plains nearby, and this finger of land is very popular with Greek tourists and more discerning foreign visitors drawn to its pretty **villages**, excellent **beaches** and **hiking routes** (see box above).

The peninsula is dominated by **Mount Pelion** (Mount Pílio; 1651m), below which villages are spread out widely, linked by cobbled paths. The best concentration of traditional communities lies just north and east of **Vólos**, the main gateway to the region. The **west coast** down from Vólos to Áfyssos is less memorable, with concentrated development along the Pagasitic Gulf despite no decent beaches. The **far south**, relatively low-lying and sparsely populated, has just two major resorts – Plataniás and Milína – plu a few inland villages and the picturesque fishing port of Ayía Kyriakí at the extreme southwestern tip.

## ARRIVAL AND DEPARTURE                                    THE PELION PENINSULA

Vólos (see opposite) is the natural gateway to the Pelion, and there are buses from there to most towns, if slow an infrequent. The southern part of the Pelion can also be reached via speedboats to Ayía Kyriakí (Tríkeri) from Vólos or fron northern Évvia. To take full advantage of the place in all its variety, one's own transport is essential.

**By air** Arriving fairly directly in the Pelion from overseas is possible, thanks to May–October charter flights to either Skiáthos (frequent) or Néa Anhíalos (see p.670).

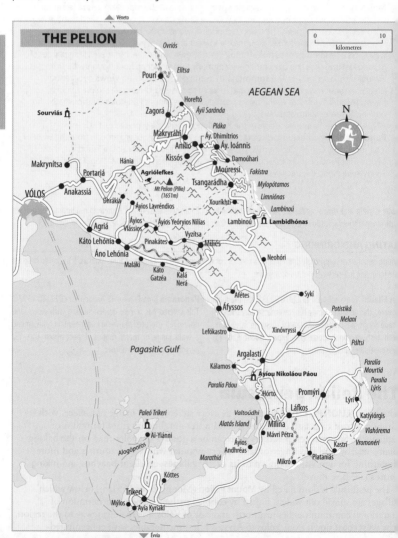

## GETTING AROUND

**By bus** Buses to the east cover two main routes: Vólos–Hánia–Zagorá and Vólos–Tsangarádha–Áyios Ioánnis (see below), with scarce services linking Zagorá and Tsangarádha to complete a loop. The far south is equally infrequently served with departures to Milína, Tríkeri, Plataniá and Katiyiórgis, though the respective northern and western highlights Makrynítsa and Vyzítsa both have more frequent connections, as does Áfyssos.

**By car** Given patchy bus services, a rental car is your best option. Note that driving is slow progress, since perilously narrow, often rock-strewn roads snake around ravine contours, seemingly never getting closer to villages just across the way. Car rental is available in Vólos (see p.224) and from Pelion Rent (☎ 24230 54365, ⚓ pelionrent.com) in Áfyssos and Milína.

## INFORMATION

**Services** Banks and petrol stations are found along the commercialized coastal road just out from Vólos. Otherwise, there are post offices in Zagorá, Tsangarádha and Áyios Yeóryios, ATMs in Zagorá, Tsangarádha, Ayía Kyriakí and Argalastí, and petrol stations in Zagorá, Argalastí, Ayía Kyriakí and elsewhere.

# Vólos

Sitting at the northwest corner of the Pagasitic Gulf, the city of **VÓLOS** is a major port and looks promising enough based on the glittering view from the hillside as you approach. Close-up, however, the resolutely industrial outskirts and the mostly lacklustre centre evoke nothing of its mythological past as the spot from which Jason and the Argonauts embarked on their quest for the Golden Fleece.

With a population approaching 150,000, Vólos ranks as the fifth-largest Greek city, rebuilt in utilitarian style after a series of devastating earthquakes between 1947 and 1957, and now edging to its natural limits against the Pelion foothills. University of Thessaly students make it a lively place, and you could do worse than spend a few hours or even a night here while waiting for a bus into the Pelion or a boat to the Sporades islands, for which Vólos is the **main port**. The most attractive place to linger is along the eastern **waterfront esplanade**, between landscaped **Platía Yeoryíou** and the **archeological museum**.

## Archeological museum

Athanasaki 1 • Tues–Sun 8am–8pm; Mon 1.30–8pm • €2

Vólos's **archeological museum** boasts exemplary labelling and well-lit galleries, one reserved for changing exhibits. Highlights of the permanent collection include one of the best European assemblages of Neolithic (6500–3500 BC) figurines from various surrounding sites; faint but expressive painted grave stelae from Hellenistic Dimitrias depicting everyday scenarios of fifth-century BC life, with some inscriptions helpfully translated; and a massive quantity of items, including superb stone and gold jewellery, from tombs of all eras across Thessaly.

## ARRIVAL AND DEPARTURE

VÓLOS

**By air** The nearest airport, receiving overseas flights (but not domestic flights), is 26km southwest of the city, beyond Néa Anhíalos (Almyrós). Buses generally meet flights and transfer passengers to Vólos. Package companies monopolize most such flights while Ryanair also offer flights from Germany, Belgium and Italy.

**By train** The train station is just off Platía Ríga Feréou.

Destinations Athens (1 daily express service via Lárissa; 4hr 30min); Lárissa (15 daily; 52min).

**By bus** The KTEL city bus terminal is on Sekéri, just off Grigoríou Lambráki, a 10min walk southwest of the main square, Platía Ríga Feréou. There is a taxi rank outside.

Destinations Áfyssos (6 daily Mon–Fri, 5 Sat & Sun; 1hr); Áyios Ioánnis (2 daily Mon–Fri, 1 Sun; 2hr 15min); Katiyiórgis (2 daily Mon–Fri, 1 Sat & Sun; 2hr); Makrynítsa (9 daily Mon–Fri, 7 Sat & Sun; 50min); Miliés (6 daily Mon–Fri, 4 Sat & Sun; 1hr); Milína via Hórto (4 daily; 1hr 30min); Plataniás (3 daily Mon–Fri, 2 Sat & Sun; 2hr); Thessaloníki (8–9 daily; 3hr); Tríkala (4 daily; 2hr 30min); Tríkeri (2 daily Mon–Fri, 1 Sat & Sun; 2hr 30min); Tsangarádha (2 daily; 1hr 45min); Vyzítsa (6 daily Mon–Fri, 4 Sat & Sun; 1hr 10min); Zagorá (3 daily Mon–Fri, 2 Sat & Sun; 2hr–2hr 30min).

**Parking** The city centre has pay-and-display parking – or try the covered car park on Ogl.

**By ferry** Vólos has daily car ferries and – in summer – frequent hydrofoils or catamarans to the Sporades. *Sporades Travel* at Argonaftón 33 (☎ 24210 23400) is the central agent for *Hellenic Seaways*; *Vis Travel* around the corner at Andonopoúlou 3 (☎ 24210 25666) represents *Saos Ferries*.
Destinations Alónissos (1 daily car ferry in summer, 3 weekly spring and autumn; 4hr 45min–5hr; daily summer catamaran, 3hr); Ayía Kyriakí (summer jet boat 3–4 daily 1hr 10min); Oreí, Évvia (1hr 45min); Skiáthos (1–2 daily car ferries; 2hr 15min; daily summer catamaran/hydrofoil 1hr 20min); Skópelos, both ports (1–2 daily car ferries depending on season; 3hr 30min; daily catamaran/hydrofoil in summer, 2hr–2hr 30min).

## INFORMATION

**Tourist office** Opposite the KTEL (April–Oct daily 8am–9pm, Nov–March Mon–Sat 8am–8pm, Sun 8am–3.30pm; ⓦ volos.gr.
**Car rental** Agents include Avis, Argonaftón 41 (☎ 24210 28880); Budget, Polyméri 27 (☎ 693 61 13 027); or helpful and efficient Hertz, Iássonos 90 (☎ 24210 22544).

## ACCOMMODATION

**Iasson** Pávlou Melá 1 ☎ 24210 26075. Facing the waterfront, this basic, bright, plainly modern choice offers double-glazed windows, a/c, a small elevator and balconies. Rooms and bathrooms are generally on the small side but clean, but ask to see them before choosing. Look for the sunny yellow building. No breakfast. €35
**Park** Platía Yeoryíou at Dheliyióryi 2 ☎ 24210 36511, ⓦ amhotels.gr. Comfortable enough and nicely situated, just behind a large park and with port views from most balconies, this is a classic business hotel. Rooms are slightly on the small side, but well appointed, with marble trim and state-of-the-art baths. Free wi-fi. Breakfast included. €100

**Roussas** Iatroú Tzánou 1 ☎ 24210 21732, ☎ 24210 22987. A very basic option with en-suite accommodation, proximity to the waterfront and the archeological museum, with a/c, relatively easy parking, and convenience to tavernas, though no breakfast facilities. €40
**Xenia Domotel** Plastíra 1 ☎ 24210 92700, ⓦ domotelxeniavolouhotel.gr. This crisply modern seafront luxury resort has a pool, spa, fitness centre, plush rooms in Grecian blue and white, with state-of-the-art technology, including free wi-fi and free use of a laptop, as well as a range of other amenities and a copious buffet breakfast. €130

## EATING AND DRINKING

Vólos specializes in one of Greece's most endearing and enduring institutions – the authentic ouzerí or *tsipourádhiko* serving various mezédhes washed down not necessarily with ouzo but with *tsípouro*, the all-but identical spirit of the northern mainland.

**Haliambalias** (aka Zafíris) Kondarátou 8 corner Skýrou. Founded in 1947 and the place to go for affordable *mayireftá*; the menu never varies much from vegetarian *tourloú*, baked *pérka* fish and a few stews. Closed Sun.
**Monosandalos** Tsopotoú 1 ☎ 24210 37525. Located near Nikifórou Plastíra and the enormous Áyios Konstandínos church. Come here for the waterside seating and seafood, including the house special, *garidhokrokétes* (shrimp patties). A full meal should run about €15. Daily lunch & dinner.
**Nikos** Iasonos 118. You can always count on the freshly grilled souvlákis, chicken or pork, served here. You'll find it near the Art Deco cinema back from the port. €10/person or less for a freshly prepared, simple meal. Daily, noon to midnight.

## NIGHTLIFE AND ENTERTAINMENT

The most central nightlife zone, comprising intimate live-music venues and café-bars where conversation is possible, fill the grid of pedestrianized lanes east of Koumoundoúrou and north of Dhimitriádhos; a few indoor clubs survive at the west edge of town near the KTEL, particularly on Lahaná.

**Cinemas** There's a summer cinema off Platía Yeoryíou, the Exoraïstiki, unusually specializing in art-house fare; in winter film action moves to the Art Deco Ahilleion multiplex on Koumoundoúrou.
**Theatre** Concerts and plays are performed at either the open-air or covered theatres on Platía Ríga Feréou.

# The northern Pelion

The **northern Pelion** features the region's best (and most popular) beaches, and its lushest scenery, particularly along the Aegean-facing **northeast coast**. A relatively humid climate and shady dells nurture exotic flowers such as hydrangeas, gardenias and camellias, locally bred and sold at the roadside. The "county town" of the region is **Zagorá**, self-proclaimed apple capital of Greece, but the first hamlet of interest you're likely to meet, if approaching from Vólos, is **Anakassiá**, which boasts a unique art museum.

## Anakassiá

The village of **ANAKASSIÁ** (Iolkós), 4km out of Vólos, is still essentially a suburb, but it does offer a museum dedicated to the "naive" painter **Theophilos** (1873–1934). A prize eccentric, originally from Lésvos, Theophilos lived for long periods in Vólos, where he wandered around, often dressed as a historical hero, painting frescoes in exchange for a meal or pocket money. On the Pelion you find his murals in unlikely places, such as village tavernas, bakeries and *kafenía*.

### Theophilos Museum

Tues–Sun 8am–3pm • Free • Turn off at Anakassiá's roadside platía.

The **Theophilos Museum** occupies the **Arhondikó Kondoú**, an eighteenth-century mansion whose first floor preserves much of Theophilos's earliest (1912–27) work, with unusually vivid colours thanks to restoration in recent decades. The Greek War of Independence – one of his favourite themes – features often, including such scenes as Patriarch Gregory's body being dumped into the Bosphorus, Admiral Tombazis setting the Ottoman flagship alight, and the taking of Tripoli, with the attendant massacre of Turkish civilians graphically shown. Nearer floor level, a bestiary features a bear-headed hippo (the painter never saw most of his animal subjects in the flesh).

## Makrynítsa

From Anakassiá you can detour 4km northwest to **MAKRYNÍTSA**, 17km from Vólos, where stone houses straggle picturesquely 200m down the mountainside. Founded in 1204 by refugees from the Fourth Crusade's sacking of Constantinople, it comprises six churches plus a monastery, and various **traditional mansions** – many restored as accommodation. From most spots the views are splendid.

Most impressive of the churches are **Áyios Ioánnis**, next to the fountain on the shady main platía, and the beautiful eighteenth-century **monastery of Panayía Makrynítissa**, beneath the clock tower. The marble relief work on Áyios Ioánnis' apse, plus that on the fountain opposite, is among the best of its type in Greece. A few paces above the Áyios Ioánnis square there's a **Theophilos fresco** in the right-hand café, showing revolutionary chieftain Katsandonis and his men merry-making.

If you are looking for a **challenging walk**, Makrynítsa is the starting point for the three-and-a-half-hour trek to the deserted, frescoed **monastery of Sourviás**, mostly on *kalderími* and path surface. The route starts from a steep cement track west of the monastery of Ayíou Yerasímou, though trail resumes for most of the way once Makrynítsa is out of sight.

## Zagorá

The largest Pelion village, **ZAGORÁ** has a life more independent of tourism than others, though studies give the fruit orchards only until the year 2020 to survive, owing to depleted soil and overuse of pesticides. Other crops (kiwis, raspberries) are being considered as a potential breakaway from apple monoculture.

Visitors often jump to unfavourable conclusions from the workaday main street where the bus calls; in fact, there are four well-preserved and architecturally varied parishes with handsome Neoclassical mansions, arrayed around the squares of **Ayía Paraskeví, Ayía Kyriakí, Áyios Yeóryios** and **Metamórfosis (Sotíra)**, strung out over 5km.

Coming from Vólos, turn left at the first filling station to find Ayía Paraskeví (Perahóra), with its pleasant, unvisited platía. Ayía Kyriakí is effectively the centre of Zagorá. Bearing left away from the turning for Horeftó will bring you to the broad platía of Áyios Yeóryios, in the shadow of its plane tree and beautiful eighteenth-century church, while Sotíra lies beyond this, above the road to Pourí.

### Horeftó
Eight twisting kilometres down the mountain, **HOREFTÓ** (infrequent bus from Zagorá) makes an excellent coastal base. There is ample choice of **beaches**: a long, decent one in front of this former fishing village; secluded Áyii Saránda 2km south and two coves at Análipsi, just north – a brief hike brings you to the first cove, a little paradise popular with nudists and rough campers taking advantage of a spring behind the sand. Determined explorers can follow the coastal path for twenty minutes more to the northerly cove, road-accessible and rockier. There are also two hour-long *kalderímia* up to Zagorá, which can be combined to make an enjoyable loop.

### Áyios Ioánnis
**ÁYIOS IOÁNNIS** is eastern Pelion's main resort. Numerous hotels and *dhomátia* were erected during the 1980s to a density no longer allowed, but despite this, finding a bed here in peak season is as problematic as anywhere on the peninsula.

The **beach** at Áyios Ioánnis, though of average quality, is equipped with windsurf boards for rent. For more ambitious activities, such as sea-kayaking or mountain-biking, contact local travel agency Les Hirondelles (☎24260 31181, ⊛les-hirondelles .gr), which also represents most of the ocean-view studios in the area.

### Damoúhari
South of Áyios Ioánnis, a narrow paved road leads up over a low ridge and down through olive groves to **DAMOÚHARI** hamlet, bordering a stageset-perfect port indeed used for film shoots. The construction of a broader road down from Moúressi ended its seclusion, and villas have sprung up mushroom-like among the olive trees. However, cars are excluded from the shoreline, which offers a large pebble beach, the overgrown ruins of a Venetian castle, and several **tavernas**.

From Damoúhari, you can **walk to Tsangarádha** in 75 minutes, a popular and rewarding trip (though most folk do it downhill in under an hour). At the mouth of the ravine descending to the larger bay, a spectacular *kalderími* begins its steep ascent, allowing glimpses of up to six villages simultaneously, plus the Sporades on a clear day, from points en route. Then there is deep shade, and a potable spring approaching Ayía Kyriakí; the path emerges in the Ayía Paraskeví quarter of Tsangarádha, just downhill from the post office.

### Tsangarádha
**TSANGARÁDHA** is the largest northeastern village after Zagorá, though it may not seem so at first, since it's also divided into four distinct quarters – south to north, **Taxiárhes**, **Ayía Paraskeví** (**post office** and bank **ATM**), **Ayía Kyriakí** and **Áyios Stéfanos** – strung along several kilometres of road. Each of these focuses on a namesake church and

---

## PELION LEGENDS AND FOOD

For the ancients, the lushness of the Pelion made this the site of revelries by the gods and haunt of the mythical **centaurs** – thus the name *Kentavros* (Centaur) for various hotels and bars, as well as the rowdy creature's depictions everywhere.

With its orchards of apple, pear and nut, the Pelion is still one of the most agriculturally prolific areas of Greece. Herbs, fruit, home-made preserves and honey are likely souvenirs. The Pelion boasts a distinct regional **cuisine**: *spedzofáï* (sausage and pepper casserole) and *gídha lemonáti* (goat stew with lemon sauce); seafood is often garnished with *krítamo* (pickled rock samphire) or *tsitsíravla* (pickled April-shrubbery shoots), and wine from the Dhimitra Co-op at Néa Anhíalos is widely available.

platía, the finest being **Ayía Paraskeví**, shaded by reputedly the heftiest plane tree in Greece – about a thousand years old, and requiring eighteen men to encircle it – and Taxiárhes, with a tree nearly as large and a four-spouted fountain from 1909. More Taxiárhes botanical prodigies are found at the **Serpentin Garden** (visits by appointment only, ☎ 24260 49060, ⓦ serpentin-garden.com), a hillside Eden featuring many heirloom roses and other rare plants.

## Moúressi
There are more **hotels** and **tavernas** in MOÚRESSI, 3km northwest of Áyios Stéfanos. An excellent short stroll, very useful for reaching the beach or completing a loop via Áyios Ioánnis, is the 45-minute descent to Damoúhari; look for the sign-posted start of the trail on the bend in the road just past the minimarket/newsagent.

## Mylopótamos
From Taxiárhes Tsangarádha, a ninety-minute path, or a 7km hairpin road, snake down to **Mylopótamos** and its two attractive if hugely popular pebble coves, with afternoon shade from caves and overhangs. The pair are separated by a naturally tunnelled rock, with a music bar just above.

## Limniónas Beach
Southeast of Mylopótamos lies the attractive Limniónas **beach**. You can arrive on foot from Mylopótamos, but most people get there via Lambinoú village (no reliable facilities), from where a paved road leads 3km down past the restored eighteenth-century **Lambidhónas monastery**, sporting fine frescoes over the doors. Scenic **Limniónas** has a fresh-water shower but no other reliable amenities. There's a romantic, out-of-the-way hotel option here (see p.228).

## ACCOMMODATION NORTHERN PELION

A great accommodation pleasure of the Pelion is staying in one of the many traditional mansions, a number of them now beautifully and authentically restored. The northern part of the peninsula is especially rich in these architectural treasures, but if you plan on visiting out of high season, be sure to contact the owner well in advance. If they are not expecting guests, they may be in Vólos or even Athens.

### MAKRYNÍTSA
**Arhondiko Pandora** ☎ 24280 99404, ⓦ pandora mansion.gr. Just before Platía Bráni, about 300m along on the right, the spacious large grounds behind the gate include a café-restaurant serving meals in a lovely courtyard. Each of the seven rooms and suites are unique and tastefully appointed, as you'd expect from an architect-owner. Breakfast included. **€150**
**Arhondiko Repana** ☎ 24280 99067, ⓦ repana.gr. Along the pedestrian-only street, this is one of the finest of the traditional mansions in the Pelion, its rooms edging a bit toward twee but the best value here. Great views. Breakfast included. **€70**

### ZAGORÁ
★ **Arhondiko Gayanni** ☎ 24260 23391, ⓦ villagayannis.gr. This property is a gorgeous three-storey mansion dating from 1770, all impeccably restored, with beautiful gardens, ample parking, genial hosts, large rooms with antiques and wood-beamed ceilings, and copious breakfasts, included. **€70**

**Xenonas Stefania** ☎ 24260 23666, ⓦ stefania-zagora .gr. Families should head here for air-conditioned studios with full kitchens, fireplaces and terraces. Lots of extras available, such as drinks and games. **€60**

### HOREFTÓ
**Hagiati** ☎ 24260 22405, ⓦ hagiati.com. Near the quieter, south end of the shoreline road you'll find this excellent beachside hotel. There's off-street parking, a spacious garden bar, wheelchair access and fridges in the comfortable sea-view rooms with balconies. **€55**
★ **La Dhelfinia** ☎ 24260 23644. Toward the north end of the beach, this large establishment, just metres from the sand, is a popular and very reasonable *mayireftá* taverna, with grills at weekends. Choose from an extensive menu and expect portions big enough to share (€10–20). Daily lunch & dinner.

### ÁYIOS IOÁNNIS
**Anesis** ☎ 24260 31123, ⓦ www.hotelanesis.gr. Set back from the street so quieter, but still handy to the beach,

this hotel has a slightly alternative ambience and large, pastel-coloured rooms. Breakfast (€7/person extra) is served on a terrace with sea views. **€70**

**Sofokles** ☎ 24260 31230, ⊕ sofokleshotel.com. Slightly bland hotel located towards the northern end of the beachfront. Plus points include sea views from most of the rooms, and an attractive terrace-pool. Breakfast €7.50/person extra. **€60**

### DAMOÚHARI

★ **Damouhari** ☎ 24260 49840, ⊕ pelion.com.gr. This place is actually a "village" of stone-built, creatively decorated studio cottages and rooms below a small infinity pool, with antiques and wood trim in the rooms and *objet-trouvé* decor in its *Kleopatra Miramare* bar. There's an excellent waterside annexe of five state-of-the-art rooms, as well. **€85**

### TSANGARÁDHA

**Konaki** ☎ 24260 49481. Located just south of the Ayía Paraskeví square but set back from the road. All rooms have fridges and views, some have balconies, and there's a pleasant basement breakfast area. **€50**

★ **The Lost Unicorn** ☎ 24260 49930, ⊕ lostunicorn .com. Under the sympathetic management of Clare and Christos Martzos, this place scores as much for its common areas – kitted out like a British gentlemen's club – as for the eight antique-furnished, terrazzo-floored rooms in the 1890s building. Continental or full English breakfast extra.

The hotel also offers a pricey on-site "continental cuisine" restaurant, turning the freshest local products into French- and Italian-inspired dishes. Restaurant open for dinner only weekends and holidays. Shut one month in winter. **€90**

### MOÚRESSI

★ **The Old Silk Store** ☎ 24260 49086 or 693 71 56 780, ⊕ pelionet.gr. Set in a beautiful, lightly restored nineteenth-century mansion with a lush garden, barbecue area and high-ceilinged, wood-floored rooms (plus a self-catering studio cottage). Breakfasts change daily but always include excellent bread and home-made preserves. Closed Feb. **€65**

### MYLOPÓTAMOS

**Diakoumis** ☎ 24260 49203, ⊕ diakoumis.gr. On the approach to Mylopótamos these are the first rooms you come to and among the best, just 1km from the beach. Accommodation is spread over two rambling buildings; each studio (2–3 persons) or apartment (up to 5 persons) is brightly decorated and has kitchen, a/c and spectacular views of the sea from a private wooden balcony. **€70**

### LIMNIÓNAS

**Faros** ☎ 24260 49194, ⊕ faros.pelionet.gr. North of Limniónas, at the very end of a rough, precipitous road, stands this small, very welcoming, family-run operation, in a secluded, leafy spot popular with hikers, beachgoers and horseriders. Breakfast €8 extra. **€45**

## EATING

### MAKRYNÍTSA

**Alfa ke Vita** ☎ 24280 99355. About 30m beyond the platía tavernas, along a gravel path, look for a romantic flowery terrace and enjoy carefully prepared dishes employing fresh family-farm produce. Full meals for as little as €10/pers. Lunch & dinner; closed Mon.

### ÁYIOS IOÁNNIS

**Ostria** ☎ 24260 32132. Hillside taverna featuring Mediterranean recipes making use of herbs and strong flavourings – proprietress Hariklia spent years in Florence, so pasta dishes are prominent; reserve tables in season. €10–15/person. Daily lunch & dinner.

**Poseidhonas** ☎ 24260 31222. Run by a fishing family, this is the best seafood choice in the Pelion. They only sell their own fresh catch of the day so can run out of food quickly. Main courses run to about €6–8. Daily lunch & dinner.

### DAMOÚHARI

**Karagatsi** ☎ 24260 49841. One of the best tavernas in the area. Personable chef/owner Apostolis (who also runs the unique hotel *Damouhari*) puts together big Greek salads and fresh fish creations, including his own *taramasalata*. Seating features bay views, especially romantic at sunset. Dishes €4–10. Daily lunch & dinner.

**To Kalyvi** ☎ 24260 49578. This traditional taverna has tables on the platía, and features grilled meats and stews, as well as fresh wild greens and local veggies, depending on the season. €10–15/person. Daily lunch & dinner.

### MYLOPÓTAMOS

**Angelika** ☎ 24260 49588. Welcoming and efficient taverna where the fresh fish is, as usual, expensive, but other seafood, *mezédhes* and *mayireftá* are tasty and reasonably priced. €10–15/person. Daily lunch & dinner, Easter–Oct, otherwise weekends only.

# The western Pelion

Lying in the rain shadow of the mountain, the **western Pelion** has a drier, more Mediterranean climate, with olives and arbutus predominating except in shady, damp

## THE PELION TRENÁKI

A prime west-Pelion attraction is the *trenáki*, or **narrow-gauge railway**, which originally ran between Vólos and Miliés. The 60km line, in normal service until 1971, was laid out between 1894 and 1903 under the supervision of engineer Evaristo de Chirico, father of famous artist Giorgio de Chirico (which accounts for the little trains which chug across several of his paintings). To conquer the 2.8-percent gradient and numerous ravines between Áno Lehónia and Miliés, the elder de Chirico designed six multiple-span stone viaducts, tunnels and a riveted **iron trestle bridge**, all justly considered masterpieces of form and function. The bridge, some 700m west of the terminus below Miliés, spans a particularly deep gorge and can be crossed on a **pedestrian catwalk**; indeed, following the entire route down to Áno Lehónia is a popular 5hr 30min walk, with occasional springs en route.

You can ride on one of the original Belgian steam locomotives (since converted to diesel), during weekends and holidays Easter–October (daily July–Aug), and several of the *belle epoque* stations have been restored. The **train** leaves Áno Lehónia (city bus #5 from Vólos) on the coast at 11am, taking 95min to reach Miliés, from where it returns at 4pm. **Tickets** are currently €13 adults, €8.50 kids, one-way or round trip, and go on sale at 10.30am (start queuing at 10am), at either Vólos or Áno Lehónia. However, groups often book out the three carriages, so best make enquiries at Vólos station a few days in advance.

ravines. The beaches, at least until Kalá Nerá, are far more developed than their natural endowments merit and lack the character of those on the east shore. Inland it is a different story, with pleasant foothill villages and decent bus services. **Vyzítsa** and **Pinakátes** in particular both make good bases for car-touring or hiking.

## Miliés

The sizeable village of **MILIÉS** (sometimes Miléës or Mileai) was an important cultural refuge during the eighteenth century. It retains some imposing mansions and the Pelion's most interesting church, **Taxiárhis** (usually open around 6pm). Its narthex frescoes are the oldest (eighteenth century) and most unusual, including scenes from Noah's Flood (with two elephants boarding the Ark) and, in one corner, a three-ringed mandala showing the seasons, the zodiac and the cycle of human existence. With five wells under the floor and 48 clay urns secreted in the walls, the church's acoustics are superb, so it's occasionally used for concerts of sacred music.

## Vyzítsa

**VYZÍTSA**, 3km west of Miliés and alive with water in streams and aqueducts, has a more open and less lived-in feel than either Makrynítsa or Miliés, though it, too, draws crowds of day-trippers in summer. It's also the nexus of pleasant trails, some of which can be combined into half-day **loop-hikes**. One that leads down to the sea in about two hours starts from the chapel of Zoödhóhou Piyís, just below Vyzítsa's platía, and follows a sporadically marked route that takes you around a vast landslip zone, and then across two ravines (bridges provided) followed by a brief stretch of farm track until dropping down to Kalá Nerá. Whatever your penchant for exploring the area, the famously picturesque hamlet makes an excellent base, with several **accommodation** options in converted mansions.

## Pinakátes

**PINAKÁTES**, at the top of a densely forested ravine, was once among the least visited and most desolate of the west Pelion villages, following a 1955 phylloxera outbreak that ended its status as vineyard capital of the Pelion. No longer: the surfacing of roads in from three directions and trendy Greeks buying up crumbling mansions for restoration have seen to that. For now it remains a superbly atmospheric spot, with just enough food and accommodation to make it practicable for a sojourn.

You'll find more antique mansions to be found in this part of the Pelion, but also quite a few modern copycats, no less comfortable or charming for that. Be sure not to turn up unannounced: in high season they're likely to be booked up, and off-season the owners will be elsewhere.

## MILIÉS

**Eskitzi** ☎ 24230 86789, ⊛ eskitziroomspelion.com. Just east of town these country-style rooms have a cosy feel despite the plain modern building. All have views of the surrounding mountain scenery, but ask for one with a balcony. Free parking; basic breakfast included. **€50**

**Othon Korbas** ☎ 24230 86219. This bakery, down by the bus stop, sells every kind of bread, pie and turnover imaginable, including *eleópsomo* and *tyrópsomo* suitable for hikers. Prices start at as little as €1. Daily, lunch early evening.

**O Palios Stathmos** ☎ 24230 86425, ⊛ paliosstathmos .com. "The Old Station" is located, as the name implies, out by the old train station. The colourful, simple rooms here are worth it if you get a balconied front unit with a nostalgic view of the quaint tracks. Breakfast included, in their own traditional restaurant, which is also open for lunch and dinner (€10–15/person). **€60**

**Panorama** ☎ 24230 86128. This simple grill occupies a vine-covered wedge-shaped building just above the platía, and is consistently good. Fresh vegetable pies and meats, average price/dish €6. Daily lunch & dinner.

## VYZÍTSA

★ **Arhondiko Karagianopoulou** ☎ 24230 86717, ⊛ karagiannopoulou.com. A very handsome eighteenth-century mansion, with touches such as painted ceilings and stained-glass windows, located 200m uphill from the village through-road. Rooms are elegant and impressive and breakfast is served in the courtyard. **€70**

**O Yiorgaras** ☎ 24230 86359. Located next to the *Stoïkos* this taverna is the place to come for traditional dishes featuring game and wild mushrooms and whatever is in season. Expect about €15 and up, per person. Daily lunch & dinner.

**Stoïkos** ☎ 24230 86406, ⊛ stoikoshotel.com. The approach road from Miliés to the village is lined with inns including this modern option constructed in the traditional way, where most of the well-executed rooms have wood-beam ceilings and views. Breakfast included. **€70**

## PINAKÁTES

**Alatinou** ☎ 24230 86995 or 697 28 38 28, ⊜ demileon@mailbox.gr. A few steps below the square, this hotel offers rather monastic, but comfortably renovated, en-suite rooms with dark-wood decor and terrace for breakfast, included. Open summer only. **€70**

★ **Dhrosia** (alias Taverna tou Papa) ☎ 24230 86777. Taverna at the far western edge of Pinakátes. The food here – including *dolmádhes* and *gídha lemonáti* (goat stew with lemon sauce) – uses free-range meat and poultry. Washed down with a jug of the deceptively potent red wine from some of the few surviving local vineyards. Expect about €15/person. Daily, dinner only.

# The southern Pelion

The **southern Pelion** is drier, lower and more stereotypically Mediterranean; the terrain overall is less dramatic, the villages more scattered. The region has been hit hard by forest fires – in particular a June 2007 blaze that burnt the entire coast from Argalastí to Áfyssos, and across the peninsula to Potistiká – such that the only undamaged pines grow around Neohóri, southeast of Miliés, and above Katiyiórgis. There are, however, interesting corners, and considerably less tourism inland, while a number of busy coastal resorts attract a mixed clientele of foreigners and Greeks. The area can be reached a little tortuously by bus or car from Vólos, or more directly by sea, via speedboats from Vólos.

## Áfyssos

The first village you come to in the deep south, **ÁFYSSOS**, is by far the prettiest Pagasitic resort, laid out like a theatre, on hillside slopes with a shady waterfront square and a fairly broad, long crescent beach, lined with consistently vernacular structures: tavernas, private bungalows, small hotels and rooms. It's packed out in summer – with Greeks, especially – and you can forget about the teeming weekends. Its main claim to fame is that this was the very spot from which Jason and the Argonauts embarked in pursuit of the Golden Fleece.

## rgalastí

**RGALASTÍ**, an inland junction point, is the biggest place in the south, with a **post ffice**, **bank** ATM by the church, petrol stations and shops, as well as car rental. rgalastí is close to the Pagasitic Gulf, with two **beaches** just a brief drive (or short walk) est. **Kálamos** is about the longest and sandiest on the Pagasitic side, but the road runs st behind it; there are dozens of apartments and two tavernas. Secluded **Paralía Páou**, ached by a different, dead-end road, is by contrast fine gravel, one of the best on the agasitic, but without amenities. En route there, stop at **Ayíou Nikoláou Páou monastery**, estored as a conference and New-Age seminar centre but usually open to permit iewing its **frescoes** dated to 1794; particularly fine are an Ancient of Days in the arthex dome, townscapes with ships and a *Pandokrátor* in the sanctuary dome.

## Hórto and Milína

Continuing south from Argalastí, you reach the sea again after 7km at **HÓRTO**, a quiet ttle resort largely ensured against exploitation by its mediocre beaches. Just 3km urther, **MILÍNA** seems far more commercialized; the beach is scanty, the norm for agasitic beaches, making it mostly a place to watch magnificent sunsets over the ffshore islets and distant mainland ridges from one of the waterside **bar-cafés**. Beyond Milína to the south and west, there are no more shoreline villages, and the arren landscape becomes increasingly empty, with only the occasional weekend villa r moored boat to vary the horizon.

## Plataniás

Heading south eventually brings you to **PLATANIÁS** (or "Plataniá"), on the Pelion's outh coast. One of the earliest Pelion beach resorts, Plataniás is essentially a collection f low-rises interspersed with restored vernacular houses. Named for the robust plane rees in the stream valley meeting the sea here, this is the biggest southern resort after Milína, with bus service from Vólos, and excursion *kaïkia* – on which you can arrange assage – calling most days from Skiáthos. The small beach is fine, but always busy; rom the olive grove just inland, an obvious path, threading spectacularly above the oast, leads twelve minutes west to the much bigger and better strand of **Mikró**, with aturist covelets in between.

## Tríkeri and Ayía Kyriakí

Until 1974 no road linked southwesterly **TRÍKERI** with the rest of the Pelion; though a road highway now connects it with Milína in less than 45 minutes, this crab-claw-haped peninsula still feels remote and insular. The hilltop village of **Tríkeri** ("Horió" in ocal parlance) has few amenities for outsiders so best to pass on down the hill to its ort town, **AYÍA KYRIAKÍ**. Transport by donkeys and mules is on the wane, but the 500m *kalderími* that connects the two is still well used (drivers tackle a winding, 6km oad). Ayía Kyriakí is still very much a working port with multicoloured fishing smacks t anchor, and much the most attractive spot on this coast. It's also a very active hipbuilding centre; in the boatyard, a variety of craft are still built as they always have een, continuing the local seafaring tradition. Tourist facilities are few, perhaps because here's no really good beach nearby.

## ACCOMMODATION AND EATING                                        SOUTHERN PELION

here are few more restored eighteenth-century mansions here, but mostly the south features modern, self-catering esorts and modest rooms for rent, more in keeping with the arid, more typically "Greek" landscape.

### ARGALASTÍ

★ **Agamemnon** ☎ 24230 54557, ⌨ agamemnon.gr. his well-restored, eighteenth-century mansion-hotel has swimming pool, common areas stuffed with antiques, a restaurant and wi-fi access; rooms, some with fireplaces, feature lots of stone, some with wood floors. Self-catering studios, too. **€60**

### HÓRTO

**Diplomats' Holidays** ☎ 24230 65497, ⓦ diplomats holidays.com. A mock-traditional complex of white, red-tile-roofed houses set amid garden greenery. Excellent facilities include a pool, tennis court and private beach, pebbly and small, but all yours. All accommodation is self-catering and comes with a/c and private verandas. April–Oct. €65

### MILÍNA

**Accommodation** in this resort is largely self-catering, and handled by tour companies. Check with the *Houses of Pelion* agency (☎ 24230 65471, ⓦ pelion.co.uk), which can fix you up with one of their premises here.

★ **O Sakis** ☎ 24230 66078. This seafront taverna is the best in the area and has the most genuinely Greek feel. You can assemble a tasty meal of seafood, two mezédhes and local wine for €14 – or scaly fish for a bit more. Lots of meat dishes, too. Daily lunch & dinner.

**Xenon Athina** ☎ 24230 65473, ⓦ athina-pelion.com. Located directly on the seafront, the fully self-catering accommodation here is simple but clean and comfortable; all rooms feature a/c and balconies, some with sea view. April–Oct. €55

### PLATANIÁS

**Camping Louisa** ☎ 24230 71260, ⓦ camplouisa.com. Located on the access road 600m inland, set amid forest and flowers and a certified organic farm, you'll find this rustic campsite. They offer full kitchen use as well as their own taverna, plus 24hr hot showers and laundry facilitie Full range of information on activities that includ kayaking, area hikes, spelunking, rock-climbing, hors riding, mountain-biking and fishing. Some sites have se views. May–Sept. €6/person; €3/car.

**Platanias** ☎ 24230 71240, ⓦ hotelplatanias.con Located east of the river mouth, right on the waterfron this is the best and quietest option in Plataniás. Set in rambling complex, all rooms have a kitchenette an balcony, and mostly mountain rather than sea views; the are also family units suitable for four. They also have the own sea-front taverna (*To Steki*) on the ground floor. €50

### AYÍA KYRIAKÍ

★ **Argo-Mythos** Mylos ☎ 24230 91032, ⓦ argomythc .gr. This beautiful, well-managed hilltop resort, just 4k over the hill from Ayía Kyriakí, has it all: rooms and sel catering apartments with a/c and balconies, a swimmin pool, a restaurant, and proximity to a cove with beach – plu fine views. €45

**Mouragio** ☎ 24210 45791. This traditional taverna, on of three lined up here, is the most likely to be open all yea and offers the usual Greek dishes, temptingly prepared an at excellent prices (€10–15/person), with fresh catch-o the-day. Daily lunch & dinner.

**Paradhosiakós Xenónas** ☎ 24230 91112 or 697 87 7 831. This is one of the agents that coordinate room renta in buildings all over the village. Accommodation is bas but clean, and they usually include breakfast. €40

# Lárissa and around

**LÁRISSA**, approached across a prosperous but dull landscape of wheat and corn fields, is a major transport hub, as well as both marketplace and major garrison: army camps ring it, the airport remains monopolized by the Greek Air Force, and the southwestern part of the city – with over 160,000 inhabitants – is dominated by ranks of military housing. There's no real reason to stay here, unless your transport scheduling requires it, and, if that happens, you'll find a city centre with an ancient theatre and the remains of an acropolis with archeological layers dating 8000 years back to Neolithic times. In the modern centre, life focuses around three main squares and a park.

Travelling **north** from Lárissa, the motorway heads towards Thessaloníki via the renowned **Vale of Témbi**, between mounts Olympus and Óssa, before emerging on the coast. **West from Lárissa**, the road follows the River Piniós to **Tríkala**, a provincial capital with a fairly attractive centre and important Byzantine monuments nearby.

### ARRIVAL AND ACTIVITIES

**By train** The train station (☎ 24105 90143) is located south of the city centre, at Oktourou Square.
Destinations Athens (hourly; 3hr 15min–4hr 30min); Thessaloníki (hourly; 1hr 10min–2hr); Tríkala (2 daily; 1hr 15min); Vólos (hourly; 50min).

**By bus** The main KTEL station (☎ 24105 37777) is or Yeoryiádhou at the far north end of Olýmbou, 200m east o the acropolis, but all buses towards Tríkala leave from a station on Iróön Polytekhníou southwest of the centre (☎ 24105 90143).

estinations Athens (6 daily; 4hr 15min); Kalambáka via rikala (hourly; 1hr 15min); Lamía (six daily; 2hr); hessaloníki (hourly; 2hr); Tríkala (hourly; 1hr); Vólos almost hourly; 1hr).

**Olympos Trek** ☎ 24109 21244, ⓦ olympostrek.gr. Lárissa-based operator offering rafting trips along the Vale of Témbi gorge with Grade IV rapids at Vernézi (€60 for 3hrs).

## ACCOMMODATION AND EATING

**Metropol** Roosevelt 14 ☎ 24105 37161, ⓦ hotel metropol.gr. Large, popular, cheerfully decorated hotel; its 80-place basement garage is a blessing in a town with difficult parking. Rooms are spacious, soundproofed, and have a/c. You can have your breakfast (included) in your room, or in their full-service restaurant, where meals go for 10–15. Non-smoking rooms are available. **€60**

**To Syndrivani** Protopapadháki 8 ☎ 24105 35933. On the south side of tree-filled Platía Makaríou – one of the main squares, where the central post office is – this classic taverna purveys a variety of *mayireftá*, with tables outside in summer. €10–15 for a full meal. Daily lunch & dinner.

# The Vale of Témbi

The **Vale of Témbi**, for millennia inspiration to poets, is a gorge-like valley cut over the eons by the Piniós River, which runs for nearly 10km between steep cliffs of the Olympus (Ólymbos) and Óssa ranges. In antiquity it was sacred to Apollo and constituted one of the few practicable approaches into central Greece – being the route taken by both Xerxes and Alexander the Great.

At the beginning of the vale, on the northern side, a notable landmark is the **Hasa Baba Tekkés**, the domed remnant of a Turkish Dervish monastery (not open to visitors). Halfway through the vale (on the southeast flank) another ruin is the **Kástro tís Oreás** ("Castle of the Beautiful Maiden"), one of four local Frankish guardposts, while marking the northern end – and the border with Macedonia – is the Platamónas Crusader-built **fortress** (Summer Tues–Fri 8am–7pm; winter Tues–Fri 8.30am–5pm; all year Sat & Sun 8.30am–3pm).

# Tríkala and around

**TRÍKALA** (population 50,000) has a fairly charming centre and is reasonably easy to manoeuvre, although like so many Greek municipalities it's generally shabby and seems to be dusty even when it's raining. The town is evenly divided by the Lethéos River, a tributary of the Piniós – clean enough to harbour trout – and backed by the Kóziakas mountain range rising abruptly to the west. For most travellers, it's merely a staging post en route to the Metéora, with the rail line connecting Lárissa and Tríkala continuing to Kalambáka. Frequent buses also call from Lárissa, with additional services heading west over the mountains.

Tríkala was the capital of a nineteenth-century Ottoman province, and in the **Varoúsi** district – below the fortress clock tower at the north end of town – there are lanes with variably restored houses from that era.

The town's inner **fortress**, a Turkish and Byzantine adaptation of a fourth-century BC citadel, hosts attractive gardens and a terrace café. The liveliest part of town, encompassing what remains of the **old bazaar**, is the streets around the central, riverside **Platía Iróön Polytekhníou** with its statue of local hero Stefanos Sarafis, commander of ELAS from 1943 to 1945. Rembétika great Vassilis Tsitsanis (see Contexts p.797) also hailed from here, and he, too, is honoured by the street bearing his name, heading east from the platía.

## ARRIVAL AND DEPARTURE                                    TRÍKALA

**By train** The picturesque nineteenth-century station (☎ 24310 27214) is still used and has been upgraded. It's on Asklipiou, all the way at the southern edge of town.

Destinations Athens (2 daily; 4–5hr); Kalambáka (8 daily; 15min); Lárissa (2 daily; 1hr); Thessaloníki (1 daily; 2hr 30min).

**By bus** The KTEL is on Óthonos on the southwest bank of the river, 300m southeast of the square.

Destinations Athens (7 daily; 4hr 30min); Eláti (2 daily Mon–Fri, 1 Sat & Sun; 1hr); Ioánnina (2 daily; 2hr 30min); Kalambáka (hourly, 6am–10pm; 30min); Lárissa (hourly;

1hr); Métsovo (2 daily; 2hr); Pýli (hourly; 20min).

**By car** Drivers should be mindful of the prevailing pa and-display parking scheme, easily enough avoided parking slightly out of the centre – or following signs attended fee car parks.

## ACCOMMODATION AND EATING

★ **Palia Istoria** Ypsilanti 3 ☎ 24310 77627. A popular taverna (the name means the "Old Story") in the Manavika district, with good prices (€10–12) for dishes such as sardines, grilled mushrooms, ostrich steak, *imám baildí* and hot peppers. Daily lunch & dinner.

**Panellinion** Platía Ríga Feréou ☎ 24310 73545, ⓦ panellinion.com. There are three mid-range hotels in town but the *Panellinion* is the most distinctive and historic. This Neoclassical beauty is away from traffic noise, gracing a mostly pedestrian area. It dates from 1914 and hosted leading Greek politicians and artists of the era; during World

War II it served as the Italian and German HQ. En-sui rooms are parquet-floored and a/c, some with balconies ar small tubs; there's a mezzanine bar and a decent groun floor restaurant, the *Aigli*, where breakfast is offered. **€60**

**Selemekos** Óthonos 10 ☎ 24310 22118. Come here f an excellent *mayireftá* meal and rub elbows with wh passes for the town's young and stylish set. Located ne the KTEL station, in the hub of daytime café society c pedestrianized Asklipíou. Dishes start at just €3. Dai lunch & dinner.

# Pýli

It takes some exercise of will to delay immediate progress from Tríkala to the Metéora. Byzantine aficionados, however, should make a detour to **PÝLI**, 19km southwest, for the thirteenth-century church of **Pórta Panayía**, one of the unsung beauties of the region, in a superb setting at the mouth of a gorge.

A kilometre upstream from Pórta Panayía, easiest reached along the Pýli bank of the river, a graceful **medieval bridge**, built in 1514 by St Vissarionos, spans the Portaïkós a the point where it exits a narrow gorge.

## Pórta Panayía

Daily: summer 8am–noon & 4–8pm; winter 9am–noon & 3–5pm • €2

Much of the current church of **Pórta Panayía** was completed in 1283 by Prince Ioannis Doukas of the Despotate of Epirus, atop an ancient Athena temple (its masonry liberall recycled into the walls); the domed narthex, Serbian built, was added a century later. In the three-aisled Doukas section, perpendicular barrel vaults over a narrow transept and more generous nave lend antiseismic properties, with further support from six columns.

The highlights of the interior are two **mosaic icons** depicting the adult Christ plus the Virgin holding the Child right-handedly, contrary to the usual iconography. Slightly later **frescoes** have fared less well, either blackened by fires or long covered by plaster. The most interesting is the *Metastási* (Assumption) of the Virgin on the west wall, reflecting the church's August 23 festival and a late medieval Holy Trinity over the apse showing Renaissance influence.

## ARRIVAL AND DEPARTURE

**By bus** Pórta Panayía church is a 10min walk from the bus stop in Pýli village. Cross the Portaïkós River on the footbridge, then bear left on the far bank until you see the dome.

**By car** Cars must use a slightly longer route via a one-lan vehicle bridge.

## ACCOMMODATION AND EATING

The church caretaker is often found in the excellent, reasonable café/bar just upstream from the church, and may admit yo outside of the stated hours.

**Pyli** ☎ 24310 23510, ⓦ hotelpyli.gr. A comfortable, traditional hotel upstream from the church, with a mix of wood- and tile-floored balconied rooms, from which there

are superb views of the gorge and river. Substantia breakfast included featuring home-made jams, cheese an ham. **€40**

# The Metéora

The **monasteries of the METÉORA** are indisputably one of the great sights of Greece. These extraordinary buildings, perched on seemingly inaccessible rock pinnacles, occupy a valley just north of **Kalambáka**; *metéora* means "suspended in mid-air", while *alabak* is an Ottoman Turkish word meaning cliff or pinnacle. Arriving at the town, you glimpse the closest of the monasteries, Ayíou Stefánou, firmly ensconced on a massive pedestal; beyond stretches a forest of greyish pinnacles, cones and stubbier, rounded cliffs. These are remnants of river sediment which flowed into a prehistoric sea that covered the plain of Thessaly around 25 million years ago, subsequently moulded into bizarre shapes by the combined action of fissuring from tectonic-plate pressures and erosion by the infant River Piniós.

## Brief history

Legend credits **St Athanasios**, founder of the earliest hermitage here (late 900s), with flying up the rocks on the back of an eagle. More prosaically, local villagers may have helped the original hermits up – with ropes and pulleys. Centuries later, in 1336 they were joined by two Athonite monks: **Gregorios** and his disciple **Athanasios**. Gregorios soon returned to Áthos, having ordered Athanasios to found a monastery. This Athanasios did around 1344, establishing Megálou Meteórou. Despite imposing a

**3**

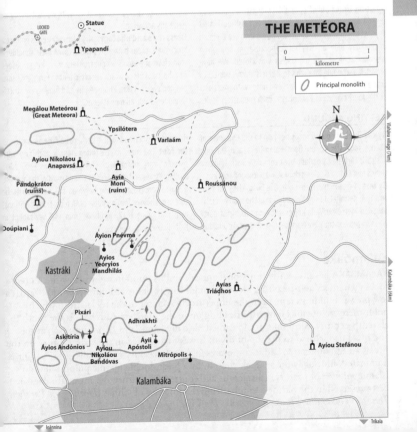

THE METÉORA

0          1
kilometre

◯ Principal monolith

N

LOCKED GATE

◉ Statue

Ypapandí

Megálou Meteórou (Great Meteora)

Ypsilótera

Varlaám

Ayíou Nikoláou Anapavsá

Ayía Moní (ruins)

Roússanou

Pandokrátor (ruins)

Doúpiani

Áyion Pnévma

Ayios Yeóryios Mandhilás

Kastráki

Ayías Triádhos

Pixári

Adhrakhtí

Askitíria

Ayios Andónios

Ayíou Nikoláou Bandóvas

Ayii Apóstoli

Mitrópolis

Ayíou Stefánou

Kalambáka

Ioánnina

Trikala

Vlahává village (7km)

Kalambáka (4km)

particularly austere rule he was quickly joined by other brothers, including (in 1381) **John Urod**, who renounced the throne of Serbia to become the monk Ioasaph.

Royal patronage was instrumental in endowing monasteries and hermitages, which multiplied on all the (relatively) accessible rocks to 24 institutions during the reign of Ottoman sultan Süleyman the Magnificent (1520–66). Money was provided by estates in distant Wallachia and Moldavia, as well as in Thessaly itself. It was largely the loss of land and revenues (particularly after the Greco-Turkish war) that brought about the **ruin of the monasteries** – although some were simply not built to withstand the centuries and gradually disintegrated in the harsh climatic conditions here.

By the late 1950s, there were just four active monasteries, struggling along with barely a dozen monks between them – an era chronicled in Patrick Leigh Fermor's *Roumeli*. Ironically, before being overtaken by **tourism** in the 1970s, the monasteries had begun to revive, attracting younger and more educated brothers; today about sixty monks and fifteen nuns dwell in the six extant foundations.

## INFORMATION                                                          THE METÉORA

Seeing the six inhabited monasteries of the Metéora requires at least a full day, which means staying at least one night, in either **Kalambáka** or **Kastráki**. Perhaps the ideal time to visit is out of season, when the leaves turn or snow blankets the pinnacles. During midsummer, the commercialization, traffic and crowds detract from the wild, spiritual aspect of the valley. In this period you're better off heading for less visited monasteries such as Ayíou Nikoláou or Ayías Triádhos.

**Opening times** Out of 24 original monasteries, there are six still functioning, all keeping different visiting hours/days. At the time of writing it was possible to see them all in one day only on weekends, because on any given weekday at least one monastery was closed. We have provided a schedule for each site, but it is always subject to change, so confirm opening days and times with your hotel or the tourist office in Kalambáka. Each monastery levies an admission charge – currently €2, with student discount generally not given.

**Dress code and photography** All monasteries enforce a strict dress code: both sexes must cover their shoulders; women wear a long skirt not trousers; men, long trousers not shorts. Skirts or wraps are often lent to female visitors but don't rely on this. Photography and filming are strictly forbidden inside all monasteries.

## GETTING AROUND

**By car** There are paved roads right up to the entrances of all the monasteries, up from Kalambáka and through Kastráki. Each has a parking area complete with souvenir stands and *kantínas* selling drinks and packaged snacks.

**By bus** In season there are up to five buses daily (at 9am and 1pm definitely) from Kalambáka up the road as far as Megálou Meteórou/Varlaám; even being taken just part-way will provide the necessary head start to make a hiking day manageable, and to fit in perhaps half the monasteries.

**On foot** The main road is often narrow and busy with speeding cars, so follow the hiking directions – by using available trails and dirt tracks you avoid most of the asphalt. If you're considering hiking between the monasteries be sure to get hold of *The Footpaths of Meteora* (Kritiki Editions), map and guide (€12) available from the newsagent in Kalambáka's main square.

# Kalambáka

**KALAMBÁKA** has pleasantly functional appeal, and its position right below the **Metéora** rocks guarantees awe-inspiring views. Though largely destroyed during World War II, a few prewar buildings remain in the upper reaches, closer to the rocks, from which point there are obvious footpaths heading up in the Metéora. Also here is the ninth to eleventh-century **Mitrópolis** or old cathedral (daily 8am–1pm & 4–6pm; €2), at the end of a bucolic road to the top of town. It was first erected in the sixth century on the site of an Apollo temple and incorporates Classical masonry in its walls. The interior is dominated, unusually for a Greek church, by a great double marble pulpit – like an Islamic *mimber* or oratory. Thirteenth- and fourteenth-century Byzantine frescoes are best preserved in the narthex, emphasizing the miracles of Christ (*Healing the Paralytic*, *The Storm on Galilee*, *Raising Lazarus*, *The Wedding at Cana*).

## ARRIVAL AND INFORMATION
## KALAMBÁKA

**By train** The train station is on the ring road three blocks south of the centre.

Destinations Athens (2 direct daily, 2 with connections; 4hr 30min–5hr 30min); Laríssa (2 daily; 1hr); Thessaloníki (2 daily; 4hr).

**By bus** Incoming buses stop at the central Platía Dhimarhíou, and the KTEL station is just downhill from there, two blocks down Ródhon.

Destinations Athens (7 daily; 5hr): Ioánnina (2 daily; 2hr 30min); Kastráki (hourly, 6am–10pm; 10min); Métsovo (2 daily; 1hr 30min); Tríkala (hourly, 6am–10pm; 30min); Vólos (4 daily; 2hr 30min).

**Taxi ☎** 24320 22310.

**Tourist office** Diagonally opposite the KTEL (☎ 24320 77734), with maps and foreign-language guides.

## ACCOMMODATION

Arrivals may be met by **accommodation touts**; you are advised to ignore them, following numerous complaints about substandard rooms and price-fiddling. It's also best to avoid hotels on the main street, which are usually filled with coach tours and plagued by traffic noise despite double glazing.

★ **Monastiri** Nea Dimotiki Odos ☎ 24320 23952, ⓦ monastiri-guesthouse.gr. Located on the lower side of the train station, with views of the pinnacles, everything in this handsome stone mansion is done with perfect taste and sumptuous style. Spiros and Dita are most welcoming hosts and speak perfect English. Plus, Spiros is extremely knowledgeable about hiking trails throughout the Metéora. Wonderful home-made breakfast included, in the sunny parlour, with views. **€60**

★ **Mythos Guesthouse & Restaurant** Vlachavas 20 (Platanos Square) ☎ 24320 23952, ⓦ mythos-guesthouse.com. Situated near the upper, old part of the town, the

very cosy rooms in this fresh new property have balconies with Metéora views. Facilities include en-suite bathrooms, free wi-fi, flat screen TV, a/c and free parking. The atmospheric taverna on the ground floor serves fresh traditional dishes using only local produce. Local, high-quality wines, too. About €10/person. Breakfast included. **€50**

**Odysseon** ☎ 24320 22320, ⓦ hotelodysseon.gr. Hotel set on the main through road at the Kastráki end of things, but fairly quiet since set back. Rooms feature a mix of tile or parquet floors, and showers or tubs. There's a bright salon for breakfast (included). **€45**

## EATING AND DRINKING

**O Skaros** ☎ 24320 24152. Not many tourists find it (it's on the west edge of town), but locals certainly know about the excellent *kebáb*, chops and own-grown vegetables served here. About €10/person. Daily lunch & dinner.

★ **Panellinion** ☎ 24320 24735. Located right on the central square, this large restaurant has cheery rustic-kitsch decor and average prices (around €15–20).

High-quality ingredients, home cooking, and good brown bread, plus superb fresh-cut chips. Forget the menu and choose from among the dishes of the day, which may include lamb with oregano, lemon chicken, vegetable stews or casseroles, or another of the chef's family recipes – always based on whatever's in season. Seating inside and out. Daily lunch & dinner.

---

## METÉORA ACTIVITIES

Beyond visits to the monasteries themselves, the dramatic setting makes for exciting outdoor activities, especially hiking. In all, there are nearly 700 different trails among and around the monoliths, though many of them are far from an easy stroll and some are crumbling outright. In any case, if you go off-road, a good map is essential (see p.52), and don't hesitate to ask the locals about current conditions.

### USEFUL CONTACTS

**No Limits** ☎ 24320 78180, ⓦ nolimits.com.gr. Long-established Greek operator focusing on mountain and river adventures in Metéora and areas of the Píndhos range, especially the Zagóri. Activities include trekking, rappelling, rafting and mountain biking.

**Summit Post** ⓦ summitpost.org/meteora/150984. Excellent website providing everything you might need to know about climbing and hiking in the Metéora.

# Kastráki

**KASTRÁKI** is a smaller, sloping village located on the way up to the pinnacles, twenty minutes' walk out of Kalambáka, although along the busy and narrow road; in season (May 15–Sept 15) there's regular bus service throughout the day. Like Kalambáka, it's mostly modern, but even more low-key and arguably a better springboard for hiking among and/or rock-climbing the 50-odd pinnacles all around here.

## ACCOMMODATION AND EATING

Kastráki has scores of mid-range *dhomátia*, mostly high standard, as well as several hotels. As at Kalambáka it's worth avoiding the main road, where coaches rumble through much of the day (and scooters buzz along by night).

**Camping Vrachos** ☎ 24320 22293, �🌐 campingkastraki .gr. Entering the downhill end of the village, you pass this well-equipped facility, with a pool, minimarket, a restaurant, and fairly reliable facilities (hot water for showers can run out). **€10**

★ **Doupiani House** ☎ 24320 77555, �🌐 doupianihouse .com. Well sign posted left of the road, with superb views from the front-facing rooms; proprietors Thanassis and Toula serve breakfast (included) in the finest hotel garden of Kastráki, and can point walkers to the start of various hikes. Closed Dec–Feb. **€50**

★ **Paradhisos** ☎ 24320 22723. This place is on the through road, with views, and besides excellent *kokorétsi* and *biftéki* features *moussakás*, starters and *ravaní* by award-winning owner-chef Koula, long experienced

cooking abroad and in Thessaloníki. Everything is fresh and local. €10–15/person. Daily lunch & dinner.

**Pyrgos Adrachti** ☎ 24320 22275, �🌐 hotel-adrachti.gr. Built in 2007, this cosy, family-run property sits at the top of the old quarter – a steep drive up but ample parking on arrival. Features some of the best views in the area from their comfortable wood and stone rooms with a/c. Free wi-fi and parking. Breakfast included. **€70**

**Vassiliki Zioga** ☎ 24320 24037, �🌐 ziogasrooms.com. Located downhill and well back from the road, this family offers simple balconied, marble-floored rooms with a/c and wi-fi, most with superb views, above a huge restaurant (their own farm produce; €10/person), where guests have breakfast (included). Free parking. **€40**

# The monasteries

The four most visited monasteries and convents – **Megálou Meteórou**, **Ayíou Nikoláou**, **Varlaám** and **Roussánou** – are essentially museum-monuments. Only **Ayías Triádhos** and **Ayíou Stefánou** still function with a primarily religious purpose, though there has been a notable increase in pilgrimage by devout Romanian and Russian Orthodox. Handy service elevators have now been installed to take care of both deliveries and visiting dignitaries. However, access for most visitors is by extensive **stairways** carved into the rock in the early twentieth century.

Each monastery consists essentially of monks' cells focused round a central space, with chapels and refectories added on as possible – up, down and sideways – given the physical limitations of constructing on a rock pinnacle. The central church of each monastery, the *katholikón*, is usually elaborately decorated with beautiful and often quirky sixteenth- and seventeenth-century frescoes.

## Ayíou Nikoláou Anapafsá

☎ 24320 22375 • Daily except Fri: April–Oct 9am–5pm; Nov–March 9am–1pm

The diminutive **Ayíou Nikoláou Anapafsá** is the closest monastery to Kastráki (20min on foot or 5min by car). The road leads to the base of the stairway-path (150 steps). This tiny, multi-levelled structure has superb frescoes from 1527 by the Cretan painter Theophanes in its *katholikón* (main chapel). On the east wall of the naos over the window, a shocked disciple somersaults backwards at the *Transfiguration*, an ingenious use of the cramped space; in the *Denial of Peter* on the left door-arch as you enter the naos, the protagonists warm their hands over a fire in the pre-dawn, while above the *ierón* window is the *Sacrifice of Abraham*. On the west wall of the narthex, a stylite (column-dwelling hermit) perches in a wilderness populated by wild beasts, while an acolyte

---

**HEALING HEADSCARVES**

Visitors to Kastráki are often puzzled by the sight of brightly coloured rags hanging in a cave high above the village. This is the shrine of **Áyios Yeóryios Mandhilás** (Saint George of the Kerchiefs), and the "rags" are votive cloths, offerings to the saint. Legend has it that in the seventeenth century, during the Turkish occupation of Greece, a local Muslim landowner cut down some trees in the saint's sacred grove. As punishment, Saint George paralyzed the man's hand; and he was only cured after he offered the saint his wife's veil or *yashmak*, the most precious gift a Muslim can give. In memory of that donation, once a year on April 23, a couple of hundred daredevil youth from neighbouring villages clamber up to hang new pieces of cloth and retrieve the old ones, a guarantee of good luck and good health in the coming year.

---

prepares to hoist up a supply basket – as would have been done just outside when the fresco was new. Other Desert Fathers rush to attend the funeral of St Ephraim the Syrian: some riding beasts, others – crippled or infirm – on litters or piggyback on the strong.

**3**

### Megálou Meteórou

🕿 24320 22278 • Daily except Tues in summer; Tues & Wed in winter: April–Oct 9am–5pm; Nov–March 9am–4pm

The **Megálou Meteórou** (aka Great Meteoron & Metamorphosis) is the highest monastery – requiring a climb of nearly 300 steps from its entrance – built on the Platýs Líthos ("Broad Rock") 615m above sea level. It enjoyed extensive privileges and dominated the area for centuries: in an eighteenth-century engraving (sold as a reproduction) it dwarfs its neighbours.

The monastery's cross-in-square **katholikón**, dedicated to the Transfiguration, is Metéora's most imposing; columns and beams support a lofty dome with a *Pandokrátor*. It was enlarged in the 1500s and 1600s, with the original chapel, constructed by the Serbian Ioasaph in 1383, now the *ierón* behind the intricately carved *témblon*. Frescoes, however, are much later (mid-sixteenth century) than at most other monasteries and artistically undistinguished; those in the narthex concentrate almost exclusively on grisly martyrdoms.

Elsewhere in this vast, arcaded cluster of buildings, the *kellári* (cellar) hosts an exhibit of rural impedimenta; in the domed, vaulted refectory, still set with the traditional silver/pewter table service for monastic meals, a **museum** features exquisite carved-wood crosses and rare icons. The ancient smoke-blackened kitchen adjacent preserves its bread oven and soup-hearth.

### Varlaám (Barlaam)

🕿 24320 22277 • Daily except Thurs; also closed Fri in winter: April–Oct 9am–4pm; Nov–March 9am–4pm

**Varlaám** is among the oldest monasteries, replacing a hermitage established by St Varlaam shortly after Athanasios' arrival. The present building, now home to a handful of monks and one of the most beautiful in the valley, was constructed by the Apsaras brothers from Ioánnina in 1540–44. To get up to it from the entrance point means climbing about 150 steps.

The monastery's *katholikón*, dedicated to Ayíon Pándon (All Saints), is small but glorious, supported by painted beams, its walls and pillars totally covered by frescoes (painted 1544–66), dominated by the great *Pandokrátor* of the inner dome. Among the more unusual are a beardless Christ Emmanuel in the right transept conch, and the Parliament of Angels on the left; on one pier, the Souls of the Righteous nestle in the Bosom of Abraham, while the Good Thief is admitted to Paradise. On the inner sanctuary wall, there's a vivid Crucifixion and a Dormition of the Virgin with, lower down, an angel severing the hands of the Impious Jew attempting to overturn her funeral bier. The treasury-museum features crucifixes and silver items; elsewhere the monks' original water barrel is on show.

Varlaám prominently displays its old **ascent tower**, comprising a reception platform, well-worn windlass and original rope-basket. Until the 1930s the only way of reaching most Metéoran monasteries was by being hauled up in said rope-basket, or by equally perilous retractable ladders. A nineteenth-century abbot, asked how often the rope was changed, replied, "Only when it breaks." Steel cables eventually replaced ropes, and then steps were cut to all monasteries by order of the Bishop of Tríkala, unnerved by the vulnerability of his authority on visits. Today rope-baskets figure only as museum exhibits, supplanted by metal cage-buckets, as well as a hidden elevator or two.

## Roussánou

🕾 24320 22649 • Daily except Wed: April–Oct 9am–6pm; Nov–March 9am–2pm

The convent of **Roussánou**, founded in 1545, has an extraordinary, much-photographed situation, its walls edging to sheer drops all around. After some 150 steps up, the final approach to the convent (today housing about a dozen nuns) is across a vertiginous bridge from an adjacent rock.

Inside, the narthex of its main chapel has particularly gruesome frescoes (1560) of martyrdom and judgement, the only respite from sundry beheadings, spearings, crushings, roastings and mutilations being the lions licking Daniel's feet in his imprisonment (left of the window); diagonally across the room, two not-so-friendly lions proceed to devour Saint Ignatios Theoforos. On the right of the transept there's a vivid *Transfiguration* and *Entry to Jerusalem*, while to the left are events after Christ's Resurrection. On the east of the wall dividing naos from narthex is an exceptionally vivid Apocalypse.

## Ayías Triádhos

🕾 24320 22220 • Daily except Thurs in summer; Wed & Thurs in winter: April–Oct 9am–5pm; Nov–March 9am–3pm

Few tour buses stop at **Ayías Triádhos** (Holy Trinity) – despite it famously featuring in the 1981 James Bond film, *For Your Eyes Only* – and life remains essentially monastic, even if there are only three brothers to maintain it. The approach from the parking area consists of some 150 steps down and then another roughly 150 back up the other side of the sheer ravine that separates its pinnacle from the road. You finally emerge into a cheerful compound with small displays of kitchen/farm implements, plus an old ascent windlass.

The seventeenth-century frescoes in the *katholikón* have been completely cleaned and restored, fully justifying a visit. On the west wall, the *Dormition* is flanked by the *Judgement of Pilate* and the *Transaction of Judas*, complete with the thirty pieces of silver and subsequent self-hanging. Like others at the Metéora, this church was built in two phases, as evidenced by two domes, each with a *Pandokrátor* (the one above the *témblon* very fine), and two complete sets of Evangelists on the squinches. In the arch right of the *témblon* is a rare portrait of a beardless Christ Emmanuel, borne aloft by four seraphs; on the arch supports to the left appear the *Hospitality of Abraham* and *Christ the Righteous Judge*.

Although Ayías Triádhos teeters above its deep ravine and the little garden ends in a precipitous drop, an obvious, well-signposted path leads from the bottom of the monastery's access steps back to the upper quarter of **Kalambáka**. This 1km descent is a partly cobbled, all-weather surface in good shape, ending adjacent to Kalambáka's fine, very early cathedral (see p.236).

## Ayíou Stefánou

🕾 24320 22279 • Daily except Mon: April–Oct 9am–1.30pm & 3.30–5.30pm; Nov–March 9.30am–1pm & 3–5pm

**Ayíou Stefánou**, the last, easternmost monastery, is 1.5km along the road beyond Ayías Triádhos (no path short cuts), and it's the only one that requires no staircase climb to

get to. Note that it's also the only one that closes during lunch. It's occupied by nuns keen to peddle trinkets and memorabilia, but the buildings – bombed during World War II and then raided during the civil war – are disappointing: the obvious one to miss if you're short of time. That said, the fifteenth-century refectory contains an apsidal fresco of the Virgin, beyond the museum graced by a fine *Epitáfios* (Good Friday bier) covering embroidered in gold thread. The trail towards Kalambáka from Ayíou Stefánou is disused and dangerous – return to Ayías Triádhos to use the descending path described above.

# The Píndhos Mountains

Continuing west from Meteóra, you soon encounter the rugged peaks, forested ravines and turbulent rivers of the **Píndhos Mountains**. Over the centuries, this range has insulated the communities and culture here from outside interference, securing a large measure of autonomy even under Ottoman rule. Yet, today it's the mountains themselves that provide the strongest attraction. Their physical beauty is stunning, with limestone peaks, dramatic **gorges** and dense forest contrasting with stone-built **villages** and arched packhorse **bridges**.

Roughly halfway over the mountains stands **Métsovo**, the most convenient venue for alpine life Greek-style, plus a taste of the local **Vlach** culture. Down on the plain below is the fascinating lakeside city of **Ioánnina**, capital of **Epirus**, the last region of Greece to be liberated from the Turks. Farther to the north, back up in the Píndhos mountains, authentic stone hamlets and the stunning **Víkos Gorge** provide unforgettable scenery and hiking opportunities.

## Métsovo

**MÉTSOVO** lies just west of the Katára pass, 1km off the Vía Egnatía. It's a small, touristy alpine town of some 8,000 inhabitants, occupying two sides of a plunging ravine and guarded by the forbidding peaks of the Píndhos range to the south and east. It's pretty enough, with tiers of eighteenth- and nineteenth-century stone houses spilling downhill to and past the main platía, where a few old men still loiter after Sunday Mass in traditional dress (black caps and pompom-topped shoes).

If you avoid the high seasons (midsummer and Christmas/Easter weeks), stay overnight and take in the surroundings, the place can seem magical. In season, Métsovo makes a favourite target for tour buses full of Greeks, who are catered for by shops selling kitsch wooden souvenirs and "traditional" weavings (mostly mass-produced these days). Even the roof tiles of many traditional houses have been replaced with garish modern versions.

Nonetheless, it would be a shame to omit Métsovo altogether, for its history and status as the **Vlach "capital"** make it unique. Positioned astride the most viable route over the Píndhos, it secured a measure of independence, both political and economic,

---

### TAKE THE HIGH ROAD: THE KATÁRA PASS

West of Kalambáka, the 1694-m **Katára Pass** carries the only high-altitude paved road across the central Píndhos Mountains to link the regions of Thessaly and Epirus, which lie on either side. One of the most spectacular drives in the country, this centuries-old route switchbacks through folds in the enormous peaks rising more than 2300m around **Métsovo**. From November to April the pass is snowploughed – although these days the old, twisty road is entirely optional. Sixty enormous tunnels linked by long viaducts have been bored through the ridges here as part of the recently completed **Vía Egnatía** expressway, which now smoothly flows all the way to the west coast.

> ## THE VLACHS
>
> Europe's last semi-nomadic peoples the **Vlachs** have lived in the Píndhos Mountains for centuries. Each summer, the melting of the winter snows finds the vast slopes here coming alive with the sound of bells, as the Vlachs bring their flocks up from the plains to graze in the mountains. Though the ethnicity of the Vlachs (from the ancient Germanic word for "foreigner" *Walh*) is a subject of much scholarly debate, most claim to be descendants of Roman soldiers stationed here in Classical times, and they speak a Latin-derived, unwritten language similar to modern Romanian. Today, although the Greek government keeps no records of ethnicity, it is estimated that perhaps 40,000 Vlachs live in small communities scattered throughout the Píndhos range, where you can still see shepherds wearing the distinctive goat-skin cape and wielding their fanciful crook. In the remotest areas, traditional Vlach pagan beliefs are only thinly overlaid with the Orthodox faith; many elderly women still have a black cross tattooed on their foreheads, to ward off the evil eye, and their gossip is rife with folktales of sorcery and curses.

**3**

in the earliest days of Ottoman rule. Métsovo's continued prosperity and preservation of some traditions is largely due to Baron Mihaïl Tositsas (1888–1950), Swiss-banker offspring of a local family, who left his colossal fortune to an endowment that supports industries, crafts and restoration work in and around the town.

## Áyios Nikólaos

Daily 8.30am–1.30pm & 4–7.30pm • donation and/or purchase expected

The main attraction in Métsovo's surroundings is the stone monastery of **Áyios Nikólaos**, signposted from the main platía but in fact thirty minutes' walk down just south of town; it is reached just off the path toward Anílio, in a dramatic position on a steep ravine. The monastery's *katholikón*, topped by a simple barrel vault, was built in the fourteenth century to an unconventional plan; what might once have been the narthex eventually became a *yinaikonítis* or women's gallery. Inside are some brilliantly coloured **frescoes** dating from 1702, cleaned and illuminated courtesy of the Tosítsa Foundation. A guardian family lives on the premises and receives visitors. You'll also be shown the monks' former cells, with insulating walls of mud and straw, and the abbot's less austere quarters.

## ARRIVAL AND INFORMATION                                    MÉTSOVO

**By bus** Métsovo is on the route between Tríkala and Ioánnina. The bus stop is on the main platía.
Destinations Ioánnina (4 daily; 1hr 30min); Tríkala (2 daily; 3hr 30min).
**By car** The old Kalambáka–Ioánnina highway is now superseded by the Vía Egnatía, seamlessly extending all the

way to the coast, linking Métsovo with Ioánnina and Igoumenítsa.
**Services** The post office is on the main street 200m uphill from the bus stop, with several bank ATMs scattered between the two. There is no tourist office, so to some extent hotel receptions provide that service.

## ACCOMMODATION

Métsovo has a wide range of **accommodation**, with some 20 hotels plus quite a few *dhomátia*, nearly all en suite. Outside Christmas/Easter weeks, the local festival (July 26) or August, you should have little trouble in getting a bed or even bargaining indicated prices down.

**Adonis** ☎ 26560 42300, ⊕ metsovohotels.com. Though recently constructed, this hotel, just above the main square, is a very successful re-creation of the local chalet style, with thick stone walls and lots of woodwork. It offers some of the largest, plushest rooms (almost all with fireplace) in town, some with hydromassage. Free wi-fi. **€60**
**Bitouni** ☎ 26560 41217, ⊕ hotelbitouni.com. At the

top of the main street, the affable proprietor here speaks fluent English, the result of eight years' residence in London. Most rooms are wood-panelled and have balconies with valley views; there are attic suites suitable for four, plus a sauna. Home-made breakfast included. **€50**
**Filoxenia** ☎ 26560 41021, ⊕ jsp@hol.gr. Just behind the grassy central-park hillock, these *dhomátia* (rooms) are

en-suite units and excellent value, with valley views out of the rear rooms and some pricier, plusher units. The manager/owner is very helpful and full of information about the area. Breakfast €4/person. **€40**

**Galaxias** ☎ 26560 41202, � hotel-galaxias-metsovo .gr. This hotel is very traditional, slate-roofed, with lots of natural wood in eight large, comfortable rooms, three with fireplaces. The hotel restaurant is the main option for vegetarians, where a limited but tasty menu is served on the lawn under giant trees. Daily lunch & dinner; full meal about €13. **€60**

## EATING

Restaurants here are generally part of hotels and *dhomátia*, and menus often feature traditional mountain dishes. **Wine** buffs may want to try the fabled Katóyi, available at restaurants, local shops and indeed across Greece. It's a moderately expensive limited bottling from vineyards along the Árakhthos River, though quality of the main Averoff label varies (the Ktima line is best).

**Katoi** ☎ 26560 42040. Named after the noted Métsovo red wine, this popular taverna occupies several wood-panelled rooms on the main square and is good for grills and all the Greek standards. Greek salads go for €6, grills start at €9. Daily lunch & dinner.

# Ioánnina and around

**IOÁNNINA**, the provincial capital of Epirus, with some 130,000 inhabitants, boasts an idyllic setting, its old town jutting out into the great **Lake Pamvótis** along a rocky promontory, its fortifications punctuated by spindly minarets. From this base, **Ali Pasha** "the Lion of Ioánnina" carved from the Turkish domains a personal fiefdom that encompassed much of western Greece and present-day Albania: an act of rebellion that prefigured wider defiance in the Greeks' own **War of Independence**.

Although much of the city is modern and undistinguished (albeit home to a thriving **university**), the old town remains one of the most interesting in Greece. There are stone-built **mosques** (and a **synagogue**) that evoke the Ottoman era, and Ali Pasha's citadel, the **kástro**, survives more or less intact, its **inner citadel**, the **Its Kale**, now a museum park. In the lake, **Nissí island** has a car-free if overly prettified village, and frescoed **monasteries**. Ioánnina is also a springboard for visits to the **caves of Pérama**, among the country's largest, on the western shore of the lake, and a slightly longer excursion to the very ancient Oracle of Zeus at **Dodona**. Finally, the city is also the gateway to what is possibly the area's most rewarding corner, **Zagóri** (see p.250).

## The kástro

In its heyday the **Kástro's** walls dropped abruptly to the lake, and were moated on their landward (southwest) side. The moat has been filled in, and a quay-esplanade now extends below the lakeside ramparts, but there is still the sense of a citadel, with narrow alleys and bazaar-like shops.

### Municipal Ethnographic Museum

Daily: May–Sept 8am–8pm; Oct–April 9am–4pm • €4.40

Signs inside point to the **ethnographic museum**, an elegantly arranged collection of Epirot costumes, guns, silver-work and Islamic art, housed in the well-preserved, floodlit **Aslan Pasha Tzamí**, allowing a rare glimpse inside an intact Greek mosque. It dates from 1618, built on the site of an Orthodox cathedral pulled down in reprisal for a failed local revolt of 1611. The interior retains painted decoration in its dome and *mihrab* (niche indicating direction of Mecca), as well as a vividly coloured *mimber* or pulpit, nicely complementing a walnut and mother-of-pearl suite on display in the "Muslim section".

More poignant is a section devoted to synagogue rugs and tapestries donated by the dwindling Jewish community of about fifty.

IOÁNNINA

**3**

● **EATING & DRINKING**
| | |
|---|---|
| Byzantine Museum Cafe | 3 |
| Fysa Roufa | 5 |
| Limni | 1 |
| Paleopanos | 6 |
| Select | 7 |
| Stin Ithaki | 2 |
| To Manteio | 4 |
| Vrettanía | 8 |

■ **ACCOMMODATION**
| | |
|---|---|
| Galaxy | 6 |
| Kastro | 2 |
| Kentrikon | 4 |
| Olympic | 5 |
| Sotiris & Evangelos Dellas | 1 |
| Tourist | 3 |

## The inner citadel (the Its Kale)

**Its Kale** daily 8am–10pm • Free • **Byzantine Museum** and **Silverwork Hall** summer Mon 12.30–7pm, Tues–Sun 8am–7pm; winter Tues–Sun 8am–5pm • €3

Southeast of the Aslan Pasha Tzamí lies the **inner citadel**, signposted as **Its Kale**, a transliteration of its Turkish name – a kind of fortress within the fortress. The park-like grounds, with wonderful mountain views from this elevated spot, are occasionally used for concerts after-hours, and there's a large and pleasant terrace café-restaurant near the entrance, occupying the garrison's former mess.

Next to the old **Fethiye Tzamí** ("Victory Mosque") and its slim, rocket-like minaret – which occupy an upper corner – one of the two Ottoman graves, surmounted by an elegant wrought-iron cage, is probably that of Ali Pasha, while the other contains his first wife Emine and one son. The mosque itself, remodelled by Ali, was built atop the remains of a thirteenth-century cathedral.

Next to the mosque, on the site of Ali's vanished palace, where Byron was entertained, stands the arcaded so-called **Byzantine Museum**, a thin, largely post-Byzantine collection. The displays comprise masonry, coins, pottery, icons and colour prints of frescoes from various ages; the only actually Byzantine painting is a fresco fragment of *The Betrayal*.

## ALI PASHA – THE LION OF IOÁNNINA

As an "heroic rebel", the Muslim Albanian **Ali Pasha** assumes an ambivalent role – for his only consistent policy was that of ambition and self-interest. As frequent as his attacks on the Ottoman authorities were, he also engaged in acts of appalling savagery against his Greek subjects. Despite this, he is still held in some regard by locals for his perceived role as a **defier of Istanbul**, the common enemy – folk postcards of the man abound, and a platía in the citadel is named after him.

Ali was born in 1741 in Tepelene, now in modern Albania, and by 1787 had been made pasha of Tríkala as a reward for his efforts in the war against Austria. His ambitions, however, were larger, and the following year he **seized Ioánnina**, an important town since the thirteenth century, with a population of 30,000 – probably the largest in Greece at the time. Paying perfunctory and sporadic tribute to the sultan, he operated from here for the next 33 years, allying himself in turn, as strategy required, with the Ottomans, the French or the British.

In 1809, when his dependence upon the sultan was nominal, Ali was visited by the young **Lord Byron**, whom he overwhelmed with hospitality and attention. Byron, impressed for his part with the rebel's daring and stature, and the lively revival of Greek culture in Ioánnina, commemorated the meeting in *Childe Harold*. This portrait that he draws, however, is ambiguous, since Byron well knew that behind Ali's splendid court and deceptively mild countenance were "deeds that lurk" and "stain him with disgrace".

Ali met a suitably grisly end. In 1821, the Ottoman sultan resolved to eliminate Ali's threat to his authority before tackling the Greek insurgency, and he sent an army of 50,000 to capture him. Lured from the security of Ioánnina citadel with false promises of lenient surrender terms, he was ambushed, shot and decapitated, his head sent to Istanbul. The rest of Ali supposedly lies in the northeast corner of the inner citadel.

A few paces down the hill, in the presumed treasury of Ali Pasha's seraglio, is the **Silverwork Hall**, containing important masterpieces of Ioánnina's centuries-old silver-working tradition.

### The old bazaar and Jewish quarter

Apart from the kástro, the town's most enjoyable district is the **old bazaar and Jewish quarter**, a warren of narrow lanes and alleys between the citadel's main gate and Anexartissías avenue bounding it on the south. It retains a cluster of Ottoman-era buildings (including imposing mansions with ornate window grilles and founding inscriptions), as well as a scattering of copper- and tinsmiths, plus the silversmiths who were long a mainstay of the town's economy. Retail **silver** outlets cluster either side of kástro's gate; you'll find the last traditional **tinsmiths** at Anexartissías 84, and the last **copper-mongers** at no. 118–122. *Stoas* off Anexartissías serving old warehouses, now being gentrified, can also be rewardingly explored.

### Nissí island

Water buses half-hourly in summer, otherwise hourly; 8am–11pm, return journey 6.30am–11pm; €1.50 each way

The island of **Nissí** in **Lake Pamvótis** is connected by water buses from the Mólos quay on Platía Mavíli. Only islanders' cars are allowed, hauled across on a chain-barge to the mainland opposite. The pretty island village, founded during the sixteenth century by refugees from the Máni, is flanked by several **monasteries**, worthy targets for an afternoon's visit. By day the main lane leading up from the boat dock is crammed with stalls selling jewellery and kitsch souvenirs. Except at three overpriced waterfront restaurants and another cluster by Pandelímonos, quiet descends with the sun setting vividly over the reed beds that fringe the island.

Lake Pamvótis itself is certainly idyllic-looking enough, and it's the region's largest lake, but runoff **pollution** is an ongoing problem and most locals do not advise either swimming in its waters or eating its fish.

## ARRIVAL AND INFORMATION

**By air** Ioánnina airport is on the road to Pérama, 5km from the centre (city bus #7 links it with town).

**Destinations** Athens (2 daily on Olympic, plus 1 daily on Aegean; 1hr).

**By bus** KTEL buses currently arrive at the station at Zozimadhon 4 (❶ 26510 26404). The bus station on Bizaniou is for local services, such as to the Perama Caves and Dodona.

**Destinations** Athens (9 daily; 7hr 30min); Igoumenítsa (8 daily; 2hr 30min); Métsovo (4 daily; 1hr); Monodhéndhri (Mon, Wed & Fri early morning & early afternoon; 1hr); Pápingo (Mon, Wed & Fri early morning & early afternoon; 2hr); Párga (1 daily; 3hr); Pátra (2 daily; 3hr 30min); Préveza (6 daily; 2hr); Tríkala via Kalambáka (2 daily, 3 Fri &

## IOÁNNINA

Sun; 3hr 15min); Víkos (Wed only early morning & early afternoon; 1hr).

**By car** Most drivers arrive from the south via the new Vía Egnatía expressway. The city's pay-and-display parking scheme only allows two hours at a time – it's easiest to use the car park shown on the map, or try for unregulated spaces in the kástro. The best solution is to choose a hotel with private parking.

**Tourist office** The EOT is at Hodhónis 39 (❶ 26510 41142; Mon–Fri 7.30am–2.30pm) – good for information on current KTEL timetables as well as hiking tips for the Zagóri and Víkos Gorge. Alpine Zone (see p.253) are also worth contacting if you're interested in activities.

## GETTING AROUND

**By bus** Blue-and-white city buses leave from a cluster of stops below the central Platía Pýrrou, mostly on Bizaniou; buy tickets from adjacent booths beforehand, and cancel them when boarding.

**By taxi** Local taxis are dark green; central ranks are marked on the map.

## ACCOMMODATION

Most hotels are located along the main drag Avéroff which leads from central Platía Pýrrou north past the dense grid of lanes in the old bazaar area to the gate of the lakeside kástro.

### CENTRAL IOÁNNINA

**Galaxy** Platía Pýrrou ❶ 26510 25432, ❷ 26510 25032. Comfortable and quiet rooms with spectacular mountain/lake views from the balconies, a/c and small tubs in the bathrooms. You don't get much more central; limited street parking. Breakfast included. **€70**

★ **Kastro** Andhroníkou Paleológou 57 ❶ 26510 22866, ⓦ ameliko.gr. Located at the base of the ramp up to the Its Kale is this freshly restored and very classy inn, with seven individually decorated rooms done in plush fabrics and soft tones. All rooms have a/c; one room has three beds, the others two. Adequate street parking. Breakfast included. **€90**

**Kentrikon** Kollétti 5a ❶ 26510 71771, ⓦ hotel-kentrikon.gr. As the name says, "central": a boutique hotel in a restored building, with exposed stonework, flat-screen TVs and quality furnishings in variably sized rooms (doubles and two galleried family suites). There's a small

salon for breakfast (included) and a pleasant rear courtyard. Parking garage included. **€65**

**Olympic** Melanídhis 2 ❶ 26510 25888, ⓦ hotelolymp.gr. The highest-standard hotel in the city centre, in a fairly quiet spot. Well-appointed rooms (plus a few suites) have music systems, safes, small but well-executed designer bathrooms with tubs, and balconies or large terraces. Full-service restaurant on-site, breakfast included; private parking. **€100**

**Tourist** Kolétti 18 cnr Krystálli ❶ 26510 25070, ⓦ hoteltourist.gr. The only recommendable quasi-budget digs in town, though admittedly in a drab location. Rooms are clean and basic, all with a/c and en suite. There are a few with balconies, although the views are of other high-rise buildings. No parking. **€40**

### CAMPING

**Camping Limnopoula** Yachting Club of Ioánnina Kanari 10 ❶ 26510 25265, ⓦ camping.gr/limnopoula.

---

### SWEET TREATS IN IOÁNNINA

Ioánnina is the original home of **bougátsa** (custard tart; served with a salty *kouloúra* or round biscuit), fresh at breakfast time with sweet or savoury fillings from *Select* at Platía Dhimokratías 2, its decor of terrazzo floor and marble tables unchanged for forty years. Its rival, with a more updated design sense, is *Paleopanos* at Avéroff 3. The patisserie *Vrettania*, under the eponymous hotel at Platía Dhimokratías 11A, has excellent own-brand ice cream as well as all imaginable sticky cakes.

Unusual for in-town is this attractive option, located lakeside, well equipped and mosquito-free, though a bit cramped and more geared towards camper vans than tents. To get here, take city bus #8 or do the 20min walk 1500m west of Platía Mavíli. For two adults, comes to about €25

**NISSÍ**
**Sotiris & Evangelos Dellas** ☎ 26510 81494. Simple *pension* with several rooms sharing bathrooms; you'll find the proprietors at the house right next to the school, or in the ground-floor café-bar of the inn-building (can be noisy at night). Breakfast included. €25

## EATING AND DRINKING

Ioánnina offers numerous **restaurants**. The most obvious concentration lines part-pedestrianized Pamvótidhas northwest of Mólos quay (though addresses are cited as Stratigoú Papágou, the parallel back alley (see map). Just outside the *kástro* gate are a few traditional Greek tavernas and *psistariés*. On Nissí Island, the obvious dockside **tavernas** are atmospheric venues for freshwater specialities like eel (*héli*), crayfish (*karavídhes*), carp (*kyprínos*) and frog legs.

★ **Byzantine Museum Cafe** Its Kale. This is a bustling, atmospheric spot, with fine views, ideal for a meal, or just a drink, before or after you check out the museums here – or any time, really. Expect to pay a little more, about €15/person, €3–4 for a drink. Daily 9am–10pm.
**Fysa Roufa** Avéroff 55 ☎ 26510 70705. Traditional *mayireftá* such as *patsás*, *mayirítsa*, baked fish, suckling pig and *spetzofäï*, whose slightly higher prices are amply justified by the calibre of the cooking, the service, a pleasantly upmarket environment, and the large portions; unusually, there's a full line of desserts too. Cosy loft seating for winter, and a decor of archival photos from Párga, the proprietor's birthplace, and Greek theatre actors. Open 24hr.
**Limni** Stratigoú Papágou 26 ☎ 26510 78988. More likely than its neighbours to have seafood (its name means "lake"), and its slightly elevated prices are compensated for by large portions and the rather luxurious standard, with

both indoor and lakeside terrace seating. Expect to pay about €20/person, depending very much on the fish you choose. Daily lunch & dinner.
★ **Stin Ithaki** Stratigoú Papágou 20A ☎ 26510 73012. The most ambitious menu on the lakefront, encompassing Turkish-style kebabs, Cypriot specialities and Smyrna recipes as well as Epirot standards such as trout, *píttes*, cheeses and mushrooms in various guises. Starters are big, and even better value than main courses, which run €7–10. Try the traditional walnut cake, *karythopita* for dessert. Daily lunch & dinner.
**To Manteio** Karamanlis ☎ 26510 25452. Facing the old ramparts, this simple taverna is very popular with locals, serving all manner of authentically earthy food, including great tztaziki (€3.50) and perfect souvláki, chicken or pork (€8), with home-made chips and secret sauce, all washed down with good house wine. Daily lunch & dinner.

## NIGHTLIFE

Nightlife oscillates between the calmer **cafés** on pedestrian-only lanes on either side of Platía Pýrrou and along nearby Dhodhónis, and the more nocturnal **café-bars**, patisseries and ice-cream parlours on Platía Mavíli, heart of the Mólos or lakefront, where a gas-lantern-lit carnival atmosphere prevails. There are more wine bars, crêperies and the odd cheerfully painted "pub" scattered across the approaches to the castle, especially along Karamanlí. Posters announce hangar-like summer **music clubs** out on the lakeshore.

**Café Avli** Pamvotidhos/Platía Mavíli ☎ 26510 35416. This is a quieter choice in the lakeside café zone, focused on a colourful, tree-shaded courtyard. Primarily frequented by students, as are all the spots around here. Drinks €2–5. Daily, morning till late.
**Presveia** Karamanlí 17 ☎ 26510 26309. Come to this

pub to sample the "new" heartier style of beer now being produced locally in northern Greece. Much appreciated by the evidently well-heeled students who throng here (beers go for €4–10), the place has some 100 varieties on offer, as well as food to go with it (€5–14 for various options with cheese, ham and the like). Daily, evenings till late.

## ENTERTAINMENT

**Cinemas** There are three cinemas around Platía Pýrrou, which usually host first-run films (nearly all in English, with subtitles), as does the Odeon five-screen at the Paralimnio Centre, out in Votanikós district.

**Theatre and music** Various formal music/theatre events occur in midsummer; get information and tickets from the EOT office.

## DIRECTORY

**Books, maps and newspapers** For quality maps and a respectable stock of books in English, head for Papasotiriou

bookshop at Mihaïl Angélou 6, just off Platía Pýrrou; the newsstand at Pyrsinélla 14 has foreign newspapers.

**Car rental** Most rental offices are on Dhodhónis: *Avis*, no. 71 ☎ 26510 46333; *Budget*, no. 109 ☎ 26510 43901; *Tomaso*, no. 42 ☎ 26510 66900; *National/Alamo*, no. 10 cnr Kaliáfa 3G ☎ 26510 47444; and *Hertz*, no. 105 ☎ 693 70 96 377. *Hertz* and *Avis* also have booths at the airport.

**Internet** *On-Line*, on Pyrsinélla, behind the provincial government HQ; open 24hr with cheap rates.
**Post office** Both the central post office (Mon–Fri 7.30am–8pm) and the secondary one (normal hours) have long queues; take a number and wait.

### The Pérama caves

Daily 9am–7pm • €6 • #8 blue city bus runs from the terminal below Platía Pýrrou to Pérama village; the caves are a 10min walk from here

Some 5km north of Ioánnina, the village of **PÉRAMA** claims to have Greece's largest system of **caves**, extending for kilometres beneath a low hill. They were discovered during late 1940 by locals attempting to find shelter from Italian bombing raids. The one-hour mandatory tours of the complex are primarily in Greek (commentary repeated in passable English) and make some effort to educate, though there are the inevitable bawdy nicknames for various suggestively shaped formations.

### Dodona: the Oracle of Zeus

Daily 8.30am–3pm, may close 6pm midsummer • €2 • Dodona is best visited with your own transport – take the Vía Egnatía west and follow the signs (exit "Dhodhóni"). A round-trip by taxi from Ioánnina should cost about €40 per carload, including waiting time

**DODONA**, 22km southwest of Ioánnina in a broad, mountain-ringed valley, comprises the ruins and large **theatre** of the ancient **Oracle of Zeus**, Greece's first oracle, some of the site dating back as far as four millennia.

The impressive theatre was built during the reign of King Pyrrhus (297–272 BC), and was one of the largest in Greece, rivalled only by those at Argos and Megalopolis. The Romans added a protective wall and a drainage channel around the orchestra as adaptations for their blood sports. What's now visible is a meticulous late nineteenth-century reconstruction. Almost all except the stage area is now off-limits, though it's worth following a path around to the top of the *cavea* (seating curve) to fully savour the glorious setting, looking across a green, silent valley to Mount Tómaros. A grand entrance gate leads into the overgrown **acropolis**, with Hellenistic foundations up to 5m wide.

Beside the theatre, tiered against the same slope, are the foundations of a *bouleuterion*, beyond which lie the complex ruins of the **Sanctuary of Zeus**, site of the oracle itself. There was no temple per se until late in the fifth century BC; until then, worship had centred upon the **sacred oak**, inside a circle of votive tripods and cauldrons. The remains you can see today are adorned with a modern oak tree planted by a helpfully reverent archeologist. Nearby is a useful placard detailing the entire site.

Dodona occasionally hosts **musical and ancient drama performances** on summer weekends, though sadly since 2000 these are staged on modern wooden bleachers rather than in the ancient theatre.

---

#### THE OAK TREE ORACLE

"Wintry Dodona" was mentioned by Homer, and religious activities here appear to have begun with the first Hellenic tribes who arrived in Epirus around 1900 BC. Herodotus records that the oracle was founded after the mythic arrival of a *peleiae* (either "dove" or "old woman" in ancient Greek) from Egypt, said to have alighted on an oak tree. In any case, the **oak tree** was certainly central to the cult with the oracle speaking through the rustling of its leaves, amplified by copper vessels suspended from its branches. These sounds would then be interpreted by frenzied priestesses and/or priests, who allegedly slept on the ground and never washed their feet.

Many **oracular inscriptions** were found when the site was first systematically dug in 1952, demonstrating not only the oracle's lingering influence even after its eclipse by Delphi, but also the fears and inadequacies motivating pilgrims of the era in such questions as: "Am I her children's father?" and "Has Peistos stolen the wool from the mattress?"

## Zagóri and the Víkos Gorge

Few parts of Greece are more surprising or more beguiling than the part of the Píndhos mountains known as **ZAGÓRI**. A wild, thinly populated region, it lies just to the north of Ioánnina. The beauty of its landscape is unquestionable: dense forest and rugged mountains are furrowed by foaming rivers and dotted with **traditional villages** (the Zagorohória), many sporting grand stone houses or *arhondiká*, dating from the late eighteenth century. Here, also, you can seek out evocative ancient **monasteries** set in improbably remote spots. **Wildlife** is impressive too: there's good birdwatching, increasing numbers of wolves, plus legally protected brown bears.

The best way to enjoy the countryside is by **hiking** the numerous paths connecting the villages. The most accessible and rewarding target is the magnificent UNESCO-protected **Víkos Gorge** (see box opposite), while **mounts Gamíla** and **Smólikas** provide several days of serious trekking. Even if you don't plan on hiking, the area deserves some time. Its remoteness, traditional architecture and scenery all constitute a very different Greece to the popular tourist stereotype and, despite growing popularity, the area remains relatively unspoilt.

### Monodhéndhri

Near the south end of the gorge, at 1150m elevation, stands handsome **MONODHÉNDHRI**, the main accommodation base in the area. The village survived World War II more or less intact – though it's now slightly spoilt by tourist shops and

ZAGÓRI & AROUND

parked coaches. Just before the flagstoned platía with its giant tree, the seventeenth-century church of **Áyios Minás** is locked, but the narthex, with fine eighteenth-century frescoes, is open. The wide, artlessly modern *kalderími* leading from the far end of the platía reaches, after 900m (not "600m" as signed) the eagle's-nest monastery of **Ayía Paraskeví** (built 1412), teetering on the brink of the gorge (there's a small viewing platform just behind) and now empty, though left open. If you're extremely sure-footed and have a head for heights, continue around the adjacent cliff face along an exceedingly narrow and dangerous path to a stair-trail climbing to **Megáli Spiliá**, a secluded cave where villagers once barricaded themselves in times of danger. The views

## HIKING THE VÍKOS GORGE

The **Víkos Gorge** cuts right through the limestone uplands of Mount Gamíla for 20km, separating the villages of western and central Zagóri. With walls almost 1000m high in places, it's quite equal to the famous Samarian gorge in Crete, and a **hike** through or around it is probably the highlight of a visit to the Zagóri.

Despite the gorge's popularity with hikers, and periodic bouts of trail maintenance, it's worth emphasizing that it is not a Sunday stroll. Bring proper, over-the-ankle **boots** and a leak-proof water container and walking poles or a stick (also useful for warding off guard dogs and belligerent cows). The best **maps** for the region are produced by Anavasi Editions (see p.52). Check **conditions** in advance of setting out. During April or early May, snowmelt often makes the Monodhéndhri end impassable, and during a rainstorm the sides of the gorge are prone to landslides.

### THE ROUTE

The most-used **path down to the gorge** begins beside the Áyios Athanásios church in Monodhéndhri; a sign promises fairly accurate walking times of four-and-a-half hours to Víkos village, six hours to either of the Pápingo villages. Once past Monodhéndhri's municipal amphitheatre, the path is cobbled for most of the forty minutes down to the riverbed, whose stony course you follow for another few minutes before shifting up the west (true left) bank, reaching the best viewpoint at a saddle ninety minutes from the village.

The entire route is waymarked, sometimes faintly, by red-paint dots and white-on-red stencilled metal diamonds with the legend "**O3**". This refers to a long-distance path, which begins south of Kípi at Lynkiádhes on Mount Mitsikéli, traverses Mount Gamíla and ends beyond Mount Smólikas. However, the surface underfoot is arduous, with some boulder-hopping in the gorge bed, metal or felled-branch ladders getting you over tricky bits on the bank, plus slippery, land-slid patches.

About two hours out of Monodhéndhri you draw even with the **Mégas Lákkos ravine**, the only major breach in the east wall of the gorge; a spring here has been piped to make it more usable in summer. Another thirty minutes' level walking takes you past the small, white shrine of **Ayía Triádha**; a further half-hour (around 3hr from Monodhéndhri) sees the gorge begin to open out and the sheer walls recede.

As the gorge widens you must make a choice. Continuing straight, the best-defined path takes you past the side trail to the beautifully set eighteenth-century **Kímisis Theotókou** chapel (unlocked; excellent frescoes well worth the 15min round-trip detour). Beyond here, the route becomes a well-paved *kalderími*, climbing up and left to **Víkos** (**Vitsikó**; 870m elevation), four-plus hours from Monodhéndhri and also accessible by a 5km paved road from Arísti. This underrated village has two inns, and up on the square, with its exceptionally handsome church of **Áyios Trýfon**, a good restaurant.

Most walkers, however, prefer to follow the marked O3 route to the two **Pápingo villages**, crossing the gorge bed at the **Voïdhomátis springs**, some three-and-a-half hours from Monodhéndhri. It's about two hours' walk from the springs up to Mikró Pápingo, slightly less to Megálo, with the divide in the trail nearly ninety minutes above the riverbed crossing. After an initial steep climb, there's a fine view down into the gorge near some weathered, tooth-like pinnacles, before the trail traverses a stable rockslide to the fork. Should you be reversing this route, the path-start in Mikró Pápingo village is signposted bilingually, and marked by a fancy stone archway in Megálo Pápingo.

3

over the gorge en route are spectacular from a natural balcony, with all of Víkos spread vertiginously at your feet.

### The Pápingo villages

**MEGÁLO PÁPINGO** is the larger of the two paired **Pápingo villages**, comprising two distinct quarters of 25 or so houses each along a tributary of the Voïdhomátis. It has served as the location for Jonathan Nossiter's 2000 film *Signs and Wonders*, starring Charlotte Rampling, plus countless Greek advertising shoots. Even before this, Megálo was a haunt of wealthy, trendy Greeks, making it a dubious target in peak season, though it is still delightful at other times. The fact that large coaches can't scale the steep hairpin road from the Voïdhomátis valley has made all the difference between here and Monodhéndhri; in peak season you must leave cars at the outskirts.

Megálo Pápingo is linked to its smaller namesake, **Mikró Pápingo**, by a 3km surfaced road; walkers should take the marked path off the road, via a historic bridge, which short-cuts the journey to half an hour. If you do take the road, just before the bend – at an obvious spot adorned by low masoned walls – you can detour to some natural swimming pools. Just below the church, in Mikró Pápingo, the WWF maintains an **information centre** (Mon, Tues, Thurs & Sun 10.30am–5.30pm; Fri, Sat & hols 11am–6pm; free) with worthwhile exhibits on the human and natural history of Pápingo and environs.

### Vítsa and the Skála Vítsas

**VÍTSA** (Vezítsa), 2km below Monodhéndhri, is to many tastes less claustrophobic and more attractive than Monodhéndhri. There's also access to the gorge via the signposted **Skála Vítsas**, a half-hour's gentle descent from the platía along the **Z9** – mostly on engineered stair-path – to the handsome single-arched **Misíou bridge**; from there one can continue upstream to Kípi village via the O3 path, or downstream along the heart of the gorge.

### Dhílofo

From either Vítsa or the Misíou bridge, the **Z15** leads south to **DHÍLOFO**, one of the most handsome Zagorian villages. The village has road access (though cars must be left at the outskirts). Alternatively it makes for a rewarding hike. The path-start in Vítsa is trickier to find than the branch leading from the bridge, but once done it's a twenty-minute descent to a stream bed, where the Misíou branch links up, then a climb along a crumbled *kalderími* which peters out in flysch badlands. After another stream crossing, the path resumes before becoming a track to the outskirts of Dhílofo, just over an hour along.

### Eláti

The village of **ELÁTI** (Boúltzi) is rather distant from the gorge, but there are fine views north to the peaks of Gamíla. From Dhílofo, walkers can continue down to Áyios Minás chapel on the main road and thence to Eláti on the **Z24**, but nearly half the way (90min) is along asphalt or bulldozer track, so you may as well come by car.

### Dhíkorfo and the Kaloutás bridge

**DHÍKORFO** (Tzódhila) proves a beauty with its grand houses and unusual, minaret-like belfry of Áyios Minás church. Beyond the village the chief attraction is the enormous **triple-arched bridge** below **Kaloutás**, about 250m off the paved road by dirt track. All villages past Kaloutás were destroyed during World War II, but the road continues paved to Miliotádhes and thence the old Ioánnina–Métsovo highway – a useful short cut.

## Áno Pedhiná

**ÁNO PEDHINÁ** (Soudhená), 3km west of Vítsa and Monodhéndhri, offers a few places with **rooms** and some superior **hotels**. At the base of the village stands the restored **convent of Evangelístria**, currently untenanted. Should you gain admission, you'll see the *katholikón*'s magnificent carved *témblon* and vivid, cleaned frescoes from 1793, though the structure is much older. Nearby Káto Pedhiná is headquarters for worthwhile **activity organizer** *Compass Adventures* (see below).

### ARRIVAL AND DEPARTURE

**By bus** From Ioánnina to Vítsa and Monodhéndhri, the bus leaves on Mon & Fri, at 6.15am and 2pm. Buses leave Ioánnina for Áno Pedhiná, and Dhílofo on Mon, Wed & Fri, at 6.15am and 4.15pm. On the same days, another bus leaves Ioánnina for the Pápingo villages and Áno Klidhoniá

### ZAGÓRI AND THE VÍKOS GORGE

at 5.15am and 2.30pm. Each trip takes about an hour, and all services then make immediate return trips.

**By taxi** A taxi from Ioánnina to Monodhéndhri will cost about €45.

### ACTIVITIES

**Alpine Zone** Ioséf Eliyía 16 ☎ 26510 23222, ⓦ alpinezone.gr. This Ioánnina-based operator offers rafting, canyoning, trekking and a full range of other activities in the Píndhos. Weekend springtime rafting packages, with an overnight stay in Pápingo, start at €100 for two persons, equipment and breakfast included.

**Compass Adventures** Káto Pedhiná ☎ 26530 71770, ⓦ compassadventures.gr. This operator offers primarily hiking/trekking and mountain biking, plus ski trips. For example, their hike of Víkos Gorge lasts 6–7 hours, includes an English-speaking guide and equipment and goes for €30, plus transport if provided for under 3 persons.

### ACCOMMODATION AND EATING

Monodhéndhri is the most popular accommodation base, but far from the only one. Every hamlet within spitting distance of the gorge has some form of rooms, and at least one taverna or snack bar. But you won't get a room anywhere without prior booking from mid-July through to late August; during the rest of the year, this applies also to weekends and official holidays.

### MONODHÉNDHRI

★ **Monodendri** ☎ 26530 71300, ⓦ monodendrihotel.com. Newly done up in sumptuous style and as close to a real luxury hotel as the area will ever see. There's also a very nice restaurant here (mains €6.50), with terrace-view seating. Breakfast included. **€50**

**Pítes tis Thrósos** ☎ 26530 71320. Located just up from the platía, one of three tavernas with seating all around the big tree, this friendly, family-run place has standard Greek fare as well as such local specialities as *alevrópitta* (a heavy dish made from dough, egg and cheese). About €12 for a full meal. Daily lunch & dinner.

### VÍTSA

**O Troas** ☎ 26530 71123. This restored-mansion inn, just below the fine platía, features five large rooms with modern baths, an old mural of Sebastopol in the upstairs lounge, and a pleasant café/courtyard for breakfast (included). **€50**

### DHÍLOFO

**Arhondiko Dhilofo** ☎ 26530 22455, ⓦ dilofo.com. Centuries old and filled with treasures, about which the owner will be happy to hold forth, this sumptuous mansion

house is worth a side-trip. Breakfast, included, consists of all local products. **€90**

### ELÁTI

**Elati** ☎ 26530 71181, ⓦ hotelelati.gr. Run by Canadian-Greek Alex Yiannakopoulos, this replica stone mansion has every comfort, including home-made meals on the panoramic veranda. Rooms are simple and colourful, with private bath. Breakfast included. **€85**

★ **Sta Riza** ☎ 26530 71550. This traditional taverna offers local *píttes*, vegetarian choices, such as the cheese ramekin with aubergine, and grills and casseroles, with good house wines and local *tsipouro*, too. Local specialities include various game dishes, stewed with nuts and fruit. Great views over the gorge from the balconies. About €12/person. Daily lunch & dinner.

### ÁNO PEDHINÁ

**Ameliko** ☎ 26530 71501 or 694 47 72 638, ⓦ ameliko.gr. Hotel consisting of three buildings, featuring stylishly appointed rooms with working fireplaces and views of either the village or the garden; there's also an on-site restaurant (meals about €15). Breakfast included. **€90**

3

★ **Porfyron** ☎ 26530 71579, ⊛ porfyron.com. Located beside Áyios Dhimítrios church, this lovingly restored mansion has very large rooms with painted or carved ceilings, antique furnishings and fireplaces; there's also a large garden and a taverna (about €15/person). Breakfast included. **€100**

#### VÍKOS
**Faraggi Vikou** ☎ 26530 42112. This inn is kept by Ioannis Dinoulis and located right where the gorge trail arrives, with modern, comfortable rooms and a small restaurant-bar. Breakfast included. **€40**

#### MEGÁLO PÁPINGO
**Kalliopi** ☎ 26530 41081. On the south side of the village, this place offers dated but cheerful en-suite rooms, and home-style meals at their year-round taverna, about €15 for a full meal. Breakfast included. **€60**

**Kouli** ☎ 26530 41115 or 693 28 47 752. This is *the* historic original inn, with en-suite rooms fitted with TVs and fridges; English-speaking Nikos and Vangelis

Khristodhoulou manage both it and the lively café-bar ou front. Breakfast included. **€60**

★ **Papaevangelou** ☎ 26530 41135, ⊛ papaevangelo .gr. Located at the far north end of the village, this hote features homely, non-institutional rooms – many wit fireplace – and four self-catering studios amid well-tende gardens, family-friendly common areas and a genia multilingual proprietor, Yiorgos. Breakfast included. **€75**

★ **Tsoumanis** ☎ 26530 12108. This restaurant is the best in the village, with tasty soufflés, lamb and regiona dishes, an understatedly classy dining room (the old barn for winter, plus an unbeatable view of Mount Astráka from the summer terrace. Expect €15–20/person. Daily lunch & dinner.

#### MIKRÓ PÁPINGO
★ **Xenon O Dhias** ☎ 26530 41257. Kostas Tsoumanis twelve rustic rooms are distributed over two building bracketing a decent, sometimes lively, bar-restaurant (abou €12/person). Discount for trekkers. Breakfast included. **€70**

# The west coast

Starting just south of where the Vía Egnatía expressway ends, the **west coast** has some attractive **beaches** between Igoumenítsa and Préveza, among the best on the mainland outside of Mount Pílio. **Igoumenítsa** itself, the capital of Thesprotía province, is a purely functional ferry port. Attractive **Párga**, the most established beach resort heading south, gets super packed-out in summer and at Easter, so is best left for June or September visits. Just inland, there are worthwhile detours from the main route south: the intriguing **Nekromanteion of Acheron** evokes the legendary entrance to Hades; and the vast ruins of **Nikopolis** break the journey to **Préveza**, a low-key provincial capital at the mouth of the marshy Amvrakikós gulf. Down along the south coast, **Mesolónghi** is considered by Greeks as a sacred spot for being where Lord Byron died while doing his part to liberate Greece from the Ottomans.

## Igoumenítsa and around

**IGOUMENÍTSA** is Greece's third passenger port after Pireás and Pátra, with frequent ferries to **Corfu** and **Italy**. With the completion of the Vía Egnatía from Grevená to here, this unloved provincial capital has become the country's leading cargo port; a mega-terminal – part of the **New Port Egnatía** – for lorries dominates the harbour, and all shipping agencies have branches nearby, plus embarkation booths inside.

Seagoing functions and waterfront apart, Igoumenítsa is decidedly unappealing, levelled during World War II and rebuilt in bland utilitarian style. You should hopefully be able to get a ferry out immediately; every day in season there are sailings to Italy in the morning, and throughout the evening. If you end up stuck for the day, you're better off taking an excursion out of Igoumenítsa than hanging around this rather dodgy port town.

### ARRIVAL AND INFORMATION                                    IGOUMENÍTSA

**BY BUS**
The KTEL is inland from the Corfu/Paxí quay on Minermoú, corner Arhilóhou.

Destinations Athens (5 daily, 8hr); Ioánnina (9 daily; 2hr); Párga (5 daily; 1hr); Préveza (2 daily; 2hr 30min).

## BY FERRY

**International ferries** Almost all international ferries (see p.27) depart from the New Port Egnatía at the far south end of town, with its own exit from the Vía Egnatía – so most drivers bound for Italy can skip the town altogether, although a few ferries do still use the old port. You must check in with the appropriate official agent's embarkation booth in the Egnatía Port at least 2hr before departure. There's a good spread of departure times across the day for Italy-bound ferries, which leave between 7.30am and 10am, with a larger cluster of evening departures between 8pm and 1am (especially 11pm–midnight). During high season, make advance reservations for cabins or vehicles.

Destinations Ancona (1–2 daily; 15hr–15hr 30min); Bari (1–2 daily; 9hr–10hr 30min); Brindisi (1–3 daily; 6hr 30min–8hr); Venice (every day except Wed) 22–25hr.

**Local ferries** to Corfu (with connections to Paxí) operate from the domestic ferry quay just north of the new terminal; tickets for these services are purchased at waterside booths. Destinations Corfu (5 daily; 1hr 15min–1hr 45min); Patra, 11 weekly (5hr 45min); Zakynthos, 1 weekly (6hr 15min).

## BY CAR

**Orientation and parking** With the completion of the new expressway, accessing the town and the port areas by car couldn't be easier, all of the routes and ramps being very well signed in English. Drivers can use the free car park at the waterfront's north end.

## INFORMATION

**Services** Numerous ATMs line the south end of the front. The post office is at the north end.

3

## ACCOMMODATION AND EATING

**Egnatia** Eleftherías 2 ☎ 26650 23648. Inland, at the southeast corner of the main platía, stands this comfortable, air-conditioned hotel. Ask for a rear room facing the pine grove, and take advantage of unrestricted street parking out back. **€50**

**Family Akti** Roudou 13 cnr Agion Apostolon ☎ 26650 23763. This simple taverna is much more authentic than the usual choices along the strip. The menu has all the

Greek standards, plus fresh catch of the day, of course. Expect just €10/meal. Daily lunch & dinner.

**Stavrodhromi** Soulíou 16 ☎ 26650 22343, ⓦ stavrodromihotel.gr. The best budget choice – it's on the street leading diagonally uphill and northeast from the square. En-suite, air-conditioned rooms, as well as an in-house restaurant. **€45**

# Párga and around

**PÁRGA**, 53km south of Igoumenítsa, has prospered thanks to its alluring setting on a lush coastline with a string of rocky islets offshore. Though concrete development has spread to the outskirts, the old centre, an arc of tiered houses set below a Norman-Venetian **kástro**, retains plenty of charm. Greeks love Párga for their own holidays and the little alleyways of the centre can become impossibly crowded with cars and people in midsummer and at Easter. That said, normal life just about continues, exemplified by older ladies in the traditional garb of black veil, braids and dark blue kerchiefs. Visit in spring or autumn and you'll be able truly to appreciate the atmosphere.

## Brief history

Párga has an idiosyncratic history, being linked with the Ionian islands as much as with the mainland. From the 1300s to the 1700s, the port was a lone **Venetian** toehold in Epirus – the Venetian Lion of St Mark still adorns the kástro keep – and during this time a small Jewish community flourished here producing citrons (a lemon-like fruit used in Jewish ceremonies).

Later, the Napoleonic **French** briefly took Párga, leaving additional fortifications on the largest islet guarding the harbour. At the start of the nineteenth century, the town enjoyed autonomy under **Russian** protection, and lived from olive export, before being acquired by the **British**, who sold it on to **Ali Pasha**. Ali Pasha rebuilt all the local castles, while the townspeople, knowing his reputation, decamped to the Ionian islands on Good Friday 1819. The area was subsequently resettled by **Muslim Turks** who remained until the exchange of populations in 1923, when they were replaced in part by **Orthodox Greek** refugees.

## The kástro

8am–midnight • Free

The blufftop Venetian **kástro** provides a haven from Párga's bustle; a long stair-street leads up to the crumbled, cypress-tufted ramparts, which offer excellent views. Restored barracks inside the castle boundary house a recommended café; you can continue up a cobbled way to one of Ali Pasha's summer palaces, a warren of vaulted rooms and cisterns, with ruined, domed baths at the very summit.

## The beaches

Párga's **beaches** line several **consecutive bays**, split by various headlands. The small, spring-chilled bay of **Kryonéri** lies opposite the islet studded with a monastery and Napoleonic fortifications, a 200m swim or pedalo from the town quay. Tiny but scenic **Gólfo beach**, the next (less clean) cove southeast, is reached by a narrow lane signposted for its eponymous taverna. Immediately northwest beyond the kástro (reached on foot by the long ramp from the kástro gate, or frequent water-taxis from the town dock) lies **Váltos beach**, more than 1km in length as it arcs around to the eponymous hamlet. **Lýkhnos beach**, 3km in the opposite (southeast) direction, is similarly huge; a shaded path through the olive groves from the far end of Kyronéri short-cuts the winding road in, or again taxi-boats spare you the walk.

## Castle of Ayiá

8am–midnight • Free

A short, 5km excursion (covered several times daily by tourist train from Kyronéri quay) leads to the diminutive **castle of Ayiá** (actually between Anthoússa and Ayiá), illuminated at night. Head west on the main road through and beyond Anthoússa, then turn off at the side road for Tríkorfo hamlet. The castle is more elaborate and intact than apparent from a distance, having been rebuilt in 1814 by Ali Pasha's Italian engineers. There's unrestricted access to the dungeons, the upper gallery and the roof with its rusty cannons and superb views encompassing Paxí, Váltos beach, Ammoudhiá and Lefkádha.

### ARRIVAL AND INFORMATION

PÁRGA

**By bus** The KTEL station – just a small booth – is up on the bypass road, near the start of Spýrou Livadhá (the way to Váltos).

**Destinations** Athens (3 daily; 7hr); Igoumenítsa (5 daily; 1hr); Préveza (4 daily; 2hr).

**Services** The post office is on Alexándhrrou Bánga, start of the main market street, which also has two ATMs. *Kanaris Travel* on the quay sells a few maps and English-language books/magazines. *Parga.net* at the jetty bas provides internet access (wi-fi signal for laptops); there no tourist office, though ⓦ parga.gr is a useful source of information.

### GETTING AROUND

**Taxis** The main taxi rank is at the corner of Spýrou Livadhá and Alexándhrou Bánga.

**Car and scooter rental** Established car rental outlets include *Parga Hire* at Spýrou Livadhá 4 (ⓣ 26840 31833, ⓦ pargahire.com); *Synthesis* at Alexándhrou Bánga 6 (ⓣ 26840 31700) and *Budget/National* in Kyronéri at Ayío Athanasíou 4 (ⓣ 26840 32584). Waterfront travel agencie rent scooters.

**Parking** There is only one free lot at Kryonéri and a fre olive grove.

### ACCOMMODATION

Tour operators and regular visitors monopolize most of Párga's accommodation between mid-June and early Septembe Outside these seasons, however, you'll have ample choice on spec. **Rooms/studios** cluster in the lanes inland from Kryonéri, and the ridge of Tourkopázaro (officially Odhós Patatoúka), where premises have unbeatable views over Váltc beach. **Camping** options also exist handy to several of the beach areas.

**Galini** Kryonéri ⓣ 26840 31581, ⓦ hotel-galini.com. On the edge of town below Váltos road, this hotel is set in a small garden and is as quiet as the name ("Serenity") implies, with 25 large, though spartan rooms with a/c and balconies. Breakfast included. Easte to Oct. **€80**

**Lichnos Beach** Lýkhnos ☎ 26840 31257, ⓦ lichnos beach.gr. With free private parking, this place makes a good-value choice for the car-bound or families. There's a mix of standard rooms, studios and bungalows set in lush grounds, big enough that packages don't completely monopolize it. Tennis court, pool and "private" beach with watersport facility. Breakfast included. **€110**

**Lichnos Camping** ☎ 26840 31371, ⓦ www.njoy-lichnos.net. Centred right on less congested Lýkhnos beach, this site offers both camping and self-catering apartments with sea-view balconies. They have their own taverna, as well, and the beach and watersports are handy. Campsites are in shady groves and some have views, too. Camping from **€15**; apartments from **€35**

★ **Magda's Apartments** Váltos ☎ 26840 31228,

ⓦ magdas-hotel.com. On Váltos road just before lane to the kástro. A mix of studios, and six superior apartments (let by the week), in a hillside garden with partial sea views, plus a terrace pool and two spas. Good breakfasts (extra), easy parking, quality acoustic music sessions and free internet. English-speaking hosts Kostas and Spyros are ever-helpful; not surprisingly, three-month advance booking is usually necessary if you want high season. Greek Easter to late Oct. **€90**

**Villa Coralli** Kryonéri ☎ 26840 31069, ⓦ villacoralli .com. This large and spacious hotel is right on the beach and has clean, well-appointed rooms and self-catering studios and apartments, all with balconies and either sea or hillside views. Parking options not far away; free wi-fi. Large sea-view terrace for dining; breakfast extra. Easter–Nov. **€80**

**3**

## EATING AND DRINKING

There are some thirty full-service tavernas around town, though cooking is usually aimed squarely at the package trade. Most Párga tavernas offer local wine from the barrel; the red is generally excellent. Plenty of café society, too, nearly all places vying to offer all things to all people: restaurant, taverna, café, bar, breakfast spot.

**Golfo Beach** Kyronéri ☎ 26840 32336. Evangelia is heart and soul of one of Párga's oldest tavernas, with a cult following for her sustaining *mayireftá*; three courses and a beer won't much exceed €16; live music some nights. Located just steps away from the beach. Daily, breakfast, lunch and dinner, till late.

★ **Kastro 1380** Restored kástro ☎ 26840 32164. The most romantic chill-out place in Párga, with perfect views, especially port lighting at night. This terrace restaurant has a full bar, and 30 kinds of coffee and flavoured Italian chocolate. Live Greek music some nights. About €20/person. Daily, breakfast, lunch and dinner, till late.

**Oskar** Grigoríou Lambráki (north side of waterfront) ⓦ oskar-parga.gr. Friendly and tiny – thus seasonally packed – Italian place with the freshest pizza and pasta (some with seafood), as well as baked *plevrótous* mushrooms and huge salads (real caprese) with prosciutto, home-baked bread and sun-dried tomatoes. About €10/person. Daily lunch & dinner.

★ **Porto Lichnos** ☎ 26840 32684. Located at the top of the road to Lichnos Beach, this large, friendly and efficient restaurant offers an extensive menu and panoramic views all the way down to the beach. Mains include chicken fillet in mushroom sauce or grilled swordfish steak, €8, both including sides of chips and fresh salad garnish. Daily, breakfast, lunch and dinner.

**Sakis** Turkopázaro Located by the fountain and plane trees, this is the place for a cheap-and-cheerful, village-style feed. Despite the constant hum of street traffic it's a huge favourite with visitors, featuring reliable grills and a few *mayireftá*. About €10/person. Daily lunch & dinner.

**To Souli** Anexartisias 45 ☎ 26840 31658. Oldest taverna in town; its *mayireftá* standards are renowned, plus grilled options (house speciality grilled feta with tomatoes and herbs) and casseroles, often featuring lamb; but ask to see what's cooking today. About €15/person. Daily lunch & dinner.

## NIGHTLIFE AND ENTERTAINMENT

Nightlife centres around annually changing, semi-open-air bars on the east quay pumping out 1960s and 1970s sounds to match a thirty to fifty-something crowd; there's a more youthful vibe along the steps to the kástro, where *Blue Bar* and adjacent *Sail In* get a less sedate, more Greek clientele.

## The Nekromanteion of Acheron

Daily 8.30am–3pm, may close later summer • €2 • The site is best visited with your own transport; Mesopótamos is well signed, just 1km off the main coast highway

The **Nekromanteion of Acheron** stands 22km southeast of Párga on a rocky hill just above the village of **Mesopótamos**. According to mythology, the Underworld rivers Styx, Acheron and Cocytus flowed into a marshy lake here across which Charon rowed the dead to the gates of Hades. From Mycenaean to Roman times an elaborate oracle for consulting the departed existed somewhere nearby. The Acheron sanctuary never achieved the stature of Delphi or Dodona, but its fame was sufficient to warrant a mention in Homer where it becomes the site of Odysseus's visit to Hades.

A stand of trees marks the ostensible netherworld gateway. Homer spoke of poplars and willows, but today's cypresses are appropriate enough, being emblems of the dead across the Mediterranean. The ancient lake, which once made this spot an island, has now receded, though the mythological rivers still flow in the area, under different names.

The **ruins** in some ways correspond with descriptions of the oracle by ancient chroniclers, but based on archeological finds here, including such things as domestic pottery and catapult parts, the site is actually consistent with a fairly large agricultural enterprise that had occasion to defend itself against invaders – and, in fact, it has been dated to only Hellenistic times, the third or fourth century BC at the earliest, nearly a thousand years after Homer's account.

## Préveza and around

At the mouth of the Amvrakikós Gulf, modern **PRÉVEZA** is fairly scruffy and undistinguished, but its **old bazaar quarter and waterfront**, now pedestrianized and full of appealing tavernas, are worth a look. Since international flights began serving Áktio airport, the town has had a partial facelift, and more character remains in the old quarter than at Párga. Préveza merits a stopover also for the nearby ruined Roman city of **Nikopolis**.

### ARRIVAL AND INFORMATION

**By air** Charters from London and Manchester arriving at nearby Áktio airport generally have transport laid on to the various resorts; otherwise there are only taxis for the 7km trip to town. The airport itself is a cheerless, overcrowded shed at the edge of an air-force base, with two car-rental booths, snacks at the bar, and no banking facilities or anywhere to sit.

Destinations Corfu (3 weekly; 25min); Kefalonia (3 weekly; 20min); Sitia (2 weekly; 1hr 40min); Zakynthos (3 weekly; 1hr).

**By bus** The bus station in Préveza is at the north edge of town, 1km out at the start of the road to Párga; there are sporadic shuttles into the centre.

### PRÉVEZA AND AROUND

Destinations Athens (5 daily; 6hr); Ioánnina (8 daily; 2hr); Lefkádha (5 daily; 25min); Párga (4 daily; 2hr); Igoumenítsa (2 daily; 2hr 30min).

**By car** A high-tech tunnel under the straits links Préveza and Áktio (3min; €3 cars, €5 camper vans; no cyclists). Drivers arriving from Párga or Préveza should follow signposting for "Áktio" to find the entrance.

**Tourist office** Bálkou near the waterfront (☎ 26820 21078; Mon–Fri 8am–2.30pm).

**Services** The post office is on Spiliádhou, near the castle. Several banks with ATMs are found at the north end of the waterfront. There's a taxi rank on the waterfront.

### ACCOMMODATION AND EATING

None of the four in-town **hotels** is especially inviting or great value, though if you do stay after dark there is fairly lively nightlife on offer. A dozen **tavernas** (many dinner only) are scattered around the inland lanes and alleyways of old Préveza, with **cafés and bars** mostly lined up along the pedestrianized waterfront esplanade Venizélou.

**Avra** Venizélou 19 ☎ 26820 21230, ⓦ hotelavra.net. This comfortable though quite spartan hotel is on the seafront just steps away from the picturesque pedestrian zone. It's run by two brothers, both very helpful and friendly. Breakfast €5/person extra. €45

**Psatha** Dhardhanellíon 4–6 ☎ 26820 23051. One block south of the Venetian clock tower along the main shopping thoroughfare, this is the place to come for standard *mayireftá*. In addition, they do fish and grills, and the kitchen always has something special on the stove, so have a look. €15 or so for a full meal – in fact, you might have to be careful not to order too much. Daily lunch & dinner.

### NIGHTLIFE AND ENTERTAINMENT

By night, the pedestrianized alleys of the **old bazaar district**, particularly around the fish-market building and the clock tower, come alive with assorted **bars and cafés** patronized by locals, guests from surrounding resorts and denizens of yachts moored at the esplanade. There's a summer outdoor **cinema** south of town on the road to Pandokrátoras; the central winter one's on Ethnikís Andístasis.

# Nikopolis

Summer daily 8am–7.30pm; winter daily 8.30am–3pm • €3 • The site is best visited by car; buses from Préveza pass by the museum, but there is no regular stop

**NIKOPOLIS** ("Victory City") was founded by Octavian on the site where his army had camped prior to the Battle of Actium: an ill-considered gesture that made little geographical sense. The settlement was on unstable ground, water had to be transported by aqueduct from the distant Loúros springs, and a population had to be forcibly imported from various towns. However, such a *folie de grandeur* was understandable. At **Actium** (modern Áktio), Octavian had first blockaded and then annihilated the combined fleets of Antony and Cleopatra, gathered there for the invasion of Italy. These events culminated in Octavian the general becoming Roman Emperor Augustus.

The subsequent history of Nikopolis is undistinguished, with much of its population drifting back to their homes, and the town suffering barbarian sackings as Rome declined. During the sixth century AD, it flourished briefly as a Byzantine city, but within four centuries it had vanished from the combined effect of earthquakes and Bulgar raids.

## Archeological Museum

Architecturally minimalist, the small museum offers good lighting and informative labelling for its finds, which include impressive marble carvings, stelae and inscriptions, as well as mosaics and a variety of pottery. Highlights include a marble relief depicting an erotic banquet scene and a fourth-century BC seated lion, life-size.

## The site

The far-flung monuments begin 8km north of Préveza, on either side of the main road. The 2220-acre site is really too scattered to tour on foot or by bus; hire a taxi in Préveza, or come by car.

Nikopolis is bounded on the south by a formidable stretch of sixth-century Byzantine **walls**, beyond which lie the **Dhométios basilica** (with covered-over mosaics) and the Roman **odeion** dating from the original construction of the city, well restored for use in the local summer festival. From the foundations of the sixth-century **basilica of Alkýsonos** just north of the main **baths**, it's 2km to the main **theatre**, west of which you can discern the sunken outline of the **stadium**, below Smyrtoúna village.

# Astakós

**ASTAKÓS** ("Lobster") is a small port on the western mainland with a ferry to Kefaloniá every weekday lunchtime, plus a Sunday evening departure to Itháki and Kefaloniá. Despite the name there's no lobster served at any of the mediocre tavernas lining the quay; around the marketplace many Neoclassical buildings from the 1870s hint a a more prosperous past.

## LH1 ARRIVAL AND DEPARTURE                    ASTAKÓS

**By bus** The KTEL is at the end of the quay; buses from Athens should coincide with the ferry.
**By ferry** Weekday departures to Kefaloniá at around noon

(Sámi; early May to mid-Sept only), Sun evening to Itháki and Kefaloniá; ☎ 26460 38020 for current details.

## ACCOMMODATION

**Stratos** By the quay ☎ 26460 41911. The only hotel, overlooking the tiny, gravelly town beach, is overpriced; in

peak season cheaper rooms are available elsewhere. **€80**

## Mesolóngi and around

**Mesolóngi** (Missolongi), for most visitors, is irrevocably associated with **Lord Byron**, who died here to dramatic effect during the War of Independence (see box below). Otherwise it's a fairly shabby and unromantic place: rainy from autumn to spring, and comprised largely of drab, modern buildings between which locals enthusiastically cycle along a flat grid plan. To be fair, the town has been spruced up, especially in the centre, but if you come here on pilgrimage, it's still best to move on the same day, most likely to Lefkádha island or the Peloponnese.

### Gate of the Sortie

You enter the town from the northeast through the **Gate of the Sortie**, named after the April 12, 1826 break-out by nine thousand Greeks, ending the Ottomans' year-long siege. In one desperate dash they quit Mesolóngi, leaving a group of defenders to destroy it – and some three thousand civilians not capable of leaving – by firing the powder magazines. But those fleeing were betrayed, ambushed on nearby Mount Zygós; fewer than two thousand evaded massacre or capture and enslavement by an Albanian mercenary force.

### Garden of Heroes

Daily: summer 8am–9pm; winter 8am–6pm, but sometimes unaccountably closed • Free

Just inside this gate, on the right, partly bounded by the remaining fortifications, is the **Kípos Iróön**, or "Garden of Heroes" – signposted in English as "Heroes' Tombs" – where a tumulus covers the bodies of the town's anonymous defenders. Beside the tomb of Souliot commander Markos Botsaris is a **statue of Byron**, erected in 1881, under which – despite apocryphal traditions – is buried neither the poet's heart nor lungs. Byron might conceivably have been offered the throne of an independent Greece: thus the relief of his coat of arms with a royal crown above. Among the palm trees and rusty cannon loom busts, obelisks and cenotaphs to an astonishing range of American, German and French Philhellenes, those Romantics who strove to free the Classical Greece of their ideals from the barbaric thrall of the Ottomans.

---

### BYRON IN MESOLÓNGI

Byron has been a Greek national **hero** ever since he became involved in the country's struggle for independence. Almost every town in the country has a street – Výronos – named after him; not a few men still answer to "Vyron" as a first name. He first passed through in 1809 when tyrannical local ruler Ali Pasha was at the height of his power, and the poet's tales of intrigue sent a shiver down romantic Western spines.

Later, in January 1824, Byron made his way to **Mesolóngi**, a squalid, inhospitable southwestern port amid lagoons – but also the western centre of **resistance** against the Ottomans. The poet, who had by then contributed his personal fame and fortune to the war effort, was enthusiastically greeted with a 21-gun salute, and made **commander** of the five-thousand-strong garrison, a role as much political as military. The Greek forces were divided into factions whose brigand-chieftains separately and persistently petitioned him for money. Occasionally Byron despaired: "Here we sit in this realm of mud and discord", read one of his journal entries. But while other Philhellenes returned home, disillusioned by the fractious, larcenous Greeks, or worn out by quasi-tropical Mesolóngi, he stayed.

On February 15 Byron caught a **fever**, possibly malaria, and two months later **died**; ironically, he became more valuable to the Greek cause dead than alive. News of the poet's demise, embellished to heroic proportions, reverberated across northern Europe; arguably it changed the course of the war in Greece. When Mesolóngi fell again to the Ottomans in spring 1826, there was outcry in the European press, and French and English forces were finally galvanized into sending a naval force that unintentionally engaged an Egyptian fleet at Navarino, striking a fatal blow against the Ottoman navy.

## Museum of History and Art

Platía Bótsari • Mon–Fri 9am–1.30pm & 4–7pm, Sat & Sun 9am–1pm & 4–7pm, closes 6pm winter • Free

Back on the central square, the Neoclassical town hall houses the small **Museum of History and Art** devoted to the revolution, with some emotive paintings on the upper floor (including a copy of Delacroix's *Gate of the Sortie*), reproductions of period lithographs and a rather disparate (and desperate) collection of Byronia on the ground floor. Pride of place, by the entrance, goes to an original edition of Solomos's poem *Hymn to Liberty*, now the words of the national anthem.

## The lagoon

More interesting than any town sight is a walk across the **Klísova lagoon**, past two **forts** that were vital defences against the Ottoman navy. The lagoon, with its salt-evaporation ponds and fish farms, attracts a variety of wading birds, especially in spring.

## ARRIVAL AND INFORMATION

MESOLÓNGI

**By bus** Travelling here by bus will probably involve changing at Agrínio, a grim transport hub and the hottest town in Greece in summer. KTEL buses arrive in Mesolóngi at Mavrokordhátou 5, by Platía Bótsari, while local blue-and-white ones call just a few paces away.

Destinations Agrínio (hourly; 35min); Athens (12 daily; 3hr 30min); Náfpaktos (3 daily Mon–Fri; 50min); Pátra (9 daily; 1hr). From Agrínio services run to: Corfu (bus/ferry, 2 daily in season; 4hr); Ioánnina (6 daily; 2hr 20min); Karpeníssi (1 daily; 3hr 30min); Mesolóngi (hourly; 35min); Préveza (5 daily Mon–Fri, 2 Sat & Sun; 1hr).

**By car** Mesolóngi is linked to Ioánnina by the modern Ionian Highway.

**Services** ATMs surround the square; the post office stands a block east on Spyrídhona Moustaklí.

## ACCOMMODATION

**Avra** Hariláou Trikoúpi 5 ☎ 26310 22284. A good budget option just off the central platía and close to the best of Mesolóngi's eating and drinking venues. For quiet, ask for a room at the back. Breakfast included. **€45**

**Theoxenia** ☎ 26310 22493, ⓦ theoxenia-hotel.gr. An upmarket, if impersonal, choice is this small, landscaped complex just south of town on the lagoon shore – convenient if you're driving, though the 1970s-vintage rooms are ripe for an overhaul. Nice bathrooms. Free wi-fi. Breakfast included. **€55**

## EATING

The main concentration of **tavernas**, interspersed with a few **bars**, is along and around Athanasíou Razikótsika, a pedestrianized street one block south of similarly car-free Hariláou Trikoúpi. In the narrow alleys linking these two broader streets are too many **bars** and **kafenía** to detail – you'll find something to suit. Mesolóngi is especially noted for its eels, smoked or grilled; also famous is the local *avgotáraho* or *haviára*, caviar made from grey mullet roe.

★ **Filoxenos** Razikótsika 7 ☎ 26310 28008. The poshest restaurant in town is worth the extra expense, with exemplary presentation of generous portions and a pleasant interior. The local eel, grilled, is the signature dish. Daily, lunch & dinner.

## Tourlídha

A causeway extends 4km from Mesolóngi to the open sea at **TOURLÍDHA**, a hamlet of wood-plank and prefab summer cottages on stilts, plus a few **tavernas**. If you can stomach the intermittent stench from the nearby salt-ponds, there's a packed-sand beach to swim from, with showers and a few café-bars. Makes a picturesque, funky outing if you're visiting Mesolóngi.

## EATING

TOURLÍDHA

**Alykés** ☎ 26310 24327. Nicely placed with tables facing the beach, this large taverna is a pleasant, family-run place for lunch, with fresh fish always on offer. A meal centred round a large grilled squid, big enough for three persons, will cost you about €25. Daily lunch & dinner.

# The northern mainland

**266** Thessaloníki and around

**280** Mount Olympus and around

**284** Véria and Vergina

**288** Northwest Macedonia

**296** Halkidhikí

**310** Northeastern Macedonia

**312** Kavála and around

**315** Thrace

WHITE TOWER, THESSALONÍKI

# The northern mainland

Greece's northern mainland is dominated by the provinces of MACEDONIA and THRACE. Each has been part of the Greek state for less than a century – Macedonia (Makedhonía) was surrendered by the Turks in 1913 while Greek sovereignty over western Thrace (Thráki) was not confirmed until 1923 and there is still a sizeable ethnic minority population (see box, p.315). Consequently, they stand slightly apart from the rest of the country, an impression reinforced for visitors by architecture and scenery, customs and climate that seem more Balkan than typically Mediterranean. In fact the region is relatively little known to outsiders, perhaps thanks to its capricious climate, lack of beach resorts and few charter flights. Yet northern Greece is one of the country's most rewarding areas to visit.

**Mount Olympus**, mythical abode of the gods, is a tempting target for hikers, while **Mount Áthos**, a Byzantine ecclesiastical idyll, is an unmissable attraction (at least for men, who are the only ones allowed here). The sybaritic capital of Macedonia, **Thessaloníki**, and the region's other main city, **Kavála**, are also intriguing places to visit, the former providing access to the beach-fringed peninsula of **Halkidhikí**. The north also has more outstandingly beautiful spots, especially the **Préspa National Park** in rugged western Macedonia and the birdwatchers' heaven of the **Kerkíni wetlands** to the east. The lakeside city of **Kastoriá** and the clifftop town of **Édhessa** are among Greece's most beguiling urban centres, thanks to a belated but determined attempt to restore some fine old buildings. Admittedly, the region's ancient sites are relatively modest, though there is one notable exception: the awe-inspiring Macedonian tombs discovered at **Vergina** in the 1970s, near the pleasant city of **Véria**. Not so well known are the Macedonian and Roman sites at **Pella**, with its fabulous mosaics, and at **Philippi**, St Paul's first stop in Greece. Few travellers on their way to Bulgaria or Turkey stray from the dull trunk road through Thrace, but the well-preserved town of **Xánthi**, a trio of minor archeological sites, the waterfowl reserves of the **Évros Delta** and the **Dhadhiá Forest**, with its black vultures, deserve more than just a meal stop. **Alexandhroúpoli** is dull but rewards the curious with one of the best ethnological museums in the whole of Greece.

## GETTING AROUND                                        NORTHERN MAINLAND

**By train and bus** Public transport in the north is somewhat limited. A few trains link some of the urban centres, but the railway line east from Thessaloníki curls unhelpfully inland, bypassing Kavála altogether and leaving buses or your own transport as the only alternatives for travelling along the coast.

**By car** The road system has improved beyond recognition in recent years, however, with the completion of the "Via Egnatia" highway, which now provides an uninterrupted link between the west coast and the Bulgarian and Turkish borders, as well as connecting to the upgraded Athens–Thessaloníki motorway.

Ottoman Thessaloníki p.272
Byzantine churches p.273
The Jews of Thessaloníki p.274
The fire-walkers of Langadhás p.279
Climbing Mount Olympus p.283
Little Jerusalem p.286

The birds of Préspa p.291
Kastoriá's churches p.294
Macedonian cavemen p.296
Mount Athos time p.305
Athos etiquette p.308
1923 and all that p.315

HIKING, MOUNT OLYMPUS

# Highlights

**❶ Thessaloníki** Balkan in atmosphere, Greece's second city offers historic monuments and a vibrant nightlife. **See p.266**

**❷ Mount Olympus** The mythical home of the gods; a three-day hike to the summit and back offers pristine scenery and riots of wild flowers. **See p.280**

**❸ Vergina** Beguiling treasures unearthed in the poignant burial chambers of Macedonia's royal dynasty. **See p.287**

**❹ Édhessa** Clifftop wooden houses and impeccably restored water mills make this one of Greece's most inviting towns. **See p.288**

**❺ The Préspa lakes** Forming the leading ornithological reserve in the region, the reed-fringed shores are a haven for nature lovers. **See p.290**

**❻ Kastoriá** Situated on a wooded headland jutting into the pewter-coloured Lake Orestiádha, this unusual resort is the country's fur capital. **See p.292**

**❼ Mount Athos** Timeless Orthodox monasteries set among unspoilt landscapes in a semi-independent republic run by monks. **See p.304**

**❽ Dhadhiá** Oak and pine forests draped over volcanic ridges, home to black vultures and other rare raptors. **See p.322**

**HIGHLIGHTS ARE MARKED ON THE MAP ON P.266–267**

# Thessaloníki and around

Home to three quarters of a million people, Greece's second city, **THESSALONÍKI** – or **Salonica**, as it is was once known – stands apart from the rest of the country. Situated at the head of the Gulf of Thessaloník, it seems open to the rest of the world, with a wide ethnic mix and an air of general prosperity, stimulated by a major university and a famously avant-garde live music and entertainment scene. The food is better here too and there are some very sophisticated restaurants, but also wholesome traditional food on offer in a great number of old-fashioned Turkish-influenced ouzerís and tavernas.

The city has enough to offer the visitor for two or three days, at least. There are substantial **Roman remains** and the many **churches** (see box, p.273) constitute a showcase of Orthodox architecture through the ages, while you can catch glimpses of the Turkish city both in the walled Upper City and in the modern grid of streets below: isolated pockets of **Ottoman buildings**, many of them Islamic monuments, which miraculously survived the 1917 fire (see p.268). Modern Greek architecture is exemplified by Art Deco piles dating from the city's twentieth-century heyday, around the time of the first **International Trade Fair** in 1926, an event that continues to this day. Thessaloníki's many and often excellent **museums** cover subjects as varied as Byzantine culture, the city's Jewish heritage, folklife, musical instruments, Atatürk (who was born here) and, more recently, modern art and photography.

## Brief history

When King Cassander of Macedonia founded the city in 315 BC, he named it after his wife Thessalonike, **Alexander the Great's** half-sister, whose name in turn derived from the Macedons' decisive victory (*nike*) over the Thessalians. It soon became the region's cultural and trading centre, issuing its own coins, and when Rome conquered Macedonia in 146 BC, the city (under the name **Salonica**) became the natural and immediate choice of capital. Its fortunes and significance were boosted by the building of the Via Egnatia, the great road linking Rome (via Brindisi) with Byzantium and the East.

**Christianity** had slow beginnings in the city. St Paul visited twice, and on the second occasion, in 56 AD, he stayed long enough to found a church, later writing the two Epistles to the Thessalonians, his congregation there. It was another three centuries,

**HIGHLIGHTS**
1. Thessaloníki
2. Mount Olympus
3. Vergina
4. Édhessa
5. Préspa Lakes
6. Kastoriá
7. Mount Athos
8. Dhadhiá

**NORTHERN MAINLAND**

---

### ORIENTATION

Most of central Thessaloníki's principal sights are within easy walking distance of each other, many located on either side of Egnatía. Perpendicular to the avenues that run parallel to the seafront, **Aristotélous** is a partly pedestrianized street with Italianate porticoes on either side and lined with freshly painted, pale ochre buildings, housing offices, shops and facilities such as the post office and the national railways bureau. It slopes down from Egnatía and opens out at the seaside end into completely pedestrianized **Platía Aristotélous**, where you can enjoy views across to Mount Olympus on clear days. The divide between the older and newer parts of town is marked by the exhibition grounds and the start of the seaside park strip, known locally as Zoo Park and dominated by the **White Tower** (Lefkós Pýrgos).

---

however, before the new religion took full root. **Galerius**, who acceded as eastern emperor upon Byzantium's break with Rome, provided the city with virtually all its surviving late Roman monuments. The first resident Christian emperor was **Theodosius** (reigned 379–95), who after his conversion issued the Edict of Salonica, officially ending paganism.

Under Justinian's rule (527–65) Salonica became the second city of **Byzantium** after Constantinople, which it remained – under constant pressure from Goths and Slavs – until its sacking by Saracens in 904. The storming and sacking continued under the Normans of Sicily (1185) and with the Fourth Crusade (1204), when the city became for a time capital of the Latin Kingdom of Salonica. It was, however, restored to the Byzantine Empire of Nicea in 1246, reaching a cultural "**golden age**" until Turkish conquest and occupation in 1430.

Thessaloníki was the premier **Ottoman Balkan city** when Athens was still a backwater. Its population was as varied as any in the region, with Greek Orthodox Christians in a distinct minority. Besides Ottoman Muslims, who called the city "Selanik", there were Slavs (who still know it as "Solun"), Albanians, Armenians and, following the Iberian expulsions after 1492, the largest European **Jewish community** of the age (see box, p.274).

The modern quality of Thessaloníki is due largely to a disastrous **fire** in 1917 which levelled most of the old plaster houses along a labyrinth of Ottoman lanes, including the entire Jewish quarter. The city was rebuilt, often in a special form of Art Deco style, over the following eight years on a grid plan prepared under the supervision of French architect Ernest Hébrard, with long central avenues running parallel to the seafront and cross-streets densely planted with trees. During **World War II** the city was occupied by the Nazis, who decimated the Jewish community. After the war more reconstruction was necessary to repair bomb damage, though this was interrupted in 1978 by a severe **earthquake** that damaged many older buildings.

Thessaloníki's opulence has traditionally been epitomized by the locals' sartorial elegance, but the boom of the 1990s is long gone and an increasing number of boarded-up shops indicate that Greece's economic malaise has taken hold here. A permanent underclass lives in shantytowns near the port, consisting of Pontic or Black Sea Greeks, Albanians and eastern European refugees, as well as a growing community of Afghans and Africans.

## The archeological museum

Platía H.A.N.TH.; June–Oct Mon 10.30am–8pm, Tues–Sun 8am–8pm; Nov–May Tues–Sun 8.30am–3pm • €6 • ☎ 2310 830 538, ⓦ amth.gr

The refurbished **archeological museum** is undoubtedly the city's leading museum. Star billing goes to the marvellous **Gold of Macedon exhibition** in the south hall, which displays – and clearly labels in both English and Greek – many of the finds from the royal tombs of Philip II of Macedon (father of Alexander the Great) and others at the ancient Macedonian capital of Aegae, in Vergina (see p.287). They include startling amounts of gold and silver – masks, crowns, necklaces, earrings and bracelets – all of extraordinarily imaginative craftsmanship, both beautiful and practical, as well as pieces in ivory and bronze. Other highlights include the central gallery (opposite as you enter), which is devoted to rich grave **finds from ancient Sindos**, a few kilometres north of the modern city, while the left-hand wing is taken up by **Hellenistic and Roman art**, in particular some exquisite blown-glass birds, found in the tumuli or *toúmbes* which stud the plain around Thessaloníki.

## The Museum of Byzantine Culture

Stratoú 2; June–Oct Mon 10.30am–8pm, Tues–Sun 8am–8pm; Nov–May Mon 10.30am–5pm, Tues–Sun 8.30am–3pm • €4 • ☎ 2313 306 400, ⓦ mbp.gr

The prize-winning **Museum of Byzantine Culture**, in a handsome brick structure just east of the Archeological Museum, does a fine job of displaying the early Christian tombs and graves excavated in the city, featuring rescued wall paintings depicting, among others, *Susannah and the Elders*, and a naked rower surrounded by sea creatures. Despite this and the faultless lighting and display techniques, most of the displays will appeal more to specialists than to lay visitors.

## The White Tower

East end of Leofóros Níkis; Tues–Sun 8.30am–3pm • €3 • ☎ 2310 267 832

Dominating the seafront promenade, the **White Tower (Lefkós Pýrgos)** is the city's graceful symbol. Originally known as the Lions' Tower and the Fortress of Kalamariá, it formed a corner of the city's Byzantine and Ottoman defences before most of the walls were demolished late in the nineteenth century. In 1890 a Jewish prisoner was given the task of whitewashing the tower, in exchange for his freedom, hence the new name, which stuck, even though it is now more of a buff colour. It was restored in 1985 for the city's 2300th birthday celebrations and has since been converted into a moderately interesting historical museum.

## Roman remains

The **Arch of Galerius** dominates a pedestrianized square just off the eastern end of Egnatía. Along with the nearby Rotónda (see below), it originally formed part of a larger Roman complex which included palaces and a hippodrome. The mighty arch is the surviving span of a dome-surmounted arcade that once led towards the palaces. Built to commemorate the emperor's victories over the Persians in 297 AD, its piers contain weathered reliefs of the battle scenes interspersed with glorified poses of Galerius himself. The well-displayed remains of **Galerius's palace** can be viewed, below the modern street level, along pedestrianized Dhimitríou Goúnari towards its southern extension, Platía Navarínou.

### Rotónda (Áyios Yeóryios)

Platía Ayíou Yeoryíou • Tues–Sun 8.30am–3pm • Free • ☎ 2310 968 860

North of the great arch, the **Rotónda**, later converted into the church of **Áyios Yeóryios**, is the most striking single Roman monument in the city. It was designed, but never used, as an imperial mausoleum, possibly for Galerius himself. Consecrated for Christian use in the late fourth century, by the addition of a sanctuary, an apse, a narthex and rich mosaics, it later became one of the city's major mosques, from which period the minaret remains. The cavernous interior is stark but some of the stunning mosaics remain in place.

## Roman Forum

Daily: summer 8am–8pm; winter 8.30am–3pm • Free

Just north of leafy Platía Dhikastiríon, the **Roman Forum** has been undergoing gradual excavation for over a decade so access is limited. In many ways, its layout is best observed from the road behind, where the shape of the *stoa*, with several remaining columns, is clear. The restored amphitheatre is used for occasional summer performances.

## Atatürk's house

Apostólou Pávlou 17 • Daily 10am–5pm • Free • For admission contact the Turkish Consulate at Ayíou Dhimitríou 151 (Mon–Fri 9.30am–12.30pm; ☎ 2310 248 452)

In **Kástra**, as the lower fringes of the Upper Town are known, stands a pink nineteenth-century building in which **Kemal Atatürk**, creator and first president of the modern secular state of Turkey, was born in 1881. The consulate maintains the house as a small

## OTTOMAN THESSALONÍKI

Despite years of neglect, the 1917 fire and the 1978 quake, Thessaloníki has quite a number of vestiges of **Ottoman architecture** to show, mostly within walking distance of Platía Dhikastiríon. At the eastern corner of the square itself stands the disused but well-preserved Bey Hammam or **Parádhisos Baths** (Mon–Fri 9am–9pm, Sat & Sun 8.30am–3pm; free), the oldest Turkish bathhouse in the city (1444) and in use until 1968. The doorway is surmounted by elaborate ornamentation, while inside art exhibitions – often paradoxically with Byzantine themes – are held from time to time.

To the south of Platía Dhikastiríon lies the main **Turkish bazaar area**, bounded roughly by Egnatía, Dhragoúmi, Ayías Sofías and Tsimiskí. Much the most interesting bit, and a quiet midtown oasis, is a grid of lanes between Ayías Sofías and Aristotélous, devoted to selling animals, crafts and cane furniture. Nearby Ottoman monuments include the six-domed Bezesténi or covered valuables market at the corner of Venizélou and Egnatía, now housing jewellery and other shops. Directly opposite, on the north side of Egnatía, rather more modest stores occupy a prominent mosque, the fifteenth-century purpose-built Hamza Bey Tzamí (most mosques in Ottoman Thessaloníki were converted churches), now looking decidedly ramshackle.

Well to the north of Platía Dhikastiríon, beyond Áyios Dhimítrios basilica, is the seventeenth-century **Yeni Hammam**, now a summer cinema and music venue serving basic food, and better known as the Aigli (see p.278); the fifteenth-century Altaza Imaret, tucked away in a quiet square diagonally opposite, sports a handsome portico and multiple domes.

**museum**, with its original fixtures and an interesting selection of Atatürk memorabilia. Due to tight security, you must apply for admission with your passport to the Turkish consulate, next door.

## Ayía Sofía

Between Egnatía and Platía Navarínou • Daily 7am–1pm & 5–6.30pm • Free • ☎ 2310 270 253

The heavily restored eighth-century church of **Ayía Sofía** is the finest of its kind in the city. Modelled on its more illustrious namesake in Constantinople, it replaced an older basilica, the only trace of which remains a few paces south: the below-street-level holy well of John the Baptist, originally a Roman *nymphaeum* (sacred fountain). Ayía Sofía's dome, 10m in diameter, bears a splendid **mosaic** of the *Ascension*, for which you'll need binoculars. Christ, borne up to the heavens by two angels, sits resplendent on a rainbow throne, right hand extended in blessing; below, a wry inscription quotes Acts 1:11: "Ye men of galilee, why stand ye gazing up into heaven?" The whole is ringed by fifteen figures: the Virgin attended by two angels, and the twelve Apostles reacting to the miracle. The dome was restored late in the 1980s; the rest of the interior decoration was plastered over after the 1917 fire.

## Áyios Dhimítrios

Ayíou Dhimítríou; Mon 12.30–7pm, Tues–Sat 8am–8pm, Sun 10.30am–8pm • Free • ☎ 2310 968 843

The massive yet simple church of **Áyios Dhimítrios** was conceived in the fifth century but heavily restored subsequently. Far more impressive than the official cathedral down at Mitropóleos, it is the de facto cathedral of the city, with pride of place in Thessalonian hearts, and was almost entirely rebuilt after the 1917 fire. The church is dedicated to the city's patron saint and stands on the site of his martyrdom.

As the largest basilica in Greece, its immense interior cannot fail to inspire awe. Amid the multicoloured marble columns and vast extents of off-white plaster, six small surviving **mosaics**, mostly on the columns flanking the altar, make an easy focal point; of these, four date back to the church's second reconstruction after the fire of 620. The astonishing seventh-century mosaic of *Áyios Dhimítrios Flanked by the Church's Two Founders*, on the inside of the south (right-hand) pier beside the steps to the crypt, and the adjacent mosaics of *Áyios Sérgios* and *Áyios Dhimítrios with a Deacon*, contrast well with their contemporary on the north column, a warm and humane mosaic of the saint with two young children.

The **crypt** (same hours; free) contains the *martyrion* of the saint – probably an adaptation of the Roman baths in which he was imprisoned – and a whole exhibit of beautifully carved column-capitals, labelled in Greek only and arrayed around a seven-columned fountain and collecting basin.

# Áno Póli (Upper Town)

Above Odhós Kassándhrou, the street parallel to Ayíou Dhimitríou, rises the Upper Town or **Áno Póli**, the main surviving quarter of Ottoman Thessaloníki. Although the streets here have long been swamped by new apartment buildings, they remain ramshackle and atmospheric, a labyrinth of timber-framed houses and winding steps. In the past few years many of the older houses have been bought up and restored and it is justifiably one of the city's favourite after-dark destinations. Sections of the fourteenth-century **Byzantine ramparts**, constructed with brick and rubble on top of old Roman foundations, crop up all around the northern part of town.

## BYZANTINE CHURCHES

Almost all the Byzantine churches in Thessaloníki are located in the central districts or on the slopes heading up towards the Upper Town. Under the Turks most of the buildings were converted for use as mosques, a process that obscured many of their original features and destroyed the majority of their frescoes and mosaics. Further damage came with the 1917 fire and, more recently, with the 1978 earthquake. Restoration seems a glacially slow process, meaning that many sanctuaries remain locked. Nevertheless, those below are all worth a visit and free to enter.

One of the most central is the eleventh-century **Panayía Halkéon** church (daily 7.30am–noon), a classic though rather unimaginative example of the "cross-in-square" form, nestling at the lush southwestern corner of Platía Dhikastiríon. Its interior contains fragmentary frescoes in the cupola and some fine icons.

Several blocks east, and tucked away just out of sight north of Egnatía, the restored, fifth-century, three-aisled basilica of **Panayía Ahirópiitos** (daily 7am–noon & 4.30–6.30pm) is the oldest in the city. It features arcades, monolithic columns and highly elaborate capitals – a popular development begun under Theodosius. Only the mosaics inside the arches survive, depicting birds, fruits and vegetation in a rich Alexandrian style.

Around Áyios Dhimítrios (see opposite) are several more churches, utterly different in feel. To the west along Ayíou Dhimitríou is the church of **Dhódheka Apóstoli** (daily 8.30am–noon & 4–6pm), built in the twelfth century with the bold Renaissance influence of Mystra. Its five domes rise in perfect symmetry above walls of fine brickwork, while inside are glorious fourteenth-century mosaics, among the last executed in the Byzantine empire. High up in the arches to the south, west and north of the dome respectively are a *Nativity*, an *Entry into Jerusalem*, a *Resurrection* and a *Transfiguration*.

A short climb up Ayías Sofías is **Ósios Dhavíd** (Mon–Sat 9am–noon & 4–6pm), a tiny fifth-century church on Odhós Timothéou. It doesn't really fit into any architectural progression, since the Ottomans demolished much of the building when converting it to a mosque. However, it has arguably the finest mosaic in the city, depicting a clean-shaven Christ Emmanuel appearing in a vision, with the four Rivers of Paradise, replete with fish, flowing beneath and lapping the feet of the prophets Ezekiel and Habakkuk.

Farther east in Kástra, on Irodhótou, fourteenth-century **Áyios Nikólaos Orfanós** (Tues–Sun 8.30am–2.45pm) is a diminutive, much-altered basilica; the imaginative and well-preserved frescoes inside are the most accessible and expressive in the city. It also houses the unusual *Áyion Mandílion*, an image of Christ's head superimposed on a legendary Turin-style veil sent to an ancient king of Anatolian Edessa. Around the apse is a wonderful *Niptir* (Christ Washing the Disciple's Feet), in which the image top right of a man riding a horse is thought to be the painter himself.

4

The best-preserved portion begins at a large circular keep, the Trigónion or **Chain Tower** (so called for its encircling ornamental moulding), in the northeast angle where the easterly city walls veer west. A much smaller circuit of walls rambles around the district of **Eptapýrgio** (Seven Towers), enclosing the old eponymous acropolis at the top end. For centuries it served as the city's **prison** until abandoned as too inhumane in 1989; it is described as a sort of Greek Devil's Island in a number of plaintive old songs entitled *Yedi Küle*, the Turkish name for Eptapýrgio.

## The Jewish Museum

Ayíou Miná 13 • Tues, Fri & Sun 11am–2pm, Wed & Thurs 11am–2pm & 5–8pm • €3 • ☎ 2310 250 406, ⊕ jmth.gr

Way down in the Bazaar quarter, an early twentieth-century house, once belonging to a Jewish family, has been beautifully renovated to accommodate the impressive **Jewish Museum**. On the ground floor are a few precious remains and some moving photographic documentation of the city's Jewish cemetery, which contained half a million graves until it was vandalized by the Nazis. Outstanding is a marble Roman stele from the third century, recycled as a Jewish tombstone for a member of the post-1492 Sephardic community from Iberia. In the middle of the courtyard is a finely sculpted fountain that once stood in a city synagogue. Upstairs, a well-presented exhibition, clearly labelled in Greek and English, traces the history of the Jewish presence from around 140 BC to the present day and displays some of the few religious and secular items that miraculously survived the 1917 fire and the Holocaust.

## The portside museums

If you cross busy Koundouriótou, the harbour-end extension of Níkis, to the city's **port**, through Gate A you'll find a set of dockside warehouses that have been converted into the city's latest arts complex, complete with bars and, perhaps bizarrely, a kindergarten. Sharing the same warehouse as the hermetic Cinema Museum, only of interest to Greek film buffs, the outstanding **Museum of Photography** (Tues–Fri 11am–7pm, Sat–Sun 11am–9pm; €2; ☎ 2310 566 716, ⊕ thmphoto.gr) stages exhibitions by Greek and international photographers. Across the road in an unprepossessing breeze-block bunker, the **State Museum of Contemporary Art** (Tues–Fri 10am–6pm, Sat & Sun 11am–7pm; €3) hosts exhibitions of paintings, often related to the city and its history.

---

### THE JEWS OF THESSALONÍKI

In the early sixteenth century, after virtually all the Jews were expelled from Spain and Portugal, nearly half of the inhabitants of Thessaloníki, over 80,000 people, were Jewish. For them "Salonik" or "Salonicco" ranked as a "Mother of Israel" and the community dominated the city's commercial, social and cultural life for some four hundred years, mostly tolerated by the Ottoman authorities but often resented by the Greeks. The first waves of Jewish emigration to Palestine, western Europe and the United States began after World War I. Numbers had dropped to fewer than 60,000 at the onset of World War II, during which all but a tiny fraction were **deported** from Platía Eleftherías to the concentration camps and immediate gassing. The vast Jewish cemeteries east of the city centre, among the world's largest, were desecrated in 1944; to add insult to injury, the area was later covered over by the new university and expanded trade-fair grounds in 1948. Thessaloníki's only surviving pre-Holocaust **synagogue** is the Monastiriótou at Syngroú 35, with an imposing, if austere, facade; it's usually open for Friday-evening and Saturday-morning worship. At the very heart of the former Jewish district sprawls the Modhiáno, the still-functioning central meat, fish and produce market, named after the wealthy Jewish Modiano family which long owned it.

# The Folk & Ethnological Museum of Macedonia

Vasilíssis Ólgas 68 • Mon–Tues & Fri–Sat 9am–3pm, Wed 9am–9pm • €2 • ☎ 2310 830 591 • Bus #5

In the southeast of the city, the **Folk & Ethnological museum** is housed in the elegant early twentieth-century mansion of the **Modiano** family, one of several Jewish-built residences in the district. It is one of the best of its kind in Greece, with well-written commentaries (English and Greek) accompanying temporary exhibitions on housing, costumes, day-to-day work and crafts.

## ARRIVAL AND DEPARTURE | THESSALONÍKI

**By plane** Thessaloníki "Makedonía" airport (☎ 2310 985 000, ☎ 2310 411 977 for flight information, ⓦ thessalonikiairport.gr) is located 15km south of the city centre. City bus #78 shuttles back and forth from the airport to the KTEL bus terminal via the town centre once or twice hourly all day, and #78N goes once an hour through the night. A taxi ride into town comes to €14, plus extras. There are numerous flight connections with major European cities and destinations all over Greece.

Domestic flights Athens (12–14 daily; 50min); Corfu (4 weekly; 1hr); Haniá, Crete (1–2 daily; 1hr 30min); Híos (4 weekly; 1hr 10min–2hr 45min); Iráklion, Crete (2–4 daily; 1hr 15min); Lésvos (1–2 daily; 1hr–1hr 50min); Límnos (5 weekly; 50min); Rhodes (2–4 daily; 50min); Sámos (4 weekly; 1hr 20min).

**By train** The train station is on the west side of town, with convenient bus links and a taxi rank. If you want to buy tickets or make reservations in advance, the OSE office at Aristotélous 18 (Mon & Sat 8am–3pm, Tues–Fri 8am–9pm) is far more central and helpful than the station ticket-windows.

Destinations Alexandhroúpoli (2 daily; 5hr 45min–6hr 15min); Athens (7 daily; 4hr 15min–7hr); Édhessa (8 daily; 1hr 35min); Lárissa (20 daily; 1hr 20min–1hr 45min); Litóhoro (13 daily; 1hr); Véria (8 daily; 1hr); Xánthi (2 daily; 4hr 15min–4hr 50min).

**By bus** Most KTEL buses arrive at the main terminal ("Makedonía"), 3km west of the city centre at Yiannitsón 194 (☎ 2310 500 111, ⓦ ktel-thes.gr); local buses #1, #31 & #78 go to the train station and Egnatía. All Halkidhikí buses leave from the dedicated KTEL Halkidhikís (☎ 2310 316 555, ⓦ ktel-chalkidikis.gr), 8km east of the city; take #36 from the Voulgári terminal at the eastern end of the #31 route or from IKEA, the terminal for a number of routes.

Destinations Alexandhroúpoli (6 daily; 5hr); Athens (11 daily; 7hr); Édhessa (hourly; 1hr 30min); Ierissós (7–8 daily; 2hr 30min); Ioánnina (6 daily; 7hr); Kalambáka (4 daily; 4hr 30min); Kassándhra (various resorts; 3–10 daily; 2–3hr); Kastoriá (8 daily; 3hr); Kavála (hourly; 2hr 15min); Litóhoro (5 daily; 1hr 30min); Ouranoúpoli (7–8 daily; 2hr 45min); Pélla (hourly; 1hr); Sithonía (various resorts; 3–6 daily; 2hr 30min–3hr 30min); Véria (half-hourly; 1hr 15min); Vólos (4 daily; 4hr).

**By ferry** All ferries leave from the port located at the western end of the seafront. The most convenient all-round agent, selling tickets for all companies, is Zorpidis, near the port at Salamínas 4 ☎ 2310 555 995, ⓦ www.zorpidis.gr. Currently, only one reliable route operates to: Límnos, Lésvos, Híos and Sámos (1 weekly).

## INFORMATION

**Tourist office** Visit Greece at Tsimiskí 136 (Mon–Fri 8am–3pm; ☎ 2310 221 100) gives away adequate maps of the city and Greece, as well as timetables and brochures. The websites ⓦ saloniki.org and ⓦ travelthessaliniki.org are reasonable resources. The tourist police (daily 8am–2pm; plus Tues, Thurs & Fri 5–9pm; ☎ 2310 554 871) are at Dhodhekaníssou 4, off Platía Dhimokratías.

## GETTING AROUND

**By bus** The local bus system (ⓦ oasth.gr) is very comprehensive and user-friendly; from a booth or *períptero* single-ride tickets cost €0.80, while a €0.90 ticket allows multiple transfers for up to ninety minutes; each ticket type costs €0.10 extra from machines on board; a 24hr pass costs €3. Useful lines include #10 and #11, both of which ply the length of Egnatía/Karamanlí. From Platía Eleftherías, just behind the seafront, buses initially run east along Mitropóleos; line #5 takes you to the archeological and folklore museums, and #23 heads north through Kástra to the highest quarter, known as Eptapýrgio.

**By taxi** Taxis are plentiful and reliable; an average trip across the town centre will cost €3–5.

**By car** If you have a car, it's best to use the attended fee-parking area that occupies all of Platía Eleftherías, where you pay on exit. Otherwise, finding a kerbside space is tough, even in the suburbs; most city-centre street parking costs €1.70 per hour from 8am–8pm Mon–Fri and 8am–3pm Sat – buy stripcards from a *períptero*. Nearly all streets are one way. Most car rental agencies are clustered near the fairgrounds and archeological museum on Angeláki, which is a good place to compare prices. The leading multinationals here have kiosks at the airport too, but you will get better deals from local firms,

**4**

such as Macedonia at no. 9 ☎ 2310 241 119, ⓦ automotorental .gr; or Avance at no. 7 ☎ 2310 279 888, ⓦ avance.gr.

**By metro** A metro is under construction but seems unlikely to achieve its 2013 opening date.

## ACCOMMODATION

For most of the year, reasonably priced **hotel** rooms are fairly easy to find, especially in the busy area at the western end of Egnatía. During the **International Trade Fair** (Sept) hotels are allowed to add a **twenty-percent surcharge** to the standard rate. Low season runs from June to August, this being a business-oriented city.

The closest **campsites**, both run by EOT, are at the small resorts of Ayía Triádha (24km; bus #73) and Órmos Epanomís (33km; #69); the latter is better, as is the beach there.

### WESTERN EGNATÍA AREA

**Atlantis** Egnatía 14 ☎ 2310 540 131, ⓦ www .atlantishotel.com.gr. Old-style joint with high ceilings and period decor. Some rooms have shared bathrooms and the ones at the back are the best deals. **€30**

★ **Augustos** Ptoleméon 1 ☎ 2310 522 550, ⓦ augustos .gr. Charming if slightly faded 1920s hotel on a quiet corner near Egnatía, with all en-suite high-ceilinged rooms and wi-fi in the spacious lounge. **€30**

**Kinissi Palace** Egnatía 41 ☎ 2310 508 081, ⓦ kinissipalace.gr. The smartest hotel in the area, its comfortable rooms have all mod cons but cramped bathrooms and noisy a/c. There's a sauna, *hammam* and massage service, plus a bar and a decent restaurant, the *Averof*. Breakfast included. **€70**

**Nea Mitropolis** Syngroú 22 ☎ 2310 525 540, ⓦ neametropolis.gr. Clean, reasonable value and well maintained.; all rooms are brightly furnished with fridges and TV. Relatively quiet for the location. Good online deals. **€45**

**Pella** Íonos Dhragoúmi 63 ☎ 2310 524 222, ⓦ pella -hotel.gr. A tall, narrow, modern hotel on a moderately quiet street; pleasant, impeccably clean minimalist rooms and modern if smallish bathrooms. **€45**

**The Tobacco Hotel (Davitel)** Ayíou Dhimitríou 25 ☎ 2310 515 002, ⓦ www.davitel.gr. This former tobacco warehouse has sleek double-glazed rooms with contemporary decor and efficient a/c; complimentary breakfasts served in a designer-rustic mezzanine salon. **€75**

### REST OF THE CITY

★ **Capsis Bristol** Oplopíou 2 ☎ 2310 506 500, ⓦ capsisbristol.gr. Thessaloníki's ooriginal boutique hotel, with twenty period-furnished rooms and suites in an impeccably restored 1870 building. Good Italian/Argentinian restaurant and lavish buffet breakfast included; best booked online. **€130**

**Egnatia Palace** Egnatía 61 ☎ 2310 222 900, ⓦ egnatiapalace.gr. A smart hotel in a modern building with some Art Deco flourishes, it has spacious rooms whose modish decor ranges from kitsch to stylish; includes a spa. Breakfast included. **€120**

**Electra Palace** Platía Aristotélous 9 ☎ 2310 294 000, ⓦ electrahotels.gr. In one of the town's most prestigious positions and as palatial inside out, this five-star large, lavishly furnished rooms and a good restaurant, albeit with a slightly dated air. **€175**

**Les Lazaristes (Domotel)** Kolokotróni 16, Stavroúpoli ☎ 2310 647 400, ⓦ domotel.gr. Opposite the Moní Lazaristón arts complex (see p.278), this handsome new hotel, in a converted tobacco factory, is a long way out but has free parking. Beautiful magazine interiors and a gorgeous pool, plus the *Fred and Ginger* gourmet restaurant. Breakfast included. **€100**

**Le Palace** Tsimiskí 12 ☎ 2310 257 400, ⓦ lepalace.gr. This Art Deco hotel offers spacious, stylishly decorated rooms with modern baths and double glazing. Lovely common areas comprise a mezzanine lounge, a ground-floor café and a restaurant. Good online deals. Outstanding buffet breakfast iincluded. **€95**

## EATING

There is a wealth of interesting **places to eat** in Thessaloníki, from authentic tavernas and eclectic ouzerís to quite sophisticated international restaurants. Areas particularly worth investigating are trendy **Ladhádhika**, near the port, and the web of streets between **Syngroú** and Platía Athónos. Dozens of prominent bakeries, *zaharoplastía* and *souvladtzídhika*, dotted all across town, provide a range of snacks and breakfast possibilities. All the places listed are within walking distance, though to reach the Áno Póli establishments you may well choose to jump on the handy #23 bus.

### CITY CENTRE

**Aristotelous** Aristotélous 8 ☎ 2310 230 762. Tucked off the road behind wrought-iron gates, this stylish ouzerí with its fine, arcaded interior and courtyard specializes in excellent *mezédhes* for €4–8. Great *tsípouro* too. Daily noon–1am; closed Sun pm and 1 week mid-Aug.

★ **ly Gonia tou Merakli** Avyerinoú, alley off Platía Áthonos ☎ 2310 287 726. Inexpensive seafood, better than average portions, a quality free dessert and highly palatable barrelled wine make this the best of several ouzerís in these atmospheric surrounding lanes. Daily noon–2am.

**Kamares** Platía Ayíou Yeoryíou 11, by the Rotónda ☎ 2310 219 686. Excellent seafood, salads and grilled meat at standard prices (€7–8), washed down by bulk wine from Límnos. Summer outdoor seating beside the park. Mon–Sat 10am–1am, Sun 10am–6pm.

**Koumbarakia** Egnatía 140 ☎ 2310 271 905. Tucked behind a tiny Byzantine chapel, the outdoor tables of this durable, budget ouzerí groan with Macedonian-style grills for €8–10, seafood and salads, including *túrsi* (pickled vegetables). Mon–Sat noon–midnight, Sun noon–6pm.

**Krasodhikio** Filíppou 18 ☎ 2310 239 031. Another fine ouzerí, serving a range of ample meat and seafood meals and *mezédhes* for under €10 on the pavement in summer or in the cosy interior when it's cold. Daily noon–1.15am.

**Molyvos** Kapodhistríou 1 ☎ 2310 555 952, ⓦ molyvos .gr. Ouzo and *mezédhes* combos for €12–15 from Crete, Lesvos, Cyclades and Istanbul are among the regional specialities served at this first-floor taverna-ouzerí, with an attached shop selling ouzo and olive oils. Daily 11am–2am.

★ **Myrovolos Smyrni** In arcade in the Modhiáno off Komninón 32 ☎ 2310 274 170. Friendly, crowded ouzerí, also known as *Tou Thanassi*. Typical dishes include cheese-stuffed squid, Smyrna-style meatballs, stuffed potatoes and grilled baby fish. Reservations recommended. Daily noon–2am, closed Sun eves.

★ **Nea Ilyssia** Sófou 17 ☎ 2310 514 162. Just below Egnatía, this popular restaurant is great for *mayireftá*, such as beef in tomato sauce and lamb fricassé for €7–8, as well as filling souvlaki. Daily 8.30am–2am, Fri–Sat till 4am.

**Ta Bakaliarakia tou Aristou** Katoúni 3, Ladhádhika ☎ 2310 542 906. Heapings of cod and chips, served on greaseproof paper for around €6–7, make this joint in a pedestrianized portside alley quite memorable. Second branch one block away. Daily 9am–7pm.

**Tre Marie** P.P. Yermanoú 13 ☎ 2310 240 051. This smart trattoria serves a selection of risotto and pasta dishes for €15–20 in a marble- and- dark- wood dining room with stained-glass ceiling panels and sparkling chandeliers. Small outside terrace. Daily 11am–midnight.

**Tsarouhas** Olýmbou 78 ☎ 2310 271 621. Reputedly the best and certainly the most famous of the city's *patsatzídhika*, churning out rich tripe-and-trotter soup for €8. Lots of other tasty *mayireftá* and Anatolian puddings. Open 24hr; closed mid-July to mid-Aug.

**Vrotos** Mitropolítou Yennadhíou 6, Platía Áthonos ☎ 2310 223 958. One of the most popular ouzerís here, with something for all tastes: elaborate vegetable dishes with or without cheese, plus creative meat and seafood recipes for €6–10. Reservations recommended. Daily 11am–2am; closed Sun eves.

**Zythos** Platía Katoúni 5, Ladhádhika ☎ 2310 540 284, ⓦ zithos.gr. Imaginative Greek *mezédhes* plus a range of sausages and pasta dishes for around €10, along with an excellent selection of wines and beers, both draught and bottled. Reservations recommended at weekends. Food served daily noon–9.30pm, bar 10am–2am.

## ÁNO PÓLI

**Kreonidis** Leofóros Óhi 4 ☎ 2310 206 006. This *psistariá*/ouzerí has tables overlooking the city and sea, where you can eat grills or *mezédhes* for under €10 while enjoying the splendid view. Daily noon–1am.

**Ladhokolla me Thea** Kýprou 2 ☎ 2310 210 805. The increasingly popular trend of eating chunks of pork or lamb on greaseproof paper for around €8 has reached Áno Póli with this otherwise smart taverna. Daily noon–midnight.

★ **O Volos sta...Kastra!** Gravías 1 ☎ 2310 210 819. A range of dips, salads, meats and fish, as well as seafood risotto and shrimp spaghetti, can be enjoyed for €12 or under along with organic Cretan wine in this taverna cum ouzerí. Daily noon–2am.

★ **To Makedhoniko** Y Papadhopoúlou 32, Sykiés ☎ 2310 627 438. Tucked inside the western city gate, this old-fashioned taverna with a triangular courtyard serves an excellent but limited range of grills, dips, salads and barrelled retsina. Stuff yourself and drink merrily for little over €10 in total. Tues–Sun noon–midnight.

## NIGHTLIFE

Apart from the almost unbroken line of expensive café-bars on the seafront **Leofóros Níkis** and around **Platía Aristotélous**, the most fashionable nightlife is to be found in **Ladhádhika**, near the port. Bustling **Platía Navarínou** and the nearby pedestrianized streets, **Iktínou** and **Zefxídhou**, also contain some of the trendiest establishments in the city. During the warmer months, action mostly shifts to various glitzy, barn-like establishments lining the coast road out to **Kalamariá**, for which you'll need to take taxis.

**A Votre Santé** Mitropóleos 70 ☎ 2310 239 494. Low-key café-bar that offers a wide range of range of imported beers and cocktails, as well as quality chocolates. The musical genre shifts from Greek *éntekhno* to jazz and ethnic. Daily 8.30am–2.30am.

**Decadence** A Yeoryíou 21, near the Mylos centre. The most highly rated of the big clubs for cutting-edge dance,

techno and progressive house music. Oct–May Wed–Sun 10pm–late.

**Dizzy** Eyíptou 5, Ladhádhika. Full-on rock/goth sounds abound in this lively bar with motorbikes hanging from sturdy wooden beams and Guinness or other beers on tap. Daily 9pm–late.

**Kissfish** Fokéas 1, Ladhádhika ☎ 2310 550 636. Spread

over two floors, this chic portside club hosts regular live acts and lively DJ nights upstairs, while the ground-floor café is more for chilling. Daily 6pm–late.

**Kitchen Bar** 2nd Port Warehouse, ☎ 2310 502 241, ⓦ kitchenbar.com.gr. This cavernous warehouse conversion is now a top hangout, with a hi-tech indoor space and breezy seafront terrace with sweeping city views as you sip a cocktail, eat a full-blown meal or just relax with a coffee. Daily 10am–2am.

**Kourdhisto Gourouni** Ayías Sofías 31 ☎ 2310 274 672. Several foreign brews on tap and a bewildering range of bottled beers at this stylish bar with indoor and outdoor seating; expensive food menu also. Daily 11am–2am.

**Pasta Flora Darling** Zefxídhou 6 ☎ 2310 261 518. This small, crowded student favourite retains touches of eccentricity in its decor with the odd gnome and abstract painting; good cocktails and vegetarian snacks too. Daily 10am–2am.

## ENTERTAINMENT

### THEATRE

**Moní Lazaristón** Kolokotróni 25, Stavroúpoli ☎ 2310 652 020, ⓦ monilazariston.gr. Arts complex and theatre converted from a deconsecrated Catholic monastery. It's 2km north of the centre along Langadhá. Buses #34 and #38 go there from Platía Dhikastiríon.

**Mylos** at Andhréou Yeoryíou 56 ☎ 2310 551 836, ⓦ mylos.gr. A multifunctional cultural complex housed in an old flour mill some way west of the centre. Here you'll find a couple of bars, a live jazz café, a popular *tsipourádhiko*, a summer cinema, a theatre, concert halls and exhibition galleries.

**State Theatre of Northern Greece** Multiple venues ☎ 2315 200 200, ⓦ ntng.gr. Hosts winter events at Etería Makedhonikón Spoudhón or the ultramodern Vassilikó Théatro, both near the White Tower. In summer, things move to one of a number of outdoor venues: the Théatro Kípou, near the archeological museum; well up the hill at

the Théatro Dhássous, in the pines east of the upper town, with events from late June to mid-September; or the Théatro Damári in Triandhría district.

### CINEMA

Thessaloníki is a cinephile city, never more so than during its annual film festival (ⓦ filmfestival.gr), and while open-air cinemas are now thin on the ground, they are worth seeking out in summer.

**Indoor cinemas** Aristotelion, Ethnikís Ámynas 2 (open in summer); Kolosseon, V Olgas 150 (open in summer); Makedhonikon, corner Ethnikís Ámynas and A Svólou; Olympion, Platía Aristotélous 9; and Vakoura, Ioánnou Mihaïl 10.

**Open-air cinemas** Aigli, outside the Yeni Hammam; and Natali, at the start of Megálou Alexándhrou, by the *Macedonia Palace* hotel. Listings are given in *About* and the daily Greek papers.

## SHOPPING

Thessaloníki is not a major shopping destination but has the mixture of independent and big brand outlets you would expect for any European city of its size, mostly along or just off Tsimiskí, as well as suburban malls. Travellers are most likely to hunt for books, music or the odd souvenir.

**The Artware Shop** Avyerinoú 14 Platía Áthonos, ☎ 2314 313 844. Handmade jewellery and crafts, as well as imaginative T-shirts and other clothes. Daily 10am–9pm.

**Bravos** Egnatías 43 ☎ 2310 539 383. This is the place to buy your bouzouki or choose from a range of other quality traditional instruments. Mon–Fri 10am–7.30pm, Sat 10am–2pm.

**Konstandinidis** P Melá 11 ☎ 2310 256 173. Excellent stocks of English-language books on a huge range of topics

from art and fiction to philosophy and natural history. Mon–Fri 10am–8.30pm, Sat 10am–2.30pm.

**Metropolis** Tsimiskí 33 ☎ 2310 250 074. Northern outpost of the popular Athenian chain, offering a wide selection of Greek CDs, as well as international rock, dance, jazz and ethnic sounds. Also films on DVD and concert tickets. Daily 10.30am–10pm.

**Studio 52** D Goúnari 46 ☎ 2310 271 301. Basement music shop, with lots of out-of-print vinyl and even cassettes plus well-sorted CDs. Mon–Fri 11am–9pm, Sat 11am–3pm.

**Traveler** P Koromilá 48 ☎ 2310 275 215. The best source of travel literature, guidebooks and maps in the city. Mon–Fri 10am–8pm, Sat 10am–2.30pm.

## DIRECTORY

**Consulates** Australia, Kifissías 46, Kalamaria ☎ 2310 482 322; Canada, Tsimiskí 17 ☎ 2310 256 350; UK/Commonwealth, Aristotélous 21 ☎ 2310 278 006; US, Tsimiskí 43, 7th floor ☎ 2310 242 905.

**Cultural institutes** British Council, Ethnikís Amynis 9, cnr Tsimiskí ☎ 2310 378 300; free library and reading room, plus various events in the winter months.

**Exchange** For changing notes, use the 24hr automatic exchange machine at the National Bank on Platía Aristotélous 6. Thessaloníki has hundreds of reliable ATMs accepting international cards.

**Football** Thessaloníki's main team is PAOK, whose stadium is in the east of the city at Toúmba. Its two big rivals are Aris, who play in Hariláou, also east of the centre, and Iraklis, whose

## THE FIRE-WALKERS OF LANGADHÁS

On May 21, the feast day of SS Constantine and Helen, villagers at **LANGADHÁS**, 20km north of Thessaloníki, perform a ritual barefoot dance across a bed of burning coals known as the **anastenária**. While it has been suggested that they are remnants of a Dionysiac cult, devotees fiercely assert a purely Christian tradition. This seems to relate to a fire, around 1250, in the Thracian village of Kostí (now in Bulgaria), from where many of the inhabitants of Langadhás originate. Holy icons were heard groaning from the flames and were rescued by villagers, who emerged miraculously unburnt from the blazing church. The icons, passed down by their families, are believed to ensure protection during the fire walking. Equally important is piety and purity of heart: it is said that no one with any harboured grudges or unconfessed sins can pass through the coals unscathed.

Whatever the origin, the rite is still performed most years – lately as something of a tourist attraction, with an admission charge and repeat performances over the next two days. It is nevertheless eerie and impressive, beginning around 7pm with the lighting of a cone of hardwood logs. A couple of hours later their embers are raked into a circle and, just before complete darkness, a traditional Macedonian *daoúli* drummer and two lyra players precede a group of about sixteen women and men into the arena. These *anastenáridhes* (literally "groaners"), in partial trance, then shuffle across the coals for about a quarter of an hour, somehow without requring a trip to hospital at the end.

---

Kaftantzoglou stadium is both the largest and most central.

**Hospitals** For minor trauma, use the Yeniko Kendriko at Ethnikís Amynis 41; otherwise, head for the Ippokration at Konstandinopóleos 49, in the eastern part of town.

**Internet access** Most hotels and many cafés offer free wi-fi and there are still a good few cafés with terminals; two of the least noisy are *Enterprise* at Dhimitríou Goúnari 52 and *Planet* at Svólou 55.

**Laundries** Bianca, Antoniádhou 3, near the Arch of Galerius (quick service and long hours); Freskadha, Filíppou 105, beside the Rotónda; Ion, Karaóli Dhimitríou 52 (good dry cleaning).

**Post office** Main branch is at V Iraklíou 38 (Mon–Fri 7.30am–8pm, Sat 7.30am–2pm, Sun 9am–1.30pm). There are other post offices around the city: the most useful ones are at Koundouriótou (by the port), Ethnikís Amynis 9A and Ayíou Dhimitríou 98.

**Travel agents** Most general sales agents and consolidators cluster around Platía Eleftherías, especially on Kalapotháki, Komninón, Níkis and Mitropóleos. Students and under-27s should try Nouvelles Frontières at Kalapotháki 8 (☎2310 237 700) or Sunflight at Tsimiskí 114 (☎2310 280 500). For cheap buses to Turkey, try Bus and Atlantic Tours, Aristotélous 10, 4th Floor (☎2310 226 036). Mountain trekking and other outdoor expeditions are offered by Trekking Hellas, Mitropóleos 60 (☎2310 264 082).

# Pella

**PELLA**, 40km west of Thessaloníki, was the capital of Macedonia throughout its greatest period and the first capital of Greece after Philip II forcibly unified the country around 338 BC. It was founded some sixty years earlier by King Archelaos, who transferred the royal Macedonian court here from Aegae (see p.287). At that time it lay at the head of a broad lake, connected to the Thermaïkós gulf by a navigable river. The royal palace was decorated by the painter **Zeuxis** and was said to be the greatest artistic showplace since the time of Classical Athens. **Euripides** wrote and produced his last plays at the court, and here, too, **Aristotle** was to tutor the young Alexander the Great – born, like his father Philip II, in the city.

The site today is a worthwhile stopover en route to Édhessa and western Macedonia or as a day-trip from Thessaloníki. Its main treasures are a series of pebble mosaics, some in the museum, others *in situ*.

## The site

June–Sept Mon 1.30–8pm, Tues–Sun 8am–8pm; Oct–May Tues–Sun 8.30am–3pm • €6 including museum • ☎23820 31160 • The site of Pella lies on the main Thessaloníki–Édhessa road and is served by half-hourly buses

Today Pella's **ruins** stand in the middle of a broad expanse of plain. It was located by chance finds in 1957 and as yet has only been partially excavated. The **acropolis** at Pella is a low hill to the west of the modern village of Pélla. To the north of the road, at the main site, stand the low remains of a grand official building, probably a government office; it is divided into three large open courts, each enclosed by a *peristyle*, or portico (the columns of the central one have been re-erected), and bordered by wide streets with a sophisticated drainage system.

In the third court three late fourth-century BC **mosaics** have been left *in situ* under sheltering canopies; one, a stag hunt, is complete, and astounding in its dynamism and use of perspective. The others represent, respectively, the rape of Helen by Paris and his friends Phorbas and Theseus, and a fight between a Greek and an Amazon.

### The museum
Same hours and admission as site • ☎ 23820 32963

The excellent new **museum**, designed on the rectangular model of the ancient dwellings, stands up at the back of the modern village of Pélla. It showcases more spectacular **pebble mosaics** taken from the site, as well as rich grave finds from the two local necropolises, delicately worked terracotta figurines from a sanctuary of Aphrodite and Cybele, a large hoard of late Classical/early Hellenistic coins, and – on the rarely seen domestic level – metal door fittings: pivots, knocker plates and crude keys. The finds are all set within the context of life in the ancient capital, with detailed contextual displays, all well translated.

# 4

# Mount Olympus and around

The highest, most magical and most dramatic of all Greek mountains, **MOUNT OLYMPUS** – Ólymbos in Greek – rears straight up to 2917m from the coast and, when pollution allows, is visible from Thessaloníki, some 100km away to the northeast. Its summit was believed by the ancient Greeks to be the home of the gods and it seems that quite a few locals still follow the old religion. Dense forests cover its lower slopes, and its **wild flowers** are without parallel even by Greek standards.

**Climbing the mountain** requires an early start (certainly pre-8am) for the 3hr ascent to Mýtikas, the highest peak, so it's best to stay overnight at one of the **refuges**. The peaks frequently cloud up by midday and you lose the view, to say nothing of the danger of catching one of Zeus's thunderbolts. Besides, nights at the refuge are fantastic: a log fire blazes, you watch the sun set on the peaks and dawn break over the Aegean, and you can usually see a multitude of stars.

**ARRIVAL AND INFORMATION**                                      **MOUNT OLYMPUS**

To make the most of the mountain, you need to allow two to three days' hiking. You should go equipped with decent boots and warm clothing. No special expertise is necessary to get to the top in summer (mid-June to Oct), but it's a long hard pull, requiring a good deal of stamina; winter climbs, of course, are another matter, with heavy snowfall adding to the challenge. At any time of year Olympus is a mountain to be treated with respect: its weather is notoriously fickle, with sudden fogs or storms, and it regularly claims lives.

**By car and on foot** To reach alpine Olympus, you've a choice of road or foot routes via Litóhoro (see p.282), the main village nearby. With your own vehicle, you can drive deep into the mountain along a fairly decent road, the first 11km of which is paved.
**Maps and guides** The best and most easily available commercial trekking map is Road Editions' *Olymbos* at 1:50,000, available from specialist map shops abroad or in

Athens or Thessaloníki; a good alternative is one of the same scale that is co-produced by *Korfes* magazine. One or other is usually available at local shops in Litóhoro, but they sometimes run out. Two organizations, EOS and SEO (see p.282), can provide limited advice, as can 2917 in Thessaloníki (☎ 2310 914 654, ⓦ 2917.gr) but their website is in Greek only.

**MOUNT OLYMPUS**

Contour
Cross-country route
Refuge
Spring

Litóhoro

Refuge D
(Takis Boundolos)

Petróstrounga

Old Ayíou Dhionysíou
Monastery

Priónia (Taverna)

Mandhres
(2247m)

Skolio
(2485m)

Refuge C
(Khristos Kakalos)

Refuge A
(Spílios Agapitós)

Profítis Ilías
(2803m)

Yíosos Apostolídhis
(SEO) Refuge

Stefáni
(2909m)

Mýtikas
(2917m)

Skála
(2866m)

Skolió
(2911m)

Ayíos Andónios
(2817m)

Kalóyeros
(2701m)

Símedions
(2381m)

Livadháki

Áno Tsouknídha
(1498m)

Páter Dhionysíou

Gólna
(926m)

Délí

Dhlakláthasi (Gortsiá)

Páter Dhionysíou

Pápa Alóni Ravine

Oropédhio Mouzón

Zonária

Loúki

Metamórfosi
(2699m)

Páges
(2676m)

Frángou Aláni
(2677m)

MACEDONIA

THESSALY

Kokkinóplos

N

kilometres

## ACCOMMODATION AND EATING

**Refuges** Accommodation on Mount Olympus itself is better organized than on any other mountain in Greece. There are two staffed refuges: the EOS-run *Spílios Agapitós* at 2100m, commonly known as Refuge A (May–Oct, reservations recommended in summer; ☎ 23520 81800, ⓦ www.mountolympus.gr), and the SEO-managed *Yíosos Apostolídhis* hut at 2700m (July–Sept, though its glassed-in porch is always available for climbers in need; ☎ 2310 224 710). Both charge around €10 for a bunk and you can camp at Refuge A for around €5, including use of

their bathroom; lights-out and outer door locked at 10pm, so bring a torch.

**Meals** at either shelter are relatively expensive, and mandatory since no cooking is allowed inside; bring more money than you think you'll require, as bad weather can ground you a day or two longer than planned. For sustenance while walking, you'll need to buy food at the well-stocked grocery stores in Litóhoro, though water can wait until you're in the vicinity of the main trailhead at Priónia (see opposite).

# Litóhoro

By far the best base for a walk up the mountain, if only part of the way for the views, is the small town of **LITÓHORO** on the eastern side. A fairly pleasant garrison town with two huge army camps on the approach road, its setting, in good weather, affords intoxicating vistas into the heart of the range. Facilities have also improved greatly in recent years, as it has become a popular weekend getaway for Thessalonians.

## ARRIVAL AND DEPARTURE

**By train** The train station is 5km away, down by the motorway, where you'll find taxis are sometimes waiting or you can walk 500m and pick up a bus just west of the motorway. There are 13 trains daily from Thessaloníki.

**By bus** There are frequent buses to the central platía KTEL

from Thessaloníki (5 daily; 1hr 30min) or the nearby market town of Kateríni (hourly; 30min).

**By car** Litóhoro has its own motorway turn-off. Parking is not a problem.

## ACCOMMODATION

Litóhoro has a range of reasonable accommodation and there's a seaside hostel not far away. The nearest campsites are on the beach at Varikó, 11km away: *Stani* (☎ 23520 61277) and *Niteas* (☎ 23520 61290), both open all year round.

**Enipeas** right behind Xenios Dias ☎ 23520 84328, ⓦ hotel-enipeas.gr. Very welcoming and spotless place, its upper rear rooms have fine views, while attic rooms with skylight only are cheaper. €40

**Olympus Mediterranean** Dhionýsou 5 ☎ 23520 81831, ⓦ olympusmed.gr. Boasting a smart new lobby in modernist style and twenty beautifully refurbished rooms, this is the town's poshest option; breakfast included. €75

**Seaside Hostel, Gríitsa** ☎ 23520 81800, ⓦ summitzero.gr. Set right on the beach only 5km from Litóhoro, this friendly family-run hostel provides bunk-beds for 20 people in four rooms and spotless shared facilities. Dorm beds €15

**Villa Drosos** Arheláou 18 ☎ 23520 84561, ⓦ villadrosos .gr. Tucked away behind Ayíou Yeoryíou church, two or

three streets back from Ayíou Nikoláou, the *Villa* boasts smart rooms, an enticing swimming pool and an open fire in winter, plus parking space; breakfast included. €65

**Xenios Dias** On the main square ☎ 23520 81234, ⓦ hotel-xeniosdias.gr. With views to equal those of the *Enipeas*, this place has smarter rooms and a cosy bar. Breakfast included. €60

★ **Xenonas Papanikolaou** NE Kítrous 1, signposted 100m from square ☎ 23520 81236, ⓦ xenonas -papanikolaou.gr. Very central but tucked in a quiet side street, this friendly and excellently appointed hostel offers modernized, yet traditionally decorated en-suite rooms with central a/c/heating and cable TV. Superb value. €40

## EATING

★ **Gastrodromio "En Olymbo"** Main square ☎ 23520 21300, ⓦ gastrodromio.gr. Main courses such as rabbit or suckling pig cost €8.50–18 and there are starters like potato salad with herring and apple in a mustard yoghurt dressing. Fine wine list too. Daily 12.30–11.30pm.

**Meze Meze** Ayíou Nikoláou 40 ☎ 23520 82721. Bright

and colourfully decorated new restaurant serving a range of tasty mezédhes and some baked items like lamb with potatoes. Daily noon–1am.

**Neromylos** By the start of the path into the canyon ☎ 23520 84141. The food at this place is solid taverna fare, with salads, dips and grills, but the spectacular setting,

## CLIMBING MOUNT OLYMPUS

The main trailhead for the ascent of Mount Olympus starts from **Priónia** – just under 18km up the mountain on the sealed road from Litóhoro (€20 taxi ride). There is an information booth at km3, where (in high season, anyway) your nationality is recorded and you're given some literature advising you of the park rules, but so far there's no admission charge. At the Priónia car park there's a a spring, toilets and a primitive taverna (May–Oct).

If you're up for a real challenge and an early start, it's possible to **walk** from Litóhoro to Priónia via the monastery of **Ayíou Dhionysíou**. It's a delightful route (allow 4hrs) along the **E4 overland trail**, but you'll need basic hiking skills, as there are some scrambles over steep terrain, and a few water crossings. From Ayíou Dhionysíou it's just under an hour more upstream along the riverside E4 to **Priónia**.

### PRIÓNIA TO THE SUMMIT

From the Priónia car park the E4 trail carries on just uphill by a signpost giving the time to Refuge A (see opposite) as 2hrs 30min, though it actually takes more like three, even at a brisk pace. You cross a stream (last water before Refuge A; purification advisable) and start to climb steeply up through woods of beech and black pine. This path, the continuation of the E4, is well trodden and marked, so there is no danger of getting lost. As you gain height there are majestic views across the Enipéas (Mavrólogos) canyon to your left and to the peaks towering above you. **Refuge A** perches on the edge of an abrupt spur, surrounded by huge storm-beaten trees.

The E4 path continues behind the refuge (your last **water source** on the ascent), climbing to the left up a steep spur among the last of the trees. Having ignored an initial right fork towards the usually unstaffed *Khristos Kakalos* hut (Refuge C), within about an hour you reach a signposted **fork** above the tree line. Continuing straight on takes you across the range to Kokkinopylós village with the E4 waymarks, or with a slight deviation right to Mýtikas, via the ridge known as Kakí Skála (1hr 30min–2hr). An immediate right turn leads to the *Yiosos Apostolidhis* hut in one hour along the so-called Zonária trail, with the option after 45min of taking the very steep Loúki couloir left up to Mýtikas; if you do this, be wary of rock falls.

For the safer **Kakí Skála route**, continue up the right flank of the stony, featureless valley in front of you, with the Áyios Andónios peak up to your left. An hour's dull climb brings you to the summit ridge between the peaks of Skolió on the left and Skála on the right. You know you're there when one more step would tip you over a 500m sheer drop into the Kazánia chasm; take great care. The Kakí Skála ("Evil Stairway") begins in a narrow cleft on the right just short of the ridge; paint splashes mark the way. The route keeps just below the ridge, so you are protected from the drop into Kazánia. Even so, it's a tough scramble and not for those who don't like heights.

You start with a slightly descending rightward traverse to a narrow nick in the ridge revealing the drop to Kazánia – easily negotiated. Continue traversing right, skirting the base of the Skála peak, then climb leftwards up a steepish gully made a little awkward by loose rock on sloping footholds. Bear right at the top over steep but reassuringly solid rock, and across a narrow neck. Step left around an awkward corner and there in front of you, scarcely 100m away, is **Mýtikas summit**, an airy, boulder-strewn platform with a trigonometric point, tin Greek flag and visitors' book. In reasonable conditions it's about 40min to the summit from the start of Kakí Skála; three hours from the refuge; five and a half hours from Priónia. **Descending** from Mýtikas, most climbers go back the way they came, with the option of turning left at the signpost for the *Yiosos Apostolidhis* hut (2hr 30min from Mýtikas by this route).

4

---

with canyon views, is unsurpassed. May–Sept daily 11am–11pm; Oct–Apr Fri–Sun only.
**Pazari** Platía 3-Martíou ☎23520 82540. Extremely friendly ouzerí serving locally caught octopus and squid, as well as other fish and various mezédhes. Daily noon–midnight.

# Dion

Ancient **DION**, in the foothills of Mount Olympus outside the modern village of **Dhíon**, was the Macedonians' sacred city. At this site – a harbour before the river mouth silted up – the kingdom maintained its principal sanctuaries: to Zeus (from which the name Dion, or Dios, is derived) above all, but also to Demeter, Artemis, Asklepios and, later on, to foreign gods such as the Egyptian Isis and Serapis. Philip II and Alexander both came to sacrifice to Zeus here before their expeditions and battles. Inscriptions found at the sanctuaries referring to boundary disputes, treaties and other affairs of state suggest that the political and social importance of the city's festivals exceeded a purely Macedonian domain.

Most exciting for visitors, however, are the finds of **mosaics, temples and baths** that have been excavated since 1990 – work that remains in progress whenever funds allow. These are not quite on a par with the Vergina tombs (see p.287), but still rank among the major discoveries of ancient Macedonian culture.

### The site

June–Sept daily 8am–7pm; Oct–May Tues–Sun 8.30am–3pm • €4, €6 including the museum

The integrity of the site and its finds is due to the nature of the city's demise. At some point in the fifth century AD, a series of earthquakes prompted an evacuation of Dion, which was then swallowed up by a mudslide from the mountain. The place is still quite waterlogged, and constant pumping against the local aquifer is necessary; indeed the surrounding frog ponds and grazing geese lend it a delightfuly bucolic air. The main visible excavations are of the vast **public baths** complex and, outside the city walls, the **sanctuaries** of Demeter and Aphrodite-Isis. In the latter, a small temple has been unearthed, along with its cult statue – a copy of which remains *in situ*. Two Christian **basilicas** attest to the town's later years as a Byzantine bishopric in the fourth and fifth centuries AD. An observation platform allows you to view the layout of the site more clearly.

### The museum

Same hours as site • €3, €6 including the site

In Dhíon village the well-laid-out and refurbished **museum** houses most of the finds. In the basement there are fascinating displays on **daily life**, including many tools and household goods such as pottery. The ground floor features **sculptures**, perfectly preserved by the mud, accompanied by various tombstones and altars. Finds from the villa of Dionysos are highlighted upstairs, along with the finest **mosaics** yet discovered at the site, including one of Medusa.

### ARRIVAL AND DEPARTURE                                                      DION

**By bus** Dhíon is 7km inland from Litóhoro beach and can be reached by #14 bus from Kateríni. A direct, signposted, paved road links Dion to Litóhoro (see p.282).

### ACCOMMODATION

**Safetis Apartments** 100m from the museum ☎ 23510 46272, ⓦ safetis.gr. Smart and comfortable studios of different sizes are available in this modern place with a leafy courtyard. Breakfast included. **€60**

# Véria and Vergina

West of Thessaloníki, **VÉRIA** (ancient Berrhoea or Berea) is one of the more interesting northern Greek communities, thanks to its mixed Jewish, Muslim and Christian heritage. In the nineteenth century the town became an important industrial centre, growing prosperous from flour and sesame milling as well as hide tanning. The pleasant modern town boasts an excellent new Byzantine Museum and a smattering of appealing religious edifices. There are also enough facilities to make it a reasonable base for visits to the excavations of ancient Aegae at **Vergina**.

## The archeological museum

Leofóros Aníxeos 47; Tues–Sun 8.30am–3pm • €2 • ☎ 23310 24972

The town's modest **archeological museum** has three rooms on a single floor. Two of these display finds from the **Hellenistic** period, with funerary relics in the shape of vases, weapons and jewellery in the first, while the second concentrates on sculptures, inscriptions and figurines. The third room is devoted to sculptures and other remains from the **Roman** period, while the garden at the back has an impressive array of columns.

## Byzantine Museum

Thomaidhos 26; Tues–Sun 8.30am–3pm • €2 • ☎ 23310 25847

Véria's outstanding **Byzantine Museum** is housed in a beautifully restored nineteenth-century flour mill. It mostly comprises an exquisite display of icons – Véria was renowned for its painting workshops in the late Middle Ages – along with other treasures mostly from the Byzantine era, including coins. On the ground floor, a highly moving video, with English subtitles, records the history of the mill, its demise and its exemplary refurbishment.

## Ottoman and Jewish Véria

What remains of the old **bazaar** straddles central Kendrikís, while downhill and to the west tumbles the riverside Ottoman quarter of **Barboúta** (aka Barboúti). Largely **Jewish** before the 1944 deportations annihilated the thousand-strong community, it is today being swiftly gentrified. The disused **synagogue** can be reached via Odhós Dhekátis Merarhías, past the conspicuous officers' club near Platía Oroloyíou. Situated on a plaza with a small amphitheatre, it is a long stone building with an awning over the door, which is sometimes left ajar, allowing you to look at the rambling, arcaded interior. Of the many handsome nineteenth-century mansions hereabouts, the impeccably restored **Arhondikó Béka** currently houses the International Institute of Traditional Architecture.

Survivals of the **Muslim** presence in Véria are more numerous and conspicuous, but less well restored. It is worth hunting down the twin hammam complex, **Dhídhymi Loutrónes**, at the end of Loutroú, the small **Ortá Tzamí** mosque just off Kendrikís, and the splendid **Medresé Tzamí** mosque on Márkou Bótsari, but do not expect to enter them or be impressed by their state of conservation.

### ARRIVAL AND DEPARTURE
### VÉRIA

**By bus** The KTEL station is just off Venizélou at the northern end of central Véria.

Destinations Édhessa (Mon–Fri 3 daily; 1hr); Thessaloníki (every 15min–1hr; 1hr 15min); Vergina (8–10 daily; 20min).

### LITTLE JERUSALEM

**Christianity** has a venerable and long history in Véria: St Paul preached here (Acts 17:10–14) on two occasions, between 50 and 60 AD, and a gaudy alcove shrine or "altar" of modern mosaics at the base of Mavromiháli marks the supposed spot of his sermons. Four dozen or so small **churches**, some medieval but mostly dating from the sixteenth to eighteenth centuries, are scattered around the town, earning it the moniker of **Little Jerusalem**. Under Ottoman rule, many were disguised as barns or warehouses, with little dormer windows rather than domes to admit light; but today, often surrounded by cleared spaces and well labelled, they're not hard to find. The only church regularly open, however, is the well-signposted **Resurrection of Christ**, or **Anastásseos Christoú** (Tues–Sun 8.30am–3pm; free), with cleaned fourteenth-century frescoes, near the fork end of Mitropóleos. The most striking images here are a *Dormition/Assumption* over the west door and a rare image of Christ mounting the Cross on a ladder on the north wall.

## ACCOMMODATION

**Aiges Melathron** ☎ 23310 77777, ⓦ www.aigesmelathron.gr. On the Véria–Náoussa ring road, 3km east of the centre, this sizeable 4-star is really aimed at business travellers; bright rooms, a good restaurant and a swimming pool. Breakfast included. **€80**

**Makedonia** Kondoyeorgáki 50 ☎ 23310 66902, ⓦ www.makedoniahotel.gr. Modern four-storey hotel with smart, functional rooms and a pleasant roof garden affording admirable views. Substantial breakfast included. **€60**

**Veroi** Platía Oroloyíou 1 ☎ 23310 22866. Spruced up but still with an old-fashioned feel, this is the best budget option in town. The compact but comfortable rooms are all en suite. **€45**

## EATING AND DRINKING

Véria has a respectable if not stellar smattering of decent **tavernas**. The trendy **bars** along Eliás and around the Belvedere heave with locals sporting tight shirts, bare midriffs and the very latest in mobile phones. If you crave more action after dark, the pedestrianized area around Patriárhou Ioakeím is crammed full of noisy bars and comes into its own.

**Elia** Belvedere park ☎ 23310 24676. Pleasant café with a shady terrace overlooking the plain. A good place to sample the local speciality sweet, *revaní*, a syrup-soaked sponge cake. 8am–midnight.

★ **Kostalar** Afrodhítis 2/D, Papákia district ☎ 23310 61801. Set in a lovely location by a plane-tree-shaded square with rivulets, this place specializes in tasty grills and fine mezédhes for €5–10. Tues–Sun noon–2am.

**Veryiotiko** Thomaïdhos 2 ☎ 23310 74139. Mostly predictable taverna menu, though in winter it occasionally comes up with the likes of wild boar with quinces; the summer terrace suffers from road noise. Daily noon–late.

# Vergina: ancient Aegae

June–Sept Mon noon–7.30pm, Tues–Sun 8am–7.30pm; Oct–May daily 8.30am–3pm • €8 • no photography • ☎ 23310 92347 • There are buses from Véria every hour or two, taking 20min. Parking around the site costs €1.50

The site of **VERGINA**, 16km southeast of Véria, undoubtedly qualifies as one of Greece's most memorable attractions. This was the site of **Aegae**, the original **Macedonian royal capital** before the shift to Pella, and later the sanctuary and royal burial place of the Macedonian kings. It was here that **Philip II**, father of Alexander the Great, was assassinated, cremated and buried; tradition maintained that the dynasty would be destroyed if any king were buried elsewhere, as indeed happened after the death of Alexander in Asia. Until the site was unearthed in 1977 after decades of work by **Professor Manolis Andronikos**, Aegae had long been assumed to be lost beneath modern Édhessa. The ruins of the **Palace of Palatítsia** are currently closed for renovations until at least 2017.

## The Royal Tombs

Under a tumulus, then just outside modern Veryína, Andronikos discovered several large Macedonian chamber tombs, known simply as the **Royal Tombs**. From outside, all that's visible is a low hillock with skylights and long ramps leading inside, but once underground in the climate-controlled bunker you can admire the facades and doorways of the tombs *in situ*, well illuminated behind glass. Finds from the site and tombs, the richest Greek trove since the discovery of Mycenae, are exhibited in the complex along with erudite texts in Greek and English. It's best to try and get here very early or visit at siesta time in order to avoid the crowds.

A clockwise tour takes you round the tombs in the order IV-I-II-III. Tomb IV, the so-called Doric, was looted in antiquity; so too was **Tomb I**, or the **Persephone tomb**, but it retained a delicate and exquisitely crafted **mural** of the rape of Persephone by Hades, the only complete example of an ancient Greek painting that has yet been found. **Tomb II**, that of **Philip II**, is a much grander vaulted affair with a Doric facade adorned by a sumptuous painted **frieze** of Philip, Alexander and their retinue on a lion hunt. Incredibly, the tomb was discovered intact. Among its treasures on display are a marble sarcophagus containing a **gold ossuary** (*larnax*), its cover embossed with the sixteen-pointed star symbol of the royal line, and, more significantly, five small **ivory heads**, among them representations of both Philip II and Alexander. It was this clue, as well as the fact that the skull bore marks of a facial wound Philip was known to have sustained, that led to the identification of the tomb as his. Also on view are a fabulous **gold oak-leaf wreath** – so delicate it quivers – and a modest *larnax* (small coffin) found in the antechamber, presumed to contain the carefully wrapped bones and ashes of a Thracian queen or concubine.

**Tomb III** is thought to be that of Alexander IV, "the Great's" son, murdered in adolescence – thus the moniker **Prince's Tomb**. His bones were discovered in a silver vase. From the tomb frieze, a superb **miniature of Dionysos and his consort** is highlighted. You should also spare a moment or two to view the excellent **video**, subtitled in English, which brings the archeological finds to life.

### The Macedonian Tomb

The so-called **Macedonian Tomb**, actually five adjacent tombs, can also be visited after a fashion. They are about 500m uphill, above the large parking lot, left of the main road. Like the Royal Tombs, they lie well below ground level, protected by a vast tin roof. Excavated by the French in 1861, the most prominent one, thought to be that of Philip's mother Eurydike, is in the form of a temple, with an Ionic facade of half-columns breached by two successive marble portals opening onto ante- and main chambers. Inside you can just make out an imposing marble throne with sphinxes carved on the sides, armrests and footstool. The neighbouring two pairs of tombs, still undergoing snail-paced excavation, are said to be similar in design.

**ACCOMMODATION AND EATING**                                                                 **VERGINA**

**Hotel Aigon** 250m from the Royal Tombs, on parallel road ☎23310 92524, ⊕hotel-aigon.gr. Pleasantly designed hotel with comfortable rooms and a quiet courtyard. Breakfast included. **€50**

**Xenonas Evridiki** Just below the Macedonian Tomb ☎23310 92502, ⊕www.evridiki.com.gr. The splendid location adds immmeasurably to the attraction of these simple rooms above a fine taverna that is much more authentic than those on the main drag. **€40**

# Northwest Macedonia

This intriguing corner of the province includes the handsome towns of **Édhessa** and **Kozáni**. West of Édhessa is the handsome mountain village of **Nymféo**, where some of the attractive stone houses have been converted into classy accommodation, and the bird-rich **Préspa lakes**, both of which nestle in a strategic spot where Greece, Albania and the Republic of Macedonia meet. **Flórina**, the area's main urban centre, is of limited appeal but does have two notable museums. Seeing the area properly is really only viable if you have your own transport.

## Édhessa

The main gateway to northwest Macedonia, **ÉDHESSA** is a delightful place atop an escarpment. Its modest fame is attributed to the waters that flow through the town; descending from the mountains to the north, which eventually cascade down a dramatic ravine, luxuriant with vegetation, to the plain below. Most of the town's architecture is humdrum, but the various stream-side parks and wide pedestrian pavements are a rare pleasure in Greece (Édhessa was a pioneer in pedestrianization) and it's an increasingly important centre for regional tourism.

### Édhessa aquarium

Mon & Wed–Sun 10am–6pm • €2

This unusual freshwater **aquarium** is the centrepiece of a so-called open-air water museum, built from converted watermills in the **Varósi** district just west of the waterfalls.

The surrounding mills and Balkan-style houses, some decorously decaying, others tastefully renovated, reward aimless wanderings – though everything is well signposted.

## The folklore museum

Megálou Alexándhrou • Tues–Sun 10am–6pm • €1.50

The only real sight as such is a delightful little **folklore museum** near Ayía Paraskeví church; it displays various household objects and other traditional items of the kind that would once have graced every home in the district.

### ARRIVAL AND INFORMATION                                    ÉDHESSA

**By train** The train station is in the north of town and has 8 daily services to Thessaloníki.

**By bus** The main KTEL station is on the corner of Filíppou and Pávlou Melá and serves Thessaloníki (hourly; 1hr 30min); Véria (Mon–Fri 3 daily; 1hr), as well as local destinations.

**Tourist office** This excellent new visitor centre in the

park at Garéfi and Pérdhika (daily 10am–6pm; ☎ 23810 20300, ⓦ edessacity.gr) is far and away the best in the region. English-speaking staff can provide useful bilingual leaflets and all manner of information about activities, such as trekking, rafting, kayaking and skiing in the surrounding region.

### ACCOMMODATION

**Olympia** 18-Oktovríou 51 ☎ 23810 23544. Typical 1960s-era hotel with simply furnished and quiet rooms; very convenient for the train station. Scantily manned so you may have to wait a while for service. **€40**

★ **Varosi** Arhieréos Meletíou 45–47, Varósi ☎ 23810 21865, ⓦ varosi.gr. For some real old-fashioned hospitality, this beautifully converted stone mansion boasts

open fires, cosy en-suite rooms decorated in a vernacular style and delicious complimentary breakfasts. The even plusher *Varosi Four Seasons* is just up the road. **€60**

**Xenia** Párko Merarhías Filíppou 35 ☎ 23810 21898, ⓦ xeniaedessa.gr. The town's most expensive hotel, yet its deluxe facilities, such as the only swimming pool, and great views make it reasonable value. **€80**

### EATING AND DRINKING

There are few standout restaurants but a surplus of excellent *souvláki* joints all over town. Café and bar life is concentrated in the pedestrian zones flanking the rivulets, especially on Angelí Gátsou.

**Fysiolatrikos Omilos Edhessas** No phone. Superbly sited among the woods, 2km out of town on the road to Aridhéa, this local nature club puts more effort into its decor than its food, but the latter is appetizingly presented and has some adventurous Gallic touches. Daily 10am–midnight.

**Ladhokolla** Thessaloníkis 3 ☎ 23810 6946 690 360. Beside the first stream going north from the centre, this cosy joint specializes in tastily seasoned meat dishes such as chops, sausage and *seftaliá*, served on greaseproof paper for €7–9. Mon–Sat 11am–1am.

**Psilos Vrahos** Megaálou Aléxandhrou 2 ☎ 23810 26793. Perched atop its namesake vantage point, this municipal café is worth a visit for a beer, coffee or fruit juice and the superb view. Daily 8am–midnight.

★ **Stathmos** At the train station ☎ 23810 21110. The name means "Station" but this is no railway canteen. Rather it is a superb taverna serving meaty delights like tender *gourounopoulo* for only €7, plus the full gamut of tasty *mezédhes*. Highly entertaining proprietor too. Daily noon–2am.

## Nymféo

Perched at 1300m on the eastern flank of Mount Vítsi, some 85km southwest of Édhessa and 60km northeast of Kastoriá, lies the well-groomed mountain village of **NYMFÉO**, popular of late with prosperous young Greek professionals looking for alternative recreational activities in retreats far from the city.

### ACCOMMODATION AND EATING                                    NYMFÉO

As a trendy getaway, Nymféo accommodation tends to be on the pricey side, especially at weekends, so try to visit during the week. The hotel restaurants also tend to be pricey but there are cheaper tavernas in the village centre.

**Ederne** On road into village ☎ 23860 31230, ⓦ enterne .gr. This professionally run inn offers simple, traditionally

decorated rustic rooms, a welcoming lounge and self-catering facilities. Breakfast included. **€60**

4

★ **La Moara** Uphill at the back of the village ☎ 2310 287 626, ⓦ lamoara.gr. A luxurious mansion with tastefully appointed rooms and state-of-the-art bathrooms. Run by nationally renowned wine-makers, the Boutari family, its refined cuisine matches the cellar.

Breakfast included. **€110**

**Xenonas Neveska** Village centre ☎ 23860 31442, ⓦ neveska.gr. This attractive ochre-coloured guesthouse provides some of the best-value rooms in Nymféo. There is also a reasonably priced restaurant. **€40**

# Flórina

Surrounded by steep hills carpeted with beech woods, **FLÓRINA** lies only 13km from the border with the Macedonian Republic and is the nearest town with any transport connections to the Préspa lakes (see below). Although the only attractive part of town is the immediate environs of the Sakouléva River, two museums warrant a visit.

## Museum of Modern Art
Leofóros Eleftherías 103 • Daily May–Sept 6–9pm; Oct–April 5–8pm • Free • ☎ 23850 29444

Flórina's impressive **Museum of Modern Art** is housed in a refurbished Neoclassical building beside the river. With nearly five hundred works by over two hundred and fifty Greek painters, sculptors and engravers of the twentieth century, it boasts the best collection of contemporary art outside of Athens.

## Archeological museum
Tues–Sun 8.30am–3pm • €2 • ☎ 23850 28206

Just opposite the defunct railway station, the **Archeological museum** has a modest collection of scuplture, votive reliefs and some artefacts from the Préspa lakeshores.

### ARRIVAL AND DEPARTURE     FLÓRINA

**By bus** The KTEL bus station is at Makedhonomákou 10 (☎ 23850 22430), just north of the centre. There are two buses on Mon, Wed & Fri to Áyios Yermanós in Préspes and connections to Thessaloníki (6 daily; 2hr 30min).

### ACCOMMODATION AND EATING

**Hotel Hellinis** Pávlou Melá 31 ☎ 23850 22671, ⓦ hotel-hellinis.gr. Classic sixties-style town hotel but upgraded to make the rooms more comfortable and contemporary. Very central and good value. **€35**

**To Petrino** Pávlou Melá 2 ☎ 23850 22560. Very popular *estiatório* by day and night, serving healthy heapings of mostly oven-baked goodies such as *pastiísio* or beef *stifádho* for around €7–8. Some grills too. Daily till late.

# The Préspa lakes

A shimmering expanse of water riven by islets and ridges, the **PRÉSPA LAKES** are one of the Balkans' most important wildlife sanctuaries. Though not postcard-pretty, the basin, in the far northwest of Macedonia, has an eerie beauty that grows on you with further acquaintance. It also has a surprisingly turbulent history as a place of exile for troublesome noblemen during the Byzantine era and the scene of vicious local battles during the 1947–49 Greek civil war.

**Mikrí Préspa**, the southerly lake, is mostly shallow (9m maximum depth) and reedy, with a narrow fjord curling west and just penetrating Albanian territory. The borders of Greece, Albania and the Republic of Macedonia meet in the middle of deeper **Megáli Préspa** and, especially during the early 1990s, it became a major exit corridor into Greece for Albanian refugees, who found work as illegal agricultural workers in the local bean and hay industry.

The core of the **national park**, established in 1971, barely encompasses Mikrí Préspa and its shores, but the peripheral zone extends well into the surrounding mountains, affording protection of sorts to foxes, wolves and even bears, which inhabit the area. The lakes have a dozen resident fish species, including *tsiróni*, a sort of freshwater sardine, and *grivádhi*, a kind of carp, but it's **birdlife** for which the Préspa basin is most famous.

## THE BIRDS OF PRÉSPA

The lakes are home to relatively few birds of prey but you should see a fair number of egrets, cormorants, crested grebes and pelicans. This is one of the few breeding sites of both the white and Dalmatian pelican, which nest in the spring, with the chicks out and about by summer. They feed partly on the large numbers of snakes, which include vipers, whip snakes and harmless water snakes which you may encounter while swimming. Observation towers are available at Vromolímni and near Áyios Ahíllios, but dawn spent anywhere at the edge of the reedbeds with a pair of binoculars will be immensely rewarding, though bear in mind that you are not allowed to boat or wade into the reeds.

## Mikrolímni

**MIKROLÍMNI**, 5km up a side road off the main route into the valley, is an extremely sleepy hamlet that might be your first conceivable stop. In the evening, you can look towards sunsets over reedbeds and the snake-infested Vidhronísi (or Vitrinítsi) islet, though swimming isn't good here, or anywhere else on Mikrí Préspa for that matter.

Return to the main road, which reaches a T-junction 16km from the main Flórina–Kastoriá highway, on the spit which separates the larger and smaller lakes. It's probable that at one time there was just one lake here, but now there's a 4m elevation difference. Bearing right at the junction leads within 4km to Áyios Yermanós; the left option splits again at the west end of the spit, bearing south towards the islet of Áyios Ahíllios or northwest towards the hamlet of Psarádhes.

## Áyios Yermanós

**ÁYIOS YERMANÓS**, 4km to the right at the T-junction when the main road reaches Megáli Préspa, is a large village of tile-roofed houses, overlooking a patch of the lake in the distance and adjoining the hamlet of **Lemós**. It's worth making the trip up just to see two tiny late Byzantine churches, whose frescoes, dating from the time when the place belonged to the bishopric of Ohrid, display a marked Macedonian influence. Inside the lower church, **Áyios Athanásios**, seldom open, you can glimpse a dog-faced *St Christopher* among a line of saints opposite the door. Far more impressive, however, is the tiny, eleventh-century parish church of **Áyios Yermanós** up on the square, hidden behind a new monster awkwardly tacked onto it in 1882. The Byzantine structure has its own entrance, and the frescoes, skilfully retouched in 1743, can be lit; the switch is hidden in the narthex.

## Koúla beach

At the far end of the wide causeway dividing the two lakes, 4km to the left from the T-junction, is **Koúla beach**, a motley cluster of what passes for tourist development hereabouts: a patch of reed-free sand from where you can swim in Megáli Préspa; a free but basic camping area, now bereft of its water tap; plus an army post.

## Psarádhes

Reached by 6km of panoramic corniche road from a signposted turning near Koúla beach, the rickety village of **PSARÁDHES** makes for a pleasant stroll. Unfortunately, the wonderful old houses lining the lanes are increasingly derelict. It is sometimes possible to take a short **boat excursion** out onto the lake to see some of the lakeside monuments and churches, but this is not the best way to spot birdlife; there is no fixed schedule, so ask around.

## Áyios Ahíllios

Two kilometres directly south of Koúla beach, the road soon brings you to a floating footbridge, 1500m in length, which leads across to the islet of **Áyios Ahíllios** and its impoverished, almost deserted hamlet. A five-minute walk from the footbridge is the ruined Byzantine basilica of **Áyios Ahíllios,** while another ruin, a sixteenth-century monastery, Panayía Porfaras, lies at the southern end of the islet. For unrivalled views of Mikrí Préspa climb up to the summit of the islet's hill.

## ARRIVAL AND INFORMATION

PRÉSPA LAKES

**By bus** Although there are two buses on Mon, Wed and Fri from Flórina (1hr), in order to explore the region, you really need a vehicle.
**Tourist office** Áyios Yermanós has the helpful Préspa information centre (daily 9.30am–7.30pm, staff permitting; ☎23850 51211, ⓦwww.spp.gr), focusing on the wildlife of the national park; given sufficient warning, the centre can arrange guides for birdwatching trips into the park. The area's only post office is here too.

## ACCOMMODATION

Although facilities are basic, Préspa is becoming increasingly popular, so you'd be wise to reserve a room in advance during midsummer, especially at weekends. Free camping is available near the *Plaz Prespon* taverna (see below).

**Mimallones** Lemós ☎23850 51422, ⓦmimallones.gr. Undoubtedly Préspa's smartest accommodation, this spacious modern hotel has large, comfortably furnished rooms, a massive bar-cum-lounge and firendly management. Breakfast included. **€60**
**O Yiorgos** Mikrolímni ☎23850 23622. Very basic en-suite rooms in an unattractive concrete block, but it's all about the location, as the lake lies mere metres away. **€30**

**To Arhontiko** Psarádhes ☎23850 46260. An effectively converted old stone house, this place offers decent en-suite rooms, the upper ones with lake views, and a warm welcome. **€40**
**Xenonas ly Paradosi** Opposite the church, Áyios Yermanós ☎23850 51266. Plain yet cosy guesthouse with friendly owners and simple but clean rooms. The best base for a variety of food and other facilities. Breakfast included. **€40**

## EATING

**Plaz Prespon** Koúla beach ☎23850 46220. A fairly run-of-the-mill taverna which is nonetheless the best option in the immediate area and can rustle up simple grills for around €7, the odd fish and basic salads. Daily 11am–10pm.
**Taverna Syndrofia** Psarádhes ☎23850 46107, ⓔtinaxr10@gmail.com. A good spot to sample *fassoládha* (bean soup), lake fish, unavailable elsewhere in Greece, and the proprietor's wine. There are also a few rooms. **€40**
**To Tzaki** Near the church, Áyios Yermanós ☎23850 51470. The best taverna in the whole region offers a good range of tasty *mayireftá* such as pork in wine sauce and baked aubergines, as well as succulent meat cooked in the *gástra* (clay oven). Daily noon–11pm.

# Kastoriá

Set on a hilly, wooded peninsula extending deep into slate-coloured Lake Orestiádha, **KASTORIÁ** is one of the most interesting and attractive towns of mainland Greece. For centuries it grew rich on the **fur trade**, using the pelts of local wild beavers (*kastóri* in Greek). Though these animals were trapped to extinction by the nineteenth century, Kastoriá still supports a considerable industry of furriers using a mixture of imported pelts and locally farmed beavers. You'll see pelts drying on racks, and fur megastores with profuse Russian signposting hinting at the target market. The town also has a strong tradition of **rowing**, and rowers can be seen out on the lake most days. Even the Oxford and Cambridge Blues have been known to practise their strokes here.

For most visitors, however, Kastoriá's main appeal lies in traces of its former prosperity: dozens of splendid *arhondiká* – **mansions** of the old fur families – dating from the seventeenth to nineteenth centuries, plus some fifty Byzantine and medieval **churches**. About the only reminder of Muslim settlement is the minaret-less Koursoún Tzamí, marooned in a ridgetop car park; there's also a patch of an originally Byzantine fortification wall down on the neck of the peninsula.

## Karýdhis

For a sense of what Kastoriá must once have been during its heyday, head for the former lakeside quarter officially called **Karýdhis** but better known as Dóltso. Among

Flórina (70km)

Fish Market

**KASTORIÁ**

Bus Station

Byzantine Wall

PLATIA VAN FLEET

PLATIA DHAVAKI

Olympic Airways

Lake Orestiádha

Lake Orestiádha

LEOFOROS NIKIS

**ACCOMMODATION**

| | |
|---|---|
| Allahou Guesthouse | 2 |
| Arhondiko tou Vergoula | 6 |
| Idiston | 4 |
| Kastoria | 3 |
| Keletron | 1 |
| Pension Filoxenia | 5 |

Koursoún Tzamí

PLATIA DHEXAMENIS

**Byzantine Museum**

Panayía Koumbelidhikí

PLATIA OMONIAS

**EATING**

| | |
|---|---|
| Faros | 1 |
| Krondiri | 4 |
| Leskhi Filon Perivalondos | 3 |
| Sanies | 5 |
| Ta Ladhokolla | 2 |

**Áyii Anáryiri**

**Áyios Stéfanos**

**Áyios Nikólaos Kasnítzi**

**Taxiárhes tis Mitropóleos**

PLATIA PAVLOU MELA

**Áyios Athanássios**

**Cathedral**

**KARYDHIS (DÓLTSO)**

**Traditional Costume Museum**

**Arhondikó Bassáras**

**Arhondikó Natzís**

**Folklore Museum**

Lake Orestiádha

0    200
metres

The Dragon's Cave (1km) & Mavriótissa monastery (1.3km)

4

the notable mansions in the area are **Bassáras** and **Natzís**, close together on Vyzandíon; the latter was admirably restored in the 1990s. A third, also close by, on Platía Dóltso, now houses the **Traditional Costume Museum** (open by appointment; free; ☎24670 22697), a magical display of traditional clothing from western Macedonia and a chance to see another magnificent interior.

## KASTORIÁ'S CHURCHES

Of the town's many Byzantine churches, a handful are well worth seeking out. The excellent frescoes of the twelfth-century church of **Áyios Nikólaos Kasnítzi** were returned to their former glory during the late 1980s. The unusual epithet stems from the donor, who is shown with his wife on the narthex wall presenting a model of the church to Christ. Lower down are ranks of exclusively female saints, to console the women congregated in the narthex which long served as a women's gallery. High up on the west wall of the nave, the *Dormition* and the *Transfiguration* are in good condition, the former inexplicably backwards (the Virgin's head is usually to the left). **Taxiárhes tís Mitropóleos**, the oldest (ninth-century) church, was built on the foundations of an earlier pagan temple, of which recycled columns and capitals are visible. Its more prominent frescoes, such as that of the *Virgin Platytera and Adoring Archangels* in the conch of the apse, and a conventional *Dormition* on the west wall, are fourteenth century. In the north aisle is the tomb of Greek nationalist Pavlos Melas, assassinated by Bulgarians at a nearby village in 1906, and commemorated by street names across northern Greece. Lastly, the **Panayía Koumbelidhikí**, so named because of its unusual dome (*kübe* in Turkish), retains one startling and well-illuminated fresco: a portrayal – almost unique in Greece – of God the Father in a ceiling mural of the *Holy Trinity*. The building was constructed in stages, with the apse completed in the tenth century and the narthex in the fifteenth. The cylindrical dome was meticulously restored after being destroyed by Italian bombing in 1940.

## Folklore Museum

Kapetán Lázou 10 • Mon–Sat 9.30am–1pm & 4–7pm, Sun 11am–1pm & 4–7pm • €2

The splendidly opulent seventeenth-century Aïvazís family mansion has been turned into a **Folklore Museum**. The house was inhabited until 1972 and its furnishings and most of its ceilings are in excellent repair, having miraculously survived German shelling; the Ottoman-style kiosk sports a set of stained-glass windows, three of them original, the others replaced by a local craftsman. Other features are an oriental fireplace in the master bedroom and the kitchen with all the original pots and pans.

## Byzantine Museum

Platía Dhexamenís • Tues–Sun 8.30am–3pm • Free

The **Byzantine Museum**, up on Platía Dhexamenís, wisely goes for quality over quantity in this well-lit if unimaginatively displayed collection spanning the twelfth to the sixteenth centuries. Highlights include an unusually expressive thirteenth-century icon of Áyios Nikólaos and a fourteenth-century Ayii Anaryiri, plus a later one depicting the life of St George. There are also a few double-sided icons, including a rare *Deposition*, intended for use in religious processions. Captions are in Greek only.

## Lake Orestiádha

One of the most pleasant things to do in Kastoriá is to follow the narrow road along **Lake Orestiádha** to the **peninsula** to the east of town; at the tip vehicles must circulate anticlockwise, but the route is mainly used by joggers and the odd walker. Although the lake itself is visibly polluted, wildlife still abounds – pelicans, swans, frogs, tortoises and water snakes especially, and on a spring day numerous fish break water.

### Mavriótissa monastery

Near the southeastern tip of the peninsula, some 3km along from the *Hotel Kastoria*, stands the **Mavriótissa monastery**, flanked by peacocks and a fair-value restaurant. Two churches are all that remains of the monastery: a smaller fourteenth-century chapel, with fine frescoes of scenes from Christ's life, abutting the larger, wood-roofed eleventh-century *katholikón* on whose outer wall looms a well-preserved *Tree of Jesse*, showing the genealogy of the Saviour.

## The Dragon's Cave (Spiliá tou Dhrákou)

1km along the anticlockwise lakeshore route • Tues–Sun 10am–5pm • €5

Given its name because the entrance resembles the mouth of a dragon and an old legend claimed there was a resident one that spouted fire if anyone approached, the **Dragon's Cave** was discovered in 1940 but only opened to the public in 2010. The interior is festooned with an impressive array of stalgmites and stalactites and there are some patches of lake within, around which walkways have been carefully constructed.

## Dhispílio prehistoric lake settlement

5km from Kastoriá in the village of Dhispílio • Museum daily 9am–2pm & 5–8pm • €3

On the southern shore of the lake lie the remains of a fascinating **prehistoric lake settlement**, which is thought to date from around 5500–5000 BC during the Neolithic Period. First excavated in 1992, finds include a range of household goods and a wooden tablet, inscribed with an early linear script. A modern re-creation of the original huts and an eco-museum help bring to life what the area must have looked like in these distant times.

## ARRIVAL AND INFORMATION                                          KASTORIÁ

**By plane** The airport is 10km south of town, while the Olympic Airways office, connected by an airport bus, is at Megálou Alexándhrou 15. The only destination served is Athens (2 weekly; 1hr 15min).

**By bus** The KTEL bus station is at A Dhiákou 14 (☎ 24670 83633, ⍰ ktel-kastorias.gr), near the western edge of the peninsula. There are services to: Ioánnina (6 weekly; 2hr) and Thessaloníki (6 daily; 2hr 30min).

**By car** Coming by car, beware of the fee-parking scheme in effect across much of the city centre, operated by ticket machines; only a couple of the more expensive hotels have free or off-street parking.

**Tourist office** There is a municipal tourist kiosk (May–Sept 9am–9pm; ☎ 24670 26777, ⍰ kastoriacity.gr) in the lakeside park, 150m from KTEL, but staffing problems mean it is often shut.

## ACCOMMODATION

Many of Kastoriá's hotels, especially those within easy walking distance of the bus station, are rather noisy with prices above average. Advance booking is a good idea for weekends, although a string of identikit modern business hotels along the airport road takes care of the overspill.

**Allahou Guesthouse** Panayiás Faneroménis 18 ☎ 24670 27058, ⍰ kastoria.allahou.gr. Beautifully converted mansion with five comfortable, brightly decorated rooms and an airy conservatory for breakfast, which is included. **€55**

★ **Arhondiko tou Vergoula** Aïdhítras 14, Dóltso ☎ 24670 23416, ⍰ vergoulas.gr. Delightful boutique hotel, housed in a handsome mid-nineteenth-century mansion. Rooms with a view are pricier but all are faultlessly done out in traditional yet comfortable style, albeit with midget bathrooms. Breakfast included. **€55**

**Idiston** Megálou Alexándhrou 91 ☎ 24670 22250, ⍰ idiston.gr. Self-catering apartments in a prime location over one of the town's trendy bars, with lake views. Run by a returnee from Canada whose passion for his native town is contagious. Book well ahead. **€50**

**Kastoria** Leofóros Níkis 122 ☎ 24670 29453, ⍰ hotel-kastoria.gr. At the far end of the northern waterfront, the town's smartest hotel offers lake views from its balconied, air-conditioned front rooms, plus free parking. Breakfast included. **€60**

**Keletron** 11-Noemvríou 52 ☎ 24670 22676, ⍰ www .anastassiou-hotels.gr. Simple but perfectly adequate hotel with its entrance on a side street and some rooms overlooking leafy Platía Van Fleet. Breakfast included. **€35**

**Pension Filoxenia** Y Paleológou 23 ☎ 24670 22162, ⍰ filoxeniakastoria.gr. Well located and thoughtfully decorated, this welcoming place has rooms of varying sizes, the pricier ones with lake views. Breakfast included. **€50**

## EATING AND DRINKING

★ **Faros** Leofóros Níkis 6 ☎ 24670 23501. Seafood taverna with very cheap *gávros*, sardines and mussels, as well as lots of grilled meat and a fine pork *tianiá*. Nice harbour view from the long covered courtyard. Daily noon–2am.

**Krondiri** Orestiádhos 13 ☎ 24670 28258. This slightly upmarket taverna dishes up some of the town's best food, especially fancy mezédhes, gratins and "soufflés" in attractive clay pots for €5–12, and has tables on the lake shore. Daily 11am–1am.

4

**Leskhi Filon Perivalondos** Tsardháki ☎ 24670 26300. The café of the Friends of the Environment is a great spot for a drink, as it affords fine views of the northeastern lakeshore from its vantage point up near Profítis Ilías. Daily noon–midnight.

**Sanies** Orestiádhos 79 ☎ 693 65 68. Pleasant, unpretentious taverna that offers tasty fish, such as trout

for €10, as well as a range of meat, salads and vegetable dishes. Daily noon–1am.

**Ta Ladhokolla** Megálou Aléxandrou 125 ☎ 24670 29659. As the name suggests, this restaurant follows the recent trend of serving meat and fish dishes on greaseproof paper for under €10. Best of the southern lakefront establishments. Daily 11am–midnight.

# Halkidhikí

HALKIDHIKÍ begins at a perforated edge of shallow lakes east of Thessaloníki, then extends into three prongs of land – Kassándhra, Sithonía and Athos – trailing like tentacles into the northern Aegean Sea. **Kassándhra** and **Sithonía** host some of the busiest holiday resorts in Greece, drawing hordes from Thessaloníki and other parts of the north, as well as increasing numbers from eastern Europe. The beaches themselves consist of white sand, ranging in consistency from powder to coarse-grained.

**Mount Athos**, the easternmost peninsula, is in all ways separate, a "Holy Mountain" whose monastic population, semi-autonomous within the Greek state, **excludes all females** – even as visitors. The most that women can do is to glimpse the buildings from offshore cruise *kaïkia* sailing from the two small resorts on the periphery of the peninsula – Ierissós and Ouranoúpoli – on the "secular" part of the Athos peninsula.

## ARRIVAL AND INFORMATION

**By car** Both Kassándhra and Sithonía are connected to Thessaloníki by a four-lane expressway which ends at Néa Moudhaniá, a dull town and minor passenger port, from where a network of fast two-lane roads extends around their coastlines.

**By bus** Buses run frequently to all the larger resorts. In spite of this, neither peninsula is that easy to travel around if you are dependent on public transport. You really have to pick a place and stay there, perhaps renting a motorbike or car for excursions.

**Useful website** ⓦ halkidiki.com

## Kassándhra

Vaguely boot-shaped **KASSÁNDHRA**, the nearest of Halkidhikí's three peninsulas to Thessaloníki, is also by far the most developed and its appearance has been done no favours by the extensive 2006 fires that decimated almost the entire forest once covering the central section of its spine. Most of the attractive inland villages date from the mid-nineteenth century, as the earlier ones were left deserted after their inhabitants were massacred during the 1821 War of Independence. On the coast, there were only a few small fishing hamlets here until after 1923, when the peninsula was resettled by refugees from around the Sea of Marmara – these have since burgeoned into holiday venues. Many travellers choose to bypass Kassándhra and keep going to Sithonía or the top end of Athos.

### MACEDONIAN CAVEMEN

Fifty kilometres southeast of Thessaloníki, en route to the Kassándhra peninsula, and set among handsome mountain scenery, is the cave of **Kókkines Pétres** (daily 9am–5pm; guided tours only €7; ☎ 23730 71671). The name means "Red Stones", and they were discovered in 1959 by villagers from nearby Petrálona looking for water. Besides an impressive display of stalagmites and stalactites, the villagers – and, later, academics – found the fossilized remains of prehistoric animals and, most dramatic of all, a **Neanderthal skull**, all of which are displayed in a decent museum near the cave entrance. No photography is allowed, but there is a small museum and onsite café.

# HALKIDHIKÍ: KASSÁNDHRA, SITHONÍA & SECULAR ATHOS

## Néa Fókea

Bypassing the eyesore of Néa Potídhea, some 6km beyond Néa Moudhaniá and across the ancient canal, the first place you might consider stopping at is **NÉA FÓKEA**, a modest place consisting mostly of holiday apartments for Greeks, rendered picturesque by a Byzantine watchtower on a grassy headland. From the harbour a long beach heads north under cliffs, improving as you distance yourself from the tower.

## Sáni

Just north of Néa Fókea, an 8km paved side road takes you westwards through bucolic countryside to **SÁNI** on the west coast, with a British-operated manicured marina full of boutiques and chic restaurants. Sáni is also noted for its summer **festival**, which boasts a cosmopolitan billing of world music, salsa, jazz and cutting-edge Greek stars. This takes place up by another quaint Byzantine watchtower on the headland.

## Áfytos

Some 5km south of Néa Fókea, you reach the turning east for **ÁFYTOS** (or Áthytos), by far the most attractive spot on Kassándhra. This large village of tile-roofed traditional houses spreads over a series of ravines that punctuate the bluff here, which ends in a sharp drop to the sea. Near the cliff bottom, a series of springs bubbles from a rock overhang, nurturing a little oasis – doubtless a spur in the founding of Aphytis, the village's ancient predecessor. Both beaches (turn left for Paralía Várkes, right for Paralía Moudhoúnou) are marred by rock sills with lots of sea urchins. On the square, the focus of a mesh of slightly twee cobbled lanes closed to traffic for the nightly promenade, stands a handsome church in post-Byzantine style, dating only from 1850 but seeming much older.

## Kallithéa and around

The modern and rather ugly resort of **KALLITHÉA** is useful only for its **ATMs** and **car, motorbike and windsurfer rental**. At **KRYOPIYÍ**, just under 6km further, most of the development is concentrated along the steep roads that cascade down to the water, where there's a beach, but Kryopiyí has managed to preserve its old village core up the hill, on the land side of the main road.

Beyond Kryopiyí, you head towards the "toe" of the Kassandhrian boot via a trio of tacky and missable coastal resorts – Polýkhrono, Haniótis and Pefkohóri – and the far more scenic and deserted bay of **Khroussoú**. From here, rather than continuing to the disappointing "toe"-cape at Kánistro, you're better off heading west and inland along the main road to the rambling ridge-top village of **PALIOÚRI**.

## The southwestern shore

The southwestern shore of Kassándhra is, in general, developed more for Greek weekenders. Some 6km beyond hilltop Palioúri lies **Ayía Paraskeví**, a delightful village with sea views, a little way beyond which you emerge on the coast at the **Loutrá Ayías Paraskevís**, where a popular **spa** complex (☏23740 71810) contains a hot sulphurous pool and offers various treatments from €6. **NÉA SKIÓNI**, 4km northwest, can be a decent base, with its good clean beach and appealing seafront.

Tucked on the cape beyond droll Mála Kalýva is **POSÍDHI**, which covers a hill and spills down onto a harbour and fine stretch of beach. At the far end of the **beach**, beyond the lively *Bouda* beach bar, the rock reef abates and you can skinny-dip from the tapering sand spit. On the opposite side of the promontory, the splendid beach of **Eyeopelayítiko** is one of the finest on the whole peninsula, with the seasonal *Oramabar* providing refreshments. From here you can return to the main road and complete the clockwise coastal circuit, happily ignoring the unappealing resort of Síviri, although if time allows, you may choose to detour back to this coast for a peep at the yachting haven of **Sáni**.

### ACCOMMODATION, EATING AND DRINKING                                       KASSÁNDHRA

You should have no trouble getting **accommodation** outside the busy midsummer period, though places start closing down in September, and few remain open between October and April. Large signs at the entrance to both peninsulas remind you that camping outside authorized sites is strictly prohibited. If you avoid the identikit tavernas at the most heavily touristic resorts, Kassándhra has a decent sprinkling of reasonable **places to eat**. The liveliest nightlife is in Áfytos, with Greek musicians often playing the bars at summer weekends, sometimes under the aegis of the **Kassándhra Festival** which Áfytos shares with Síviri: performances include blues, soul, classical and traditional Greek music.

### NÉA FÓKEA

**Seryiani** ☏23740 81677. Delightfully positioned seafood taverna on the little harbour. Prices are kept low – fresh fish can cost under €50 per kilo. Good mezédhes and barrelled wine too. May–Oct daily noon–1am.

**Villa Madeleine** ☏23740 81991, ✉valasaki@ freemail.gr. Smart modern studios on hill behind the tower, comfortably furnished, with kitchenettes, and balconies overlooking the bay. Mid-June to mid-Sept. **€30**

### SÁNI

**Blue Dream** ☏23740 31435. Municipal campsite just north of the harbour with adequate space but not a great deal of shade or facilities. May–Sept.

**Tomata** On the marina ☏23740 99465. The expensive but imaginative menu at this taverna is aimed at the yachters who moor here, but look out for the €15-per-person "Dine Around" options. April–Oct noon–midnight.

## ÁFYTOS

**Aloni Apartments** Start of the Kallithéa road ☎ 23740 91637. An attractively designed and decorated building, with simple, spotlessly clean rooms and apartments of varying sizes. May–Sept. €35

**Hotel Afitis** Paralía Várkes ☎ 23740 91233, ⓦ afitis -hotel.gr. Smart resort hotel with a vast pool and range of facilities. Huge difference in price between the modest rooms at the back and those with balconies facing the sea. April–Oct. €55

★ **Ta Bakaliarakia tou Pirati** Centre of village ☎ 23740 31001. Slightly above-average prices but still a good place for quality fish and meat dishes, mainly around €10, and a convivial atmosphere. May–Oct daily, Nov– April Fri–Sun noon–2am.

**Ta Harakia** Paralía Várkes ☎ 23740 91211. Best of the seaside tavernas, offering a range of daily specials for only €6–7 on the chalk board outside, such as baked swordfish. May–Oct daily 9am–1am.

## KALLITHÉA AND AROUND

**Iy Platia Tis Anthoulas** Kryopiyí ☎ 23740 53001. Cosy traditional taverna serving delights such as stuffed chicken for €8 and artichokes in an egg and lemon sauce. April– Oct daily, Nov–March Fri–Sun 10am–midnight.

**Paliouri Camping** Just above Khroussoú bay ☎ 23740 92169. This is an organized and shady spot with a minimarket and plenty of sites for your tent. May–Oct.

## SOUTHWESTERN SHORE

★ **Kyani Akti** Néa Skióni ☎ 23740 71184, ⓦ kyaniakti .com. Complete with a courtyard of palms and bougainvillea, this appealing little hotel at the south end of the beach offers cosy rooms with sea views. May–Sept. €40

★ **Kyparissis** Posídhi ☎ 23740 42264. By far the friendliest and best of the half-dozen places along the front, it serves mainly grilled meat and fish, plus some oven dishes. There are some newly decorated rooms behind (€35). April–Oct daily, Nov–Mar Fri–Sun 10am–midnight.

**O Kleon** Néa Skióni ☎ 23740 71266. This inexpensive ouzerí-style restaurant a block back from the seafront is extremely popular with the locals for its wide range of mezédhes such as vegetable fritters and small fish. May– Oct daily, Nov–April Fri–Sun noon–1am.

**Possidi Paradise** Posídhi ☎ 23740 42030, ⓦ possidi paradise.gr. Sparkling new upmarket hotel with a swimming pool and large rooms looking out onto the seafront. Breakfast included. May–mid-Oct. €85

# Sithonía

As you move east across Halkidhikí and away from the frontline of tourism, the landscape becomes increasingly green and hilly, culminating in the isolated and spectacular scenery of Mount Athos, looming across the gulf. The **SITHONÍA** peninsula is more rugged but better cultivated than Kassándhra, though here there are even fewer true villages, mostly dating from the 1920s resettlement era. Pine forests cover many of the slopes, particularly in the south, giving way to olive groves on the coast. Small sandy inlets with relatively discreet pockets of campsites and tavernas make a welcome change. It's a good idea to follow the loop road clockwise around the east coast, so that the peak of Athos is always before you.

## Ancient Olynthos

Daily: summer 8am–7.30pm, winter closes 3pm • €3

If you're travelling under your own steam, some 6km past the last motorway exit at Néa Moudhaniá en route to Sithonía, it's worth making the slight detour to splendidly located ancient Olynthos, atop a hill offering mountain and sea views. This is a rare example of an unmodified Classical town laid out to the geometric grid plan of Hippodamus – the fifth-century BC architect who designed Pireás and Rhodes. There's an initially off-putting walk of 700m, partly up a slope, from the ticket booth, but well-excavated streets, houses and even some mosaics to see once you arrive, most notably one of Bellerophon riding Pegasus and killing the Chimaira. Like the new, informative museum near the entrance, everything is clearly labelled in Greek and English. The modern village of Ólynthos, 1km west across the riverbed here, offers limited facilities.

## Órmos Panayías

**ÓRMOS PANAYÍAS**, first of the east-coast resorts, is heavily developed; ranks of villas dwarf the picturesque hamlet and tiny harbour, while the nearest decent beaches lie 4km north en route to Pyrgadhíkia, below the inland village of Áyios Nikólaos, whose square is a traffic-free haven for diners and drinkers. The only real reason to stop at Órmos would be to catch one of the excursion boats that sail around Athos from here, but these are better value from Ouranoúpoli (see p.303).

## Vourvouroú

**VOURVOUROÚ**, 8km down the coast from Órmos Panayías, is not a typical resort, since it stands on land expropriated from Vatopedhíou monastery on Athos. Islets astride the mouth of the bay make for a fine setting, but the beach, while sandy, is extremely narrow, and Vourvouroú is really more of a yachters' haven.

## Onwards to Sárti

Some of Sithonía's best **beaches** lie off the 30km of corniche road between Vourvouroú and the busy tourist resort of **SÁRTI**: five signposted sandy coves, each with a **campsite** and little else. The names of the bays, such as Koutloumousíou or Zográfou, reflect the fact that most of the land here belonged to various Athonite monasteries until confiscated by the Greek government to resettle Anatolian refugees. A short way beyond **Armenistís**, a dirt track leads down to a pair of idyllic coves, almost tropical in appearance. Sárti itself may not ooze charm but does offer a good choice of facilities and one of the widest beaches in a major enclave.

## Paralía Sykiás

**PARALÍA SYKIÁS**, 8km past Sárti, is a well-appointed beach, with just a few tavernas well back from the sea along 2km of coastal highway. The best strategy here is to follow the side road at the south end of the beach towards the more scenic coves and smattering of restaurants at **Pigadháki** or **Paleó Fánaro**. For a **post office** and shops head for **SYKIÁ**, 2km inland, hemmed in by a bowl of rocky hills.

## Kalamítsi

**KALAMÍTSI**, another 8km south of Paralía Sykiás, consists of a beautiful double bay, now rather spoilt by development. The small strand at the sheltered north bay of Pórto can get cramped in summer, at which time you can easily swim out to the main islet for less company or head over the rocks to the north, where there's an informal nudist beach.

## Pórto Koufó

The forest cover gets progressively thinner the further south you go from Sárti, until you reach the recently replanted tip of the peninsula, where the hills spill into the sea to create a handful of deep bays. **PÓRTO KOUFÓ**, just northwest of the cape, is the most dramatic of these, almost completely cut off from the open sea by high cliffs. The name Koufó ("deaf" in Greek) is said to come from one's inability to hear the sea within the confines of this inlet, which served as an Axis submarine shelter during World War II. There are a few fine **stretches of sand** around the bay, especially where the road drops down from the east. The north end of the inlet, 1km from the beach area, is a picturesque yacht and fishing harbour. Overall this area is one of the star attractions on the whole peninsula as a place to base oneself.

## Toróni and Tristiníka

**TORÓNI**, 3km north of Pórto Koufó, is an exposed, 2km-long crescent of sand with wooded hills behind. It makes another plausible base and for a little stimulation there is a minimal **archeological site** on the southern cape, sporting the remains of a Byzantine fortress, while nearby is an early Christian basilica. Just 2km north is the turning for less-developed **TRISTINÍKA**, with another outstanding 2km beach.

## Pórto Carrás and around

Beyond Tristiníka, you edge back into high-tech-resort territory, epitomized by Greece's largest planned holiday complex, **PÓRTO CARRÁS** (ⓦportocarras.com), comprising four upmarket hotels that range from mock-Byzantine to futuristic and 3-star to luxury. Established by the Carras wine and shipping dynasty, it features an in-house shopping centre, golf course and vineyards, while from the expansive private beach in front, you can indulge in every imaginable watersport.

The nearest proper town to all this, with **banks** (ATMs) and a **post office**, is **Néos Marmarás**, a little fishing port with a small beach. Nowadays, it's popular with Greeks who stay in a score of modest hotels and apartments.

## Parthenónas

A detour inland to **PARTHENÓNAS**, the lone traditional village on Sithonía, will give you some idea of what Sithonía must have looked like before the developers moved in. Crouched at the base of 808m Mount Ítamos, it's 5km up from Néos Marmarás and reached via a good road lined with pine and olive groves. Parthenónas was abandoned in the 1960s in favour of the shore, and never even provided with mains electricity; its appealing houses have now largely been restored into chic residences.

## Nikíti

The clockwise loop is completed back at the neck of the peninsula in the pleasant resort of **NIKÍTI**, which can of course be used as a reasonable first base. Although there is nothing too spectacular about the seafront here, the old village on the inland side of the main road is full of venerable old stone houses and contains a few decent options for staying and dining.

**4**

### GETTING AROUND                                                     SITHONÍA

**By bus** Services are sparse: depending on the season, there are up to five daily around the west coast to Sárti, and up to three a day direct to Vourvouroú, but just a single daily KTEL connection, in August only, between these two endpoints. A complete circuit is only really feasible with your own transport.

### ACCOMMODATION AND EATING

As with Kassándhra, finding somewhere to stay is only ever a problem during the short peak season in August, and there is plenty of choice for campers. Locating a hotel open off-season can be more of a challenge. Sithonía presents the best eating options of anywhere in Halkidhikí.

#### VOURVOUROÚ

**Diaporos** ☎23750 91313, ⓦhotel-diaporos.com. Rather grand edifice with lush gardens and huge, well-appointed rooms, as well as its own rooftop restaurant. May–Sept. **€70**

**Dionysos** Behind the beach ☎23750 91214. Reasonable campsite, part of which faces the beach, with ample space and good shared facilities, including a shop and café. April–Oct.

**Ekies All Senses Resort** ☎23750 91000, ⓦekies.gr. Ecologically minded, high-luxury resort, set in vast landscaped grounds at the southern end of the village, with designer rooms, a gourmet restaurant and enticing pool. **€100**

**Itamos** ☎23750 90429. With a manicured courtyard, this taverna offers a wider menu at fairer prices than the seafront joints. Try the pork in wine sauce for €7.50 and the smooth barrelled wine. May–Oct noon–2am.

#### ONWARDS TO SÁRTI

★ **Armenistis** ☎23750 91487, ⓦarmenistis.com.gr. One of the best-developed campsites on the peninsula and a major hangout for ravers from Thessaloníki. Often stages gigs and festivals. May–Sept.

#### PÓRTO KOUFÓ

★ **Boukadoura** On main road ☎23750 51012, ⓦboukadoura.gr. The menu contains over 100 dishes, among which are some unusual creations like seafood *spetsofáï* and a rich lobster *makaronádha* for only €15. June–Aug daily and some weekends Sept–May noon–1am.

★ **Porto Koufo** On the beach ☎23750 51207, ⓦportokoufohotel.gr. Attractive whitewashed complex of spacious rooms with subtle decoration, large bathtubs and bay-view balconies. Buffet breakfast included. May–Sept. **€50**

## TORÓNI AND TRISTINÍKA

**Barracuda** Toróni. Lively beach bar that serves a range of soft drinks, coffees, beers and snacks, while keeping everyone entertained with a fair selection of music, mostly in English. Daily 11am–1am.

**Camping Isa** Tristiníka ☎ 23750 51235. Campsite at the southern end of the beach. Besides tent space in well-landscaped olive groves, there are also wood chalets (€40) with all amenities. May–Sept.

**Ethnik** Tristiníka ☎ 694 43 56 830. Imaginatively painted solid wooden beach bar, offering a range of drinks and snacks, as well as a laidback vibe, aided and abetted by the cool world sounds. June to early Sept 10am–2am.

★ **Haus Sakis** Toróni ☎ 23750 51261, ⓦ haus-sakis .de. Towards the northernmost end of the seafront, this place has comfortable rooms and a warm welcome guaranteed, plus good food and German beer on tap in the restaurant below. Breakfast included. €40

★ **Villa Sithonia** Tristiníka ☎ 23750 51118. Lovely, well-furnished and great-value rooms and more spacious apartments in two buildings set in lush gardens amid olive groves 500m from the beach. €25

## PARTHENÓNAS

**Pension Parthenon** ☎ 23750 72225, ⓦ parthenonas -chalkidiki.com. This beautifully decorated stone house on high ground above the village centre offers some of the peninsula's most charming accommodation. All rooms have kitchens. Buffet breakfast included. €60

★ **To Steki tou Meniou** ☎ 694 54 14 052. Friendly and very traditional restaurant beside the village square that dishes up copious amounts of tasty oven recipes for €6–8, plus grills and occasionally even delicacies like quail. Daily 11am–midnight.

## NIKÍTI

**Danai Beach Resort** 4km northwest of Nikíti ☎ 23750 20400, ⓦ dbr.gr. Occupying its own patch of beach, this is one of Greece's most exclusive resorts; the decor mixes shiny white marble with soft-coloured quality furnishings. There's a spa, two restaurants, a bar and sports facilities. Breakfast included. April–Oct. €435

**Ta Tria Skalopatia** ☎ 697 48 30 330. Family-run taverna which has partial sea views from its patio and offers traditional cuisine like shrimp *saganáki* and *papoutsáki* for around €6–7. May–mid-Oct 9am–midnight.

# Secular Athos

From Sithonía a road winds around the coast and up over a ridge to Halkidhikí's third peninsula, the upper part of which is **secular Athos**. The principal place you'd think to stop for refreshment is **Pyrgadhíkia**, a ravine-set fishing village jutting out into the Sigitikós gulf. There's little beach to speak of, although there are some good ones dotted along the stretch leading towards it. From Pyrgadhíkia the main road heads back inland, while a turn-off via Gomáti takes you through unspoilt moors to Ierissós at the neck of the Athos peninsula. This route has no public transport links, however; to travel between Sithonía and Athos by bus you will have to backtrack via Halkidhikí's inland capital, **Políyiros**.

### Ierissós and around

With its good, long beach and a vast, promontory-flanked gulf, **IERISSÓS** is the most Greek-patronized of the secular Athos resorts, although the sizeable town itself, built well back from the shore and with room to expand, is a sterile concrete grid dating from after a devastating 1932 earthquake. The only hint of pre-touristic life is the vast boat-building area on the sand, at the back of the wide beach to the south.

The road beyond Ierissós passes through mundane **Néa Ródha** before veering inland to follow a boggy depression that is the remaining stretch of **Xerxes' canal**, cut by the Persian invader in 480 BC to spare his fleet the shipwreck at the tip of Athos that had befallen the previous expedition eleven years before.

### Ammouliani

Apart from Thássos (see p.412) **AMMOULIANÍ** (ⓦ visitammouliani.com) is Macedonia's only inhabited Aegean island, and after decades of eking out an existence from fishing, the island's population, originally refugees from the Sea of Marmara, has in recent years had to adjust to an influx of holiday-makers. Like anywhere else in Halkidhikí, it can get very busy in late July and August, but in early or late summer this low-lying, scrub- and olive-covered islet can make an idyllic hideaway.

The island is accessed from the ferry jetty at **Trypití**. The main village, where the ferries dock, is an unprepossessing grid of concrete slung over a ridge, with few pre-1960s buildings remaining; it is, however, chock-a-block with **rooms**, many self-catering, and a few tavernas.

Beaches

Two kilometres southwest of Ammoulianí village is **Alykés**, the islet's most famous beach, named after the salt-marsh just behind. The island's best beaches, however, lie in the far southeast, facing the straits with the Athos peninsula. To reach them, bear left onto the newly paved road 1500m out of town and follow the signs some 2km along this to **Áyios Yeóryios**, whose tiny **chapel** overlooks the excellent beach. You can continue a final 500m to the even more enticing **Megáli Ámmos** beach, which has the island's only campsite. Still other, less accessible, beaches beckon in the northwest of the island, served in season by excursion boats from the town; a popular map-postcard on sale will give necessary hints on how to reach them on foot or by bicycle.

## Ouranoúpoli

Fifteen kilometres beyond Ierissós, **OURANOÚPOLI** is the last community before the restricted monastic domains, with a centre that's downright tatty, showing the effects of too much tourism. Somewhat mysteriously, it has become a major resort aside from its function as the main gateway to Mount Athos; local beaches, stretching intermittently for several kilometres to the north, are sandy enough but narrow and cramped. If you're compelled to stay the night while waiting for passage to Athos, the best temporary escape would be either to take a cruise, or to **rent a motorboat**, to the mini-archipelago of **Dhrénia** just opposite, with almost tropical sandy bays and tavernas on the larger islets. Modern craft also offer three-hour **cruises** (from €18 per person, depending on the season; hours vary), which skim along the Athonite coast, keeping any female passengers 500m offshore as required by the monastic authorities.

**4**

## ARRIVAL AND DEPARTURE                     SECULAR ATHOS

**By bus** There are 8 daily buses down to Ouranoúpoli via all points mentioned above from Thessaloníki and 7 in the opposite direction.

**By ferry** Ferries run to Mount Athos from Ierissós and

Ouranoúpoli (see above). Ferries to Ammoulianí leave from Trypití (15min; hourly in summer, less frequently off season; €2, car €10).

## ACCOMMODATION AND EATING

### AMMOULIANÍ

**Camping Alikes Alykés beach** ☎ 23770 51379, ⓦ alikescamping.gr. Set right behind the beach but with plenty of shade and good cooking and washing facilities, the site also offers the *Metochi* restaurant and *Big Fish* beach bar. May–Sept.

★ **Gripos** Áyios Yeóryios beach ☎ 23770 51049 or 697 39 88 161. Has rooms of considerable charm with copper antiques, beam ceilings, terracotta floor tiles, large balconies and a swimming pool in the garden, full of pheasants and other exotic fowl. Great meals and mezédhes at its ouzerí too. May–Oct 11am–midnight. **€30**

**Janis** Facing the rear Limanáki port ☎ 23770 51322. Good all-round taverna, serving the usual range of dips, salads, grills and the odd oven dish at around €7–8. May–Oct daily 10am–late.

**Megali Ammos** Megáli Ámmos beach ☎ 23770 51183. The superb location is matched by the fresh fish served at

this taverna: quality catches such as *barboúni* or *tsipoúra* should only work out at around €12–15 per portion. Mid-May to Sept daily 11am–1am.

**Philippos** In the centre of the main village ☎ 23770 51326. Compact but cosy rooms, decorated in rustic style, all with kitchen facilities and balconies with at least partial sea views. **€30**

**Sun Rise** Left from the harbour ☎ 23770 51273, ☎ 23770 51174. With its own swimming jetty and a surprisingly snazzy cocktail bar in the lobby, this is one of the island's largest hotels, yet intimate. **€40**

### IERISSÓS

**Delfini** 2km along road to Néa Ródha ☎ 698 41 24 606. Well-developed private campsite with ample shade, good shared facilities and a minimarket. June–Sept.

**Marcos** 3 blocks back from south end of seafront ☎ 23770 22518, ⓦ hotelmarkos.gr. Overlooking its own garden and car park, the two-storey hotel has medium-sized comfortable rooms. May–Oct. **€45**

**To Kolatsi** Behind the landscaped promenade ☎ 23770 22487. A cross between a grill house and fish taverna, serving both succulent meats and fresh fish like for gavros or sardines for €7–8. Daily noon–midnight.

### OURANOÚPOLI

**Akroyali** On the southern seafront ☎ 23770 71201, ⓦ ouranoupolis-akrogiali.gr. Standard hotel with perfectly adequate rooms, some with sea-facing balconies, that provide the best value around. Open all year. **€35**

**Sorokadha** Behind the main beach ☎ 23770 71332.

Offers a wide range of meat dishes such as roast lamb, pork chops or beef *kokkinistó* for only €6, plus plenty of vegetarian choices. Daily 9am–midnight.

**Tou Apostoli To Koutouki** On the south waterfront ☎ 23770 71172. A decent choice for both grilled and oven dishes, all under €10, which can be washed down with the palatable house wine. Daily 11am–1am.

**Xenia** Nearly 500m north along the beach ☎ 23770 71412, ⓦ xeniaouranoupolis.com. The area's swishest hotel, with good off-season deals. Sixties-style rooms in the main block or larger bungalows available, plus a decent restaurant and other facilities. Open all year. **€75**

## Mount Athos: the monks' republic

Known in Greek as the *Áyion Óros* (Holy Mountain), **MOUNT ATHOS** is an autonomous province of the country – a "**monks' republic**" – on whose slopes are gathered twenty monasteries populated exclusively by men. Women and even female farm animals have been banned here since an edict by the Byzantine emperor in 1060. Most of the **monasteries** were founded in the tenth and eleventh centuries; today, all survive in a state of comparative decline but they remain unsurpassed in their general and architectural interest and for the art treasures they contain.

If you are male, over 18 years old and have a genuine interest in monasticism or Greek Orthodoxy, sacred music or simply in Byzantine and medieval architecture, a

## MOUNT ATHOS TIME

The traditional Byzantine **daily schedule** observed on Athos is somewhat disorienting. On the northeast side of the peninsula the "12 o'clock" position on monastery clocks indicates neither noon nor midnight but sunrise, whereas on the opposite side of Athos it coincides with sunset. Yet Vatopedhíou, the largest monastery, keeps "worldly" time, as do most monks' wristwatches, and in many monasteries two wall clocks are mounted side by side, one showing secular, the other "Byzantine" time. However, the **Julian calendar**, a fortnight behind the outside world, is observed throughout Athos. Bedtime is shortly after sunset and in the small hours your hosts will awake for solitary meditation and study, followed by *órthros*, or matins. Around sunrise there is another quiet period, just before the *akolouthía*, or main liturgy, that precedes the morning meal. The rest of the day is devoted to manual labour until the *esperinós*, or vespers, followed immediately by the afternoon meal and the short *apódhipno*, or compline service.

visit is strongly recommended; this requires a **permit** (see p.306) which can be easily arranged in Thessaloníki. In addition to the religious and architectural aspects of Athos, it should be added that the peninsula remains one of the most beautiful parts of Greece. For many visitors, this – as much as the experience of monasticism – is the highlight of time spent on the Holy Mountain.

### Brief history

The **development of monasticism** on Athos is a matter of some controversy, and foundation legends abound. The most popular asserts that the **Virgin Mary** was blown ashore here on her way to Cyprus. The earliest historical reference to Athonite monks is to their attendance at a council of the Empress Theodora in 843; probably there were some monks here by the end of the seventh century. In 885 an edict of Emperor Basil I recognized Athos as the sole preserve of monks, and gradually hermits came together to form communities known in church Greek as *koinobia* (literally "common life"). The year 963 is the traditional date for the **foundation of the first monastery**, Meyístis Lávras, by Athanasios the Athonite, largely financed by Emperor Nikiforos Fokas. Over the next two centuries foundations were frequent, the monasteries reaching forty in number, alongside many smaller communities.

Troubles for Athos began at the end of the eleventh century. The monasteries suffered sporadically from pirate raids and from the settlement of three hundred Vlach shepherd families on the mountain. After a reputedly scandalous episode between the monks and the shepherdesses, the Vlachs were ejected and a new imperial edict was issued, confirming that **no female** mammal, human or animal, be allowed to set foot on Athos. This edict, called the *ávaton*, remains in force today, excepting cats to control rodents.

During the twelfth century, the monasteries gained an international – or at least, a **pan-Orthodox** – aspect, as Romanian, Russian and Serbian monks flocked to the mountain in retreat from the turbulence of the age, although the peninsula itself was subject to raids by Franks and Catalans over the next two centuries. After the fall of the Byzantine Empire to the Ottomans, the fathers wisely declined to resist, maintaining good relations with the early sultans, one of whom paid a state visit.

The mountain's real decline came after the early nineteenth-century **War of Independence**, in which many of the monks fought alongside the Greek revolutionary forces but paid the price when Macedonia was easily subdued. This led to a permanent Turkish garrison and the first drastic reduction in the monastic population, which did not increase even when Macedonia returned to Greece in 1912. The Athonite fathers, however, resisted diluting the Greek nature of the Holy Mountain with too many foreign (mainly Russian) monks. By the early 1960s numbers were at their lowest, barely a thousand, compared to 20,000 in Athos's heyday. Today, however, the monastic population has climbed to about two thousand, its average age has dropped significantly and the number of well-educated monks has increased markedly. While Athos remains a part of Greece, all foreign monks must adopt Greek citizenship and the Greek civil government is represented by an appointed governor and a small police force.

## The monasteries

Obviously you can't hope to visit all twenty monasteries during a short stay, though if you're able to extend the basic four-day permit period you can see the most prominent foundations. Each monastery has a distinct place in the **Athonite hierarchy**: Meyístis Lávras holds the prestigious first place, Konstamonítou ranks twentieth. All other settlements are attached to one or other of the twenty "ruling" monasteries; the dependencies range from a *skíti*, or minor monastic community (either a group of houses, or a cloister-like compound scarcely distinguishable from a monastery), through a *kellí* (a sort of farmhouse) to an *isyhastírio* (a solitary hermitage, often a cave). Numerous laymen – including many Muslim Albanians of late – also live on Athos, mostly employed as agricultural or manual labourers by the monasteries.

For simplicity's sake it is easiest to divide the monasteries according to which coast of the peninsula they belong to, southwestern or northeastern; our listings (see p.308), which give brief descriptions of the main highlights, reflect this division. The institutions of each coast are described in geographical order, starting with those closest to the mainland. Apart from the four *skítes* that accept overnight visitors and thus merit their own entry, all other dependencies are mentioned in the account of their ruling monastery.

### ARRIVAL AND DEPARTURE                                  MOUNT ATHOS

**By ferry** All boats to Athos are run by Ayiorítikes Grammés (☎ 23770 71149, ⊛ www.agioreitikes-grammes.com). Most visitors arrive at the main port of Dháfni on the southwest coast. From here the small *Ayia Anna* sails round the southern tip of the peninsula as far as Kafsokalývia, stopping at all the monastic communities en route; advance booking is advisable. Each monastery has a small harbour annexe (*arsanás*) which can be a considerable distance from the monastery itself.

From Ouranoúpoli The regular ferry sails at 9.45am as far as Dháfni (90 min; €7), stopping at each harbour or coastal monastery en route. There are also faster boats at 8.45am and 10.40am (45min; €12) direct to Dháfni.

From Ierissós From Ierissós, a single fast boat leaves at 8.35am daily and travels along the northeast shore as far as the monastery of Megístis Lavras (2hr; €18); it may not stop at every harbour on the way but is guaranteed to halt at the Hilandharíou police post for the issue of permits.

From Thessaloníki To reach Athos from Thessaloníki, first take a Halkidhikí KTEL bus (see p.275) to Ouranoúpoli or Ierissós (see p.302).

### INFORMATION

**Permits** Only ten permits per day are issued to non-Orthodox visitors to Athos (120 for baptized Greek Orthodox), so it is wise to apply as far in advance as possible (six months maximum), especially for summer or Easter visits. The first step is to contact the Pilgrims' Bureau in Thessaloníki (☎ 2310 252 578, ☎ 2310 222 424, ☎ pilgrimsbureau @c-lab.gr) at Egnatía 109. Staff speak English but walk-in visits are not encouraged. Once you have your booking you must reconfirm two weeks before the intended date of entry. Last-minute permits can sometimes be obtained if there's a cancellation, but that leaves you with the problem of not having a reservation at any of the monasteries.

**Fees and extensions** You pay for and receive your permit (€30; students €20) on the day of entry itself, either from the pilgrims' bureau in Ouranoúpoli, if sailing from there, or at the police post at Hilandharíou, if sailing from Ierissós; make sure you have your passport with you. The permit entitles you to stay for three nights and four days, during which time board and meals at the monasteries are free. Many visitors apply for an extension. This can theoretically be done at the Ayía Epistasía (Holy Superintendancy) in Karyés, the picturesque administrative capital; two or three extra days are normally granted, and your chances are much better out of season.

### GETTING AROUND

**By car** Landrover minibuses meet the larger ferries at Dháfni and other harbours, to carry people to Karyés and the more inland monasteries accessible by road; they can be expensive and, if they're driven by lay-workers, you should establish a price beforehand.

**By foot** Most foreign visitors prefer to walk between monasteries, preferably armed with the excellent map by Road Editions (1:50,000), which includes an informative 48-page booklet. Even with that, it's wise to check the current condition of trails at each monastery.

**FROM TOP** ÉDHESSA (P.288), KARYÉS, MOUNT ATHOS (ABOVE) >

## ATHOS ETIQUETTE

It's worth remembering that the monks on Athos are expecting **religious pilgrims**, not tourists. Each monastery varies a good deal in their handling of visitors; signs at some institutions specifically forbid you from attending services or sharing meals with the monks. Others put themselves at the disposal of visitors of whatever creed (though you may well find yourself being encouraged to switch to Greek Orthodoxy!). Yet, wherever you stay there's a certain amount of etiquette to observe.

You must reach the monastery where you will overnight **before dark**, since they all lock their front gates at sunset – which would leave you outside with the wild boars. Upon arrival you should ask for the **guestmaster** (*arhondáris*), who will proffer the traditional welcome of a *tsípouro*, *loukoúmi* (Turkish delight) and often a Greek coffee, before showing you to your bed. Most guestmasters speak good English.

You should be **fully dressed** at all times, even when going from dormitory to bathroom; shorts should not be worn anywhere on the peninsula, nor hats inside monasteries. Swimming is officially prohibited, so if you are tempted, choose a cove where nobody can see you, and certainly don't skinny-dip. Smoking is forbidden, though it is often tolerated outside the monastery walls; it would be criminal to smoke on the trail, however, given the chronic fire danger. Singing, whistling and raised voices are taboo; as is standing with your hands behind your back or in your pockets. If you want to photograph monks you should always ask permission, though photography is forbidden altogether in many monasteries, and video cameras are completely banned from the Mountain.

## MONASTERY ACCOMMODATION

Theoretically, all of the twenty major and four minor monasteries that receive guests require advance reservations, although there are several that do not apply this rule strictly. This is noted, along with contact details for all the institutions below. Just about all the most interesting monasteries, however, do require booking, which can be done up to six months in advance. Where hours are denoted, it is best to call during these times on Monday to Saturday but you may have to persevere for an answer, and don't even bother trying on Sunday or any major holy day.

Accommodation is typically in **dormitories**, and fairly spartan, but there's invariably a shower down the hall (often hot) and you're always given sheets and blankets.

### THE SOUTHWESTERN COAST MONASTERIES

**Zográfou** ☎&📠23770 23247. Almost an hour from its harbour, the most inland monastery is inhabited by Bulgarian and Macedonian monks. The name derives from a legend that the founders left out a wooden panel, upon which a painting of St George appeared. Non-Orthodox and believers are segregated but walk-in guests are usually accepted.

**Konstamonítou** ☎&📠23770 23228. Nearly 2hr from Zográfou and 45min from its own harbour. Set amid thick woodland, it's as humble, bare and poor as you'd expect from the last-ranking monastery. Non-Orthodox and believers are segregated but guests are happily taken on spec.

**Dhohiaríou** ☎&📠23770 23245. Nearly 2hr from Konstamonítou. Picturesque monastery with lofty church nearly filling the courtyard. The best frescoes are in the long, narrow refectory, which has sea views.

**Xenofóndos** ☎23770 23633, 📠23770 23631. Only 30min from Dhohiaríou. The enormous, sloping, irregularly shaped court, expanded upwards in the nineteenth century, is unique in possessing two main churches. The small, older

one, decorated with exterior frescoes of the Cretan school, was usurped during the 1830s by the huge upper one.

**Ayíou Pandeleïmonos** ☎&📠23770 23252; 10am–noon. Nearly 2hr from Dháfni and 1hr from Xenofóndos. Also known as "Róssiko", as many of its monks are Russian and it sports onion-shaped domes. The main attraction is the enormous bell over the refectory, the second largest in the world.

**Xiropotámou** ☎23770 23251, 📠23770 23733; 10am–12.30pm. Under an hour from Dháfni. Most of its construction and church frescoes date from the eighteenth century. Here again non-Orthodox are kept segregated from the faithful at meal times.

**Símonos Pétras** ☎23770 23254, 📠23770 23707; 1–3pm. Best reached by boat. Though entirely rebuilt after an early twentieth-century fire, "Simópetra", as it is known, is perhaps the most visually striking monastery on Athos. With its multiple storeys, ringed by wooden balconies overhanging sheer 300m drops, it resembles a Tibetan lamasery.

**Osíou Grigoríou** ☎23770 23668, 📠23770 23671; 11am–1pm. An hour and a half from Símonos Pétras. Hovering closely above the sea and renowned for the quality of its chanting, it has a fine common room/library with literature on Orthodoxy and an extra guest hostel outside the gate.

**Ayíou Dhionysíou** ✆ 23770 23687, 🖷 23770 23686. Around an hour from Osíou Grigoríou, this fortified structure, perched spectacularly on a coastal cliff, is among the most richly endowed monasteries. The best icons are in the refectory rather than the dim church. Non-orthodox must eat separately.

**Ayíou Pávlou** ✆ 23770 23741, 🖷 23770 23355; 10am–12.30pm. About an hour from Ayíou Dhionysíou, this edifice actually looks more imposing from afar; many Cypriot monks in residence.

**Néa Skíti** ✆ 23770 23572; 10am–noon. Under an hour from Ayíou Pávlou. Nothing too special about this dependency, except that it serves as a handy base for Athos peak.

**Skíti Ayías Ánnas** ✆ 23770 23320. An hour and a half from Ayíou Pávlou. Pleasant location with buildings tumbling down to the shore. Used as the most common "base camp" for climbing Athos peak (2030m).

## THE NORTHEASTERN COAST MONASTERIES

**Hilandharíou** ✆ 23770 23797, 🖷 23770 23108. A beacon of Serbian culture since the thirteenth century, with monks on rotation from Serbia. The fourteenth-century church in the triangular courtyard has attractive frescoes – look out for the *Ouranóskala* or "Stairway to Heaven". Boasts the most salubrious guest quarters on the Mountain.

**Esfigménou** ✆ 23770 23229. Built fortress-like right on the coast but little visited due to its reputation as the strictest institution on Athos. It refuses to accept Patriarch Bartholemew because of his ecumenical initiatives. Banners proclaim "Orthodoxy or death!"

**Vatopedhíou** ✆ 23770 41480, 🖷 23770 41462; 9am–1pm. Great 3.5hr walk from Esfigménou. The largest and second most important monastery, home to over three hundred monks, many of them English-speaking. The cobbled, slanting courtyard with its freestanding belfry resembles a town plaza. The *katholikón* contains exceptional fourteenth-century frescoes and three exquisite mosaics.

**Pandokrátoros** ✆ 23770 23880, 🖷 23770 23685. Nearly a 3hr walk from Vatopedhíou, its best features are the guest rooms overlooking its own picturesque fishing harbour and the citrus-laden courtyard. In a valley above looms its imposing dependency, Profítis Ilías.

**Stavronikíta** ✆&🖷 23770 23255; 10am–noon. An hour's walk from both Pandokrátoros and Ivíron, this offers some of the best views of Athos peak and is the most distinct example of an Athonite coastal fortress-monastery. The narrow church occupies virtually all the gloomy courtyard. Orthodox and infidel alike are roused for 3.30am matins.

**Skíti Ayíou Andhréou** ✆ 23770 23810. A former Russian dependency of the great Vatopedhíou monastery, erected in the nineteenth century. Almost deserted today but close to Karyés and may take walk-in overnighters.

**Koutloumousíou** ✆ 23770 23226, 🖷 23770 23731. Small and tidy monastery on the edge of Karyés. Its name is said to derive from a Seljuk chieftain who converted to Christianity.

**Ivíron** ✆ 23770 23643, 🖷 23770 23248; noon–2pm. Vast place housing around 40 monks. Pilgrims flock to the miraculous icon of the *Portaítissa*, the Virgin Guarding the Gate, inside its own chapel. The huge main church has an elaborate mosaic floor dating from 1030 and interesting pagan touches such as ram's-head column capitals. There is also an immensely rich library and treasury-museum.

**Filothéou** ✆ 23770 23256, 🖷 23770 23674; noon–3pm. Around 1hr walk uphill from Ivíron. Lively place, which was at the forefront of the monastic revival in the early 1980s but not too attractive apart from the expansive lawn. Non-Orthodox visitors are barred from services and dining with the faithful.

**Karakálou** ✆ 23770 23225, 🖷 23770 23746. Under an hour's walk downhill from Filothéou. The lofty keep is typical of the fortress-monasteries built to deter pirate attacks. Non-Orthodox barred from services and dining with the faithful.

**Meyístis Lávras** ✆ 23770 23754, 🖷 23770 23013. The oldest and foremost of the ruling monasteries, as well as the most imposing complex on Athos, with fifteen chapels within its walls. At mealtimes you can enjoy the frescoes in the refectory, executed by Theophanes the Cretan in 1535. Among its many dependencies, just 10min away by marked path there's the hermitage-cave of Ayios Athanasios, watched over by five skulls.

**Skíti Prodhrómou** ✆ 23770 23294. A good 2hr walk from Meyístis Lávras, this large dependency is run by welcoming young Romanian monks, who may well take you in on spec. Other dependencies further along the southern tip include the *kellí* of Áyios Nílos and the frescoed chapel of Kafsokalývia, from where boats depart to the southwestern coast.

## EATING AND DRINKING

Athos grows much of its own **food** and the monastic diet is based on tomatoes, beans, olives, green vegetables, coarse bread, cheese and pasta, with occasional meat dishes or treats like *halvás* and fruit; a glass of wine is commonly served and fish of some description is standard after Sunday morning service. Only two meals are served daily in the *trápeza* (refectory or dining room), the first, more substantial one any time between 8am and 11am, the latter about an hour and a half to two and a half hours before sunset, depending on the time of year. It's a good idea to bring supplementary provisions with you. There are a few shops in Karyés and Dháfni, but for a better selection you should stock up before coming to Athos.

# Northeastern Macedonia

Few people ever venture into the arable plains of **northeastern Macedonia**, where attractions are sparsely spread among golden fields of corn and tobacco and incredible numbers of storks' nests. Up near the craggy mountains that form the frontier with Bulgaria, artificial **Lake Kerkíni** is home to masses of birds, some of them extremely rare in Europe, making it as interesting to ornithologists as the Préspa lakes much farther west. The tranquil setting and rich flora mean it is not only for avid twitchers.

An alternative route to the Egnatía Odhós for reaching Kavála is the scenic route that climbs northeast out of Thessaloníki, first taking you via Sérres before passing **Alistráti**, worth visiting for its memorable caves, and then heading towards Dhráma and ancient **Philippi** along a quieter road that offers majestic panoramas of Mount Meníkio (1963m), Mount Pangéo (1956m) and Mount Falakró (2230m). Regular **buses** from Thessaloníki and between Sérres and Dhráma ply this road.

## The Kerkíni Wetlands

Artificial, marsh-fringed **Lake Kerkíni**, tucked up near the mountainous Bulgarian border some 80km northeast of Thessaloníki, enjoys international protected status, thanks to the 300-plus species of **birds** that spend at least part of the year here, some of them on the endangered species list. Huge expanses of water lilies stretch across the large anvil-shaped lake, out of which the River Strymónas flows to the northern Aegean near ancient Amphipolis, while a herd of water buffalo wallows and grazes the eastern banks, and local fishermen compete with every type of heron known to inhabit Europe. Other birds breeding in the Kerkíni wetlands include various species of grebes, terns, egrets, ducks, geese, ibis, spoonbills, avocets and pelicans, plus raptors such as the black kite, the short-toed eagle and the Levant sparrowhawk.

### Kerkíni

Two kilometres from the lake's northern shore lies the village of **KERKÍNI**, where you will find the **Kerkíni Wetlands Information Centre** (hours vary; ☎23270 28004, ✉ wkerkini@otenet.gr). You can also negotiate **birdwatching** trips in a *pláva*, a traditional punt-like fishing boat. The surroundings reward exploration with their abundance of flora and fauna, with huge numbers of wildflowers in the spring and early summer.

#### ARRIVAL AND DEPARTURE                                                    KERKÍNI

**By bus** Although you can get a bus from Thessaloníki or Sérres to Livadhiá, 7km north of the lake, you're pretty hamstrung coming up here without your own vehicle.

#### ACCOMMODATION AND EATING

★ **Oikoperiigitis** Kerkíni village ☎23270 41450, ⓦ oikoperiigitis.gr. By far the best place to stay: in addition to comfortable rooms, a decent restaurant and camping facilities, the eco-minded lodge offers local tours by boat, canoe, bike, jeep or on horseback. **€55**

**O Harisis** Kerkíni village ☎23270 41232. Simple *psarotavérna* that serves fresh fish from the lake, such as trout for around €10, and a fair range of accompanying salads and vegetable dishes. Daily noon–midnight.

## Alistráti

Just over 20km before you reach the dull market town Dhráma, on the road from Sérres, you come to the large village of **ALISTRÁTI**, which is well placed for exploring the nearby mountains, although the main reason to stop here is to visit the impressive caves nearby.

# Alistráti caves

Daily: Easter–Sept 9am–7pm, until 8pm in Aug; rest of year 9am–5pm; 1hr guided tours only • €8 • No photography • ☎ 23240 82045, ⓦ alistraticave.gr

Reached down a scenic side road 6km southeast of the village, the **Alistráti caves** were first explored in the mid-1970s and surpass those at Pérama; indeed they are claimed to be the most extensive of their kind in Europe not requiring special equipment or training to visit. These gigantic limestone cavities are over two million years old, and bristle with a variety of wonderful formations, including the relatively rare eccentrites and helictites, respectively stalactites sticking out at angles, rather than hanging vertically, and twisted forms resembling sticks of barley sugar. The entrance, a long tunnel bored into the hillside, takes you right into the caverns, and a winding path weaves its way through masses of stalagmites, many of them outstandingly beautiful, and some exceeding 15m in height.

## ACCOMMODATION AND EATING                                    ALISTRÁTI

★ **Arhondiko Voziki** Signposted from main road ☎ 23240 20400, ⓦ hotelboziki.gr. A delightfully restored tobacco factory-cum-mansion, painted a rich yellow, with beautifully furnished period rooms and a swimming pool. Breakfast included. €50

**Ifiyenia** On main road ☎ 23240 31886. The comfy cushioned chairs and gingham tablecloths are deceptive: this cheap local taverna does an interesting range of salads, seafood pasta and pork chops for a mere €6. Daily noon–1am.

# Philippi

Tues–Sun: June–Oct 8am–7pm; Nov–May 8.30am–3pm • €3 • half-hourly buses from Kavála or Dhráma

Just 14km short of Kavála on the busy road from Dhráma, you come to **PHILIPPI** (Filippoi on some maps and signs), a famous battlefield during the civil wars of Ancient Rome and the subject of one of St Paul's Epistles. Apart from the scattered Roman ruins, the principal remains of the site are several impressive, although derelict, **basilican churches**.

## Brief history

Philippi was named after Philip II of Macedon, who wrested it from the Thracians in 356 BC for the sake of nearby gold mines on Mount Pangéo. However, it owed its later importance and prosperity to the Roman construction of the Via Egnatía. With Kavála/Neapolis as its port, Philippi was essentially the easternmost town of Roman-occupied Europe. Here, as at Actium (see p.259), the fate of the Roman Empire was decided, at the **Battle of Philippi** in 42 BC. After assassinating Julius Caesar, Brutus and Cassius had fled east of the Adriatic and, against their better judgement, were forced into confrontation on the Philippi plains with the pursuing armies of Antony and Octavian and were comprehensively beaten in two successive battles.

**St Paul** landed at Kavála and visited Philippi in 49 AD, and so began his religious mission in Europe. Despite being cast into prison, he retained a special affection for the Philippians, his first converts, and the congregation that he established was one of the earliest to flourish in Greece.

## The site

The most conspicuous of the churches at the site is the **Direkler** (Turkish for "columns" or "piers"), to the south of the modern road which here follows the line of the Via Egnatía. Also known as Basilica B, this was an unsuccessful attempt by its sixth-century architect to improve the basilica design by adding a dome. The central arch of its west wall and a few pillars of reused antique drums stand amid remains of the Roman **forum**. A line of second-century porticoes spreads outwards in front of the church, and on their east side are the foundations of a colonnaded octagonal church, which was approached from the Via Egnatía by a great gate. Behind the Direkler and, perversely, the most interesting and best-preserved building of the site, is a huge monumental **public latrine** with nearly fifty of its original marble seats still intact.

Across the road on the northern side, stone steps climb up to a terrace, passing on the right a Roman crypt, reputed to have been the **prison of St Paul** and appropriately frescoed. The terrace flattens out onto a huge paved atrium that extends to the foundations of another extremely large basilica, designated Basilica A. Continuing in the same direction around the base of a hill you emerge above a **theatre** cut into its side. Though dating from the same period as the original town, it was heavily remodelled as an amphitheatre by the Romans – the bas-reliefs of Nemesis, Mars and Victory all belong to this period. It is now used for performances during the annual summer Philippi-Thássos Festival. The best general impression of the site – which is extensive despite a lack of obviously notable buildings – and of the battlefield behind it can be gained from the **acropolis**, whose own remains are predominantly medieval. This can be reached by a steep climb along a path from the museum.

# Kavála and around

Backing onto the easterly foothills of Mount Sýmvolo, **KAVÁLA** is the second-largest city of Macedonia and the second port for northern Greece; it was an extremely wealthy place in the nineteenth century when the region's **tobacco** crop was shipped from its docks to the rest of the world. Known in ancient times as **Neapolis**, the town was the first European port of call for merchants and travellers from the Middle East. It was here that **St Paul** landed en route to Philippi (see p.311), on his initial mission to Europe. In later years, the port and citadel were occupied in turn by the Byzantines, Normans, Franks, Venetians, Ottomans and (during both world wars) Bulgarians.

Although its attempt to style itself as the "Azure City", on account of its position at the head of a wide bay, is going a little overboard, it does have an interesting **historic centre**, focused on the harbour area and the few remaining tobacco warehouses. A picturesque **citadel** looks down from a rocky promontory to the east, and an elegant Ottoman aqueduct leaps over modern buildings into the old quarter on the bluff. Kavála is also one of the main departure points for Thássos (see p.660), as well as Límnos (see p.650) and other northeast Aegean islands.

## Panayía

Although the remnants of Kavála's Ottoman past are mostly neglected, the wedge-shaped **Panayía** quarter to the east of the port preserves a scattering of eighteenth- and nineteenth-century buildings with atmospheric lanes wandering up towards the citadel. The most conspicuous and interesting of its buildings is the splendid **Imaret**, overlooking the harbour on Poulídhou. A long, multi-domed structure, it was originally a hostel for theological students. After many decades of dereliction it was lovingly refurbished and, in 2004, opened as a luxury **hotel** (see p.314). Undoubtedly the best-preserved Islamic building on Greek territory, it was built in 1817 and endowed to the city by **Mehmet (or Mohammed) Ali**, pasha of Egypt and founder of the dynasty which ended with King Farouk; it still officially belongs to the Egyptian government. Further up the promontory, near the corner of Poulídhou and Mohámet Alí, you can see the prestigious **Ottoman-style house** where Mehmet Ali was born to an Albanian family in 1769. Nearby rears an elegant equestrian bronze **statue** of the great man, one of the finest of its kind in Greece.

## The citadel

Daily: June–Sept 8am–7pm, sometimes closed for siesta; Oct–May 8am–5pm • Free

Wonderful views can be had from the Byzantine **citadel**, signposted "castle". You can explore the ramparts, towers, dungeon and cistern, and in season it co-hosts the Philippi-Thássos Festival of drama and music in its main court.

## The aqueduct

Sweeping imperiously across the traffic in Platía Nikotsára as it enters the centre below Panayía, the towering **Kamáres aqueduct** was built on a Roman model during the reign of Süleyman the Magnificent (1520–66).

## The archeological museum

Erythroú Stavroú 17 • Tues–Sun 8.30am–3pm • €2 • ☎ 2510 222 335

Kavála's **archeological museum** contains a fine dolphin and lily mosaic upstairs in the Abdera room (when the floor reopens), plus painted sarcophagi in the adjacent section devoted to Thassian colonies. Downstairs there are many terracotta figurines still decorated in their original paint and gold ornaments from tombs at Amphipolis.

## The Tobacco Museum

Paleológou 4 • Mon–Sat 9am–1pm • Free • ☎ 2510 223 344, ⓦ tobaccomuseum.gr

The potentially interesting **Tobacco Museum** falls down on presentation and the lack of explanations in Greek, let alone English, though some of the exhibits, including historic photographs and antique cigarette packets, are worthwhile. A refurbishment is planned, however, to incorporate displays from the now defunct Municipal Folklore Museum, so it is to be hoped that there will be an all-round improvement. For a more impressive taste of the town's tobacco history check out the fabulous facade of the **Municipal Tobacco Warehouse** (Dhimotikí Kapnapothíki), at Platía Kapnergáti.

## ARRIVAL AND DEPARTURE
KAVÁLA AND AROUND

**By plane** Megas Alexandhros airport is about 25km east of Kavála. There is no airport or convenient local bus. Taxis cost at least €40. There are frequent flights to the UK (Thomsonfly) and Athens (3–4 daily; 1hr).

**By bus** The main bus station is on the corner of Mitropolítou Khryssostómou and Filikís Eterías. Destinations Alexandhroúpoli (4 daily; 3hr); Keramotí (hourly; 1hr); Komotiní (hourly; 2hr); Philippi (half-hourly; 20min); Thessaloníki (hourly; 2hr); Xánthi (half-hourly; 1hr).

**By ferry** Details for the following services are available

from the port authority (☎ 2510 223 716) and tickets from agencies such as Zolotas (☎ 2510 835 671), around the harbourfront towards the terminal/customs house.

Destinations Híos (2–3 weekly; 12hr); Ikaría (1 weekly 17hr); Lésvos (2–3 weekly; 10hr); Límnos (2–3 weekly 5hr); Sámos (2 weekly; 15hr); Thássos (Skála Prínou; 6 daily; 1hr 15min).

**By car** If you're driving in, you can usually find a space on the quay car park near the Thássos dock or the one next to the Archeological Museum.

## INFORMATION

**Tourist office** The municipal tourist office (summer daily 8am–9pm; ☎ 2510 231 011) in the main square, Platía Eleftherías, has a host of brochures and sells

tickets for the summer Philippi-Thássos Festival; it is often unmanned, however.

## ACCOMMODATION

**Acropolis** Venizélou 29 ☎ 2510 223 543, ✉ hotel -acropolis@hotmail.com. Basic old-fashioned guest house. The one single with shared bath (€30) is the cheapest acceptable place to stay in town, but the plain en-suite rooms are overpriced. €50

**Esperia** Erythroú Stavroú 42 ☎ 2510 229 621, 🌐 esperiakavala.gr. A decent hotel offering comfortable rooms with a/c – ask for the quieter side or back ones. Breakfast, served on a terrace, included. €55

★ **Imaret** Poulídhou 6 ☎ 2510 620 151, 🌐 imaret.gr. This expertly refurbished Ottoman medrese offers rooms

and suites that have been faultlessly fashioned, while keeping the original building intact. Services include a traditional hammam with massage, a restaurant serving Ottoman dishes and a womb-like indoor pool. €300

**Irini** ☎ 2510 229 785. On the shore 3km east of the port and served by city bus #2, this is the nearest campsite to town, with reasonable facilities. March–Oct.

**Nefeli** Erythroú Stavroú 50 ☎ 2510 227 441, 🌐 nefeli .com.gr. This nondescript modern hotel nonetheless has the best-value en-suite rooms in town and the roof garden is pleasant. €50

## EATING

Eating out in Kavála offers a good deal of variety, although most places are on the waterfront. The most fruitful area for exploration is the Panayía district, with its row of moderately priced tavernas and ouzerís.

★ **O Kanadhos** Poulídhou 27 ☎ 2510 835 172. Grilled meat for around €6 is the speciality at this friendly and exceptionally cheap place run by returnees from Toronto – hence the name and the English-speaking management. Daily 11am–1am.

**Orea Mytilini Zafira** Karaolí Dhimitríou 36 ☎ 2510 224 749. The most reliable of the waterfront eateries, most items on the menu for under €10, as long as you avoid the top-quality fish. Daily 11am–2am.

**Tembelhanio** Poulídhou 33b ☎ 2510 232 502. Cosy ouzerí serving a tasty range of mezédhes, involving both meat and seafood, to a soundtrack of eclectic Greek and Middle Eastern sounds. Daily noon–2am; Sun closes 6pm.

**To Araliki** Poulídhou 33 ☎ 697 23 39 033. Just about all the main dishes are meaty ones from the grill and cost under €10. There is also a fair range of salads and dips, plus fine Limniot wine. Daily 10am–late.

## DRINKING AND NIGHTLIFE

As a student town, Kavála has plenty of lively bars and night spots, especially around pedestrianized Ayíou Nikoláou, behind the eponymous church. A string of trendy café-bars also lurks on pedestrianized Palamá, parallel to Venizélou street.

**Café Briki** Poulídhou 76 ☎ 694 43 33 220. This popular café-bar is newly converted from a large stone mansion beside the citadel and provides a chic venue for admiring the splendid bay view over a coffee or cocktail. Daily 10am–late.

★ **Mao** Ayíou Nikoláou 10–12 ☎ 2510 831 300. This lively hangout draws the leftist student crowd and other mavericks with its murals of the chairman and cutting-edge recorded and occasional live sounds. Daily noon–late.

## Keramotí

**KERAMOTÍ**, 46km southeast of Kavála, offers a more frequent, shorter and marginally cheaper ferry crossing to Thássos (8–12 daily; 40min), especially between September and April. Keramotí is a small, rather drab village, 9km beyond the Kavála airport turn-off, with a decent enough beach backed by pines, a few rooms and a half-dozen hotels which you shouldn't have to patronize.

# Thrace

The ethnically diverse Greek province of **THRACE** (Thráki) was once part of a much larger region now split between the modern states of Greece, Turkey and Bulgaria. Heading across the Néstos River, the border with Macedonia, the change in population is obvious: Turkish settlements with their tiled, whitewashed houses and pencil-thin minarets contrast sharply with modern Greek villages built for the refugees of the 1920s (see box below). The same features are combined in the region's biggest urban centre, the attractive market town of **Xánthi**. Of the mountain villages north of Xánthi, **Stavroúpoli** stands out as the most worth visiting, while to the south and east a trio of **archeological sites** is to be found along the coast near **Komotiní**. Beyond the service town of **Alexandhroúpoli** lies the Évros River, which forms the heavily guarded land border with Turkey.

## Xánthi

**XÁNTHI** is the most interesting point to break a journey in Thrace. There is a busy market area, good food and, up the hill to the north of the **Kendrikí Platía**, the main café-lined square, a very attractive old Ottoman quarter. The town is also home to the University of Thrace, which lends a lively air to the place, particularly in the

---

### 1923 AND ALL THAT

Separated from the Turkish territory of eastern Thrace by the Évros River and its delta, western Thrace is the Greek state's most recent acquisition, under effective Greek control only since 1920. While Muslims throughout the rest of the country were evacuated by force under the **Treaty of Lausanne in 1923** (see p.778), the Muslims of western Thrace were exempted and continue to live in the region in return for a continued Greek presence in and around Constantinople (Istanbul).

Nowadays, out of a total population of 360,000, there are officially around 120,000 **Muslims**, about half of them Turkish-speakers, while the rest are **Pomaks** and Roma. Although there are dozens of functioning mosques, some Turkish-language newspapers and a Turkish-language radio station in Komotiní, only graduates from a special Academy in Thessaloníki have been allowed to teach in the Turkish-language schools here – thus isolating Thracian Turks from mainstream Turkish culture. Local Turks and Pomaks claim that they are the victims of discrimination, but despite violence in the past, relationships have improved with each decade and as an outsider you will probably not notice the tensions. In mixed villages Muslims and Greeks appear to coexist quite amicably and this harmony reaches its zenith in Xánthi. All Thracians, both Muslim and Orthodox, have a deserved reputation for hospitality.

area between the bazaar and the campus, where bars, cinemas and bistros are busy in term time.

The main south–north thoroughfare is 28-Oktovríou, lined with fast-food outlets and sundry shops. One end is marked by the Kendrikí Platía, recognizable by its distinguished clocktower. Try, if you can, to visit on Saturday, the day of Xánthi's **street fair** – a huge affair, attended equally by Greeks, Pomaks and ethnic Turks, held in an open space near the fire station on the eastern side of the town.

## The old town

The narrow cobbled streets of the **old town** are home to a number of very fine mansions – some restored, some derelict – with colourful exteriors, bay windows and wrought-iron balconies; most date from the mid-nineteenth century when Xánthi's tobacco merchants made their fortunes.

Further up, the roads become increasingly narrow and steep, and the Turkish presence (about fifteen percent of the total urban population) is more noticeable: most of the women have their heads covered, and the more religious ones wear full-length cloaks. Churches and mosques hide behind whitewashed houses with tiled roofs and orange-brown tobacco leaves are strung along drying frames. Numerous houses, no matter how modest, sport a dish for tuning in to Turkish satellite television.

### The folk museum

Odhós Antíka 7 • Tues–Sun 9am–2.30pm • €2

Two adjacent mansions at the bottom of the hill up into the right-bank quarter of the old town, originally built for two tobacco magnate brothers, have been turned into an excellent **folk museum**. Worth seeing for the imposing exterior alone, some years ago the interior was lovingly restored with painted wooden panels, decorated plaster and floral designs on the walls and ceilings. The interesting displays include Thracian clothes and jewellery, numerous household objects and historical displays on the tobacco industry and society in general; entry includes an enthusiastic guided tour if requested.

## ARRIVAL AND DEPARTURE

**By bus** The KTEL station (📞 25410 22684, 🌐 ktelxanthis .gr) is at Dhimokrítou 6, about 300m south of the main square. If heading to Alexandhroúpoli it is better to travel by train, as you will have to change bus in Komotiní.
Destinations Alexandhroúpoli (hourly; 2hr); Kavála (half-hourly; 1hr); Komotiní (every 45min–1hr; 1hr); Thessaloníki (6–7 daily; 3hr 30min).

**By train** The train station lies just off the Kavála road, 2km south of the centre.
Destinations Alexandhroúpoli (2 daily; 2hr); Thessaloník (2 daily; 4hr).

**By car** Xánthi's pay-and-display parking scheme is pretty comprehensive, with fees payable in the centre Mon–Sat 8.30am–8.30pm.

## ACCOMMODATION

Town-centre hotel choices are limited and rather overpriced, and disappointingly there's no official accommodation in the atmospheric old town.

**Elisso** Vasilíssis Sofías 9 📞 25410 84400, 🌐 hotelelisso .gr. Conveniently placed for the university, the town's newest and smartest hotel contains slick, well-furnished rooms with state-of-the-art facilities. Breakfast included. **€65**

★ **Orfeas** Mihaïl Karaolí 40 📞 25410 20121,

🌐 orfeashotel.gr. A short stroll south of Kendrikí Platía, the spacious, bright, en-suite rooms here constitute the best value in town. The atmosphere is also warmer than the average business hotel. Breakfast included. **€55**

## EATING

★ **Erkolos** Bahtzetzí 18A, off Mihaïl Karaolí 📞 25410 67735. Here you can wash down inexpensive dishes, such as tenderly fried liver for €6 and copious dips, with lashings

of tsípouro, often to the tune of traditional music. Daily 8pm–late.

**Erodhios** Ayíou Athanasíou 2 📞 25410 66379. Quality

taverna two blocks north of the clocktower, with a delightful summer garden enclosed by old town walls. Excellent main courses include lamb *exohikó* for €8–10. Daily 8pm–2am.

**Ta Fanarakia** Yeoryíou Stavroú 18 ☏ 25410 73606. Good all-round taverna just north of Kendrikí Platía where you can tuck into meat or fish on its pavement seating. Daily 11am–2am.

## DRINKING AND NIGHTLIFE

Xánthi's **nightlife** is focused on Vasilíssis Sofías, which forks off Paleológou at the little park sporting a bust of war hero Antíkas, and around the Kendrikí Platía itself. There's a new multiplex **cinema** in the Cosmos Centre on Mihaïl Karaolí, 200m down from the square.

**Kyverneio** Vassilíssis Sofías 4 ☏ 25410 77577. Boasting a huge, rambling terrace and enormous interior, this bar is the place to be for Xánthi's trendy crowd. Occasional DJ sets. Daily 11am–late.

# North of Xánthi

Much of the countryside north of Xánthi, towards the Bulgarian border, is a military controlled area, dotted with signs denoting the fact. If you venture up into the western Rodhópi range here, the main reward is some magnificent scenery around **Stavroúpoli**. There's not much arable land amid the wild, forested hills, and what there is – down in the river valleys – is devoted entirely to tobacco, hand-tilled by the **Pomaks**, who tend to keep themselves to themselves. Owing to the modest increase in material prosperity since the 1980s, the Pomak villages have mostly lost their traditional architecture to concrete multistorey apartments, although the mosque at rambling **Smínthi**, 14km due north of Xánthi, is still blessed with a tall, graceful minaret. **Oréo**, 6km up a side road northwest of Smínthi, is dramatically set on a steep hillside with cloud-covered peaks behind and terraces falling away to the riverbed.

## Stavroúpoli

Set among some of the region's most inviting scenery – deep gorges, fir-draped crags and high waterfalls, more like the French Jura than a typically Greek landscape – neat little **STAVROÚPOLI**, 27km northwest of Xánthi, is doing its very best to attract tourists, so far mainly Greeks. Having suffered a major population drain during the decades of mass emigration, the village, with its immaculate cobbled streets, shady central platía, complete with traditional café, and well-restored Thracian-style houses, is showing sure signs of a revival. Some 30km northwest of Xánthi along the scenic Dhráma road, it is conveniently placed for visiting the most spectacular stretch of the Néstos River, whose meanders and rapids lend themselves to safe rafting and canoeing. The town has a delightful little **Folklore Museum** (ask around for the curator; no fixed opening hours), signposted from the town centre, a proudly displayed collection in a restored house full of local memorabilia donated by residents – everything from embroidered bodices to an ancient record player.

### ARRIVAL AND ACTIVITIES                                   STAVROÚPOLI

**By bus** From Xánthi (Mon–Sat 6, Sun 4; 35min).

**Activities** The best source of information about kayaking, mountain bikes and horseriding in the region is the *Oinos* taverna (see p.318).

### ACCOMMODATION

**Nemesis** 2km south of Stavroúpoli ☏ 25420 21005, ⊛ hotelnemesis.gr. Oddly resembling a medieval castle, this hotel has simple but comfortable rooms and a swimming pool. Breakfast included. **€60**

★ **Xenios Zeus** Just off the main square ☏ &☏ 25420 22444. An old Thracian house with traditional decor. A roaring fireplace in the lounge keeps guests warm during winter. Breakfast included. **€45**

4

### EATING AND DRINKING

★ **Oinos** Near the main square ☏ 25420 22115. Excellent taverna which serves up delicious game – try the quail or hare – and vegetable dishes, washed down with aromatic barrelled wine or fiery *tsípouro*. Daily 11am–midnight.

## South of Xánthi

South of Xánthi, the coastal plain, bright with fields of cotton, tobacco and cereals, stretches to the sea. Heading towards modern **Ávdhira**, 31km away, you'll pass through **Yenisséa**, an unspectacular farming village with one of the oldest **mosques** in Thrace, dating from the sixteenth century. Now derelict, it's a low whitewashed building with a tiled roof, crumbled wooden portico and truncated minaret.

### Ancient Abdera

Daily: June–Sept 8am–7.30pm, Oct–May 8.30am–3pm • Free • ☏ 25310 21517 • 2–5 daily buses serve the village of Ávdhira, 3km west of the site, and, in summer, pass it en route to the beach of Paralía Avdhíron

**Ancient Abdera** was founded in the seventh century BC by Clazomenians from Asia Minor. The walls of the ancient acropolis are visible on a low headland above the sea, and there are fragmentary traces of Roman baths, a theatre and an ancient acropolis. The remains are unspectacular, and the setting not particularly attractive, but the **archeological museum** (same hours as site; free), located in the village, puts it all into context with a beautifully presented exhibition, accompanied by extensive English texts. A rich collection of ceramics, coins, oil lamps, mosaics and jewellery is dominated by a moving section devoted to burial customs, including some spectacular reconstructions of graves dating from the seventh to fifth centuries BC.

## East of Xánthi

The fertile central plains of Thrace, with their large ethnic Turkish population, are one of the least visited areas of the country, but are not without some appeal. Though outwardly unattractive, the market town of **Komotiní** rewards a brief visit, with its two well-presented museums, one folk, the other archeological. The contents of the latter are complemented by the delightful ancient site of **Maroneia**, on the coast, and **Mesembria**, further east.

### Komotiní

Lying 48km east of Xánthi along the direct road skirting the Rodhópi foothills, **KOMOTINÍ** is larger and markedly more Turkish than Xánthi but lacks its charm. Unlike Xánthi, social mixing between the different ethnic groups – roughly at parity population-wise – is almost nonexistent, although Orthodox and Muslims live in the same neighbourhoods. Since the 1990s the town has become even more polyglot, with an influx of Greek, Armenian and Georgian Christians from the Caucasus.

The old **bazaar**, to the north of Platía Irínis, is a little bit of Istanbul, lodged between fine mosques and an elegant Ottoman-era **clocktower**. Alongside shady cafés, tiny shops sell everything from dried apricots to iron buckets; it's especially busy on Tuesdays when the villagers from the surrounding area come into town to sell their wares. Behind this old quarter, you can see the remains of Komotiní's **Byzantine walls**.

Greek influence has been in the ascendant since the waning years of the Ottoman empire, when rich Greeks funded schools in the city. Some of these educational foundations still survive: one, a handsome half-timbered building at Ayíou Yeoryíou 13, has become the **Museum of Folk Life and History** (Mon–Sat 10am–1pm; free), displaying examples of Thracian embroidery, traditional Thracian dress, silverware, copperware and a collection of religious seals, but avoiding any mention of the ethnic Turkish community. The **archeological museum** at Simeonídhi 4 (daily

9am–6pm; free; ☎ 25310 22411) is also worth a visit, giving a lucid overview of Thracian history, by means of plans and finds from local sites, from its beginnings up to the Byzantine era.

## ARRIVAL AND DEPARTURE KOMOTINÍ

**By train** The train station is over 1km to the southwest of the centre; there are 2 daily trains in each direction: Thessaloníki (5hr); Xánthi (1hr).

**By bus** The KTEL bus station (☎ 25310 22912) is some way to the south of central Platía Irínis, via Énou; there are hourly services to Alexandhroúpoli (1hr 15min), Thessaloníki (4hr 30min) and Xánthi (1hr).

## ACCOMMODATION

**Chris & Eve Mansion** 3km on Alexandhroúpoli road ☎ 25310 33560, ⍟ chris-eve.com. The best hotel in the area (not saying much), this place has spacious, well-equipped rooms, a swimming pool and a reasonable restaurant. **€80**

**Hellas** Dhimokrítou 31, 250m from main square ☎ 25310 22055, ⍟ hotelhellas.com.gr. A 1950s hotel, a short walk from the main square. Refurbished in 2008, it's still on the basic side but all rooms are now en suite with wi-fi. Can suffer from traffic noise. **€35**

## EATING AND DRINKING

**Giaxis** Kilkís 8, amid the narrow bazaar lanes ☎ 25310 32000. Traditional ouzerí with a wide range of tasty mezédhes from cheese dips to mussels *saganáki*, plus fine ouzo and *tsípouro*, of course. Daily noon–2am.

**Inopion** Platía Irínis 67 ☎ 25310 36082. Conventional, impeccably prepared dishes such as moussakás and lamb fricassé for €7.50, served with considerable style and washed down with good local wine. Daily noon–1am.

# Maróna

Not far off the E90 motorway, southeast of Komotiní, lie two archeological sites that make an excellent break in the journey to Alexandhroúpoli or a refreshingly rural alternative base for the area. Clearly indicated from the Sápes turn-off is **ancient Maroneia**, a set of ancient and Byzantine ruins scattered among seaside olive groves. It's just below the modern village of **MARÓNIA**, which has held onto a few surviving old Thracian mansions with balconies.

## Ancient Maroneia

To get to the ruins of ancient Maroneia, attractively situated at the foot of Mount Ísmaros, follow the signs to Maróna's harbour of **Áyios Harálambos**, taking care not to enter the air-force camp nearby. The founder of the city is reckoned to be Maron, the son of the god of wine, Dionysos, and the city became one of the most powerful in all of ancient Thrace. Mostly unexcavated, the remains can be explored at will but are badly signposted. Even so, you should be able to track down traces of a theatre, a sanctuary of Dionysos and various buildings including a house with a well-preserved mosaic floor. The land walls of the city are preserved to a height of 2m, together with a Roman tower above the harbour. Over time, the sea has done its own excavation, eroding the crumbling cliffs and revealing shards of pottery and ancient walls.

## ARRIVAL AND DEPARTURE MARÓNIA

**By bus** Maróna is served by 7 daily buses from Komotiní via the old road.

## ACCOMMODATION AND EATING

**Ly Lola** ☎ 25330 41484. Under the thick shade of plane trees in the village square, this wonderful traditional taverna serves up succulent grills for €6–8, some oven dishes and excellent barrelled wine. Daily noon–1am.

**Pension Petran** ☎ 25330 41564. Good year-round fallback when Roxani is closed, this old-fashioned place run by a friendly old non-English-speaking couple has simple rooms with distant sea views from the balconies. **€25**

★ **Roxani** ☎ 25330 21501, ⍟ roxani.com. Large complex on the edge of the village whose spacious rooms look out on fabulous views. Can arrange all manner of activities, from birdwatching and astronomy to sea-canoeing and archery. Breakfast included and other meals available. June–mid-Sept. **€65**

## Mesimvría

Daily 8am–7.30pm, winter closes 3pm • €2

**Ancient Mesembria**, or **Mesimvría** in modern Greek, is clearly signposted from the motorway and is reached via the nondescript village of Dhíkela. Thanks to its unspoilt seaside location, fruitful recent excavations and a well-thought-out display, it easily qualifies as the most appealing of the three ancient sites on the Thracian coastline.

# Alexandhroúpoli

Some 120km southeast of Xánthi, the modern city of **ALEXANDHROÚPOLI** (Dedeagaç in Turkish) was designed by Russian military architects during the Russo-Turkish war of 1878. The town only became Greek in 1920, when it was renamed after a visit from Greece's King Alexander. It does not, on first acquaintance, have much to recommend it: a border town and military garrison with Greek holiday-makers competing in summer for limited space in the few hotels and the campsite. There is, however, an excellent **museum** and a lively seafront promenade. The town also provides access to two excellent **birdwatching** sites, the nearby **Évros Delta** and further north the **Dhadhiá Forest Reserve**. No village nearby is complete without its stork's nest, dominating the landscape like a watchtower.

## Ethnological Museum of Thrace

14-Maïoú 63, around 10 blocks north of the ferry terminal • March–Sept Tues–Wed 9am–3pm, Thurs–Fri 9am–3pm & 6–9pm, Sat–Sun 10am–3pm; Oct–Feb Tues–Sat 9am–3pm, Sun 10am–3pm • €3 • ☎ 25510 36663, ⓦ emthrace.org

The excellent **Ethnological Museum of Thrace** is one of the best of its kind in the country and can easily fill an hour or so. Housed in a tastefully restored Neoclassical mansion, its eye-catching modern displays cover almost every aspect of traditional life in Thrace. For once every ethnic group is covered: Pomaks, Turks, Armenians, Jews and Roma as well as Greeks. Professionally produced videos, with commentaries in Greek only, complement the beautifully lit cabinets. A delightful café, serving local specialities, and a good museum shop complete the picture.

## The seafront

Alexandhroúpoli's **seafront** is dominated by the 1880 **lighthouse**, the town's symbol; it comes alive at dusk when the locals begin their evening promenade. In summer, café tables spill out onto the road and around the lighthouse; makeshift stalls on the pavements sell pumpkin seeds and grilled sweetcorn as well as pirate DVDs and the like. Looking south, you can usually see the dramatic silhouette of the island of Samothráki, over 40km off the coast.

### ARRIVAL AND DEPARTURE                     ALEXANDHROÚPOLI

**By plane** The airport is 4km west of town. There is no dedicated airport bus but the terminal is right off the main road where frequent buses from local villages stop en route to town.
Destinations Athens (3–4 daily; 1hr); Sitía, Crete (3 weekly; 1hr40min).

**By train** The train station is next to the port; there are 2 daily services to Thessaloníki (6hr), via Komotiní (1hr) and Xánthi (2hr).

**By bus** The KTEL station is at Venizélou 36 (☎ 25510 26479), several blocks inland from the port.

Destinations Dhadhiá (2 daily; 1hr); Dhidhymótiho (every 30min–1hr; 1hr 30min); Komotiní (hourly; 1hr 15min); Thessaloníki (6 daily; 5hr).

**By ferry** Alexandhroúpoli is now the only access port for ferries to Samothráki (see p.656; 1–3 daily; 2hr 30min).

**By car** Drivers will find it prudent to enter town from the west along coastal Megálou Alexándhrou and park in the huge non-fee area beside the port, since pedestrianization one-way systems and fee parking effectively block movement further inland.

## ACCOMMODATION

Booking ahead is wise in high summer even though there are a number of choices, ranging from no-frills hotels to a string of luxurious resort-cum-conference hotels, well west of town. There is also a large municipal campsite on the main road at the western edge of town (☎ 25510 28735).

**Erika** K Dhimitríou 110, just east of the port entrance ☎ 25510 34115, ⓦ hotel-erika.gr. Smart seafront hotel, recently upgraded, with comfortable rooms and a decent breakfast included. **€60**

**Okeanis** K Paleológou 20–22, six blocks northwest of the port ☎ 25510 28830. Renovated hotel, stylishly furnished in dark wood and fabrics, with comfortable, average-sized rooms. **€55**

★ **Thraki Palace** Paleológou 20, 5km west of town ☎ 25510 89100, ⓦ thrakipalace.gr. This sleek, modern five-star establishment has a sea-view swimming pool, a swish restaurant, piano bar, fitness centre and spacious, contemporary rooms, though the surroundings lack any character. Breakfast included. **€120**

**Vergina** K Dhimitríou 74, opposite train station ☎ 25510 27583, ☎ 25510 27580. Simple, plainly decorated rooms, some with sea-view balconies. Among the best-value options in town. **€35**

## EATING AND DRINKING

The standard of restaurants in town is pretty good, especially in the streets just behind the seafront and near the train station. The trendiest bars and cafés are, unsurprisingly, strung along the seafront.

★ **Kyra Dimitra** Kounouriotou 2 ☎ 25510 34434. A wide range of vegetable dishes accompanies fried fish for around €7–8 in this welcoming local favourite near the train station. Daily noon–1am.

**Naftikos Omilos** Next to the ferry terminal ☎ 25510 28577. This café-patisserie draws people from all over the area for a coffee or cake with a great view of the lapping waves and seafront promenade. Daily 9am–late.

**Nea Klimataria** Platía Polytekhníou 18 ☎ 25510 26288. Taverna offering an appealing variety of dishes from soups and starters like *saganáki* to oven-baked and grilled meat and fish. It's one block behind the seafront west of the port. Daily 11am–midnight.

**O Glaros** K Dhimitríou 126, opposite port entrance ☎ 25510 32899. The one surviving seafront *kafenío*-cum-ouzerí is a great spot to wait for a ferry with a glass of ouzo and a few cheap *mezédhes*, mostly under €5. Daily 10am–midnight.

# The Évros Delta

The **Évros Delta** is one of Europe's most important wetland areas for birds – and one of Greece's most sensitive military areas. Among more than 250 different bird species are sea eagles, pygmy cormorants and the lesser white-fronted goose. The delta is crisscrossed with tracks along the dykes used by farmers taking advantage of the plentiful water supply for growing sweet corn and cotton. The south is the most inspiring part, well away from the army installations to the north; as you go further into the wetlands, the landscape becomes utterly desolate, with decrepit clusters of fishing huts among the sandbars and inlets. At the mouth of the delta sprawls a huge saltwater lake called **Límni Dhrakónda**. Obviously what you see depends on the time of year, but even if birdlife is a bit thin on the ground, the atmosphere of the place is worth experiencing.

## ARRIVAL AND DEPARTURE                   ÉVROS DELTA

**By car** Leave Alexandhroúpoli on the main road towards Turkey and Bulgaria; some 10km after the airport, you'll reach the turn-off to Loutra Traianopolis, the site of an ancient Roman spa and its modern continuation Loutrós.

The delta is best approached by turning right off the main road, opposite the side road to the hotels; the lane is paved only as far as the level crossing but remains good thereafter.

## ACCOMMODATION

**Athina** Loutrós village ☎ 25510 61208. This relatively basic medium-sized hotel offers pleasant rooms and makes a decent base for exploring the delta. Breakfast included. **€40**

# Dhadhiá Forest Reserve

A little under 40km northeast of Alexandhroúpoli, the **Dhadhiá Forest Reserve** stretches over 352 square kilometres of protected oak and pine forest covering a succession of volcanic ridges in the Évros Valley. The diversity of landscape and vegetation and the proximity of important migration routes make for an extremely diverse flora and fauna, but raptors are the star attraction, and main impetus for this WWF-backed project. In all, 36 of Europe's 38 species of diurnal birds of prey, including eagles, falcons, hawks and buzzards, can be sighted at least part of the year. The region is also one of two remaining European homes of the majestic **black vulture**, the other being the Extremadura region of Spain.

## The reserve complex

March–May & Sept–Nov daily 9am–7pm; June–Aug daily 8.30am–8.30pm; Dec–Feb Mon–Thurs 10am–4pm, Fri–Sun 9am–6pm

After a drive of 7km through the rolling, forested hills, you reach the reserve complex, with its information centre and exhibition about the region's wildlife. All cars – except for a tour van which makes sorties several times daily (€3) – are banned from core areas totalling 72 square kilometres, and foot access is restricted to two marked trails: a two-hour route up to the reserve's highest point, 520m **Gíbrena** with its ruined Byzantine castle, and another ninety-minute loop-route to an observation hide overlooking **Mavrórema** canyon from where griffon vultures and other raptors make up the bulk of sightings.

## ARRIVAL AND DEPARTURE                                    DHADHIÁ FOREST RESERVE

**By car** The reserve is reached by a clearly marked road off to the left, 1km after passing the second right-hand turn-

off to Likófi (Likófos).

## ACCOMMODATION AND EATING

It's a good idea to stay the night, as the best raptor viewing is in the early morning or evening in summer (but virtually all day Oct–March).

★ **Ecotourism Lodge** Dhadhiá village ☏ 25540 32263, ⓦ ecoclub.com/dadia. The cosy, suitably rustic en-suite rooms have been given bird names instead of numbers at this lodge run by the ecotourism centre, which also has a café and restaurant. **€43**

**Pelargos** Dhadhiá village square ☏ 25540 32481 Simple *psistariá* that churns out cheap and tasty grills plus a few salad and vegetable items for hungry twitchers. Daily 11am–11pm.

# Souflí

The nearest town to Dhadhiá, 7km north of the side turning and set among lush mulberry groves, is **SOUFLÍ**, renowned for a now all-but-vanished silk industry. The town's history as Greece's silk centre in Byzantine and Ottoman times, and a fascinating explanation of the whole silk-making process, are documented (with English text) in the **Folk and Silk Museum** (Wed–Mon: Easter to mid-Oct 10am–2pm & 5–7pm; rest of year 10am–4pm; €1.50), a little way uphill and west of the main through road. It's lodged in a fine old yellow mansion, one of a number of surviving vernacular houses, including semi-ruined *bitziklíkia*, or *koukoulóspita* in Greek (cocoon-houses), which lend Souflí some distinction.

## ACCOMMODATION AND EATING                                                SOUFLÍ

**Egnatia** Egnatía 225 ☏ 25540 24124. This small, simple hotel offers rudimentary comforts and gets some noise from the main road outside but is still the best-value option in town. **€35**

**Lagotrofio** Yiannoúli village, 4km from Souflí ☏ 25540

22001. Excellent taverna serving wild boar and other game for under €10, plus *mayireftá* standards, at a wonderfully shady hilltop location with panoramic views. Daily: June–Sept noon–midnight, Oct–May 8pm–midnight.

# Dhidhymótiho

**DHIDHYMÓTIHO**, 30km northeast of Souflí, is the last place on the trunk route into Turkey of any interest. The old part of town is still partially enclosed by the remains of double Byzantine fortifications, and some old houses and churches survive, but the area has a feeling of decay despite continuing efforts at restoration. Below the fortified hill, on the central platía, stands the most important surviving monument, a fourteenth-century **mosque**, the oldest and second largest in the Balkans. A great square box of a building with a pyramidal metal roof, its design harks back to Seljuk and other pre-Ottoman prototypes in central Anatolia, and you'll see nothing else like it between here and Divriui or Erzurum in Turkey. Unfortunately, the interior is closed indefinitely for restoration, though you can still admire the ornate west portal.

## ACCOMMODATION AND EATING                    DHIDHYMÓTIHO

**Plotini** 1km south of town ☎ 25530 23400, ☎ 25530 22251. A rather gaudy labyrinthine building set back from the main road. Rooms have slightly anachronistic decor but are generously sized. **€40**

**Zythestiatorio Kypselaki**. This small restaurant In the central market hall, just above the mosque, is the best choice in town for some home-cooked favourites like baked beef and potatoes or fried aubergines. Daily 11am–midnight.

# The Argo-Saronic Islands

**328** Salamína

**329** Égina

**335** Angístri

**338** Póros

**341** Ýdhra

**347** Spétses

ÝDHRA TOWN

**5**

# The Argo-Saronic Islands

The rocky, partly volcanic Argo-Saronic islands, most of them barely an olive's throw from the mainland, differ to a surprising extent not just from the land they face but also from one another. The northernmost island of the Argo-Saronic group, Salamína, is effectively a suburb of Pireás, with its narrow strait, barely a kilometre across, crossed by a constant stream of ferries. There's little to attract you on the other side, however, and the island is covered only briefly here. Égina, important in antiquity and more or less continually inhabited since then, is infinitely preferable: the most fertile of the group, it is famous for its pistachio nuts and home to one of the finest ancient temples in Greece. Tiny Angístri is often treated as little more than an adjunct of Égina, but it's a lovely place in its own right, ideal for a few days' complete relaxation. The three southerly islands – green Póros, tiny, car-free Ýdhra and upmarket Spétses – are comparatively infertile, and rely on water piped or transported in rusting freighters from the mainland.

Given their proximity to Athens and their beauty, the Argo-Saronics are hugely popular destinations, with Égina (Aegina) almost becoming a city suburb at weekends. Póros, Ýdhra (Hydra) and Spétses are similar in the summer, though their visitors include a higher proportion of foreign tourists. More than any other group, these islands are best out of season and midweek, when visitors (and prices) fall dramatically and the port towns return to a quieter, more provincial pace. You'll also notice a significant difference between Ýdhra and Spétses, the furthest of the islands, and those closer to Athens – because of the distance, and because they're accessible only by hydrofoil and catamaran rather than the cheaper conventional ferries, they're markedly more expensive and exclusive, with significant expat populations. The islands were not extensively settled until medieval times, when refugees from the mainland established themselves here, adopting seagoing commerce (and piracy) as livelihoods. Today, foreigners and Athenians have replaced locals in the depopulated harbour towns; windsurfers, water-taxis and yachts are faint echoes of the massed warships, schooners and *kaïkia* once at anchor.

## GETTING THERE

**By ferry** Virtually all services from Pireás to the Argo-Saronic islands leave from between gates E8 and E9; there are ticket booths here. For all of these islands, hydrofoil or catamaran services are faster and more frequent than ferries, though they cost around twice as much. Friday evening and Saturday morning sailings, as well as the returns on Sunday night, can be very busy; for these, or if you hope to bring a vehicle for the weekend on a regular ferry, reserve your trip well in advance.

## THE ARGO-SARONIC

**Tickets and agencies** Contact details for Pireás are as follows (local island agencies are given in the island accounts). Aegean Flying Dolphins (to Égina and Angístri) ☎ 210 41. 1654, ⓦ aegeanflyingdolphins.gr; Alexandros (fast ferry to Souvála and Ayía Marína, Égina) ☎ 210 482 1002 ⓦ alexcruises.com; Ayios Nektarios Eginas (ferry to Égina ☎ 210 422 5625, ⓦ anes.gr; Hellenic Seaways (ferries hydrofoils and Flying Cat to all points) ☎ 210 419 9000, ⓦ hsw .gr; Nova (ferry to Égina) ☎ 210 412 6181, ⓦ novaferries.gr.

The Battle of Salamis p.329
Excursions to the Peloponnese p.340
Ýdhra's festivals p.345
Ýdhra's inland walks p.346
Sotírios Anáryiros p.348
Hiking across Spétses p.351

PÓROS TOWN

# Highlights

**❶ Temple of Aphaea, Égina** The best-preserved ancient temple on any island, in an evocative setting on a wooded hill with magnificent views towards the mainland and Athens. **See p.333**

**❷ Angístri Island** Little known to outsiders, this dot of land is less than an hour from Athens by hydrofoil, yet preserves the feel of an unspoilt hideaway. **See p.335**

**❸ Póros Town** Climb to the clocktower of this small island's capital to look down over the Argo-Saronic Gulf and the Peloponnese; the shipping in the narrow strait between here and

the mainland offers an ever-changing spectacle. **See p.339**

**❹ Ýdhra Town** Ydhra's perfect, horseshoe-shaped harbour, surrounded by grand eighteenth-century mansions and genuinely traffic-free streets, is one of the most perfect in all of Greece. **See p.343**

**❺ Zoyeriá Beach, Spétses** Some of the most alluring beaches in the Argo-Saronics can be found along Spétses' pine-speckled coastline; at hard-to-reach Zoyeriá is a wonderful, isolated taverna, most of whose customers arrive by boat. **See p.350**

**HIGHLIGHTS ARE MARKED ON THE MAP ON P.328**

5

# Salamína

**SALAMÍNA** is the quickest possible island-hop from Pireás, and indeed much of its population commutes to the city to work. The island itself, however, is highly developed, has few tourist facilities, and is close enough to the Athenian dockyards to make swimming unappealing. The island's port is at **Paloúkia**, facing the mainland, just a short hop across a narrow, built-up isthmus to **Salamína Town** on the west coast. Five kilometres or so beyond Salamína Town, **Eándio** has the island's cleanest and most attractive beaches. A similar distance from Salamína Town to the north, the **monastery of Faneroméni** (daily 8.30am–12.30pm & 4pm–sunset) is a working nunnery with impressive frescoes, beautifully sited amid pine woods overlooking the mainland.

THE AGRO-SARONIC

**HIGHLIGHTS**
1. Temple of Aphaea
2. Angístri
3. Póros Town
4. Ýdhra Town
5. Zoyeriá Beach, Spétses

## THE BATTLE OF SALAMIS

Perhaps the main reason for heading to Salamína is for the boat trip itself, through an extraordinary industrial seascape of docks and shipworks. The waters you cross were the site of one of the most significant **sea battles** of ancient times; some would say of all time, given that this was a decisive blow in preventing a Persian invasion and allowing the development of Classical Athens, and with it modern Western culture.

In 480 BC, the Greeks were in full retreat from the vast Persian army under Xerxes, following the defeat of the Spartans at Thermopylae. Many Greek cities, including Athens, had been sacked and burned by the invaders – indeed smoke from the ruins on the Acropolis probably formed a backdrop to the **Battle of Salamis**. The Greeks had roughly 370 triremes supplied by around twenty cities, the bulk from Athens, Corinth and Aegina; the Persian fleet was twice the size, with heavier ships, but even more diverse, with many from subject nations whose loyalty was questionable.

Through false information and strategic retreats, the Greeks managed first to tire many of the Persian crews – who rowed all night to cut off a non-existent escape attempt – and then to lure them into the narrow strait off Salamína. Crowded in and unable to manoeuvre, and with the wind in the wrong direction, the Persians found themselves at the mercy of the more nimble Greek triremes, and the battle eventually became a rout. Some two hundred Persian ships were sunk, against forty-odd on the Greek side, and few of their heavily armoured crews or marines survived.

### ARRIVAL AND DEPARTURE
SALAMÍNA

**By boat** There are half-hourly small passenger boats from Pireás throughout the day (Gate E8; 45min), and a constant stream of small boats and roll-on, roll-off car ferries, day and night, from Pérama, on the mainland directly opposite (5min). Pérama is easily reached by bus: #843 from Pireás, G18 or B18 from Omónia in central Athens. There are also ferries every 20min or so between Faneroméni and Néa Péramos (aka Megára) on the mainland.

### GETTING AROUND

**By bus** Salamína has a pretty impressive bus system, with departures from the ferry dock in Paloúkia to Salamína Town every fifteen minutes. Buses also run hourly to numerous other destinations on the island, including Eándio and Faneroméni.

# Égina

A substantial and attractive island with a proud history, less than an hour from Pireás, **ÉGINA (Aegina)** is not surprisingly a popular weekend escape from Athens. Despite the holiday homes, though, it retains a laidback, island atmosphere, especially if you visit midweek or out of season. Famous for its **pistachio orchards** – the nuts are hawked from stalls all around the harbour – the island can also boast substantial ancient remains, the finest of which is the beautiful fifth-century BC **Temple of Aphaea**, commanding superb views towards Athens from high above the northeast coast.

### ARRIVAL AND DEPARTURE
ÉGINA

**By ferry and hydrofoils** Those to Égina Town dock at parallel quays, pretty much at the heart of things; the *Angístri Express* (☎ 694 71 18863) can be found among the pleasure and fishing boats a short distance to the south. The schedule summaries below are for summer weekday services; sailings are more frequent and significantly busier at weekends (Fri–Sun), less regular from mid-Sept to June. Ayía Marína and Souvála are linked to Pireás once or twice daily, with an extra early morning run to Souvála only in high season.

**Tickets and agencies** Immediately in front of the docks in Égina Town is a row of cabins selling tickets for Aegean Flying Dolphins (to Pireás and Angístri ☎ 22970 25800, ⊚ aegeanflyingdolphins.gr), Ayios Nektarios Eginas (ferry to Pireás ☎ 22970 25625, ⊚ anes.gr), Hellenic Seaways (ferries, hydrofoils and Flying Cat to Pireás and Angístri, ferry to Póros ☎ 22970 24456, ⊚ hsw.gr) and Nova (ferry to Pireás ☎ 22970 24200, ⊚ novaferries.gr). Alexandros Ferries (to Pireás from Ayía Marína ☎ 22970 52210 and Souvála ☎ 22970 32234, ⊚ alexcruises.gr) has quayside booths open an hour or so before departure.

ÉGINA

Destinations Angístri (6 hydrofoils and 1 or 2 ferries daily, plus Angístri Express 2–3 daily except Sun; 15min); Pireás (from Égina Town 12 hydrofoils and 15 ferries daily, 40min–1hr 30min; from Ayía Marína 1–2 ferries daily, 1hr 15min; from Souvála 1–3 daily, 40 min); Póros (via Méthana 2–3 ferries daily; 1hr 15min).

## INFORMATION

**Services** There are numerous banks around Égina Town harbour, many with ATMs. The post office is at the rear of Platía Ethneyersías, where the buses stop. Most of the harbourfront cafés have wi-fi; Global Internet Café at Fanerómenis 7, just off the southern end of the waterfront, has plenty of terminals and fast connections.
**Newspapers** Foreign-language papers and a few books from Kendrou Typou, on Eákou at the corner of Spýrou Ródhi.

**Useful website** There's no tourist office, but ⓦ aeginagreece.com is a useful resource.
**Travel agent** Aegina Island Holidays (☎ 22970 26430, ⓦ aeginaislandgreece.com), on the Égina Town waterfront near the church of Panayítsa, offers excursions to the mainland and islands, including to the Epidaurus festival, as well as help with accommodation should you need it.

## GETTING AROUND

**By bus** The bus station is on Platía Ethneyersías, immediately north of the dock; buy your tickets at the little booth, in summer located on the waterfront, the rest of the year in the square by the bus stop. At least five buses a day (mostly in the morning) head to Souvála and to Ayía Marína, at least six along the coast to Pérdhika; on arrival they turn round and head straight back. All buses towards Ayía Marína stop at Áyios Nektários and most at the Temple of Aphaea; on the return journey, they all stop at both.
**By car and motorcycle** Several places on and behind Égina Town's main waterfront rent scooters, cars,

motorbikes and mountain bikes – Égina is large and hilly enough to make a motor worthwhile for anything other than a pedal to the local beaches: Trust (☎ 22970 27010), one of the first you come to behind the harbour, has the best prices, though some of their mopeds are fairly battered. There are also hire places in Ayía Marína.
**By taxi** The taxi rank is at the base of the ferry jetty, opposite the ticket cabins; taxis meet ferry arrivals in Ayía Marína and Souvála too.

# Brief history

Inhabited from the earliest times, ancient **Aegina** was a significant regional power as early as the Bronze Age. It traded to the limits of the known world, maintained a sophisticated silver coinage system (the first in Greece) and fostered prominent athletes and craftsmen. The Aeginian fleet played a major role in the Battle of Salamis (see p.329). After this, however, the islanders made the political mistake of siding with the Spartans, giving Athens a pretext to act on long-standing jealousy; her fleets defeated those of the islanders in two separate sea battles and, after the second, the population was expelled and replaced by more tractable colonists.

Subsequent history was less distinguished, with a familiar pattern of occupation – by Romans, Franks, Venetians, Catalans and Ottomans – before the War of Independence brought a brief period of glory as seat of government for the fledgling Greek nation, from 1826 to 1828. For many decades afterwards Égina was a penal island, and you can still see the **enormous jail** undergoing restoration on the edge of town; the building was originally an **orphanage** for victims of the independence struggle, founded by first president Kapodhístrias in 1828.

# Égina Town

**ÉGINA TOWN**, the island's capital, makes an attractive base, with some grand old buildings around a large, busy harbour. The Neoclassical architecture is matched by a sophisticated ethos: by island standards this is a large town, with plenty of shopping and no shortage of tempting places to eat and drink. Life revolves around the **waterfront**, where ferries come and go, yachts moor, fishermen tend their nets and *kaïkia* tie up to sell produce from the mainland.

## The Markellos Tower

The restored **Pýrgos Markéllou**, or Markellos Tower, is an extraordinary miniature castle which was the seat of the first Greek government after independence. Despite appearances, it was built only around 1800 by members of the Friendly Society (see p.776) and the local politician Spýros Márkellos. You can't go inside except during the occasional special exhibition, but walking here, through the cramped inland streets, is enjoyable in itself.

## Folklore Museum

Spýrou Ródhi 16 • Wed & Thurs 8.30am–2.30pm, Fri 8.30am–2.30pm & 4.30–7.30pm, Sat 10am–1pm & 4.30–7.30pm, Sun 10am–1pm • Free

Égina's **Folklore Museum** is a lovely example of its type, housed in a nineteenth-century mansion. Its upper rooms are packed with fine old furniture, traditional costumes, and many of the trappings of island life a century ago, along with a small local historical archive. Downstairs are rooms devoted to fishing, with model boats and fishing gear, and to agricultural life, with a collection of the basics of village life.

## Ancient Aegina

Daily 8.30am–3pm, museum closed Mon • €3

The site of **Ancient Aegina** lies north of the centre on a promontory known as **Kolóna**, after the lone column that stands there. The extensive remains, centring on a Temple of Apollo at the highest point, are well signed, and some reconstruction makes it easier to make out the various layers of settlement from different eras. Near the entrance, a small but worthwhile **archeological museum** houses finds from the site, along with information on the island's ancient history. Highlights of the display include a room of Minoan-influenced Middle Bronze Age pottery, rescued from a nearby building site.

## The beaches

On the north edge of town, between the port and Kolóna, there's a tiny but popular **beach** with remarkably shallow water. This was the site of the ancient city's

**5**

harbour, of which various underwater remains are clearly visible. You can swim south of town, too, but there are more enticing spots further north – immediately beyond Kolóna there's an attractive bay with a small, sandy **beach**, while other small coves lie off the road heading further out of town in this direction. Just a couple have any facilities, with loungers and beach bars; **Kamares Paradise** is among the more attractive.

## ACCOMMODATION
ÉGINA TOWN

**Aeginitiko Archontiko** Thomaïdhou and Ayíou Nikólaou **☎** 22970 24968, **ⓦ** aeginitikoarchontiko.gr. Brick-red Neoclassical mansion opposite the Markellos Tower, lovingly restored with period furnishings and a conscious attempt to preserve traditional island culture. About as far from a bland business hotel as you can get – there's lots of lace, old pictures on the walls, creaking, springy beds and a wonderful breakfast (included) with home-made preserves, cakes and pastries. The suite has painted ceilings; other rooms can be pretty basic, though all have a/c, TV and fridge. **€70**

**Brown** Waterfront **☎** 22970 22271, **ⓦ** hotelbrown .gr. Rather dated 3-star hotel, housed in a former sponge factory dating from 1886, on the southern part of the harbour. Some rooms have great views of the harbour activity, though the garden bungalows are quieter; a galleried family suite sleeps four. Breakfast included. **€65**

**Elektra** Leonándrou Ladhá 25 **☎** 22970 26715, **ⓦ** aegina-electra.gr. Friendly, quiet establishment, directly inland from the ferry quay on the street with Piraeus Bank on the corner, whose compact but comfortable rooms come with small balconies and free wi-fi. **€55**

**Pavlou** Eyinítou 21 **☎** 22970 22795. Old-school rooms establishment set behind Panayítsa church, with very plain, stone-floored rooms not all of which are en suite; they do all have fans, a/c (extra charge), fridge and TV though. **€40**

**★ Plaza** Kazantzáki 4 **☎** 22970 25600, **ⓦ** plaza -aegina.gr. One of a series of small waterfront hotels close to the town beach. Rooms have been newly refurbished, with quality bathrooms and elegant dark-wood decor, plus double-glazing, a/c and TV. There are great sea views from the marginally more expensive rooms at the front, and little balconies from which to appreciate them. **€55**

## EATING AND DRINKING

There are plenty of good places to eat and drink in Égina, particularly at the south end of pedestrianized Panayióti Irióti behind the fish market, and at the far ends of the waterfront – fussy Athenian patronage keeps the standards fairly high. The cafés near the ferry jetty and in the centre of the waterfront tend to be less good value. Numerous bakeries are in the backstreets – Papayionis, by Trust motorbike hire up the first alley off the seafront, is excellent, while Melenio, close to the Markellos Tower, is an exceptional modern *zaharoplastío*, with fine ice cream and beautiful displays of cakes and sweets.

**★ Agora** (also known as Yeladhakis) Panayióti Irióti **☎** 22970 27308. The best of three rival seafood ouzerís behind the fish market (the others are very good too). Not the most attractive location, but serves wonderful, inexpensive (around €8 per fish plate), authentic Greek food: accordingly it's usually mobbed and you may have to wait for a table. Summer seating in the cobbled lane, winter up in the loft inside. Daily, evening only.

**Avli** Panayióti Irióti 17 **☎** 22970 26438. Big place in an alley behind the harbour, popular with expats and open all day serving coffee, breakfast (€4–8), lunch and dinner (mains €6–9; spaghetti and pizza as well as Greek dishes and pricier steaks), while in the early hours it transforms into a bar with Latin/jazz sounds. Daily 10am–late.

**Elia** Koumoundhoúrou 5 **☎** 22975 00205. Modern taverna in an alley that emerges close to the Markellos Tower with a Mediterranean menu including salads, pasta (carbonara

€7.50) and unusual meze (chicken satay €6.50) as well as traditional Greek dishes (daily special €8.50); live music many evenings. Wed–Sat lunch and dinner, Sun lunch only.

**Flisvos** Kazantzáki 8 **☎** 22970 26459. An excellent spot for grilled fresh fish and traditional dishes at fair prices (moussaka or *souvláki* €7.50, swordfish steak €12), towards the end of a line of similar establishments behind the town beach. Good-value lunchtime specials. Daily lunch & dinner.

**Posto Grillo** Panayióti Irióti **☎** 22970 28687. A modern kebab place behind the fish market with a wide variety of grills, from excellent *yíros píta* (€1.70) to chops and *souvláki*; takeaway or eat in. Daily 11am–midnight.

**Skotadis** Harbourfront **☎** 22970 24014. The best of a cluster of taverna-ouzerís just south of the market, popular with locals. A short menu, predominantly fish and meze at €6–7 a dish, but what it does it does well. Daily 10am–1am.

## NIGHTLIFE AND ENTERTAINMENT

Athenian visitors are largely responsible for a surprisingly ample choice of nightlife given a town of about nine thousand souls. As well as bars and clubs there are three summer open-air cinemas – Anesis on Eákou close to the Pýrgos Markéllou,

Olympia on Faneroménis opposite the football ground, and Akroyiali out beyond this on the Pérdhika road; indoor Titina, opposite the Pýrgos Markéllou, is open year-round.

**Ellinikon Seaside** Aktí Hatzí 10 ☎ 22976 00448 or 693 61 11 213. A big, enjoyable, somewhat touristy club on the southern fringe of town, near the Cine Akroyiali, with mainstream and Greek dance music. Nightly in summer from 10pm.

**En Aigini** Spýrou Ródhi 44 ☎ 22970 22483 or 694 85 33 060. Upstairs bar with live Greek music from around 11pm

every weekend; they also host big-name visiting artists – look out for posters, and book if you want to secure a table. Fri–Sat from around 9pm, plus special events.

**Maska** Mitropóleos 8 ☎ 22970 22280. Restored stone-walled, high-ceilinged building that makes a pleasant spot for a quiet, early drink – later there's often a DJ playing oldies and classic dance tracks. Daily from 9pm.

# Across the island

Two main routes lead east towards Ayía Marína and the Temple of Aphaea: you can head directly **inland** from Égina Town across the centre of the island or follow the **north coast** road via Souvála. Along this north coast there are plenty of scruffy beaches and clusters of second-home development, between which is a surprisingly industrial landscape, with boatyards and working ports. Souvála itself is something of an Athenian resort, with a couple of direct daily ferries to Pireás but little other reason to stop.

## Áyios Nektários

On the route inland you'll pass the modern convent of **Áyios Nektários**, whose vast church is said to be the largest in Greece. The convent was founded by Saint Nektarios, who died in 1920 and was canonized in 1961. His tomb lies in the chapel of the original monastery, Ayía Triádha. Miracles surrounded Nektarios from the moment of his death, when nurses put some of his clothing on an adjacent bed, occupied by a man who was paralyzed; the patient promptly leapt up, praising God.

## Paleohóra

Unrestricted • Free

On the hillside opposite Áyios Nektários is the ghost-town of **PALEOHÓRA**, the island capital through the Middle Ages. Established in early Christian times as a refuge against piracy, it thrived under the Venetians (1451–1540) but was destroyed by Barbarossa in 1537. The Turks took over and rebuilt the town, but it was again destroyed, this time by the Venetians, in 1654, and finally abandoned altogether in the early nineteenth century. The place now consists of some thirty stone chapels dotted across a rocky outcrop, an extraordinary sight from a distance. Little remains of the town itself – when the islanders left, they simply dismantled their houses and moved the masonry to newly founded Égina Town (see p.331). At the entrance a helpful map shows the churches and the paths that lead up the hill between them; many are semi-derelict or locked, but plenty are open too, and several preserve remains of frescoes. Despite their apparent abandonment, many have candles burning inside, and prayers left alongside the icons. If you climb right to the top you're rewarded with wonderful views in all directions – you can also appreciate the defensive qualities of the site, from which both coasts can be watched, yet which is almost invisible from the sea.

## The Temple of Aphaea

Summer daily 8am–7pm, winter Tues–Sun 8am–5pm; museum Tues–Sun 8am–2.15pm • €4

The Doric **Temple of Aphaea** stands on a pine-covered hill 12km east of Égina Town, with stunning views all around: Athens, Cape Soúnio, the Peloponnese and Ýdhra are all easily made out. Built between 500 and 480 BC, it slightly predates the Parthenon, and is one of the most complete and visually complex ancient buildings in Greece, its superimposed arrays of columns and lintels evocative of an Escher drawing. Aphaea was a Cretan nymph who, fleeing from the lust of King Minos, fell into the sea, was caught by some fishermen

**5**

and brought to ancient Aegina; her cult, virtually unknown anywhere else, was established on the island as early as 1300 BC. Two hundred years ago the temple's pediments were intact and essentially in perfect condition. However, like the Elgin marbles, they were "purchased" from the Turks – this time by Ludwig I of Bavaria – and they currently reside in Munich's Glyptothek museum. A small **museum** offers a great deal of information about the history and architecture of the temple. A well-signed path leads from the temple to Ayía Marína; an easy walk down, slightly tougher coming up.

## Ayía Marína and around

The island's major beach resort, **AYÍA MARÍNA**, lies steeply below the Temple of Aphaea on the east coast. There's a good, clean, sandy beach that shelves very gently, pedaloes to rent and plenty of places to eat, many of them catering to day-trippers – direct boats arrive from Pireás daily. The place has clearly seen better days, as the number of empty premises and the ugly, half-built hotel overshadowing the beach attest, but package tourism seems to be on the up, and it can be lively and enjoyable in a bucket-and-spade sort of way, with plenty of hotels and rooms, and a main street lined with shops, bars and pubs; the occasional summer beach party sees an overnight invasion of young Athenians.

### Pórtes

**PÓRTES**, 8km south of Ayía Marína, is a hamlet with a distinctly end-of-the-road feel, a partly sandy beach with decent snorkelling and a couple of good tavernas. From here, the road climbs steeply inland, beneath the island's highest peak, heading back towards Égina Town via the villages of **Anitséou** and **Pahiá Ráhi**. The latter, with fine views eastwards, has been almost entirely rebuilt in traditional style by foreign and Athenian owners.

**ACCOMMODATION AND EATING**                               **AYÍA MARÍNA AND AROUND**

#### AYÍA MARÍNA

**Argo Spa Hotel** ☎ 22970 32266, ⊛ argohotel.com. With a great position directly above the bay as you come into town, the *Argo* has a pool and small "spa" (sauna, hot tub) and often offers good, all-in deals; refurbished, modern rooms mostly have sea views. **€65**

**Barracuda Beach Bar** ☎ 694 55 33 693. With a precarious wooden terrace hanging over the beach, the *Barracuda* also offers service on the beach itself. Milkshakes, coffee and sandwiches by day; cocktails and a DJ at night. Daily 11am–3am.

**Hotel Liberty 2** ☎ 22970 32105, ⊛ hotelliberty2.gr. An ochre-coloured building overlooking the end of the beach; simple and old-fashioned, with marble floors, but

all rooms have sea views as well as a/c and TV. **€40**

**Neromilos** ☎ 22970 32198. Just above the tiny fishing harbour, Neromilos (the "Watermill") is a big, popular place with a terrace above the water serving inexpensive no-nonsense Greek food – starters €3–5, mains €5–9. Daily lunch & dinner.

#### PÓRTES

**Akroyiali** ☎ 22970 31335. A fine *psarotavérna* with a terrace above the sea, close to the beach. Good fish and mezédhes attract visitors from around the island at weekends. Nearby *Thanasis* offers a slightly more meaty menu. May–Sept lunch & dinner daily, plus winter weekends.

## The west coast

The road south of Égina Town, along the **west coast** of the island, is flat and easy. Sprawling **Marathónas**, 5km from Égina, has the biggest if not the prettiest of the west coast's sandy beaches, offering fine views and loungers, along with a scattering of rooms, tavernas and cafés. The next settlement, **Eyinítissa**, has a popular, sheltered cove backed by eucalypts and a beach bar.

### Pérdhika

**PÉRDHIKA**, scenically set on a little bay packed with yachts at the end of the coastal road, is the most picturesque village on the island. The pedestrianized waterfront esplanade at the southern edge of the village, overlooking Moní islet and the

Peloponnese, is the heart of tourist life. From the harbour, you can take a boat to **Moní** (10min; €5 return), most of which is fenced off as a nature conservation area and is worth the trip for a swim in wonderfully clear water. Pérdhika Bay itself is shallow and yacht-tainted, though you can swim from the rocky shore further round.

On the headland opposite the harbour, along with crumbling wartime bunkers, is a **Camera Obscura** built by two Austrian artists. In the darkened interior twelve narrow slits project an inverted 360 degree image of the landscape outside. If you have your own transport, a couple more **cove beaches** are accessible beyond Pérdhika, where new holiday homes are reached by steep concrete tracks.

## ACCOMMODATION AND EATING                     THE WEST COAST

### MARATHÓNAS

**Ostria** ☎ 22970 26738. An idyllic setting, with tables set out under the trees at the southern end of the beach and the water lapping almost to your feet. The food is great too, especially the calamari and the cheese pies. Daily lunch & dinner.

### PÉRDHIKA

**Andonis** ☎ 22970 61443. One of a long line of tavernas along the front, this is the best of the bunch for fish; plenty of Athenian and yachtie patronage, so prices are a little higher than its neighbours – fish is priced by the kilo. Daily lunch & dinner.

**Antzi Studios** ☎ 22970 61446, ⓦ antzistudios.gr. Large studio and apartment complex with a good-sized pool. The modern apartment units with separate kitchens,

some for four people, are greatly preferable to the older studios. €50, new apartments €90

**Hermes** At the furthest extremity of the esplanade, this café-bar is Pérdhika's busiest late-night spot, probably because its position means it can afford to turn the music up louder than its neighbours. Daily 10am–late.

**Hotel Hippocampus** ☎ 22970 61363, ⓦ hippocampus -hotel-greece.com. Friendly, simple two-star hotel built around a garden courtyard. All rooms have balcony, a/c and TV, and there's a small roof terrace. €50

**To Proreon** ☎ 22970 61577. Proreon stands out thanks to its many potted plants and old-fashioned atmosphere. Excellent Greek food including home-made cheese (€3.50) or pumpkin (€6) pies, standards like moussaka (€6) and fish by the kilo. Daily lunch & dinner.

# Angístri

ANGÍSTRI, fifteen minutes by fast boat from Égina, is a tiny island, obscure enough to be overlooked by most island-hoppers, though the visitors it does have are a diverse mix: Athenian weekenders, retirees who bought and restored property here years ago, plus a few British and Scandinavian package holidaymakers. There's a small, not terribly attractive strip of development on the north coast facing Égina, but the rest of the island is pine-covered, timeless and beautiful – albeit with very few beaches. It's also strangely schizophrenic: holiday weekends can see hordes of young Greeks camping out on otherwise empty beaches, while in Skála a few small, classy hotels are juxtaposed with cafés serving English breakfasts to the package-trippers.

## ARRIVAL AND DEPARTURE                            ANGÍSTRI

**By ferry** There are ferries and hydrofoils to and from Pireás via Égina; ferries dock at Skála (twice daily in the week, three from Fri–Sun; 25min/1hr 30min); hydrofoils at Mýlos (12 daily in summer, 6 out of season; 10min/1hr). The Angístri Express (☎ 694 71 18 863) calls at both on its route

to and from Égina (2–3 daily; 15min).
**Ferry operators** Hellenic Seaways (ferry and hydrofoils; ☎ 22970 91171, ⓦ hsw.gr) and Aegean Flying Dolphins (hydrofoils; ☎ 22970 91221, ⓦ aegeanflyingdolphins.gr).

## GETTING AROUND

**By bus** In summer, the island bus connects Skála and Mýlos with Dhragonéra, Limenária and Apónissos several times a day; the day's timetable (timed to match ferry and hydrofoil arrivals) is chalked up at its starting point, outside the church in Skála.

**By scooter and bike** Scooters and mountain bikes are available for rent from several outlets in Skála and Mýlos; Kostas Motorent in Skála (☎ 22970 91021) is particularly helpful. It is less than 10km to the furthest point of the island, so in cooler weather you can comfortably cross Angístri by

5

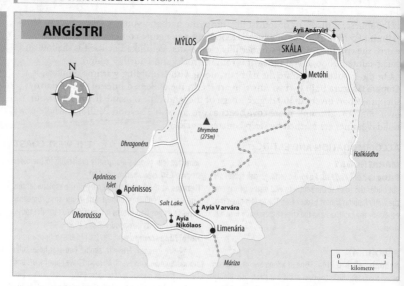

pedal power – albeit with a couple of steep climbs.
**On foot** The island is small enough to cross on foot, via Metóhi along a winding dirt track through the pines.

**By water-taxi** Water-taxis (☎ 697 76 18 040; about €30 per boat from Skála to Dhragonéra, for example) serve the beaches and Égina.

## Skála and around

**SKÁLA** is Angístri's main tourist centre, its sandy beach backed by a straggle of modern development. Thanks to the weekending Athenian youth, there are lively bars and cafés here, and an unexpectedly busy nightlife; in summer, there's even an open-air cinema. The beach, and most of the new development, lies to the right (west) from the jetty, beyond the big church, but there are some far more attractive places to stay, looking out over a rocky coastline, if you turn left.

From the paved road's end in this direction, beyond the *Alkyoni Hotel*, a path leads along the clifftop to secluded **Halikiádha**. This pebble beach, backed by crumbling cliffs, is predominantly nudist; at busy weekends there may be crowds of young Greeks camping nearby, the rest of the time it's almost deserted. The scary scramble down is rewarded by the island's best swimming in crystalline water. On the main town beach, you can rent sun-loungers, pedaloes and kayaks.

**METÓHI**, the hillside hamlet just above Skála, was once the island's main village, but now consists chiefly of holiday homes. If you can face the steep climb there are wonderful views out towards Égina.

### ACCOMMODATION                                    SKÁLA

**Aktaion Hotel** ☎ 22970 91222, ⓦ hotelaktaion.gr. Close to the jetty and the best of the options in town, with a small swimming pool. Most rooms have sea views and big balconies; some are a little dilapidated, others refurbished. Also small apartments with kitchen. **€55**

★ **Alkyoni Hotel** ☎ 22970 91377, ⓦ alkyoni-agistri.gr. Turn left (southeast) from the jetty to find these large, stone-floored rooms; those on the seafront side have balconies directly above the water with stunning views. Best of all are

the duplex rooms on the upper floor, big enough for a family with a raised sleeping area and kitchenette below. There's also a friendly coffee/breakfast bar. **€50**

**Rosy's Little Village** ☎ 22970 91610, ⓦ rosyslittle village.com. Delightful spot on the rocks southeast of the jetty with a variety of rooms, most with sea view, direct access to its own rocky swimming spot, free kayaks and bikes for guests, and a small sail-boat and motorboat for hire, plus a good restaurant. **€60**

## EATING, DRINKING AND NIGHTLIFE

**Quattro** ☎ 22970 91447. Beachside café/bar that trumps its neighbours by offering not just free wi-fi, but a laptop brought to your table. Open all day for breakfast, coffee and cocktails, plus good, chilled out sounds at night. Daily 10am–late.

**Saronis** ☎ 22970 91394. Blue-and-white checked tablecloths lend a relaxed feel to this long-established restaurant beside the church, with a more interesting and authentic menu than many here; stuffed mushrooms, horta and saganaki feature, as well as fresh fish, prawns and octopus. Daily lunch & dinner.

**Taboo** Main road on the western edge of town ☎ 22970 91181. The one real club on the island, which can be packed, sweaty and thumping or can be deserted, depending on the visiting crowds – watch out for posters advertising special events like beach parties and funk and soul nights. Summer Fri–Sun from 11pm, plus special events year-round.

**Taverna Parnassos** Metóhi ☎ 22970 91539. The roof terrace here, close to the village's highest point, has perhaps the best views on the whole island, and there's excellent, home-cooked traditional food to appreciate while you enjoy them. Daily lunch & dinner.

**To Kyma** ☎ 22970 91622. Behind the beach in the midst of the beachfront cafés, To Kyma has a charcoal grill out front where kebabs and squid are grilled, plus a good, traditional Greek menu with plenty of vegetable dishes. Daily lunch & dinner.

# Mýlos (Megalohóri)

The least attractive aspect of Angístri is the windblown road along the coast between Skála and **MÝLOS**. Mýlos itself has an attractive, traditional village centre with a church and platía, but there's only a tiny beach, so relatively few people stay here. Access to the rest of the island is easy, however, and there are plenty of rooms and tavernas.

## ACCOMMODATION AND EATING MÝLOS

**Fotis** ☎ 22970 91325. This year-round taverna on the main street in the village centre is also the local butcher, so the meat here is particularly good. It's worth checking out the day's specials in the kitchen – they're often absolutely delicious. Daily lunch & dinner.

**Kouros** Café with a lovely position looking out over the goings-on of the harbour; breakfast, ice cream and waffles served as well as full meals, and there's free wi-fi. Daily 10am–10pm.

**Meltemi Studios** ☎ 22970 91057, ⓦ meltemistudios .gr. Purpose-built studios in a prime position with views back along the coast towards Skála as well as over the harbour. Rooms are clean and cheerful, and there's a tiny deep pool that operates as a pool bar in high season. €50

# Rest of the island

There's basically just one road on Angístri, running from Skála and Mýlos round the west coast to the bottom of the island. Midway around, **Dhragonéra** is a beautiful but rocky pine-fringed beach with a dramatic panorama across to the mainland; other small coves are accessible across the rocks. Despite the warning signs, many people camp in the woods around these beaches. **LIMENÁRIA**, a small farming community at the edge of a fertile plateau in the southern corner of the island, is largely unaffected by tourism. The closest swimming is a few hundred metres east down a cement drive, then steps, at **Máriza**, where a diminutive concrete lido gives access to deep, ice-clear water. The little anchorage of **Apónissos** lies 2km west, past a shallow salt marsh; there's lovely swimming here in a tiny, warm lagoon, idyllic when uncrowded, or off the rocks in deeper, cooler water.

## EATING AND DRINKING REST OF THE ISLAND

**Aponisos Taverna** Apónissos. A matchless beachside setting for this simple ouzerí, whose wooden chairs are set on a terrace above the water. Simple meze dishes are the order of the day. June–Sept lunch & dinner daily.

**O Tasos** Limenária ☎ 22970 91362. Hugely popular with visiting mainlanders – and hence packed at weekend lunchtimes – O Tasos produces traditional cooking using local produce. Pricier than you'd expect for the location. Daily lunch & dinner.

5

# Póros

Separated from the mainland by a 350m strait, **PÓROS** ("the ford") barely qualifies as an island at all. Popular with Brits and Scandinavians – more than any other Argo-Saronic island, Póros attracts package-holiday operators – it is also busy with weekending Athenians, who can get here by road (via Galatás) or on cheap ferries from Pireás, and with yachties taking advantage of the extensive mooring. There are in fact two islands, **Sferiá** (Póros Town) and the far larger **Kalávria**, separated from each other by a miniature canal spanned by a bridge. The town is a busy place, with constant traffic of shipping and people: if your stay is longer than a couple of nights you may want to base yourself on Kalávria for a little more peace, coming into town for the food, nightlife and shopping.

## ARRIVAL AND DEPARTURE                                            PÓROS

**By ferry** In addition to regular ferry and hydrofoil connections with Pireás and the other Argo-Saronics, Póros has frequent, almost round-the-clock passenger boats shuttling across from the mainland port of Galatás (5min; €1) to Póros Town, plus a car ferry every half-hour. Small passenger boats tie up among the yachts and other small vessels on the southerly side facing Galatás, hydrofoils next to them near the northwestern end of the waterfront, ferries further round at the northern end of town.
**Destinations** Pireás via Méthana and Égina (2–3 ferries daily; 2hr 15min; plus 4–6 hydrofoils and flying cats; 1hr); Spétses (4–6 hydrofoils and flying cats; 1hr 30min); Ýdhra (4–6 hydrofoils and flying cats; 35min).
**Tickets and agents** All hydrofoils and catamarans serving the island are operated by Hellenic Seaways (ⓦ hsw.gr), whose local agents, both on the waterfront, are Marinos Tours (☎ 22980 23423) for hydrofoils, and Askeli Travel (☎ 22980 24900, ⓦ poros-accommodation .gr) for conventional ferries.

## INFORMATION

**Services** A couple of banks with ATMs and the post office are on Platía Iroön in the centre of Póros Town. Many of the waterfront cafés have free wi-fi; terminals at Kendrou Typou (see below) or Fight Club, on the southeastern waterfront beyond *Taverna Naftis*.
**Newspapers and books** Available in English from Kendro Typou, opposite the ferry dock.
**Useful website** Check ⓦ poros.com.gr for information on the island, and for accommodation listings.

## GETTING AROUND

**By bus** Buses (€1.50) depart to Kalávria, west to Russian Bay or east to the monastery, hourly on the hour from the road across from Platía Iroón (less frequent out of season).

**By taxi** The taxi rank is close to Platía Iroón; a taxi to the beaches is less than €5.

**By car or bike** Travel agents in town can rent you a car, or a quad-bike or scooter, though for the latter much the best service and prices are from Fotis (☎ 22980 25873); their office is over the bridge, on the road towards Askéli, but if you call they can deliver a bike to you.

**Island tours** In high season, thrice-weekly boat trips around the island depart from the central waterfront while a *trenaki* offers a variety of tours from the car park by the ferry dock, including a regular evening haul all the way up to the Temple of Poseidon.

# Póros Town

**PÓROS TOWN** rises steeply across the western half of tiny volcanic Sferiá, a landmark clocktower at its summit. There's a two-room **archeological museum** on the waterfront (Tues–Sun 8.30am–3pm; €2) whose local finds will fill a spare half-hour, but otherwise few sights. This is a place to eat, drink, shop and watch the world go by. Away from the waterfront you'll quickly get lost in the labyrinth of steep, narrow streets, but nowhere is far away and most of the restaurants reasonably well signed. For a fine view over the rooftops and the strait, climb up to the **clocktower** (signed Roloï) – the tower itself is structurally suspect and fenced off, but you can still enjoy the outlook.

## ACCOMMODATION                                                                 PÓROS TOWN

Rooms in Póros Town itself can be in very short supply at weekends and holiday times, when prices are inevitably high (they can be dramatically lower out of season); some noise is always likely too. Over on Kalávria (see p.340) there's considerably more choice, with plenty of apartments and small hotels in the touristy enclaves of Askéli – close to good beaches – or less attractive Mikró Neório.

**Dionysos** ☎ 22980 23511, ⓦ hoteldionysos.eu. An imposing mansion on the waterfront directly opposite the ferry dock, with large, newly refurbished rooms; most have bare stone walls, some with four-poster beds and wonderful old baths. Great value. **€50**

**Manessi** ☎ 22980 22273, ⓦ manessi.com. Classy place on the waterfront in the centre of town, with lots of dark wood and designery touches. The larger rooms have impressive power showers, while those at the front have fabulous views; new windows mean they're well soundproofed too. **€60**

**Nikos Douros** ☎ 22980 22633, ⓦ poros.com.gr /nikos-studios. Rooms and apartments in a number of houses, which means facilities and quality vary, but all are clean and comfortable, with a/c and TV, and prices are good. Try to see the room before you check in. **€40**

**Villa Tryfon** ☎ 22980 25854, ⓦ poros.com.gr/tryfon -villa. Cheerful blue-and-white studio rooms with kitchenette, near the main square on the clocktower side of the hill. Facilities are somewhat basic, but they do all have a/c, stunning views and an exceptionally friendly welcome. **€50**

## EATING, DRINKING AND NIGHTLIFE

The central waterfront is mostly given over to competing cafés, all of which are open from breakfast till late, bars and souvenir shops: the better tavernas lie towards the southeastern end of the waterfront or up in the steep streets of the hilltop town. The southeastern end of the waterfront is also the place for good-value cafés – on Platía Dhimarhíou, for example, or next to the archeological museum. The better bars and clubs are in this direction too, becoming livelier as you head out along the coast road, though nightlife is highly seasonal. The open-air Cine Diana, functioning in the summer only, is on the northern waterfront towards the ferry dock.

★ **Karavolos** ☎ 22980 26158. Rightly popular with locals and expats, friendly *Karavolos*, above and directly behind Cine Diana (see above), serves excellent traditional cuisine such as *kolokythokeftédhes* (courgette and cheese fritters) or pork roasted with garlic; the name means snail, and you'll also find these on the menu. Daily, evenings only.

**Kyma** ☎ 22980 22793. Simple, good-value kebab and grill place on the waterfront just beyond the archeological museum. There are plenty of *yíros* joints in town, but this has a waterfront terrace with a setting to match the fanciest restaurant. Daily 11am–1am.

**Luna Piena** Platía Iroón ☎ 694 85 94 928. Greek-influenced Italian food, a step up in price and quality from its neighbours; try the excellent spaghetti with king prawns (€16.50), for example. Also pasta and pizzas. Daily lunch & dinner.

**Malibu** ☎ 22980 22491. One of the first of the bars you

5

come to on the southeastern harbourfront, and the most reliably open year-round. Popular with expats and tourists, and a good place to start your evening. Daily 9pm–late.

**Naftis** ☎ 22980 23096. Excellent *psarotavérna* with an attractive waterside terrace overlooking the yachts, south of the centre. As the evening wears on, the owners have been known to put on an impromptu Greek dancing display. Daily, evenings only.

**Platanos** ☎ 22980 25409. On the main square of the upper town, *Platanos* serves earthy, rural food on a vine-covered terrace, washed down with powerful retsina. The owners also have a butcher's shop, so charcoal-grilled meat is the speciality – *kondosoúvli* (hunks of pork roasted on a spit) or pricier steaks. Daily, evenings only.

★ **Yiahni Sokaki** ☎ 693 64 48 568. Old-fashioned *mayireftá* establishment in the alley behind the fish market. Take a look at the kitchen to see what's been prepared that day – meatballs, moussaka or more original dishes like chicken roasted with potatoes and cherry tomatoes, all for €6–7. When it's all gone, they close. Daily, lunchtime only.

# Kalávria

**KALÁVRIA**, Póros's "mainland", is covered in pine forest and barely inhabited, though there are a couple of fertile plateaus on the northern side with olive terraces, vineyards and magnificent panoramic views.

## Western Kalávria

**Kanáli** and **Míkro Neório**, immediately across the canal from Póros Town, are overdeveloped, though they do have some good seafront restaurants looking back toward town. The first place worth a stop in its own right, though, is **MEGÁLO NEÓRIO**, arguably the island's most pleasant resort, small-scale, with a sandy beach, an excellent waterski centre with courses to professional level (☎ 22980 42540, ⓦ passage.gr), and some fine beachside tavernas. **Love Bay**, immediately west, has a lovely sandy beach, but is unfortunately tiny and always packed; there's a friendly seasonal *kantína*, and kayaks and snorkel gear can be hired here.

The **Rossikós Navstathmós** on Russian Bay, a crumbling Russian naval base dating from the early nineteenth century, marks the end of the route for the westward bus. There's a hard-packed, mostly shadeless beach here, with lots of small craft anchored offshore.

## Askéli

**Askéli**, with its strip of hotels and villas, is the first place you reach as you head east on Kalávria. There are plenty of cafés and places to eat, many overlooking the narrow, crowded beach. A good watersports centre hires out kayaks and small sailing boats, and they also have a powerboat for ringo rides and the like.

---

### EXCURSIONS TO THE PELOPONNESE

Take one of the boats shuttling constantly to and from Galatás and you're on the mainland Peloponnese, where there are numerous potential excursions. Local travel agents run a variety of tours, or you'll see hire cars on offer in Galatás from around €25 a day.

**Troezen** Ancient Troezen is an unenclosed site near the modern village of Trizína, barely 10km from Galatás. Legendary birthplace of Theseus, the scattered site is most easily understood if you purchase a map in the village – this also recounts the stories of Theseus's life. A short walk up a gorge from the site takes you to the spectacular natural rock arch of the Dhiavoloyéfyro, the Devil's Bridge.

**Epidaurus** (Epídhavros) Most famous for its fourth-century BC theatre, one of the finest ancient monuments in Greece, Epidaurus is also an extensive sanctuary to Asklepios, god of healing. The theatre is used for productions of Classical Greek drama on Friday and Saturday nights from June to August as part of the annual Athens & Epidaurus Festival (ⓦ greekfestival.gr; organized excursions from many island travel agents). Daily summer 8am–7.30pm, winter 8am–5pm; €6.

**Náfplio** A long day-trip, but arguably the most rewarding destination in the Peloponnese, Náfplio is a gorgeous nineteenth-century town in a stunning coastal setting protected by forbidding fortresses. There are plenty of excellent restaurants and cafés.

## Monastiríou

The eighteenth-century **monastery of Zoödhóhou Piyís** (daily sunrise–1.30pm & 4.30pm–sunset), next to the island's only spring, is the terminus of Póros's eastward bus. Steps from the bus stop lead down to the pleasant sandy beach of **Monastiríou**, overlooked by pine-covered slopes. Perhaps the island's best beach, it is, surprisingly, usually one of the least crowded – though hardly empty as the two tavernas here will testify.

## Temple of Poseidon

Daily 8am–2.30pm • Free • ⓦ kalaureia.org

The remains of the **Temple of Poseidon** overlook the island's northern and western coasts, with great views towards Égina. The temple lay at the heart of ancient Kalaureia, whose heyday was in the fourth century BC, and it's an extensive site. Despite plenty of new signage and an ongoing Swedish excavation there's not a great deal to see above ground level, however – many of the stones were carted off to be used as building materials in the seventeenth and eighteenth centuries (much of it ended up on Ýdhra), and some of the more interesting sections are roped off while they are excavated. It was here that Demosthenes, fleeing from the Macedonians after encouraging the Athenians to resist their rule, took poison rather than surrender.

## Vayioniá

**Vayioniá**, just about the only accessible beach on the island's north shore, was the port of ancient Kalaureia. The bay is beautiful when viewed from above; close up the pebbly beach is narrow and can be windy, but it's still a very pleasant spot, with a seasonal beach bar/café, and loungers to rent.

### ACCOMMODATION AND EATING · KALÁVRIA

#### MEGÁLO NEÓRIO

★ **Pavlou** ⓣ 22980 22734, ⓦ pavlouhotel.gr. Family-run hotel with pool, tennis court and restaurant, right on one of the island's best beaches (where they also have a great restaurant). The decor is plain but comfortable, with big balconies, half of which have great sea views. Breakfast included. **€50**

#### MIKRÓ NEÓRIO

**Aspros Gatos** Waterfront ⓣ 22980 25650. Friendly taverna serving good seafood on a waterfront terrace with views back over Póros Town; try the rice pilaf with mussels and pine nuts, for example. Only about twenty minutes walk from town, or they offer free water-taxi service for groups of five or more. Daily lunch & dinner.

#### MONASTIRÍOU

**Sirene** ⓣ 22980 22741, ⓦ sireneblueresort.gr. Large, modern hotel with pool and tennis courts, spectacularly sited on a steep slope above the sea, with a small private beach below. The stunning location ensures fabulous views from the balconies, though the refurbished rooms are small. Good off-peak deals. **€140**

#### VAYIONIÁ

**Paradisos** ⓣ 22980 23419. Well signed on the main road just east of the turning down to Vayioniá, this rural taverna serves plenty of local produce, including rabbit stifado or spit-roasted pork, plus charcoal-grilled squid or lamb, washed down with local retsina and home-made bread. Daily noon–midnight.

# Ýdhra

The island of **ÝDHRA (Hydra)** is one of the most atmospheric destinations in Greece. Its harbour and main town preserved as a national monument, it feels like a Greek island should, entirely traffic-free (even bicycles are banned) with a bustling harbour and narrow stone streets climbing steeply above it. Away from the main settlement the rest of the island is roadless, rugged and barely inhabited. The charm has not gone unnoticed – Ýdhra became fashionable as early as the 1950s, and in the Sixties characters ranging from Greek painter Nikos Hatzikyriakos-Ghikas to Canadian songster Leonard Cohen bought and restored grand old houses here. There's still a sizeable expat community, which contributes to a relatively sophisticated atmosphere, and also noticeably high

5

## ÝDHRA (HYDRA)

prices. But even the seasonal and weekend crowds, and a very limited number of beaches, can't seriously detract from the appeal. When the town is overrun, it's easy enough to leave it all behind on foot or by excursion boat. The interior is mountainous and little-visited, so with a little walking you can find a dramatically different kind of island – one of rural cottages, terraces of grain to feed the donkeys, hilltop monasteries and pine forest.

## ARRIVAL AND DEPARTURE                                                  ÝDHRA

**By ferry** Hellenic Seaways hydrofoils and flying cats connect Ýdhra to Pireás (1hr 20min) via Póros (35min) at least 5 times a day, more in midsummer. In the other direction they continue to Spétses (5 daily; 45min), some via Ermióni or on to Pórto Héli on the mainland. Small passenger boats also cross to Metóhi (4 daily; 15 min) on the nearby mainland.

**Tickets and agencies** The local agent for Hellenic Seaways tickets (ⓦhsw.gr) is Hydreoniki Travel (ⓣ22980 54007, ⓦhydreoniki.gr), located in an alley at the eastern end of the harbour. Metóhi boats are operated by Hydra Lines (ⓣ694 73 25 263, ⓦhydralines.gr).

## INFORMATION

**Services** Several banks with ATMs can be found round the waterfront, while the post office is on the market square just inland. There's free wi-fi at many cafés; terminals at the shop immediately behind the waterfront Alpha Bank.

**Newspapers** Foreign-language papers, and some books, are sold at a shop on N. Votsi, off the waterfront between the church and Pirate bar.

## GETTING AROUND

**On foot** There's only one paved road on Ýdhra, leading east from the harbour to Mandhráki just a couple of kilometres away, so to explore the island you either walk or take a boat (see below). The largely shadeless trails mean that in midsummer walking can be a mercilessly hot experience. There are excellent, part-cobbled tracks leading west of town to the beaches at Kamíni (about 20min), Vlyhós (30min) and Plákes (40min). Steeper, rougher paths lead into the interior and towards the south coast (see box, p.346).

**By boat** Small boats shuttle constantly from the harbour to the beaches, at prices ranging from about €2.50 per person one-way to Mandhráki or Vlyhós, to €12 return to Bísti. You can also hire private water-taxis – good value for groups at around €15 per boat to Vlyhós or €55 to Bísti, for example.

**By mule** If you are carrying luggage, or might struggle on the sometimes steep cobbles in Ýdhra Town, you can hire a mule at the harbour; fixed prices for various destinations are posted. The fancier hotels may provide a mule if they know when you are arriving – or more likely a porter with a handcart for your luggage.

# Ýdhra Town

**ÝDHRA TOWN**, with tiers of grey-stone mansions and humbler white-walled, red-tiled houses rising from a perfect horseshoe harbour, makes a beautiful spectacle. Around the harbour, trippers flock to cafés and chic boutiques, but it's also worth spending time wandering the backstreets and narrow alleys – one thing you may notice while doing so is that even more than most Greek island towns, Ýdhra is overrun with wild cats, probably because there are so many "cat ladies" who feed them.

The waterfront mansions were mostly built during the eighteenth century on the accumulated wealth of a remarkable merchant fleet, which traded as far afield as America and – during the Napoleonic Wars – broke the British blockade to sell grain to France. In the 1820s the town's population was nearly 20,000 – an incredible figure when you reflect that today it is under 3000 – and Ýdhra's merchants provided many of the ships for the Greek forces during the War of Independence, and consequently many of the commanders. At each side of the harbour, cannons facing out to sea and statues of the heroes of independence remind you of this place in history.

## The mansions

The **mansions** of the wealthy eighteenth-century merchant families are still the great monuments of the town; some labelled at the entrance with "*Oikía*" ("Residence of …") followed by the family name. Among the finest are the two **Koundouriótis mansions**, built by two brothers: Yíoryios, whose former home is periodically open for art exhibitions, was a leading politician of the fledgling Greek nation and grandfather of Pávlos, president of Republican Greece in the 1920s; older brother Lázaros was prominent in the independence wars.

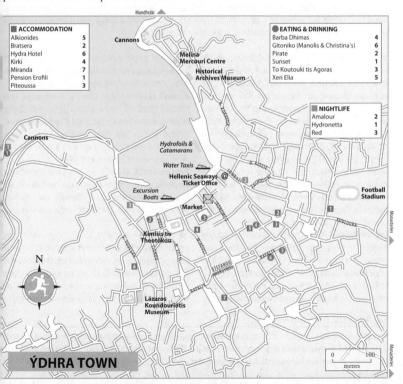

ÝDHRA TOWN

**5**

Lázaros Koundouriótis Museum

Daily 10am–2pm, July & Aug also 5.30–8.30pm • €4

The **Lázaros Koundouriótis Museum** is the large ochre building high on the western side of town. The hot climb up the stepped alleyways is rewarded with great views down over the town and port, and a lovingly restored interior that looks ready to move into. The red-tiled floors, panelled wooden ceilings and period furnishings outshine the contents of the museum – paintings, folk costume and independence paraphernalia.

Historical Archives Museum

Daily 9am–4pm, July & Aug also 7.30–9.30pm; €5

On the eastern waterfront, the **Historical Archives Museum** occupies one of Ýdhra's great houses. It's a small, crowded and enjoyable display of clothing, period engravings, and ships' prows and sidearms from the independence struggle. The **Melina Mercouri Centre**, next door, often has interesting temporary art exhibitions.

## Kímisis tís Theotókou

**Museum** Tues–Sun 10am–2pm, Aug also 7–9pm • €2

The most obvious and important of Ýdhra's many churches is **Kímisis tís Theotókou** by the port, with its distinctive clocktower. The cloistered courtyard houses the small but rich collection of the **ecclesiastical museum** – silver-bound books, icons, vestments, bejewelled crosses and the like.

**ACCOMMODATION**                                                    **ÝDHRA TOWN**

Most accommodation in Ýdhra Town is high quality, though prices tend to be equally high. Midweek or out of season you should be able to negotiate significant reductions on the official rates. The nature of the old buildings and the closely packed streets mean that some noise is inevitable, especially near the waterfront. Addresses and street signs are almost nonexistent, so ask for directions when you book, or refer to our map.

★ **Alkionides** ☎ 22980 54055, ⓦ alkionidespension .com. Lovely pension, quietly tucked away yet central, with an attractive courtyard and helpful management; the rooms are extremely comfortable and well equipped, especially the slightly more expensive ones that have been newly refurbished, and there's a wonderful studio apartment with its own roof terrace. €65, studio €100

★ **Bratsera** ☎ 22980 53971, ⓦ bratserahotel.com. Classy four-star hotel that occupies a stylishly renovated former sponge factory; the extensive common areas (including bar, restaurant and courtyard pool) serve as a museum of the industry with photos and artefacts. Lovely rooms have flagstone floors and beamed ceilings, though only superior and above have balconies. €150

**Hydra Hotel** ☎ 22980 53420, ⓦ hydra-hotel.gr. Stunning boutique hotel in a mansion high above the harbour, with glorious views from many rooms. Each room is different, from simple doubles up to a split-level family apartment. €150

**Kirki** ☎ 22980 53181, ⓦ hydrakirki.gr. Unprepossessing entry leads to a delightful old house, with a small courtyard

garden and simple, island-style rooms; all have a/c and balconies, though the attractive large terraces at the back do get some early morning noise from the market. €60

**Miranda** ☎ 22980 52230, ⓦ mirandahotel.gr. An 1810 mansion converted into a popular hotel, with highly individual rooms; best are nos. 2 and 3, both with painted, coffered ceilings and large sea-view terraces. Large breakfasts in the shaded courtyard are another big plus; there is a basement bar for winter. €120

**Pension Erofili** ☎ 22980 54049, ⓦ pensionerofili.gr. Simple but spacious rooms around a courtyard, all with a/c, fridge and television; quiet, friendly and relatively inexpensive. A small apartment upstairs has its own kitchen. €55

★ **Piteoussa** ☎ 22980 52810, ⓦ piteoussa.com. Named after the three giant pines at the front, this small inn is exceptional value, with modern units equipped with iPod speakers, CD and DVD players and Korres toiletries in the marble-floored bathrooms. Downstairs rooms are larger, but all have balconies and designer touches. €65

**EATING AND DRINKING**

The permanently busy quayside cafés and bars offer an incomparable people-watching experience – albeit at a price – but there are few worthwhile restaurants on the harbour. If you want something to take down to the beach with you, there's an excellent bakery, with *tyrópittes* and cakes, tucked into the western corner of the harbour by the *Pirate* bar.

**Barba Dhimas** ☎ 22980 53306. Tiny place with just half a dozen tables set out in an alley. There's a short, daily menu of Italian food; mixed antipasto (€8) or spaghetti *vongole* (€18), for example. May–Sept 7pm–midnight.

★ **Gitoniko (Manolis & Christina's)** ☎ 22980 53615. Hidden away inland, near Áyios Konstandínos church, this traditional taverna serves excellent, well-priced *mayireftá* at lunch (stuffed marrow €7) – which runs out early – plus grills (including succulent fish) in the evening; extensive roof-terrace in summer. Daily lunch & dinner.

**Pirate** ☎ 22980 52711. Café by day and an increasingly lively bar as the evening wears on, *Pirate* has a young crowd and Western music. Among the best prices on the waterfront for coffee, breakfast and sandwiches. Daily 10am–2am.

**Sunset** ☎ 22980 52067. Behind the cannons on the western edge of town, *Sunset* offers an incomparable setting for an end-of-holiday treat or romantic tryst; the modern Greek and Italian cuisine is on the pricey side (pasta dishes €10–18, steak €25), but the views justify the cost. Daily lunch & dinner.

**To Koutouki tis Agoras**. Rickety-tabled, inexpensive tradesmen's ouzerí behind the market. The place makes no concessions at all to tourists, but the titbits served with drinks, ranging from *pastourmás* (cured meat) to octopus, can be exceptional. At its best in the early evening. Daily noon–9pm.

**Xeri Elia** ☎ 22980 52886. Large, busy taverna with a lovely setting in a vine-shaded inland platía. All the standards are served, along with good seafood, and there's often live music in the evenings. Daily lunch & dinner.

### NIGHTLIFE

Nightlife is tame on the whole, though a number of bars do play music into the early hours; there's also an open-air cinema in summer.

**Amalour** Laidback cocktail bar with an eclectic playlist – plenty of Latin and jazz – and 30-to-40-something crowd. Almost always the busiest place in town in the early evening; sometimes hosts special events or theme nights. Daily 6pm–2am.

**Hydronetta** The classic sunset-watching bar, with steps down the rocks into the water, where the music carries on into the small hours. Limited seating gives it an exclusive,

chill-out vibe. The place is also open during the day, for swimming, coffee and an early start on the drinking. Daily 9am–2am.

**Red** The closest thing you'll find to a dance club in town, *Red* is a late-night joint right on the waterfront playing sixties and seventies rock plus a few dance tunes and the odd Greek number. Fri–Sun 10pm–3am, plus some weekdays in summer.

## Beaches

There's no big sandy beach on Ýdhra, just a series of small, mainly shingly, coves. **Mandhráki** is the closest to town, dominated by the *Miramare Hotel* which occupies the imposing former shipyard of independence war hero Admiral Miaoulis. Despite appearances, the sandy beach is open to all, with windsurfing, waterskiing, pedaloes to hire and floating trampolines.

Walk west from Ýdhra Town and you'll find several spots where you can clamber down to swim from the rocks in crystal-clear water, but the first tiny pebble beach lies just beyond the picturesque village of **Kamíni**. Next up is a popular swimming cove at **Kastéllo** and then **Vlyhós**, a small hamlet with a rebuilt nineteenth-century bridge and a shingle beach with loungers and umbrellas; there's pleasant swimming in the lee of an offshore islet here. **Plákes**, a long, pebbly stretch with loungers, palapa shelters and a

### ÝDHRA'S FESTIVALS

Over the weekend closest to June 21, Ýdhra Town celebrates the **Miaoulia**, in honour of Admiral Andreas Miaoulis whose fire boats, packed with explosives, were set adrift downwind of the Turkish fleet during the War of Independence. The highlight of the celebrations is the burning of a boat at sea as a tribute to the sailors who risked their lives in this dangerous enterprise.

**Orthodox Easter** is also a colourful and moving experience, especially on the evening of Good Friday when the fishermen's parish of Áyios Ioánnnis at Kamíni carries its *Epitáfios*, or symbolic bier of Christ, into the shallows to bless the boats and ensure calm seas.

**5**

## ÝDHRA'S INLAND WALKS

To explore the island's interior and south coast, head out of Ýdhra Town on the street that leads past the *Miranda* hotel or around the eastern edge past the *Piteoussa*: as you start to climb, a left turn leads to Áyios Nikólaos, keeping right heads to Profítis Ilías.

**Profítis Ilías and Mount Éros** The monastery of Profítis Ilías and nearby convent of Ayía Efpraxía are about an hour's climb above Ýdhra Town. What must be the longest stairway in Greece (or alternatively a zigzag path) constitutes the final approach to Profítis Ilías (closed noon–4pm, but water and *loukoúm* are hospitably left at the gate). If you want to go further, a rather tougher, harder-to-follow trail continues left behind the monastery to a saddle overlooking the south coast. From here a pathless scramble brings you within twenty minutes to the 590m summit of Mount Éros, the Argo-Saronic islands' highest point, but the path itself branches: right to the chapel of Áyios Mámas, on whose feast day of September 2 there's a pilgrimage of people and animals to be blessed; left eventually circles down to the sea at the tiny hamlet of Klimáki, a couple of hours' walk in all.

**Áyios Nikólaos** The path from Ýdhra Town towards deserted Áyios Nikólaos monastery offers spectacular views back down over the harbour before reaching, at the top, a broad, easy dirt track heading straight across a high plateau towards the monastery. Just beyond Áyios Nikólaos is a small settlement, from where you can in theory head down to Limnióniza, a scenic cove on the south coast an hour and a quarter from Ýdhra Town. However, it's a steep scramble on a path which is hard to find and there are no boats back unless you arrange to be picked up by water-taxi. A far easier alternative is to follow the broad track down from Áyios Nikólaos to Mandhráki, where you can have a swim before taking the boat back to town.

**Cape Zoúrva** This is Ýdhra's eastern tip and is about three hours' walk from town, on a path that heads east from Áyios Nikólaos. There are several small chapels along the way, along with the substantial Moní Zoúrvas. Perhaps the best way to do this trip is to take an early morning water-taxi to the cape, and walk back to town along the island's spine.

small resort hotel, marks the end of the easy path. At the western tip of the island, virtually inaccessible except by boat, are two coves sheltering perhaps the island's best beaches: **Bísti** has a smallish, white-pebbled beach surrounded by pine trees that offer shade; **Áyios Nikólaos** is larger and sandier, but with less shade and fewer boats. A path leads over the cape between the two; both have seasonal snack bars as well as loungers and kayaks to rent.

## ACCOMMODATION, EATING AND DRINKING                                          BEACHES

### MANDHRÁKI

**Mandraki 1800** ☎ 22980 52112. Above a tiny cove as you enter Mandhráki, where they have loungers and umbrellas, free for customers, this café/ouzerí serves good fresh fish as well as beer and drinks.

**Miramare Hotel** ☎ 22980 52300, ⊕ miramare.gr. Restaurant, beach-bar and hotel right on the beach. The rather crude beachside bungalows are not great value, but you can eat or simply have a coffee on a beautiful waterside terrace, and they have their own boat to town. **€70**

### KAMÍNI

**Antonia** ☎ 22980 52481. Just one delightfully old-fashioned room and one apartment for up to five people, both with balconies hanging right over the sea; with no frills at all (though there is a/c), and virtually no English spoken, this feels like the Greece of thirty years ago. **€60**

**Pension Petrolekka** ☎ 22980 52701. Immediately

behind Antonia, with just a couple of well-equipped apartments, simply furnished but with wi-fi and a/c; the larger and more expensive one has two rooms with separate bathroom and kitchen and huge balcony. **€80**

**Taverna Kodylenia** ☎ 22980 53520. With a beautiful terrace overlooking the little harbour, *Kodylenia* is famous for its seafood and wonderful sunset views. Crowds of weekend trippers mean slightly higher-than-average prices: moussaka for €9, seafood spaghetti €15, pork with mushroom and wine sauce €12.

### VLYHÓS

**Antigone** ☎ 22980 53228, ✉ antigone@freemail.gr. Just above the jetty where the boats drop you, *Antigone* has good-value apartments; small ones with bedroom and living room/kitchenette, larger with two bedrooms and separate kitchen. There's also a decent restaurant and snack bar. **€65**

## PLÁKES

**Four Seasons** ☎ 22980 53698, ⓦ fourseasonshydra .gr. An incongruously luxurious small suite hotel in this isolated spot, complete with a decent restaurant and organized beach. Accommodation is in beautiful, spacious suites and studio apartments, sleeping up to four people, with modern facilities including wi-fi and satellite TV. **€170**

# Spétses

A popular, upmarket escape for Athenians, **SPÉTSES** had brief fame and a vogue as a package destination, largely thanks to John Fowles, who lived here in the early 1950s and used the place, thinly disguised, as the setting for his cult novel *The Magus*. But the island never developed the mass infrastructure – or the convenient beaches – to match. Today, the town is much the biggest in the Saronic islands, with apartments and villas spreading for several kilometres along the northeast coast, while the rest of the island remains almost entirely uninhabited, with pine forest inland and numerous excellent small beaches around the coast.

## ARRIVAL AND DEPARTURE                                      SPÉTSES

**By ferry** At least five daily Hellenic Seaways hydrofoils and flying cats connect Spétses with Pireás (2hr 20min) via Ýdhra (45min) and Póros (1hr 25min). Around three a day call at mainland Ermióni en route, and in the other direction continue to Pórto Héli. A car ferry and seasonal passenger boats also run several times daily to Kósta on the nearby mainland (though you can't bring a car to the island). All of them dock pretty much in the heart of town at the cannon-studded main harbour known as the Dápia.

**Tickets** The local agent for Hellenic Seaways is Bardakos (☎ 22980 73141, ⓦ hsw.gr), on the east side of the Dápia.

## INFORMATION

**Services** There are banks with ATMs all around the Dápia. Many of the harbour cafés have free wi-fi, but *Café 1800*, on the waterfront towards Kounoupítsa, is the only central internet café.

**Travel agents** Mimoza Travel (☎ 22980 75170) and Alasia Travel (☎ 22980 74098, ⓦ alasiatravel.gr), both on the waterfront immediately east of the Dápia, can help with accommodation and local information.

**5**

## GETTING AROUND

**By bus** There are two bus services to the beaches in high season: west to Kounoupítsa, Ligonéri and Vréllos from the waterfront by the *Hotel Poseidonion*; east and then around the island to Áyii Anáryiri and Ayía Paraskévi from behind the town beach.

**By boat** Seasonal *kaïkia* offer shuttles to the beaches (€9 return to Áyii Anáryiri, for example) or round-the-island trips, and there are plentiful water-taxis (€15–80 per boatload depending on destination).

**By bike** Bike Center (☎ 22980 74009), about halfway along the shopping street behind the seafront hotels, has good mountain bikes for €6 a day, plus maps and suggested routes.

**By scooter and motorbike** Several rental places can be found behind the town beach; try Labros (☎ 693 23 33 014), often the cheapest if you bargain (from €15 a day), or Nautilus (☎ 22980 72107). Stanathiotis (☎ 22980 75364) on Bótasi, the main street inland, generally has the newest machines.

## Spétses Town

**SPÉTSES TOWN** shares with Ýdhra a history of late eighteenth-century mercantile adventure and prosperity, and a leading role in the War of Independence, which made its foremost citizens the aristocrats of the new Greek state. Plenty of fine old homes and public buildings survive, but here there's been little restriction on new building, which spreads along the shore in both directions. And although most cars are banned in town you won't notice it, as they're replaced by thousands of mopeds and scooters that pay little attention to whether a street is pedestrianized or not. In short, it's much less pretty than Ýdhra Town, but also a great deal more lively and earthy, and full of pricey shops, bars and restaurants.

For most visitors, shopping, eating and drinking are the principal attractions of Spétses, but it's a very enjoyable place to wander, with majestic old houses and gardens scattered through the narrow streets. The harbour, the **Dápia**, marks pretty much the centre of town, with the main square tucked in behind. To the east lies the **town beach** of Áyios Mámas and beyond that – a lovely walk around the point – the **Old Harbour**, upmarket focus of the island's nightlife, where private yachts moor up. West of the Dápia is **Kounoupítsa** – much of the simpler accommodation is here, and there are small beaches and waterfront tavernas. It's a big place; to walk from Kounoupítsa to the far end of the Old Harbour will take at least forty minutes.

### Bouboulína's Mansion

Guided tours (30min) up to a dozen times daily; times are posted outside and on boards around town • €6

Local heroine **Laskarína Bouboulína** was a wealthy widow who commanded her own small fleet in the War of Independence, reputedly seduced her lovers at gunpoint, and was shot in 1825 by the father of a girl her son had eloped with. Her former home – the so-called **Bouboulína's Mansion** – signed not far behind the Dápia, is now a private museum. On the entertaining tour you'll hear the story of how she spent much of her fortune on ships and men for the independence struggle, while highlights among the arms, furniture, pictures and correspondence are a gorgeous wooden ceiling in the main room and a model of Bouboulína's flagship, the *Agamemnon*.

---

### SOTÍRIOS ANÁRYIROS

The man most responsible for Spétses' appearance today is **Sotírios Anáryiros**, a descendant of a once grand Spetsiot family who emigrated in 1868 and returned, thirty years later, having made a fortune selling Turkish tobacco in the United States. His most obvious legacy is the landmark waterfront **Hotel Poseidonion**, but he also built and endowed **Anáryiros Koryalénos College**, a curious Greek re-creation of an English public school, where John Fowles taught (behind College beach), and a kitsch, Neoclassical private residence, now gradually falling into disrepair alongside the Bouboulína mansion. Most importantly, however, he was responsible for replanting the island's **pine forests**, depleted by generations of shipbuilders.

## Spétses Museum

Tues–Sun 8.30am–2.30pm • €3

Spétses' enjoyable local **museum** is housed in one of the town's grandest mansions, the Hatziyánnis Méxis family home above the east side of town. Apart from the house itself, highlights include magnificent polychrome wooden ships' prows from the revolutionary fleet, as well as its flag, plus (out of sight in a plain wooden ossuary) the bones of Laskarína Bouboulína.

## ACCOMMODATION                                           SPÉTSES TOWN

Accommodation, especially at the cheaper end of the range, tends to be widely scattered. On busy weekends and in August it can be in short supply, so it may make life easier to arrange it through an agency (see p.347). The rest of the season, though, you're likely to be met off the hydrofoil by people offering rooms. In town prices range from high, at comfortable studio complexes, to jaw-droppingly expensive at some of the boutique hotels; at quiet times, big discounts can be negotiated.

**Kastro Apartments** ☏22980 75152, ⓦkastro -margarita.com. An attractive complex of studios and duplex apartments towards Kounoupítsa, behind Café 1800. Comfy accommodation with kitchen, a/c, TV and balcony is arranged around a small pool and bar. **€100**

**Klimis** ☏22980 72334, ✉klimishotel@hol.gr. Right on the front, 200m east of the Dápia, *Klimis* may be a little run-down, but is convenient, open all year and excellent value given its position, with wonderful views from the balconied rooms at the front and some kind of sea view from almost every room. Downstairs there's a superb, old-fashioned *zaharoplastío* with excellent ice cream, where breakfast (included) is served. **€60**

**Poseidonion** ☏22980 74553, ⓦposeidonion.com. Vast, imposing, fin-de-siècle edifice immediately west of the Dápia which reopened in 2009 after years of meticulous refurbishment. Grand, high-ceilinged rooms in the main building, many with free-standing, claw-foot baths; bungalows at the back, behind the pool, and an amazing cupola suite in the tower. Prices to match, unfortunately. **€200**

**Roumani** ☏22980 72244, ⓦhotelroumani.gr. Prime location right on the Dápia, which means rooms at the front have stunning views – though they can also be noisy

and are overdue for a refurb. Hence the reasonable prices. **€65**

★ **Villa Christina** ☏22980 72218, ⓦvillachristina hotel.com. Friendly, well-maintained restored inn occupying a rambling old building with two courtyards, in a quiet location 200m inland from the Dápia, just off Bótasi. A/c rooms and studios (with kitchens) for up to four people; breakfast in the courtyard usually included. **€60**

**Villa Orizontes** ☏22980 72509, ⓦvillaorizontes.gr. Simple hotel in a quiet spot, high up (500m directly uphill from the back of Platía Oroloyíou – look for the large veranda and blue shutters), with a variety of different-sized rooms and apartments with fridge, a/c and TV; more than half have knockout views across town and out to sea. **€50**

**Zoe's Club** ☏22980 74447, ⓦzoesclub.gr. Lovely, designer-decorated studios, apartments and houses around a large pool, 200m east of the Dápia on a quiet inland corner. All have flat-screen satellite TV, DVD players and espresso machines in the fully equipped kitchens, and almost all have a great sea view. Fully booked for Aug and summer weekends and almost empty the rest of the time, though few bargains even then. **€195**

## EATING AND DRINKING

Brace yourself for some of the steepest food and drink prices in the Greek islands outside of Mýkonos and Rhodes – especially in the cafés around the Dápia and romantic spots on the old harbour.

★ **Akroyialia** ☏22980 74749. Excellent seafood taverna on the waterfront towards Kounoupítsa with reasonable prices (cheese-stuffed biftékia €9, grilled prawns €16) and a wonderful setting, with candlelit tables on the beach and the water lapping almost to your feet as you eat. Daily lunch & dinner.

**Cockatoo** ☏22980 74085. Basic kebab and *yíros* place in a narrow alley between the Dápia and Platía Oroloyíou, serving some of the cheapest food in town; stick to the basics, and it's delicious. Daily noon–midnight.

**Exedra** Old Harbour ☏22980 73497. A smarter, older crowd enjoys standard dishes like moussaka, *angináres ala políta* (artichokes with dill sauce, both €7.50) and fresh fish in an unbeatable waterside seating. Despite the upmarket image, prices are just a little higher than at neighbouring establishments. Daily noon–4pm & 7pm–midnight.

**Kafeneion** Dápia. Pebble mosaics underfoot and sepia photos indicate that this was the island's first watering hole; a prime people-watching spot, open all day for coffee and snacks, progressing later to a full range of mezédhes, or

**5**

just a drink while waiting for a hydrofoil. Daily 10am–1am.

**Lazaros** Bótasi ☎ 22980 72600. A stiff climb 500m uphill leads to this most traditional of tavernas, its cavernous interior decked out with an old jukebox, dangling gourds and wine barrels; it serves a limited but savoury menu of grills, goat in lemon sauce, superior *taramás* and decent barrelled wine. Evening only, late March–early Oct.

**Patralis** Kounoupítsa ☎ 22980 75380. Old-fashioned, bourgeois *psarotavérna*, very popular with Greek visitors, which can mean slow service and a wait for a table. The fish is excellent, though, and there are plenty of less expensive meaty alternatives (lamb chops €7) plus good barrelled wine if you don't like the prices on the extensive wine list. Better value for fish and sea views than the Old Harbour. Daily lunch & dinner.

**To Liotrivi** Old Harbour ☎ 22980 72269. The "old olive oil press" offers an upmarket, Greek-Mediterranean menu – pirate risotto, grilled prawns, *Spetsiot fish* – to a Latin and jazz soundtrack, with occasional live music. Some tables enjoy a stunning position on a jetty that extends right out into the harbour. Daily lunch & dinner.

**To Nero tis Agapis** Kounoupítsa ☎ 22980 74009. Virtually adjacent to *Patralis* (see above) and with a similar seafood-based menu (excellent seafood spaghetti), "The Water of Love" could hardly be a greater contrast in style and decor – self-consciously modern, island-style, with decent music and enthusiastic young staff. Crayfish €17, black tagliatelle with squid €15, zarzuela fish stew €18. Daily lunch & dinner.

## NIGHTLIFE

Late-night nightlife is mostly centred on Baltíza, the furthest of the inlets at the old harbour – here there are several seasonal clubs, though even in August they only really come to life at the weekend. Closer to town, Áyios Mámas beach also has a couple of lively music bars. Two cinemas operate in summer, close to the main square – Titania (with a roof for shelter, but open sides) and open-air, rooftop Marina.

**Balkoni** The elegant alternative to nearby *Socrates*; sip your wine or cocktails on a candlelit balcony overlooking the waterfront east of the Dápia; also open for coffee during the day. Daily 10am–2am.

**Bar Spetsa** Áyios Mámas. Chilled-out bar playing decent retro rock, mainly 60s and 70s. Strong drinks and a great craic most nights. Nightly 8pm–3am.

**La Luz** Old harbour. Classy music bar spreading over two storeys floors in a beautifully restored mansion with plenty of exposed brickwork. Open from 4pm for coffee and drinks, but the main action is late at night

– live music or DJs most weekends from 11.45pm. Daily 4pm–late.

**Mama's Beach Café** Áyios Mámas beach. Lively café and lunch spot by day, with sandwiches, milkshakes and waffles, while at night the upstairs music bar (playing summer party stuff) takes over. Daily 10.30am–2am.

**Socrates** English-pub-style bar on the waterfront east of the Dápia (main entry from the shopping street behind) serving draught beer, including Guinness, and showing big-screen sports. A popular hangout for local expats, especially on football nights. Daily 7pm–2am.

# The beaches

A single paved road circles Spétses, mostly high above a rocky coast but with access to beaches at various points. You can also get to many of the beaches by excursion boat.

Kaïki or **College Beach** is just twenty minutes' walk west of town, with a frequent bus service and extensive facilities including loungers, bars and a waterski outfit that also rents jet-skis. **Vréllos**, a small, pebbly cove in a pretty, wooded bay, is the end of the line for buses heading west out of Spétses. Thanks to paved access and a beach cocktail bar pumping out loud Greek rock it's almost always packed at weekends.

At the western extremity of the island, **Zoyeriá** is reached down a track that soon degenerates into a path (which doesn't stop locals riding their scooters) past a series of rocky coves – following this you eventually climb over a small headland to arrive at a sandy beach with a large and popular summer-only taverna, *Loula*. Many of the patrons here arrive the easy way, by boat.

The bay of **Ayía Paraskeví**, on the southwest coast, shelters a part-sand beach that is almost always quieter than its near neighbour, Áyii Anáryiri. The end of the eastern bus route, it has a seasonal café/bar, but no other development at all.

**Áyii Anáryiri** is the largest and most popular beach on Spétses: a long, sheltered, partly sandy bay, with an offshore swimming pontoon and a watersports centre offering kayaks, pedaloes, windsurfers and catamarans to rent, as well as a waterski boat. At the

## HIKING ACROSS SPÉTSES

If you want to explore Spétses on foot, you can strike directly across the island to many of the beaches. Follow Bótasi out of town, past the *Lazaros* taverna, and as you leave town a sign (the only one you'll see) points you up a paved road. The paving soon runs out, but a good broad track heads up towards the heights. At the top there are no signs at all: one track leads directly down the other side, to rejoin the road halfway between Áyii Anáryiri and Xylokériza (the other end of this track is optimistically signposted "Profítis Ilías 5", but in practice is virtually impassable, on two wheels or four). The better option is to turn right along the spine of the island, with increasingly impressive views across towards the mainland over both coasts; before long there's an obvious (unsigned) path heading down towards Áyii Anáryiri. Continue beyond this and there's a less obvious path to Ayía Paraskeví, while the main trail curls back around towards the north, eventually descending to the coast road near Vréllos.

end of the beach concrete steps lead round to the Bekiris Cave, a low-ceilinged, shallow cavern; you can clamber in through a narrow entrance at the back and then swim out, though best to have something on your feet for the sharp rocks.

Almost at the southern tip of the island a long, steep concrete track leads down to a cove of pale-coloured pebbles at **Xylokériza**. There's no sand at all here, but it's a beautiful spot, surrounded by pines and phoenix palms, and rarely crowded. There's a café and volleyball court.

**Ayía Marína** or Paradise Beach is a busy, almost suburban beach, within walking distance of the eastern edge of Spétses Town. Packed with loungers, it also has a popular bar-restaurant and a watersports operation offering kayaks and waterski and ringo rides. There are views offshore towards the tempting but off-limits islet of **Spetsopoúla**, the private property of the heirs of shipping magnate Stavros Niarchos.

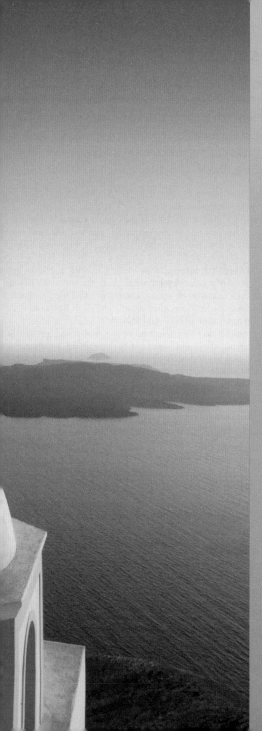

# The Cyclades

**357** Kéa

**360** Kýthnos

**363** Sérifos

**366** Sífnos

**372** Mílos

**377** Kímolos

**380** Ándhros

**384** Tínos

**388** Mýkonos

**394** Delos

**397** Sýros

**402** Páros

**410** Náxos

**418** Lesser Cyclades

**421** Amorgós

**425** Íos

**428** Síkinos

**430** Folégandhros

**434** Santoríni

**442** Anáfi

SANTORÍNI AT SUNSET

# The Cyclades

Named from the circle they form around the sacred island of Delos, the Cyclades (Kykládhes) offer Greece's best island-hopping. Each island has a strong, distinct character based on traditions, customs, topography and its historical development. Most are compact enough for a few days' exploration to show you a major part of their scenery and personality in a way that is impossible in Crete, Rhodes or most of the Ionian islands.

The islands do have some features in common. The majority (Ándhros, Kéa, Náxos and Tínos excepted) are arid and rocky, and most also share the "Cycladic" style of brilliant-white cuboid architecture, a feature of which is the central **kástro** of the old island capitals. The typical kástro has just one or two entrances, and a continuous outer ring of houses with all their doors and windows on the inner side, so forming a single protective perimeter wall.

The impact of mass tourism has been felt more severely in the Cyclades than anywhere else in Greece; yet whatever the level of tourist development, there are only three islands where it completely dominates their character in season: **Íos**, the original hippie island and still a paradise for hard-drinking backpackers, the volcanic cluster of **Santoríni** – a dramatic natural backdrop for luxury cruise liners – and **Mýkonos**, by far the most popular of the group, with its teeming old town, selection of gay, nudist and gay-nudist beaches, and sophisticated restaurants, clubs and hotels. After these, **Páros**, **Náxos** and **Mílos** are the most popular, their beaches and main towns packed at the height of the season. The once-tranquil **Lesser Cyclades** southeast of Náxos have become fashionable destinations in recent years, as have nearby **Amorgós**, and **Folégandhros** to the west. To avoid the hordes altogether the most promising islands are **Kýthnos** or **Sérifos** and for an even more remote experience **Síkinos**, **Kímolos** or **Anáfi**. For a completely different picture of the Cyclades, try the islands of **Tínos** with its imposing pilgrimage church and **Sýros** with its elegant Italianate townscape, both with a substantial Catholic minority. Due to their proximity to Attica, **Ándhros** and **Kéa** are predictably popular weekend havens for Athenian families, while **Sífnos** remains a smart, chic destination for tourists of all nationalities. The one UNESCO site, **Delos** – once a great religious centre for the Cyclades – is certainly worth making time for, visited most easily on a day-trip from Mýkonos. One consideration for the timing of your visit is that the Cyclades is the group worst affected by the *meltémi*, which scatters sand and tablecloths with ease between mid-July and mid-August. Delayed or cancelled ferries are not uncommon, so if you're heading back to Athens to catch a flight, leave yourself a day's leeway.

## ARRIVAL AND DEPARTURE

THE CYCLADES

### BY PLANE

There are airports on Páros, Mýkonos, Santoríni, Sýros, Mílos and Náxos. In season, or during storms when ferries are idle, you have little chance of getting a seat on any flight at less than three days' notice, and tickets are predictably expensive. Expect off-season (Nov–April) frequencies to drop by at least eighty percent.

---

A brief history p.357
Ancient Karthaia p.359
The Monastery of Khryssopiyí p.370
Mílos boat tour p.373
Panayía Panakhrándou p.383
The Dovecote Trail p.387

Old Delos Days p.396
Náxos Music Festival p.412
Climbing Mount Zas p.417
Homer's tomb p.428
The wineries p.440

TSIGRÁDHO BEACH, MÍLOS

# Highlights

**①Beaches of Mílos** Spectacular shorelines characterized by multicoloured rocks and volcanically heated sand. **See p.375**

**②Mýkonos Town** Labyrinthine lanes crammed with restaurants, boutiques and nightlife. **See p.390**

**③Delos** The Cyclades' sacred centre and holiest ancient site, birthplace of Apollo and Artemis. **See p.394**

**④Ermoúpolis, Sýros** The elegant capital of the Cyclades, an Italianate architectural jewel and once Greece's busiest port. **See p.398**

**⑤Church of Ekatondapylianí, Parikiá** An imposing and ornate Paleochristian church on Páros, incorporating a number of impressive architectural styles. **See p.404**

**⑥Mount Zas, Náxos** The only must-do trek in the Cyclades: climb the archipelago's highest mountain. **See p.417**

**⑦Hóra, Folégandhros** The "town of five squares", free of traffic and sitting atop a spectacular cliff, arguably the most beautiful inland island capital. **See p.431**

**⑧Caldera of Santoríni** The geological wonder of a crater left by a colossal volcanic explosion, offering unforgettable sunset views. **See p.436**

**HIGHLIGHTS ARE MARKED ON THE MAP ON P.356**

**6**

## BY FERRY

Most of the Cyclades are served by main-line ferries from Pireás. Boats for Kéa, and seasonally elsewhere, depart from Lávrio. There are regular services from Rafína to Ándhros, Tínos and Mýkonos, with seasonal sailings elsewhere. All three ports are easily reached by bus from Athens. Between May and Sept there are also a few weekly sailings to the most popular islands from Crete and the eastern Aegean.

**Agents and tickets** Routes are covered by Aegean Speed Lines (w aegeanspeedlines.gr), ANEK lines (w anek.gr), Blue Star ferries (w bluestarferries.gr), Hellenic Seaways (w hsw.gr), SeaJets (w seajets.gr) and NEL (w nel.gr). All agents are required to issue computerized tickets, to conform to EU regulations and prevent the ferry overcrowding. In high season (particularly Easter, August and during elections),

popular routes will be booked up, so it is important to check availability upon arrival in Greece and book your outward and inbound pre-flight ferry tickets well ahead (particularly those returning to Pireás from the most popular islands). That said, agents may have little advance information on ferry schedules, and purchasing a ticket too far in advance can lead to problems with delayed or cancelled boats. There is usually more space on ferries sailing between islands than to and from Pireás.

**Timetables** The frequency of Pireás, Lávrio and Rafína sailings given in the chapter is from June to August, and the timings are for both direct and indirect services. For other islands the listings are intended to give an idea of services from late June to early Sept, when most visitors tour the islands. During other months, expect schedules to be at or below the minimum level listed, with some ferries cancelled entirely.

## HIGHLIGHTS
1. Beaches of Milos
2. Mýkonos Town
3. Delos
4. Ermoúpolis, Sýros
5. Church of Ekatondapylianí, Parikiá
6. Mount Zas, Náxos
7. Hóra, Folégandhros
8. Caldera of Santoríni

**THE CYCLADES**

## A BRIEF HISTORY

The Cyclades are the most quintessentially Greek of all the islands and their long history reflects that. The mining of **obsidian**, the black, sharp-edged volcanic glass used for making implements, originated on **Mílos**; shards dating to 11,000 BC have been found deep in the Peloponnese, demonstrating early seaborne Paleolithic trade. The Bronze Age started here around 2800 BC and with it came the **Cycladic civilization**, notable for its sought-after geometric, minimalist figurines made of marble from **Páros** or **Náxos**. **Mining** for copper, silver and gold, combined with the islands' strategic position, turned them into trading centres.

By 2000 BC the Cretan Minoans had become influential in the area, particularly on **Santoríni**. Such influence, however, came to an end with a catastrophic volcanic eruption around 1600 BC. The Ionian Greeks arrived around 1000 BC and within two hundred years the first cities had appeared. **Delos** became a great religious centre in antiquity.

During and after the Persian wars, **Athens** gradually stripped away the wealth and influence of the **Delian Confederacy**. The Cyclades only regained prosperity during the Hellenistic period, as demonstrated by the construction of numerous large, impressive watchtowers, most notably on Náxos. The subsequent Roman occupation converted Delos back into a successful commercial centre, until a series of raids from the east eventually destroyed it. Under **Byzantine** rule, with little control or support from distant Constantinople, the islands were vulnerable to **pirates**, and settlements moved from the open coast to inland, defensive **Kástros**, where you find them today.

With the fall of Constantinople to the Crusaders in 1204, the Cyclades came under **Venetian** control and were divided up by adventurers under **Marco Sanudo** who set up the Náxos-based Duchy of the Aegean. Catholicism prospered, some vestiges of which are still found today on Sýros and Tínos. Most of the islands were taken by the **Ottomans** from the 1530s onwards, though Tínos held out until 1715. As they rightly considered the West a bigger threat, the Turks encouraged the Orthodox Church to fight a resurgence against the former Catholic majority.

After the revolution against the Ottoman Empire in 1821, the Cyclades became part of the Greek state in 1832 and **Sýros**, in particular, prospered, as the new state's largest port and a major industrial base. However, the development of **Pireás** and the 1893 opening of the **Corinth Canal** led to a sharp industrial and commercial decline. This was only reversed in the 1960s when the discovery of the pleasures of **Mýkonos** kick-started the tourism boom that continues unabated today.

**Catamaran and small-boat services** These operate during the summer season from Pireás and Rafína, replacing winter ferries on some routes. Catamaran travel is expensive, but when time is an issue these high-speed craft are a welcome addition to the conventional fleet. The slower *Express Skopelitis* sails daily in season between Náxos and Amorgós, overnighting at the latter and connecting Irakliá, Skhinoússa, Koufoníssi and Dhonoússa – for current info call ☎ 22850 71256.

# Kéa

**KÉA (Tziá)**, the nearest of the Cyclades to the mainland, is extremely popular with Athenian families in August and at weekends year-round; their impact has spread beyond the small resorts, and much of the coastline is peppered with holiday homes built with the locally quarried green-brown stone. Because so many visitors self-cater, there is a preponderance of villa accommodation and not as many tavernas as you might expect. However, outside August or weekends, the island, with its rocky, forbidding perimeter and inland oak and almond groves, is an enticing destination for those who enjoy a rural ramble: ten separate walking paths have been earmarked and are well signposted.

## ARRIVAL AND DEPARTURE                                                         KÉA

**By ferry** There are regular ferry connections to and from Lávrio on the mainland; ferries dock at Korissía. Only a few agents in Athens sell ferry tickets from Lávrio to Kéa, so you will probably need to get these in Lávrio.

**Destinations** Ándhros (1 weekly; 5hr 40min); Folégandhros (1 weekly; 12hr); Kýthnos (1–4 weekly; 1hr 15min); Lávrio (2–4 daily; 1hr); Mílos (1 weekly; 12hr 20min); Náxos (1 weekly; 6hr 40min); Páros (1 weekly; 5hr 20min); Sýros (1–4 weekly; 3hr 40min); Tínos ( weekly; 3hr 50min).

## INFORMATION

**Tourist office** At the seafront in Korissía (Mon–Fri 8.30am–2pm).

**Services** There are two banks and three ATMs in Korissía. Ioulídha has one bank and three ATMs. The island's only post office is opposite the archeological museum (see opposite) in Ioulídha.

**Travel agents** Kea Paths (☎22880 22651, ✆keapath .gr) in Korissía offers a different walking tour or excursion around the island every day; €8–15 per person depending on the length of the trip.

## GETTING AROUND

**By bus** Buses always meet the boats, and from mid-June to September there's a regular fixed schedule around the island (every 30–45min). Most visitors bring their cars along, so there are not many extensive bus services. You may need one of the six taxis available.

**By car and motorcycle** There is only one, expensive rental outlet, so it's best to rent a car or motorcycle in Athens (see p.113) – or the airport, which is very close to Lávrio – and take it to Kéa, like Athenians do. The island has three petrol stations, all on the road to the port.

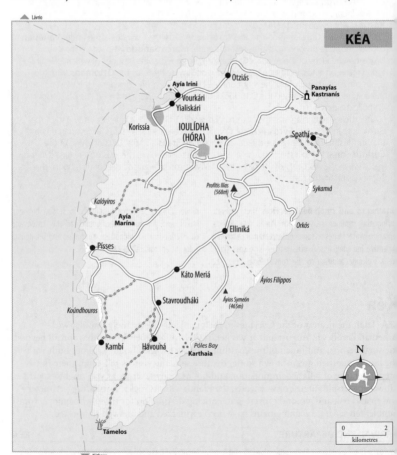

**ANCIENT KARTHAIA**

The only remains of any real significance from Kéa's past are fragments of temples of Apollo and Athena at **ancient Karthaia**, tucked away on the southeastern edge of the island above Póles Bay, with an excellent deserted twin beach. It is a good ninety-minute round-trip walk from the hamlet of Stavroudháki (on the paved road linking Ioulídha and Havouná), and the inland paved road is worth following along the island's summit from Ioulídha, as it affords fine views over the thousands of magnificent oaks, Kéa's most distinctive feature. Kea Paths (see opposite) offers a walking trip (June–Sept Sat only).

# Korissía

The small port of **KORISSÍA** is unlike any other in the Cyclades; with its red-tiled roofs and Neoclassical houses, it could be Pláka-by-the-Sea. It is very convenient as a base; from there you can easily get by bus to Otziás (6km), Ioulídha (6km) or Písses (16km). Although the port beach, **Áyios Yeóryios**, is adequate, there is better swimming at **Yialiskári**, a small, eucalyptus-fringed cove after the eastern promontory on the road to Vourkári.

## ACCOMMODATION
KORISSÍA

**Brillante Zoi** ☎ 22880 22685/86, ⓦ hotelbrillante.gr. A comfortable hotel on the middle of the port beach, with a beautifully overgrown garden, idiosyncratic furnishings, spacious rooms and a sumptuous breakfast. The chatty, welcoming owner will feel more like an old acquaintance than your landlady. **€70**

**Karthea** ☎ 22880 21204, ⓦ hotelkarthea.gr. Dated 1970s hotel, but very centrally located at the beginning of the port beach. Followers of modern history would be interested to learn that this is where Greek junta leaders were held under house arrest in 1974. Breakfast included. **€75**

★ **Keos Katoikies** ☎ 22880 84002, ⓦ keos.gr. Cool, contemporary minimalist studios, each one with its own large balcony in a dramatic setting overlooking Korissía bay. Make sure you watch the sunset in the adjoining café. The room price includes an excellent English buffet breakfast. Free wi-fi at reception. Easter–Oct. **€120**

**Porto Kea** ☎ 22880 22870, ⓦ portokea-suites.com. Luxurious hotel behind the main road and by the church of Áyios Yeóryios, with a large swimming pool and complimentary internet access. It has its own trendy bar, Ammos, on the beach in front offering free chairs for hotel clients. Breakfast included. Easter–Oct. **€160**

## EATING AND DRINKING

**En Plo** ☎ 694 86 05 176. Opposite the ferry disembarkation point, this snack bar-café serves delicious desserts. Try the chocolate soufflé with a cappuccino for €5 while watching the world go by and the ferries dock. It's a lively spot in the early evening. April–Oct daily 8am–1am; Nov–March Fri–Sat 8am–1am.

★ **Fillipas** ☎ 22880 21690. Built in local Kéa stone and sitting on the hill above Keos Katoikies, this is the best grill restaurant on the island. Although often booked for functions, they will always find you a table

and serve you promptly. Try the giant steaks or its signature beefburger filled with local cheese (€8). April–Oct daily 6pm–1am; Nov–March Fri–Sat 6pm–1am.

**Magazés** ☎ 22880 21104. The best in the cluster of the port restaurants, this traditional taverna with a small but tasty range of Greek dishes also offers fresh fish, often caught by the speargun of the owner. If you crave meat instead, try the baked pork with potatoes for €9. April–Oct daily 9am–midnight.

# Ioulídha

Kéa's capital, **IOULÍDHA** (Hóra), with its winding flagstoned paths, is beautifully situated in an amphitheatric fold in the hills. It is by no means a typical Cycladic town, but is architecturally the most interesting settlement on the island. Accordingly it has numerous bars and bistros, much patronized in August and at weekends, but during other times the town is quiet, its atmospheric, labyrinthine lanes excluding vehicles.

The lower reaches of the town stretch across a spur to the **kástro**, a tumbledown Venetian fortress incorporating stones from an ancient temple of Apollo. Ioulídha's **archeological museum** (Tues–Sun 8.30am–2.30pm; €3) displays extensive finds from the four ancient city-states of Kéa, its highlight being thirteen female Minoan-style statues. Fifteen-minutes' walk northeast of Ioulídha on the path toward Otziás, you pass the **Lion of Kéa**, a sixth-century BC sculpture carved out of an outcrop of rock, 6m long and 3m high – the effect is most striking from a distance.

**En Lefko** ☏ 22880 22155. On the street between Hóra's two squares, this coffee shop has one of the most romantic gardens, suspended over the cliffs and overlooking the port and beyond. Dimly lit, this is the perfect place to snuggle up with a cappuccino (€4). April–Oct daily 8am–2am.

**Hotel Serie** ☏ 22880 22355, ⊕ serie.gr. Only 100m from the Ioulídha bus stop and employing a tasteful colour combination of blue and orange throughout – from the stone building itself to the furnishings – this is maybe the best-situated boutique hotel on the island with views both of Ioulídha itself and the valley below. Easter–Oct. **€80**

★ **Rolandos** Main square ☏ 22880 22224. The chef, Rolandos, comes from Corfu and serves a traditional Greek menu with an Ionian flavour. His moussaka (€8) – using courgettes instead of potatoes – is as famed as his house wine. Easter–Oct daily 10am–2am.

## The northwest coast

Kéa's northwest coast attracts the most visitors. **VOURKÁRI**, strung out around the next bay, a couple of kilometres northeast of Korissía, is a fishing village, arguably more attractive than Korissía, serving as a hangout for the yachting set. Another 4km further **OTZIÁS** has a beach that's bigger and better than any on the northern shore, though more exposed to prevailing meltémi winds.

The eighteenth-century monastery of **Panayías Kastrianís** (June–Sept sunrise–sunset) is 7km along a surfaced road from Otziás. From here you can take the pleasant walk on dirt tracks and occasional paths to Ioulídha in another two hours. Further on, **Spathí**, only reachable by car 3km away from the monastery on a dirt road, is by far the island's finest beach.

**Anemousa** Otziás ☏ 22880 21335. A modern cluster of villas alternating the brown-gold Kéa stone with whitewashed walls. The colour scheme extends to the tasteful furnishings inside the spacious studios. April–Oct. **€55**

**Aristos** Vourkári ☏ 22880 21475. Don't be fooled by the look of this sleepy fish and seafood taverna at the entrance to the village; it is renowned for its crayfish spaghetti (€20–30) drawing customers from all over the island. April–Oct daily noon–midnight; Nov–March Fri–Sat noon–midnight.

**Otziás** Otziás beach ☏ 22887 70500. You can relax in the taverna's beach deckchairs for €4/day in the morning before retiring under its roof to sample a variety of grilled meat and fish from only €8 for lunch when the sun gets really scorching. Easter–Oct daily noon–8.30pm.

**Strofi tou Mimi** Vourkári ☏ 22880 21480. The locals are almost equally divided on whether this place, on the corner of the road towards Otziás, or *Aristos* (see above) is the best fish taverna on the island. You'll have to make up your own mind by dining in both. *Strofi tou Mimi* is only slightly cheaper. April–Oct daily 7pm–midnight.

## The south

The road southwest of Ioulídha twists around a scenic agricultural valley and emerges at a large sandy beach at **Písses**. Beyond here, the asphalt peters out at the end of the 5km road south to **Koúndhouros beach**, consisting of two sheltered coves popular with yachters. A further 2km south, at **Kambí**, there's a nice little beach and a good taverna of the same name.

# Kýthnos

One of the lesser known and most low-key of the larger Cyclades, **KÝTHNOS** is an antidote to the overdevelopment you may encounter elsewhere, so much so that credit cards are still not accepted in many places. Few foreigners visit, and the island – known also as Thermiá, after its renowned hot springs – is even quieter than Kéa, particularly to the south where drives or long hikes from **Dhryopídha** to its coastal coves are the primary diversion. This is truly a place to sprawl on sunbed-free beaches without having to jostle for space.

## ARRIVAL AND DEPARTURE

**KÝTHNOS**

**By ferry** Boats dock at the west-coast in Mérihas. There is frequent service to Lávrio and Pireás, but ferries to nearby Kéa, Sérifos or other islands are sparse.

**Destinations** Ándhros (0–1 weekly 4hr 30min); Folégandhros (1–2 weekly; 8hr 30min); Íos (1–2 weekly; 8hr); Kéa (2–4 weekly; 1hr 10min); Kímolos (3–5 weekly; 3hr); Lávrio (1–2 daily; 1hr 40min–2hr 30min); Mílos (1–2 daily; 4hr); Náxos (1 weekly; 5hr); Páros (1 weekly; 4hr); Pireás (4–5 weekly; 3hr); Sérifos (4–8 weekly; 1hr 30min); Sífnos (4–8 weekly; 2hr 15min); Síkinos (1 weekly; 7hr 30min); Sýros (2–4 weekly; 2hr 20min); Tínos (1 weekly; 2hr 30min).

## INFORMATION

**Tourist office** A good and helpful information office is open by the jetty during ferry arrivals even on Sundays or late at night.

**Services** There is one bank and two ATMs in Mérihas: one up the steps near the disembarkation point, and a second on the harbour road. These are the only ATMs on the island, and hotels or restaurants do not as a rule accept credit cards. Hóra has the island's only post office (Mon–Fri 9.30am–2pm).

**Activities** Aqua Team (☎22810 31333, ⓦaquakythnos .com), opposite the spa in Loutrá, offer PADI, ANDI and IAHD diving courses.

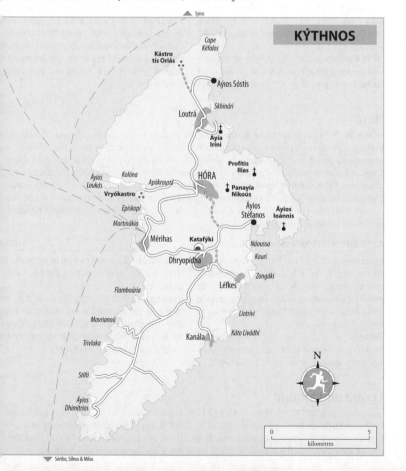

## GETTING AROUND

**By bus** Buses run from Mérihas port around six times daily from early June to September, serving Hóra (15min), Loutrá (30min), Dhryopídha (30min) and Kanála (45min).
**By boat** There is a *kaïki* from Mérihas (4 daily; ☎ 22810 32104) to the northern beaches of Apókrousi and Kolóna.
**By car and motorcycle** Halivelakis rental agency (☎ 22810 32506, ⊚ halivelakis.gr) operate a manne stand at the port during ship arrivals.

# Mérihas and around

**MÉRIHAS** is an attractive ferry and fishing port – but not really the place to base your stay. The closest beach of any repute is the fine sandy cove of **Martinakia**, a ten-minute stroll north of the port, while **Episkopí**, a 500m stretch of clean grey sand, is thirty minutes' walk further north. About an hour's walk northwest of Episkopí are the vastly better and more popular beaches of **Apókroussi** and **Kolóna**, the latter a very picturesque sand spit joining Kýthnos to the islet of **Áyios Loukás**.

## ACCOMMODATION AND EATING                        MÉRIHAS AND AROUND

**Martinos Studios** ☎ 22810 3246, ⊚ martinos-studios .com. Good-sized rooms, only 30m from the sea and overlooking the harbour, with local Kýthnos furnishings, stone floors, fridge, a/c, TV, kitchenette and phone. Reception is closed in the afternoon. Breakfast included. May–Sept. **€50**
★ **To Kandouni** ☎ 22810 32220. For those who fancy meat in a sea of fish tavernas: here is an excellent grill – situated near the port police – with many different starters

and salads as well as specialities such as *sfoungáto* (loca cheese croquettes) for €6. The owners also rent studios above the restaurant. April–Oct daily noon–1am. Studios **€50**
**Villa Elena** Martinakia ☎ 22810 32275, ⊚ villa-elen .gr. Two-storey self-catering maisonettes situated on slope with superb sea views over the Aegean and a stone throw away from the best beach near Mérihas. Full equipped kitchenette, TV, parking and port transfer available. April–Sept. **€70**

# Hóra

**HÓRA** lies 7.5km northeast of Mérihas, in the middle of the island. Though the town looks unpromising at first sight, wander into the narrow streets beyond the initial square and you'll find a wonderful network of alleyways, weaving their way past shops, churches and through tiny squares with colourful cafés. The early nineteenth-century church of **Áyios Ioánnis Theológos** is worth a visit for its elaborate wooden iconostasis. However, its most valuable possession is a miraculous seventeenth-century icon of the three matriarchs (Elisabeth, Anne and Virgin Mary), said to have been found floating in the sea by local fishermen.

## ACCOMMODATION AND EATING                                    HÓRA

**Apocalypse** ☎ 22810 31272. Relatively cheap (beer €3) café-bar, next to the main church of – appropriately enough – St John. When the bar closes at midnight, the club of the same name opposite – which plays anything from trance to Greek popular tunes – opens its doors till 6am. Daily 7am–midnight.
**Filoxenia** ☎ 22810 31644, ⊚ filoxenia-kythnos.gr. Welcoming *pension* next to the main square with clean, basic rooms arranged around a flowery courtyard. It's a

convenient base if you want to travel by bus around th island, but still sample whatever nightlife there i afterwards. **€50**
**Messaria** ☎ 22810 31620. Large restaurant that offer the Hóra speciality of rabbit in wine sauce for €9. Unlik other establishments in Hóra that close during the day a the clients are out on the beaches, this one's open for lunch as well as dinner. Daily noon–midnight.

# Loutrá and around

The resort of **LOUTRÁ**, 4.5km north of Hóra, is named after its mineral thermal baths. Its nineteenth-century spa was designed by Ernst Ziller, the architect of many of Greece's finest Neoclassical public buildings. There is a small beach at Loutrá, but the bay of **Ayía Iríni**, just 1km east, is much nicer for a dip. Just north of Loutrá, at

**Maroula**, Mesolithic graves dating to about the eighth millennium BC suggest Kýthnos may have been one of the earliest inhabited Cycladic islands; other sites indicate copper mining and smelting. About a ninety-minute walk from Loutrá, on Cape Kéfalos, lie the picturesque ruins of the medieval capital **Kástro tís Oriás**, once home to around 5000 people, but now abandoned.

## ACCOMMODATION

**LOUTRÁ AND AROUND**

**Meltemi** ☎ 22810 31271, ⊛ meltemihotel-kythnos.gr. Fully renovated hotel on the road out of Loutrá that offers dependable good value, with beautifully tiled walls, a landscaped garden and different colour schemes in each room. It organizes daily excursions all over Kýthnos. Credit cards accepted; breakfast included; free wi-fi available; free pick-ups from Mérihas offered. April–Oct. **€65**

★ **Porto Klaras** ☎ 22810 31276, ⊛ porto-klaras.gr. A hotel worth making the trip to Loutrá just to stay in; its rooms are huge, with decorated carved recesses and large, sculpted beds, while its balconies – some of which come with sofas – have great port views. Free wi-fi, safebox, and, for those who dislike a/c, there are ceiling fans, as well. April–Oct. **€70**

## EATING AND DRINKING

**Araxovóli** ☎ 22810 31082. A fish taverna conveniently situated in the middle of the quay that also offers tasty cooked meals (dish of the day €10). If you want to eat calamari, octopus, crayfish or lobster on the island, this is the place to make a beeline for. Daily 8am–1am.

**Sofrano** ☎ 22810 31436. A waterfront restaurant for the yachting jet-set, this is the most romantic establishment on the island complete with candle-lit tables, flower-filled vases, pink tablecloths and bundles of atmosphere. Thankfully the food (mains €12) matches the decor. March–Nov daily 9am–midnight.

# Dhryopídha and the south

From Hóra you can drive south to **DHRYOPÍDHA**; more visually appealing than Hóra by virtue of spanning a well-watered valley, its red-tiled roofs are reminiscent of Spain or Tuscany. It was once the island's capital, built around one of Greece's largest **caves**, the Katafýki, that served as a hiding place from corsairs. South of Dhryopídha, **KANÁLA** is a relaxed alternative to Loutrá, with its **Panayía Kanála** church set in a tiny but pleasant pine woodland and home to a miracle-working icon by the seventeenth-century Cretan master, Skordhilis.

## ACCOMMODATION AND EATING

**DHRYOPÍDHA AND THE SOUTH**

**Bouritis** Kanála ☎ 22810 32350. Large self-catering apartments and studios on the beach, all with balcony sea views, a/c, TV and kitchen, sharing a delightfully tended garden with a BBQ. There is also a well-stocked supermarket in the premises. **€60**

**Mílas Rooms** Áyios Dhimítrios ☎ 22810 32815.

Modern villa complex at the end of Áyios Dhimítrios beach decorated in schist stone and marble and comprising large suites with separate, fully equipped kitchens. The owners also operate a restaurant nearby, whose *sfougata* (€6) have won a Greek gourmet prize. May–Sept. **€40**

# Sérifos

**SÉRIFOS** has long languished outside the mainstream of history and modern tourism. Little has happened here since Perseus returned with Medusa's head in time to save his mother, Danaë, from being ravished by the local king Polydectes – turning him, his court and the green island into stone. Many would-be visitors are deterred by the apparently barren, hilly interior, which, with the stark, rocky coastline, makes Sérifos appear uninhabited until the ferry turns into postcard-picturesque Livádhi Bay. This element of surprise continues as you slowly discover a number of lovely **beaches** around the island.

Sérifos is also great for serious **walkers**, who can head for several small villages in the under-explored interior, plus some isolated coves. Many people still keep livestock and produce their own cognac-red wines, which are an acquired taste.

6

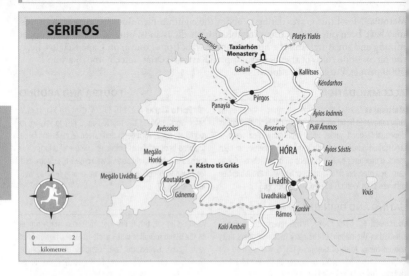

SÉRIFOS

N

0    2
kilometres

## ARRIVAL AND DEPARTURE

SÉRIFOS

**By ferry** There is a fast catamaran service to Pireás taking only two hours and there are good connections in the summer to many other islands. The port is at the Livádhi promontory.

Destinations Ándhros (1 weekly; 4hr); Folégandhros (2–4 weekly; 2hr); Íos (1–2 weekly; 2hr); Kímolos (3–5 weekly; 3hr 30min); Kýthnos (4–8 weekly; 1hr 20min); Mílos (4–6 weekly; 1hr 45min); Mýkonos (1 weekly; 3hr 45min); Páros (1 weekly; 2hr 40min); Pireás (6–8 weekly 4hr); Sífnos (1–3daily; 45min); Síkinos (1–2 weekly; 3hr 10min); Sýros (1–3 weekly; 3hr 20min); Tínos (1 weekly; 3hr).

## INFORMATION

**Services** There are two ATMs along the seafront in Livádhi. The island's post office is in the lowest quarter of Hóra. For internet access try *Malabar* pub (☎ 22810 52333) in Livádhi inside the shopping arcade (€4/hr); it also attracts the local youth in numbers because of its pool table (daily 10am–1.30pm & 6pm–1am).

**Travel agents** Krinas Travel (☎ 22810 51488; daily

9am–9pm) opposite the disembarkation point has become by default the starting point for help to visitors on the island.

**Activities** Avlómonas beach (see opposite) is the headquarters of Sérifos Scuba Divers (☎ 693 25 70 552, ⓦ serifosscubadivers.gr), who operate scuba-diving and snorkelling trips plus day-long boat excursions during July and August.

## GETTING AROUND

**By bus** The bus stop and timetable are at the base of the yacht- and fishing-boat jetty. There is a circular bus route serving Panayía–Galaní–Kéndarhos–Áyios Ioánnis–Psilí Ámmos (2–7 daily; circular route 1hr), Hóra (every 30min in summer; 15min; the last weekend bus from Hóra is after midnight) and Panayía–Galaní–Kéndarhos–Áyios

Ioánnis–Psilí Ámmos–Méga Livádhi–Koutalás (2 daily; 30min).

**By car and motorcycle** For car and motorcycle rental try Blue Bird (☎ 22810 51511, ⓦ rentacar-bluebird.gr), next to the filling station on the main street of Livádhi, or from Kartsonaki Bros (☎ 22810 51534) at Livadhákia.

## Livádhi and around

Most visitors stay in the port, **LIVÁDHI**, set in a wide greenery-fringed bay and handy for most of the island's beaches. The usually calm bay here is a magnet for island-hopping yachts, to take on fresh water which, despite its barren appearance, Sérifos has in abundance. Livádhi and the neighbouring cove of Livadhákia are certainly the easiest places to find rooms in, along with any amenities you might need, which are scarce elsewhere.

## Beaches

The very attractive curve of **Avlómonas**, the long Livádhi town beach, has the advantage of overlooking the inland capital, so that when you are swimming in the sea you have a great inland view. Heading away from the dock, climb over the southerly headland to reach **Livadhákia**, a golden-sand beach, shaded by tamarisk trees. A further ten-minutes' stroll across the low headland to the south brings you to the smaller **Karávi** beach, with its blue-green clear waters, but which has no shade or facilities.

North of Livádhi Bay and accessible by bus in summer – or a 45-minute walk (3km) along a (mostly) surfaced road – is **Psilí Ámmos**, a long, sheltered, award-winning white-sand beach, backed by a large reservoir, and considered the island's best. It is possible to continue on the road, then by path for ten minutes to the larger, but more exposed, **Áyios Ioánnis** beach. Additionally, two more sandy coves, **Liá** (naturist) and **Áyios Sóstis**, hide at the far eastern flank of the island opposite the islet Voús; they are popular with the locals, and accessible via a dirt track off the road to Psilí Ámmos.

**6**

## ACCOMMODATION                                                  LIVÁDHI

**Areti ⊕** 22810 51479, **ⓦ** aretihotel.com. Attractively positioned hotel on the headland overlooking Livádhi, with a lovely communal terrace fronting a tiny beach and the entrance to the bay. They also have studios and apartments further out for around €50. April–Oct. **€60**

**Coralli Camping at Livadhákia Beach ⊕** 22810 51500, **ⓦ** coralli.gr. Superbly located and managed camping with a communal pool, restaurant, bar, mini-market and free wi-fi. This has been named by the Greek *Vima* newspaper as the best campsite in Greece. They also run the more modern four-person *Coralli Studios* for €100, closer to town. April–Oct. **€11**

**★ Maïstráli ⊕** 22810 51220, **ⓦ** hotelmaistrali .com. Seventies-built and furnished hotel but, being the tallest building in town, it has balconies (many frequented by nesting birds) with the best views. At the start of the beach, it is situated conveniently for everything: nightlife, beach and restaurants. Breakfast included. April–Oct. **€55**

**Naïás ⊕** 22810 51749, **ⓦ** naiasserifos.gr. A slightly dated, but comfortable, good-value hotel on the headland between Livádhi and Livadhákia, with a sociable owner; come here to make friends, not just pass through. All rooms with balconies, some with sea views. Breakfast included. **€55**

**Vasso ⊕** 22810 51346. Very spacious, spotless rooms – some with kitchens – looking inwards into a common courtyard, right on the asphalted road from Livádhi to Livadhákia. If airiness and roominess is your thing, look no further – these are simply exceptional value. **€40**

## EATING AND DRINKING

**Kalís** Waterfront **⊕** 694 24 67 987. One of the most popular ouzerí, where you may have to queue to get a table; you may be tempted to stuff yourself with just its excellent mezédhes, but hang on and try the delicious crayfish spaghetti for €14. Daily 1am–1am.

**Metalleio** Livádhi **⊕** 22810 51755. Hidden behind the coastal road, this is one of the few restaurants in the Cyclades where you may have to book. Great service and food without having to break the bank; imaginative mains from €12; and desserts that can't be finished. After midnight it becomes a nightclub with occasional live bands. Easter–Oct daily 6pm–1am.

**★ Sail ⊕** 22810 52242. German-managed beach café-bar in the middle of Livádhi beach that transforms itself into a sophisticated first-rate restaurant at night, with a chef from Salonika who cooks excellent and varied European or Greek food (mains €9). Easter–Oct daily 8am–2am.

## NIGHTLIFE

Nightlife is lively and mostly clustered in or near the Livádhi seafront mini-mall.

**Shark** Livádhi **⊕** 693 24 11 657. Set in a conspicuous roof garden above the mini-mall, where all nightlife seems to be clustered, this is an institution on the island playing mostly Top 10 hits. It has a good selection of bottled beers for €5 and some strong cocktails for €7. April–Oct daily 9pm–5am.

**Yacht club** Livádhi Beach **⊕** 22810 51888, **ⓦ** yachtclubserifos.gr. Hard to imagine that this was the first and only taverna in Livádhi back in 1938. It seems that every person under 30 on the island will come here to be seen at some point during the night, every night. Easter–Oct daily 8am–4am.

## Hóra

Quiet and atmospheric, **HÓRA** – only 2km from Livádhi – is one of the most unspoilt villages of the Cyclades. The best sights are in the precarious upper town: follow signs to the kástro to reach the top via steep and occasionally overgrown stairways. The central square, Ayíou Athanasíou, just northwest of the summit, has an attractive church and a small but colourful Neoclassical town hall. From the main bus stop, starting from the *Tap Bar* (see below), a circular signposted loop "route A" takes you to Áyios Konstandínos where on a clear day you can see as far as Sífnos.

### EATING AND DRINKING                      HÓRA

**Alóni** ☎ 22810 52603. A restaurant with superb westerly views over Livádhi that offers tasty Mediterranean specialities (including rabbit in lemon sauce for €8). More locals than tourists frequent it at weekends because of its live Greek music evenings. Daily 6pm–1am.

**Stou Stratou** ☎ 22810 52566, ⓦ stoustratou.com. An atmospheric café on the main square with a poetry-strewn menu which offers a nice alternative to eating on the busy seafront down below. Its chocolate cake (€5) is renowned all over the island. Daily noon–2am.

**Tap** ☎ 22810 52513. Just up from the final bus stop, this is a cosy alternative rock pub for people who just want to drink cold beer, sit at the bar and listen to the bass bouncing off the walls and down their solar plexus. June–Sept daily 9am–5am.

## The north and west

If you venture north from Psili Ámmos (p.365) your best bet for a swim is the sheltered cove of **Platýs Yialós** at the extreme northeastern tip of the island, reached easily by a partly paved road. Immediately after the Platýs Yialós turn is the fortified fifteenth-century monastery of **Taxiarhón**, once home to sixty monks but currently inhabited by only one. Treasures of the monastic **catholicon** include an ivory-inlaid bishop's throne, silver lamps from Egypt (to where many Serifiots emigrated during the nineteenth century) and the finely carved **iconostasis**. Call before you arrive (☎ 22810 51027) to arrange a visit; a donation is expected.

If you drive north from Hóra, you reach a junction in the road; follow the signs west for Megálo Horió and on to **Megálo Livádhi**, a remote but lovely beach resort 10km west of Hóra. Iron and copper ores were once exported from here, via a loading bridge that still hangs over the water. At the north end of the beach, there is a monument to four workers killed in 1916 in one of Greece's first protest strikes for better pay and conditions.

An alternative turning just below Megálo Horió leads 3.5km to the small mining and fishing port of **Koutalás**, a pretty sweep of bay with a church-tipped rock and a long, if narrow, beach. Above the port are the scant ruins of the medieval **Kástro tís Griás**. The winding track above the village leads east back to Livádhi, but there are no places to buy refreshments on the two-hour journey back. A side-track en route leads down to the very pretty but shadeless **Kaló Ambéli** beach.

# Sífnos

**SÍFNOS** is prettier, tidier and more cultivated than its northern neighbours. In keeping with the island's somewhat high-class clientele, camping rough is forbidden, while nude sunbathing is not tolerated. The island's modest size makes it eminently explorable. The areas to head for are the port, **Kamáres**, the island's capital **Apollonía**, as well as the east and south coasts. There is nothing in the north worth a peek, except maybe the small fishing village of **Herrónisos**, but even that is too far and offers too little for the first-time visitor. Sífnos has a strong tradition of pottery (as early as the third century BC) and has long been esteemed for its distinctive cuisine, with sophisticated casseroles baked in the clay-fired *gástres* (pots), from where the word gastronomy derives. The island is perhaps best appreciated today, however, for its many beautifully situated **churches** and **monasteries**, and for the beautiful scenery around **Vathý** in the far southwest (see p.371).

## ARRIVAL AND DEPARTURE

SÍFNOS

**By ferry** Sífnos is better connected with the mainland and with the rest of the Cyclades than its northern neighbours. Ferries dock at the port in Kamáres.

Destinations Ándhros (1 weekly; 5hr 30min); Folégandhros (1–2 weekly; 1hr 30min–4hr); Íos (1–3 weekly; 3hr); Kímolos (2–5 weekly; 1hr 45min); Kýthnos (1–3 weekly;

2hr–15min); Mílos (5–7 weekly; 1hr); Mýkonos (1 weekly; 5hr); Páros (2 weekly; 3hr); Pireás (2–4 daily; 3–5hr); Santoríni (2 weekly; 4hr 30min); Sérifos (1–3 daily; 40min–1hr); Síkinos (2 weekly; 2hr); Sýros (2–3 weekly; 2hr 30min–5hr 30min).

## INFORMATION

**Tourist office** There is an information centre opposite the disembarkation point (Mon–Fri 8am–3.30pm).
**Services** There are three banks and four ATMs in Apollonía; the post office is beside the central square. *Stavros Hotel* (see p.368) in Kamáres operates an internet and fax hub available to non-residents at €4/hr.

**Travel agents** Katsoularis Travel on Stenó in Apollonía (daily 9.30am–2pm & 6–9.30pm; ☎ 22840 31004) can help you find accommodation, tours and ferry tickets. Aegean Thesaurus (☎ 22840 33527), on Kamáres main street, can arrange accommodation across the island.

## GETTING AROUND

**By bus** The bus service is excellent, most of the roads are good, and there's a vast network of paths that are mostly easy to follow. Buses leave regularly from Kamáres to Apollonía/Artemónas (8–10/day; 20min); for all other destinations you have to change at Apollonía. Buses leave for Kamáres (8–10 daily) from Apollonía's central square, Platía Iróon. There is a second station by the *Anthousa* (see p.369) hotel for Platys Gialós (6–8 daily; 30min), Fáros

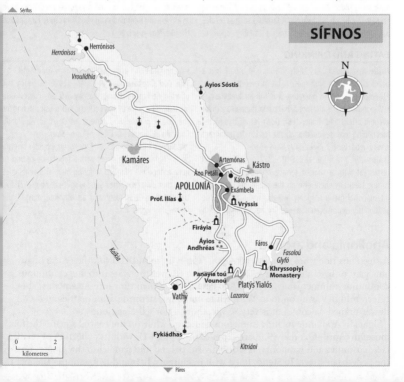

(5–6 daily; 20min), Kastro (5–6 daily; 20min), Vathý (3–4 daily; 50min) and Herrónisos (3 daily; 1hr).

**By car and motorcycle** For rental try Stavros Hotel (see below) and No1 (☎ 22840 33791/33793, ⦿ protomotocar .gr) right by the disembarkation point in Kamáres.

# Kamáres

**KAMÁRES**, the island's port, with its gorgeous, clean beach, is tucked away in a long, steep-sided valley that cuts into the cliffs of the island's western side. A compact resort, though with concrete blocks of accommodations edging up to the base of the hill-slopes, Kamáres' seafront road is crammed with bars, travel agencies, ice-cream shops and restaurants.

## ACCOMMODATION                                          KAMÁRES

**Boulis** ☎ 22840 32122, ⦿ hotelboulis.gr. If you want to wake up and head straight for a swim, this hotel – arranged around a hedged and vine-covered courtyard in the middle of Kamáres beach – is the place for you. Optional breakfast (€8) in the adjoining, atmospheric café. Easter–Oct. **€65**

**Dina's rooms** Ayía Marína ☎ 22840 32364. On the furthest side of the beach, these spotless rooms have the best views in Kamáres and are suited for those who prefer quieter, more secluded accommodation. "Rooms" here is a misnomer – there are hotels that offer much less. May–Sept. **€60**

**Makis** ☎ 22840 32366, ⦿ makiscamping.gr. A campsite on Kamáres beach with excellent facilities such as a café-bar, free wi-fi, minimarket and a laundry open to

non-guests. The obliging, friendly owner is a mine of information about the island. There are also on-site double studios. May–Sept. Camping **€10**, studios **€50**

**Myrtó bungalows** ☎ 22840 32055 ⦿ hotel-myrto.gr. Opposite the junction to Ayía Marína, this is what you envisage as the ultimate Cycladic hotel: whitewashed, stone-paved, comfortable rooms with balconies and, up from the port as it stands overlooking Ayía María, beautiful beach views. Breakfast included. April–Oct. **€60**

★ **Stavros** ☎ 22840 33383, ⦿ sifnostravel.com. A first-class, extremely helpful and reasonably priced hotel on the harbourfront with spacious rooms, free wi-fi and internet facilities. With a wide range of services, it can serve as a one-point information and booking centre for trips and the like. May–Sept. **€60**

## EATING AND DRINKING

**Follie** Ayía Marína ☎ 22840 31183. Is it a bar? Is it a beach club? Is it a nightspot? A bit of everything really; Athenian-owned and operated, it is full for breakfast, is rather muted in the afternoon, but packs them in again for evening drinks and dinner (€8). Don't let all this multi-functioning confuse you, though; the food in the restaurant is very good. Easter–Sept daily 8am–3am.

**Ísalos** Ayía Marina ☎ 22840 33716. Café-bar and restaurant with a shaded terrace offering more classy cuisine than anywhere else on the island. Its Greek and International menu is highly imaginative, matching the assiduously sophisticated decor. Try its marinated fish

selection for €10. Easter–Sept daily 8am–midnight.

**The Old Captain Bar** ☎ 22840 31990. A beach bar offering deckchairs during the day, it really comes alive after sunset when a DJ plays eclectic rock music catering for the young people who haven't made it to Apollonía. Cocktails €8. Easter–Oct daily 11am–3am.

★ **Simos** ☎ 22840 32353. Family-run, popular taverna on the Kamáres main street with a reputation second to none among the islanders, offering meat and vegetables from their own farm. Their Sunday split-pea soup (€7) is as traditional as it is tasty and an absolute must. Daily noon–midnight.

# Apollonía and around

A steep bus ride from Kamáres takes you 5.5km up to **APOLLONÍA**, the centre of an amalgam of five hilltop villages that have merged over the years into one continuous community: immediately north is **Áno Petáli**, which then runs into **Artemónas**, about fifteen minutes away on foot. With white buildings, stepped paths, belfries and flower-draped balconies, it is very scenic, though not self-consciously so.

Sights in Apollonía include numerous churches, while on the central square, the **folk museum** (April–Oct daily 9.30am–2pm & 6–10pm; €1), with its collection of textiles, lace, costumes and weaponry, is worth a visit. Behind and parallel to the square runs the pedestrian street, **To Stenó**, lined with restaurants, bars and fancy shops. The main pedestrian street north from the square leads via Áno Petáli to Artemónas, past the eighteenth-century church of **Panayía Ouranofóra**, incorporating fragments of a seventh-century BC temple of Apollo and a relief of St George over the door.

Taking the road south to **Katavatí** you'll pass, after a few minutes, the beautiful empty monastery of Firáyia and – fifteen minutes further along– there is a turning to a vast Mycenaean archeological site (Tues–Sun 8.30am–3pm; free). Next to it, there is the church of **Áyios Andhréas**, from where there are tremendous views over the neighbouring islands.

## ACCOMMODATION                                           APOLLONÍA AND AROUND

**Anthoússa Hotel** ☎ 22840 31431, ⊚ hotelanthousa -sifnos.gr. A good and solid enough hotel with comfortable rooms, balconies with views and tasteful light blue decor, plus a terrific patisserie below: try its home-made cakes, chocolates and ice cream for breakfast, if you dare. Free wi-fi. Easter–Nov. **€60**

**Mrs Dina** ☎ 22840 31125. A string of well-furnished rooms and studios in a peaceful position with panoramic views, next to the four-star *Petali Village* (see below) in the

cathedral area but at a fraction of the price. The landlady is almost never there and will leave you to chill out in peace. May–Oct. **€45**

★ **Petali Village** Áno Petáli ☎ 22840 33024, ⊚ hotelpetali.gr. A luxurious hotel in a quiet position, easy to fall in love with, offering parking, jacuzzi, pool and free wi-fi. Its nautical decoration and verandas overlooking the east of the island offer relaxation worth the price tag. Breakfast included. **€125**

## EATING AND DRINKING

**Mamma Mia** ☎ 22840 33086. On the Ano Petali steps, this is the surprising meeting point of the island's teenage youth, but don't let that put you off. If you find yourself tired of moussaka and pastitsio and, of course, fish, then have a large wood-fired pizza here for €10; that's what the Sifniots themselves do. June–Sept daily 7pm–2am.

**Okýalos** ☎ 22840 32060. Established as the in-place to dine, with Hard Rock Café-style music while you eat, this restaurant on the main street is worth making a reservation

for the roof garden – if you can. The casseroles here (€15) are worth sampling, especially if they are the dish of the day. Daily 7pm–late.

**Tou Apostóli to Koutoúki** To Stenó ☎ 22840 33186. One of the better eating establishments but rather pricey, offering island and other Greek specialities. This is the best place to try the Sifniot casseroles; choose either from its selection of veal- or pork-baked dishes (€13). April–Sept daily 7am–11am.

## NIGHTLIFE

**Argó** Stenó ☎ 22840 31114, ⊚ argobar.gr. Long-standing island club, refurbished in 2009 and playing everything from classical music to modern rock. While weekdays are mostly the realm of young tourists with their drink antics, the live music shows on Fridays and Saturdays attract all ages and are considerably better behaved. April–Oct daily 11pm–late.

**Cosí** Stenó ⊚ cosisifnos@gmail.com. Club with live DJs playing soul and R&B. Its mostly 18–30 clientele tends to sit down outside, where you can hardly walk through the chairs and tables sometimes, but there is much less of a crush on the large indoors dancefloor, should you want to boogie. June–Sept daily 11pm–late.

# The east coast

Most of Sífnos's coastal settlements are along the less precipitous **east coast**, within a modest distance of Apollonía and its surrounding cultivated plateau. **Kástro** may be more appealing than the resorts of **Fáros** and **Platýs Yialós**, which can get very overcrowded in July and August.

## Kástro

**KÁSTRO**, the ancient capital of the island, retains much of its medieval character. It's essentially a sinuous main street along the ridge of a hilltop, the houses on either side, all of the same height, forming the outer defence wall. Their roofs slope inwards in order to collect rainwater inside in case of siege. There are some fine sixteenth- and seventeenth-century churches with ornamental floors; Venetian coats of arms, ancient wall fragments and cunningly recycled Classical columns are still on some of the older dwellings, while the occasional ancient sarcophagus lies incongruously on the pavement. In addition, there are the remains of the ancient acropolis, as well as a small **archeological museum** (Tues–Sun 9am–3pm; free) operating in a former Catholic church in the higher part of the village.

You can walk along Kástro's northeastern peripheral path overlooking the picture-postcard church of the **Eptá Martyres** (Seven Martyrs), which juts out into the sea. There's nothing approximating a **beach** near Kástro, as defence and not easy access was the aim of the inhabitants. For a swim you can use the Eptá Martyres rocks, or possibly the rocky cove of **Serália**, just south of Kástro, or the small shore at **Panayía Pouláti**, 1.3km to the northwest; both have facilities.

The fantastic views over the valley below might inspire you to tackle two well-signposted walks to Fáros (1hr 30min) and to Vrússis monastery (50min) that start from the Konáki snack bar (see below).

### ACCOMMODATION AND EATING                                KÁSTRO

**Aris & Maria** ☎22840 31161, ⓦarismaria-traditional.com. Rooms and studios in six century-old houses all over Kástro, fully renovated, but retaining all of the traditional Cycladic features such as wooden ceilings and stone floors. As no cars are allowed inside Kástro, you will need to carry your luggage for about 100m uphill to the reception following the signs to "Ancient Wall". €55

★ **Konáki** ☎22840 33165. With a striking pink decor, this café-cum-snack bar has good, strong cappuccino and home-made local pastries (€5). Shaded and with comfortable seats, it is the perfect place to laze about and gaze across to Apollonía beyond the valley below. April–Oct daily 9am–10pm.

**To Astro** ☎22840 31476. The oldest taverna in the village, feeding people since 1969. Enjoy your food slowly and unhurriedly to match the service, but you can speed it up by choosing from the day's *gastra* dishes (€12) that should already have been prepared. May–Sept daily noon–midnight.

## Fáros

To the south of Kástro, the small fishing village of **FÁROS** is a possible fall-back base, though the beaches are relatively small. The main beach is partly shaded and crowded in season while **Fasoloú**, a 400m walk to the southeast past the headland is better and shaded by many tamarisk trees. Head off west through the older part of the village to find the picturesque **GLYFÓ** beach, arguably the best of the three.

### ACCOMMODATION                                           FÁROS

**Sifnéïko Arhontikó** Fáros ☎22840 71422, ⓦsifneiko-arxontiko.gr. Don't be taken in by its Greek name (Sífnos Manor); this modern hotel is not housed in an old mansion, but was built in 1992 in typical Cycladic style. Rather hard to find because it's not signposted, but worth tracking down, as it offers the most comfortable option in Fáros – convenient both for the buses and the beach. April–Sept. €50

**Thalatta** Glyfó ☎22840 71485. Built on a slope and inaccessible to vehicles, this villa complex is as close to pure solitude as you can hope for – although you do have access to a minimarket, bars and several tavernas within 200m. Four nights minimum stay. May–Sept. €65

---

### THE MONASTERY OF KHRYSSOPIYÍ

From the beach at Glyfó (see above), a fifteen-minute hillside path leads to the longer beach of **Apokoftó**, with a couple of good grill tavernas. Flanking Apokoftó to the south, marooned on a sea-washed promontory, the seventeenth-century **Khryssopiyí Monastery** features on every poster of the island. According to legend, the cleft in the rock (under the entrance bridge) appeared when two village girls, fleeing to the spit to escape the attentions of menacing pirates, prayed to the Virgin to defend their virtue. To celebrate the story, a large festival takes place forty days after Easter and involves the spectacular arrival of a holy icon on a large high-speed ferry, and its – often dramatic – transfer to a small boat to be brought ashore.

## EATING AND DRINKING

**Gorgóna** ☎22840 71461. A lively hippy and alternative commune that also offers rooms. Don't be put off by the tattooed arms on display, or the rock music blasting out of the speaker; this is the hangout of mellow souls who welcome strangers. May–Sept daily noon–late. Rooms €60

**Yórgos-Dimítris** Fasoloú ☎22840 71493. An excellent and well-priced taverna offering only produce from its own farm and good house wine. The shady location under the tamarisk trees and the nearby parking facilities make it the best beach eating option in this part of the island (mains start from €5). Easter–Sept daily noon–midnight.

## Platýs Yialós

PLATÝS YIALÓS is 12km away from Apollonía, near the southern tip of the island, and has a long stretch of beach that takes four bus stops to cross in its entirety. Buffeted by occasional strong winds, a continuous row of buildings – many of them pottery workshops – lines the entire stretch of beach, which can be slightly off-putting. Still, it should be on everyone's radar, because it offers some of the best food on the island. A five-minute walk from the last bus stop over the southwestern headland brings you to **Lazárou Beach**, a tiny pebble bay entirely occupied by the eponymous beach bar and restaurant behind the water's edge.

## ACCOMMODATION AND EATING                                      PLATÝS YIALÓS

**Alexandros** ☎22840 71300, ⓦhotelalexandros.gr. Getting off at the first bus stop at Platýs Yialós, you encounter this unmistakeably luxurious – as the large swimming pool indicates – but surprisingly affordable hotel where the focus is on room size rather than elaborate reception areas. Large, home-made buffet breakfast included. May–Sept. €70

★ **Ariadne Beach** ☎22840 71277. An excellent restaurant in a shady courtyard under the beach salt cedar trees near bus stop #3. It is featured regularly in every

Greek gourmet publication, specializing in octopus macaroni, lobster spaghetti and seafood risotto (€11). March–Oct daily noon–midnight.

**Cyclades Beach** ☎22840 71276, ⓦcycladesbeach.gr. Reputable hotel by the third beach bus stop that has been operating since 1979 and offering the best-priced rooms on the island. Its restaurant, open to non-residents, has a good buffet breakfast for €4 and, later, traditional Greek food for €8 till midnight. The owners also organize trips around Sífnos. €45

## Vathý

A fishing village on the shore of an almost circular, almost enclosed bay, VATHÝ is the most attractive base on the island, with little to do but relax on the beach or in a waterfront taverna. Even the surfaced road and the opening of the luxury *Elies* resort (see below) seems not to have destroyed the character of this previously remote spot; a character accentuated by the poster-pretty all-white monastery of Taxiárhis on the promontory bisecting the beach.

## ACCOMMODATION                                                        VATHÝ

**Elies Resort** ☎22840 34000, ⓦeliesresorts.com. Gated, and protected by its own security staff, this top-class resort – where every employee is disconcertingly attired in white clothes, giving it a semblance of the village in the *Prisoner* TV series – offers luxurious surroundings and claims to have the largest pool in the Cyclades. Drop in to play spot-the-VIP, as it is frequented by celebrities, politicians and industrialists. May–Oct. €250

**Studios Nikos** ☎22840 33244, ⓦsifnosrooms.com. A villa compound dead on the beach with attractive, comfortable studios sharing a front grass garden with uninterrupted views to the sea. With large balconies and verandas, separate kitchens and a lot of room inside for three or four people, they are great value for a family self-catering stay. April–Nov. €50

## EATING AND DRINKING

**To Tsikali** ☎22840 71177. One of the better-known family tavernas on Sífnos, it has the best spot on the seafront beyond the monastery and can occasionally surprise the

most discerning of palates with its home-made cheese, mezédhes, chunky chips, goat *gástres* and lemony rabbit dishes (€7). Easter–Oct daily noon–midnight.

**Tou Koutsouná** ☎ 22840 71156. Signposted just before the hairpin that descends to the village, this is a grill restaurant that claims with good reason to have the best views over Vathý. It has some imaginative croquettes based on courgettes, tomatoes and chick peas (€6) which are all worth sampling before moving to its traditional lamb stew *mastélo*. Take it easy and don't hurry the two old dears who own it. Daily noon–midnight.

# Mílos

Volcanic **MÍLOS** is a geologically diverse island with weird rock formations, hot springs and odd outcrops off the coast. Minoan settlers were attracted by obsidian; this and other products of its volcanic soil made it one of the most important of the Cyclades in the ancient world. Today, the quarrying of many rare minerals has left huge scars on the landscape but has given the island a relative prosperity which today translates into several gourmet restaurants with better wine lists than many of its neighbours. With some 75-odd **beaches** and sensational views Mílos hasn't had to tart itself up to court tourism – indeed, the wealthy mining companies that employ a quarter of the population are happy to see tourism stay at low levels. It helps that the western half of Mílos, as well the other islands around it, including **Kímolos**, is a nature reserve protecting three endemic species: the extremely rare **Mediterranean seal**, the **Mílos viper** and the one you are most likely to encounter, the long, crocodile-shaped **Mílos wall lizard**. Note that the importance of the archeological finds, museums and sites here is only surpassed by Delos and Santoríni.

MÍLOS & KÍMOLOS

## ARRIVAL AND DEPARTURE

MÍLOS

**By plane** The tiny airport is 5km southeast of the port and served by Olympic with flights to Athens (1–2 daily; 45min).
**By ferry** Ferries dock at the port of Adhámas. A small car ferry to Kímolos leaves from Pollónia, a quicker and cheaper option than the larger ferries.
Destinations Amorgós (1 weekly; 5hr 30min); Anáfi (1–2 weekly; 7hr); Ándhros (1 weekly; 6hr); Iráklion/Lassithi (2 weekly; 9hr); Folégandhros (1–3 daily; 2hr); Íos (3–5 weekly; 3hr 30min); Kárpathos and Kássos (2 weekly; 14–26hr); Kímolos (5–7 daily from Pollónia; 20min); Kýthnos (1 daily; 3hr); Mýkonos (3–4 weekly; 6–9hr); Náxos (1–2 daily; 6hr); Páros (3 weekly; 6hr 30min); Pireás (1–3 daily; 6hr); Rhodes and Hálki (1–2 weekly; 27–36hr); Santoríni (1–2 daily; 2–5hr); Sérifos (1–3 daily; 1hr 30min); Sífnos (1 daily; 2hr); Síkinos (2–3 weekly; 3hr 30min); Sýros (2–3 weekly; 5–10hr); Tínos (1 weekly; 6hr).

## INFORMATION

**Tourist office** Situated opposite the ferry dock (☎ 22870 22445, ⓦ milos.gr; daily 9am–5pm & 7–11pm), with daily updated list of available rooms around the island, maps, plus detailed bus and ferry timetables.
**Services** There are several banks and ATMs behind the main square in Adhámas, while the post office is by the main square. Internet Café (April–Oct daily 9am–5pm & 7–11pm), at the start of the Pláka road, is well priced at €1.50/hr. Pláka has a post office near the archeological museum.

## GETTING AROUND

**By bus** Services start from the main square by *Hotel Portiani* and are sometimes inconveniently timed in the shoulder season: Pláka/Tripití (9–10 daily; 20min), Pollónia (2–3 daily; 30min), Paleohóri via Zefyría (2–4 daily; 30min), Hivadholímni (8–10 daily; 15 min), Sarakíniko (1–2 daily; 30min).
**By taxi** Taxis seem to be used on Mílos more than on other islands. The taxi rank is near the bus stop (☎ 22870 22219). The fare to Pollónia is around €12.
**By car and motorcycle** Rental is available on the waterfront near the jetty from many places including Sophia (☎ 22870 21994) and Tomaso (☎ 22870 24100, ⓦ tomaso.gr).

# Adhámas

The lively main port of **ADHÁMAS** was a small hamlet until it was populated by refugees from a failed rebellion in Crete in the 1840s. Because it is so recent, you may find it architecturally disappointing compared to some of the Cycladic ports, despite the marble-paved esplanade around its natural headland. There is an ill-defined centre just inland of the esplanade, at the junction of the Pláka road and the Mílos Bay coastal road, where restaurants, cafés and shops abound.

## Ecclesiastical Museum

April–Oct Mon–Sat 9.15am–1.15pm & 6.15–10.15pm • Free
The unmissable **Ecclesiastical Museum** is housed in the ninth-century church of Ayía Triádha just behind the quayside. It has a superb collection of liturgical paraphernalia and rare icons that arrived in Adhámas when the inland capital, Zefyría, was

---

### MÍLOS BOAT TOUR

One of the absolute must-dos on Mílos is a **boat tour**, either down the bizarre western coastline, making several stops at otherwise inaccessible swimming spots like the magnificent **Kléftiko**, or to **Kímolos** and **Períaigos** to spot the rare Mediterranean seal. Weather permitting, the boats normally leave at 10am from the Adhámas quayside and return at 6–7pm.

**Chrysovalándou** ☎ 6944 587 574. Offers two shorter excursions per day.
**Excellent Yachting** ☎ 22870 41292, ⓦ e-y.com. Provides alternative "snorkel safaris" aimed at younger travellers for €50 including lunch and free drinks.
★ **Panormos** ☎ 694 57 78 809, ✉ skipper20@in.gr. Excursions to sheltered coves whatever the weather and the wind direction.

**6**

abandoned. This is the place to admire the work of the Cretans Emmanouel Skordhílis and his son, Antonis, two of the prime icon makers in eighteenth-century Greece.

## Mining Museum of Mílos

Daily 9am–2pm & 5.30–9.30pm · €3 · ⓦ milosminingmuseum.gr

On the seafront east of town, about 500m from the centre, the well-organized **Mining Museum of Mílos** gives an interesting insight into how mining has shaped the island, with an extensive collection of mining equipment, mineral samples and geological maps of Mílos, plus informative displays on the extraction, processing and uses of minerals. The museum is well worth a visit at the start of your stay in order to make more sense of the island's appearance and economy. Don't miss the two moving short films where old miners describe their working conditions (English subtitles).

### ACCOMMODATION

ADHÁMAS

★ **Aeolis** ☏ 22870 23985, ⓦ aeolis-hotel.com. Great-value hotel with palatial rooms and designer furniture but a bit difficult to find: behind the main square, in the street by the dry rivulet. Built with modern specifications, it provides baby cots on request and has two rooms specially adapted for disabled travellers. Minimum stay two nights in the summer. €70

**Meltémi** ☏ 22860 41425, ⓦ hotelmeltemi.gr. Basic, centrally positioned hotel behind the main square, clean, a bit noisy (ask for a room at the back) but with all amenities, this is the cheapest option in town. Suffers from occasional water pump pressure, so your showers may be quite lengthy. €60

**Ostria** ☏ 22870 28127, ⓦ ostria-hotel.gr. A beautiful and comfortable hotel in a quiet position to the east of town (near the mining museum) with excellent breakfast. The ivy-covered common areas and its candle-lit roof garden are as relaxing as the rooms themselves. May–Sept. €120

**Portiani** ☏ 22870 22940, ⓦ hotelportiani.gr. The most central hotel (in the main square), partly renovated, with excellent buffet breakfast, free wi-fi and a spectacular seaview terrace. The reception can organize everything for you, from car rental to daily excursions. It can be a bit noisy, though, if you are an early sleeper. €100

### EATING AND DRINKING

**Aggeliki** ☏ 694 24 75 162. A waterfront café that will appeal to lovers of ice cream, with its selection of extremely delicious home-made products. Turn your back on your hotel breakfast to have a strong cup of cappuccino (€3) and a piece of mouthwatering chocolate cake. Daily 9am–2am.

★ **Flisvos** ☏ 22870 22275. An award-winning restaurant in the same family for three generations. Wide menu offering everything from fried calamari to grilled

meats (€8) and a variety of savoury filo pastries accompanied by a good wine list of Santoríni vintages. April–Oct daily noon–midnight.

**Kinigós** ☏ 22870 22349. A popular place to eat, with a varied menu and excellent people-watching potential. Its specialities are the various meatball dishes (€7) made with a secret house recipe, as well as its famed moussaka (€6.50). Come early to find a table. April–Oct daily noon–midnight.

## Pláka and around

**PLÁKA**, the capital of the island, is the largest of a cluster of traditional villages that huddle beneath a small crag on the road northwest of Adhámas. Steps beginning near the *Fóras* taverna lead up to the **kástro**, its upper slopes clad in stone and cement to channel precious rainwater into cisterns. The **Folk Museum** (Tues–Sat 10am–2pm & 6–9pm, Sun 10am–2pm; €3) has a well-presented array of artefacts related to the history of arts, crafts and daily life on Mílos. The small church of the **Dormition** nearby offers one of the best views in the Aegean, particularly at sunset.

On a long ridge 1km south of Pláka, the narrow, attractive village of **Trypití** ("perforated"), which takes its name from the cliffside catacombs nearby, is less busy with traffic than lower Pláka. At the very bottom of the cliff edge and accessed via a road from the southern end of Trypití or steps down from the catacombs, **Klíma** is the most photogenic of the island's fishing hamlets, with its picturesque boathouses tucked underneath the colourful village dwellings.

## Archeological Museum

Tues–Sun 8.30am–3pm – it does not always look open, even when it is • €3

Behind the lower car park in Pláka, this Neoclassical jewel of a building, built by Ernst Ziller (see p.362) in the 1840s, contains numerous Neolithic obsidian implements, plus a whole wing of finds from ancient Phylakope (see p.376); highlights include a votive lamp in the form of a bull and a Minoan-looking terracotta idol, the **Lady of Phylakope**. You'll also recognize the plaster-cast copy of the **Venus de Milo**, the original of which was found on the island in 1820. It is not clear whether it was discovered with the arms already separated from the torso, or if they were broken off in a skirmish between French sailors and locals.

## Catacombs and Ancient Melos

Tues–Sun 8am–3pm • €2 • Groups of ten allowed at a time

From Pláka's archeological museum, signs point you towards the **early Christian catacombs**, 1km south of Pláka and just 400m from Trypití; steps lead down from the road to the inconspicuous entrance. Some 5000 bodies were buried in three tomb-lined corridors with side galleries, stretching 200m into the soft volcanic rock, making these the largest catacombs in Greece. Bear in mind that only the first 50m are illuminated and accessible by boardwalk and the guided tour lasts only about fifteen minutes.

Just above the catacombs, extending down from Pláka almost to the sea, are the ruins of **Ancient Melos** whose focal point is a well-preserved Roman **amphitheatre**. En route to the theatre from the surfaced road is the signposted spot where the *Venus de Milo* was found in what may have been the compound's gymnasium.

### ACCOMMODATION                                                      PLÁKA AND AROUND

★ **Mýlos tou Markétou** Tripití ☎ 22870 22147, ⓦ marketoswindmill.gr. A sixteenth-century windmill on the furthest, eastern side of the village that has been fully adapted to a four-bed apartment (€170). The adjoining auxiliary buildings have been converted to more conventional studios; all with a fantastic view of the Mílos bay. May–Oct. **€70**

**Spíti tis Mákhis** ☎ 22870 41353/22129. A hotel with refurbished rooms employing cherry-wood furniture and bright orange colours that make a difference from the Cycladic blue, it occupies the house where the *Venus de Milo* was hidden following its discovery. Conveniently situated for the bus, but set back from the main road, it also has plenty of parking space. June–Oct. **€75**

### EATING AND DRINKING

**Arhontoúla** ☎ 22870 21384, ✉ arhontoula3@yahoo .gr. One of the oldest and more reputable family restaurants in Pláka occupying the same spot for over 100 years offering Greek and International cuisine – even Indian curry dishes – plus a carefully selected wine list. Mains start from €7. April–Nov daily noon–midnight.

**Foras** ☎ 22870 23954. An old-style *mezedhopolío* like they don't make them any more. Greek coffee, a variety of ouzo bottles, many small-plate mezédhes (€6) and an elderly clientele that has been coming here to enjoy the food for decades. Daily noon–midnight.

# The south

The main road to **SOUTHERN MÍLOS** splits at Kánava junction, near the large power station. The sea there contains underwater hot vents resulting in fizzy hotspots that locals use for jacuzzi-like baths. The eastern fork leads to **Zefyría**, which was briefly the capital until an eighteenth-century earthquake (and subsequent plague) drove out the population. There is little to see in the old town, but a magnificent seventeenth-century church with beautifully painted walls and ceilings. The original iconostasis was transferred to the church of the Dormition in Adhámas, while the icons are displayed in the Ecclesiastical museum.

South of Zefyría, it's a further 8km down a winding, surfaced road to the coarse sand of **Paleohóri**, one of the island's best beaches, warmed by underground volcanism. A little rock tunnel leads west to a second beach, which is backed by extraordinarily coloured cliffs and where steam vents heat the shallow water. **Ayía Kyriakí**, further to the west of Paleohóri, is a pebble beach under imposing sulphurous and red oxide cliffs.

### ACCOMMODATION AND EATING                                    THE SOUTH

**Artémis** Paleohóri ☎ 22870 31222. A restaurant and apartment complex, difficult to categorize because its fish taverna (with an excellent wine list) is as good and as well known as its comfortable lodgings. May–Oct daily 9am–6pm. Apartments for 2–3 people **€100**

★ **Sirocco** Paleohóri ☎ 22870 31201. An institution on the island, using the hot volcanic sand – that reaches a constant temperature of 100°C only 30cm below the surface – to bake casseroles of lamb, veal, pork and fish (€10) in clay pots overnight. May–Oct daily noon–10pm.

## Hivadholímni and the west

The westerly road from the Kánava junction leads past the airport entrance to **HIVADHOLÍMNI**, the best beach on Mílos bay itself. Behind the beach is a salty lagoon, where in May and September you can observe migrating birdlife. Just before Hivadholímni, you can fork south to **Provatás**, a short beach, closed off by multicoloured cliffs to the east. It's easy to get to so it hasn't escaped development.

Forking to the east before Provatás, the road leads to the trendy and very popular beach of **Firipláka**. Further east, on a dirt road, sandy **Tsigrádho** is excellent for swimming and usually uncrowded. Going west from the Kanava junction the surfaced road ends at **Ayía Marína**, although a dirt road continues into **Hálakas** and the small fishing village of **Embourió** with a perfectly acceptable beach.

For the most part, the southwestern peninsula of Hálakas centred on the wilderness of Mount Profítis Ilías (748m) is an uninhabited nature reserve with unsurfaced, dirt tracks, two of which lead to the fine, unspoilt beaches of **Triádhes** and **Ammoudharáki Kléftiko** in the southwest corner. It is only reachable by boat, but repays the effort to get there with its stunning rock formations and semi-submerged tunnels.

### ACCOMMODATION                                                HIVADHOLÍMNI

**Milos Camping** ☎ 22870 31410, ⊕ miloscamping.gr. Large campsite overlooking Mílos Bay and above Hivadholímni beach; its minibus meets ferries, and in summer there are frequent buses to and from Adhámas. There is a decent restaurant next door with a swimming pool. Ask for special deals (five days get a sixth free). May–Sept. **€13**

## The north coast

From either Adhámas or the Pláka area, good roads run roughly parallel to the **NORTH COAST** which, despite being windswept and sparsely inhabited, is not devoid of geological interest. **Sarakíniko**, in particular, is an astonishing sculpted inlet with a sandy sea bed and gleaming white rocks popular with sunbathing local youth. Nearby **Mýtakas** is another good beach, accessible via a 500m dirt road, with dramatic views west along the rocky coastline.

Eastwards you reach another of Mílos's coastal wonders, **Papáfranga**, a short ravine into which the sea flows under a rock arch – the tiny beach at its inland end is accessed by rock-carved steps. To the right of the Papáfranga car park, the remains of three superimposed Neolithic settlements crown a small knoll at **Phylakope** (Tues–Sun 8.30am–3pm; free). **Pollónia**, the end of the road 12km northeast of Adhámas, is a small harbour within a semicircular bay with a long, curved, tamarisk-lined beach. This is where you take the small ferry to Kímolos (see opposite) opposite.

### INFORMATION                                                  THE NORTH COAST

**Activities** Pollónia is immensely popular with windsurfers and divers; the Apollon Dive Centre (☎ 22870 41451) offers PADI courses, snorkelling trips and equipment rental.

## ACCOMMODATION

**Andréas** ☎ 22870 41262, ⓦ andreas-rooms.gr. Villa complex at the western edge of Pollónia with triple studios, stunning views and easy access to the quiet neighbouring bay, plus its own boat, *Perseas*, bookable for trips and fishing expeditions to nearby islands. Help yourself to vegetables from the garden. **€60**

**Kapetán Tásos** ☎ 22870 41287, ⓦ kapetantasos.gr. One of the more luxurious options in the quay area that has been fully renovated; the "superior" suites are as big as a two-bedroom flat. Free transfers, wi-fi, mini-gym and optional breakfast until 2pm. April–Oct. **€110**

## EATING AND DRINKING

★ **Armenáki** Pollónia ☎ 22870 41061. Claiming never to use anything frozen and nothing but olive oil, this is one of the best restaurants on Mílos, packed day and night, so it is wise to make a reservation. Its fish casseroles (€12) and seafood pasta go down well with its diligently chosen white wines. April–Oct daily noon–late.

**Yialós** Pollónia ☎ 22870 41208. Small but stylish restaurant with a well-thought-out menu and a wide range of seafood and fish dishes. Try the fish soup, or crab (€18), and follow that with an imaginative dessert such as caramelized strawberries. April–Oct daily noon–midnight.

# Kímolos

Of the three islands off the coast of Mílos, only rugged, scenic **KÍMOLOS** is inhabited. Volcanic like Mílos, it profits from its geology and used to export chalk (*kimolía* in Greek) until the supply was exhausted. Bentonite is still extracted locally, and the fine dust of this clay is a familiar sight on the northeastern corner of the island, where mining still outstrips fishing and farming as an occupation. Apart from the inhabited southeast, the rest of the island is a nature reserve, which explains the lack of surfaced roads.

Even in August Kímolos isn't swamped by visitors. Just as well, since, although there are around 450-odd beds on the whole island, there is little in the way of other amenities. There is only one bus, no car or motorbike rental (rent your vehicle from Mílos) and few restaurants. Those visitors who venture here come for the tranquillity and for trekking in pristine nature.

## ARRIVAL AND INFORMATION                     KÍMOLOS

**By ferry** Whether you arrive from Adhámas or from Pollónia on Mílos (see p.375), you'll dock at the tiny port of Psáthi. Ferry tickets for onward journeys – unless bought in advance up in Hóra (see below) – are only sold an hour or so before the arrival of the boat. Larger ferries call briefly on their way to and from Adhámas, but the best option for Mílos is the ferry *Panagia Faneromeni* (☎ 22870 51184, ⓦ kimolos-link.gr) that serves Pollónia (see opposite).
**Destinations** Folégandhros (2 weekly; 1hr); Kýthnos (2–5

weekly; 3hr 30min); Mílos, Adhámas (2–8 weekly; 1hr); Mílos, Pollónia (7 daily; 20min); Santoríni (2 weekly; 3hr); Sérifos (2–5 weekly; 2hr 30min); Sífnos (2–5 weekly; 2hr); Síkinos (2 weekly; 1hr 30min).
**Travel agents** There are two shipping agencies, both highly reputable: Kimolos Travel (☎ 22870 51219) and Maganiotis (☎ 22870 51000).
**Services** There is one bank and one ATM in Hóra; the island's post office is in the west of the village.

## GETTING AROUND

**By bus** There is one regular bus in high season to Hóra (8–10 daily; 10min) from the port as well as connecting with the ferries.

**On foot** The capital, Hóra, can be reached on foot in about thirty minutes from the port. Other destinations around the island are on paths that are 2–3 hours on foot from Hóra.

## Hóra

Dazzlingly white **HÓRA** (known locally as Horió) is perched on the ridge above Psáthi behind a few old windmills overlooking the bay. The magnificent, two-gated, sixteenth-century **kástro** was built against marauding pirates. The perimeter houses are still intact and inhabited, though its heart is a jumble of ruins except for the small church of **Christós** (1592) and the chapel of the island's own saint **Ayía Methodhía**, beatified in

**6**

1991. Just outside the kástro to the north stands the conspicuously unwhitewashed, late seventeenth-century church of **Khryssóstomos**, the most beautiful on the island. Near the church is the **archeological museum** (July–Sept Tues–Sun 8.30am–3pm; free), displaying pottery from the Geometric to the Roman period. In a restored house near the eastern gateway is the privately run **Folk and Maritime Museum** (July–Sept daily 9am–1.30pm; €1).

## ACCOMMODATION                                             HÓRA

★ **Meltemi** ☎ 22870 51360. A superlative option in the west of the village, with modern, recently renovated rooms, airy balconies and an excellent view across to Hóra. The owner is the captain of the *Panagia Faneromeni* and can arrange for your pickup at Psáthi. There is also an excellent restaurant below where you can taste island dishes such as *tomatokeftédhes* (€6), something like tomato bhajis. **€50**

**Villa Maria** ☎ 22870 51392. Central hotel, right by the entrance to Hóra, with rooms and studios that are up there with the most comfortable in the Cyclades; however, check carefully (and then reconfirm) whether it is block-booked, something that happens often. **€50**

## EATING AND DRINKING

★ **Panorama** ☎ 22870 51351. This is the best place to eat on the island near the northeastern gate of the kástro. It offers well-cooked dishes (mains €6) with fresh ingredients, a tasteful marine decor and a pretty veranda. Most importantly in an island as sleepy as this, the place is consistently open. Daily noon–midnight.

**To Kyma** Psáthi ☎ 22870 51001. An excellent taverna midway along the beach, specializing in fresh seafood (€8) and vegetarian dishes that come directly from their own farm. This is the place to try fried rather than the normally grilled octopus. April–Oct daily noon–late.

# Rest of the island

The hamlet of **Alykí** on the south coast is about thirty minutes' walk on the paved road that forks left from Psáthi; it is named after the saltpan that sprawls behind a pebbly beach. Here you can indulge in some serious birdwatching or to spot the rare, endemic Mílos wall lizard. If you stroll west one cove, you arrive at **Bonátsa** which has better sand and shallower water. Passing another cove you come to the even more attractive beach of **Kalamítsi**, with decent shade.

There are three clearly signposted beaches next to each other starting from the dirt track at the end of the asphalted road off **Fykiádha**, a 45-minute walk west of Alykí. The first one, dotted with caves and ancient tombs, is **Dhékas**. It is divided by a low bluff from the long coarse-sand beach of **Elliniká**, itself divided by a rocky promontory from **Mavrospiliá**, which provides the best spot to watch the sunset. There are no facilities on any beach.

Some 7km northeast from Hóra is **Prása**, arguably the best easily accessible beach on the island, with crystal-clear water, fine sand and, to top it all, radioactive thermal springs. The route takes in impressive views across the straits to the island of **Políaigos**, and there are several peaceful coves where it's possible to swim in solitude. In the northwest, on Kímolos's 361m summit, are the scant ruins of a Venetian fortress known as **Paleókastro** which can be reached after a reasonable trek (2hr 30min) from the dirt road off Prása. The road forks by the peak to Sklavos with one branch leading to **Skiadhi**, an odd rock formation like a mushroom which has been adopted as the island landmark.

## ACCOMMODATION AND EATING                       REST OF THE ISLAND

**Bonátsa Studios** Bonátsa ☎ 22870 51429, ⊛ bonatsa .gr. Right behind a string of salt cedars, this apartment complex offers studios of exceptional quality in bright red and yellow colours. A good restaurant belonging to the owner operates next door. June–Sept. **€90**

**Kimolía Yi** Prássa ☎ 22870 51192, ⊛ kimoliagi.gr. Set

at 200m from the beach, this is the only, but still pretty good, accommodation option here, eye-catchingly decorated, with much ornamental bric-a-brac on show. Children under the age of four pay nothing. Breakfast included. April–Sept. **€90**

**Sardis** Alykí ☎ 22870 51458. Comfortable hotel with

enormous rooms 50m from the sea. Recommended for birdwatchers especially outside the peak season as the

saltpan (Alykí) that gives the beach its name attracts mar waders. Good restaurant on-site. June–Sept. **€60**

# Ándhros

**ÁNDHROS**, the second largest and northernmost of the Cyclades, is also one of the most verdant, its fertile, well-watered valleys and hillsides sprouting scores of holiday villas. Stil home to a very hospitable people, an attractive capital, numerous good beaches, plus some idiosyncratic reminders of the Venetian period – such as the *peristereónes* (dovecote towers) and the *frákhtes* (dry-stone walls) – Ándhros has a special charm. Driving is also a joy, with precipitous coastal roads offering panoramic views over the Aegean.

The only cloud in your enjoyment of the island may be the current shutdown of all state museums on Ándhros; check if they have opened before you visit.

## ARRIVAL AND INFORMATION                                    ÁNDHRO

**By ferry** All ferries and catamarans arrive at the main port, Gávrio.

Destinations Lávrio via Kéa/Kýthnos (1 weekly; 5–6hr); Mýkonos (1–3 daily; 2hr 30min); Náxos (4 weekly; 4hr); Rafína (2–3 daily; 1–2hr); Sýros (4 weekly; 3hr); Tínos (1–3 daily; 1hr 30min).

**Tourist offices** A tiny converted dovecote by the disembarkation point in Gávrio houses an unmanned information booth. There's also an unmanned but signposted info kiosk by the jewellers' in Batsí.

**Services** There are two banks and three ATMs on the

waterfront in Gávrio, and the post office is at the souther end. *Carlito's* café-bar (☎ 22820 71442; daily 9am–3am also at the waterfront offers free wi-fi as well as interne facilities (€2.50/hr). Batsí has an ATM behind the *Dodó* café-bar. There are several banks and ATMs in Hóra, and th post office is on the main street. There is one ATM Southern Ándhros, on Yeoryíou Psálti, parallel to th esplanade.

**Travel agents** Batis (☎ 22820 71489), Kyklades Trave (☎ 22820 72363) and Porto Andros (☎ 22820 71222), a operate near the centre of the port.

## GETTING AROUND

**By bus** Buses run from the port's waterfront where the schedules are posted: Batsí (6–8 daily; 20min); Hóra (4–6 daily; 50 min); Kórthi (2–3 daily; 1hr).

**By car and motorcycle** Gávrio is the easiest place on the island for car rental, with several competing

establishments. Try the reliable and friendly Euro Ca (☎ 22820 71312, ⓦ rentacareuro.com) right in front of th disembarkation point. As the island is very large and trick to explore, and the bus services limited, you are advised book your transport before arriving.

## Gávrio and around

**GÁVRIO** is a pleasant enough small town set in an oval bay, but it has more tavernas and bars than good hotels, which generally tend to be out of town. There is an adjacent town beach, but there are more attractive alternatives 5km northwest of the port: beautiful **Fellós** is very popular with the self-catering holiday community, while **Kourtáli** hidden beyond the headland is as popular but with fewer facilities.

Head inland and south from Gávrio, and you reach the best beaches on the island in a row: **Áyios Pétros** attracts the young because of the lively beach bar; **Khryssí Ammos** is long, sandy and very popular with families; **Kyprí** is a long stretch of fine sand; and **Áyios Kyprianós**, just before you reach the major resort of **Batsí**, is located in a small sheltered cove of the same name.

## ACCOMMODATION                                        GÁVRIO AND AROUNI

**Andros** ☎ 22820 71444, ⓦ campingandros.gr. A very pleasant campsite, 300m behind the centre of town, with a minimarket, café and excellent communal kitchen facilities. The swimming pool partly compensates for the fact that it is not very close to the sea. Free pickups to and

from the port. As the reception is not always open, mak sure they are waiting for you. May–Oct. **€10**

★ **Andros Holidays** ☎ 22820 71384, ⓦ androsholida hotel.com. Luxury hotel on the headland side road sout of town with lovely sea views from its garden terraces an

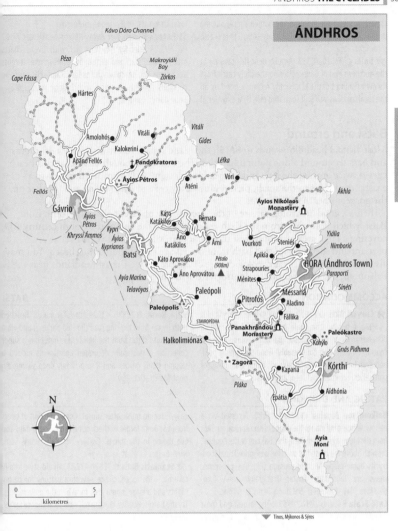

**ÁNDHROS**

6

arched verandas. With a large pool, a bar, and a private cove in front, its rooms are exceptional value. Breakfast included. During the last week of June it holds a renowned English Creative Writing workshop. April–Oct. **€80**

**Galaxias** ☎ 22820 71228. Labelled "basic but clean", this hotel right at the centre of the port feels like living in one of the faceless blocks of flats in Central Athens. However, it is very cheap and, due to its location, it can serve as a late-arrival fallback. **€35**

**Perrakis** ☎ 22820 71456, ⓦ hotelperrakis.com. Top hotel in white and gold – matching the local stone it is built with – that offers great views from even its standard-rate rooms. Situated between Khryssí Ámmos and Kyprí, it houses the headquarters of Andros Surf Club (ⓦ windsurfingingreece.com) as well as one of the most creative restaurants on the island (open to non-residents) with mains around €15. April–Oct. **€80**

## EATING, DRINKING AND NIGHTLIFE

**Marabou** Áyios Pétros beach ☎ 693 71 01 695, ⓦ marabouclub.gr. High on a promontory and facing

west, this is the main late-night option for a predominantly young crowd dancing to Western pop, although many choose to spend the nights in the garden simply sipping drinks (€6–8). Fri–Sat, plus July–Aug Thurs–Sun midnight–late.

★ **Sails** ☎ 22820 71333. An excellent fish taverna at the northern end of Gávrio offering the daily catch from its own fishing boat (€12). Highly recommended by all the locals and, as you will soon find out, by a clowder of

local stray cats. Daily noon–midnight.

**St Peter's Beach Bar** Áyios Pétros beach ☎ 697 03 06 792. A friendly, youthful bar with lively, chatty international staff and a studenty atmosphere. It rents deckchairs and beach umbrellas for €6 and sells beer and cocktails while lulling you with lounge music. May–Sept daily 10am–8pm.

# Batsí and around

Most visitors head 8km south to **BATSÍ**, the island's main resort with its hotels, rooms and bars set around a fine natural harbour. The beautiful though often crowded beach curves twice around the bay, and the sea is cold, calm and clean. South of town, a coastal road leads to the small, picturesque sandy cove of **Ayía Marína** and, further on, the gorgeous beach of **Telavóyas**.

There's a good archeological site of the ancient city of **Paleópolis**, 8km south from Batsí, which flourished from the sixth century BC to the end of the eighth century AD, covering a large area just southwest of the modern village. It is reached via a very pleasant and shady signposted path from the village to the eponymous beach. You may also be interested in the archeological site of **Zagorá** on west-coast headlands near Paleópolis, but access is not straightforward without a map.

## ACCOMMODATION                                                                                           BATSÍ

★ **Chryssí Akti** ☎ 22820 41236, 🌐 hotel-chryssiakti .gr. Right behind the main beach, this hotel, which depends mainly on domestic package tours, is solid, central, efficient and comfortable. Good swimming pool, and even better interior café-bar with a first-class range of patisseries. Breakfast included. April–Oct. **€60**

**Villa Rena** ☎ 22820 41024, 🌐 villarena.gr. Reached both by car from the ring road (limited parking) and via a five-minute climb from the beach, this hotel has a super collection of tastefully decorated apartments around a sloping shady garden and a surprisingly deep swimming pool. March–Oct. **€60**

## EATING AND DRINKING

**Balkoni tou Aigaiou** ☎ 22820 41020. Accessed via a narrow, winding hill road to the village of Áno Aprovátou, 3km from the highway south of Batsí, the "Balcony of the Aegean", set high above the coast, has superior, well-priced rural food; try its home-made Ándhros sausage (€9). The panoramic views are legendary. Easter–Oct daily noon–4pm, 6–11pm, Nov–Easter Fri–Sat noon–4pm, 6–11pm.

**Café Scala** Batsí ☎ 22820 41656. The largest and most popular hangout in the village with a DJ playing

easy-listening music after sunset. Good selection of beers from €5. Don't forget to check out the hilarious Adam and Eve theme in the toilets. Easter–Oct daily 9am–5am, Nov–Easter Fri–Sat 9am–5am.

★ **Stamátis** Batsí ☎ 22820 41283. An old-style family taverna – the locals' choice – with a balcony for balmy nights and a large indoor area for when the *meltémi* hits. Try the Batsí speciality, chicken roll with local cheese for €9. Daily noon–1am.

# Hóra and around

Stretched along a rocky spur that divides a huge bay 32km from Gávrio, the capital **HÓRA** (also known as **ÁNDHROS TOWN**) is the most attractive town on the island. Paved in marble and schist from the still-active local quarries, the buildings near the bus station are grand nineteenth-century edifices, and the squares with their ornate wall fountains and gateways are equally elegant. The old port, Plakoúra, on the west side of the headland, has a yacht supply station and a former ferry landing from where occasional boats run to the isolated but superbly idyllic **Ákhla** beach in summer. More locally, there are beaches on both sides of the town headland, **Nimborió** to the north and the less developed **Parapórti** to the southeast, though both are exposed to the *meltémi* winds in summer – the reason Gávrio (see p.380), on the other side of the island, became the main port instead.

From the Theófilou Kaïri square, right at the end of Hóra's main street, Embiríkou (aka "Agorá"), you pass through an archway and down through the residential area of Paleá Póli past the town theatre to **Ríva Square**, with its Soviet-donated statue of an unknown sailor scanning the sea.

The tidy village of **Apikía**, north of Hóra, is the source of the Sáriza mineral water brand. An uphill turn at the southwestern end of the village leads, via a signed fifteen-minute path, to the **Rematiá Pytháras**, a pretty wooded stream with small waterfalls. The road continues to **Vourkotí** and, after a turn-off to *Ákhla* (a dirt track continuing for 8km), it then becomes a broad, mostly unused highway, via Árni, to the west coast. There are some wonderful views of the northeast from along this road, particularly where it crosses the **Kouvára ridge** at an altitude of 700m.

**6**

## Archeological museum
Currently closed; check if open

Inside the **archeological museum**, on the main street near Kaïri, the displays, mostly from Paleópolis (see opposite), are well laid-out and clearly labelled: there are funerary stellae, a kouros and a torso of Artemis, but its prize item is the fourth-century *Hermes of Ándhros*, reclaimed from a prominent position in the Athens archeological museum. This is a remarkably preserved Roman copy of the Hermes of Praxiteles, one of antiquity's greatest sculptors.

## Goulandhrís Museum of Contemporary Art
June–Sept Wed–Mon 10am–2pm • €6 • Oct–May Sat–Mon 10am–2pm • €3 • Temporary exhibitions also open evenings 6–8pm • W moca-andros.gr

Behind the archeological museum (see above) there is the private **Goulandhrís Museum of Contemporary Art** in the street of the same name. A four-storey mansion, it has a permanent collection with works by prominent Greek sculptors as well as international artists such as Hundertwasser, Warhol, Rodin and Giacometti, plus regular temporary exhibitions.

## ACCOMMODATION
### HÓRA AND AROUND

**Alcióni** 📞 22820 23652/23805, W alcioni.gr. These pink-and-cyan studios right by Nimborió beach have been expanded to fill all available space, cutting down on common areas, such as reception; consequently they are on the large side, with local wooden furniture, though some tend to be a bit noisy from the traffic in front. April–Oct. **€70**

**ró** 📞 22820 22905. Just one block away from the main road, behind Nimborió beach, you can hear a pin drop in these huge, well-furnished studios with their own kitchenette – the best priced in Hóra. Easter–Oct. **€50**

**Onar Residence** Áchla beach 📞 693 25 63 707, W onar andros.gr. Extremely difficult to reach and a pain to get to

– 40km from Gávrio including 8km on a dirt road – but worth it. This is an eco-lodge in the middle of one of the best beaches of Ándhros with self-catering bungalows composed of stone, wood and reeds, but supplied with all modern facilities; as close to feeling stranded on a desert island as you could dream of. May–Oct. **€150**

**Paradise Hotel** 📞 22820 22187, W paradiseandros.gr. If you have your own transport, this hotel, though far from the beach and the town centre, is an exclusive holiday sanctuary with modern art paintings in the common areas, a striking swimming pool, a tennis court, free wi-fi, regal furnishings and even a small folklore museum next door. Easter–Sept. **€90**

### PANAYÍA PANAKHRÁNDOU
Two hours' pleasant walk from Hóra via the village of Fállika, or via a signposted turn-off on the road to Kórthi, you arrive at the finest monastery on the island, **Panayía Panakhrándou** (closed 1–4.30pm). Founded around 961 and with an icon said to be by St Luke, it's still defended by massive walls but is occupied these days by just one monk. From the entrance door, a long passageway leads in past gushing springs to the atmospheric catholicon dedicated to the Dormition of the Virgin with its impressive and colourful iconostasis. Its lower decoration with **Ottoman Iznik tiles** is unique in the Aegean and it represents a gift to the monastery by Patriarch Dionysius III in the 1660s.

## EATING AND DRINKING

**Madoúris** Nimborió ☎22820 24620. Simple and unassuming, you'll wonder why its tables are all taken while the surrounding tavernas are empty. Then you'll taste the fresh fried calamari with portions that feed two adults (€9) and you'll understand. April–Sept daily noon–midnight.

**Vegéra** Nimborió ☎698 02 20 171. You've heard it before: an establishment that starts as a beach bar at 10am continues as a pretty decent restaurant after 2pm (mains €8) and ends up as a club with a live DJ after 10pm (drinks €7). Yes, there may be many bars like that, but not as stylish in each incarnation. May–Sept daily 10am–late.

## The south

If you're exploring **the south** from Hóra, take the road that runs through the dramatic **Dipotámata** valley; at the seaward end, the fine, sheltered cove of **Sinéti** is worth a detour, though the access road is somewhat steep. Two kilometres further, the entry road to Kohýlo village forks: the left goes 2km (partly surfaced) to **Paleókastro** (aka Kástro Faneroménis), a ruined Venetian castle perched on a rocky crest at 586m, with amazing views overlooking Kórthi Bay. Legend has it that an old woman, who betrayed the stronghold to the Turks, jumped from the top in remorse, and she remains as a column of rock in the sea off **Griás Pídhima** beach where she landed. A short distance further south, the resort of **Kórthi** (or Órmos Korthíou or simply Órmos) is a small town, with a new seafront esplanade, waking up to its tourist potential and popular with windsurfers; this is where the Greek Olympic team practises. Set on a large bay, isolated from the rest of the island by the high ridge and relatively unspoilt, it is pleasant enough to merit a stay. Lovely Griás Pídhima beach is accessible via a signed road and dirt track from near the northern end of the esplanade, while **Kandoúni** beach covers the southern half of the main bay.

## EATING AND DRINKING                                                    THE SOUTH

**Lithodhomí** ☎22820 61130. One of those surprise finds that make your heart beat faster with excitement: a restaurant in the middle of the Kórthi esplanade with great rustic stone decor, an inventive menu offering many vegetarian options (€10), good service, fresh ingredients and a great wine list. A must if you've come all this way. Daily 8am–1am.

# Tínos

**TÍNOS** still feels like one of the most Greek of the larger islands in the Cyclades. A few foreigners have discovered its beaches and unspoilt villages, but most visitors are Greek, here to see the church of **Panayía Evangelístria**, a grandiose shrine erected on the spot where a miraculous icon with healing powers was found in 1822. A local nun, now canonized as Ayía Pelayía, was directed in a vision to unearth the relic just as the War of Independence was getting under way, a timely coincidence that served to underscore the links between the Orthodox Church and Greek nationalism. Today, there are two major annual pilgrimages, on March 25 and August 15, when Tínos is inundated by the faithful, and at 11am, the icon bearing the Virgin's image is carried in state down to the harbour.

The Ottoman tenure here, and on adjoining Sýros, was the most fleeting in the Aegean. **Exóbourgo**, the craggy mount dominating southern Tínos and surrounded by most of the island's sixty-odd villages, is studded with the ruins of a Venetian citadel that defied the Turks until 1715, long after the rest of Greece had fallen; an enduring legacy of the long Venetian rule is a **Catholic minority**, which accounts for almost half the population. Hills are dotted with distinctive and ornate **dovecotes**, even more in evidence here than on Ándhros. Aside from all this, the inland village architecture is striking, and there's a flourishing folk-art tradition that finds expression in the abundant local marble.

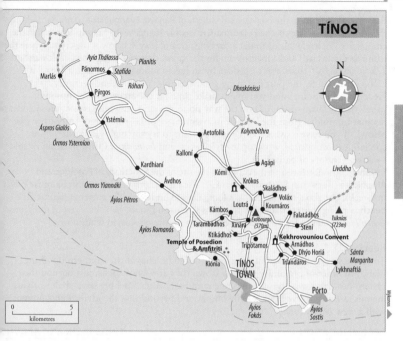

TÍNOS

TÍNOS

## ARRIVAL AND DEPARTURE

**By ferry** All ferries dock at Tínos Town at any one of three different marinas; one for yachts, one for catamarans and one for normal ferries, all next to each other.

**Destinations** Ándhros (2–6 daily; 1hr 30min); Iráklion (0–1 weekly; 4hr); Íos (2–4 weekly; 2hr); Lávrio via Kéa/

Kýthnos (1 weekly; 5hr 30min); Mýkonos (2–6 daily; 30min); Náxos (5–6 weekly; 1hr 30min); Páros (1–2 daily; 1hr); Pireás (2–4 daily; 4–5hr); Rafína (3–5 daily; 2–4hr); Santoríni (5 weekly; 3hr); Sýros (2–4 daily; 30min–1hr 20min).

## TOURS AND INFORMATION

**Services** There is no shortage of banks or ATMs in Tínos town.

**Travel agents** Windmills Travel (☎ 22830 23398, ✪ windmillstravel.com) on the front towards the new jetty can help with information as well as tour bookings to Delos and hotel bookings both here and on Mýkonos.

**Day-trip to Delos** In season (July–Sept) there are day-trips by boat to Delos (Tues–Sun; €50 round trip); this makes it possible to see Delos without the expense of staying overnight on Mýkonos (see p.394). The time on Delos itself (about 2hr 30min) is the same from wherever you sail off.

## GETTING AROUND

**By bus** Buses leave from a small parking area on the inner quay and serve: Áyios Fokás (5 daily; 15min); Falatádos/Stení (6 daily; 20min); Kalloní via Xinára (3 daily; 20min); Kiónia (hourly; 10min); Pánormos via Pýrgos (5 daily; 45min); Kalloní (3 daily; 45min); Pórto (6 daily; 20min).

**By car and motorcycle** Not only a much more reliable

means of exploring the island than bus, especially in the shoulder season, but also the only way to reach some of the beaches of the island. Vidalis at 2 Ierarhon St (☎ 22830 23400, ✪ vidalis-rentacar.gr) is an excellent rental agency – there are four other rental outlets in Tínos Town.

# Tínos Town and around

**Tínos Town** is large and commercial, possessing a unique mixture of religion and commerce: trafficking in devotional articles certainly dominates the streets leading up from

6

the busy waterfront to the Neoclassical church of **Panayía Evangelístria** (daily 8am–8pm) that towers above. Approached via a massive marble staircase, the famous **icon** inside the church is completely buried under a dazzling array of jewels; below is the crypt (where the icon was discovered) and a mausoleum for the sailors drowned when the Greek warship *Elli*, at anchor off Tínos, was torpedoed by an Italian submarine on August 15, 1940.

The shrine aside, the port has many good examples of nineteenth-century Neoclassical buildings and you might make time for the **archeological museum** (Tues–Sun 8.30am–3pm; €2) on the way up to the church, whose collection includes a fascinating sundial from the local Roman sanctuary of Poseidon and Amphitrite (see below). If you have a sweet tooth you may want to try the highly calorific Tiniot specialities: *amygdalotó*, a marzipan-style sweet, and *loukoumia* (Turkish delight), sold by street vendors or patisseries.

**Kiónia**, 3km northwest of the capital, is the site of the **Sanctuary of Poseidon and Amphitrite** (Tues–Sun 8.30am–3pm; free). The excavations yielded many columns (*kiónia* in Greek), but also a temple, baths, a fountain and hostels for the ancient pilgrims. The **beach** is a long thin strip, lined with rooms to rent and snack-bars, but west of the *Tinos Beach Hotel* you can follow an unpaved road to a series of isolated sandy coves.

## Beaches

There are several first-class but mostly unshaded beaches at the southern tip of the island. In order of proximity to Tínos Town they are: **Áyios Fokás**, just beyond the eastern headland, which is a good, fine sand beach after a pebbly start, shallow **Áyios Ioánnis** at Pórto (served by six daily buses), and beyond that the idyllic **Pahiá Ámmos**, with a view of Mýkonos.

### ACCOMMODATION

### TÍNOS TOWN AND AROUND

**Ávra** Konstandínou 4–6 ☎22830 22242, ⓦavrahoteltinos.gr. Charming Neoclassical building on the waterfront with fully renovated spacious rooms with modern bathrooms, some with balconies and an attractive plant-filled communal atrium area. Port transfers, breakfast and free wi-fi included. May–Oct. **€55**

**Cávos** Áyios Sóstis ☎22830 24224, ⓦcavos-tinos.com. Well situated for the beach and adorned with flowers and palm trees, these large apartments and suites can sleep up to four people and are ideal for families; everything from a baby cot to laundry services can be provided. April–Nov. **€80**

**Favie Suzanne** Antoníou Sókhou 22 ☎22830 22693, ⓦfaviesuzanne.gr. An attractive hotel about 200m from the waterfront fully renovated with facilities for disabled guests, marble balconies, large swimming pool plus free jacuzzi and wi-fi. Breakfast included. March–Oct. **€70**

★ **Tínion Hotel** Alavánou 1 ☎22830 22261, ⓦtinionhotel.gr. A 1920s Neoclassical hotel just back

from the waterfront, full of faded grandeur an[d] resonating with history; a Greek prime minister onc[e] resigned in the dining room in a fit of pique. Spaciou[s] rooms, some with balconies. Port transfers, free wi-[fi] and breakfast included. March–Nov. **€55**

**Tinos Beach** Kiónia ☎22830 22626, ⓦtinosbeach.g[r]. Typical 1970s-built hotel that dominates the beach, offerin[g] comfortable rooms with verandas. Good swimming poo[l,] large breakfast, fair pricing, a range of facilities and regula[r] shuttle into town makes this rather anonymous resort a mo[re] attractive option than expected. April–Oct. **€75**

**Tinos Camping** Ten-minute walk south of por[t] ☎22830 22344, ⓦcamping.gr/tinos.html. One o[f] the nicer and more laidback campsites in the Cyclade[s,] shady and roomy very close to the centre of town, bu[t] reception only open 8am–4pm. En-suite double[s] studios are also on offer. May–Oct. Camping **€11** studios **€40**

### EATING AND DRINKING

**Symposion** Evangelistrias 13 ☎22830 24368, ⓦsymposion.gr. Sophisticated restaurant at the top of a converted Neoclassical house offering an imaginative menu (€14) that makes no concessions to normal meagre pilgrim fare as is usual around town. It's worth trying its huge English brunch for €17 at least once during your stay. April–Oct daily 9am–4pm & 7.30pm–midnight.

★ **To Koutouki tis Elenis** G. Gafou 5 ☎22830 2485[7] A gem of a restaurant with a creative chef who mixe[s] international and traditional cooking with superb result[s.] Try its artichoke pie for a starter, the pork with feta (€9) fo[r] a main and finish with its irresistible cheesecake with Tini[ot] sour cheese. Daily noon–midnight.

**6**

### THE DOVECOTE TRAIL

Drive up Evangelistrías, turn right and follow the signs to **Tripótamos** where you can visit the only still functioning clay pot workshop on the island. Nearby **Ktikádhos** is a fine village with two superb churches and a very good taverna. Heading northwest from the main road junction beyond Ktikádhos, you can see several beautifully restored **dovecote houses** on the turn-off to **Tarambádho**– it's worth stopping there and following an hour-long signed path through the village, to get as close to these dovecotes as possible, as they are the most photogenic you are likely to encounter.

Driving further north from the Tarambádho turn-off, you can break your trip at **Ystérnia** by turning off to **Órmos Ysterníon**, a pretty compact beach, and even prettier Skhináki beach at the far end.

There are a number of eating options en route; here are the best:

**Drosia** Ktikádhos ☎22830 21087. A good, vine-shaded, sea-view taverna with mains around €8. One of the few that still offers baked pigeons (*pitsounia*), the age-old traditional Tínos staple food and the *raison d'être* of the dovecotes, if booked in advance. April–Oct daily noon–midnight.

**To Thalassaki** Órmos Ysterníon ☎22830 31366, ✉tothalassaki@gmail.com. Award-winning fish taverna right on the beach providing exceptional range and quality of food for something so out of the way. Most dishes (€13) are marinated in an infusion of herbs before cooking. Just its extensive ouzo selection is worth making a detour for. March–Oct daily noon–midnight.

## The north

A good beginning to a foray into **NORTHERN TÍNOS** is to drive the so-called **Dovecote Trail** (see box above). The ornate dovecotes are mostly found in the villages off the main road between **Tínos Town** and **Ystérnia**.

### Pýrgos and around

Five daily buses along the Dovecote Trail (see box above) finish up at **PÝRGOS**, a few kilometres beyond Ystérnia and in the middle of the island's marble-quarrying district, as can be surmised by the magnificently crafted marble bus stop. The artisans of this beautiful village are renowned throughout Greece for their skill in producing marble ornamentation; ornate fanlights and bas-relief plaques fashioned here adorn houses throughout Tínos. Pýrgos is also home to a School of Fine Arts, and the **museum of Tiniot artists** (daily 10.30am–2.30pm & 5.30–7pm) contains numerous representative works from some of the island's finest pupils. Nearby, the **Yiannoúlis Halepás museum** (same hours; €3 for both) is devoted exclusively to the work of the artist who spent many years here and is generally recognized as the most important Neoclassical Greek sculptor. The small cemetery up and left from the main square offers a free showcase of the villagers' talent over the ages.

The marble products were once exported from **Pánormos** harbour, 4km northeast of Pýrgos, with its small, shaded **Stafída** beach. The village itself gives access to a number of good beaches reachable on foot: **Róhari** is to the southeast, facing north with deep clear waters and massive waves, while **Ayía Thálassa** and **Kaválargos** are much more sheltered on the northwest side of the bay.

### EATING

PÝRGOS AND AROUND

**Marina** Pánormos ☎22830 31314. A seaside ouzerí with a great ouzo and mezédhes selection; spoilt for choice, you may want to order a starters platter (€7) but, unless there are two of you, wait until you've finished before you venture into a main; the portions are quite large. May–Sept daily 10am–midnight.

**Myrónia** Pýrgos ☎22830 31229. The best of the tavernas and patisseries on the attractive main village square, with seats around the 150-year-old plane tree. It still serves baked pigeon with pasta (€8) if you pre-order; but there are some excellent vealburgers if you want something more conventional. Easter–Oct daily noon–midnight.

**Tis Irinis** Pýrgos ☎ 22830 31165. A friendly, popular taverna opposite the stunning marble bus stop that offers good, traditional family favourites such as pastitsio (€6) and a quick turnaround service for those pressed for time to visit the museums opposite. Easter–Oct daily noon–midnight.

## Around Exóbourgo

The ring of villages around the mountain of **EXÓBOURGO** is a worthwhile visit. The fortified pinnacle itself (570m), with the ruins of three Venetian churches and a fountain, is reached by steep steps from **Xinára** (near the island's major road junction), the old seat of the island's Roman Catholic bishop. Most villages in north-central Tínos have mixed populations, but Xinára and its immediate neighbours are purely Catholic; the inland villages also tend to have a more sheltered position, with better farmland nearby – the Venetians' way of rewarding converts and their descendants.

At **Loutrá**, an almost deserted village north of Xinára (population 7), there's an Ursuline convent, and a small **folk art museum** (daily 9.30am–2.30pm; free) in the seventeenth-century Jesuit monastery. From Krókos, 1km northwest of Loutrá, you can turn to tiny **Voláx**, the most spectacular village on the island: a windswept oasis surrounded by hundreds of giant granite boulders, as far from a typical Greek landscape as you can get in the Cyclades. Alternatively you can continue to **Kómi**, 5km beyond Krókos, where you can take a detour for **Kolymbíthra**, a magnificent double beach: one part wild, huge and windswept and the other balmy and sheltered.

From either Skaládho or Voláx you go on to **Koúmaros**, towards the agricultural villages of **Falatádhos** and **Stení**, which appear as white speckles against the fertile Livádhia valley. Falatádhos has a number of whitewashed churches, including Áyios Ioánnis, notable for its marble decoration. From Stení, which has fewer amenities but plenty of postcard-perfect whitewashed buildings to admire, you can catch the bus back to Tínos Town.

### EATING AND DRINKING                                    AROUND EXÓBOURGO

**To Katóï** Falatádhos ☎ 22830 41000. A good restaurant that draws customers from all around the island, based in a low-ceilinged old warehouse that reminds you of Central European Bierkellers; specializes in grills (€12) and meat on the spit. June–Sept daily 7pm–midnight.

# Mýkonos

**MÝKONOS** has become the most popular, the most high profile and the most expensive of the Cyclades. Boosted by direct air links with Europe, it sees several million tourists a year pass through, producing some spectacular August overcrowding on the island's 85 square kilometres. But if you don't mind the tourist hordes, or you come in the shoulder season, its striking capital is still one of the most photogenic Cycladic towns with whitewashed houses concealing a dozen little churches, shrines and chapels.

The sophisticated nightlife is hectic, amply stimulated by Mýkonos's former reputation as *the* gay resort of the Mediterranean, although today gay tourists are well in the minority. While everywhere on the island is at least gay-friendly, gay tourists prefer to congregate in Mýkonos Town itself or the beaches of Super Paradise and Eliá. The locals take it all in their stride, ever conscious of the important revenue generated by their laissez-faire attitude. When they first opened up to the hippy tourists who began appearing on Mýkonos in the 1960s, they assumed their eccentric visitors were sharing cigarettes due to lack of funds. Since then, a lot of the innocence has evaporated, and you shouldn't come for scenery, solitude or tradition, but Mýkonos offers lively beaches and a party lifestyle next to none.

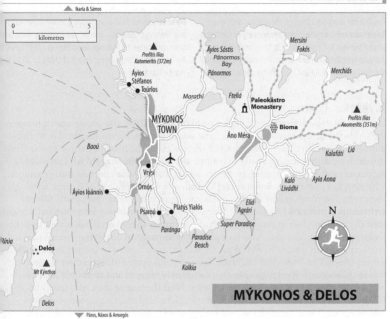

## ARRIVAL AND DEPARTURE

MÝKONOS

**By plane** The airport is twenty minutes outside Mýkonos Town in the centre of the island.

**Destinations** Athens (2–5 daily with Aegean and Olympic; 55min); Thessaloníki (1–2 daily with Aegean; 1hr); Santoríni (daily with Sky Express; 30min); Vólos (2 daily; 1hr with Sky Express).

**By ferry** Most visitors arrive by ferry at the old port jetty at the north end of town. Cruise ships and the occasional overflow anchor at the new port, which is 2km further out. Check your ticket before leaving to see if you have an old or a new port stamp. Boats for Delos leave from the waterfront in town.

**Destinations** Amorgós (0–1 weekly; 2hr 15min); Ándhros (1–2 daily; 2hr 15min); Folégandhros (1 daily; 5hr); Irāklion (1 weekly; 4h 30min); Ikaría (1 weekly; 2hr min); Íos (6 weekly; 1hr 15min–5hr 30min); Mílos (1–2 weekly; 6hr); Náxos (2–3 daily; 45min–3hr); Páros (2–3 daily; 1hr 30min); Pireás (3–4 daily; 4hr–5hr 30min); Rafína (1–3 daily; 2hr 10min–3hr); Sámos (6–7 weekly; 4hr 40min); Santoríni (2–4 daily; 2hr 15min–7hr); Sérifos (1 weekly; 3hr 30min); Sífnos (1 weekly; 3hr 30min); Sýros (2–5 daily; 45min–1hr 15min); Tínos (2–5 daily; 30min).

## INFORMATION

**Services** There is no shortage of banks or ATMs in Mýkonos Town. The island post office is near the south bus station. There are countless advertiser-based tourist publications circulating throughout Mýkonos during high season, the best of which is the free Mýkonos Sky Map, available from some agents and hotels.

**Activities** Kalafati (see p.394) is the activity centre of the island with no less than three watersports facilities based

there: Kalafati Watersports for waterskiing and wake-boarding (☎694 52 61 242 ⊛mykonoswatersports .t35.com), Kalafati Dive Center (☎22890 71677, ⊛mykonos-diving.com) for scuba diving, and Pezi-Huber (☎22890 72345, ⊛pezi-huber.com) for windsurfing. Alternatively, behind Paradise beach (see p.393), Dive Adventures (☎22890 26539, ⊛diveadventures.gr and ⊛divemykonos.gr; April–Oct) offer introductory scuba and a full range of PADI.

## GETTING AROUND

**By bus** The north bus station for Toúrlos, Áyios Stéfanos, Kalafáti, Eliá and Áno Méra is located by the old port; the south bus station for all western and the popular southern beaches is just outside the pedestrianized area at the other

end of town. If you choose to use public transport to the beaches from Paránga to Paradise, you certainly won't be alone – on any sunny day in season the beaches and transport range from busy to overcrowded. Buses to

Paradise run every hour through the night in high season. **By car and motorcycle** Rental agencies are concentrated around the two bus stops. The only free parking area near the town is by the north bus station. Parking spaces at most beaches are inadequate and signposting surprisingly poor.

**By taxi** Taxis run from Mantó square on the main seafront and from the south bus station; the rates are fixed and quite reasonable; try Mykonos Radio Taxi (☎ 22890 22400)
**By boat** *Kaïkia* head from town and Orkós to all of the southern beaches.

## Mýkonos Town

Don't let the crowds put you off exploring **MÝKONOS TOWN**, the quintessential image of the Cyclades. In summer most people head out to the beaches during the day, so early morning or late afternoon are the best times to wander the maze of narrow streets. The labyrinthine design was supposed to confuse the pirates who plagued Mýkonos in the eighteenth and early nineteenth centuries, and it has the same effect on today's visitors.

Getting lost in the convoluted streets and alleys is half the fun of Mýkonos, although there are a few places worth seeking out. Coming from the ferry quay you'll pass the **archeological museum** (Tues–Sun 9.30am–3pm; €2) on your way into town, which was specially built in 1905 to display artefacts from the cemeteries on Rínia island, opposite Delos (see p.396). The town also boasts a **Maritime museum** displaying various nautical artefacts and ship models as well as an 1890 lighthouse lantern re-erected in the back garden (April–Oct Tues–Sun 10.30am–1pm & 6.30–9pm; €4). Next door is **Lena's House** (Mon–Sat 4.30–8.30pm; free), a completely restored and furnished merchant home from the turn of the twentieth century. Near the base of the Delos jetty, the **Folklore museum** (Mon–Sat 4.30–8.30pm; free), housed in an eighteenth-century mansion, crams in a larger-than-usual collection of bric-a-brac, including a basement dedicated to Mýkonos's maritime past. The museum shares the promontory with Mýkonos's oldest and best-known church, **Paraportianí**, a fascinating asymmetrical hodgepodge of four chapels amalgamated into one (and a gay cruising area after dark).

Beyond the church, the shoreline leads to the area known as **Little Venice** because of the high, arcaded Venetian houses built right up to the water's edge on its southwest side. Together with the adjoining **Alefkándhra** district, this is a dense area packed with art galleries, trendy bars, shops and clubs. Beyond Little Venice, the famous **windmills** look over the area, renovated and ripe for photo opportunities.

### ACCOMMODATION                                          MÝKONOS TOWN

The scrum of room-owners by the old port jetty can be intimidating, so if you arrive by ferry press on 100m further, where you will find two accommodation offices; one deals with hotels (☎ 22890 24540, ⓦ mha.gr) and the other with rented rooms (☎ 22890 24860).

**K Group** Vrýsi ☎ 22890 23415, ⓦ myconiancollection .gr. A cluster of hotels, *Kalypso*, *Kochyli*, *Korali* and *Kyma* about 1km south of town. Many of the comfortable rooms have wonderful views and there's also a pool and restaurant. Often available when smaller places are fully booked. Breakfast included. Easter–Oct. **€150**
★ **Leto** Old Port ☎ 22890 22207/22918, ⓦ letohotel .com. The best of the luxury town hotels, slightly raised above the small town beach with a large swimming pool that becomes the focus both in the daytime and, fully lit, at night when the hotel restaurant – one of the best on the island – lays its tables around it. Breakfast included. **€250**
**Mantó** Evangelistrías 1 ☎ 22890 22330, ⓔ mantohotel1@yahoo.gr. Situated in a small side street, the hotel's exterior belies its Tardis-like interior expanse. Good, simple rooms with a/c and fridge for those who are

always on the move and just want a comfortable bed to crash in afterwards. March–Nov. **€75**
**Matogianni** Matogianni Str ☎ 22890 22217 ⓦ matogianni.gr. Living proof that it's possible to stay in Mýkonos Town without mortgaging your home, this is a comfortable hotel with classically minimalist decor and as peaceful as can be in the buzz of the backstreets. **€60**
**Stelios** Above the old port ☎ 22890 24641. This whitewashed Mykoniot-style building is an excellent-value pension in a prime location overlooking the old port. One hitch may be hauling your luggage up the steep steps behind the OTE office. April–Oct. **€90**
**Tagoo** Tangoú ☎ 22890 22611, ⓦ hoteltagoo.gr. Top quality hotel overlooking the sea, about a 700m walk north of the archeological museum. Attentive service, spacious rooms, roof pool with panoramic views and

# MÝKONOS TOWN

**ACCOMMODATION**
| | |
|---|---|
| Elysium | 6 |
| K Group | 7 |
| Leto | 3 |
| Mantó | 4 |
| Matogianni | 5 |
| Stelios | 2 |
| Tagoo | 1 |

**EATING & DRINKING**
| | |
|---|---|
| Baboulas | 1 |
| Kostas | 4 |
| Kounelas | 3 |
| Nikos | 2 |
| Yiavroutas | 5 |

**NIGHTLIFE**
| | |
|---|---|
| Jackie O' | 2 |
| Katerina's | 5 |
| Montparnasse | 6 |
| Pierro's Bar | 3 |
| Remezzo Kaminaki Waterfront | 1 |
| Skandinavian Bar | 4 |
| Space | 7 |

New Port, Toúrlos, Áyios Stéfanos & 1

Car Park

Accommodation Centre

North Bus Station

Island Ferries

Archeological Museum

Buses Áno Mera/Kalafati

Scooter Rental

Boats to Delos

Delos Ferry Ticket Kiosk

Taxis

ATM

PLATIA M. MAVROYENOUS

WC

Folklore Museum

Paraportianí

Port Police

LITTLE VENICE

KAMBANI

ALEFKÁNDHRA

WC

Cine Manti

ATM

Maritime Museum

Mýkonos Accommodation Centre

ATM

LÁKKA

School

Summer Theatre

Car Park

Laundry

VIDHA

South Bus Station/Taxis

ATM
ATM

Scooter Rental

Scooter Rental

ATM

Scooter Rental

Scooter Rental

ATM

SKHOLI KALÓN TEKHNÓN

Áno Mera

Áno Mera & By-pass

N

0       100
metres

Megáli Ámmos & Ornós

Airport, Vrýsi, Southern Beaches & 7

6

392 THE CYCLADES MÝKONOS

restaurant with specialist sushi chef. Booking for a minimum four nights in July–Aug. Breakfast included. May–Oct. **€450**

## GAY AND LESBIAN
**Elysium** By the School of Fine Arts ☎ 22890 23952,

w elysiumhotel.com. Exclusively gay hotel with beautiful views, boasting a poolside bar open to non-residents, a popular setting for an early evening party complete with go-go dancers and drag shows. Occasional all-night parties in conjunction with international DJs. Breakfast included. May–Oct. **€250**

## EATING AND DRINKING

★ **Baboúlas** Kaminaki Waterfront ☎ 22890 26804. Ouzerí that offers the best coal-grilled seafood mezédhes on Mýkonos, all personally supervised by Petroúla, the owner and chef. Try the mussels cooked in seawater (€13) and marvel. April–Nov daily noon–midnight.

**Kostas** Mitropoléos 5 ☎ 22890 23326. Buried deep within Alefkándhra, this restaurant serves everything from seafood to grills with a good wine list including wine straight from the barrel. Competitive prices for mains start at €12. Daily 6pm–2am.

**Kounelas** Svorónou ☎ 22890 28220. Seafood taverna set in an appealing garden, with a reputation for offering the freshest fish on the island. Very popular with the gay crowd, it is tucked away in a narrow street but easily signposted. May–Oct daily 8pm–2am.

**Nikos** Ayías Monís square ☎ 22890 28220. One of the most famous tavernas on the island, strong on the catch of the day but also serving traditional Greek cuisine (€15). Every centimetre of its side of the square is packed with customers after 10pm, which sometimes has a detrimental effect on service. April–Oct daily noon–2am.

**Yiavroutas** Mitropoléos 11 ☎ 22890 23063. Open until the early morning, this basic taverna has been serving clubbers with the munchies for decades with Greek dishes around €8. For those who prefer, above all, quantity over quality. April–Oct daily noon–7am.

## NIGHTLIFE

**Katerina's** Little Venice ☎ 22890 23084. Owned by the first female captain in the Greek navy, Katerina, this low-key bar-restaurant with sea and sunset views from the balcony is one of the most laidback places for a drink (cocktails €10). April–Oct daily noon–late.

**Remezzo** Kaminaki Waterfront ☎ 22890 28999. Stylish music club, offering alternative sunset views to those at Little Venice. Split into two sections and bars: one for the early birds with lounge music outside, and a second one with stronger beats for the night owls indoors. April–Oct daily 8pm–late.

**Skandinavian Bar** Áyios Ioánnis Barkiá ☎ 22890 22669, w skandinavianbar.com. For some serious drinking, head for the *Skandinavian*, which has been thumping out dance music and cocktails (€8) until the early hours since 1978. VIP table service can be booked. May–Sept daily 8pm–late.

**Space** Lákka w spacemykonos.com. The largest dance club in town, Space Mykonos has become a world brand in dance circles. Resident DJs from Greece and Italy play feelgood house tunes with the best sound system this side of Ibiza. Entrance €8 includes first drink. May, June & Sept Fri–Sat midnight–8am; July–Aug daily midnight–8am.

## GAY AND LESBIAN
**Jackie O'** Near Paraportianí ☎ 22890 17968, w jackieomykonos.com. The busiest gay club in town, it attracts a crowd of all sexual persuasions who like to dance to relentless funky house mixed with the occasional disco hit. On two floors, although trying to reach the top bar through the crowd is sometimes impossible. Daily 10pm–6am.

**Montparnasse** Ayíon Anargýron 24, Little Venice ☎ 22890 23719 w pianobar.com. With great cocktails (€8) and a balcony over the sea, this gay piano bar is a very good place to warm up for the night ahead. Sunset views followed by cabaret and live music. May–Oct daily 8pm–3.30am.

**Pierro's Bar** Ayías Kyriakís Square ☎ 22890 22177 w pierrosbar.gr. Legendary gay bar and club that has thrived since the 1960s, with innovative dance music. Despite its longevity, it is still trendy with its finger on the pulse of the gay scene. May–Sept daily 9pm–late.

# Around Mýkonos Town

The closest **beaches** around Mýkonos Town are those to the north, at **Toúrlos** (only 2km away but not up to the usual standard) and **Áyios Stéfanos** (3km away, much better), both developed resorts and connected by a very regular bus service to Mýkonos Town. There are tavernas and rooms (as well as package hotels) at Áyios Stéfanos. You'll need your own transport, a bus or *kaïki*, to get to most of them.

The undistinguished but popular beaches southwest of the town are tucked into pretty bays. The nearest, 1km away, is **Megáli Ámmos**, a good but often windy beach backed by flat rocks and pricey rooms, but nearby Kórfos Bay is unpleasant, thanks to the town dump and machine noise. Buses serve **Ornós**, a package resort on a low-lying area between the rest of the island and the Áyios Ioánnis peninsula. The south side has a reasonable beach, plus *kaïkia* to other beaches, a handful of tavernas, and numerous accommodation options.

Two kilometres west is **Áyios Ioánnis**, the island's westernmost bay and small, namesake church, overlooking Delos – the tiny public beach achieved a moment of fame as a location for the film *Shirley Valentine*. Accessed by a 500m dirt track northwest from Áyios Ioánnis is the small but popular beach at **Kápari**, with good views of Delos and the sunset.

6

## ACCOMMODATION · AROUND MÝKONOS TOWN

**Best Western Dionysos** Ornós ☎ 22890 23313, ⓦ dionysoshotel.gr. Easily the most comfortable hotel in the area with a pool and adjoining bar, free wi-fi, satellite TV, children's area and a fitness room, as well as parking space – mission impossible in Ornós. Breakfast included. May–Oct. **€100**

**Manoúlas Beach** Áyios Ioánnis ☎ 22890 22900, ⓦ hotelmanoulas.gr. A surprisingly affordable high-class hotel, blindingly set in white against the background of the deep blue of the Aegean. The panoramic view of its restaurant (€12) across to Delos is breathtaking. Breakfast included. May–Oct. **€120**

# The south coast

The western half of the south coast is the busiest part of the island. *Kaïkia* and buses head from town to all of its beaches; drivers will find that car-parking spaces at most beaches are inadequate and signposting surprisingly poor. You might begin with **Platýs Yialós**, 4km south of town: one of the longest-established resorts on the island, where the sand is monopolized by end-to-end hotels. **Psaroú**, just a steep hairpin road away to the west, is much prettier – 150m of white sand backed by foliage and reeds.

Just over the headland to the east of Platýs Yialós lies **Paránga**, actually two beaches separated by a smaller headland, the first of which is quieter than its neighbour. Next is the golden crescent of **Paradise beach**. Here, as on many of Mýkonos's most popular beaches, it can be difficult to find an opening big enough to fit a towel in high season, and any space clear of people is likely to be taken up by straw umbrellas, rentable (usually along with two accompanying loungers) for about €16 per day.

The next bay east contains **Super Paradise beach**, accessible by *kaïki*, or by a surfaced but extremely steep access road. It is one of the most fun spots on the island with its main beach bar staging a party every evening at 6pm. The eastern half gets progressively more gay as you walk towards the hills, below which the beach is almost exclusively gay and nudist. The more secluded **Agrári** beach is 300m to the east.

One of the more scenically attractive beaches on Mýkonos is **Eliá**, the last port of call east for the *kaïkia*, also reachable via an inland road. A broad, sandy stretch, with plenty of parking and a mountainous backdrop at the eastern end, it's the longest beach on the island, though divided by a rocky area, and almost exclusively gay later in the season.

East from the Eliá road is **Kaló Livádhi** (seasonal bus service), long and sandy, fronting an agricultural valley scattered with little farmhouses.

## ACCOMMODATION · THE SOUTH COAST

★ **Mykonos Camping** Paránga ☎ 22890 24915/6, ⓦ mycamp.gr. This small campsite, a short distance from the second Paránga beach, has one of the most pleasant settings on the island. It offers a wood-fired pizzeria, a pool with an adjoining cocktail bar and a minimarket, as well as

relative peace and quiet from the relentless Mykoniot buzz. May–Oct. **€7.50**

**Paradise Beach Resort** Paradise ☎ 22890 22852, ⓦ paradise-greece.com. An industrial-size (and feel) campsite operating since 1969, also offering cabins for

€30 and bungalows for €54. Totally self-sufficient with a restaurant, various bars, a clothes shop and its own club

with resident DJs. April–Oct. €15

## NIGHTLIFE

★ **Cavo Paradiso** Paradise ☎ 22890 27205, ⓦ www .cavoparadiso.gr. The after-hours club in the Cyclades, regularly voted as one of the Top 10 in the world, where die-hard party animals of all persuasions come together,

united by world-famous DJs. €20 entrance includes first drink, but check for discounts/guest list online. June–Sept (opening nights vary during the week) 12.30am–9am.

## The east and north

The main road **east** via the unexciting village of **Áno Méra** leads to **Ayía Ánna**, on a double-headed headland with a shingle beach and taverna, just before the larger, more attractive **Kalafáti**, the island's cleanest beach. **Liá**, roughly 4.6km east by road from Áno Méra, is smaller than Kalafáti, but as pleasant and with as clear water.

The **north coast** suffers persistent battering from the *meltémi* and for the most part is bare, brown and exposed. The deep inlet of **Pánormos Bay** is the exception to this, with the lovely, relatively sheltered beaches of **Pánormos** and **Áyios Sóstis**; although not served by buses, they are becoming increasingly popular, but still remain among the least crowded on the island. At the southern, inner end of the bay, **Fteliá** is a good windsurfers' beach and legendary burial site of Ajax, one of *The Iliad*'s mythical heroes. If you are driving there, stop by at the only – but excellent – vineyard on the island, **Bíoma** (☎ 22890 71883), for some wine tasting.

### ACCOMMODATION AND EATING                                    THE EAST AND NORTH

★ **Aphrodite Beach** Kalafáti ☎ 22890 71367, ⓦ aphrodite-mykonos.gr. A four-star hotel 18km from Mýkonos Town, and completely self-sufficient should you want to sample Mýkonos without the crowds. There is also a selection of hostel-style accommodation with four bunk beds per room, so it draws a very hip young crowd. April–Nov. Dorms €35, doubles €120

**La Luna** Liá ☎ 22890 72150. The furthest restaurant east, but don't let that deter you if you have your own transport.

Once there, you will be surprised as to how busy it is, but once you sample the Italian menu (€12) you'll understand. April–Sept daily 10am–9pm.

**Thalassa** Kalafáti beach ☎ 22890 72081. One of the best places to eat on Mýkonos and worth making the trip for dinner only. Its pork in thyme-honey (€18) is one of the top gastronomic experiences on the island. All this and free wi-fi, too. May–Sept daily noon–midnight.

# Delos

The remains of **ANCIENT DELOS** (Dhílos), the Cyclades' sole UNESCO Heritage Site, manage to convey the past grandeur of this small, sacred isle a few kilometres west of Mýkonos. The ancient town lies on the west coast on flat, sometimes marshy ground that rises in the south to **Mount Kýnthos**.

### ARRIVAL AND DEPARTURE                                                   DELOS

**By boat** In season, excursion boats to Delos leave from the west end of Mýkonos harbour Tues–Sun at 9am, 10am and 11am, returning from the site at 1pm, 2pm and 3pm (€17 return from a kiosk at the front). Guided day-trips are also

possible from Tínos (see p.385). Note that it is illegal to remove anything from Delos – not even a stone as a souvenir – as well as anchor, swim or dive at or near the island.

## The site

Tues–Sun 9am–3pm • €5

As you disembark from the boat, the Sacred Harbour is on your left, the Commercial Harbour on your right and straight ahead lies the **Agora of the Competaliasts**. The

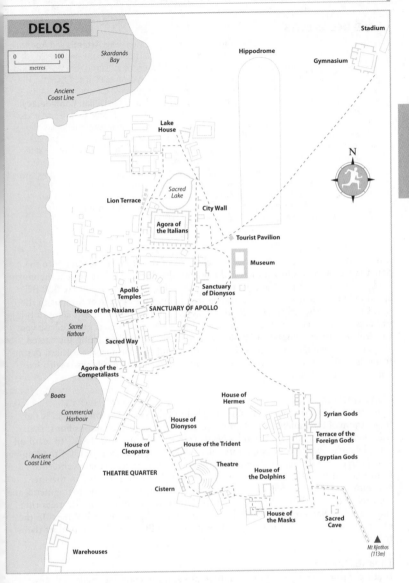

Competaliasts were Roman merchants who worshipped the Lares Competales, the guardian spirits of crossroads; offerings to Hermes would once have been placed in the middle of the agora (market square), their positions now marked by one round and one square base.

### Sacred Way and Sanctuary of Apollo

The **Sacred Way** leads north from the far left corner of the Agora of the Competaliasts. Formerly lined with statues and the grandiose monuments of rival

**6**

## OLD DELOS DAYS

Delos's ancient fame arose because **Leto** gave birth to the divine twins **Artemis** and **Apollo** here, although the island's fine, sheltered harbour and central position in the Aegean did nothing to hamper development from around 2500 BC. When the Ionians colonized the island about 1000 BC it was already a cult centre, and by the seventh century BC it had also become a major commercial and religious port. Unfortunately Delos attracted the attention of Athens, which sought dominion over this prestigious island; the wealth of the **Delian Confederacy**, founded after the Persian Wars to protect the Aegean cities, was harnessed to Athenian ends, and for a while Athens controlled the Sanctuary of Apollo. Athenian attempts to "purify" the island began with a decree (426 BC) that no one could die or give birth on Delos – the sick and the pregnant were shipped to the neighbouring island of **Rínia** – and culminated in the simple expedient of banishing the native population.

Delos recovered in Roman times and reached its peak of prosperity in the third and second centuries BC, after being declared a free port by its Roman overlords; by the start of the first century BC, its population was around 25,000. In the end, though, its undefended wealth brought ruin: first **Mithridates**, of Pontus (88 BC), then the pirate **Athenodorus** (69 BC) plundered the treasures, and the island never recovered since.

kings, walk up it to reach the three marble steps of the **Propýlaia** leading into the **Sanctuary of Apollo**. On your left is the Stoá of the Naxians, while against the north wall of the House of the Naxians, to the right, a huge statue of Apollo (c.600 BC) stood in ancient times; parts of it can be seen behind the **Temple of Artemis** to the left. In 417 BC the Athenian general Nikias led a procession of priests across a bridge of boats from Rínia to dedicate a bronze palm tree whose circular granite base you can still see. Three **Temples to Apollo** stand in a row to the right along the Sacred Way: the massive Delian Temple, the Athenian, and the Porinos, the earliest, dating from the sixth century BC. To the east stands the **Sanctuary of Dionysus** with its colossal marble phallus.

### Lions' Quarter

Northwest of the Sanctuary of Dionysus, behind the small **Letóön** temple, is the huge **Agora of the Italians**, while on the left are replicas of the famous **lions**, their lean bodies masterfully executed by Naxians in the seventh century BC to ward off intruders who would have been unfamiliar with the fearful creatures. Of the original lions, three have disappeared and one – looted by Venetians in the seventeenth century– adorns the Arsenale in Venice. The remaining originals are in the site **museum** whose nine rooms include a marble statue of Apollo, mosaic fragments and an extensive collection of phallic artefacts. Opposite the lions, tamarisk trees ring the site of the **Sacred Lake**, where Leto gave birth, clinging to a palm tree. On the other side of the lake is the City Wall, built – in 69 BC – too late to protect the treasures.

### Theatre Quarter

Bear right from the Agora of the Competaliasts and you enter the residential area, known as the **Theatre Quarter**. The remnants of impressive private mansions are now named after their colourful main **mosaic** – Dionysus, Trident, Masks and Dolphins. The **theatre** itself seated no fewer than 5500 spectators; just below it and structurally almost as spectacular is a huge underground cistern with arched roof supports. Behind the theatre, a path leads towards the **Sanctuaries of the Foreign Gods**, serving the immigrant population. It then rises steeply up Mount Kýnthos for a **Sanctuary of Zeus and Athena** with spectacular views out to the surrounding islands. Near its base, a small side path leads to the **Sacred Cave**, a rock cleft covered with a remarkable roof of giant stone slabs – a Hellenistic shrine to Hercules.

# Sýros

**SÝROS** is a living, working island with only a fleeting history of tourism, rendering it the most Greek of the Cyclades. There's a thriving, permanent community, the beaches are busy but not overflowing and the villages don't sprawl widely with new developments. As well as being home to a number of excellent restaurants, the island is known for its numerous shops selling *loukoúmia* (Turkish delight), *mandoláta* (nougat) and *halvadhópita* (soft nougat between disc-shaped wafers). In addition Sýros still honours its contribution to the development of **rebétika** music: Markos Vamvakaris, one of its prime proponents, hailed from Áno Sýros where a square has been named after him.

The island's sights – including the best beaches – are concentrated in the south and west; the north is unpopulated and barren, offering little interest. Most people tend to stay in Ermoúpolis, which offers better connections to a variety of beaches, none further than 15km away.

## ARRIVAL AND DEPARTURE

**By plane** The island is served by Athens (via Olympic, 1 daily; 45min). There is no bus service from the airport, and you will have to take a taxi.

**By ferry** All ferries dock at Ermoúpolis.

Destinations Amorgós (3–4 weekly; 5–6hr); Anáfi (3 weekly; 10hr); Ándhros (2–3 weekly; 2hr 30min); Astypálea (1 weekly; 6hr 30min); Folégandhros (5 weekly; 5hr 30min); Ikaría (6–7 weekly; 3hr); Íos (3–5 weekly; 4hr); Koufoníssi/Lesser Cyclades (3 weekly; 3hr–7hr 30min); Lávrio via Kéa/Kýthnos (2–4 weekly; 4hr); Mílos/Kímolos (3–5 weekly; 5–7hr); Mýkonos (2–5 daily; 1hr); Náxos (2–5 weekly; 2hr); Páros (2–5 weekly; 1hr 10min–1hr 30min); Pátmos (1 weekly; 3hr 30min); Pireás (2–3 daily; 3–4hr); Sámos (6 weekly; 4hr 30min); Santoríni (3–5 weekly; 5–7hr); Sérifos (3 weekly; 2–5hr); Sífnos (3 weekly; 2hr 30min–6hr); Síkinos (3–5 weekly; 5hr); Tínos (2–6 daily; 30–50min).

## INFORMATION AND TOURS

**Tourist office** TeamWork (☎ 22810 83400, ⊛ teamwork .gr), at Aktí Papágou 18 on the waterfront in Ermoúpolis, is a useful source of information and is able to help with your accommodation, excursion and ticket needs. In the summer there is an accommodation kiosk on the waterfront open during ferry arrivals.

**Services** There are several banks and about a dozen ATMs in Ermoúpolis, mostly around the waterfront. The post office is on Protopapadháki street. Laundry facilities are available at Krinos, Protopapadháki 34 (☎ 22810 88554). In Spot, on the seafront at Papágou, has internet but requires that you become a member, the cheapest option being €5 for 3hr. It is open 24/7.

**Tours** Starting from Platía Miaoúli in Ermoúpolis a small tourist train runs a 40min tour of the town's main sights (€4), while horse-drawn carriages (☎ 22810 81517) start from the centre of the waterfront in season, doing city tours of various durations (€10–50).

## GETTING AROUND

**By bus** The buses inside the city are free, but there are moves to start charging soon. Buses run on the main beach loop road south (to Galissás, Fínikas, Mégas Yialós, Akhládi, Vári and Azólimno) hourly in high season, until late.

**By taxi** Sýros drivers tend not to use the taximeter, so insist. If you are unsuccessful, a fare inside the city should cost around

€3 and from the port to Áno Sýros €5 (☎ 22810 86222).
**By car and motorcycle** There are many car and motorbike rental agencies on the waterfront such as

Gaviotis, Papagou 20 ☎ 22810 86610. Note that the police are pretty stringent here about giving drivers alcohol tests or fines for speeding.

# Ermoúpolis

Possessing an elegant collection of grand townhouses that rise majestically from the bustling, café-lined waterfront, **ERMOÚPOLIS** – once Greece's chief port – is one of the most striking towns in the Cyclades, and is certainly worth at least a night's stay.

Medieval Sýros was largely a Catholic island, but the influx of refugees from Psará and Híos during the nineteenth century created two distinct communities. Today, the Orthodox community accounts for two thirds of the population; Lower Ermoúpolis is mostly Orthodox while the Catholics live in the Upper Town and in the majority of the villages. They do, however, commonly celebrate each other's festivals (including Easter on the Orthodox dates only), lending a vibrant mix of cultures that gives the island its colour.

## Platía Miaoúli and around

The long, central square, **Platía Miaoúli**, is named after an admiral of the War of Independence whose statue stands there, and in the evenings the population parades in front of its arcades. The bougainvillea-covered pedestrian street of Roïdi and side streets east of Miaoúli square are peppered with most of the better eating options.

Up the stepped street (Benáki) to the left of the town hall is the small **archeological museum** (Tues–Sun 8.30am–3pm; free), with three rooms of finds from Sýros, Páros and Amorgós. To the left of the clock tower more steps climb up to **Vrondádho**, the hill that hosts the Orthodox quarter. The wonderful church of the **Anástasis** stands atop the hill, with its domed roof and panoramic views over Tínos and Mýkonos.

Below Miaoúli square, and down a side street you can find the elaborate **Casino** and the **Church of the Dormition** (Sept–March 7.30am–12.30pm & 4.30–5.30pm; April–Aug 7.30am–noon, 5.30–6.30pm; free), which contains the town's top art treasure: a painting of the Assumption by **El Greco**, executed while he was around 20 years old.

## Vapória

Up from the right of Miaoúli square is the **Apollon Theatre**, built like an Italian provincial opera house, which occasionally hosts performances (during morning rehearsals you can enter and watch for free or visit its small museum for €1.50). Further on up, the handsome Neoclassical Orthodox church of **Áyios Nikólaos** was built in 1848–70, with an impressive marble iconostasis (7am–2pm & 5–8pm). Beyond it lies the **Vapória** district, where the island's wealthiest shipowners, merchants and bankers built their mansions.

## Áno Sýros

On the taller hill to the left from Miaoúli square is the intricate medieval quarter of **Áno Sýros**, with a clutch of Catholic churches below the cathedral of St George. Just below it lies the **Capuchin monastery of St Jean**, founded in 1535 to do duty as a poorhouse. Once up here it's worth visiting the local art and rembétika exhibitions, as well as personal items of the man himself at the **Markos Vamvakaris museum** (June–Sept daily 11am–2pm & 7–10pm; €1.50).

**ACCOMMODATION**                                                                **ERMOÚPOLIS**

**Hermes** Kanári Square ☎ 22810 88011, ⓦ hermes -syros.com. Modernist sixties hotel in a prime location, overlooking the port and home to a very popular seafront restaurant (mains €10). Ask specifically for a room with sea views. Breakfast included. **€85**

**Kastro** Kalomenopóulou 12 ☎ 22810 88064. Spacious rooms in a beautiful old mansion near the main square, with access to a communal kitchen. These are the

# ERMOÚPOLIS

**EATING**

| Amvix | 6 |
| Archontariki tis Maritsas | 2 |
| Cotton Fresh | 3 |
| Lilis | 1 |
| Stin Ithaki tou Aï | 4 |
| Yiánnena | 5 |

**NIGHTLIFE**

| Casino Aigeou | 3 |
| Piramatikó | 2 |
| Theia Methi | 1 |

**ACCOMMODATION**

| Hermes | 6 |
| Kastro | 4 |
| Omiros | 3 |
| Palladion | 7 |
| Paradise | 5 |
| Sea Colours Apartments | 2 |
| Syrou Melathron | 1 |

cheapest – but far from disagreeable – lodgings in town. **€35**

**Omiros** Omírou 43 ☎ 22810 84910, ⓦ hotel-omiros.gr. One of the most romantic options in town, on a quiet road above the Orthodox Cathedral, in the direction of Áno Sýros. Classically styled rooms set in an elegant nineteenth-century mansion once owned by Tiniot sculptor Yeóryios Vitalis. Breakfast €7.50. **€80**

**Palladion** Proïou 3 ☎ 22810 86400, ⓦ palladion-hotel .com. Not far from the Casino, yet quiet, clean, recently renovated and with rooms overlooking a garden; overall excellent value. **€55**

**Paradise** Omírou 3 ☎ 22810 83204, ⓦ hotel-paradise -syros.com. Basic en-suite rooms in a quiet part of town. All rooms have access to a pleasant shaded courtyard, while rooms on the top floor have good views. Breakfast €7. **€45**

**Sea Colours Apartments** Athinás 10 ☎ 22810 81181. Traditionally decorated apartments for up to six people, with sea views, just above the swimming platforms of Áyios Nikólaos, a 5min walk from Platía Miaoúli. April–Nov. **€65**

★ **Sýrou Mélathron** Babayiótou 5 ☎ 22810 85963, ⓦ syroumelathron.gr. Regal hotel, recently renovated, set in a restored 1856 mansion in the quieter Áyios Nikólaos area of town. Has suites as well as spacious rooms, some with sea views. **€100**

### EATING

**Amvix** Aktí Papágou 26 ☎ 22810 83989. Owned by Roberto, an Italian chef from Padua, since 1995, this trattoria offers a taste of real Italy. Best pizzas on the island for €12. Daily noon–midnight.

**Archontariki tis Maritsas** Roïdi 8 ☎ 22810 86771. Very popular rustic taverna that serves island specialities, including its signature dish of casserole of mushrooms and spicy local sausage with peppers (€8). Daily noon–midnight.

**Cotton Fresh** Platía Miaouli ☎ 22810 82781. The best of the central square cafés, this is one to visit for a coffee and a snack, and it even uses its own home-made filo pastry for sweet and savoury pies (€4). Try a piece of the *karydhópita* (walnut pie with honey). Daily 8am–3am.

**Lilis** Ano Syros ☎ 22810 82100. An institution in the old town, with an unmatched view by the Kamares entrance, this is the taverna where Vamvakaris (see p.397) played. It's still going since 1953, offering Greek specialities from Asia Minor (€9). March–Oct daily noon–midnight.

★ **Stin Ithaki tou Aï** ☎ 22810 82060, ⓦ ithakitouai .gr. Welcoming taverna at Klonos and Stefanou corner, serving traditional ladherá dishes (various vegetables cooked in oil), as well as a good, cheap *souvláki* (€10). Daily noon–midnight.

**Yiánnena** Kanári Square ☎ 22810 87865. Popular, friendly spot, seemingly unchanged since the 1950s, serving great seafood and other Greek standards (€7). A smaller branch is on Venizelou 2. March–Oct daily 11am–1am.

### NIGHTLIFE

**Casino Aigeou** Proïou 74 ☎ 22810 84400, ⓦ casinosyros .gr. Large casino that draws in well-dressed punters (no T-shirts, shorts or flip-flops) from as far as Russia. Minimum bid roulette €2.50; Black Jack €5; slot machines open 24/7. Sun–Thurs 8pm–3.30am, Fri–Sat 8pm–5.30am.

**Piramatikó** Platía Miaoúli ☎ 22810 83734. Busy, sophisticated bar, playing a varied and eclectic mix from

indie rock to house music. Starts off as a café and ends up as a club. Cheap beers start at €3. Daily 9am–4am.

**Theia Meth** Chiou 43 ☎ 690 85 20 165. If you want to hear rembétika now, then take an early seat at this *mezedhopolío* on the western side of Platía Miaoúli, which has free live music most days after 9.30pm, order your mains (€8) and enjoy the show. Daily 7pm–late.

## Beaches

The first stop on the beach round-trip from Ermoúpolis is well-developed **Galissás**, the largest beach on the island, and the home of its only **campsite** (see p.402). If you feel the urge to escape the crowds, you can rent a scooter, or walk ten minutes over the southern headland to the small nudist beach of **Armeós**. A longer walk (1hr 15min plus) goes, rather steeply, over the ridge to the southeast and down to the **sea-cave** of Áyios Stéfanos.

A rural forty-minute walk, or a ten-minute bus ride south from Galissás, brings you to the more mainstream resort of **Fínikas**, with its long and narrow beach protected from the road by a row of tamarisk trees. Fínikas is separated by a small headland from its neighbour **Posidhonía** (or Delagrazia after the local Madonna della Grazia church), a nicer spot with some idiosyncratically ornate mansions and a bright-blue church right on the edge of the village. It's worth walking ten minutes further south, past the naval yacht club and its patrol boat, to **Agathopés**. This is the best sandy beach on the island, facing a little islet, Skhinónisi, just offshore. **Komitó**, at the end of the road leading south 500m from **Agathopés**, is a small, quiet sandy bay below a private olive grove.

From Posidhonía the road swings southeast to **Mégas Yialós**, a diffuse, elongated resort. There are two beaches, Mégas Yialós and Ambélia; the long, eponymous beach is lined with shady trees and there are pedal boats for hire.

The cove of **Akhládhi** is sheltered and family-friendly, while **Vári**, just beyond, is more – though not much more – of a town, with its own small fishing fleet. As it is the most sheltered of the island's bays – something to remember when the *meltémi* is up – it

attracts mostly families and little children; the younger crowd are attracted by the beach bars of Agathopés and Komito above.

The final resort on the circular tour is **Azólimnos**, accessed by a narrow road from Vári, or a wider one from the northern end.

### ACCOMMODATION                                                        BEACHES

**Brazzera** Fínikas ☎ 22810 79173, ⓦ www.brazzera.gr. Modern, well-situated hotel close to the beach, whose green furnishings tastefully match the green of the salt cedars in front. Large rooms with tiled floors adorned with flowers make this one of the most pleasant stays outside Ermoúpolis. April–Oct. **€85**

**Dolphin Bay** Galissás ☎ 22810 42924, ⓦ dolphin-bay .gr. Luxurious hotel, amphitheatrically built with impressive views over the bay from its large swimming

pool and bar. The complex includes an excellent restaurant (mains €15). Breakfast included. May–Oct. **€90**

**Two Hearts** Galissás ☎ 22810 42052, ⓦ ww.twohearts -camping.com. The only camping on the island, it is well organized with a minimarket, internet access, a currency exchange plus a car and motorcycle rental office. It offers bungalows that sleep two and have their own WCs, as well as pickups from the ferries. May–Sept. Camping **€8**, bungalows **€20**

### EATING AND DRINKING

**Niriídhes** Akhládhi ☎ 697 88 30 332. Fish taverna, the beach offshoot of the Archontariki tis Maritsas (see p.400) in Ermoúpolis, which specializes in imaginative seafood dishes such as shrimp omelette, yet still has a place for time-honoured platters like grilled octopus (€9). May–Oct noon–midnight.

**To Iliovasilema** Galissás ☎ 22810 43325. A small

seaside taverna with an inventive menu, it punches well above its weight in the reputation stakes. The owner has his own boat and nothing from the catch goes to waste: small fish are used for the bouillabaisse, shellfish are added to the pasta sauce, while the larger items are grilled with lemon and herbs. April–Oct noon–midnight, Nov– March 7pm–midnight.

# Páros

With a gentle and undramatic landscape arranged around the central peak of Profítis Ilías, **PÁROS** has a little of everything one expects from a Greek island: old villages, monasteries, fishing harbours, nice beaches and varied nightlife. However, Parikiá, the capital, can be touristy and expensive, and it is very difficult finding rooms and beach space here in August, when the other settlements, the port of **Náoussa** and the satellite island of **Andíparos**, handle most of the overflow. Drinking and carousing is many people's idea of a holiday on Páros, so it's not surprising that both Parikiá and Náoussa have a wealth of pubs, bars and discos, offering staggered happy hours.

### ARRIVAL AND DEPARTURE                                                 PÁROS

**By plane** The island is served by regular flights from Athens (via Olympic; 2–3 daily; 55min). The airport is 12km south of Parikiá. There are buses waiting for the flights during the summer months.

**By ferry** Parikiá is a major hub for inter-island ferry services and serves almost all islands in the Cyclades. There are two ferries to Andíparos: the first is a passenger ferry from Parikiá and the second is a car ferry from Poúnda, 7km south of Parikiá (see opposite). The latter leaves every 30–45min during the summer months; 7.15am–1.30am (€1.15 per person, €6.15 per car).

Destinations Amorgós (2–3 weekly; 3hr); Anáfi (1–3

weekly; 6hr 30min); Andíparos (hourly in season; 40min); Astypálea (1–4 weekly; 4hr 50min); Iráklion (5–6 weekly; 3hr 30min); Dhonoússa (daily; 2hr); Folégandhros (2–4 weekly; 3hr 30min); Íos (2–3 weekly; 2hr–3hr 45min); Lávrio via Kéa/Kýthnos (1 weekly; 8hr); Mílos (2–3 weekly; 5hr); Mýkonos (1–2 daily; 45min–1hr 40min); Náxos (2–3 daily; 35min–1hr); Pireás (3–5 daily; 3–4hr); Santoríni (1–3 daily; 3hr); Sérifos (1–2 weekly; 3–5hr); Sífnos (2 weekly; 2hr 30min); Síkinos (2–4 weekly; 3hr); Skhinoússa (2–4 weekly; 2hr 20min–6hr); Sýros (6–8 weekly; 2hr 40min); Tínos (1–2 daily; 1hr 10min).

### INFORMATION

**Tourist office** There is no official tourist office on the island; bus timetables are posted by the bus station in

Parikiá and there is a kiosk by the windmill with general accommodation information on the island. Your best bet is to go to a travel agent (see below).

**services** There is no shortage of banks or ATMs in Parikiá. The island's only post office is west of the windmill, past the ancient cemetery. Cybercookies (☎ 22840 21610, ⓦ cybercookies.gr; €3/hr) off the main square is the best internet café. Luggage can be left at various travel agents

(look for signs) along Parikiá's watefront.

**Travel agents** Polos Tours (☎ 22840 22092, ⓦ polostours .gr) in Parikiá is one of the friendlier travel agencies, issuing air tickets for Olympic, and acting as agents for virtually all the boats.

## GETTING AROUND

**By bus** The bus station is 100m or so west of the ferry dock. Note that there are two places called Poúnda on Páros, one being the west-coast port, the other a beach on the east coast (see p.408). Náoussa (hourly through the night in high season; 20min), Poúnda for Andíparos (20min), Dhryós (1hr). **By car and motorcycle** Rental outfits include European

(☎ 22840 21771, ⓦ paroscars.gr) and Avant Travel (☎ 22840 22302, ⓦ europcar-paros.com) on the western and eastern waterfronts respectively. Note that traffic rules are strictly enforced, and that various streets are one-way. Parking is only allowed in designated areas and parts of the Parikiá seafront are closed to traffic during summer evenings.

## Parikiá and around

Bustling **PARIKIÁ** sets the tone architecturally for the rest of Páros, its ranks of typically Cycladic white houses punctuated by the occasional Venetian-style building and church domes. The town's sights apart, the real attraction of Parikiá is simply to wander the town itself, especially along the meandering **old market street** (Agorá) and adjoining Grávari. Arcaded lanes lead past Venetian-influenced villas, traditional island dwellings, ornate wall-fountains and trendy shops. The market street culminates in a formidable **kástro** (1260), whose surviving east wall incorporates a fifth-century BC round tower and is constructed using masonry pillaged from a nearby temple of Athena which is still highly visible. On the seafront behind the port police are the exposed, excavated ruins of an **ancient cemetery** used from the eighth century BC until the third century AD.

## The Ekatondapylianí
Daily 7am–9pm • Free

Just beyond the central clutter of the ferry port, Parikiá has the most architecturally interesting church in the Aegean – the **Katopoliani** (facing the town). Later Greek scholars purified the name and connected it with past glories, so they changed it to **Ekatondapylianí** ("The One Hundred Gated"), a nickname that baffles today's visitors. Tradition, supported by excavations, claims that it was originally founded in 326 AD by St Helen, mother of Emperor Constantine, but what's visible today stems from a sixth century Justinian reconstruction.

Enclosed by a great front wall, sign of an Imperial-built church, the church is in fact three interlocking buildings. The oldest, the chapel of **Áyios Nikólaos** to the left of the apse, is an adaptation of a pagan building dating from the early fourth century BC. On the right, there is another building attached, housing a Paleochristian **baptistry**, where the initiate used to dip in a cross-shaped pool. Inside the church courtyard, there is a small **Byzantine museum** (church hours; €2) displaying a collection of icons. Look through the iconostasis (which still retains its ancient marble frame) to observe two unique features: at the back, a set of amphitheatric steps, the **synthronon**, where the priests used to chant, and, at the front, the **ciborium**, a marble canopy over the altar.

## Archeological Museum
Tues–Sun 8.30am–2.30pm • €2

Behind Ekatondapylianí, the **archeological museum** has a good collection and is definitely worth a visit. Its prize exhibits are a large Gorgon, a fifth-century winged Nike by **Skopas** and – hidden at the back of the main room – a piece of the **Parian Chronicle**, a social and cultural history of Greece up to 264 BC engraved in marble.

## Áyii Anárgyiri monastery

If you're staying in Parikiá, you'll want to get out at some stage. The shortest **excursion** is the 2.5km along the road starting from the northern end of the ring-road up to the **Áyii Anárgyiri** monastery. Perched on the bluff above town, this makes a great picnic spot, with cypress groves, a gushing fountain and some splendid views.

## Beaches near Parikiá

Less than 1km north of the harbour lies the twin crescent of **Livádhia** beach, with shallow waters and shaded by salt cedars; further on lies **Kriós** beach, much better, served by *kaïki* from just to the right of the ferry terminal (€4). The beaches south along the asphalt road are even better: the first unsurfaced side-track leads to the small, sheltered **Dhelfíni**; fifteen minutes further on is **Paraspóros** near the remains of an ancient temple to Asklepios, the god of healing. Continuing for 45 minutes (or a short hop by bus) brings you to arguably the best of the bunch, **Ayía Iríni**, a palm-fringed beach with fine sand, a taverna and a beautiful **campsite** (see p.406).

## Petaloúdhes

Not far from the turning to Ayía Iríni, is the "Valley of the Butterflies", a walled-in private oasis where millions of Jersey tiger moths perch on the foliage in summer

# PARIKIÁ

| | | |
|---|---|---|
| **EATING** | | |
| Apollon | | 3 |
| Boudaraki | | 5 |
| Happy Green Cows | | 2 |
| Hibiscus | | 4 |
| Trata | | 1 |

| | | |
|---|---|---|
| **ACCOMMODATION** | | |
| Anna Platanou | | 9 |
| Argonauta | | 5 |
| Camping Ayía Iríni | | 10 |
| Captain Manolis | | 6 |
| Dina | | 7 |
| Koula Camping | | 1 |
| Krios Camping | | 2 |
| Mike's Rooms | | 3/4 |
| Pándrossos | | 8 |

| | | |
|---|---|---|
| **NIGHTLIFE** | | |
| Alexandros | | 4 |
| Dubliner | | 6 |
| Paros Rock | | 5 |
| Pebbles | | 1 |
| Pirate Bar | | 3 |
| Saloon D'Or | | 2 |

(May–Sept 9am–8pm; €2). The trip can be combined with a visit to the eighteenth-century nunnery of **Áyios Arsenios**, at the crest of a ridge 1km to the north. Only women are allowed in the sanctuary, although men can wait in the courtyard. Petaloúdhes can also be reached from Parikiá by bus during the summer months.

## ACCOMMODATION
PARIKIÁ AND AROUND

**Anna Platanou** ☎ 22840 21751, ⓦ annaplatanou.gr. This smart, family-run and family-friendly hotel 600m southwest of the port has clean, refurbished rooms in a peaceful location overlooking a garden. The owners also have much larger studios, and apartments at the junction of the Alykí-Poúnda roads for €50. Port transfers available. April–Oct. **€60**

**Argonauta** ☎ 22840 21440, ⓦ argonauta.gr. Stylish hotel in the white-and-blue Cycladic fashion with smart rooms arranged around a beautiful stone courtyard next to the National Bank. There is a good restaurant underneath. April–Oct. **€70**

**Camping Agia Iríni** Ayía Iríni ☎ 22840 91496,

ⓦ campingai.gr. One of the most atmospheric campsites in the Cyclades: you are right on the beach, but it feels like you are camping in someone's overgrown garden. It has its own cheap taverna, although the olive, citrus and summer-ripening fruit trees can provide you with free sustenance. Bus transfers organized. May–Sept. **€18**

★ **Captain Manolis** ☎ 22840 21244, ⓦ paroswelcome .com. Central – behind the National Bank – but unbelievably quiet; all rooms have ivy-covered balconies facing the garden, as well as a/c and fridge. Free wi-fi. May–Oct. **€40**

**Dina** ☎ 22840 21325, ⓦ hoteldina.com. Small family pension, right in the middle of the night action in the Agorá opposite the Ayía Triádha church. There is only occasional

**6**

noise from the *Pirate's Bar* opposite, so either come home when they close at 3am or ask for a room at the back. May–Oct. **€50**

**Koula Camping** ☎ 22840 22081, ⊛ campingkoula.gr. For those who need to be very close to the town, this campsite, 900m along the seafront east of the bus stop, is a reasonable choice for a night or two, with 24/7 reception, a wide range of cabins or bungalows, and even a covered area for just sleeping bags. The owners also operate a cheap but good restaurant next door. April–Oct. **€6**

★ **Krios Beach Camping** ☎ 22840 21705, ⊛ krios -camping.gr. Excellent facilities in a shady, flat site, 2km east from Parikiá, supplemented by a cool beach bar next door. Occasional Greek parties, which include plate

smashing, see crowds specially bussed in from Parikiá; they finish early enough so that you can enjoy your sleep. Free wi-fi, pool. May–Sept. **€8**

**Mike's Rooms** ☎ 22840 22856, ⊛ roomsmike.com. Clean, comfortable studios opposite the ferry dock with hospitable staff, and a recommendations diary as long as the Encyclopedia Britannica. Mike, the owner, is a tirelessly enthusiastic source of information and assistance. May–Sept. **€35**

**Pándrossos** ☎ 22840 22903, ⊛ pandrossoshotel.com. Perched magnificently on a high hill overlooking the port and beyond, this four-star hotel has a good restaurant, a deep swimming pool and colourful rooms with balconies offering exceptional sunset views. March–Oct. **€75**

### EATING

**Apollon** Off Agorá ☎ 22840 24691. Housed in a converted 1920s olive press with a large garden near the market, this is one of the island's classiest restaurants. Despite high prices, its popularity never wanes. Try the chicken with prunes (€18), highly recommended. April–Oct daily 7pm–late.

★ **Boudaraki** ☎ 22840 22297. The locals rate this restaurant at the southern beachfront by the bridge as the best one on Páros. Expect good service even when packed, an excellent selection of mezédhes and mains (€12), as well as home-made baklava to finish the meal off. Easter–Sept daily noon–1am.

**Happy Green Cows** ☎ 22840 24691. Remarkably eclectic vegetarian restaurant in a side street behind the National Bank with some concessions to carnivores that

include chicken and fish. Not cheap (mains around €17), yet imaginative, with unexpected local ingredients that make you want to play "name that vegetable". April–Oct daily 7pm–2am.

**Hibiscus** ☎ 22840 24691. One of the oldest restaurants on the island, in a great, central spot on the waterfront south of the windmill, overlooking the sea; it offers the usual Greek dishes, but is famed mainly for its selection of generous-sized, wood-oven-baked pizzas for €10. April–Oct daily 6pm–2am.

**Trata** ☎ 22840 24651. Behind the ancient cemetery off the road heading out of town, this popular, family-run taverna specializes in serving large plates of tasty seafood and grilled meats (€12) in a vine-covered patio. April–Oct daily noon–midnight.

### NIGHTLIFE

**Alexandros** The best possible location for a sophisticated evening drink in a fabulously romantic spot around a real windmill. Set apart from the town, on an elevated promontory at the southern end of the promenade, it has wonderful sunset views which you can enjoy while listening to classical music. Cocktails €9. June–Sept daily 6.30pm–3am.

**Dubliner/Paros Rock** ☎ 22840 21113. Large, brash and youthful dance complex thankfully set back from the main drag just off the seafront bridge, thus avoiding scrutiny of the antics of the 18–30 crowd dancing to mainstream hits. It comprises four loud bars – opening gradually as the summer hots up – a main club and an outdoors chillout area. Entrance with first drink €5. June–Sept daily 11pm–6am.

★ **Pebbles** Upstairs bar at the seafront, east of the

windmill and up the steps from the kiosk, playing jazz and lounge music, with good sunset views and excellent cocktails (€7). It attracts a mixed-age crowd, who pack the place to watch the sunset around 8pm and then return after midnight. Daily noon–3am.

**Pirate Bar** Popular, established jazz and blues bar near the town hall, opposite Dina's. It is rather small, so it's convenient for smokers as most of its clientele tend to stand outside. Cocktails €8. April–Oct daily 10am–2pm & 6.30pm–3am.

**Saloon D'Or** Rowdy but fun spot on the seafront south of the windmill, with cheap drinks and lounge/chillout music. It offers shishas in various flavours, as well as comfortable Oriental divans and settees to sink in and enjoy them. Cocktails €7. May–Sept daily 8.30pm–3.30am.

## The southwest

There's little to stop for southwest of Parikiá until **Poúnda**, 6km away, the watersports centre of the island. A further 6km south, past the airport, you reach **Alykí**, a pretty resort on a picturesque bay with two beach sections: one pebbly and bare and the other sandy and shaded.

## Skorpios Cycladic Folk Museum

Daily May–Sept 9.30am–2pm • Free

A fascinating and deeply idiosyncratic private museum with a collection of model boats and miniatures of various typical buildings from the Cyclades. You can find here painstakingly reconstructed examples, from the dovecotes of Tínos to Náxos cereal grinding mills, and from the Lion Avenue of Delos to the windmills of Mýkonos.

### INFORMATION

THE SOUTHWEST

6

**Activities** Paros Watersports in Poúnda (☏ 22840 92229, ☷ paros-watersports.gr) offers courses and rents

equipment for all levels of kitesurfing, wakeboarding and scuba diving leading to a PADI certification course.

### ACCOMMODATION AND EATING

**Galatis** Alykí ☏ 22840 91355, ☷ galatishotel.com. This is the best hotel outside Parikiá and Náoussa, several notches up from merely comfortable, offering a pool, a

restaurant and (mostly) sea-view rooms. Free wi-fi. Breakfast included. April–Nov. €75

## Náoussa and around

Many consider **Náoussa** as a more fashionable alternative to Parikiá. Although a major resort town, with modern concrete hotels and attendant trappings, it has developed around a charming little port whose layout has not been adversely affected. The local festivals are still celebrated with enthusiasm, especially the re-enactment on August 23 of a naval victory over the pirates, followed by a fireworks display.

Although the nightlife is on a par with that of Parikiá, most people are here for the local beaches. **Áyii Anárgyri** is just off the path that goes east of Náoussa's harbour, while **Piperí** is a couple of minutes' walk west. To the northwest, 4km on the road around the bay brings you to **Kolymbíthres**, with its wind- and sea-sculpted rock formations. A few minutes beyond, **Monastíri beach**, below the abandoned Pródhromos monastery, is similarly attractive for diving and snorkelling. A regular summer *kaïki* service connects them for €6 return.

Go northeast of town and the sands are better still: after the glorious sandbank of **Kínari** you reach the barren **Viglákia** headland, also reached by *kaïki*. It is dotted with good surfing beaches such as **Platiá Ámmos** that lies on the northeastern tip of the island and **Lángeri** which is backed by dunes; a walk ten minutes south of the main beach brings you to the mostly gay section. The best surfing beach, though, is at **Sánta María**, an expanse of sand 6km by road from Náoussa.

**Ambelás**, 3km southeast of Náoussa, has a safe, sheltered beach, as you might guess from the number of fishing boats moored here. It is also the start of a long, rough coastal 6km track that leads south, passing several undeveloped shady coves on the way such as **Glyfádha** and the almost deserted **Tsoukália** until you reach the impressive spread of **Mólos beach**, never particularly crowded. From here you can pick up again the asphalted road straight back to Náoussa or through the **inland villages** back to Parikiá.

### ACCOMMODATION

NÁOUSSA AND AROUND

**Astir of Paros** ☏ 22840 51976, ☷ www.astirofparos.gr. Superb and lavish five-star resort on the road to Kolymbíthres with marble baths, huge balconies and excellent service. Its sixteen-acre site includes two restaurants, large pool, tennis court, three-hole golf course, heliport and even two small chapels for weddings. April–Oct. €250

**Christiana** Ambelás ☏ 22840 51573, ☷ christiana hotel.gr. A good-value hotel, with great fresh fish and local wine in the in-house restaurant and extremely friendly proprietors; they have both rooms and fully equipped

apartments, all with balconies facing the beach. Breakfast included. May–Sept. €45

★ **Heaven** ☏ 22840 51549, ☷ heaven-naoussa.com. As it is difficult to find (walk up the steps above the bus station car park), this feels like a true discovery: an elegant, cool, gay-friendly and spotlessly clean boutique hotel belonging to a Scandinavian Greek and his family. Internet and parking available. May–Sept. €60

**Sea House** ☏ 22840 52198. This was one of the first places in Náoussa to let rooms and has one of the best locations above Pipéri beach with beautiful views from all of its balconies. Recommended for those who prize location over extravagance. April–Oct. €60

**Stella** ☎ 22840 53617, ⓦ hotelstella.gr. Out of season, you should be able to haggle for reduced prices at this basic but well-located hotel with rooms arranged around its own garden, several blocks inland from the old harbour. €55

**Surfing Beach Village** Sánta María ☎ 22840 52493, ⓦ surfbeach.gr. A well-organized campsite where surfers rub shoulders with families. In late June–July it runs a summer camp for 7–14-year-olds. Also offers beach huts and bungalows with a/c and private WC (€55). Courtesy minibus to and from Parikiá. June–Sept. Camping **€8**, beach huts **€15**

### EATING AND DRINKING

**Meltemi** ☎ 22840 51263. On the quiet side of the bridge, this excellent grill restaurant offers Cretan specialities (€12) with a smile. The owner is friendly and chatty and you'll undoubtedly be offered a free shot of *tsikoudiá* "for digestion". Easter–Oct daily 6pm–late.

**Ouzerí ton Naftikón** ☎ 22840 51662. Probably the best *mezedhopolio* in the harbour area. Offers fresh fish and a rather standard Greek menu (mains €8), but has a

reputation second to none. Come before 9pm or else you won't find a seat. April–Oct daily 6.30pm–late.

**Yeméni** ☎ 22840 51445, ⓦ yemeni.gr. Popular family restaurant in the winding streets of central Náoussa, offering well-cooked, traditional Greek dishes for around €10. Everything comes from the family farm – from the pork and chicken to the oil you will pour on your salad. Easter–Oct daily 6pm–late.

### NIGHTLIFE

**Barbarossa** ☎ 22840 51391. Chic bar bathed in candlelight at the far end of the harbour (not to be confused with the expensive restaurant at the opposite end). Frequented mostly by twenty-something Greeks, this may be the place to try your language skills. Cocktails €10. April–Oct daily 6pm–4am.

**Shark** ☎ 693 73 06 037. On a first-floor balcony overlooking the harbour, this is a bar for alternative rockers

and where ale rather than cocktails is the drink of choice. A good selection of bottled beers on offer (€5). May–Sept daily 9pm–3am.

**Vareladhiko** Potami. Classic club playing pop hits and frequented mainly by under-thirties. The script is predictable: beer will flow, patrons will dance on the tables and holiday romances will blossom. It's still great fun, though. Mid-June to mid-Sept (days vary) 11pm–6am.

## The southeast coast

The coast southeast of the inland junction at **Marpíssa** – itself a maze of winding alleys and ageing archways overhung by floral balconies – is comparatively off the tourist radar, yet it is easily reachable by regular buses during the summer and boasts some magnificent beaches.

The first resort you reach, **Píso Livádhi**, was once a quiet fishing village, but it is now dominated by open-air car parks and relatively indifferent tavernas. However, between here and **Dhryós** to the south there are no fewer than four excellent beaches. **Logarás** just over the promontory from Píso Livádhi has a superb stretch of sand, while the next

### THE INLAND VILLAGES

Most people bypass Páros interior, but on a cooler day try walking the **medieval flagstoned path** that once linked both sides of the island. Start from the main square of the village of **Mármara** and go west. First up is **Pródhromos**, an old fortified farming settlement with defensive walls girding its nearby monastery. **Léfkes** itself, 5km from Pródhromos, is perhaps the most unspoilt settlement on Páros. The town flourished from the seventeenth century on, its population swollen by refugees fleeing from coastal piracy; indeed it was the island's capital during most of the Ottoman period. Léfkes's marbled alleyways and amphitheatrical setting are unparalleled – and undisturbed by motor vehicles, which are forbidden in the middle of town. Another 5km towards Parikiá and you hit **Maráthi**, from where Parian marble was supplied to much of Europe. Considered second only to Carrara marble, the last slabs were mined here by the French in 1844 for **Napoleon's tomb** in Les Invalides. Just east of the village, marked paths lead to two huge entrances of ancient marble mines which can be visited with an organized tour only. From Maráthi, it's easy enough to pick up the bus on to Parikiá.

beach, **Poúnda** (not to be confused with the port of the same name on the west coast), is home to a beach club with parties that go on well into the night. The final two are the twin windsurfing beaches of **New** and **Old Khrissí Akti** (Golden Beach), which have been established as the main resorts of the southeast.

**Dhryós**, the end of the bus routes, is the only settlement of any size in this part of Páros. Although the village is mostly modern and characterless, it has an attractive, quiet beach.

## ACCOMMODATION AND EATING — THE SOUTHEAST COAST

**Fisilánis** Logarás ☏ 22840 41734, ✉ fysilanisgr@hol
.gr. In operation since 1964, this is an outstanding value
family hotel and taverna (mains €6) worth experiencing
if only for a few days. Well-stocked rooms with
sea views, friendly service and unbeatable prices. April–
Oct. **€40**

**Golden Beach** Khrissí Aktí ☏ 22840 41366,
🌐 goldenbeach.gr. The dominant hotel on the "Old"
Golden Beach with windsurfing facilities available next
door, an adjoining restaurant open for breakfast through to
dinner and a beach bar open until 2am (beer €3). Free wi-fi
and breakfast included. April–Oct. **€80**

# Andíparos

**ANDÍPAROS** is no longer a secret destination: the waterfront is lined with new hotels and apartments, and in high season it can be full, though in recent years families have displaced the former young, international crowd. However, the island has retained its friendly backwoods atmosphere and has a lot going for it, including good sandy beaches and a remarkable cave. Furthermore, rooms and hotels here are much less expensive than on Páros.

## ARRIVAL AND INFORMATION — ANDÍPAROS

**By ferry** There are two ferries going to two different
places on Páros: the passenger-only ferry goes to Parikiá
(see p.403) and the car ferry goes to Poúnda, 7km below
Parikiá (see p.406).
**Destinations** To Páros, Parikiá (hourly in season; 40min);
Páros, Poúnda (every 30min in season; 20min).
**Services** There is a bank at the waterfront, as well as a
small post office.

**Travel agents** Oliaros Tours (☏ 22840 61231,
🌐 antiparostravel.gr) in the main shopping street can help
with accommodation, boat and plane tickets, excursions
and car rental. They also operate a currency exchange and a
postal courier service.
**Activities** Blue Island Divers (☏ 22840 61767, 🌐 blueisland
-divers.gr) on the waterfront offer two-day PADI diving
courses (€200). They also rent underwater scooters.

## GETTING AROUND

**By bus** The stop is by the disembarkation point. Cave
(30min); Áyios Yeóryios (50min).
**By car and motorcycle** Europecar (☏ 22840 61346,

🌐 antiparos-cars.com) is a good rental outlet near the ferry
dock.

## Andíparos Town

Most of the population live in the large low-lying **ANDÍPAROS TOWN**, across the narrow straits from Páros, the new development on the outskirts concealing an attractive traditional settlement. A long, flagstoned pedestrian street forms its backbone, leading from the jetty to the Cycladic houses around the outer wall of the kástro. It was built by Leonardo Loredano in the 1440s as a fortified settlement safe from pirate raids – his family coat of arms can still be seen on a house in the courtyard. The only way in is through a pointed archway from the main square, where several cafés are shaded by a giant eucalyptus. Inside, more whitewashed houses surround two churches and a cistern built into the surviving base of the central tower. The town has also developed into a prime diving centre.

## ACCOMMODATION — ANDÍPAROS TOWN

**Camping Antiparos** ☏ 22840 61221, 🌐 camping
-antiparos.gr. This fully equipped campsite is a 10min

walk northeast of town along a track, next to its own nudist
beach; the water here is shallow enough for campers to

6

wade across to the neighbouring islet of Dhipló. June–Sept. €8

**Koúros Village** ☎ 22840 61084/5, ⓦ kouros-village.gr. If any proof were needed that Andíparos is value for money you need only visit this extensive resort. Large, clean pool, a restaurant with a panoramic view (mains €6), an open-air dancefloor and apartment-sized rooms. Breakfast included. Easter–Oct. €70

**Mantaléna** ☎ 22840 61206, ⓦ hotelmantalena.gr. In 1960 a Greek film, *Mantalena*, was shot on Andíparos by director George Roussos. Three years later his brother built this hotel north of the jetty, which is still run by his family. This is one of the more exclusive places on Andíparos and offers large rooms and balconies with wi-fi and satellite TV – plus some apartments in the old town. Breakfast included. Easter–Oct. €70

### EATING AND DRINKING

**Anárgyros** ☎ 22840 61204. Taverna with the most central location in the port where you can rest assured that the daily special (around €8) will be also be consumed by the owner's family later. Also offers basic, clean rooms at the back for €50. June–Sept daily 10am–midnight.

**Yannis Place** ☎ 22840 61469. A restaurant that mutates into a late-night bar. This is a laidback place for the young and the very young and will make you feel nostalgic for your salad days, if you are but over 30. June–Sept daily 8pm–midnight.

## Beaches

Andíparos's **beaches** begin right outside town: **Psaralíki**, just to the south with golden sand and tamarisks for shade, is much better than **Sifnéïko** on the opposite side of the island. Villa development is starting to follow the surfaced road down the east coast, but has yet to get out of hand. **Glýfa**, 4km down, is another good beach, while, in the southeast of the island, **Sorós** is by far the most bewitching beach on the island. On the southwest coast there are some fine sand dunes at **Áyios Yeóryios**, the end of the surfaced road. From there, one *kaïki* makes an 11am daily trip to the uninhabited, but archeologically rich, island of **Dhespotikó**, opposite.

### ACCOMMODATION AND EATING                                    BEACHES

**Delfini** Áyios Yeóryios ☎ 22840 24506, ⓦ dolphinantiparos.gr. Newly renovated studios sleeping up to four people, with large verandas. There is a café-bar for breakfast and lunch as well as a grill for dinner. Although off the beaten track, this is a lively establishment, offering a range of excursions and activities. May–Sept. €80

### The Great Cave

Summer daily 11am–3pm • €3

The great **cave** in the south of the island is the chief attraction for day-trippers. In these eerie chambers the Marquis de Nointel, Louis XIV's ambassador to Constantinople, celebrated Christmas Mass in 1673 while a retinue of five hundred, including painters, pirates, Jesuits and Turks, looked on; at the exact moment of midnight explosives were detonated to emphasize the enormity of the event. Although electric lights and cement steps have diminished its mystery and grandeur, the cave remains impressive. Check out the historical graffiti carved over the centuries.

# Náxos

**NÁXOS** is the largest and most fertile of all the Cyclades islands and with its green and mountainous highland scenery it appears immediately dissimilar to its neighbours. The difference is accentuated by the **unique architecture** of many of the interior villages: the Venetian Duchy of the Aegean, headquartered here from 1204 to 1537, left towers and fortified mansions scattered throughout the island, while medieval Cretan refugees bestowed a singular character upon Náxos's eastern settlements.

Today Náxos could easily support itself without visitors by relying on its production of potatoes, olives, grapes and lemons, but it has thrown in its lot with mass tourism, so that parts of the island are now almost as busy as Páros (see p.402) in season. The and has plenty to see if you know where to look: the highest mountains in the Cyclades, intriguing central valleys, a spectacular north coast and long, marvellously sandy beaches in the southwest. It is also renowned for its wines, cheese and *kítron*, a sweet liqueur distilled from the leaves of this citrus tree and available in green, yellow or clear varieties depending on strength and sugar level.

## ARRIVAL AND DEPARTURE
## NÁXOS

**By plane** Náxos is served by regular flights from Athens (via Olympic, 1–2 daily; 45min). The airport is a 10min bus ride south from Náxos Town (€12).

**By ferry** Ferries dock in the northern harbour quay of Náxos Town.

**Destinations** Amorgós (7–9 weekly; 3–4hr); Anáfi (3 weekly; 7hr); Ándhros (2–4 weekly; 4hr); Astypálea (2–4 weekly; 3hr); Dhonoússa (3–7 weekly; 1hr 30min); Folégandhros (1–4 daily; 4hr); Íos (4–5 weekly; 1hr

30min); Iráklia (2–5 weekly; 1hr 30min); Koufoníssi (3–7 weekly; 2hr 30min); Mýkonos (1–3 daily; 3hr); Páros (2–3 daily; 45min); Pireás (2–3 daily; 4hr–5hr 30min); Rafína (4–8 weekly 3–6hr); Santoríni (1–2 daily; 1hr 30min–3hr 30min); Sérifos (1 weekly; 2hr 30min); Sífnos (1 weekly; 3hr 30min); Síkinos (3–5 weekly; 2–5hr); Skhinoússa (2–4 weekly; 2hr); Sýros (4–5 weekly; 2hr 30min); Tínos (4–8 weekly; 1–2hr 30min).

6

NÁXOS

6

## INFORMATION

**Services** The post office is north of the Town Hall square in Náxos Town.

**Travel agents** Excursions around Náxos and to other islands are conveniently booked at Zas Travel (☎ 22850 23330) on the seafront near the jetty. Further down the promenade Naxos Tours (☎ 22850 23043, ⓦ naxostou .net) can also help with all kinds of arrangements.

**Activities** Flisvos Sportsclub (☎ 22850 22935, ⓦ flisv -sportclub.com) is based at Áyios Yeóryios beach, offerii windsurfing courses and other activities.

## GETTING AROUND

**By bus** The bus station (☎ 22850 22291) is opposite the main dock. Printed timetables are available.
Destinations Aperáthou via Filóti and Halkí (4–5 daily; 1hr); Apóllonas (2–3 daily; 1hr; 2hr via scenic coastal route); Ayía Marína – Zas (4–5 daily; 1hr); Áyios Prokópios/ Ayía Ánna (half hourly; 7.30am–midnight; 15min); Pláka (half hourly; 7.30am–midnight; 30min); Kastráki-Pyrgáki (3 daily; 45min).

**By car and motorcycle** Auto Tour Rent-a-Car by the bi station in Náxos Town (☎ 22850 25480) rents cars ai offers a wealth of information as well as accommodatii advice. In town parking immediately next accommodation is not always possible. The best one-d drive is Halkí–Filóti–Aperáthou–Apóllonas returning v the northern coastal route.
**By taxi** The central taxi call number is ☎ 22850 22444.

# Náxos Town

As your ferry approaches **NÁXOS TOWN**, you can't help sensing that this a really special place, if only because of the looming, fortified **kástro**. Indeed, this is where Marco Sanudo – the thirteenth-century Venetian who founded the town and established the Duchy of th Aegean – and his descendants ruled over the Cyclades. A superficial glance at the waterfront may be enough to convince you that most of the town's life occurs by the crowded port esplanade, but don't be deceived. There is a lot more life in Náxos Town in the vast network of backstreets and low-arched narrow alleys that lead up through the old town, **Boúrgo**, to the **Kastro** itself. And don't miss out on the second centre of activity to the south, around the main square, **Platía Evripéous**, with more tavernas, shops and cafés.

## Portára

A long causeway, built to protect the harbour to the north, connects Náxos Town with the islet of Palátia – the place where, according to legend, Theseus was duped by Dionysos into abandoning Ariadne on his way home from Crete. The famous stone **Portára** that has greeted visitors for 2500 years is the portal of a temple of Apollo, buil on the orders of the tyrant Lygdamis around 530 BC, but never completed.

## The Kástro

Tours offered by the Venetian museum at 11am Tues–Sun in season • €15, includes entrance to all the kástro museums

The kástro is normally entered through the **north gate** (also known as the Traní Pórta o "Majestic Gate"), a splendid example of a medieval fort entrance. A few of the Venetians' Catholic descendants still live in the old mansions that encircle the site, man with ancient coats of arms above the doorways. In the centre of the kástro are the plain stone remains of a rectangular tower, said to have been the residence of Marco Sanudo. Opposite the tower stands the restored Catholic cathedral, still displaying a thirteenth-century crest inside. Behind the tower you can find the seventeenth-century Ursuline convent. Nearby is what was to become one of Ottoman Greece's first schools, the

### NÁXOS MUSIC FESTIVAL

One of the highlights of Naxiot evenings is the Domus Festival of classical, jazz, choral, Byzantine and traditional music held at the Venetian Museum in either the garden or the basement, depending on the season and weather (ⓦ naxosfestival.com/naxos-domus-festival). Tickets should be booked in advance at the museum (☎ 22850 22387) and include a glass of local wine or *kítron*.

# NÁXOS TOWN

0 _____ 100
metres

Portára
(Temple of Apollo)

RING ROAD

GRÓTTA

NEOFYTOU

Bus
Station

RING ROAD

Mitropoleos
Museum

Orthodox
Mitrópolis

BOURGO

Ferry Jetty

PARALIA

Panayía
Myrtidhiótissa

Palátia

Small Ferry
Jetty

Port Police

Venetian
Museum

Catholic
Mitrópolis

Archeological
Museum

KÁSTRO

PARALIA

PIGADHÁKIA

PRANTOÚNA

Road to interior

PAPAVASSILIOU

PARALIA

ARIADNIS

P

SKHINOUSSAS

DAMBANAKI

ARISTOTÉLOUS PRÓTOPAPADHÁKI

DHONOUSSAS

PLATIA
EVRIPEOU

BRAGANAS

KOMIAKIS

AY. YEORYIOU

PRÓTOPAPADHÁKI

MONÍS

MELANÓN

SANGRIOÚ

POTAMIÁS

FILOTIOÚ

ENGARÓN

TRÍPODHON

APEIRÁNTHOU

KÓRONOU

KÓRTHOU

Police

N

Áyios Yeóryios

6

### ACCOMMODATION
| | |
|---|---|
| Apollon | 2 |
| Despina's Rooms | 3 |
| Grotta | 1 |
| Naxos Camping | 5 |
| Nissaki Beach | 4 |
| Porto Naxos | 6 |

### EATING
| | |
|---|---|
| Apostolis | 1 |
| Manolis' Garden | 3 |
| Metaxí Mas | 2 |
| Scirocco | 5 |
| Typografio | 4 |

### NIGHTLIFE
| | |
|---|---|
| Cosa Nostra | 4 |
| Escoba Waterfront | 5 |
| Jazz and Blues | 3 |
| Soul | 2 |
| Villa del Mare | 1 |

French Commercial School; opened by Jesuits in 1627 for Catholic and Orthodox students alike, its pupils included, briefly, writer Nikos Kazantzakis (see p.449).

### The Venetian Museum

Daily 10am–3pm & 7–10pm (to 11pm in July–Aug) • €3

A mansion next to the Traní Pórta, the **Venetian Museum** (Domus Della-Rocca-Barozzi), is open to the public and offers the best views from the kástro, with concerts (see box, p.412); the guided tour includes a tasting from the family's wine cellar.

### The Archeological Museum

Tues–Sun 8.30am–2.30pm • €3

The French Commercial School building now houses an excellent **archeological museum**, which includes an important collection of Early Cycladic figurines (note how most of the throats were cut in some kind of ritual), Archaic and Classical sculpture, pottery dating from Neolithic to Roman times, as well as obsidian knives and spectacular gold rosettes. Sadly, labelling is mostly in Greek. On the terrace, a Hellenistic period mosaic floor shows a Nereid (sea nymph) astride a bull surrounded by deer and peacocks.

## Mitropóleos Museum

Tues–Sun 8.30am–3pm • Free

In front of the Orthodox cathedral, the **Mitropóleos Museum** has walkways over a recently excavated tumulus cemetery from the Mycenaean era – thirteenth to eleventh century BC – with funerary remnants including a *hermax*, a pile of the stones that were traditionally thrown behind on leaving a cemetery. In the general area, items dating from the early Cycladic period (3200 BC) right through to late Roman (300 AD) have been found.

## Town beaches

**Grótta**, just to the northeast of the town, is the easiest beach to reach. It's not ideal for swimming but snorkellers can see the remains of submerged Mycenaean buildings. The other town beach, **Áyios Yeóryios**, is an improvement: a long sandy bay fringed by the town's southern accommodation area, within ten minutes' walking distance from Platía Evripéous.

### ACCOMMODATION                                                          NÁXOS

**Apollon** Fontana ☎ 22850 22468, ⓦ apollonhotel -naxos.gr. Comfortable, modern doubles, all with balconies, in a quiet spot near the Mitropóleos Museum (see above) and convenient for the port, the nightlife and Grótta beach. Breakfast included. **€60**

**Despina's Rooms** Boúrgo ☎ 22850 22356. Hidden (but well signposted) beneath the castle; you'll need to climb some distance to reach it. The rooms are small but clean and airy, some with shared bathroom, and balconies with sea views. The owner organizes boat trips to the Lesser Cyclades. **€35**

★ **Grotta** Grótta ☎ 22850 22215, ⓦ hotelgrotta.gr. Welcoming hotel in a good location, with fabulous sunset views. Offers comfortable rooms, with an indoor jacuzzi, a fantastic breakfast (included) with pies cooked fresh daily, free pickups plus free wi-fi and cable internet access. **€75**

**Naxos Camping** Áyios Yeóryios ☎ 22850 23500, ⓦ naxos-camping.gr. At the southern end of Áyios Yeóryios – but close to the highway – this is the cheapest option for those who want to combine the beach with nightlife. They also offer wooden cabins for two. June–Sept. Camping **€7**, cabins **€30**

**Nissaki Beach** Áyios Yeóryios ☎ 22850 25710, ⓦ nissaki-beach.com. One of the most luxurious options on the island, oozing minimalist but comfortable Cycladic elegance. If the palm trees around the pool area don't tempt you, then the boundless views to the Aegean surely will. Buffet breakfast included. April–Oct. **€240**

**Porto Naxos** Áyios Yeóryios ☎ 22850 25710, ⓦ porto -naxos.gr. If you have your own transport, this five-star hotel with parking space, a swimming pool and a tennis court by the Náxos circular road – but only 200m from the beach – is highly recommended. Breakfast included. April–Oct. **€90**

## EATING

⭐ **Apostolis** Old Market, Hóra ☎ 22850 26777. Always busy, a sign of its regard in the town, with invariably excellent family dishes and grills (€8). Good selection of local wines. Beware its side salads (€5) – they are a meal in themselves. Daily noon–midnight.

**Manolis' Garden** Boúrgo ☎ 22850 25168. Popular taverna, located in a large yet cosy garden in the old town, with a small but well-considered menu (mains €8). Although not vegetarian it has many vegetable-only options. May–Oct daily 6pm–1am.

**Metaxí Mas** Boúrgo ☎ 22850 26425. Friendly ouzerí serving excellent, well-priced food (€7) on a little street heading up to the kástro. Service is friendly and unhurried, and even the fussiest demands are met with a smile. April–Oct daily noon–midnight.

**Scirocco** Platía Evripéous ☎ 22850 25931, ⊛ scirocco -naxos.gr. Well-known restaurant popular with locals and tourists alike for its well-priced traditional dishes such as meatballs in tomato sauce (€7) – hence the occasional long queue to get in. Daily noon–midnight.

**Typografío** Hóra ☎ 22850 22375. Superb central location, delicious local cuisine and reasonable prices for a menu (mains €9) as imaginative as the wine list. This is the place to go for a romantic tête-à-tête (book in advance one of the tables with the best views in front). Daily 6pm–midnight.

## NIGHTLIFE

**Cosa Nostra** Old Market. On a huge balcony above the harbourfront but entered from Old Market street, this bar plays funk/soul/rock and attracts a young clientele all year long. It's often difficult to find standing space, let alone a seat, after 11pm. Wide range of cocktails starting from €8. April–Oct daily 8pm–5am.

**Escoba Waterfront** ☎ 22850 23567. The best option in the cluster of bars and clubs in the southern waterfront, it serves large cocktails (€8), and is bigger than its neighbours, so there is less of a crush. Normally plays Latin music, but it has a popular rock night on Tuesdays. June–Sept daily 6pm–1am.

**Jazz and Blues** ☎ 694 47 01 215. A petite jazz bar, with the occasional live performance thrown in, tucked away on a street behind the port police. It has classy drinks much cheaper (€5) than the rest of the surrounding bars. April–Oct daily 10am–2pm & 8.30pm–3am.

**Soul** Halfway up the road to Grótta, this is the town's biggest and most cavernous club, but also managing to contain intimate corners, nooks and crannies. It is frequented by a regular, mixed-age crowd dancing to European hits. Entrance €10 with a free first drink. June–Aug Fri & Sat midnight–6am.

**Villa del Mare** With a large terrace facing west, *Villa del Mare* opens just before the sunset and closes earlier than most, dumping its clientele in the bigger club, *Soul*, below. Good value cocktails at €7 and a relaxed pre-dinner atmosphere. June–Sept daily 8pm–3.30am.

# Beaches

Lying just 4km from Náxos Town, **Áyios Prokópios** is a long line of sand dotted with lagoons that's regularly voted among Greece's top beaches. The village itself lies in the southern part of the main road and on the bus route, but the best and quieter part of the beach is closer to Náxos Town, at the base of the distinct double cone of Stelídha hill. Rapid development along the southwestern stretch means that Áyios Prokópios has blended into the next village, **Ayía Ánna**, further along the busy southern highway. Beyond the Ayía Ánna headland is 5km-long **Pláka beach**, a vegetation-fringed expanse of white sand accessed by a flat, unsurfaced road from the north where purely for convenience this part of the beach is called **Marágas**. Some parts of Pláka are naturist where shielded from the road by dunes, and at the southern end is **Orkós**, the playground of the young and intrepid with plenty of wind- and kitesurfers in high season. You'll find more windsurfers along the coastal stretch from Pláka through remote **Glyfádha** down to **Alykó** and nearby **Pyrgáki**, where the coastal road ends and the asphalted highway to Náxos begins. On the juniper-covered promontory by **Alykó** there is another nudist beach, known locally as **Hawaii** for the vibrant blue colour of its waters, while 4km beyond by unsurfaced road is the **Ayiassós** beach – this is where Marco Sanudo landed, in 1207 to conquer the island from the Byzantines and promptly burned his ships so that there could be no way back.

## ACCOMMODATION

**Finikas** Pyrgáki ☎ 22850 75230, ⊛ hotelfinikas.gr. At the end of the coastal dirt road and away from it all, this is a fully self-sufficient hotel, offering everything from a restaurant and free wi-fi to a sauna and a gym. It also organizes watersports activities. Breakfast included. May–Sept. **€165**

**Marágas** Ayía Anna ☎ 22850 24552, ⊛ maragas camping.gr. A suitably laidback shaded campsite with a taverna, beach bar and watersports facilities. There is a regular bus service to Náxos. April–Oct. Camping **€7**, cabins **€45**

**Naxos Imperial Resort and Spa** Stelídha ☎ 22850 26620, ⊛ naxosimperial.com. The best deluxe hotel of many on the Stelídha peninsula, it is also close to the best section of Áyios Prokópios beach. There's volleyball, gym, spa, restaurant, bar and a pool. Breakfast included. May–Nov. **€160**

## BEACHES

**Orkos Beach** Orkós ☎ 22850 75194, ⊛ orkosbeach.gr. Next to the Flisvos Kite Center (see p.413), with a cool pool and even cooler customers. Its garden alone is perfect to laze in. Internet, wi-fi, parking and breakfast included. May–Oct. **€70**

**Plaka** Pláka ☎ 22850 42700, ⊛ plakacamping.gr. Near the beginning of the Cyclades' longest beach, this is the newest camping on Náxos with a swimming pool, restaurant and café. It is flanked by its imaginatively named Plaka I and Plaka II sister hotels (€45–60). Bus service to Náxos Town available. April–Oct. **€9**

**Stella** Ayía Anna ☎ 22850 42526, ⊛ stella-apartments -naxos.gr. Clean and close to the sea but not far from the village itself, these studios with kitchenette and bougainvillea-bursting balconies are possibly the best option south of Náxos Town. Wi-fi in the reception only. May–Oct. **€50**

## EATING AND DRINKING

**Gorgóna** Ayía Anna ☎ 22850 41007. Cool, large, shaded, family-run beach bar that becomes a fish restaurant with reasonable prices (€10) in the evening and continues functioning as a late-night bar until the morning. Known locally for its delicious home-made *rizógalo*, a spiced rice pudding. Daily 8am–3am.

**Mólos** Áyios Prokópios ☎ 22850 26980. Fish taverna offering only fresh fish caught on the day and assorted seafood – which tends to be fried, however, rather than grilled. Occupying the best spot on the beach, it is unsurprisingly popular. Two deckchairs plus one umbrella €10. May–Oct daily 9am–1am.

# Central Náxos

After its beaches, **Central Náxos** is the island's second unique selling point with lush green valleys, mountains, painfully picturesque villages, historic churches, old forts and Classical sites. Because of the sheer size of the island these are best enjoyed via two day-long drives: one short and one much longer. The short drive is Náxos–Galanádho–Sangrí–Halkí–Moní–Kinídharos–Flério–Náxos, while the longer drive is Náxos–Galanádho–Sangrí–Halkí–Filóti–Aperáthou–Apóllonas–Náxos via the northern coastal road.

### Galanádho and Sangrí

From Náxos Town, head for the market village of **Galanádho** to reach the twin villages of **Sangrí**, on a vast plateau at the head of a long valley. On the way have a look at the domed eighth-century church of **Áyios Mámas**, neglected since the Ottoman conquest. Káto Sangrí has the ruins of a Venetian castle, while Áno Sangrí is an attractive little place, all cobbled streets and fragrant courtyards. It's also only about ninety minutes' walk to the Byzantine castle of **Apalírou**, at 474m, which held out for two months against the besieging Marco Sanudo. Its fortifications are relatively intact and the views magnificent. Thirty minutes' stroll away, on a path leading south out of the village, or 3km by surfaced lane, are the partially rebuilt remains of a **Classical temple of Demeter** (Tues–Sun 8.30am–3pm; free) from 530 BC, over which was constructed an early Christian basilica.

### The Tragéa and Halkí

From Sangrí, the road twists northeast into the **Tragéa** region, scattered with olive trees and occupying a vast highland valley. The area is the only part of the Cyclades to have a regular winter snowfall, and the only part with traditional songs about snow. It's a good umping-off point for all sorts of exploratory rambling. **Halkí**, 16km from Náxos Town, s a fine introduction of what is to come; set high up, it's a quiet town with some lovely churches, including the **Panayía Protóthronis** church (daily 10am–1pm; free), with its eleventh- to thirteenth-century frescoes. Just behind is the restored seventeenth-century Venetian **Grazia-Barozzi Tower**, and nearby is the distillery (1896) and shop of **Vallindras Naxos Citron**, whose charming proprietors explain the process of producing *kítron* followed by a little tasting session.

## Moní, Kinídharos and Flério

Driving from Halkí to Moní you pass the sixth-century church of **Panayía Dhrosianí** (daily 11am–5pm, donation expected), historically the most important church on the island with some of the oldest frescoes in Greece. Moní itself, at an altitude of 550m, enjoys an outstanding view of the Tragéa and Mount Zas, and has numerous woodcarving workshops. From Moní you can loop back to Náxos Town, and the first village you encounter on the way is **Kinídharos**, with its marble quarries and daily folk evenings; it has a reputation of staging one of the best carnivals in the Cyclades. Five kilometres beyond is the village of **Flério**. Nearby is the most interesting of the ancient marble quarries of the seventh- to sixth-century BC on Náxos, home to two famous **koúroi**, left recumbent and unfinished; even so, they're finely detailed figures, over 5m in length. The Koúros Flerioú (Koúros Melánon), from around 570 BC, is a short walk along the stream valley; the Koúros Farangioú (Koúros Potamiás) is a steeper walk up the hillside. Both are well signposted.

## Aperáthou and the south

At the far side of the gorgeous Tragéa valley, Filóti, the largest village in the region, lies on the northwestern slopes of Mount Zas, which at 1001m is the highest point in the Cyclades. **APERÁTHOU** (officially Apíranthos), 8km beyond Filóti, is hilly, winding and highly picturesque; it shows the most Cretan influence of all interior villages and gave Greece one of its prime ministers, **Petros Protopapadakis** (it's unfortunate that he was executed for high treason in 1922). Its location high in the mountains means it is noticeably cooler and greener than the coast. There are two Venetian fortified mansions, Bardáni and Zevgóli, and, amazingly, four small private museums: Natural History, Geological, Fine Arts and a Folklore museum (April–Oct daily 10.30am–2.30pm; 7.30pm June–July; 9pm Aug; €2 for all); as well as a state Archeological museum (Tues–Sun 8.30am–3pm; free). There is some good **shopping** in Aperáthou, as well: **Epilekton** in the main street is an excellent delicatessen with a selection of local cheeses, hot peppers and sun-dried aubergines.

A turning at the southern end of Filóti is signposted to the **Pýrgos Himárrou** (12.5km), a remote 20m-high Hellenistic watchtower – one of the tourist landmarks of the island – and onward (another 12km) to the deserted but excellent in all respects **Kalandó** beach on the south coast. Bring your own water and food supplies if you're planning to stop here.

---

### CLIMBING MOUNT ZAS

If you are arriving by bus and intend to climb **Mount Zas** you should start from the steps opposite the taverna *Baboulas* at the main square. This is a round-trip walk of three to four hours on partly marked trails to the summit, a climb that rewards you with an astounding panorama of virtually the whole of Náxos and its Cycladic neighbours. The initial path out of the village climbs up to rejoin the road to Apóllonas. The final approach trail begins beside the small Ayía Marína chapel. You can return to Filóti via the trail to the 150m-deep Zas Cave, which is also accessed by a separate route through **Ariés**, ten minutes' drive from Filóti.

If you have your own transport, you can drive all the way to Ayía Marína and continue on from there.

**6**

**Leftéris** Aperáthou ☎ 22850 61333. A restaurant with an unmatched reputation on Náxos and, as a bonus, not as full as others closer to the main road, which are always busy. At the end of your meal (mains €13) try the home-made *glyká koutalioú*, stewed syrupy fruit which are so sweet that a few teaspoonfuls constitute a serving. April–Oct daily 10am–1am.

**Panorama** Moní ☎ 22850 31070. Small family restaurant with exceptional views. Whatever the dish of the day is (€6), order it; it will most likely involve some kind of meat, as this part of Náxos is famous for its tender beef and veal. Daily 11am–11pm.

**Plátanos** Aperáthou ☎ 22850 61192. Rare mountain decor, good balcony views and food standards to rival *Leftéris* (see above). This is one of those old-fashioned Greek restaurants where you can go in the kitchen to check what's available (mains €9) and whether you like the look of it. April–Oct daily 9am–11pm.

**Yannis** Halkí ☎ 22850 31214. A traditional grill, under a vine-covered roof, which is always busy with customers stopping at the nearby Vallindras distillery. Try the local mountain sausage in tomato sauce (€7) or order the locally sourced beefburger. Daily noon–midnight.

## Northern Náxos

The route to **Northern Náxos** through the mountains from Aperáthou to Apóllonas is very scenic, and the road surface is in reasonable condition all the way. Jagged ranges and hairpin bends confront you after **Kóronos**, past **Skadhó**, to the remote emery-miners' village of **Koronídha** – the highest village on the island.

**Apóllonas** is a small resort with two good beaches: a tiny and crowded stretch of sand backed by a line of cafés and restaurants, and a longer and quieter stretch of shingle, where *Kouros Hotel* lies. The major attraction in Apóllonas is a 12m-long **koúros**, approached by a path from the main road just above the village. Lying *in situ* at a former marble quarry, this is the largest of Náxos's abandoned stone figures, but less detailed than those at Flério. The return to Náxos Town is via the northern coastal road which is spectacularly beautiful, set high above the sea for most of the way.

**Kouros Apóllonas** ☎ 22850 67000, ⊚ hotelkouros .blogspot.com. Relaxing, dreamy hotel standing alone in the middle of the shingle beach with spacious, quiet rooms and a well-stocked beach bar. Despite it being out of the way, it attracts a surprisingly young clientele. May–Sept. **€60**

# Lesser Cyclades

Four of the six small islands in the patch of the Aegean between Náxos and Amorgós have slid from obscurity into fashion in recent years. Inhabited since prehistoric times, the group is known commonly as the **Lesser Cyclades** and includes **Irakliá, Skhinoússa, Áno Koufoníssi** and **Dhonoússa**. The islands' popularity has hastened the development of better facilities and higher prices, but, with only limited ferry services, they've managed to avoid mass tourism.

**By ferry** Apart from slower direct connections to Pireás, the fast Blue Star ferries call at Náxos linking up with the smaller *Express Skopelitis* which serves the Lesser Cyclades and Amorgós.

**Day-trip from Náxos** A boat trip from Náxos takes in Iraklá and Áno Koufonísi. If you stay in the latter, you can travel by boat for a swim to the uninhabited Káto Koufonísi but not to Kéros which is out of bounds; the whole island is an archeological area (much like Delos) which is still being excavated.

## INFORMATION

**Health** Note that there are no pharmacies on any island, but some drugs are dispensed from the rural GP practices. In case of emergency there are speedboats on call 24/7, so make sure you have good travel insurance.

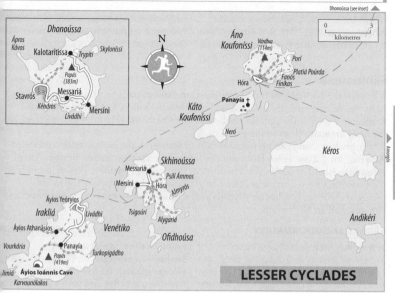

# raklliá

**raklliá**, the westernmost of the Lesser Cyclades, and with the least spoilt scenery, has ust over 150 permanent residents. As the first stop on the ferry service from Náxos, the sland is hardly undiscovered by tourists, but with fewer amenities than some of its eighbours, it retains the feel of a more secluded retreat.

  The port of **Áyios Yeóryios** is a small but sprawling settlement behind a sandy amarisk-backed beach that gets quite crowded in August. **Livádhi**, a big, shallow each, is 2km southeast of the port and its crystal-clear waters are the main tourist ttraction of the island. The asphalted road continues 3km on to the tiny capital **anayía (Hóra)**, which has no lodgings to speak of. In season, a local boat sails from the ort at 11am to make a tour of the island, stopping at the small sandy beach at **Alimiá** nd the nearby pebble beach of **Karvounólakos**.

## RRIVAL AND INFORMATION

**IRAKLIÁ**

**y ferry** Ferries call at Áyios Yeóryios.
**estinations** Áno Koufonísi (1–2 daily; 2hr); Amorgós –2 daily; 1hr 45min); Dhonoússa (1–2 daily; 3hr 30min); áxos (1–2 daily; 1hr); Páros (2–4 weekly; 2hr 15min); ireás (2–3 weekly; 7hr); Skhinoússa (2–3 daily; 15min); ros (2 weekly; 7hr 10min).

**Services** There are no banks in Irakliá, but there is an ATM at Áyios Yeóryios. The post office is a short distance above the *Perigiali* taverna (see p.420).
**Travel agents** Aegeon (☎ 22850 71561) should take care of all your travel and ticket needs.

## CCOMMODATION

**nna's** ☎ 22850 74234. Family lodgings on the slope at e back of the village with great views offering rooms with wn bathroom, plus some luxurious studios (€60) higher up e hill. Not all rooms have air conditioning, so check. **€35**

**Iliovasílema** ☎ 22850 71486, ⓦ sunset-iraklia.gr. Four very large apartments on top of a small hill 500m from the port and with magnificent sunset views, a/c, TV, fridge and WC; cooking facilities are shared. May–Sept. **€35**

## ATING AND DRINKING

**aïstrali** ☎ 22850 71807. The best place to eat on the land with a menu of seafood, goat stew – the Lesser

Cyclades' signature dish – and moussaka (€6). The veranda has a good view of the port below and there is free internet

available for clients. May–Sept daily 6pm–midnight.
**Perigiali** port ☎ 22850 71118. Small ouzerí with great
fish and seafood meze platters (€15) caught daily by the

family boat; nice, cosy atmosphere with tables around a
large central salt cedar tree and friendly service. Daily
noon–midnight.

## Skhinoússa

A little to the northeast of Irakliá, the island of **Skhinoússa** is just beginning to awaken
to its tourist potential. Its indented outline, sweeping valleys and partly submerged
headlands – such as the sinuous, snake-like islet Ofidhoúsa (Fidoú) – provide some of
the most dramatic views in the group.

An asphalted road leads up from the port of **Mersíni** to the capital, **Hóra** (also called
**Panayía**), for 1.2km. From Hóra you can reach no fewer than sixteen beaches dotted
around the island, accessible by a network of dirt tracks. **Tsigoúri** is a ten-minute track
walk downhill from northwest Hóra and gradually being developed. The locals'
preferred choice of beaches are **Alygariá** to the south, **Psilí Ámmos** to the northeast, and
**Almyrós**, half an hour southeast.

### ARRIVAL AND INFORMATION
SKHINOÚSSA

**By ferry** Boats dock at the small port of Mersíni.
Destinations Amorgós (1–2 daily; 1hr 30min); Áno
Koufonísi (6–8 weekly; 30min); Dhonoússa (1–2 daily;
3hr 40min); Irakliá (2–3 daily; 15min); Náxos (1–2 daily;
1hr 45min); Páros (4 weekly; 4hr 30min); Pireás (2–3

weekly; 7hr 45min); Sýros (3 weekly; 5hr).
**Services** There are no banks, but there is an ATM at Hóra
and four minimarkets, four bars and several tourist shops.
There's also a post office and a Western Union branch at
Hóra.

### GETTING AROUND

There are no buses or taxis on the island; hotels will organize your transport to and from the port. There is also no car rental.

### ACCOMMODATION AND EATING

**Grispos Villas** Tsigoúri ☎ 22850 71930, ⓦ grisposvillas
.com. Perched above Tsigoúri beach at the northwest end,
this complex offers everything – from rooms with
continental breakfast to large studios with cooking
facilities; they also sell ferry tickets in season. There's a half-
board option for €14 per adult, €10 per child. **€60**

**Iliovasilema** ☎ 22850 71948, ⓦ iliovasilemahotel.gr.
Well-priced friendly hotel, comfortable rather than
luxurious, whose veranda bar enjoys spectacular views of
the harbour. They operate a free shuttle to and from every
beach for their customers. May–Oct. **€60**

## Áno Koufoníssi

**ÁNO KOUFONÍSSI** (usually referred to simply as Koufoníssi) is the flattest, most
developed and most densely inhabited island of the group. With some of the least-
spoilt beaches in the Cyclades, the island is attracting increasing numbers of Greek and
foreign holidaymakers and as it's small enough to walk round in a day, it can feel
overcrowded in July and August. The best views are not of Koufoníssi itself, but out
across the water to mountainous Kéros island.

The old pedestrian street of **HÓRA**, crossing a low hill behind the ferry harbour, has
been engulfed by new room and hotel development, but the town still retains its
affable, small-island atmosphere. All the good **beaches** are in the southeast of the
island, improving as you go east along a road that skirts the gradually developing
coastline along the edge of low cliffs. **Fínikas**, a fifteen-minute walk from town, is the
first of four wide coves with gently shelving golden sand. The next beach, **Fanós**, is the
youngsters' favourite, because of the beach bar that dominates the stretch of sand. Next
is **Platiá Poúnda**, where caves have been hollowed out of the cliffs. Further east, the
path rounds a rocky headland to **Porí**, a much longer and wilder beach, backed by
dunes and set in a deep bay. It can be reached more easily from the town by following a
dirt road heading inland through the scrub-covered hills.

## ARRIVAL AND INFORMATION

**By ferry** Boats dock at the jetty below Hóra.

**Destinations** Amorgós (1–3 daily; 1hr); Dhonoússa (4–5 daily; 2hr 30min); Irakliá (2–4 daily; 45min); Mílos (1–2 weekly; 4hr 15min); Mýkonos (3 weekly; 2hr); Náxos (1–2 daily; 2hr 20min); Páros (4–5 weekly; 5hr); Pireás (6–8 weekly; 7–8hr); Skhinoússa (1–2 daily; 30min); Sýros (3

weekly; 6hr).

**Services** There is a post office up a street by the *Hotel Roussetos*, with an ATM.

**Travel agents** The Koufonissia Tours ticket agency (☏ 22850 74091, ⊛ koufonissiatours.gr) is on the main pedestrian street.

## ACCOMMODATION

**Aeolos** ☏ 22850 74206, ⊛ aeoloshotel.com. Modern, exceptionally well-designed hotel with a great pool overlooked by bougainvillea-draped balconies and large rooms in bright colour schemes. Free wi-fi and big breakfast buffet included. June–Sept. **€100**

**Kéros Icons** ☏ 22850 71600, ⊛ keroshotel.gr. Smart

hotel complex, technologically up to date with intelligent a/c, electronic card keys, memory mattresses and massage showers. Even if the cherry and ebony furniture doesn't satisfy your romantic streak, the rooms with four-poster beds will. Breakfast included. June–Oct. **€110**

## EATING AND DRINKING

**Capetan Nicolas** ☏ 22850 71690. Cheaper than most, but still the best place to eat on the island. At the west of the bay, it offers a fine array of fresh, grilled seafood and home-made taramasalata that bears no resemblance to any supermarket varieties. May–Oct daily noon–late.

**Remezzo** ☏ 22850 74203. Family fish taverna above the ferry jetty with excellent food, not all seafood-based – try the chef's delicious savoury pastries (€6) – and a cosy atmosphere. The terrace tables have an incomparable view to Kato Koufoníssi. June–Sept daily noon–late.

# Dhonoússa

Dhonoússa is a little out on a limb compared with the other Lesser Cyclades, and ferries call less frequently. Island life centres on the pleasant port settlement of **Stavrós**, spread out behind the harbour and the village beach. Most sunbathers head for **Kéndros**, a long and attractive stretch of shadeless sand twenty minutes over the ridge to the east; a World War II wreck can be easily spotted by snorkellers. The village of **Mersíni** is an hour's walk from Stavrós, while a nearby path leads down to **Livádhi**, an idyllic white-sand beach with tamarisks for shade. In high season a beach-boat runs from the port to all beaches, many of which are nudist; the locals don't seem to mind.

## ARRIVAL AND DEPARTURE

**By ferry** Ferries dock at Stavrós.

**Destinations** Amorgós (1–2 daily; 1hr); Áno Koufoníssi (2–4 weekly; 1–3hr); Irakliá (1–2 daily; 3hr); Náxos (1–2

daily; 1hr 10min–5hr); Páros (4–5 weekly; 2hr 30min–5hr); Pireás (4 weekly; 7hr); Skhinoússa (1–2 daily; 30min); Sýros (3 weekly; 6hr).

## ACCOMMODATION AND EATING

**Chrýssa** ☏ 22850 51575, ⊛ donoussarooms.gr. Set back from Stavrós, a pension with basic but large rooms and balconies overlooking the port. Every room has its own kitchenette and cooking implements but not all have a/c. May–Oct. **€45**

**Corona Borealis** Beach bar that slowly becomes the soul of the party in Stavrós playing alternative indie rock until the early hours. Young clientele, because, well, there are not many other places to go. June–Sept daily 10am–3am.

# Amorgós

**AMORGÓS**, with its dramatic mountain scenery and laidback atmosphere, is attracting visitors in increasing numbers. The island can get extremely crowded in midsummer, the numbers swollen by film buffs paying their respects to the film location of Luc Besson's *The Big Blue*, although fewer venture out to Líveros at the island's western end to see the wreck of the *Olympia* which figures so prominently in the film. In general it's a low-key, escapist clientele, happy to have found a relatively large, interesting, uncommercialized and hospitable island with excellent walking. Families tend to stay around Katápola, while younger tourists prefer Aigiáli.

This is the island to try *rakómelo* – a kind of fermented grappa with honey, herbs and spices, drunk in shots as an aperitif.

## ARRIVAL AND DEPARTURE                                      AMORGÓS

Most ferries and catamarans call either to Katápola in the southwest or Aigiáli in the north, while some dock at both. Be aware that it is those destinations, rather than "Amorgós", that are named on ferry schedules. There are more onward connections from Katápola than Aigiáli.

### KATÁPOLA

**By ferry** The ferries stop at the town jetty; some continue on to Aigiáli (15min).

Destinations Áno Koufoníssi (1–2 daily; 40min); Dhonoússa (3–4 weekly; 1hr 30min); Irakliá (1–2 daily; 1hr 50min); Folégandhros (6–7 weekly; 2hr 30min); Íos (1 weekly; 5hr 20min); Kos (1 weekly; 5hr); Léros (1 weekly; 3hr 20min); Mílos (0–3 weekly; 3hr 30min); Mýkonos (0–3 weekly; 2hr 20min); Náxos (1–2 daily; 3hr); Páros (4–5 weekly; 4hr 15min); Pátmos (0–1 weekly; 2hr); Pireás (1–2 daily; 9hr); Rhodes (1 weekly; 8hr); Skhinoússa (5–6 weekly; 1hr 25min); Sýros (3 weekly; 7hr).

### AIGIÁLI

**By ferry** Ferries stop at the town jetty; some continue on to Katápola (15min).

Destinations Áno Koufoníssi (4–5 weekly; 25min); Astypálea (4 weekly; 1hr 30min); Dhonoússa (1–2 daily; 50min); Irakliá (1 daily; 2hr 45min); Náxos (1–2 daily; 3–4hr); Páros (4–5 weekly; 4hr 30min); Pireás (4 weekly; 6hr); Skhinoússa (5 weekly; 2hr 20min); Sýros (2 weekly; 7hr 30min).

## INFORMATION

**Services** Internet is available at the Teloneio rock café in Katápola.The island's main post office is in the upper square in Hóra. There's no bank in Aigiáli, but you'll find an ATM near the ferry dock.

**Travel agents** Prekas (☏ 22850 71256) in Katápola, just along from the ferry dock, is the one-stop boat-ticket agency (as well as an ouzerí). Aegialis Tours (☏ 22850 73393, ⓦ www.aegialistours.com) in Aigiáli can help you with tickets, transfers, car rental and accommodation.

## GETTING AROUND

**By bus** A bus shuttles between Katápola and Hóra, the island capital; several times daily it continues to Ayía Ánna via Hozoviótissas monastery, and 2–7 times weekly (9.45am) out to the "Káto Meriá", made up of the hamlets

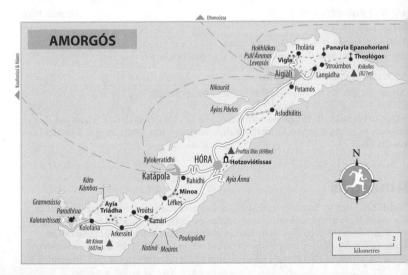

Kamári-Vroútsi, Arkessíni and Kolofána. From Aigiáli there is a bus service up to Langádha and Tholária, the two villages east of and 200m above Aigiáli bay, with 3–8 departures daily up and down (a timetable is posted by the harbour bus stop).

**By boat** There's a *kaïki* service from Katápola to the nearby beaches at Maltézi and Plákes (€3 return) and a daily excursion *kaïki* to the islet of Gramvoússa off the western end of Amorgós (€8 return).

**By car and motorcycle** There are several car/bike-rental outfits, but the one that has been around the longest is Thomas (☎ 22850 71777, ⊕ thomas-rental.gr) in Katápola. In Aigiáli, Aigialis Tours (see opposite) can help; Thomas Rental also has a branch here (☎ 22850 73444, ⊕ thomas-rental.gr).

## Katápola and around

**KATÁPOLA**, set at the head of a deep inlet, is actually three separate villages: **Katápola** proper on the south side, **Xylokeratídhi** on the north shore, and **Rahídhi** on the central ridge. There is a beach in front of Rahídhi, but Káto Krotíri beach to the west of Katápola is better, though not up to the standards of Aigiáli in the northeast.

### ACCOMMODATION                                            KATÁPOLA AND AROUND

**Anna Studios** ☎ 22850 71218, ⊕ studioanna -amorgos.com. Well signed and difficult to miss because of its height, this hospitable *pension* with a garden setting has some very good views to the sea from the top floors. Laptops with internet connections available. **€45**

**Camping Kastanis** ☎ 22850 71012, ⊕ kastanis.com .gr. 1km up towards Hóra this is a fully modern, shaded campsite with free wi-fi, offering a scale of accommodation that includes studios with their own WC, kitchenette and balcony with sea views. Camping **€8**, studio **€35**

**Minoa-Landéris** ☎ 22850 71480, ⊕ hotelminoa.gr. Twin neighbouring two-star hotels in the waterfront square under the same management with smart, comfortable and contemporary rooms, as well as internet access. *Minoa* is the older, traditional one, *Landéris* the modern one (built 2006). **€55**

**Sofia** ☎ 22850 71493, ⊕ pensionsofia.gr. Super little pension in the east of Katápola with large, bright rooms; the ones on the top floor have balconies with views while those on the ground floor have individual garden yards. Free wi-fi. **€40**

### EATING AND DRINKING

**Mourayio** Katápola ☎ 22850 71518. The most popular taverna in town, cooking a wide range of seafood including a good fish soup, cheap lobster and marinated octopus (€12), all worth the wait while you sample the waterfront views. April–Oct daily noon–late.

**Vitzentzos** Xylokeratídhi ☎ 22850 71011. Traditional Amorgós dishes that include island goat in the oven with potatoes and a range of vegetable dishes cooked in oil and tomato sauce (€6). Daily noon–midnight.

### NIGHTLIFE

**Teloneio Café Bar** ☎ 22850 71721. A loud, youthful alternative rock café on the main town drag with live DJ, this is the life and soul of Katápola. Atmospheric interior with local quarried stone if it's too windy, and tables outside for those with a low decibel threshold. Daily 11am–late.

## Hóra and around

**HÓRA** is one of the better-preserved settlements in the Cyclades, with a scattering of tourist shops, cafés, tavernas and rooms. Dominated by an upright volcanic rock plug, wrapped with a chapel or two, the thirteenth-century Venetian fortifications look down on nearly thirty other churches, some domed, and a line of decapitated windmills beyond. The nearest beach at **Ayía Ánna** is small but more than adequate. If you skip the first tiny coves, where the car park is larger than the sand, the path will take you to the nudist bay of Kambí; bring food and water for the day. For alternatives to Ayía Ánna, head west to **Kamári** and down to the adjacent beaches of **Notiná**, **Moúros** and **Poulopódhi**, all of them clean, crystal clear and calm.

Three kilometres further west of Kamári is **Kolofána**. From here the surfaced road leads towards the far western tip of the island, branching north to Ayía Paraskeví above **Paradhísia beach** (20km from Hóra), or 3km further west to spectacular **Kalotarítissas**

**Bay**, its tiny fishing jetty and small sand and pebble beach partly enclosed and sheltered by a rocky headland and the islet of **Gramvoússa**. About 1.8km before Kalotarítissas, the **wreck of the Olympia** is visible down to the right, in **Líveros Bay**.

### Monastery of Hotzoviótissas
Daily 8.30am–1pm & 5–7pm • Donation expected

The spectacular **Monastery of Hotzoviótissas**, gleaming white at the base of a towering, vertical orange cliff, can be reached by bus or on foot from a wide cobbled 8km-path by the upper telecoms tower. Modest dress is required; the sign advises that trousers are not suitable for women, but you will find that most female Greek visitors wear them. Only a handful of monks occupy the fifty rooms now, but they are quite welcoming considering the crowds who file through; you can see the miraculous icon around which the monastery was founded, along with other treasures. Tradition has it that between the ninth and eleventh centuries AD, a precious icon of the Virgin was brought here by beleaguered monks from the monastery of **Khotziba** in Palestine, who settled here to escape Arab raids. Sitting and admiring the view from the *katholikón*'s terrace while being treated to a shot of *rakómelo* and a sweet by the monks is one of the highlights of visiting Amorgós.

#### ACCOMMODATION AND EATING                                    HÓRA AND AROUND

**Liotrivi** ☎ 22850 71700. With a roof terrace facing the kástro, this taverna, down the steps from the bus stop, is where you should try the local casseroles such as veal with aubergines (€8) or lamb pie. Its home-made *rakómelo* makes it the most popular in Hóra. May–Oct daily noon–midnight.

**Panorama** ☎ 22850 74016, ⊛ panorama-studios .amorgos.net. Rooms and studios in two different sites in Hóra, large and comfortable with fitted and kitted kitchens; some have balconies with western views towards the kástro. €50

## Aigiáli and around

The road from Hóra to **Aigiáli** (Eyiáli),15km away, is one of the most impressive in the Cyclades, overlooking several beautiful small coves. The town itself is smaller and more picturesque than Katápola, and so tends to be more popular. The main Aigiáli beach is more than satisfactory, getting better and better as you stroll further north. A trail here leads over various headlands to three bays: **Levrosós**, which is sandy and nudist (20min walk), **Psilí Ámmos** (30min walk), which is mixed sand and gravel, and **Hokhlákas** (20min) where naturism is also tolerated; there are no facilities here so bring along what you need. The best of all beaches north, however, is **Áyios Pávlos**, 5km away, reachable by bus.

#### ACCOMMODATION                                               AIGIÁLI AND AROUND

★ **Aegialis** ☎ 22850 73393, ⊛ amorgos-aegialis.com. High on the hillside on the far side of the bay, this is the largest hotel on the island with an Olympic-size pool, spa with thalassotherapy treatments, using salt water and natural marine products, sauna, jacuzzi, gym and a superb

restaurant (mains €15). €130

**Aegiali Camping** ☎ 22850 73500, ⊛ aegialicamping.gr. Usually busier than the one in Katápola but not necessarily better, this is a huge, tree-covered campsite with spots to suit everybody, 100m from the beach on the road to Tholária.

---

### A WALK INLAND

Climb up the well-made cobblestone path that starts by the tiny cave-church of Ayía Triádha in Aigiáli to reach the picturesque village of **Langádha** about 200m above. Beyond Langádha, turn left off the main onward path towards the pretty, monastery-like Panayía Epanohorianí, then continue around the hillside to **Tholária**, named after vaulted Roman tombs. They were found around Vígla, the site of ancient Aegiale, on a hill opposite the village, where you can still see the bases of statues and traces of city walls incorporated into later terracing. A descending cobblestone path from the village car park towards Aigiáli goes back to the end of the town beach. The whole walk should take 2–3 hours.

Free wi-fi in the restaurant next door. April–Oct. **€9.50**

**Karkisia** ☎ 22850 73180, ⊛ karkisia-hotel.gr. Well-priced option that's very comfortable and easy on the eye, near the Aigiáli beach over which all studio balconies have views. Every double room has a sofabed that can be used to sleep a third person at no extra cost. Breakfast buffet €5 per person. April–Oct. **€40**

**Pension Christina** ☎ 22850 73236, ⊛ christina-pension.amorgos.net. A family pension 200m from Aigiáli beach offering bright, cheerfully painted rooms and simple furnishings, as well as studios with fully equipped kitchens. April–Oct. **€45**

## EATING AND DRINKING

**Barba Yánnis** Áyios Pávlos ☎ 22850 73011. Fish taverna on the beach offering generous portions of salads and seafood spaghetti as well as at least one meat or vegetable casserole as a dish of the day. The owner bakes his own bread in a traditional wood-fired oven. June–Sept daily noon–9pm.

# Íos

Though not terribly different – geographically or architecturally – from its immediate neighbours, no other Greek island attracts the same vast crowds of young people as **Íos**. Although it has worked hard to shake off its late-twentieth-century reputation for alcohol excesses and to move the island's tourism one class up with some success, Íos is still extremely popular with the young backpacker set who take over the island in July and August.

The only real villages – **Yialós** (for families), **Hóra** and **Mylopótas** (for the 18–25s) – are clustered in a western corner of the island, and development elsewhere is restricted by poor roads. As a result there are still some very quiet beaches with just a few rooms to rent. Most visitors stay along the arc delineated by the port – at Yialós, where you'll arrive, in Hóra above it, or by the beach at Mylopótas. Despite its past popularity, sleeping on the beach on Íos is strictly banned these days and so is nudism.

## ARRIVAL AND DEPARTURE                                          ÍOS

**By ferry** Ferries dock in Yialós, an easy 20min trek from the capital, Hóra.

**Destinations** Amorgós (1 weekly; 3hr); Anáfi (1–2 weekly; 4hr); Folégandhros (4–6 weekly; 1hr); Kéa/Lávrio (1 weekly; 11–12hr); Kímolos (3–4 weekly; 3hr); Kýthnos (1–2 weekly; 8hr 30min); Mílos (3 weekly; 4hr); Mýkonos

(1–2 daily; 1hr 40min); Náxos (4–5 weekly; 45min–3hr); Páros (2–4 weekly; 5hr); Pireás (1–2 daily; 3hr 20min); Rafína (1 weekly; 4hr); Santoríni (2–3 daily; 1hr 30min); Sérifos (1 weekly; 6hr 30min); Sífnos (3 weekly; 3hr 30min–5hr 30min); Síkinos (1–2 daily; 20min); Sýros (3–5 weekly; 5hr 30min); Tínos (5 weekly; 2hr).

## INFORMATION AND TOURS

**Tourist office** The unofficial tourist information office is Aktaion right in the middle of the port (daily 9am–2pm & 5–9pm), which also has a branch in Hóra.

**Services** An ATM is near the quay. The post office is in the new town of Hóra, a block behind the town hall.

**Travel agents** Aktaion Travel (☎ 22860 91343) has a

branch (closed 2–5pm) in the main church square in Yialós.

**Tours** For a quick escape from the packed beaches at the height of the season, try one of the daily excursions around quieter nearby beaches on the wooden Leigh Browne sailing vessel moored in the harbour (€25), available on demand.

## GETTING AROUND

**By bus** Buses constantly shuttle between Yialós, Hóra and Mylopótas (every 20–30min 8am–midnight). There are occasional public and private buses running to the beaches at Manganári and Ayía Theodhóti; they sell return tickets only and are quite pricey (€6).

**By boat** From Yialós, daily boats depart at around 10am (returning in the late afternoon; €12 return) to the beaches

on the south coast

**By car and motorcycle** Hiring cars is not as necessary as on other islands; the main strip, Yialós to Mylopótas, is walkable and a very nice stroll. To rent your own transport in Hóra try Vangelis Bike Rental (☎ 22860 91919) or Jacob's Car & Bike Rental (☎ 22860 91700, ⊛ jacobs-los.gr) in Yialós.

6

6

ÍOS

0 2
kilometres

Plakotós
"Homer's" Tomb
Vouní (417m)
Ayia Theodhóti
Paleókastro
Psáthi
Koumbára
Yialós
HÓRA
Plákes
Megálo Vouní (704m)
Valmás
Mylopótas
Kálamos
Kolitsáni
Klíma
N
Mangandrí
Santoríni & Anáfi          Crete

Náxos & Páros
Mílos
Alopronia (Síkinos)

## Hóra and around

**HÓRA** (also called Íos Town) is a twenty-minute walk up behind Yialós port, and is one of the more accessible picturesque towns in the Cyclades, filled with meandering arcaded lanes and whitewashed chapels. Still, it gets pretty raunchy when the younger crowd moves in for the high season, and the laddish logos and inscriptions available on T-shirts and at tattoo parlours clash with its superior aspirations. The main road divides it naturally into two parts: the old town climbing the hillside to the left as you arrive, and the newer development to the right. The **archeological museum** (Tues–Sun 8.30am–3pm; free), in the yellow town hall, is part of an attempt to attract a more diverse range of visitors to the island. It contains some interesting finds from ancient **Skárkos**, a few kilometres inland from Yialós.

**Yialós** – with its surprisingly peaceful and uncrowded beach – isn't in the same league as Hóra above, but it provides a refreshing, breezy escape from the hot, noisy capital. Alternatively there's the popular **Mylopótas**, the site of a magnificent beach, lots of water activity outlets and surprisingly little nightlife.

### ACTIVITIES                                                        HÓRA AND AROUND

**Meltemi Watersports** ☎ 693 21 53 912, ⊛ meltemi watersports.com. Outlets on Mylopótas and Manganári beaches, offering waterskiing, windsurfing and

wakeboarding lessons. They also hire out canoes, pedaloes, snorkelling equipment and sailboats.

### ACCOMMODATION

#### HÓRA

★ **Francesco's** ☎ 22860 91223, ⊛ francescos.net. An excellent hostel made up mostly with super-clean doubles (€40) and relatively few dorm beds. With free pickups and wi-fi, a bar, a pool and jacuzzi plus spectacular views over the port, it offers the best value for money on the island. May–Sept. **€17**

**Lofos** new quarter ☎ 22860 91481. Right up from the archeological site, this family-owned, shaded room complex, with simple but well-furnished rooms, is very convenient for access both to the bus stop and Hóra's nightlife opposite. Best of all, for something so close to the action, it's quiet. May–Oct. **€40**

**Lofos Village** new quarter ☎ 22860 92481, ⊜ lofosvillagehotel@yahoo.com. A luxurious set of modern villas further up the hill with panoramic views over Hóra from its common swimming pool. Currency exchange, free port transfers, jacuzzi and parking are some of the many facilities on offer. May–Oct. **€80**

#### YIALÓS

**Brothers' Hotel** ☎ 22860 91508, ⊛ brothershotel .com. A relaxed family-friendly option set far back from the beach with spacious rooms, studios and a pool; it is co-managed by a Geordie lady who has made her Shirley Valentine dream come true. Free wi-fi. April–Oct. **€70**

**Galini Rooms** ☎ 22860 91115, ⊛ galini-ios.com. A good, quiet choice, in a rural setting just over 200m down the lane by the centre of the beach; relaxing in the well-tended large garden is as big a delight as lying on the beach. April–Oct. **€70**

**Golden Sun** ☎ 22860 91110, ⊛ www.iosgoldensun .com. Family-owned hotel about 300m up the road to Hóra with meticulously clean, brightly painted rooms offering nice views over the bay and large, well thought-out common areas around a swimming pool. Mid-May to Sept. **€60**

**Yialós Beach** ☎ 22860 91421, ⊛ yialosbeach.gr. Stylish hotel, just behind the hospital, offering smart doubles and

udios with their own private gardens, built around a large
ool with a children's pool nearby. Minimum two nights
ay in high season. May–Oct. **€65**

## YLOPÓTAS

**ionysos** ☏ 22860 91215, ⓦ dionysos-ios.gr. Both
ttractive and luxurious, with buildings arranged around a
vimming pool, this complex has rooms rather on the
mall side, but it comes up trumps on location and services
ffered including free wi-fi, children's pool, a fitness studio
nd tennis courts. May–Oct. **€120**

**ar Out Beach Club** ☏ 22860 91468, ⓦ faroutclub
om. Large campsite with well-organized facilities, including
pool, laundry, internet, bungalows and a good-value

cafeteria. However, it can get very noisy and crowded in
August. May–Sept. Camping **€9**, dorm **€18**, bungalow **€50**
**Íos Palace** ☏ 22860 92000, ⓦ iospalacehotel.com.
Luxury hotel that has appropriated part of the beach with
its own deckchairs (free to residents). Despite its opulent
looks, this is a place for all budgets offering a range of
differently priced rooms from basic and undersized, to
massive suites with their own balcony pool. May–Oct. **€90**
**Purple Pig (ex-Stars)** ☏ 22860 91302, ⓦ purple
pigstars.com. A friendly, laidback hostel and camping
complex by the road up to Hóra, with a range of facilities,
including its own club, minimarket, pool and poolside bar.
It offers film shows, twice-weekly live music and
watersports rental. Call to check the latest rates.

## ATING

### ÓRA

**ord Byron** ☏ 22860 92125. A *mezedhopolío* off the main
quare that tries hard to re-create a traditional atmosphere,
ith old rembétika music, a good, Greek menu (mains €12)
nd a well-chosen Santoríni wine list. Extremely popular, so
ake a booking or come early. Daily 6pm–1am.
★ **The Nest** Old Town ☏ 22860 91778. Signposted from
verywhere in Hóra, this is where the locals go to eat and you
ill soon find out why: from the moment you sit down the
ervice and sociability are exceptional. Try the *yiuvétsi* (veal
aked in pasta), a snip at €7. April–Oct daily noon–1am.

### IALÓS

**ctopus Tree** ☏ 697 27 54 365. A warm, intimate space a
t out of the way by the fishing boats on the Yialós

waterfront, which serves fresh seafood caught by the owner.
With mains starting at €12 it is not exactly cheap but you
pay for the freshness. Daily 9am–3pm & 7pm–1am.

### MYLOPÓTAS

**Drákos** ☏ 22860 91281. Right at the water's edge, this is
the best fish taverna on Mylopótas offering mostly fried
seafood dishes (€10). If you want to challenge your
tastebuds, try its cod in garlic sauce, which is thankfully
based mostly on mashed potato. May–Sept daily
noon–2am.
**Mários** ☏ 22860 91130. Perched alone on a curve on the
road to Hóra at the top of the steps to the beach, this chalet-
like restaurant has spectacular views, excellent service and
enormous pizzas for €9. Daily noon–midnight.

## IGHTLIFE AND ENTERTAINMENT

very evening during the summer, Hóra is the centre of the island's nightlife, its streets throbbing with music from ranks of
ompeting discos and clubs – mostly free, or with a nominal entrance charge, and inexpensive drinks. Most of the smaller
ars and pubs are tucked into the narrow streets of the old village on the hill, offering something for everyone, and you'll
ave no trouble finding them.

### LUBS

**un Pub** Old Hóra ⓦ funpubios.com. An early starter
nd late finisher, this is a lively, Irish-themed and Irish-
wned pub in the narrow backstreets of Hóra. From
araoke, quiz nights and internet to free films and a pool
ble, you can come here seven nights a week and still be
ntertained. April–Oct daily 6pm–3am.
**s Club** ⓦ iosclub.gr. Since 1969, this snack bar at the top of
e stairs leading to Yialós starts off the evening with classical
usic while the clients sit back and enjoy the sweeping sunset
ews over Yialós. May–Sept daily 6pm–late.

**Skorpion** Cavernous club on the road to Mylopótas, with
an excellent sound and lighting system; its frenetic
atmosphere is up there with the best on Mýkonos. This is
where everyone ends up when the clubs in Hóra close, so
large queues start forming around 3am. €10 with first
drink. June–Sept daily midnight–8am.

### THEATRE

**Odysséas Elýtis** ⓦ ios.gr. An outdoor theatre behind the
windmills provides a beautiful setting in which to enjoy
concerts and plays (July & Aug).

## Beaches

he best beach on the Yialós side is **Koumbára**, a twenty-minute stroll over the
eadland, where the scenery is rockier and more remote. There is also a smaller beach

## HOMER'S TOMB

**Homer's tomb** can be reached by car or motorbike (signposted from the road to Ayía Theodhóti, 4.5km from Hóra). An ancient town has long since slipped down the side of the cliff, but the rocky ruins of the entrance to a tomb remain, as well as some graves. There is certainly an ancient tradition, from Pausanias and Pliny, that Homer was buried on the island; furthermore, Hellenistic coins from Íos bear his name and his head. However, it was Dutch archeologist Pasch van Krienen who first discovered these tombs in 1771 and immediately claimed one of them as Homer's – in reality, though, it probably dates only to the Byzantine era.

further on with a cove backed by extraordinary green cliffs and a rocky islet to explore. Its western-facing setting and string of palm trees makes it ideal to watch the sunset, and attracts many amateur photographers.

On the south coast, there's a superb beach at **Manganári** easily reached by boat or bus (see p.425). Another decent beach is at **Kálamos**: get off the Manganári bus at the turning for Kálamos, which leaves you with a 4km walk, else take a *kaïki* from Yialós. There's more to see, and a better atmosphere, at **Ayía Theodhóti** up on the east coast. You can get there on a paved road across the island – the daily excursion bus costs €6 return. A couple of kilometres south of Ayía Theodhóti is **Paleókastro**, a ruined Venetian castle which encompasses the remains of a marble-finished town and a Byzantine church.

In the unlikely event that the beach is too crowded, try the one at **Psáthi**, 14km to the southeast, although you may need your own transport.

### EATING

BEACHE

#### KUMBÁRA
**Polídoros** 📞 22860 92072. This grill taverna is one of the better places to eat on Íos offering coal-grilled meats and local specialities such as pork with celery casserole (€12). Unfortunately, it has a very short opening season. Mid-June to mid-Sept daily noon–10pm.

#### AYÍA THEODHÓTI
**Koukos** 📞 22860 92420. A very good family restaurar rated highly by the locals, because it offers produce such a honey, milk products, eggs and chickens from its own far next door (mains €8). Accompanied by bread baked in wood-fired oven, organic food never tasted so good. May Sept daily noon–8pm.

# Síkinos

**SÍKINOS** has so small a population – around 240 – that the mule ride or walk from the port up to the capital was only replaced by a bus in the late 1980s. At roughly the sam time the new jetty was completed; until then Síkinos was the last major Greek island where ferry passengers were still taken ashore in launches. With no dramatic characteristics and no nightlife to speak of, few foreigners make the short trip over her from neighbouring Folégandhros or Íos. The end result, however, is the most unspoilt rural countryside in the Cyclades where the clichéd image of a priest riding a donkey can suddenly materialize from over a hill.

### ARRIVAL AND INFORMATION

SÍKINO

**By ferry** Ferries dock at the far end of the port of Aloprónia. There are fewer connection options than in many of the neighbouring islands.
Destinations Anáfi (2–4 weekly; 3hr); Folégandhros (6–8 weekly; 40min); Íos (4–6 weekly; 30min); Kéa/Kýthnos/Lávrio (1 weekly; 8–12hr); Kímolos (1–2 weekly; 2hr); Kýthnos (2 weekly; 7hr 30min); Mílos (3 weekly; 3hr);

Mýkonos (2 weekly; 5hr 30min); Náxos (3–5 weekly; 2 30min); Páros (3–6 weekly; 3hr); Pireás (2–3 weekl 6–7hr); Santoríni (5–7 weekly; 2hr); Sífnos (2 weekly; 2 30min); Sýros (3–5 weekly; 4–7hr).
**Services** There is a bank with an ATM in Kástro, while th post office is at the entrance to Kástro.

## GETTING AROUND

**By bus** There is a single island bus, which shuttles in the high season regularly (4–8 daily; 7.15am–11.45pm) between the harbour and Hóra. Note that the bus changes to a normal four-seater car out of season.

**By car and motorcycle** The island's only rental office is at the Eko petrol station 50m back from Aloprónia; it mostly rents scooters.

# Aloprónia

Such tourist facilities that exist are concentrated in the little harbour of **Aloprónia**, with its crystal-clear water, sandy beach, breakwaters and jetty. Many of the few dozen houses around the bay are summer holiday homes owned by expat Sikiniots now resident in Athens or beyond.

## ACCOMMODATION AND EATING

ALOPRÓNIA

**Lucas** ☎ 22860 51076, 🌐 sikinoslucas.gr. Family studios at the water's edge on the opposite side of the bay, as well as rooms and studios among a cluster of buildings at the back of the village, 700m from the harbour along the road to Hóra. The family also operate a taverna which in May and June is your only eating option in the port (mains €10). April–Oct. €50

**Maïstrali** 22860 51087, 🌐 maistrali-sikinos.gr. Modern hotel behind the lighthouse, unimaginatively built like a square, urban two-storey house, but offering large, well-furnished rooms with the best views over the port. April–Oct. €80

★ **Porto Sikinos** ☎ 22860 51220, 🌐 portosikinos.gr. The place to stay in Aloprónia, a pricey option but on the swish side, offering free wi-fi, fridge, TV, a/c, island furnishings and everything else you might require for a restful stay. May–Sept. €95

# Hóra

**HÓRA** consists of the double village of **Kástro** and **Horió**. As you slowly drive or walk up from Aloprónia, the scenery turns out to be less desolate than initial views from the ferry suggest, while the village itself, draped across a ridge overlooking the sea, is a delightfully unspoilt settlement. Most of the facilities are in the larger, northeastern Kástro, whereas Horió is mainly residential. A partly ruined fortress-monastery,

**6**

Zoödhóhou Piyís ("Life-giving Fountain"), crowns the cliff-edged hill above, and is accessed by a stepped path out of the top of Kástro. The architectural highlight of the village is the **kástro** itself, a quadrangle of eighteenth-century mansions arrayed defensively around the blue-domed church of **Panayía Pantánassa** which opens for evensong at around 6pm. Although tourists don't tend to stay here, eating options cater for the locals and are surprisingly varied and better than in Aloprónia.

## EATING AND DRINKING                                                    HÓRA

★ **Anémelo** ☎ 22860 51216. A friendly café-bar with the only shade in town; it has only a few tables outside, but you can share a table with strangers. Good cup of coffee and a snack menu from omelettes (€5) to home-made syrupy desserts. May–Oct daily 10am–midnight.

**To Stéki tou Garbí** ☎ 22860 51215. Unpretentious and cheap with a first-class selection of traditional Greek island cooking (€6), along with its own barrel wine, which is still made in the same traditional way for generations. March–Nov daily noon–midnight.

## Around the island

Ninety minutes' walk northeast from Hóra lies **Paleókastro**, the patchy remains of an ancient fortress. In the opposite direction, another ninety-minute walk takes you by an old path or higher road through a steeply terraced landscape to **Episkopí**, where elements of an ancient temple-tomb have been incorporated into a seventh-century church – the structure is known formally as the Héroön, though it is now thought to have been a Roman mausoleum rather than a temple of Hera. Note the weathered wooden door, and the cistern under long stone slabs in the courtyard.

The beaches of **Dhialiskári** and **Áyios Yeóryios** are reachable by road – though only the latter is asphalted – while **Málta** is only reachable by *kaïki* from Aloprónia. A more feasible journey by foot is to the pebble beach at **Áyios Pandeleïmonas**: just under an hour's trail walk southwest of Aloprónia, it is the most sheltered on the island, and is also served by a small boat in season.

# Folégandhros

The sheer cliffs of **FOLÉGANDHROS** rise 300m from the sea in places, and until the early 1980s they were as effective a deterrent to tourists as they had historically been to pirates. Folégandhros was used now and then as an island of political exile from Roman times right up until 1969, and life in the high, barren interior was only eased in 1974 by the arrival of electricity and the subsequent construction of a road running from the harbour to Hóra and beyond. Development has been given further impetus by the recent increase in tourism and the ensuing commercialization. The island is becoming so trendy that Greek journalists speak of a new Mýkonos in the making, a fact that is reflected in its swish jewellery and clothes shops. Yet away from showcase Hóra and the beaches, the countryside remains mostly pristine. Donkeys are also still very much in evidence, since the terrain on much of the island is too steep for vehicles.

## ARRIVAL AND INFORMATION                                          FOLÉGANDHROS

**By ferry** The recent popularity of Folégandhros has resulted in a slew of new ferry routes to almost every other port in the Cyclades. Ferries dock at Karavostási.
Destinations Amorgós (1–2 weekly; 2hr 15min–4hr); Anáfi (2–4 weekly; 4hr); Íos (4–8 weekly; 15min); Kéa/Lávrio (1 weekly; 10–11hr); Kýthnos (3 weekly; 9hr); Mílos (3–5 weekly; 2hr 30min); Mýkonos (0–2 weekly; 4hr); Náxos (3–6 weekly; 1hr 30min–2hr); Páros (2–4 weekly; 1hr 15min); Pireás (2–6 weekly; 3hr 30min–10hr);

Santoríni (3–5 weekly; 3hr); Sérifos (0–2 weekly; 2hr 30min); Sífnos (1–3 weekly; 1hr 30min); Síkinos (3–5 weekly; 40min); Sýros (3–4 weekly; 3hr 30min).
**Services** There is an ATM at Doúnavi square and the island's post office is at Poúnda square.
**Travel agents** Diaplous (☎ 22860 41158) and Maraki (☎ 22860 41211) – both closed 2–5pm – are between Doúnavi and Poúnda squares.

## GETTING AROUND

**By bus** There are hourly buses daily in summer from Karavostási to Hóra, from where further buses run to Áno Meriá (6 daily; 30min) or Angáli beach (4 daily; 30min). Off-season the bus to Angáli leaves you 1km away on the road to Áno Meriá.

**By car and motorcycle** It may be worthwhile renting a car for a day – try Spyros's Motorbike Rental at Karavostási (📞 22860 41448), which is cheaper than its counterparts in Hóra – but generally the buses will, as a rule, take you where you want to be. Lignós (📞 22860 41346) rents motorcycles at the northern end of Hóra.

# Karavostási and around

**Karavostási**, the port, serves really as a last-resort base. There are several hotels and plenty of rooms but compared to the beauty of Hóra, just above, hardly any atmosphere. The closest **beach**, other than the narrow main shingle strip, is the smallish, sand-and-pebble **Várdhia**, signposted just north over the tiny headland. Some fifteen minutes' walk south lies **Livádhi**, a family beach with tamarisk trees. Just before Livádhi are the much smaller but more romantic beaches of **Vitséntzou** and **Poundáki**, reached by steep paths.

Touted as the island's most scenic beach, **Kátergo** is a 300m stretch of pea-gravel with two offshore islets, on the southeastern tip of the island. Most visitors come on a boat excursion from Karavostási or Angáli, but you can also get there on foot (20min) from the hamlet of Livádhi, itself a fifteen-minute dirt-road walk inland from Livádhi beach. Be warned, though, that it's a rather arduous and stony trek, with a final 80m descent on loose-surfaced paths; there is no shade on the walk or the beach. The narrow sea passage between the beach's southern cliffs and the right-hand islet, **Makrí**, has very strong currents and swimming through is not recommended.

## ACCOMMODATION AND EATING | KARAVOSTÁSI AND AROUND

**Kalýmnios** 📞 22860 41146. Fish taverna said to have the freshest seafood on the island. Whether crab claws, fried calamari (€10) or lobster spaghetti, you order and pay by the kilo. Also open for breakfast. April–Oct daily 7am–1am.

**Livadhi Camping** Livádhi 📞 22860 41204, 🌐 www .folegandros.org. A friendly and more than adequate campsite with a café-restaurant, minimarket, and a rental office for cars and motorbikes. They also rent apartments for two people (€50). June–Sept. **€9**

**Vardia Bay** Várdhia 📞 22860 41277, 🌐 vardiabay.com. Grand hotel with luxurious rooms and studios in a great location above the jetty, right on the beach of the same name. Everything is on the large side: from the rooms and the verandas with their stupendous seaviews to the breakfast buffet. **€80**

# Hóra

The island's real character and appeal are rooted in the spectacular **HÓRA**, perched on a cliff-edge plateau, a steep 3km from the port. Locals and foreigners mingle at the cafés and tavernas under the trees of the five adjacent squares, passing the time undisturbed by traffic, which is banned from the village centre. Towards the northern cliff-edge and entered through two arcades, the defensive core of the medieval **kástro** neighbourhood is marked by ranks of two-storey residential houses, with almost identical stairways and slightly recessed doors.

From the cliff-edge Poúnda square, where the bus stops, a path zigzags up – with views along the northern coastline – to the wedding-cake church of **Kímisis tis Theotókou**, whose unusual design includes two little fake chapels mounted astride the roof. The church, formerly part of a nunnery, is on the gentlest slope of a pyramidal hill with 360m cliffs dropping to the sea on the northwest side and is a favourite spot for watching some of the Aegean's most spectacular sunsets. Beyond and below it hides the **Khryssospiliá**, a large cave with stalactites and ancient inscriptions, centre of a strange ancient youth cult, but closed to the public for archeological excavations. However, a minor, lower grotto can still be visited by excursion boat from the port. Towards the top of the hill are a few fragments of the ancient Paleókastro.

**6**

Hóra is inevitably beginning to sprawl at the edges, and the burgeoning **nightlife** – a few dance bars along with a number of music pubs and ouzerís – is to the south, away from most accommodation.

## ACCOMMODATION HÓRA

**Aegeo** ☎ 22860 41468, ⒲ aegeohotel.com. A reasonably priced hotel option, just before Poúnda square, which includes free wi-fi and breakfast, but gets booked quickly. The same family manages a more basic option at *Evgenía* rooms (☎ 22860 41006) right next to the hotel; basic but immaculately clean. April–Sept. **€60**

**Anemómilos Apartments** ☎ 22860 41309, ⒲ anemomilosapartments.com. Wonderfully appointed at the cliff's edge with dramatic vistas, these are super-luxurious apartments from which watching the sunset becomes an artistic experience. "Blue" coded rooms have better views and are more expensive than "green" ones. April–Sept. **€190**

**Chora Resort** ☎ 22860 41590–4, ⒲ choraresort.com. Grand luxury resort at the northern end of town, spanning a couple of acres, that offers a large pool, fitness centre, designer rooms, minigolf and even its own church for weddings and baptisms. Larger rooms have their own jacuzzi. April–Sept. **€190**

★ **Polikandia** ☎ 22860 41322, ⒲ polikandia -folegandros.gr. Centred around a large swimming pool, this is a superbly designed boutique hotel before Poúnda square, paying great attention to detail: free wi-fi, communal jacuzzi and individual massage showers that have to be seen to be believed. April–Sept. **€110**

## EATING AND DRINKING

**Eva's Garden** ☎ 22860 41110. If proof be needed that Folégandhros is sophisticated, this elegant restaurant-bar provides it with an unusually inventive menu (mains €8) in a very romantic atmosphere. Easter–Oct daily 6am–1am.

**Kritikós** ☎ 22860 41219. A Cretan grill in the fourth square with the best *dakos* (feta, crispy roll and tomato salad) in the

Cyclades and some good Cretan wines. Excellent barbecued and broiled steaks from €8. April–Oct daily noon–1am.

★ **Piazza** ☎ 22860 41274. By the third square, this is the best restaurant to try the local *matsáta* (hand-drawn tagliatelle with veal, chicken or goat) for €10. May–Oct daily noon–1am.

## NIGHTLIFE

**Astarti** A very popular bar in the third square with an alternative feel, elegant furnishings, carefully chosen wooden decor and large cocktails. The clubbers come here and then continue to Beez, a few doors down, its sister club that stays open after everything else has closed. May–Sept daily 6pm–3am.

★ **BaRaki** On the same road as Astarti, this is a cosy, friendly bar with a good selection of cocktails for €7. Occasional music with a DJ whose booth takes up almost half the space inside – but, who cares, as everyone is out enjoying the pleasant nights. June–Sept daily 10pm–3am.

# Áno Meriá and around

West of Hóra, a paved road threads its way along the spine of the island towards sprawling **Áno Meriá** – in fact a multitude of tiny hamlets. In the middle of the settlement stands the large parish church of Áyios Yeóryios (1905), with an unusual white, carved iconostasis. Ask the bus driver to drop you off at the long footpaths down to the beaches on the western half of the island. Muleteers await the buses here and will, for €5, transport tourists down dirt roads to the beaches at **Ambéli**, **Ligariá** and **Áyios Yeóryios**; the former are small and can get crowded, the latter is a much better beach but faces north and is only comfortable when the wind blows from the south. **Livadháki beach** is accessed by signed path from just beyond Taxiárhis.

The best swimming in this part of the island is at the attractive and popular sheltered south-coast beach of **Angáli**, where there are several tavernas. (Off-season the bus leaves you 1km away on the road to Áno Meriá.) Naturists should take the paths which lead twenty minutes east to **Firá** or west to **Áyios Nikólaos** beaches respectively. The latter is particularly fine, with many tamarisks, coarse sand and views back over the island. Although at Áyios Nikólaos, a lone taverna operates up by the namesake chapel, while Firá has no facilities.

**FROM TOP** LIONS IN THE DELOS MUSEUMS (P.396); SANTORÍNI'S BLUE DOMES (P.434) >

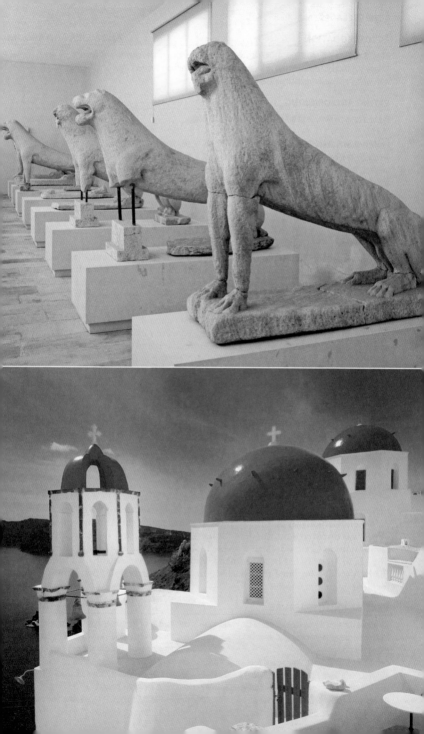

6

## ACCOMMODATION ÁNO MERIÁ AND AROUND

**Blue Sand** Angáli ☎ 22860 41042, ⓦ bluesand.gr. A three-star boutique option in this well-connected beach with white, minimalist undulating staircases and rooms with verandas offering mesmerizing sea views. Free wi-fi and port transfers. May–Sept. €120

## EATING AND DRINKING

The best eating options lie at the end of the bus line at Taxiárhis.

**Profítis Ilías Bakery** At Profítis Ilías, a well-concealed, yet signposted, bakery is along a short lane to the left of the road. It offers the local cheese-and-onion pie called *kalasoúna* for €2. Mon–Sat 8am–3pm.

**Synandisi** ☎ 22860 41208. A taverna at the last but one bus stop in Áno Meriá with a bit of everything: fresh fish, home-grown vegetables and hotpots of local meat such as rabbit, goat or chicken (€9). This is the easiest place to find and try the local *kalasoúna* pies. May–Sept 10am–midnight.

# Santoríni

As the ferry manoeuvres into the great caldera of **SANTORÍNI (Thíra)**, the land seems to rise up and clamp around it. Gaunt, sheer cliffs loom hundreds of metres above the deep blue sea, nothing grows or grazes to soften the awesome view, and the only colours are the reddish-brown, black and grey pumice layers on the cliff face of Santoríni, the largest island in this mini-archipelago. The landscape tells of a history so dramatic and turbulent that legend hangs as fact upon it.

These apocalyptic events, though, scarcely concern modern tourists, who come here to take in the spectacular views, stretch out on the island's dark-sand beaches and absorb the peculiar, infernal geographic features. The tourism industry has changed traditional island life, creating a rather expensive playground. There is one time-honoured local industry, however, that has benefited from all the outside attention: **wine**. Santoríni is one of Greece's most important producers, and the fresh, dry white wines it is known for (most from the *assýrtiko* grape for which the region is known) are the perfect accompaniment to the seafood served in the many restaurants and tavernas that hug the island's cliffs.

## Brief history

From as early as 3000 BC, Ancient Thíra developed as a sophisticated outpost of Minoan civilization, until sometime between 1650–1600 BC when catastrophe struck: the volcano-island erupted some 60 cubic kilometres of magma over a period of months. The island's heart sank below the sea, leaving a caldera 10km in diameter. Earthquakes and tsunami reverberated across the Aegean – one full metre of ash was discovered on Rhodes – Thíra was destroyed, and the great Minoan civilization on Crete was dealt a severe blow by the ensuing ash fallout and tsunami. The island's history has become linked with the legend of Atlantis, all because of Plato. Although he dated the cataclysm to approximately 9500 BC, he was perhaps inspired by folk memories.

## ARRIVAL AND DEPARTURE SANTORÍNI

**By plane** The airport is on the east side of the island, near Monólithos. Buses are not frequent, so make sure you have arranged a pickup.

Destinations Athens (both Olympic and Aegean; 3–8 daily; 45min); Crete, Iráklion (Olympic, 1 daily; 30min); Rhodes (4–5 weekly; 45min); Thessaloníki (Aegean 1–2 daily; 1hr 5min).

**By ferry** All ferries dock at the port of Athiniós. The old ports of Skála Firás and Ammoúdhi for Ía in the north are only used by local excursion boats and cruise ships. The old, traditional route of 580 steps from Skála up to Firá is a difficult 45min walk; you can also go by mule (€5) or cable car (April–Oct daily 6.30am–11pm, every 20min; Nov–March daily 7.30am–10.30am & 2.30–4.30pm, every 30min; €4, luggage €2 extra).

Destinations Amorgós (1–3 weekly; 3hr); Anáfi (2–5 weekly; 1hr 20min); Astypálea (1 weekly; 3hr); Chálki (2 weekly, 11hr); Iráklion (1–2 daily; 1hr 30min–5hr); Folégandhros (1–2 daily; 1hr 30min); Íos (1–3 daily; 30min–1hr); Kálymnos/Tílos (2 weekly; 5hr 30min–10hr); Kárpathos/Kássos (3 weekly; 6–8hr); Kéa/Lávrio (2 weekly; 13–14hr); Kímolos (2 weekly; 4hr); Mílos (4–6 weekly; 2hr); Mýkonos (1–3 daily; 2hr 30min); Náxos (2–4 daily;

1hr 30min); Níssyros (2 weekly; 8hr); Páros (1 daily; 3hr 30min–7hr); Pireás (3–5 daily; 4hr 30min–9hr); Rhodes (5–6 weekly; 9–12hr); Sífnos (1–2 weekly; 5hr); Síkinos (6–8 weekly; 2hr); Sýros (5–6 weekly; 5–8hr); Thirassía (4–6 daily from Órmos and 2–3 daily from Ammoúdhi; 15 min); Tínos (5 weekly; 3hr).

## INFORMATION

**Services** There are many cafés clustered on Firá's main square; others offer free wi-fi to their customers all over the island. Penguin (☎ 22860 22168; 9am–9pm) laundry is on the main road to Ía about 100m up from the main square (from €6).

**Travel agents** There are many travel agents clustered around Firá's main square. Santo Star (☎ 22860 23082,

ⓦ santostar.gr) and Kamari Tours (☎ 22860 31390, ⓦ kamaritours.gr) organize excursions and trips to ancient Thíra, as well as day tours to Nea and Paleá Kaméni and Thirassía. Prices for the latter range from €10 for simple transport to about €30 for a more intimate guided tour on a traditional *kaïki*.

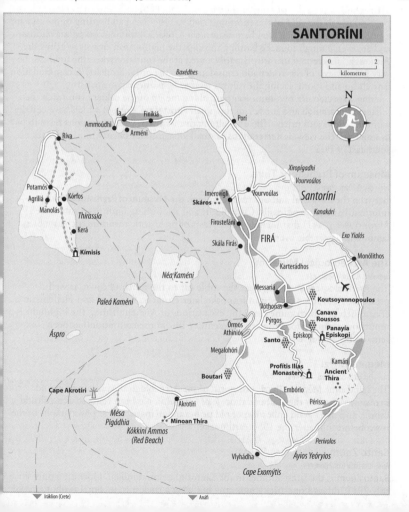

6

## GETTING AROUND

**By bus** Buses leave Firá from just south of Theotokopoúlou Square to Períssa, Perívolos, Kamári, Monólithos (via the airport), Akrotíri, Órmos Athiniós and Vliháda. For the timetable consult ⓦ ktel-santorini.gr.

**By taxi** The island's taxi base (☎ 22860 22555) is near the Firá bus station, within steps of the main square. There are fewer than forty in the whole island, so make sure you have your onward transport arranged well in advance.

**By car and motorcycle** If you want to see the whole island in a couple of days, a rented motorbike or car will be essential. There are many rental places all over the island

and your hotel or any travel agent can arrange it for you. Nomikos Travel (☎ 22860 24940, ⓦ nomikostravel.gr) opposite the OTE building in Firá is a good, reliable agency.

**Day-trips** The glass-bottom *Calypso* (☎ 22860 22958, ⓦ dakoutrostravel.gr) makes an excursion to the islands of the archipelago daily at 10.45am (€28) and hovers over the volcanic reefs at the end of each journey to allow passengers a peek into the dark depths of Santoríni's flooded crater. Ancient Thira Tours (☎ 22860 32474; €8; 2hr stopping time at site) also operate guided tours of the ruins of Ancient Thíra from Kamári (p.439).

# Firá and around

Half-rebuilt after a devastating earthquake in 1956, **FIRÁ** (also known as Hóra) clings precariously to the edge of the enormous caldera. The rising and setting of the sun are especially beautiful when seen here against the Cycladic buildings lining the clifftop, and are even enough to make battling through the high-season crowds worthwhile. Although Firá's restaurants are primarily aimed at the tourist market, the food can be very good; views of the crater add considerably to the price. Similarly accommodation isn't cheap and rooms facing the caldera tend to be particularly expensive.

Using a spectacular two-hour footpath along the lip of the caldera you reach the village of **Imerovígli** and further to the north **Firostefáni**, both of which have equally stunning views and prices. The only alternative location, where you don't have to pay as much for the view, is **Karterádhos**, a small village about twenty minutes' walk southeast of Firá.

## Museum of Prehistoric Thira

Tues–Sun 8.30am–8pm • €3

Between the cathedral and bus station in Firá, the **Museum of Prehistoric Thira** has informative displays of fossils, Cycladic art and astonishing finds from submerged Akrotíri (see p.441) that include plaster casts of prehistoric furniture such as tables, lamps and a portable oven.

## The Archeological Museum

Tues–Sun 8.30am–3pm • €3

The **Archeological Museum**, near the cable car to the north of town, is well presented, and has a collection from the later Homeric Classical and Hellenistic eras, much of which came from the excavations of Ancient Thira. The highlight is a mourning woman from the seventh century BC whose coloration has been remarkably preserved.

## Mégaro Ghýzi

May–Oct Mon–Sat 10am–4pm • €3

The handsome **Mégaro Ghýzi**, just north of the Archeological Museum in an old mansion owned by the Catholic diocese of Santoríni, has been restored as a cultural centre, and has a good collection of old prints and maps as well as photographs of the town before and after the 1956 earthquake.

## Santo Zeum

April–Oct daily 9am–8pm • €5

**Santo Zeum** is the latest stunner in the Santoríni cultural milieu. Operating only since July 2011, this is a one-trick museum – but what a trick it is: it contains photographic reproductions (using a technique specially invented by Kodak) of the Akrotíri murals, which can be reasonably assumed to mark the beginning of the art of painting per se.

## Lignós Folklore Museum

Daily 10am–2pm • €2

In a part of Firá called Kondohóri the extensive **Lignós Folklore Museum** features a completely furnished local "cave home" with period winery, chapel, garden and workshops, as well as a gallery and historical archive.

**6**

## ACCOMMODATION                                                                                      FIRÁ

**Galini** Firostefáni ☎ 22860 22095, ⓦ hotelgalini.gr. Possibly the cheapest hotel with a caldera view, situated in a relatively quiet spot a 10min walk from Firá. March–Nov. €100

**Loucas** ☎ 22860 22480, ⓦ www.loucashotel

-santorini.com. Traditional caldera-side hotel below Ypapandís with rooms in caves carved into the cliffside with 180-degree views of the precipice below and a beautiful pool and jacuzzi. Breakfast included. April–Oct. €150

FIRÁ

**ACCOMMODATION**
| | |
|---|---|
| Galini | 1 |
| Loucas | 6 |
| Pelican | 5 |
| Pension George | 7 |
| San Giorgio | 3 |
| Santorini Camping | 4 |
| Villa Rena | 2 |

**EATING & DRINKING**
| | |
|---|---|
| Aris | 3 |
| Mama's House | 4 |
| Naoussa | 1 |
| Nikolas | 2 |
| Sphinx | 5 |

**NIGHTLIFE**
| | |
|---|---|
| Enigma | 2 |
| Franco's | 5 |
| Kirá Thira | 4 |
| Koo | 1 |
| Murphy's Bar | 3 |

6

**Pelican** ☎ 22860 23113, ⍾ pelicanhotel.gr. Large hotel off the central square with spacious rooms; it's owned by a travel agency a few blocks away, so they can organize your stay completely. Free wi-fi, satellite TV, 24/7 reception, parking possible nearby. €85

**Pension George** Karterádhos ☎ 22860 22351, ⍾ pensiongeorge.com. Comfortable rooms and studios, pool and a good welcome, just a 15min walk from Firá. Unlike other hotels, this one also has a well-attended garden where you can relax among the palm trees. Free transfers. €70

★ **San Giorgio** ☎ 22860 23516, ⍾ sangiorgiovilla.gr. Tucked away to the left of parking next to the main square, you can find this hospitable, clean, hotel with simple rooms, all with balconies; excellent value for budget travellers. Also offers a ten percent discount for Rough Guide readers. April–Nov. €50

**Santorini Camping** ☎ 22860 22944, ⍾ santorini camping.gr. A shady campsite 300m east of the centre, with a pool, restaurant, games room, 24/7 reception, own security and free internet access. March–Nov. €9

**Villa Rena** ☎ 22860 28130, ⍾ renasplace.gr. Comfortable, friendly hotel, a 10min walk towards the Folklore Museum, whose rooms are furnished individually in bright, non-standard Cycladic colours, some overlooking a large pool. Minibus transfers available for a charge. April–Oct. €70

## EATING AND DRINKING

**Aris** ☎ 22860 22480. Dependably good Greek and international food plus an excellent wine list in a relaxed, unhurried atmosphere, with a sensational view – and prices to match (€20); not always busy, as the steep steps down below *Hotel Loucas* act as a deterrent to some customers. April–Oct daily noon–midnight.

**Mama's House** Right below the main square, this is a cheap, backpacker-friendly spot with hearty Continental and English breakfasts, filling dishes (€8), a shaggy dog and the overwhelming chatty presence of Mama herself, a distinguished old lady straight out of the photo album of Greek stereotypes. March–Nov daily 8am–1am.

**Naoussa** ☎ 22860 24869, ⍾ naoussa-restaurant.gr. Good traditional Greek cuisine on the first floor of the shopping centre Lagoudhéra opposite the steps to old port.

Dishes as close to home-made as you'll get anywhere on Firá; start with the celebrated moussaka for €10. Easter–Oct daily noon–late.

**Nikolas** Erythroú Stavroú ☎ 22860 24550. An old and defiantly traditional taverna, insisting on using nothing frozen or not in season; the locals know this and prefer it, so it can be very hard to get a table. Mains around €15. Daily noon–midnight.

**Sphinx** Mitropóleos (Via d'Oro) ☎ 22860 23823, ⍾ sphinx.gr. On terraces overlooking the caldera, and offering home-made pasta dishes with a Greek twist, such as the addition of lobster, crayfish or octopus, at a price (€20). Its cellar boasts 150 different wines. April–Oct daily noon–1am.

## NIGHTLIFE

Most of the first-rate nightlife is northwest of the central square, on Erythroú Stavroú, often not starting long before midnight and busiest between 1am and 4am.

**Enigma** Erythroú Stavroú ⍾ www.enigmaclub.gr. Long-established dance club with three large barrel-roofed arches and outdoor area with a palm-tree bar and facecheck security. Its VIP room has seen some of the most famous world celebrities and still attracts the island's *beau monde*. June–Sept daily midnight–late.

**Franco's** ☎ 22860 24428, ⍾ www.francos.gr. Exclusive, expensive cocktail bar in a fabulous location by the steps to the old port offering opera, champagne and sunbeds. Try the Maria Callas cocktail (€9) and watch the sunset listening to the Diva herself singing Norma. Easter–Oct daily 5pm–late.

**Kirá Thíra** Erythroú Stavroú. Going back more than three decades, this small, laidback venue with live DJs and music

has fanatic followers who pack the place to the rafters year after year, despite its less-than-ideal acoustics: it's cut in a cave so its sound is on the echoey side. May–Oct daily 8pm–late.

**Koo** Erythroú Stavroú ☎ 22860 22025, ⍾ kooclub.gr. In direct competition with *Enigma* (see above), it offers less frenetic chill-out and trance music, with candles and cocktails, three bars, and a reservation service if you want to book a table in the VIP room. June–Sept daily midnight–late.

**Murphy's Bar** Erythroú Stavroú ☎ 22860 22248. Reasonably priced Irish pub with all the obligatory hilarity; established in 1999 and hasn't looked back since. The wall of drinks behind the bar reaches to the ceiling and this is a rather tall venue. April–Oct daily noon–3am.

# Ía

Ía (Oía), the most photographed town on the island, was once a major commercial centre in the Aegean, but it has declined in the wake of economic depression, wars, earthquakes and depleted fish stocks. Partly destroyed in the 1956 earthquake, the town has been sympathetically reconstructed, its white and cyan houses clinging to the cliff face. Apart from the caldera and the town itself, there are a couple of things to see, including the **Naval Museum** (Mon & Wed–Sun 10am–2pm & 5–8pm; €3) and the very modest remains of a Venetian castle. It is a quieter, though still touristy, alternative to Firá except during sunset, for which people are coached in from all over the island, creating traffic chaos and driving up prices. Public buses are extremely full around this time (after 6pm, although in the summer the sunset occurs around 8.30pm).

Below the town, two sets of 220-odd steps lead to two small harbours: one to **Arméni** for the fishermen, and the other to **Ammoúdi**, where the excursion boats dock.

6

## ACCOMMODATION                                                                                      ÍA

Much of the town's accommodation is in restored cave houses, with caldera views adding at least €100 to the rooms.

**Andronis Suites** ☎ 22860 72041, ⓦ andronis-suites .com. With its central location, superlative views, spa, apartments carved deep into the cliffs, and balconies that can induce vertigo, this may well be the most prestigious spot in the Cyclades and the price reflects it. The apartments sleep up to five, mind you. April–Oct. **€600**

**Oia Youth Hostel** ☎ 22860 71465, ⓦ santorinihostel .gr. Well signposted from the bus terminal, this excellent hostel has a terrace and a shady courtyard, laundry, a good café-bar and clean dormitories, but with a very short season, so call to check it's open. Mid-June to Sept. **€16**

**Pension Delfini** ☎ 22860 23016, ⓦ delfinihotel.net. By far the best middle-price option, this small boutique hotel offers rooms with jacuzzis and private balconies with caldera views. April–Nov. Doubles **€110**, 4-person suite **€180**

## EATING AND DRINKING

Restaurant prices can be as steep as the cliffs, at the older, western end of town. In general the further east you go along the central ridge the better the price.

**1800** ☎ 22860 71485. Regarded as one of the best restaurants on the island, and serving highly refined, French-inspired cuisine, its interiors have a fin-de-siècle feel and the roof garden offers unique unhindered views over the caldera. Its wines are excellent and, like the food (mains around €30), accordingly expensive. May–Oct daily 6.30pm–midnight.

**King Neptune** ☎ 22860 71294. With a rooftop bar to rival the best for views and dishes for €15 that don't break the bank, this is the best-value combination of good food, view and atmosphere in Ía. Come early for dinner before the sunset buses invade, get a front-row table and chill. April–Nov daily noon–late.

# The east coast

Santoríni's **beaches**, on the island's east coast, are long black stretches of volcanic sand that get blisteringly hot in the afternoon sun. They're no secret, and in the summer the crowds can be a bit overpowering. Among the resorts lie the substantial and beautifully sited remains of **ancient Thira**.

In the southeast, the family resort of **Kamári** is popular with package-tour operators, and hence more touristy. Nonetheless it's quieter and cleaner than most, with a well-maintained seafront promenade.

Things are considerably scruffier at **Períssa**, around the cape. Because of its beach and abundance of cheap rooms, it's crowded with backpackers. The beach itself extends several kilometres to the west, through Perívolos to Áyios Yeóryios, sheltered by the occasional tamarisk tree and with beach bars dotted along at intervals. A new attraction in Períssa is the **Museum of Minerals and Fossils** (summer, daily 10am–2pm, winter Sun only; free), with exhibits that include rare palm tree fossils from pre-eruption Santoríni.

## Ancient Thira

Tues–Sun 8.30am–2.30pm • €1.50 • Excursion minibuses depart from Kamári (see above); there are also donkey rides up (€20).
Alternatively, walk the interminably looping cobbled road – Archaias Thiras – starting from Ancient Thira Tours

Kamári and Períssa are separated by the Mésa Vounó headland, on which stood **ancient Thira**, the post-eruption settlement, dating from 915 BC through to the Venetian period. Starting from Períssa a stony shadeless path to the site passes a chapel dating back to the fourth century AD before skirting round to the Temenos of Artemidoros with bas-relief carvings of a dolphin, eagle and lion representing Poseidon, Zeus and Apollo. Next, the trail follows the sacred way of the ancient city through the remains of the agora and past the theatre. The path meets the paved road to Kamári at a saddle between Mésa Vounó and Profítis Ilías, the only remaining visible components of the pre-eruption landscape.

## INFORMATION
THE EAST COAST

**Activities** Kamári is the base of Navy's Diving Centre (☎ 22860 31006, ⊛ navys.gr), which offers PADI courses for beginners and volcanic reef diving for certified divers.

## ACCOMMODATION

★ **Chez Sophie** Kamári ☎ 22860 32912, ⊛ chezsophie.gr. A stunningly designed boutique hotel with large rooms set around a swimming pool towards the southern end of the beach. Superb service that includes free wi-fi, parking, free air and ferry transfers, plus a delicious home-made buffet breakfast. May–Oct. **€90**

**Ostria** Kamári ☎ 22860 31727, ⊛ villaostria.gr. A friendly, family-run oasis of studios and apartments at the foot of Mount Profítis Ilías that stands in pleasant contrast to the resort's many large hotel blocks. Parking available. April–Oct. **€100**

**Perissa Beach** Períssa ☎ 22860 81343. Right behind the coastal road, this campsite has plenty of space and shade, but is also next to a couple of noisy late-night bars, but if you choose to stay here you are more likely to be carousing rather than resting. Has special overflow space for sleeping bags only. **€9**

**Rose Bay Hotel** Kamári ☎ 22860 33650, ⊛ rosebay.gr. A less pricey option than other luxurious hotels in the north part of town, with a pleasant pool setting, set back from the beach. Single rooms are as big as the doubles, too. April–Oct. **€120**

## EATING AND DRINKING

Kamári is the centre of nightlife in the east coast: the best of the bars are towards the southern end of the beach offering staggered happy hours 8pm–midnight, and there is a good open-air cinema at the north end of the town, which is licensed and offers cocktails and drinks at reasonable prices during the film.

**Kritikos** Kamári ☎ 22460 4170. A taverna much frequented by locals, this is one of the better grill places to eat on the island (mains €15). It's a long way out of Kamári on the road up to Messariá, and too far to walk, but the bus stops outside. April–Nov daily noon–midnight.

**Mistral** Kamári ☎ 22860 32108, ⊛ www.mistral -fishtavern.gr. Set in a quiet alley with tables in a large, tree-covered garden, this is rumoured to offer the best lobster spaghetti on the island (€30–40 for a platter for two). Also try the tomato salad with caper leaves, a Santoríni special. April–Nov daily noon–late.

## THE WINERIES

Some of Santoríni's most important **wineries** are scattered around Pýrgos and the south, and offer excellent-value tours. Whichever tour you go on, none is complete without a taste of Santoríni's prized dessert wine, **vinsánto** (reminiscent of the Tuscan *vin santo*), which is among the finest wines produced in Greece and used by the Orthodox Church in Holy Communion. Tour prices at the smaller wineries usually include tastings, while samples are available from the larger wineries for a nominal fee.

**Boutari** Just out of Megalohóri ⊛ boutari.gr. This is the Santorini branch of one of the largest wineries of Greece with an exceptional Estate Argyros Vinsanto, named Best Greek Wine 2009.

**Canava Roussos** Episkopí ⊛ canavaroussos.gr. Making wines since 1836, this is one of the most traditional Greek family wineries producing a famed white called Nyktéri. May–Oct.

**Koutsoyannopoulos** Just outside Kamári ⊛ volcanwines.gr. The best-known winery, it has a 300m-long cellar that's home to a wine museum offering a more intimate glimpse at the wine-making process (April–Oct daily noon–8pm; €4 includes tasting; on Fri evenings there are buffet meals with Greek dancing).

**Santo** Near Pýrgos. April–Nov, 10am–sunset; ⊛ santowines.gr. Offers the most comprehensive tours (€2–3), complete with multimedia presentations.

# Pýrgos

As you drive west of Kamári towards **PÝRGOS** you can't miss the sight of **Panayía Episkopí**, the most important Byzantine monument on the island. Built in the eleventh century, it was the setting of centuries of conflict between Orthodox Greeks and Catholics, but is most notable today for its carved iconostasis of light blue marble with a white grain.

Further west, Pýrgos is one of the oldest settlements on the island, a jumble of weather-beaten houses and alleys that form several concentric circles around the village kástro. It climbs to another Venetian fortress crowned by the seventeenth-century church of the **Presentation of the Virgin**. You can clamber around the battlements for sweeping views over the entire island and its Aegean neighbours.

**6**

### EATING AND DRINKING
### PÝRGOS

**Kallisti** Pýrgos ☎ 22860 34108. If you can't get a table at *Selene* (see below), worry not. This cosy, covered taverna on the main square has excellent cheap food and a tradition of good service; its lamb casserole (€6) literally melts in the mouth. April–Oct daily noon–midnight.

★ **Selene** Pýrgos ☎ 22860 22249, ⊛ selene.gr. Santoríni's most famous restaurant, awarded Greece's top gastronomic accolade in 2011, has moved to Pýrgos from Firá, but still serves delicious, inventive food. Choose from dishes such as rabbit confit, piglet cheeks, cuttlefish in its own ink, vegetable risotto with feta powder (all around €20–€30) or the taster menu from €60 per person. Booking essential. April–Oct daily noon–11pm.

# Akrotíri and the south coast

Evidence of the Minoan colony that once thrived here has been uncovered at the ancient site of Minoan Thira at **AKROTÍRI** (closed since 2005; check with the Museum

---

### THE ARCHIPELAGO

The best and most popular day-trip from Firá is to the three islands of the inner archipelago. Most people stick to the still volcanically active Paleá and Néa Kaméni, although, if you have time, it is worth staying overnight in Thirassía for a glimpse of what Santoríni used to feel like before the cruise ships arrived.

#### PALEÁ AND NÉA KAMÉNI

Local ferries from either Skála Firás or Ía (Ammoúdhi), venture to the charred volcanic islets of **Paleá Kaméni** (active 46–1458 AD) and **Néa Kaméni** (active 1707–1950). At Paleá Kaméni you can swim from the boat to warm mineral-laden springs, while Néa Kaméni (€2 entrance fee), with its own mud-clouded hot springs, features a demanding hike to a smouldering, volcanically active crater.

#### THIRASSÍA

The boat excursions also continue to the relatively unspoilt islet of **Thirassía** (⊛ thirasia.gr), which was once part of Santoríni until sliced off by an eruption in the third century BC. It's an excellent destination, except during the tour-boat rush of lunch hour. At other times, the island is one of the quietest in the Cyclades, with views as dramatic as any on Santoríni. The downside is that there is no proper beach and the tavernas in Kórfos close early after the last ferry has gone. There is an ATM at the Citizen's Service office (KEP) and credit cards are normally not accepted on the island.

Tour boats head for the village of **Kórfos**, a stretch of shingle backed by fishermen's houses and high cliffs while ferries dock at **Ríva**. There should be no problem taking a car or rental bike over, but fill up with petrol first. From Kórfos a steep, stepped path climbs up to **Manolás**, nearly 200m above, where donkeys are still used for transport. Manolás straggles along the edge of the caldera, an attractive small village that gives an idea of what Santoríni was like before tourism arrived there.

### ACCOMMODATION

**Zacharo Rooms** Manolás ☎ 22860 29102. All rooms have a/c, private bathroom and TV with amazing views over both Manolás, Kórfos and Santoríni itself. No credit cards accepted. Easter–Oct. **€45**

---

of Prehistoric Thira in Firá; see p.436), at the southwestern tip of the island; the site was inhabited from the Late Neolithic period through to the seventeenth century BC.

**Kókkini Ámmos** (Red Beach) is about 500m from the site and is quite spectacular, with high reddish-brown cliffs above sand of the same colour. It's a better beach than the one below the site, but gets crowded in season. More secluded black-sand beaches lie under the surreal, pockmarked pumice stone that dominates the lunar coast around **Cape Exomýtis** at the island's southern extremity. Both **Vlyhádha** to the west and **Áyios Yeóryios** to the east of the cape are accessed by decent roads branching off from the main one to Embório, though no buses run here and there are no amenities to speak of. An hour's walk west of ancient Akrotíri, a lighthouse marks the tip of **Cape Akrotíri**, which offers better views of the caldera than even Ía itself.

### ACCOMMODATION AND EATING                                    AKROTÍRI AND THE SOUTH COAST

**Caldera View Resort Megalohóri** ☎ 22860 82010, ⓦ calderaview-santorini.com. Situated 2km from Akrotíri and very near the Red Beach, this modern bungalow complex, only opened in May 2011, has arguably better sunset and caldera views than any other location on the island. June–Sept. **€90**

**Delfinia** Akrotíri ☎ 22860 81151. Wonderfully situated at the water's edge, just below the bus stop, this is a grill taverna that offers fresh seafood and the catch of the day. Try the lightly fried calamari (€15), which is perfectly cooked. Daily noon–10pm.

# Anáfi

A ninety-minute boat ride to the east of Santoríni, **ANÁFI** is the last stop for ferries and is something of a travellers' dead end. It was so for the Argonauts who prayed to Apollo for some land to rest; he let the island emerge from the sea for their repose. If rest is what you crave, you'll have it here in abundance. Not that this is likely to bother most of the visitors, who come here for weeks in midsummer to enjoy exactly that: its seclusion. Although idyllic geographically, Anáfi is a harsh place, its mixed granite and limestone core overlaid by volcanic rock spewed out by Santoríni's eruptions. Apart from the few olive trees and vines grown in the valleys, the only plants that seem to thrive are prickly pears. The quiet, unassuming capital, **Hóra**, provides a daring dash of white in a treeless, shrub-strewn hillock, its narrow, winding streets offering protection from the occasionally squally *gharbís* wind that comes unencumbered from the southwest.

## The beaches

The glory of Anáfi is a string of south-facing beaches starting under the cliffs at

**Áyios Nikólaos**. These – along with two nearby monasteries – are accessible by bus, although walking is still an option. The nearest beach is **Klisídhi**, east of the harbour, which has 200m of gently shelving sand. The next big beach is **Roúkounas** with some 500m of broad sand rising to tamarisk-stabilized dunes; the craggy hill of **Kastélli**, an hour's scramble above the beach, is the site both of ancient Anáfi and a ruined Venetian castle. Beyond Roúkounas, it's another half-hour on foot to the first of the exquisite half-dozen coves at **Kateloumátsa**, of all shapes and sizes, and forty-five minutes to **Monastíri**, where the bus stops – all without facilities, so come prepared.

# The monasteries

**Monastíri** in Anáfi means the **monastery of Zoödhóhou Piyís**. The bus stops only a few hundred metres before the building. A ruined temple of Apollo, supposedly built by the grateful Argonauts, is incorporated into the monastery, while the courtyard, with a welcome cistern, is the venue for the island's major festivals, celebrated eleven days after Easter and September 7–8. Go left immediately before the monastery to join the spectacular onward path to **Kalamiótissa**, another monastery perched atop the abrupt limestone pinnacle at the extreme southeast of the island. It takes another hour to reach, but is eminently worthwhile for the stunning scenery and views over the entire south coast – there is no accessible water up here, so bring enough with you.

**6**

## ARRIVAL AND INFORMATION             ANÁFI

**By ferry** All ferries dock at the small port of Áyios Nikólaos. Buses always wait for ferries to take them to Hóra (5min). Destinations Chalki (1 weekly; 10hr); Iráklion (1 weekly; 3hr 30min); Folégandhros (4 weekly; 4hr 30min); Íos (4 weekly; 3hr); Kárpathos/Kássos (2–3 weekly; 5–10hr); Kéa/Lávrio (2 weekly; 14–15hr); Mílos (1 weekly; 7hr 30min); Mýkonos (1 weekly; 6hr 30min); Náxos (2–3 weekly; 5hr 30min); Páros (3 weekly; 6–7hr); Pireás (2 weekly; 9–11hr); Rhodes (2 weekly; 12hr); Santoríni (5–6 weekly; 1hr 30min); Síkinos (2–3 weekly; 3hr); Sýros (2–3 weekly; 7hr).

**Pharmacy** There is no pharmacy on the island (some drugs are dispensed from the GP's practice).

**Services** There is an ATM in Hóra, and the island's only post office.

**Travel agents** Jeyzed Travel (☎ 22860 61253, ✉ jeyzed @san.forthnet.gr) sell boat tickets and arrange excursions around the island.

## GETTING AROUND

**By bus** There are buses from Hóra to Áyios Nikólaos (7–8 daily; 15min) and Monastíri (3–4 daily) via the beaches.

**By car and motorcycle** You can rent both cars and motorbikes at Margarita's (☎ 22860 61292) or Panorama (☎ 22860 61292).

## ACCOMMODATION

**Apollon** Village Klisídhi ☎ 22860 28739, ⓦ apollonvillage.gr. Fifteen minutes outside Hóra, this complex has twelve elegant maisonettes on the hillside overlooking Klisídhi beach each named after the 12 Olympian gods and every one designed accordingly. Breakfast included. May–Sept. **€70**

**Ta Plágia Hóra** ☎ 22860 61308, ⓦ taplagia.gr. Rooms (with ceiling fans) and studios with kitchenette (and a/c) for up to four people (€70) with own balconies and unhindered pelagic views. Internet and good home-made breakfasts charged separately. May–Sept. **€40**

## EATING AND DRINKING

**Alexandhra** Hóra ☎ 22860 61212. A good, solid restaurant, as laidback as the island itself, offering both grilled fresh fish and seafood by the kilo as well as casseroles and prepared dishes (€6). Daily 9am–11pm.

**Liotrivi** Hóra ☎ 22860 61209. A good family taverna where you are invited to come to the kitchen and choose among the prepared dishes (€9) or pick up the fresh ingredients for your own individual fish soup, which is then cooked on the spot. May–Sept daily noon–midnight.

# Crete

**448** Central Crete

**467** Eastern Crete

**482** Réthymnon and around

**492** Western Crete

SITÍA HARBOUR

# Crete

Crete (Kríti) is a great deal more than just another Greek island. In many places, especially in the cities or along the developed north coast, it doesn't feel like an island at all, but rather a substantial land in its own right. Which of course it is – a precipitous, wealthy and at times surprisingly cosmopolitan one with a tremendous and unique history. At the same time, it has everything you could want of a Greek island and more: great beaches, remote hinterlands and hospitable people.

With enough land for agriculture (and some surprisingly good vineyards), it's one of the few Greek islands that could probably support itself without visitors. Nevertheless, tourism is an important part of the economy, particularly exploited along the **north coast**, where many resorts cater almost exclusively to rowdy young revellers lured by thumping bars and cheap booze. The quieter, less commercialized resorts and villages lie at either end of the island – west, towards **Haniá** and the smaller, less well-connected places along the south and west coasts, or east around Sitía. The **high mountains** of the interior are still barely touched by tourism.

Of the cities, sprawling **Iráklion** often gives a poor first impression of the island but is well worth a visit for its excellent archeological museum. It's also close to the fabulous Minoan sites of **Knossos**, **Phaestos** and **Ayía Triádha** to the south (with Roman Gortys to provide contrast). Further east, the upmarket resort of **Áyios Nikólaos** provides sophisticated restaurants and hotels, while quiet, lazy **Sitía** is a perfect base for exploring the eastern coastline. Heading west, **Réthymnon** boasts a pretty old town and an excellent beach, though **Haniá** in the extreme west arguably beats it in terms of style and atmosphere. South of here is the **Samariá Gorge**, one of the best hikes in the country.

In terms of **climate**, Crete has by far the longest summers in Greece, and you can get a decent tan here right into October and swim at least from May until early November. The one seasonal blight is the *meltémi*, a northerly wind, which regularly blows harder and more continuously here than anywhere else in Greece – the locals may welcome its cooling effects, but it's another reason (along with crowds and heat) to avoid an August visit if you can.

### Brief history

Crete is distinguished above all as the home of Europe's earliest civilization, the **Minoans**. They had a remarkably advanced society, and formed the centre of a maritime trading empire as early as 2000 BC (see p.761). The island's strategic position between east and west has since continued to play a major role in its history. Control of the island passed from **Greeks** to **Romans** to **Saracens**, through the **Byzantine empire** to **Venice**, and finally to Turkey for more than two centuries. During **World War II**, Crete was occupied by the Germans and attained the dubious distinction of being the first place to be successfully invaded by paratroops.

Adventure sports p.450
The legend of the Minotaur p.457
Wine tasting in Crete p.462
Climbing Mount Psilorítis p.467

Island escape: Gaidhouronísi p.481
Hiking the Amári valley p.490
Festival island p.499
Ecotourism in Crete p.504

SAMARIÁ GORGE

# Highlights

**Archeological Museum, Iráklion** The world's foremost Minoan museum. Following a substantial renovation, the museum is set to reopen in 2012. **See p.452**

**Knossos** The Minoan palace of Knossos is the standout archeological site on the island. **See p.457**

**Paleóhora** With bags of charm and excellent strands, this resort in the far east of the island is well worth seeking out. **See p.502**

**Lasíthi Plateau** This fertile high mountain plateau has picturesque agricultural villages and unique white-cloth-sailed windmills. **See p.473**

**The Dhiktean Cave** Mythological birthplace of Zeus, stunningly situated on the Lasíthi Plateau. **See p.473**

**Haniá old town** Atmospheric city centre where vibrant modern life coexists with the beautiful architectural legacies of Venetian and Turkish history. **See p.492**

**Samariá Gorge** A magnificent gorge, offering a chance to see brilliant wild flowers, golden eagles and perhaps a Cretan ibex. **See p.499**

**Southwest coast** Having made it through the Samariá Gorge, some of Crete's least-visited coastline awaits. **See p.501**

HIGHLIGHTS ARE MARKED ON THE MAP ON PP.448–449

## ARRIVAL AND DEPARTURE

**By plane** Crete has two international airports, Iráklion (Heraklion) and Haniá (Chania), both served by direct flights from the UK and Europe between April and October. Daily flights from mainland Athens operate year-round to Iráklion, Haniá and Sitía with Aegean Airways and Olympic Air.

**By ferry** There are daily year-round ferry connections from Pireás to both Iráklion and Haniá with ANEK Lines and Minoan Lines, and there are also ferries to Kastélli in the west and Sitía in the east.

## GETTING AROUND

**By bus** There are excellent connections across most of Crete, regular fast buses run along the north-coast highway, and the south coast is served, less frequently, with connections from the main hubs of Iráklion, Áyios Nikólaos, Réthymnon and Haniá.

**By car or motorcycle** The main routes across the island and south are generally well surfaced and fairly well signposted. Beware of heading off on unsurfaced roads, particularly on mountain tracks, which often just peter out before coming to a dead end.

## INFORMATION

**Maps** The best maps for driving are the German-produced Harms-Verlag (wharms-ic-verlag.de), which cover the island (east and west) in two separate maps at a scale of 1:100,000. For hiking try the 1:25,000-scale Crete Hiking Maps series (Anavasi; wmountains.gr); both are widely available from bookshops on the island.

# Central Crete

The hub of central Crete is the capital city, **Iráklion**, a busy but convenient base for visits to the nearby Minoan palace of **Knossos**. The area immediately around the city is

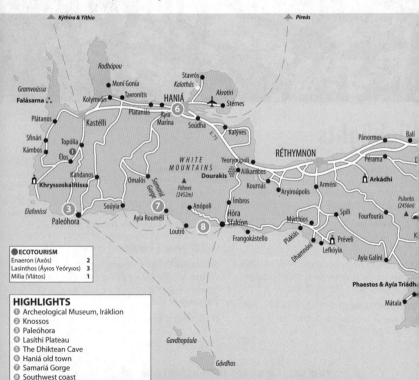

**ECOTOURISM**
Enaeron (Axós)  2
Lasinthos (Áyios Yeóryios)  3
Milia (Vlátos)  1

**HIGHLIGHTS**
1 Archeological Museum, Iráklion
2 Knossos
3 Paleóhora
4 Lasíthi Plateau
5 The Dhiktean Cave
6 Haniá old town
7 Samariá Gorge
8 Southwest coast

ess touristy than you might expect, mainly because there are few decent beaches of any
ize on the adjacent coast. To the west, mountains drop straight into the sea virtually all
he way to Réthymnon, with just two significant coastal settlements: **Ayia Pelayia**, and
he more attractive **Bali**. Eastwards, the main resorts are at least 30km away, at
Iersónissos and beyond, although there is a string of rather unattractive developments
ll the way there. **Inland**, there's agricultural country, some of the richest on the island,
 cluster of Crete's better vineyards and a series of wealthy villages. To the south lie the
ites of **Gortys**, **Phaestos** and **Ayía Triádha** which can all be visited in a day, with a
unchtime swim on the south coast at **Mátala** or Léndas thrown in.

# ráklion

Crete's biggest city, **IRÁKLION** (Heraklion) is a hectic place, a maelstrom of bustle,
oise and traffic-congested thoroughfares. On the positive side, though, the city
oes have superb fortifications, a fine market, atmospheric old alleys and some
nteresting lesser museums. Virtually everything you're likely to want to see lies
vithin the northeastern corner of the walled city. The most vital thoroughfare,
5-Avgoústou, links the harbour with the commercial city centre. Further up
5-Avgoústou, **Kalokerinoú** leads down to Haniá Gate and westwards out of the
ity; straight ahead, **Odhós-1821** is a major shopping street, and adjacent **Odhós-
866** is given over to the animated street market, perhaps the best on the island. To
he left, **Dhikeosínis** heads for the city's main square, **Platía Eleftherías**, paralleled by
he pedestrian alley, **Dedhálou**, lined with many of the city's swankier fashion stores
nd the direct link between the two squares.

## ADVENTURE SPORTS

With its temperate climate and varied topography Crete is a great place for **adventure holidays**, and there are numerous companies across the island offering everything from mountain biking and canyoning to trekking and horseriding. Here's a selection of what's on offer. Watersports and diving operators are also listed throughout the chapter.

### CLIMBING/ADRENALINE SPORTS

**Liquid Bungy** ☎ 693 76 15 191, ⓦ bungy.gr. White-knuckle bungee jumping (Europe's second highest) at the Arádhena Gorge, Haniá.

**Trekking Plan** ☎ 28210 60861, ⓦ cycling.gr. Rock climbing, mountaineering, canyoning, rapelling, kayaking and mountain biking in Haniá province.

### HORSERIDING

**Melanouri** ☎ 28920 45040, ⓦ melanouri.com. Horseriding holidays (one to seven days) from a stable near Mátala.

**Odysseia** ☎ 28970 51080, ⓦ horseriding.gr. One-to six-day guided and unguided horse treks from their base at Avdhoú near the Lasíthi Plateau.

**Zoraïda's Horseriding** ☎ 28250 61745, ⓦ zoraidas -horseriding.com. Horseriding holidays and treks from their stables in Yeoryoúpoli, Haniá.

### WALKING AND CYCLING

**Alpine Travel** ☎ 28210 50939, ⓦ alpine.gr. Hiking, rock climbing, sea kayaking and biking holidays (or combinations thereof) in Haniá province.

**Cretan Adventures** ☎ 28103 33772, ⓦ cretan adventures.gr. Hiking, horseriding and jeep safaris throughout Crete.

**The Happy Walker** Tombázi 56, Réthymnon ☎ 28310 52920, ⓦ happywalker.com. Walking tours from one day to two weeks from €30 (for the day-hike which includes minibus from your hotel to start point).

**Hellas Bike** ☎ 28210 60858, ⓦ hellasbike.net. One- to seven-day bike tours from Ayía Marína in Haniá province.

**Korifi Tours** ☎ 28930 41440, ⓦ korifi.de. Hiking and climbing holidays in central, southern and western Crete.

**Olympic Bike** Adelianos Kampos 32, Réthymnon ☎ 28310 72383, ⓦ olympicbike.com. Guided bike tours from €139 for three one-day trips, or bike rental only from €20 per day.

**Strata Walking Tours** ☎ 28220 24336, ⓦ stratatours.com. Guided trekking holidays in the Kastélli Kissamou area of Haniá.

## City walls and fortifications

The massive **Venetian walls**, in places up to 15m thick, are the most obvious evidence of Iráklion's history. Though their fabric is incredibly well preserved, access is virtually nonexistent. It is possible to scramble up and walk along them from Áyios Andhréas Bastion over the sea in the west, as far as the Martinengo Bastion and the **tomb of Nikos Kazantzakis**, Cretan author of *Zorba the Greek*, whose epitaph reads: "I believe in nothing, I hope for nothing, I am free." If the walls seem altogether too much effort, the **port fortifications** are much easier to see; the Venetian **arsenáli** (arsenals), their arches rather lost amid the concrete road system all around, and, opposite, the **fortress** at the harbour entrance.

## Venetian fortress

The impressive sixteenth-century **Venetian fortress**, known by its Turkish name of **Koúles**, stands at the harbour entrance; emblazoned with the Venetian Lion of St Mark it withstood a 22-year siege before finally falling to the Ottomans. Unfortunately the siege of time has caught up with the underwater foundations – in early 2011 the building was deemed unsafe and closed to visitors for an expected two- to three-year renovation programme; once completed, it should once again be possible to stroll out along the jetty, explore the interior and enjoy the views from the top floor.

## 25-Avgoústou Street and around

Heading inland from the harbour the pedestrianized **25-Avgoústou Street** is lined with shipping and travel agencies, a few restaurants, banks and stores. **El Greco Park**, to the right as you approach Platía Venizélou, is crowded with cafés and bars, while opposite, on the left, are some of the more interesting of Iráklion's older buildings including the

CENTRAL IRÁKLION

**ACCOMMODATION**

| | |
|---|---|
| Atrion | 4 |
| Creta Camping | 8 |
| Galaxy Hotel | 11 |
| Hellas Rooms | 9 |
| Kastro | 6 |
| Kronos | 1 |
| Lato | 3 |
| Lena | 2 |
| Olympic | 10 |
| Rea | 7 |
| Youth Hostel | 5 |

**DRINKING & NIGHTLIFE**

| | |
|---|---|
| Big Fish | 3 |
| Fashion | 10 |
| Korais | 9 |
| Mayo | 8 |
| Pagopiion | 7 |
| Privilege | 5 |
| Room 109 | 2 |
| Route 66 | 4 |
| Senses Club | 1 |
| Take Five | 6 |

**EATING**

| | |
|---|---|
| I Avli tou Deikaliona | 4 |
| Giakoumis | 9 |
| Ippokampos | 2 |
| Ta Ladadika | 10 |
| Liasti | 11 |
| Ligo Thalassa | 7 |
| Loukoulos | 5 |
| The Mexican | 1 |
| Pagopiion | 6 |
| Peri Orexeos | 8 |
| Ouzerie Terzaki | 3 |

7

**church of Áyios Títos** and the Venetian city hall with its famous **loggia**, both almost entirely rebuilt. Just above this, facing Platía Venizélou, stands the **church of San Marco**, its steps usually crowded with sightseers spilling over from the nearby platía. Neither of these last two buildings has found a permanent role in its refurbished state, but both are generally open to house some kind of exhibition or craft show.

Platía Venizélou

The focal **Platía Venizélou**, also known as **Liontária** or Lion Square, is crowded most of the day with locals patronizing its café terraces. The **Morosini Fountain** is not particularly spectacular at first glance, but on closer inspection is really a very beautiful work; it was built by Venetian governor Francesco Morosini in the seventeenth century, incorporating four lions which were some three hundred years old even then.

Platía Eleftherías

**Platía Eleftherías**, with seats shaded by palms and eucalyptuses, is the traditional heart of the city; traffic swirls around it constantly, on summer evenings crowds of strolling locals come to fill its café terraces, and most of Iráklion's more expensive shops are in the streets leading off here. At the southeastern corner of the platía an underground entrance to the **Gateway of St George** – a recently restored sixteenth-century tunnel and vault housing small art exhibitions – connects the platía with Ikárou Avenue.

## The archeological museum

Xanthoudhídhou and Hatzidhaki, off Platía Eleftherías • May, June, Oct Mon noon–5pm; Tues–Sun 8.30am–5pm; July–Sept Mon 1–8pm, Tues–Sun 8am–8pm; Nov–April Mon noon–3pm, Tues–Sun 8.30am–3pm (check times with the tourist office) • €4 • ☎ 2810 224 630

Iráklion's **archeological museum** is one of Greece's largest; almost every important prehistoric and Minoan find on Crete is included in this fabulous, if bewilderingly large, collection. Hopefully, the current refurbishment (see box below) will be a huge improvement on the museum's previously dreary presentation. The size of the collection means that it's not possible to see everything in one visit, and the museum tends to be crowded – especially when guided tours stampede through – but it's certainly worth taking time over.

A number of the main exhibits from the collection are on display in the temporary museum annexe; highlights include the "**Town Mosaic**" and fragments of the spectacular "**Bull Leaping**" from Knossos, the famous **Festos disc** from Festos Palace, a **bull's head rhyton** (drinking vessel), the **snake goddess**, and a collection of jewellery including the **pendant of the two bees** from the Palace of Mália.

## Church of Ayía Ekateríni

Ayía Ekateríni Square • Museum daily 9.30am–3.30pm • €2

The **church of Ayía Ekateríni**, an ancient building just below the new **Áyios Minas cathedral** off Kalokerinoú, has an excellent collection of icons in its **Ecclesiastical Museum**. The finest here are six large scenes by Mihaïl Damaskinos (a near contemporary of Cretan painter Doménikos Theotokópoulos, better known as El Greco), who fused Byzantine and Renaissance influences. Supposedly both Damaskinos and El Greco studied at Ayía Ekateríni in the sixteenth century, before the latter moved to Spain, when it functioned as a sort of monastic art school.

Iráklion's archeological museum closed in 2007 for complete **refurbishment**, with a temporary exhibition established at the rear of the building while work took place. The proposed two-year completion date proved hopelessly optimistic (it took four years just to approve the plans) but a section of the new museum is expected to open sometime during 2012 with full reopening pencilled in for 2013.

## Historical Museum

Sofokli Venizélou 27 • May–Oct Mon–Sat 9am–5pm, Nov–April Mon–Sat 9am–3pm • €5 • ☎ 2810 283 219, ⊛ historical-museum.gr

The **Historical Museum** lies some 300m west of the harbour, on the waterfront. Its display gives a comprehensive view of Cretan history, incorporating sculptures and architectural pieces from the Byzantine, Venetian and Turkish periods as well as documents and photos of the German invasion of Crete, and folklore exhibits. Local memorabilia include the reconstructed studies of both Nikos Kazantzakis and Emanuel Tsouderos (the latter both Cretan statesman and former Greek prime minister). There's enough variety to satisfy just about anyone, including the only **El Greco** paintings on Crete, the small *View of Mount Sinai and the Monastery of St Catherine* and the even smaller *Baptism of Christ*.

## Natural History Museum

Sofokli Venizélou • Mon–Fri 9am–4pm, Sat–Sun 10am–6pm • €6 • ☎ 2810 282 740, ⊛ www.nhmc.uoc.gr

Rehoused in a converted old power plant overlooking the bay of Dermatás, is the excellent **Natural History Museum**, operated under the framework of the University of Crete, and definitely worth a visit. Covering the ecosystems of the eastern Mediterranean, flora and fauna, exhibits over four floors detail the island's geological evolution, the arrival of man and the environment as it would have appeared to the Minoans. There's also an earthquake simulator and a planetarium, as well as a child-oriented Discovery Centre with interactive exhibits.

## The beaches

Iráklion's **beaches** are a short way out, to both the east and west of town. **Ammoudhára** to the west has a large sandy beach that has been subjected to a degree of development, with hotels lining much of the coastal strip; at the far end there's an ugly power station and cement works. **Amnissós**, to the east, is the better choice, with several tavernas and the added amusement of planes swooping in immediately overhead to land at the nearby airport. This is where most locals go on their afternoons off; the furthest of the beaches is the best, although new hotels are encroaching. Little remains to indicate the once-flourishing port of Knossos here, aside from a rather dull, fenced-in dig.

## ARRIVAL AND DEPARTURE                                                    IRÁKLION

### BY PLANE

**Iráklion airport** (Heraklion) (☎ 2810 397 111, ⊛ heraklion-airport.info) is right on the coast, 4km east of the city. Bus #1 goes to the city (every 20min until 11pm; €1.10); buy your ticket at the booth before boarding. Taxis can be found at the airport rank (about €14 into town); prices to all major destinations are posted here.

**Airlines** Aegean, Airport office (☎ 2810 330 475, ⊛ aegeanair.com), and Olympic, 25-Avgoústou 27 (☎ 2810 245 644, ⊛ olympic-airways.com), are the main scheduled airlines with connecting flights to Athens and other parts of Greece. EasyJet and Jet2 operate direct flights from the UK in summer. Charter airlines flying into Iráklion mostly use local travel agents as their representatives.

**Domestic destinations** Athens (12 daily with Olympic and Aegean; 50min); Rhodes (at least 2 daily on Olympic and Sky Express; 1hr); Thessaloníki (at least 2 daily on Olympic, Aegean or Sky Express; 1hr 15min).

**International destinations** Bristol, Leeds-Bradford, London Gatwick and Manchester (easyJet and Jet2 April–Oct).

### BY FERRY

From the port cut straight up the stepped alleys behind the bus station onto Dhoúkos Bofór to Platía Eleftherías (about a 15min walk) or follow the main road west along the coast, past the bus station and the Venetian harbour, then cut up towards the centre along 25-Avgoústou.

**Tickets** Available from Minoan Lines, 25-Avgoústou 78 (☎ 2810 399 800, ⊛ minoan.gr), which handles the islands and Athens; and ANEK Lines, Dhimokratías 11 (☎ 2810 223 067, ⊛ anek.gr), for Athens only; or from any of the travel agents listed on p.451. For the latest timetables for domestic and international ferries to and from Crete visit ⊛ cretetravel.com, ⊛ ferries.gr or ⊛ greekislands.gr.

**Destinations** 2 ferries daily to Pireás (9hr); 1 daily fast catamaran to Thíra-Santorini (April–Oct; 2hr), also fast boats and hydrofoils (2hr 30min); 4–5 weekly ferries to Páros, Mýkonos, Íos and Náxos in season.

### BY BUS

**Bus station A** Near the Venetian harbour. Use this station for buses to: west to Réthymnon, Haniá, east to Hersónissos, Mália, Áyios Nikólaos, Sitía, southeast to Ierápetra and

**7**

points en route. Local bus #2 to Knossos also leaves from here.

**Bus Station B** Haniá Gate, at the beginning of 62-Martyrs street (a very long walk from the centre up Kalokerinoú, or jump on any bus heading down this street). Buses to: southwest to Phaestos, Mátala and Ayía Galíni, inland west to Týlissos, Anóyia.

Destinations Ayía Galíni (7 daily 6.30am–4.30pm; 2hr

15min); Áyios Nikólaos (19 daily 6.30am–10.30pm; 1h 30min); Haniá (16 daily 5.30am–9pm; 2hr 50min, Ierápetra (8 daily 6.45am–7.30pm; 2hr 30min); Mátala daily 7.30am–3.30pm; 2hr 30min); Phaestos (8 dail 7.30am–4.30pm; 1hr 30min); Réthymnon (16 dail 5.30am–9.30pm; 1hr 30min); Sitía (4 daily 7am–5.45pm 3hr 15min).

## GETTING AROUND

**By bus** Local buses serve the beaches: (see p.453)to get to Ammoudhára, take #6 from the stop outside the *Astoria* hotel in Platía Eleftherías; for Amnissós, take #7 from the stop opposite this, under the trees of the platía.

**By car** Driving in busy Iráklion can be stressful. Follow the signs for car parking as soon as you enter the city centre; there's parking at the Museum car park (with another car

park next door if this is full), just off Platía Eleftherías (we signed). There are plenty of car rental offices in town (se p.456).

**Taxis** Major taxi ranks are in Platía Eleftherías, Platí Kornarou and at the bus stations. Alternatively call ☎ 281 210 102 or ☎ 2810 210 168. Prices should be displayed o boards at the taxi stands.

## INFORMATION

**Tourist office** Xanthoudhídhou 1, just below Platía Eleftherías and opposite the Archeological Museum (Mon–Fri: May–Sept 9am–5pm; Oct–April

9am–2.30pm; ☎ 2810 246 298, ⓦ heraklion-city.gr. There's a secondary office at the airport (May–Sept dail 8am–8pm).

## ACCOMMODATION

Finding a room can be difficult in high season. Inexpensive places cluster around Platía Venizélou, along Hándhakos an towards the harbour to the west of 25-Avgoústou. Other concentrations of affordable places are around El Greco Park an in the streets above the Venetian harbour. More luxurious hotels mostly lie closer to Platía Eleftherías and near the east and westbound bus stations.

**Atrion** Hronáki 9 ☎ 2810 246 000, ⓦ atrion.gr. This attractive, modern, minimalistic-style hotel is in a handy location between the port and the centre, rooms are well-equipped with fridge, satellite TV, wi-fi and balcony. Breakfast included. **€80**

**Galaxy Hotel** Dimokratías 75 ☎ 2810 238 812, ⓦ galaxy-hotel.com. Located outside the old city wall, a 10min walk to the centre, this sleek, modern five-star hotel boasts a large pool, two gourmet restaurants and a wellness centre. Rooms are luxurious, with balcony, although some are rather small; allergy-friendly rooms are also available. Excellent buffet breakfast included. **€145**

**Hellas Rooms** Hándhakos 24 ☎ 2810 288 851, ⓔ hellasrooms24@yahoo.gr. A central hostel-type place, clean and friendly, with simple doubles, and dormitory rooms favoured by younger travellers. Facilities include a roof garden (with sea view) and snack-bar. The hotel is open May–Oct. Dorms **€14**

**Kastro** Theotokopoúlou 22 ☎ 82810 284185, ⓦ kastro-hotel.gr. The Kastro has undergone a contemporary restyle with comfortable a/c rooms, flat-screen TV and modern en-suite bathrooms. It's handily located on a side street behind El Greco park, but lacks decent views. Breakfast included. **€80**

**Kronos** Agárthou 2, west of 25-Avgoústou ☎ 2810 28 240, ⓦ kronoshotel.gr. Refurbished in 2011, this friendl two-star hotel is located on a busy street (so some traffi noise) by the central seafront. En-suite rooms with a/c, T fridge and balcony, some with sea view. **€50**

★ **Lato** Epomenídhou 15 ☎ 2810 228 103, ⓦ lato.g Stylish boutique hotel in a great central location opposit the Venetian harbour, with luxurious rooms sporting a/ minibar, TV and fine balcony views over the port (th higher floors have better views). Breakfast included. **€103**

**Lena** Lahaná 10 ☎ 2810 223 280, ⓦ lena-hotel.gr. In quiet, yet central, area, this efficient small hotel, north of E Greco park, offers rooms with balconies, both a/c en-suit rooms and rooms with shared bath and ceiling fan. TV an wi-fi. **€45**

**Olympic** Platía Kornárou, west of Platía Eleftherí ☎ 2810 288 861, ⓦ hotelolympic.com. One of the man hotels built in the 1960s, this one has been beautifull refurbished, and overlooks the busy platía and the famou Bembo fountain; facilities include a/c, TV, minibar an strongbox. Breakfast included. **€78**

**Rea** Kalimeráki 1 ☎ 2810 223 638. A good budge option, this friendly, comfortable and clean *pension* is in quiet area just off Hándakos street. Some rooms wit vashbasin, others en suite. May–Oct. €35

**'outh Hostel** Vyronos 5 @ 2810 286 281, @ heraklio
'outhhostel@yahoo.gr. Formerly Iraklión's official youth
ostel, now privately operated, this is a reasonable and
conomical option. There's plenty of space, some private
ooms as well as dormitories, with hot showers, breakfast
nd other meals available. May–Oct. Dorms €10

**CAMPING**

**Creta Camping** Káto Goúves, 16km east of the city
@ 2897 041 400. Sits at the western end of the long sandy
Káto Goúves beach, and offers some shady pitches (not all)
and simple facilities. If you don't have your own equipment
you can rent a tent or a cabin. €25

**EATING**

t's best to avoid the main tourist cafés around the platíes Venizélou and Eleftherias, which are generally both expensive
nd mediocre. Authentic and inexpensive **ouzerís** huddle near the 1866 market street and round Platía Dhaskaloyiánni
near the archeological museum), while other good **restaurants** are on, and just off, the seafront. For **snacks** and
akeaways, a group of *souvláki* and other fast-food joints clusters around the top of 25-Avgoústou, and for *tyrópita* and
panakópita* (cheese or spinach pies) and other pastries there is no shortage of bakery shops.

★ **Giakoumis** Fótiou Theodosáki 5, in the market
@ 2810 284 039. Established in 1935, this is the city's
oldest taverna and locals claim it serves up the best
païdhákia (lamb chops) on the island – some tribute given
he competition. You can wash them down with the hyma
house) wine produced by Lyrarakis, a noted Pezá vineyard.
Païdhákia €7.50. Mon–Sat 10am–late.

★ **I Avli tou Deikaliona** Kalokairinoú 8, at the rear of
he Historical Museum @ 2810 244 215. Popular taverna,
with a lovely little terrace fronting the Idomeneus
Fountain, serving up well-prepared meat and fish dishes. In
high summer you may need to book to ensure an outdoor
table. Grills from €6.50. Daily, dinner only.

★ **Ippokampos** Sófokli Venizélou, west of
25-Avgoústou, close to the Kronos hotel @ 2810 280 240.
Deservedly popular with locals for lunch mezédhes as well as
dinner, this fish taverna is often crowded late into the evening;
turn up early to snag a table. Has a pleasant shaded terrace
over the road on the seafront. Mon–Sat, lunch & dinner.

**Liasti** Miliara 7, south of the central zone @ 2810 343
490. At the end of an alley with a terrace under the trees
– in the centre of town, just off Evans, yet away from the
main hustle and bustle of traffic. This new *mezedhopolío*
(formerly *Embolo*) produces many original dishes, with
reasonable prices; try the pork shank with honey (€8), the
house speciality. There's also indoor dining for the cooler
months. Mon–Sat 1pm–1am.

**Ligo Thálassa** At the foot of Marinéli near the Venetian
fort @ 2810 300 501. This small ouzerí is very popular
with locals and serves up a good selection of seafood
mezédhes, with a small street terrace facing the harbour.
Daily 1pm–1am.

**Loukoulos** Koraí 5 @ 2810 224 435. With a leafy
courtyard terrace and an Italian slant to its international
menu, this is one of the better tavernas in Iráklion.
However, the pricey food (mains from €15) and wine list
seem aimed more at luring Iráklion's smart set than the
casual visitor. Daily noon–1am.

**The Mexican** Hándhakos 71 @ 2810 220 334. The red
and orange ethnic decor creates a warm atmosphere in this
eatery, which serves inexpensive Mexican tacos, beers and
jugs of sangria, complemented by salads and bean dishes.
Daily lunch & dinner.

**Ouzerie Terzáki** Marinéli 17 @ 2810 221 444. This place
is a favourite among local city-types, and serves mezédhes,
pasta dishes and mains such as chicken fillet stuffed with
spinach and mushrooms, on the outdoor street terrace.
Mezédhes from €6. Daily noon–late.

★ **Pagopiion** Platía Áyios Títos @ 2810 346 028. This
is the pricier restaurant of Iráklion's most original bar,
serving Cretan and international dishes to a high standard;
the wine list includes interesting bottles from little-known
but excellent small vineyards around the island. Mains
€15–20. Daily noon–late.

**Peri Orexeos** Koraí 10, almost opposite Loukoulos
@ 2810 222 679. This popular small taverna is a good bet
for creative Cretan cooking, with dishes such as burger
stuffed with feta, red pepper and olives. Mains from €7.
Daily noon–1am.

**Ta Ladádika** Tzikritzi 5, near the market @ 2810 346
135. Welcoming little ouzerí in a small pedestrianized
street, with outdoor tables. Excellent mezédhes – try their
dolmadhákia €4.50 – and local house wine from the barrel.
Mon–Sat, 10am–late.

**7**

**DRINKING AND NIGHTLIFE**

As a university town, Iráklion has plenty of places to let your hair down. Young Cretans tend to be more into sitting
and chatting over background music than energetic dancing; consequently large areas of **Koráï** and the surrounding
pedestrianized streets are packed with alfresco cafés which transform into bars as the lights dim and the volume
ramps up. In addition to the central zone nightlife, venues are also in the suburbs and out along the hotel strip to the
west at Amoudhára.

## BARS

**Fashion** Perdhíkari 3 ☎ 2810 241 903. A large, trendy music café-bar that's cloned numerous similar places nearby. On summer weekends, this is the place to be if you're under 30. Daily 9am–3am.

**Korais** Koraí 3 ☎ 2810 346 336. Glitzy open-air café with spacious plant-festooned terraces, overhead movie screens and soft rock music – highly popular with Iráklion's smart set. Daily 10am–3am.

**Mayo** Milátou 11, just north of Korai ☎ 2810 336 000. This extravaganza of a bar with spotlights, screens and music under a big canopy terrace is one of the places to be seen if you're part of Iráklion's student set. Its arrival has spawned a whole new set of bars and cafés along the same street. Daily 9am–3am.

**Pagopiion** (Ice Factory) Platía Áyios Títos ☎ 2810 346 028. Stunning bar with arty decor inside Iráklion's former ice factory. Much of the old building has been preserved, including a lift for hauling the ice from the basement freezer and a fascistic call to duty in German Gothic script on one wall – a remnant of Nazi occupation of the factory in World War II. Make sure to visit the toilets, which are in an artistic league of their own. Daily 9am–late.

**Route 66** Hándakos 46. This small rock bar attracts a slightly older crowd, and blasts out rock classics into the night. Also opens as a café during the day, with a couple of tables on the pedestrianized street outside. Daily noon–late.

**Take Five** Arkoléontos 7, El Greco Park ☎ 2810 226 564.

One of the oldest bars in Iráklion, it began as a rock bar i[n] the 1980s and is now a slick pavement café with an indo[or] bar, playing mainstream music that ramps up the volum[e] as the night goes on. Daily 9am–4am.

## CLUBS AND DISCOS

Discos and clubs proper tend to play Western music (and lo[ts] of techno) interspersed with Greek pop. Some of the club[s] proper don't open their doors before 11pm, with the crowd[s] drifting in after 1am and dancing until dawn. For livelier, an[d] earlier, partying head to one of the nearby resorts.

**Big Fish** Corner of Sófokli Venizélou & Makarios 1[?] ☎ 697 32 36 922. Popular late-night dance club, wit[h] theme evenings, international and Greek music, an[d] occasional live performers. Daily 9pm–late.

**Privilege** Dhoúkos Bofór 7, down towards the harbou[r] below the archeological museum ☎ 2810 244 850. [A] glitzy mainstream club, which opens at midnight in th[e] summer months – you can dance until the sun rise[s.] Entrance €10 including a drink.

**Room 109** Sófokli Venizélou 109 ☎ 2810 261 615[.] Fashionable and cool late-night bar on the seafront road[,] hosting various dance-themed nights, including Latin an[d] house nights. Daily 9pm–late.

**Senses Club** Papandréou 277, Ammoudára ☎ 2810 82[?] 059. A lively summer club with a party atmosphere, 5km wes[t] of the city, by Ammoudára beach, playing variou[s] international music including dance & R&B. Daily 9pm–late[.]

## DIRECTORY

**Banks** There are ATMs all over town, but the main bank branches are on 25-Avgoústou.

**Car and motorbike rental** 25-Avgoústou is lined with rental companies, but you'll often find good deals on the backstreets nearby; it's always worth asking for discounts. For cars and bikes try: Blue Sea, Kosmá Zótou 7, just off the bottom of 25-Avgoústou (☎ 2810 241 097, ⓦ bluesea rentals.com), Kosmos, 25-Avgoústou 15 (☎ 2810 241 357, ⓦ cosmos-sa.gr), or the nearby Caravel, 25-Avgoústou 39 (☎ 2810 245 345, ⓦ caravel.gr); and Ritz in the *Hotel Rea*, Kalimeráki 1 (☎ 2810 223 638). All offer free delivery to hotels and airport.

**Hospital** The closest is the Venizélou Hospital, on the Knossós road south out of town (☎ 2810 368 000).

**Internet** Two central cafés are Netcafé, Odhós-1878 4 (daily 10am–2am), and Gallery Games, Koráï 14. Many cafés and hotels offer free wi-fi.

**Laundry** Washsalon, Hándhakos 18 (Mon–Sat 8.30am–9pm), is reliable and also does service washes (around €7 for 6kg). The slightly cheaper (around €6 for 6kg) Laundry Perfect at Malikoúti 32, north of the archeological museum, is also good (Mon–Sat 9am–9pm).

**Left luggage** Offices in (bus) Station A (daily 6.30am–8pm; €2 per bag per day), but not Station B, as well as a commercial

agency at Hándhakos 18 (daily 9am–9pm; €3 per larg[e] locker per day). Blue Sea, Kotzia 3 off Epimenidhou, near th[e] Venetian harbour (daily 7am–11pm), is a reliable and simila[r] outfit and stores bags for €3 per day. You can also leave bag[s] at the youth hostel (see p.455); €3 per bag per day for guests[,] €5 per bag per day for non-guests.

**Newspapers and books** For English-languag[e] newspapers and novels, Bibliopoleio, almost opposite th[e] Morosini Fountain on Platía Venizélou, is the most centra[l.] The excellent Planet International Bookstore, near th[e] seafront at Hándhakos 73, has the island's biggest stock o[f] English-language titles and is a great place to browse.

**Pharmacies** Plentiful on the main shopping streets – a[t] least one is open 24hr on a rota basis; the others will have [a] sign on the door indicating which it is. There are tradition[al] herbalists in the market.

**Post office** Platía Dhaskaloyiánnis, off Platía Eleftherí[as] (Mon–Fri 7.30am–8pm, Sat 7.30am–2pm).

**Travel agencies** Budget operators and student specialist[s] include the extremely helpful Blavakis Travel, Platí[a] Kallergón 8, just off 25-Avgoústou by the entrance to E[l] Greco Park (☎ 2810 282 541). Ferry information and ticket[s] from Paleologos Travel, 25-Avgoústou 5 (☎ 2810 346 185[,] ⓦ ferries.gr).

# Knossos

Daily: May–June 8am–5pm; July–Sept 8am–8pm; Oct–April 8.30am–3pm • €6 • ☎ 2810 231 940

KNOSSOS, the largest and most important of the **Minoan palaces**, and the most visited, lies some 5km southeast of Iráklion. The mythological home of King Minos and the Minotaur, it dates from the second millennium BC, and its vast interconnected rooms and corridors provide a fitting backdrop to the legend.

The discovery of the palace is among the most amazing tales of modern archeology. **Heinrich Schliemann**, the German excavator of Troy, suspected that a major Minoan palace lay under the various tumuli here, but was denied the permission to dig by the local Ottoman authorities. It was left for **Sir Arthur Evans** who excavated and liberally "restored" the palace from 1900 onwards. His restorations have been the source of furious controversy among archeologists ever since. Even so, his guess as to what the palace might have looked like is certainly as good as anyone's, and it makes Crete's other Minoan sites infinitely more meaningful if you have seen Knossos first.

## ARRIVAL AND INFORMATION KNOSSOS

**7**

To avoid the hordes get to the site early morning, before the coach tours arrive, or late afternoon when they've left

**By bus** Local buses #2 and #4. Set off (every 10min) from Iráklion's city bus stands (adjacent to the eastbound Bus Station A), then proceed to Platía Eleftherías and out of town along Odhós-1821 and Evans).
From the centre of Iráklion a taxi will cost around €10.
**By car** There's a free car park immediately before the site entrance, which will enable you to avoid paying exorbitant rates for the private car parks dotting the road immediately before this (and whose touts will attempt to wave you in).

**Guided tours** Official guides can be hired at the site entrance; they are self-employed and expensive, but you can usually negotiate the price a little if you wish to use their services, and rope in other visitors to share the cost.
**Websites** The British School at Athens has a useful website dedicated to Knossos, with detail on its history and excavations in addition to a virtual tour; check out ⓦ bsa.gla.ac.uk/knossos/vrtour.

## The site

As soon as you enter the **Palace of Knossos** through the West Court, the ancient ceremonial entrance, it is clear how the legends of the labyrinth grew up around it. Even with a detailed plan, it's almost impossible to find your way around the complex with any success, although a series of **timber walkways** channels visitors around the site, severely restricting the scope for independent exploration. If you haven't hired a guide and are worried about missing the highlights, you can always tag along with a group

---

### THE LEGEND OF THE MINOTAUR

Knossos was the court of the legendary **King Minos**, whose wife Pasiphae, cursed by Poseidon, bore the **Minotaur**, half-bull, half-man. The **labyrinth** was constructed by Daedalus to contain the monster, and every nine years seven youths and seven maidens were brought from Athens as human sacrifice. Hearing of this, the Greek hero **Theseus** arrived on Crete vowing to venture into the labyrinth and slay the beast. **Ariadne**, daughter of the king, promptly fell in love with him and, as every cub scout knows, showed Theseus how to find his way back using a simple ball of thread. The legend has inspired writers from Homer to Dante, who famously depicts the best in his vision of Hell:

*Into the chasm was that descent: and there*
*At point of the disparted ridge lay stretch'd*
*The infamy of Crete, detested brood*
*Of the feign'd heifer: and at sight of us*
*It gnaw'd itself, as one with rage distract.*

Dante, Inferno, Canto XII

**PALACE OF KNOSSOS**

Royal Road

Theatral Area

N

North Entrance

Lustral Basin

Bull Relief

West Court

Giant "Pithoi"

Storage Pits

Throne Room

Piano
Nobile

Workshops

Site Entrance

Statue

Central Court

West Entrance

Grand
Stairway

Royal Apartments

Priest-King
Fresco

Storerooms

South House

0    25
metres

Southeast House

for a while, catching the patter and then backtracking to absorb the detail when the crowd has moved on. You won't get the place to yourself, whenever you come, but exploring on your own does give you the opportunity to appreciate individual parts of the palace in the brief lulls between groups.

For some idea of the size and complexity of the palace in its original state, take a look at the cutaway drawings (wholly imaginary but probably not too far off) on sale outside.

### Royal Apartments

The superb **Royal Apartments** around the central staircase are not guesswork, and they are plainly the finest of the rooms at Knossos. The **Grand Stairway** itself is a masterpiece of design, its large well bringing light into the lower storeys.

In the **Queen's Suite**, off the grand **Hall of the Colonnades** at the bottom of the staircase, the main living room is decorated with the celebrated **dolphin fresco** – it's a reproduction; the original is now in the Iráklion Archeological Museum (see p.452) – and with running friezes of flowers and abstract spirals. Remember, though, that all this is speculation; the dolphin fresco, for example, was found on the courtyard floor, not in the room itself, and would have been viewed from an upper balcony as a sort of trompe l'oeil like looking through a glass-bottomed boat. A dark passage leads around to the queen's **bathroom** and a clay tub, the famous "flushing" toilet (a hole in the ground with drains to take the waste away – it was flushed by throwing a bucket of water down).

The much-perused **drainage system** was a series of interconnecting terracotta pipes running underneath most of the palace. Guides to the site never fail to point these out as evidence of the advanced state of Minoan civilization.

The Grand Stairway ascends to the floor above the queen's domain, and the **King's Quarters**; the staircase opens into a grandiose reception chamber known as the **Hall of the Royal Guard**, its walls decorated in repeated shield patterns. Immediately off here is the **Hall of the Double Axes** (or the King's Room); believed to have been the ruler's personal chamber, its name comes from the double-axe symbol carved into every block of masonry.

### The Throne Room

At the top of the Grand Stairway you emerge onto the broad **Central Court**; on the far side, in the northwestern corner, is the entrance to another of Knossos's most atmospheric survivals, the **Throne Room**. Here, a worn stone throne – with its hollowed shaping for the posterior – sits against the wall of a surprisingly small chamber; along the walls around it are ranged stone benches, suggesting a king ruling in council, and behind there's a reconstructed fresco of two griffins.

### The rest of the palace

Try not to miss the giant *pithoi* in the northeast quadrant of the site, an area known as the palace workshops; other must-see areas and features include the storage chambers (which you see from behind the Throne Room), the reproduced frescoes in the reconstructed room above it, the fresco of the Priest-King looking down on the south side of the central court, and the relief of a charging bull on its north side. Just outside the North Entrance is the **theatral area** (another Evans designation), an open space a little like a stepped amphitheatre, which may have been used for ritual performances or dances. From here the **Royal Road**, claimed as the oldest road in Europe, sets out. Circling back around the outside of the palace, you can get an idea of its scale by looking up at it; on the south side are a couple of small reconstructed Minoan houses which are worth exploring.

## Inland from Iráklion

Heading south from Knossos, the zone around **Arhánes** and **Péza** is one of Crete's major wine-producing areas (see box, p.462). Nearby are some more Minoan sites at **Anemospiliá** and **Vathýpetro**, plus a few diverting villages. The main inland route southwest from Iráklion climbs through the mountains before winding down to **Áyii Dhéka** and the Messará plain. Here on the Messará, all within a 40km range of each other, lie the three major archeological sites of **Phaestos**, **Ayía Triádha** and **Gortys**. Once you get this far south you're within a short drive of the coastal resorts of **Mátala** and (accessed via a mountain road) **Léndas**.

**GETTING AROUND**       **INLAND FROM IRÁKLION**

**By bus** Iráklion (Bus station A) to: Arhánes (Mon–Fri hourly 6am–9pm, Sat hourly 7am–7pm, Sun 8am, 11am, 2pm, 5pm); Houdhétsi (Mon–Thur 6 daily 7am–3pm, Fri 7 daily 7am–8.15pm, Sat 4 daily 9.30am–3pm, Sun 7.30am only); Mátala – some change at Mires (4 daily 7.30am–3.30pm; 2hr 30min); Léndas (Mon–Fri; 12.30pm; 2hr). Iráklion (Bus station B) to: Phaestos (8 daily 7.30am–4.30pm; 1hr 30min).

**By car** When heading south from the Messará plain, the Asteroussia hills, which divide the plain from the coast, are surprisingly precipitous and the roads in these parts are slow going.

### Myrtiá

**MYRTIÁ** is an attractive village, 15km south of Iráklion, and home to the small **Kazantzakis Museum** (March–Oct daily 9am–5pm; Nov–Feb Sun only 10am–3pm; €3), dedicated to the famous writer and philosopher, Nikos Kazantzakis (see p.450). The museum, a cluster of buildings in the village square, displays manuscripts, notes and first editions of the writer's works, as well as photographs and personal effects – expect to see plenty of models, costumes and other material from theatre productions of his works in Greece and abroad.

## Arhánes

**ARHÁNES**, at the foot of Mount Yioúhtas, is a sizeable, wealthy farming town that was reasonably heavily populated in Minoan times. The main square has several tavernas, cafés and bars, while 100m to the north is the excellent **archeological museum** (Wed–Mon 8.30am–2.30pm; free), which displays finds from here and other excavations in the area, including a strange ceremonial dagger seemingly used for human sacrifice. The nearby site of **Anemospiliá**, 2km northwest of the town (directions are available from the archeological museum), is visitable, and has experienced huge controversy since its excavation in the 1980s: many traditional views of the Minoans, particularly that of Minoan life as peaceful and idyllic, have had to be rethought in the light of the discovery of an apparent human sacrifice. From Arhánes you can also drive (or walk with a couple of hours to spare) to the summit of Mount Yoúktas to see the imposing remains of a Minoan **peak sanctuary** and enjoy spectacular panoramic **views** towards Knossos (with which it was linked) and the northern coast beyond.

## Vathýpetro

At **VATHÝPETRO**, some 4km south of Mount Yoúktas, is a **Minoan villa and vineyard** (Tues–Sun 8.30am–2pm; free), which once controlled the rich farmland south of Arhánes. Inside, a remarkable collection of farming implements was found, as well as a unique **wine press**, which remains *in situ*. Substantial portions of the farm's buildings remain, and it's still surrounded by fertile vines three-and-a-half-thousand years later – making it probably the oldest still-functioning vineyard in Europe, if not the world.

## Houdhétsi

Some 2km southeast of **Vathýpetro** brings you to the agricultural village of **HOUDHÉTSI**, where you'll find the remarkable **Museum of Musical Instruments of the World** (March–Oct daily 8am–4pm; Nov–Feb Sun 10am–3pm; €3; ☎2810 741 027, ⓦlabyrinthmusic.gr). Founded by Irish *lýra* player Ross Daly, who is famed in Crete and lives in the village, the museum consists of a collection of mainly string and percussion instruments (many very rare) from across the globe. To get to the museum head for the pharmacy on the main road by the central square – the museum is opposite, housed in a mansion.

## Áyii Dhéka

**ÁYII DHÉKA** is the first village on the fertile Messará plain on the main route south from Iráklion and for religious Cretans a place of pilgrimage; its name, "The Ten Saints", refers to ten early Christians martyred here under the Romans. The old Byzantine church in the centre of the village preserves the stone block on which they are supposed to have been decapitated, and in a crypt below the modern church on the village's western edge you can see the martyrs' (now empty) tombs. It's an attractive village to wander around, with several places to eat.

## Gortys

Daily: July–Sept 8am–8pm; Oct–June 8am–3pm • €3 • ☎ 2810 226 470

Within easy walking distance of Áyii Dhéka (1km), sprawls the site of **Gortys**, ruined capital of the Roman province that included not only Crete but also much of North Africa. Evidence of a Minoan site has been unearthed on the acropolis, but the extant ruins date almost entirely from the Roman era.

At the main entrance to the **fenced site**, to the north of the road, are the ruins of the still impressive sixth-century **basilica of Áyios Títos**, and beyond this is the **odeion**, which houses the most important discovery on the site, the **Law Code**. Written in an obscure early Doric-Cretan dialect, they are, at 9m by 3m, the largest Greek inscription ever found. The laws set forth reflect a strictly hierarchical society: five witnesses were needed to convict a free man of a crime, only one for a slave; raping a free man or woman carried a fine of a hundred *staters*, a serf only five. A small **museum** in a loggia (also within the fenced area) holds a number of large and finely worked sculptures found at Gortys, more evidence of the city's importance. Next to the museum is a **café** (same hours as site).

## Phaestos

Daily: June–Sept daily 8am–8pm; Oct–May 8.30am–3pm • €4, joint ticket with Ayía Triádha €6

The **Palace of Phaestos**, 35km west of Gortys, was excavated by the Italian Federico Halbherr (also responsible for the early work at Gortys) at almost exactly the same time as Evans was working at Knossos. Here, however, to the approval of most traditional archeologists, reconstruction was kept to an absolute minimum – it's all bare foundations, and walls which rise at most 1m above ground level. This means that, despite a magnificent setting overlooking the plain of Messará, the palace at Phaestos is not as immediately arresting as those at Knossos or Mália, but no less fascinating.

It's interesting to speculate why the palace was built halfway up a hill rather than on the plain below – certainly not for defence, for this is in no way a good defensive position. Psychological superiority over the peasants or reasons of health are both possible, but it seems quite likely that it was simply the magnificent view that finally swayed the decision. The site looks over Psilorítis to the north and the huge plain, with the Lasíthi mountains beyond it, to the east.

On the ground closer at hand, you can hardly fail to notice the strong similarities between Phaestos and the other palaces: the same huge rows of storage jars, the great courtyard with its monumental stairway, and the theatre area. Unique to Phaestos,

7

**PALACE OF PHAESTOS**

Tourist Pavilion

Entrance

Lustral Basin

Royal Apartments

Archive

Peristyle Hall

Peristyle House

North Court

Theatral Area and West Court

Propylon

Grand Stairway

Storage Pits

Workshops

Storerooms

Furnace

Office

Prince's rooms

Steep bank

Central Court

First Palace Remains

Classical Temple

Steep bank

N

0    25
metres

**7**

---

## WINE TASTING IN CRETE

As well as the large Péza region near Knossos and the ancient vineyard at Vathýpetro (see p.460), there are also vineyards in eastern Crete, around Sitía, another major producer, and smaller vineyards in the west around Haniá. The main grape varieties grown on the island are the white Vilana and the red Mantilari, Kotsifari and Syrah grapes. Wine tasting and cellar tours can be undertaken during the summer months.

**Boutari** Skaláni, Iráklion ☎ 2810 731617, ⓦ boutari .gr. On the road towards the village of Myrtiá lies the Fantaxometocho estate of the privately owned Boutari vineyard. Specializing in organic production methods, they make excellent wines. Tours €5. May–Oct daily 10am–4pm.

**Dourakis** Alíkambos, Vrýsses, near Haniá ☎ 28250 51761. On the main road, 4km from Vrýsses towards Hóra Sfákion, this small, friendly family-owned winery offers tasting and tours, and there's a small one-room museum of old farming implements. Tours €3. May–Oct Mon–Sat 10am–2pm & 4–6pm.

**Minos Wines** Péza, Iráklion ☎ 2810 741213, ⓦ minoswines.gr. Milliarakis is the estate of another privately owned producer, Minos Wines. Tasting takes place in their large wine-tasting room, which is furnished as a traditional *kafenío*. Tours €2. May–Oct Mon–Fri 9am–4pm.

**Peza Union** Kalloní, Iráklion ☎ 2810 741945, ⓦ pezaunion.gr. Beyond Péza village, 2km. The union of agricultural cooperatives of Péza produces olive oil as well as wine. A tour of their exhibition centre is followed by wine tasting and a small meze. Tours free. May–Oct Mon–Sat 9am–5pm.

**Sitia Co-operative** Géla, Sitía ☎ 28430 29991. On the main road towards Áyios Nikólaos, 1km from Sitía. The famous wines of Sitía OPAP are produced here. Tours include a tasting in the cellar and an audiovisual presentation. Tours €2. Mon–Fri 9am–3pm.

---

however, is the third courtyard, in the middle of which are the remains of a **furnace** used for metalworking. Oddly enough, Phaestos was much less ornately decorated than Knossos; there is no evidence, for example, of any of the dramatic Minoan wall-paintings.

### Ayía Triádha
Daily: May–Sept 10am–4pm; Oct–April 8.30am–3pm • €4, joint ticket with Phaestos €6

Some of the finest artworks in the museum at Iráklion came from **Ayía Triádha**, 4km west of Phaestos. No one is quite sure what this site is, but the most common theory has it as some kind of royal summer villa. It's smaller than the palaces but, if anything, even more lavishly appointed and beautifully situated. In any event, it's an attractive place to visit, far less crowded than Phaestos, with a wealth of interesting little details. Look out in particular for the row of **stores** in front of what was apparently a marketplace, and the remains of a **paved road** that probably led down to a harbour on the Gulf of Messará. There's a fourteenth-century **chapel** – dedicated to Áyios Yeóryios – at the site, worth visiting in its own right for the remains of ancient frescoes.

### Míres
The large market town of **MÍRES**, 20km west of Gortys, serves as a transport hub for buses further west and to the beaches of the south coast; if you're travelling to Mátala, or west beyond Phaistos, then you'll normally switch buses here. There are good facilities including a **bank**, a few **restaurants**, a couple of **rooms** places and a handy **internet** café, *Sirvitis*, right opposite the bus stop, though there's no particular reason to stay unless you are waiting for a bus.

### Mátala
**MÁTALA** is best-known for its famous caves cut into the cliffs above beautiful sands. These are ancient tombs first used by Romans or early Christians, but more recently inhabited by a sizeable hippie community in the 1960s and 1970s (including some famous names such as Bob Dylan and Joni Mitchell). The caves have long since been

eared and cleaned up, and these days they are an archeological site, fenced off at ight, but you can still wander around them freely in the daytime.

The resort still has a laidback feel outside of high summer, but July and August see he beach packed to overflowing in the early afternoon, when the tour buses pull in for heir swimming stop. The town beach is beautiful, and if the crowds get excessive, you an climb over the rocks in about twenty minutes to another excellent stretch of sand, nown locally as "Red Beach". It's best to stay a night here and enjoy the waterside bars nd restaurants in peace once the tour buses have left.

## RRIVAL AND INFORMATION                                                    MÁTALA

**y bus** Buses arrive by the beach car park. There are 5 rvices per day to Iráklion (2hr 30min).

**y car** In Mátala, park in the car park at the beach

(€2 per day), on the right as you reach the town proper.
**Services** Internet is available at *Zafiria Café* opposite the main square.

## CCOMMODATION

cluster of rooms places lies near to the *Zafiria* hotel, and the street to the left is known as "Hotel Street"; here you'll find veral options.

**iaki** Hotel Street ☏28920 45110, ⊛matala holidays.gr. A small, immaculate *pension* with recently ecorated rooms. All have a/c, TV, fridge and free wi-fi. A vo-bedroomed apartment within the *pension* with its wn patio garden is also available to rent (€75). May– ct. €45

**latala Camping** Next to the main beach, behind the ar park ☏28920 45720. There's plenty of shade here to itch your tent in the sand under the tamarisk trees, close the beach, but the shower/wc facilities are very basic. ne–Oct. €12

**latala View** Hotel Street ☏28920 45114, ⊛matala partments.com. Simple and clean rooms, studios and

apartments (sleeps 4) with private bathroom, fan and fridge. Studios and apartments have kitchenette and some with a/c (€5/day extra). May–Oct. €40

★ **Nikos** Hotel Street ☏28920 45375, ⊛matala -nikos.com. The friendly *Nikos* has pleasant a/c rooms with en-suite bathroom, TV and fridge, off a plant-filled patio. The "penthouse" room, which stands alone on the roof, has a stunning view. Some rooms with cooking facilities. Free wi-fi. May–Oct. €45

**Zafiria** Main street, just beyond the car park turn-off ☏28920 45112, ⊛zafiria-matala.com. Here rooms (some with a sea view) come with a/c but no TV, and there's a pool. May–Oct. €45

## ATING AND DRINKING

**lex and Anna** A popular, simple taverna serving fresh ome-cooked food, daily specials and grills, with tables on e road-side terrace in the main square. Mains from €5.50. lay–Oct daily lunch & dinner.

**afeneio** Stylish café at the entrance to town, serving offees, snacks, drinks and cocktails throughout the day

and evening, and with wi-fi access. April–Oct daily 8am–1am.

**Skala** ☏28920 45489. A good fish taverna, perched above the sea at the far south end of the bay with a great view. Fresh fish, with seafood dishes from €7. May–Oct daily lunch & dinner.

## IGHTLIFE

**ort Side** ☏694 59 83 886. A cocktail bar with an nviable location, great views across the bay from the bar rrace, perched above the beach, and a café by day. May– ct daily 9am–late.

**Tommy's Music Bar** Just beyond Port Side, this popular bar gets lively later on, with the crowds spilling into the street. May–Sept daily 8pm–late.

## éndas

**ÉNDAS**, east of Mátala, has a partly justified reputation for being peaceful though it uffers from considerable summer weekend crowds. From the ramshackle outskirts f the village take the cobbled paths leading down to the village square and to the mall, grey-sand beach. The main attraction, however, is the vast and sandy beach n the other (west) side of the headland, **Ditikós** (or Diskós) beach; part of it is sually taken over by nudists, with a number of taverna/bars overlooking it from he road side.

## ACCOMMODATION AND EATING

**Akti** Léndas beach. Excellent, friendly taverna in a great location on the beach, serving freshly prepared meat, fish and Cretan dishes. April–Oct daily 11am–1am.

**El Greco** Léndas village ☎ 28920 95322. A particularly good restaurant with a large leafy terrace, serving home-made Greek dishes, as well as fresh fish and seafood. Try their *oktapódhi* (octopus; €8), or prime Messará beef pepper steak. April–Oct daily lunch & dinner.

**Villa Tsapakis** Ditikós Beach ☎ 28920 95378, ⊚ villa tsapakis.gr. These bougainvillea-fronted rooms above Ditikós beach come with a sea view, fridge and TV, and reductions for longer stays. They have their own decent taverna, *Odysseas*, nearby. April–Oct. €35

# East of Iráklion: the package-tour coast

East of Iráklion, the main package-tour resorts are at least 30km away, at **Hersónissos** and **Mália**, although there is a string of rather unattractive developments all the way there; the merest hint of a beach is an excuse to build hotel and apartment complexes. That said, there are one or two highlights amid the dross, which are well worth a visit: the impressive **Cretaquarium** at Goúrnes, the **old villages** in the hills behind Hersónissos, and, beyond the clubbing resort of Mália, a fine **Minoan palace** that will transport you back three and a half millennia.

## GETTING AROUND

**By bus** Iráklion (Bus station B) to: Hersónissos and Mália (daily, every 30min 6am–10.30pm; 40min); Palace of Malia (2 daily 9.15am, 3.15pm; 45min).

## Cretaquarium

Daily: May–Sept 9.30am–9pm; Oct–Apr 9.30am–5pm • €8, children aged 5–17 €6 • ☎ 28103 37788, ⊚ cretaquarium.gr • Goúrnes, 15km from Iráklion

The only reason to visit the resort of Goúrnes is the **Cretaquarium**, a spectacular and sizeable marine aquarium converted from a US air base. Boasting thirty tanks (some huge), it houses everything from menacing sharks to dazzling jellyfish. Part of the Hellenic Centre for Marine Research, the venture is purely educational, scientific and non-profit making. Most of the island's fish and crustaceans are included among the 250 species and over 2500 specimens on display, and unless you're a marine biologist the audio-guide (€3; easily shared between two or three) is pretty well indispensable and gives loads of fascinating background information on the creatures you're looking at. The aquarium is well signposted on the road leading from Iráklion.

## Hersónissos

The first of the really big resorts, **HERSÓNISSOS** was once just a small fishing village (Límin Hersoníssou); today it's one of the most popular of Crete's package resorts, a brash, sprawling place overrun with hotels, bars, touristy tavernas and nightclubs. Beach and clubs excepted, the main attractions are the **Lychnostatis Open-air Museum of Folklore** (Mon–Fri & Sun 9am–2pm; €5), a surprisingly rewarding museum of traditional Crete with imaginative reconstructions of island life past and present, and **Aqua World** (April–Oct daily 10am–6pm; €6 adults, €4 under-12s), a small aquarium. A short distance inland, the three pretty **hill villages** of Koutoulafári, Piskopianó and "old" Hersónissos present a glimpse of more traditional Crete and offer some attractive rooms and good tavernas.

## Mália

Eight kilometres east of Hersónissos lies the package-resort town of **MÁLIA,** renowned for its wild, teenage, bar and clubbing scene. The town's focus is a T-junction, from where the beach road – a kilometre-long strip lined with bars, clubs, games arcades, tavernas and souvenir shops – heads north to the sea and beaches. South of this junction the **old town** presents a saner image of what Mália used to be; a labyrinth of narrow streets and whitewashed walls, but even here commercialism is making inroads.

## The Palace of Malia

Tues–Sun 8.30am–3pm • €4 • ☎ 28970 31957

Much less imposing than either Knossos or Phaestos, the **Palace of Malia**, 2km east of Mália town, in some ways surpasses both. For a start, it's a great deal emptier and you can wander among the remains in relative peace. While no reconstruction has been attempted, the palace was never reoccupied after its second destruction in the fifteenth century BC, so the ground plan is virtually intact.

From this site came the famous **gold pendant** of two bees and the beautiful **leopard-head axe**, both of which are displayed in Iráklion's archeological museum. At the site, look out for the strange indented stone in the central court (which probably held ritual offerings), for the remains of ceremonial stairways and for the giant *pithoi*, which stand like sentinels around the palace. To the north and west of the main site, archeological digs are still going on as the large town which surrounded the palace comes slowly to light (part of this can be viewed via an overhead walkway).

Any passing **bus** should stop at the site, or you could even rent a **bike** for a couple of hours as it's a pleasant, flat ride from Mália town. Leaving the archeological zone and turning immediately right, you can follow the road down to a lovely stretch of clean and relatively peaceful **beach**.

# West of Iráklion

Leaving Iráklion city to the west, the fast **E75 coastal highway** winds all the way to Réthymnon, a spectacular drive, the road being hacked into the sides of mountains which for the most part drop straight to the sea, though there are no more than a handful of places where you might consider stopping: the coastal settlements of **Ayía Pelayía** and the more attractive **Balí**, both sizeable resorts, and the smaller village of **Fódhele**, which claims to be the birthplace of **El Greco**. By contrast, the old roads inland are agonizingly slow, but they do pass through a whole string of **attractive villages** beneath the heights of the **Psilorítis** range.

## Ayía Pelayía

Some 20km west along the highway from Iráklion lies the resort of **AYÍA PELAYÍA**. It looks extremely attractive from above but, once there, and especially in July and August, you're likely to find the narrow, taverna-lined beach packed to full capacity. Despite the high-season crowds, the resort maintains a dignity long since lost in Mália and Hersónissos, and even a certain exclusivity; one of Crete's most luxurious hotel resorts nestles on the headlands just beyond the main town beach.

## Fódhele

Beyond Ayía Pelayía, there's a turning inland to the village of **FÓDHELE**, allegedly El Greco's birthplace. A plaque from the University of Valladolid (in Spain) acknowledges the claim and, true or not, the community has built a small tourist industry on that basis. There are a number of craft shops and some pleasant tavernas where you can sit outside along the river. A peaceful 1km walk (or drive) takes you to the spuriously titled **El Greco's House** (aka Museum of El Greco; May–Oct Tues–Sun 9am–7pm; €2), exhibiting a few poor reproductions of his works and not much more, while the picturesque fourteenth-century Byzantine **church of the Panayía** is opposite (usually locked). None of this amounts to very much, but it is a pleasant, relatively unspoilt village if you simply want to sit in peace for a while.

## Balí

**BALÍ**, on the coast about halfway between Iráklion and Réthymnon, is a charming small resort with a beautiful setting and sandy beaches. The village is built around a trio of small coves, some 2km from the highway, and is similar to Ayía Pelayía except that the beaches are not quite as good and there are no big hotels, just an ever-growing proliferation of apartment buildings, rooms for rent and a number of smaller hotels. You'll have plenty of company here, and it has to be said that Balí has become a package resort too popular for its own good; it's a beautiful place to splash about, surrounded by mountains rising straight from the sea, but there's rarely a spare inch on the sand in high season.

## Týlissos

Daily 8.30am–3pm • €2

**TÝLISSOS**, 11km inland and west of Iráklion, has a significant archeological site where three Minoan houses were excavated; unfortunately, its reputation is based more on what was found here (many pieces in the Iráklion Archeological Museum) and on its significance for archeologists than on anything which remains to be seen. Still, it's worth a look, if you're passing, for a glimpse of Minoan life away from the big palaces, and for the tranquillity of the pine-shaded remains.

## Anóyia

**ANÓYIA** is a tempting place to stay, especially if the summer heat is becoming oppressive. It's a large village, with two centres, spilling prettily down a hillside below **Mount Psilorítis**. It looks traditional, but closer inspection shows that most of the buildings are actually concrete; the village was destroyed during World War II and the local men were rounded up and shot – one of the German reprisals for the abduction of General Kreipe by the Cretan resistance. The town has a reputation as a centre of **lýra** playing (many famous exponents were born here, most notably the late Nikos Xylouris) and also as a **handicrafts** centre. It's a thriving place today thanks to a buoyant sheep farming sector – farmers here are some of the richest in Greece; don't miss the **spit-roast lamb** if you're carnivorously inclined.

### GETTING AROUND                                          WEST OF IRÁKLION

**By bus** Iráklion–Réthymnon line buses, running hourly along the main coastal highway, stop at the exit roads to Ayía Pelayía, Balí and Fódhele; you'll then have a 2–3km (hot) walk down to each village. Ayía Pelayía also has a limited direct service from Iráklion to the centre of the resort (3 daily, 8.30am, 9.15am, 2.30pm; 30min).

### ACCOMMODATION AND EATING

#### AYÍA PELAYÍA

Most accommodation here is block-booked by package holiday companies, although in quieter times you shouldn't have any problems finding a bed. The Pangosmio travel agency (☎ 28108 11402) may be able to come up with something at the last minute.

**Irini** Beach road ☎ 28108 11455, ⓦ irini-hotel -apartments.gr. Cheery apartments, above a good snack-bar and café of the same name, and just a few metres from the beach. Apartments sleep 2–6, with a/c, balcony, TV, and kitchen. April–Oct. **€45**

**Out of the Blue, Capsis Elite Resort** ☎ 28108 11112, ⓦ capsis.gr. This five-star luxury resort complex sits on a private peninsula, comprising four hotels, seven pools, luxury villas with private pools and three private beaches. It even has its own zoo. April–Oct. From **€200**

**Zorba's** Beach road, near the beach ☎ 28102 56072, ⓦ zorbas.gr. Pleasant apartments and studios with balcony, located above a shop just seconds from the beach. Facilities include a/c, kitchenette and fridge. Wi-fi is also available. May–Oct. **€45**

#### BALÍ

**Mira Mare** ☎ 28340 94256. Good-value rooms located on the main thoroughfare, a short, but steep, walk from the beach, and above a supermarket, with a/c, fridge and balcony with sea views. May–Oct. **€35**

#### ANÓYIA

**Aetos** Upper village. A popular local meat taverna, specializing in lamb and goat (€7–8) cooked on the outdoor barbecue. Some good local cheeses too. Daily lunch & dinner.

**CLIMBING MOUNT PSILORÍTIS**

Climbing to the summit of **Mount Psilorítis**, for experienced and properly equipped hikers, is not at all arduous. The route, which diverts from the path to the Idean Cave just beyond a small chapel, forms a stretch of the E4 Pan-European footpath and is marked with the red arrows and the E4 waymarkers. It should be a 6–8hr return journey to the summit, although in spring, thick snow may slow you down. Don't attempt the walk alone as you could face a very long wait should you run into trouble, and mobile phones may not have a signal in places.

If you're prepared to camp on the Nídha plateau (it can be very cold), or rent a room at the *Taverna Nida*, you could continue on foot the next day down to the southern slopes of the range. It's a beautiful hike and also relatively easy, four hours or so down a fairly clear path to **Vorízia** where there is no food or accommodation, although **Kamáres**, 4km west, has both.

**Aristea** Upper village ☏ 28340 31459, ⓦhotelaristea .gr. Simple en-suite rooms with TV and spectacular valley views from the terrace; also has studios and apartments, with open fireplace for winter stays, which sleep up to six. Breakfast included. **€45**

**Rooms Aris** Upper village ☏28340 31817, ⓦaris .anogia.info. The flower-bedecked Aris has pleasant en-suite rooms with fabulous valley and mountain views. Facilities include fridge, balcony and central heating for winter stays. **€40**

**Taverna Skalomata** Upper village, east. ☏ 28340 31316. Offers well-prepared taverna standards, including the usual barbecued meats and spit-roast lamb, with a fine view. Grills from €6. Daily lunch & dinner.

## Mount Psilorítis

Heading for the mountains from Anóyia, a smooth road ascends 21km to an altitude of 1400m on the **Nídha Plateau** at the base of Mount Psilorítis. Here, at the end of the road and opposite the *Taverna Nida*, is the path up to the celebrated **Idean cave** (about a 15min walk) and the start of the way to the top of **Mount Psilorítis** (2456m), Crete's highest mountain.

### Idean cave

The **Idean cave** (Idhéon Ándhron), a rival of that on Mount Dhíkti (see p.473) for the title of Zeus's birthplace, is certainly associated from the earliest of times with the cult of Zeus. The remnants of a major archeological dig carried out inside – including a miniature railway used by archeologists to remove tonnes of rock and rubble – still litter the site, giving the place a rather unattractive prospect. When you enter the cave down concrete steps into the depths, it turns out to be a rather shallow affair, with little to see.

**ACCOMMODATION AND EATING**                                        **MOUNT PSILORÍTIS**

**Taverna Nida** Nihda plateau ☏28340 31141. Serves up hearty mountain dishes featuring lamb, pork and chicken, and has a couple of simple rooms, which makes it a good base for hikes in the surrounding mountains. June–Sept daily; Oct–May Sat & Sun only. Breakfast included. **€30**

# Eastern Crete

**Eastern Crete** is dominated by **Áyios Nikólaos**, a small cosmopolitan town and resort, and its close neighbour Eloúnda, the home of luxury hotel and villa complexes, and the gateway to the mysterious islet of **Spinalónga**. Inland from Áyios Nikólaos, **Kritsá** with its famous frescoed church and textile sellers and the imposing ruins of **ancient Lato** make for good excursions. Further inland, the extraordinary **Lasíthi Plateau** is worth a night's stay if only to observe its abidingly rural life. Far fewer people venture beyond the road south to **Ierápetra** and east to **Sitía,** where only the famous beach at **Váï** ever sees anything approaching a crowd.

## Áyios Nikólaos

**ÁYIOS NIKÓLAOS**, known simply as "Áyios" to the locals, is set around a supposedly bottomless salt lake, now connected to the sea to form an inner harbour. It is supremely picturesque and has some style and charm, which it exploits to the full. The excellent **archeological museum** (Tues–Sun 8.30am–3pm; €3) on Paleológou north of the lake, and an interesting **Folk Museum** (Tues–Sun April–Oct 10am–2pm and 5–7pm; €3) near the tourist office are both worth seeking out. Both the lake and the harbour area are surrounded by charming restaurants and bars.

The small and busy **Kitroplatía beach** lies just around the southwest corner of the port and is lined with tavernas and cafés, while 1km beyond here, past the marina, lies the much larger, and well-kept, municipal beach. There are further swimming opportunities to the north around Eloúnda, and some great backcountry inland – perfect to explore on a scooter.

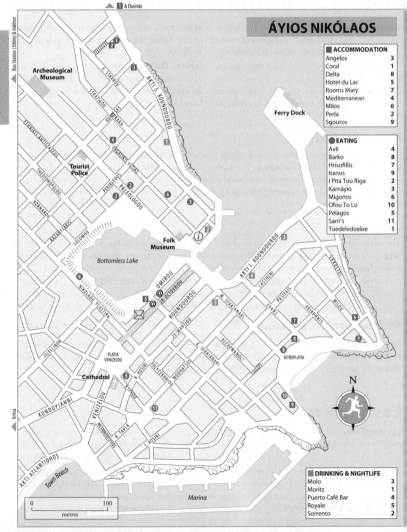

### ÁYIOS NIKÓLAOS

**ACCOMMODATION**

| | |
|---|---|
| Angelos | 3 |
| Coral | 1 |
| Delta | 8 |
| Hotel du Lac | 5 |
| Rooms Mary | 7 |
| Mediterranean | 4 |
| Milos | 6 |
| Perla | 2 |
| Sgouros | 9 |

**EATING**

| | |
|---|---|
| Avlí | 4 |
| Barko | 8 |
| Hrisofillís | 7 |
| Itanos | 9 |
| I Pita Tou Riga | 2 |
| Karnáyio | 3 |
| Migomis | 6 |
| Ofou To Lo | 10 |
| Pelagos | 5 |
| Sarri's | 11 |
| Toedeledoekie | 1 |

**DRINKING & NIGHTLIFE**

| | |
|---|---|
| Molo | 3 |
| Moritz | 1 |
| Puerto Café Bar | 4 |
| Royale | 5 |
| Sorrento | 2 |

## ARRIVAL AND DEPARTURE

## ÁYIOS NIKÓLAOS

**By bus** The station is situated to the northwest end of town near the archeological museum.
Destinations Eloúnda (20 daily; 20min); Iráklion (at least 20 daily, 6 via Iráklion Airport 6.15am–9.30pm; 1hr

30min); Kritsá (9 daily 6am–8.15pm; 20min); Lasíthi plateau (2 daily; 2hr); Pláka (7 daily 6am–7pm; 30min); Sitía (7 daily 6.15am–8.30pm; 1hr 45min).

## INFORMATION AND ACTIVITIES

**Tourist office** Between the lake and the port (April–June & Oct 9am–5pm, July–Sept 8.30am–9.30pm; closed Sat; ☎ 28410 22357, ⊛ aghiosnikolaos.gr). One of the best on the island for accommodation information, they also exchange currency.
**Boat trips** Leave from the west side of the harbour to

Spinalónga and Eloúnda (about €12–20 depending on the company, some include lunch).
**Diving** Pelagos Minos Beach Hotel, Eloúnda road, Áyios Nikólaos ☎ 28410 24376, ⊛ divecrete.com. This company also rents out sailing dinghies by the hour.

## ACCOMMODATION

★ **Angelos** Aktí S. Koundoúrou 16 ☎ 28410 23501. Welcoming small hotel located on the seafront, offering excellent a/c balconied rooms with TV and fridge plus fine views over the Gulf. No breakfast but a supermarket sits directly beneath. **€40**

**Coral** Aktí S. Koundoúrou ☎ 28410 28363, ⊛ mhotels .gr. One of the best in-town hotels offering a/c rooms with sea view, fridge, balcony and satellite TV, plus a rooftop pool and bar. Out of high season, prices can fall by up to fifty percent. Breakfast included. **€115**

**Delta** Tselepi 1 Kitroplatía ☎ 28410 28893, ⊛ agiosnikolaos-hotels.gr. Modern, refurbished a/c studios and apartments overlooking Kitroplatía beach, a 5min walk from the centre of town. Rooms at the front have sea-view balconies. Facilities include full kitchen and TV. **€55**

★ **Hotel du Lac** 28-Octovríou ☎ 28410 22711, ⊛ dulachotel.gr. Perhaps the most unexpected bargain in town, with classily renovated rooms and studios in designer style with all facilities including a/c, TV, wi-fi and (in studios) kitchenette in a prime location overlooking the lake. However, it's also in the heart of things so night-time noise is the only downside. **€60**

**Mediterranean** S. Dhávaki 27 ☎ 28410 23611. On a hill

between the lake and the seafront, run by an Anglo-Greek couple, these clean, economical en-suite rooms come with fridges, a/c, TV, use of communal kitchen and some rooms with balcony. **€30**

★ **Milos** Sarolídi 2 ☎ 28410 23783. Sweet little pension east of the Kitroplatía beach, with some of the best rooms in town for the price. The spotless en-suite balcony rooms (number 2 is a dream) with a/c have spectacular sea views over the gulf. April–Oct. **€35**

**Perla** Salaminos 4 ☎ 28410 23379, ⊛ apartments -perla.gr. Chic en-suite apartments, close to the sea, on a hill to the north of the harbour, recently refurbished, with a/c, cooker, fridge, TV and wi-fi, and front rooms have sea-view balconies. **€50**

★ **Rooms Mary** Evans 13, near the Kitroplatía ☎ 28410 23760. Very friendly place with a/c (€5 extra) en-suite balcony rooms (some with sea view), access to fridge and use of kitchen. Also has some apartments nearby sleeping up to four. **€35**

**Sgouros** Kitroplatía ☎ 28410 28931, ⊛ sgourosgroup hotels.com. Good-value modern hotel with a/c, TV, fridge, balcony rooms overlooking one of the town's beaches, and close to plenty of tavernas. Breakfast included. **€70**

## EATING

The places around the Kitroplatía are generally good, but you are paying for the location – the more authentic establishments tend to be less obvious, on the streets behind the tourist office, and near Platia Venizelou.

**Avlí** Odhós P. Georgíou 12 ☎ 28410 82479. Delightful garden ouzerí offering a wide mezédhes selection as well as more elaborate dishes. May–Oct daily 12.30–2.30pm & 7–11pm.

**Barko** Kitroplatía ☎ 28410 24610. This hip restaurant and bar, with a large terrace overlooking the beach, serves Greek dishes with flair; share a mix of mezédhes such as feta-stuffed red peppers, courgette pie and pork in wine. There's indoor seating too, in the smartly renovated building. Daily lunch & dinner.

**Hrisofillís** Aktí Themistokléous ☎ 28410 22705.

Attractive, stylish and creative *mezedhopolío* with reasonably priced fish, meat and veggie mezédhes served on a pleasant sea-facing terrace fronting the east side of the Kitroplatía beach. Meze from €4.50. Daily lunch & dinner.

**I Pita Tou Riga** Paleológou 24, close to the lake. Excellent Lilliputian snack-bar/restaurant serving imaginative fare – salads, filled pitta breads and some Asian dishes; has a small terrace up steps across the road, shared with its sister restaurant, *Karnáyio* (below). Pitta club sandwich with pork €5.50. Daily noon–2am.

7

**Itanos** Kýprou 1. Popular with locals, this traditional taverna serves reasonably priced Cretan food such as *yemista* (rice-stuffed vegetables; €5), and barrel wine. It also has a terrace across the road. Daily 11am–midnight.

★ **Karnáyio** Paleológou 21 ☎ 28410 25968. Atmospheric traditional *kafenío* popular with a younger crowd and serving tasty *mezédhes* – try the *fava* (mashed split peas) – inside or on its pleasant terrace with lake view. A bonus here is some great *lýra* and *lauto* (lute) music most Fri and Sat evenings. Daily noon–3am.

**Migomis** Nikoláou Plastíra 22 ☎ 28410 24353. Pleasant café high above the bottomless lake with a stunning view. Perfect (if pricey) place for breakfast, afternoon or evening drinks. Their next-door restaurant enjoys the same vista and is pricier than the norm, but perhaps worth it if you've booked a table to feast on that view. Daily 9am–1am.

★ **Ofou To Lo** Kitroplatía ☎ 28410 24819. Best of the moderately priced places on the seafront here: the food is consistently good. Try their *loukánika me tirí* (spicy sausages with cheese; €5) starter. Daily lunch & dinner.

★ **Pelagos** Stratigoú Kóraka, behind the tourist office ☎ 28410 25737. Housed in an elegant mansion, this stylish fish taverna has an attractive leafy garden terrace which complements the excellent food. Pricey, but worth it. April–Oct daily lunch & dinner.

**Sarri's** Kýprou 15. Great little economical neighbourhood café-diner especially good for breakfast, also grills and *souvláki*, all served on a leafy terrace. Daily 9am–midnight.

**Toedeledoekie** Aktí S. Koundoúrou 24. Friendly, low-key Dutch-run café with international press to read; great sandwiches and milkshakes by day, chilled bar at night. Daily 9am–late.

## DRINKING AND NIGHTLIFE

The one thing which Áyios Nikólaos undeniably does well is bars and nightlife. Music bars with terraces spread along Aktí Koundoúrou on the harbourfront. More raucous bars and clubs crowd the bottom of 25-Martíou (known as "Soho Street") as it heads up the hill.

**Molo** Aktí Koundoúrou 6. One of a bunch of popular glitzy café-bars looking out over the ferry dock on the east side of the harbour. A relaxed café during the day and a bar at night, open until the early hours. Daily 9am–late.

**Moritz** Aktí Koundoúrou 10. West of the harbour. Cosy, laidback café-bar along the seafront with a dressy clientele and jazz and soft-rock sounds. Daily 9am–late.

**Puerto Café Bar** Aktí I Koundoúrou. One of the row of café-bars on the harbourfront, with outdoor harbourside

seating and an indoor bar which pumps up the volume after dark. Daily 9am–late.

**Royale** 25-Martiou. The first of a row of bars proper, at the bottom of 25-Martíou, near the harbour. Daily 11pm- late.

**Sorrento** Aktí I Koundoúrou 23. On the west side of the harbour, near the tourist office. A long-established haunt of expats, loud and fun, if that's what you're in the mood for. Daily 9pm–late.

## DIRECTORY

**Car rental** Good deals are available at Club Cars, 28-Oktovríou 24 (☎ 28410 25868), near the post office, or Economy (☎ 28410 22013) under the *Hotel Angelos*.

**Internet access** Peripou, 28-Oktovríou 25 (daily 9.30am–2am), and Café du Lac at no. 17 on the same street.

**Travel agents** Plora Travel, Corner of 28-Oktovríou and K. Sfakianáki (☎ 28410 82804).

**Post office** 28-Oktovríou (Mon–Sat 7.30am–2pm), halfway up, on the right.

# Eloúnda and around

The village of **ELOÚNDA**, now a small-scale resort, lies about 8km from Áyios Nikólaos, along the coast road. Just before the centre of the village, a road (signposted) leads downhill to a natural causeway leading to the ancient "sunken city" of **Olous**. Here you'll find restored windmills, a short length of canal, Venetian salt pans and a well-preserved dolphin **mosaic**, inside a former Roman basilica, but nothing of the sunken city itself beyond a couple of walls in about 70cm of water. Swimming here is good – but watch out for sea urchins. Life in **Eloúnda** village focuses around the large square lined with cafés, tavernas and shops, in front of the picturesque harbour. Right next to the harbour is the sandy town **beach**, with other patches of sand stretching out north along the coast.

**CLOCKWISE FROM TOP LEFT** STAVRÓS BEACH (P.499); AYÍA TRIÁDHA (P.498); MOUNT PSILORÍTIS (P.467) >

## Pláka

**PLÁKA**, some 5km north of Eloúnda, stands on the shore directly across the sea from Spinalónga and used to be the colony's supply point. This small seaside village consists of a few **rooms** and a clutch of fish **tavernas** – a couple of which arrange boats excursions across to Spinalónga. The *Taverna Spinalonga*'s proprietor Aris also does boat trips to isolated beaches not reachable by road and fishing trips (€80/hr, up to four people). A small pebble beach lies to the north of the village.

## Spinalónga

Daily: June–Sept 9am–7pm, Oct & April–May 9am–3pm, Nov–March Sat & Sun 9am–3pm • €2 • ☎ 28410 41773 • Boats run to Spinalónga every 30min in high season from Eloúnda (€10 return) and Pláka (€8 return); tickets can be bought at the signed dockside

As a bastion of the Venetian defence, the fortress-rock of **Spinalónga** withstood the Turkish invaders for 45 years after the mainland had fallen; the infamous part of the islet's history, however, is more recent; it served as a **leper colony** for five decades until 1957. Even today, despite the crowds of visitors, there's a real sense of the desolation of those years as you walk through the gated tunnel entrance and emerge on a narrow street below the castle, with the roofless shells of houses once inhabited by the unfortunate lepers all around. A short row of buildings here, which were once stores, has been restored and houses a small **museum** with photos and artefacts.

### ARRIVAL AND INFORMATION

**By bus** Services run from Áyios Nikólaos to Eloúnda and Pláka from 6am to 7.30pm, every 2hr.

**Services** The friendly Olous Travel (☎ 28410 41324) on the

### ELOÚNDA AND AROUND

main square in Eloúnda gives out information, can help with accommodation and changes money.

### ACTIVITIES

**Watersports** Driros Beach ☎ 694 49 37 760, ⓦ spinalonga-windsurf.com. Windsurfing, waterskiing, kayaking and sailing courses at Driros Beach near Eloúnda. Also rents out outboard dinghies.

### ACCOMMODATION

#### ELOÚNDA

★ **Akti Olous** On the Olous road, seafront ☎ 28410 41270, ⓦ greekhotels.net/aktiolous. This is one of the good mid-range hotel options, with a beach bar, restaurant and roof garden pool with panoramic view. Rooms have a/c, fridge and TV. May–Oct. **€70**

**Elounda Bay Palace** ☎ 28410 67000, ⓦ eloundabay .gr. If you fancy indulging in a little luxury this swanky hotel has en-suite a/c rooms, suites and bungalows with TV, mini bar, three pools, spa and two private beaches with watersports. May–Oct. **€260**

**Milos** Upper part of town ☎ 28410 41641, ⓦ pediaditis .gr. Ask at "The Bookshop" on the main square. Attractive,

clean and comfortable rooms, studios and apartments which come with sea views and a pool. May–Oct. Rooms **€45**, apartment **€60**

**Oasis** Off the square, on the road heading inland ☎ 28410 41076, ⓦ pensionoasis.gr. This friendly place, just 100m from the centre in a rural setting, has en-suite rooms with kitchenette, fridge and TV. June–Oct. **€40**

#### PLÁKA

**Taverna Spinalonga** On the main street ☎ 28410 41804. Clean, simple rooms in the heart of the village, across the street from the taverna and with a view to the island. En-suite bath and fridge. Ask Aris at the taverna. **€40**

### EATING, DRINKING AND NIGHTLIFE

#### ELOÚNDA

**Aligos** On the square. One of the livelier café-bars, open throughout the day until late, for drinks and snacks and, later, loud music. Daily 9am–late.

**Ferryman** ☎ 28410 41230. The ultra-chic *Ferryman* is one of the town's best (and priciest) tavernas. Freshly prepared starters, fish and meat dishes, and a lovely waterfront setting. April–Oct daily lunch & dinner.

★ **Megaro** ☎ 28410 42220. This friendly place serves

fresh, well-prepared fish, seafood and steaks, inside or on a pontoon terrace on the water. Salads and starters are delicious too – try the halloumi and aubergine salad, €6. April–Oct daily noon–late.

**Vritomartes** ☎ 28410 41325. Situated in a plum spot in the centre of the harbour, noted for the fish, which can be a bit pricey, but they also have more economical options such as the fish dish for two at €18.50. April–Oct daily lunch & dinner.

**PLÁKA**

**Taverna Giorgos** ☎ 28410 41353, ⓦ giorgos-plaka.gr.
Serves good seafood, fish and traditional Cretan dishes on a large terrace facing out to sea opposite Spinalónga island. Daily lunch & dinner.

**Taverna Spinalonga** ☎ 28410 41804. With an outdoor terrace facing the sea and island, this taverna has perhaps the most economical fish meals, fresh from the day's catch. Daily lunch & dinner.

## SHOPPING

**Eklektos** Papandreou 13. Guide books and reading matter in English, it also stocks walking guides and maps for the area. Located 100m uphill from the square in the direction of Áyios Nikólaos.

# Lasíthi Plateau

Scores of daily tour buses visit the **LASÍTHI PLATEAU** to view the "thousands of white-cloth-sailed windmills" which irrigate the high plain. In fact there are very few working windmills left, although most roadside tavernas seem to have adopted many of those made redundant as marketing features. The drive alone is worthwhile, however, and the plain is a fine example of rural Crete at work, every inch devoted to the cultivation of potatoes, apples, figs, olives and a host of other crops; stay in one of the villages for a night or two and you'll see real life return as the tourists leave.

## Lasíthi villages

**Tzermiádho** is the largest village on the plateau, on the northern edge, and one of the least touristy; here there's a number of tavernas and *kafenía* and a couple of places to stay. Travelling clockwise around the plateau, **Áyios Yeóryios** has a couple of tavernas and rooms and a lovely little-visited Folk Museum, while **Psykhró** is the most visited village on the plateau, as it's the base for visiting Lasíthi's other chief attraction: the birthplace of Zeus, the **Dhiktean Cave**.

## The Dhiktean Cave

Daily: June–Sept 8am–7pm; Oct–May 8.30am–3pm • €4

In legend, Zeus's father, the Titan Kronos, was warned that he would be overthrown by a son, and accordingly ate all his offspring; however, when Rhea gave birth to Zeus in the **Dhiktean Cave**, she fed Kronos a stone and left the child concealed, protected by the Kouretes, who beat their shields outside to disguise his cries. The rest, as they say, is history (or at least myth).

The cave lies 1km southwest of Psykhró, where a signed road takes you up to a car park (€2); from here the cave is a ten-minute climb, or you can go up by mule (€15). The cave has been made more "visitor friendly" in recent years, with the introduction of concrete steps and electric lighting, so inevitably some of the magic and mystery have been lost, but it's still a worthwhile visit. The steps meander down to the bottom of the cave where there is a small lake surrounded by impressive stalactites and stalagmites.

## ARRIVAL AND TOURS

LASÍTHI PLATEAU

**By bus** Services run around the plateau to Psykhró direct from Iráklion and from Áyios Nikólaos via Neápoli. Both roads offer spectacular views, coiling through a succession of passes guarded by lines of ruined windmills.

**Wildlife tours** Petros Zarvakis is a wildlife expert and

leads guided wild-flower and bird-spotting hikes (April–Sept) into the mountains surrounding the plain, and also to the summit of Mount Dhíkti; Ask for him at the *Taverna Petros* at the Dhiktean Cave or call direct on ☎ 28440 31600 or 694 56 16 074.

## ACCOMMODATION AND EATING

**Dias Village** Áyios Yeóryios ☎ 28440 31207. This economical and friendly hotel can offer basic rooms with shared bath, and there's a small taverna below with

wholesome home-cooked food. The same family also rent out more superior en-suite rooms at their nearby sister hotel, *Maria*. April–Oct. **€25**

**Zeus** Psykhró ☎ 28440 31284 (or enquire at Taverna Halavro close to the cave car park). This small, seven-room hotel offers simple rooms just outside the main village, with views across the plateau. April–Oct. **€35**

# Kritsá

**KRITSÁ** is a pretty mountain village about 10km inland from Áyios Nikólaos and despite some commercialization is a welcome break from resort life. On the way you'll find the **Church of Panayía Kyrá** and the ancient site of **Lato**, both worth a visit.

Kritsá is known for its local **crafts**, particularly weaving, ceramics, embroidery and olive wood carvings, which are sold along the main-street shops by the village women. Once you get past the touristy shops and explore the maze of streets winding up the hillside, and their wonderful valley views, you get a real sense of a genuinely Cretan village. The small platía at the centre of the village is the focus of life.

## Church of Panayía Kyrá

Daily 8.30am–3pm • €3

On the approach road, about 1km before Kritsá, is the lovely Byzantine **church of Panayía Kyrá**, inside which survives perhaps the most complete set of Byzantine frescoes in Crete. The fourteenth- and fifteenth-century works have been much retouched, but they're still worth the visit. Excellent (and expensive) reproductions are sold from a shop alongside.

## Lato

Tues–Sun 8.30am–3pm • €2

Just before Kritsá a surfaced road leads off for about 4km to the archeological site of **Lato**, where the substantial remains of a Doric city are coupled with a grand hilltop setting. The city itself is extensive, but largely neglected, presumably because visitors and archeologists on Crete are more concerned with the Minoan era. If you're interested in knowing more about the site and its history an informative booklet is on sale at the ticket office. Ruins aside, you could come here just for the views: west over Áyios Nikólaos and beyond to the bay and Olous (which was Lato's port), and inland to the Lasíthi mountains.

### ARRIVAL AND DEPARTURE                                                    KRITSÁ

**By Bus** Áyios Nikólaos to Kritsá (8 daily; 7am–8.15pm; 15min).

### ACCOMMODATION

**Argyro** On the way into the village ☎ 28410 51174, ⓦ argyrorentrooms.gr. Clean, pleasant and economical en-suite rooms, some with TV and wi-fi – around a courtyard, with open views across the olive tree-lined valley. A/c €5 extra. **€35**

⭐ **The Olive Press** Close to the main church ☎ 28410 51296, ⓦ www.olivepress.centerall.com. A most attractive place to stay, this is a Belgian-run venture with pleasant rooms and apartments in a beautifully restored, stone-built olive-oil mill. Breakfast included. **€50**

### EATING AND DRINKING

There are a number of decent places to eat in the small platía at the centre of the village, with more alternatives further up, as well as a couple of bakeries for tempting *tyrópita* (cheese pies) or currant breads.

# East to Sitía

From Áyios Nikólaos the main road heads south and then east, a drive through barren hills sprinkled with villas and skirting above the occasional sandy cove. A newly completed stretch of the E75 continues past the site of **Gourniá**, slumped in the saddle between two low peaks, and from here on the road to **Sitía** is one of the most exhilarating in Crete. Carved into cliffs and mountain-sides, the road teeters above the coast before plunging inland at Kavoúsi. Of the beaches you see below, only the one at **Mókhlos** is at all accessible, some 5km below the main road.

# Gourniá

Tues–Sun 8.30am–3pm • €3 • ☎ 28410 22462

GOURNIÁ, 20km east of Áyios Nikólaos, is the most completely preserved **Minoan town**. Its narrow alleys and stairways intersect a throng of one-roomed houses centred on a main square, and the rather grand house of what may have been a local ruler or governor. Although less impressive than the great palaces, the site is strong on revelations about the lives of the ordinary people – many of the dwellings housed craftsmen, who left behind their tools and materials to be found by the excavators. Its desolation today (you are likely to be alone save for a dozing guardian) only serves to heighten the contrast with what must have been a cramped and raucous community 3500 years ago.

# Mókhlos

MÓKHLOS is a sleepy seaside village with a few rooms, a hotel or two and a number of **tavernas** along its tiny harbour. The village beach is very small and pebbly, but there's a slightly larger beach (also pebble) to the west. For those who stay there's not a great deal to do – hang out in the harbour taverna-cafés or swim out to the **islet of Mókhlos** just offshore, where there are remains of Minoan houses – but it's very easy to do nothing here in this laidback place.

## ACCOMMODATION AND EATING                                MÓKHLOS

**Hermes** ☎ 28430 94074. This clean and simple pension behind the waterfront offers the cheapest rooms in the village. Some en-suite rooms with a/c, others sharing bath. April–Oct. €28

**Sofia Hotel** ☎ 28430 94738. For a bit more en-suite luxury, and a harbourfront view, this friendly hotel has a/c rooms with fridge and TV, and is situated above its waterside taverna which serves good home-cooked dishes. April–Oct. €40

# Sitía

SITÍA is the port and main town of the relatively unexploited eastern edge of Crete. It's a pleasantly scenic, offering a plethora of waterside restaurants, a long sandy beach and a lazy lifestyle little affected even by the thousands of visitors in peak season. The town attracts a number of French, Italian and Greek tourists, and it grows on you, perhaps inviting a longer stay than intended. For entertainment there's the **town beach**, providing good swimming, windsurfing and diving. In town there's a small **folklore museum** (Mon–Fri 10am–1pm; €2), an excellent **archeological museum** (Tues–Sun 8.30am–3pm; €2) and a Venetian fort to explore. A colourful weekly **market** takes place on Tuesdays between 7am and 2pm along Odhós Itanou near the archeological museum.

## ARRIVAL AND DEPARTURE                                      SITÍA

**By plane** Sitía's airport lies 1km north of the town and is currently served by domestic flights only, with Aegean Airways and Olympic Air.
Destinations Athens (5 weekly; 50min), Kárpathos (5 weekly; 1hr), Kássos (6 weekly; 25min), Rhodes (5 weekly; 1hr).
**By ferry** The ferry port lies 500m north of the town. Sitía to: Pireás via Iráklion (2 weekly; 16hr). Tue–Wed to: Kássos (2hr 30min), Kárpathos (4hr 20min), Mílos (9hr) Rhodes

(9hr), Santoríni (7hr).
**By bus** The station is at the south end of Venizélou – the main entry road into town from the west.
Destinations Áyios Nikólaos (7 daily; 6.15am–8.30pm; 1hr 45min), Iráklion (6 daily; 5.30am–7.45pm; 3hr 15min), Ierápetra (5 daily; 6.15am–8pm; 1hr 30min), Palékastro (5 daily; 6am–2.30pm; 40min), Vái Beach (3 daily 9.30am–2.30pm; 1hr), Zákros (2 daily 6am & 2pm; 1hr 20min).

## INFORMATION AND ACTIVITIES

**Tourist office** On the seafront, at the start of the beach road (Mon–Fri 9.30am–2.30pm & 5–9pm, Sat 9am–2.30pm; ☎ 28430 28300, ⊛ sitia.gr). Supplies accommodation lists, maps and local information.

**Diving** Universal Diver, Kornárou 140 (☎ 28430 23489, ⊕ pavlossimos@yahoo.gr). PADI-certified dive centre with courses for all levels.

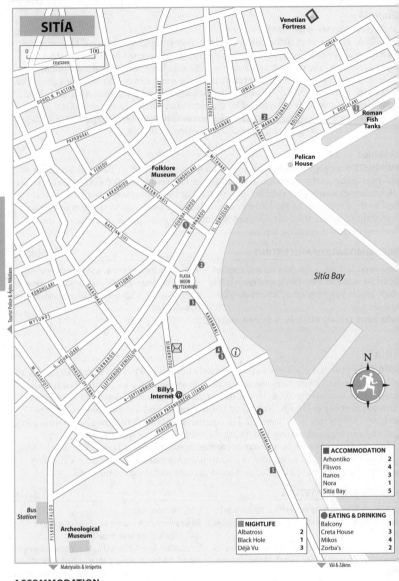

SITÍA

0     100
metres

Venetian Fortress

Roman Fish Tanks

Folklore Museum

Pelican House

Sitía Bay

PLATIA IROON POLYTEKHNIOU

Billy's Internet @

N

Bus Station

Archeological Museum

■ **ACCOMMODATION**
| | |
|---|---|
| Arhontiko | 2 |
| Flisvos | 4 |
| Itanos | 3 |
| Nora | 1 |
| Sitia Bay | 5 |

■ **NIGHTLIFE**
| | |
|---|---|
| Albatross | 2 |
| Black Hole | 1 |
| Déjà Vu | 3 |

● **EATING & DRINKING**
| | |
|---|---|
| Balcony | 1 |
| Creta House | 3 |
| Mikos | 4 |
| Zorba's | 2 |

Tourist Police & Áyios Nikólaos

Makriyialós & Ierápetra

Vái & Zákros

## ACCOMMODATION

**Arhontiko** Kondhiláki 16 ☎ 28430 28172. One of the best budget places in town, a couple of blocks back from the seafront (10min walk to beach), with clean, attractive rooms and a garden with communal terrace. One of the rooms is en suite. **€30**

**Flisvos** Karamanlí 4 ☎ 28430 27135, ⓦ flisvos-sitia .com. Refurbished hotel fronting the sea at the start of the Beach Road; simple, clean a/c rooms with TV, wi-fi and

fridge face either the sea or a patio garden behind. Breakfast included. **€60**

★ **Itanos** Platía Iroon Polytekhníou ☎ 28430 22900 ⓦ itanoshotel.com. Upmarket hotel by the town's main sea-front square, 200m along the harbour to the beach, with smart, a/c balcony rooms (those at the front with sea view), satellite TV and there's a rooftop bar. Breakfast included. **€60**

**Sitia Bay** Karamanlí ☏ 28430 24800, ⊚ sitiabay.com. A stone's throw from the town beach, this modern hotel-apartment complex offers tastefully furnished, comfortable a/c rooms and studios with kitchenette; all rooms have sea-view balcony and there's a pool. Optional breakfast is extra. **€90**

**Nora** Rouseláki 31 ☏ 28430 23017, ✉ norahotel@yahoo .gr. Near the ferry port, this small female-run hotel has basic rooms with a/c, TV, balcony and shower and fine views over the bay. A 10min walk to the town centre. April–Oct. **€35**

## EATING AND DRINKING

A line of enticing outdoor tavernas crowds the harbourfront, many displaying dishes and fresh fish to lure you in – though these places can be relatively expensive. Away from the water you'll find cheaper (and often more interesting) places to dine.

★ **Balcony** Kazantzákis & Foundalídhou ☏ 28430 25084. Stylish restaurant in the upper floor of an elegant townhouse. An eclectic menu has Mexican- and Asian-influenced dishes as well as Greek fusion cooking, such as the pork fillet with yoghurt and pilaf rice. Mains from €10. May–Oct daily lunch & dinner; Nov–March daily dinner only.

**Creta House** Karamanlí, next to the Hotel Flisvos. A reliable, if somewhat touristy, traditional taverna specializing in Cretan dishes; try the moussaka or lamb, all served on the large harbourside terrace. April–Oct daily lunch & dinner.

**Mikos** Karamanlí 14 ☏ 28430 22416. Tasty charcoal-grill meats (from €6) plus traditional Greek dishes are served up with very strong local wine at this popular diner with a seafront terrace. Daily lunch & dinner.

**Zorba's** Cnr El Venizélou & Kazantzákis. The oldest, biggest and most popular place on the seafront. Serves up much more authentic food than you might expect from its touristy appearance and is regularly frequented by locals. Daily lunch & dinner.

## DRINKING AND NIGHTLIFE

Sitía's nightlife, mostly conducted at an easy pace, centres on the music bars and cafés at the northern end of Venizélou and along the beach road.

**Albatross** Venizélou 185. This modern café and bar is one of many along the harbourfront strip, with street and terrace seating. Daily 10am–late.

**Black Hole** Venizélou, far end. One of Sitía's most popular summer music bars, playing house and rock, a lively place with a large outdoor terrace and indoor bar. May–Sept 9pm–late.

**Déjà Vu** Venizélou 183. Glitzy, neon café-bar on the harbourfront, with comfy terrace seating, popular with young Sitians. Daily 10am–late.

# The far east

Not long after leaving Sitía along the new main road a signed side road up to the left leads to **Váï** and the **Monastery of Toploú**. **Palékastro**, some 9km south of Váï, is a good place to stopover, with good beaches to explore and a **Minoan site**. Palékastro is also the crossroads for the winding road south to **Zákros** and **Xerókambos**, a beautiful drive, and having your own transport presents all kinds of beach and exploration possibilities.

## Monastery of Toploú

Daily 9am–1pm & 2–6pm, Oct–March closes 4pm • €3

The **Monasterty of Toploú**'s forbidding exterior reflects a history of resistance to invaders, and doesn't prepare you for the gorgeous flower-decked cloister within. The blue-robed monks keep out of the way as far as possible, but in quieter periods their cells and refectory are left discreetly on view. In the church is one of the masterpieces of Cretan art, the **eighteenth-century icon** *Lord Thou Art Great* by Ioannis Kornaros, incorporating 61 small scenes full of amazing detail inspired by the Orthodox prayer "Lord thou art great …" In the monastery's shop you can buy enormously expensive reproductions of the work as well as olive oil and wine made by the monks.

Recently a €1 billion tourist resort and golf course was set to be built on monastery-owned land at Cape Sideros. The project, approved by the Abbot, was abandoned after vehement opposition by local residents and environmentalists.

7

**7**

## Vái

**Vái beach** itself features alongside Knossos or the Lasíthi Plateau on almost every Cretan travel agent's list of excursions. Not surprisingly, it is now covered in sunbeds and umbrellas, though it is still a superb beach. Above all, it is famous for its **palm trees**, and the sudden appearance of the grove is indeed an exotic shock; lying on the fine sand in the early morning, the illusion is of a Caribbean island. There's a car park (€3), a café and an expensive taverna at the beach, plus toilets and showers. By day you can find a bit more solitude by climbing the rocks or swimming to one of the smaller beaches which surround Vái. **Ítanos**, twenty minutes' walk north by an obvious trail, has a couple of tiny beaches and some modest ruins from the Classical era.

## Palékastro

**PALÉKASTRO** is an attractive large farming village with a good choice of tavernas, shops, a few bars and a small **folk museum** (May–Oct Tues–Sun 10am–1pm & 5–8pm; €2). The sea is a couple of kilometres to the east of town, where you'll find fine beaches which are highly popular with windsurfers. **ANGÁTHIA** village, smaller and quieter, lies less than 1km to the east of its neighbour, and closer to the beaches.

### The beaches

**Hióna beach**, a good stretch of EU blue-flagged pebble and sand, to the south of a flat-topped hill named Kastrí which dominates the coastal landscape, lies a kilometre east of Angáthia and is the most popular local beach, though still far from crowded. The better sands are around the bay further to the south of Hióna, where for most of the year you can easily claim a cove to yourself. Also south of Hióna beach along the track running beside the sea, about 200m down on the right (signed "Peak Sanctuary"), a walking track will take you to the nearby **Petsofas peak** – a pleasant 3km hike. The best beach of all, **Kouréménos**, lies to the north of the Kastrí bluff and is one of Crete's top **windsurfing** spots. The long golden sand beach here has a number of tavernas and rooms along the beachfront road.

### Palékastro Minoan site

Open daily during daylight hours • Free

Behind Hióna beach lies the main excavation area – known as Roussolákkos and left open – of Palékastro's **Minoan site**, one of the most important in eastern Crete. Only partly excavated (digging continues and new finds are coming to light) surveys indicate that the largest Minoan town yet discovered lies underground here, as well as a very large building which could be a palace.

## Áno Zákros

**ÁNO ZÁKROS** (Upper Zákros) lies a little under 20km from Palékastro, a slow-moving country town with a couple of cafés, tavernas and one hotel. The beach and the Minoan palace of Zákros are actually at Káto ("lower") Zákros, eight winding kilometres further down an asphalted road towards the sea. If you prefer to walk, there's a magnificent hike down the impressive **Valley of the Dead gorge** (named after ancient Minoan tombs in its sides); follow the signs from the south end of town, opposite the *Taverna Napoleon*.

## Káto Zákros

The delightful village of **KÁTO ZÁKROS** is little more than a collection of tavernas, some of which rent out rooms, around a peaceful beach with a minuscule fishing anchorage and another interesting Minoan palace. It's a wonderfully restful place, quiet most of the time, except in high season when rooms are rarely to be had on spec; at such times you'd be wise to ring ahead if you wish to stay.

## Palace of Zákros

Daily: June–Oct 8am–5pm; Nov–May 8am–3pm • €3 • ☎ 28430 26897 • 100m behind Káto Zákros beach

The **Palace of Zákros** was an important find for archeologists; it had been occupied from about 1600 BC to 1450 BC, when it was abandoned hurriedly and completely. Later, it was forgotten almost entirely and as a result was never plundered. The first major excavation began only in 1960; all sorts of everyday objects, such as tools, raw materials, food and pottery, were thus discovered intact among the ruins. Although the site is set back from the sea, in places it is often marshy and waterlogged – partly the fault of a spring which once supplied fresh water to a cistern beside the royal apartments. In wetter periods you can keep your feet dry and get an excellent view down over the central court and royal apartments by climbing up the remains of narrow streets of the town which occupied the hill higher up.

## Xerókambos

The newly asphalted road south of Áno Zákros descends through olive groves and giant greenhouses to run along a deep ravine. After 10km a brilliant turquoise sea and white sandy beaches divided by rocky outcrops appear below; here lies **XERÓKAMBOS**, as tranquil a getaway as you could wish for. This coastal settlement consists of one long "main" street, in the midst of fields and olive groves, with a few rooms and tavernas and a couple of minimarkets, but nothing at all in the way of after-dark diversions. The main beach is 2km of pristine shimmering sand, long enough to find seclusion should you want it, and if that isn't escapist enough, to the north and especially the south are wonderful isolated coves.

7

## GETTING AROUND                                                    THE FAR EAST

**By bus** Sitía to: Palékastro (5 daily 6am–2.30pm; 40min), Váï Beach (3 daily 9.30am–2.30pm; 1hr), Zákros (2 daily 6am & 2pm;1hr 20min), Káto Zákros site (2 daily 11am & 2pm; 1hr 30 min). There is no public transport south of Zákros.

**By car and scooter** Rental is available in Palékastro at Moto Kastri (☎ 28430 61477), on the eastern edge of the village along the Váï road.

## INFORMATION AND ACTIVITIES

**Tourist office** On the Sitía road 50m from the square (April–Oct Mon–Fri 9am–9pm, Sat 9am–2pm ☎ 28430 61546).

**Windsurfing** Freak Windsurf ☎ 697 92 53 861,

ⓦ freak-surf.com. Courses and board hire from a reliable company based at Kouremenos, Crete's best windsurfing locale, at the extreme east end of the island.

## ACCOMMODATION

### PALÉKASTRO

**Hellas Hotel** ☎ 28430 61240, ⓦ palaikastro.com. Comfortable en-suite rooms in the village centre with a/c, balcony, TV, fridge, and there's a taverna below. Reductions for longer stays. April–Oct. **€36**

★ **Marina Village** Between Angathia and Kouremenos beach ☎ 28430 61284, ⓦ palaikastro .com/marinavillage. A peaceful haven 800m from the beach with well-furnished, a/c balcony rooms, surrounded by a garden of bougainvillea and banana plants. Buffet breakfast included. May–Oct. **€68**

**Metochi Vai Village** On the Váï–Palékastro road ☎ 28430 61546, ⓦ palaikastro.com/metohivai. Here shepherds' shelters, owned by the Monastery of Toploú, have been converted into well-furnished, traditional-style apartments, which retain many original features including Cretan stone arches, fireplaces and wooden beams. Rooms

come with a/c, fridge, cooker and TV. **€55**

**Ostria** ☎ 28430 61022, ⓦ ostria-itanos.gr. This brightly furbished hotel is set in gardens on the outskirts of the village on the Váï road. The modern, clean rooms have a/c, fridge and balcony. March–Oct. **€45**

### ÁNO ZÁKROS

**Hotel Zakros** ☎ 28430 93379. A plain hotel with simple, economical rooms, some en-suite, with a/c, TV and great views across the Valley of the Dead gorge from its rear rooms; it also offers guests a free minibus service to the Minoan palace at Káto Zákros and beach. **€35**

### KÁTO ZÁKROS

**Coral & Athina** ☎ 28430 26893, ⓦ kato-zakros.gr. These rooms sit right above the beach, with great sea views from their large communal terraces; en suites are clean, simply furnished and come with a/c, fridge and TV. March–Nov. €45

**George Villas** ☎ 28430 23739. George has spacious a/c studios in a lovely stone building with mature gardens, in a quiet spot at the back of the village (600m behind the archeological site, along a driveable track). Rooms come with kitchenette, terrace and views over the bay. April–Oct. €60

★ **Zakros Palace Apartments** ☎ 28430 29550, ⓦ katozakros-apts.gr. An attractive option on the hill, with superb views; all balconies overlook both the bay and gorge, rooms and studios are all a/c with large terraces, TV and kitchen corner. €50

### XERÓKAMBOS

**Asteras** ☎ 28430 26787. Set in their own garden, above the olive groves, these modern a/c studio rooms and apartments all come with kitchenette, fridge and good sea views. April–Oct. €45

**Liviko View** ☎ 28430 27001, ⓦ livikoview.gr. These excellent rooms (and taverna below) are run by a couple of Greek-Australians. Rooms come with a/c and balcony sea view, and there are some more expensive apartments sleeping up to four. Internet access available. April–Oct. €35

## EATING AND DRINKING

When it comes to eating, there are plenty of tavernas in the area. With the exception of Palékastro, there are few, if any bars in these quiet villages.

### PALÉKASTRO

**Hellas Hotel Taverna** On the main square ☎ 28430 61240. A good traditional taverna on the terrace beneath the hotel, in the heart of the village, serving Greek and Cretan dishes. April–Oct daily 10am–late.

**Mythos** On the main square ☎ 28430 61243. This popular family-run taverna serves good traditional food, with meat, fish and plenty of vegetarian options. Friendly service and economical prices. Daily 10am–late.

**Taverna Vaios** Angáthia ☎ 28430 61043. Up the hill from the bridge leading into the village, on the right. Makes a good lunch stop; their home-cooked food and charcoal-grilled meats (from €5.50) are served on a large roadside terrace in this quiet village. May–Oct daily lunch & dinner.

**To Botsalo** Kouremenos beach. Cretan dishes, fish and grills served on a large pleasant terrace facing the sea and shaded by tamarisk trees. May–Oct daily lunch & dinner.

★ **Xiona Taverna** Hióna beach ☎ 28430 61228. A great spot at the northern end of the beach; fresh fish and seafood (try the kalamari €7) are served on a shady terrace perched on the rocks above the sea. May–Oct daily lunch & dinner.

### ÁNO ZÁKROS

**Napoleon** ☎ 28430 93252. This taverna serves

traditional Greek food and home-cooked pizza on a small road-side terrace overlooking the valley, with great views. Daily noon–1am.

**Xyloporto** Next to the petrol station. A good place for coffee, breakfast or a snack. If you need to check email there's internet and wi-fi. Daily 8am–midnight.

### KÁTO ZÁKROS

★ **Akrogiali** On the beachfront ☎ 28430 26893. With a large shady terrace by the water's edge, this relaxed taverna serves good fish, seafood and charcoal-grill meats (€6). The friendly owner, Nikos, also acts as an agent for many room options nearby. March–Nov daily 9am–late.

### XERÓKAMBOS

**Akrogiali** On the beachfront, at the south end. This taverna serves up fresh fish, seafood, salads and Cretan dishes on a large terrace set back from the beach with good sea views. April–Oct daily lunch & dinner.

**Liviko View** Below the apartments of the same name (see above). The cooking here, with organic ingredients grown on the family farm, is recommended and there is a wonderful terrace. Vegetarian dishes from €4. April–Oct daily lunch & dinner.

# Ierápetra and the southeast coast

The main road across the island from Sitía to the south coast runs between the east and west ranges of the **Sitía mountains**. One of the first places it hits on the south coast is the sprawling resort of **Makryialós**, but from here to the bustling town and resort of **Ierápetra** there's little reason to stop; the few beaches are rocky and the coastal plain submerged under ranks of polythene-covered greenhouses. A more tranquil hideaway lies just west of Ierápetra, the charming resort of **Mýrtos**.

## Ierápetra

**IERÁPETRA** itself is a bustling modern supply centre for the region's farmers, but despite an ongoing modernization programme, which has cleaned up the centre and revamped

## ISLAND ESCAPE: GAIDHOURONÍSI

One way to escape the urban hubbub for a few hours is to take a boat to the **island of Gaidhouronísi** (aka Donkey Island or Chrissi Island ) some 10km out to sea from Ierápetra. No one seems to know how the 5km-long island got its name as there are no donkeys; instead you'll find a cedar forest, the fabulous "**Shell Beach**" covered with millions of multicoloured mollusc shells, some good sandy beaches and a couple of tavernas. Excursion **boats** (May–Sept daily 10.30am & 12.30pm out, 4pm & 7pm return; €24, under-12s €12) leave from Ierápetra seafront harbour, and you can buy tickets on the boat or at any of the town travel agents in advance. The voyage to the island takes fifty minutes and the boats have an on-board bar.

..e seafront, as a town, most people find it pretty uninspiring. The tavernas along the
..ee-lined seafront are scenic enough and there is a decent EU blue-flagged beach
..hich stretches a couple of kilometres east. Although there has been a port here since
..oman times, only the **Venetian fort** guarding the harbour and a crumbling Turkish
..inaret remain as reminders of better days. What little else has been salvaged is in the
..ne-room **archeological museum** (Tues–Sun 8.30am–3pm; €2) near the post office.

7

### ..akryialós

..AKRYIALÓS, some 27km east of Ierápetra, was originally composed of two distinct
..llages. It has gobbled up its neighbour Análipsi to form a single resort, strung out along
..e coastal road. There are still quiet spots along the long beach, one of the best in the east,
..strand of fine sand which shelves so gently you feel you could walk the two hundred
..autical miles to Africa. To the west lies the village's small harbour, lined with tavernas.
..[M]any rooms and apartment places here are pre-booked by package tours, so while still a
..ry pleasant place to stop for a swim or a bite, it can get pretty busy in high summer.

### ..ýrtos

..ÝRTOS, 15km west of Ierápetra, lies just off the main road, and although developed
..  a degree, it nonetheless remains a tranquil and charming white-walled village kept
..[cl]ean as a whistle by its house-proud inhabitants, and most of the summer you'll find
..[pl]enty of space on the long shingle-and-sand beach. A village **museum** (April–Oct
..[M]on–Fri 3.30–7.30pm), located to the side of the church, houses some of the finds
..[fr]om a couple of excavated hilltop **Minoan villas**, Fournoú Korifí and Pýrgos (which
..[ca]n be found just off the road from Ierápetra a couple of kilometres east of the village,
..[an]d signed), in addition to a folklore section.

### ..RRIVAL AND DEPARTURE

### IERÁPETRA AND THE SOUTHEAST COAST

..**y bus** Ierápetra bus station is on Lasthenous, north of
..wn.
..[De]stinations Áyios Nikólaos (8 daily 6.30am–8.30pm;
..[1h]r), Iráklion (8 daily 6.30am–8.30pm; 2hr 30min),

Makrigialos (8 daily, 6.15am–8.15pm; 30 min), Mýrtos (6
daily 6.30am–8.15pm; 30min), Sitía (6 daily
6.15am–6.15pm; 1hr 30min).

### ..FORMATION AND TOURS

..[To]urist office In the seafront car park in Ierápetra. (Mon–
..[Sa]t 9am–1pm ⓦ ierapetra.gr). Provides a detailed town
..[m]ap and leaflets.
..[Se]rvices Ierápetra Express travel agency, 100m north of

the town hall on Platía Eleftherías, is a good source of
information.
**Tours** Prima Tours in Mýrtos (☎ 28420 51530, ⓦ sunbudget
.net) offer guided walks and provide internet access.

### ..CCOMMODATION

#### ..RÁPETRA

..[Ca]mping Koutsounari 7km east of Ierápetra on the
..[M]akriyialós road ☎ 28420 61213. Offers plenty of shade on

fixed camping positions right next to a long sandy beach,
with access to the new pool bar next door. May–Sept. **€18**
★ **Cretan Villa** Lakérdha 16 ☎ 28420 28522,

ⓦ cretan-villa.com. Close to the bus station; sparkling a/c rooms with TV and fridge overlook the flower-bedecked patio of a beautiful 180-year-old stone house. **€54**

**Ersi** Platía Eleftherías 20 ☎ 28420 23208. Central hotel, recently refurbished, offering good-value rooms with fridge, TV, balcony; the owner also rents out seafront apartments nearby for not much more than the cost of a room. **€35**

**Katerina** Eastern seafront ☎ 28420 28345, ⓦ katerina-rooms.gr. Recently refurbished inside (but in need of an outside refurbishment at the time of writing), smart rooms and studios with a/c, TV, wi-fi, fridge and balcony with sea view. **€50**

### MAKRYIALÓS

★ **Maria Tsanakalioti Apartments** ☎ 28430 51557, ⓦ makrigialos-crete.com. The friendly proprietor offers bright beach-front studio rooms and apartments – some with sea view and terrace – with kitchenette, a/c and TV. April–Oct. **€50**

**Oasis Rooms** Beachfront, before the harbour ☎ 28430 51918. Simple sea-view en-suite rooms with a/c, fridge and balcony, just 10m from the beach (just after the Rom villa). May–Oct. **€40**

★ **White River Cottages** ☎ 28430 51120, ⓔ wri @otenet.gr. An abandoned hamlet of traditional sto dwellings (originally *Áspro Pótamos* or "White River" h been restored as a warren of charming a/c studios a apartments with kitchen and private terraces, set arou a pool. It's located 900m up a signed track on the right you enter the village from the east. April–Oct. **€68**

### MÝRTOS

**Big Blue** West village, near the beach ☎ 28420 5109 ⓦ big-blue.gr. Spacious studios and pricier apartmer above the beach, sleeping two to four with en-su bathrooms, a/c, kitchenette and sea view. April–Nov. **€4**

**Mirtos Hotel** Main thoroughfare behind the bea ☎ 28420 51227, ⓦ mirtoshotel.com. Friendly and goo value small hotel with comfortable a/c, en-suite roo with balcony. They own the excellent taverna below, whe breakfast (included) is served. Jan–Nov. **€42**

### EATING AND DRINKING

### IERÁPETRA

★ **Gorgona** Stratigou Samouil 12 ☎ 28420 26619. Near the harbour and fort, directly on the beach, this reliable, well-known taverna serves good fish, seafood (try the octopus €8) and Cretan dishes at reasonable prices and is very popular among the locals. March–Nov daily, breakfast, lunch & dinner.

**Napoleon** Stratigou Samouil 26 ☎ 28420 22410. Close to the *Gorgona* this is one of Ierápetra's oldest tavernas. Freshly cooked dishes, a good choice of appetizers and reasonable prices make this another favourite with locals. Daily lunch & dinner.

### MAKRYIALÓS

**Faros** ☎ 28430 52456. Set in a great position overlooking

the harbourfront, this taverna serves good fish ("fresh fro our boat") as well as the usual taverna offerings. May–O daily lunch & dinner.

**To Limani** ☎ 28430 52457. This taverna serves fis seafood and meat dishes on the waterfront terra overlooking a tiny strip of beach by the harbour. May–O daily lunch & dinner.

### MÝRTOS

**Mirtos Taverna** Main thoroughfare, below the Hot Mirtos ☎ 28420 51227. An excellent, family-run tavern offering a range of home-cooked dishes and tas mezédhes, with some outdoor tables along the pavemer Jan–Nov daily breakfast, lunch & dinner.

# Réthymnon and around

The province of **Réthymnon** reaches to Mount Psilorítis in the east and towards the White Mountains in the west. The fertile **Amari Valley**, with its pretty villages, lies in the central plain, while on the south coast, in particular around **Plakiás**, there are beaches as fine as any Crete can offer.

Réthymnon itself is an attractive and lively city, with some excellent beaches nearby, although the coastline to the east has seen a great influx of tourists, with the development of a whole series of large hotels extending almost 10km along the beach.

## Réthymnon

**RÉTHYMNON** remains one of the most beautiful of Crete's major cities (only Haniá is a serious rival), with an enduringly provincial air. A wide sandy beach and palm-lined promenade border the old town, a labyrinthine tangle of Venetian and Turkish houses where ancient minarets lend an exotic air to the skyline. Dominating everything from the west is the superbly preserved outline of the **fortress** built by the Venetians after a series of pirate raids had devastated the town.

## The beach

With a large sandy **beach** right in the heart of town, lined with cafés and tavernas, you don't need to stir too far. The sea here is dead calm, being protected by the breakwaters in front of the town, but there are disadvantages – the beach can be crowded and the

# RÉTHYMNON

| ■ NIGHTLIFE | |
|---|---|
| Envy | 3 |
| Kenzo | 1 |
| Metropolis | 5 |
| Nuvel | 4 |
| Opera Club | 2 |

| ● EATING | |
|---|---|
| Castelvecchio | 2 |
| Fanari | 7 |
| Kyria Maria | 6 |
| Mesostrati | 9 |
| O Gounas | 1 |
| Stella's Kitchen | 8 |
| Tapas y Vinos | 4 |
| Thalassografia | 3 |
| To Pigadi | 5 |

| ■ ACCOMMODATION | |
|---|---|
| Atelier | 1 |
| Barbara Dokimaki | 5 |
| Camping Elizabeth | 10 |
| Fortezza | 2 |
| Ideon | 4 |
| Leo | 7 |
| Pension Castello | 8 |
| Vecchio | 3 |
| Youth Hostel | 6 |
| Zania | 9 |

water none too clean. Less sheltered sands stretch for many kilometres to the east, crowded at first but progressively less so further out.

## The Old Town

Away from the beach, the atmospheric **old town** lies immediately behind the attractive **inner** harbour. Almost anywhere here, you'll find unexpected old buildings, wall fountains, overhanging wooden balconies, heavy, carved doors and rickety shops, some still with local craftsmen – such as the lýra makers, the "national" instrument of Crete – sitting out front. Look out for the **Venetian loggia** which houses a shop selling Classical art reproductions; the **Rimóndi Fountain**, another of the more elegant Venetian survivals; and the **Nerandzés mosque**, the best preserved in Réthymnon but currently serving as a music school and closed to the public, with its **minaret**. Ethnikís Andístasis, the street leading straight up from the fountain, is the town's **market** area.

## The Venetian fortress

Daily: May–Sept 8am–7pm; 10am–5.30pm Oct–April • €4 • ☎ 28310 28101

The massive Fortezza or **Venetian fortress** dominates the town from the west. Said to be the largest Venetian castle ever built, this was a response, in the last quarter of the sixteenth century, to a series of **pirate raids** (by Barbarossa among others) that had devastated the town. Inside is now a vast open space dotted with the remains of all sorts of barracks, arsenals, officers' houses, earthworks and deep shafts, and at the centre a large domed **mosque** complete with surviving *mihrab* (a niche indicating the direction of Mecca). The fortress was designed to be large enough for the entire population to take shelter within the walls. Although much is ruined, it remains thoroughly atmospheric, and you can look out from the walls over the town and harbour, and along the coast to the west.

## The archeological museum

Top end of Himáras • Tues–Sun 8.30am–3pm • €3 • ☎ 28310 54668

The **archeological museum** occupies a building almost directly opposite the entrance to the fortress. This was built by the Turks as an extra defence, and later served as a prison; it's now entirely modern inside: cool, spacious and airy. Unfortunately, the collection is not particularly exciting, but worth seeing if you're going to miss the bigger museums elsewhere on the island.

## Historical and Folk Art Museum

M. Vernárdhou 28 • Mon–Sat 9am–2.15pm • €3 • ☎ 28310 23398

A beautifully restored seventeenth-century Venetian mansion is the home of the small but tremendously enjoyable **Historical and Folk Art Museum**, close to the Nerandzés mosque. Gathered within four, cool, airy rooms are musical instruments, old photos, basketry, farm implements, traditional costumes and jewellery, lace, weaving and embroidery (look out for a traditional-style tapestry made in 1941 depicting German parachutists landing at Máleme), pottery, knives and old wooden chests. It makes for a fascinating insight into a fast-disappearing lifestyle, which survived virtually unchanged from Venetian times to the 1960s.

### The public gardens

The old city ends at the Porta Guora at the top of Ethnikís Andístasis, the only surviving remnant of the city walls. Almost opposite are the quiet and shady **public gardens**. These are a soothing place to stroll, and in the latter half of July the **Réthymnon Wine Festival** is staged here; an enjoyable event, with local dancing as the evening progresses and the barrels empty. The nominal entrance fee includes all the wine you can drink.

## ARRIVAL AND DEPARTURE

**By bus** The bus station in Réthymnon is by the sea to the west of the town centre just off Periferiakós, the road which skirts the waterfront around the fortress.

**Destinations** Arkádhi monastery (3 daily; 40min); Ayía Galíni via Spíli (4 daily 5.30am–2.15pm; 45min–1hr 30min); Haniá (16 daily 7.30–10.30pm; 1hr 30min); Iráklion (18 daily 6.30am–10.15pm; 1hr 30min); Plakiás (4 daily 6.15am–7.30pm; 50min).

## INFORMATION

**Tourist office** Delfini Building, on the seafront (Mon–Fri 8am–2.30pm, Sat 10am–4pm; ☎ 28310 29148, ⓦ rethymnon.com), provides maps, timetables and accommodation lists.

**Services** Galero Internet Café, Rimóndi fountain (daily 9am–midnight). Ellotia Tours, Arkhadíou 155, behind the seafront (☎ 28310 51981, ⓦ rethymnoatcrete.com), is a reliable source of travel information and tickets.

## ACCOMMODATION

There's a great number of places to stay in Réthymnon, and only at the height of the season are you likely to have difficulty finding somewhere, though you may get weary looking. The greatest concentration of rooms is in the tangled streets west of the inner harbour, between the Rimóndi fountain and the museums; there are also quite a few places on and around Arkadhíou and Platía Plastíra.

★ **Atelier** Himáras 25 ☎ 28310 24440, ⓦ frosso-bora .com/rooms. Attractive en-suite balcony rooms with a/c, fridge and plasma TV run by a talented potter, who has her studio in the basement and sells her wares in a shop on the other side of the building. **€45**

**Barbara Dokimaki** Platía Plastíra 14 ☎ 28310 24581, ⓔ alicedokk@yahoo.gr. Strange warren of a place, with one entrance at the above address, just off the seafront behind the Ideon, and another on Dambérgi; ask for the refurbished top-floor studio rooms, which have balconies and kitchenettes. April–Oct. **€45**

★ **Fortezza** Melissinoú 16, near the fortress ☎ 28310 55551, ⓦ fortezza.gr. Fully renovated in 2011, this top-range hotel is styled with a mix of marble, chrome and wood, while cream furnishings complement the traditional wooden furniture in the rooms and suites, which have a/c, satellite TV and balcony. There is a swimming pool, two bars and a restaurant. Breakfast included. April–Oct. **€88**

**Ideon** Platía Plastíra 10 ☎ 28310 28667, ⓦ hotelideon .gr. High-class hotel with a brilliant position just north of the ferry dock; little chance of getting one of their superior balcony sea-view rooms without prebooking in high season, though. Facilities include a swimming pool, bar and restaurant. Breakfast included. April–Oct. **€88**

**Leo** Vafé 2 ☎ 28310 26197, ⓦ leohotel.gr. This elegant boutique hotel in a restored Venetian mansion offers luxurious individually styled rooms featuring exposed stonework and beautiful wooden floors, equipped with a/c, fridge, satellite TV and wi-fi. Breakfast included. **€95**

**Pension Castello** Karaoli 10 ☎ 28310 23570, ⓦ castello-rethymno.gr. An attractive small pension in a renovated sixteenth-century Venetian-Turkish mansion; a/c en-suite rooms with fridge, TV and a delightful patio garden. Breakfast included. **€60**

**Vecchio** Daliani 4, near the Rimóndi Fountain ☎ 28310 54985, ⓦ vecchio.gr. Elegant Venetian mansion tastefully transformed into an enchanting small hotel with a/c rooms (some with balcony) set around a pool. Breakfast included. May–Oct. **€85**

**Youth Hostel** Tombázi 41 ☎ 28310 22848, ⓦ yhrethymno.com. The cheapest beds in town. Large, clean, very friendly and popular, it has food, showers, clothes-washing facilities, internet access and a multilingual library. **€11**

**Zania** Pávlou Vlástou 3 ☎ 28310 28169. Pension right on the corner of Arkadhíou in a well-adapted and atmospheric Venetian mansion. The airy high-ceilinged rooms come with a/c and fridge, but bathrooms are shared. May–Oct. **€40**

### CAMPING

**Camping Elizabeth** 4km east of town ☎ 28310 28694, ⓦ camping-elizabeth.com. A pleasant, large site on the beach with all facilities and wi-fi. Special rates for long-term stays in autumn/winter. To get here take the bus for the out-of-town hotels (marked Scaleta/El Greco). **€20**

## EATING AND DRINKING

The most touristy restaurants are arrayed immediately behind the town beach with menu picture boards outside – many of them overpriced and mediocre – and around the inner harbour there's a cluster of expensive and intimate fish tavernas. The most inviting and best-value places to eat tend to be scattered in less obvious parts of the old town.

**Castelvecchio** Himáras 29 ☎ 28310 55163. This long-established family taverna next to the fortress has a large pleasant terrace with stylish seating and a great view over the town. Try the succulent *kléftiko* lamb (€8). Offers quite a

**7**

few vegetarian choices as well. May–Oct daily 1pm–late.

**Fanari** Makedhonías 5 ☎28310 50070. A good-value little taverna, below the fortress on a seafront terrace with wonderful open sea views, serves up tasty lamb and chicken dishes. Daily lunch & dinner.

**Kyria Maria** Moskhovítou 20 ☎28310 29078. Tucked down an alley behind the Rimóndi Fountain, this quaint, unassuming little taverna serves tasty mezédhes and good-value fish and meat dishes; after the meal, everyone gets a couple of Maria's delicious *tyropitákia* with honey on the house. May–Oct daily noon–late.

★ **Mesostrati** Yerakári 1. Just behind the church on Platía Martíron, this is a pleasant little neighbourhood ouzeri/taverna serving Cretan country dishes and mezédhes, on a small terrace. It's frequented by some of Réthymnon's (and Crete's) top lýra and lauto players who often hold impromptu jam sessions. Mon–Sat 11am–3pm & 6pm–2am, Sun 6pm–2am.

**O Gounas** Koronaiou 6 ☎28310 28816. Hearty, no-frills traditional cooking by a family who leave the stove to perform lýra every night, and when things get really lively the dancing starts. May–Oct daily dinner only.

**Stella's Kitchen** Soulíou 55 ☎28310 28665. Great-value little diner tucked away in an alleyway, serving healthy, home-baked food and six daily specials (at least two of which are vegetarian, from €4); also good for breakfasts. Daily 9am–9pm.

**Tapas y Vinos** Melissinoú 14 ☎28310 58554. An expat from Málaga runs Réthymnon's authentic Spanish tapas bar, complete with ethnic decor, a great tapas range, excellent *jamón serrano* and superb Spanish wines. Daily 1pm–late.

★ **Thalassografia** Kefalogiánidon 33 ☎28310 52569. Near the fortress, this modish taverna perched on a cliff overlooking the sea is one of the "in" places for locals to dine out. Tables have sensational views, service is slick and dishes such as *arní sti stamna* (jugged lamb; €8) hit the spot. May–Oct daily 11am–late.

★ **To Pigadi** Xanthoudhídhou 31 ☎28310 27522. Excellent taverna in the old town serving traditional dishes with a twist, such as pork with wild greens and lemon (€8). Reasonably priced and efficient service. The name is a reference to the ancient well (*pigádi*) on the attractive terrace. May–Oct daily lunch & dinner.

## NIGHTLIFE

Nightlife is concentrated in the streets immediately behind the inner harbour. A relatively new café-bar scene popular with the local university student community has taken root around Platía Plastíra, above the inner harbour.

**Envy** Archadiou 226. Music and dance bar with a mix of house, techno and rock with a fun, casual atmosphere. Watch out for the explosive cocktail shots. Daily 11pm–dawn.

**Kenzo** Platía Plastíra ☎28310 51488. One of the row of trendy cafés above the Platía, with a young crowd, one of the sitting cafés rather than a bar. The large terrace looks out to sea, making it a good spot for a sunset drink. Daily 10am–late.

**Metropolis** Neárchou 24. In the small alley between the inner harbour and Arkhadíou, this loud music and dance

bar plays 70s, 80s and rock music, with occasional performances by live bands. Mar–Nov daily 10pm–late.

**Nuvel** Inner harbour. Chic café bar with a large terrace by the harbourfront. Open all day, the music gets louder as night falls. Daily 9am–late.

**Opera Club** Salamínos 12 ☎694 43 33 282. One of the town's bigger dance clubs with an eclectic mix of Greek and western rock and lots of strobe pyrotechnics. May–Oct daily 11pm–dawn; Nov–April weekends only.

# Around Réthymnon

To the southeast of the city the best-known, and still the most worthwhile, short trip that can be made is to the **monastery of Arkádhi**, some 25km and immaculately situated in the foothills of the Psilorítis range. Leaving Réthymnon to the west, the main road climbs for a while above a rocky coastline before descending to the sea, where it runs alongside sandy **beaches** for perhaps 14km. About 7km before **Yeoryioúpoli**, the beach widens and scattered hotel development appears along the coast. If you have your own vehicle, there are plenty of places to stop for a swim, some with hardly anyone else around – but beware of some very strong currents.

## Monastery of Arkádhi

Daily 9am–8pm • €2 • ☎28310 83136

The **monastery of Arkádhi** is also something of a national Cretan shrine. During the 1866 rebellion against the Turks, the monastery became a rebel strongpoint in which, as the Turks gained the upper hand, hundreds of Cretan independence fighters and their families took refuge. Surrounded and on the point of defeat, the defenders ignited a powder magazine just as the Turks entered. Hundreds were killed, Cretan and Turk alike, and the tragedy did much to promote international sympathy for the cause of Cretan independence. Nowadays, you can peer into the roofless vault where the explosion occurred and wander about the rest of the well-restored grounds. The sixteenth-century **church** survived, and is one of the finest Venetian structures left on Crete; other buildings house a small **museum** devoted to the exploits of the defenders of the faith.

## Yeoryioúpoli and around

On the coastal route, midway between Haniá and Réthymnon (on the provincial border of Haniá), **YEORYOÚPOLI** (Georgioúpoli) is very much a resort, packed with rooms to rent, small hotels, apartment buildings, tavernas and travel agencies, but everything remains on a small scale. As long as you don't expect to find too many vestiges of traditional Crete, it's a very pleasant place to pass a few days. Yeoryioúpoli's central beach is narrow and busy; walk east a few hundred metres for the quieter and wider sands.

### Lake Kournás

**KOURNÁS**, Crete's only natural freshwater lake, is set deep in a bowl of hills just 4km inland from Yeoryioúpoli. The best scenic route is via the hamlet of **MATHÉS**, and if you are on foot there is a ramblers' path from here leading to the lake's northern edge. **Kournás** village proper lies 4km uphill from the lake. Spring is the best time to visit the lake; the peacefulness and the profusion of wild flowers are stunning. In high summer you could be in a completely different place, as the winter waters recede and the lake-shore "beach" is packed with umbrellas and sunloungers.

| | |
|---|---|
| **ARRIVAL AND DEPARTURE** | **YEORYIOÚPOLI AND AROUND** |

**By bus** Yeoryioúpoli is easily reached from both Réthymnon and Haniá; the main-line buses running hourly (6.30am–10.30pm) along the main highway stop here.

### ACTIVITIES

**Cycling** Adventure Bikes (☎ 28250 61830, ⓦ adventurebikes.org) organize easy bike tours all around the western end of the island with transport to get you up the steep bits.

**Diving** Paradise Dive Centre, Petres Geraniou ☎ 28310 26317, ⓦ diving-center.gr. Beginners' and advanced scuba

diving based near Yeoryioúpoli to the west of town. Will pick up from hotels in Réthymnon. PADI certificated.

**Horseriding** Zoraïda's (☎ 28250 61745, ⓦ zoraidas -horseriding.com), for horseriding, including organized rides along the beach or up to Lake Kournás.

### ACCOMMODATION

#### YEORYIOÚPOLI

**Andy's Rooms** ☎ 28250 61394. Friendly place, shaded by eucalyptus trees, offering large good-value rooms and apartments with balcony, a/c, fridge and TV. Take the road towards the beach from the south end of the square and you'll find it opposite the church. **€45**

**Anna** ☎ 28250 61556, ⓦ annashouse.gr. Just across the river, this upgraded complex of stylish rooms, studios and apartments (sleeping up to seven) with balcony is set around a large pool. Facilities include fridge and satellite TV. May–Oct. **€85**

**River House** ☎ 28250 61141, ⓦ riverhouse.gr. A pleasant family-run complex of rooms and studios with balcony, kitchenette, a/c, satellite TV and free wi-fi access. There's also a pool and garden. May–Oct. **€48**

#### LAKE KOURNÁS

**Villa Kapasa** ☎ 28250 61050, ⓦ villa-kapasas.com. Comfortable, spacious, en-suite, a/c rooms in a restored old building which retains a number of its original stone features, with a cool, leafy garden. 50m uphill from *Taverna Mathés* (see p.488). May–Oct. **€40**

### EATING AND DRINKING

#### YEORYIOÚPOLI

**Taverna Babis-Fontas** ☎ 28250 61760. This friendly traditional taverna down towards the beach is good for

simple Greek and Cretan dishes; try their excellent rabbit stifado (€7.50). May–Oct daily lunch & dinner.

**Taverna Paradise** ☎ 28250 61313. A good taverna

with a large terrace garden, home-cooked Greek and Cretan dishes such as lamb stifado and pork with peppers (€8). May–Oct daily 7pm–late.

**LAKE KOURNÁS**

**Eye of the Lake** The lakeside view here is peaceful and the food is good; fresh starters and salads, grilled meats and home-cooked dishes. Well frequented by locals. May–Oct daily 10am–late, Nov–Apr weekends only.

★ **Kali Kardia** Kournás ☎ 28250 96278. This is a wonderful, simple but popular place. Sample the local lamb (€7) and *loukánika* (sausages), accompanied by fresh home-grown salad. All the produce is their own. May–Oct daily 10am–late, Nov–April weekends only.

**Taverna Mathes** Mathés ☎ 28250 61514. This peaceful place offers great terrace views over the bay of Yeoryioúpoli. Good food with traditional dishes, many made from their own produce. May–Oct daily 10am–late.

# South from Réthymnon

There are a couple of alternative routes south from Réthymnon, but the main one heads straight out from the centre of town, an initially featureless road due south across the middle of the island towards the south coast and **Ayía Galíni**. About 23km out, a turning cuts off to the right for **Plakiás** and **Mýrthios**, following the course of the spectacular Kourtaliótiko ravine.

## Plakiás

**PLAKIÁS** is an established, yet still quite low-key, resort with a satisfactory beach and a string of good tavernas around the dock. Relax and soak up the atmosphere, or if you're looking for **walks** there's plenty to explore along the coastline and inland. Some of the most tempting beaches in central Crete hide just to the east of Plakiás, though unfortunately they're now a very poorly kept secret. These three splashes of yellow sand, divided by rocky promontories, are within walking distance (40min) and together go by the name **Dhamnóni**.

## Mýrthios

For a stay of more than a day or two, **MÝRTHIOS**, in the hills just behind Plakiás, also deserves consideration. There are some great apartments and wonderful views, and you'll generally find locals still outnumbering the tourists. It takes twenty minutes to walk down to the beach at Plakiás, a little longer to Dhamnóni.

## Préveli monastery

April & May daily 9am–7pm; June–Oct Mon–Sat 9am–1.30pm & 3.30–7pm, Sun 9am–7pm; in winter, knock for admission • €3 • ⓦ preveli.org

**PRÉVELI**, lying some 7km southeast of Plakiás, takes its name from the **monastery** set high above the sea which, like every other in Crete, has a proud history of resistance, in this case accentuated by its role in World War II as a shelter for marooned Allied soldiers awaiting evacuation. There are fine views and a new monument commemorating the rescue operations and depicting a startling life-size, rifle-toting abbot and an Allied soldier cast in bronze.

## Préveli "Palm Beach"

Préveli "Palm Beach" is a sandy cove with a small date-palm grove (recovering from fire damage in 2010) where an estuary feeds a little oasis. Although beautiful, the beach is often crowded with day-trip boats from Plakiás and Ayía Galíni. The turn-off for the beach is the newly asphalted road 1km before Préveli monastery (if travelling by bus you'll be dropped at this junction). This leads to a pay car park (€2) from where the beach is accessed via a steep climb down a path over the rocks (about a 10min descent and a sweaty 20min haul back up). Another path from the east side of the beach follows the river valley 2km back to a stone bridge, by the main road, where there are cafés.

**FROM TOP** LOUTRÓ (P.502); IRÁKLION ARCHEOLOGICAL MUSEUM (P.452) >

## Spíli

The pleasant country town of **SPÍLI** lies about 30km south of Réthymnon. A popular coffee break for coach tours passing this way, Spíli warrants a visit and there's some good hiking country in the nearby hills. Sheltered under a cliff are narrow alleys of ancient houses, all leading up from a platía with a famous 25-spouted **fountain** that replaced a Venetian original. It's a worthwhile place to stay, peacefully rural at night and with several good **rooms** for rent.

## Ayía Galíni

**AYÍA GALÍNI** is a picturesque place nestling in a fold in the mountains. Once a small "fishing village", it is now so busy in high season that you can't see it for the tour buses, hotel billboards and package tourists. It also has a beach that is much too small for the crowds that congregate here. Even so, there are a few saving graces – mainly some excellent restaurants and bars, a lively nightlife scene, plenty of rooms and a friendly atmosphere that survives and even thrives on all the visitors. Out of season, when the climate is mild and the crowds have departed, it can be quite enjoyable too.

## The Amári valley

An alternative route south from Réthymnon, and a far less travelled one, is the road which turns off on the eastern fringe of town to run via the **Amári valley**. There's little specifically to see or do (though a number of richly frescoed Byzantine churches are hidden away en route), but it's an impressive drive under the flanks of the mountains and a reminder of how, in places, rural Crete continues to exist regardless of visitors. The countryside here is delightfully green even in summer, with rich groves of olive and assorted fruit trees, and if you **stay** you'll find the nights are cool and quiet. It may seem odd that many of the villages along the way are modern: they were systematically destroyed by the German army in reprisal for the 1944 kidnapping of General Kreipeo, and many have poignant roadside monuments commemorating those tragic events.

**GETTING AROUND**                                    **SOUTH FROM RÉTHYMNON**

**By bus** Réthymnon to: Ayía Galíni via Spíli (4 daily; 1hr), Plakiás (4 daily; 1hr), Préveli (2 daily; 1hr).

---

### HIKING THE AMÁRI VALLEY

A good base for touring the **Amári valley** is Thrónos, a sizeable village at the valley's northern end with an inviting place to stay, *Rooms Aravanes* (see below). The proprietor here – Lambros Papoutsakis – is a keen walker and conducts guided treks to the peak of **Mount Psilorítis**, which at 2456m is Crete's highest. Although he does guide groups up in the daytime, his preferred approach is during the full moons of June, July and August, which avoids the extreme summer temperatures. Phone in advance for details; it's not a difficult climb, but you'll need sturdy footwear and a sleeping bag. The summit is reached at around dawn, and the sunrise is always spectacular: on clear days the mountain offers a breathtaking view of the whole island and its four seas spreading in all directions.

Other hikes from Thrónos include a relatively easy path leading north through the foothills in a couple of hours to the monastery of Arkádhi (see p.486), while south from Thrónos is an easy stroll on a paved road running back into the main valley via Kalóyerosa. A map detailing these walks is available from *Rooms Aravanes*.

**Rooms Aravanes** Thrónos ☎ 28330 22760, ✉ aravanesthronos@yahoo.gr. The stone-built *Aravanes* has amazing panoramic views across the valley to Mount Psilorítis. The owners rent five en-suite rooms with large balconies and run the taverna below, together with a small shop selling mountain herbs and home-made honey. **€35**

## ACTIVITIES

**Boat trips** from Plakiás and Ayía Galíni will get you to réveli "Palm Beach" with a great deal less fuss.

**Diving Kalypso Rock Palace** Plakiás ☎ 28310, 20990, ⓦ kalypsodivingcenter.com. This PADI-certificated diving centre offers advanced and learner courses.

## ACCOMMODATION

### PLAKIÁS

**Afrodite** Off the inland road to the hostel ☎ 28320 31266, ⓔ kasel@hol.gr. The bougainvillea-draped *Afrodite* is in a quiet spot, 150m from the beach, and offers pleasant a/c rooms and apartments, with TV, fridge and large balconies with mountain views, plus a garden. April–Oct. **€30**

★ **Gio-ma** Western end of the seafront ⓦ gioma.gr. In a prime position on the seafront by the harbour, opposite the taverna of the same name, sea-view balcony rooms and studios with a/c, fridge and TV. April–Oct. **€40**

**Ippokambos** On the inland road parallel to the sea ☎ 28320 31525, ⓔ amoutsos@otenet.gr. Excellent simple and friendly rooms place with modern en-suite balcony rooms and fridge, along the backstreet, 200m from the beach. April–Oct. **€35**

**Youth Hostel** 500m inland, signed from the seafront ☎ 28320 32118, ⓦ yhplakias.com. A friendly, well-run hostel with gardens and a large shady terrace for breakfast, evening drinks and barbecues. Accommodation is in dorm bungalows sleeping four. April–Oct. Dorms **€10**

### MÝRTHIOS

★ **Anna Apartments** Mýrthios ☎ 697 33 24 775, ⓦ annaview.com. These classy apartments, built with traditional stone and wood, are beautifully furnished and have fantastic views over Plakiás Bay. All come with kitchenette, balcony, a/c, satellite TV and wi-fi. **€48**

### SPÍLI

**Green Hotel** On the main road, north of the square. ☎ 28320 22225. Comfortable en-suite rooms with TV and wi-fi. Rooms at the back have great valley views and the hotel has a small sauna and fitness room. Breakfast included. **€40**

**Herakles Rooms** Off the main road, below the Green Hotel ☎ 28320 22111, ⓔ heraclespapadakis@hotmail.com. This friendly pension has a/c en-suite balcony rooms with valley views and internet, situated in a quiet spot. The genial proprietor can advise on some superb walks in the surrounding hills and also rents out mountain bikes. **€35**

### AYÍA GALÍNI

**Camping No Problem** ☎ 28320 91386. A big site with shady pitches, down by the river. Good facilities include a supermarket, taverna and large pool. A 10min walk from town along the beach. May–Oct. **€18**

**Idi** Opposite Minos Hotel ☎ 28320 91152. Friendly rooms place, simple and clean a/c rooms with TV, fridge and balcony – some of which have sea view. June–Oct. **€35**

**Minos Hotel** ☎ 28320 91292. Economical and great value with en-suite rooms, with TV and fridge, the south-facing rooms have superb views from the terrace. May–Oct. **€35**

★ **Neos Ikaros** ☎ 28320 91447, ⓦ neosikaros.gr. A more upmarket option towards the harbour; modern rooms come with a/c, fridge, satellite TV and large balconies, and there's a superb pool and gardens. Breakfast included. April–Oct. **€53**

## EATING AND DRINKING

### PLAKIÁS

**Gio-ma** ☎ 28320 32003. Right on the water's edge, this taverna is good for fish, seafood, home-cooked specials and grills. The kalamári is excellent (€7.50). April–Oct daily 9am–late.

**Medousa** At the east end of town. ☎ 28320 31521. Reached up the road inland from the post office and then right. A splendid traditional taverna with prices lower than those on the seafront, and they also serve breakfast. May–Oct daily 9am–11pm.

**Nikos Souvlaki** On the road inland from the post office ☎ 28320 31921. Dishes up the least expensive meals in town – excellent *souvláki* (€2) or even fish and chips, to eat in, at one of the small pavement tables, or take away. March–Oct Tues–Sun 6pm–11.30pm.

★ **Sofia** ☎ 28320 31226, ⓦ tavernasofia.gr. A long-established taverna, friendly with a good reputation. Try their fresh daily specials (€5.50–8) or choose from the range of starters, fish and grills on their large menu. April–Oct daily 10am–late.

**Tassomanolis** ☎ 28320 31129. One of a line of waterfront places enjoying spectacular sunsets; this one has a blue-and-white nautical theme and specializes in fish caught by the proprietor from his own boat (from €22 /kg – there are many more economical dishes too). April–Oct daily lunch & dinner.

### MÝRTHIOS

**Taverna Plateia** ☎ 28320 31560. This long-established taverna on the central square has had a complete makeover but still serves up excellent traditional Cretan cooking, great wines, and has arguably the most spectacular terrace view of any taverna on the island. May–Oct daily lunch & dinner.

7

### AYÍA GALÍNI

**Onar** Taverna Street ☎ 28320 91121. One of the best tavernas on this row, at the harbour end with a great rooftop terrace and views over the harbour, serving wholesome food; try their excellent charcoal-grilled fish and meat or specials such as meatballs with feta cheese (€6). May–Oct daily 10am–late.

**To Petrino** Off the harbour platía ☎ 28320 91504. A charming little stone-built (*Petrino*) street café-ouzerí serving up breakfasts, coffees and drinks during the day and tasty mezédhes at night. April–Oct daily 9am–late.

# Western Crete

Crete's westernmost quarter is one of its least visited, partly because there are no big sandy beaches to accommodate resort hotels, and partly because it's so far from the great archeological sites. But for mountains, scattered coves and unexploited villages, it's unrivalled.

The city of **Haniá** (Chania) is an excellent reason to come here, but the immediately adjacent coast, especially to the west of the city, is overdeveloped and not particularly exciting; if you want beaches head for the south coast or the far west. Here, Paleóhora is the only place which could really be described as a resort, and even this is on a thoroughly human scale; others are emptier still. Elsewhere on the south coast, **Ayía Rouméli** and **Loutró** can be reached only on foot or by boat; **Hóra Sfakíon** sees hordes passing through but few who stay; **Frangokástello**, nearby, has a beautiful castle and the first stirrings of development. Behind these lie the **White Mountains** (Lefká Óri) and the famed walk through the **Samariá Gorge**. In the far west, great beaches at **Falásarna** and **Elafoníssi** are mostly visited only as day-trips.

## Haniá

**HANIÁ**, as any of its residents will tell you, is spiritually the capital of Crete, even if the political title was passed back to Iráklion. It is also the island's most attractive city, especially if you can catch it in spring, when the White Mountains' snowcapped peaks seem to hover above the roofs. Although it is for the most part a modern city, you might never know it as a tourist. Surrounding the harbour is a wonderful jumble of **Venetian streets** that survived the wartime bombardments, while simply wandering the old town you will discover old city walls, Ottoman, Byzantine and Minoan ruins. Restoration and gentrification, consequences of the tourist boom, have made inroads of late, but it remains an atmospheric place.

### The harbour

The **harbour** area is the oldest and the most interesting part of town, at its busiest and most attractive at night, when the lights from bars and restaurants reflect in the water and crowds of visitors and locals turn out to promenade. By day, things are quieter. Straight ahead from Platía Sindriváni (also known as Harbour Square) lies the curious domed shape of the **Mosque of the Janissaries**, built in 1645 (though heavily restored since) and the oldest Ottoman building on the island. It is usually open as a gallery, housing temporary exhibitions. Further east, on the inner harbour, the arches of sixteenth-century **Venetian arsenals**, a couple of them beautifully restored (and one housing a reconstructed Minoan ship), survive alongside remains of the outer walls.

#### Kastélli

The little hill that rises behind the mosque is **Kastélli**, site of the earliest habitation and core of the Minoan, Venetian and Turkish towns. There's not a great deal left, but archeologists believe that they may have found the remains of a Minoan palace, and the "lost" city of **Kydonia**, in the excavations being carried out – and open to view – along

# HANIÁ

**Airport & Akrotiri**

**KOÚM KÁPI**

Stadium

Public Gardens

Platía Eleftherías

Platía Eleftherías

New Road, Soúdha, Réthymnon & Iráklion

**7**

Dhimarhío

Bus Station

**Market**

Minaret

Ayios Nikólaos

**SPLANTZIA**

San Rocco

**KASTÉLLI**

Arsenáli

Port Police

Minoan Excavation

Inner Harbour

Mosque of the Janissaries

Outer Harbour

**N**

Frikás & Naval Museum

Byzantine Museum

Café Notos

Renieri Gate

Center of Traditional Folk Art

Archeological Museum

Folklore Museum

Cathedral

Schiavo Bastion

Supermarket

Camping & City Beach

Beaches, Plataniás, Kastélli & 

metres 0    200

**■ ACCOMMODATION**

| | |
|---|---|
| Amphora | 4 |
| Casa Veneta | 3 |
| To Dhíporto | 13 |
| El Greco | 7 |
| Ionas | 9 |
| Kastélli | 5 |
| Lucia | 8 |
| Maro | 11 |
| Palazzo | 6 |
| Pension Nora | 1 |
| Splanzia Hotel | 10 |
| Thereza | 2 |
| Vranas Studios | 12 |

**■ DRINKING & NIGHTLIFE**

| | |
|---|---|
| Ta Duo Lux | 1 |
| El Mondo | 7 |
| Ellinikon | 6 |
| Fagotto | 3 |
| Café Kriti | 5 |
| Mylos | 8 |
| Pallas | 2 |
| Rudi's Bierhaus | 4 |

**■ EATING**

| | |
|---|---|
| Akrogiali | 6 |
| Akanea | 2 |
| Amphora | 7 |
| Apostolis | 1 |
| Doloma | 5 |
| Faka | 3 |
| Iordanis Bougatsa | 13/14 |
| Karnayio | 4 |
| Kormoranos | 8 |
| Muses | 9 |
| To Pigadi tou Tourkou | 11 |
| Portes | 12 |
| Tamam | 10 |

Kanevárou. It's also here that you'll find traces of the oldest **walls**; there were two rings, one defending Kastélli alone, a later set encompassing the whole of the medieval city.

### The Naval Museum
Daily: April–Oct 9am–4pm, Nov–March 9am–2pm • €3 • ☎ 28210 91875

The hefty bastion at the western end of the harbour now houses Crete's **Naval Museum**. The collection consists of model ships and other naval ephemera tracing the history of Greek navigation, plus a section on the 1941 **Battle of Crete** with fascinating artefacts, and poignant photos depicting the suffering here under the Nazis. From the **Fírkas**, the fortress behind the museum, the modern Greek flag was first flown on Crete, in 1913.

### Byzantine Museum
Tues–Sun 8.30am–3pm • €2, combined ticket with Archeological Museum €3 • ☎ 28210 96046

At the back of the Naval Museum lies the **Byzantine Museum** (entrance at the top of Theotokopoúlou), located in the Venetian Chapel of San Salvatore, with an interesting collection of mosaics, icons and jewellery from the various periods of Byzantine rule.

### City walls and backstreets
Beyond the Byzantine museum, follow Pireós inland outside the best-preserved stretch of the old city walls. Following the walls around on the inside is rather trickier, but far more enjoyable. This is where you'll stumble on some of the most picturesque little alleyways and finest Venetian houses in Haniá. Keep your eyes open for details on the houses, such as old wooden balconies or stone coats of arms. The arch of the **Renieri Gate**, at the bottom of Moschón, is particularly elegant. There are also lots of interesting art and craft stores around here, along Theotokopoúlou and the many alleys that run off, while between the Renieri Gate and Hálidhon are more such alleys, though here the emphasis is more on tavernas, bars and cafés.

### The synagogue
Mon–Fri 10am–6pm • Free • Ⓦ www.etz-hayyim-hania.org

At the end of a small alley off the west side of Kóndhilaki is Haniá's fifteenth-century Etz Hayyim **synagogue**, recently renovated. All but one of the city's Jews were rounded up by the Nazi occupation forces in 1944, but they met their end (along with around 500 members of the captured Cretan resistance) when the transport ship taking them to Auschwitz was torpedoed by a British submarine off the island of Mílos.

### Odhós Hálidhon and beyond
Behind the harbour lie the less picturesque but more lively sections of the old city. **Odhós Hálidhon** is lined with touristy shops, in the midst of which you'll find the **archeological museum**, **folklore museum** and the modern **cathedral**. Behind the cathedral square are cafés and some of the more animated shopping areas, leading up to the back of the market: on **Odhós Skrídhlof** ("Leather Street") traditional leathermakers plied their trade, but today just one small workshop remains, the rest having been replaced with imported leather goods and souvenirs, but there are still leather bargains (shoes, bags and more) to be had. Further east behind the market, the **Splántzia** quarter is a maze of ancient alleys with tumbledown Venetian stonework and wooden balconies; there are a couple of **minarets** here, one on Dhaliáni, and the other attached to the church of Áyios Nikólaos in Platía 1821. A clutch of new, popular *mezedhopolía* and *ouzerís* along Dhaliáni have revitalized this area.

### Archeological Museum
Odhós Hálidhon 28 • Tues–Sun 8am–3pm • €2, combined ticket with Byzantine Museum €3 • ☎ 28210 90334

A short way up Hálidhon, on the right, is Haniá's **Archeological Museum**, housed in the Venetian-built church of San Francesco. The building has been substantially restored and contains a fine display, covering the local area from Minoan through to Roman times. In the courtyard garden, a huge fountain and the base of a minaret survive from the period when the Ottomans converted the church into a mosque; around them are scattered various other sculptures and architectural remnants.

### Folklore Museum

Odhós Hálidhon 46b • Mon–Sat 9.30am–3pm & 6–9pm • €2 • ☎ 28210 90816

The nearby **Folklore Museum** is worth a look as much for its setting, on a fine courtyard that is also home to Haniá's Roman Catholic church, as for its contents. This small museum replicates a "traditional" Cretan house, with furnishings, tapestries and artefacts on display.

## The beaches

Haniá's beaches lie to the west of the city and on the Akrotíri peninsula to the northeast. The clean **city beach** (Néa Hóra) is no more than a ten-minute walk west, following the shoreline from the Naval Museum, but for more extensive spaces you're better off heading further west along the coast to the beaches of **Khrissi Akti**, **Áyios Apostólis** and **Kalamáki**. These beaches can get pretty crowded but they may be a considerable improvement over the beach in Haniá itself. Further afield there are even finer beaches at **Áyía Marína** (see p.499) to the west, or **Kalathás** and **Stavrós** (p.499) out on the Akrotíri peninsula, all of which can be reached by KTEL buses from the main station.

**7**

### ARRIVAL AND DEPARTURE

HANIÁ

#### BY PLANE

**Haniá Airport** (Chania) lies 15km east of town on the Akrotíri peninsula and is served by domestic flights (Aegean Airways ☎ 28210 63366 and Olympic Air ☎ 28210 63264 and international flights with easyJet and charter airlines in the summer only. Airport buses to the city run frequently during the summer, less regularly in winter months (April–Oct 15 daily 6.40am–9.45pm, Nov–March 6 daily 6.40am–9.20pm; 25min; €2.40). Taxis (€20) are plentiful, from the airport taxi rank.

Destinations Athens (6 daily on Aegean and Olympic; 50min); Thessaloníki (1 daily on Aegean; 1hr 15min). London (easyJet – summer only).

#### BY FERRY

Arriving by ferry, you'll anchor about 10km east of Haniá at the port of Soúdha: take a bus (every 15 min; 20min; €1.60) or taxi (around €12) to the city. Tickets are available from

ANEK line office (on Venizélou, right opposite the market; ☎ 28210 27500) or any travel agent.

Destinations Daily overnight (8hr 30min), with ANEK lines (Ⓦ anek.gr), extra daytime sailing in July and Aug.

#### BY BUS

The bus station is on Kydhonías. For the latest timetables and complete route and fare information for Haniá buses, visit Ⓦ bus-service-crete-ktel.com.

Destinations Elafonísi (daily at 9am; 2hr 30min); Falásarna (3 daily 8.30am–3.30pm; 1hr 30min); Frangokástello (daily at 2pm; 2hr 30min); Hóra Sfakíon (2 daily 8.30am & 2pm; 2hr); Iráklion via Réthymnon (hourly 5.30am–6.30pm, then 8pm & 9pm; 3hr); Kastélli (14 daily 6.30am–9.15pm; 1hr); Omalós (Samariá Gorge; 4 daily 6.15am–2pm; 1hr); Paleóhora (4 daily 5am–4pm; 1hr 30min); Soúyia (2 daily 5am & 2pm; 2hr); Stavrós (5 daily 6.50am–8.20pm; 30min).

### INFORMATION, TOURS AND ACTIVITIES

**Tourist office** Kydhonías 29 (Mon–Fri 8am–2.30pm ☎ 28210 36155, Ⓦ chania.gr). In the *dhimarhío* (town hall), with entrance at the side of the building, four blocks east of the bus station.

**Boat tours** A number of boats run trips from the harbour (around €10–12 for 2hr), mainly to the nearby islands of Áyii Theódori and Lazarétta, for swimming and *krí-krí* (ibex) spotting, also evening sunset cruises.

**Diving** Blue Adventures Diving, Arholéon 11, near the inner harbour (☎ 28210 40608, Ⓦ blueadventuresdiving .gr), runs daily diving and snorkelling trips.

**Waterpark** Limnoupolis (Ⓦ limnoupolis.gr), located close to the village of Varípetro, 8km southwest of the city, with slides taking advantage of a natural hillside (€11–23). Buses from the bus station depart daily at 10.45am and return at 6.30pm.

## GETTING AROUND

**Bike and car rental** For bikes, Summertime, Dhaskaloyiánnis 7, slightly northeast of the market (📞 28210 45797, 🌐 strentals.gr), including mountain bikes. For cars, try around the top of Hálidhon where Tellus Rent a Car (📞 28210 91500, 🌐 tellustravel.gr) is one of many. El Greco Cars at the *El Greco* hotel (📞 28210 60883, 🌐 elgreco.gr; see below) offer ten percent off to Rough Guide readers.

**Taxis** The main taxi ranks are on Platía 1866 and at the junction of Yiánnari and Karaiskáki. For radio taxis call 📞 18300, 📞 28210 94300 or 28210 98700.

## ACCOMMODATION

There are thousands of rooms to rent in Haniá, as well as a number of pricey boutique hotels. Though you may face a long search for a bed at the height of the season, eventually everyone does seem to find something. Perhaps the most desirable rooms of all are those overlooking the **harbour**. Most are approached not direct from the harbourside itself but from the streets behind; those further back are likely to be more peaceful. Theotokopoúlou and the alleys off it make a good starting point. In the eastern half of the old town, rooms are far more scattered and in the height of the season your chances are much better over here. Try **Kastélli**, immediately east of the harbour, or around **Splántzia** and the streets around the cathedral.

### HARBOUR AREA

★ **Amphora** 2 Párodos Theotokopoúlou 20 📞 28210 93224, 🌐 amphora.gr. Traditional hotel in a beautifully renovated Venetian mansion; the entrance is via a small alley but the hotel faces the harbour and lighthouse. Rooms and suites come with a/c, TV, fridge and some with balcony and sea view. Good harbourfront restaurant below. March–Nov. **€110**

**Casa Veneta** Theotokopoúlou 57 📞 28210 90007, 🌐 casa-veneta.gr. Well-equipped, comfortable studios and apartments with a/c, fridge, kitchenette, some with balcony, behind a Venetian facade along the quaint Theotokopoúlou street, and with a friendly owner. April–Oct. **€60**

**El Greco** Theotokopoúlou 47–49 📞 28210 94030, 🌐 elgreco.gr. Comfortable hotel with nicely furnished if rather compact rooms which include fridge, a/c, TV and wi-fi. Some have balconies and there's a seasonal roof terrace. Breakfast included. April–Oct. **€50**

**Lucia** Aktí Koundouriótou 📞 28210 90302, 🌐 loukiahotel.gr. Harbourfront hotel with a/c rooms with TV and fridge; furnishing is basic at best, hence much less expensive than you might expect for one of the best views in town, and – thanks to double-glazing – reasonably soundproof. May–Oct. **€45**

**Maro** Párodos Portoú 5 📞 28210 97913. Probably the cheapest en-suite rooms in the old town, hidden away in a quiet, unmarked alley off Portou not far from the Schiavo bastion. Basic but friendly and clean; with a/c. May–Oct. **€35**

**Palazzo** Theotokopoúlou 54 📞 28210 93227, 🌐 palazzohotel.gr. This old converted mansion has wood-beamed ceilings and wooden floors. Good-sized, simply furnished rooms with a/c, TV, fridge, and most rooms come with balcony, plus there is a pretty roof terrace with harbour views and tasty breakfasts. Breakfast included. May–Oct. **€80**

**Pension Nora** Theotokopoúlou 60 📞 28210 72265, 🌐 pension-nora.com. Charming a/c rooms in a ramshackle wooden Turkish house, some very basic with shared bath, others relatively fancy, so look first. Pleasant breakfast café below. **€40**

**Thereza** Angélou 8 📞 28210 92798, 🌐 pensiontheresa.gr. Beautiful old house in a great position, with stunning views from the roof terrace and en-suite a/c rooms (some with TV); classy decor, too; unlikely to have room in high season unless you book. **€60**

### THE OLD TOWN

**Ionas** Sarpáki, cnr Sórvolou 📞 28210 55090, 🌐 ionashotel.com. Small boutique hotel in a lovingly restored Venetian mansion, set at the end of a small square in the heart of the old Splántzia quarter. Very comfortable rooms and beautiful architectural detail. May–Oct. **€90**

**Kastelli** Kanevárou 39 📞 28210 57057, 🌐 kastelistudios.gr. A comfortable, modern, reasonably priced *pension* that's very quiet at the back. All rooms come with a/c, TV, fridge, balcony and wi-fi. The owner is exceptionally helpful and also has a few apartments and a beautiful house (for up to five people) to rent nearby. **€45**

★ **Splanzia Hotel** Dhaskaloyiánnis 58 📞 28210 45313, 🌐 splanzia.com. Small friendly boutique hotel in a beautiful restored Venetian building, comfortable stylish en-suite rooms come with a/c, satellite TV and wi-fi. Breakfast, served in the pretty courtyard, is included. **€115**

**To Dhiporto** Betólo 41 📞 28210 40570, 🌐 todiporto.gr. In the alley one block in front of Odhós Skrídhlof (Leather Street). Refurbished, good-value en-suite rooms in a traditional renovated building, with a/c, TV, fridge and balcony; some triples and singles too. **€40**

**Vranas Studios** Ayíon Dhéka, cnr Sarpáki 📞 28210 58618, 🌐 vranas.gr. Tucked away in a narrow street below the cathedral, these traditional-style, spacious, studio rooms have TV, a/c, kitchenette and wi-fi, with an internet café below. **€55**

## CAMPING

**Camping Hania** Áyios Apostólis, 4km west of Haniá ☎ 28210 31138, ⓦ camping-chania.gr. Served by local bus. The site is rather small, and hemmed in by new development, but it has a pool and all the usual facilities just a short walk from some of the better beaches. May–Oct. **€20**

## EATING

The harbour is encircled by a succession of pricey restaurants, tavernas and cafés which are usually better for a drink than a meal. Away from the water, there are plenty of slightly cheaper possibilities on Kondhiláki, Zambelíou and most of the streets off Hálidhon.

### CAFÉS

★ **Alcanea** Angélou 2 ☎ 28210 75370. Small, relaxed terrace café at the quieter western tip of the harbour, beneath the hotel of the same name, next to the naval museum. Good for breakfast, coffee or evening drinks. Daily 9am–late.

**Iordanis Bougatsa** Branches at Kydhonías 96 and Apokorónou 24. Specializes in traditional creamy *bougátsa*, a sugar-coated cream-cheese pie to eat in or take away. Mon–Sat 8am–3pm.

**Kormoranos** Theotokopoúlou. This bakery/café/ouzerí serves pastries washed down by juices, herb teas and coffee during the day, and an ouzerí serving delicious meze to go with your drinks at night. May–Oct daily 9am–late.

**Muses** Platía Sindriváni. Pleasant café on the harbour square, in a prime position for people-watching, serves breakfasts, coffees, snacks and late drinks. May–Oct daily 7am–late.

### RESTAURANTS

★ **Akrogiali** Aktí Papanikolí 19, Néa Hóra ☎ 28210 73110. Opposite the city beach, with a summer terrace, this excellent, reasonably priced fish and seafood taverna is well worth the 15min walk or short taxi ride. Always packed with locals, so may be worth booking – though there are plenty of alternatives along the same street. Daily lunch & dinner.

**Amphora** Aktí Koundouriótou, under Hotel Amphora ☎ 28210 93224. One of the most reliable places on the outer seafront, across from the lighthouse, with good, simple home-cooked Greek food, fish and seafood. Mains €5.50–10. March–Nov daily 10am–late.

**Apostolis 1 and 2** Aktí Enóseos 6 & 10, inner harbour ☎ 28210 43470. The fish tavernas at the inner end of the harbour are rated much more highly by locals than those further round – some locals claim *Apostolis 2* is the best of all. The fish is excellent, but pricey. Daily lunch & dinner.

★ **Doloma** Kapsokályvon 5, behind the Arsenali ☎ 28210 51196. Excellent little taverna set back off the street, with a shady terrace, serving well-prepared and economical Cretan dishes with good local wine. Mains such as rice-stuffed tomatoes or *pastitsio* (spaghetti pie) from €4. Daily lunch & dinner.

**Faka** Arholéon 15 ☎ 28210 42341. Set back from the harbour in the small square behind the *Arsenali* building, this is significantly less touristy and less expensive than many near neighbours. Excellent traditional local food, often with live Greek music. May–Oct daily lunch & dinner.

**Karnayio** Platía Katehákí 8, next to the Arsenali ☎ 28210 53366. Not right on the water, but one of the best harbour restaurants nonetheless. Excellent fish, traditional Cretan cooking and a fine selection of wines – all served on an inviting terrace – make this a winner. Mains from €5.50. May–Oct daily lunch & dinner.

★ **Portes** Portoú 48 ☎ 28210 76261. A small group of restaurants nestles under the walls along Portoú. *Portes* is smarter than most, with a particularly adventurous menu putting a modern twist on age-old dishes: rabbit with prunes (€9.50), cuttlefish with fennel (€8.50), and traditional pies with unusual fillings. April–Oct lunch & dinner.

**To Pigadi tou Tourkou** Sarpáki 1 ☎ 28210 54547, ⓦ welloftheturk.com. Greco-Moroccan restaurant (the name translates to "Well of the Turk") with an interesting menu combining the two cuisines along with dishes from the Middle East. Mains from €8. Wed–Sun dinner only; closed Dec.

★ **Tamam** Zambelíou ☎ 28210 96080, ⓦ tamamrestaurant.com. Popular place where the adventurous Greek menu includes much vegetarian food, with added spices giving an eastern flavour. The original restaurant is housed in an old Turkish baths, while opposite is the less atmospheric annexe, *Tamam II*; tables are squeezed into the alley between the two. Mains from €6. Daily noon–1am.

## DRINKING AND NIGHTLIFE

The harbour area contains dozens of beautifully set but touristy bars. Locals head east, to the inner harbour and beyond to Koum Kápi, where the scores of bars and cafés lining Aktí Miaoúli are heaving by 11pm. In summer the action moves to the vibrant club scene on the coast west of town.

**Café Kriti (Lyrakia)** Kalergón 22, cnr Andhroyíou. Cretan music and dancing virtually every night at what is basically an old-fashioned *kafenío*. Daily 7.30pm–late.

**El Mondo** Kondiláki 35 ☎ 28210 88044, ⓦ elmondo

bar.com. An old favourite, popular with tourists and occasional visiting military, this small but lively bar belts out a mixture of rock classics, dance music and latest tracks. May–Oct daily 9pm–4am, Nov–April Wed–Mon 8pm–2am.

**Elliniko** Aktí Miaoúli ☎ 28210 27729. One of the more popular and consistent of the bar-cafés on the Koum Kápi strip to the east, beyond the harbour, packed nightly with young locals: if this doesn't appeal, take your pick from its dozens of neighbours. Daily 10am–late.

★ **Fagotto** Angélou 16 ☎ 28210 71877. Laidback, indoor jazz bar off the quieter end of the harbour, often with live performances. Daily 8pm–late.

**Mylos** Main street, Plataniás ☎ 28210 60449. Large, buzzing summer nightclub with four indoor bars and a large dancefloor, on the coast 10km out of town, in the busy resort of Plataniás, popular with both locals and tourists. June–Sept midnight–6am.

**Pallas** Aktí Tombázi 15, near Port Police ☎ 28210 45688. Popular harbourfront café-bar with a terrace that's ideally placed to admire the sunset over the harbour. In winter the action moves indoors to the first-floor music bar. Daily 9am–late.

★ **Rudi's Bierhaus** Kalergón 16 ☎ 28210 50824. Austrian – and long-time Haniá resident – Rudi Riegler's bar stocks more than a hundred of Europe's finest beers. Excellent mezédhes to accompany them. Daily 8pm–late.

**Ta Duo Lux** Sarpidhónos ☎ 28210 52519. Comfy bar-café in a street full of similar places, just off the inner harbour, that attracts a slightly older crowd than nearby Aktí Miaoúli. Daily 10am–late.

## DIRECTORY

**Banks and exchange** The National Bank of Greece is directly opposite the market with three ATMs, and there's a cluster of banks with more ATMs around the top of Halídhon. You'll also find plenty of out-of-hours exchange places on Hálidhon, in the travel agencies.

**Internet access** There are plenty of internet cafés including Vranas, Ayíon Dhéka beneath Vranas Studios (see p.499), Triple W, Odhós Balantínou just off the top of Hálidhon, and Café Notos (May–Oct) on the outer harbour under the *Hotel Lucia*.

**Laundry** Speedy Laundry (☎ 28210 88411), junction of Koronéou and Korkídhi, just west of Platía 1866, will collect and deliver your load if you call; the Old Town Laundromat, Karaóli 40; Oscar, Kanevárou, just off Platía Syndriváni.

**Left luggage** The bus station has a left-luggage office (6am–8.30pm).

**Market and supermarkets** The central indoor market has fresh fruit and vegetables, meat and fish, dairy stalls and a baker; on Saturday mornings there is a farmer's market (*laíki*) with a wonderful line of stalls along Mínoos, inside the eastern city wall, selling local produce. Several small stores by the harbour platía sell cold drinks and food; they are expensive but open late. Small supermarkets can be found on Platía 1866, and the larger Carrefour supermarket is at the top of Pireós, outside the western wall, close to the Schiavo bastion.

**Post office** The main post office is on Odhs Perídou just off the bottom of Kydhonías (Mon–Fri 7.30am–8pm, Sat 9am–1pm).

**Travel agencies** Concentrated around the top of Hálidhon and on Platía 1866, as well as around the bus station. Try Tellus Travel, Hálidhon 108 (☎ 28210 91500, ⓦ tellustravel .gr), or in the old town El Greco Travel, Theotokopoúlou 50 (☎ 28210 86015, ⓦ elgreco.gr).

# Around Haniá

Northeast of Haniá, the **Akrotíri peninsula** loops around, protecting the Bay of Soúdha. The peninsula has a number of sandy beaches and coves on the northeast side; beyond the suburb of Kounoupidhianá lies the excellent sandy beach of **Kalathás** and, further out, lies **Stavrós** with its magnificent mountain soaring up out of the bay, while inland are the **monasteries** of **Ayía Triádha** and **Gouvernétou**.

The coast west of Haniá has considerable tourist development along much of the shore to Áyía Marína and **Plataniás**. Beyond, the road to **Kolymvári** runs through mixed groves of calamus reed (Crete's bamboo) and oranges; the windbreaks fashioned from the reeds protect the ripening oranges from the *meltémi*. You'll still find long, quiet stretches of sand here, between hotels and villages.

## Ayía Triádha
Daily 7.30am–2pm & 5–7pm · €2 · ☎ 28210 63572

The majestic three-domed **Ayía Triádha** monastery, originally built in the seventeenth century on the ruins of an old church, is approached via an avenue of cypress trees and surrounded by olive groves and vines – all property of the monastery; it's a thriving commercial place, producing and selling organic olive oil and wine from its vast landholdings. By the entrance a small museum houses ecclesiastical heirlooms, including valuable sixteenth- and seventeenth-century icons.

### Gouvernétou and Katholikó

Easter–Sept Mon, Tues & Thurs 9am–noon & 5–8pm, Sat & Sun 8–11am & 5–8pm • Oct–Easter afternoon hours are 4–7pm • Free

**Gouvernétou** is one of the oldest monasteries on Crete, dating back to around 1537, and it's a rather isolated, contemplative and strict place; visitors are expected to respect this. The monastery looks more like a fortress from the outside where two towers stand guard; originally there were four – one on each corner – but two have collapsed. Inside, there are fine frescoes in the ancient church, and a small museum. Next to the monastery a paved path followed by steep steps leads down to the amazing abandoned ruins of the **monastery of Katholikó** (25min walk down – longer to climb back up), built into a craggy ravine and, further on, the remains of its narrow harbour.

### Stavrós

**Stavrós** beach, 15km from Haniá, is superb if you like the calm, shallow water of an almost completely enclosed lagoon; this one sits right beneath the imposing "Zorbas" mountain (*Zorba the Greek* was filmed here). It's not very large, so it does get crowded, but rarely overpoweringly so. There's a makeshift café/*kantína* on the beach, and a couple of tavernas across the road. For accommodation search 1km west of here, in the area around *Blue Beach* and beyond where there are plenty of apartment complexes.

### Ayía Marína

**AYÍA MARÍNA**, 8km west of Haniá, is a developed resort of some size with many hotels, shops, tavernas and nightlife; it's also known for its trendy beach bars, pumping out sounds which attract hordes of young locals and tourists. The west end of the long sandy beach is quieter and there are good **watersports** facilities here, including jet skiing and paragliding. Just offshore, **Theodorou** island is said to be a sea monster petrified by Zeus before it could swallow Crete. Seen from the west, its "mouth" still gapes open.

## The Samariá Gorge

May–Oct (in the first and last few weeks of opening period it may close if there's a danger of flash floods) • €6 • ☎ 28210 67179

From Haniá the spectacular **SAMARIÁ GORGE**, which claims to be Europe's longest (it's a 16km hike), can be visited as a day-trip or as part of a longer excursion to the south. It's strenuous – you'll know all about it next day – the path is rough and it's not a walk to be undertaken lightly, particularly in the heat of summer, and walking boots or solid shoes are vital.

The **gorge** begins at the *xylóskalo*, or "wooden staircase", a stepped path plunging steeply down from the southern lip of the Omalós plain. The descent is at first through almost alpine scenery: pine forest, wild flowers and greenery – a verdant shock in the spring, when the stream is at its liveliest. About halfway down you pass the abandoned village of **Samariá**, now home to a wardens' station, with picnic facilities and toilets. Further down, the path levels out and the gorge walls close in until, at the narrowest

SAMARIÁ GORGE

Omalós

E4 Variant

2000M
Melídaou
(2133m)

1500M

Kallérgi Hut

1500M

Tourist Lodge

Áyios
Nikólaos

1000M

Xylóskalo

500M

1000M

1500M

Samariá

Gingílos
(2080m)

Volakiás
(2116m)

2000M

E4 VARIANT

N

1500M

Kéfala
(1700m)

Katsoprínes
(1400m)

Sidherespórtes

1500M

1000M

1000M

1000M

500M

1000M

Old Ayía Rouméli

500M

500M

500M

Ayía Rouméli

Site of
Tarrha

Áyios
Pávlos

E4

E4

0    2
kilometres

Soúyia & Palèohóra

point (the *sidherespórtes* or "iron gates"), one can practically touch both tortured rock faces at once and, looking up, see them rising sheer for well over 300m.

At an average pace, with regular stops, the walk down takes between five and seven hours (though you can do it quicker); beware of the kilometre markers: these mark only distances within the **National Park** and it's a further 2km of hot walking before your reach the sea at **Ayía Rouméli**. On the way down there is plenty of water from springs and streams, but nothing to eat. The park that surrounds the gorge is a refuge of the Cretan wild ibex, the *krí-krí*, but don't expect to see one; there are usually far too many people around.

**ARRIVAL AND DEPARTURE**                                              **THE SAMARIÁ GORGE**

Tours to Samariá Gorge run from virtually everywhere on the island. The gorge walk ends on the south coast at Ayía Rouméli; from here you need to take a boat to Hóra Sfakíon, Soúyia or Paleóhora (see p.502) then catch a connecting bus. Return bus journeys are timed to coincide with the ferries and will wait for them – theoretically, no one gets left behind.

**By bus** From Haniá (4 daily at 6.15am, 7.30am, 8.30am & 2pm); from Soúyia (Mon, Wed, Sat; 6.15am); from      Paleóhora (Mon, Wed, Sat; 7am).

**7**

**ACCOMMODATION**

Wardens ensure that no one remains in the gorge overnight, where camping is strictly forbidden. The nearest accommodation is at Omalós where you'll find the hotels listed below. Both have tavernas and also offer lifts to the top of the gorge in the morning if you stay overnight.

**Hotel Gingilos** ☎ 28210 67181. Slightly cheaper than the neighbouring *Neos Omalos* hotel and also very friendly. Modern en-suite rooms come with bath and balcony view. €30

**Hotel Neos Omalos** ☎ 28210 67269, ⓦ neos-omalos .gr. This is perhaps the best hotel; en-suite rooms all have balcony with views of the Lefká Óri, TV and central heating. €35

## Omalós

**OMALÓS** lies in the middle of the mountain plain from which the Samariá gorge descends. The climate is cooler here all year round and the many paths into the hills surrounding the plateau are a welcome bonus; in season a profusion of wild flowers and birdlife is to be seen. There are plenty of **tavernas** and some surprisingly fancy **rooms** with all facilities, should you want to stay overnight to get an early start into the gorge. Another significant advantage to staying up here would be if you wanted to undertake some other **climbs** in the White Mountains; the **Kallérgi mountain hut** (☎ 28210 33199 or 697 34 00 777; €12 per person) is about ninety minutes' hike (signed) from Omalós or the top of the gorge.

# The southwest coast

The ancient capital of the Sfakiá region, **Hóra Sfakíon**, lies 70km south of Haniá, reached via a spectacular twisting asphalted road over the mountains. It's the main terminus for gorge walkers, with a regular boat service west along the coast to **Ayía Rouméli** and **Loutro**, which are accessible only by foot or boat. **Frangokastello**, with its castle fortress and sandy **beaches**, lies a few kilometres east of Hóra Sfakíon, along the coastal road. Other main routes south over the mountains from Haniá are those to the small town of **Paleóhora** (from the north-coast highway at Tavronítis) and to the laidback seaside village of Soúyia (via Alikianós on the Omalós road).

## Hóra Sfakíon

**HÓRA SFAKÍON** sees thousands of people passing through daily; those who have walked Samariá Gorge come striding, or staggering, off the boat from Ayía Rouméli to pile onto onward buses or waiting coaches. Relatively few stay, although there are plenty of great-value **rooms** and some excellent waterfront **tavernas**. Though there are a couple of pebbly coves, what is missing in Hóra Sfakíon is a decent beach. You could walk (or for much of the year take an excursion boat) west to Sweetwater, or there are numerous opportunities for a dip along the coast road east towards Frangokástello and beyond.

## Loutró

For tranquillity, it's hard to beat **LOUTRÓ**, one-third of the way from Hóra Sfakíon to Ayía Rouméli and accessible only by boat or on foot. Like Hóra Sfakíon, the small pebbly bay in front of the village soon gets crowded. If you're prepared to walk, however, there are plenty of lovely **beaches** along the coast in each direction; these can also be reached by hired **canoe**, and some (particularly Sweetwater to the east and Mármara to the west) by regular excursion boats. For walkers, the **coastal trail** through Loutró covers the entire distance between Ayía Rouméli and Hóra Sfakíon (part of the E4 Pan-European footpath), and there's also a daunting zigzag path up the cliff behind to the mountain village of **Anópoli**.

Loutró itself has a number of excellent **tavernas** and a fair few **rooms**, though not always enough of the latter in peak season. The season in Loutró runs from April to October, but in the winter months everything is closed.

## Ayía Rouméli

**AYÍA ROUMÉLI**, a small coastal settlement lying at the end of Samariá Gorge, is visited daily by hundreds of weary walkers for whom the sea is a welcome shimmering mirage after their long hike. After an iced drink, a plunge in the sea to cool the aching limbs, and lunch at one of the cluster of tavernas, there's nothing much else to stay for, although you'll have no choice if you've missed the last boat, in which case you'll need to seek out one of the many **rooms** for rent along the beach.

## Frangokástello

**FRANGOKÁSTELLO** is named after a crumbling Venetian attempt to bring law and order to a district that went on to defy both Turks and Germans. The four-square, crenellated thirteenth-century **castle**, isolated a few kilometres below a chiselled wall of mountains, looks as though it's been spirited out of the High Atlas or Tibet. The place is said to be haunted by ghosts of Greek rebels massacred here in 1829: every May, these *dhrossoulítes* ("dewy ones") march at dawn across the coastal plain and disappear into the sea near the fort. The rest of the time Frangokástello is peaceful enough, with a lovely beach and a number of tavernas and rooms scattered for some distance along the coast.

## Paleóhora

The easiest route to the southwest leaves the north coast at Tavronítis, 22km west of Haniá, heading for **PALEÓHORA**, and although this road also has to wind through the western outriders of the White Mountains, it lacks the excitement of the alternatives to either side.

The little town is built across the base of a peninsula, its harbour and a beach known as Pebble Beach on the eastern side, the wide sands (Sandy Beach) on the west. Above, on the outcrop, ruined Venetian ramparts stand sentinel. Though a resort of some size, Paleóhora remains thoroughly enjoyable, with a narrow main street that closes to traffic in the evenings so diners can spill out of the restaurants, and with a pleasantly chaotic social life.

## Soúyia

A small village slowly on its way to becoming a resort, **SOÚYIA** is not, in all honesty, a particularly attractive place on first sight but it does grow on you; its best feature is the enormous swathe of bay with a long, grey pebble beach and sparkling clean water. At the far end of this bay most summers there's something of a nudist and camping community – known locally as the Bay of Pigs. Otherwise, sights are few – the local

hurch has a sixth-century Byzantine mosaic as the foundation, although most of it is
n Haniá's archeological museum – but there are a couple of fabulous walks: down the
beautiful **Ayía Iríni Gorge** or a wonderful hour-long hike over to the nearby ancient site
of **Lissós** with temples and mosaics.

There are a number of good tavernas, cafés and a couple of minimarkets in the village;
he latter will exchange money.

## GETTING AROUND

**By bus** Haniá to: Frangokástello (1 daily; 2hr 30min), Hóra
Fakíon (2 daily; 2hr), Paleóhora (4 daily 5am–4pm; 1hr
10min), Soúyia (2 daily 5am & 2pm; 2hr).

**By boat** Hóra Sfakíon to: Loutró/Ayía Rouméli (3 daily
April–Oct; 15min/45min), Gávdhos (2–3 weekly; 3hr).

## THE SOUTHWEST COAST

Ayía Rouméli to: Soúyia (2 daily April–Oct; 45min),
Paleóhora (1 daily May–Oct; 1hr 20min). Paleóhora to:
Elafoníssi (daily May–Oct), Soúyia (daily May–Oct; 30min).
**Taxi boats** can be hired in Loutró and Hóra Sfakíon to take
you to local beaches and coves.

## INFORMATION

**Tourist office** Paleóhora Pebble Beach, close to the ferry
harbour (June–Sept, Mon & Wed–Sun 10am–1pm &
6–9pm; ☎ 28230 41507) provides accommodation lists
and a useful map with listings.

**Services** Notos Travel, Odhós Venizélou, Paleóhora (☎ 28230
42110), can book ferry tickets. There are also plenty of other
travel agents along and around central Venizélos. There's a
post office on the road behind Sandy Beach.

## ACCOMMODATION

### HÓRA SFAKÍON

**Livikon** ☎ 28250 91211, ⓦ sfakia-livikon.com. Has
great views from the upper-floor rooms though some noise
from the tavernas below. All rooms are en suite with a/c,
balcony, sea view and TV. **€40**

**Stavris** ☎ 28250 91220, ⓦ hotel-stavris-chora-sfakion
.com. Plain but comfortable en-suite rooms with balcony,
some with side sea view. They also have smarter
apartments on the edge of town. **€35**

**Xenia** ☎ 28250 91202, ⓦ xenia-crete.com. Has the best
location in town with amazing views across the Libyan Sea.
This former state-owned hotel, now refurbished, has
en-suite rooms with a/c, fridge, satellite TV and balcony
with sea view. April–Oct. **€50**

### LOUTRÓ

**Blue House** ☎ 28250 91127, ⓦ bluehouse.loutro.gr.
Simple, yet comfortable, sea-front en-suite rooms with
balcony and a wonderful (slightly pricier) top-floor
extension as well as a great taverna. April–Oct. **€45**

**Nikolas** ☎ 28250 91352. Thanks to its position right at
the eastern end of the seafront, the simple rooms with a/c
are probably the quietest you'll find in Loutró, some with
balcony and sea view. April–Oct. **€40**

**Porto Loutro** ☎ 28250 91433, ⓦ hotelportoloutro
.com. The only place with any pretensions at all, whose
comfortable rooms with a/c and balcony spread across
several attractive cubist white buildings by the beach (and
more rooms by the ferry dock). Breakfast included. April–
Oct. **€60**

### AYÍA ROUMÉLI

**Hotel Kalypso** Western end of the village ☎ 28250

91231, ⓦ agiaroumeli.gr. Simple, airy rooms with a/c,
fridge, TV and balcony, most with sea view, and there's a
café below for coffee and breakfast (not included). April–
Oct. **€40**

### PALEÓHORA

**Anonymous Homestay** Off Odhós Venizélos ☎ 28230
42098, ⓦ anonymoushomestay.gr. Among the least
expensive places in town, and something of a travellers'
meeting place, with simple, en-suite rooms around a
courtyard garden and a very friendly, far from anonymous,
atmosphere. **€25**

**Camping Paleohora** 1km north of Pebble Beach
☎ 28230 41120. Set in a large olive grove with plenty of
shade and decent facilities, next to a rather desolate stretch
of beach. Opposite is the Paleochora Club (see p.505);
although indoors and soundproofed, some noise from late-
night revellers is inevitable when the club is open. May–
Oct. **€16**

★ **Castello** Overlooking the southern end of Sandy
Beach ☎ 28230 41143. Exceptionally friendly place, most
of whose simple rooms have balconies overlooking the
beach; otherwise enjoy the view from the excellent café.
The alleys behind here, beneath the castle, have many
more simple rooms places. April–Oct. **€30**

**Sandy Beach** Seafront at the southern end of Sandy
Beach ☎ 28230 42138. The town's chicest hotel option,
right opposite the beach, its a/c balcony rooms equipped
with fridge, TV and sea view. Breakfast included. **€55**

**Scorpios** North end of Pebble Beach ☎ 28230 41058,
ⓦ scorpios-rooms.gr. Comfortable rooms, most with sea
views, and quieter than most thanks to a position near the
end of the beach. Breakfast included. April–Oct. **€50**

7

**Villa Marise** Sandy beach ☎ 28230 41162, ⓦ villamarise.com. One of the best locations in town, right on the main beach and boasting a variety of good apartments and studios. The pool is shared with accommodation next door. April–Oct. **€60**

### SOÚYIA

★ **Captain George** ☎ 28230 51133, ⓦ sougia.info /hotels/captain_george. Clean and comfortable en-suite rooms, studios and apartments, set in gardens, a few hundred metres from the beach, with a/c, balcony, TV, fridge and kettle (kitchenette in studios/apartments). The owner also owns a couple of small cruise boats and books day-trips. April–Oct. **€45**

**El Greco** ☎ 28230 51186, ⓦ www.elgreco.sougia .info. The *El Greco* is tucked away off the main street in a peaceful location, 200m from the beach (behind *Captain George*). It offers a/c balcony rooms with fridge and kettle, wi-fi, and some studios with kitchenette. April–Oct. **€40**

**Santa Irene** ☎ 28230 51342, ⓦ santa-irene.gr. Smart modern studios and apartments in probably the best location. Rooms come with a/c, TV, kitchenette and balcony (some with sea view). Long-stay deals available in winter. **€50**

**Syia** ☎ 28230 51174, ⓦ syiahotel.gr. This modern hotel is the fanciest place in the village, although it doesn't boast the best location, bang on the noisy main street. Spacious boutique-style studios and apartments with a/c, TV, fridge and coffee maker. Breakfast included. April–Oct **€80**

## EATING AND DRINKING

### LOUTRÓ

**Blue House** ☎ 28250 91127. This friendly taverna, beneath the rooms of the same name, has a good choice of fresh home-cooked Cretan and Greek dishes, all at reasonable prices. April–Oct daily 10am–late.

**Ilios** ☎ 28250 91160. Good seafood and fish, which is caught from their own boat, and reasonable prices. Try the excellent swordfish (€9). Standard taverna fare is also served. Located at the far eastern end of the bay, just beyond the beach. April–Oct daily 10am–late.

### AYÍA ROUMÉLI

**Taverna Tara** ☎ 28250 91231. Under the same management as the *Hotel Kalypso*, this taverna offers the usual suspects – oven-baked lamb and stuffed aubergines, from €5, on a large seafront terrace by the ferry dock. April–Oct daily 10am–11pm.

### PALEÓHORA

**Atoli** ☎ 28230 41645. Lively café-bar serving drinks and snacks – a good spot to catch the sunset – that has occasional live music, both Greek traditional and modern. Southern end of Sandy Beach. Daily 10am–late.

★ **Caravella** ☎ 28230 41131. Overlooking the harbour, this is Paleóhora's flagship seafood restaurant. The cooking and service are outstanding, as is their chilled *hýma* (barrelled wine) from a vineyard in the Kastélli Kissámou area. April–Oct daily lunch & dinner.

★ **The Third Eye** ☎ 28230 41234. An excellent vegetarian restaurant which includes plenty of Asian spices and ingredients you won't find anywhere else on the island, as well as the usual Greek veggie dishes and vegetarian curry (€7). Inland from sandy beach. April–Oct Daily breakfast, lunch & dinner.

## ECOTOURISM IN CRETE

Crete has an incredibly diverse landscape, flora and fauna, and a number of environmentally aware locals have set about preserving its natural and cultural heritage. A range of retreats and lodges has sprung up across the island, offering the chance to experience sustainable, eco-friendly living and participate in everything from hiking to making the local firewater *tsikoudhiá*.

**Enagron** Axós, Réthymnon ☎ 28340 61611, ⓦ enagron.gr. These traditional-style, stone-built houses stand in the hills at the foot of Mount Psilorítis, surrounded by olive groves and vines. There's a farm and taverna, with activities including grape harvesting, cooking courses and botanical walks. **€95**

**Lasinthos** Áyios Yeóryios, Lasíthi Plateau ☎ 28440 89101, ⓦ lasinthos.gr. At the foot of the Dikti mountains, this newly constructed eco-park and village rents traditionally furnished and well-equipped guest rooms. The farm cultivates olives, grapes and vegetables, and there are workshops for ceramics, weaving and woodcarving, plus a still for making *tsikoudhiá*. **€60**

**Miliá** Vlátos, Haniá ☎ 28210 46774, ⓦ milia.gr. The most authentic of Crete's eco retreats, this renovated seventeenth-century settlement in the White Mountains uses only renewable energy sources, accommodation is in small cottages with solar power and candles, while the taverna uses fresh organic ingredients. Activities include walking and cooking. Breakfast included. **€75**

## SOÚYIA

**Omikron** On the seafront ☎ 28230 51492. This French-run café and taverna has a more northern European flavour and offers some vegetarian choices. Snacks, salads, curry and pepper steak, among other offerings, are usually on the menu. April–Oct daily breakfast, lunch & dinner.

★ **Rembetiko** ☎ 28230 51510. Home-cooked traditional dishes including plenty of vegetarian options such as rice-stuffed tomatoes and peppers (€5) are served on a pleasant garden terrace (halfway up the main street). April–Oct daily lunch & dinner.

### NIGHTLIFE

## PALEÓHORA

**Nostos** Pebble Beach, by the tourist office ☎ 697 48 93 355. Open as a café and bar throughout the day, Nostos is also the liveliest late-night joint in town, with a chilled club atmosphere. May–Oct daily 10am–late, Nov–March

weekends and bank holidays 10am–late.
**Paleohora Club** North end of Pebble Beach close to the campsite. The one real dance place, far enough from town to be able to make some noise, though still fairly restrained and mainstream. June–Sept daily 11pm–6am.

# Kastélli and the far west

7

Apart from being Crete's most westerly town, and the end of the main coastal highway, **KASTÉLLI** (Kíssamos, or Kastélli Kissámou, as it's variously known) has little obvious appeal. It's a busy small town and port with a long seafront and a rocky central **beach** (there's also a small sandy beach to the west). The very ordinariness of Kastélli, however, can be attractive: life goes on pretty much regardless of outsiders, and there's every facility you might need. The town was important in antiquity, when the Greco-Roman city-state of **Kísamos** was a major regional power.

To the west of Kastélli lies some of Crete's loneliest and, for many visitors, finest coastline. On the far western tip, **Falásarna** has beautiful beaches and ancient ruins, while **Elafonísi's** "pink" beaches and lagoon lie in the southwest corner; the coastal road connecting them has little development along the way, just a couple of villages, rocky coves and patches of sand.

## The archeological museum

Platía Tzanakáki • Tues–Sun 8.30am–3pm • €3 • ☎ 28220 83308

Kastélli's superb **archeological museum** houses stunning Roman-era **mosaics** on the upper floor; mosaic production was a local speciality, and many more are being excavated around town. Other exhibits include prehistoric and Minoan relics from excavations in the town and from nearby Ancient Polyrínia.

## Falásarna

The ruins of an ancient city and port are ignored by most visitors to **FALÁSARNA** in favour of some of the best beaches on Crete, wide and sandy with clean water, though far from undiscovered. There's a handful of **tavernas** and an increasing number of **rooms** for rent, and plenty of people **camp** out here too. Although the beach can occasionally be afflicted by washed-up tar and discarded rubbish, this doesn't detract from the overall beauty of the place. Crowds of locals on summer weekends can always be escaped if you're prepared to walk, and the beaches are worth it.

## Sfinári and Kámbos

Further south, the western coastline is far less discovered. **SFINÁRI** is a sleepy village with a number of rooms to rent on the road down to a quiet pebble beach, sandy in patches. At the bottom is a cluster of tavernas which offer free sunloungers to customers.

**KÁMBOS** is similar to Sfinári, but even less visited. Its stony beach is a good hour's walk down a well-marked gorge path – a branch of the E4 – starting from the village square. Alternatively there's a steep asphalted track, which is driveable.

## Monastery of Khryssoskalítissa

Daily 8am–8pm • €2

Some 5km before Elafonísi the **monastery of Khryssoskalítissa** sits perched on a cliff with amazing views along the coastline. It is increasingly visited by tours from Haniá and Paleóhora, but worth the effort for its isolation. The name Khryssoskalítissa translates as **golden step**, and the faithful here believe that one of the 90 steps leading up to the monastery appears gold to those who are pure of spirit.

## Elafonísi

The tiny uninhabited islet of **Elafonísi** lies marooned on the edge of a gloriously scenic turquoise lagoon that shares its name. The pinky-white sand, the warm, clear lagoon and the islet to which you can easily wade are magnificent, but you certainly won't have them to yourself unless you visit out of season.

There are a number of stalls selling cold drinks and basic food on the beach, but perhaps the best option is to bring your own supplies and have a picnic on the beach.

### ARRIVAL AND DEPARTURE

### KASTÉLLI AND THE FAR WEST

**By bus** Kastélli bus station is on Platía Tzanakáki. Destinations Haniá (14 daily 6.30am–9.30pm; 1hr 15min), Elafonísi (May–Sept 1 daily; 1hr 40min), Falásarna (May–Sept 3 daily; 40min), Sfinári (1 daily; 1hr).

**By ferry** The port of Kastélli lies some 3km to the west of town.
Destinations Weekly (Thurs) to Andikýthira (2hr), Kýthira (4hr), Yíthio (8hr).

### INFORMATION AND TOURS

**Tours** Daily boat trips run from Kastélli port to the beautiful beaches at Gramvoússa and Bálos Bay, at the far northwestern tip of Crete.
**Services** Travel agents (for ferry tickets, boat tours or car

rental) lie east of the square along Skalídhi; another group can be found around nearby Platía Venizélou, on the main road through town.

### ACCOMMODATION

#### KASTÉLLI

**Argo** Telonio beach ☎28220 23322, ⓦpapadaki.biz. Simply furnished rooms on the seafront with a/c, TV, fridge and balconies with sea view. April–Oct. **€45**
**Galini Beach Hotel** ☎28220 23288, ⓦgalinibeach .com. Located right by the beach near the football pitch, this family-run hotel has sparkling a/c, sea-view rooms with TV, balconies and free wi-fi in communal areas. April–Oct. **€50**
**Vergerakis** (aka Jimmy's) Platía Tzanakáki ☎28220 22663. Central rooms place, a few hundred metres from the beach; simple, clean rooms with shared bath and use of kitchen facilities, plus a few en suites. April–Oct. **€25**

#### FALÁSARNA

**Pension Anastasia Stathis** ☎28220 41480, ⓦstathisanastasia.com. Spacious, modern, but simple, rooms with sea and mountain views from the balconies, located 300m from the beach (on the main road down to Falásarna). Facilities include a/c, fridge, and some rooms with kitchenette. April–Oct. **€45**

**Sunset** ☎28220 41204, ⓦsunsethotel.biz. One of the best locations right above the beach. Basic rooms with a/c, fridge and balcony with great sea views – and sunsets – with a good taverna below. April–Oct. **€40**

#### KÁMBOS

**Rooms Hartzulakis** On the edge of the village ☎28220 44445. Friendly rooms with taverna and dramatic views overlooking the gorge. A map here gives details of local walking routes around the area and coast, and the owner can provide further information. April–Oct. **€30**

#### ELAFONÍSI

**Elafonísi** 1km before the beach ☎28220 61274. Probably the best of Elafonísi's few rooms places, with a/c balcony rooms, TV and fridge. There is a good taverna below which uses many home-grown ingredients, and a minimarket. May–Oct. **€40**

### EATING AND DRINKING

There are a number of tavernas on Kastélli's beach promenade. Around them are numerous cafés and bars, popular with young locals and hence livelier than you might expect, particularly at weekends.

★ **Kellari (The Cellar)** Telenio beach, eastern seafront ☎ 28220 23700. Popular seafront taverna with friendly service and delicious fresh dishes – such as beef *kritiko* (beef in a red wine and ouzo sauce; €8) – all cooked with their own olive oil. April–Oct daily lunch & dinner.

**Papadakis** ☎ 28220 22340. Good taverna with a large seafront terrace (same owner as the *Argo* rooms), serving fish, seafood and meat dishes. Try the excellent fish soup, the speciality of the house. April–Oct daily lunch & dinner.

# Gávdhos

**GÁVDHOS**, some 50km of rough sea south of Hóra Sfakíon, is the southernmost island in Greece (and Europe if you don't count Spain's Canary Islands). Gávdhos is small (about 10km by 7km) and barren, but it has one major attraction: the enduring **isolation** which its inaccessible position has helped preserve. If all you want is a beach and a taverna to grill your fish, this remains the place for you. There's a semi-permanent community of campers and would-be "Robinson Crusoes" resident on the island year-round, swelling to thousands in August – but just six indigenous families.

Most people choose to base themselves near to one of the three largest beaches; at the most popular of all, **Sarakíniko**, there's a number of beachfront tavernas and cafés and a few rooms places. At **Áyios Ioánnis**, 2km to the northwest, there's a thriving hippy-type community of nudist campers. The third choice is pebbly **Kórfos**, south of the port and capital at **Karabé**.

## ARRIVAL AND INFORMATION

**By ferry** Check in advance, as the schedules change year to year, and be aware that in windy or bad weather the ferry will not go at all – even in high summer. The summer timetable is currently as follows: From Hóra Sfakíon: June–Aug; Fri, Sat & Sun 11.30am. From Paleóhora: via Soúyia and Ayía Rouméli May–Oct; Mon, Wed 8.30am.

**Services** There are well-stocked minimarkets at Sarakíniko and Áyios Ioánnis, but no banks on the island so remember to bring cash with you, and more than you might normally need, in case you get stuck on the island due to the weather.

## GETTING AROUND

**By bus** From the harbour at Karabé, local buses head north towards Sarakíniko and south to Kórfos.

## ACCOMMODATION AND EATING

If you turn up in August without a booking you may well find yourself camping on the beach. Travel agents in Paleóhora (see p.502) or Hóra Sfakíon (p.501) will arrange rooms.

**Sarakiniko Studios** Sarakíniko ☎ 28230 42182, ⓦ gavdostudios.gr. A collection of rooms and studios on the hillside above the bay, with kitchen, fridge and terrace. They will pick you up from the ferry if you've pre-booked. Satellite TV and internet are available at their taverna. May–Oct. **€45**

**Vailakakis (Gerti & Manolis)** Sarakíniko ☎ 28230 41103. Simple en-suite rooms with a/c. They also have some new stone villas, split into apartments, for rent. Their taverna has probably the best food on the beach, with good-value seafood caught daily by Manolis. May–Oct. **€45**

**Yiorgos and Maria's** Kórfos ☎ 28230 42166, ⓦ gavdos -online.com. Friendly place with comfortable a/c rooms and an excellent taverna. Breakfast included. May–Oct. **€48**

# The Dodecanese

**512** Rhodes

**530** Kastellórizo

**533** Hálki

**535** Kássos

**537** Kárpathos

**543** Sými

**550** Tílos

**554** Níssyros

**560** Kos

**569** Psérimos

**569** Astypálea

**574** Kálymnos

**580** Léros

**585** Pátmos

**590** Lipsí

**592** Arkí

**592** Agathoníssi

SNORKELLING OFF KÁRPATHOS

# The Dodecanese

Curving tightly against the Turkish coast, almost within hailing distance of Anatolia, the Dodecanese (Dhodhekánisos) are the furthest island group from the Greek mainland. They're hardly a homogeneous bunch. The two largest, Rhodes (Ródhos) and Kos, are fertile giants where traditional agriculture has almost entirely been displaced by a tourist industry focused on beaches and nightlife. Kastellórizo, Sými, Hálki, Kássos and Kálymnos, on the other hand, are essentially dry limestone outcrops that grew rich enough from the sea – especially during the nineteenth century – to build attractive port towns. Níssyros is a real anomaly, created by a still-steaming volcano that cradles lush vegetation, while Kárpathos is more variegated, its forested north grafted onto a rocky limestone south. Tílos, despite its lack of trees, has ample water, Léros shelters soft contours and amenable terrain, and further-flung Pátmos and Astypálea offer architecture and landscapes more reminiscent of the Cyclades.

**8**

Major Dodecanese attractions include the beaches on Rhodes and Kos; the wonderful medieval enclave of Rhodes Old Town; the gorgeous ensemble of Neoclassical mansions that surrounds the harbour on Sými; the rugged landscapes of Kálymnos, Kárpathos and Níssyros; the cave and monastery on Pátmos, where St John had his vision of the Apocalypse; and the hilltop village of Hóra on Astypálea. Each island has its own subtler pleasures, however; every visitor seems to find one where the pace of life, and friendly ambience, strikes a particular chord.

Thanks to their position en route to the Middle East, the Dodecanese – too rich and strategic to be ignored, but never powerful enough to rule themselves – have had a turbulent history. The scene of ferocious battles between German and British forces in 1943–44, they only joined the modern Greek state in 1948 after centuries of rule by Crusaders, Ottomans and Italians.

That historical legacy has given the islands a wonderful blend of **architectural styles** and **cultures**; almost all hold Classical remains, a Crusaders' castle, a clutch of vernacular villages and whimsical or grandiose public buildings. For these last the Italians, who held the Dodecanese from 1912 to 1943, are responsible. Determined to turn them into a showplace for Fascism, they undertook ambitious public works, excavations and reconstruction.

## GETTING AROUND

The largest islands in the group are connected by regular ferries and catamarans, as well as flights; only Kastellórizo and Tílos are relatively difficult to reach. Rhodes is the main transport hub, with connections for Crete, the northeastern Aegean, the Cyclades and the mainland too. The fastest, most useful connections are provided by twin catamarans, the *Dodekanisos Express* and the *Dodekanisos Pride*, which follow a busy schedule between Rhodes and Pátmos; see ⓦ 12ne.c

| | |
|---|---|
| Windsurfing at Prassoníssi p.528 | Sponges and sponge-diving p.576 |
| Hiking in northern Kárpathos p.543 | Italian architecture in |
| Hiking on Sými p.549 | the Dodecanese p.582 |
| Hiking on Níssyros Island p.559 | Saint John on Pátmos p.588 |
| Hippocrates p.566 | |

SÝMI HARBOUR

# Highlights

**1** **Rhodes Old Town** One of Europe's most magnificently preserved medieval towns. See p.514

**2** **Lindos Acropolis, Rhodes** Occupied for over 3000 years, this hilltop citadel enjoys great views over the town and coast. See p.526

**3** **Northern Kárpathos** Old walking trails thread through a spectacular mountainous landscape to reach isolated villages. See p.542

**4** **Sými** Graceful Neoclassical mansions soar to all sides of Sými's gorgeous harbour. See p.543

**5** **Níssyros Volcano** Explore the still-bubbling craters of the volcano that created the island. See p.558

**6** **Brós Thermá, Kos** Relax in shoreline hot springs, which flow into the sea, protected by a boulder ring. See p.566

**7** **Hóra, Astypálea** Wrapped around a beautiful Venetian kástro, the windswept island capital perches proudly above the sea. See p.571

**8** **Télendhos islet**, **Kálymnos** Whether admired at sunset from western Kálymnos, or visited via local ferries, beach-fringed little Télendhos should not be missed. See p.578

**9** **Hóra, Pátmos** With its fortified monastery dedicated to St John of the Apocalypse, this is the Dodecanese's most atmospheric village. See p.588

HIGHLIGHTS ARE MARKED ON THE MAP ON P.512

# Rhodes

**Rhodes (Ródhos)** is deservedly among the most visited of all Greek islands. Its star attraction is the beautiful **medieval Old Town** that lies at the heart of its capital, Rhodes Town – a legacy of the crusading Knights of St John, who used the island as their main base from 1309 until 1522. Elsewhere, the ravishing hillside village of **Líndhos**, topped by

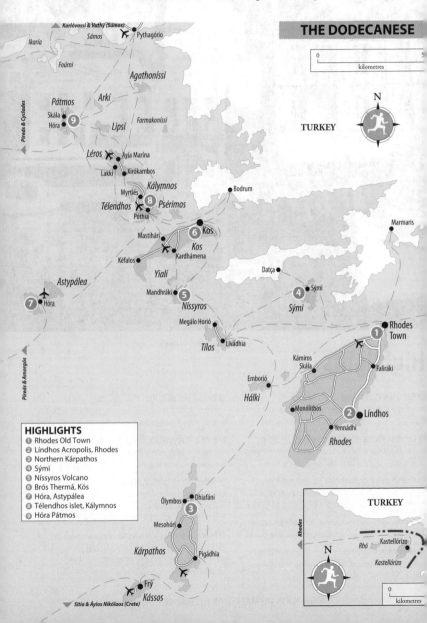

## THE DODECANESE

0 _____ kilometres

N

TURKEY

**HIGHLIGHTS**
1. Rhodes Old Town
2. Líndhos Acropolis, Rhodes
3. Northern Kárpathos
4. Sými
5. Níssyros Volcano
6. Brós Thermá, Kós
7. Hóra, Astypálea
8. Télendhos islet, Kálymnos
9. Hóra Pátmos

TURKEY

Rhodes

Rhó    Kastellórizo

Kastellórizo

N

0 _____ kilometres

n ancient acropolis, should not be missed. It marks the midpoint of the island's long astern shoreline, adorned with numerous sandy **beaches** that have attracted considerable esort development. At the southern cape, **Prassoníssi** is one of the best windsurfing spots n Europe. If you want to escape the summer crowds, take a road trip into the island's raggy and partly forested interior: worthwhile targets include the castles near **Monólithos** nd **Kritinía**, and frescoed churches at **Thárri**, **Asklipió** and **Áyios Yeóryios Várdhas**.

## Brief history

Blessed with an equable climate and strategic position, Rhodes, despite its lack of good arbours, was important from the very earliest times. The finest natural port served the ncient town of **Lindos** which, together with the other Dorian city-states **Kameiros** and alyssos, united in 408 BC to found a new capital, **Rodos** (Rhodes), at the windswept orthern tip of the island. The cities allied themselves with Alexander, the Persians, Athenians or Spartans as conditions suited them, generally escaping retribution for backing the wrong side by a combination of seafaring audacity, sycophancy and urgeoning wealth as a trade centre. Following the failed siege of Macedonian general Demetrios Polyorketes in 305 BC, Rhodes prospered even further, displacing Athens as he major venue for rhetoric and the arts in the east Mediterranean.

Decline set in when the island became involved in the Roman civil wars and was sacked by Cassius; by late imperial times, it was a backwater. The Byzantines ceded Rhodes to he Genoese, who in turn surrendered it to the Knights of St John. After the second great **siege** of Rhodes, in 1522–23, when Ottoman Sultan Süleyman the Magnificent ousted he stubborn knights, the island once again lapsed into relative obscurity, though heavily colonized and garrisoned, until its seizure by the Italians in 1912.

**8**

## ARRIVAL AND DEPARTURE

**RHODES**

### BY PLANE

hodes' airport lies on the island's west coast, 14km outhwest of Rhodes Town alongside Paradhísi village. Buses to and from town stop between the two terminals (turn left out of arrivals; frequent services 6.30am–midnight; €2.30). A taxi ride into town should cost around €22.

**Destinations** Olympic fly to and from the following Islands: Astypálea (2–3 weekly); Athens (4–5 daily); Iráklion, Crete (2 daily); Kos (2–3 weekly); Léros (2–3 weekly); Thessaloníki (2 weekly); Kárpathos (1–2 daily); Kássos (1–2 daily); Sitía (1–2 daily). Aegean fly to Athens (4–7 daily) and Thessaloníki (1–2 daily).

### BY FERRY

erries to Rhodes use two separate harbours in Rhodes own. Large boats and catamarans dock at Kolóna, immediately outside the Old Town, while smaller vessels nd excursion craft use the yacht harbour of Mandhráki acing the New Town.

**Ticket offices** ANES 88 Australis St (☎22410 37769, anes.gr) for catamarans and hydrofoil to Sými; odhekanisos Seaways have a kiosk at their departure

point in Kolóna Harbour (☎22410 70590, ⓦ12ne.gr); Tsangaris (☎22410 36170) for GA boats; Skevos, 111 Amerikis St (☎22410 22461, ⓦbluestarferries.gr), for Blue Star; Zorpidhis (☎22410 20625) for LANE; Stefanakis, Alex Diakou St, for Sea Star and *Panayia Spiliani* (☎22410 78052, ⓦtils.gr).

**Destinations** The following islands have regular connections: Anáfi (1 weekly; 17hr); Astypálea (1 weekly; 9hr 10min); Crete (2 weekly; 12hr 30min); Hálki (4 weekly; 1hr 25min–2hr); Kálymnos (2–4 daily; 2hr 40min–8hr 15min); Kárpathos (4 weekly; 5hr); Kássos (4 weekly; 6hr 30min); Kastellórizo (3 weekly; 2hr 20min–3hr 40min); Kos (1–5 daily; 2hr 10min–6hr 15min); Léros (1–2 daily; 4hr–5hr 15min); Lipsí (6 weekly; 5hr 10min–8hr 20min); Milos (2 weekly; 23hr); Níssyros (4 weekly; 3hr 10min–4hr 45min); Pátmos (1–3 daily; 4hr 45min–9hr 45min); Pireás (1–4 daily; 12hr 30min–17hr); Santoríni (7 weekly; 7–20hr); Sitía (2 weekly; 9hr 20min); Sými (3–4 daily; 50min–1hr 40min); Sýros (2 weekly; 9hr); Tílos (7 weekly; 1hr 20min–2hr 15min). The tiny port at Kámiros Skála, 45km southwest of Rhodes Town, is used only by regular boats to Hálki (daily except Sun; 1hr 15min).

## INFORMATION

**Tourist offices** The municipal tourist office is at Platía Rimíni, just north of the Old Town (June–Sept Mon–Sat 9.30am–9.30pm, Sun 9am–3pm; Oct–May daily 9.30am–3pm). A short walk from here up Papágou, on the

corner of Makaríou, the Greek National Tourist Office (Mon–Fri 8.30am–2.45pm) dispenses bus and ferry schedules.

**Hospital/clinic** The modern state hospital, just northwest of town, is understaffed and has a deservedly poor reputation;

especially if you're insured, head for the well-signed Euromedica clinic in Koskinoú, 6.5km south (24hr; English-speaking staff; ☏ 22410 45000 for their ambulances).

**Activities** For scuba diving, contact Waterhoppers (ⓦwaterhoppers.com) at Mandhráki quay; as well as running beginners' courses in the bay at Kallithéas beach, they offer more challenging deep-wall dives at Ladhikó just south of Faliraki, and near Líndhos.

### GETTING AROUND

**By bus** Buses from Rhodes Town to the west and east coasts leave from adjacent terminals on Avérof in New Town, immediately north of the Old Town just outside the Italian-built New Market. The main local operator is KTEL (☏ 22410 27706, ⓦ ktelrodou.gr).

**By taxi** The main taxi rank is at Platía Rimínis, immediately north of Rhodes Old Town, across from the bus stops. A taxi to the airport officially costs €22; the fare to Líndhos is €44. Taxi drivers won't normally enter Rhodes Old Town; expect to walk to your hotel from the nearest gate.

**By car** Major car rental chains have outlets at the airport. In Rhodes Town, try Just, Mandhilará 70 (☏ 22410 31811, ⓦ just-rentacar.gr); Etos, Venizelou 33 (☏ 22410 22511 ⓦ etos.gr); or Kosmos, Papaloúka 31 (☏ 22410 74374 ⓦ cosmos-sa.gr). Driving is not permitted in Rhodes Old Town, while parking outside can be hard to find; the best bet is along Filellínon on the south side, between the Ayíou Athanasíou and Koskinoú gates.

**By bike and motorcycle** Outlets that rent bikes, scooters and motorcycles include Kiriakos, Apodhímon Amerikís 1 (☏ 22410 36047, ⓦ motorclubkiriakos.gr), which will deliver to Rhodes Old Town and shuttle you back once you've finished; Bicycle Centre, Griva 39 (☏ 22410 28315), and Mike's Motor Club, Ioánni Kazoúli 23 (☏ 22410 37420).

# Rhodes Town

By far the largest town on the island, **Rhodes Town** straddles its northernmost headland, in full view of Turkey less than 20km north. The ancient city that occupied this site, laid out during the fifth century BC by Hippodamos of Miletos, was almost twice the size of its modern counterpart, and at over 100,000 held more than double its population.

While the fortified enclave now known as the **Old Town** is of more recent construction, created by the Knights Hospitaller in the fourteenth century, it's one of the finest medieval walled cities you could ever hope to see. Yes, it gets hideously overcrowded with day-trippers in high season, but at night it's quite magical, and well worth an extended stay. It makes sense to think of it as an entirely separate destination to the **New Town**, or **Neohóri**, the mélange of unremarkable suburbs and dreary resort that sprawls out from it in three directions.

It was the entrance to **Mandhráki** harbour, incidentally, that was supposedly straddled by the **Colossus**, an ancient statue of Apollo erected to commemorate the 305 BC siege. In front of the New Town, the harbour is today used largely by yachts and excursion boats.

## Rhodes Old Town

**Rhodes Old Town** is an absolute gem, a superbly preserved medieval ensemble that's all but unique in retaining the feel of a genuine lived-in village, having neither grown to become a city nor been overly prettified for visitors. Still entirely enclosed within a double ring of mighty sandstone walls, it stands utterly aloof from the modern world.

Although the newly arrived Knights encircled the local population as well as their own castle within their fourteenth-century walls, they took the precaution of keeping whatever they needed for survival north of the straight-line street of **Sokrátous**, which could be sealed off in times of emergency. Broadly speaking that distinction remains, with the monumental district, now also scattered with Ottoman mosques and minarets, set somewhat apart.

While it does hold some fascinating sights and museums, however, what makes the Old Town so special is the sheer vibrancy of the place as a whole. Its busiest commercial lanes, packed with restaurants, cafés, and souvenir stores selling anything from T-shirts to fur coats, and gelati to jewellery, can be overpowering congested in summer – Sokrátous itself is the worst culprit – but it's always possible to escape into the time-forgotten tangle of cobbled alleyways that lie further south, and away from the sea

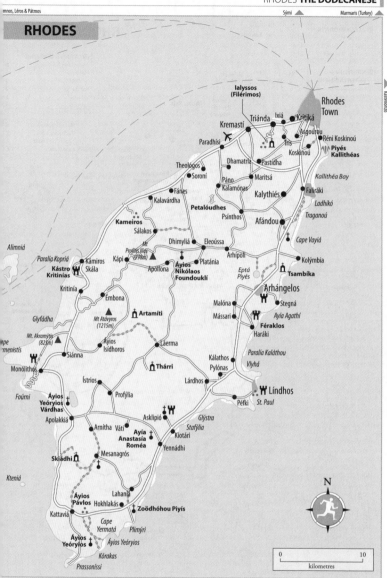

No map can do justice to what a labyrinth it all is, or quite how much is missing;
mysterious ruins lie half-buried, amok with cats or wildflowers, while isolated Cyclopean
arches suddenly rear into view, without a trace of the buildings they used to hold up.

## Palace of the Grand Masters

Summer Mon 12.30–7.30pm, Tues–Sun 8am–7.30pm; winter Tues–Sun 8.30am–3pm • €6, free Sun Nov–March

The **Palace of the Grand Masters** dominates the northwestern corner of the Old Town's
walls. Destroyed by an ammunition explosion in 1856, it was reconstructed by the

# RHODES TOWN

**KUMBURNU**

Aquarium

**ACCOMMODATION**

| | |
|---|---|
| Anastasia | 3 |
| Cactus | 1 |
| Plaza Best Western | 2 |

**NIGHTLIFE & ENTERTAINMENT**

| | |
|---|---|
| Christos' Garden | 2 |
| Colorado Club | 1 |

**EATING & DRINKING**

| | |
|---|---|
| Anatolikes Nostimies | 6 |
| Meltemi | 1 |
| Niohori | 3 |
| Ronda | 2 |
| Sakis | 5 |
| Tamam | 4 |

| | |
|---|---|
| Hydrofoil docking | H |
| Yacht docking | Y |
| Excursion boats | E |
| Catamaran | C |

Museum of Modern Greek Art

Casino (Hotel Rodon)

Murad Reis Mosque

Villa Cleobolus

Santa Maria della Vittoria

ELLI Beach

PL. KOUNDOURIOTI

Rodon Cinema

Municipal Theatre

Provincial Government

Áyios Nikólaos Tower

**NEOHORI**

Town Hall

Basilica of Evangelismós

Port Police

Manodhráki Harbour

Windmills

Ferry Mooring Points

Hospital

New Market

Roda Bus Stop

KTEL Bus Stop

PL. RIMINIS

Customs & Passport Control

Kolóna (Commercial Harbour)

Agency Booths

SEE MAP OF RHODES OLD TOWN FOR DETAIL

University of the Aegean

STREETS BLOCKED PERMANENTLY

Áyios Frangískos

Stadium

Pallas Cinema

Metropol Cinema

**AMMOS**

N

8

Airport

Monte Smith

0    100
metres

Rodhini Park, Lindhos & Koskinoú

Cemeteries

Italians as a summer home for Mussolini and King Vittore Emmanuele III, although either one ever visited Rhodes. While its external appearance, based on medieval engravings and accounts, remains reasonably authentic, free rein was given in its interior to Fascist delusions of grandeur.

The two splendid ground-floor galleries jointly constitute the best **museums** in town. They often close due to staff shortages; check whether they're open before you pay for admission, because otherwise there's precious little to see. One covers ancient Rhodes, documenting everyday life around 250 BC; highlights include a Hellenistic floor mosaic of a comedic mask. The other, across the courtyard, covers the medieval era, stressing the importance of Christian Rhodes as a trade centre. The Knights are represented with a display on their sugar-refining industry and a gravestone of a Grand Master; precious manuscripts and books precede a wing of post-Byzantine icons.

## Street of the Knights

The Gothic, heavily restored **Street of the Knights** (Odhós Ippotón) leads east from Platía Kleovoúlou in front of the Palace of the Grand Masters. The various "Inns" along the way lodged the Knights of St John, according to linguistic and ethnic affiliation, until the Ottoman Turks forced them to leave for Malta in 1523. Today the Inns house government offices, foreign consulates or cultural institutions vaguely appropriate to their past. Several stage occasional exhibitions, but the overall effect of the Italian renovation is sterile and stagey.

## Archeological Museum

Summer Tues–Sun 8am–7.30pm; winter Tues–Sun 8.30am–3pm • €6

At the foot of the Street of the Knights, the Knights' Hospital now houses the town's **archeological museum**. A very lovely complex in its own right, which takes at least an hour to explore, it consists of several galleries in the medieval hospital itself, plus a delightful raised and walled garden where extensions and outbuildings hold further displays. Rather too many rooms simply hold glass cases filled with small artefacts, displayed with little contextual information, but there's a lot of interesting stuff, including votive offerings from Egypt and Cyprus found in the Kamiros acropolis, and an amazing array of ancient painted pottery. The grandest hall upstairs is lined with the tomb slabs of fourteenth- and fifteenth-century Knights, but the light-filled gallery of **Hellenistic statues** nearby is the true highlight. *Aphrodite Adioumene*, the so-called "Marine Venus" beloved of Lawrence Durrell, stands in a rear corner, lent a sinister aspect by her sea-dissolved face that makes a striking contrast to the friendlier *Aphrodite Bathing*.

## Decorative Arts Collection

Platía Aryirokastrou • Daily except Mon 8.30am–3pm • €2

The vernacular treasures in the **Decorative Arts Collection**, which occupies a single large room at the northern edge of the old town, were gleaned from old houses throughout the Dodecanese. Redolent of Byzantine and Italian influences, they reflect the islands' cosmopolitan past. Amid the fading embroidery and brightly painted plates, the most compelling artefacts are the carved cupboard doors and chest lids, depicting mythological or historical episodes.

## Turkish Rhodes

Many of the mosques and *mescids* (the Islamic equivalent of a chapel) in which the old town abounds were converted from Byzantine churches after the Christians were expelled in 1522. The most conspicuous of all is the rust-coloured, candy-striped **Süleymaniye Mosque**, rebuilt during the nineteenth century on 300-year-old foundations. Like most local Ottoman monuments, it's not open to visitors, though the purpose-built (1531) **Ibrahim Pasha Mosque** on Plátonos, for example, is still used by the sizeable Turkish-speaking minority.

# RHODES OLD TOWN

N

Akándia

Moat Exit ▲

Southern limit of Kollákio

PROMITHEOS

Customs & Passport Control

Port Police

Akándia Gate

Moat Entry

Bastion of Italy (Carreto Bastion)

Ayia Ekaterini Gate

Services to Turkey

Hospitaller
Panayía Hospice
Panayía Tou
OLD JEWISH QUARTER
Synagogue

Mylon (or Jews') Gate

Kolóna (Commercial Harbour)

Dodekanisos Express

Theátro Táfros

Moat Entry

PERIKLEOUS

Marine Gate

Kastellanía

Arnaldo Gate

Fishing Boats

Inn of England

Ibrahim Pasha Mosque

PYTHAGORA

Arsenal Gate

Inn of Auvergne

ERMOU

EVRIPIDHOU

SOFOKLEOUS

Rejep Pasha Mosque

Koskinoú Gate (Kókkini Pylí)

Moat Entry

St Paul's Gate

Tower of Naíllac

Eleftherías Gate

Aphrodite Temple

Museum of Modern Greek Art (Annexe)

Decorative Arts Collection

Inn of France

Archeological Museum

APPELOU

Ayios Fanoúrios

ESKHILOU

FILELLINON

French Chapel

Inn of Provence

STREET OF THE KNIGHTS (IPPOTON)

Villaragut Mansion

Süleymaniye Mosque

Imaret

Hamam

Folk Dance Theatre

Ayiou Athanasíou Gate

Palace of the Grand Masters

Ayios Andónios Gate

Ottoman Library

Clocktower

THEOFILISKOU

Tower of Spain

Moat Entry

D'Amboise Gate

Moat Entry

Ayios Yeóryios Bastion

RIGA FEREOU

ROMANOÚ MELODHOÚ

metres 0 200

### ■ ACCOMMODATION

| | |
|---|---|
| Andreas | 8 |
| Avalon Boutique Hotel | 1 |
| Marco Polo Mansion | 5 |
| Niki's | 7 |
| Nikos Takis | 2 |
| Spirit of the Knights | 6 |
| Spot | 4 |
| Via-Via | 3 |

### ● EATING & DRINKING

| | |
|---|---|
| Fotis Melathron | 2 |
| La Varka | 5 |
| Mama Sofia | 1 |
| Marco Polo Café | 6 |
| Nireas | 7 |
| O Meraklis | 8 |
| Sea Star | 4 |
| Ta Kioupia | 3 |

### ■ NIGHTLIFE & ENTERTAINMENT

| | |
|---|---|
| Bekir Karakuzu | 1 |
| Besara Kafé | 4 |
| Rogmi tou Kronou | 3 |
| Santana Music Bar | 2 |

### KEY

Moat

Southern limit of Kollákio

The Ottomans' most enduring civic contributions are the **Ottoman Library**, opposite the Süleymaniye (Mon–Sat 9.30am–4pm; tip custodian), which has a rich collection of early medieval manuscripts and Korans; the **imaret** (mess-hall) at Sokrátous 179, now an exceptionally pleasant café (*Palio Syssitio*); and the imposing 1558 **Mustafa Hammam** (Turkish bath) on Platía Aríonos (Mon–Fri 10am–5pm, Sat 8am–5pm, last admission 4pm; €5). Bring everything you need – soap, shampoo, towel, loofah – to enjoy separate, *au naturel* men's and women's sections.

### Jewish Rhodes

Beyond the tiled central fountain in Platía Ippokrátous, Odhós Aristotélous leads to **Platía tón Evréon Martýron** ("Square of the Jewish Martyrs"), named in memory of the 2100 Jews of Rhodes and Kos who were sent to the concentration camps in 1944; a black granite column honours them. Of four synagogues that once graced the nearby Jewish quarter, only ornate, arcaded, pebble-floored **Kal Kadosh Shalom** (Mon–Fri & Sun 10am–3pm; donation) on Odhós Simíou, just south, survives. To one side, a well-labelled, three-room **museum** thematically chronicles the community's life on Rhodes.

## The New Town (Neohóri)

What's now known as the New Town – in Greek, **Neohóri** – dates originally to the Ottoman era, when Orthodox Greeks excluded from the fortified city built their own residential districts outside the walls. Only **Kumburnú**, the area immediately north of the Old Town, at the tip of the headland, bears any relevance to visitors. On its eastern side, Mandhráki yacht harbour serves as the base for excursion boats and some ferry companies, while the streets immediately inland hold the workaday shops, offices and agencies that keep the town as a whole ticking along. The headland itself is surrounded by a continuous **beach** of gritty shingle (loungers, parasols and showers), particularly at **Élli**, the more sheltered east-facing section. Despite being so close to the city, the water offshore is exceptionally clean. That explains the many hotels and restaurants hereabouts, but judged on its own merits the New Town makes a poor holiday destination.

### Aquarium

Daily: April–Oct 9am–8.30pm; Nov–March 9am–4.30pm • €5.50 • Ⓦ hcmr.gr

Perched at the northernmost point of the island, Rhodes' **Aquarium** is as much a museum as a conventional aquarium. It does hold tanks of live fish, not necessarily captioned correctly, but most of its space is taken up with displays on the history and function of the building itself, as well as a monk seal buried as an ancient family's pet, and a stuffed Cuvier's beaked whale.

### Museum of Modern Greek Art

Pl. G. Harítou • Tues–Thurs & Sat 8am–2pm, Fri 8am–2pm & 5–8pm • €3 • Ⓦ mgamuseum.gr

Near the northernmost tip of the New Town, on what's colloquially known as "100 Palms Square", Rhodes' **Museum of Modern Greek Art** holds the most important collection of twentieth-century Greek painting outside Athens. All the heavy hitters – Hatzikyriakos-Ghikas, surrealist Nikos Engonopoulos, naïve artist Theophilos, neo-Byzantinist Fotis Kontoglou – are amply represented. Some of Kontoglou's greatest frescoes, dating from 1951–61, are in the **Evangelismós basilica** at Mandhráki.

What used to be the main, cramped home of the museum, on Platía Sými 2 in the Old Town, is now the **annexe** (Tues–Sat 8am–2pm, same ticket), devoted to maps, prints and special exhibits. Both premises have excellent gift shops.

## Hellenistic Rhodes

A half-hour, 2km walk west and uphill from the Old Town – a hike best undertaken just before sunset, both for the views and the temperature – leads to the unenclosed remains of the **acropolis of Hellenistic Rhodes**, atop Monte Smith. Formerly known as Áyios Stéfanos, this hill was renamed for a British admiral during the Napoleonic Wars. While the ruins cover an extensive area, there's not really all that much to see – a restored theatre and stadium, plus three columns of a temple to **Apollo Pythios**. It's striking to realize that the ancient city stretched from here all the way down to the sea, however.

### The cemeteries

While the vast **municipal cemeteries** at Korakónero, just inland from Zéfyros beach 2km southeast of the centre, might not sound like a hot tourist destination, they can be strangely compelling. This is one of the very few remaining spots in the Balkans where the dead of four faiths lie in proximity, albeit separated by high walls. The easterly **Greek Orthodox section**, the largest, holds the fewest surprises. The small **Catholic section** is not only the last home of various north European expatriates, but also demonstrates that a fair number of Italians elected to accept Greek nationality and stay on after the 1948 unification with Greece. The **Jewish section** (Mon–Fri 8am–1pm) has, understandably, seen little activity since 1944, and is full of memorials in French to those who were deported. Opposite its gate, across the busy road, a small **Allied War graves** plot holds 142 burials. Just south of the Jewish section, the "**Muslim**" **section** (ie Turkish) is the most heavily used and best maintained of the three minority cemeteries.

## ACCOMMODATION                                                    RHODES TOWN

**8**

### OLD TOWN

★ **Andreas** Omírou 28D ☎ 22410 34156, ⓦ hotelandreas.com; see map, p.518. Perennially popular *pension*, imaginatively converted from an old Turkish mansion, with switched-on, international management. The eleven rooms vary in size and price; some sleep four, and there's a fabulous "penthouse". All have a/c; eight have en-suite bathrooms, while each of the other three has the key to its own dedicated bathroom, down the corridor. Excellent breakfasts (€6–8 extra) and evening drinks are served on the terrace bar, which has free wi-fi and great views. Two-night minimum stay, reservations essential. **€55**

**Avalon Boutique Hotel** Hárnós 9 ☎ 22410 31438, ⓦ avalonrhodes.gr; see map, p.518. Fourteenth-century manor house, tucked into a quiet courtyard very near the Grand Masters' palace, and stylishly re-modelled to hold six bright, modern and very luxurious suites, each with an open-air terrace. The friendly family team serve breakfast in your unit, the courtyard café, or the vaulted bar. **€215**

★ **Marco Polo Mansion** Ayíou Fanouríou 42 ☎ 22410 25562, ⓦ marcopolomansion.gr; see map, p.518. Superb conversion of an old Turkish mansion, opening off one of the old town's most charming lanes, with a hammam on site. All rooms are en suite, exquisitely furnished with antiques from the nearby eponymous gallery, and equipped with cotton pillows and handmade mattresses. The cheapest rooms face the garden. Large buffet breakfasts are provided in the garden snack bar, open to all later in the day (see

opposite). Reservations and credit-card deposit mandatory. Closed Nov–March. **€100**

**Niki's** Sofokléous 39 ☎ 22410 25115, ⓦ nikishotel.gr; see map, p.518. Attractive and very welcoming little hotel. All rooms are en suite, most have a/c, and those on the upper storey have fine views; there's also a shared roof terrace, and guests use use of a washing machine. Pay a little extra for a private balcony, or a room that sleeps three. Someone will wait up for late-night arrivals. Rates include breakfast. **€50**

**Nikos Takis** Panetíou 26 ☎ 22410 70773, ⓦ nikostakishotel.com; see map, p.518. Miniature "fashion hotel" in a restored mansion close to the Grand Masters' palace. Set up by two of Greece's most celebrated fashion designers, whose flamboyant 1960s work is on show throughout (and sold in the ground-floor boutique), its eight rather extraordinary units range through themes from Moroccan to medieval, with opulent furnishings, plush fabrics everywhere, stone arches and painted ceilings. Pebble-mosaic courtyard with fine views over town, for breakfast and drinks. **€170**

★ **Spirit of the Knights** Alexandridou 14 ☎ 22410 39765, ⓦ rhodesluxuryhotel.com; see map, p.518. Gorgeous traditional home in a very quiet back alleyway of the old town, in full view of a peaceful stretch of walls. Sensitively converted to create a lovely boutique hotel, it holds six exquisitely furnished and very distinct suites. Breakfast served in a pleasant garden courtyard that also holds a large jacuzzi. The front desk remains open around the clock, and nothing is too much trouble.

or the extended English family who own and run the place. **€200**

**pot** Perikléous 21 @22410 34737, @spothotel hodes.gr; see map, p.518. The cheerfully painted a/c n-suite rooms in this custard-yellow modern building re festooned with artworks and textiles, and offer xcellent value; triples available. An unlimited buffet reakfast, charged extra, is served on the rear patio, and here's also a roof terrace and free luggage storage. losed Dec–Feb. **€90**

**Via-Via** Lysipoú 2 @22410 77027, @hotel-via-via com; see map, p.518. Efficiently but congenially run otel on an alleyway off Pythagóra; most of the one-to-our-person rooms, all a/c, are en suite, but two share aths across the hall. All are simply and tastefully urnished with bedding and throw rugs in pastel hues. Roof terrace with pergola and divans for three grades of reakfast and an eyeful of the Ibrahim Pasha mosque opposite. **€70**

## NEW TOWN

**Anastasia** 28-Oktovríou 46 @22410 28007, @anastasia-hotel.com; see map, p.516. Italian-era mansion, with high ceilings and tiled floors, that's been converted to a congenial, family-run guesthouse. The rooms, which sleep up to four, are simple but have a/c and en-suite facilities; there's a bar in the garden, with its resident tortoises. Breakfast costs extra. **€45**

**Cactus** Kó 14 @22410 26100, @cactus-hotel.gr; see map, p.516. The best-value beachfront hotel in the new town, an updated 1960s high-rise with graceful curving glass-fronted balconies, facing the best stretch of Élli beach near the tip of the headland and offering a street-side pool of its own. **€110**

**Plaza Best Western** Ieroú Lóhou 7 @22410 22501, @rhodesplazahotel.com; see map, p.516. Crisp, modern four-star hotel, convenient for Mandhráki harbour, with a pool, garden and sauna. There's also a restaurant, and they offer buffet English breakfasts. **€115**

## EATING AND DRINKING

While the Old Town holds a quite staggering number of restaurants, prices tend to be high, and both value and quality tend to improve away from the main commercial lanes. Most places are open long hours every night, serving couples with children from about 6.30pm, then tourists until perhaps 10pm, and Greeks until midnight or later.

**8**

## OLD TOWN

**Fotis Melathron** Sokrátous 41 @22410 24272, @fotisgroup.com; see map, p.518. Despite the address, this large restaurant opens onto a small square just south of the main pedestrian drag. Come at lunchtime, when the tables in the flowery gardens that surround the compound are all but irresistible, and you might never realize that the interior's charming too, rambling through an old town house that holds assorted dining rooms. Reckon on €70 for dinner for two. A good mixed *mezédhes* plate costs €10.50, while the sliced-up whole stuffed squid is excellent. Daily noon–10pm.

**La Varka** Sofokléous 5; see map, p.518. Indoor-outdoor ouzerí, with a table-filled terrace right on a busy bar-filled alleyway, and live Greek music of its own. The interior makes a cosy retreat in the cooler months. Good salads, *pikilíes* for 2 at €30, grilled *thrápsalo*, fried or salt-cured seafood titbits, cheapish ouzo and *soúma* by the carafe. Daily 11.30am–1am.

**Mama Sofia** Orfeos 28 @22410 24469; see map, p.518. Good, reasonably priced home cooking in a very friendly atmosphere, across from the clocktower and minaret in the northwest corner of the Old Town. Choose between the roof terrace or the plentiful street-level tables, which make for perfect people-watching. Open until 10pm nightly.

★ **Marco Polo Café** Ayíou Fanouríou 42 @22410 25562; see map, p.518. Very lovely, deservedly popular hotel restaurant, filling a garden courtyard; don't worry about the lack of a street sign, they just want to keep the crowds down. Traditional adapted recipes, adeptly blending subtle flavours, include pilaf with lamb and raisins, turnovers with *pastourmá*, and *psaronéfri* with *manoúri* cheese, fig and red peppercorn sauce. Excellent wine list and desserts of the day. Closed Nov–March. Dinner only, daily until midnight.

★ **Nireas** Sofokléous 22 @22410 21703; see map, p.518. This long-standing, family-run fish specialist, on a quiet square just away from the bustle, has earned its sky-high reputation thanks to the hard work and friendly professionalism of its owners, its still-reasonable prices, and its atmospheric indoor/outdoor seating, making this a good choice for a treat. Individual seafood dishes, like mussels saganaki, cost around €10, and unusually they have a range of Italian desserts too. Around €70 for two including dessert and wine. Daily lunch & dinner.

**O Meraklis** Aristotélous 30; see map, p.518. One of the last Rhodian rough edges not yet filed smooth, this *pátsatzídhiko* (tripe-and-trotter-soup kitchen) caters for a pre-dawn clientele of clubbers, Turkish shopkeepers, gangsters and nightclub singers. Great free entertainment, including famously rude staff, and the soup's good, too: the traditional working man's breakfast and hangover cure. Open 1–8am only, at its peak 3–4am.

**Sea Star** Sofokléous 24 @22410 31884; see map, p.518. Quality seafood restaurant that's somewhat overshadowed by Nireas (see p.518) next door, but deserves mention in its own right for its perfectly grilled fresh fish – the bream, at around €12.50, is out of this world – and mezédhes like kápari and salt-cured mackerel. Indoor seating in winter, otherwise outside on the little square. Daily lunch & dinner.

**Ta Kioupia** Menekleous 22 ☎ 22410 30192; see map, p.518. Friendly, high-quality restaurant, perched towards the top of the Old Town, slightly south of Sokrátous. Its contemporary twists on classic Greek cuisine are consistently delicious – you'll remember the smoked aubergine with feta, and the blue cheese mousse, for a long time. It all works out expensive, though, especially as they make a habit of charging for the various little bonus extra plates they bring to your table. Expect to pay around €40 per head. Daily lunch & dinner, closes 6pm Sun.

### NEW TOWN

**Anatolikes Nostimies** Klavdhíou Pépper 109, Zéfyros Beach ☎ 22410 29516; see map, p.516. The name means "Anatolian Delicacies": Thracian Pomak/Middle Eastern dips and starters, plus beef-based kebabs. Beach-hut atmosphere, but friendly, popular and reasonably priced; post-prandial hubble-bubble on request. Daily noon–midnight.

★ **Meltemi** Platía Koundourióti 8, Élli beach ☎ 22410 30480; see map, p.516. Beachfront ouzerí, with a nicely shaded beach-level patio, offering such delights as karavidhópsyha (crayfish nuggets), octopus croquettes, chunky hummus, and superb roast aubergine with beans and onions to a local crowd; pleasant winter salon inside. Daily lunch & dinner.

**Niohori** Ioánni Kazoúli 29, Neohóri ☎ 22410 35116 see map, p.516. Alias "Kiki's" after the jolly proprietress this homely, inexpensive local, across from the Franciscan monastery, is tops for meat grills, sourced from their own butcher/farm; veal liver costs €6, a mixed grill €8. There's usually a cooked vegetable dish like okra for the salad averse. Most seating is indoors, but there's a little shade courtyard at the side. Daily lunch & dinner.

**Ronda** Platía Koundourióti 6, Neohóri ☎ 22410 76944 see map, p.516. Built by the Italians as a waterfront spa complex, and every bit as round as the name implies, this large-domed room now houses a very spacious and rather expensive café. There's nothing remarkable about the food or drink, but it's a lovely place to sit, with views through its huge arched windows of the beach to one side and the harbour to the other. Daily 9am–1am.

**Sakis** Kanadhá 95, cnr Apostólou Papaïoánnou, Zéfyros ☎ 22410 21537, ⊛ tavernasakis.gr; see map, p.516. A friendly old favourite with pleasant patio and indoor seating, equally popular with Rhodians and foreigners. Known for its shellfish (such as limpets and snails), meat (chops, Cypriot seftaliés) and the usual starters. Mon–Sat 5pm–1am, Sun 12.30pm–12.30am.

**Tamam** Yeoryíou Leondos 1, Neohóri ☎ 22410 73522 see map, p.516. This small but enormously popular New Town newcomer serves good but expensive traditional cuisine. Steaks cost €25–30 each, and there's a wine list to match. If you're happy to spend a lot, you'll have a real feast; show any reluctance, and the charming service turns off like a tap. Daily lunch & dinner.

### NIGHTLIFE AND ENTERTAINMENT

In the Old Town, an entire alley (Miltiádhou) off Apellóu is home to a score of loud, annually changing music bars and clubs extending towards Plátonos and Platía Dhamayítou, and frequented mostly by Greeks (in winter too). Two a/c cinemas show first-run action films year-round: the Metropol multiplex, at the corner of Venetokléon and Výronos (☎ 22410 28410) southeast of the Old Town opposite the stadium, and the nearby Pallas multiplex on Dhimokratías (☎ 22410 24475).

**Bekir Karakuzu** Sokrátous 76, Old Town; see map, p.518. The last traditional Turkish kafenío in the Old Town simply oozes atmosphere; its Oriental-fantasy interior is filled with wooden screens and has an ornate votsalotó floor. Yoghurt, loukoúmi, alisfakiá tea and coffees are on the expensive side – consider it admission to an informal museum. Daily 11am–midnight.

**Besara Kafé** Sofokléous 11–13, Old Town; see map, p.518. Congenial breakfast-snack café-cum-low-key bar run by Australian-Texan Besara Harris, with a mixed clientele and live jazz two nights weekly Oct–May. Daily 9am until late.

**Christos' Garden** Dhilberáki 59, Neohóri; see map, p.516. This combination art gallery/bar/café occupies a carefully restored old house and courtyard with pebble-mosaic floors throughout. Daily 10pm until late.

**Colorado Club** Orfanídhou 57, cnr Aktí Miaouli, Neohóri ☎ 22410 75120, ⊛ colorado.com.gr; see map,

p.516. Triple venue, just back from the sea on the west side of the New Town, and comprising a "disco-house" dance club, a live music venue, and "Heaven", the top-floor chill-out bar. Daily 9pm until late.

**Rogmi tou Kronou** Platía Aríonos 4, Old Town ☎ 22410 25202; see map, p.518. Rock-oriented bar and music venue, taking up two storeys of a fine old house on one of the Old Town's most attractive squares – outside tables make this a great spot for a drink. Live music or DJs every night until late. Daily noon until late.

**Santana Music Bar** Miltiadou 4–8, Old Town ☎ 695 5 12 251; see map, p.518. Somewhat garish bar and music venue, on an alleyway just off Sokrátous – look out for the creeping flowers – which unlikely as it may seem is the one Old-Town spot where you may catch live, late-night rembétika and local music. Daily 9am until late, closed Sun–Thurs in winter.

# The east coast

From the capital as far south as Líndhos, the **east coast** of Rhodes has been built up with a succession of sprawling towns and resorts. Some, such as **Faliráki**, have long since lost any charm they may once have possessed, but there are still some pleasant lower-key alternatives, including **Stegná** and **Haráki**.

## Piyés Kallithéas

Daily 8am–8pm • €2.50

A prize example of orientalized Art Deco from 1929, the former spa at **Piyés Kallithéas**, 7km south of Rhodes Town, was the work of a young Pietro Lombardi who, in his old age, designed Strasbourg's European Parliament building. Accessed via a short side road through pines, the complex has an upmarket bar serving from inside artificial grottoes at the swimming lido, just below the dome of the **Mikrí Rotónda** in its clump of palms. The main **Megáli Rotónda** higher up is now a small **museum**, with changing modern art exhibits.

## Faliráki

The overblown and unappealing resort of **Faliráki**, 10km south of the capital, is a town of two halves. The half-dozen high-rise family hotels in its northerly zone sit uneasily alongside the cheap-and-nasty southern zone, notorious for its drink-fuelled brawls, rapes and even murder. Since the island police forcefully curbed the local club-crawling culture, the place is now a shadow of its former self.

Faliráki's sandy sweep is closed off on the south by the cape of **Ladhikó**. For the best swimming, head for the main cove, south of the promontory. The scenic bay of "**Anthony Quinn**", on its northern flank, is named after the late Mexican American actor, whom Greeks took to their hearts following his roles in *Zorba the Greek* and *The Guns of Navarone*. Quinn bought much of this area and constructed the first road to the beach, but during the 1980s the Greek government swindled him out of his claim; legal battles continue to this day.

## Afándou Bay

South of Ladhikó, the coastline is adorned, all the way to Líndhos, by striking limestone turrets that punctuate long stretches of beach. The first is the pebble-and-sand expanse of **Afándou Bay**, the least developed large east-coast beach, with just a few showers and clusters of inexpensive sunbeds. Spare a moment, heading down the main access road to mid-beach, for the atmospheric sixteenth-century church of **Panayía Katholikí**, paved with a *votsalotó* floor and decorated with frescoes.

## Kolýmbia

Immediately north of the Tsambíka headland, 25km south of Rhodes Town, **Kolýmbia** was laid out by the Italians, not long before World War II, as a model farming village. Its original little grid of streets now serves a fast-growing resort that's become a favourite with more upscale package travellers. Reasonable beaches lie to either side of the low hill at road's end; the northern one holds more facilities.

## Tsambíka and Stegná

The enormous promontory of **Tsambíka**, 26km south of town, offers unrivalled views along some 50km of coastline. From the main highway, a steep, 1500m cement drive leads to a small car park from where steps mount to the summit. On its September 8 festival childless women climb up – on their hands and knees in the final stretches – to an otherwise unremarkable **monastery** to be cured of their barrenness. Shallow **Tsambíka Bay**, south of the headland (2km access road), has an excellent if packed beach.

A kilometre or so south of Tsambíka Bay, a steep road drops for 3.5km down to the sea from the main highway, in huge sweeping curves. It ends at the scruffy but appealing semicircular bay of **Stegná**, where for once no large hotels lurk behind the fine-gravel shore, just some relatively tasteful apartment complexes.

## Haráki and around
**Haráki** is a very likeable little crescent bay, overlooked by the stubby ruins of **Feraklós castle**, the last Knights' citadel to fall to the Turks. There's no road along the shoreline, just a walkway beside a part pebble, part grey-sand **beach** that's backed by a solid row of small two- or three-storey studios, interspersed with the occasional café. It couldn't really be called a port, or a village, but it's a nice self-contained enclave.

The long straight shoreline south of Haráki is lined with beaches of sand and fine gravel, such as **Paralía Kaláthou**. It ends after 8km, just short of Líndhos, at the little cove of **Vlyhá**, which holds a couple of enormous hotels.

### ACCOMMODATION                                    THE EAST COAST

**Atrium Palace** Paralía Kaláthou ☎ 22440 31601, ⓦ atrium.gr. Surprisingly unobtrusive despite its 300-plus luxurious rooms, this upscale hotel is one of the few developments on Kaláthou Beach, not far north of Líndhos. Its expensively landscaped grounds are dotted with pools, and the lawns extend down to the beach; the remoter villa wings, towards the spa, are best. Closed Nov–March. **€180**

**Haraki Village** Haráki ☎ 694 63 50 401, ⓦ haraki village.gr. Eight little pastel-coloured studios and apartments, all with balconies or outdoor space, at the north end of the beach below the castle. **€100**

**Lindos Blu** Vlyhá ☎ 22440 32110, ⓦ lindosblu.gr. Very opulent, very stylish modern resort hotel, tumbling down the slopes of a pretty bay immediately north of Líndhos, with a spa, infinity pools, and on-site restaurants. All seventy units have sea views, and are intended for adults only – villas/maisonettes have private pools. Minimum stay 4 nights in high season. **€420**

**Panorama B&B** Stegná ☎ 22440 22516, ⓦ stegna.gr. Laidback B&B, in a peaceful setting a short walk back from Stegná beach, with simple good-value a/c studios and rooms and a breezy shared terrace. **€50**

### EATING AND DRINKING

**Argo Restaurant** Haráki ☎ 694 63 51 410. Behind its weathered, custard-yellow exterior, this seafront restaurant, squeezed among the toothy rocks at the southern end of Haráki beach, is surprisingly smart, and serves a good Greek menu, with mussels, chicken or shrimp main dishes priced at €8–12, with views across to the castle thrown in. Daily noon–10pm.

★ **To Periyiali** Stegná ☎ 22440 23444. The best taverna in Stegná, down by the fish anchorage. Greeks flock here for seafood, hand-cut round chips, home-made *yaprákia* and substantial salads ("Periyali" has caper greens and grilled aubergine) washed down by good bulk wine; the travertine-clad loos must be the wackiest, yet most charming, on the island. Daily lunch & dinner.

## Líndhos
Set on a stark headland 50km south of Rhodes Town, **LÍNDHOS** is almost too good to be true. A classic Greek village of crazily stacked whitewashed houses, poised between a stupendous castle-topped acropolis above and sandy crescent beaches below, it's the island's number-two tourist attraction. Inevitably, it's so tightly packed with day-trippers in summer that you can barely breathe, let alone move along its impossibly narrow lanes. Almost all its immaculately whitewashed houses have long since been bought up by foreigners; most of those along the ancient agora, or serpentine main alleyway, are now run as restaurants, cafés and souvenir stores, while discreetly advertised rental properties lie to either side.

Arrive outside peak season, or if that's not possible at least in the early morning, and strolling through the village is still hugely atmospheric. The belfried, post-Byzantine **Panayía church** (Mon–Sat 9am–3pm & 6.30–8pm, Sun 9am–3pm) is covered inside with well-preserved eighteenth-century frescoes. The most imposing **medieval captains' residences** are built around *votsalotó* courtyards, their monumental doorways often fringed by intricate stone braids or cables supposedly corresponding in number to the fleet owned.

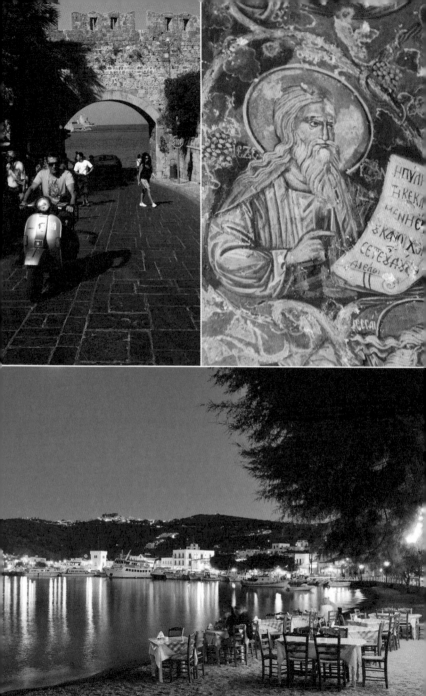

## The acropolis

Mid-June to mid-Sept Mon 12.30–7.10pm, Tues–Sun 8am–7.10pm; mid-Sept to mid-June Tues–Sun 8.30am–2.40pm • €6

Although the dramatic battlements that circle the **acropolis** on the bluff directly above Líndhos belong to a **Knights' castle**, the precinct they enclose is much more ancient. A sanctuary dedicated to local deity Lindia was founded here in the ninth century BC, while the surviving structures were started by local ruler Kleoboulos three hundred years later.

A short climb up steep steps from the centre of the village, or a longer walk (or even donkey ride) up a gentler but more exposed pathway, brings you to the stairway to the castle itself. The relief sculpture of a ship's prow at its foot dates from the second century BC. Once you pass through the sole gateway, restrain the impulse to head straight for the summit, and explore the site from the bottom upwards instead. That way the temple of Athena Lindia at the top, set on a level platform that commands magnificent coastline views to both north and south, comes as a stunning climax. Almost all the buildings are recent reconstructions, replacing older restoration work now deemed inaccurate, though some ancient stones have been incorporated.

Come early or late in the day if you can, to avoid the crowds and enjoy the best light. And be warned that many of the stairways, parapets and platforms have precipitous, unrailed drop-offs.

## Beaches

Líndhos's main **beach**, once the principal ancient harbour, tends to get very overcrowded; quieter options lie one cove beyond at **Pállas beach**. The small, perfectly sheltered **St Paul's harbour**, south of the acropolis and well away from town, has excellent swimming. According to legend, the Apostle landed here in 58 AD on a mission to evangelize the island.

## ARRIVAL AND INFORMATION LÍNDHOS

**By car** No cars are allowed in the village itself, and there's no vehicle access to the acropolis. Arriving drivers instead have to perform an elaborate U-turn at the tiny main square to reach car parks towards the beach, some of which, as clearly signposted, are free.

## ACCOMMODATION

★ **Melenos** ☎ 22440 32222, ⓦ melenoslindos.com. The only hotel in Líndhos itself is an absolute gem, exquisite and highly exclusive, discreetly sited on the second lane above the north beach, by the school. No expense has been spared in laying out the twelve luxurious suites with semi-private, *votsalotó* terraces and tasteful furnishings; there's also a swanky garden-bar and restaurant. Open all year round. **€310**

## EATING AND DRINKING

The lanes of Líndhos are crammed with run-of-the-mill restaurants, with a rapid turnover in ownership, but there are still a few stand-outs. Almost all have roof terraces, offering views up to the castle; whatever the decor may look like inside, most diners end up sitting on bare concrete patios in a parallel rooftop world.

**Acropolis Roof Garden** Trapeza 26 ☎ 22440 32160, ⓦ lindostreasures.com/village. The best option along the lanes, with a solid menu of Greek specialities such as rabbit stifhádo (€9.50) and a fine array of mezhédes, including tasty *dolmádhes*, all served on a castle-view terrace. Daily lunch & dinner.

★ **Mavrikos** Main Square ☎ 22440 31232. Prominent restaurant, on the fig-tree square where all traffic has to turn around. Starters such as *yígandes* in carob syrup (€7.50), sweet marinated sardines, or beets in goat-cheese sauce, are accomplished, as are fish mains such as skate timbale with sweetened balsamic, or superior traditional recipes like *dolmádhes* and *tyrokafterí*. Typical food charge of €23–30 per person. Daily noon–midnight.

**Village Café** ☎ 22440 31554, ⓦ lindostreasures.com/village. Friendly café and snack bar, set around a little pebbled courtyard, with a fine array of pastries, juices, sandwiches and snacks. Daily 10am–5pm.

# The southeast coast

Until recently, tourist development petered out south of Líndhos, but these days Rhodes' **southeast coast** holds plenty of facilities for travellers seeking to escape the hectic atmosphere of the northern resorts. **Péfki** and **Yennádhi** are the best overnight stops, while **Prassoníssi** at the southern tip is popular with windsurfers. Even if you're not staying down here, it's worth touring in your own vehicle, stopping off perhaps in the villages just inland, like **Asklipió**, with its wonderful church.

## Péfki

A couple of kilometres around the headland beyond Líndhos, **PÉFKI** was originally the garden annexe of its illustrious neighbour, but has now burgeoned as a resort in its own right. Its principal **beach**, a gorgeous little cove lined with sand and lapped by sparkling clear waters, inevitably becomes very crowded in summer, but other, more secluded little beaches are tucked at the base of the low cliffs to the west.

## Lárdhos

Although the village of **LÁRDHOS** stands well in from the sea, it has lent its name to dense beachfront development a little further south. Its main beach, 2km south of the centre, is gravelly and heavily impinged upon by hotels; Glýstra cove, 3km south, is a small and more sheltered crescent that's at its best in low season.

## Asklipió

Nine kilometres south of Lárdhos, close to the unexciting resort of Kiotári, a side road heads 3.5km inland to **ASKLIPIÓ**, a sleepy village enlivened by a crumbling Knights' castle and Byzantine **Kímisis Theotókou church**. Asklipió's central **Kímisis Theotókou church** (daily: summer 9am–6pm, spring/autumn 9am–5pm; €1) dates from 1060, and has a pebble-floored ground plan, to which two apses were added during the eighteenth century. Thanks to the dry local climate, the **frescoes** inside remain in breathtaking condition. Didactic "cartoon strips" extend completely around the church and up onto the ceiling, featuring Old Testament stories alongside the more usual lives of Christ and the Virgin. Half of the adjacent **Asklipió Museum** (same hours and ticket) is devoted to ecclesiastical treasures; the other, housed in a former olive mill, holds a folklore gallery, full of craft tools and antiquated machinery.

## Yennádhi and Lahaniá

The drab outskirts of **YENNÁDHI**, 13km south of Lárdhos and the only sizeable settlement on the southeast coast, mask the attractive older village core inland. Though the present, barrel-vaulted structure of the village cemetery-church, **Ayía Anastasía Roméa**, dates from the fifteenth century, it's built on sixth-century foundations, and covered inside with post-Byzantine **frescoes**. Yennádhi's dark-sand-and-gravel **beach**, clean and offering the usual amenities, extends for kilometres in either direction.

Some 10km south of Yennádhi, then 2km inland, the tiny and picturesque village of **LAHANIÁ** was abandoned after a postwar earthquake, though since the 1980s its older houses have been mostly occupied and renovated by foreigners.

## Prassoníssi

The main circular island highway doesn't run all the way down its southernmost tip. Branch south at Kattaviá, however, and a paved 8km spur road will bring you to **Prassoníssi**, a two-hour, 90km drive south of Rhodes Town. This gloriously desolate spot has become a major rendezvous for **windsurfers** (see box, p.528).

**8**

**WINDSURFING AT PRASSONÍSSI**

Situated at the very southern tip of Rhodes, **Prassoníssi** is regarded as one of the finest **windsurfing** sites in Europe. Strictly speaking the name refers to "Leek Island", the sturdy little islet just offshore, which is connected to the mainland by a long, low and very narrow sandspit through which a small natural channel frequently opens.

Not only do the waters here belong to different seas – the **Aegean** to the west of the spit, and the **Mediterranean** to the east – but in season they usually offer dramatically contrasting conditions. Thanks to the prevailing **meltémi** wind, and the funnelling effect of the islet, the Aegean side is generally much rougher, with head-high waves. On summer days it therefore becomes the area for expert windsurfers and daredevil kitesurfers. The Mediterranean side, meanwhile, tends to be much calmer, almost lagoon-like, and its shallow sandbars make it especially ideal for beginners.

The **season** at Prassoníssi lasts from May until mid-October. Of the three **windsurfing schools** that operate here, the Polish-run Prasonisi Center (late April–Oct; ☎ 22440 91044, ⓦ prasonisicenter.com) is the keenest and friendliest.

## ACCOMMODATION                                              THE SOUTHEAST COAST

**Effie's Dreams** Yennádhi ☎ 22440 43410, ⓦ effiesdreams.com. Six serviceable, good-value a/c studios, overlooking a fountain-fed oasis at the northern end of Yennádhi, plus free wi-fi and a bar. **€55**

**Lindian Village** Lárdhos ☎ 22440 35900, ⓦ lindian village.gr. Sumptuous beachfront resort, 5km south of Lárdhos, and consisting of an attractive complex of individual bungalows that hold three grades of units (suites have their own plunge-pools), plus several gourmet restaurants, a spa/gym and a private beach. **€500**

**Pefkos Blue Hotel** Péfki ☎ 22440 48017,

ⓦ dimitristudiospefkos.com. Good-value all-studio hotel on the hillside just above Péfki. 35 clean, comfortable apartments sleeping two to four, with kitchens, a/c and panoramic views. **€80**

**Prasoni Light House** Prassoníssi ☎ 22440 91030, ⓦ prasonisilighthouse.com. Marginally the better of the two accommodation options at the island's southernmost tip, with a wide range of possibilities, from simple good-value "eco rooms" to larger rooms with sea-view balconies and fully-fledged apartments. Rates include breakfast and dinner in the reasonable on-site restaurant. **€92**

## EATING AND DRINKING

**Kyma Beach Restaurant** Péfki ☎ 22440 48213. High-class restaurant at the midpoint of Péfki beach, with lovely sunset views, and serving delicious Greek specialities with a creative twist; try the octopus carpaccio. Reserve ahead in summer. Daily noon–10pm.

★ **Platanos** Lahaniá Prassoníssi ☎ 694 41 99 991,

ⓦ achaniaplatanostaverna.com. On the tiny little main platía at the lower, eastern end of Lahaniá village, this welcoming rural taverna has superb mezédhes platters like hummus and *dolmadhákia*. Sit outside at the front, under the eponymous plane tree, or in the indoors dining room, overlooking a deep wooded valley. Daily lunch & dinner.

# The west coast

While Rhodes' windward **west coast** is damp, fertile and forested, its beaches are exposed and often rocky. None of this has deterred development and, as on the east coast, the first few kilometres of the busy main road have been surrendered entirely to tourism. From Rhodes Town to the airport, the shore is lined with generic hotels, though **Triánda**, **Kremastí** and **Paradhísi** are still nominally villages, with real centres.

## Kameiros

Tues–Sun: summer 8am–7.10pm; winter 8.30am–2.40pm • €4

The site of ancient **KAMEIROS**, which united with Lindos and Ialyssos to found the city-state of Rhodes, stands above the coast 30km southwest of Rhodes Town. Soon eclipsed by the new capital, Kameiros was only rediscovered in 1859, leaving a well-preserved Doric townscape in a beautiful hillside setting. Visitors can make out the foundations of two small temples, the re-erected pillars of a Hellenistic house, a Classical fountain, and the *stoa* of the upper agora, complete with a water cistern.

Kameiros had no fortifications, nor even an acropolis – partly owing to the gentle slope of the site, and also to the likely settlement here by peaceable Minoans.

## Kámiros Skála

The tiny anchorage of **KÁMIROS SKÁLA** (aka Skála Kamírou), 45km southwest of Rhodes Town, is noteworthy only as the home port for a regular ferry service to the island of Hálki (see p.533). It does hold a handful of restaurants, however, while the off-puttingly named **Paralía Kopriá** ("Manure Beach") is 400m southwest.

## Kástro Kritinías

From afar, **Kástro Kritinías**, 2km south of Kámiros Skála, is the most impressive of the Knights' rural strongholds; the paved access road is too narrow and steep for tour buses. Close up, it proves to be no more than a shell, albeit a glorious one, with fine views west to Hálki, Alimniá, Tílos and Níssyros.

## Monólithos

The tiered, flat-roofed houses of **MONÓLITHOS**, high atop the cliffs 22km south of Kámiros Skála, don't themselves justify the long trip out, but the view over the Aegean is striking. Local diversions include yet another **Knights' castle**, out of sight of town 2km west, which is photogenically perched on its own pinnacle but encloses very little, and the sand-and-gravel beaches at **Foúrni**, five paved but curvy kilometres below the castle.

### ACCOMMODATION AND EATING                                      MONÓLITHOS

**Hotel Thomas** ☎ 22460 61291 or 697 30 38 494, ⓦ thomashotel.gr. Behind its somewhat grim exterior, this welcoming village hotel holds plain, fair-sized rooms with kitchen facilities and panoramic balconies. **€85**

**O Palios Monolithos** ☎ 22460 61276. The best of several tavernas in the village, opposite the church. Mains are a bit pricey but it's known for grilled meat and starters like wild mushrooms, *tyrokafterí* and mixed *dolmádhes*, accompanied by good bread and non-CAIR bulk wine. Open all year, weekends only off season.

# Inland Rhodes

**Inland Rhodes** is hilly and still part-forested, despite the ongoing efforts of arsonists. You'll need a vehicle to take in the soft-contoured, undulating scenery, along with the last vestiges of agrarian life in the villages; no single spot justifies the expense of a taxi or battling with inconveniently sparse bus schedules. Most people under retirement age are away working in the tourist industry, returning only at weekends and during winter.

## Ialyssos

Summer Tues–Sat 8am–7.10pm, Sun 8.30am–2.40pm; winter Tues–Sun 8.30am–2.40pm • €3

From the scanty acropolis of ancient **Ialyssos**, 10km southwest of Rhodes Town on flat-topped Filérimos hill, Süleyman the Magnificent directed the 1522 siege of Rhodes. Filérimos means "lover of solitude", after tenth-century Byzantine hermits who dwelt here; **Filérimos monastery** is the most substantial structure. Directly in front of the church sprawl the foundations of third-century temples to Zeus and Athena, built atop a far older Phoenician shrine.

## Petaloúdhes

Daily: May–Sept 9am–6pm; April & Oct 9am–5pm • Oct to mid-June free, mid-June to Sept €5

The one "tourist attraction" in the island's interior, **Petaloúdhes** ("Butterfly Valley"), is reached by a 7km side road that bears inland between Paradhísi and Theológos. It's actually a rest stop for Jersey tiger moths, which congregate here between mid-June and September, attracted for unknown reasons by the abundant *Liquidambar orientalis* trees growing abundantly in this stream canyon. The moths, which roost in droves on the tree trunks and cannot eat during this final phase of their life cycle, rest to conserve energy, and die of starvation soon after mating. When stationary, the moths are a well-camouflaged black and yellow, but they flash cherry-red overwings in flight.

### Eptá Piyés to Profítis Ilías

**Eptá Piyés** ("Seven Springs"), 4km inland from Kolýmbia junction on the main east-coast highway, is an oasis with a tiny irrigation dam created by the Italians. A trail and a rather claustrophobic Italian aqueduct-tunnel both lead from the vicinity of the springs to the reservoir. Continuing on the same road, you reach **ELEOÚSSA** after another 9km, in the shade of dense forest. Built as the planned agricultural colony of Campochiaro in the mid-1930s, it's now a bizarre **ghost town**, with a central square lined by eerily derelict Italian structures that visitors can wander through at will. From the vast, yellow-trimmed Art Deco fountain-cum-pool just west of the village, stocked with endangered *gizáni* fish, keep straight 3km further to the gorgeous little late-Byzantine church of **Áyios Nikólaos Foundouklí** ("St Nicholas of the Hazelnuts").

### Émbona

All tracks and roads west across Profítis Ilías converge on the road from Kalavárdha bound for **ÉMBONA**, a large but unremarkable village backed up against the north slope of 1215m **Mount Atávyros**. Émbona lies at the heart of the island's most important wine-producing districts. The small, family-run **Emery winery** (daily 9.30am–3.30pm; ⓦemery.gr) is highly regarded.

### Thárri monastery

Accessible from Apóllona and Laerma to the north, or via a rough but passable road from Asklipió 11km south, the Byzantine monastery of **Thárri** is the oldest religious foundation on Rhodes, re-established as a vital community in 1990 by charismatic abbot Amfilohios. In the striking *katholikón* (daily, all day), successive cleanings have restored damp-smudged frescoes dated 1300–1450 to a pale approximation of their original glory.

#### ACCOMMODATION AND EATING                                        INLAND RHODES

★ **Elafos Hotel** Profítis Ilías ☎ 22460 22402, ⓦhotel -elafos.gr. Rather splendid, restored Italian, 1929-vintage chalet-hotel, in a village west of Áyios Nikólaos church, where the high-ceilinged rooms ooze retro charm, and the arcaded ground-floor common areas include a restaurant and a sauna. **€95**

★ **Piyi Fasouli** Psínthos ☎ 22410 50071. Excellent taverna, at the edge of Psínthos village, 6km southeast of Butterfly Valley (see p.529), serving excellent grills and appetizers as well as a few tasty *mayireftá* at tables overlooking the namesake spring. Daily lunch & dinner.

# Kastellórizo

Although **KASTELLÓRIZO**'s official name of Meyísti means "Biggest", it's actually among the very smallest Dodecanese islands; it's just the biggest of a local archipelago of islets. It's also extremely remote, located more than 100km east of Rhodes and barely more than a nautical mile off mainland Asia. At night its lights are outnumbered by those of the Turkish town of Kaş opposite, with which Kastellórizo has excellent relations.

The island's population has dwindled from around ten thousand a century ago to perhaps three hundred now. Having been an Ottoman possession since 1552, it was occupied by the French from 1915 until 1921, and then by the Italians. When Italy capitulated to the Allies in 1943, 1500 Commonwealth commandos occupied Kastellórizo. Most departed that November, after the Germans captured the other Dodecanese, which left the island vulnerable to looters, both Greek and British. By the time a fuel fire in 1944 triggered the explosion of an adjacent arsenal, demolishing half the houses on Kastellórizo, most islanders had already left. Those who remain are

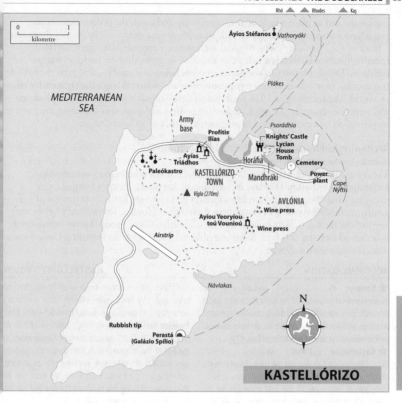

KASTELLÓRIZO

8

supported by remittances from more than 30,000 emigrants, as well as subsidies from the Greek government to prevent the island reverting to Turkey.

Yet Kastellórizo has a future of sorts, thanks partly to repatriating "Kassies" returning each summer to renovate their crumbling ancestral houses as second homes. Visitors tend either to love Kastellórizo and stay a week, or crave escape after a day; detractors dismiss it as a human zoo maintained by the Greek government to placate nationalists, while devotees celebrate an atmospheric, little-commercialized outpost of Hellenism.

## ARRIVAL AND DEPARTURE
KASTELLÓRIZO

**By air** Kastellórizo's airport, 1km above the harbour, is served by regular Olympic Air flights from Rhodes (4–6 weekly). A minibus shuttles once between town and airstrip at flight times (€2); excess passengers are accommodated in the island's lone taxi, at €6 per passenger.

**By ferry** Kastellórizo is connected to: Astypálea (1 weekly; 16hr); Kalymnós (2 weekly; 11hr 40min); Kos (2 weekly; 10hr);

Naxós (1 weekly; 20hr 30min); Níssyros (2 weekly; 8hr 30min); Páros (1 weekly; 22hr); Pireás (2 weekly; 28hr); Rhodes (3 weekly; 2hr 20min–3hr 40min); Sými (2 weekly; 3hr 50min–6hr 25min); Tílos (2 weekly; 7hr). Day-trips to Turkey leave regularly from the port in summer, for around €20.

**Travel agents** Papoutsis Travel sells all sea and air tickets (☎ 22410 70630, ⊛ kastelorizo.gr).

## Kastellórizo Town

The island's population is concentrated in **KASTELLÓRIZO TOWN** on the north coast – neatly arrayed around what's said to be the finest natural harbour between Beirut and Fethiye on the Turkish coast – and its "suburb" of Mandhráki, just over the fire-blasted hill and boasting a half-ruined Knights' castle. In summer, it's what Greeks call a *klouví* (bird cage) – the sort of place where, after two strolls up and down the pedestrianized quay, you'll have a nodding acquaintance with your fellow visitors and all the island's characters.

Most of the town's surviving original **mansions** are ranged along the waterfront, sporting tiled roofs, wooden balconies and blue or green shutters on long, narrow windows. Derelict houses in the backstreets are being attended to, and even the hillside is sprouting new constructions in unconventional colours, though the cumulative effect of World War I shelling, a 1926 earthquake, 1943 air-raids and the 1944 explosions will never be reversed. The black-and-white posters and postcards depicting the town in its prime, on sale everywhere, are poignant evidence of its later decline.

### Archeological Museum and Lycian house-tomb

Mandhráki • Tues–Sun 8.30am–3pm • Free

The outer bulwark of Mandhráki's clifftop castle houses the island's worthwhile **archeological museum**. Displays include Byzantine plates, frescoes rescued from decaying rural churches and a reconstruction of an ancient basilica on the site of today's gaudy, crumbling Áyios Yeóryios Santrapé church at Horáfia. Immediately below and beyond the museum, facing across to Psorádhia islet, Greece's only **Lycian house-tomb** is hollowed into the cliff face. Steep unrailed steps lead up to its imposing Doric facade from the shoreline walkway.

## ACCOMMODATION                                                                    KASTELLÓRIZO TOWN

★ **Karnayo** ☎ 22460 49266, ⓦ karnayo.gr. An excellent mid-range choice, off the platía at the west end of the south quay, spread over two quiet, sensitively restored buildings, and offering four double a/c en-suite rooms as well as two studios, one of which sleeps four. **€70**

★ **Kastellorizo Hotel** ☎ 22460 49044, ⓦ kastellorizohotel.gr. Right in the thick of things in the middle of west quay, this lovely hotel has friendly management and some of the best amenities on the island. All its fourteen individually styled suites have kitchenettes, four have balconies, and there's a thalasso-spa-pool as well as waterfront lido. March–Nov. **€130**

★ **Megisti Hotel** ☎ 22460 49219, ⓦ megistihotel.gr. Beautiful hotel in an unbeatable location, at the northwest corner of the harbour, with fabulous views

and fifteen spotless, attractively decorated rooms plus four large and very lavish suites. There's great swimming immediately off the spacious patio. Closed Oct–April. **€160**

**Pension Mediterraneo** ☎ 22460 49007 or 697 36 76 038, ⓦ mediterraneo-kastelorizo.com. Simple rooms at the end of the northwest quay, furnished with mosquito nets and wall art, some with sea view, plus an arcaded, waterside basement suite that's worth the extra cost for the privilege of being able to roll out the door and into the sea. Rates include breakfast. **€80**

**Poseidon** ☎ 22460 49257, ⓦ kastelorizo-poseidon.gr. Newly built houses in traditional style, set back from the platía at the west end of the south quay, and offering a total of sixteen well-appointed studios similar to the neighbouring Karnayo, some with balcony. **€70**

## EATING AND DRINKING

Kastellórizo's harbour quayside is a wonderfully romantic spot to enjoy a leisurely meal, though taverna prices are significantly higher than elsewhere. The island has its own fish, goat meat and wild-fig preserves, and assorted produce is smuggled over from Kaş, but otherwise food and drinking water have to be shipped here from Rhodes. Incidentally, the mains water is contaminated by goat droppings, and not safe to drink.

★ **Akrothalassi** ☎ 22460 49052. The best of the waterfront tavernas, near the west end of the quay, dishing out large, great-value grills and salads. It's especially popular at lunch, as it offers the only shaded quayside seating. Daily lunch & dinner.

**Iy Ypomoni** Cheap, cheerful and popular waterfront taverna, two doors to the left of the arcaded market. Open for dinner only, it serves a limited seafood menu. Daily 7pm–late.

**Ta Platania** ☎ 22460 49206. Set well back from the sea, up the hill on the Horáfia platía, this welcoming place is festooned with film posters, and a good option for

daily-changing *mayireftá* and desserts, though the prices are much the same as down by the port. June–Sept only, daily lunch & dinner.

**To Mikro Parisi** ☎ 22460 49282. Long-established seafood specialist alongside the port, with succulent soups and stews and zestful meat and fish grills. Not the cheapest by any means, but good for a special occasion. Daily lunch & dinner.

**Zaharoplastio Iy Meyisti** Sweet shop and café by the harbour, serving a fine array of fresh-baked pastries and cakes. Just the place to linger over a fine breakfast or pudding. Daily 8am–6pm.

## NIGHTLIFE

**Faros ☎** 22460 49370. Bright yellow café-bar, jutting into the harbour alongside the mosque, where the roof terrace is the coolest place in town on long summer nights. While the sun's up, it's a "day-bar" with sunbeds on the quay. Daily noon–late.

**Radio Café ☎** 22460 49029. Café with great views, close to the ferry jetty, which as well as coffee and breakfast offers internet access and *ouzomezédhes*. Daily 9am–late.

## The rest of the island

Kastellórizo's austere **hinterland** is predominantly bare rock, flecked with stunted vegetation; incredibly, until 1900 this was carefully tended, producing abundant wine of some quality. A rudimentary paved road system links points between Mandhráki and the airstrip, and a dirt track heads towards Áyios Stéfanos, but there are few specific attractions, and no scooters for rent. Karstic cliffs drop sheer to the sea, offering no anchorage except at the main town, Mandhráki and Návlakas fjord (see below).

### The shoreline

**Swimming** on Kastellórizo is made difficult by the total lack of beaches, and the abundance of sea urchins and razor-sharp limestone reefs. Once clear of the shoreline, however, you're rewarded by clear waters with a rich variety of marine life, and amphora shards that testify to the ancient wine trade. Many visitors simply dive in from the lidos on the northwest quay; otherwise the safest entries near town lie beyond the graveyard at Mandhráki and the cement jetty below the power plant at road's end. **Taxi-boats** can take you to otherwise inaccessible coves such as **Plákes**, along the western shoreline of the town bay, where the flat surfaces of a former quarry are equally good for sunbathing on, or swimming off.

### Návlakas fjord and Perastá grotto

Halfway along Kastellórizo's southeastern coast, **Návlakas fjord** is a favourite mooring spot for yachts and fishing boats. Uniquely for the island, Návlakas is free of sea urchins. Freshwater seeps keep the temperature brisk, and there's superb snorkelling to 20m depths off the south wall.

Another popular stop for boat excursions, a little further south, **Perastá grotto** (Galázio Spílio) deserves a visit for its stalactites and strange blue-light effects. The low entrance, negotiable only by inflatable raft, gives little hint of the enormous chamber within, with monk seals occasionally sheltering in an adjacent cave.

# Hálki

The little island of **Hálki**, a waterless limestone speck west of Rhodes, continues to count as a fully fledged member of the Dodecanese, even if its population has dwindled from three thousand to barely three hundred in the century since its Italian rulers imposed restrictions on sponge-fishing.

While visitation has brought the island back to life, except at the height of summer Hálki tends to be very quiet indeed. That said, in the middle of the day in high season, when day-trippers from Rhodes vastly outnumber locals in its broad quayside-cum-square, Emborió can feel more like a stage set than a genuine town.

## ARRIVAL AND INFORMATION                                      HÁLKI

**By ferry** Hálki's port, Emborió, is connected with the following ports: Anáfi (2 weekly; 9hr 50min); Crete (2 weekly; Sítia 4hr 10min, Iráklion 7hr 20min); Kárpathos (2 weekly; 2hr 40min); Kássos (2 weekly; 5hr); Kos (2 weekly; 2hr 45min); Níssyros (2 weekly; 1hr 40min); Pireás (2

weekly; 20–24hr); Rhodes Kámiros Skála (daily except Sun; 1hr 15min); Rhodes Town (4 weekly; 1hr 25min–2hr); Santoríni (2 weekly; 11hr 20min); Sými (2 weekly; 2hr 20min); Tílos (2 weekly; 35min).
**Ticket agency** Zifos (☎ 22460 45028, ⓦ zifostravel.gr).

## GETTING AROUND

**By bus** A sixteen-seat bus shuttles between the waterfront, Póndamos and Ftenáya.

# Emborió

With its photogenic ensemble of restored Italianate houses rising from the waterfront, **EMBORIÓ**, facing east towards Rhodes from the head of a large bay, is a sort of miniature version of Sými (see p.543). Hálki's port as well as the only inhabited town, its skyline is pierced by the tallest freestanding **clocktower** in the Dodecanese, as well – a bit further north – as the **belfry** of Áyios Nikólaos, which holds a fine *votsalotó* (pebble-mosaic) courtyard. The waterfront has been paved with fieldstones, generally prettified and declared off-limits to vehicles in season.

Although there's no **beach** at Emborió, many visitors swim anyway, simply lowering themselves into the water from the quayside or shoreline rocks. If that doesn't suit you, two beaches lie within easy walking distance, both equipped with good seaside tavernas. The island's only sandy beach, long narrow **Póndamos**, a fifteen-minute walk west over the hilltop, along the grandly named Tarpon Springs Boulevard, fills with day-trippers in summer. The best alternative, the tiny pebble cove and the gravel sunbed-lido at **Ftenáya**, lies a few minutes south of Emborió, along a well-signposted path that starts behind the *Hiona Art Hotel*. It too can get heavily subscribed.

## ACCOMMODATION                                                        EMBORIÓ

Reserve accommodation in high season, whether in one of Emborió's handful of hotels, or in the many rental houses and villas. Some are divided into individual studios, while several perch right over the sea, with access ladders for swimmers. Both ⓦ nissiaholidays.com and ⓦ zifostravel.gr offer an extensive selection of properties.

★ **Captain's House** ☏ 2246 045201, ⓦ chalkiholidays .gr. Three delightful en-suite a/c rooms, with a sea-view terrace, a shady garden, and the feel of an old French country hotel. Closed Nov–March. **€50**
**Hiona Art Hotel** ☏ 22460 45244, ⓦ hionaart.gr. Nicely refurbished, municipally owned hotel, in the splendid-looking old sponge factory on the south side of the bay, barely 5m from the sea. Tasteful en-suite rooms with

sea-view balconies, but haphazard service. Closed Nov–March. **€130**
**Mouthouria House** ☏ 22460 45061, ⓦ halki mouthouria.com. Fine old pastel-orange mansion, perched above the harbour and decorated in rich antique flair, and rented out for longer stays. Sleeps four, in two bedrooms. **€90**

**EATING AND DRINKING**

The quayside at Emborió is lined with six full-service tavernas, bars and cafés, filled with leisurely holiday-makers every night in summer. There are also four well-stocked stores and a bakery.

★ **Lefkosia's Paradosiako** Known for her TV appearances, chef Lefkosia believes in making everything – from her cheese to her pasta – from scratch. Baked dishes are the highlights at her waterfront taverna, including a delicious moussaka as well as her speciality "Halki pasta", baked with onions and feta. Daily lunch & dinner.
**Maria ✆ 22460 45300.** Well-shaded café, tucked behind the post office, that's dependable for substantial portions of island staples such as lamb stew, or pasta baked with bubbling feta cheese. Daily lunch & dinner.

**Remezzo ✆ 22460 45010.** Simple little green-painted taverna, with a cluster of little tables outside, which as well as excellent *mayireftá* serves pretty much the gamut of tourist-favoured cuisines, from pizzas to Mexican. Daily noon–late.
**Theodosia's Zaharoplastio ✆ 22460 45218.** Also known as "The Parrot Café" on account of its resident bird, this friendly café, with a cushioned wooden bench facing the base of the jetty, serves puddings and home-made ice cream to die for, as well as good breakfasts. Daily 9am–late.

## Horió and beyond

Still crowned by its Knights' castle, the old pirate-safe village of **HORIÓ**, looming 3km west of Emborió, beyond Pondamos, was abandoned in the 1950s. Except during the August 14–15 festival, the church here is locked to protect its frescoes. Across the valley, little **Stavrós monastery** hosts another big bash on September 14. There's little else inland, though Tarpon Springs Boulevard continues all the way across the island to reach the monastery of **Ayíou Ioánnou Prodhrómou** (festival Aug 28–29; *kantína* otherwise). The terrain en route is bleak, but compensated for by views over half the Dodecanese and Turkey. The monastery itself has a certain charm, with its central courtyard dominated by a huge juniper, and surrounded by an array of cells.

## Trahiá and Aréta

Hálki's remotest **beaches** can be reached either on boat excursions from Emborió quay – for example, aboard the *Kiristani* (✆ 693 61 16 229) – or via demanding hiking trails. **Trahiá**, directly below Horió's castle, and served by a very rough path from Yialí, consists of two coves to either side of an isthmus.

On the north coast, **Aréta fjord** is an impressive, cliff-girt place where seabirds roost and soar. There's some morning and afternoon shade, but only a brackish well for the inquisitive sheep with which you may share the small-pebble beach, so bring plenty of water. Experienced hillwalkers can get here on foot in around 1hr 30min.

# Kássos

The southernmost Dodecanese island, less than 48km northeast of Crete, **KÁSSOS** is very much off the beaten tourist track. Ever since 1824, when an Egyptian fleet punished Kássos for its active participation in the Greek revolution by slaughtering most of the 11,000 Kassiots, the island has remained barren and depopulated. Sheer gorges slash through lunar terrain relieved only by fenced smallholdings of midget olive trees; spring grain crops briefly soften usually fallow terraces, and livestock somehow survives on a thin furze of scrub. The remaining population occupies five villages facing Kárpathos, leaving most of the island uninhabited and uncultivated, with crumbling old houses poignantly recalling better days.

**ARRIVAL AND INFORMATION**                                                          **KÁSSOS**

**By air** The island's airport, 1km west of Frý, is connected to Kárpathos (1–2 daily); Rhodes (1–2 daily); and Sitía on
Crete (1–2 daily).
**By ferry** The island's port, Frý, is connected with: Anáfi

8

(2 weekly; 4hr 30min–10hr 30min); Crete (2 weekly; Sítia 2hr 30min, Iráklion 5hr 40min); Hálki (2 weekly; 4hr 30min); Karpathós (4 weekly; 1hr 20min); Mílos (2 weekly; 14hr 20min); Pireás (3 weekly; 14–20hr); Rhodes (4 weekly; 6hr 30min); Santoríni (2 weekly; 6–12hr). In season, to no fixed schedule, excursion boats also run to Frý from tiny Finíki on Kárpathos's west coast.

**Tourist information** The official island website is ⓦ kasos.gr.

**Travel agent** The main agent for ferry tickets is Kasos Maritime & Travel Agency (☎ 22450 41495, ⓦ kassos-island.gr).

## GETTING AROUND

**By bus** A Mercedes van connects all the island's villages several times daily in summer, for a flat fare of €0.80.

**By car and scooter** Oasis in Frý rents out cars and scooters between June and September (☎ 22450 41746).

# Frý

The capital of Kássos, **FRÝ** (pronounced "free"), is halfway along the island's north coast, with views towards northwest Kárpathos. It's a low-key little place, with most of its appeal concentrated in the **Boúka** fishing port, protected by two crab-claws of breakwater and overlooked by Áyios Spyrídhon cathedral. Inland, Frý is engagingly unpretentious, even down-at-heel in spots; there are few concessions to tourism, though some attempts have been made to prettify a scruffy little town that's quite desolate out of season.

There's no beach in Frý itself: what's generally regarded as the town beach is the sandy cove at **Ammoúá**, a half-hour walk along the coastal track west, beyond the airstrip. The first section you reach is often caked with seaweed and tar, but keep going another five minutes and you'll find cleaner pea-gravel coves.

Determined swimmers also use the little patch of sand at **Emboriós**, fifteen minutes' walk east from Frý, where there's also a more private pebble stretch off to the right. Once you've got this far, however, it's worth continuing ten minutes along the shore, first along an old track, then on a path past the last house, for a final scramble to the base of the **Pouthená ravine**, which cradles another secluded pebble cove.

In high season, boat excursions head to far better beaches on two islets visible to the northwest, **Armáthia** and **Makrá**. Armáthia has five white-sand beaches to choose from, while Makrá has just one large cove. There are no amenities on either islet, so bring all you need.

## ACCOMMODATION

**Angelica's** ☎ 22450 41268, ⓦ angelicas.gr. Four bright, roomy kitchenette apartments in a converted mansion 200m above Boúka harbour, with traditional furnishings, and, courtesy of the owner's mother, some rather extraordinary floor-paintings. All have outside space, but only two enjoy sea views. **€50**

★ **Evita Village** ☎ 22450 41731, ⓦ evita-village.gr. Small complex of five impeccable and very spacious modern studios, 200m uphill from Emboriós, with comfortable new furnishings and plenty of room to spread out. **€60**

**Fantasis Apartments** ☎ 22450 41695, ⓦ fantasis -hotel.gr. Six plain en-suite rooms, four equipped with sea-view balconies, in a prominent yellow-trimmed modern structure five minutes' climb up from the port towards Panayía. **€40**

**Flisvos** ☎ 22450 41284. Very basic hotel, right on the seafront 150m beyond the harbour towards Emboriós. All rooms are en suite with sea-view balconies, and share use of a kitchen. **€50**

## EATING AND DRINKING

**Iy Orea Bouka** Summer-only taverna with a small terrace overlooking the port at Boúka, and a good range of inventive and tasty Kassiot dishes, which you select by visiting the kitchen. June–Sept only, daily lunch & dinner.

**O Mylos** ☎ 22450 41825. Frý's finest full-service taverna, overlooking the ferry port, is also the only one that stays open year-round. Excellent food, with a selection of slow-cooked *mayireftá* at lunch, and grilled meat or fish by night. Daily lunch & dinner.

**Taverna Emborios** ☎ 22450 41586, ⓦ emborios.com. This lively and very welcoming taverna, facing the eponymous cove, is renowned for its fresh-caught seafood, supplemented with hand-picked local herbs and vegetables. Summer only, daily 11am–2am.

**To Koutouki** ☎ 22450 41545. This bustling little place, up the steps from the quayside at Boúka, deserves its reputation for sizeable servings of old-fashioned Greek cooking; succulent lamb is the house speciality. June–Sept only, daily lunch & dinner.

## Ayía Marína and around

Several villages are scattered around the edges of the agricultural plain inland from Frý, linked to each other by road; all can be toured on foot in a single day. Larger and yet more rural than Frý, **AYÍA MARÍNA**, 1500m inland and uphill, is best admired from the south, arrayed above olive groves; its two belfried churches are the focus of lively **festivals**, on July 16–17 and September 13–14. Fifteen minutes beyond the hamlet of **Kathístres**, a further 500m southwest, the cave of **Ellinokamára** has a late Classical, polygonal wall blocking the entrance; it may have been a cult shrine or tomb complex.

## Ayíou Yeoryíou Hadhión

Between Ayía Marína and Arvanitohóri, a paved road veers southwest towards the rural monastery of **Ayíou Yeoryíou Hadhión**. The entire route is 12km, and best tackled by scooter. Once you've skirted the dramatic gorge early on, you're unlikely to see another living thing aside from goats, sheep or an occasional falcon. Soon the Mediterranean appears; when you reach a fork, take the upper, right-hand turning, following the phone lines. Cistern water is always available in the monastery grounds, which only come to life around the April 23 festival.

# Kárpathos

Despite being the third-largest Dodecanese island, poised halfway between Rhodes and Crete, long, narrow **KÁRPATHOS** has always been a wild and underpopulated backwater. The island's usually cloud-capped mountainous spine, which rises to over 1200m, divides it into two very distinct sections – the low-lying **south**, with its pretty bays and long beaches, and the exceptionally rugged **north**, where deeply traditional villages nest atop towering cliffs. If you prefer to stay in a sizeable town, then **Pigádhia** on the east coast, Kárpathos's capital and largest port, is a good choice, with a wide range of hotels

8

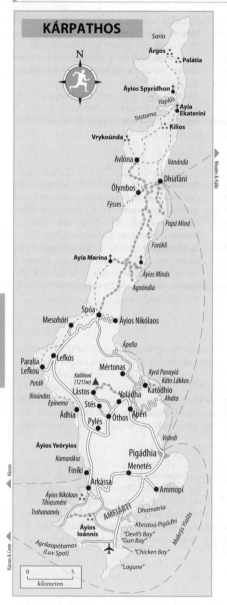

**KÁRPATHOS**

*Saría*

Árgos

★ Palátia

Áyios Spyrídhon †

*Yaplós*

† Ayía Ekateríni

*Trístomo*

Kílios

Vrykoúnda

*Vanánda*

Avlóna

Dhiafáni

Ólymbos

*Fýsses*

*Papá Miná*

*Forókli*

Ayía Marína †

† 

*Áyios Minás*

*Agnóndia*

Spóa

Mesohóri

Áyios Nikólaos

*Ápella*

Paralía Lefkoú

Lefkós

Mértonas

*Kyrá Panayiá*

*Káto Lákkos*

*Potáli*

*Kalilímni (1215m)* ▲

Lástos

Voládha

Katódhio

*Aháta*

*Ilioúndas*

*Epínemo*

Stés

Áperi

Ádhia

Pylés

Óthos

*Vrándi*

Áyios Yeóryios

Pigádhia

*Kamarákia*

Menetés

Finíki

Arkássa

*Áyios Nikólaos Tihiasméni*

Ammopí

*Trahanamós*

AMFIÁRTI

*Dhamatría*

*Khristoú Pigádhi*

Áyios Ioánnis

*"Devil's Bay" "Gun Bay"*

*Makrý Yialós*

*Agrilaopótamos (Luv Spot)*

*"Chicken Bay"*

*"Lagune"*

0 — 5
kilometres

*Rhodes & Háki*

*Kássos*

*Kássos & Crete*

as well as a good beach, but several smaller resorts and isolated coves also hold lovely beachfront accommodation.

Touring Kárpathos's magnificent, windswept **coastline** is consistently superb, with its verdant meadows, high peaks, isolated promontories and secluded **beaches**, lapped by crystalline waters. The **interior**, however, isn't always as alluring: the central and northern forests have been scorched by repeated fires, while agriculture plays a minor role. The Karpathians are too well off to bother much with farming; emigration to North America and the resulting remittances have made this one of Greece's wealthiest islands.

Although the Minoans and Mycenaeans established trading posts on what they called Krapathos, the island's four Classical cities figure little in ancient **history**. Kárpathos was held by the Genoese and Venetians after the Byzantine collapse and so has no castle of the Knights of St John, nor any surviving medieval fortresses of note.

### ARRIVAL AND DEPARTURE
### KÁRPATHOS

**By air** Kárpathos's airport is on the flatlands at the island's extreme southern tip, 14km south of Pigádhia. It's served by Olympic Air flights to Athens (1 daily), Rhodes (1–2 daily), and Sitía at the eastern tip of Crete, via Kássos (daily except Fri). There's no bus service, so renting a car at the airport can save you a steep taxi fare (from €18 to Pigádhia).

**By ferry** The port at Pigádhia is connected with the following ports: Anáfi (2 weekly; 6hr 15min–12hr); Crete (2 weekly; Sitía 4hr 10min, Iráklion 7hr 20min); Hálki (2 weekly; 2hr 40min); Kássos (4 weekly; 1hr 20min); Mílos (2 weekly; 17hr 30min); Pireás (3 weekly; 21hr); Rhodes (4 weekly; 5hr); Santoríni (2 weekly; 12hr). One weekly ferry in each direction also calls at Dhiafáni on Kárpathos's north coast.

**Travel agents** The main ferry agent in Pigádhia is Possi Travel (☎ 22450 22235, ✉ possitvl@hotmail.com), who also sell day-trips to Hálki by ferry (Tues), and Kássos by air and ferry (Sat).

### GETTING AROUND

**By car** The airport's only car rental outlet, Houvarda Maria (☎ 22450 61249), is the agent for Budget (✉ budgetkarpathos@yahoo.gr) and Drive (✉ drivekarpathos@yahoo.gr). Several more agencies are based in Pigádhia. The only petrol stations are immediately north and south of Pigádhia, so it's impossible to tour the whole island on a scooter.

**By bus** Pigádhia's "bus station" is a car park at the western edge of the town centre. Regular buses, run by KTEL (☎ 22450 22338), go to Pylés, via Apéri, Voládha and Óthos (3–4 daily); Ammopí (5–6 daily). Less frequent services run to Menetés, Arkássa, Finíki and Lefkos, with some continuing to Mesohóri; and to Kyrá Panayía, Ápella and Spóa.

**By taxi** Set-rate, unmetered taxis congregate two blocks inland from the harbour. Typical fares range from €10 to Ammopí up to €42 to Lefkos.

**Boat excursions** Boats offer day-trips from Pigádhia to isolated east-coast beaches. In addition, *Chrisovalandou III* (☎ 02410 51292) sails to and from Dhiafáni every day, typically leaving Pigádhia at 8.30am and Dhiafáni around 4.30pm, for a one-way fare of €15.

# Pigádhia

The island capital of **PIGÁDHIA** (**Kárpathos Town**) lies on the southeast coast, at the southern end of scenic, 3km-long **Vróndi Bay**. The town itself makes little of its spectacular setting, typically reaching just one or two streets back from its long curving waterfront. All the main action is concentrated along its southernmost section. From the jetty where ferries and excursion boats dock, at the far end, the quayside curls north, lined initially by seafood restaurants and then an increasing number of cafés and music bars. The only buildings that catch the eye are a group of stately but fading Italian-era port police and county-government buildings, overlooking the port from a low bluff at its northern end. Beyond them, another hotel or two, most large but reasonably tasteful, seem to join the procession along the bay each year, stretching Pigádhia ever further northwards. While there's nothing special to see, Pigádhia does offer most conceivable facilities, albeit with a package-tourism slant.

8

## ACCOMMODATION PIGÁDHIA

A long line of beach hotels is snaking ever northwards along Vróndi Bay; the larger and newer ones tend to be dominated by package clients, but in any case you're likely to enjoy Pigádhia more if you stay closer to the harbour.

**Amarylis Hotel** ☎ 22450 22375, ⓦ amarylis.gr. Nice little budget hotel, on the hillside just above the bus terminal and central car park, with sixteen clean, whitewashed and surprisingly large studios and apartments. All have a/c, showers and kitchenettes, half have sea-view balconies. **€30**

**Atlantis Hotel** ☎ 22450 22777, ⓦ atlantis hotelkarpathos.gr. Welcoming little hotel in a great central location, facing the Italian "palace" just up from the port. Helpful management, and nice rooms. Cheaper rooms overlook the pool; pay €9 extra for a port view. **€63**

**Electra Beach Hotel** ☎ 22450 23256, ⓦ electra beachhotel.gr. Imposing modern hotel a 5min walk along the beach from the harbour. Each of its somewhat small but very neat and tastefully modernized rooms has its own balcony, with dazzling views of the bay, and there's also a good pool. Buffet breakfasts included. In summer it tends to be filled with Scandinavian groups, but look for bargain low-season rates. **€100**

**Elias Rooms** ☎ 22450 22446 or 697 85 87 924, ⓦ eliasrooms.com. Simple little converted house, perched just above the *Hotel Karpathos* in the heart of town, with sea views from the balconies. Three plain little en-suite double rooms, two larger and slightly more expensive apartments that sleep four. Closed Nov–March. **€35**

## EATING AND DRINKING

★ **Mezedhopolio To Ellinikon** ☎ 22450 23932. Serving what's unquestionably Pigádhia's finest food, this cosy indoor dining room is set back a block inland from the middle of the harbour. Diners are invited up to the raised kitchen to choose from daily specials like a fabulous stuffed aubergine for €5, or a substantial grilled bream for €12; expect free trimmings such as a rich tapenade. Open all year, daily lunch & dinner.

**Orea Karpathos** ☎ 22450 22501. The best all-round restaurant along the harbourfront strip, near the southern end; almost nothing costs more than €10. *Trahanádhes* soup for €4.50, spicy sausages for €7.50, marinated artichokes, great spinach pie, and palatable local bulk wine. Locals use it as an ouzerí, ordering just mezédhes. Evenings only, closed Dec–Feb.

**Sofia's Place** ☎ 22450 23152. Sit and enjoy the life of the port from the blue chairs on the terrace of this pretty little restaurant in the heart of the action. Friendly service, good local seafood at above-average prices, and tasty grilled-meat specials. Daily noon–late.

# The south

Immediately south of Pigádhia, reached by a detour off the main road down the other side of a low headland, the purpose-built resort of **AMMOPÍ** (also known as "Amoopi") is not so much a town as a succession of sand-and-gravel, tree- or cliff-fringed coves. There's no commercial centre to it, let alone anything that could be called authentic, but for a beach-side holiday any of the hotels here could make an appealing base. Keep going beyond them all to find some delightful little turquoise bays, usually deserted except at the height of summer.

Back on the main road, the further south you go, the flatter and more desolate Kárpathos becomes. The long windswept beach that leads all the way down to the airport has become popular with foreign **windsurfers**, who take advantage of the prevailing northwesterlies, especially during the annual summer European championships. As such, different segments are known these days by their windsurfing nicknames, such as Gun Bay.

For non-surfers, the best beach here is **Chicken Bay**, the southernmost, though it's a bit too exposed to spend a whole day here. Its shallow, impossibly turquoise waters begin within a few metres of the airport runway.

## INFORMATION                                                    THE SOUTH

**Activities** The most established surf school in southern Kárpathos is Pro Center Kárpathos (☎ 22450 91063 or 697 78 86 289, ⓦ Chris-Schill.com), which makes use of three separate bays, catering to different ability levels.

## ACCOMMODATION AND EATING

**Esperida** Ammopí ☎ 22450 81002, ⓦ esperida.gr. Large, very welcoming taverna, set well back from the sea halfway down the approach road to Ammopí. Delicious local food, including island cheese, wine and sausage, roast aubergine, and pickled wild vegetables (look out for what they call "capers"). Main dishes cost around €8, mezes half that. They also offer clean, good-value rooms and apartments. **€50**

**Irini Beach Hotel** Gun Bay ☎ 22450 91000, ⓦ hotelirini24.com. Upscale hotel complex on the island's prime windsurfing beach, with large comfortable rooms, a good pool, equipment rental and instruction. **€65**

★ **Vardes Studios** Ammopí ☎ 22450 81111 or 697 21 52 901, ⓦ hotelvardes.com. Ammopí's most peaceful studios, set amid orchards 400m back from the beach. Ten comfortable units, all with shower and balcony; some sleep up to five. House fruit and jam for breakfast, plus a bar but no restaurant. **€73**

# The west

Although it's much less developed than the area around Pigádhia, the western shoreline of Kárpathos holds several of the island's most attractive **beaches**. Small resorts such as Finíki and Lefkós make great bases for low-key holiday relaxation, amid scintillating scenery.

## Arkássa

The main road from Pigádhia reaches the west coast at the little town of **ARKÁSSA**. Hardly anything survives of the original village, the rocky coastal frontage now consisting of unremarkable studios and tavernas. Head a few hundred metres south, and you'll come to the signposted side-road that leads to the whitewashed chapel of **Ayía Sofía**. Remains of a much larger Byzantine basilica here feature several mosaic floors with geometric patterns.

The finest beach hereabouts is also located just south of Arkássa. The broad 100m stretch of good-quality sand known as **Áyios Nikólaos beach** still feels pleasantly rural, even though a newly built hotel has just joined its long-standing taverna.

## Finíki

A couple of kilometres north of Arkássa, facing it from the northern end of a long bay, the even smaller resort of **FINÍKI** is still very recognizable as the fishing village it used to be. A brief detour down from the main road, the port is arrayed along the curve of a minuscule beach, and holds several welcoming tavernas. In summer, excursion boats head across from here to Kássos.

## Lefkos

To reach the attractive resort of **LEFKÓS** – also known as **Paralía Lefkoú** – take a side turning that drops back down from the main road as it climbs through the dense forest around 10km north of Finíki. While considerably more developed than Finíki, it started out as a fishing village. Its best tavernas are concentrated around the harbour, which also holds a great sheltered beach, and accommodation is plentiful too. Several more beaches lie nearby, separated by a striking topography of cliffs, islets and sandspits.

## Mesohóri

The main road climbs northeast from Lefkos through the pine forest to the dramatically sited village of **MESOHÓRI**. Tumbling seaward along narrow, stepped alleys, Mesohóri comes to a halt at the edge of a bluff that's dotted with three tiny, ancient chapels, separated from the village proper by extensive orchards.

### ACCOMMODATION                                    THE WEST

**Arhontiko Studios** Finíki ☏ 22450 61473, ⓦ hotel arhontiko.gr. Simple, well-run hotel on the main coast road just above Finíki, where all six comfortable studios and six larger apartments have sea-view balconies. **€60**

**Finiki View Hotel** Finíki ☏ 22450 61400, ⓦ finikiview.gr. Pleasant modern hotel, dropping down towards the port from the coast road. Eighteen well-equipped studios and two apartments, set in attractive gardens and sharing use of a pool. Great views at sunset. Closed Nov–April. **€70**

**Glaros** Áyios Nikólaos, Arkássa ☏ 22450 61015, ⓦ glarosrestaurant-karpathos.com. Classic little beach taverna beside one of Kárpathos' nicest beaches, run by returned Karpathian-Virginians. Good open-air dining, plus

five tastefully furnished, good-value studios. **€60**

**Hotel Krinos** Lefkos ☏ 22450 71410, ⓦ hotel-krinos .com. Low-rise complex, just before the road reaches the centre of town, that's especially popular with returning German guests. All its mix of rooms, studios and apartments are en suite and have either balcony or terrace. Closed Nov–April. **€55**

★ **Pine Tree** Ádhia ☏ 697 73 69 948, ⓦ pinetree -karpathos.gr. Simple but very attractive and inexpensive rooms in an utterly gorgeous rural location, a short walk up the hillside from the *Pine Tree Restaurant* (see below), and enjoying long-range sea views. There's also a lovely stand-alone studio, complete with traditional sleeping platform, a little higher up, and free camping. **€35**

### EATING AND DRINKING

**Dhramoundana 1** Mesohóri ☏ 22450 71373. The finest eating option in this hillside village, but fiendishly difficult to find; it's near the church of Panayía Vryssianí, low down at the far north end. A couple of outdoor tables enjoy fabulous views, but the food indoors is the main attraction, featuring capers, sausages, home-made *dolmadhes* and marinated "sardines". Daily lunch & dinner.

**Dhramoundana 2** Lefkos ☏ 22450 71373. The pick of the three restaurants grouped together at the western end of Lefkos's harbour is slap in the middle. Its friendly owner, whose wife runs the sister restaurant *Dhramoundana 1* (see above), is a Greek-American who lived in Baltimore – hence the fabulous crab cakes. Daily lunch & dinner.

**Marina** Finíki ☏ 22450 61100. Finíki's finest waterfront taverna, with a shady patio right by the beach. €5 buys a quarter chicken, otherwise most meat and fish dishes cost €8, though you'll pay more when there's fresh lobster. Live Greek music on summer evenings. Daily 9am–late.

**Pine Tree Restaurant** Ádhia ☏ 697 73 69 948, ⓦ pinetree-karpathos.gr. Delightful restaurant, set amid orchards and lush gardens in an isolated spot, just up from the sea, 7km north of Finíki. Relax on the flower-decked terrace and sample such delights as home-baked bread, lentil soup and octopus *makaronádha* (plus other *mayireftá*), washed down by sweet Óthos wine. Daily noon–9pm.

## The centre

**Central Kárpathos** supports a group of villages blessed with commanding hillside settings, ample running water and a cool climate, even in August. Nearly everyone here has "done time" in North America before returning home with their nest eggs; the area is said to have the highest per capita income in Greece.

You're more likely to take a driving tour through the interior than to spend much time in any one place. Villages to look out for include **ÓTHOS**, which is the highest (around 400m) and the chilliest, on the flanks of 1215m Mount Kalilímni, and is noted for its bread, sausages and sweet, tawny-amber wine. **VOLÁDHA**, downhill to the east, cradles a tiny Venetian citadel, while the most attractive, **PYLÉS**, faces west atop a steeply switchbacking road that branches from the main west-coast road 6km north of Finíki.

## The north

**Northern Kárpathos** still feels very much a world apart. Despite repeated promises, the road north from Spóa has not been fully paved, and remains a hair-raising prospect for all but the hardiest mountain drivers. Most visitors therefore still arrive by boat at the little port of **Dhiafáni**, and then take a bus up to the traditional hilltop village of **Ólymbos**.

### Spóa

The gateway to northern Kárpathos, where the unpaved road to Ólymbos branches off the main circle-island road, is the village of **SPÓA**, just east of the island's central spine. No road enters the village itself.

If you're heading this way along the east coast, you might prefer to take a break at the best beach in these parts, down at **Ápella**, though from the taverna at the road's end you still have to walk a short pathway to reach the scenic 300m gravel strand.

### Dhiafáni

The sleepy seafront village of **DHIAFÁNI** only springs to life twice a week, when its rare mainline ferries – one heading towards Rhodes, the other towards Crete – call in. Otherwise, the daily excursion boats from Pigádhia (see p.539) keep a low-key tourist industry, including several tavernas and lodging options, ticking along.

All the **beaches** in northern Kárpathos are made of pebbles. Dhiafáni itself has a reasonable fringe of shingle, or there's a quieter alternative at **Vanánda** cove; follow the pleasant signposted path north through the pines for thirty minutes, short-cutting the road. Naturist **Papá Miná**, with a few trees and cliff-shade, lies an hour's walk distant via the cairned trail taking off from the road to the ferry dock.

### Ólymbos

Founded in Byzantine times as a refuge from pirates, the windswept village of **ÓLYMBOS** straddles a long ridge below slopes studded with ruined windmills. Isolated for centuries, the villagers speak a unique dialect, with traces of its Doric and Phrygian origins. Their home has long attracted foreign and Greek ethnologists for **traditional dress, crafts, dialect and music** that have vanished elsewhere in Greece. Here too the traditions are dwindling by the year; only older women, or those who work in the tourist shops, now wear striking, colourful clothing – while flogging trinkets imported from much further afield.

Women still play a prominent role in daily life, however: tending gardens, carrying goods on their shoulders or herding goats. Nearly all Ólymbos men historically emigrated to Baltimore or work outside the village, sending money home and returning only on holidays.

Live folk music is still played regularly, especially at festival times (Easter and Aug 15), when visitors have little hope of finding a bed.

### ACCOMMODATION AND EATING

★ **Gorgona** Dhiafáni ☎ 22450 51509, ⓦ gorgona karpathos.it. Behind the seafront fountain, this Italian-run place is a favourite local rendezvous, featuring light dishes, wonderful desserts, proper coffees and *limoncello* digestif. Daily 9am–late.

**Hotel Aphrodite** Ólymbos ☎ 22450 51307. Little hotel, run by the same management as the nearby Parthenonas restaurant, with just four spacious double rooms, one of

## HIKING IN NORTHERN KÁRPATHOS

Northern Kárpathos is renowned for excellent **hiking**. While the most popular walk of all simply follows the jeep track down from Ólymbos to the superb west-coast beach at **Fýsses**, a sharp drop below the village, most local trails head more gently north or east, on waymarked paths.

**Ólymbos to Dhiafáni** An easy ninety-minute walk leads back down to Dhiafáni, starting just below the two working windmills. The way is well marked, with water twenty minutes along, and eventually drops to a ravine amid extensive forest. The final half-hour, unfortunately, follows a bulldozed riverbed.

**Ólymbos to Vrykoúnda** Heading north from Ólymbos, it takes around 1hr 30min to reach sparsely inhabited Avlóna, set on a high upland devoted to grain. From there, less than an hour more of descending first moderately, then steeply, along an ancient walled-in path that takes off from the valley-floor track, will bring you to the ruins and beach at Vrykoúnda. Once you've seen the Hellenistic/Roman masonry courses and rock-cut tombs here, and the remote cave-shrine of John the Baptist on the promontory (focus of a major Aug 28–29 festival), there's good swimming in the pebble coves to one side.

**Avlóna to Trístomo** Starting just above Avlóna, a magnificent cobbled way leads in 2hr 30min, via the abandoned agricultural hamlets of Ahordhéa and Kílios, to Trístomo, a Byzantine anchorage in the far northeast of Kárpathos. The views en route, and the path itself, are the thing; Trístomo itself is dreary, with not even a beach.

**Trístomo to Vanánda** If you've already hiked to Trístomo, and would prefer not to retrace your steps to Avlóna, you can hook up, via a shortish link trail east from Trístomo, with a spectacular coastal path back to Vanánda (3hr 30min). Once clear of abandoned agricultural valleys and over a pine-tufted pass, it's often a corniche route through the trees, with distant glimpses of Dhiafáni and no real challenge except at the steep rock-stairs known as Xylóskala.

**8**

which has a kitchen. All have phenomenal views, to the windmills and the sea. **€50**

**Hotel Astro** Ólymbos ☎ 22450 51421. Smart en-suite rooms, with traditional furnishings, and a warm welcome from its owners, the two sisters who run Café-Restaurant Zefiros on the other side of the village, where breakfast is taken. **€55**

**Hotel Studios Glaros** Dhiafáni ☎ 22450 51501, ⍟ hotel-glaros.gr. Run by the very welcoming George and Anna Niotis, these sixteen huge units, some of which sleep four, are top of the heap in all senses in Dhiafáni, ranged in tiers up the southern slope. Closed Nov–March. **€45**

**Pension Olymbos** Ólymbos ☎ 22450 51009. This friendly little place, near the village entrance, offers modern units with baths as well as unplumbed ones with traditional furnishings. It also holds an excellent, inexpensive restaurant, specializing in traditional home cooking, including unusual shellfish. **€30**

**Restaurant Avlona** Ávlona ☎ 694 60 18 521. On a spur road away from the Dhiafáni–Ólymbos road, this offshoot of the restaurant at Pension Olymbos (see above) features artichoke hearts with eggs in spring. The signature dish is makaroúnes, home-made pasta with onions and cheese. Four en-suite rooms make it an ideal base for walkers. Daily lunch & dinner.

**Studios Delfini** Dhiafáni ☎ 22450 51354, ⍟ studiosdelfini.wordpress.com. Very pleasant ground-floor studios, with kitchenettes, bathrooms and air conditioning, just a few metres from the sea. Upstairs, the Dolphins restaurant serves vegetables from the garden, and good fish. Closed Nov–March. **€45**

# Sými

For sheer breathtaking beauty, the Greek islands can offer nothing to beat arriving at SÝMI. While the island as a whole is largely barren, its one significant population centre, **Sými Town**, is gorgeous, a magnificent steep-walled bay lined with Italian-era mansions.

With its shortage of fresh water and relative lack of sandy beaches, Sými has never developed a major tourist industry. Sými Town however holds a wide range of small hotels, as well as abundant delightful rental properties, while day-trippers from Rhodes – and yachties lured by the wonderful harbour – mean it can support some very good restaurants too. In the height – and searing heat – of summer it can get uncomfortably crowded, with a large influx of Italian visitors as well as mainland Greeks, but in spring and autumn it's wonderful, and even in winter a substantial expat community keeps many businesses open.

Visitors who venture beyond the inhabited areas find an attractive island that has retained some **forest** of junipers, valonea oaks and even a few pines – ideal walking country in the cooler months. Dozens of tiny, privately owned **monasteries** dot the landscape; though generally locked except on their patron saint's day, freshwater cisterns are usually accessible. Near the southern tip of the island, the much larger monastery of **Panormítis** is an important pilgrimage destination.

Little more than a century ago, Sými Town was home to more people than Rhodes Town, thanks to the wealth generated by its twin ancient skills of shipbuilding and sponge-diving. Many of the mansions built during that age of prosperity have long since tumbled into decay – a process hastened in September 1944, when an ammunition blast set off by the retreating Germans levelled hundreds of houses up in Horió. While restoration is gradually bringing them back to life, the scattered ruins lend the island an appealing sense of time-forgotten mystery.

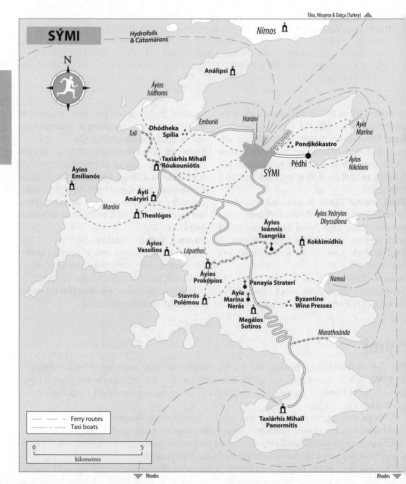

Ferry routes
Taxi boats

## ARRIVAL AND INFORMATION

## SÝMI

**By ferry** Ferries from the following islands use the main harbour in Sými Town: Astypálea (1 weekly; 9hr); Hálki (2 weekly; 2hr 20min); Kálymnos (9 weekly; 2hr 10min–6hr 20min); Kastellórizo (3 weekly; 3hr 20min–6hr); Kos (11 weekly; 1hr 30min–4hr 50min); Léros (6 weekly; 3hr 20min–5hr 50min); Lipsí (6 weekly; 3hr 45min–7hr); Náxos (1 weekly; 14hr); Níssyros (3 weekly; 3–4hr); Páros (1 weekly; 15hr 20min); Pátmos (6 weekly; 5hr 10min–8hr 10min); Pireás (2 weekly; 17–21hr); Rhodes (3–4 daily; 50min–1hr 40min); Tílos (3 weekly; 1hr 30min–3hr 10min). Ferries also call in Panormítis monastery at the island's southern tip, but most stop there en route from Rhodes to Sými Town; only the Proteus sails from Sými Town to Panormítis, three times weekly.

**Ticket agents** Kalodoukas Holidays at the foot of the Kalí Stráta (☎ 22460 71077, ⊛ kalodoukas.gr), and Sými Tours on the harbourfront (☎ 22460 71307, ⊛ symitours. com).

**Tourist office** Sými does not have an official tourist office, but Sými Visitor, based above Pahos café by the taxi-boat jetty, sells books and maps of local interest, and runs a very helpful website, ⊛ symivisitor.com.

## GETTING AROUND

**Boat excursions** Between late May and late Sept, taxi-boats from Yialós harbour run south to the beaches detailed on p.548 onwards, and north to Emborió (see p.546). In Aug, several a day make it possible to beach-hop; in lower season, pick a single day-trip destination. Fares range up to €15 for the round-trip to Marathoúnda. Larger boats offer circle-island cruises in summer, with snorkelling and picnic stops, or day-trips to Turkey, for around €40. You can also take a day-trip to Kastellórizo aboard the Dodekanisos Express catamaran (Mon only; €36; ⊛ 12ne.gr). On Saturdays only, the same catamaran makes a day-trip to Datca in Turkey; excursion boats run that route to no fixed schedule in summer.

**By bus** A year-round bus service operates from a tiny car park on the south side of the harbour. A coach shuttles at regular intervals between Yialós and Horió via Pédhi, and a minibus makes two or three round-trips daily all the way south to Panormítis monastery; both charge €1 flat fare.

**By taxi** Sými's six taxis, based alongside the bus stop, serve the entire island. Expect to pay €5 to get between Yialós and Horió with baggage.

**By car and scooter** Scooters and/or cars – not that there's much point renting a car on Sými, with its minimal road network – are available from Glaros (☎ 22460 71926, ⊛ glarosrentacar.gr), Katsaras (☎ 22460 72203) and Sými Tours (⊛ symitours.com).

**8**

# Sými Town

**SÝMI**, the capital and only town, is arrayed around a superb natural harbour in an east-facing inlet on the island's north shore. Inter-island ferries arrive right in the heart of town, while excursion boats jostle for room in summer with mighty Mediterranean cruisers. Immediately behind the straight-line quaysides that enclose the main segment of the port, scattered with sponge stalls and souvenir stores targeted at day-trippers, the lowest row of Italian-era mansions clings to the foot of the hillsides. Each is painted in the officially ordained palette of ochres, terracotta, cream or the occasional pastel blue, and topped by a neat triangular pediment and roof of ochre tiles. The hills are steep enough that the houses seem to stand one above the other, to create a gloriously harmonious ensemble.

The lower level of the town, known as **Yialós**, extends northwards to incorporate the smaller curving **Haráni Bay**. Traditionally this was the island's shipbuilding area, and you'll still see large wooden boats hauled out of the water. Yialós also stretches some way inland from the head of the harbour, beyond the main town square, which is used for classical and popular Greek performances during the summer-long **Sými Festival**.

On top of the high hill on the south side of the port, the old village of **Horió** stands aloof from the tourist bustle below. It's hard to say quite where Yialós ends and Horió begins, however; the massive **Kalí Stráta** stair-path, which climbs up from the harbour, is lined with grand mansions, even if some are no more than owl-haunted shells. Another similar stairway, the **Katarráktes**, climbs the west side of the hill, from further back in Yialós, but it's more exposed, and used largely by locals.

## Horió

As the 350-plus steps of Kali Stráta deter most day-trippers from attempting to reach **Horió**, the old hilltop village makes a great refuge whenever Yialós is too hot or crowded. It too holds its fair share of Italianate splendours and impressive basilicas. Once you venture away from the main pedestrian lane, it can be quite a tangle to explore – the part you can see from the harbour is just a small portion of the village, which stretches a long way back above Pédhi Bay. At the very pinnacle of things, a **Knights' castle**, largely destroyed by the wartime explosion, occupies the site of Sými's ancient acropolis; you may glimpse a stretch of Classical polygonal wall on one side. The **church of the Assumption**, inside the fortifications, is a modern replacement. One of the bells in the new belfry is the nose-cone of a thousand-pound bomb, hung as a memorial.

A series of arrows leads deep into Horió to the excellent local **museum** (Tues–Sun 8am–2.30pm; €2). Housed in a fine old mansion, its collection highlights Byzantine and medieval Sými, particularly frescoes in isolated, often locked churches. Displays continue in the eighteenth-century **Hatziagapitos mansion** below, with wonderful carved wooden chests and allegorical wall-paintings.

## Beaches

There's no beach in Sými Town. Some visitors clamber into the sea from the harbour wall in Haráni Bay, but neither there nor at the tiny, man-made **Sými Paradise** "beach", adjoining a restaurant just around the headland beyond Haráni, is the water clean enough for swimming to be advisable.

Keep walking along the paved coast road from Haráni, however – there's no shade, but the views are nice, and there's seldom any traffic – and in around half an hour you'll come to quiet **Emborió** (Nimborió) Bay. The beach is just a narrow strip of coarse shingle, but it's a great place to while away an afternoon of swimming, snorkelling, and eating at the friendly taverna (see opposite). In summer, the beach is served by regular taxi boats, so you're not obliged to walk both ways.

**Albatros** Marketplace, Yialós ☎22460 71707, ⊛albatrosymi.gr. This pretty little hotel has five a/c rooms, a pleasant second-floor breakfast salon, and distant sea views. The website is also the booking venue for a number of magnificent Neoclassical villas divided into apartments. **€65**

**Aliki** Haráni quay, Yialós ☎22460 71665, ⊛hotelaliki .gr. Upscale waterfront hotel, housed in a renovated 1895 mansion, just around the corner from the main harbour. The tasteful rooms have wood floors and some antique furnishings, plus a/c and large bathrooms. All have at least partial sea views, some have balconies, and there's a very nice suite. Closed early Nov to mid-April. **€130**

**Fiona** Horió ☎22460 72088, ⊛fionahotel.com. Village hotel near the top of the Kalí Stráta; turn left at *George & Maria's*. The large, simply furnished but attractive and airy rooms upstairs enjoy stunning views and have small balconies; breakfast, included in the price, is taken on the bigger shared harbour-view terrace below. Also three studios next door. A three-person room costs €5 extra. **€65**

**Iapetos Village** Yialós ☎22460 72777, ⊛iapetos -village.gr. Tucked into walled, landscaped grounds just back from the main square at the head of the harbour, this smart complex also includes a roofed-over pool. All its 29 units, variously categorized as rooms, studios and apartments, are exceptionally large, and have kitchens, some sleep up to six. A good buffet breakfast is offered either in cool basement premises or by the pool bar. **€162**

**Kalodoukas Holidays** ☎22460 71077, ⊛kalodoukas .gr. Rental agents for a wide array of generally irresistible houses and apartments, all with kitchen facilities and many featuring traditional furnishings plus harbour-view balconies and/or courtyard gardens. Some sleep up to six guests. They also offer five beachfront apartments at Marathoúnda Bay; see p.544. Two-person apartments **€100**, four-person houses **€140**

**Les Catherinettes** north quay, Yialós ☎22460 71671, ⊚marina-epe@rho.forthnet.r. Spotless en-suite *pension*, above the eponymous restaurant, in a historic harbourfront building. Six simple rooms, with painted ceilings, fridges, fans and sea-view balconies. The same owners also offer three studios in Haráni, plus a family apartment. **€90**

**Nireus Hotel** Yialós ☎22460 72400, ⊛nireus-hotel .gr. Sými's most conspicuous hotel, in prime position near the clocktower at the harbour entrance, with a lovely waterfront bar and a decent restaurant. The stunning sea views from the adequate but unexceptional seafront rooms just about justify the high prices; don't even consider the cheaper rear-facing ones. Closed mid-Oct to March. **€115**

**Niriides Apartments** Emborió ☎22460 71784, ⓦniriideshotel.com. Ten simply furnished, spacious and quiet rental units, spread over five hillside buildings on the hillside just above the nice little beach at Emborió, 2km from Yialós in the next bay north. All sleep four, and have a/c; friendly management, on-site "lounge-café", and a good taverna immediately below. **€100**

**The Old Markets** Kali Stráta, Yialós ☎22460 71440, ⓦtheoldmarkets.com. Boutique B&B hotel, housed in an imposing and very elegant converted mansion a short way up the Kali Stráta, with magnificent harbour views. Each of its four en-suite rooms is luxuriously furnished; the Sými Suite, which costs double the rest, is quite superb. **€225**

**Opera House** Yialós platía ☎22460 72034, ⓦsymioperahouse.gr. This unexpectedly large complex, a short walk inland from Yialós' main square, consists of several separate houses, newly built in traditional style, perfunctorily furnished, and owned by a Greek-Australian. They're divided into apartment suites holding from two to six people; few have views to speak of, though they do have balconies, but the rates for the sheer space you get are remarkably low, especially off season. **€70**

★ **Sými Visitor Accommodation** ☎22460 71785, ⓦsymivisitor.com. Wendy Wilcox and Adriana Shum offer great-value rental stays in restored houses in Yialós and Horió, with maid service every three days. Ranging from simple studios to family mansions, these are private homes let in their owners' absence, and come with full kitchens, book/DVD collections – and all sorts of idiosyncrasies. Typical four-person house **€115**, two-person **€85**

## EATING AND DRINKING

### RESTAURANTS

**Dhimitris** South quay, Yialós ☎22460 72207. This family-run ouzerí, with open-air tables near the main island bus stop, offers exotic seafood items like *hokhlióalo* (sea snails), tasty octopus fritters, and the miniature local shrimps, along with grilled local sausages and chops and vegetarian starters. Daily lunch & dinner.

**George & Maria's** Top of Kalí Stráta, Horió. Jolly, much-loved Sými institution, with summer seating on a pebble-mosaic courtyard. Expect to be invited to inspect the pots in the kitchen before making your choice – perennial dishes, costing around €10, include feta-stuffed peppers, beans with sausage, lemon chicken, and a full range of grills. Dinner daily, plus random lunchtimes in season.

**Metapontis Taverna** Emborió ☎22460 71820. Lovely little taverna, right beside the beach at Emborió, a half-hour walk along the coast from Yialós. Open for all meals daily; some beachgoers hang on to a table all day, with fresh-grilled meat or fish for lunch and then ice creams and snacks later on. Daily 10am–7pm.

★ **Muses** Yialós Platía ☎695 87 34 503. The up-and-coming star of the Sými scene, *Muses* offers a distinctive, delicious, very contemporary and rather pricey take on Greek cuisine. The cucumber salad is a deconstructed tsatsiki, while the octopus with ouzo foam and orange is fabulously succulent; like most dishes, it's available as a meze (€10) or a main (€20). They've made the best of their setting on the drab village square, just back from the harbour, with lovely open-air seating beneath trailing vines. Daily 7.30–11.30pm.

★ **Mythos** South quay, Yialós ☎22460 71488. This dinner-only, harbour-view roof terrace near the bus stop serves some of the best food on the island. Chef-owner Stavros's specialities include *psaronéfri* with mushrooms

and sweet wine sauce, lamb *stifádho*, feta *saganáki* in fig sauce, and good desserts like lemon pie or panna cotta. Best value of all is the phenomenal meze menu, designed to share and costing around €15 per head; the dishes just keep on coming. Late May to late Sept, daily 7.30–11pm.

**Syllogos** Platía Syllógou, Horió. Vast but not impersonal place with indoor/outdoor seating, great for taverna standards like *skordhaliá*, *arní lemonáto*, fried fish and aubergine *imám*, with good *hýma* wine on offer – only skimpy portion sizes deprive it of an "author pick" symbol. Daily lunch & dinner.

**Tholos** Haráni quay ☎22460 70203. The last restaurant you come to as you walk around Haráni bay, with waterside tables laid out right on the headland. A fabulously romantic spot for a fine meal of grilled fresh fish; the cheese-topped aubergine is pretty good too. May–Oct, daily lunch & dinner.

**Trata** Platía Trata, Yialós ☎22460 71411. This lively, very informal local hangout fills most of the small square at the foot of the Kalí Stráta. As you might expect from a place called "The Trawler", the fresh seafood is great, but it's also a place to go off piste, and simply see what delights – especially vegetable dishes – may be lurking in the kitchen. Daily 9am–late.

### BARS AND CAFÉS

**The 2 As** Horió. Named for owners Alex and Astrid, but still widely known by its former tag of Jean & Tonic, this convivial place is the heart and soul of the expat bar scene in Horió, and caters to a mixed clientele with 1960s music. Daily 6pm–late.

**Bar Tsati** Harani quay ☎22460 72498. You can't get any closer to the water than this friendly, Italian-run little café-bar, a short walk from the clocktower around Haráni bay. A

**8**

cluster of pastel-coloured tables and chairs in a harbourfront nook, plus cushions on the seawall itself – people go swimming right here. The wi-fi access reaches to the quayside, while there's a computer inside. Proper Italian espresso and tasty tidbits, and a lively late-night scene. Daily 11am–1am or later.

**Evoi Evan** Yialós platía. With a large terrace sprawling beneath the spreading ficus trees, and a cavernous interior that includes a pool table upstairs, *Evoi Evan* is open from breakfast onwards, serving coffee, smoothies and juices first thing, and a full drinks menu later on. Daily 8am–late.

**Kalí Stráta** Horió. The perfect place for a (pricey) sunset cocktail, with its canvas chairs and comfy cushions arrayed where the Kalí Stráta makes its final right-angle bend before reaching Horió. The best views on the island, with a jazz/world soundtrack. Daily noon until late.

**Lefteris** Top of the Kalí Stráta, Horió. The local characters' *kafenío*, in the second shopfront on Platía Syllógou, and attended by all. Coffee or ice cream at any hour; also simple *mezédhes*.

**Nikolas** Yialós. The first-ever *zaharoplastío* on the island, tucked into a back alley just south of Yialós bridge, and still the only one making its sweeties on site rather than importing from Rhodes. They also have a freezer-full of the best ice cream on the island.

**The Olive Tree** Horió ☎ 22460 72683, ⊚ olivetreesymi .eu. Friendly English-run café, across from the *Fiona* hotel (see p.546), that's a meeting place for energetic local expats. Top-quality coffee, really well-priced juices and smoothies using Greek fruits and Greek yoghurt, sandwiches (including to go), big healthy breakfasts. Also open for dinner on Saturdays in spring and autumn. Daily 8am–3pm.

★ **Pahos** Yialós. Classic *kafenío*, in operation since World War II. Facing the west quay south of Yialós bridge, it's still the spot for an evening ouzo or coffee and people-watching. Pahos himself has retired and can often be found sitting out front as a customer; otherwise it's hardly changed – including the prices, significantly lower than elsewhere. Daily 8am–late.

**Sunrise Café/Anatoli Iliou** Horió. Cosy English/German-run café, near the windmill on the eastern edge of Horió. Well-priced drinks, breakfasts, good salads and light snacks. Open all day until the small hours.

# The rest of the island

Away from Sými Town, the only other settlements on the island are little **Pédhi**, on the shoreline below Horió, and **Panormítis** down at the southern tip. The main attractions for visitors are isolated pebbly **beaches** that stand at the heads of the deeply indented bays along the eastern coast – accessible by taxi-boat in summer – and the tiny scattered **monasteries** that make great targets for hikers.

## Pédhi

The hugely indented bay lying south of Sými Town, on the far side of the ridge that stretches away from Horió, is home to the separate little community of **PÉDHI**. Somewhat further than it may look from Horió – it takes about half an hour to walk down the hillside – it's served by regular buses.

Originally a fishing hamlet with a sideline in boatbuilding, Pédhi has slowly expanded over the past twenty years. Much of the waterfront is now lined with new houses built in the standard Italian-influenced Sými style. Even if there's nothing authentic about it, it's reasonably pretty; locals fear the construction of an ugly new marina may spoil things, but there's been little progress so far. While the waterfront holds a hotel and a couple of tavernas, Pédhi doesn't have a beach.

## Ayía Marína

A small indentation in the headland that separates Sými Town from Pédhi Bay, known as **Ayía Marína**, has been developed as a miniature beach. With wonderful turquoise water, and a monastery-capped islet within easy swimming distance just offshore, it's an attractive spot, but in summer it tends to fill up (largely with Italians) the moment the day's first taxi boat arrives. The waterfront is an unbroken row of sunbeds, and the one taverna does a brisk trade.

It's possible to beat the crowds by walking here, either along a paint-splodge-marked path from Pédhi or over the top of the ridge from the east end of Horió, but the best time to hike is in low season, when the taxi boats aren't running and you may have the place to yourself.

## Áyios Nikólaos

An exposed fifteen-minute footpath along the south side of Pédhi Bay – simply push your way through the gate at the end of the quayside, then follow the cairns along the slope – leads to **Áyios Nikólaos**, the only all-sand cove on Sými. Also served by regular taxi-boats in season, this offers sheltered swimming, shady tamarisks, a bar, beach volleyball and a relaxing taverna.

## Áyios Yeóryios Dhyssálona

The first significant bay to interrupt Sými's eastern coastline south of Pédhi is **Áyios Yeóryios Dhyssálona**. This spectacular fjord can only be accessed by boat. No path could find a foothold in the smooth limestone that soars at its inland end. There's no taverna, and the whole place falls into shade in the early afternoon.

## Nanoú

The largest east-coast bay, **Nanoú**, holds the most popular beach for boat-trippers. A 200m stretch of gravel, sand and small pebbles, with a scenic backdrop of pines, it offers good snorkelling, and has a decent, seafood-strong **taverna**. Nanoú isn't on a paved road, but it is possible to hike down here, from the main trans-island road; see box below.

## Marathoúnda

The southernmost taxi-boat stop, **Marathoúnda**, is a magnificent bay, fringed by a long beach of coarse pebbles and ideal for tranquil swimming. It's also accessible via a paved road, which branches off the main road just after it switchbacks down from the island's central spine towards the monastery at Panormítis. Just back from the beach, the valley floor is flat enough to support a few fields, as well as goats who regularly stroll along the waterfront in search of tidbits.

**8**

### HIKING ON SÝMI

Sými has become an extremely popular **hiking** destination. With midsummer temperatures high even by Greek-island standards, spring and autumn are much the best seasons to come. Most trails lead through depopulated and waterless areas, so you need to have good equipment and provisions, and ideally relevant experience. Lance Chilton's *Walks in Sými*, sold locally packaged with his "Walker's Map of Sými", is a very good investment for all hikers. Guiding **walking tours**, from €10 per person, can be arranged through ⦿ symidream.com (Neil Gosling, ☎ 693 64 21 715), ⦿ symivisitor.com, or ⦿ kalodoukas.gr.

One excellent trail takes three hours (one-way) to cross the island from Yialós to its westernmost tip, where the tiny monastery of **Áyios Emilianós** is tethered to the mainland by a slender causeway. Some of the route lies through forest. Along the way there, you'll pass Sými's oldest monastery, **Taxiárhis Mihaïl Roukouniótis** (daily 9–11am & 5–6pm), which holds naïve eighteenth-century frescoes. For a shorter walk, you can drop down a dirt track from the monastery to reach small, pebbly **Tolí Bay**, which holds a summer-only taverna. An eastward trail over the hilltop from there drops down to **Emborió**, to complete a potential loop back to Yialós.

Another meaty hike crosses the island from Horió in ninety minutes to scenic **Áyios Vassílios** gulf; for the final forty minutes follow a paint-splodge-marked path from the road's end. Immediately above **Lápathos beach** here, the little monastery (which has accessible water) has some interesting frescoes.

The finest frescoes on the island are at hilltop, 1697-vintage **Kokkimídhis monastery** (usually open), reached by a steep track off the Panormítis road, where a complete cycle shows the acts of the Archangel and the risen Christ.

It's also possible to hike all the way from Horió to **Nanoú beach** (see above) in around three hours. That leaves you with time for a meal and swim before catching the boat back to Yialós. Alternatively, as the route leads first, mostly along an ancient footpath, to the chapel at **Panayía Stratterí** on the main road, you could take a scooter that far and only walk the final 45 minutes from there, through a scenic forested gorge, down to the beach.

## Panormítis monastery

Museums daily 8.30am–2pm & 3–4pm • €1.50 combined admission

In summer, at least one daily inter-island ferry, as well as countless excursion boats from Rhodes, calls in at the large **Taxiárhis Mihaïl Panormítis** monastery, located in a gorgeous (albeit beachless), almost entirely closed little bay in the far south of Sými. You can also get here by road, with daily buses heading down from Yialós. A shop, bakery and simple taverna cater to the needs of day-trippers.

Built in honour of the Archangel Michael (*Taxiárhis* in Greek), patron saint of the island, the monastery was thoroughly pillaged during World War II, so – except for its lofty belfry – don't expect much of the building or its contents. Away from its spruce main courtyard, which has an attractive pebble-mosaic floor, most of the complex is gently fading. Lit by an improbable number of oil lamps, the central *katholikón* is also graced by a fine *témblon* and of course the cult icon, though frescoes are unremarkable.

The monastery courtyard holds two small **museums**. One, devoted entirely to artefacts related to the monastery's religious significance, contains a strange mix of precious antiques, exotic junk, and votive offerings including bodybuilding and motocross trophies. A small boat is piled with messages-in-bottles carried here by the Aegean currents – the idea is that if the bottle or toy boat arrives, the sender's prayer is answered. In the opposite corner, a folklore museum holds displays on costumes, weaving, and domestic activities.

### ACCOMMODATION AND EATING                    THE REST OF THE ISLAND

**Katsaras** Pédhi ☎ 22460 71417. With a shaded terrace right at water's edge, this large taverna, in the middle of Pédhi Bay, makes a great place for a full meal or a sunset drink. Vegetable and seafood mezes cost around €8, grilled meat more like €12. Daily noon–9pm.

**Pédhi Beach Hotel** Pédhi ☎ 22460 71981, ⓦ pedibeachhotel.gr. Large, simply furnished a/c rooms in the middle of the bay, with a patio laid out with sunbeds. Around ten of the 56 rooms have sea-view balconies; rates include dinner at the on-site restaurant,

and drop significantly outside August. There's no beach here, but for lovers of the quiet life it's not a bad alternative. €120

★ **Taverna** Marathoúnda Run by the Kalodouka family, who also offer rental studios here, and supplied with fresh organic produce from their adjoining fields, this excellent waterfront taverna makes a wonderful lunch spot. Top-quality mezes for around €8, or beautifully prepared fish from around €12.50. Daily lunch & dinner mid-May to mid-Sept only.

# Tílos

Stranded midway between Kos and Rhodes, the small, usually quiet island of **TÍLOS** is among the least frequented and most unpredictably connected of the Dodecanese. For visitors, however, it's a great place simply to rest on the beach, or hike in the craggy hinterland.

Tílos shares the characteristics of its closest neighbours: limestone **mountains** like those of Hálki, plus volcanic lowlands, pumice beds and red-lava sand as on Níssyros. With ample groundwater and rich volcanic soil, the islanders could afford to turn their backs on the sea, and made Tílos the **breadbasket** of the Dodecanese. Until the 1970s, travellers were greeted by the sight of shimmering fields of grain bowing in the wind. Nowadays the hillside terraces languish abandoned, and the population of five hundred dwindles to barely a hundred in winter.

While recent development has turned the port of **Livádhia** ever more towards tourism, Tílos remains low-key. This is still a place where visitors come to get away from it all, often for extended stays. If you're here to **walk**, little may seem striking at first glance, but after a few days you may have stumbled on several small Knights' **castles** studding the crags, or found some of the inconspicuous, often frescoed, often locked **medieval chapels** that cling to the hillsides.

**By ferry** The port of Livádhia is connected with the following islands: Astypálea (1 weekly; 7hr 15min); Hálki (2 weekly; 45min); Kálymnos (1 weekly; 5hr 30min); Kastellórizo (2 weekly; 6hr 35min–10hr); Kos (2 weekly; 2hr–3hr); Náxos (1 weekly; 12hr); Níssyros (3 weekly; 50min); Páros (1 weekly; 13hr 30min); Pireás (2 weekly; 14–19hr); Rhodes (7 weekly; 1hr 20min–2hr 15min); Sými (3 weekly; 1hr 30min–3hr 10min).

**Travel agents** Buy ferry tickets from Stefanakis, close to the jetty (☏ 22460 44310, ⊚ tilos-travel.com). English-run Tilos Travel nearby offers boat excursions, accommodation, used-book swap and vehicle rental (☏ 22460 44294 or 694 65 59 697, ⊚ tilostravel.co.uk).

**Maps** The best maps on Tílos are published by SKAI, while walking guides Iain and Lyn Fulton (☏ 22460 44128 or 694 60 54 593, ⊚ tilostrails.com) offer itineraries geared towards all levels.

**By bus** A blue-and-white bus, charging €1.20, links Livádhia and Megálo Horió, to coincide with ferry arrivals. It also makes up to five runs daily between Livádhia and the beaches at Áyios Andónios and Éristos, plus a €4 round trip to Ayíou Pandelímona monastery on Sunday mornings.

**By taxi** The island has one taxi (☏ 22460 44059).

**By car and scooter** Tilos Travel (☏ 22460 44294, ⊚ tilostravel.co.uk) and Drive (☏ 22460 44173) in Livádhia.

# Livádhia

At its core, the port-cum-resort of **LIVÁDHIA**, at the head of a splendid bay on the island's north shore, is still recognizable as a traditional harbourfront village. A row of little tavernas, hotels and studios stretches away to the east, however, taking advantage of a narrow strip of beach that offers pleasant family swimming. The entire seafront is now lined by a broad pedestrian promenade, which is great for visitors even if it does diminish the "authentic" feel of the place. The bypass road that was supposed to take all vehicles around the back of the village hasn't quite materialized, however, so even the shortest journey by road can require labyrinthine detours. Once you're settled in you'll almost certainly walk everywhere local anyway.

**8**

## ACCOMMODATION

**Anna's Studios** ☎ 22460 44334, ⊕ tilosrooms.gr. The immaculate units in this bright whitewashed building, on the west hillside immediately above the jetty, vary in size, but all have pastel-hued furnishings and kitchenettes, and several have enormous sea-view balconies. **€60**

**Blue Sky** ☎ 22460 44294, ⊕ tilostravel.co.uk. Nine well-appointed apartments, right on the harbour just above the ferry jetty, and available year-round through Tilos Travel. Each is designed for three, with a galleried sleeping area, kitchen, and sea-view balcony. **€60**

**Dream Island Hotel** ☎ 22460 70707, ⊕ dreamisland .gr. Assorted very spacious one- and two-bedroom apartments, within a few metres of the water roughly two-thirds of the way around the bay. All have at least partial sea views, and are decorated in cool contemporary colours. Rates include breakfast and sunbeds. **€130**

★ **Eleni Beach Hotel** ☎ 22460 44062, ⊕ elenihoteltilos.gr. The best value on the shoreline, about halfway around the bay just as the continuous strip peters out. 36 airy, whitewashed rooms in four separate blocks; 31 have full-on sea views, five partial, and there's wheelchair access. Superbly attentive and sympathetic management. Rates include breakfast and sunbeds. **€60**

**Faros Hotel** ☎ 22460 44068, ✉ dimkouk@otenet.gr Friendly hotel-cum-taverna, out on its own at the far east end of the bay. A dozen or so peaceful, well-cared-for three-bedded rooms, plus what's effectively its own beach It's a ten-minute walk back to the main strip of restaurants but the food here is perfectly good. **€70**

**Ilidi Rock** ☎ 22410 44293, ⊕ tilosholidays.gr. Tílos largest and newest hotel, dropping in bright-white tiers to water's edge at the west end of the bay, five minutes' walk from the ferry. State-of-the-art studios and apartments sleeping up to four; one wing has disabled access. Two little private pocket beaches, plus gym facilities. Open all year, breakfast served summer only. A/c available at extra cost. **€100**

**Irini Hotel** ☎ 22410 44293, ⊕ tilosholidays.gr. Lushly landscaped low-rise hotel, 200m inland from the middle of the beach. The large pool, good breakfasts from the onsite café, wi-fi signal and pleasant gardens make up for somewhat small, mock-antique furnished rooms. **€60**

**Tilos Fantasy** ☎ 22460 44425, ⊕ tilosfantasy.gr. Substantial modern complex of studios, in a quiet hillside location 400m back from the sea. They're perfectly presentable, though the furnishings look straight from IKEA and there are two single beds in each room. **€55**

## EATING AND DRINKING

**CaféBar Georges** ☎ 22460 44257. Traditional old bar on the main square, where the outdoor tables are filled nightly with locals watching the world go by. Daily 8am–late.

**Iy Omonoia** ☎ 22460 44287. Enduringly popular traditional café, also known as *Tou Mihali*, stretching under trees strung with light bulbs beside the square, just up from the sea. A good venue for a sundowner, breakfast or a drink while waiting for a ferry; its inexpensive, tasty, generous mezédhes will stand in for a formal meal. Daily 8am–late.

**Mihalis** ☎ 22460 44359. Welcoming taverna, set in attractive gardens a short walk back from the sea, 50m east of the central square. No-nonsense fish for around €10, roast goat for a little less, as well as good vegetable platters and non-CAIR bulk wine. Daily 8am–late.

★ **Oneiro/Dream** Very popular "Grill and Fish House", open to the sea breezes near the centre of the beachfront promenade. Excellent grills and spit-roasts, typically

costing €8 for meat and €12 for fish. Be prepared to wait for your food in high season. Daily lunch & dinner.

**Taverna Trata** ☎ 22460 44364. Relaxed taverna, 100m inland from the beach at the first bend in the road, serving good local food on a nice open-air terrace. Check in the kitchen to see what's cooking, or sample grilled meat or fish for around €10. Daily lunch & dinner.

**To Armenon** ☎ 22460 44134. Professionally run and salubrious beach-taverna-cum-ouzerí, right by the sea in the middle of the bay, with large portions of octopus salad (€8.50), white beans, meaty mains and fish platters (typically €12.50), plus pasta and pizza, all washed down by Alfa beer on tap. Daily 10am–late.

**To Mikro Kafé** Pretty little shoreline cottage, nicely restored to create a buzzing, music-oriented bar and café that also offers a reasonable snack menu. The rooftop terrace is a great spot for late-night stargazing. Daily 5pm–late.

## Beaches near Livádhia

It's easy to spend days on end lazing on the beach at Livádhia itself but quieter alternatives lies within easy walking distance. An obvious trail heads north to the pebble bay of **Lethrá**, a walk that takes around an hour one-way. Two-thirds of the way along, a side-path drops to the tiny red-sand beach of **Ammóhosti**, which you're unlikely to have to yourself.

Another hour-long hike, to the secluded south-shore cove of **Stavrós**, starts between the *Tilos Mare Hotel* and the *Castellania Apartments*; once up to the saddle with its paved road, you've a sharp drop to the beach. Ignore the cairns in the ravine bed; the true path is up on the right bank.

The trail to the similar cove of **Thólos**, also an hour's walk away on the south coast, begins by the cemetery and the chapel of **Áyios Pandelímon**, then curls under the seemingly impregnable castle of **Agriosykiá**. From the saddle on the paved road overlooking the descent to Thólos (25min; also red-marked), a cairned route leads northwest to the citadel in twenty minutes. Head east a couple of curves along that paved road to the trailhead for **Áyios Séryis Bay**, Tílos's most pristine beach but also the hardest to reach (30min from the road).

## Mikró Horió

The ghost village of **Mikró Horió**, whose 1200 inhabitants left for Livádhia during the 1950s, is less than an hour's walk west of the port, with some surviving path sections short-cutting the road curves. Its only intact structures are churches (locked to protect their frescoes) and an old house restored as a small-hours **music bar** (July–Aug).

## Megálo Horió

Tílos's capital, the village of **MEGÁLO HORIÓ**, lies 7km west of Livádhia along the main road. The only other significant settlement on the island, it enjoys sweeping views over the vast agricultural plain that stretches down to Éristos, and is overlooked in turn by a prominent **Knights' castle**. Reaching the castle requires a stiff thirty-minute climb, which threads its way through a vast jumble of cisterns, house foundations and derelict chapels.

A little **museum** in the town hall (summer only, daily 8.30am–2.30pm; free) displays the bones of midget elephants, found in the **Harkadhió cave** not far east in 1971. Such remains have been found on a number of Mediterranean islands, but Tílos's group may have been the last to survive, until as recently as 4000 BC.

Long, pink-grey-sand **Éristos beach**, 3km south of Megálo Horió, ranks among the island's finest, though swimmers have to cross a reef to reach open sea. The far south end, where the reef recedes, is nudist, as are the two secluded all-naturist coves at **Kókkino** beyond the headland (accessible by path from the obvious military pillbox).

### ACCOMMODATION AND EATING

MEGÁLO HORIÓ

**Eden Villas** Megálo Horió ☎ 22460 44094, ⓦ eden -villas.com. Choice option run by Brits, this comfortable three-bedroom villa, with pool and wi-fi, is nicely located 500m north of Megálo Horió in the valley that leads towards Skáfi beach. Available for extended stays all year round. **€200**

**Eristos Beach Hotel** Éristos ☎ 22460 44025. Crisp modern complex facing the large, barely developed beach at Éristos on the southwest, with lots of outdoor space, including a pleasant terrace. Hotel rooms with big

balconies, and sizeable apartments suitable for four. **€60**

**Kastro** Megálo Horió ☎ 22460 44232. While the interior of Megálo's only taverna can be a little gloomy, its patio has lovely long-range views, and the food is good, with meat and goat cheese from their own flock, and home-made *dolmádhes*. Daily lunch & dinner.

**Milios Apartments** Megálo Horió ☎ 22460 44204. Attractive rooms and apartments set in pleasant flowery gardens in the heart of Megálo Horió. All have balconies offering (distant) sea views. **€50**

## The far northwest

The main road west of Megálo Horió hits the coast again at somewhat grim **ÁYIOS ANDÓNIOS**, which has an exposed, truncated beach and two tavernas. There's better, warm-water swimming at isolated, sandy **Pláka beach**, another 2km west, where people camp rough despite a total lack of facilities.

### Ayíou Pandelímona monastery

Daily: May–Sept 10am–7pm, may close briefly at noon; Oct–April 10am–4pm

The paved road ends 8km west of Megálo Horió at fortified **Ayíou Pandelímona monastery**, founded in the fifteenth century for the sake of its miraculous spring, still the best water on the island. A fitfully operating drinks café hosts the island's major **festival** of July 25–27. The monastery's tower-gate and oasis setting, high above the forbidding west coast, are its most memorable features, though a photogenic inner courtyard boasts a *votsalotó* surface, and the church a fine tesselated mosaic floor.

# Níssyros

The volcanic island of **Níssyros** is unlike its neighbours in almost every respect. It's much lusher and greener than dry Tílos and Hálki to the south, blessed with rich soil that nurtures a distinctive flora, and it supported a large agricultural population in ancient times. In contrast to long flat Kos to the north, Níssyros is round and tall, with the high walls of its central caldera rising abruptly from the shoreline around its entire perimeter. And Níssyros conceals a startling secret; behind those encircling hills, the interior of the island is **hollow**, centring on a huge crater floor that's dotted with still-steaming vents and cones.

For most visitors, the volcano is Níssyros' main attraction. It's easy enough to see it on a day-trip from Kos, so few bother to spend the night. That's a shame, because it's a genuinely lovely island, very short on beaches but abounding in spectacular scenery. The port and sole large town, **Mandhráki** on the northwest coast, is an appealing tight-knit community with some fine ancient ruins, while two delightful villages, Emboriós and Nikiá, straddle the crater ridge.

These days, much of the island's income is derived from the offshore islet of **Yialí**, a vast lump of pumice, all too clearly visible just north of Mandhráki, that's slowly being quarried away. Substantial concession fees have given the islanders economic security.

Níssyros also offers good **walking**, on trails that lead through a countryside studded with oak and terebinth (pigs gorge themselves on the abundant acorns, and pork figures prominently on menus).

## ARRIVAL AND DEPARTURE                                NÍSSYROS

**By ferry** Ferries moor at a concrete jetty a few hundred metres east of Mandhráki, out of sight of town. Níssyros is connected with the following ports: Astypálea (1 weekly; 5hr 30min); Hálki (2 weekly; 1hr 40min); Kálymnos (2 weekly; 2hr 50min); Kastellórizo (2 weekly; 8hr 30min); Kos Kardamena (3 weekly; 40min); Kos Town (8 weekly; 1hr–1hr 40min); Náxos (1 weekly; 10hr); Páros (1 weekly; 12hr); Pireás (1 weekly; 17hr 30min); Rhodes (4 weekly; 3hr 10min–4hr 45min); Sými (3 weekly; 3–4hr); Tílos (3 weekly; 50min).

**Travel agencies** Dhiakomihalis (☎22240 31459) or Kendris (☎22240 31227).

## GETTING AROUND

**By bus** Buses from the jetty head up to six times daily to Emboriós and Nikiá, via Páli.

**By taxi** For fixed-rate taxi service, call ☎22420 31460.

**By car and scooter** Rental outlets include Manos K on Mandhráki harbour (☎22420 31029), and Dhiakomihalis in town (☎22240 31459).

**By coach** Several coach trips daily set off from the jetty to visit the volcano. English-run Enetikon Travel, nearby on the road into town (☎22420 31180, ☎agiosnis@otenet .gr), are typical in offering €8 round trips every morning from 10.30am onwards, each of which takes a total of 1hr 45min.

## Mandhráki

The ancient harbour of **MANDHRÁKI**, the capital of Níssyros, silted up centuries ago, creating a fertile patch that now serves as the *kámbos* (community orchard), surrounded in turn by the modern town. Nonetheless this remains the island's sole

ferry port – boats pull in at a concrete jetty to the east, out of sight of the centre.
Mandhráki's a nice little place, stretching along the seashore slightly further than
appears at first glance. Behind the pedestrianized waterfront promenade, to some
extent overwhelmed by poor tavernas and souvenir stores aimed at day-trippers, the
tangled narrow lanes are lined with whitewashed houses, whose brightly painted
balconies and shutters are mandated by law. The ensemble is punctuated by
appealing little squares, and offers repeated glimpses of fruit trees to one side, and
blue sea to the other.

At its western end, Mandhráki comes to an abrupt halt at a low bluff that's topped by
the stout walls of a **Knights' castle**. Though records have been lost, the Knights
Hospitaller occupied Níssyros from 1314 until 1522, and it's thought to have reached
its heyday around 1400. You can't access any more of the castle itself than the corner
staircase and gateway that leads to the little **Panayía Spilianí monastery**, generally open
daylight hours.

**Langadháki**, the district immediately below the castle, was badly hit by
earthquakes in the 1990s, but little damage is now visible. At sea level, an attractive
mosaic footpath leads further west around the headland to reach the short,
black-rock beach of **Hokhláki**, which is seldom suitable for swimming.

## Archeological Museum

Daily 8.30am–3pm • Free

Níssyros's modern **Archeological Museum**, a couple of blocks back from the sea on the
main lane, holds assorted treasures from the island's past. The main floor focuses on the
pre-Christian era, starting with six-thousand-year-old artefacts created using obsidian
from nearby Yialí. Ceramic pieces range from delicate winged figurines of Eros, dating

from 350 BC but closely conforming to modern depictions of angels, to a colossal funerary pithos (urn) from the sixth century BC. Stelae in the downstairs galleries reveal a Christian presence on the island in the third century.

## Paleókastro
Unrestricted access

From the Langadháki district, beneath the cliffs at the west end of the Mandhráki waterfront, a well-signposted twenty-minute walk climbs up to the hugely impressive **Paleókastro**, a mighty ancient fortress that's one of the most underrated ancient sites in Greece.

On its way up, the path through the fields passes numerous ancient stairways and ruins. Once you meet a cement road – also accessible on a much more circuitous drive up from town – turn right and you're confronted by massive black fortifications. This hilltop was occupied from the eighth century BC onwards. Around four centuries later, Mausolus of Halicarnassus, the Persian satrap who left us the word "mausoleum", enclosed its inland slopes within 3m-thick walls – the cliffs on the seaward side already formed a natural boundary. If you think of ancient Greek ruins as all graceful white marble columns, this is something different – much older and vaster. Slotted chinklessly together, the colossal trapezoid blocks are reminiscent of Inca masonry. Only the barest outlines of the buildings within the enclosure survive, but visitors can clamber onto the ramparts by means of broad staircases to either side of the still-intact gateway.

## ACCOMMODATION
MANDHRÁKI

**Haritos** ☎ 22420 31322. Small hotel, a short walk from the ferry landing; head left along the coast road rather than towards town. Its eleven rooms have marble-trimmed baths and veneer floors, while the seafront across the road holds a terrace restaurant and a hot-spring pool. Open all year. **€60**

**Porfyris** ☎ 22420 31376, ⬢ porfyris-nisyros.com. Large, somewhat old-fashioned hotel, well back from the sea in the town centre, overlooking the common orchards. Most of the 38 spruce a/c rooms have sea views from private balconies and terraces, and there's also a large swimming pool and breakfast terrace. **€65**

**Romantzo** ☎ 22420 31340, ⬢ nisyros-romantzo.gr. Good-value family-run hotel, up to the left of the ferry jetty out of sight of the town, with simple but comfortable a/c en-suite rooms and apartments. While the rooms themselves have rear-view windows, all benefit from the broad, shared and very pleasant sea-view terrace on the first floor. **€35**

★ **Ta Liotridia** ☎ 22420 31580, ⬢ liotridia@nisyrosnet.gr. Two incongruously gorgeous suites, above a rough-and-ready bar just metres from the sea on the oceanfront footpath in the centre of town. Exposed stone walls, incorporating lava boulders; fine wooden furnishings and head-on sea views. Each sleeps up to four. **€150**

**Xenon Polyvotis** ☎ 22420 31011. Municipally owned hotel, on the quayside facing the ferry port; its en-suite rooms are large but utterly unremarkable, but there's no faulting the sea views. June–Sept only. **€60**

## EATING AND DRINKING

**Irini** Platía Ilikiomenis ☎ 22420 31365. Lively restaurant, in a busy little tree-shaded square, inland at the west end of town, that's all but entirely filled with bar and taverna tables. Hearty traditional dishes like aubergine and mince, or pepper stuffed with rice for €6–8. In truth the food isn't exceptional, but it's a convivial and involving place to spend an evening. Daily lunch & dinner.

**Kali Katsou** Cheap and cheerful local specialities poised immediately above the water on the quayside, including seafood such as mussels or squid as well as tasty island sausages for just €6. Daily lunch & dinner.

**Kleanthis** ☎ 22420 31484. The best seafood restaurant along the waterfront, with bright blue tables and chairs set out on the quayside, and busy for lunch and dinner. Tasty pittiá (chickpea croquettes) and other mezes, followed by fish dishes ranging from fried shrimps for €8 up to stuffed squid with cheese or swordfish for €16. Daily lunch & dinner.

**Proveza** ☎ 22420 31618, ⬢ proveza.net. Lively café-bar with extensive comfortable seating on the seafront promenade near Ta Liotridia. Besides being great for a sunset drink, with an appropriate soundtrack, it also offers free wi-fi and a row of internet-access computers indoors. Daily 11am–late.

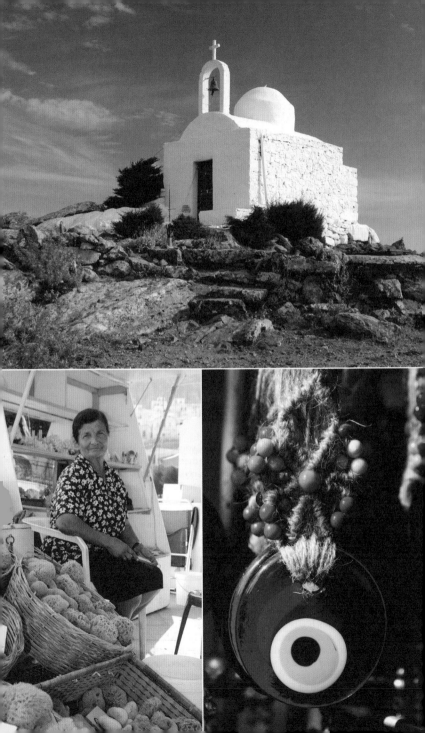

# The coast

Níssyros is almost entirely devoid of **beaches**, and only a small proportion of its coast – along the north and northwest shoreline – is even accessible to visitors. While the coast road east from Mandhráki peters out after barely 10km, it does make a pretty drive – and you'll have to come this way anyway if you're heading for the volcano. The largest structures en route are a couple of huge abandoned spas, dating back to the Italian era.

Four kilometres along, **PÁLLI** is a fishing village turned low-key resort that can be a welcome retreat when Mandhráki fills with trippers. All summer, the little harbour here is busy enough with pleasure boats – which can't moor at Mandhráki – to support several tavernas. Pálli also has an excellent **bakery**, cranking out tasty brown bread and pies. A reasonable tamarisk-shaded **beach** of reddish-grey sand, kept well groomed, extends east to the derelict Pantelídhi spa, behind which the little grotto-chapel of **Panayía Thermianí** is tucked inside the vaulted remains of a Roman baths complex.

Keep going beyond Pálli, along an initially bleak stretch of shore, to the pleasant cove of **Liés**, home to the summer-only Oasis snack-bar. The paved road ends at a car park a little further on, a spot that can also be reached in summer by taxi boats from Mandhráki. There's a grey-sand beach right here, while another fifteen minutes by trail over the headland brings you to the idyllic, 300m expanse of **Pahiá Ámmos**, with grey-pink sand heaped in dunes, limited shade at the far end and a large colony of rough campers and naturists in summer.

## ACCOMMODATION AND EATING — THE COAST

**Ellinis** Pálli ☎22420 31397. This long-established taverna is the best in Pálli, serving spit-roasted meat by night and grilled fish in season, all at reasonable prices, and offering a handful of simple rooms upstairs. **€45**

★ **Limenari** Limenari valley ☎22420 310233. Excellent traditional cooking, in an attractive location just below the main road 1km west of Pálli, halfway down a terraced valley towards its little namesake bay. Fair prices for big portions of home-style food. Daily lunch & dinner.

**Mammis Apartments** Pálli ☎22420 31453. A dozen tasteful self-contained a/c apartments, capable of sleeping four and equipped with large sea-view balconies and their own separate entrances, perched amid hillside gardens a short walk west of Pálli. **€60**

# The interior

If you've come to Níssyros to see the **volcano**, you're already there – the whole island is the volcano. Beyond and behind the steep slopes that climb from the shoreline, the entire centre of the island consists of a vast bowl-shaped depression. The hills end in a slender ridge that's the rim of the caldera, meaning that the two hilltop villages that survive, **Emboriós** and **Nikía**, are long thin strips that enjoy stupendous views both out to sea and down into the maw. The interior is etched almost in its entirety with ancient agricultural terraces, mostly long abandoned but giving a very real sense of the much greater population in antiquity. A side road just beyond Emboriós offers the only road access, and continues south to the craters at the far end.

## Emboriós

The road up from Pálli winds first past the village of **EMBORIÓS**. As is obvious from the copious ruins that stretch high above the current village centre, the population here once numbered in the thousands; in winter these days it dwindles to just twenty. It's a gorgeous spot though, which is being bought up and restored by Athenians and foreigners. New owners often discover natural volcanic saunas in the basements of the crumbling houses; at the outskirts of the village there's a signposted public **steam bath** in a grotto, its entrance outlined in white paint. One can hike down to the caldera floor from Emboriós; a trail drops from behind the little platía and it's another fifteen-minute walk to the craters.

Some 3km south of Emboriós, a paved drive leads down from the main road to **Panayía Kyrá**, the island's oldest and most venerable monastery, worth a stop for its enchanting, arcaded festival courtyard as much as its church.

### HIKING ON NÍSSYROS ISLAND

Níssyros is a fabulous destination for hikers, with enticing trails to suit all abilities. The one drawback is that hiking to and from the volcano from Mandhráki is for most walkers too much to attempt in a single day. It's not so much the distance that's the problem as the fact that you have to climb back out of the island interior on your way home. SKAI publish a good topographical **map** (w shop.skai.gr).

#### VOLCANO TO MANDHRÁKI

About 1km north of the volcano admission booth, a clear, crudely marked path climbs to a pass, then maintains altitude along the north flank of **Káto Lákki** gulch, emerging after ninety minutes at the important monastery of **Evangelístra** with its giant terebinth tree just outside. Beyond Evangelístra, you have to walk about 1km on the paved access road before the old path kicks in for the final half-hour down to Mandhráki. Look sharp at curves to find the old walled-in path. At first it just short-cuts the road, then for quite a long stretch it loops above the port well away from the road, before finally curling around to emerge above the local school.

#### NIKIÁ TO EMBORIÓS

Hiking from **Nikiá to Emboriós** takes just under ninety minutes, with a short stretch of road-walking towards the end. Descend from Nikiá towards the volcano and bear right towards Theológos monastery, then take the left fork by the wooden gate before reaching it. The path ambles along through neglected terraces, without much altitude change, occasionally obstructed by debris and vegetation. You eventually emerge after just under an hour by some utility poles on the modern Emboriós–Nikiá road. Follow the road from there for about 1km (15min) to the turn-off for Lakkí, where the onward trail continues conspicuously uphill into Emboriós.

## Nikiá

The village of **NIKIÁ**, overlooking the caldera from high on its southeastern rim, is a gorgeous little place that should figure on any island itinerary. Its spectacular location, 14km from Mandhráki, enjoys panoramic views out to Tílos as well as across the volcano. Tiny lanes lead from the bus turnaround at road's end to railed volcano viewpoints as well as to the diminutive, engagingly round central platía called Pórta. Paved in pebble mosaic, ringed by stone seating for folk dances, and facing a pretty little church, it's all so dazzlingly white that it's hard to keep your eyes open.

A 45-minute trail descends from the end of the road to the crater floor. A few minutes downhill, detour briefly to the eyrie-like monastery of **Áyios Ioánnis Theológos**, whose festival grounds come to life at the September 25–26 evening festival.

### EATING AND DRINKING   THE INTERIOR

**Andriotis** Nikiá ☎ 22420 31027. The only taverna in Nikiá, at the village entrance, with huge views out over the sea, serves a good menu of meaty €6 specials, including rabbit or chicken stews, and succulent chocolatey desserts. Summer only, daily lunch & dinner.

★ **Apyria** Emboriós ☎ 22420 31377. Excellent little taverna, which spreads out into the platía by the church in peak season, and otherwise has a couple of tables crammed into a tiny alleyway, and a breezy indoor dining room. Delicious local food at great prices, including spit-roasted suckling pig in summer as well as grills and mezédhes. The friendly owner is also a beekeeper; be sure to sample fresh honey if you're here in July. Dinner daily all year, lunch daily in summer, Sunday only in winter.

**Porta Pangiotis** Nikiá ☎ 22420 31285. This welcoming village café, one of a matching pair on Nikiá's tiny, delightful circular platía, is an irresistible spot to pause for a snack, juice or coffee. Daily 10am–8pm.

## Visiting the volcano

What's loosely referred to as being the "volcano" is the eerie conglomeration of cinder cones and deep craters at the far southern end of the summit caldera, reached by a single road that drops down beyond Emboriós. Although the volcano is dormant, and you won't therefore see fiery eruptions or flowing lava, it's disconcertingly alive, with sulphurous steam sprouting from holes and fissures on all sides. Access is unrestricted, though occasionally a ticket booth charges €2.50 admission. A snack bar opens at peak times only.

A steady procession of coach trips from Mandhráki (see p.555) usually keeps the area busy between 11am and 3pm; to enjoy it in solitude, make your own way up early or late in the day. Either rent a vehicle, or choose from the hiking possibilities on p.555.

As soon as you follow the short trail from the road's-end car park to the fenced overlook, you realize that while the main crater – officially named **Stéfanos** – may look small from a distance, close-up it's a massive, hissing, stinking pit. Its striated walls, yellow with sulphur, drop straight down 40m to a flat stained floor that's pockmarked with bubbling fumaroles. You can venture down there via an easy trail that winds along a timeworn groove in the crater wall. Don't get too close to the boiling mud-pots, which sound as though there's a huge cauldron bubbling away beneath you. In legend this is the groaning of the titan Polyvotis, crushed by Poseidon under a huge rock torn from Kos.

The hillside immediately west holds several steep-sided cones, accessible via an obvious and undemanding trail. Climbing up lets you escape the crowds, and also offers a greater thrill of discovery. It seems a shame to reveal what awaits you at the top, but rest assured it's worth it.

# Kos

After Rhodes, **KOS** ranks second among the Dodecanese islands for both size and visitor numbers. Here too the harbour in **Kos Town** is guarded by an imposing castle of the Knights of St John, the streets are lined with Italian-built public buildings, and minarets and palm trees punctuate extensive Hellenistic and Roman remains. And while its hinterland mostly lacks the wild beauty of Rhodes' interior, Kos is the most fertile island in the archipelago, blessed with rich soil and abundant ground water.

Mass **tourism**, however, has largely displaced the old agrarian way of life; all-inclusive complexes comprising tens of thousands of beds are a blight that contribute little to the local economy, and have forced many restaurants and more modest hotels out of business. Except in Kos Town and Mastihári, there are few independent travellers, and from mid-July to mid-September you'll be lucky to find a room without reserving far in advance, while the tourist industry itself is juxtaposed rather bizarrely with cows munching amid baled hay near olive groves, and Greek Army tanks exercising in the volcanic badlands around the airport. Like Tílos further south, Kos never had to earn its living from the sea and consequently has little in the way of a maritime tradition or a contemporary fishing fleet. All these peculiarities acknowledged, Kos is still worth a few days' time while island-hopping: its few **mountain villages** are appealing, the tourist infrastructure excellent and **swimming** opportunities limitless – about half the island's perimeter is fringed by beaches of various sizes, colours and consistencies.

## ARRIVAL AND INFORMATION                                        KOS

**By plane** The local airport is just outside Andimahía in the very centre of the island, 24km southwest of Kos Town. Destinations served include Astypálea (2–3 weekly); Athens (5–7 daily); Iráklio, Crete (3 weekly); Léros (2–3 weekly); Rhodes (2–3 weekly); and Thessaloníki (2 weekly). Taxis (☏ 22420 23333, ⓦ kostaxi.eu) charge around €35 to Kos Town, and more like €20 to Mastihári or Kardhámena. Bus services are detailed below.

**By ferry** Kos Town is connected by ferry to Agathoníssi (1 weekly; 2hr 40min); Astypálea (1 weekly; 4hr 30min); Hálki (2 weekly; 2hr 45min); Kálymnos (2–5 daily; 30min–1hr); Kastellórizo (1 weekly; 9hr 45min); Léros (1–3 daily; 1hr 25min–3hr); Lipsí (2–3 daily; 2hr 10min–4hr 10min); Níssyros

(8 weekly; 1hr–1hr 40min); Pátmos (2–4 daily; 1hr 35min–5hr); Pireás (12 weekly; 10–14hr); Rhodes (1–5 daily; 2hr 10min–6hr 15min); Samos (1 daily; 3hr 30min); Sými (11 weekly; 1hr 30min–4hr 50min); Syros (1 weekly; 5hr 30min); Thíra (2 weekly; 5hr); and Tílos (2 weekly; 1hr 50min–2hr 50min). In addition, Mastihári on the north coast has frequent connections with Kálymnos (6 daily; 20min–1hr), and Kardhámena is connected with Níssyros (2 weekly; 40min).

**International ferries** Kos Town also has frequent ferry and excursion-boat connections to Bodrum in Turkey (30–45min).

**Tourist office** Akti Koundouriotou 7 in Kos Town (Mon–Fri 7.30am–2.45pm; ☏ 22420 24460, ⓦ kosinfo.gr).

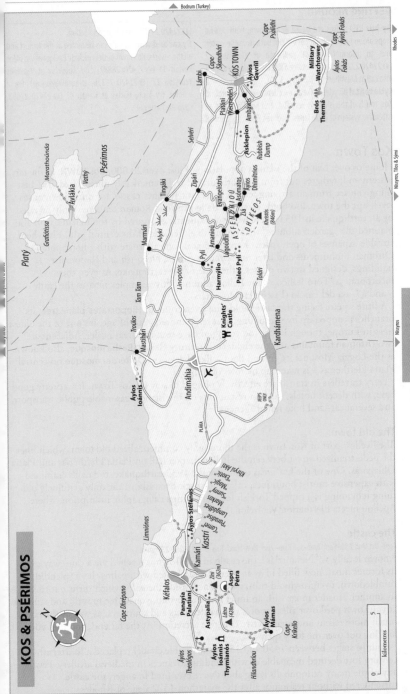

**KOS & PSÉRIMOS**

N

Bodrum (Turkey)

Cape Psalídhi

Cape Ayios Fokás

Rhodes

Military Watchtower

Brós Thermá

Ayios Fokás

Ayios Gavríl

Cape Skandhári

KOS TOWN

Lámbi

Platáni (Kermedés)

Ambávris

Asklepion

Rubbish Dump

Nísyros, Tílos & Sými

Sélveri

Tingáki

Zipári

Evangelístria

Kýos Dhimitríos

Ásomatos

ASFENDIOU

Zía

DHÍKEOS

Khristós (846m)

Nísyros

Marmári

Alykí

Amaníou

Lagoúdhi

Linopótis

Amaníou

Pylí

Paleó Pylí

Toláni

Harmýlio

Kardhámena

Tam Tam

Troúlos

Mastihári

Knights' Castle

Andimáhia

JETS ONLY

PLÁKA

Ayios Ioánnis

Limniónas

Kéfalos

Kamári

Ayios Stéfanos

Kástri

'Camel'

'Paradise'

Langádhes

Markos

Sunny

'Magic'

'Exotic'

Khrysí Aktí

Cape Dhrépano

Panayía Palatianí

Astypalia

Aspri Pétra

Zíni (36m)

Líthra (428m)

Ayios Ioánnis Thymianós

Ayios Mámas

Cape Kríkello

Ayios Theológos

Hilandhríou

Psérimos

Marathoúnda

Avlákia

Vathý

Grafiótissa

Platý

Nísyros, Tílos & Sými

0   5
kilometres

8

## GETTING AROUND

**By bus** KTEL buses are based in Kos Town, with several stops around a triangular park 400m back from the water, and an information booth adjacent at Kleopátras 7 (☎ 22420 22292). Buses between Kos Town and the airport also call at Mastihári (3–6 daily; €3.20).

**Cycle rental** Bicycles make an excellent way to get around Kos; much of the island is very flat, and Kos Town has an extensive system of cycle lanes. George's Bikes, Spetson 48

(☎ 22420 24157), has a good selection.

**By car and scooter** Cars can be rented at the airport and all the resorts. Kos Town outlets include Budget at Vassiléos Pávlou 31 (☎ 22420 28882) and AutoWay at Vassiléos Yeoryíou 22 (☎ 22420 25326, ⓦ autowaykos.gr). For a scooter, try Moto Harley at Kanári 42 (☎ 22420 27693, ⓦ moto-harley.nl).

# Kos Town

Home to over half of the island's population of just over 28,000, **Kos TOWN**, at the far eastern end, radiates out from the harbour and feels remarkably uncluttered. The first thing you see from an arriving ferry is a majestic **Knights' castle**, for once down at sea level, but the town also holds extensive **Hellenistic** and **Roman** remains. Only revealed by an earthquake in 1933, these were subsequently excavated by the Italians, who also planned the "garden suburbs" that extend to either side of the central grid. Elsewhere, sizeable expanses of open space or archeological zone alternate with a hotchpotch of Ottoman monuments and later mock-medieval, Art Deco-ish and Rationalist buildings, designed in two phases either side of the earthquake. As ever, they incorporate a "Foro Italico" – the Italian administrative complex next to the castle – and a Casa del Fascio (Fascist Headquarters).

A little square facing the castle holds the riven trunk of **Hippocrates' plane tree**, its branches propped up by scaffolding; at seven hundred years of age, it's one of the oldest trees in Europe, though it's far too young to have seen the great healer. Adjacent are two **Ottoman fountains** and the eighteenth-century **Hassan Pasha mosque**, also known as the Loggia Mosque; its ground floor – like that of the **Defterdar mosque** on central Platía Eleftherías – is taken up by rows of shops.

Ferry travellers in transit are effectively obliged to stay in Kos Town. It's a pretty good base, with decent hotels, the best restaurants on the island, reasonable public transport, and several car- and bike-rental agencies.

## The old town

The liveliest part of Kos Town is the thoroughly commercialized **old town**, which lines the pedestrianized street between the Italian market hall on Platía Eleftherías and Platía Dhiagóras. One of the few areas to survive the 1933 earthquake, today it's crammed with expensive tourist boutiques, cafés and snack-bars. About the only genuinely old thing remaining is a capped Turkish fountain with a calligraphic inscription, where Apéllou meets Eleftheríou Venizélou.

## The castle

April–Oct Mon 3.30–8pm, Tues–Sun 8am–7pm; Nov–March Tues–Sun 8.30am–2.30pm • €3

Known locally as "Nerantziás", the **castle** in Kos Town is reached via a causeway over its former moat, now filled in as an avenue and planted with palms. It's a splendid, tumbledown, overgrown old ruin, where once inside the gate, which turns out to lead to another broader moat with an inner fortress beyond, you're free to walk and stumble at your own peril over all sorts of walls, battlements and stairways, as well as the odd much more recent and unattractive concrete accretion. At the far end, you find yourself looking out over the ferry quays.

Built in stages between 1450 and 1514, the double citadel replaced a fourteenth-century fort deemed incapable of withstanding advances in medieval artillery. Few if any of the many cannonballs lying about were ever fired in anger; the castle surrendered without resistance after the marathon 1522 siege of Rhodes.

**5** (200m), Psalidhi, Áyios Fokás & Brós Thermá

# KOS TOWN

0 metres 200

**PLATÍAS**

| | |
|---|---|
| Ayías Paraskevís | D |
| Dhiagóras | F |
| "Dolphin" | A |
| Eleftherías | C |
| Kazoúli | B |
| K. Paeologou | E |

**■ ACCOMMODATION**

| | |
|---|---|
| Afendoulis | 4 |
| Aktis Art | 2 |
| Hotel Sonia | 1 |
| Theodhorou Beach | 5 |
| Triton | 3 |

**■ EATING & DRINKING**

| | |
|---|---|
| Aenaos | 3 |
| Ambavris | 9 |
| Barbas | 6 |
| Koako | 8 |
| Law-Court Café | 1 |
| Petrino | 4 |
| Pote tin Kyriaki | 5 |
| Special (arvanitakis) | 2 |
| Swedco | 7 |

**■ NIGHTLIFE**

| | |
|---|---|
| Fashion Club | 2 |
| Hamam Club | 3 |
| Mylos | 1 |

Yacht Marina

Trenáki to Asklepíon

Hydrofoil Jetty

Ferry & Catamaran Dock

Knights' Castle (Nerantziás)

Excursion Boats

Hippocrates' Plane Tree

Loggia

Turkish Bath

Agora

Old Synagogue

Porta tou Forou

Defterdar

Market

PUB LANES

PLESSA

DHIAKOU

Hippocrates Park

Port Police

Archeological Museum

Winter Cinema

Turkish Fountain

KTEL

Casa Romana

Hellenistic Baths

Ancient Stadium

Atik Nymphaíon

Western Excavations

Roman Odeion

Catholic Cemetery

Summer Cinema

ITALIAN QUARTER

ITALIAN QUARTER

8

Villages, Airport & Asklepíon

Ambavris & Platáni

## Archeological Museum

Platía Eleftherías • April–Oct Tues–Sun 8am–8pm; Nov–March Tues–Sun 8.30am–2.30pm • €3

Kos Town's Italian-built **archeological museum** has a predictable Latin bias. Centred on an atrium that holds a mosaic of Hippocrates welcoming Asklepios to Kos, it's almost entirely devoted to statuary, of which the best preserved and most prominently displayed are Roman rather than Greek. That said, the single most famous item, said to be a statue of Hippocrates, is indeed Hellenistic. With no captions to put the displays in historical context, the whole thing takes around fifteen minutes to explore.

### The agora

Unrestricted access in daylight hours

The largest single relic of ancient Kos, the **agora**, occupies a huge open site just back from the harbour. The man who laid it out in 366 BC, Hippodamus, was credited by Aristotle as having "invented the division of cities into blocks". Thanks to earthquakes between the second and sixth centuries AD, it's now a confusing jumble of ruins. Scattered through a delightful public park, however, abounding in bougainvillea and palmettos, it's a lovely area in which to stroll, admiring the crumbling walls, standing columns, and exposed mosaics.

### The western excavations

Unrestricted access in daylight hours

Set in pit-like gardens up to 4m below the street level of modern Kos Town, the so-called **western excavations** consist of two intersecting marble-paved streets as well as the Xystos or colonnade of a covered running track. Crumbling plastic canopies at either end of the L-shaped complex shelter **floor mosaics**.

Across Grigoríou toú Pémptou to the south, a small, restored Roman-era **odeion**, capable of seating 750 spectators in 14 rows, was built on the site of a similar Greek theatre.

### ACCOMMODATION

KOS TOWN

★ **Afendoulis** Evrypýlou 1 ☎ 22420 25321, ⓦ afendoulishotel.com. Large, balconied en-suite rooms – including a few family quads – with fridges, a/c and wi-fi, all at excellent prices. Alexis Zikas, brother Ippokrates and wife Dionysia really look after their guests, winning a loyal repeat clientele; top-quality breakfast at any reasonable hour. Credit cards accepted. Closed mid-Nov to mid-March. **€50**

**Aktis Art** Vassiléos Yeoryíou 7 ☎ 22420 47200, ⓦ kosaktis.gr. Designer hotel whose futuristic standard doubles or suites, in brown, grey and beige, all face the water. Bathrooms are naturally lit and have butler sinks. There's wi-fi, gym, conference area, seaside bar and affiliated restaurant. All year. **€200**

**Hotel Sonia** Irodhótou 9, cnr Omírou ☎ 22420 25594. Popular, friendly little hotel, across from the agora and formerly known as *Pension Alexis*. Its eleven wood-floored rooms have been thoroughly renovated with en-suite bathrooms, a/c and wi-fi; there's also a pleasant courtyard and bar. Run by the sister and niece of Alexis of the *Afendoulis*. Closed early Nov to April. **€60**

**Theodhorou Beach** 1200m from the centre, towards Psalídhi ☎ 22420 22280, ⓦ theodorouhotel.com. Generous-sized units with disabled access, including suites and a wing of self-catering studios. A leafy environment includes a lawn-pool at the back and a small "private" beach with the *Nostos* day-and-night café-bar. **€80**

**Triton** Vassiléos Yeoryíou 4 ☎ 22420 20040, ⓦ maritina.gr. Moderately upmarket, town-centre seafront hotel, part of a small local chain, with veneered floored rooms (not all with sea view) in a neutral decor. Bathrooms somewhat small; the ground-floor *Avanti* Italian restaurant and breakfast café is popular. **€80**

### EATING AND DRINKING

#### CAFÉS

**Aenaos** Platía Eleftherías ☎ 22420 26044. Join the largely local crowd at this café under the Defterdar mosque, and people-watch while refilling your Greek coffee from the traditional *bríki* used to brew it. They also serve a range of teas and flavoured hot chocolates. Daily 9am–late.

**Law-Court Café** Finikon. Some of the cheapest and best-brewed coffees in Kos are available (along with cold drinks) under the arches at the rear of the courthouse, a few paces from Hippocrates' plane tree; no sign outside, mostly civil-servant clientele. Daily 8am–8pm.

**Special (Arvanitakis)** Vassiléos Yeoryíou ☎22420 22087. This tiny hole-in-the-wall pastry and cake shop, right by the sea, also serves dynamite gelato. Daily 10am–7pm.

**Swedco** Vassiléos Pávlou 20 ☎22420 24154. Ultra-sleek outlet of the Rhodes café chain, with (pricey) sandwiches, hot drinks and decadent desserts, as well as internet access. Daily 10am–11pm.

## RESTAURANTS

★ **Ambavris** Vourína ☎22420 25696, ⓦampvris.gr. Top-notch restaurant, 500m south of the edge of town, in the eponymous suburb village. Skip the English-only à la carte menu, take the hint about mezédhes and let the house bring on their best. This changes seasonally but won't much exceed €25 (drink extra) for six plates – typically pinigoúri (bulgur pilaf), pikhtí (brawn), little fish, spicy loukánika, stuffed squash flowers and fáva. May–Oct, dinner only.

**Barbas** Evrypýlou 6 ☎693 71 42 802. Friendly restaurant, opposite Hotel Afendoulis (see opposite). Excellent grills, with giros at €6–7.50 and lamb for €9, as well as the odd seafood choice like octopus salad for €6, all served at cosy outdoor tables. Closed Nov–March. Daily

10am–12.30pm & 5pm–12.30am.

**Koako** Vassílios Yeoryíou 56 ☎22420 25645. This spartan-looking place, with a crisp minimalist terrace just steps from the sea at the south end of Kos Town, is a versatile all-rounder, handling grilled meat and fish, mezédhes and a few daily mayireftá with equal aplomb – all priced below €10 – without the usual multinational flags and photo-menus. Daily lunch & dinner, all year.

**Petrino** Platía Theológou 1 ☎22420 27251, ⓦpetrino .kosweb.com. Elegant garden-set place, which has recently re-invented itself as a "meze restaurant", with a menu that ranges through fish, shellfish, meat and the local hard cheese. Almost nothing costs over €10, though share a few plates and the bill mounts up. As well as the extensive outdoor seating, two cosy indoor salons allow year-round operation (dinner only); large groups should reserve. Dinner only, 6–11pm.

★ **Pote tin Kyriaki** Pissándhrou 9 ☎22420 27872. Kos's sole genuine ouzerí, whose creatively assembled menu (painstakingly written out in school exercise books) has delights such as shrimps, fried mussels or gávros, monastiriakí (Cretan "monk's" salad), as well as grilled chops and loukánika. Look out for the couscous-like pinigoúri, served with pork for €4. Summer Mon–Sat evenings only, winter Thurs–Sat evenings plus lunch.

**8**

## NIGHTLIFE AND ENTERTAINMENT

Kos Town has a hyperactive nightlife. Visitors from all over the island congregate each night in the so-called "Pub Lanes", Nafklírou and Dhiákou, filled with an ever-changing array of generally mediocre bars and clubs. There are newer, better nightlife areas around Platía Dhiagóra (mostly Greeks) and out at Aktí Zouroúdhi towards Lambi.

**Fashion Club** Kanari 2 ☎22420 22592. Beyond its large and very shiny front terrace on the west side of the inner port, this cavernous club is still among the very hottest on the island, noted for its light shows. Daily 8pm–late.

**Hammam Club** Platía Dhiagóra ☎22420 21444. The most stable and classy music bar in town, installed in a former Turkish bath that still holds its original oriental

decor. Chill-out sofas and outdoor seating, until a midnight noise curfew moves everyone indoors. Daily 6pm–late.

**Mylos** Aktí Zouroúdhi ☎22420 23235. Sprawling around an old seafront windmill, with some tables out on Lambi beach, Mylos is Kos Town's top day-and-night-bar, with both live music and DJs. Daily noon–late.

# The Asklepion

Tues–Sun: May–Oct 8am–6pm; Nov–April 8.30am–2.30pm • €3

Native son **Hippocrates** is justly celebrated on Kos; not only does he have a tree, a street, a park, a statue and an international medical institute named after him, but his purported **Asklepion**, 4km south of town and one of three in Greece, is a major attraction.

Although the Asklepion was in fact founded just after Hippocrates' death, the methods used and taught here were probably his. Both a sanctuary of Asklepios (god of healing, son of Apollo) and a renowned curative centre, its magnificent setting on three artificial terraces overlooking Anatolia reflects early concern with the therapeutic environment. Little now remains standing, owing to periodic earthquakes and the Knights filching masonry to build their castle. The lower terrace never held many buildings, being instead the venue for the observance of the Asklepieia – quadrennial athletic/musical competitions in honour of the god. Sacrifices to Asklepios were conducted at an **altar**, the oldest structure here, whose foundations are found near the

## HIPPOCRATES

**Hippocrates** (c.460–370 BC) is generally regarded as the father of scientific medicine, even if the Hippocratic oath, much altered from its original form, may well have nothing to do with him. Hippocrates was certainly born on Kos, probably at Astypalia near present-day Kéfalos, but otherwise confirmed details of his life are few. A great physician who travelled throughout the Classical Greek world, he spent at least part of his career teaching and practising on his native island. Numerous medical writings have been attributed to Hippocrates; *Airs, Waters and Places*, a treatise on the importance of environment on health, is generally thought to be his, but others are reckoned to be a compilation found in a medical library in Alexandria during the second century BC. His emphasis on good air and water, and the holistic approach of ancient Greek medicine, now seem positively contemporary.

middle of the second terrace. Just east, the Corinthian columns of a second-century-AD **Roman temple** were partially re-erected by nationalistic Italians. A monumental **staircase** leads from the altar to a second-century-BC **Doric temple** of Asklepios on the highest terrace, the last and grandest of the deity's local shrines.

# The east

The shoreline of the **eastern** half of Kos, in both directions from Kos Town, is fringed with good **beaches**, albeit interspersed with marshlands. The best, around Cape Psalídhi to the east and Lámbi, Tingáki and Marmári to the southwest, have attracted resort development, but with a bike especially (thanks to the coastal bike paths) it's usually possible to find a stretch of sand to yourself. Inland, the rugged **hills** cradle some delightful villages, though many are now sadly empty.

### Brós Thermá

East of Kos Town, beyond the huge hotels of Cape Psalídhi, the paved coast road ends after 12km. A dirt track continues for the final kilometre to the massively popular **hot springs** known as **Brós Thermá**. Best experienced at sunset or on moonlit nights, they issue from a grotto and flow through a trench into a shoreline pool formed by boulders, heating the seawater to an enjoyable temperature.

### Tingáki and Marmári

The coast southwest of Kos Town is home to the twin beach resorts of Tingáki and Marmári. There's almost always a breeze along this stretch, which makes it popular with windsurfers, while the profiles of Kálymnos, Psérimos and Turkey's Bodrum peninsula all make for spectacular offshore scenery. Heading for either resort from town, especially on a bike, the nicest and safest route is the minor road from the southwest corner of town.

A favourite with British travellers, **TINGÁKI** is 12km west of the harbour. Its long narrow beach of white sand improves, and becomes more separated from the frontage road, the further southwest you go. Thanks to the island of Psérimos just offshore, waves tend to stay small, and the warm shallow waters are ideal for children. There's little accommodation near the beach itself, though medium-sized hotels and studios are scattered amid the fields and cow pastures inland.

**MARMÁRI** lies another 3km along, beyond the **Alykí** salt marsh, which retains water – and throngs of migratory birds, including flamingos – until June after a wet winter. Marmári has a smaller built-up area than Tingáki, and the beach is broader, especially to the west where it forms little dunes.

### The Asfendhioú villages

The inland villages of **Mount Dhíkeos**, a handful of settlements collectively referred to as **Asfendhioú**, nestle amid the island's only natural forest. Together these communities give a good idea of what Kos looked like before tourism arrived, and all have been severely depopulated by the mad rush to the coast. They are accessible via the curvy side road from Zipári, 8km from Kos Town; an inconspicuous minor road to Lagoúdhi; or by the shorter access road for Pylí.

### Ziá

There's precious little left of the original village of **ZIÁ**, 7km inland from Tingáki, which now holds barely a dozen resident families. Instead, its heavily commercialized main street and spectacular sunsets make it the target of dozens of tour buses daily, and the general tattiness seems to increase year on year.

### Pylí

Both the contemporary village of **Pylí** and the separate ruins of the medieval town can be reached via the road through Lagoúdhi and Amanioú, or from beside the duck-patrolled Linopótis pond on the main island trunk road. Apart from its giant, lion-spouted cistern-fountain (the *piyí*), Pylí's other attraction is the **Harmýlio** ("Tomb of Harmylos"), a fenced-off, subterranean, niched vault that was probably a Hellenistic family tomb. **Paleó** (medieval) **Pylí**, 3km southeast of its modern descendant, was the Byzantine capital of Kos. It's an absolutely wonderful spot, perched on what's now a very isolated peak but still well below the crest of the island's central ridge. Opposite the end of the paved road up, a stair-path leads within fifteen minutes to the roof of the fort. En route you pass the remains of the abandoned town tumbling southwards down the slope.

### ACCOMMODATION                                                     THE EAST

**Grecotel Kos Imperial** Psalídhi ☎22420 58000, ⓦgrecotel.com. A superbly designed garden complex with tropical-river novelty pool and spa, where standard doubles and bungalows share decor (including music systems) and size (large). **€160**

**Oceanis Beach & Spa Resort** Psalídhi ☎22420 24641, ⓦoceanis-hotel.gr. Enormous beachfront hotel, very much geared towards families, with almost four hundred rooms, three pools (two saltwater), kids' club, on-site windsurf school, and an opulent garden environment. **€160**

### EATING AND DRINKING

⭐ **Ambeli** Tingáki ☎22420 69682. The "Vineyard" is a great local taverna, in a rural setting 2.5km east of the main beachfront crossroads. Pleasant seating indoors and out, and dishes including *pinigoúri*, *bekrí mezé*, *pikhtí*, *yaprákia* (the local *dolmádhes*) and *arnáki ambelourgoú*, washed down with wine from their own vineyard. Book ahead in peak season. Nov–April Fri & Sat dinner, Sun lunch; May–Oct lunch & dinner daily.

**Iy Palia Piyi** Pylí ☎22420 41510. Excellent taverna, in a superb setting beside a fountain fed by a natural

year-round spring in the upper part of Pylí, 100m west of the partly pedestrianized square and church. Inexpensive *soutzoukákia* grilled with onions, home-made *tzatzíki*, fried-vegetable mezédhes and local sweet red wine. Daily lunch & dinner.

⭐ **Oromedon** Ziá ☎22420 69983, ⓦpragmata.info /Oromedon_gb.htm. The best of Ziá's dozen tavernas, this Greek-patronized place serves good *pinigoúri*, mushrooms and local sausage on a roof terrace. Bill Clinton and the Greek and Turkish presidents have all eaten here. May–Oct daily lunch & dinner.

## The west

Near the desolate centre of the island, well sown with military installations, a pair of giant, adjacent roundabouts by the airport funnels traffic northwest towards **Mastihári**, northeast back towards town, southwest towards **Kéfalos** and southeast to **Kardhámena**. Most visitors are bound for the south-coast **beaches**, reached from the Kéfalos-bound turning.

### Mastihári

The least "packaged" and least expensive of the north-shore resorts, **MASTIHÁRI**, 8km north of the airport, has a shortish, broad beach extending west, with less frequented

dunes (and no sunbeds) towards the far end. Ferries and excursion boats from
Kálymnos (see p.574) moor close to the centre, which has the feel of a genuine town.

## Kardhámena
**KARDHÁMENA**, 31km from Kos Town and 8km southeast of the airport, is the island's
largest package resort after the capital itself. In summer, locals are vastly outnumbered
by boozing-and-bonking visitors, predominantly young Brits. A beach stretches to
either side – sandier to the southwest, intermittently reefy and hemmed in by a road
towards the northeast – but runaway development has banished any redeeming
qualities the place might have had. The main reason anyone not staying here would
bother to visit is to catch a boat to Níssyros (see p.554).

## South-coast beaches
The coastline west of Kardhámena boasts a series of scenic and secluded **south-facing
beaches**. Though each has a fanciful English name, they form essentially one long
stretch at the base of a cliff, accessed by successive footpaths down from the main road.
As the prevailing wind on the island is usually from the north, the water as a rule is
gloriously calm.

The longest, broadest and wildest of the beaches, "**Magic**", officially Polémi, has a
proper taverna above the car park, no jet-skis and a nudist zone ("**Exotic**") at its eastern
end. "**Sunny**", signposted as Psilós Gremmós and easily walkable from "Magic", has
another taverna and jet-skis; **Langádhes** is the cleanest and most picturesque, with
junipers tumbling off its dunes and more jet-skis. "**Paradise**", alias "**Bubble Beach**"
because of volcanic gas-vents in the tidal zone, is small and oversubscribed, with
wall-to-wall sunbeds and a large restaurant just above. Jet-ski-free "**Camel**" (Kamíla) is
the shortest and loneliest, protected by the steep, unpaved drive in past its hillside
taverna; the shore here is pure, fine sand, with good snorkelling to either side.

## Kamári
The westernmost resort on Kos, **KAMÁRI**, comes just before the high headland at the
island's western tip, and is essentially the shoreline annexe of the old town of Kéfalos.
More popular with families and older visitors than Kardhámena, Kamári may look
from the main road like a long and rather dispiriting strip, but the beach itself is good.

There's also a very lovely spot at its western end, 3km from the centre, where the
tiny **Kastrí** islet, topped by a little chapel, stands just off the **Áyios Stéfanos** headland.
A public access road, close to an abandoned Club Med, leads down to beaches either
side of a small peninsula, crowned with the remains of two triple-aisled, sixth-
century **basilicas**.

## The far west
The village of **KÉFALOS**, 43km from Kos Town, covers a bluff looking down the length
of the island. Aside from some lively **cafés** at the south end, it's a dull little place
mainly of note as a staging point for expeditions into the rugged **peninsula** that
terminates at **Cape Kríkello**.

The main highlights of a visit there, along the ridge road south, include **Panayía
Palatianí** Byzantine church amid the ruins of a larger ancient temple, 1km beyond the
village, and the Classical theatre (unrestricted access) and Hellenistic temple of **ancient
Astypalia**, 500m further via the side-path starting from an unlocked gate. A paved road
west just beyond Astypalia leads to windy **Áyios Theológos beach**, 7km from Kéfalos.

### ACCOMMODATION AND EATING — THE WEST

**Ayios Theologos Taverna** Ayios Theologos ☎697 45
03 556. High-quality taverna at the far western tip of the
island, enjoying incredible sunsets. A vast selection of fresh
home-grown produce brings in the crowds at weekends.
Lunch & dinner daily in summer, weekends only in
winter.

**Grand Café** Kamári ☎ 22420 71290. Large and very comfortable café, at the point where Kamári beach briefly disappears and the sea laps directly against the road, which as well as drinks serves top-quality pastries and sweets from the adjoining bakery. Winter weekends only, summer all day every day.

**Kali Kardia** Mastihári ☎ 22420 59289. Reliable taverna,

facing the ferry jetty, that's good for fresh fish and mezédhes as well as standards like stifádho, and great desserts. Almost all mains cost €8–10. All meals daily.

**Panorama Studios** Mastihári ☎ 22420 59019, ⓦ kospanorama.eu. Simple studio apartments with a/c, kitchenettes and sea-view balconies, above a nice little restaurant just steps from the beach. **€60**

# Psérimos

Were it not so close to Kos and Kálymnos, the little island of **PSÉRIMOS**, filled with remote beaches, might be idyllic. Throughout the season, so many excursion boats arrive that they've had to build a second jetty at little **AVLÁKIA** port. In midsummer, day-trippers blanket the main sandy beach that curves in front of Avlákia's thirty-odd houses and huge communal olive grove; even during May or late September you're guaranteed at least eighty outsiders daily (versus a permanent population of 25). Three other **beaches** are within easy reach: the clean sand-and-gravel strand at **Vathý** is a well-marked, thirty-minute walk east, starting from behind the *Taverna Iy Psérimos*. It takes 45 minutes of walking north along the main trans-island track to get to grubbier **Marathoúnda**, composed of pebbles. Best of all is **Grafiótissa**, a 300m-long beach of near-Caribbean quality half an hour's walk west of town.

## ARRIVAL AND DEPARTURE
PSÉRIMOS

**By ferry from Kálymnos** To spend the entire day on Psérimos, you'll have to take a day-trip from Póthia (Kálymnos); boats usually leave at 9.30am daily, and return at 5–6pm.

**By ferry from Kos** Boats from Kos Town operate triangle tours to Platý islet and somewhere on Kálymnos with only a brief stop on Psérimos.

## ACCOMMODATION AND EATING

**Studios Kalliston** Avlákia ☎ 22430 51540. Ten reasonable studios, most with sea views and some with a/c, facing a very broad segment of the beach from its eastern end. **€60**

**Taverna Manola** Avlákia ☎ 22430 51540. Although it looks more like a bar, and stays open late as the island's main social hub, this beachfront taverna, run by the same

management as *Studios Kalliston* (see above), serves good Greek standards and fresh seafood. Daily 9am–late.

**Tripolitis** Avlákia ☎ 22430 23196. Six simple en-suite studio apartments, three of which have sea views, upstairs from English-speaking *Anna's* café/snack-bar and directly across from the beach. Closed Nov–April. **€40**

# Astypálea

Geographically, historically and architecturally, **Astypálea** really belongs to the Cyclades – on a clear day you can see Anáfi or Amorgós far more easily than any of the other Dodecanese. Its inhabitants are descended from colonists brought from the Cyclades during the fifteenth century, after pirate raids had left the island depopulated, and supposedly Astypálea was only reassigned to the Ottomans after the Greek Revolution because the Great Powers had such a poor map at the 1830 and 1832 peace conferences.

Astypálea's main visitor attractions include a beautiful old **citadel** – not just the castle itself, but also the whitewashed village of **Hóra** beneath it – as well as several good, easily accessible **beaches**. The island may not immediately strike you as especially beautiful: many beaches along its heavily indented coastline have reef underfoot and periodic seaweed, while the windswept heights are covered in thornbush or dwarf juniper. Hundreds of sheep and goats manage to survive, while citrus groves and vegetable patches in the valleys signal a relative abundance of

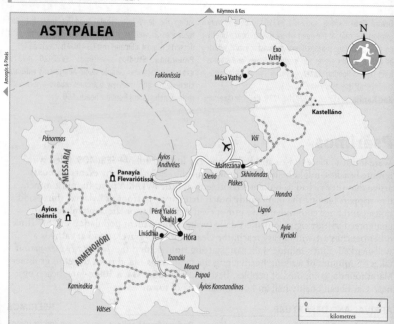

water. Besides the excellent local **cheese**, Astypálea is renowned for its **honey**, **fish** and **lobster**.

There is no **package tourism** on Astypálea, and its remoteness discourages casual trade. During the short, intense **midsummer season** (mid-July to early Sept), however, visitors vastly outnumber the 1500 permanent inhabitants. The one real drawback is that **transport** connections are so poor.

## ARRIVAL AND INFORMATION
ASTYPÁLEA

**By air** Astypálea's tiny airport, 8km east of Hóra and Péra Yialós, has infrequent connections to Athens (1 weekly) and to Léros, Kos and Rhodes, all on the same plane (2–3 weekly). Many hotels will pick up and drop off guests, and buses and taxis are available (see below).

**By ferry** Astypálea's main ferry port, at Áyios Andhréas, 7km north of Péra Yialós, is extremely inconvenient. There are no facilities whatsoever, and almost all boats arrive and depart in the dead of night. It's connected to Amorgós (2 weekly; 1hr 25min); Dhonoússa (3 weekly; 2hr 20min); Kálymnos (1 weekly; 2hr 15min); Kastellórizo (1 weekly; 15hr 10min); Kos (1 weekly; 3hr 35min); Náxos (3 weekly;

3hr 45min); Páros (3 weekly; 5hr); Pireás (4 weekly; 9hr 45min–11hr 35min); Rhodes (1 weekly; 9hr 10min); Sými (1 weekly; 8hr 25min); Tílos (1 weekly; 6hr 35min). In addition, just one boat, the *Nissos Kalymnos,* calls in at Péra Yialós, with connections to Kálymnos only (3 weekly; 2hr 45min).

**Travel agencies** Ferry tickets can be bought in Péra Yialós from Astypalea Tours (☎22430 61571) and Paradise (☎22430 61224).

**Tourist office** There's an information office in one of the windmills at the approach to Hóra (June–Sept daily 6–9pm; ☎22430 61412, �🌐astypalia.gr).

## GETTING AROUND

**By bus** Ten buses daily connect Péra Yialós with Hóra, Livádhia and Maltezána, and drop passengers at beaches along the way. A connecting bus takes passengers from the airport to Péra Yialós or Maltezána.

**By taxi** The island's only taxi (☎22430 61087) can't cope with passenger numbers in season. Fares are reasonable, at

around €10 from the airport to Péra Yialós.

**By car and scooter** In Péra Yialós from Lakis and Manolis (☎22430 61263), Tomaso (☎22430 61000, �🌐tomaso.gr) and Vergoulis (☎22430 61351), or through several island hotels.

# The west

The shape of Astypálea is often compared to a butterfly, in that it consists of two separate "wings" joined by a low narrow isthmus. The only major population centre, made up of the built-up strip that joins the waterfront villages of **Péra Yialós** and **Livádhia** by way of hilltop **Hóra**, is on the southeast coast of its **western** half, well away from both the ferry port and the airport.

## Péra Yialós

Astypálea was the first Dodecanese island occupied by the Italians, and the little harbour town of **PÉRA YIALÓS**, also known as **SKÁLA**, dates from the Italian era. Set in a deeply indented, steep-sided little bay, it's not where most inter-island ferries arrive (see opposite). Only at the head of the harbour, where a broadish gravel beach – fine for families with young children – fronts a row of seafront cafés and restaurants, is there much life or activity. A broad and uninteresting concrete quayside stretches along its southern shore, below Hóra, while the hillsides are dotted with houses and the odd small hotel.

### Archeological museum

June–Sept Tues–Sun 9am–1pm & 6–8.30pm; Oct–May Tues–Sun 8.30am–2.30pm • Free

Just back from the waterfront in the centre of Péra Yialós, the local **archeological museum** consists of a single room. Many of its local finds, spanning the Bronze Age to medieval times, are little more than fragments, but it does hold impressive goblets and vases unearthed from two Mycenaean tombs.

## Hóra

The delightful, very photogenic ensemble of **HÓRA**, accessible by road as well as steep stair-paths from Péra Yialós, neatly caps a high headland. Beneath the grey walls of the hilltop castle, the village itself is comprised of dazzling bright houses – many restored as holiday homes – threaded along intriguing narrow alleyways. The main approach road is lined with eight picturesque orange-roofed **windmills**.

### Kástro

Unrestricted access • Free

Astypálea's thirteenth-century **kástro**, among the finest in the Aegean, was erected not by the Knights of St John, but by the Venetian Quirini clan, and modified by the Ottomans after 1537. Rather than purpose-built battlements, its unique "walls" consisted instead of the stacked-up frontages of private houses. Until well into the twentieth century more than three hundred people lived inside, but depopulation and a severe 1956 earthquake combined to leave only a shell. Reached via a brightly whitewashed passageway beneath its main church of **Evangelístria Kastrianí**, the interior has been laid out with new pathways.

## Livádhia

The little resort village of **LIVÁDHIA** occupies the next bay along from Hóra. A long, straight and pleasant **beach**, albeit scruffy with dried vegetation, lines the waterfront, fringed by cafés, restaurants and low-key hotels. You can walk there from Hóra in fifteen minutes; be sure to take the road that drops down to the sea just beyond the Pylaia Boutique Hotel (see p.572). If you simply go down to the beach you won't realize quite how far this fertile valley stretches inland.

## Beyond Livádhia

When the beach at Livádhia is too busy, press on southwest for fifteen minutes on foot to reach the three small fine-pebble coves at **Tzanáki**. Beyond these, **Papoú** is an 80m fine-gravel strand accessible overland by a horrifically steep side track, and then a final path approach around a fenced-off farm.

8

The third large bay beyond Livádhia, **Áyios Konstandínos**, is a partly shaded, sand-and-gravel cove with a good seasonal taverna. Further afield, lonely **Vátses** and **Kaminákia** beaches are visited by a seasonal excursion boat from Péra Yialós. By land, **Vátses** has the easier dirt road and is 25 minutes by scooter from Livádhia; sandy, with a basic *kantína*, it's often windy. The track to **Kaminákia**, 8.5km from Livádhia, is rough and steep for the final 2km – best to go in a jeep – but the sheltered, clean and scenic cove, Astypálea's best, repays the effort.

## ACCOMMODATION

### PÉRA YIALÓS

**Akti Rooms** ☎ 22430 61114, ⓦ aktirooms.gr. Rather faded hotel in a beautiful hillside location near the Thalassa, offering cheap but minimally equipped rooms, not all with sea views, above a gorgeous terrace restaurant. **€55**

**Hotel Australia** ☎ 22430 61275 or 22430 61855, ⓔ pmariaki@hotmail.com. Plain but perfectly adequate en-suite rooms, with fans or a/c and balconies, just back from the harbourfront above a friendly little restaurant. **€60**

**Hotel Thalassa** ☎ 22430 59840, ⓦ stampalia.gr. The best accommodation in Péra Yialós, spilling down the hillside across from the castle, where the first access road down to the harbour drops from the coastal road. Open all year, it consists entirely of very comfortable suites and studios, with fabulous views but no direct access to the sea. **€125**

### HÓRA

**Kalderimi** ☎ 22430 59843, ⓦ kalderimi.gr. Smart modern complex, just beyond the *Pylaia Boutique Hotel* (see below) on the road out of Hóra, where the eleven impeccably appointed mock-trad a/c cottages (some large enough for families) hold all the lastest electronic gadgets. **€140**

**Kallichoron Studios** ☎ 22430 61934, ⓦ astypalea .com. Tasteful, upscale studios and one-bed apartments, close to the windmills at the edge of Hóra at the start of the road to Livádhia, all with flagstoned terrace and magnificent views of the citadel. Open all year, rates include breakfast. **€120**

**Pylaia Boutique Hotel** ☎ 22430 61070, ⓦ pylaiahotel .gr. Rather sumptuous new hotel, spilling down the hillside

### WESTERN ASTYPÁLEA

200m out of Hóra towards Livádhia, with friendly young management. Slightly too large to be really "boutique", it holds 25 spacious, stylish rooms and suites, most with outdoor space and great views, plus a pool and summer-only rooftop restaurant. Open all year, rates include breakfast. **€170**

★ **Studios Kilindra** ☎ 22430 61131, ⓦ astipalea .com.gr. Plush studios and galleried maisonettes, on the quiet west slope of Hóra, with a swimming pool and good breakfasts – units accommodate two to three people. Closed Jan–March. **€150**

### LIVÁDHIA

**Maganas** ☎ 22430 61468, ⓦ maganas.gr. Small, neat hotel, directly across from the beach on the frontage road, where the eight stiudios have a/c, kitchenettes and even tiny washing machines. **€60**

**Mouras Studios** ☎ 697 24 53 571, ⓔ mourass@otenet .gr. Very nice little set of individual rental units, right by the beach, each with its own kitchen and balcony, and arranged around a courtyard. Reserve ahead for best rates. **€50**

**To Yerani Studios** ☎ 22430 61484, ⓔ gerani72 @hotmail.com. Ten nicely maintained and very comfortable marble-floored studios, with kitchens and little terraces facing flower-filled gardens, a short walk from the sea behind the village's best taverna. Closed Nov–April. **€60**

**Venetos Studios** ☎ 22430 61490, ⓦ venetosstudios .gr. Several buildings scattered inland from the beach in a pleasant orchard at the base of the westerly hillside, and holding well-furnished studios and apartments of varying sizes. Closed Oct–April. **€60**

## EATING AND DRINKING

### PÉRA YIALÓS

**Akroyiali** ☎ 22430 61863. While the food here is pretty good, with a wide range of mezhédes and tasty cheese dishes, the prime reason this beachfront taverna is so full every night is its unbeatable setting, with tables spreading out onto the sand. Daily lunch & dinner.

**Australia** ☎ 22430 61275. Dependable, long-established favourite, beneath the eponymous hotel (see above) just back from the waterfront, with delicious seafood, and superbly prepared home-grown vegetable dishes. April–Nov daily lunch & dinner.

**Dapia Café** ☎ 22430 61590. The pick of the waterfront cafés, with a large well-shaded terrace overlooking the harbour and free wi-fi. Good for full breakfasts, crêpes, juices and infusions, as well as sunset drinks. Daily 10am–late.

★ **Maïstrali** ☎ 22430 61691. Welcoming, high-quality restaurant, with oblique sea views from the corner of the harbour. As well as rich stews like rabbit with tomato or chicken with yoghurt and mustard, for under €10, they also serve seafood dishes like lobster, scaly fish or shrimp saganaki. Daily lunch & dinner.

## HÓRA

**Barbarossa** ☎ 22430 61577. The only serious taverna in Hóra, just as the main street starts to climb towards the kástro. Popular for its warm, pleasant interior, and nice terrace, it serves hearty but generally unexceptional food, with rich meaty dishes like chicken with okra for €7.50 as well as more substantial seafood; the salads are disappointing. Daily noon–midnight.

## LIVÁDHIA

**Astropelos** ☎ 22430 61473. With its large shaded patio, this beachside taverna is a great place to linger over vegetable dishes like stuffed tomatoes, but the seafood can be expensive. June–Sept daily 11am–late.

★ **To Yerani** ☎ 22430 61484. Livádhia's best food, set inland from the little bridge in the middle of the beach, but still enjoying sea views from its large tiled terrace. Home-cooked specialities range from delicious courgette flowers with cheese for €4 or moussaka for €6 up to large meat grills. May–Oct daily 11am–late.

## KAMINÁKIA

**Linda** ☎ 697 21 29 088. Well-run beach taverna, which as well as offering honest, rustic fare (salads, fresh fish and a dish of the day) oversees a handful of sunbeds. Late June to early Sept, daily noon–6pm.

# The east

Astypálea's wilder and less populated **eastern** half is home to the island's airport and a small resort, **Maltezána**, but little else. Apart from a couple of south-coast beaches, the only day-trip worth making over here is the bumpy but spectacular drive out to the huge bay at **Mésa Vathý**.

## Stenó and Plákes

Two good but isolated beaches stand on the southern shore of Astypálea's slender central isthmus. At **Stenó** (meaning "narrow", in reference to the isthmus), inviting turquoise shallows stretch away from a sandy shore. There's only limited shade, courtesy of a few tamarisks, but a *kantína* opens up in high summer.

Another kilometre east, the much quieter beach at **Plákes** has no facilities and can only be accessed by walking a few hundred metres down from the main road. It's at the end of the airport runways, but with barely a plane a day that's no problem.

## Maltezána

The little resort of **MALTEZÁNA**, Astypálea's second-largest settlement, is 9km east of Péra Yialós, under 1km from the airport. Its official name is **ANÁLIPSI**, but it's universally known by the nickname it acquired thanks to medieval Maltese pirates. It's a nice enough spot, with a narrow, exposed, packed-sand beach, a small fishing port at its eastern end, and a good view south to islets.

### ACCOMMODATION AND EATING                                      MALTEZÁNA

**Analipsi** ☎ 22430 61446. Maltezána's best taverna, also known as *Ilias-Irini's*, is a tranquil little space facing the jetty that doubles as the fishermen's *kafenío*. The food – fried squid, bean soup – is simple but wholesome; confirm prices and portion size of the often frozen seafood. Feb–Dec daily 11am–9pm.

**Maltezana Beach** ☎ 22430 61558, 🌐 maltezanabeach.gr. Astypálea's largest hotel, with 48 large, well-appointed bungalow-rooms – five of which are family-sized apartments – plus a pool and on-site restaurant. Closed mid-Sept to Easter. **€100**

**Villa Barbara** ☎ 22430 61448. A dozen very spruce blue-and-white studios, all with kitchen and balcony and sleeping 2–3, set a short way back from the beach. Closed Oct to mid-May. **€50**

## Mésa Vathý

Although the main road turns to dirt east of Maltezána, it remains just about passable in an ordinary car, and snakes its way onwards across the exposed hillsides all the way to **MÉSA VATHÝ**, at the head of an utterly magnificent west-facing bay 23km out from Hóra. Much the best way to arrive at this sleepy fishing hamlet would be by boat; it's a popular anchorage for pleasure yachts in summer. There's no town, just one little taverna; walk onwards from the end of the road to reach a small beach.

# Kálymnos

Despite its size and beauty, the island of **KÁLYMNOS** has long been overshadowed by Kos. Kálymnos fought in the Trojan War as a vassal of its southern neighbour, and to this day its tourist industry remains largely dependent on the overspill – and the airport – of Kos.

In most respects, however, Kálymnos is very unlike Kos. It's much more mountainous, consisting of three high limestone ridges that fan away from the continuous rugged cliffs of its west coast, to create two long sloping valleys that hold most of its settlements and agricultural land.

The island's capital and largest town, the busy port of **Póthia**, faces Kos from the midpoint of its southern shoreline. Most visitors head instead for the west coast, where a handful of small resorts have struggled to survive the collapse of a short-lived experiment in mass tourism. The pick of the pack, **Myrtiés**, stands close to some attractive little beaches. This craggy shoreline has found deserved fame among **climbers** and **hikers**, who keep businesses ticking along in the cooler spring and autumn months.

For a beach holiday, you'd do better to head for the separate islet of **Télendhos**, (a spectacular sight at sunset), or further north up the coast to **Emboriós**.

The prosperity of Kálymnos traditionally rested on its **sponge industry** (see box, p.576), but blights have now wiped out almost all of the eastern Mediterranean's sponges. Only a few boats of the island's thirty-strong fleet remain in use, and most of the sponges sold behind the harbour are imported from Asia and the Caribbean.

## ARRIVAL AND INFORMATION
KÁLYMNOS

**By air** Kálymnos's small airport, 6km northwest of Póthia, is served only by Olympic Air flights to and from Athens (1–2 daily).

**By ferry** Ferries from Póthia serve the following islands: Agathoníssi (5 weekly; 2hr 15min–5hr 30min); Arkioi (4 weekly; 4hr 20min); Astypálea (3 weekly; 2hr 15min–2hr 45min); Kastelórizo (2 weekly; 10hr 15min–13hr); Kos (Kos Town) (2–5 daily; 30min–1hr); Kos (Mastihari) (6 daily; 20min–1hr); Léros (1–2 daily; 50min–1hr 20min); Lipsi (2–3 daily; 1hr 20min); Náxos (1 weekly; 6hr 55min); Níssyros (2 weekly; 2hr 50min); Páros (1 weekly; 8hr 30min);

Pátmos (2–4 daily; 1hr 40min–3hr 25min); Pireás (5 weekly; 9hr 40min–14hr 10min); Pserimos (3 weekly; 20min); Rhodes (2–4 daily; 2hr 40min–8hr 15min); Sámos (1–2 daily; 2hr 50min–6hr 50min); Sými (11 weekly; 10min–6hr 20min); Tílos (2 weekly; 4hr 20min). There are frequent ferries to Télendhos from Myrtiés (see above).

**Travel agents** Sofia Kouremeti (☎22430 23700) and Mahias Travel (☎22430 22909).

**Tourist office** The municipal tourist office faces the ferry jetty in Póthia (Mon–Fri 8am–3pm; ☎22430 50956, ⓦ kalymnos-isl.gr).

## GETTING AROUND

**By bus** Buses to the west-coast resorts (6 daily in season; 30min), and also northwest to Emboriós (2 daily; 50min) and east to Vathýs (4 daily; 30min), run from two terminals beside the municipal "palace".

**Taxis** Shared taxis, available at Platía Kyprou, cost less

than normal taxis.

**By car and scooter** Car rental outlets along Póthia quay include the recommended Auto Market (☎22430 51780, ⓦ kalymnoscars.gr), while for scooters check out Kostas (☎22430 50110), very close to the tourist office.

# Póthia

The long curving waterfront of **PÓTHIA**, Kálymnos's main town and port, may not be architecturally distinguished, but arrayed around a huge curving bay it looks fabulous at sunset. The town itself remains vibrant year-round, even if it's not really a tourist destination in its own right. With its houses marching up the valley inland or arrayed in tiers along the surrounding hillsides, it forms a natural amphitheatre that readily fills with noise, whether from souped-up motorbikes or summer sound-systems. As well as the usual Italian-era "palace", at the centre of the bay, Póthia also boasts backstreets lined with elegant **Neoclassical houses**, painted the traditional pink or ochre.

Sprawled to either side of the road to the west coast, the built-up area of Póthia stretches northwest up the valley to the suburb of **Mýli**. The whitewashed battlements of the Knights' **Kástro Khryssoheriás** (unrestricted access), 1.2km along, offer wonderful views over town towards Kos. Another 1.5km up, the former island capital, **Hóra**, is still a large, busy village.

## Archeological Museum of Kálymnos

Evangelístria • Daily except Mon: May to mid-Sept 8.30am–3pm; mid-Sept to May 9.30am–12.30pm • €3

Tucked away in an unremarkable and hard-to-find new building on Póthia's western hillside, Kálymnos's **Archeological Museum** provides an excellent overview of local history. Everything is beautifully displayed, with very helpful captions in both Greek and English, and many of its artefacts are quite stunning. Its greatest treasures, discovered underwater during the 1990s, are a larger-than-life cast bronze figure of a woman draped in a chiton, thought to date from the second century BC, and the well-preserved bronze head of a ruler, which may have formed part of a colossal equestrian statue.

## Municipal Nautical and Folklore Museum

Daily 10am–1pm • €2

Kálymnos's **Municipal Nautical and Folklore Museum**, very near the ferry port on the seaward side of Khristós cathedral, focuses on the sponge-fishing past. A large photo shows Póthia in the 1880s, with no quay, jetty, roads or sumptuous mansions, and with most of the population still up in Hóra. You can also see horribly primitive divers' breathing apparatuses, and "cages" designed to keep propellers from cutting air lines.

## Péra Kástro

Hóra • Unrestricted daylight access • Free

The thirteenth-century Byzantine citadel-town of **Péra Kástro**, a magnificent fortified enclave atop the impressive crag that towers over Hóra, originally served as a refuge from seaborne raiders. Appropriated by the Knights of St John, it remained inhabited until the late 1700s. It's now reached by a steep stair-path that climbs from the eastern edge of the village.

Once you've passed through the massive gate and perimeter walls, you're faced with yet more stiff climbing, now through a jumble of overgrown ruins, tumbled stonework, and wildflowers, interspersed with the odd paved walkway. The views are tremendous, but the true highlights are the nine scattered **medieval chapels**, the only complete buildings to survive. Re-roofed and freshly whitewashed, several still hold faded frescoes.

## ACCOMMODATION
### PÓTHIA

**Arhondiko** Áyios Nikólaos ☎ 22430 24051. Much the most basic option near the port, this refurbished mansion on the southwest quay is the family home of an elderly couple who speak little English, and remains open year-round. Plain rooms with pleasant views. **€45**

**Hotel Panorama** Amoudhára ☎ 22430 23138, ⓦ panorama-kalymnos.gr. Simple, well-kept hotel, high on the hillside west of the harbour, where all thirteen en-suite rooms have air conditioning and balconies overlooking the port. There's also a pleasant breakfast salon. Closed Nov–March. **€50**

★ **Villa Melina** Enoria Evangelístria ☎ 22430 22682, ⓦ villa-melina.com. Póthia's quietest and most elegant hotel, set in attractive gardens near the archeological

## SPONGES AND SPONGE-DIVING

**Sponges** are colonies of microscopic marine organisms that excrete a fibrous skeleton. The living sponges that can be seen throughout the Aegean as black, melon-sized blobs, anchored to rocks in three to ten metres of water, are mostly "wild" sponges, impossible to clean or shape with shears. Kalymnian divers seek out "tame" sponges, which are much softer, more pliable, and dwell thirty to forty metres deep.

Sponge-fishers were originally **free divers**; weighted with a rock, they'd collect sponges from the seabed on a single breath before being hauled back up to the surface. Starting in the late nineteenth century, however, divers were fitted with heavy, insulated suits (*skáfandhro*). Breathing through an air-feed line connected to compressors aboard the factory boats, they could now attain depths of up to 70m. However, this resulted in the first cases of the "bends". When divers came up too quickly, the dissolved air in their bloodstream bubbled out of solution – with catastrophic results. Roughly half of those early pioneers would leave with the fleets in spring but fail to return in autumn. Some were buried at sea, others, it's said, buried alive, up to their necks in hot sand, to provide slight relief from the excruciating pain of nitrogen bubbles in the joints.

By the time the malady became understood, during World War I, thousands of Kalymnians had died, with many survivors paralyzed, deaf or blind. Even though the *skáfandhro* was banned elsewhere as the obvious culprit, it remained in use here until after World War II. After the first **decompression chambers** and diving schools reached Greece, in the 1950s, the seabed was stripped with ruthless efficiency, and the sponge fleets forced to hunt further from home.

Even the "tame" sponge is unusable until **processed**. The smelly organic matter and external membrane is thrashed out of them, traditionally by being trodden on the boat deck, and then they're tossed for a day or so in a vat of hot sea-water. Visitors to Póthia's remaining handful of workshops can still watch the sponge-vats spin; in the old days, the divers simply made a "necklace" of their catch and trailed it in the sea behind the boat.

To suit modern tastes, some sponges are bleached to a pale yellow colour with nitric acid. That weakens the fibres, however, so it's best to buy the more durable, natural-brown ones.

museum, just inland from the eastern side of the port. The pink, century-old Italianate villa holds seven high-ceilinged, bug-screened, wood-floored rooms, while a further thirteen studios and apartments, sleeping up to six, are laid out around the large swimming pool behind. There's a friendly and very helpful family atmosphere, especially around the communal, outdoor breakfast table. Open all year. **€60**

### EATING AND DRINKING

**Kafenes** Khristós ☎ 22430 28727. This pavement café, close to the county "palace" in the centre of the harbour, is always held thanks to its generous, tasty salads, seafood, local goat cheese and bulk wine. Be sure to try the €6 "crab balls". Daily 8am–late.

**Taverna Pandelis** Áyios Nikólaos ☎ 22430 51508. Large but inconspicuous restaurant, tucked into a cul-de-sac behind the waterfront *Olympic Hotel*. Dependably good meat and fish grills – ask for the daily catch – as well as *mezédhes*. Daily lunch & dinner.

★ **Xefteris Khristós** ☎ 22430 28642. Century-old, family-run restaurant, a block inland from the waterfront east of the Italian "palace". The dining room is utterly plain, more like a large garage, and it's next to the same owners' loud garden-set music bar, but the traditional local food is superb, with dishes including stewed chickpeas, and *mouourí*, shredded lamb with rice. Daily lunch & dinner.

**Zaharoplastio O Mihalaras** Áyios Nikólaos. This wonderful local cake shop, a must for any fan of Greek sweetmeats, has two premises in Póthia. The traditional original is on the harbourfront close to the "palace", while there's *a* modern annexe near the ferry jetty. Daily 8am–6pm.

## Vathýs and Rína

Ten kilometres northeast of Póthia, and accessed via an initially dispiriting coastal road, the long, fertile valley known as **VATHÝS** is Kálymnos' agricultural heartland. Its orange and tangerine groves make a startling contrast to the mineral greys and ochres of the surrounding hills, but visitors only pass this way to visit the fjord port of **RÍNA** at its southeastern end. Set at the end of a long slender inlet, Rína remains a popular stopover with yachties, and can also be reached by taxi-boats from Póthia. It's a very scenic spot, with tiny little Christian basilicas perched on the cliffs to either side, while the total lack of a beach keeps the crowds down. This safe anchorage has been in use since Neolithic times; several caves show signs of ancient occupation.

| ACCOMMODATION AND EATING | VATHÝS AND RÍNA |
|---|---|

**Galini Hotel Restaurant** Rína ☎ 22430 31241, ⓦ galinihotelvathikalymnou.com. Of the three similar, largely open-air seafood restaurants clustered around the harbour at Rína, only the friendly *Galina* also doubles as a hotel, charging bargain B&B rates for its clean, simple sea-view rooms. €30

# Northern Kálymnos

Fringed with wildflowers, and backed by mighty cliffs, it's great **hiking** and **climbing** territory. **Emboriós** at road's end makes a great overnight stop, or you can simply complete a round-island car or scooter tour by heading inland from **Aryinónda**, further south, and making your way back to Póthia via Vathýs (see p.576).

### Aryinónda to Emboriós

**ARYINÓNDA** itself, 5km beyond Massoúri at the head of its own deeply indented bay, has a clean pebble beach, plus a couple of small tavernas. Keep heading north along the west coast from here to find several more splendid, isolated beaches, including **Áyios Nikólaos** and **Kalamiés**. The village of **EMBORIÓS**, at the end of the bus line 20km out from Póthia, is a pretty little spot that offers a reasonable gravel-and-sand beach, and a scattering of apartments and tavernas. The little jetty in the middle is served by excursion boats from Myrtiés, which only run when demand is high enough.

A hundred metres beyond Emboriós, reached by a detour inland of the church, the next cove along holds the similar, goat-patrolled **Asprokykliá beach**. Follow the rough dirt track above Asprokykliá to the isthmus by the fish farm, then walk fifteen minutes north on path and track to reach **Aptíki**, a smallish but perfectly formed pea-gravel cove.

### Paliónissos and around

From Skália, 1km or so short of Emboriós, a newly paved road – signposted only in Greek – switchbacks up the west flank of the island and back down the other side. A steep but safe 5km drive, it stops short of the eastern shoreline, leaving visitors to walk the final couple of hundred metres along a rough track.

Set at the head of another extravagantly indented fjord-like bay, the yacht anchorage of **Paliónissos** is more usually reached by excursion boats from Rína (see p.576). It boasts an ample crescent of shingle beach, with a taverna to either side.

| ACCOMMODATION AND EATING | NORTHERN KÁLYMNOS |
|---|---|

★ **Harry's Paradise** Emboriós ☎ 22430 40062, ⓦ harrys-paradise.gr. This lovely taverna, set behind gorgeous flower-filled gardens a short walk from the beach, serves delicious home-cooked traditional food for all meals, using produce from their own fields. Their small hotel annex alongside offers simple but great-value air-conditioned en-suite studios, each individually themed and equipped with a kitchenette and balcony, and they rent out a slightly more expensive renovated cottage. Closed Dec–March. Daily 9am–9pm. €45

# The west coast

The mountainous headland that fills Kálymnos's southwest corner is largely inaccessible to visitors. From the moment the island's **west coast** can be reached by road, however, the shoreline is lined by a succession of small beach communities. Although several set out to turn themselves into beach resorts around the turn of the millennium, only **Myrtiés** and **Massoúri** have thrived enough to make worthwhile bases.

## Myrtiés to Armeós

Beach tourism on Kálymnos is most heavily concentrated in the twin resorts of **MYRTIÉS** and **MASSOÚRI**. Occupying neighbouring coves that start 8km northwest of Póthia, they face across to towering Télendhos islet (see below), and enjoy dramatic **sunsets**.

They're easy enough to reach on the island's main road, though once it's crossed the island to Pánormos the road has to climb the Kamári pass before it can zigzag back down to the sea. A lengthy one-way loop then leads drivers through the two resorts. There's no significant gap in the commercial strip of restaurants and hotels that runs through them both, 50m up from the beach, and neither has a historic core or town centre.

The narrow, pebbly **beach** at Myrtiés has a marina at its southern end and the small concrete jetty used by the Télendhos ferries in the middle. The beach at Massoúri, ten minutes' walk north, is broader and sandier; the largest and liveliest on the island, it has a noisy beach-bar vibe in summer. There's also an all-sand beach at **Melitsáhas** cove, 500m south of Myrtiés, but its surroundings have become very run-down; don't reckon on staying there.

Another kilometre north of Massoúri, the coastal village of **Armeós** is the terminus for most local buses. In low season especially, it tends to be dominated by European **rock-climbers**. Several popular cliffs soar overhead – look for the route-inscribed columns at their base – and various businesses cater to climbers' needs.

### ACCOMMODATION                                                    THE WEST COAST

★ **Acroyali** Myrtiés ☎ 22430 47521 or 21036 22688, ⓦ acroyali.gr. Six clean, well-designed apartments, right on the beach, with unfussy furnishings and spacious sea-view balconies. Each sleeps two adults and two kids; book well in advance. There's also an on-site restaurant. Closed Dec–March. **€60**

**Apollonia Hotel Apartments** Massoúri ☎ 22430 48094, ⓦ apollonia-kalymnos.gr. Large, very spruce studio-format hotel, close to the beach at Massoúri. The units are slightly bland, but they're air-conditioned, and have nice big balconies with great views. Closed Dec–Feb. **€50**

**Hotel Atlantis** Myrtiés ☎ 22430 47497, ⓦ atlantis-kalymnos.gr. Eighteen pleasant and well-located studios and apartments, with living room, kitchen and balconies looking across to Télendhos. Closed Nov–March. **€50**

**Hotel Philoxenia** Armeós ☎ 22430 59310, ⓦ philoxenia-kalymnos.com. Simple but good-value hotel, in prime climbing territory at the foot of the roadside hills ten minutes' walk north of Massoúri. Plain clean rooms with large balconies, plus a nice pool with snack bar; ask in advance if you want dinner. Closed Nov–April. **€50**

### EATING AND DRINKING

**Kokkinidis** Massoúri. Terrace restaurant, perched just above the main road in the centre of Massoúri, with nice views and a good menu of Greek and Mediterranean dishes, including a whole roast chicken for two at €15. Daily lunch & dinner.

**To Steki tis Fanis** Linária ☎ 22430 47317. Friendly family restaurant, in an old mansion on the hillside overlooking Linária beach. Local specialities such as *mermizéli* (salad of greens, *kopanistí* and barley rusks) and ample vegetarian starters, but mains quality varies. May–Oct, dinner only.

**Tsopanakos** Armeós ☎ 22430 47929. This friendly meat specialist is the best old-school taverna to survive on the west coast. Whether on the lovely terrace in summer, or in the cosy indoor dining room in winter, feast on fresh meat and cheese dishes from island-grazed goats. Daily noon–9pm.

## Télendhos

The towering pyramid-shaped islet of **TÉLENDHOS**, silhouetted at sunset a few hundred metres west of Myrtiés, was severed from Kálymnos by a cataclysmic earthquake in 554 AD. Car-free, home to a mere handful of year-round inhabitants, and blissfully tranquil, it's the single most compelling destination for Kálymnos visitors, and the short row of hotels and restaurants on its east-facing shore makes it a great place to spend a few nights. Regular little boat-buses shuttle across the narrow straits between Myrtiés and Télendhos (every 30min 8am–midnight; €2); it's said that somewhere far below, an ancient town lies submerged.

It only takes a few minutes to explore the little built-up strip that stretches in both directions from the boat landing. A narrow beach of reasonable sand runs along the straight seafront, and the calm shallow water is ideal for kids. Kayaks and beach toys are available for rent, while tousled tamarisks provide shade.

To find a more secluded beach, simply keep walking. A few hundred metres north – head right from the boat landing, and keep going after the paved coastal roadway peters out to become a dirt path – nudist **Paradise** beach is peaceful and sheltered, but at its best in the morning, before the sun disappears for good behind the mountain. A ten-minute walk southwest of the village, following a footpath over the ridge, will bring you to the pebble beach at **Hokhlakás**, a scenic but more exposed spot where the sea tends to be much rougher.

While all the shoreline buildings are of modern construction, abundant ruins are scattered slightly further afield. Closest to the village, north of the boat landing, a seafront field holds the ruined outline of the thirteenth-century monastery of **Áyios Vassílios**. On the hillside immediately above Hokhlakás, **Ayía Triádha** was originally an enormous basilica, though now just a few stones survive. Further up the slopes, wherever you look, giant Cyclopean caves burrow deep into the foot of the central massif. Setting out to hike right round Télendhos would be a mistake; it's a long and exposed walk with little reward. Devote an hour or two, however, to investigating the islet's southwest corner, a little low-lying afterthought. Follow the footpaths through the woods, signed to "Early Christian Necropolis", and in addition to some intact arched sixth-century tombs you'll come to a perfectly sheltered sandy cove that's ideal for swimming and snorkelling.

**8**

## ACCOMMODATION
TÉLENDHOS

**Hotel Porto Potha** ☎ 22430 47321, ⊛ telendoshotel.gr. Friendly hotel on the hillside just north of *On The Rocks* (see p.574), with twelve comfortable and spacious guest rooms, eight self-catering studios alongside, and a large pool, plus what amounts to a private beach. Special offers for hikers and climbers in low season. Closed late Oct to March. **€50**

**On the Rocks** ☎ 22430 48260, ⊛ otr.telendos.com. Three superbly appointed en-suite rooms, with balconies and sea views, above the beachfront restaurant 200m

north of the ferry jetty (see p.574). One can hold a family of four. Breakfast – and kayaks – available. The same friendly owners also rent a studio near Hokhlakás beach, with double-glazing, kitchen, bug screens and internet. Free boat connection from Mastihári on Kos. Closed Dec–March. **€50**

**Zorba's** ☎ 22430 48660. Very simple en-suite rooms at bargain prices, above a reasonable taverna a short walk south from the ferry jetty. **€30**

## EATING AND DRINKING

**Barba Stathis** ☎ 22430 47953. Also known as *Tassia's*, this welcoming place is just behind *Zorba's* (see p.574) en route to Hokhlakás. Barbecue every night, and daily specials like flounder fillet or fresh-made dolmades. Daily 11am–late.

**On the Rocks** ☎ 22430 48260, ⊛ otr.telendos.com. Very pleasant restaurant, with a shaded patio overlooking the beach not far north of the ferry jetty, and run by a very friendly Greek-Australian family. A full menu of fresh fish

and meat dishes, typically costing around €10, plus pizzas and burgers, Greek specialities, and lovely home-made desserts. Wednesday night is Greek barbecue, with music and dancing. It also holds a lively bar. Daily 9am–late.

**Plaka** Next door to, and slightly cheaper than, *On the Rocks* (see p.574), this large vine-covered terrace, poised just above the beach, is a great place to enjoy inexpensive local dishes such as goat with tomato sauce, or fresh octopus, for under €10. Daily lunch & dinner.

# Léros

As the island of **LÉROS** is indented with deep, sheltered bays, lined with little settlements, it doesn't have an obvious "capital". Ferries arrive at both **Lakkí** on the west coast and **Ayía Marína** on the east, but neither is recommended as a place to stay. Instead visitors congregate in the resorts of **Pandélli** and **Álinda**, and in more refined

**Plátanos** up on the hillside. While Léros can be very attractive, however, it doesn't hold spectacular **beaches**, so tourism remains relatively low-key.

The island still bears traces of the **Battle of Léros** of November 1943, when German paratroops displaced a Commonwealth division that had occupied Léros following the Italian capitulation. Bomb nose-cones and shell casings turn up as gaily painted garden ornaments, or do duty as gateposts. After the war, the local economy relied on prisons and sanatoria in former Italian military buildings. During the civil war and the later junta, leftists were confined to a notorious **detention centre** at Parthéni, while **hospitals** warehoused intractable psychiatric cases and mentally handicapped children. In 1989, a major scandal exposed conditions in the asylums; most wards were eventually closed.

## ARRIVAL AND DEPARTURE
LÉROS

**By air** A tiny airport near the island's northern tip is served by twice-weekly flights to Astypálea, Kos and Rhodes.

**By ferry** Large ferries and the *Dodekanisos Pride* catamaran arrive at Lakkí; smaller ferries and the *Dodekanisos Express* arrive at Ayía Marína. Destinations served: Agathoníssi (5 weekly; 1hr 10min–4hr); Arkí (5 weekly; 2hr 50min); Kálymnos (1–2 daily; 45min–1hr 15min); Kos (1–3 daily; 1hr 25min–3hr); Lipsí (2–3 daily;

20min–1hr); Pátmos (2–4 daily; 40min–1hr 55min); Pireás (3 weekly; 9–11hr); Rhodes (1–2 daily; 4hr–5hr 15min); Samos (1–2 daily; 1hr 55min–5hr 20min); Sými (6 weekly; 3hr 10min–5hr 50min); Syros (2 weekly; 5hr 30min).

**Travel agencies** Aegean Travel, 9 King George Ave, Lakkí (☎ 22470 26000, ☻ aegeantravel.gr); Kastis Travel, Ayía Marína (☎ 22470 22140).

## GETTING AROUND

**By bus** Regular buses from the main taxi rank in Platanós run north via Ayía Marína, Álinda and the airport to Parthéni, and south to Lakkí and Xirókambos.

**Car and scooter rental** Motoland (Pandélli, ☎ 22470

24103; Álinda, ☎ 22470 24584) and Rent A Car Léros (Lakkí, ☎ 22470 22330). Take care if you rent a scooter – Lerian roads are particularly narrow, potholed and gravel-strewn, and the low-slung, fat-tyred bikes on offer don't cope well.

# Lakkí

Set in a hugely indented bay on Léros's southwest coast, the unusual town of **LAKKÍ** is the arrival port for all the island's large **ferries**. Built in the 1930s as a model town to house 7500 civilian dependants of an adjacent Italian naval base, it's now an incongruous under-populated relic. Sweeping boulevards, out of all proportion to the traffic they ever see, are lined with Stream Line Modern edifices (see box, p.582) including a round-fronted cinema, but the entire seafront tends to be devoid of life even in high season. It does have a handful of hotels and restaurants, but none is worth recommending.

Lakkí's nearest approximation to a beach, sand-and-gravel **Kouloúki** 500m west, holds ample trees for shade and supports a seasonal taverna. A kilometre or so beyond, **Merikiá** is a little nicer, and has two tavernas.

## War Museum
Merikiá • Daily 10am–1pm • €3

An interesting little **War Museum**, set in two long arched tunnels that burrow deep into the hillside close to Merikiá beach, 2km west of Lakkí, commemorates the 1943 Battle of Léros. Part of an enormous Italian-built subterranean complex, the

## ITALIAN ARCHITECTURE IN THE DODECANESE

The architectural heritage left by the Italian domination in the Dodecanese has only recently begun to be appreciated. Many structures had been allowed to deteriorate, if not abandoned, by Greeks who would rather forget the entire Italian legacy.

Although the buildings are often dubbed "Art Deco", and some contain elements of that style, most are properly classed as **Rationalist** (or in the case of Léros, **Stream Line Modern**). They drew on various post-World War I architectural, artistic and political trends across Europe, particularly Novecento (a sort of Neoclassicism), the collectivist ideologies of the time, and the paintings of Giorgio di Chirico. The school's purest expressions tended to have grid-arrays of windows (or walls entirely of glass); tall, narrow ground-level arcades; rounded-off bulwarks; and either a uniform brick surface or grooved/patterned concrete. As well as in Italy and Greece, examples can still be found as far afield as Moscow or London (underground stations and blocks of flats), Los Angeles (apartment buildings) and Ethiopia (cinemas).

Italy initially attempted to create a hybrid of Rationalist style and local vernacular elements in the Dodecanese, both real and semi-mythical, to evoke a supposed generic "Mediterranean-ness". Every Italian-claimed island had at least one specimen in this "**protectorate**" style, usually the gendarme station, post office, covered market or governor's mansion, but only on the most populous or strategic islands were plans drawn up for sweeping urban re-ordering.

The years from 1936 to 1941 saw an intensified Fascist imperial ideology, an increased reference to the heritage of the Romans and their purported successors the Knights, and the replacement of the "protectorate" style with that of the "**conqueror**". This involved "**purification**", the stripping of many public buildings in Rhodes (though not, curiously, in Kos) of their orientalist ornamentation, its replacement with a cladding of porous stone to match medieval buildings in the old town, plus a monumental severity – blending Neoclassicism and modernism – and rigid symmetry to match institutional buildings (especially Fascist Party headquarters) and public squares across Italy.

tunnels are crammed with barely labelled World War II documents, models, machine guns and assorted military hardware. To make sense of it all, head first to the far end and watch the archival footage.

## Xirókambos

The fishing port of **XIRÓKAMBOS**, 5km south of Lakkí, is served by regular *kaiki* from Myrtiés on Kálymnos. It's a pretty spot, and many visitors swim, but the beach itself is unremarkable, improving as you head west.

In the hillside village of **LEPÍDHA**, 1km short of Xirókambos, a side turning north of the island's campsite leads up to a tiny **acropolis**. Behind the modern summit chapel, you can admire stretches of restored ancient masonry, while the views across to Kálymnos are superb.

### ACCOMMODATION AND EATING

**Hotel Efstathia** Xirókambos ☎ 22470 24099, ⊛ hotel -efstathia.gr. Studio apartments set 50m back from the beach. Huge, well-furnished doubles (with rather basic bathrooms) as well as family four-plexes facing a large pool. **€60**

**To Aloni** Xirókambos ☎ 22470 26048. Xirókambos's best waterfront taverna, right of where the road meets the sea. Enjoy *mayireftá*, souvláki and barbecued meats as well as fish, at beachside tables shaded by jacarandas. Daily 11am–9pm.

## Plátanos, Pandélli and around

Five kilometres north of Lakkí, across the island, a continuous built-up strip climbing across a low ridge to connect two east-coast bays nominally consists of three distinct villages. On the shore of the northern bay, **Ayía Marína** stretches along a quayside used by smaller inter-island ferries (see p.581). Immediately above it, older **Plátanos** stands beneath a Knight's castle, while on the bay to the south **Pandélli** is a busy but attractive little resort.

## Plátanos

Draped over the saddle between Ayía Marína and Pandélli, a one-minute taxi ride or five-minute walk up from the ferry dock, **PLÁTANOS** is a residential community full of fine Neoclassical and vernacular houses. A good central base for exploring the island, it's short on restaurants or nightlife.

### Kástro

May–Oct Mon, Tues, Thurs & Fri 8.30am–12.30pm; Wed, Sat & Sun 8.30am–12.30pm & 2.30–6.30pm; Nov–April daily 8.30am–12.30pm • €1

Atop the mighty headland northeast of Plátanos, Léros's **kástro** overlooks virtually the entire island – which was of course why the Knights sited a castle up here. Reach it either via a steep stair-path from the central square, or along a zigzagging road that starts its climb 100m back from the beach in Pandélli.

   Although the castle's walls and staircases have been stabilized and/or restored, there's little to see; the reason to come is to enjoy the stupendous views from the battlements, especially dramatic at sunset.

### Archeological Museum

Tues–Sun 8am–2.30pm • Free

Léros's **archeological museum**, a short way down towards Ayía Marína, is little more than a single room. Its few artefacts are however well laid out, with good explanation of where each was found, and a clear account of Lerian history.

## Pandélli

Ten minutes' walk down from Plátanos, the former fishing village of **PANDÉLLI** has been transformed into a smart, rather upscale but still very pleasant little resort. In summer, there's little room on its small but reef-free, pea-gravel **beach** for anyone other than guests at its beachfront hotels, but it holds a good crop of cafés and tavernas. A short way east around the bay, a long cement jetty still serves local fishermen rather than yachts, which in high season must anchor offshore.

## Southern beaches

Sadly, the prominent coastal footpath that heads south from Pandélli peters out as soon as it curves out of sight. To reach **VROMÓLITHOS**, 1km south, pedestrians and drivers alike have to follow a higher road, through the village of Spília.

   Although the **beach** at Vromólithos is usually less crowded than Pandélli, it's no place to linger, consisting of a long narrow strip of exposed gravel squashed up against the high walls of beachfront properties. The sea is clean, but you have to cross rock seabed at most points to reach deeper water. There's a more secluded, sandier cove southeast towards **Tourkopígadho**, and an even better duo at the end of the side-road to Aï Yiórgi.

| ACCOMMODATION | PLÁTANOS, PANDÉLLI AND AROUND |
|---|---|

**Castelo Beach** Pandélli beach ☏ 22470 23030, ⓦ castelo.gr. With its castellated tiers dominating the west end of Pandélli beach, this hotel is an eyesore, but once you're inside – whether in the spacious en-suite rooms, many of which have four-poster beds, or in the terrace café, perched just above water – it's a great place to take it easy. **€120**

★ **Hotel des Couleurs** Plátanos ☏ 22470 23341, ⓦ hotel-des-couleurs.com. This gorgeous Italianate mansion, tucked up on the hillside just a few steps from the centre of Plátanos, holds six irresistibly stylish suites, each decorated in a different colour and featuring antique furnishings such as four-poster beds or clawfoot tubs. Charming and very helpful hosts, and superb breakfasts out on the terrace. **€90**

**Panteli Beach Studios** Pandélli beach ☏ 22470 26450, ⓦ panteli-beach.gr. Dutch-owned complex of very tasteful and comfortable studios and apartments, all with balcony or terrace. There's no pool, but it opens directly onto the beach. €90

**Studios Happiness** Pandélli beach ☎ 22470 23498, Ⓦ studios-happiness-leros.gr. Attractive blue-trimmed house, just short of the sea, that's been divided into a mixture of good-value rooms, studios and apartments,

with plentiful outdoor space. €45

★ **Windmills/Anemomyli** Pandélli ☎ 22470 25549, Ⓦ leros-windmills.com. Lovely little B&B complex, poised above Pandélli on the road up to the castle, and consisting of two galleried windmill apartments and a long cottage, all with stone floors and great views from rear terraces. Closed Nov–April. €100

## EATING AND DRINKING

★ **Mezedhopolio O Dimitris O Karaflas** Spília ☎ 22470 25626. One of the best-sited ouzerís on the island, adjoining the *Hotel Rodon* up in Spília, between Pandélli and Vromólithos. Ample portions of delicacies such as chunky local sausages, onion rings and *floyéres*, or dairy-based dips like *galotýri* and *batíris*. Daily lunch & dinner, all year.

★ **Mylos** Ayía Marína ☎ 22470 24894. Excellent restaurant, with a romantic setting by the wave-lapped windmill at the western edge of Ayía Marína. The menu has a strong Italian leaning, featuring risotto and panacotta as

well as specialities like expertly home-made *garidhopílafo* (shrimp-rice, for €12), grilled *mastéllo* cheese, seasonal fresh fish, and *kolokythokeftédhes* (courgette patties). Reserve in summer. March–Sept only, daily lunch & dinner.

**Zorba's** Pandélli beach ☎ 22470 22027. Pandélli's best seafront restaurant, with tables on the beach itself, as well as on a long terrace. The food is consistently good, with grills for €8 and steak or fish for €12–15 – choose your own fish in the kitchen – but service can be slow at peak times. Reserve ahead in summer. Daily lunch & dinner.

## NIGHTLIFE

**Café del Mar** Vromólithos ☎ 22470 24766. Stylish, laidback bar, nestling along a shelf in the hillside just above the north end of Vromólithos beach. Very relaxing in the daytime, it hots up at night. Daily noon–late.

**Enallaktiko** Ayía Marína ☎ 22470 25746. As well as offering a handful of tables right on the quayside, this friendly local café also offers internet access. Daily

10am–midnight.

**Savana** Pandélli beach Ⓦ savanabar-leros.com. Long-standing and very civilized English-Danish bar at the far end of the port, which despite its shaded seafront terrace retains a laidback rural feel. The perfect spot for a late-night musical nightcap (request your favourites); things get going from 10pm nightly. Daily noon–late.

# Álinda and around

**ÁLINDA**, 3km northwest around the bay from Ayía Marína, is the longest-established resort on Léros, with development fringing a long, narrow strip of pea-gravel beach. It's also the first area to open in spring, and the last to shut in autumn.

## Historical and Ethnographic Museum

Álinda • May–Sept Tues–Sun 9am–1pm & 6–8pm • €3

Housed in a castle-like seafront mansion, the island's **Historical and Ethnographic Museum** concentrates on the Battle of Léros. Displays include relics from the sunken *Queen Olga*, a wheel from a Junkers bomber, and a stove made from a bomb casing. There's also a grisly mocked-up clinic (mostly gynaecological tools), assorted rural implements, costumes and antiques.

## Beaches near Álinda

**Beaches** near Álinda include **Krithóni**, 1.5km south, where the pretty cove gets very crowded in summer. Several more gravelly inlets lie alongside the road that curves around the bay further north, collectively known as **Dhýo Liskária**. From the dead end of the road, a 25-minute scramble north on a faint path brings you to pebbly **Kryfós** cove.

## ACCOMMODATION AND EATING

★ **Archontiko Angelou** Álinda ☎ 22470 22749, Ⓦ hotel-angelou-leros.com. Grand, marvellously atmospheric if slightly faded Italianate villa, a few hundred

metres inland from the beach. Eight pretty and very different rooms, with Victorian bath fittings, beamed ceilings and antique furnishings; some have balconies, but the views are of

the lovely gardens, not the sea. Closed mid-Oct to April. **€100**
**Crithoni's Paradise** Krithóni ☎22470 25120, ⓦcrithonisparadisehotel.gr. Luxurious hotel, halfway between Ayía Marína and Álinda. The low-rise complex holds well over a hundred fair-sized a/c rooms; all have outdoor space, those on the top floor enjoy bay views. The vast common areas include a large pool, gym, sauna and wi-fi zone. **€140**
**Hotel Alinda** Álinda ☎22470 23266. Very friendly family-run hotel, also known as *Xenonas Mavrakis*, set just

back from the middle of Álinda beach behind the good eponymous taverna, and offering good-value well-kept a/c rooms with fridges. **€60**
**Vareladiko** Dhýo Liskária ☎22470 23726. The last beachfront taverna you come to, at road's end east of Álinda. The owners have playfully painted walls and the hillside itself to make it look like it's a hotel, but all the "rooms" are just facades. As a restaurant, with seaside seating, it's fine, with inexpensive options like meatballs or mussels for just €6–7. Daily lunch & dinner.

## Goúrna and Dhrymónas

The best beach on Léros's west coast is **Goúrna**, at the head of a large bay 2km southwest of Álinda or 3km north of Lakkí. It's the longest sandy beach on the island, hard-packed and gently shelving, if wind-buffeted and somewhat scruffy. A road along the southern shore of the bay ends beside a jetty at little **Dhrymónas**.

### ACCOMMODATION AND EATING                          GOÚRNA AND DHRYMÓNAS

**Gourna Taverna** Goúrna ☎22470 25120. Friendly taverna, with sunbed rental, slap in the middle of Goúrna beach. Grills include chicken on a spit, wild fish and tasty mezédhes. Summer only, daily noon–7pm.
**Ouzerí Sotos** Dhrymónas ☎22470 24546. This quayside restaurant is so close to the sea that they plant some tables right in the water. Very good food at good prices, with mezédhes at €2–4, unusual shellfish for €8–10, and fresh

fish daily courtesy of owner Sotos himself. May–Oct daily lunch & dinner.
**Psilalonia** Dhrymónas ☎22470 25283, ⓦpsilalonia .com. Lovely French-owned little B&B, up on the hillside above the far end of the bay at Dhrymónas (turn left at the little chapel where the coast road stops). Three nice en-suite rooms, set in a row with fabulous views. **€70**

# Pátmos

Arguably the most beautiful, certainly the best known of the smaller Dodecanese, **PÁTMOS** has a distinctive, immediately palpable atmosphere. In a cave here, St John the Divine (known in Greek as *O Theológos*, "The Theologian", and author of one of the four Gospels) set down the **Book of Revelation**, the final book of the New Testament. The huge fortified **monastery** that honours him remains the island's dominant feature; its monks owned all of Pátmos until the eighteenth century, and their influence remains strong.

For those visitors not motivated by religion, Pátmos's greatest strength is its **beaches**. With so many attractive strands, you can usually escape the crowds even in high season, though you may need a vehicle to do so. **Day-trippers** exceed overnighters, thanks in part to the island's lack of an airport, and Pátmos feels a different place once the last excursion boat has left after sunset. Among those staying, no single nationality predominates, lending Pátmos a **cosmopolitan** feel almost unique in the Dodecanese. The steady clientele can be very **posh** indeed, with assorted royal and ex-royal families among repeat visitors.

### ARRIVAL AND INFORMATION                                        PÁTMOS

**By ferry** All ferries arrive in the heart of Skála. Agathonisi (4 weekly; 1hr 50min–2hr 50min); Arkí (4 weekly; 40min); Kálymnos (2–4 daily; 1hr 35min–4hr); Kos (2–4 daily; 1hr 35min–5hr); Léros (2–4 daily; 40min–1hr 55min); Lipsi (1–3 daily; 25–50min); Pireás (4 weekly; 8hr 10min); Rhodes (1–3 daily; 4hr 45min–9hr 45min); Samos (1–2 daily; 1hr–3hr 10min); Sými (6 weekly; 4hr–8hr); Syros (2 weekly; 4hr).
**Travel agencies** Astoria Travel (☎22470 31324,

ⓦastoriatravel.com) and Apollon Travel (☎22470 31324), both on Skála's main waterfront street.
**Tourist office** Pátmos has no tourist office, though ⓦpatmos-island.com and ⓦpatmosweb.gr are useful. However, the Orthodox Culture and Information Center facing the ferry landing (Mon, Tues, Thurs & Fri 9am–1pm & 6–9pm, Sat & Sun 6–9pm) aims to make visitors aware of the island's religious sites, and posts current opening hours.

8

## GETTING AROUND

**By bus** Island buses leave from the quayside to Hóra (7 daily), Gríkou (3 daily) and Kámbos (3 daily).
**Car and scooter rental** Outfits include Tom & Gerry (☎ 22470 31357) and Astoria Travel (☎ 22470 31324,

ⓦ astoriatravel.com).
**Excursion boats** Boats to Psilí Ámmos and Arkí/Maráthi leave the quayside at 9.30–10am (7.30–10am to Léros and Lipsí depending on day/season).

## Skála

Home to most of Pátmos's 3200 official residents, **SKÁLA** seems initially to contradict any solemn image of the island; the commercial district with its gift boutiques is incongruously sophisticated for such a small town. During peak season, the quay and inland lanes throng with trippers, and visitors still tend to be arriving after dark, including from the huge, humming cruisers that weigh anchor around midnight. Skála becomes a ghost town in winter (which here means by early October), when most shops and restaurants close.

Given time, Skála reveals more enticing corners in the residential fringes to its east and west, where vernacular mansions hem in pedestrian lanes creeping up the hillsides. At the summit of the westerly rise, **Kastélli**, masonry courses from an ancient acropolis enclose a more recent chapel. An easy ten-minute walk southwest across the flat isthmus, starting from the central market street, brings you to pebbly **Hokhlakás Bay** on the island's west coast. More of a quiet seafront suburb than a beach, it enjoys wonderful sunset views.

**8**

PÁTMOS

Livádhi Kaloyíron
Lámbi
Kambí
Léfkes
Kámbos
Kámbos    Vayiá
Livádhi
Linginóu    Yeranóu    Apolloú
Agriolivadho    Áyios
Yeóryios    Panayiá
Yeranoú
Mérihas
Kastélli    Melóï
Netiá
Skála    Áspri
Hokhlakás    Konsoláto
Bay
Apokálypsis    Sápsila
Ayíou
Ioánnou    Hóra
Theológou    Gríkou    Hiliomódhi
Evangelismoú    Pétra
Traoníssi
Alykí    Dhiakófti Isthmus
Cape    Stavrós
Yénoupa    Psilí
Ámmos

Piréás & select Cyclades
Lipsí, Arkí, Agathonissí & Sámos

N

0        1
kilometre

▼ Léros, Kálymnos & Kós

## ACCOMMODATION                SKÁLA

**Asteri** near Mérihas cove, Nétia ☎ 22470 32465, ⓦ asteripatmos.gr. The best option in Nétia, set in spacious grounds on a knoll overlooking the bay, just under ten minutes' walk from the ferry. 37 simply furnished en-suite rooms of varying sizes, with sea-view balconies; many have a/c, two have wheelchair access. Breakfasts, available outdoors, feature own-grown produce. Breakfast included. **€80**

**Australis** Nétia ☎ 22470 31576, ⓦ patmosaustralis .gr. Very friendly, somewhat spartan en-suite hotel, owned by a helpful Greek-Australian family; an affiliated scooter-rental business saves you traipses into town. Units in the better-standard apartment annexe accommodate up to six. Breakfast included. **€70**

**Blue Bay** ☎ 22470 31165, ⓦ bluebay.50g.com. Multi-tiered Australian-Greek-run hotel on the hillside just above the sea, a short walk south from the jetty just out of sight of Skála. There's no beach, but all the a/c en-suite rooms have substantial sea-view balconies, and there's a small internet café. Credit cards accepted for stays of over two days. Breakfast included. **€116**

**Captain's House** Konsoláto ☎ 22470 31793, ⓦ captains-house.gr. A hotel not a house, with 17 a/c rooms, moments from the jetty and facing a tiny beach dotted with café tables. The quiet rooms in the rear wing overlook a fair-sized pool and shady terrace. Friendly management, nice furnishings and on-site car rental. B&B **€85**

**Galini** Skála ☎ 22470 31240, ⓦ galinipatmos.gr. Good-value hotel, at the end of a cul-de-sac just a few metres inland from the jetty, with pleasant furnishings in its eleven large rooms, most of which have balconies. €75

**Hellenis** Netiá ☎ 22470 31275, ⓦ hotelhellinis patmos.gr. This whitewashed 40-room hotel is very close to the sea path (paved at this point) and just north of a new yacht marina, and has bright, airy common areas, a lift (rather superfluous for just two storeys) and better-than-average rooms offering fridges, balconies and baths. The same management has six superior apartments in contemporary style out back. €90

**Maria** Hokhlakás flatlands ☎ 22470 31201, ⓦ hotelmariapatmos.com. Quietly set small hotel, 150m from the sea, where the pleasant front garden, a/c, lobby internet facility and big sea-view balconies offset tiny bathrooms. Breakfast included. €80

★ **Porto Scoutari** Melóï hillside ☎ 22470 33124, ⓦ portoscoutari.com. Pátmos's premier hotel, this bungalow complex overlooks the beach and islets. The common areas and spacious a/c units, with TV and phone, are arrayed around a large pool and small spa. Unparalleled personal service from owner Elina Scoutari and her staff. Rates shown apply for stays of two or more nights. Breakfast included. €126

**Skala Hotel** Skála ☎ 22470 31343, ⓦ skalahotel.gr. Smart, large, bougainvillea-drenched hotel, set a short way back from the quayside in the heart of the village, and accessed via a flowery gateway-gazebo. 78 comfortable renovated rooms, with sea-view balconies and a large pool. €130

**Studios Mathios** Sápsila beach ☎ 22470 32583, ⓦ mathiosapartments.gr. Superior rural accommodation, ranging from small studios to an entire house, beside an unremarkable beach 2km southeast of Skála, with creative decor and extensive gardens. Owners Iakoumina and Theologos are exceptionally welcoming. €60

## EATING AND DRINKING

**Benetos** Sápsila beach ☎ 22470 33089, ⓦ benetosrestaurant.com. High-class Mediterranean fusion, 2km southeast of Skála, with idyllic conservatory seating and a menu encompassing the likes of smoked sardine, bean and salmon croustade, *astakomakaronádha* and decadent desserts; budget €35–40 for three courses plus drink. Reservations recommended. Dinner only, June to early Oct, Tues–Sun from 7.30pm.

**Ostria** Skála ☎ 22470 33254. The food tends to be run-of-the-mill at this central, mid-priced, year-round ouzerí, facing the excursion-boat quay, but – late ferry arrivals take note – it's the only place serving after 11pm. Daily 10am–late.

**To Hiliomodhi** Skála ☎ 22470 34080. Cheap and crowded ouzerí, a few metres from the waterfront at the start of the road to Hóra, which offers vegetarian mezédhes (typically €3) and seafood delicacies such as limpets (served live) or grilled octopus (€7.50), plus decent *hýma* wine from Mégara.

There's outdoor seating at the back, in an unremarkable pedestrian lane. Open all year. Daily noon–late.

**Tzivaeri** Skála ☎ 22470 31170. Quality outfit, facing Theológos town beach a short walk along the quayside from the excursion boats, featuring delicate Cretan-style mezédhes and seafood such as boiled or grilled octopus (€8.50). As well as the enticing tables on the beach itself, seating is on the upstairs sea-view veranda, and there's live music courtesy of the owner in the large room inside. Dinner only, from 6pm nightly all year.

★ **Vegghera** Skála ☎ 22470 32988, ⓦ patmosweb .gr/vegghera.htm. The best all-rounder, opposite the yacht marina, with flawlessly presented stuffed scorpion fish, vegetarian or seafood salads, superb desserts, and per-head bills of €40–45 plus drink. It's the last place you come to as you walk north from the port. Reservations recommended. Easter to early Sept, daily 7.30pm–late.

## NIGHTLIFE

**Café Arion** ☎ 22470 31595. This appealing wood-panelled, barn-like place, in the centre of the quayside, is Pátmos's most durable café-bar; all sorts sit outside, dance inside or prop up the long bar. Daily 9am–late.

**Koukoumavla** Konsoláta ☎ 22470 32325. The "Owl" is a perennially popular, hippy-ish bar near the foot of the main road up to Hóra. Run by a friendly Italian-Greek couple, it has garden seating, wacky decor and live music, and sells crafts as well as snacks and drinks. Daily noon–late.

## Apokálypsis monastery

Daily 8am–1.30pm, also Tues, Thurs & Sun 4–6pm • Free

A ten-minute walk up the hill from Skála, halfway to Hóra, the **Apokálypsis monastery** is built around the cave where St John heard the voice of God issuing from a cleft in the rock, and where he sat dictating to his disciple Prohoros. The cave itself, of course, was once open to the elements, but it's now enclosed within an eleventh-century chapel. In a recess in the rock, the place where the saint is said to have rested his head at night is fenced off and outlined in beaten silver. Only if you come first thing in the morning, before the cacophonous tour groups arrive, can you hope to get a sense of the contemplative peace that inspired St John.

## Ayíou Ioánnou Theológou monastery

Daily 8am–1.30pm, also Tues, Thurs & Sun 4–6pm • Free, museum €6

In 1088, the soldier-cleric **Ioannis "The Blessed" Khristodhoulos** (1021–93) was granted title to Pátmos by Byzantine emperor Alexios Komnenos. Within three years, he and his followers had completed most of what's now **Ayíou Ioánnou Theológou monastery**. Enclosed within its stout hilltop walls, a warren of courtyards, chapels, stairways, arcades, and roof terraces offers a rare glimpse of a Patmian interior. In antiquity, this site held a temple of Artemis, marble columns from which were incorporated here and there in the monastery.

As most of the complex is closed to outsiders – it remains home to a community of around a dozen monks – few visitors spend more than half an hour up here. The diminutive flower-bedecked courtyard just inside the gate opens onto the church itself, where frescoes depict the Apocalypse. Off to one side, the **museum** has a magnificent array of religious treasures, including medieval icons of the Cretan school, and several later donations from Russia. Manuscripts date as far back as a shrivelled parchment copy of the Gospel of St Mark, from the fifth or sixth century, though pride of place goes to the original chrysobull (edict) signed by Emperor Alexios Komnenos in the eleventh century, granting the island to Khristodhoulos. The upper floor also holds some archeological relics, including a statue of Dionysos from Paros.

### Hóra

St John's promise of shelter from pirates spurred the growth of **HÓRA** outside the stout fortifications of the monastery. A magnificent ensemble, it remains architecturally homogeneous, its cobbled lanes sheltering shipowners' mansions from the island's seventeenth to eighteenth-century heyday. High, windowless walls and imposing wooden doors betray nothing of the painted ceilings, *votsalotó* terraces, flagstone kitchens and carved furniture inside. Inevitably, touristic tattiness disfigures the main approaches to the monastery, but by night, when the ramparts are startlingly floodlit, it's hard to think of a more beautiful Dodecanesian village. Neither should you miss the view from **Platía Lótza**, particularly at dawn or dusk.

### SAINT JOHN ON PÁTMOS

Pátmos has been intimately associated with Christianity since **John the Evangelist** – later John the Divine – was exiled here from Ephesus by emperor Domitian in about 95 AD. John is said to have written his **Gospel** on Pátmos, but his sojourn is better remembered for the otherworldly voice that he heard coming from a cleft in the ceiling of his hillside grotto, which bid him to set down its words in writing. By the time John was allowed to return home, that disturbing finale to the New Testament, the **Book of Revelation** (aka the Apocalypse), had been disseminated as a pastoral letter to the Seven Churches of Asia Minor.

Revelation followed the standard Judeo-Christian tradition of apocalyptic books, with titanic battles in heaven and on earth, supernatural visions, plus lurid descriptions of the fates awaiting the saved and the damned following the **Last Judgement**. Hugely open to subjective interpretation, Revelation was being wielded as a rhetorical and theological weapon within a century of appearing. Its vivid imagery lent itself to depiction in frescoes adorning the refectories of Byzantine monasteries and the narthexes of Orthodox churches, conveying a salutary message to illiterate medieval parishioners.

John also combated paganism on Pátmos, in the person of an evil wizard, **Kynops**, who challenged him to a duel of miracles. As the magician's stock trick involved retrieving effigies of the deceased from the seabed, John responded by petrifying Kynops while he was under water. A buoy just off Theológos beach in Skála today marks the relevant submerged rock.

Forever after in the Orthodox world, heights amid desolate and especially **volcanic topography** have become associated with John. Pátmos, with its eerie landscape of igneous outcrops, is an excellent example, as is Níssyros, where one of the saint's monasteries overlooks the volcano's caldera.

Numerous "minor" churches and monasteries around Hóra contain beautiful icons and examples of local woodcarving; almost all are locked to prevent thefts, but key-keepers generally live nearby. Among the best are the church of **Dhiasózousa**; the convent of **Zoödhóhou Piyís** (daily except Sat 9am–noon), and the convent of **Evangelismoú**, at the edge of Hóra (daily 9–11am).

## ARRIVAL AND INFORMATION

HÓRA

**By bus** Seven buses from Skála serve Hóra daily, from 7.30am until 7pm.

**On foot** The 40min walk from Skála to Hóra follows a beautiful old cobbled path. Don't try it in the full heat of the day, and whatever you do, don't walk up the much longer, switchbacking main road. To find the path, head through Skála towards Hokhlakás, then turn left onto a lane that leads uphill to the main road – you'll see the cobbles ahead of you.

**Festivals** The best dates to visit, besides the Easter observances, are September 25–26 (Feast of John the Theologian) and October 20–21 (Feast of Khristodhoulos), both featuring solemn liturgies and processions. The annual Festival of Religious Music (late Aug/early Sept) is held in the grounds of the Apokálypsis monastery (see p.587).

## ACCOMMODATION AND EATING

★ **Archontariki** Hóra ☎ 22470 29368, ⊛ archontariki -patmos.gr. Very gorgeous B&B, concealed behind high walls in a traditional village house that's been beautifully converted to hold five exquisitely furnished, exceptionally comfortable suites. As well as the lovely central courtyard, there's a garden and roof terrace; rates include a superb breakfast. Closed Oct–Easter. **€200**

**Loza** Platía Loza, Hóra ☎ 22470 32405. Nicely positioned café/restaurant just below the eponymous platía, close to the main road, where the broad terrace offers sweeping views, and as well as hot and alcoholic drinks you can get mezédhes for €7–8, salads and pasta dishes for under €10, and pricier steaks. Open for all meals daily.

**Pantheon** Hóra ☎ 22470 31226. The village's most authentic restaurant, at the start of the monastery approach. Good atmosphere and music, a lovely old interior or terrace views over the village and friendly management offset somewhat run-of-the-mill, pricey mezédhes. Easter–Dec all meals daily, until late.

# The rest of the island

Pátmos's **best beaches** are concentrated north of Skála, tucked into the startling eastern shoreline, and accessible from side roads off the main road. Most of the island's west-facing bays are unusable, owing to the prevailing wind and washed-up debris.

## Gríkou and Pétra

Not far south of uninspiring Sapsila beach, roads converge at the sandiest part of **Gríkou**. The beach itself, far from the island's best, forms a narrow strip of hard-packed sand, yielding to sand and gravel, then large pebbles at **Pétra** immediately south. It's not possible to drive any further south along the coast.

## Melóï and Agriolívadho

A couple of kilometres northeast of Skála, the large crescent beach at **Melóï** is handy and quite appealing, with tamarisks behind the slender belt of sand, and good snorkelling offshore. It's accessible by road at its southern end, which is home to a taverna. North of Melóï, **Agriolívadho** (Agriolivádhi) is another attractive sheltered bay. Most of the beach is pebbly gravel, but there's a reasonable amount of sand at its broad centre.

## Kámbos

Hilltop **KÁMBOS**, 4km north of Skála, is the island's only other real village. Originally built to house the wives and children of lay workers at the monastery, it's surrounded by scattered farms.

Kámbos **beach**, 600m downhill to the east, is a strong contender for the best beach on the island, although it fills with local kids in summer. Too deeply indented to be seen from the rest of Pátmos, it offers peaceful sheltered swimming, along with plentiful sunbeds, two tavernas, and beach toys to rent.

### Beyond Kámbos

A succession of less busy coves lies **east** of Kámbos. **Vayiá** is a little bay where a few trees overhang a beach of pebbles and coarse sand, there's a snack bar, and the sea is a particularly enticing shade of turquoise. The double bay at **Lingínou** can only be reached on foot, but has a *kantína*. **Livádhi Yeranoú** is a long stretch of mingled sand and gravel, shaded by tamarisks, and with a delightful islet offshore as a target for swimmers.

### ACCOMMODATION                                                THE REST OF PÁTMOS

**Patmos Aktis** Gríkou Beach ⊕ 22470 32800, ⊕ patmosasktis.gr. This very upscale, dazzling white 56-room luxury hotel opened in 2011; as a style statement it's incongruous for Pátmos, but there's no disputing the opulence of its rooms, spa and restaurant. The same management has also taken over and renovated the cheaper *Silver Beach* hotel nearby, bookable via the same website. Closed Oct–Easter. **€200**

### EATING AND DRINKING

**George's Place** Kámbos Beach ⊕ 22470 31881. Friendly snack and café bar, spreading out onto the sand at the broader eastern end of Kámbos Beach. Pies and salads €5–7, plus juices, milkshakes and a full bar, and free wi-fi access. Mid-May to Sept, daily 10am–10pm.

★ **Ktima Petra** Petra Beach ⊕ 22470 33207. The best rural taverna on Pátmos, set back slightly behind the trees at the north end of Petra beach, with its own large greenhouse. Lush salads, home-made *dolmádhes*, carefully cooked *mayireftá*, plus grills after dark; little on the menu costs over €10. Reservations advised in summer. Easter–Oct daily 1–10pm.

**Lambi** Lámbi Bay ⊕ 22470 31490. Lovely little seafront taverna, founded in 1958, where the roof is held up by elderly tamarisk trees, and some tables are on the beach itself. The fish is recommended; the menu is very brief off-season. Easter to mid-Oct, daily noon–8pm.

**Livádhi Yeranoú Taverna** Livádhi Yeranoú Beach ⊕ 22470 32046. Good-value taverna, just short of the beach, with a nice terrace and a reasonable menu of seafood, chops, *tzatzíki*, *hórta* and salads. May–Nov daily noon–late.

**Tarsanas** Patmos Marine boatyard, Dhiakoftí isthmus. The boatyard near the southern tip of the island might not seem the obvious place to find a smart, good-value taverna, but *Tarsanas* is a favourite (all-year) "power lunch" spot for locals. Mountainous salads, quiche-like *píttes* and Greek standards; the nicest tables are in a permanently grounded boat. Daily lunch & dinner.

# Lipsí

The largest, most interesting and most populated of the islets north and east of Pátmos, **LIPSÍ** also has the most significant tourist trade. Returning regulars make showing up in peak season without reservations unwise. During quieter months, however, Lipsí still provides an idyllic halt, its sleepy pace almost making plausible a dubious link with **Calypso**, the nymph who held Odysseus in thrall. Once a dependency of the monastery on Pátmos, Lipsí is still conspicuously sown with blue-domed churches. Deep wells water small farms and vineyards, but there's only one flowing spring, and although plenty of livestock can be seen, the non-tourist economy is far from thriving.

### ARRIVAL AND DEPARTURE                                                        LIPSÍ

**By ferry** Agathoníssi (4 weekly; 2hr 45min); Arkí (4 weekly; 1hr 35min); Kálymnos (2–3 daily; 1hr 20min–2hr 50min); Kos (2–3 daily; 1hr 40min–4hr 10min); Léros (2–3 daily; 25min–1hr 5min); Pátmos (2–3 daily; 20min); Pireás (1 weekly; 9hr 45min); Rhodes (6 weekly; 5hr 10min–8hr 20min); Samos (1 daily; 1hr 30min–4hr 5min); Sými (6 weekly; 4hr 20min–7hr).

## Lipsí Village and around

Lipsí's only significant population centre, known as **LIPSÍ VILLAGE**, stretches around its large south-facing harbour. From the ferry jetty at its northwestern extremity, the hilltop centre of town is a 600m walk.

None of the **beaches** is more than an hour's walk from the port. The closest, and sandiest, are crowded **Liendoú** and **Kámbos**, but many prefer attractive **Katsadhiá**

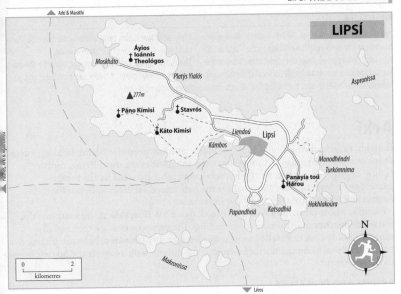

(sand) and **Papandhriá** (coarse sand-and-gravel), adjacent coves 2km south of the port. Another paved road leads 4km west from town to protected **Platýs Yialós**, a shallow, sandy bay, continuing to sumpy Moskháto fjord (no beach).

To reach the isolated east-coast beaches, which lack facilities, rent a **scooter** at the port. **Hokhlakoúra** consists of coarse shingle (finer pebbles at mid-strand); nearby **Turkómnima** is sandy and much shadier, if mercilessly exposed to the *meltémi*.

## ACCOMMODATION
## LIPSÍ VILLAGE AND AROUND

**Aphroditi** Lipsí Village ☏ 22470 41000, ⓦ hotel-aphroditi.com. Complex of large, tiled-floor studios and apartments, some with kitchens and two double bedrooms, set slightly back across the road from Liendoú beach. Closed Dec–April. **€75**

**Galini Apartments** Lipsí Village ☏ 22470 41212. The first building you see on disembarking, right above the ferry jetty, is a prime budget choice in all respects, run by the hospitable Matsouris family. Units have kitchens and balconies. Nikos may take guests fishing on request. Closed Nov–Easter. **€60**

**Helios Apartments** Lipsí Village ☏ 694 54 60 534, ⓦ helioslipsi.gr. Five variably sized units, just off the road to Hokhlakoúra and Katsadhiá. All have two bedrooms and two bathrooms, and are tastefully decorated with terracotta tiles, rounded corners and quality furnishings like wrought-iron

beds and even washing machines. Some have galleries, but there are no sea views. Closed Nov–Easter. **€80**

★ **Nefeli Hotel** Kámbos beach ☏ 22470 41120, ⓦ nefelihotels.com. This modern bungalow-hotel complex, overlooking the beach, offers a range of huge studios plus one- and two-bedroom apartments in the same pastel colours. Ground-floor studios are cave-like, breezier upstairs units are preferable. Open all year. **€100**

★ **Poseidon Apartments** Lipsí Village ☏ 22470 41130, ⓦ lipsi-poseidon.gr. Impeccable, roomy, modern studios with large balconies, 150m from the jetty, as well as a one-bedroom apartment; the decor may be IKEA-on-steroids but everything has been thought of. On the ground floor, handy scooter rental and a convenient *psistariá* with roast chicken. Closed Nov–Easter. **€65**

## EATING AND DRINKING

**Café du Moulin** ☏ 22470 41316. The main daytime hub for travellers, in the central square. Hearty lashings of *mayireftá* at shaded tables, as well as inexpensive breakfasts. Daily 8am–late.

★ **Karnayio** ☏ 22470 41422. This good-value restaurant, adjoining a blue-domed church on the far side of the bay,

serves hefty salads and ample helpings of *mayireftá* such as pork with celery and carrots. Daily lunch and dinner, all year.

★ **To Pefko** ☏ 22470 41404. Classic Greek cuisine overlooking the main jetty, strong on baked aubergine recipes and lamb-based hotpots like *ambelourgoú*, and with efficient service. May to late Sept, daily lunch and dinner.

## NIGHTLIFE

★ **Dilaila** Katsadhiá ☎22470 41041. Garden-set beachfront taverna-café, overlooking the strand at Katsadhiá. While pricier than the island norm, it's worth it for such delights as salad with bits of local cheese, chunky aubergine dip or *fáva* and marinated fish dishes; from 11pm until 4am it hots up as a late-night music bar. June to mid-Sept, noon until very late indeed.

**The Rock** Lipsí's longest-lasting bar, right by the port, with a congenial crowd, boulder-like host Babis and good tunes. Daily 6pm–late.

# Arkí

Roughly two-thirds the size of Lipsí, **ARKÍ** is a far more primitive island, lacking proper shops or a coherent village. A mere fifty or so inhabitants eke out a living, mostly fishing or goat/sheep-herding, though servicing yachts attracted by the superb anchorage at Avgoústa Bay – named for the half-ruined Hellenistic/Byzantine **Avgoustínis fortress** overhead – is also important.

Excursion-boat clients swim at the "Blue Lagoon" of **Tiganákia** at the southeast tip, but other **beaches** on Arkí take some finding. The more obvious are the carefully nurtured sandy cove at **Pateliá** by the outer jetty, or tiny **Limnári** pebble-bay (fitting five bathers at a pinch) on the northeast coast, a 25-minute walk away via the highest house in the settlement.

## ARRIVAL AND DEPARTURE ARKÍ

**By ferry** Agathoníssi (4 weekly; 1hr); Kálymnos (4 weekly; 4hr 20min); Lipsí (4 weekly; 1hr 35min); Léros (4 weekly; 2hr 50min); Pátmos (4 weekly; 40min); Samos (4 weekly; 2hr 20min).

## ACCOMMODATION AND EATING

**Nikolas** ☎22470 32477. Friendly taverna on the flagstoned harbourside platía, where a mother/son team serve home-made puddings and *mayireftá* such as peppers with goat's cheese, and offer pleasant west-facing rooms. **€40**

**O Trypas** ☎22470 32230. Also known as *Tou Manoli*, this waterfront taverna is renowned for its very decent fish meals and *mezédhes*; has mock-trad, stone-floored rental units just up the hillside; and doubles as the island's most happening music bar. Daily 1pm–late.

## Maráthi

The nearest large, sandy, tamarisk-shaded beach is a ten-minute boat trip away on **Maráthi**, the only inhabited islet (permanent population 3) of the mini-archipelago around Arkí.

## ACCOMMODATION AND EATING MARÁTHI

**Pantelis** ☎22470 32609, ⓦ marathi-island.gr. The most elaborate and "resort"-like establishment on Maráthi. The beachfront tables outside make a perfect venue to enjoy local free-range goat, fresh-caught fish, or vegetables from the adjacent garden, while the rooms are spacious, airy and tastefully furnished. Closed Nov–April. **€45**

**Piratis** ☎22470 31580 or 69739 62462, ⓦ marathi-island.com. Full-service taverna with waterside seating and a menu of home-baked classic as well as fresh fish, plus ten simple, adequate a/c en-suite rooms. Barefoot proprietor Mihalis emphasizes his comic-book-pirate persona with a Jolly Roger flag and speedboat named *Piratis*. **€35**

# Agathoníssi

The small, steep-sided, waterless islet of **AGATHONÍSSI** is too remote – closer to Turkey than Pátmos, in fact – to be a popular day-trip target. Intrepid Greeks and Italians form its main tourist clientele, along with yachts attracted by excellent anchorage. Even though the *Nissos Kalymnos* (and a summer catamaran) appear regularly, schedules mean you should count on staying at least two days.

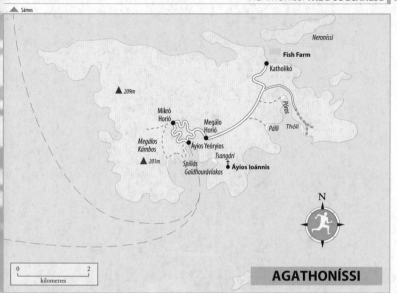

Despite the lack of springs, the island is greener and more fertile than apparent from the sea; lentisc, carob and scrub oak on the heights overlook two arable plains in the west. Fewer than a hundred people live here full time, but they make a go of stock-raising or fishing (or rather, fish-farming), and few dwellings are abandoned or neglected.

Most of the population lives in **Megálo Horió** hamlet, just visible on the ridge above the harbour hamlet of **ÁYIOS YEÓRYIOS** and at eye level with tiny **Mikró Horió** opposite. Except for a small shop and two café-restaurants working peak-season nights only in Megálo Horió, all amenities are in the port.

With no rental scooters, exploring involves **walking** along the cement-road network, or following a very few tracks and paths – bring plenty of water. If you won't swim at the port, home to the largest sandy **beach**, hike ten minutes southwest to shingle-gravel **Spiliás**, or continue another quarter-hour by path over the ridge to **Gaïdhourávlakos**, another gravel cove.

Bays in the east, all reached by paved roads, include tiny **Póros** (45min distant), fine sand with lentisc-tree shade at the back; **Thóli** (25min further) in the far southeast, with good snorkelling and some morning shade; and **Pálli** across the same bay, a small but pristine fine-pebble cove reached by a fifteen-minute walk down from the trans-island road.

## ARRIVAL AND DEPARTURE                                      AGATHONÍSSI

**By ferry** Arkí (4 weekly; 1hr); Kálymnos (4 weekly; 5hr 30min); Lipsí (4 weekly; 2hr 45min); Léros (4 weekly; 4hr); Pátmos (4 weekly; 1hr 50min); Samos (4 weekly; 1hr 5min).

## ACCOMMODATION AND EATING

**Rooms Maria Kamitsi** ☎ 22470 29065, or 693 25 75 121. Thirteen pleasant a/c rooms at the centre of the beach, sharing use of a kitchen and fridges, with a vine-covered patio outside. **€40**

**Seagull** ☎ 22470 29062. Central taverna, close to the yacht moorings, where the romantic waterside tables are filled every night for a full menu of baked and grilled dishes. Daily lunch & dinner.

**To Agnanti** ☎ 22470 29019 or 697 48 14 013. Good-value rooms, the newest on the island, above the popular *Memento Bar*, which has a wooden deck reaching out over the water. **€50**

# The East and North Aegean

**599** Sámos

**612** Foúrni

**614** Ikaría

**620** Híos

**630** Inoússes

**631** Psará

**632** Lésvos

**649** Áyios Efstrátios

**650** Límnos

**656** Samothráki

**660** Thássos

IKARÍA

**9**

# The East and North Aegean

The seven substantial islands and four minor islets scattered off the Aegean coast of Asia Minor form a rather arbitrary archipelago. While there are similarities in architecture and landscape, the strong individual character of each island is far more striking and thus they do not form an immediately recognizable group, and neither are they all connected with each other by ferries. What they do have in common, with the possible exception of Sámos and Thássos, is that they receive fewer visitors than other island groups and so generally provide a more authentic Greek atmosphere. Yet the existence of magnificent beaches, dramatic mountain scenery, interesting sights and ample facilities makes them a highly attractive region of Greece to explore.

Verdant **Sámos** ranks as the most visited island of the group but, once you leave its crowded resorts behind, is still arguably the most beautiful, even after a devastating fire in 2000. **Ikaría** to the west remains relatively unspoilt, if a minority choice, and nearby **Foúrni** is (except in summer) a haven for determined solitaries, as are the Híos satellites **Psará** and **Inoússes**. **Híos** proper offers far more cultural interest than its neighbours to the south, but far fewer tourist facilities. **Lésvos** may not impress initially, though once you get a feel for its old-fashioned Anatolian ambience you may find it hard to leave. By contrast, few foreigners visit **Áyios Efstrátios**, and for good reason, though **Límnos** to the north is much busier, particularly in its western half. In the far north Aegean, Samothráki and Thássos are relatively isolated and easier to visit from northern Greece, which administers them. **Samothráki** has one of the most dramatic seaward approaches of any Greek island, and one of the more important ancient sites. **Thássos** is more varied, with sandy beaches, mountain villages and minor archeological sites.

## Brief history

Despite their proximity to modern Turkey, only Lésvos, Límnos and Híos bear significant signs of an **Ottoman** heritage, in the form of old mosques, hammams and fountains, plus some domestic architecture betraying obvious influences from Constantinople, Macedonia and further north in the Balkans. The limited degree of this heritage has in the past been duly referred to by Greece in an intermittent **propaganda war** with Turkey over the sovereignty of these far-flung outposts – as well as the disputed boundary between them and the Turkish mainland. Ironically, this friction gave these long-neglected islands a new lease of life from the 1960s onward, insomuch as their sudden **strategic importance** prompted infrastructure improvements to support garrisoning, and gave a mild spur to local economies, engaged in providing goods and services to soldiers, something predating the advent of tourism. Yet the region has remained one of the **poorest regions** in western Europe. Tensions with Turkey have occasionally been aggravated by disagreements over suspected undersea oil

Climbing Mount Kérkis p.611
Walking in western Ikaría p.618
Day-trips from Híos p.622
Mastic mastication p.626
Theophilos Hadzimihaḯl: the Rousseau of Greece? p.638

Polikhnítos Spa p.640
The olives of Lésvos p.642
The war cemeteries p.655
The Samothracian mysteries p.658
Climbing the moon p.659

MÓLYVOS, LÉSVOS

# Highlights

**①Vathý, Sámos** The two-wing archeological museum is among the best in the islands, while there are atmospheric tavernas in the upper town of Áno Póli. **See p.601**

**②Foúrni** This small fishing island offers numerous deserted coves, a surprisingly lively port and a lovely main street lined with mulberry trees. **See p.612**

**③Ikaría** Western Ikaría has superb beaches and you can participate in the idiosyncratic nocturnal lifestyle of the Ráhes villages. **See p.614**

**④Southern Híos** The architecturally unique *mastihohoriá* (mastic villages) have a distinct Middle Eastern feel. **See p.625**

**⑤Mólyvos, northern Lésvos** This castle-crowned resort village is undoubtedly the most beautiful on the island, perhaps in the whole island group. **See p.646**

**⑥Límnos villages** Atmospheric basalt-built villages with lively central tavernas and great local wines to sample. **See p.650**

**⑦Sanctuary of the Great Gods, Samothráki** With Mount Fengári as a backdrop, the remote Sanctuary of the Great Gods is blessed with a natural grandeur. **See p.656**

**⑧Alykí, Thássos** A beautifully situated resort, with fine beaches flanked by ancient and Byzantine archeological sites. **See p.660**

**HIGHLIGHTS ARE MARKED ON THE MAP ON P.598**

# THE EAST & NORTH AEGEAN

Kavála
Keramotí
Thássos
Skála
Prínou
Thássos
Limenária ⑧

Alexandhroúpoli

**TURKEY**

0        kilometres

Kamariótissa ⑦
Hóra    *Samothráki*

Gökçeada

Çanakkale

Bozcaada

Thessaloníki →

*Límnos*
⑥
Mýrina
Kondiás  Moúdhros

**HIGHLIGHTS**
① Vathý, Sámos
② Foúrni
③ Ikaría
④ Southern Híos
⑤ Mólyvos, Lésvos
⑥ Límnos villages
⑦ Sanctuary of the Great Gods
⑧ Alykí, Thássos

*Ay. Efstrátios*

Mólyvos ⑤
Sígri
Eressós
Polikhnítos  Ayiássos
Mytilíni
*Lésvos*
Plomári

Ayvalık

**TURKEY**

*Skýros*

*Kými*

*Psará*

Mármaro
Volissós  *Inoússes*
Inoússes
*Híos*
Híos
Mestá ④
Pyrgí
Çeşme

İzmir

*Ándhros*

*Rafína*

*Lávrio*

*Tínos*

*Pireás*

*Sýros*

*Mýkonos*

Áy. Kírykos
Évdhilos
*Ikaría* ③
②
*Foúrni*

*Pátmos*  *Arkí*  *Agathoníssi*

Efes
(Ephesus)
Karlóvassi  ① Vathý  Kuşada
Pythagório
*Sámos*

deposits in the straits between the islands and Anatolia. The Turks have also persistently demanded that Límnos, astride the sea lanes to the Dardanelles, be demilitarized, and in the last decade Greece has finally complied, with garrisons also much reduced on Sámos and Lésvos, as part of the increasing **détente** between the traditional enemies.

# Sámos

Lush, seductive and shaped like a pregnant guppy, **SÁMOS** seems to swim away from Asia Minor, to which the island was joined until Ice Age cataclysms sundered it from Mount Mykáli (Mycale) on the Turkish mainland. The resulting 2.5km strait provides the narrowest maritime distance between Greece and Turkey, except at Kastellórizo. In its variety of mountainous terrain, beaches and vegetation, Sámos has the feel of a much larger island, and despite recent development and wildfires taking their toll, it remains indisputably among the most beautiful in the Aegean.

## Brief history

Sámos was during the Archaic era among the **wealthiest** islands in the Aegean and, under the patronage of tyrant Polykrates, home to a thriving intellectual community that included Epicurus, Pythagoras, Aristarcus and Aesop. Decline set in when Classical Athens rose, though Sámos's status improved in Byzantine times when it formed its own imperial administrative district. Late in the fifteenth century, the ruling Genoese **abandoned** the island to the mercies of pirates and Sámos remained almost uninhabited until 1562, when it was repopulated with Greek Orthodox settlers from various corners of the empire.

The new Samians **fought** fiercely for independence during the **1820s**, but despite notable land and sea victories against the Turks, the Great Powers handed the island back to the Ottomans in 1830, with the consoling proviso that it be semi-autonomous, ruled by an appointed Christian prince. This period, known as the **Iyimonía** (Hegemony), was marked by a renaissance in fortunes, courtesy of the hemp, leather-tanning and (especially) tobacco trades. However, union with Greece in 1912, an influx of refugees from Asia Minor in 1923 and the ravages of a bitter World War II occupation followed by mass emigration effectively reversed this recovery until tourism took over during the 1980s.

---

**ARRIVAL AND DEPARTURE**                                        **SÁMOS**

**By plane** Sámos's airport lies 14km southwest of Vathý and 3km west of Pythagório. There is no airport bus; taxi fares to all points are posted on placards, and in summer taxis to the airport or ferry docks must be booked in advance. There are flights on Olympic Airlines, Aegean or Sky Express to the following destinations (frequencies are for June–Oct):

Destinations Athens (3–4 daily; 50min–1hr 20min); Iráklio, Crete (2 weekly; 1hr); Lésvos (2 weekly; 40min–1hr 20min); Límnos (2 weekly; 1hr 40min–2hr 20min); Rhodes (2 weekly; 45min); Thessaloníki (4 weekly; 1hr 10min).

**By ferry/hydrofoil** There are three ferry ports: Karlóvassi in the west, plus Vathý and Pythagório in the east, making the island a major travel hub. All ferries between Pireás and Sámos call at both Karlóvassi and Vathý, while those from the northeast Aegean call at one or both. Small boats to Kuşadası in Turkey depart mostly from Vathý, while Karlóvassi has a small ferry to Foúrni and Ikaría. Pythagório offers ferry and hydrofoil connections to the Dodecanese islands. Here is a summary of destinations and summer frequencies:

Karlóvassi to: Áyios Kírykos, Ikaría (8 weekly; 2hr); Évdhilos, Ikaría (3 weekly; 2hr 30min); Foúrni (8 weekly; 1hr 30min–2hr 30min); Híos (1 weekly; 4hr); Kavála (1 weekly; 18hr 30min–19hr 30min); Lésvos (1 weekly; 6hr 30min); Límnos (1 weekly; 12–13hr); Mýkonos (6 weekly; 5hr–5hr 30min); Pireás (6 weekly; 11–12hr); Sýros (6 weekly; 6hr–6hr 30min).

Pythagório to: Agathónissi (4 weekly; 4hr); Lipsí (1–2 daily; 1hr 40min–4hr 30min); Pátmos (1–2 daily; 1hr–3hr 30min); Léros (1–2 daily; 2hr 15min–5hr 30min); Kálymnos (1–2 daily; 3hr 10min–6hr 45min); Kos (1 daily; 3hr 45min); Kuşadası, Turkey (2 weekly; 2hr).

Vathý to: Áyios Kírykos, Ikaría (8 weekly; 3hr); Évdhilos, Ikaría (3 weekly; 2hr 30min); Foúrni (3 weekly; 1hr 30min); Híos (2 weekly; 3hr 30min); Kavála (1 weekly; 18–19hr); Kuşadası, Turkey (1–2 daily; 1hr 30min); Lésvos (2 weekly; 6hr); Límnos (1 weekly; 11hr 30min–12hr 30min); Mýkonos (6 weekly; 5hr–5hr 30min); Pireás (6 weekly; 11–12hr); Sýros (6 weekly; 6hr–6hr 30min); Thessaloníki (1 weekly; 24hr).

SÁMOS

TURKEY

Kuşadasi (Turkey)

Kuşadasi (Turkey)

Posidhónio

Zoödhóhou Piyís

Kamára

Kérveli

Kaloúni (Klíma)

Ayía Zóni

Paleókastro

VATHY

Ano Vathý

Kalámi

Nissí

Psilí Ammos

Mykáli

Kédhros

Efpalínio Órygma

Panayía Spilianí

Pythagório

Hóra

Glyfádha

Potokáki

Kokkári

Myrtiliní

Heraíon

Iréon

Petrokáravo

Megális Panayías

Lemonákia

Tsamadoú

Mýli

Kyriakoú

Avláka

Pnáka

Vrondianís

Voutiótes

Mavratzéi

Pagóndas

Tsópela

Tsboú

Platanákia

Valeondádhes

Manolátes

Mt Ámbelos (1153m)

Pándhrossos

Koumaradhéi

Ayíos Konstandínos

Spatharéi

Ambelos

Stavrinídhes

Kondakéika

Kímisis Theotókou

Mt Karvoúnis (1160m)

Pýrgos

Neohóri

Koútsi

Pídhi

Ydhroússa

Plátanos

Koumeíka

Samiopoúla

Ayios Nikólaos

Karlóvassi

Bállos

Péfkos

Paleó Meséo

Ríva

Marathókambou

Órmos

N

Limáni

Lékka

Metamórfosis

Vótsalákia

Fourtáki

Potámi

Kosmadhéi

Kastaniá

Marathókambos

Psilí Ammos

Mikró Seïtáni

Dhrakéi

Evangelístrias

Limniónas

Mt Kérkis (1437m)

Megálo Seïtáni

Ayía Triádha

Kallithéa

Panayía Makriní

0        5

kilometres

Híos & Lésvos

Ikaría & Foúrni

Ikaría & Foúrni

**Travel agents** The most comprehensive island-wide travel agents, represented in all three ports and some resorts, are By Ship (☎ 22730 22116, ⍟ byshiptravel.gr) and ITSA (☎ 22730 23605, ⍟ itsatravelsamos.gr).

## GETTING AROUND

**By bus** The KTEL service is good between Pythagório and Vathý, with 11 services on weekdays, 9 on Saturday and 4 on Sunday, and fair on the Vathý–Kokkári–Karlóvassi route, with 8 weekday services, 5 on Sat and 3 on Sun, but poor for other destinations.

**By car or motorbike** Of the myriad scooter- and car-rental agencies dotted around the island, three to try are Aramis/Sixt (☎ 22730 23253), Avis/Reliable (☎ 22730 80445), both with branches island-wide, and Auto Union (☎ 22730 27444) at Themistoklí Sofoúli 79 in Vathý, which negotiates good long-term rates and will deliver cars to the airport.

**By kaïki** There are several weekly *kaïki* day-trips (10am–4pm; from €26) from Órmos Marathokámbou to the nearby islet of Samiopoúla and inaccessible parts of the south coast.

# Vathý

Lining the steep northeastern shore of a deep bay, beachless **VATHÝ** (often confusingly referred to as "Sámos") is a busy provincial town which grew from a minor anchorage after 1830, when it replaced Hóra as the island's capital. It's an unlikely, rather ungraceful resort and holds little of interest aside from an excellent museum, some Neoclassical mansions and the hillside suburb of **Áno Vathý**.

## Áno Vathý

The best inland target on foot, a twenty-minute walk south from town and 150m above sea level, is the atmospheric hill village of **ÁNO VATHÝ**, a nominally protected but increasingly threatened community of tottering, canal-tile-roofed houses: some buildings are being replaced by bad-taste blocks of flats, others are being defaced with aluminium windows and modern tiles. Best of several venerable **churches** is quadruple-domed **Aï Yannáki**, in the vale separating the village's two hillside neighbourhoods.

### Archeological museum

Tues–Sun 8.30am–3pm • €3 • ☎ 22730 27469

The only real must is the excellent **archeological museum**, set behind the small central park beside the nineteenth-century town hall. The collections are housed in both the old Paschalion building and a modern wing just opposite, constructed for the star exhibit: a majestic, 5m-tall *kouros* discovered out at the Heraion sanctuary. The largest freestanding effigy surviving from ancient Greece, this *kouros* was dedicated to Apollo, but found next to a devotional mirror to Mut (the Egyptian equivalent of Hera) from a Nile workshop.

In the Paschalion, more votive offerings of **Egyptian** design – a hippo, a dancer in Nilotic dress, Horus-as-Falcon, an Osiris figurine – provide evidence of trade and pilgrimage links between Sámos and the Nile valley going back to the eighth century BC. The **Mesopotamian** and **Anatolian** origins of other artwork confirm an exotic trend, most tellingly in a case full of ivory miniatures: Perseus and Medusa in relief; a kneeling, perfectly formed mini-*kouros*; a pouncing lion; and a bull's-head drinking horn. The most famous local artefacts are numerous bronze **griffin-heads**, for which Sámos was the major centre of production in the seventh century BC; they were mounted on the edge of cauldrons to ward off evil spirits. There's also an unlabelled **hoard of gold byzants**, some of more than three hundred imperial coins from the fifth to seventh centuries AD – one of the largest such troves ever discovered.

## ARRIVAL AND INFORMATION                                    VATHÝ

**By ferry** Ferries dock at the north end of the seafront.

**By bus** Buses stop on the front, just south of the centre.

**By taxi** The taxi rank is opposite the fishing harbour.

**By car** See above for details of car rental around the island. The southern seafront is the best area for free parking.

**Tourist office** Themistoklí Sofoúli 107 (May–Oct Mon–Fri

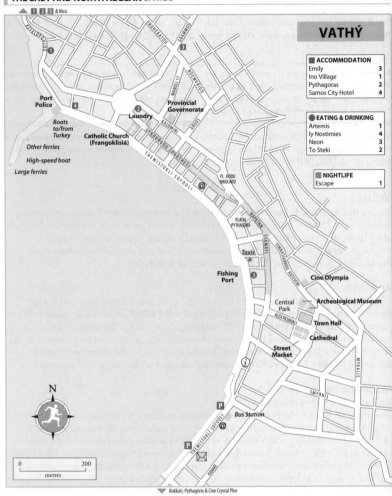

▲ ▌1▐ ▌2▐ ▌1▐ & Nissi

# VATHÝ

| ■ ACCOMMODATION | |
|---|---|
| Emily | 3 |
| Ino Village | 1 |
| Pythagoras | 2 |
| Samos City Hotel | 4 |

| ● EATING & DRINKING | |
|---|---|
| Artemis | 1 |
| Iy Nostimies | 4 |
| Neon | 3 |
| To Steki | 2 |

| ■ NIGHTLIFE | |
|---|---|
| Escape | 1 |

9am–2pm). The tourist office is minimally helpful.
**Services** Amenities include the post office, inconveniently

remote on Themistoklí Sofoúli. Internet cafés include Net House, on the front near the KTEL.

## ACCOMMODATION

**Emily** Cnr of Grámmou and 11 Noemvríou, Katsoúni ☎22730 24691, ✉emilyhotel@hotmail.com. Small, well-run two-star hotel with cheerful and comfortable rooms – there's even wall art – and a roof garden. Breakfast included. March–Nov. **€60**

**Ino Village** Kalámi ☎22730 23241, ⓦinovillagehotel.com. Surprisingly affordable three-star hotel about 1.5km north of the ferry dock, with views from most of its large, well-appointed rooms, a big pool and a decent on-site restaurant. Breakfast included. **€65**

**Pythagoras** Kalistrátou 12 ☎22730 28601, ⓦpythagorashotel.com. This medium-sized hotel, around 600m north of the ferry dock, provides the best value in town with its simple but spotless rooms. There are computers in the friendly bar/restaurant area. **€30**

**Samos City Hotel** Themistokli Soufoúli 11 ☎22730 28377, ⓦsamoshotel.gr. Refurbished behemoth by the ferry dock that's a firm favourite despite the rooms being rather small. Double-glazing against traffic noise, rooftop pool-terrace and popular café out front. Rudimentary breakfast included. **€65**

**EATING, DRINKING AND NIGHTLIFE**

Vathý's perennial nightlife venue is a "strip" at the start of Kefalopoúlou north of the jetty, with annually changing bars that boast seaside (or sea-view) terraces. Plushly fitted **Cine Olympia**, inland on Yimnasiárhou Katevéni, offers a variable programme of films (subject to unpredictable closure months), in competition with newer **Crystal Plex** at the head of the bay (mostly action films).

★ **Artemis** Kefalopoúlou 4 ☎ 22730 23639. Excellent, affordable seafood and starters like *fáva*, *hórta*, *seláhi* (ray) and *foúskes* as well as the usual mains. Good bulk *robóla* wine from the hill villages. Pleasant indoor/outdoor seating according to season. Mon–Sat 11am–1am.

**Escape** Kefalopoúlou 9. The most durable of the many clubs in the area that plays a fairly standard mixture of foreign and Greek disco favourites. Pleasant outdoor terrace and a/c dancefloor within. Daily 9pm–late.

**ly Nostimies** Áno Vathý; no phone. Popular ouzerí next to the school which features grilled chops and mackerel in summer and more imaginative items at other times. Try their *bouyiourdí* or pepper-and-cheese hotpot year-round. Mon–Sat 8pm–late; some lunches Oct–May.

**Neon** Themistoklí Sofoúli, beside Eurobank ☎ 22730 27516. A traditional *kafenío* that's good for an early-evening tipple-with-seafood-mezédhes; the waiter brings a big platter of whatever's cooking for a set price, around €6–8 per head with drink. Daily 10am–midnight.

**To Steki** ☎ 22730 23580. Family-run *inomayirío* in the shopping centre behind the seafront Catholic church that's tops for dishes like bean soup at lunch; also good fish like *gávros* and decent bulk wine. Daily 11am–1am.

# Around Vathý

Around 5km east of Vathý, the ridge-top **Zoödhóhou Piyís convent** (8am–2pm & 5–8pm) is accessible on a climbing zigzag road from Kamára, 3km east of Vathý, and gives superb views across the end of the island to Turkey. The dome of its *katholikón*, where the nuns' chanting is excellent, is upheld by four ancient columns from Miletus in Asia Minor.

Some modest **beaches** around Vathý compensate for lack of same in the capital. Striking **Kérveli Bay**, 8km southeast of Vathý, has a small but popular pebble beach and a fine taverna just inland. On the far southeast coast of the island, almost within spitting distance of Turkey and accessed from a turning 1km west of Paleókastro lie the reasonable beaches of **Mykáli** and **Psilí Ámmos**, both with a mostly mediocre range of facilities.

You'll need your own transport to reach both convent and beaches.

**ACCOMMODATION AND EATING**                                                         **AROUND VATHÝ**

★ **ly Kryfi Folia** Kérveli Bay ☎ 22730 25194. This secluded oasis, 300m uphill from the beach, offers simple but inexpensive and sustaining fare such as *kalamári* rings, the best lamb chops on Sámos and roast goat, which you can call to preorder. May to early Oct daily 11am–1am.

**Kerveli Village** Kérveli Bay ☎ 22730 23006, ⓦ kerveli .gr. One of the best hotels in eastern Sámos, located above the approach road to the beach, with sympathetic architecture, on-site car rental, pool, tennis court and private lido. April–Oct. €80

**Psili Ammos** Psilí Ámmos ☎ 693 60 69 325. You can expect excellent service, as well as good seafood, salads and meat grills at this taverna on the far right as you face the sea. May–Oct daily 9am–midnight.

**Zefiros Beach** Mykáli ☎ 22730 28532, ⓦ zefirosbeach .gr. Decent resort hotel with pleasant rooms, right behind the beach. Good for families, as it has ample watersports facilities off its patch of beach. May–Oct. €60

# Pythagório

Originally called Tigani ("frying pan"), a reference to its reputation as a heat trap, the island's premier resort, **PYTHAGÓRIO**, was renamed in 1955 to honour Pythagoras, ancient mathematician, philosopher and initiator of a rather subversive cult. Sixth-century BC tyrant Polykrates had his capital here, whose sporadic excavation has made modern Pythagório expand northeast and uphill. The village core of cobbled lanes and stone-walled mansions abuts a cosy **harbour**, fitting almost perfectly into the confines of Polykrates' ancient jetty, traces of which are still visible, but today devoted almost entirely to pleasure craft and overpriced café-bars. There are, however, several worthwhile sights in the vicinity.

**9**

## Archeological museum

Tues–Sun: June–Sept 8am–8pm; Oct–May 8.30am–3pm • €4 • ☎ 22730 62811

Finally opened to the public in 2010, the splendid new **archeological museum** has a number of fascinating and well-labelled exhibits laid out over two floors. Star billing on the ground floor goes to the stunning collection of **gold coins** from a jar found by a Dutch archeologist at the west end of the island, plus there is a substantial number of votary objects and some Greek, Hellenistic and Roman statuary. Upstairs is the home for larger statues, such as the Roman Emperor Trajan and a fine *kouros* from 540–530 BC, but the most interesting display is on the subject of **ancient Greek dwellings**. The large outdoor site behind the building contains some splendid mosaics but it is not set to open until 2013.

## The castle and around

Sámos's most complete **castle**, the nineteenth-century *pýrgos* of local chieftain Lykourgos Logothetis, overlooks both town and the shoreline where he, together with a certain "Kapetan Stamatis" and Admiral Kanaris, oversaw decisive naval and land victories against the Turks in the summer of 1824. The final battle was won on Transfiguration Day (Aug 6) – thus the dedication of the **church** by the castle – with an annual fireworks show commemorating the triumph. Also next to the castle are the remains of an early **Christian basilica**, occupying the grounds of a slightly larger Roman villa.

## Efpalínio Órygma

Tues–Sun: June–Sept 8am–8pm; Oct–May 8.30am–3pm • €4 • ☎ 22730 62813

The well-signposted **Efpalínio Órygma** is a 1036m aqueduct bored through the mountain just north of Pythagório. Designed by one Eupalinos of Mégara, and built by slave labour at the behest of Polykrates, it guaranteed the ancient town a siege-proof water supply, and remained in use until late Byzantine times. Even though the work crews started digging from opposite sides of the mountain, the horizontal deviation from true about halfway along – 8m – is remarkably slight, and the vertical error nil: a tribute to the competence of ancient surveyors. Unfortunately, only about the first 120m section of the tunnel is well lit and currently accessible to visitors.

## Panayía Spilianí

Cave open daylight hours • Free

On the way up to the Efpalínio Órygma is the well-marked turning for the monastery of **Panayía Spilianí**. The monastery itself, now bereft of nuns or monks, has been insensitively restored and the grounds are crammed with souvenir kiosks, but behind the courtyard the *raison d'être* of the place is still magnificent: a cool, illuminated, hundred-metre **cave**, at the drippy end of which is a subterranean shrine to the Virgin. This was supposedly the residence of the ancient oracular priestess Phyto, and a hiding place from medieval pirates.

## Potokáki

The local, variable **beach** stretches several kilometres west of the Logothetis castle, punctuated part-way along by the end of the airport runway and the cluster of nondescript hotels known as **POTOKÁKI**. Although you'll have to contend with the hotel crowds and low-flying jets, the western end of the sand-and-pebble beach is well groomed, the water clean and sports available.

### ARRIVAL AND INFORMATION                                  PYTHAGÓRIO

**By ferry** Ferries and hydrofoils dock at the jetty in the middle of the seafront.

**By bus** The main bus stop is on the seafront, near the jetty.

**By car** Street parking is impossible – use the pricey car park near the main T-junction or the free one just west behind the town beach.

**Tourist office** The information booth is a few paces along from the taxi rank on Lykourgoú Logothéti (June–Sept Mon–Fri 9am–1pm & 5–9pm; ☎ 22730 62274).

**Services** Several ATMs line Lykourgoú Logothéti; the post office is near the bus stop.

## ACCOMMODATION

**Doryssa Seaside Resort** Potokáki beach ☏ 22730 61360, ⊕doryssa-bay.gr. Huge complex including a hotel wing with Philippe Starck-ish rooms and a meticulously concocted fake village; each cosy bungalow is unique and there's even a platía with a pricey café. April to mid-Oct. **€130**

**Pension Dryoussa** ☏ 22730 61826, ⊕dryoussa @hotmail.com. Friendly and picturesque guesthouse, two

blocks inland from the town beach, with eight cosy, traditionally decorated rooms, most with small balconies. March–Nov. **€40**

**Studios Galini** ☏ 22730 61167. Brightly painted building, four blocks uphill from Lykoúrgou Logothéti, containing high-quality self-catering units, all with balconies and ceiling fans, most with a/c. Kindly English-speaking management. April–Oct. **€35**

## EATING, DRINKING AND ENTERTAINMENT

**Amadeus** Popular and enduring club, just in from the jetty, that showcases quality live Greek acts followed by recorded hits. Tues–Sun 9pm–late.

**Faros** ☏ 22730 62464. The best of the bunch stretching along from the harbour, where you can get basic seafood and small fish for well under €10. May–Oct daily 10am–1am.

**Rex** ☏ 22730 51236. On the outskirts of Mytilini village, 7km northwest, the Rex is one of the best-maintained

outdoor cinemas on the islands, screening quality first-run films, with free *loukoumádhes* (sweet fritters) and cheap pizza at intermission. Late May to mid-Sept.

**Souda** ☏ 698 22 79 746. Tucked down an alley off the harbour, this excellent year-round restaurant specializes in oven-baked home cooking such as moussaka and *yiouvétsi* for around €7–8. Check out the dish of the day. Daily 11am–midnight.

# Heraion

Tues–Sun: June–Sept 8am–8pm; Oct–May 8.30am–3pm • €3 • ☏ 22730 95277

Under layers of alluvial mud, plus today's runway, lies the processional Sacred Way joining ancient Samos with the **Heraion**, a massive shrine of the **Mother Goddess**, 5km west of Pythagório. Much touted in tourist literature, this assumes humbler dimensions – one surviving column and low foundations – upon approach. Yet once inside the precinct you sense the former grandeur of the temple, never completed owing to Polykrates' untimely death at the hands of the Persians. The site chosen, near the mouth of the still-active Imvrassós stream, was Hera's legendary birthplace and site of her trysts with Zeus; in the far corner of the fenced-in zone you can tread a large, exposed patch of the Sacred Way.

# Iréon

Modern **IRÉON**, barely a kilometre west of the ancient site, has a coarse-shingle beach and is at first glance a nondescript, grid-plan resort. Nonetheless its characterful pedestrianized waterfront remains popular: there are much better **tavernas** than at Pythagório, and after dark it has a more relaxed feel. The restaurants along the shore are especially busy on summer nights around the **full moon**, when Iréon is the best spot on the island to watch it rise out of the sea.

## ACCOMMODATION AND EATING                                              IRÉON

**Aegeon (Markos)** ☏ 22730 95271. Probably the most accomplished and Greek-patronized taverna, halfway along the seafront, with fresh wild fish at normal prices and good starters like potato salad and mushroom soufflé. Book ahead on moonlit nights. April–Oct daily 11am–2am.

**Glaros** ☏ 22730 95457. Cult place two-thirds of the way west along the seafront, where the atmosphere and prices

are excellent. Home-cooked delights include fish soup and okra, alongside standard grills, salads, fried vegetables and barrelled wine. May–Oct daily noon–1am.

★ **Kohili** ☏ 22730 95282. The hotel rooms at *Kohili*, just behind the western seafront, are simple but great value, especially during high season, while the taverna below is a star, offering delights such as urchins, cockles and octopus salad in the shady courtyard (daily 10am–late). **€40**

# Southern Sámos

Since island bus routes rarely pass through or near the following places, you really need your own vehicle to explore them. Three Samian "**pottery villages**" specialize in

**9**

addition to the usual wares, in the *Koúpa toú Pythagóra* or "Pythagorean cup", supposedly designed by the sage to leak over the user's lap if they were overfilled. Many of the **beaches** in this area are among the most deserted on the island, although it's not worth the effort and time involved in getting to the most remote.

## Pottery villages

The biggest concentration of retail outlets is at **KOUMARADHÉÏ**, about 7km west of Hóra, along a route dotted with the odd spot to stop for refreshment and sweeping views. From the village you can descend to the sixteenth-century monastery of **Megális Panayías** (Mon–Sat 10am–1pm & 5.30–8pm; free), containing some recently cleaned frescoes, then carry on to **PAGÓNDAS**, a large hillside community with an unusual communal fountain house on the southerly hillside. From there, a scenic road curls 15km around deforested hillside to **PÝRGOS**, at the head of a ravine draining southwest and the centre of Samian honey production.

## Kouméïka and Bállos

The western reaches of the southern Samian shoreline are approached via handsome **KOUMÉÏKA**, which has a massive inscribed marble fountain and a pair of *kafenía*-snack bars on its photogenic square. Below extends the long pebbly bay at **Bállos**, with sand and rock overhangs at the far east end. Bállos itself offers several places to stay and a few tavernas, all on the shore road.

From Kouméïka, the paved side road going west just before the village is a very useful short cut for travelling towards Órmos Marathokámbou (see p.610) and beyond.

## Plátanos

From the main road between the south coast and Karlóvassi, it's worth detouring up to **PLÁTANOS**, on the flanks of Mount Karvoúnis; at 520m this is one of Sámos's highest villages, with sweeping views west and south. The name comes from the three stout plane trees (*plátanos* in Greek) on its platía, whose spring-water in the arcaded fountain-house is immortalized in one of the most popular Samian folk songs. The only special sight is the double-naved thirteenth-century **church of Kímisis Theotókou** (key at house opposite west entrance) in the village centre.

### ACCOMMODATION, EATING AND DRINKING                          SOUTHERN SÁMOS

**Amfilissos** Bállos ☎22730 31669, ⓦamfilissos.gr. Friendly medium-sized hotel, a block behind the seafront, with functional, adequately furnished rooms, some with seaview balconies, set behind a nicely landscaped courtyard. Late May to Sept. **€36**

**Enalion** Bállos ☎22730 36444, ⓦenalionsamos.gr. The name means "on the sea", and this small white block of fully equipped studios overlooks the beach. Its taverna, *Akrogiali*, does good fish and other fare. April–Oct. **€45**

**Koutouki tou Barba Dhimitri** Central square, Pýrgos

☎22730 41060. A good range of vegetarian mezédhes, as well as the usual meaty grills, in a surprisingly chic environment for such a remote village. Daily 11am–1am.

**Leon** Central square, Plátanos ☎22730 39215. Great taverna, popular with the locals, where you can feast on goat in red sauce, *kondosoúvli* or *kokorétsi* for well under €10. Live folk music some nights. Daily noon–late.

**O Balos** Bállos ☎22730 36339. You can get grills and seafood at this seafront taverna but it's best to stick with the fine traditional baked items, such as *papoutsáki*. Pizza is also available. May to early Oct 10am–1am.

# Kokkári

**KOKKÁRI**, on Sámos's north coast, is the island's second major tourist centre. The town's coastal profile, covering two knolls behind mirror-image headlands called Dhídhymi (Twins), remains unchanged but its identity has been altered by inland expansion across old vineyards and along the west beach. The quaint harbour area is a lively place to hang out, but since the coarse-pebble **beaches** here are buffeted by near-constant winds, locals have made a virtue of necessity by developing the place as a successful **windsurfing** resort.

**INFORMATION** KOKKÁRI

**Tourist office** (May–Sept Mon–Sat 8.30am–1.30pm, Mon, Wed & Sat 7–9pm; ☎ 22730 92333). The helpful tourist office is on the main street heading inland.

**Activities** A windsurfing school thrives just west of town (☎ 22730 92102, ✆ samoswindsurfing.gr).

**ACCOMMODATION, EATING AND DRINKING**

**Athena Hotel** ☎ 22730 92030, ✉ h-athena@otenet.gr. The modern, comfortable rooms are spread over three buildings, set in beautifully landscaped grounds with a large pool, across the road from the south beach. Very helpful Greek-Canadian owner. April–Oct. €45

**Cavos** ☎ 22730 92436. This perennially popular place on the fishing harbour, run by a Greek/German couple, cranks out breakfast, snacks, coffees and cocktails according to the time of day, though the music can be rather middle-of-the-road. April–Oct daily 8am–late.

**Girasole** ☎ 22730 92037. Genuine Italian restaurant on the fishing harbour, serving quality pizza, pasta and other classic dishes in the €10–15 range. Chic decor and comfy seating too. May–Oct daily noon–1am.

★ **ly Byra** ☎ 22730 92350. Though the range is limited, the light mezédhes on offer, like *domatokeftédhes* and *keftedhákia* plus maybe seafood titbits, are superbly executed at this old favourite opposite the main church. April–Oct daily 11am–late.

★ **Tarsanas** ☎ 22730 92337. Wonderful terrazzo-floored 1980s throwback, 100m down the lane from the west beach. doing pizzas, a couple of dishes of the day, like *briám* or *dolmádhes*, and their own dynamite red wine. Daily June–Sept 11am–late, Oct–May 8pm–2am.

**Tsamadou Hotel** ☎ 22730 92314, ✆ tsamadou.com. Friendly English-run place, towards the south end of the north beach, whose simple a/c rooms have fridges. Asian snacks are available in the garden conservatory. April–Oct. €40

# The north coast

The closest sheltered **beaches** to Kokkári are about thirty minutes' walk west, fully carpeted with sunbeds and permanently anchored umbrellas. The further you move away from the resort, however, the wilder and quieter the strands become and the less-touristed the settlements.

## Lemonákia and Tzamadhoú

The first beach west of Kokkári, **Lemonákia**, is a bit close to the road, so it is better to carry on 1km to the graceful crescent of **Tzamadhoú**. It can only be accessed by a path, and the eastern third of the beach, made up of saucer-shaped pebbles, is a well-established nudist zone.

## Avlákia and Tzaboú

**AVLÁKIA**, 3km west of Tzamadhoú, is a quiet shoreline hamlet with an excellent taverna and some of the best views on the island. The nearest beach, 2km further west with a steep lane down, is **Tzaboú**, probably the most scenic north-coast beach with its rock formations but mercilessly buffeted by the prevailing wind most days – and the snack-bar tries to charge €6 for parking. There's a nudist annexe, with separate path access from Avlákia, off to the right.

## Áyios Konstandínos

**Platanákia**, the next settlement west of Tzaboú and essentially a handful of buildings at a bridge by the turning for Manolátes, is actually the eastern quarter of **ÁYIOS KONSTANDÍNOS**, whose surf-pounded esplanade has been prettified. However, there are no significant beaches within walking distance, so the collection of mostly warm-toned stone buildings constitutes a peaceful alternative to Kokkári.

## Áyios Nikólaos

West of Áyios Konstandínos the mountains hem the road in against the sea, and the terrain doesn't relent until **Áyios Nikólaos**, which is the tiny seaside annexe of more traditional Kondakéïka. A passable pebble beach, **Piáki**, lies ten minutes' walk east past the last studio units.

**9**

## Kímisis Theotókou

The Byzantine church of **Kímisis Theotókou** (left unlocked) is signposted 2.5km inland along a partly paved road from Kondakéïka. The second oldest and most artistically noteworthy on Sámos, dating from the late twelfth/early thirteenth century, it has extensive frescoes contemporaneous with the building. The deceptively simple exterior gives little hint of the glorious barrel-vaulted interior, its decoration still vivid except where damp has blurred the images.

### ACCOMMODATION, EATING AND DRINKING THE NORTH COAST

#### LEMONÁKIA AND TZAMADHOÚ

**Arion** Lemonákia ☎ 22370 92020, ⓦ arion-hotel.gr. This well-designed bungalow/hotel complex on a flattish patch of hillside 600m inland from the coastal road has dazzlingly white, minimalist rooms and a large pool. Breakfast included. May–Oct. **€100**

★ **Armonia Bay** Tzamadhoú ☎ 22730 92279, ⓦ armoniabay.gr. This hotel directly above the beach has tastefully decorated and sizeable rooms with marble-clad baths, as well as a fine pool and pleasant common areas. Good value. April–Oct. **€75**

#### AVLÁKIA AND TZABOÚ

**To Delfini** Avlákia ☎ 22730 94279. Kyra Alexandra is the heart and soul of this welcoming traditional taverna, in the middle of the village, which is strong on fresh little fish, *hórta* and chips. May–Oct daily 10am–1am.

#### ÁYIOS KONSTANDÍNOS

**Aeolos** ☎ 22730 94021. Terrific fish or grilled meat for €7–9 and a few daily oven dishes, served at tables adjoining a tiny pebble cove at the far west end of the esplanade. May–Sept daily noon–midnight.

**Akroyiali** ☎ 22730 94655. Quite pricey all-round mid-quay taverna, with some dishes such as steaks and most fish exceeding €10. Still, a reasonable atmosphere and lovely setting. April to early Oct daily 10am–midnight.

**Daphne** ☎ 22730 94003, ⓦ daphne-hotel.gr. Set against a leafy backdrop on a hill 500m back from the village, this good-value hotel has smart but compact rooms with baths and great views. Breakfast included. May–Oct. **€50**

**Hotel Apartments Agios Konstantinos** ☎ 22730 94000, ⓦ hotelagios.gr. Attractive two-storey building on the street linking Platanákia to the sea, with a red tile roof. Its sea-facing rooms are all well equipped and have small balconies. April–Oct. **€40**

#### ÁYIOS NIKÓLAOS

**Iy Psaradhes** ☎ 22730 32489. With a terrace lapped by the waves, you'll need to book in season to guarantee a fine meal of fresh fish, salads and good barrelled wine. Easter–Oct daily 11am–1am.

**Villa Eva** ☎ 22730 30020, ⓦ villaeva-samos.gr. This hotel set in lush grounds, signposted downhill from the main coastal road, is also a thriving New Age retreat centre, with reiki, yoga and Sufi seminars. Breakfast, jacuzzi and exercise session included. May–Oct. **€85**

## Northern hill villages

Inland between Kokkári and Kondakéïka, an idyllic landscape of pine, cypress and orchards is overawed by dramatic mountains. Despite bulldozer vandalism, some of the trail system linking the various **hill villages** is still intact, and walkers can return to the main highway to catch a bus back to base. Those with transport should leave it at Vourliótes and execute a **three-hour loop** via Manolátes, north and down to Aïdhónia, then back up east to your starting point. There is some waymarking, and the final stretch of trail has been rehabilitated.

### Vourliótes

**VOURLIÓTES**, closest village to Kokkári, has beaked chimneys and brightly painted shutters sprouting from its typical tile-roofed houses. But restaurateur greed has ruined the formerly photogenic central square by chopping down old mulberries and cramming in more tables.

### Manolátes

**MANOLÁTES**, an hour-plus walk uphill from Vourliótes via a deep river canyon, has several tavernas, as ever with inland locales better value than those at coastal resorts. The two high-quality *raku* ceramic workshops are anything but cheap though.

**AAA** Manolátes ☎ 22730 94472. Central taverna that makes a good fist of such dishes as *yiouvarlákia*, grilled *mastéllo*, an idiosyncratic version of aubergine *imám* and dry red wine from Stavrinídhes. March–Nov daily 11am–2am, some winter weekends from 8pm.

**Despina** Manolátes ☎ 22730 94043. Warm-hearted Despina whips up dishes of the day, *revythokeftédhes* and good *tzatziki*, which you can enjoy in a gazebo by the central fountain. Daily 10am–10pm.

**Galazio Pigadhi** Vourliótes ☎ 22730 93480. Serving up rabbit stew, *soutzoukákia* and aubergine dishes at limited pavement seating under a kangaroo vine up beyond the platía, this is a real locals' favourite. Daily 7pm–late.

★ **Iy Pera Vrysi** Vourliótes ☎ 22730 93277. This taverna at the village entrance offers a huge range of well-priced, imaginative *mezédhes* like spinach croquettes or chicken livers, as well as local *robóla* wine. March–Nov daily noon–1am.

★ **Kallisti** Manolátes ☎ 22730 94661. Excellent roast goat, courgette pie, grills and some small fish are all available for maximum €7 at this great taverna next to *AAA*, as is fine barrelled wine. Warm welcome assured too. March–Nov daily 11am–1am, some winter weekends from 8pm.

## Karlóvassi and the northwest coast

**KARLÓVASSI**, 31km west of Vathý and Sámos's second town, is sleepier and more old-fashioned than the capital, despite having roughly the same population. It's a useful base for enjoying northwestern Sámos's excellent **beaches** or taking a number of rewarding **walks**. The town divides into five straggly neighbourhoods: **Néo**, well inland, whose growth was spurred by the influx of post-1923 refugees; **Meséo**, across the usually dry riverbed, tilting appealingly off a knoll and then blending to the west with the shoreline district of **Ríva**; picturesque **Paleó** (or **Áno**) lies further west, its hundred or so houses draped either side of a leafy ravine; while below it is **Limáni**, the small harbour district. Most tourists stay at or near Limáni, which has most tourist facilities. The **port** itself is an appealing place with a working boatyard at the west end.

### Ríva

On the 1km-long street linking Meséo's Platía 8-Maïoú to **Ríva**, stands a huge, early twentieth-century **church**, topped with twin belfries and a blue-and-white dome, typical of those that dot the coastal plain here. Ríva itself is something of a ghost town, with derelict stone-built warehouses, tanneries and mansions, reminders of the defunct leather industry that flourished here until the 1960s. The epoch is immortalized in the brand-new **Tannery Museum** (Tues–Sat 9am–1pm; free), which has informative displays on the industry, as well as tobacco production.

### Potámi and around

The closest decent **beach** to Karlóvassi is **Potámi**, forty minutes' walk away via the coast road from Limáni or an hour by a more scenic, high trail from Paleó. This broad arc of sand and pebbles is presided over on the east by the striking modernist clifftop chapel of Áyios Nikólaos from 1971. A streamside path leads twenty minutes inland from Potámi, past the eleventh-century church of **Metamórfosis** – the oldest on Sámos – to a point where the river disappears into a small gorge. Just above the Metamórfosis church, a clear if precipitous path leads up to the remains of a small, contemporaneous **Byzantine fortress**.

### Mikró Seïtáni and Megálo Seïtáni

A couple of daily water-taxi services run in peak season from Karlóvassi port to both beaches

The coast west of Potámi ranks among the most beautiful and unspoilt on Sámos; since the early 1980s it has served as a protected refuge for the rare **monk seal**, still glimpsed occasionally by lucky hikers or bathers. Some twenty minutes along the dirt track at the west end of Potámi Bay takes you to the well-cairned side trail running parallel to the water. After twenty minutes more you'll arrive at **Mikró Seïtáni**, a small pebble cove guarded by sculpted rock walls. A full hour's walk from the trailhead, through olive

**9**

terraces, brings you to **Megálo Seïtáni**, the island's finest sand beach, at the mouth of the intimidating Kakopérato gorge. Bring food, water and something to shade yourself, though a swimsuit is optional.

### ARRIVAL AND DEPARTURE

**By ferry** Karlóvassi's dock is an inconvenient 3km from the centre. Buses to town are infrequent but do often meet boats.

### KARLÓVASSI AND THE NORTHWEST COAST

**By bus** Most buses call at multiple stops along the seafront before terminating near the port.

### ACCOMMODATION

**Erato** Limáni ☎ 22730 35370. Attractive smallish hotel built in Cretan style 150m east of central Limáni, with compact but spotless rooms and a warm welcome. Breakfast included. May–Oct. **€35**

**Samaina Port/Samaina Inn** Limáni ☎ 22730 30850, ⓦ samainahotels.gr. Excellent-value place on the pedestrianized old harbour, offering rooms with sea-facing balconies. You can book more luxurious rooms at the nearby sister hotel *Samaina Inn*. Breakfast included at both. April–Oct. *Samaina Port* **€40**, *Samaina Inn* **€60**

### EATING, DRINKING AND NIGHTLIFE

★ **Hippy's** Potámi beach ☎ 22730 33796. Laid-back beach bar, set behind a sunflower garden, with a distinct Indian vibe. It does a limited breakfast and meals menu, plus ample coffee and cocktails. Regular parties and musical events. June to early Sept 10am–late.

**ly Platia** Platía 8-Maïoú, Meséo ☎ 22730 34600. Busy with locals at lunchtime thanks to plentiful traditional *mayireftá* and a few grills, all served up speedily though quality varies. Daily 11am–midnight.

**O Dionysos** Platía 8-Maïoú, Meséo ☎ 22730 30120. Offers creative dishes such as asparagus in mushroom sauce and richly cooked meat dishes. Pleasant indoor and outdoor seating, plus a wine list aspiring to Athenian sophistication. Mon–Sat 11am–1am.

**Popcorn** Ríva ⓦ popcornclub.gr. With DJed events at weekends, this enduring student club, located in an old customs warehouse, has a state-of-the-art sound system pumping out international and Greek hits. 10pm–late; June–Sept daily; Oct–May Fri–Sun.

**To Kyma** Ríva ☎ 22730 34017. Great ouzerí at the main seafront T-junction, popular with students and townies alike, where you can feast on inexpensive and ample seafood and mezédhes. April–Oct daily noon–late.

## Southwestern beach resorts

The southwestern coast of Sámos boasts some of the island's best beaches, stretching in an almost unbroken line between Órmos Marathokámbou and Limniónas. These strands also offer a range of amenities.

The port of Marathókambos, **ÓRMOS MARATHOKÁMBOU**, 18km from Karlóvassi, has become something of a resort, though with ample character in its backstreets. Otherwise, the main focus of attention is the pedestrianized quay, home to several **tavernas** and starting point for excursion boats to the island of Samiopoúla and along the coast.

Two kilometres west of Órmos, **VOTSALÁKIA** (signposted as "Kámbos"), Sámos's most family-pitched resort, straggling a further 2km behind the island's longest beach. The presence of Mount Kérkis (see opposite) looming overhead rarely fails to impress too. Just to the west, **Fournáki**, the collective name for a series of sand-and-pebble **coves** backed by low cliffs, is usually less crowded.

Three kilometres west of Votsalákia, you reach 600m-long **Psilí Ámmos**, not to be confused with its namesake beach in southeastern Sámos. The sea shelves ridiculously gently here – 100m out you're still just knee-deep – but that makes it ideal for families with young children. Access to **Limniónas**, a smaller but superior cove 2km west from Psilí Ámmos, passes the *Limnionas Bay Village Hotel*. Yachts and *kaïkia* occasionally call at the protected bay, which offers decent swimming at the east end, away from a rock shelf in the middle.

### ACCOMMODATION, EATING AND DRINKING

**Evinos** Votsalákia ☎ 698 55 68 147, ✉ elsahiou@gmail.com. Standard clean but smallish rooms above a nice

### SOUTHWESTERN BEACH RESORTS

authentic taverna behind the middle of the beach, among the cheapest at this end of the island. May–Sept. **€25**

**Hotel Kerkis Bay** Órmos Marathokámbou ☏ 22730 37202, ✆ kerkis-bay.com. Fairly spacious rooms are available at this pleasant spot, one block inland from mid-quay. There are various sports facilities (though no pool) and a decent restaurant. Breakfast included. Mid-April to late Oct. €35

**Iy Trata** Órmos Marathokámbou ☏ 22730 31859. The most authentic taverna in the resort, at its eastern end just off the pedestrian zone, specializes in fresh local fish, often at under €10 per portion. April–Oct daily 10am–1am.

**Limnionas Bay Village** Limniónas ☏ 22730 37057, ✆ hotel-limnionas-bay-village.co.uk. Large rather characterless resort right behind the bay with tiered units arrayed around a garden full of olive trees and a decent pool. Breakfast included. May–Oct. €60

★ **Loukoullos** Fournáki ☏ 22730 37147. This welcoming restaurant with a lovely courtyard overlooking the first cove is better in the evening, when the full range of tasty and inexpensive *mayireftá* and home-grown veg dishes is available. May–Sept daily noon–midnight.

## Mount Kérkis and around

A limestone/volcanic oddity in a predominantly schist landscape, **Mount Kérkis** (Kerketévs) – the Aegean's second-highest summit after Mount Sáos on Samothráki – attracts legends and speculation as easily as the cloud pennants that usually wreath it. Hermits colonized and sanctified the mountain's many caves in Byzantine times; resistance guerrillas controlled it during World War II; and mariners still regard it with superstitious awe, especially when mysterious lights – presumed to be the spirits of the departed hermits, or the aura of some forgotten holy icon – are glimpsed at night near the cave-mouths. Gazing up from a supine seaside position, you may be inspired to **climb the peak** (see box below), though less ambitious walkers might want to **circle the mountain's flank**, first by vehicle and then by foot. The road beyond Limniónas through **Kallithéa** is paved all the way to **Dhrakéï**.

### Dhrakéï and Megálo Seïtáni

**DHRAKÉÏ** is a minuscule, back-of-beyond village with views across to Ikaría. A lovely trail – minimally disrupted by a track – descends ninety minutes through forest to **Megálo Seïtáni**, from where it's easy to continue on to Karlóvassi within another two-and-a-half hours. People climbing up from Seïtáni must either retrace their steps, summon a taxi or stay at a few unofficial **rooms** establishments in Dhrakéï.

### Kallithéa, Panayía Makriní, Ayía Triádha and around

During term time a vehicle leaves Karlóvassi (Mon–Fri 1.20pm) bound for Kallithéa; during summer it only operates twice a week (Mon to Dhrakéï, Fri to Kallithéa)

From **Kallithéa**, a small village 7km southwest of Dhrakéï with just a simple grill on its tiny square, a newer track (from beside the cemetery) and an older trail both lead up within 45 minutes to a spring, rural chapel and plane tree on the west flank of Kérkis, with path-only continuation for another thirty minutes to a pair of faintly frescoed cave-churches. **Panayía Makriní** stands at the mouth of a high, wide but shallow grotto, whose balcony affords terrific views. By contrast, **Ayía Triádha**, a ten-minute scramble overhead, has most of its structure made up of cave wall; just adjacent, another long, narrow, volcanic cavern can be explored with a torch some hundred metres into the mountain.

---

### CLIMBING MOUNT KÉRKIS

The classic route up Mount Kérkis begins from Votsalákia, along the paved but narrow lane leading inland towards Evangelistrías convent. After a 45-minute walk through olive groves, the path begins, more or less following power lines up to the convent. A friendly nun may proffer an ouzo and point you up the paint-marked trail, continuing even more steeply up to the peak. The views are tremendous, though the climb itself is humdrum once you're out of the trees. About an hour before the top there's a chapel with an attached cottage for sheltering in emergencies, and just beyond, a welcome spring. All told, it's a seven-hour return outing from Votsalákia, not counting rest stops.

**9**

# Foúrni

The straits between Sámos and Ikaría are speckled with a mini-archipelago – once haunted by pirates from various corners of the Mediterranean – of which only two are inhabited. Of these, the more westerly Thýmena has no tourist facilities but the largest of the group, **FOÚRNI**, has a growing reputation as a great hideaway. Unlike so many small Greek islands, it has a stable population, around 1600, as it is home to a huge fishing fleet and one of the more thriving boatyards in the Aegean.

Apart from remote **Khryssomiliá** hamlet in the north, reached by the island's longest (18km) road, Foúrni's inhabitants are concentrated in the **port** and **Kambí** hamlet just south.

## The port

The harbour community is larger than it seems from the sea, with a friendly ambience reminiscent of 1970s Greece; the historical pirate connection is reflected in the municipality's official name, Foúrni Korseón (Fourni of the Corsairs). The central main market street, field-stoned and mulberry-shaded, ends well inland at a little **platía** with two giant plane trees and a Hellenistic sarcophagus found in a nearby field.

## Southern Foúrni

From the primary school near the port, it's a fifteen-minute walk south on a flagstone lane, then over the restored windmill ridge, to **KAMBÍ**, a scattered community overlooking a pair of sandy, tamarisk-shaded coves.

A path system starting at Kambí's last house continues south around the headland to other, more secluded **bays** of varying sizes and beach consistencies. These are also favourite anchorages for passing yachts, but unlike Kambí they have substantial summer communities of rough campers and naturists. In order of appearance they are sand-and-pebble **Áspa**, fifteen minutes along, with a tiny spring seeping from the rocks just before, **Pelekaniá**, five minutes further, and equidistant **Elidháki** – both of these coarse pebble, the latter also with paved road access. The trail is slippery and steep just before Áspa so some may prefer to employ a taxi-boat service.

The side-road serving Elidháki from the main island ridge-road also has an option for **Petrokopió** (Marmári) cove, named after its role as a quarry for ancient Ephesus in Asia Minor. The quarry itself, with obvious chisel-marks and abandoned half-worked stones down by the shore, proves impressive; the beach is made of the same stone.

## Northern Foúrni

North from Foúrni harbour via steps, then path, are a pair of slightly sullied beaches. **Psilí Ámmos**, in front of a derelict fish-processing plant and equally defunct café at the end with tamarisks, is superior to **Kálamos** further along, dominated by a military watchpoint; both now have track access, while the former has a fishermen's jetty and beach bar. In the northeast of the island, **KAMÁRI** too has a beach. Without transport, it's possible to **walk** between town and Kamári on the old *kalderími*, which goes via the ridge-top monastery of Panayía.

### ARRIVAL AND GETTING AROUND

**FOÚRNI**

**By ferry** Foúrni is surprisingly well connected, with services to: Áyios Kírykos, Ikaría (8 weekly; 1hr 15min); Karlóvassi, Sámos (8 weekly; 1–3hr); Mýkonos (3 weekly; 4hr–4hr 30min); Pireás (3 weekly; 10–11hr); Sýros (3 weekly; 5hr–5hr 30min); Vathý, Sámos (3 weekly; 2hr).

**By scooter** Although much of the island is walkable, you can rent a scooter from seafront Escape at the port (☎ 22750 51514).

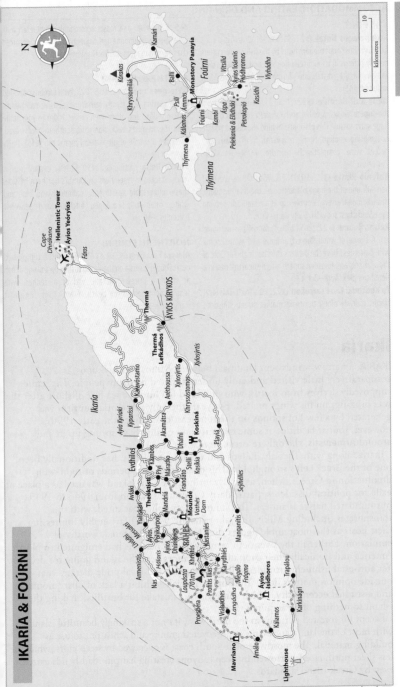

IKARÍA & FOÚRNI

Kamári
Monastery Panayia
Foúrni
Vítsiliá
Balli
Ayios Ioánnis
Pródhromos
Khryssomiliá
Kórakos
Psilí Ámmos
Vlyhádha
Foúrni
Kambí
Aspa
Petrokopió
Pelekanía & Eliúdhki
Kasídhi
Kálamos
Thímena
Thýmena

Cape
Dhrákano
Hellenistic Tower
Áyios Yeóryios
Fáros
Thermá
ÁYIOS KÍRYKOS
Thermá Lefkádhos
Xylosýrtis
Ikaría
Kyparíssi
Xylosýtis
Áyia Kyriakí
Akamátra
Xyliosýtomps
Nanoústamo
Aéthoussa
Dháfni
Koskiná
Évdhilos
Kámbos
Píyi
Maratho
Dháfni
Playiá
Theóktistí
Mandriá
Frandáto
Stelli
Kosíkia
Aváki
Tsaliskári
Messakti
Vathés
Dam
Moundé
Lívadhi
Nás
Pighí Karpoú
Áyios Dhimítrios
Armenistís
Dhrianítres
Kástanés
Kardhiés
Karkinágri
RÁHES
Halkoris
Profitis Ilías
Loupádra (701m)
Megálo Frágma
Áyios Isídhoros
Trápalou
Proespéra
Vrakádhes
Langádha
Kálamos
Mavriáno
Amálo
Lighthouse

N
kilometres
0        10

Sýros & Mýkonos

**9** ## ACCOMMODATION, EATING AND DRINKING

### THE PORT

**Archipelagos Hotel** ☎22750 51250, ⓦarchipelagos hotel.gr. This smart modern hotel by the fishing port offers quality fittings in its eighteen doubles and suites, as well as an on-site restaurant during summer. Breakfast included. **€45**

★ **Iy Kali Kardhia** ☎22750 51217. The aroma from the superb €8 *kondosoúvli* and *kokorétsi* rotating on the huge spits outside this place just behind the inland square is tempting enough. Some *mayireftá*, fresh salads and decent wine complete the picture. April–Oct daily 7pm–late.

**Kafenio Platia** ☎22750 51678. With tables crowded beneath one of the huge plane tree on the inland square, this traditional *kafenío* doubles up as a restaurant, serving the island's best *souvláki*. Daily 8am–late.

**Patras Rooms** ☎22750 51268, ⓦfourni-patrasrooms .gr. A choice of wood-floored, antique-bed rooms, some with balconies above the owner's café-bar in the middle of the seafront, and fourteen superb hillside apartments, in a tiered complex. April–Oct. **€30**

**To Koutouki tou Psarrakou** ☎22750 51670. This local staple, halfway along the main market street, still does decent *mayireftá* and roasts accompanied by Cretan bulk wine and a Peloponnesian liqueur, despite an enforced change of management. Daily noon–1am.

### SOUTHERN FOÚRNI

**O Yiorgos** Kambí ☎22750 51025. With tamarisk-shaded beach seating, the family ferries inexpensive fish plates, Ikarian *soúfiko* and other oven dishes 100m to your table from the premises back along the southern access road. There are a couple of ultra-cheap rooms too (€15). Daily noon–midnight.

**Studio Rena** Kambí ☎22750 51364, ⓦstudio-rena .com. Stacked in three tiers on Kambí's northern hillside, these comfortable apartments, painted island blue and white, offer fully equipped kitchens and sea-view balconies. **€40**

### NORTHERN FOÚRNI

**Almyra** Kamári ☎697 91 41 653. The most accomplished out-of-town taverna on the island rustles up a range of fish at standard prices, goat and various *mezédhes*, with seating right behind the beach. 11am–1am: June–Oct daily; Nov–May Fri–Sun.

# Ikaría

IKARÍA, a narrow, windswept landmass between Sámos and Mýkonos, is comparatively little visited and sadly underestimated by many people. The name supposedly derives from Icarus, who in legend fell into the sea just offshore after the wax bindings on his wings melted. For years the only substantial tourism was generated by a few **hot springs** on the southeast coast; since the early 1990s, however, tourist facilities of some quantity and quality have sprung up in and around **Armenistís**, the only resort of note.

Ikaría, along with Thessaly, Lésvos and the Ionian islands, has traditionally been one of the **Greek Left**'s strongholds. This dates from long periods of right-wing domination in Greece, when, as in Byzantine times, the island was used as a place of **exile** for political dissidents, particularly Communists, who from 1946 to 1949 outnumbered native islanders. This house-arrest policy backfired, with the transportees (including Mikis Theodhorakis in 1946–47) favourably impressing their hosts as the most noble figures they had ever encountered, worthy of emulation. Earlier in the twentieth century, many Ikarians had emigrated to North America and ironically their capitalist remittances kept the island going for decades. Yet anti-establishment attitudes still predominate and local pride dictates that outside opinion matters little. Thus many Ikarians exhibit a lack of obsequiousness and a studied **eccentricity**, which some visitors mistake for hostility, making the island something of an acquired taste.

Except for forested portions in the northwest, it's not a strikingly beautiful island, with most of the landscape being scrub-covered granite and schist put to use as building material. The mostly desolate south coast is overawed by steep cliffs, while the less sheer north face is furrowed by deep canyons creating hairpin road-bends extreme even by Greek-island standards.

## ARRIVAL AND DEPARTURE

**By plane** Ikaría airport, which can only handle small domestic planes, is around 12km northeast of Áyios Kírykos. There is just one daily flight to Athens (50min) year-round and 1–5 weekly to Iráklio (Crete; 40min), Límnos (35min) and Thessaloníki (1hr 45min).

**By ferry** Ikaría lies on the main Pireás–Sámos route and ferries alternate between calling at Áyios Kírykos and Évdhilos. Áyios Kírykos also has a weekly service on the northeast Aegean route to Kavála, as well as a small seasonal boat to Foúrni and Karlóvassi on Sámos.

**Áyios Kírykos** to: Foúrni (9 weekly; 1hr); Híos (1 weekly; 5hr); Karlóvassi, Sámos (9 weekly; 2hr–2hr 30min); Kavála (1 weekly; 21hr); Lésvos (1 weekly; 7hr 30min); Límnos (1 weekly; 13hr 30min); Mýkonos (3 weekly; 3hr); Pireás (3 weekly; 9hr–9hr 30min); Sýros (3 weekly; 4hr 30min); Vathý, Sámos (4 weekly; 2hr 30min–3hr).

**Évdhilos** to: Karlóvassi, Sámos (3 weekly; 2hr); Mýkonos (3 weekly; 2hr 30min); Pireás (3 weekly; 8hr 30min–9hr); Sýros (3 weekly; 4hr); Vathý, Sámos (3 weekly; 2hr 30min).

## GETTING AROUND

**By bus** There are 1–2 cross-island bus services between Áyios Kírykos, Évdhilos and Armenistís, with occasional erratic onward services to Khrístos. Unfortunately, the most reliable year-round service usually leaves Áyios Kírykos early morning and does not link with ferry arrivals.

**By car or motorbike** Aventura (☎ 22750 71117) and Dolihi Tours/Lemy (☎ 22750 71122) are the most prominent rental agencies, with branches in Armenistís,

Évdhilos and Áyios Kírykos.

**Taxi** Taxis can be elusive, as well as expensive, and are best booked through one of the agencies above, especially if you have a ferry or flight from the other side of the island – budget on at least €50.

**Hitching** For more leisurely travel, note that hitching is a common practice on this unconventional island.

# Áyios Kírykos and around

The south-coast port and capital of **ÁYIOS KÍRYKOS** has little to detain foreign tourists, at least until the modest archeological museum reopens in 2014. The spa of **Thérma**, just over 1km northeast of the port, saw its heyday in the 1960s, and now relies on a mostly elderly, health-service-subsidized clientele from July to early October. Of more general interest is the *spílio* or **natural sauna** on the shore (8am–8pm; €4.50), co-housed with plunge pools under the cave roof. Other good bets for informal soaks are the seaside, open-air pool (35–40°C) of the **Asklipioú hot springs**, reached by steps down from the Áyios Kírykos courthouse, or better still the natural, shoreline hot springs at **Thérma Lefkádhos**, 2km southwest of Áyios Kírykos, where 50–58°C water mixes with the sea to a pleasant temperature inside a ring of giant volcanic boulders. A further 3km brings you to another pleasant cove, below the small hamlet of **Xylosýrti**.

## Fáros and around

The longest **beach** on the south coast is at **Fáros**, 12km northeast of Áyios Kírykos along a good road which also serves the airport. A colony of summer cottages shelters under tamarisks along the sand-and-gravel strand, with a reefy zone to cross before deep water. From a signposted point just inland from Fáros beach, a dirt track leads 2km to the trailhead for the round **Hellenistic watchtower** at **Cape Dhrákano**, much the oldest and most impressive ancient ruin on the island (closed for restoration). It's part of a much larger, now mostly crumbled fort extending halfway to the cape and its pretty rustic chapel of **Áyios Yeóryios**. Right below this to the north, perfectly sheltered in most weathers, is a fantasy-image sand **beach**, with assorted rocks and islets off the cape-tip for contrast.

## ACCOMMODATION
**ÁYIOS KÍRYKOS AND AROUND**

★ **Agriolykos Pension** Thérma ☎ 22750 22433, ⓦ agriolykos.gr. Wonderful and welcoming place on the eastern bluff with original artwork, delightfully decorated rooms, use of kitchen, extensive shady grounds and direct access to a hidden cove. Breakfast included. April–Oct. **€45**

**Akti** Áyios Kírykos ☎ 22750 22694, ⓦ pensionakti.gr. Pleasant spot on a knoll above the east quay, with comfy a/c rooms, wi-fi, fluent English-speaking management and views of Foúrni from the café-garden. Breakfast included. **€40**

**Evon's Rooms** Fáros ☎ 22750 32580, ⓦ evonsrooms .com. Attractively appointed and well-equipped a/c rooms, especially the pricier galleried top-floor units. Right on the beach, with a pleasantly landscaped garden and private parking. €40

**Marina Hotel** Thérma ☎ 22750 22188, ⓦ marina -hotel.gr. All the rooms at this friendly little hotel, just above the western end of the bay, have fridges, a/c and either balconies or verandas. March–Oct. €40

**Pension Ikaria** Áyios Kírykos ☎ 22750 22108, ⓔ gmoulas@chi.forthnet.gr. Compact but cosy a/c rooms with small balconies, some above the seafront café. The entrance is on the first parallel street behind the front. €25

### EATING AND DRINKING

**Arodhou** Xylosýrti ☎ 22750 22700. This taverna on the shore, next to Ayía Paraskeví church, does excellent mezédhes and a full selection of meat and fish grills. Daily 2.30pm–midnight, closed Mon Oct–May.

**Avra** Thérma ☎ 22750 23805. The best of the handful of mostly fish tavernas set back from the beach, offering a number of seafood items for under €10, as well as fine wine. April–Oct daily 10am–midnight.

**Iy Klimataria** Áyios Kírykos ☎ 22750 23686. With tables tucked on a pedestrianized alley beneath climbing vines, two blocks back from the seafront, this old favourite does various grills, salads, dips and the odd oven dish. April–Oct daily 11am–midnight.

**To Synapandi** Áyios Kírykos ☎ 22750 22287. A new ouzeri at the start of the Évdhilos road, which serves a wide range of seafood, meat and vegetable mezédhes in a pleasant courtyard. May–Oct daily 1–11pm.

### SHOPPING

**Studio Pelagos** Áyios Kírykos ☎ 697 28 45 546, ⓦ studio-pelagos.com. You might want to take a peek or purchase one of the unique hand-painted marbles at this gallery, a block back from the seafront square. July–Sept daily 11am–2pm & 6–10pm.

## Évdhilos and around

The north-coast port of **ÉVDHILOS** is the island's second town, with most of its facilities packed around the picturesque fishing harbour, separated by a headland from the busy port. Barely 1km west, the tiny hamlet of **Fýtema** offers better dining options. There are some decent beaches and places of interest in the villages around Évdhilos.

The twisting, 37km road from Áyios Kírykos, on the south coast, to Évdhilos is one of the most hair-raising in the islands, especially as a passenger, and Ikaría's longitudinal ridge often wears a streamer of cloud, even when the rest of the Aegean is clear. So it comes as quite a relief when you reach the north coast at the pleasant fishing village of **Karavóstamo**, 8km short of Évdhilos.

### Kámbos

**KÁMBOS**, 1.5km west of Fýtema, offers a small hilltop **museum** (Tues–Sun 8.30am–3pm; €2; ☎ 22750 31300) with finds from nearby ancient Oinoe; the twelfth-century church of **Ayía Iríni** stands adjacent, with column stumps and mosaic patches of a fourth-century basilica defining the entry courtyard. Lower down still are the sparse ruins of a **Byzantine palace** used to house exiled nobles, signposted as "odeion", which earlier structure it encloses. An unmarked track below the palace leads to a 250m-long sandy **beach** with sunbeds and refreshments available.

### Monastery of Theóktisti

Ikaría's outstanding medieval monument is the **monastery of Theóktisti**, 4km up from Kámbos along a twisty road (and an easier 3km road from the cute coastal village of Avláki). The monastery looks over pines to the coast from its perch under a chaos of slanted granite slabs, under one of which is tucked the much-photographed chapel of Theoskepastí. The *katholikón* features damaged but worthwhile frescoes dated to 1688.

## ACCOMMODATION AND EATING

### ÉVDHILOS AND AROUND

**Coralli** Évdhilos ☎ 22750 31924. On the west quay, this is a good place to feast on large portions of inexpensive oven-cooked meat, such as goat done as *yiouvétsi* or *kokkinistó*, plus ample salads, dips and so on. April–Oct daily 1pm–midnight.

⭐ **Karimalis Winery** Piyí, 5km southwest of Évdhilos ☎ 22750 31151, ⊕ ikarianwine.gr. Several luxuriously restored ancient, family-sized cottages make for perhaps the classiest accommodation on the island. Half-board, bottle of wine and port/airport transfer included. Cooking courses and seminars also offered. The winery is near the junction of the two access roads to the monastery of Theóktisti. May–Sept. **€100**

**Kerame** Évdhilos ☎ 22750 31426, ⊕ atheras-kerame.gr. On the hill behind the harbour, this is the best of Évdhilos's three hotels. There are more spacious studio units 1km east overlooking the eponymous beach. April–Oct. **€45**

⭐ **Mandouvala** Karavóstamo ☎ 22750 61204. With a delightful patio set above wave-lapped schist rock, this popular taverna at the far right of the seafront provides a range of average-priced fish, *mezédhes* and veg delights such as *soúfiko* (Ikarian ratatouille). May–Oct daily noon–midnight.

⭐ **Mezedopolio tou Ilia** Avláki ☎ 22750 71009. Some 300m up the road towards Theóktisti, this is the only real ouzerí on the north coast, and very proud of its own produce and self-caught fish. Has a lovely sea-view courtyard. Noon–1am: June–Sept daily, Oct–May Fri–Sun.

**Sto Fytema** Fýtema ☎ 22750 31387. Across the coastal road from the beach, *Sto Fytema* draws crowds to its shady courtyard from all over the island for its excellent vegetable dishes and fish, much of which is under €10. May–Oct daily 11am–1am.

# Armenistís and around

Most visitors congregate at **ARMENISTÍS**, 51km from Áyios Kírykos via Évdhilos, and for good reason: this little resort lies below Ikaría's greatest, if slightly fire-diminished, forest, with two enormous sandy **beaches** battered by seasonal surf – **Livádhi** and **Messaktí** – five and fifteen minutes' walk east respectively, the latter with several reed-roofed *kantínas*. The sea between here and Mýkonos is the windiest patch in the Aegean, generating a fairly consistent summer surf. The waves, which attract Athenian boogie-boarders, are complicated by strong lateral currents, and regular summer drownings have (at Livádhi) prompted a lifeguard service and a string of safety buoys.

Armenistís itself is spectacularly set, facing northeast along the length of Ikaría towards sun- and moonrise, with Mount Kérkis on Sámos visible on a clear day. A dwindling proportion of older, schist-roofed houses and ex-warehouses, plus boats hauled up in a central sandy cove, lend the place the air of a Cornish fishing village, though in fact it started out as a smuggler's depot, with warehouses but no dwellings. Just east of Messaktí, the fishing settlement of **Yialiskári** offers alternative facilities and looks out past pines to a picturesque jetty church.

### Nas

Three kilometres west of Armenistís, **NAS**, a river canyon ending at a deceptively sheltered sand-and-pebble beach, remains a rather hippyish hangout, though it is no longer a naturist's paradise. This little bay is almost completely enclosed by weirdly sculpted rock formations, but again it's unwise to swim outside the cove's natural limits – marked here with a line of buoys. The crumbling foundations of the fifth-century BC temple of **Artemis Tavropoleio** (Artemis in Bull-Headdress) overlook the permanent deep pool at the mouth of the river. Sadly the delightful former riverside forestation further inland was swept away by heavy flooding in 2011.

## ACCOMMODATION

### ARMENISTÍS AND AROUND

### ARMENISTÍS

⭐ **Daidalos** ☎ 22750 71390, ⊕ daidaloshotel.gr. This smart place on the western edge of town has a distinct artistic flavour, with a blob-shaped pool, unusually appointed rooms and a shady breakfast terrace. Breakfast included. May–Oct. **€60**

**Erofili Beach** ☎ 22750 71058, ⊕ erofili.gr. Considered the island's best hotel, though the common area and pool, perched dramatically over Livádhi beach, impress more than the rooms. Breakfast included. April–Oct. **€90**

**Valeta Apartments** ☎ 22750 71252, ⊕ valeta.gr. The attractive and comfortable studios and quads here above the harbour offer a comparable standard and setting to the hotels, at better rates. May–Oct. €40

**NAS**

**EATING, DRINKING AND NIGHTLIFE**

**ARMENISTÍS**

**Casmir** Livádhi beach. One of the island's most enduring clubs acts as a beach bar during the day and pumps out foreign and Greek hits by night. June–Sept daily 11am–late.

★ **Kiallaris (aka tis Eleftherias)** Yialiskári ☎ 22750 71227. Mid-seafront taverna that's tops for well-executed *mayireftá* and the freshest fish, all caught locally. Especially good for fish soup and *melitzanosaláta*. May to early Oct daily 11am–2am.

**Paradhosiaka Glyka (Kioulanis)** ☎ 22750 71150. On the road down to the harbour, this is one of the Aegean's star *zaharoplastía*, featuring addictive *karydhópita* (walnut cake) with goat's-milk, mastic-flavoured ice cream and other sweet delights. May–Oct daily 8am–1am; reduced winter hours.

★ **Paskhalia** ☎ 22750 71302. With a few inexpensive

**Artemis** ☎ 22750 71485, ✉ artemis-studio@ikaria.gr. With rooms overlooking the river canyon from the cliff above, this rambling place provides great-value, comfortable and well-appointed accommodation. May–Sept. €30

rooms above (€30), this friendly taverna on the harbour approach road has a sea-view terrace, open for breakfast, where you can enjoy tasty home-cooking such as rabbit *stifádho* and roast lamb. Great barrelled wine too. April–Oct daily 8am–1am.

**NAS**

**O Nas** ☎ 22750 71486. With a huge terrace on the cliff that has the best bay views, this place offers pasta, grills and oven-baked dishes, plus there's a good bakery. May–Sept daily noon–midnight.

**Thea** ☎ 22750 71491, 🌐 theasinn.com. On the east cliff, this long-standing favourite has lots of vegetarian options like *soufikó* and pumpkin-filled *pítta*. Also has a few rooms. 6pm–1pm: May–Oct daily, Nov–April weekends; from noon in late July & Aug.

## The Ráhes villages

Armenistís was originally the port of four inland hamlets – Áyios Dhimítrios, Áyios Polýkarpos, Kastaniés and Khristós – collectively known as **Ráhes**. Curiously, these already served as "hill station" resorts during the 1920s and 1930s, with three hotels, since long-gone, and the only tourism on the island. Despite the modern, paved access roads through the pines, the settlements retain a certain Shangri-La quality, with older residents speaking a positively Homeric dialect.

On an island not short of foibles, these villages are particularly strange in that most locals sleep until 11am or so, move around until about 4pm, then have another nap until 8pm, whereupon they rise and spend most of the night shopping, eating and drinking, in particular excellent home-brewed **wine** traditionally kept in goatskins.

**EATING AND DRINKING**                    **THE RÁHES VILLAGES**

**Kapilio** Khristós ☎ 22750 41517. Right in the main pedestrian zone, this good, inexpensive carnivorous supper

option serves mainly grills, with the odd dish from the oven and some simple salads. Daily 6pm–4am.

---

### WALKING IN WESTERN IKARÍA

Although bulldozers and forest fires have reduced the number of attractive possibilities, **walking** between Ráhes and both coasts on old paths is a favourite visitor activity. A locally produced, accurate map-guide, *The Round of Ráhes on Foot*, shows most asphalt roads, tracks and trails in the west of the island, as well as a **loop-hike** taking in the best of the Ráhes villages. The well-marked route sticks partly to surviving paths; the authors suggest a full day for the circuit, with ample rests, though total walking time won't exceed six hours. The highlight is the section from Khristós to Kastaniés, which takes in the Hárakos ravine with its Spanédhon watermill.

Those wishing to traverse across Ikaría are best advised to keep on a "Round of Ráhes" sub-route from Khristós to Karydhiés, from where a historic path crosses the lunar Ammoudhiá uplands before dropping spectacularly southeast to Managanítis on the south coast, a generous half-day's outing from Armenistís.

**9**

**Platanos** Áyios Dhimítrios ☎ 22750 41472. Underneath the deep shade of the eponymous plane tree on the square, this local favourite is renowned for its *mayireftá*, like beef in wine sauce and moussaka. Daily 5pm–4am.

**Ydrohöos** Áyios Dhimítrios ☎ 22750 41526. Typically off-beat art café on the square, which has a relaxed atmosphere and showcases frequent live rock, jazz, techno or Latin bands. Wed–Sun 5pm–4am.

## The south coast

The well-paved route south from Évdhilos via Akamátra crosses the island watershed before dropping steadily towards the **south coast**; with your own vehicle this is a quicker and much less curvy way back to Áyios Kírykos compared to going via Karavóstomo. It's an eminently scenic route worth taking for its own sake, the narrow road threading corniche-like through oaks at the pass, and then olives at **Playiá** village on the steep southern slope of the island. Out to sea the islands of Pátmos and Dhonoússa are generally visible, and on really clear days Náxos and Amorgós as well. The principal potential detour, 2km past the castle turning, is the road right (west) to the secluded pebble beach of **Seÿhélles** ("Seychelles"), the best on this generally inhospitable coast, with the final approach by ten-minute hike.

With your own transport, you can visit several villages at the southwest tip of the island. **Vrahádhes** enjoys a natural-balcony setting, while a sharp drop below it, the impact of the empty convent of **Mavrianoú** lies mostly in its setting amid gardens overlooking the sea. Nearby **Langádha** is not actually a village but a lush hidden valley. Note that facilities are scarce over the whole south-coast area, with just the odd erratically opening *kafenío* or seasonal taverna providing refreshment.

# Híos

"Craggy Híos", as **Homer** aptly described his putative birthplace, has a turbulent history and a strong identity. This large island has always been prosperous: in medieval times through the export of **mastic resin** – a trade controlled by Genoese overlords between 1346 and 1566 – and later by the Ottomans, who dubbed the place Sakız Adası ("Resin Island"). Since union with Greece in 1912, several shipping dynasties have emerged here, continuing to generate wealth, and someone in almost every family still spends time in the merchant navy.

Unfortunately, the island has suffered more than its share of **catastrophes** since the 1800s. The Ottomans perpetrated their most infamous, if not their worst, anti-revolutionary atrocity here in March 1822, massacring 30,000 Hiots and enslaving or exiling even more. In 1881, much of Híos was destroyed by a violent earthquake, and throughout the 1980s the island's natural beauty was compromised by devastating forest fires, compounding the effect of generations of tree-felling by boat-builders.

Until the late 1980s, the more powerful ship-owning dynasts, local government and the military authorities discouraged **tourism** and even now it is concentrated mostly in the capital or the nearby beach resorts of Karfás and Ayía Ermióni. Despite this, various foreigners have discovered a Híos beyond its rather daunting port capital: fascinating **villages**, important **Byzantine monuments** and a respectable, if remote, complement of **beaches**. English is widely spoken courtesy of numerous returned Greek-Americans and Greek-Canadians.

### ARRIVAL AND DEPARTURE                                                         HÍOS

**By plane** There are flights to the following destinations (frequencies given for June–Oct): Athens (4–5 daily; 45–50min); Lésvos (2 weekly; 30min); Límnos (2 weekly; 1hr 30min); Rhodes (2 weekly; 1hr–1hr 45min); Thessaloníki (4 weekly; 1hr 10min–2hr 45min).

**By ferry** Híos is the only stop on the daily superfast service

between Pireás and Lésvos and is also on the much slower northern mainland to Sámos/Ikaría route, while smaller boats connect it with the satellite islands of Psará and Inoússes, as well as Çeşme in Turkey. Nearly all boats leave from Híos Town but some Psará and all Lávrio sailings go from the port of Mestá.

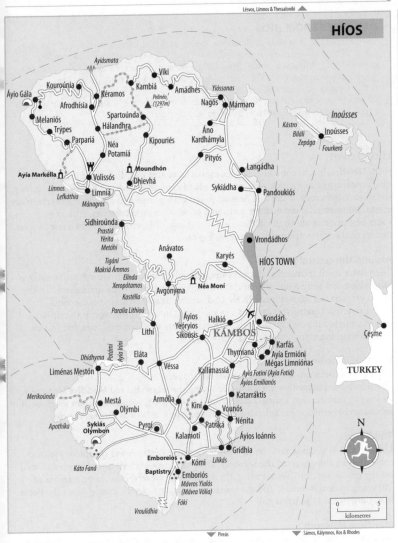

Híos Town to: Áyios Kírykos, Ikaría (1 weekly; 5hr); Çeşme (1–2 daily; 30–45min); Inoússes (1–2 daily; 30min); Karlóvassi, Sámos (1 weekly; 4hr); Kavála (2 weekly; 16hr); Lésvos (2 weekly; 3hr); Límnos (2 weekly; 9hr); Pireás (1 daily; 6hr 30min); Psará (6 weekly; 3hr); Thessaloníki (1 weekly; 19hr 45min); Vathý, Sámos (1 weekly; 4hr).

Mestá to: Lávrio (3 weekly; 6hr 30min); Psará (3–4 weekly; 1hr 15min).

## GETTING AROUND

**By bus** While services to the major destinations in the south run quite frequently (Mon–Sat 3–5, Sun 1–2), those bound for the north are much less frequent (1–4 daily) and the northwest is especially poorly served, with no schedules on Sun.

**By car or motorbike** To explore properly you'll need to rent a powerful motorbike or a car. Of the many rental agencies around the island, the best is Vassilakis/Reliable Rent a Car (☎ 22710 29300, ⊕ rentacar-chios.com), with branches at Evyenías Handhrí 3 in Híos Town (behind the eyesore *Chandris Hotel*), Karfás and Mégas Limniónas.

**9**

> ## DAY-TRIPS FROM HÍOS
> The most popular boat excursions from the main port of Híos Town are to the nearby satellite island of Inoússes (see p.630) and to the Turkish coast, as Psará is too far for a comfortable day-trip. Trips to **Inoússes** usually depart twice a week, on Thursday and Sunday, at 8.30am, returning by 6pm at a cost of €20. The longer excursions to Turkey leave daily at 8am for the port of **Çeşme**, where an optional bus transfer takes you to the city of Izmir, returning by 7.15pm. Prices vary according to demand but are often as low as €35; Kanaris Tours at Leofóros Egéou 12 (☎ 22710 42490, ⓦ kanaristours.gr) sell tickets for both.

# Híos Town

**HÍOS TOWN**, a brash, concrete-laced commercial centre with little predating the 1881 quake, will come as a shock after modest island capitals elsewhere. Yet in many ways it's the most satisfactory of the east Aegean ports, with a large and fascinating **marketplace**, several **museums**, an **old quarter** and some good, authentic **tavernas**. Although a sprawling place of about 30,000 souls, most things of interest lie within a few hundred metres of the water, fringed by Leofóros Egéou.

## Around the central platía

The town's small triangular central **platía**, officially Plastíra but known universally as **Vounakíou**, lies only a block inland from the seafront, up by the main dock. To the south extends the marvellously lively tradesmen's **bazaar**, where you can find everything from parrots to cast-iron woodstoves. Inland to the west is the urban sprawl's single lung, the attractively lush central **park**, whose most notable feature is an Ottoman fountain.

### Byzantine Museum

Opposite the Vounakíou taxi rank • Tues–Sun 8.30am–3pm • €3 • ☎ 22710 26866

The refurbished **Byzantine Museum**, occupying the renovated old **Mecidiye Mosque** with its leaning minaret, has a small but interesting collection, with sections on religious and secular architecture, some splendid murals and icons, as well as various ceramics.

## The Kástro

Until the 1881 earthquake, the Byzantine-Genoese **Kástro** stood completely intact; thereafter developers razed the seaward walls, filled in the moat to the south and sold off the real estate thus created along the waterfront. Nevertheless, large sections of imposing ramparts remain and the most dramatic entry to the citadel is via the **Porta Maggiora** behind the town hall.

## Maritime Museum

Stefánou Tsoúri 20 • Mon–Sat: May–Oct 9am–2pm; Nov–April 9am–1pm • Donation • ☎ 22710 44139, ⓦ chiosnauticalmuseum.gr

The **Maritime Museum** consists principally of model ships and nautical oil paintings, all rather overshadowed by the mansion containing them. In the foyer are enshrined the knife and glass-globe grenade of Admiral Kanaris, who partly avenged the 1822 massacre by ramming and sinking the Ottoman fleet's flagship, thus dispatching Admiral Kara Ali, architect of the atrocities.

## Argenti Folklore Museum

Koraí 2 • Mon–Thurs 8am–2pm, Fri 8am–2pm & 5–7pm, Sat 8am–12.30pm • €2 • ☎ 22710 28256

The central **Argenti Folklore Museum**, on the top floor of the Koraïs Library, features ponderous genealogical portraits of the endowing family, an adjoining wing of costumes and rural impedimenta, plus multiple replicas of Delacroix's *Massacre at Hios*, a painting which did much to arouse sympathy for the cause of Greek independence.

## Archeological museum

Mihálon • June–Aug daily 8am–7pm; Sept–May Tues–Sun 8.30am–3pm • €3 • ☎ 22710 44239

The **archeological museum** has a wide-ranging, well-lit collection from Neolithic to Roman times. Highlights include limestone column bases from the Apollo temple at Faná in the shape of lions' claws; numerous statuettes and reliefs of Cybele (an Asiatic goddess especially honoured here); Archaic faience miniatures from Emborió in the shape of a cat, a hawk and a flautist; a terracotta dwarf riding a boar; and figurines (some with articulated limbs) of *hierodouloi* or sacred prostitutes, presumably from an Aphrodite shrine. Most famous is an inscribed edict of Alexander the Great from 322 BC, setting out relations between himself and the Hiots.

## ARRIVAL AND GETTING AROUND
HÍOS TOWN

**By air** The poky airport lies 3km south of the capital at Kondári, a €4 taxi-ride away; otherwise any blue urban bus on the Híos Town–Karfás route should pass the stop opposite the airport.

**By ferry** Ferry agents cluster along the north end of waterfront Egéou and its continuation Neorión.

**By bus** Blue city buses radiate out from the terminal on the north side of Híos Town's central park and serve some nearby beaches, principally Vrondhádhos and Karfás, but also as far as Ayía Ermióni. For anywhere further afield, long-distance KTEL buses leave from just behind the passenger waiting-room on seafront Egéou.

HÍOS TOWN

**ACCOMMODATION**

| | |
|---|---|
| Chios Rooms | 3 |
| Fedra | 1 |
| Grecian Castle | 4 |
| Kyma | 2 |

**NIGHTLIFE**

| | |
|---|---|
| Bowling Club | 1 |

**EATING & DRINKING**

| | |
|---|---|
| O Hotzas | 4 |
| Ta Mylarakia | 1 |
| Tassos | 3 |
| Theodhosiou | 2 |

**SHOP**

| | |
|---|---|
| Mastiha Shop | 1 |

**9**

**By car or motorbike** Parking in town is possible only on the southern fringes and in the moat west of the kástro.

**By taxi** For shorter distances around the capital, the main taxi rank is on the central platía.

## INFORMATION

**Tourist office** Kanári 18 (Mon–Fri 7.30am–3pm; ☏ 22710 44389, ⓦ chioscity.gr).

**Online** A good general online resource for the whole island is ⓦ chiosonline.gr.

**Services** Commercial maps and a few English-language books are found at Newsstand, at the first "kink" in Egéou. The most reliable internet café is Enter, just seaward of the *Fedra Hotel*. The post office is on Omírou.

## ACCOMMODATION

Híos Town has a fair quantity of affordable accommodation, rarely full. Most places line the front or the perpendicular alleys and parallel streets behind, and almost all are plagued by traffic noise – we've listed the more peaceful establishments.

★ **Chios Rooms** Egéou 110 ☏ 22710 20198, ⓦ chiosrooms.gr. Don and Dina's lovingly restored tile- or wood-floored, high-ceilinged rooms are relatively quiet for a seafront location. Some en suite; best is the penthouse "suite" with private terrace. **€25**

**Fedra** Mihaïl Livanoú 13 ☏ 22710 41129. Well-appointed pension in a nineteenth-century mansion, with stone arches in the downstairs winter bar; in summer the bar operates outside, so get a rear room to avoid nocturnal noise. **€35**

**Grecian Castle** Bélla Vísta shore avenue ☏ 22710 44740, ⓦ greciancastle.gr. Converted factory towards the airport with lovely grounds and a sea-view pool, but the smallish main-wing rooms, despite their marble floors, wood ceilings and bug screens, are inferior to the rear "villa" suites. Breakfast included. **€100**

★ **Kyma** Evyenías Handhri ☏ 22710 44500, ⓔ kyma @chi.forthnet.gr. Variable rooms in a Neoclassical mansion or modern extension, with huge terraces on the sea-facing side; most units have new handmade wood-and-leather furniture. Owner Theo's knowledgeable service really makes the place. Breakfast included. **€65**

## EATING AND DRINKING

★ **0 Hotzas** Yeoryíou Kondhýli 3 ☏ 22710 42787. Oldest and most popular taverna in town, with an old-style interior and delightful summer garden. Menu varies seasonally, but expect a mix of vegetarian dishes and *lahanodolmádhes*, sausages, baby fish and *mydhopílafo* (rice and mussels) accompanied by own-brand ouzo or retsina. Mon–Sat 7pm–late.

**Ta Mylarakia** Tambákika district ☏ 22710 40412. A large seafood selection, every kind of Hiot ouzo (Tetteri Penindari is the best) and limited seating at the island's most romantic waterside setting at the four restored windmills. Reservations advisable in summer.

Daily April–Oct 11am–2am Nov–May 8pm–1am.

**Tassos** Stávrou Livanoú 8, Bélla Vísta district. Good all-rounder with creative salads, better-than-average bean dishes, *dolmádhes*, snails, good chips, a strong line in seafood and decent barrelled wine. There's sea-view summer garden seating and a heated gazebo for winter. Daily noon–1am.

**Theodhosiou** Neoríon 33. The oldest of three ouzerís on this quay, occupying a domed, arcaded building. There's a fair range of meat grills for this type of place, plus various seafood standards. Generally, avoid the fried platters in favour of grilled or boiled ones. Dinner only; closed Sun.

## NIGHTLIFE AND ENTERTAINMENT

Some 1400 local university students help keep things lively, especially along the waterfront between the two "kinks" in Egéou. Shooting **pool** is big here; many bars have several tables. **Film** fans are well served by Cine Kipos (late June to early Sept), in one corner of the central park, with quality/art-house first-run screenings; from October the action shifts to Cine Diana, under the eponymous hotel.

**Bowling Club** Leofóros Egéou 120 ☏ 22710 28517. This popular bar has a multitude of pool tables and seven bowling alleys as well. Daily 10am–late.

**Homerion Cultural Centre** Iroón Polytekhníou 5 ☏ 22710 44391, ⓦ homerion.gr. This large events hall on the south side of the park hosts changing exhibitions, and big-name acts, including some foreign ones, often come here after Athens concerts. Hours vary.

## SHOP

**Mastiha Shop** Egéou 36 ☏ 22710 81600, ⓦ mastihashop.com. Home base of a chain with nine branches in Greece plus others in New York, Paris and even Jeddah. Sells all things mastic from chewing gum to shower gel. Daily: July–Sept 8.30am–midnight; Oct–June 8.30am–10pm.

## Around Híos Town

Vrondádhos is served by Blue urban buses from Híos Town; most buses heading here are labelled "the Teacher's Rock"

North of Híos Town, **VRONDÁDHOS** is an elongated coastal suburb that's a favourite residence of the many local seafarers. Homer is alleged to have lived and taught here, and in terraced parkland just above the little fishing port and pebble beach you can visit his purported lectern, more likely an ancient altar of Cybele.

The locals swim at the tiny pebble coves near here or from the grubby town beach in Bélla Vísta, but really the closest decent option is at **Karfás**, 7km south beyond the airport. However, as most large Hiot resort hotels are planted here, the 500m-long beach itself, sandy only at the south end, has limited appeal. The nearby inland village of **Thymianá** offers a more authentic atmosphere and better dining options.

Some 2km further along the coast from Karfás, **Ayía Ermióni** is a fishing anchorage, adjoining the next proper beach at **Mégas Limniónas**, a few hundred metres further on, smaller than Karfás but more scenic, with low cliffs as a backdrop. Some 4km further south is the turning for **Ayía Fotiní**, also known as Ayía Fotiá, a 600m pebble **beach** with exceptionally clean water. Cars are excluded from the shore area and the pedestrian esplanade is lined with various rooms and tavernas. Five kilometres further south, back via the main road, the small fishing village of **Katarráktis** is a pleasant spot where locals in the know go to eat.

### ACCOMMODATION                                    AROUND HÍOS TOWN

**Apartments Iro** Ayía Ermióni ☎ 22710 51166. Large self-catering studios on the seafront beside the access road, with sea views from the balconies. Nicely furnished, with a/c and dedicated parking. April–Oct. **€40**

**Karatzas** Karfás ☎ 22710 31221. Typically compact but decent-value rooms above a taverna at the northern end of the seafront, which offers pricey fish but much more reasonable meat dishes. April–Oct. **€35**

★ **Markos' Place** Karfás ☎ 22710 31990, ⓦ marcos-place.gr. Markos Kostalas has lovingly created a peaceful,

leafy environment on the hillside behind the bay out of a beautiful deconsecrated monastery. Guests stay in the former pilgrims' cells, with a kitchen available or superior breakfasts provided by arrangement. April–Nov. **€35**

**Mavrokordatiko** 1.5km south of the airport ☎ 22710 32900, ⓦ mavrokordatiko.com. With enormous wood-panelled rooms and spacious communal areas, including a fine café/restaurant, this renovated mansion, 1.5km south of the airport, oozes atmosphere. Breakfast included. **€70**

### EATING AND DRINKING

**Ankyra** Mégas Limniónas ☎ 22710 32178. All-round reliable *psarotaverna* behind the middle of the beach, serving fish of all categories and an accompanying range of meat, veg and salads, as well as a fine ouzo selection. May–Oct daily 11am–midnight.

**O Tsambos** Katarráktis ☎ 22710 61601. Long-established favourite taverna on the centre of the seafront, with friendly management and a wide menu, including the cheapest pork chops on Híos at only €5. April–Oct daily 11am–1am.

★ **To Talimi** Thymianá ☎ 22710 32940. Serves excellent home-style *mayireftá* like *yiouvarlákia*, *kókoras krasáto* or bean-and-artichoke salad at friendly prices in a lovely shady courtyard in the centre of the village. Daily noon–midnight.

**The Twins** Ayía Fotiní ☎ 22710 51630. At the seaward end of the access road, this is easily the best taverna in the resort, excelling in shrimp fritters and other seafood delights, mostly for under €10. May–Oct daily 10am–2am.

## The mastihohoriá

Besides olive groves, southern Híos's gently rolling countryside is home to the **mastic bush**, and the twenty or so *mastihohoriá*, or mastic villages (see box, p.626). Since the decline of the mastic trade, the *mastihohoriá* live mainly off their tangerines, apricots and olives, though the villages, the only settlements on Híos spared by the Ottomans in 1822, retain their architectural uniqueness, designed by the Genoese but with a distinctly Middle Eastern feel. The basic plan involves a rectangular warren of tall houses, with the outer row doubling as perimeter fortification, and breached by a limited number of gateways. More recent additions, whether in traditional architectural style or not, straggle outside the original defences. Of the surviving villages, three stand out: **Pyrgí**, **Olýmbi** and **Mestá**.

> ## MASTIC MASTICATION
>
> The **mastic bush** (*Pistacia lentisca*) is found across much of Aegean Greece but only in southern Híos – pruned to an umbrella shape to facilitate harvesting – does it produce aromatic resin of any quality or quantity, scraped from incisions made on the trunk during summer. For centuries it was used as a base for paints, cosmetics and the chewable jelly beans that became an addictive staple in Ottoman harems. Indeed, the interruption of the flow of mastic from Híos to Istanbul by the revolt of spring 1822 was a main cause of the brutal Ottoman reaction. The wealth engendered by the mastic trade supported twenty *mastihohoriá* (mastic villages) from the time the Genoese set up a monopoly in the substance during the fourteenth century, but the demise of imperial Turkey and the development of petroleum-based products knocked the bottom out of the mastic market.
>
> Now it's just a curiosity, to be chewed – try the sweetened Elma-brand gum – or drunk as *mastíha* liqueur. It has had medicinal applications since ancient times; contemporary advocates claim that mastic boosts the immune system and thins the blood. High-end cosmetics, toothpaste and mouthwash are now sold at the Mastiha Shop in Híos Town (see p.624).

## Pyrgí

**PYRGÍ**, 25km south of Híos Town, is the most colourful of the *mastihohoriá*, its houses elaborately embossed with *xystá*, patterns cut into whitewash to reveal a layer of black volcanic sand underneath; in autumn, strings of sun-drying tomatoes add a further splash of colour. On the northeast corner of the central square the twelfth-century Byzantine church of **Áyii Apóstoli** (erratic hours), embellished with much later frescoes, is tucked under an arcade.

## Olýmbi and around

**OLÝMBI**, 7km west of Pyrgí along the same bus route, is one of the less visited mastic villages but not devoid of interest. The characteristic **tower-keep**, which at Pyrgí stands half-inhabited away from the modernized main square, here looms bang in the middle of the platía.

### The Sykiás Olýmbon cave

Tues–Sun: June–Aug 10am–8pm; Sept 11am–6pm • Admission every 30min • €5

From Olýmbi, a paved road leads 6km to the well-signed cave of **Sykiás Olýmbon**. For years it was just a hole in the ground where villagers disposed of dead animals, but from 1985 on speleologists explored it properly. The cavern, with a constant temperature of 18°C, evolved in two phases between 150 million and 50 million years ago, and has a maximum depth of 57m (though tours only visit the top 30m). Its formations, with fanciful names like Chinese Forest, Medusa and Organ Pipes, are among the most beautiful in the Mediterranean.

## Mestá

Sombre, monochrome **MESTÁ**, 4km west of Olýmbi, is considered the finest of the villages; despite more snack-bars and trinket shops than strictly necessary, it remains just the right side of twee. From its main square, dominated by the **church of the Taxiárhis** with its two icons of the Archangel – one dressed in Byzantine robes, the other in Genoese armour – a maze of dim lanes with anti-seismic tunnels leads off in all directions. Most streets end in blind alleys, except those leading to the six portals; the northeast one still has its original iron gate.

**ACCOMMODATION AND EATING**                                        **THE MASTIHOHORIÁ**

Tourist facilities are relatively sparse in the mastic villages. Apart from the establishments listed below, you will find a smattering of cafés, the odd tiny taverna and some signs for private rooms, usually available on spec.

**9**

**Chrysanthi Apartments** Olýmbi ☎ 22710 76196, ⓦ chrysanthi.gr. Three units suitable for two to five persons near the central platía – nicely furnished with smart kitchens – retaining many original features such as stone alcoves. €55

★ **Medieval Castle Suites** Mestá ☎ 22710 76345, ⓦ mcsuites.gr. Superbly refurbished medieval mansion on a lane just off the main square, with much of the original stone exterior, yet lavishly furnished and equipped with all modern facilities inside. Easter–Oct. €80

★ **Mesaionas (Kyra Dhespina)** Mestá ☎ 22710 76050. Excellent home-cooked dishes, such as stewed octopus, moussaka and various veg in sauces for well under €10 each, served on the square. The welcoming owner can put you in touch with places offering rooms. Daily 11am–midnight.

# The mastic coast

The most popular **beaches** at the southern end of Híos are in the vicinity of **Emboriós**, tucked in the southeast corner. Over on the southwest coast, the closest good, protected beach to Mestá lies 4.7km southwest at **Apothíka**. Others, east of ugly but functional **Liménas Mestón** port, include **Dhídhyma**, 4km away, a double cove guarded by an islet; **Potámi**, with a namesake stream feeding it; and less scenic **Ayía Iríni**, 8km distant, with a reliably open taverna.

## Emboriós

**EMBORIÓS**, an almost landlocked harbour, is 6km southeast of Pyrgí. Ancient **Emboreios**, on the hill to the northeast, has been rehabilitated as an "archeological park" (summer daily 8.30am–3pm, winter closed Mon; €2). Down in modern Emboriós a cruciform early Christian **baptistry** is signposted in a field just inland; it's protected by a later, round structure, which remains locked but everything's visible through the grating.

## Beaches around Emboriós

For **swimming**, follow the road a short way south from Emboriós to an oversubscribed car park and the beach of **Mávros Yialós**, better known as Mávra Vólia, then continue by flagstoned walkway over the headland to more dramatic **Fóki**. Twice as long and backed by impressive cliffs, this pebble strip of purple-grey volcanic stones is part nudist. If you want sand (and amenities) go to **Kómi**, 3km northeast of Emboriós, which is the main (albeit low-key) resort for the area.

**ACCOMMODATION AND EATING**             **THE MASTIC COAST**

**Bella Mare** Kómi ☎ 22710 71228. Classic beach taverna-cum-rooms-combo towards the southern end of the beach, which offers a fair selection of seafood and meat as mezédhes or main dishes, as well as simple sea-view accommodation. Restaurant May–Oct 9am–2am. €30
**Nostalgia** Kómi ☎ 22710 70070. Good all-round taverna behind the northern end of the beach, specializing in

grilled fish and meat but also offering a line in veg dishes and some decent barrelled wine. April to mid-Oct daily noon–2am.
**Porto Emborios** Emboriós ☎ 22710 71306. The best of the four tavernas clustered around the harbour offers good seafood at fair prices, a range of salads and dips, plus home-made desserts. March–Oct daily 10am–1am.

# Central Híos

The inland portion of Híos extending west and southwest from Híos Town matches the south in terms of interesting **monuments**, and good roads make touring under your own steam an easy matter. The flat **Kámbos** leads to more mountainous terrain to the west and north.

## The Kámbos

The **Kámbos**, a vast fertile plain carpeted with citrus groves, extends southwest from Híos Town almost as far as the village of Halkió. The district was originally settled by the Genoese during the fourteenth century, and remained a preserve of the local aristocracy until 1822. Exploring by two-wheeler may be less frustrating than going by

**9**

car, since the web of narrow, poorly marked lanes sandwiched between high walls guarantees disorientation and frequent backtracking. Behind the walls you catch fleeting glimpses of ornate old mansions built from locally quarried sandstone, whose courtyards are paved in pebbles or alternating light and dark tiles.

## Néa Moní

Daily 8am–1pm & 4–8pm, 5–8pm in summer • ☎ 22710 79370

Almost exactly in the middle of the island, the monastery of **Néa Moní** was founded by the Byzantine Emperor Constantine Monomahos ("The Dueller") IX in 1042 on the spot where a wonder-working icon had been discovered. It ranks among the most important monuments on any of the Greek islands; the mosaics, together with those of Dháfni and Ósios Loukás on the mainland, are the finest surviving art of their era in Greece, and the setting – high in partly forested mountains 15km west of the port – is equally memorable. Once a powerful community of six hundred monks, Néa Moní was pillaged in 1822 and most of its residents, including 3500 civilians sheltering here, were put to the sword. The 1881 tremor caused comprehensive damage, wrecking many of its outbuildings, while exactly a century later a forest fire threatened to engulf the place until the resident icon was paraded along the perimeter wall, miraculously repelling the flames.

### The site

Just inside the **main gate** stands a **chapel/ossuary** containing some of the bones of the 1822 victims; axe-clefts in children's skulls attest to the savagery of the attackers. The restored *katholikón* has a cupola resting on an octagonal drum, a design seen elsewhere only in Cyprus; the famous **mosaics** within have now been returned to their former glory. The narthex contains portrayals of various local saints sandwiched between *Christ Washing the Disciples' Feet* and the *Betrayal*, in which Judas's kiss has unfortunately been obliterated, but Peter is clearly visible lopping off the ear of the high priest's servant.

## Avgónyma

Some 5km west of Néa Moní sits **AVGÓNYMA**, a cluster of dwellings on a knoll overlooking the coast; the name means "Clutch of Eggs", an apt description when viewed from the ridge above. Since the 1980s, the place has been restored as a summer haven by descendants of the original villagers, though the permanent population is fewer than ten.

### ACCOMMODATION AND EATING                                          CENTRAL HÍOS

★ **Arhondiko Perleas** 3km south of the airport, Kámbos ☎ 22710 32217, ⊛ perleas.gr. Set in a huge organic citrus ranch, with a well-regarded in-house restaurant, this extremely classy converted mansion boasts dark wood interiors and original artwork, as well as lavish furnishings. Gourmet breakfast included. **€90**

**O Pyrgos** Avgónyma ☎ 22710 42175, ✉ pyrgosrooms @chiosnet.gr. In an attractive arcaded mansion on the main square, with ample courtyard seating, this taverna run by Greek-Americans offers both oven-cooked dishes and grills. There are some simple but adequate rooms too. **€40**

**Spitakia** Avgónyma ☎ 22710 20513, ⊛ spitakia.gr. A cluster of small stone cottages sleeping up to five people, plus some rooms, all lovingly restored and tastefully decorated, with good heating for the winter months. **€50**

# The west coast

The central section of the island's **west coast** offers a couple of picturesque villages and some not-too-crowded beaches, given that they are so easily accessible from Híos Town by way of Avgónyma, from where the main road descends 6km to the sea in well-graded loops.

## Tigáni and Makriá Ámmos

On the northern stretch of the central west coast, bypass Elínda, alluring from afar but rocky and often murky up close, in favour of the more secluded coves to either side of Metóhi – best of these are **Tigáni** and **Makriá Ámmos**, the latter nudist.

## Lithí and Paralía Lithioú
Friendly **LITHÍ** village perches on a forested ledge overlooking the sea towards the southern end of the central west coast. You can eat here but most visitors head 2km downhill to **Paralía Lithioú**, a popular weekend target of Hiot townies thanks to its large but hard-packed, windswept beach.

## Véssa
Some 5km south of Lithí, valley-bottom **VÉSSA** is an unsung gem: more open and less casbah-like than Mestá or Pyrgí, but still homogeneous, its tawny buildings are arrayed in a vast grid punctuated by numerous belfries and arcaded passages.

| ACCOMMODATION AND EATING | THE WEST COAST |
|---|---|

**Almyriki Apartments** Paralía Lithioú ☏ 22710 73124, ⓦ almiriki.gr. Smart new complex behind the middle of the beach, with modern well-appointed rooms sporting modern furniture, LCD TVs and fridges. Chic café-bar on site too. April–Oct. **€65**

**To Akroyiali** Paralía Lithioú ☏ 22710 73286. The best of the handful of tavernas here, behind the beach's north end, providing fresh fish, a variety of seafood, simple grilled meat and some tasty mezédhes. May–Sept daily 11am–1am.

# Northern Híos
**Northern Híos** never really recovered from the 1822 massacre, and between Pityós and Volissós the forest's recovery from 1980s **fires** has been partly reversed by a bad 2007 blaze. Most villages usually lie deserted, with about a third of the former population living in Híos Town, returning occasionally for major festivals or to tend smallholdings; others, based in Athens or North America, visit their ancestral homes for just a few midsummer weeks.

## Langádha and around
Some 16km north of Híos Town, **LANGÁDHA** is probably the first point on the eastern coast road you'd be tempted to stop, though there is no proper beach nearby. Set at the mouth of a deep valley, this attractive little harbour settlement looks across its bay to a pine grove, and beyond to Turkey.

Just beyond Langádha a side road leads 5km up and inland to **Pityós**, an oasis in a mountain pass presided over by a small, round castle; continuing 4km further brings you to a junction that allows quick access to the west of the island.

## Mármaro and around
**Káto Kardhámyla**, 37km out of Híos Town, is the island's second town. Better known as **MÁRMARO**, it's positioned at the edge of a fertile plain rimmed by mountains, which comes as welcome relief from the craggy coastline. However, there is little to attract casual visitors other than some Neoclassical architecture; the mercilessly exposed port is strictly businesslike and offers only a limited range of tourist facilities and mediocre beach. Swimming is much more enjoyable at the pebble bay of **Nagós**, 5km west, or at **Yióssonas**, a much longer and rockier beach, 1km further on.

## Volissós and around
**VOLISSÓS**, 42km from Híos Town, was once the market town for a dozen remote hill villages beyond. The buildings around the main square are mostly modern but a host of old stone houses still curl appealingly beneath a crumbling hilltop Byzantine-Genoese **fort**. These upper quarters, known as **Pýrgos**, are in the grip of a restoration mania, most in good taste, with ruins changing hands for stratospheric prices and usually being turned into quality accommodation.

### Beaches around Volissós
**LIMNIÁ** (or Limiá), the port of Volissós, lies 2km south of town, bracketed by the local

seemingly endless sand-and-pebble beach. More intimate, sandy **Lefkáthia** lies just a ten-minute stroll along the cement drive over the headland north of the harbour.

**Límnos**, the next protected cove 400m east of Lefkáthia, can also be accessed by a direct road from Volissós. **Ayía Markélla**, 5km further northwest of Límnos, has another long beach, fronting the eponymous, barracks-like pilgrimage **monastery** of Híos's patron saint (festival on July 22).

### Monastery of Moundhón

For access, seek out the warden, Yiorgos Fokas, in nearby Dhievhá village (☎ 22740 22011)

The engagingly set sixteenth-century **monastery of Moundhón** was second in rank to Néa Moní before its partial destruction in 1822. Best of the naïve interior frescoes of the (locked) church is one depicting the *Ouranódhromos Klímax* (Stairway to Heaven, not to be confused with Led Zeppelin's): a trial-by-ascent, in which ungodly priests are beset by demons hurling them into the mouth of a great serpent symbolizing the Devil, while the righteous clergy are assisted upwards by angels. The monastery is reached on a 2km detour north of the main Hios Town–Volissós road.

## ACCOMMODATION, EATING AND DRINKING

NORTHERN HÍOS

### LANGÁDHA AND AROUND

⭐ **Makellos** Pityós ☎ 22720 23364. Renowned all over the island for its splendid home-style lamb and beef dishes, as well as the likes of rabbit and free-range rooster. Great barrelled wine too. Noon–1am: May–Sept daily, Oct–April most weekends.

**Pandoukios (Kourtesis)** Pandoukiós ☎ 22710 74262. Excellent if rather pricey waterside taverna towards the south end of the beach, where lobster can often be had, as well as less expensive seafood, some meat dishes and plenty of salads and dips. May–Oct daily 10am–2am.

**T'Ayeri** Langádha ☎ 22710 74813. The cheapest and most traditional taverna here, serving a combination of small fish and excellent *mayireftá* for €7–8, as well as very palatable barrelled wine. Noon–2am: April–Oct daily, Nov–March Fri–Sun.

### MÁRMARO AND AROUND

**Hotel Kardamyla** Mármaro ☎ 22720 23353. Co-managed with Híos Town's *Hotel Kyma*, this friendly central hotel offers spacious, fan-equipped rooms and a few suites, all pleasantly furnished and some with sea views. The restaurant is good too. Breakfast included. April–Oct. **€50**

**Thalasses** Mármaro ☎ 22720 23888. Slightly upmarket but still good value, this *psarotavérna* on the northern seafront specializes in fresh fish and seafood, with delights such as crab and octopus salads. Daily noon–2am.

### VOLISSÓS AND AROUND

**Aigiali** Límnos ☎ 22740 21856, ⓦ aigiali.gr. Attractive, comfortably furnished apartments at the beach end of the access road, with well-equipped kitchens and sea-view balconies in a sturdy modern stone building. The café does great sweets too. May–Sept. **€35**

⭐ **Fabrika** Volissós ☎ 22740 22045. Just behind the square, this converted factory, hence the name, does superb *kondosoúvli* and *kokorétsi*, as well as a range of daily-changing oven-baked dishes. Seating in the attractive interior or leafy courtyard. Daily noon–2am.

**Limnos** Límnos ☎ 22740 22122. Good all-round taverna in the corner of the beach (near the access road) that dishes up fish grills and specials like *kókoras krasáto*, as well as delicious *mezédhes* and highly drinkable wine. May to mid-Oct daily 10am–midnight.

⭐ **Moneos A & B/Theias** Pýrgos district, Volissós ☎ 22740 21413, ⓦ volissostravel.gr. Three skilfully converted stone houses accommodating two people each – all have terraces, fully equipped kitchens, a/c and features such as tree trunks upholding sleeping lofts, reflecting proprietress Stella's background as a sculptor. May–Oct. **€45**

⭐ **O Zikos** Limniá ☎ 22740 22040. Popular local spot on the quay with good grills and a fine house salad featuring sun-dried tomatoes, plus occasional seafood, all at prices under €10, except for top-quality fish. Daily 11am–1am.

**Ta Petrina** Pýrgos district, Volissós ☎ 22740 21228, ⓦ tapetrina.gr. Half a dozen unique properties, expertly renovated by the British co-owners. They vary in size and character from a tiny stone house to a converted church. **€80**

# Inoússes

**Inoússes**, the closer and more easily accessible of Hios' two satellite islands, has a permanent population of about three hundred, less than half its 1930s figure. For generations this islet, first settled around 1750 by Hiot shepherds, provided Greece with many of her wealthiest shipping families: various members of the Livanos, Lemos and Pateras clans were born here.

## Inoússes town

Two church-tipped, privately owned islets guard the unusually well-protected harbour of **Inoússes town**, which is surprisingly large, draped over hillsides enclosing a ravine. Its illustrious maritime connections help explain the presence of large villas and visiting summer gin-palaces in an otherwise sleepy Greek backwater. Near the quay, the island's only specific sight, the impressive **Marine Museum** (daily 10am–1pm; €2), also has a nautical theme and was endowed by various shipping magnates. At the west end of the quay, the bigwigs have also funded a nautical academy, which trains future members of the merchant navy.

## Around the island

The southern slope of this tranquil island is surprisingly green and well tended; there are no springs, so water comes from a mix of fresh and brackish wells, as well as a reservoir. The sea is extremely clean and calm on the sheltered southerly shore; among its beaches, choose from **Zepága**, **Biláli** or **Kástro**, respectively five, twenty and thirty minutes' walk west of the port. More secluded **Fourkeró** (or Farkeró) lies 25 minutes east.

### ARRIVAL AND DEPARTURE                                          INOÚSSES

**By ferry** Inoússes can be reached from Híos Town either on a day-trip (see box, p.622) or on the daily ferry (30min), which usually departs from Híos in the afternoon and returns in the morning.

### ACCOMMODATION, EATING AND DRINKING

**Naftikos Omilos** ☎ 22710 55596. This yachtie near the jetty hangout provides a steady stream of coffee and snacks during the day before morphing into a fairly lively bar by night, as the music volume ramps up. May–Sept daily 9am–2am.

**Oinousses Studios** ☎ 22710 55255, ✉ oinousses studios@gmail.com. Smart modern apartments overlooking the harbour with fully equipped kitchens and large balconies facing the sea. May–Sept. €35

**Pateronisso** ☎ 22710 55311. At the base of the disembarkation jetty, this is the best of the small bunch of tavernas dotted on or around the seafront. All the usual fish, meat and salad staples are available at average prices. June–Sept daily 8am–midnight.

**Thalassoporos** ☎ 22710 55475. This modest establishment, on the main easterly hillside lane in town, is the island's only bona fide hotel, with basic clean rooms, mostly affording sea views. May–Sept. €45

# Psará

Remote **Psará** lies a good 20km west of the northwest tip of Híos and is too far from it to be visited on a day-trip. The birthplace of revolutionary war hero Admiral Konstandinos Kanaris, the island devoted its merchant fleets – the third largest in 1820s Greece – to the cause of independence, and paid dearly for it. Vexed beyond endurance, the Turks landed overwhelming forces in 1824 to stamp out this nest of resistance. Perhaps 3000 of the 30,000 inhabitants escaped in small boats to be rescued by a French fleet, but the majority retreated to a hilltop powder magazine, blowing it and themselves up rather than surrender. Today, it's a sad, bleak place fully living up to its name ("the mottled things" in ancient Greek), never really having recovered from the holocaust. The official population now barely exceeds four hundred, and, despite some revitalization since the 1980s, it has never seen a tourist boom.

**9**

## The harbour

Since few buildings in the east-facing harbour community predate the twentieth century, a strange hotchpotch of ecclesiastical and secular architecture greets you on disembarking. There's a distinctly southern feel, more like the Dodecanese or the Cyclades, and some peculiar churches, no two alike in style.

## Around the island

Psará's **beaches** are decent, improving the further northeast you walk from the port. You quickly pass **Káto Yialós**, **Katsoúni** and **Lazarétto** with its off-putting power station, before reaching **Lákka** ("narrow ravine"), fifteen minutes along, apparently named after its grooved rock formations. **Límnos**, 25 minutes from the port along the coastal path, is big and attractive, but there's no reliable taverna here, or indeed at any of the beaches.

The only other thing to do on Psará is to follow the paved road north across the island to **Kímisis (Assumption) monastery**. Uninhabited since the 1970s, it comes to life only in early August, when its revered icon is carried in ceremonial procession to town and back on the eve of August 5.

### ARRIVAL AND DEPARTURE
PSARÁ

**By ferry** Psará has decent ferry links with Híos Town (6 weekly; 3hr), Mestá in southwest Híos (3–4 weekly; 1hr 15min) and Lávrio (1–2 weekly; 6hr) during the summer months; frequencies drop drastically off season.

### ACCOMMODATION

**Kato Gialos Apartments** Behind Káto Yialós beach ☎ 22740 61201. A mixture of spotless rooms and larger apartments with kitchen facilities, all with sea views and only a minute from the water. June–Sept. **€50**

**Psara Studios** At the back of the harbour village ☎ 22740 61233. The rooms here are large and furnished well enough, and have functional kitchenettes, plus there's a pleasant garden fringed with palms. May–Sept. **€50**

### EATING AND DRINKING

**Iliovasilema** Behind Káto Yialós beach ☎ 22470 61121. As the name suggests, sunset is the best time to dine here on seafood delights such as fried kalamári or octopus with aubergines. A friendly welcome is guranteed. June–Sept daily 11am–midnight.

★ **Spitalia** Behind Katsoúnis beach ☎ 22740 61376. Located in a restored medieval hospital, this great taverna

comes up with specialities such as stuffed goat and other home-style dishes, plus grills, salads and good wine. May–Sept daily 11am–1am.

**Ta Delfinia** In the middle of the harbour ☎ 22740 61352. Probably the top place for simply but expertly grilled fish and seafood, such as lobster, *tsipoúra* and *barboúni*. Also does various *pikilíes*. May–Oct daily 7am–1am.

# Lésvos

**LÉSVOS (Mytilíni)**, the third-largest Greek island after Crete and Évvia, is the birthplace of the ancient bards Sappho, Aesop, Arion and – more recently – primitive artist Theophilos and Nobel Laureate poet Odysseus Elytis. Despite these **artistic associations**, the island may not initially strike one as particularly beautiful or interesting: much of the landscape is rocky, volcanic terrain, encompassing vast grain fields, saltpans or even near-desert. But there are also oak and pine forests as well as endless olive groves, some more than five centuries old. With its balmy climate and suggestive contours, Lésvos tends to grow on you with prolonged exposure. Lovers of medieval and Ottoman **architecture** certainly won't be disappointed, and castles survive at Mytilíni Town, Mólyvos, Eressós, Sígri and near Ándissa.

Social and political **idiosyncrasies** add to the island's appeal: anyone who has attended one of the village *paniyíria*, with hours of music and tables groaning with food and drink, will not be surprised to learn that Lésvos has the highest alcoholism rate (and some of the worst driving habits) in Greece. There is a tendency to **vote Communist**

Ayvalík, Dikili & Foça (Turkey)

**LÉSVOS**

Loutrá Eftaloú
Mólyvos (Míthymna)
Áyii Anárgyri
Ayíi Anárgyri
Kayiá
Skála Sykaminiás
Tsónia
Sykaminiá
Lepetýmnos
Lepétymnos (968m)
Kápi
Pelópi
Ypsilométopo
Mandamádhos
Taxiárhis
Panayioúdha
Pyrgí Thermís
Paralía Thermís
Pámfylla
Misteghná
Khryssomaloússa
MYTILÍNI
Vaná
Moría
Aqueduct
Akliídhou
Taxiárhes
Loutrá
Koundouroúdhiá
Áyios Ermoyénis
Harámidha
Pérama
Tárti
Áyios Isídhoros
Gulf of Yéra
Loutrá Yéras
Ípios
Skópelos
Papádhos
Paleókipos
Ayiássos
Mylélia Watermill
Megalohóri
Paleohóri
Plomári
Olympos (967m)
Ambelikó
Akrássi
Dhróta
Melínda
Páralía Dhrótas
Panayía Kryfti
Káto Stavrós
Stavrós
Vaterá
Lisvóri
Vrýssa
Skála Polikhnítou
Polikhnítou
Nyfídha
Áyios Fokás
Akhládheri
Gulf of Kalloní
Halinádhou Basilica
Ayía Paraskeví
Nápi
Kremastí Bridge
Ypsilométopo
Stýpsi
Pétri
Pétra
Lafiónas
Skoutáros
Filia
Dháfia
Limónos
Parákila
Áyios Andréas
Anáxos
Avláki
Psíridra
Tsikhránda
Ambélia
Vafiós
Aryenos
Vatoússa
Hídhira
Skalohóri
Perivolís
Lídha
Gavathás
Lápsarna
Andísa
Órdhymnos (511m)
Eressós
Mesótopos
Kroússos
Krátigos
Petrified Forest
Ypsiloú
Sígri
Líthéna
Faneroméni
Nissiópi
Skála Eressoú
Podharás

JEEPS ONLY
Ágra
Vasiliká
Apothíka

N

kilometres
0        10

(with usually at least one Red MP in office), a legacy of the Ottoman-era quasi-feudalism, 1880s conflicts between small and large olive producers and further disruption occasioned by the arrival of many refugees. Breeding livestock, especially horses, remains important, and organic production has been embraced enthusiastically as a way of making Lésvos's agricultural products more competitive.

Historically, the olive plantations, ouzo distilleries, animal husbandry and fishing industry supported those who chose not to emigrate, but when these enterprises stalled in the 1980s, **tourism** made appreciable inroads. However, it still accounts for less than ten percent of the local economy: there are few large hotels outside the capital, Skála Kallóni or Mólyvos, and visitor numbers have dropped noticeably in recent years, except for a mini-boom in Turkish weekenders.

## Brief history

In antiquity, Lésvos's importance lay in its artistic and commercial connections rather than in historical events: being on the trade route to Asia Minor, it always attracted merchants and became quite wealthy during **Roman times**. During the late fourteenth century, Lésvos was given as a dowry to a Genoese prince of the Gattilusi clan following his marriage to the sister of one of the last Byzantine emperors – it's from this period that most of its castles remain. The first two centuries of **Ottoman rule** were particularly harsh, with much of the Orthodox population sold into slavery or deported to the imperial capital – replaced by more tractable Muslim colonists, who populated even rural areas – and most physical evidence of the Genoese or Byzantine period demolished. Out in the countryside, Turks and Greeks got along, relatively speaking, right up until 1923; the Ottoman authorities favoured Greek *kahayiádhes* (overseers) to keep the peons in line. However, large numbers of the lower social classes, oppressed by the pashas and their Greek lackeys, fled across to Asia Minor during the nineteenth century, only to return again after the exchange of populations.

### ARRIVAL AND GETTING AROUND
LÉSVOS

**By plane** There are services (frequencies for June–Oct) to Athens (5–7 daily; 50min–1hr); Híos (2 weekly, 30min); Límnos (5 weekly; 30min); Rhodes (2 weekly; 1hr 40min); Sámos (2 weekly; 45min–1hr 30min); Thessaloníki (1–2 daily; 55min–1hr 50min).

**By ferry** Despite the island's size, all ferries dock in Mytilíni; there are connections to: Ayvalık (Turkey; May–Oct daily, winter sporadic; 1hr 20min); Dikili (Turkey; May–Oct daily, winter sporadic; 1hr 30min); Foça (Turkey; May–Oct 4 weekly; 1hr); Híos (1–2 daily; 2–3hr); Ikaría (1 weekly; 7hr 30min); Kavála (2 weekly; 12hr); Límnos (6hr 30min); Pireás (1–2 daily; 8hr 30min–9hr); Sámos (2 weekly; 7hr); Thessaloníki (1 weekly; 14hr 30min).

**Getting around** Public buses run once or twice daily to most major towns and resorts, but Lesvos' sheer size makes day-trips from the capital impractical. Even with a car or motorbike, it is better to choose a base and tour locally from there.

## Mytilíni Town

**MYTILÍNI**, the port and capital, sprawls between and around two bays divided by a fortified promontory, and in Greek fashion often doubles as the name of the island. Many visitors are put off by the combination of urban bustle and, in the humbler northern districts, slight seediness. However, several diversions, particularly the marketplace and a few museums within a few minutes' walk of the waterfront, can occupy you for a few hours.

### The fortress
Tues–Sun 8.30am–3pm • €2

On the promontory sits the Byzantine-Genoese-Ottoman **fortress**, its mixed pedigree reflected in the Ottoman inscription immediately above the Byzantine double eagle at the southern outer gate. Inside you can make out the variably preserved ruins of the Gattilusi palace, a Turkish *medresse* (Koranic academy), a dervish cell and a Byzantine cistern. Just below the fortress, at **Tsamákia**, is the mediocre, fee-entry town "beach".

## The bazaar area

Inland, the town skyline is dominated in turn by the Germanic-Gothic belfry spire of **Áyios Athanásios cathedral** and the mammary dome of **Áyios Therápon**, both expressions of the (post)-Baroque taste of the nineteenth-century Ottoman Greek bourgeoisie. The interior decor of Áyios Therápon in particular seems more appropriate to an opera house than a church, with gilt aplenty in the vaulting and ornate column capitals. They stand more or less at opposite ends of the **bazaar**, whose main street, Ermoú, links the town centre with the little-used north harbour of **Epáno Skála**.

## The old town

Between the bazaar and Epáno Skála, Ermoú passes various expensive antique shops near the roofless, derelict **Yéni Tzamí** at the heart of the old Muslim quarter, just a few steps east of a superb Turkish **hammam**, restored to its former glory but – like the mosque – closed

MYTILÍNI TOWN

| ■ ACCOMMODATION | |
|---|---|
| New Life | 1 |
| Orfeas | 2 |
| Pyrgos | 3 |

| ● EATING & DRINKING | |
|---|---|
| Averoff | 3 |
| Ermis | 1 |
| Kalderimi | 2 |
| Pirasmos | 4 |

| ■ NIGHTLIFE | |
|---|---|
| Hott Spott | 2 |
| Monkey Bar | 1 |

unless a special exhibition is being held. Between Ermoú and the castle lies a maze of atmospheric lanes lined with *belle époque* mansions and humbler vernacular dwellings.

## Archeological museum

**New wing** 8-Noemvríou • ☎ 22510 40223 • **Old wing** Eftalióti 7 • ☎ 22510 28032 • Tues–Sun 8.30am–3pm • €3

Mytilíni's excellent **archeological museum**, the only real must-see, is housed in two separate galleries, a few hundred metres apart. The **newer wing** is devoted to finds from wealthy Roman Mytilene, in particular three rooms of well-displayed mosaics from second/third-century AD villas. Highlights include a crude but engaging scene of Orpheus charming all manner of beasts and birds, two fishermen surrounded by clearly recognizable (and edible) sea creatures, and the arrival of baby Telephos, son of Auge and Hercules, in a seaborne box, again with amazed fishermen presiding.

Earlier eras are represented in the **older wing**, located in a former mansion just behind the ferry dock. The ground floor has Neolithic finds from Áyios Vartholoméos cave and Bronze Age Thermí, but the star exhibits are the minutely detailed late Classical terracotta figurines upstairs: a pair of acrobats, two *kourotrophoi* figures (goddesses suckling infants, predecessors of all Byzantine *Galaktotrofoússa* icons), children playing with a ball or dogs, and Aphrodite riding a dolphin. A rear annexe contains stone-cut inscriptions of various edicts and treaties, plus a Roman sculpture of a drunken satyr asleep on a wineskin.

## Byzantine Museum

Aríonos • Mon–Sat 9am–1pm • €2 • ☎ 22510 28916

The well-lit and well-laid-out **Byzantine Museum**, just opposite the entrance to Áyios Therápon, contains various icons rescued from rural island churches. The most noteworthy exhibit, and the oldest, is a fourteenth-century icon of Christ *Pandokrátor*; other highlights include a sultanic *firmáni* or grant of privileges to a local bishop, a rare sixteenth-century three-dimensional icon of *The Crucifixion* and a canvas of the *Kímisis* (*Assumption*) by Theophilos (see box, p.638).

### ARRIVAL AND DEPARTURE

MYTILÍNI TOWN

**By air** There's no bus link with the airport, so you may need to take a taxi the 7km into Mytilíni Town.

**By ferry** Nearly all agencies can make bookings for ferries within Greece, while Dimakis Tours at Koundouriótou 73 (☎ 22510 27865) or Picolo Travel at no. 73a (☎ 22510 27000) are best for tickets to Turkey.

**By bus** There are two bus terminals: the long-distance KTEL buses leave from a small station near Platía Konstandinopóleos at the southern end of the harbour, while the blue town buses depart from a stand at the top of

the harbour, or the dedicated terminal near the stadium.

**By car** Car rental is arrangeable through reputable franchises like Best at Koundouriótou 87–89 (☎ 22510 37337, ⓦ best-rentacar.com) or excellent local agency Aphrodite at the corner of Elýti & Karapanayióti (☎ 22510 48100, ⓦ aphroditehotel.gr). Drivers should use the enormous free public car park a few blocks south of the KTEL or the oval plaza near the new wing of the archeological museum. If you're driving out, 8-Noemvríou, starting just behind the ferry quay, is the quickest way.

### INFORMATION

**Tourist office** James Aristárhou 6 (Mon–Fri 8am–2.30pm). Provides excellent town and island maps, plus other brochures.

**Online** The website ⓦ lesvos.com is highly useful.

**Services** Amenities include the post office behind the central park, and numerous ATMs starting just outside the port gate.

### ACCOMMODATION

Finding accommodation can be frustrating: waterfront hotels are noisy and overpriced, but supply usually exceeds demand for the better-value rooms in the backstreets. The Lesvos Hoteliers Association at Koundouriótou 47A (☎ 22510 41787, ⓦ filoxenia.net) can book rooms in town and around the island.

★ **New Life** Olýmbou, cul-de-sac off Ermoú ☎ 22510 23400, ⓦ new-life.gr. Moderate-sized, comfy en-suite rooms (some a/c) with polished wood floors, in an old eccentrically

decorated mansion with a garden. Great value. €30

**Orfeas** Katsakoúli 3 ☎ 22510 28523, ⓦ orfeas-hotel .com. Probably the quietest of the town hotels, this well-restored nineteenth-century building has somewhat small a/c doubles with cheerfully hued modern furnishings. Some balconies; lift; breakfast included. **€50**

**Pyrgos** Eleftheríou Venizélou 49 ☎22510 25069,

ⓦpyrgoshotel.gr. Premier in-town restoration, with utterly over-the-top kitsch decor in the common areas. Most rooms have a balcony, some have bath tubs and there are three round units in the tower. **€100**

## EATING, DRINKING AND NIGHTLIFE

The trendy northeast quay is the main venue for buzzing café-bars. The summer **cinema**, Pallas, is on Vournázon near the park; the winter cinema, Arion, is near the KTEL.

**Averoff** Koundouriótou 33 ☎22510 22180. Its handy location on the west quay makes this old-fashioned *estiatório* a popular venue for *mayireftá* (including early-morning *patsás*). Most dishes €5–8. Daily 6am–11pm.

★ **Ermis** Ermoú, Epáno Skála ☎22510 26232. Best-value, and friendliest, of the ouzerís in this district. *Belle époque* decor (panelled ceiling, giant mirrors, faded oil paintings) inside and a pleasant courtyard. Best check what the "crap salad" involves though. Daily noon–2am.

**Hott Spott** Koundouriótou 63 ☎22510 22200. Named after its wi-fi connection, this perennially popular hangout also offers flashing pop videos and increasing volume as the night wears on. Daily 10am–2am.

**Kalderimi** Thássou 2 ☎22510 46577. One of the few surviving bazaar ouzerís, occupying three picturesque buildings with seating under the shade of vines; the food is abundant if a bit plainly presented. Mon–Sat 11am–2am, Sun 11am–4pm.

**Monkey Bar** Koundouriótou 57 ☎22510 37717. A favourite meeting place for students and townies alike, where fashionably dressed waitresses ferry high-quality coffees and elaborate cocktails to their equally trendy customers. Daily 10am–3am.

**Pirasmos** Fanári quay ☎22510 54970. Better value than the fish tavernas surrounding it, this unpretentious grill house specializes in delicious meat such as *kondosoúvli* and *kokorétsi*, as well as simple salads and starters. Daily 1pm–1am.

# Around Mytilíni

The road heading **north** from Mytilíni towards Mandamádhos follows a rather nondescript coastline, but offers startling views across the straits to Turkey. South of the capital, there are two fine museums at **Variá** and a couple of decent beaches further down the peninsula.

## Paralía Thermís

Just 500m beyond Pýrgi Thermís, at **PARALÍA THERMÍS**, the Roman/Byzantine **hammam** has been allowed to decay in favour of an ugly, sterile modern facility adjacent, though it still supplies the hot water, and you can stick your head in to admire the vaulted brickwork. At 12km, you're a bit far from town, but there is a decent accommodation option here.

## Loutrá Yéras

Baths daily: April–May & Oct 8am–6pm; June–Sept 8am–7pm; Nov–March 9am–5pm • €3

For a lovely warm bath near Mytilíni, make for **Loutrá Yéras**, 8km along the main road to Kallоní. These **public baths** are just the thing if you've spent a sleepless night on a ferry, with two ornate spouts that feed 38°C water to marble-lined pools in vaulted chambers; there are separate facilities for men and women (the ladies' pool is a tad smaller but has lovely masonry), and skinny-dipping is, unexpectedly in prudish Greece, obligatory.

If you take the more northerly route via Mória to Loutrá Yéras, you will pass close by the impressive remains of a second-century **Roman aqueduct**, signposted down a fertile valley.

## Variá

Accessible by hourly buses

The most rewarding sights to be visited near Mytilíni are a pair of museums at **VARIÁ**, 5km south of town, which between them hold much of the island's artistic legacy.

## THEOPHILOS HADZIMIHAÏL: THE ROUSSEAU OF GREECE?

The "naïve" painter **Theophilos Hadzimihaïl** (1873–1934) was born and died in Mytilíni Town, and both his eccentricities and talents were remarkable from an early age. After wandering across the country from Pílio to Athens and the Peloponnese, Theophilos became one of *belle époque* Greece's prize eccentrics, dressing up as Alexander the Great or various revolutionary war heroes, complete with pom-pommed shoes and pleated skirt. Theophilos was ill and living as a recluse in severely reduced circumstances back on Lésvos when he was introduced to Thériade in 1919; the latter, virtually alone among critics of the time, recognized his peculiar genius and ensured that Theophilos was supported both morally and materially for the rest of his life.

With their childlike perspective, vivid colour scheme and idealized mythical and rural subjects, Theophilos's works are unmistakeable. Relatively few of his works survive today, because he executed commissions for a pittance on ephemeral surfaces such as *kafenío* counters, horsecarts, or the walls of long-vanished houses. Facile comparisons are often made between Theophilos and Henri Rousseau, the roughly contemporaneous French "primitive" painter. Unlike "Le Douanier", however, Theophilos followed no other profession, eking out a precarious living from his art alone. And while Rousseau revelled in exoticism, Theophilos's work was principally and profoundly rooted in Greek mythology, history and daily life.

### Theophilos Museum

Tues–Sun 10am–4pm • €2 • ☎ 22510 41644

The **Theophilos Museum** honours the painter (see box above), born here in 1873, with four rooms of wonderful, little-known compositions commissioned by his patron Thériade (see below) during the years immediately preceding Theophilos's death. A wealth of detail is evident in elegiac scenes of fishing, reaping, olive-picking and baking from the pastoral Lésvos which Theophilos obviously knew best. The *Sheikh-ul-Islam* with his hubble-bubble (Room 2) seems drawn from life, as does a highly secular Madonna merely titled *Mother with Child* (also Room 2). But in the museum's scenes of classical landscapes and episodes from wars historical and contemporary Theophilos seems on shakier ground.

### Thériade Museum

Tues–Sun: April–Sept 9am–2pm & 5–8pm; Oct–March 9am–5pm • €2 • ☎ 22510 23372

Next door to the Theophilos Museum, the imposing **Thériade Museum** is the legacy of another native son, Stratis Eleftheriades (1897–1983). Leaving the island aged 18 for Paris, he Gallicized his name to Thériade and eventually became a renowned avant-garde art publisher, enlisting some of the leading artists of the twentieth century in his ventures. The displays comprise two floors of lithographs, engravings, ink drawings, wood-block prints and watercolours by the likes of Miró, Chagall, Picasso, Giacometti, Matisse, Le Corbusier, Léger, Rouault and Villon, either annotated by the painters themselves or commissioned as illustrations for the works of prominent poets and authors: an astonishing collection for a relatively remote Aegean island, deserving leisurely perusal.

## South of Variá

Heading **south** beyond the airport and Krátigos village, the paved road loops around the peninsula to **Haramídha**, 14km from town and the closest decent (pebble) **beach**; the eastern bay has a few **tavernas**. **Áyios Ermoyénis**, 3km west and directly accessible from Mytilíni via Loutrá village, is more scenic and sandy. The patron saint's chapel perches on the cliff separating two small, sandy coves from a larger, less usable easterly bay accessed by a separate track.

### ACCOMMODATION AND EATING                        AROUND MYTILÍNI

**Loriet/Laureate** Variá, 4km south of Mytilíni ☎ 22510 43111, ⓦ loriet-hotel.com. A nineteenth-century mansion with modern wings, gardens, fine restaurant and 25m saltwater pool. Rooms vary from blandly modern, marble-trimmed studios to massive suites with retro decor and big bathrooms. April–Oct. €80

**Theodora Glava (Grioules)** Haramídha ☎22510 46417. Right on the beach, legendary Theodora dishes up a great range of lovingly prepared vegetarian and seafood mezédhes, as well as more substantial meat and fish items. April–Oct daily 11am–1am.

★ **Votsala** Paralía Thermís ☎22510 71231, ⓦvotsalahotel.com. This comfortable and relaxing place offers watersports off the (somewhat scrappy) beach and well-tended gardens. It prides itself on having no TV in the rooms and no "Greek nights". May–Oct. €45

# Southern Lésvos

Southern Lésvos is indented by two great inlets, the gulfs of **Kalloní** and **Yéra**, the first curving in a northeasterly direction, the latter northwesterly, creating a fan-shaped peninsula at the heart of which looms 967m **Mount Ólymbos**. Both shallow gulfs are landlocked by very narrow outlets to the open sea, which don't – and probably never will – have bridges spanning them. This is the most verdant and productive olive-oil territory on Lésvos, and stacks of pressing-mills stab the skyline.

## Pérama

A regular kaïki service (no cars carried) links Pérama with Koundouroudhiá, which has a blue city bus service to/from Mytilíni on the far side

**PÉRAMA**, disused olive-oil warehouses dotting its oddly attractive townscape, is one of the larger places on the Gulf of Yéra. Although it feels rather forlorn and end-of-the-road, it is easily accessible by public transport from Mytilíni and offers great eating.

## Plomári and around

Due south of Mount Ólymbos, at the edge of the "fan", **PLOMÁRI** is the only sizeable coastal settlement hereabouts, and indeed the second-largest municipality on Lésvos. It presents an unlikely juxtaposition of scenic appeal and its famous ouzo industry, courtesy of several local **distilleries**. Despite a resounding lack of good **beaches** within walking distance, Plomári is popular with Scandinavian tourists; most actually stay at **Áyios Isídhoros**, 3km east.

### Varvayianni Distillery

May–Oct Mon–Fri 9am–7pm, Sat 9am–1pm; Nov–April Mon–Fri 8am–4pm • Free • ☎22520 32741, ⓦbarbayanni-ouzo.com

The largest and oldest of Plomári distilleries, **Varvayianni**, offers free tours and tasting, plus a fascinating display of old alembics, presses, storage jars and archival material. Best venues for a tipple afterwards are the old *kafenía* on central Platía Beniamín.

### Melínda

**Melínda**, a 700m sand-and-shingle beach at the mouth of a canyon lush with olive trees, lies 6km west of Plomári by paved road. It's an alluring place, with sweeping views west towards the Vaterá coast and the cape of Áyios Fokás, and south (in clear conditions) to northern Híos, Psará and the Turkish Karaburun peninsula.

### Panayía Kryftí hot springs

One of the best excursions beyond Melínda is to the **Panayía Kryftí hot springs**. From the first curve of the paved road up to Paleohóri, a dirt track goes 2.8km to a dead-end with parking space, with the final 400m on a downhill path to the little chapel just above a protected inlet. On the far side of this you'll see a rectangular cement tank, just big enough for two people, containing water at a pleasant 37–38°C.

## Ayiássos and around

**AYIÁSSOS**, 26km from Mytilíni, nestled in a remote, wooded valley under the crest of Mount Ólymbos, is the most beautiful hill town on Lésvos, its narrow cobbled streets lined by ranks of tiled-roof houses, built in part from proceeds of the trade in *tsoupiá*

**9**

(olive sacks). On the usual, northerly approach, there's no hint of the enormous village until you see huge knots of parked cars at the southern edge of town. Most visitors proceed past endless ranks of kitsch wooden and ceramic souvenirs or carved "Byzantine" furniture, aimed mostly at Greeks, and the central church of the **Panayía Vrefokratoússa** – built in the twelfth century to house an icon supposedly painted by the Evangelist Luke – to the old bazaar, with its *kafenía*, yoghurt/cheese shops and butchers' stalls. With such a venerable icon as a focus, the local August 15 *paniyíri* is one of the liveliest on Lésvos.

## Mount Ólymbos

From the southern side of Ayiássos, keen walkers can follow a network of marked paths and tracks for three hours to the **Ólymbos summit**. Approaching from Plomári, there's asphalt road and public transport only up to Megalohóri, with a good dirt surface thereafter up to some air-force radar balls, where paving resumes. The area between Megalohóri and the summit ridge was damaged by a 1994 forest fire, though once over the other side dense woods of unscathed oak and chestnut take over from the recovering pine growth.

## Mylélia water mill

Daily 9am–6pm • Ⓦ mylelia.gr

Six kilometres northeast of Ayiássos, signposted along a track near the turning for Ípio, you can visit the **Mylélia water mill**. The name means "place of the mills", and there were once several hereabouts – this is the last survivor, restored to working order in the 1990s. The keeper will show you the millrace and paddle-wheel, as well as the flour making its spasmodic exit, after which you can browse the gourmet pastas and other products at the shop, including cheeses, jams, vinegar and salted fish. They also do cooking courses.

## Polikhnítos and around

The largest settlement in the southwestern part of southern Lésvos is **POLIKHNÍTOS**, a rather dull, workaday rural centre. It is, however, the point of access to magnificent **Vaterá** beach, the seaside villages of **Skála Polikhnítou** and and **Nifídha**, each with its own smaller beach, and the Natural History Museum of **Vrýssa**.

## Vrýssa: Natural History Museum

May & June daily 9.30am–3.30pm; July–Sept daily 9.30am–3pm & 4–8pm; Oct–April Wed–Sun 9.30am–3.30pm • €2 • ☎ 22520 61890

**VRÝSSA**, 4km south of Polikhnítos, has a mildly diverting **Natural History Museum** documenting local paleontological finds. In 1997 Athenian paleontologist Michael Dermitzakis confirmed what farmers unearthing bones had long suspected when he pronounced the area a treasure-trove of **fossils**, including those of two-million-year-old gigantic horses, mastodons, monkeys and tortoises the size of a Volkswagen Beetle. Until 20,000 years ago, Lésvos (like all other east Aegean islands) was joined to the Asian mainland, and the gulf of Vaterá was a subtropical freshwater lake; the animals in question came to drink, died nearby and were trapped and preserved by successive volcanic flows.

## Vaterá and around

**VATERÁ**, 9km south of Polikhnítos, is a 7km-long sand beach, backed by vegetated hills; the sea here is delightfully calm and clean, the strand itself among the best on

---

### POLIKHNÍTOS SPA

If you're after a hot bath, head for the vaulted, well-restored **Polikhnítos Spa** complex (daily: April–Oct 9am–8pm; Nov–March 2–7pm; €4; ☎ 22520 41229, Ⓦ hotsprings.gr) 1.5km east of the town of **Polikhnítos**; there are separate, warm-hued chambers for each sex. The water actually gushes out at temperatures up to 87°C, so needs to be tempered with cold.

Lésvos. Development, mostly seasonal villas and apartments for locals, straggles for several kilometres to either side of the central T-junction but is nicely spread out, so the strip does not feel overtly commercialized.

Some 3km west at the cape of **Áyios Fokás** only the foundations remain of a temple of Dionysos and a superimposed early Christian basilica. The little tamarisk-shaded anchorage here has a superb taverna.

---

## ACCOMMODATION AND EATING                                    SOUTHERN LÉSVOS

### PÉRAMA

⭐ **Balouhanas** Pérama ☎ 22510 51948. The northern-most establishment on the front, with a wooden, cane-roofed deck jutting out over the water. Seafood is a strong point, whether grilled or as croquettes, as are regional mezédhes and home-made desserts. Daily 11am–2am.

### PLOMÁRI AND AROUND

**Maria's** Melínda ☎ 22520 93239. Right where the access road reaches the sea; the restaurant is excellent, serving a range of fish, meat and mezédhes, while the rooms are simple but extremely cheap. May–Oct. €25

**Melinda Studios** Melínda ☎ 22520 93282, ✉ melindastudios@gmail.com. Two doors along from *Maria's*, this small pension has clean, bright studios with small kitchenettes and sea-facing balconies. May–Sept. €30

**Pebble Beach** Áyios Isídhoros ☎ 22520 31651. Many of the rooms here, which are adequate in size and comfort, overlook a slightly reefy section of beach – though avoid those near the bar if you value sleep. Breakfast included. May–Oct. €60

**Pension Lida** Near Platía Beniamín, Plomári ☎ 22520 32507. An attractive restoration inn occupying two old mansions, with sea-view balconies for most units. Some of the high-ceilinged rooms share bathrooms. €30

⭐ **Taverna tou Panaï** Áyios Isídhoros ☎ 22520 31920. Set in an olive grove just beyond the northerly town limits sign; here you'll find salubrious meat, seafood and *mayireftá* dishes, and mostly Greeks in attendance. Most produce is home-grown and organic. Daily 10am–late.

### AYIÁSSOS AND AROUND

**Dhouladhellis** Ayiássos ☎ 22520 22236. Near the fork at the village's southern end, this family taverna with a huge courtyard serves various soups, meat dishes for €6–7 and plenty of *glyká koutalioú*. March–Nov daily 9am–midnight.

**Ouzerí To Stavri** Ayiássos ☎ 22520 22936. At the extreme north end of the village in Stavrí district, this quirky little place offers a warm welcome and great home-style mezédhes such as cheese croquettes and octopus in vinegar. Daily 11am–late.

### POLIKHNÍTOS AND AROUND

⭐ **Akrotiri/Angelerou** Áyios Fokás ☎ 22520 61465. Top-notch little taverna, specializing in seafood delights such as shrimp salad or *sardhélles Kallonís*, plus starters like cheese croquettes. All cost well under €10 and can be washed down with aromatic wine. April–Oct daily noon–1am.

⭐ **Aphrodite Beach** Vaterá ☎ 22520 61288, ⓦ aphroditehotel.gr. Sparkling blue-and-white complex of comfortable units with a/c, fridges and small balconies. The extremely welcoming family restaurant features tasty dishes like lamb, *briám*, very palatable wine and occasional live music sessions. Breakfast included. May to early Oct. €30

**O Grigoris** Nifídha ☎ 22520 41838. Good seafront *psarotavérna* with the usual range of fish and seafood, backed up by some salads and veg dishes. Noon–1am: March–June & mid-Sept to Nov Fri–Sun; July to mid-Sept daily.

---

# Western Lésvos

The area from the Gulf of Kalloní to the island's west coast is a mostly treeless, craggy region whose fertile valleys offer a sharp contrast to the bare ridges. River mouths form little oases behind a handful of **beach resorts** like Skála Kallonís, Sígri and Skála Eressoú. A few **monasteries** along the road west of Kalloní, plus the occasional striking **inland village**, provide monumental interest.

## Ayía Paraskeví and around

A rewarding detour en route to Kalloní is to **AYÍA PARASKEVÍ** village, midway between two important and photogenic monuments from diverse eras: the Paleo-Christian, three-aisled basilica of **Halinádhou**, its dozen basalt columns amid pine-and-olive scenery, and the large medieval bridge of **Kremastí**, the largest and best preserved such in the east Aegean, 3km west of Ayía Paraskeví.

> ## THE OLIVES OF LÉSVOS
>
> No other Greek island is as dominated by **olive production** as Lésvos, which is blanketed by approximately 11 million olive trees. Most of these vast groves date from after a lethal frost in 1851, though a few hardy survivors are thought to be over five hundred years old. During the first three centuries after the Ottoman conquest, production of olive oil was a monopoly of the ruling pasha, but following eighteenth-century reforms in the Ottoman Empire, extensive tracts of Lésvos (and thus the lucrative oil trade) passed into the hands of the new Greek bourgeoisie, who greatly expanded the industry.

## Museum of Industrial Olive Oil Production in Lésvos

Daily except Tues 10am–6pm, closes 5pm mid-Oct to Feb • €3 • ☎ 22530 32300, ⓦ piop.gr

On the southern outskirts of Ayía Paraskeví stands the eminently worthwhile **Museum of Industrial Olive Oil Production in Lésvos** (Mousío Viomihanikís Elaeouryías Lésvou), housed in a restored communal olive mill. The mill, built by public subscription in the 1920s, only ceased working under the junta; the industrial machinery has been lovingly refurbished and its function explained, while former outbuildings and warehouses are used as venues for secondary exhibits and short explanatory films.

## Kalloní and around

**KALLONÍ** is a lively agricultural and market town in the middle of the island. Some 3km south lies the town's seaside package resort, **Skála Kallonís**, backing a long, sandy but absurdly shallow beach on the lake-like gulf whose water can be turbid. It's mainly distinguished as a **birdwatching** centre during the nesting season (March–May) in the adjacent salt marshes. The local speciality is the gulf's celebrated, plankton-nurtured **sardines**, best eaten fresh-grilled from August to October, although they're available salt-cured all year round.

### ACCOMMODATION AND EATING                                   KALLONÍ AND AROUND

**Aegeon** Kalloní ☎ 22530 22398, ⓦ aegeon-lesvos.gr. Set in a leafy garden, with above-average furnishings for its class, a large pool and friendly owners, this is the best option among the hotels grouped on the west side of town. **€45**

**Medusa** Skála Kallonís ☎ 697 22 01 813. Top restaurant for sardines done Kalloní style and other super-fresh fish and seafood, much of it under €10. Pleasant location in a renovated stone house on the seafront. April–Oct daily 10am–1am.

## Limónos monastery

Museum daily 9.30am–6.30pm, may close 3pm off-season • €2

West of Kalloní, the road winds 4km uphill to **Limónos monastery**, founded in 1527 by the monk Ignatios, whose cell is maintained in the surviving medieval north wing. It's a rambling, three-storey complex around a vast, plant-filled courtyard, home to just a handful of monks and lay workers. The *katholikón*, with its ornate carved-wood ceiling and archways, is traditionally off-limits to women; a sacred spring flows from below the south foundation wall. Only the ground-floor **ecclesiastical museum** is currently functioning, with the more interesting ethnographic gallery upstairs still closed.

## Hídhira

Seven kilometres south of the beautiful settlement of **Vatoússa**, which boasts a classic plane-shaded square and some fine architecture, stands the hilltop village of **HÍDHIRA**, with a fine winery and interesting museum. The village is a dead end unless you have a jeep capable of continuing across the rough track to Eressós by way of Ágra.

### Methymneos Winery

Daily July–Sept 9am–6pm, otherwise by appointment • ☎ 22530 51518, ⓦ methymneos.gr

Just below the entrance to Hídhira, the **Methymneos Winery** has successfully revived the local ancient grape variety, decimated by phylloxera some decades ago. Because of the altitude (300m) and sulphur-rich soil (you're in a volcanic caldera), their velvety, high-alcohol, oak-aged red can be produced organically; 2007 saw the introduction of bottled white wines. Proprietor Ioannis Lambrou gives a highly worthwhile twenty-minute tour of the state-of-the-art premises in English.

## Digital Art Museum of George Jakobides
Tues–Sun: July & Aug 11am–7pm; Sept–June 9am–5pm • €2 • ☎ 22530 51128, ⊛ jakobides-digital-museum.gr

The fancy name of the **Digital Art Museum of George Jakobides** is a slight misnomer in that it is not about anything hi-tech and the artist to whom it is dedicated, a native of Hídhira who lived from 1853 to 1932, predated the computer age. Yet the short digital film and copies of seven of his most famous works, such as *Children's Concert* and *Naughty Grandson*, are worth a peep.

## Monastery of Perivolís
Daily 10am–1pm & 5–6pm • Donation • No photos

Some 8km beyond Vatoússa, a short track leads down to the thirteenth-century monastery of **Perivolís**, built amid a riverside orchard (*perivóli*), with fine if damp-damaged sixteenth-century frescoes in the narthex. An apocalyptic panel worthy of Bosch (*The Earth and Sea Yield up their Dead*) shows the Whore of Babylon riding her chimera and assorted sea monsters disgorging their victims; just to the right, towards the main door, the Three Magi are depicted approaching the Virgin enthroned with the Christ Child. On the north side there's a highly unusual iconography of Abraham, the Virgin, and the penitent thief of Calvary in paradise, with the four heavenly rivers gushing forth under their feet; just right are assembled the Hebrew kings of the Old Testament.

## Ándissa and around
**ÁNDISSA**, 11km west of Vatoússa, nestles under this parched region's only substantial pine grove; at the edge of the village a sign implores you to "Come Visit Our Square", not a bad idea for the sake of a handful of refreshment options sheltering under three sizeable plane trees.

### Gavathás and around
Directly below Ándissa a paved road leads 6km north to **GAVATHÁS**, a village with a shortish, partly protected **beach** and a few places to eat and stay. A side road leads one headland east to huge, dune-dominated, surf-battered **Kámbos** beach, which you may well have to yourself, even in August.

| ACCOMMODATION AND EATING | ÁNDISSA AND AROUND |
|---|---|

**Paradise** Gavathás ☎ 22530 56376. This pension-cum-restaurant, 300m back from the seafront, has simple but adequate rooms and serves good fish and locally grown vegetables. May–Sept. **€30**

★ **Pedhinon** Ándissa ☎ 22530 56106. The village's oldest and best taverna, shaded by the largest plane tree, is very friendly and rustles up excellent *mayireftá*, such as lamb fricassee and okra. You may even run into local octogenarian poet Panayiótis Petréllis. Daily 10am–midnight.

## Monastery of Ypsiloú
Museum daily 8.30am–3pm • Donation

Two kilometres west of Ándissa there's an important junction. Keeping straight leads you past the still-functioning, double-gated monastery of **Ypsiloú**, founded in 1101 atop an outrider of extinct Órdhymnos volcano. The *katholikón*, tucked in one corner of a large, irregular courtyard, has a fine wood-lattice ceiling but has had its frescoes repainted to detrimental effect. Exhibits in the upstairs **museum** encompass a fine collection of *epitáfios* (Good Friday) shrouds, ancient manuscripts, portable icons and – oddest of all – a *Deposition* painted in Renaissance style by a sixteenth-century Turk.

**9**

## The petrified forest

Daily: June–Sept 8am–sunset; Oct–May 8am–4pm • €2

To the west of Ypsiloú begins the 5km side road to the main concentration of Lésvos's overrated **petrified forest**, a fenced-in "reserve" toured along 3km of walkways. For once, contemporary Greek arsonists cannot be blamed for the state of the trees, created by the combined action of volcanic ash from Órdhymnos and hot springs some fifteen to twenty million years ago. The mostly horizontal sequoia trunks average 1m or less in length, save for a few poster-worthy exceptions; there's another more accessible (and free) cluster south of Sígri.

## Sígri

**SÍGRI**, near the western tip of Lésvos, has an appropriately end-of-the-line feel; its bay is guarded both by an Ottoman castle and the long island of **Nissiopí**, which protects the place somewhat from prevailing winds. The eighteenth-century **castle**, built atop an earlier one, sports the reigning sultan's monogram over the entrance, something rarely seen outside Istanbul, evidence of the high regard in which this strategic port with a good water supply was held. The odd-looking church of **Ayía Triádha** is in fact a converted **mosque**, with a huge water cistern taking up the ground floor; this supplied, among other things, the half-ruined **hammam** just south.

### Natural History Museum of the Lésvos Petrified Forest

Daily: July–Sept 8am–8pm; Oct–May 8am–5pm • €5 • ☎ 22530 54434, ⓦ lesvosmuseum.gr

At the top of town stands the well-executed but overpriced **Natural History Museum of the Lésvos Petrified Forest**, which covers pan-Aegean geology with samples and maps (including, ominously, seismic patterns), as well as the expected quota of petrified logs and plant fossils from when the surrounding hills were far more vegetated.

### The beaches

The nearest of several **beaches**, south of the castle headland, is somewhat narrow but is the only one with amenities. The far superior strand of **Faneroméni** lies 3.5km north by a coastal dirt track from the northern outskirts of town. A shorter but equally good beach, **Liména**, can be found 2km south of Sígri at another creek mouth, just off the rough, one-lane, 15km track to Eressós, passable with care in an ordinary car, in 35 minutes.

### ACCOMMODATION, EATING AND DRINKING                                    SÍGRI

**Cavo d'Oro/Blue Wave** (no sign) ☎ 22530 54221. The only taverna on the harbour itself is a classic for lobster and scaly fish; most of the restaurants around the nearby platía are run-of-the-mill in comparison. Daily 11am–2am.
**Notia** The hippest place in town, with frequent live jazz

sessions and offering the usual range of refreshments. Daily 8pm–late.
**Pyrgospito/Towerhouse** ☎ 22530 22909, ⓦ lesvos-towerhouse.gr. Four spacious antique-furnished apartments in a *belle époque* folly, 500m outside of the village, in a landscaped hillside setting with pool. May–Oct. €70

## Skála Eressoú

Most visitors to western Lésvos park themselves at **SKÁLA ERESSOÚ**, reached via a southerly turning between Ándissa and Ypsiloú. Its 3km **beach** almost rivals Vatera's as the best on the island. Behind stretches the largest and most attractive agricultural plain on Lésvos, a welcome green contrast to the volcanic ridges above.

There's not much to central Skála – just a roughly rectangular grid of perhaps five streets by twelve, angling up to the oldest cottages on the slope of Vígla hill above the east end of the beach. The waterfront pedestrian lane is divided midway by a café-lined, circular platía with a bust of **Theophrastos**. This renowned botanist hailed from **ancient Eressós** atop Vígla hill – the remaining citadel wall is still visible from a distance, and though the ruins themselves prove scanty, the views reward a scramble up.

**9**

Another famous native of ancient Eressós, honoured by a stylized statue on the platía, was **Sappho** (c.615–562 BC), poetess and reputed lesbian. There are thus always conspicuous numbers of gay women about (especially during the annual September festival), particularly in the clothing-optional zone of the **beach** west of the river mouth, also home to a small community of terrapins.

## ACCOMMODATION
SKÁLA ERESSOÚ

For accommodation, it's wise to entrust the search to Sappho Travel (☎ 22530 52202, ⓦ sapphotravel.com) who can arrange something to suit your needs; they also rent out cars.

**ly Galini** ☎ 22530 53138, ⓦ hotel-galinos.gr. Three blocks inland, this welcoming, slightly old-fashioned hotel with a colourful yard outside has cosy, spotlessly clean rooms with little balconies. Wi-fi in lobby. Breakfast included. **€40**

**Sappho the Eressia** ☎ 22530 53233, ⓦ sappho-hotel .com. With wi-fi and a pleasant ground-floor snack bar, this central seafront hotel has been spruced up to attract all comers, having dropped its previous women-only policy. **€40**

## EATING, DRINKING AND NIGHTLIFE

With about seven clubs/bars to choose from in peak season, local **nightlife** is the best on the island and all are gay-friendly. There's also a central, open-air **cinema** (July to early Sept), predictably called Sappho.

**Ioannis & Gabi** ☎ 22530 53272. Run by a Greek-Austrian couple, this garden taverna is a delightful spot to sample simple home-style cooking with a range of meat, fish and vegetarian dishes, washed down by fine barrelled wine. May–Oct daily noon–midnight.
**Kyani Sardhini/Blue Sardine** ☎ 22530 53503. A creditable seafood ouzerí at the far west end of the front, where the engaging manager will provide anything from lobster and crab at market rates to more modest small fish. April–Oct daily 11am–1am.
**Parasol** Ethnic sounds abound and exotic cocktails flow at

one of the resort's most enduring café-cum-bars, with an attractive central seafront location under a thatched bamboo roof. May to early Oct daily 10am–late.
**Samadhi** ☎ 697 62 00 799. On the east quay, this trendy and upmarket newcomer does steaks for €17, plus *pitsa*, curries, unusual salads such as niçoise and some innovative desserts. May–Sept daily 10am–2am.
**Sappho Garden** ☎ 22530 53682. Relaxed garden bar a couple of blocks inland, largely frequented by lesbians, often with live performances from poetry to music, and events like yoga sessions. April–Oct daily 11am–2am.

# Northern Lésvos

The northern part of Lésvos is largely fertile and green countryside stippled with poplars and blanketed by olive groves. Occupying the prime position on a promontory in the middle of the coast is one of the northeast Aegean's most attractive resorts, **Mólyvos**, whose castle's cockscomb silhouette is visible for many kilometres around. On either side of it, a number of **coastal resorts** offer superior bathing.

## Mólyvos (Míthymna)

**MÓLYVOS** (officially Míthymna after its ancient predecessor), 61km from Mytilíni, is the island's most beautiful village, with tiers of sturdy, red-tiled houses, some standing with their rear walls defensively towards the sea, mounting the slopes between the picturesque harbour and the Byzantine-Genoese **castle**. A score of weathered Turkish fountains, a mosque and hammam grace flower-fragrant, cobbled alleyways, reflecting the fact that before 1923 Muslims constituted more than a third of the local population and owned many of the finest dwellings.

Modern dwellings and hotels have been banned from the old core, but this hasn't prevented a steady drain of all authentic life from the upper **bazaar**; perhaps four or five "ordinary" shops ply their trade among souvenir shops vastly surplus to requirements. The shingly **town beach** is mediocre, improving considerably as you head towards the sandy southern end of the bay, called **Psiriára**.

**9**

## The castle
Daily 8.30am–3pm · €2

The imposing ramparts of the **Byzantine castle** of Mólyvos, later repaired by Genoan Francesco Gattelusi, are visible from many kilometres around. Sections can now be accessed from the inside, affording splendid views of the harbour and beyond. Entrance is via the impressive main gate, through which a set of steps leads up to the largely open interior, where a wooden **amphitheatre** is used for occasional summer performances.

## The Komninaki Kralli mansion
Daily 9am–3pm · Free

The **Komninaki Kralli mansion**, high up in the town, is worth the climb; the lower floor houses a well-signposted "School of Fine Arts", and the wall- and ceiling-murals on the upper storey (dated 1833) compare with those of the Vareltzídena mansion in Pétra (see p.648). Panels in the smallest room portray dervish musicians and women dancing to shawm and drum, while other murals depict stylized versions of Constantinople and Mytilíni Town.

### ARRIVAL AND INFORMATION
MÓLYVOS (MÍTHYMNA)

**By bus and taxi** The bus stop and taxi rank are at the southeast edge of town.

**By car and motorbike** There are numerous motorbike and car rental places near the tourist office, including Kosmos (☎22530 71710) and Best (☎22530 72145), both offering the option of pick-up here and drop-off in Mytilíni or the airport. The main car park is at the southeast edge of town;

there are further car parks above the port and up by the castle.

**Tourist office** (May–Oct Mon–Sat 10am–5pm; ☎22530 71347, ⓦmithymna.gr). The municipal tourist office, near the main junction on the south side of town, keeps lists of rented rooms.

**Services** The main post office is near the top of the upper commercial street; ATMs and wi-fi spots abound.

### ACCOMMODATION

**Delfinia** ☎22530 71315, ⓦhoteldelfinia.com. Luxury resort hotel, 1km south of town, set in 87 acres of greenery, with rooms and bungalows, a castle-view pool, tennis courts and direct access to Psiriára beach. Breakfast included. **€70**

**Hermes** ☎22530 71250, ⓦhermeshotel-molivos.com. Modern beachside single-storey hotel with variable, marble-floored rooms, all fitted with bright contemporary furnishings and set in quite lush grounds. May–Oct. **€50**

**Molyvos I** ☎22530 71496, ⓦmolyvos-hotels.com.

On the main town beach, with large balconied and comfortably furnished rooms. Complimentary breakfast served on the flagstoned terrace under the palms. Sister *Molyvos II* on nearby Eftaloú beach. April–Oct. **€60**

★ **Sun Rise Hotel** ☎22530 71713, ⓦsunrisehotel-lesvos.com. High-class hotel that sprawls in startling white tiers over a hillside 2km east of town. The rooms come in varying sizes but all are well appointed. Two pools, tennis courts, gym, sauna and classy restaurant. Breakfast included. April–Oct. **€75**

### EATING, DRINKING AND NIGHTLIFE
Apart from a selection of lively bars, there's also an outdoor **cinema** (June–Sept) next to the taxi rank.

**Bazaar** The main indoor dance hall, hidden behind an inconspicuous door on the road down to the quay, pumps out a mixture of foreign and Greek disco hits. Daily midnight–late.

★ **The Captain's Table** ☎22530 71241. Splendid quayside taverna offering squirmingly fresh seafood, including great octopus and *gávros pastós*, meat grills, plus vegetarian moussaka and mezédhes, washed down with their very palatable, own-label wine. May–Oct daily noon–2am.

**Molly's Bar** ☎22530 71772. Popular hangout, with taped music at a conversational level during the day and louder music videos by night. The cosy balcony has atmospheric harbour views. May–Oct daily 10am–late.

**To Ouzadhiko tou Baboukou** ☎22530 71776. On the south quay, this joint has an impressive array of ouzos, a bohemian atmosphere and competent, well-priced renditions of the usual mezédhes. Daily 11am–1am.

## Around Mólyvos
West of Mólyvos there is a string of decent beaches with varying degrees of commercialization, most rampant at **Pétra**. To the east, coastal development is more

measured, with some appealing beaches and yet another spa. Inland and southeast, the main paved road via Vafiós curves around 968m, poplar-tufted **Mount Lepétymnos**. You can complete a scenic loop of the mountain via Kápi and Ypsilométopo on its southern flank.

### Pétra

Given political and practical limits to expansion in Mólyvos, many package companies have shifted emphasis to **PÉTRA**, 5km due south. The modern outskirts sprawl untidily behind its broad, sandy beach, but two attractive nuclei of old stone houses, some with Levantine-style balconies overhanging the street, extend back from the part-pedestrianized seafront square. Pétra takes its name from the giant, unmissable rock monolith inland, enhanced by the eighteenth-century church of the **Panayía Glykofiloússa**, reached via 114 rock-hewn steps. Other local attractions include the sixteenth-century church of **Áyios Nikólaos**, with three phases of well-preserved frescoes up to 1721, and the intricately decorated **Vareltzídhena mansion** (Tues–Sun 8am–3pm; free), with late eighteenth-century naïve wall paintings of courting couples, a bear being trained, sailing ships and a stylized view of a naval engagement at Constantinople.

### Ánaxos

**ÁNAXOS**, 3km south of Pétra, is a higgledy-piggledy package resort fringing by far the cleanest **beach** and seawater in the area: 1km of sand well sown with sunbeds and a handful of tavernas. From anywhere along here you enjoy beautiful sunsets between and beyond three offshore islets.

### Loutrá Eftaloú

Daily: May & Oct 9am–1pm & 3–7pm; June–Sept 10am–2pm & 4–8pm; Nov–April variable access • €3.50 for group pool • Occasional summer shuttle-bus service from Mólyvos

The **Loutrá Eftaloú** thermal baths lie 5km east of Mólyvos, at the end of the paved road. Patronize the hot pool under the Ottoman-era domed structure, rather than the sterile modern tub-rooms. The spa is well looked after, with the water mixed up to a toasty 43°C, so you'll need to cool down regularly; outside stretches the long, good pebble beach of **Áyii Anáryiri**, broken up by little headlands, with the two remotest coves nudist.

### Sykaminiá

The exquisite hill village of **SYKAMINIÁ** (Sykamiá, Skamniá), just under 10km from Mólyvos, is the birthplace in 1892 of novelist Stratis Myrivilis. One of the imposing basalt-built houses below the platía, from which there are views north to Turkey, is marked as his childhood home.

### Skála Sykaminiás

A marked trail short-cuts the twisting road from just east of Sykaminiá down to **SKÁLA SYKAMINIÁS**, easily the most picturesque fishing port on Lésvos. Myrivilis used it as the setting for his best-known work, *The Mermaid Madonna*, and the tiny rock-top **chapel** at the end of the jetty will be instantly recognizable to anyone who has read the book. The only local **beach** is the one of Kayiá 1.5km east, which has a pebble-on-sand base.

### Klió and Tsónia

Some 5km east from upper Sykaminiá is **KLIÓ**, whose single main street leads down to a platía with a plane tree, fountain and more views across to Turkey. The village is set attractively on a slope, down which a wide, paved road descends 6km to **Tsónia** beach, 600m of beautiful pink volcanic sand.

**PÉTRA**

**Hotel Michaelia** ☎ 22530 41730. Good-value hotel behind the south waterfront, with smart if slightly cramped rooms, most with balconies facing the sunset. Decent buffet breakfast included. May–Sept. **€35**

**Mermaid** ☎ 22530 41275. At the far north end of the seafront, this all-round taverna provides heaps of inexpensive small and more upscale fish, as well as some meat dishes and a variety of starters. April to mid-Oct daily 9am–1am.

**Women's Agricultural Tourism Cooperative** ☎ 22530 41238, ⓦ lesvos-travel.com/womens-cooperative. The downstairs office arranges rooms or studios (from €30) in scattered premises, while the rooftop restaurant serves up tasty grills and *mayireftá*. Proceeds go to the organization's efforts. Daily 10am–midnight.

**ÁNAXOS**

**Klimataria** ☎ 22530 41864. Tucked under the cliff at the beach's northern end, the best local restaurant has a large shady courtyard, where you can enjoy healthy portions of fresh fish, meat and salads. Mid-May to Sept daily 11am–midnight.

**LOUTRÁ EFTALOÚ**

**Iy Eftalou** ☎ 22530 71649. With a shady courtyard, large meat grills, fish and *mayireftá*, if sometimes glum service, this is the nearest location to the spa to grab a snack or fuller meal. April–Oct daily 9am–midnight.

**Khrysi Akti** ☎ 22530 71879. Typical taverna plus rooms combo in the converted old spa-patrons' inn, built around a church. The en-suite rooms are quite small, while the menu offers a mixture of grills and the odd oven-baked dish. May–Sept. **€30**

**SKÁLA SYKAMINIÁS**

**Anemoessa** ☎ 22530 55360. By the chapel, this taverna has the local edge quality-wise, with imaginative starters like stuffed squash blossoms complementing fresh seafood, much of which costs under €10. April–Oct daily, some winter weekends (Fri–Sun) noon–1am.

★ **Gorgona** ☎ 22530 55301, ⓦ gorgonahotel.gr. Small, centrally located hotel run by a friendly old couple, whose simple but clean rooms have wrap-around balconies. There's a shaded terrace for the complimentary breakfast and meals are available too. May–Sept. **€35**

**Iy Mouria tou Myrivili** ☎ 22530 55319. Picturesque taverna named after the mulberry tree in which Myrivilis used to sleep on hot summer nights. You can sit under said tree and tuck into a standard range of *mezédhes*, salads, meat and fish dishes. May–Oct daily 11am–1am.

**KLIÓ AND TSÓNIA**

**Maria** Tsónia ☎ 22530 93662. No sign, oddly enough, but the first restaurant as you reach the southern end of the beach from the access road cannot be accused of serving anonymous food, as the home-style *mayireftá* are quite delicious. May–Sept daily 10am–midnight.

# Áyios Efstrátios

**Áyios Efstrátios (Aï Strátis)** is one of the quietest and loneliest islands in the Aegean, with a registered population of under 400, only half of whom live here all year round. It was only permanently settled during the sixteenth century, and land is still largely owned by three monasteries on Mount Áthos. Historically, the only outsiders to visit were those compelled to do so – political prisoners were exiled here both during the 1930s and the civil war years.

## Áyios Efstrátios village

**ÁYIOS EFSTRÁTIOS** village – the island's only habitation – is among the ugliest in Greece. Devastation caused by an earthquake on February 20, 1968, which killed 22 and injured hundreds, was compounded by the reconstruction plan: the contract went to a junta-linked company, who prevented survivors from returning to their old homes and used army bulldozers to raze even those structures – comprising one of the more beautiful ports in these islands – that could have been repaired. From the hillside, some two dozen surviving houses of the old village overlook grim rows of prefabs, a sad monument to the corruption of the junta years.

Architecture apart, Áyios Efstrátios still functions as a traditional fishing and farming community, with the prefabs set at the mouth of a wooded stream valley draining to the sandy harbour beach. There are scant tourist amenities.

**9**

## Around the island

Beyond the village – there are few vehicles and no paved roads – the hilly **landscape**, dotted with a surprising number of oak trees, is deserted apart from rabbits, sheep and the occasional shepherd. **Alonítsi**, on the north coast – ninety minutes' walk from the port following a track due east and over a low ridge – is the island's best **beach**, a 1.5km stretch of sand with rolling breakers and views across to Límnos. South of the harbour lies a series of grey-sand beaches, most with wells and drinkable water, accessible by roundabout tracks. **Áyios Dhimítrios**, an hour-plus distant, and **Lidharió**, ninety minutes away at the end of a wooded valley, are the most popular.

### ARRIVAL AND DEPARTURE
ÁYIOS EFSTRÁTIOS

**By ferry** There are ferry connections with Lávrio (4 weekly; 8hr 30min), Límnos (4 weekly; 1hr 30min) and Kavála (4 weekly; 5hr). You can also visit from Límnos on one of the overpriced day-trips (2–3 weekly; €35 return).

### ACCOMMODATION AND EATING

**Veranda** ✆ 69470 50153. The best of the island's handful of tavernas, near the port, has super-fresh though rather pricey fish and seafood, plus a limited range of salads and starters. June–Sept daily noon–midnight.

**Xenonas Aï-Stratis** ✆ 22540 93329. The only bona fide pension on the island (otherwise just look for rooms signs) offers cosy and comfortable lodgings on the north side of the village. May–Sept. **€45**

# Límnos

Bucolic **Límnos** is a sizeable agricultural and military island that has become positively trendy of late: there are upscale souvenir shops, old village houses restored by mainlanders as seasonal retreats and music bars during summer at nearly every beach. For all that, the island's remoteness and peculiar ferry schedules protected it until the mid-1990s from most aspects of the holiday trade, and conventional tourism was late in coming because hoteliers lived primarily off the visiting relatives of the numerous soldiers stationed here. Most summer visitors are still Greek, particularly from Thessaloníki, though some Brits and other Europeans now arrive on charter flights.

The island has often been the focus of **disputes** between the Greek and Turkish governments, with frequent posturing over invaded airspace, although the détente of recent years has seen such incidences cease. As a result, Límnos's **garrison** of 25,000 soldiers – at the nadir of Greco-Turkish relations during the 1970s and 1980s – is now down to about 6000, and set to fall further if, as expected, the remaining bases close.

The **bays** of **Bourniá** and **Moúdhros**, the latter one of the largest natural harbours in the Aegean, divide Límnos almost in two. The west of the island is dramatically hilly, with abundant basalt put to good use as street cobbles and house masonry. The east is low-lying and speckled with seasonal salt marshes where it's not occupied by cattle, combine harvesters and vast corn fields. There are numerous sandy **beaches** around the coast – mostly gently shelving – and it's easy to find a stretch to yourself.

Like most volcanic islands, Límnos produces excellent **wine** – good dry white, rosé and retsina – plus ouzo. The Limnians proudly tout an abundance of **natural food products**, including thyme honey and sheep's cheese, and indeed the population is almost self-sufficient in foodstuffs.

### ARRIVAL AND DEPARTURE
LÍMNOS

**By plane** The airport lies 18km east of Mýrina, almost at the geographic centre of the island; a few taxis always linger outside, there being no shuttle bus into town. Frequencies below are for June–Oct.
Destinations Athens (1–3 daily; 50min); Híos (2 weekly; 1hr 30min); Ikaría (6 weekly; 1hr 40min); Lésvos (5 weekly; 30min); Rhodes (5 weekly; 2hr–3hr 30min); Sámos (2 weekly; 1hr 45min–2hr 30min); Thessaloníki (6 weekly; 40min).
**By ferry** Límnos lies on two ferry routes, the one from Lávrio to Kavála and from the northern mainland ports down through the eastern Aegean.
Destinations Áyios Efstrátios (4 weekly; 1hr 30min); Híos

LÍMNOS

*Lávrio, Áyios Efstrátios, Lésvos & Híos*

(3 weekly; 10hr); Ikaría (1 weekly; 16hr 30min); Kavála (6 weekly; 4hr–4hr 30min); Lávrio (4 weekly; 9hr 30min); Lésvos (3 weekly; 6hr 30min); Sámos (3 weekly; 14–15hr); Thessaloníki (1 weekly; 8hr 30min).

### GETTING AROUND

**By bus** Buses are fairly infrequent on Límnos, with only afternoon departures from Mýrina to many of the more distant villages and only 1–2 daily to those nearer the capital.

**By motorbike** A vehicle is required for touring; a motorbike is quite sufficient for the more touristed western third of the island, which is a blessing as cars are expensive.

## Mýrina

**MÝRINA** (aka Kástro), the port-capital on the west coast, has the ethos of a provincial market town rather than of a resort. With about five thousand inhabitants, it's pleasantly low-key, if not especially picturesque, apart from a core neighbourhood of old stone houses dating from the Ottoman era, and the ornate Neoclassical mansions backing **Romeïkós Yialós**, the town's beach-lined esplanade. Shops and amenities are mostly found along Kydhá and its continuation Karatzá – which meanders north from the harbour to Romeïkós Yialós – or Garoufalídhi, its perpendicular offshoot, roughly halfway along.

### Mýrina castle

Unrestricted access

Mýrina's main attraction is its Byzantine **castle**, perched on a craggy headland between the ferry dock and Romeïkós Yialós. Ruinous despite later Genoese and Ottoman additions, the fortress is flatteringly lit at night and warrants a climb towards sunset for views over the town, the entire west coast and – in clear conditions – Mount Áthos, 35 nautical miles west. Skittish miniature deer, imported from Rhodes and fed by the municipality, patrol the castle grounds to the amusement of visitors.

**9**

## The Dápia

Behind the hospital in a small park is a diminutive, signposted fort, the **Dápia**, built by the Russian Orloff brothers during their abortive 1770 invasion. The fort failed spectacularly in its avowed purpose to besiege and bombard the main castle, as did the entire rebellion, and Ottoman reprisals on the island were severe.

## Archeological museum

Tues–Sun 8.30am–3pm • €2 • ☎ 22540 22900

The **archeological museum** occupies the former Ottoman governor's mansion right behind Romeïkós Yialós, not far from the site of Bronze Age **Mýrina**. Finds from all of the island's major sites are assiduously labelled in Greek, Italian and English, and the entire premises is exemplary in terms of presentation. The star upper-storey exhibits are votive lamps in the shape of sirens, found in an Archaic sanctuary at Hephaestia (Ifestía), much imitated in modern local jewellery. There are also numerous representations of the goddess Cybele/Artemis, who was revered across the island; her shrines were typically situated near a fauna-rich river mouth – on Límnos at Avlónas, now inside the grounds of the *Porto Myrina* resort. An entire room is devoted to metalwork, featuring impressive gold jewellery and bronze objects, both practical (cheese graters, door-knockers) and whimsical-naturalistic (a snail, a vulture).

## Town beaches

As town beaches go, **Romeïkós Yialós** and **Néa Mádhitos** (ex-Toúrkikos Yialós), its counterpart to the southeast of the harbour, are not bad. **Rihá Nerá**, the next bay north of Romeïkós Yialós, is even better – shallow as the name suggests and well attended by families, with watersports on offer.

### ARRIVAL AND INFORMATION

**By bus** The bus station is on Platía Eleftheríou Venizélou, at the north end of Kydhá.

**By ferry** The new jetty is on the far side of the bay. The most efficient agency for tickets is Maria Kantara Travel on Platía Eleftheríou Venizélou (☎ 22540 29570).

**By car and motorbike** Cars and motorbikes can be rented from central Limnos Car Rental (☎ 22540 23777) or Myrina Rent a Car (☎ 22540 24476), while Rent a Moto

(☎ 22540 25419), on the north side of town at Leofóros Dhimokratías 89, has good rates on two-wheelers.

**Online information** There is no tourist office but a useful site is ⓦ limnosisland.gr.

**Services** Most banks with ATMs cluster around a platía about halfway along Kydhá; the post office is around the corner on Garoufalídhi. Several cafés on the old harbour and Kydhá have wi-fi.

### ACCOMMODATION

Despite Límnos's steady gentrification, some room owners still meet arriving ferries. Otherwise the most fruitful area to search is in the northern beach suburb of Rihá Nerá.

**Apollo Pavilion** Frýnis ☎ 22540 23712, ⓦ apollopavilion.gr. In a peaceful cul-de-sac about halfway along Garoufalídhou, this mock classical hotel offers three-bed a/c studios with TV and mini-kitchen. Most have balconies, with castle or mountain views. **€60**

**Arhondiko** Cnr of Sakhtoúri and Filellínon, Romeïkós Yialós ☎ 22540 29800, ⓦ arxontikohotel.gr. Límnos's first hotel, this 1851-built mansion has three floors of small-to-medium-sized wood-trimmed rooms with all mod cons but no balconies. There's a pleasant ground-floor

bar/breakfast lounge. **€50**

**Hotel Lemnos** Limáni Mýrinas ☎ 22540 22153, ⓔ lemnos-hotel@yahoo.gr. Standard 1960s-style hotel with average-sized, simply decorated rooms, but the balconies overlooking the fishing harbour and price make it good value. **€35**

**Ifestos** Ethnikís Andístasis 17, Andhróni ☎ 22540 24960. Quiet, professionally run two-star hotel with pleasant common areas. Slightly small rooms have a/c, fridges, balconies and a mix of sea or hill views. Breakfast included. **€65**

### EATING, DRINKING AND NIGHTLIFE

**Karagiozis** Romeïkós Yialós 32. The most established watering hole on the island transforms from laidback café

by day to buzzing bar by night, which sometimes holds theme parties or hosts live bands. Daily 11am–late.

**Kosmos** Romeïkós Yialós ☎ 22540 22050. The most reasonable of the establishments on this popular but mostly overpriced strip of seafront offers fresh fish, a range of *mezédhes* and glorious sunsets across Mt Áthos. April–Oct daily noon–1am.

★ 0 **Platanos** Kydhá ☎ 22540 22070. Excellent traditional *mayireftá* such as *papoutsáki* and highly quaffable aromatic Limniot wine draw big crowds to the atmospheric little square beneath two plane trees. Daily 11am–6pm, until midnight June–Sept.

## Western Límnos

Nearly all the tourist amenities are concentrated in the western third of the island, mostly in and around the coastal stretch between Mýrina and the vast Moúdhros Bay. This area includes many of the best **beaches** and most picturesque inland **villages**.

### Coast north of Mýrina

Beyond Mýrina's respectable town beaches, the closest good sand lies 3km north at **Avlónas**, unspoilt except for the local power plant a short way inland. Just beyond, the road splits: the right-hand turning wends its way through **Káspakas**, its north-facing houses in neat tiers and a potable spring on its platía, before plunging down to **Áyios Ioánnis**, also reached directly by the left-hand bypass from the capital. The furthest of its three **beaches** is the most pleasant, a curved cove punctuated by a tiny fishing harbour and offshore islet named Vampire Island.

### Thérma and around

Daily 10am–2pm & 5–9pm • ⓦ thermaspa.gr

Six kilometres northeast of Mýrina, the old Ottoman baths at **Thérma**, complete with calligraphic plaques, have been restored as an eye-wateringly expensive contemporary health spa, with all conceivable treatments available – or you can just have a hydromassage soak (€12). Unusually for a hot spring, the water is non-sulphurous and is the tastiest on the island, so there is always a knot of cars parked nearby under the trees while their owners fill jerry cans with warm water from a **public fountain**, which has a bilingual Greek/Ottoman Turkish inscription.

Just south of Thérma is the iconic poster image of Límnos: the **chapel of Panayía Kakaviótissa**, tucked into a volcanic cave on the flank of Mt Kákavos (360m).

### Sardhés

Some 7km north of Thérma, **SARDHÉS** is the highest village on the island, with wonderfully broody sunsets and a celebrated central taverna. The handsome local houses are typical of mountain villages on Límnos in having an external staircase up to the first floor, as the ground floor was used for animals.

### Gomáti

Beyond Sardhés and 5km below Katálakkos lies the spectacular, well-signposted **dune** environment at **Gomáti**, one of the largest such in Greece. There are two zones, reached by separate dirt tracks: one at a river mouth, with a bird-rich marsh, and the other to the northwest, with a beach bar and sunbeds. The latter portion especially is a popular outing.

### Platý

**PLATÝ**, 2km southeast of Mýrina, has had its traditional profile somewhat compromised by modern villa construction, but it does have two nocturnal tavernas. The long sandy **beach**, 700m below, is popular, with non-motorized **watersports** available at the south end through Babis, below the *Lemnos Village* complex.

### Thános and its beaches

**THÁNOS** has more architectural character than smaller Platý, 2km southeast. **Paralía Thánous**, 1.5km below, is among the most scenic of southwestern beaches, flanked by volcanic crags and looking out to Áyios Efstrátios island. Beyond Thános, the road curls over to the enormous beach at **Evgátis** (**Áyios Pávlos**), reckoned the island's best, with more igneous pinnacles for definition and Áyios Efstrátios on the horizon.

## Kondiás and around

Eleven kilometres east of Mýrina, **KONDIÁS** is the island's third-largest settlement, cradled between hills tufted with Límnos's biggest pine forest. Stone-built, often elaborate houses combine with the setting to make Kondiás an attractive inland village, a fact not lost on the Greeks and foreigners restoring those houses with varying degrees of taste. Cultural interest is lent by the central **Balkan Art Gallery** (daily except Fri 10am–2pm & 7.30–9.30pm; €2), featuring works by prominent painters from across the Balkans – especially Bulgarian Svetlin Russev. **Tsimándhria**, 2.5km further east, has better dining options.

### ACCOMMODATION, EATING AND DRINKING · WESTERN LÍMNOS

#### COAST NORTH OF MÝRINA

**Aï Yiannis** Áyios Ioánnis ☎ 22540 61669. Featuring seating in the shade of piled-up volcanic boulders at the end of the first beach, this modest *psarotavérna* has fresh fish at very reasonable prices. June–Aug daily 11am–midnight.

**Aliotida Apartments** Áyios Ioánnis ☎ 22540 24406, ⓦ aliotida-apartments.gr. Bright, well-furnished studios with kitchenettes on nicely landscaped grounds up behind the third beach. May–Sept. **€40**

#### SARDHÉS

⭐ **Man-Tella** ☎ 22540 61349. Portions of rural delights such as rabbit *stifádho* and village rooster are huge, the local barrelled wine is superb and the location in the vine-trellised courtyard is atmospheric. Daily noon–1am.

#### PLATÝ

⭐ **O Sozos** ☎ 22540 25085. Just off the main platía, this local favourite serves up huge portions of succulent *kondosoúvli* and *kokorétsi*, salads and a few *mayireftá* like *dolmádhes*, washed down by *tsípouro* and local barrelled wine. Daily noon–late.

**Studios Magda** ☎ 22540 25370. Set about 100m back from the sea, this block of modern studios is well designed, with moderate-sized, comfortable rooms and friendly management. May–Sept. **€40**

⭐ **Villa Afroditi** ☎ 22540 23141, ⓦ afroditi-villa.gr.

With its spectacular topiary, welcoming owners, pleasant pool bar and mixture of spotless doubles and studios spread over two wings, this is one of the best resorts on Límnos. Free port pick-up and buffet breakfast included. Mid-May to early Oct. **€65**

#### THÁNOS AND ITS BEACHES

**Evgatis Hotel** Evgátis ☎ 22540 51700. Behind the main road some way back from the beach, this functional hotel has decent rooms, a pool and a full-service taverna serving home-cooked food. May–Oct. **€40**

**Petradi Studios** Paralía Thánous ☎ 22540 29905, ⓦ petradistudios.gr. Modern but tastefully designed two-storey building, warm ochre in colour, with spacious and comfortable rooms. There's a pleasant, relaxed beach bar on the premises. May–Sept. **€30**

**Yiannakaros** Paralía Thánous ☎ 22540 22787. Reliable taverna that covers all the bases, with simple fish and some meat dishes and a fair range of starters and salads. May to late Sept daily noon–midnight.

#### KONDIÁS AND AROUND

**O Hristos** Tsimándhria ☎ 22540 51278. Old-favourite taverna with a new name on the central square that dishes up cheap, salubrious grills and a few seafood dishes, plus great dips, salads and wine. Daily 10am–midnight.

# Eastern Límnos

The shores of **Moúdhros Bay**, glimpsed south of the trans-island road, are muddy and best avoided by serious bathers. The bay itself enjoyed strategic importance during World War I, culminating in Allied acceptance of the Ottoman surrender aboard the anchored British warship HMS *Agamemnon* on October 30, 1918. The huge chunk of Límnos east of the bay is little visited but offers some deserted **beaches** and interesting reminders of the island's recent and more distant past.

## Moúdhros

**MOÚDHROS**, the second-largest town on Límnos, is rather a dreary place, with only the wonderfully kitsch, two-belfried **Evangelismós church** to recommend it. The closest

**THE WAR CEMETERIES**

About 800m along the Roussopoúli road from Moúdhros is an unlocked **Allied military cemetery** maintained by the Commonwealth War Graves Commission, its neat lawns and rows of white headstones incongruous in such parched surroundings. During 1915, Moúdhros Bay was the principal staging area for the disastrous Gallipoli campaign. Of approximately 36,000 Allied dead, 887 are buried here – mainly battle casualties, who died after having been evacuated to the base hospital at Moúdhros. Though the deceased are mostly British, there is also a French cenotaph, and – speaking volumes about imperial sociology – a mass "Musalman" grave for Egyptian and Indian troops in one corner, with a Koranic inscription.

There are more graves at another immaculately maintained cemetery behind the hilltop church in **Portianoú**, a little over 1km from the west side of Moúdhros Bay. Among the 348 buried here are two Canadian nurses, three Egyptian labourers and three Maori soldiers. East of Portianoú and Paleó Pedhinó, signposted on a headland, lies the last and strangest of Límnos's military cemeteries: about forty 1920–21 graves of **Kuban Cossacks**, White Army refugees from the Russian civil war.

decent beaches are at **Havoúli**, 4km south by dirt track, and **Fanaráki**, 4km west, but both have muddy sand and don't really face the open sea. Until recently Moúdhros was quite literally a God-forsaken place, owing to an incident late in Ottoman rule. Certain locals killed some Muslims and threw them down a well on property belonging to the Athonite monastery of Koutloumousioú; the Ottoman authorities, holding the monks responsible, slaughtered any Koutloumousiot brethren they found on the island and set the local monastery alight. Two monks managed to escape to Áthos, where every August 23 a curse was chanted, condemning Moúdhros's inhabitants to "never sleep again"; the Athonite brothers finally relented in July 2001.

## Polyochni (Polyókhni) and around

Tues–Sun 8.30am–3pm • Free

Traces of the most advanced Neolithic Aegean civilization have been unearthed at **Polyochni (Polyókhni)**, 10km east of Moúdhros, on a bluff overlooking a long, narrow beach. Since 1930, Italian excavations have uncovered five layers of settlement, the oldest from late in the fourth millennium BC, predating Troy on the Turkish coast opposite. The town met a sudden, violent end from war or earthquake in about 2100 BC. The **ruins** are well labelled but mostly of specialist interest, though a small, well-presented **museum** behind the entrance helps bring the place to life.

The only really decent beach in the area is **Ayía Triádha**, accessed off the Polyókhni road, with blonde sand heaped in dunes.

## Kótsinas

Some 10km north of Moúdhros, reached via Repanídhi, the hard-packed beach at **KÓTSINAS** is set in the proteted western limb of Bourniá Bay. The nearby anchorage offers two busy, seafood-strong tavernas. On a knoll overlooking the jetty stands a corroded, sword-brandishing statue of **Maroula**, a Genoese-era heroine who briefly delayed the Ottoman conquest, and a large church of **Zoödhóhou Piyís** (the Life-Giving Spring), with intriguing kitsch icons, a vaulted wooden ceiling and antique floor tiles. Out front, 63 steps lead down through an illuminated tunnel in the rock to the potable (if slightly mineral) spring in question, oozing into a cool, vaulted chamber.

## Kerós beach

**Kalliópi**, 8km northeast of Moúdhros via attractive Kondopoúli, is a pleasant little village, giving direct access to **Kéros beach**, a 1.5km stretch of sand with dunes and a small pine grove, plus shallow water. It remains popular despite being exposed and often dirty, and attracts plenty of windsurfers and foreigners with camper vans.

**9**

## Hephaesia and Kabirion

Both sites Tues–Sun 8.30am–3pm • Free

Aside from Polyochni (Polyókhni), Hephaestia and Kabirion are Límnos's other significant **ancient sites**, only reachable with your own transport. **Hephaestia** (present-day Ifestía), 4.5km from Kondopoúli by rough, signposted track, offers an admirably reconstructed theatre overlooking its former harbour. The name comes from the god Hephaestos, rescued and revered by the ancient Limnians after he crash-landed on the island, hurled from Mt Olympos by Hera.

**Kabirion**, also signposted as "Kabeiroi" (modern Kavírion), on the opposite shore of Tigáni Bay and accessed by a paved road, is more evocative. The **ruins** are of a sanctuary connected with the cult of the Samothracian Kabiroi (see box, p.658), though the site here is probably older. Little survives other than eleven column stumps staking out a *stoa*, behind the *telestirio* or shrine where the cult mysteries took place. A nearby **sea grotto** has been identified as the Homeric Spiliá toú Filoktíti, where Trojan war hero Philoktetes was abandoned by his comrades-in-arms until his stinking, gangrenous leg had healed by application of *límnia yí*, a poultice of volcanic mud still prized on the island. Landward access to the cave is via steps leading down from the caretaker's shelter, though final access (from a little passage on the right as you face the sea) involves some wading.

### ACCOMMODATION AND EATING

EASTERN LÍMNOS

**Keros** Kalliópi ☎ 22540 41059. At the start of the road down to Kéros beach, this is one of the few accommodation options in the far east of Límnos. Pleasant rooms with balconies but very remote. June to mid-Sept. €30

**To Mourayio** Kótsinas ☎ 22540 41065. Easily the better, if slightly pricier, of the two tavernas here, worth the extra for the higher quality of both food and service. Good for fish, meat and veg dishes. May–Sept daily noon–midnight.

# Samothráki

**SAMOTHRÁKI** (Samothrace) has one of the most dramatic profiles of all the Greek islands, second only to Thíra (Santorini): its dark mass of granite rises abruptly from the sea, culminating in the 1611m **Mount Fengári**. Seafarers have always been guided by its imposing outline, clearly visible from the mainland, and its summit provided a vantage point for Poseidon to watch over the siege of Troy. Landing is subject to the notoriously unpredictable weather, but that did not deter pilgrims who, for hundreds of years in antiquity, journeyed to the island to visit the **Sanctuary of the Great Gods** and were initiated into its mysteries. The sanctuary remains the main archeological attraction of the island, which, too remote for most tourists, combines earthy simplicity with natural grandeur. The tourist season is relatively short – essentially (late) July and August – but you will find some facilities open as early as Easter and one or two all year round.

## Kamariótissa

Ferries dock at the dull village of **KAMARIÓTISSA**. While you're unlikely to want to spend much time here, it does make a convenient base, as some of Samothráki's best hotels lie along or just behind the tree-lined seafront and various rooms for rent can be found in the maze of streets behind; owners often meet incoming vessels.

## Hóra

**HÓRA**, also known as **Samothráki**, is the island's capital. Far larger than the portion visible from out at sea would suggest, it's an attractive town of Thracian-style stone houses, some whitewashed, clustered around a hollow in the western flanks of Mount Fengári. It is dominated by the Genoese **Gateluzzi fort**, of which little survives other than the gateway. Half an hour or so can be whiled away at the charming **folklore museum** (late May to late Sept daily 9am–2pm & 6–10pm; €1), which contains a motley collection of clothing, domestic items and miscellany.

## The Sanctuary of the Great Gods

Daily 8.30am–3pm; museum Tues–Sun only • €3 combined ticket • ☎ 22510 41474

Hidden in a stony but thickly wooded ravine between the tiny hamlet of **PALEÓPOLI** – 6km northeast from Kamariótissa, and 3km directly north from Hóra – and the plunging northwestern ridge of Mount Fengári, lie the remains of the **Sanctuary of the Great Gods**. From the late Bronze Age (around the eighth century BC) until the early Byzantine era (fifth century AD), the mysteries and sacrifices of the cult of the Great Gods (see box, p.658) were performed on Samothráki, in ancient Thracian, until the second century BC. Little is known of this dialect except that it was a very old Indo-European tongue, related to and eventually replaced by ancient Greek. The spiritual focus of the northern Aegean, the importance of the island's rituals was second only to the Mysteries of Eleusis in all the ancient world. The well-labelled site strongly evokes its proud past while commanding views of the mountains and the sea.

### Archeological museum

Closed Mon

For an explanatory introduction, it is best first to visit the **archeological museum**, whose exhibits span all eras of habitation, from the Archaic to the Byzantine. Highlights include a frieze of dancing girls from the propylaion of the Temenos, entablatures from different buildings, and Roman votive offerings such as coloured glass vials from the necropolis of the ancient town east of the sanctuary. You can also see a reproduction of the exquisitely sculpted marble statue, the *Winged Victory of Samothrace*, which once stood breasting the wind at the prow of a marble ship in the Nymphaeum. Discovered in 1863 by a French diplomat to the Sublime Porte, it was carried off to the Louvre, where it remains a major draw.

## THE SAMOTHRACIAN MYSTERIES

The **religion of the Great Gods** revolved around a hierarchy of ancient Thracian fertility figures: the Great Mother Axieros; a subordinate male deity known as Kadmilos; and the potent and ominous twin demons the Kabiroi, originally the local heroes Dardanos and Aeton. When the Aeolian colonists arrived (traditionally c.700 BC) they simply merged the resident deities with their own – the Great Mother became Cybele, while her consort Hermes and the Kabiroi were fused interchangeably with the *Dioskouroi* Castor and Pollux, patrons of seafarers. Around the nucleus of a sacred precinct the newcomers made the beginnings of what is now the sanctuary.

Despite their long observance, the mysteries of the cult were never explicitly recorded, since ancient writers feared incurring the wrath of the Kabiroi (who could reputedly brew up sudden, deadly storms), but it has been established that two levels of initiation were involved. Both ceremonies, in direct opposition to the elitism of Eleusis, were open to all, including women and slaves. The lower level of initiation, or *myesis*, may, as is speculated at Eleusis, have involved a ritual simulation of the life, death and rebirth cycle; in any case, it's known that it ended with joyous feasting, and it can be conjectured, since so many clay torches have been found, that it took place at night. The higher level of initiation, or *epopteia*, carried the unusual requirement of a moral standard – the connection of theology with morality, so strong in the later Judeo-Christian tradition, was rarely made by the early Greeks. This second level involved a full confession followed by absolution and baptism in bull's blood.

### The Anaktoron and Arsinoeion

The **Anaktoron**, or hall of initiation for the first level of the mysteries, dates in its present form from Roman times. Its inner sanctum was marked by a warning stele, now in the museum, and at the southeast corner you can make out the **Priestly Quarters**, an antechamber where candidates for initiation donned white gowns. Next to it is the **Arsinoeion**, the largest circular ancient building known in Greece, used for libations and sacrifices. Within its rotunda are the fourth-century BC walls of a double precinct where a rock altar, the earliest preserved ruin on the site, has been uncovered.

### The Temenos and Hieron

A little further south, on the same side of the path, you come to the **Temenos**, a rectangular area open to the sky where the feasting probably took place, and, edging its rear corner, the conspicuous **Hieron**, the site's most immediately impressive structure. Five columns and an architrave of the facade of this large Doric edifice, which hosted the higher level of initiation, have been re-erected; dating in part from the fourth century BC, it was heavily restored in Roman times. The stone steps have been replaced by modern blocks, but Roman benches for spectators remain *in situ*, along with the sacred stones where confession was heard.

### The Nymphaeum (Fountain) of Nike and around

To the west of the path you can just discern the outline of the **theatre**, while just above it, tucked under the ridge, is the **Nymphaeum (Fountain) of Nike**, over which the *Winged Victory* used to preside. West of the theatre, occupying a high terrace, are remains of the main **stoa**; immediately north of this is an elaborate medieval fortification made entirely of antique material.

## Loutrá and the far east

With its running streams, giant plane trees and namesake hot springs, **LOUTRÁ** (aka **Thermá**), 6km east of Paleópoli, is a pleasant enough place to stay, although in late July and August it gets packed, mainly with an incongruous mixture of foreign hippies and elderly Greeks, here to take the sulphurous waters. Far more appealing than the grim **baths** themselves (June–Oct daily 8am–6pm; €5), the low waterfalls and rock pools of **Gría Váthra** are signposted 1.5km up the paved side road leading east from the main

## CLIMBING THE MOON

Loutrá is the prime base for the tough six-hour climb up the 1611m **Mount Fengári** (known to the ancients as **Sáos**, a name found on some maps to this day), the highest peak in the Aegean islands; the path starts at the top of the village, beside a concrete water tank and a huge plane tree. Tell your accommodation proprietors that you're going. Fengári is Greek for "moon" and, according to legend, if you reach the top on the night of a full moon your wish will come true – most of those foolhardy enough to attempt this will just hope to get back down safely.

Thermá access drive. Loutrá is ghostly quiet for most of the year and its miniature harbour, built as an alternative to Kamariótissa, is never used at all.

**Beaches** on Samothráki's north shore are mostly clean but uniformly pebbly and exposed. Some 15km from Loutrá along a fine corniche road is **Kípos beach**, a long strand facing the Turkish island of Gökçeada (Ímvros to the Greeks) and backed by open pasture and picturesque crags. The water is clean and there's a rock overhang for shelter at one end, a spring, shower and seasonal *kantína* for refreshments.

## The south coast

The warmer south flank of the island, its fertile farmland dotted with olive groves, boasts fine views out to sea – as far as Gökçeada on a clear day. On the way south, beyond sleepy **Lákkoma**, the attractive hill village of **Profítis Ilías** is worth the brief detour.

From Lákkoma itself, it's less than 2km down to the eponymous **beach**. A further 6km east lies **Pahiá Ámmos**, a long, clean beach. The nearest (meagre) supplies are in Lákkoma but this doesn't deter big summer crowds who also arrive by excursion *kaïkia*. These continue east to **Vátos**, a secluded nudist beach, the **Kremastá Nerá** coastal waterfalls and finally round to Kípos beach (see above).

### ARRIVAL AND INFORMATION

SAMOTHRÁKI

**By ferry** The only current connection with Samothráki is the ferry from Alexandhroúpoli (2hr 30min); frequency varies from 2–3 daily in July & Aug to 4–5 weekly in winter.

**By kaïki** In peak season 1–2 daily excursions run from Kamariótissa to the south-coast beaches.

**By bus** There are plenty of buses from Kamariótissa along the north coast to Loutrá (6–7 daily; 20min) and inland to Hóra in season (5–6 daily; 10min), though far fewer in winter.

**By motorbike or car** You can only get to the south and

far east of the island with your own transport. The best places to rent wheels are Niki Tours (☎ 25510 41465, ✉ niki_tours@hotmail.com) and Kyrkos car rental (☎ 25510 69728, ✉ akis1kirkos@gmail.com), both on the seafront at Kamariótissa; best book in advance in high season, as supply is short. The only fuelling station on the entire island is 1km above the port, en route to Hóra.

**Services** There is no official tourist office on Samothráki. Kamariótissa has two banks with ATMs and the island's only post office.

### ACCOMMODATION, EATING AND DRINKING

#### KAMARIÓTISSA

**Aeolos** ☎ 25510 41595, ⊛ hotelaiolos.gr. Samothráki's most comfortable accommodation has a large pool and quiet, spacious rooms. There are good half-board deals in the low season. June–Sept. **€50**

**Iy Klimataria** ☎ 25510 41535. Towards the northeast end of the seafront, with a huge summer terrace, this enduring taverna serves dishes like fried aubergines, oven-baked goat and *soutsoukákia*, plus palatable barrelled wine. June–Sept daily noon–2am.

**Kyrkos Apartments** ☎ 25510 41620, ✉ akis1kirkos @gmail.com. Spacious modern studios with well-equipped kitchens, in a rural setting 500m from the port,

just off the road to Hóra. April–Oct. **€30**

**To Mouragio** ☎ 694 58 94 107. New restaurant at the southwestern end of the seafront, where you can get pizza, sandwiches and *souvláki*, as well as a range of typical taverna items. Daily 11am–1am.

#### HÓRA

★ **1900** ☎ 25510 41222. Boasting a lovely vine-shaded terrace with stunning views of the Kástro and the valley below, this friendly taverna serves stuffed goat (€8) and spicy aubergines. Mid-May to mid-Sept daily noon–1am.

**9**

### THE SANCTUARY OF THE GREAT GODS

**Samothraki Village** Paleópoli ☎25510 42300, ⓦsamothrakivillage.gr. Smart new resort, handily placed for the Sanctuary of the Great Gods, with manicured grounds, neatly furnished rooms, two pools and a bar-restaurant. **€60**

### LOUTRÁ AND THE FAR EAST

**Camping Platia** ☎25510 98244. Around 1.5km east of the village, this beachside municipal campsite is very basic, with toilets only. May–Sept. Adult plus tent **€5.50**

**Camping Voradhes** ☎25510 98258. Some 3km east of the village, the island's prime municipal campsite has hot-water showers, electricity, a minimarket, restaurant and bar. July & Aug. Adult plus tent **€8**

**O Paradhisos** ☎697 57 75 997. This place has the advantage of the village's best location, up under the plane trees. The traditional cuisine and barrelled wine also hit the spot. Mid-May to mid-Sept daily noon–1am.

**To Fengari** ☎25510 98321. Small set of adequately furnished studios, tucked in a lane east of the centre, which maintains at least a low level of operation all year, including a home-style taverna on site. **€25**

★ **To Perivoli T'Ouranou** ☎25510 98313. "Heaven's Orchard" aptly describes this leafy taverna on the lane to Gría Váthra. Various dips, types of *saganáki* and spaghetti dishes supplement the usual grills and salads. Regular live traditional music. June to mid-Oct daily 11am–2am.

### THE SOUTH COAST

**Delfini** Pahiá Ámmos ☎25510 94235. Classic taverna-cum-rooms enterprise at the west end of the beach. The rooms are fairly basic but habitable enough and the taverna is a friendly hangout with a decent range of staples. May–Sept. **€30**

**Paradisos** Profítis Ilías ☎25510 95267. Atmospheric rustic taverna, with a lovely terrace facing sunsets over Thássos. The house speciality is a selection of meats such as lamb, goat and *kondosoúvli* roast on the spit, accompanied by fiery *tsípouro* or soothing wine. June to mid-Sept daily 10am–2am.

**To Akroyiali** Lákkoma beach ☎25510 95123. Simple but clean rooms with seaview balconies are available above a friendly taverna, which serves fresh fish, some meat and a standard menu of mezédhes and salads. June–Sept. **€35**

# Thássos

Just 12km from the mainland, **Thássos** has long been a popular resort island for northern Greeks, and since the early 1990s has also attracted a cosmopolitan mix of tourists, particularly Germans and Scandinavians on packages, as well as an increasing number of people from eastern Europe. They are all entertained by vast numbers of *bouzoúkia* (music halls) and music tavernas, while nature-lovers can find some areas of outstanding beauty, especially inland. Moreover, the island's traditional industries have managed to survive the onslaught of modernity. The elite of Thássos still make a substantial living from the pure-white **marble** that constitutes two-thirds of the landmass, found only here and quarried at dozens of sites in the hills between Liménas and Panayía. Olives, especially the oil, honey, nuts and fruit (often sold candied) are also important products. The spirit *tsípouro*, rather than wine, is the main local tipple; pear extract, onions or spices like cinnamon and anise are added to home-made batches.

## Brief history

Inhabited since the Stone Age, Thássos was settled by Parians in the seventh century BC, attracted by **gold** deposits between modern Liménas and Kínyra. Buoyed by revenues from these, and from **silver** mines under Thassian control on the mainland opposite, the ancient city-state here became the seat of a medium-sized seafaring empire. Commercial acumen did not spell military invincibility, however; the Persians under Darius swept the Thassian fleets from the seas in 492 BC, and in 462 BC Athens permanently deprived Thássos of its autonomy after a three-year siege. The main port continued to thrive into Roman times, but lapsed into Byzantine and medieval obscurity.

Sadly, the salient fact of more recent history has been a series of devastating, deliberately set **fires** in the 1980s and 1990s. Only the northeastern quadrant of the island, plus the area around Astrís and Alykí, escaped, though the surviving forest is still home to numerous pine martens.

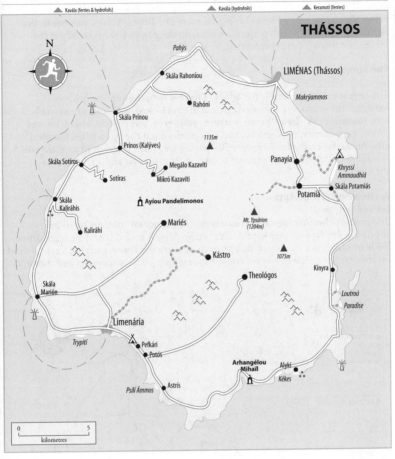

Kavála (ferries & hydrofoils)    Kavála (hydrofoils)    Keramotí (ferries)

**THÁSSOS**

Pahýs

Skála Rahoníou

LIMÉNAS (Thássos)

Rahóni

Makrýammos

Skála Prínou

1135m

Prínos (Kalýves)

Panayía

Skála Sotíros

Megálo Kazavíti

Khryssí
Ammoudhiá

Sotíras

Mikró Kazavíti

Skála Potamiás

Skála
Kaliráhis

Ayíou Pandelímonos

Potamiá

Kaliráhi

Mariés

Mt. Ypsárion
(1204m)

Skála
Marión

Kástro

1075m

Kínyra

Theológos

Loutroú
Paradise

Limenária

Trypití

Pefkári

Potós

Arhangélou
Mihaíl

Alykí

Psilí Ámmos

Astrís

Kékes

0        5
kilometres

N

## ARRIVAL AND GETTING AROUND

**By ferry/hydrofoil** Kavála-based ferries (2–6 daily; 1hr 15min) arrive at Skála Prínou, in the northwest of the island. Ferries to Liménas (8–12 daily; 40min) leave from Keramotí on the mainland opposite. Depending on the economic situation, there may be high-season hydrofoils from Kavála to Liménas.

**By bus** The service is fairly good, with frequent buses to Panayía and Skála Potamiás (7–8 daily; 15–20min), Limenária (7 daily; 45min) via Skála Prínou and Potós,

## THÁSSOS

Theológos (5 daily; 1hr) and Alykí (3 daily; 30min) via Kínyra.

**By car or motorbike** Thássos is small enough to circumnavigate in one full day by rented motorbike or car. Car rental is offered by the major international chains and local Potos Car Rentals (☎25930 23969, ⓦwww .rentacarpotos.gr), with seven branches around the island; try bargaining in the shoulder seasons.

**Water taxi** In peak season there are 2 daily services from Liménas to Khryssí Ammoudhía.

# Liménas

Largely modern **LIMÉNAS** (also signposted as Limín or Thássos) is the island's capital, though not the only port. Although it's plagued with surprisingly clogged traffic, it is partly redeemed by its picturesque fishing harbour and the impressive remains of the **ancient city**. Thanks to its mineral wealth and safe harbour, ancient Thássos prospered from Classical to Roman times. There are substantial remains which appear above and below the streets, plus a fine archeological museum. Thássos hosts a **summer festival** (ⓦthassos-festival.gr), with performances of anything from jazz to comedy at the Hellenistic theatre, funds permitting.

## The agora

Free

The largest excavated area is the **agora**, a little way back from the fishing harbour. The grassy site is fenced but not always locked, and is most enjoyably seen towards dusk. Two Roman *stoas* are prominent, but you can also make out shops, monuments, passageways and sanctuaries from the remodelled Classical city. At the far end, a fifth-century BC passageway leads through to an elaborate sanctuary of Artemis, a substantial stretch of Roman road and a few seats of the *odeion*.

## Archeological museum

Tues–Sun 8.30am–3pm • €2

The renovated **archeological museum**, close to the agora, contains small but absorbing displays on prehistoric finds, archeological methods and ancient games. Pride of place goes to the 4m-tall, seventh-century BC *kouros* carrying a ram, found on the acropolis. The courtyard contains some impressive sarcophagi and statuary.

## Other ancient remains

Free

From a **temple of Dionysos** behind the fishing port, a path curls up to a **Hellenistic theatre**, fabulously positioned above a broad sweep of sea. Sadly, it's only open for performances of the summer festival. From just before the theatre, the trail winds on the right up to the **acropolis**, where a Venetian-Byzantine-Genoese fort arose between the thirteenth and fifteenth centuries, constructed from recycled masonry of an Apollo temple. You can continue, following the remains of a massive circuit of fifth-century walls, to a high terrace supporting the foundations of the **Athena Polyouhos** (Athena Patroness of the City) temple, with Cyclopean walls.

From the temple's southern end, a short path leads to a cavity in the rock outcrop that was a **shrine of Pan**, shown in faint relief playing his pipes. Following the path to the left around the summit brings you to a precipitous rock-hewn stairway with a metal handrail, which provided a discreet escape route to the **Gate of Parmenon**, the only gate in the fortifications to have retained its lintel. From here a track, then a paved lane, descend through the southerly neighbourhoods of the modern town, completing a satisfying one-hour circuit.

## ARRIVAL AND INFORMATION

LIMÉNAS

**By bus** Buses arrive and leave from the KTEL office on the front, opposite the hydrofoil berth.

**By ferry** Ferries from Keramotí dock towards the west end of the seafront at the New Port. Hydrofoils dock much more centrally.

**By taxi** The taxi rank is just in front of the bus stop.

**By bike** Bikes can be rented from Mike's (☎ 25930 71820), opposite the *Acropolis* hotel. Car rental is also available (see p.661).

**Services** There is no official tourist office. Thassos Tours (☎ 25930 22546, ⊛ thassostours.gr) provide various services. Several banks have ATMs.

## ACCOMMODATION

**Acropolis** ☎ 25930 22488, ⊛ acropolis-hotel.com. Occupying a fine traditional house with flagstone floors, comfortable rooms decorated in traditional style and a rear garden-bar but subject to traffic noise. **€40**

**Alkyon** ☎ 25930 22148. Certainly the most pleasant harbour hotel with cosy rooms; voluble management make it a home away from home for independent British travellers. Breakfast, with English tea, included. **€40**

**Kipos Studios** ☎ 25930 22469, ⊛ kipos.gr. In a quiet cul-de-sac next to *ly Piyi* taverna, this has cool lower-ground-floor doubles and four-person galleried

apartments, plus a small pool in the garden. Late May–Sept. **€30**

★ **Lena** ☎ 25930 22933, ✉ hotel_lena@hotmail.com. The best-value budget hotel in town, with compact but clean and comfy rooms; run by a welcoming Greek-American family and young British in-law. May–Oct. **€30**

**Possidon** ☎ 25930 22690, ⊛ thassos-possidon.com. Unattractive concrete block on the seafront with a spacious lobby café and nicely refurbished rooms. The only place absolutely guaranteed to be open all year. **€50**

## EATING AND DRINKING

**ly Piyi** ☎ 25930 22941. At the south corner of the main square, this classic *estiatório* has a small terrace and is a dependable favourite for meaty *mayireftá* at only €6–7. April–Oct daily 6.30pm–midnight.

**Simi** ☎ 25930 22517. Reliable taverna behind the ancient port, offering a full menu of fish, meat and mezédhes, along with memorably good wine. Daily

11am–2am.

★ **Syrtaki** ☎ 695 53 04 897. At the far eastern end of the town beach, this just edges *Simi* as the town's most accomplished taverna, dishing up some fine seafood, an imaginative selection of dips and salads, plus the usual grills and fine barrelled wine. Daily 10am–1am.

## NIGHTLIFE

★ **Cheers** ☎ 25930 22689. Behind the ancient port, this friendly Brit-run café-bar is open for cooked breakfasts and all the way through to late-night beers or cocktails. Decent music and football on TV too. Daily 8.30am–late.

**Vertigo** Popular with trendy young Greeks and assorted tourists alike for its rocking ambience, with touches of techno and more dancy vibes as the evening draws on. Plenty of shots downed every night. Daily 10am–4am.

**9**

# The east coast

The busy **east coast** between Liménas and Alykí, occupying roughly a third of the clockwise circuit of the island – the logical way to conduct an island tour if you want to maximize the sun's presence on the beaches – contains many of the more attractive coves and best alternative bases to the capital.

## Panayía

The first place worthy of a halt southeast from Liménas is **PANAYÍA**, the attractive hillside village overlooking Potamiá Bay. It's a large, thriving place where life revolves around the central square with its huge plane trees, fountain and slate-roofed houses. Up above the village towers the island's highest peak, **Mount Ypsárion**.

## Potamiá

**POTAMIÁ**, much lower than Panayía in the river valley, is far less prepossessing – with modern red tiles instead of slates on the roofs – though it has a lively winter carnival. It also offers the modest **Polygnotos Vayis Museum** (May–Oct daily 10am–1pm & 6–8pm; €2), devoted to the locally born sculptor; though Vayis emigrated to America when young, he bequeathed most of his works to the Greek state.

## Skála Potamiás

The road from Potamiá towards the coast is lined with rooms for rent and apartment-type accommodation. A side road some 12km from Liménas takes you down to **SKÁLA POTAMIÁS**, at the southern end of the bay. From the harbourfront a road off to the left brings you to sand dunes extending all the way to the far northern end of the bay.

## Khryssí Ammoudhiá

Water taxis ply between Liménas and Khryssí Ammoudhiá twice daily in summer (10am & 4.30pm; €8)

The north end of Skála Potamiás beach, **Khryssí Ammoudhiá** – often anglicized to "**Golden Beach**" for the benefit of tourists – is quite built-up but edges the southern end in the quality of both sand and sea; it can also be approached by a direct road that spirals for 5km down from Panayía.

## Kínyra and its beaches

The dispersed hamlet of **KÍNYRA**, some 24km south of Liménas, marks the start of the burnt zone which overlooks it, though recovery is under way. Although not having much to recommend it per se, Kínyra is convenient for the superior **beaches** of Loutroú (1km south) and partly nudist Paradise (3km along) – officially called Makrýammos Kinýron – both of which can be reached down poorly signposted dirt tracks. The latter ranks as the most scenic of all Thassian beaches.

---

**ACCOMMODATION, EATING AND DRINKING**                    **THE EAST COAST**

### PANAYÍA

★ **Hotel Thassos Inn** ☎ 25930 61612, ⓦ thassosinn .gr. Up in the Tris Piyés district near the Kímisis church, with fine views over the rooftops, this hotel's bright yellow walls mirror the colour of the mature carp in its fishpond. The rooms are fine and the terrace cafeteria very relaxing. April–Oct. **€35**

**Iy Thea** ☎ 25930 61265. Excellent *psistariá* at the southeast edge of town en route to Potamiá, with fine views from the terrace, where you can enjoy simple but succulent grills and aromatic local wine. Daily noon–midnight.

### SKÁLA POTAMIÁS

**Eric's** ☎ 25930 61554, ⓦ erics.gr. On the main road 400m inland and so called after the owner who advertises his resemblance to footballer Eric Cantona widely. The rooms and studios are spotless, and there are Premiership matches on satellite TV and a swimming pool with bar. **€45**

**Hera** ☎ 25930 61467. Just inland from the far south end of the beach, this four-storey cream-coloured building contains neat rooms and larger studios, set behind a small, well-tended garden. June–Sept. **€50**

**Theagenis** ☎ 25930 61481. Popular local taverna by the fishing harbour, which serves some oven-baked meat and veg dishes, grilled meat and fish, plus decent wine. May–Oct daily 10am–midnight.

**KHRYSSÍ AMMOUDHIÁ**
**Camping Golden Beach** ☎ 25930 61472, ⓦ camping
-goldenbeach.gr. The only official campsite on this side of
the island has plenty of shaded pitches, clean baths and
laundry facilities and a minimarket. May to mid-Oct. Adult
plus tent **€8.40**
**Enavlion** ☎ 25930 58222, ⓦ enavlionhotel.com.
Cream-and-pastel-blue mock-Classical hotel on the
main road, somewhat resembling a wedding cake. Still,
the rooms are luxurious, with all mod cons. Breakfast
included. Late April–Sept. **€75**
**Golden Sand** ☎ 25930 61771, ⓦ hotel-goldensand.gr.
Backing onto the sand after which it is named, this mid-
sized resort hotel has smart rooms, most with sea-facing
balconies, and a café-bar. April–Oct. **€60**
**Sotiris** ☎ 25930 61478. Best of the tavernas dotted along
the beachfront, serving a large selection of mezédhes such as

crab salad and small cheese pies, plus more substantial
grilled fish and meat courses. May–Sept daily noon–1am.

**KÍNYRA AND ITS BEACHES**
**Agorastos** ☎ 25930 41225, ⓔ agorastoskinira
@yahoo.de. On the main road behind the village, this
colourful pension with a leafy terraced garden has cosy,
well-furnished rooms at very reasonable prices. April–
Oct. **€30**
**Paradise Beach** ☎ 25930 41248. Pleasant daytime
restaurant on the eponymous beach south of Kínyra,
serving filling breakfasts, good coffee and a full menu with
meat dishes (€8–12). May–Oct daily 8am–8pm.
**Studios Niki** ☎ 25930 25930, ⓦ studios-niki.gr.
Sparking white building just below the main road 3km
south of Kínyra, whose smart rooms have balconies
overlooking Paradise beach. May–Oct. **€35**

# Southern Thássos

The south-facing coast of Thássos has the balance of the island's best beaches, starting
with the prettiest resort, in the shape of **Alykí**. In the southwest corner, by way of
contrast, **Limenária** is rather dull and functional, although its greater local population
means it has more authentic dining choices.

## Alykí and around

**ALYKÍ** hamlet, 35km from Limenás and just below the main road, faces a perfect double
bay which almost pinches off a headland. Uniquely, it retains its original whitewashed,
slate-roofed architecture, since the presence of extensive antiquities here has led to a
ban on any modern construction. Those **ruins** include an ancient temple to an
unknown deity, and two exquisite early Christian basilicas out on the headland, with a
few columns re-erected.

Of the **beaches**, the sand-and-pebble west bay gets oversubscribed in peak season,
though you can always head off to the less crowded, rocky east cove, or snorkel in the
crystal-clear waters off the marble formations on the headland's far side. Alternatively,
head for secluded **Kékes** beach, in a pine grove 1km further southwest.

## Convent of Arhangélou Miháïl

Open during daylight hours

Some 5km southwest of Alykí, the **convent of Arhangélou Miháïl** clings spectacularly to
a cliff on the seaward side of the road. Though founded in the twelfth century above
the spot where a spring had gushed forth, the convent has been hideously renovated by
the nuns, resident here since 1974. A dependency of Filothéou on Mount Áthos, its
prize relic is a purported nail from the Crucifixion.

## Potós and around

Just 1km west of the island's southern tip is a good but crowded beach, **Psilí Ámmos**,
with watersports on offer. A few kilometres further, **POTÓS** is the island's prime
German-speaking package venue, its centre claustrophobically dense, with the few
non-block-booked rooms overlooking cramped alleys. Although the kilometre-long
beach is decent enough, there is little to warrant lingering here. **Pefkári**, with its
manicured beach and namesake pine grove, 1km west, is essentially an annexe of Potós,
with a few mid-range places to stay and better eating options.

9

## Limenária and around

**LIMENÁRIA**, the island's second town, was built to house German mining executives brought in by the Ottomans between 1890 and 1905. Their remaining mansions, scattered on the slopes above the harbour, lend some character, but despite attempts at embellishing the waterfront, it's not the most attractive place on Thássos.

The nearest good beach is **Trypití**, a couple of kilometres west – turn left into the pines at the start of a curve right. The broad, 800m-long strand is rather marred by the massed ranks of umbrellas and sun loungers for rent. The cleft to which the name refers (literally "pierced" in Greek) is a slender tunnel through the headland at the west end of the beach, leading to a tiny three-boat anchorage.

### ACCOMMODATION, EATING AND DRINKING     SOUTHERN THÁSSOS

#### ALYKÍ AND AROUND

**Beautiful Alice** ☎ 25930 31574. The oldest taverna in the village, with a lovely terrace, where you can choose from a bewildering array of reasonably priced seafood and fish, including sardines cooked in four different ways. May–Oct daily 11am–1am.

**Skidhia** ☎ 25930 31528, ⓦ kekesbeach.gr. On Kékes beach, 3km south, this traditional seaside taverna, which serves good seafood and grills, has a set of simple but adequate bungalow-style rooms. May–Sept. **€35**

#### POTÓS AND AROUND

**Camping Pefkari Beach** Pefkári ☎ 25930 51190, ⓦ camping-pefkari.gr. With its attractive wooded location and clean facilities, this is undoubtedly the best campsite on Thássos. June–Sept. Adult plus tent **€8.80**

**Thassos** Pefkári ☎ 25930 51596, ⓦ hotel-thassos.gr. Accomplished resort hotel just behind the beach with refreshingly colourful and contemporary decor, from its spacious lobby to the well-appointed rooms. Pool, tennis

and watersports available too. Breakfast included. **€65**

#### LIMENÁRIA AND AROUND

**Mouragio** ☎ 25930 51178. The most authentic of the main seafront tavernas, serving a mixture of tasty oven-baked items and grilled meat or fish, while its Street Café behind is a colourful hangout. Mid-April to mid-Oct daily noon–1am.

**Must** ☎ 25930 34795. Hip new bar with imaginative decorations and a surprisingly cutting-edge line in both rock and dance sounds, plus the usual battery of beers and spirits. May–Sept daily noon–late.

**Sgouridis** ☎ 25930 51241, ⓦ hotelsgouridis.gr. Set one block back from the seafront, this refurbished hotel, with vines creeping up the exterior, has nicely furnished if rather cramped rooms. April to mid-Oct. **€40**

★ **To Limani** ☎ 25930 52790. This old-style *tsipourádhiko* is the preferred gathering place for the savvy locals, who accompany the fiery spirit from the mainland with freshly caught fish from the adjacent sea. Daily 11am–midnight.

## The west coast

The western coast, between Limenária and Liménas, is Thrassós's most exposed and scenically least impressive, and the various *skáles* (harbours) such as Skála Kaliráhis and Skála Sotíros – originally the ports for namesake inland villages – are bleak, straggly and windy. **SKÁLA MARIÓN**, 13km from Limenária, is the exception: an attractive little bay, with fishing boats hauled up on the sandy foreshore, and the admittedly modern low-rise village arrayed in a U-shape all around. There are, most importantly, two fine beaches on either side.

**SKÁLA PRÍNOU** has little to recommend it, other than ferry connections to Kavála. **SKÁLA RAHONÍOU**, between here and Liménas, has a smattering of facilities, as well as proximity to **Pahýs beach**, 9km short of Liménas, by far the best strand on the northwest coast. Narrow dirt tracks lead past various tavernas through surviving pines to the sand, partly shaded in the morning.

### ACCOMMODATION AND EATING     THE WEST COAST

**Brian's Restaurant** Skála Prínou ☎ 25930 71445. In a huge new building 500m east of the port, this all-round taverna does daily specials and a wide standard menu. It also hosts live music every Saturday night in season. May–Sept daily 10am–1am.

**Pefkospilia** Pahýs beach, Skála Rahoníou ☎ 25930 81051. One of the oldest and most picturesque tavernas on the island, located on Pahýs beach. Great traditional cuisine is served outside the tiny whitewashed building, almost hidden by firs, as the name ("Fir cave") suggests. May–

Sept daily noon–1am.

**Pension Dimitris** Skála Marión ☎ 694 45 05 064, ⓦ pension-dimitris.gr. Perched on a hilltop behind the port, this attractively designed modern building offers smart rooms, a communal kitchen and optional breakfast for a small extra charge. May to mid-Oct. **€40**

**Ploumis** Skála Rahoníou ☎ 25930 81442. Right on the main beach, this café-taverna provides everything from breakfast through light snacks to full-blown meals of freshly grilled fish, seafood and meat. Good for sunsets especially. May to mid-Oct daily 9am–midnight.

# The interior

Few people get around to exploring inland Thássos – with the post-fire scrub still struggling to revive, it's not always rewarding – but there are several worthwhile excursions to or around the **hill villages**, which, as usual, portray a very different lifestyle to the coastal resorts.

## Theológos

**THEOLÓGOS**, 10km along a well-surfaced but poorly signposted road from Potós, was founded in the sixteenth century by refugees from Constantinople and became the island's capital under the Ottomans. Its houses, most with oversized chimneys and slate roofs, straggle in long tiers to either side of the main street, surrounded by generous kitchen gardens or walled courtyards. A stroll along the single high street, with its couple of *kafenía*, a soldiers' bar, a sandalmaker and traditional bakery, is rewarding.

## Kástro

**KÁSTRO** is the most naturally protected of the island's anti-pirate redoubts: thirty ancient houses and a church surround a rocky pinnacle, fortified by the Byzantines and the Genoese, which has a sheer drop on three sides. Summer occupation by shepherds is becoming the norm after total abandonment in the nineteenth century, when mining jobs at Limenária proved irresistible. Despite its proximity to Theológos as the crow flies, there's no straightforward route to it; especially with a car, it's best to descend to Potós before heading up a rough, 17km dirt track from Limenária.

## Sotíras

**SOTÍRAS**, a steep 3.5km up from Skála Sotíros, is the only interior village with an unobstructed view of sunset over the Aegean, and is thus popular with foreigners, who've bought up about half of the houses for restoration. On the ridge opposite are exploratory shafts left by the miners, whose ruined lodge looms above the church.

## The Kazavíti villages

From Prínos (Kalýves) on the coast road, it's a 6km journey inland to the **Kazavíti villages**, which are shrouded in greenery that escaped the fires; they're (poorly) signposted and mapped officially as Megálo and Mikró Prínos but still universally known by their Ottoman name. **MIKRÓ KAZAVÍTI** marks the start of the track for **MEGÁLO KAZAVÍTI**, where the magnificent platía is one of the prettiest spots on the whole island.

**EATING AND DRINKING**                                                        **THE INTERIOR**

★ **Kleoniki/Tou Iatrou** Theológos ☎ 25930 31000. In the village centre, this excellent traditional taverna is at its best in the evening when the roasting spits, loaded with goat and suckling pig, start turning. Great barrelled wine too. Daily noon–1am.

★ **Opos Palia** Sotíras ☎ 697 96 35 703. Wonderfully re-created old-style village *mezedhopolío* on the plane-shaded square below the old fountain, serving original recipes for dishes such as octopus in tomato sauce, *strapatsádha* and *bekri mezé*. Daily noon–midnight, except occasional winter closing.

# The Sporades and Évvia

**670** Skiáthos

**677** Skópelos

**682** Alónissos

**687** Skýros

**693** Évvia

SKÓPELOS

# The Sporades and Évvia

The Sporades lie close off Greece's eastern coast, their hilly terrain betraying their status as extensions of Mount Pílio, right opposite on the mainland. The three northern islands, Skiáthos, Skópelos and Alónissos, are archetypal Aegean holiday venues, with wonderful beaches, lush vegetation and transparent sea; they're all packed out in midsummer and close down almost entirely from October to April. Skýros, the fourth inhabited member of the group, lies well southeast, and is much more closely connected – both physically and historically – to Évvia than to its fellow Sporades. These two have less obvious attractions, and far fewer visitors.

**Skiáthos**, thanks to its international airport and extraordinary number of sandy beaches, is the busiest of the islands, though **Skópelos**, with its *Mamma Mia!* connections, extensive pine forests and idyllic pebble bays, is catching up fast. **Alónissos**, much quieter, more remote and less developed, lies at the heart of a National Marine Park, attracting more nature-lovers than night owls. Traditional **Skýros** sees fewer foreign visitors, partly because it's much harder to reach, though plenty of domestic tourism means no shortage of facilities. Between Skýros and the mainland, **Évvia** (classical Euboea) extends for nearly 200km alongside central Greece. Although in spots one of the most dramatic of Greek islands, with forested mountains and rugged stretches of little-developed coast, its sheer size and proximity to the mainland means that it rarely has much of an island feel; mainlanders have holiday homes around numerous seaside resorts, but foreigners are very thin on the ground.

An indented coastline full of bays and coves to moor in, relatively steady winds and the clear waters of the National Marine Park, also make the northern Sporades, rightly, a magnet for **yacht flotillas** and charters. Many companies have bases in Skiáthos, in particular.

## GETTING THERE
THE SPORADES AND ÉVVIA

**By plane** The airports on Skiáthos and at Vólos on the nearby mainland (see p.223) receive regular international charters as well as scheduled domestic flights. Skýros has a domestic airport, but only about three flights a week from Athens and Thessaloníki.

**By ferry** Frequent ferries and hydrofoils run from Vólos (p.223) and Áyios Konstandínos (p.217) to Skiáthos, Skópelos and Alónissos. Skýros is accessed from the port of Kými on Évvia (p.696), where ferries connect with buses from Athens. Two or three times a week in midsummer, this same ferry runs between Kými and Alónissos and Skópelos. For Évvia, local ferries shuttle from various strategic points on the mainland.

**By bus and train** Évvia is joined to central Greece by two bridges. Buses from Athens run to various points on the island, and there are trains to the island capital, Halkídha.

# Skiáthos

Undulating green countryside, some fine rural monasteries and a labyrinthine old town notwithstanding, the real business of **Skiáthos** is **beaches**: by far the best, if also the most oversubscribed, in the Sporades. There are over fifty strands (plus a few more on

Skiáthos's top ten beaches p.675
Walking on Skópelos p.681
Hiking on Alónissos p.684

The Mediterranean Monk seal p.687
Carnival on Skýros p.688
Skyrian horses p.692

LALÁRIA BEACH, SKIATHOS

# Highlights

**❶ Lalária beach, Skiáthos** Glistening white pebbles and turquoise waters, backed by steep cliffs and a natural rock arch, form a photogenic contrast to the island's other, mostly sandy, bays. **See p.675**

**❷ Skópelos Town** Wooden shutters, ornate balconies, domed churches and atmospheric passageways make this one of the most alluring island towns in Greece. **See p.678**

**❸ National Marine Park of Alónissos-Northern Sporades** Spend a day – or longer – on a boat exploring the islets of this pristine reserve, with their wildlife, monasteries and secluded bays. **See p.687**

**❹ Skýros** An outrageously pagan carnival, a striking hillside Hóra and traditional interiors are all found on one of the least spoiled islands in the Aegean. **See p.687**

**❺ Dhimosári Gorge, southern Évvia** Traverse the wildest corner of the island on a mostly cobbled path descending from Mount Óhi. **See p.699**

**❻ Límni, northern Évvia** A proud port with beautiful horizons to the west and clean pebble beaches either side. **See p.699**

**HIGHLIGHTS ARE MARKED ON THE MAP ON P.672**

satellite islets), most with fine, pale sand, though still barely enough room for the legions of visitors; Italians and Greeks in summer, Brits and Scandinavians in spring and autumn. The main road along the south and southeast coasts serves an almost unbroken line of villas, hotels, minimarkets and restaurants; although they've not impinged much on Skiáthos's natural beauty, they make it difficult to find anything particularly Greek here. But by **hiking** or using a **4WD vehicle**, you can find relative solitude, refreshing vistas and charming medieval monuments in the island's north.

## ARRIVAL AND DEPARTURE
## SKIÁTHOS

**By plane** As well as international charters, there are regular Olympic flights to Athens (April–Oct 1 daily, otherwise 2 weekly; 45min; ⓦ olympicair.com). Skiáthos airport is a tourist attraction in itself; built on reclaimed

**HIGHLIGHTS**
1. Lalária beach, Skiáthos
2. Skópelos Town, Skópelos
3. National Marine Park of Alonissos - Northen Sporades
4. Skýros
5. Dhimosári Gorge, Southern Évvia
6. Límni, Évvia Northen

THE SPORADES & ÉVVIA

land immediately outside Skiáthos Town, it has an extremely short runway, and planes come in incredibly low over the harbour. On Friday, the busiest day for charters, hundreds of people gather by the road at the end of the runway where landing planes pass just a few metres overhead, and the jet blast from those taking off can knock you over; check it out on YouTube.

**By ferry** Hellenic Seaways (ⓦhsw.gr) flying dolphins and ferries run twice daily for most of the year – more in midsummer – to and from Vólos (1hr 30min–2hr 30min), Skópelos (50min–1hr) and Alónissos (1hr 25min–1hr

45min). Flying dolphins and, in summer, a ferry (NEL Lines; ⓦnel.gr) also connect Skiáthos daily with Áyios Konstandínos (1hr 35min–2hr 45min), and with Skópelos and Alónissos. On Fridays especially it is worth booking in advance; Friday mornings into Skiáthos and evening departures to the islands are frequently full.

**Tickets and agencies** There are ticket booths on the dock at busy times; otherwise the Hellenic Seaways agent (ⓣ24270 22209) is directly opposite the jetty at the base of Papadhiamándi; NEL is handled by Panos Andritsopoulos (ⓣ24270 22018), 100m round the new harbour to the right.

**10**

## INFORMATION

**Services** In Skiáthos Town, the National Bank is on Papadhiamándi, and there are numerous others nearby and around the harbour, many with ATMs. The post office is also on Papadhiamándi. Many cafés and bars have wi-fi; i-Net internet café, on the first floor overlooking the new

harbour opposite the taxi stand, has plenty of terminals and fast connections.

**Useful website** ⓦskiathos.gr has extensive accommodation listings.

## GETTING AROUND

**By bus** A superb bus service runs along Skiáthos's coast road, from town to Koukounariés at the western end of the island, daily from 7am to midnight, with departures every fifteen minutes for most of the day (€2); the entire run takes about thirty minutes most of the time, much longer in August when traffic is chaotic. In town the terminus is at the eastern (airport) end of the new port, with further stops on the ring road. There are 26 numbered stops in all, and these numbers are often used when giving directions to a beach or restaurant. In summer a small bus also runs up to Evangelistrías monastery (8 times daily in Aug, otherwise 4 daily; 15min), departing from the car park near the Health Centre at the top of the old town.

**By taxi** The main taxi rank (ⓣ24270 24461) is at the new port just east of the ferry jetties.

**By car or scooter** Numerous rental outlets offering bicycles, motorbikes, cars and motorboats are based around the new port; Aegean Car Rental (ⓣ24270 22430, ⓦaegeancars.gr), virtually opposite the ferries, is recommended. Parking in town is impossible, except out past the yacht anchorage and at the southwest edge near the health centre.

**By boat** Dozens of boat trips are on offer, ranging from shuttles to various beaches (for example Kanapítsa roughly hourly all day; 15min; €2.50) to day-trips round the island (around €15 a head) or round Skópelos (€20). Most of these depart from the old port, but there are various interesting alternatives, on small sailing yachts for example, around the new harbour. The island tour is well worth doing – an excellent way to get your bearings and check out the beaches, including a few that can only be reached by boat.

# Skiáthos Town

**SKIÁTHOS TOWN,** the only real population centre on the island, is set on a couple of low hills around a point, with the ferry harbour and new town to the east, the picturesque old port, with the old town rising above it, in the west. You can easily get lost among the maze-like backstreets and shady platíes of the old town, but heading downhill will swiftly bring you back, either to the water or the flatter new town, where the main drag, Alexándhrou Papadhiamándi, runs directly inland from the ferry jetties.

## Alexándros Papadiamántis Museum

Just off Alexándhrou Papadhiamándi • Daily 9.30am–1.30pm & 5–7.30pm • €1.50

There are few specific sights in Skiáthos, though the **Alexándros Papadiamántis Museum**, housed in the nineteenth-century home of one of Greece's best-known writers, is worth a look. The upper storey – basically two tiny rooms – has been maintained as it was when the writer lived (and died) here, plainly enjoying a remarkably ascetic lifestyle. The ground floor operates as a bookshop-cum-exhibition area.

**10**

SKIÁTHOS

N

Kástro
Laláría
Panayía Dombón
Panayía Kardhási
Ayíou Haralámbou
Mégas Yialós
Evangelistrías
Xánemos
Panayía Kekhreás
Profítis Ilías
Kehriá
Lygariés
Mikrós Asélinos
Megálos Asélinos
Eliá
Skiáthos
Panayías Kounístras
Mandhráki
Megáli Ámmos
Cape Poúnda
Kryfí Ámmos
Ayía Eléni
Strofyliá
Ahladhiá
Banana Beaches
Koukounariés
Troúlos
Koliós
Tzaneriá
Troúlos
Ayía Paraskeví
Kanapítsa
Vromólimnos
Kalamáki Peninsula
Tsougriá
Tsoúngriaki

0    2
kilometres

▼ Vólos & Áyios Konstandínos

## The Boúrtzi

The peninsula that separates the two harbours, the **Boúrtzi**, makes for an enjoyable stroll. Surrounded by crumbling defences and a few rusty cannon – there was a castle in this obvious defensive position from at least the thirteenth century – it is today a peaceful setting for occasional exhibitions, a café with great views, and an open-air municipal theatre, with regular summertime music and drama performances.

## The rest of the island

Skiáthos's south coast is lined with beach after beach after beach, almost all of them easily accessible on the bus. If you want to explore the mountainous area north of town, though, or get to the north-coast beaches, you'll need to have your own transport or be prepared for some very hot hiking. Be warned that a moped simply won't make it up some of the exceptionally steep tracks, especially around Kástro. Thanks to the humid climate and springs fed from the mainland, the interior is exceptionally green, thick with pine, lentisc, holm oak, heather and arbutus even where (as is all too common) it has been ravaged by forest fires over the years. There are plenty of villas and tourist facilities on the coast and chapels and farms in the interior, but only **Troúlos** (with another excellent beach) really counts as a village, and even that a tiny one.

### Evangelistrías monastery

**Monastery** Daily 10am–sunset · Free **Museum** 10am–2pm · €2

From town, you can drive up to eighteenth-century **Evangelistrías monastery** in ten minutes, or walk it in just over an hour; the path takes various short-cuts from the road, mostly well signed, starting out from the ring road close to bus stop 2. A beautiful and much revered spot and the scene of major pilgrimages at Easter and on August 15, it was here that the modern Greek flag was first unfurled in 1807. Inside it's alive with the

**OPPOSITE** KOUKOUNARIÉS BEACH

## SKIÁTHOS'S TOP TEN BEACHES

Although almost all the island's beaches are sandy, some of them are very narrow. On the south coast every one will have loungers and at least one bar or taverna, often pumping out loud music; most have watersports too. If you want to get away from it all, the harder to reach sands on the north coast offer more chance of escape. These (listed clockwise from town) are our favourites:

**Tsougriá** An islet in the bay opposite Skiáthos Town, with excursion boats shuttling back and forth from the old port three or four times daily. A favourite of locals, it has two spectacular sand beaches, each with a taverna.

**Vromólimnos** The prettiest of the beaches on the Kalamáki peninsula, fine-sand Vromólimnos is a bit of a walk from bus stop 13, and hence a little quieter than many south-coast sands – it still has several cafés from which to enjoy the sunset views, though, and a busy water-ski operation.

**Koukounariés** Huge stretch of sand – at the end of the bus route – which is arguably the island's finest beach, and certainly one of its busiest. Wooden walkways traverse the sand to a series of *kantínas*, there's a harbour for excursion boats and every imaginable form of watersport including snorkelling and diving with Skiathos Diving, one of the island's best outfits (☎697 70 81 444, ⓦ skiathosdiving.gr). Behind the beach a small salt lake, Strofyliá, sits in the midst of a grove of pine trees – all of it a protected reserve. There's horseriding, too, in the forested dunes to the north, with Skiathos Riding Centre (☎24270 49548, ⓦ skiathos-horse-riding.gr).

**Big Banana** Reached by a short track over the headland from bus stop 26 at Koukounariés, Big Banana is announced before you arrive by the thumping bass tracks from three competing beach bars. It's beautifully sandy but absolutely packed, with a young crowd and a clubbing atmosphere, plus ski boats, kayaks, pedaloes and more.

**Small Banana** In the next cove beyond Big Banana, this beach is almost entirely nudist yet still thoroughly commercialized, with a café and loungers occupying almost every

centimetre. Like its neighbour, it is named not for the appendages on display but for its perfect yellow crescent of sand.

**Ayía Eléni** About 600m from bus stop 25 in Koukounariés, Ayía Eléni is a stunning, broad, sandy beach looking west towards the mountainous mainland. It is bigger and more family-oriented than the neighbouring Banana beaches, with a couple of beach bars and pedaloes and kayaks to rent.

**Mandhráki** Dunes and a protected pine forest back Mandhráki, a sandy beach with views of Mount Pílio and an exceptionally friendly snack bar serving *souvláki*, salads and omelettes. One of the island's least developed, it is accessed either by a walking path from bus stop 23 in Koukounariés, or a driveable track that follows the coast round past Ayía Eléni beach.

**Megálos Asélinos** From Troúlos village, a side-road leads 3.5km north through a lush valley to Megálos Asélinos, a large and exposed beach of gritty sand. There's a big taverna where many excursion boats stop for lunch, but it's a lovely, unspoilt spot at the end of the day when they've all headed home.

**Kástro** A small cove set steeply below Kástro (see opposite), Kástro can be very crowded in the middle of the day when the tour boats arrive, but is delightful early or late – though it loses the sun early. There's a wonderfully ramshackle snack bar with a shower of cold river water.

**Lalária** Famous beach nestling near the northernmost point of Skiáthos, and only accessible by taxi- or excursion-boat from town. With steep cliffs rising behind a white-pebble shore and an artistic natural arch, it's undeniably beautiful; three sea-grottoes just east rate a stop on most round-the-island trips.

sound of caged songbirds, there's a shop selling local wine and preserves, and an eclectic **museum** comprising ecclesiastical and rural-folklore galleries plus a vast collection of documents, posters and photos from the independence struggle and Balkan wars.

Below the monastery, another signed **path** leads north, past restored **Ayíou Haralámbou** monastery, full of cats and chickens kept by the caretaker, and on past **Panayía Dombón** chapel and then to **Panayía Kardhási** on the way to Kástro (see below).

## Kástro
Daily sunrise–sunset • Free

**Kástro**, occupying a windswept headland at the northernmost tip of Skiáthos, was the island's main population centre throughout the Middle Ages. The fortified settlement, established for security from pirate raids, thrived under Byzantine, Venetian and Turkish control until its abandonment around 1830, when the new Greek state stamped hard on piracy and the population left to build the modern capital. Most of the buildings were dismantled and the materials reused elsewhere, so all that's left now are the remains of the defences, half a dozen churches (there were once 20) and a mosque. You enter the rocky outcrop across a narrow, stone ridge – a superb natural defence once enhanced by walls and a drawbridge; inside, the remains are beautifully maintained and well signed, with tables where you can picnic and fresh spring water.

If you come by boat you're unlikely to escape the crowds; driving or walking involves an exceptionally steep, narrow cobbled track, but does give the chance to arrive early or late, and perhaps get the place to yourself.

## ACCOMMODATION                                                      SKIÁTHOS

Much of the accommodation on Skiáthos, especially villas and places out of town with pools, is block-booked by package companies. You may find it easier to check the island's website (see p.673) or go through a local agent such as Dolphin of Skiathos (☎ 24270 29910, ⓦ dolphin-skiathos.gr). There are also two local room-owners' association kiosks on the quayside (☎ 24270 22990 or 21488), operating long hours in high season. Everywhere is heavily booked in August; at other times, rates dip by as much as half.

### SKIÁTHOS TOWN
**Bourtzi** Moraïtou 8 ☎ 24270 21304, ⓦ hotelbourtzi.gr. Boutique hotel just off Papadhiamándi with designer decor and a courtyard pool; rooms boast marble floors, flat-screen TVs and all mod-cons. Impressive, though the atmosphere is more business than island. €170
**Meltemi** New harbour ☎ 24270 22493, ⓦ meltemi skiathos.com. The waterfront position is unbeatable, and rooms at the front have great sea views. Simple, island-style rooms are a bit dated, but scrupulously clean and with an exceptionally friendly welcome. Wi-fi and a/c included, and breakfast is available in the snack-bar out front. €90
**Pension Nikolas** Evangelistrías ☎ 24270 23062, ⓦ nikolaspension.gr. Very central place, off Papadhiamándi close to the port, in two buildings facing each other across an internal courtyard, tucked away off the street so reasonably quiet. The simple rooms all have

a/c, fridge and TV, with balconies overlooking the courtyard. €70
**Thymi's Home** ☎ 24270 22817, ⓦ thymishome.gr. Modern studio complex in the heart of town (signed off Papadhiamándi) with classy modern decor and every facility including wi-fi, flat-screen TVs, quiet a/c, internal balcony and tiny kitchenette. Some rooms are pretty small, and the pool is tiny. €80

### KOUKOUNARIÉS
**Mandraki Village** ☎ 24270 49301, ⓦ mandraki -skiathos.gr. Delightful garden complex near the lake, at bus stop 23, with tasteful, modern pastel-coloured rooms, family quads and junior suites (worth the small price difference), all very well equipped, spacious grounds and pool. €140

## EATING AND DRINKING

By Greek standards – just about any standards in fact – eating in Skiáthos is expensive. The best places also get very busy so, unusually, booking is often advisable.

### SKIÁTHOS TOWN
★ **Alexandhros** ☎ 24270 22431. Traditional Greek

restaurant in the old-town backstreets; signposted from Platía Trión Ierarhón but still hard to find, in an alley behind restaurant *1901*. Packed every night thanks to some of the lowest prices in town, with live Greek music most nights; service can suffer from the crowds, and book or be prepared to wait. Daily, evenings only.

★ **Amfiliki** ☎ 24270 22839. This restaurant sits opposite the health centre, high on the west side of the old town. Walk through the house and past the kitchen to find a gorgeous terrace, high above the sea. All the standard taverna recipes, skilfully prepared – and excellent seafood dishes like *seláhi* (skate), parsley and onion salad, or *bráska kípo*, monkfish covered in spicy tomato sauce. Just forty seats overlooking the sea, so book to be sure of the view (or come for breakfast). They also have some very simple rooms to rent. Daily all day. Rooms €80

**Bakaliko** ☎ 24270 24024. Probably the best of the restaurants here in a strip (the coast road beyond the new harbour) more known for nightlife, with mock decor of a traditional Greek grocer's, unimprovable seating on a deck cantilevered over the water and decently priced; Turkish-influenced food (*yogurtlu* kebab at €9.50, for example); live acoustic Greek music some nights. Daily, evenings only.

**Maria's** ☎ 24270 22292. Enjoy excellent pizza, pasta and creative salads at this restaurant behind Trís lereárhes church, up the steps from the old port. Check out the riotously eclectic decor inside, though in summer you'll prefer to sit out on the balcony, or down in the courtyard, and menus handwritten in old accounting books. The downside is price; simple pasta and pizza dishes start from around €12, though portions are large. Daily, dinner only.

**Mesoyia** ☎ 24270 21440. Cheap-and-cheerful outfit (though still around €40 for two, with house wine) in the old-town backstreets featuring the usual grilled and *mayireftá* suspects, plus daily changing seafood, such as prawn *yiouvétsi*. Tables in the lane in summer (they can usually squeeze in one more when busy); indoors during the cooler months. Daily, evenings only.

### PROFÍTIS ILÍAS

**Platanos** ☎ 693 24 13 539. Close to the island's highest point, about 4km from town, *Platanos* has fabulous views over town and towards Skópelos and Évvia. The food is almost beside the point, but there's a decent taverna menu, plus breakfast, omelettes, sandwiches or simply coffee and baklává; it's wise to book if you want a decent view in the evening. Daily 10.30am–11pm.

### KOLIÓS

**Infinity Blue** Koliós Bay ☎ 24270 49750. Hop off at bus stop 15 to get to *Infinity Blue*, with its lovely vistas from a romantic, hillside setting. The restaurant has a Greek/Mediterranean menu and a more refined ambience than most, with proper linen and wine glasses. Fine steaks (as they should be for around €23), pasta and risotto, plus Greek dishes standard and exotic (rabbit with plums) for €9 –14. Daily, evenings only.

### NIGHTLIFE

There are plenty of bars and pubs on Papadhiamándi and the nearby old-town backstreets, but the coolest places are overlooking the old port or out on the "club strip" at the start of the coast road beyond the yacht marina. The summer open-air cinema, Attikon, is at the bottom of Papadhiamándi by the museum; it has been showing *Mamma Mia!* three or four times a week since the film's release.

**BBC** ☎ 695 72 62 167. Club strip venues seem to be annually changeable, and operate only in July and August, but *BBC* – on the coast road – is bigger and longer-lived than most: riotous crowd inside and a deck jutting out over the shallows to chill out. Seasonal; from 11pm.

**Kentavros** Mitropolítou Ananíou ☎ 24270 22980. An evergreen, much-loved rock, jazz and blues bar right in the centre of town, just a few paces from the new harbour near the Papadiamántis Museum. Nightly 9.30pm–4am.

**Rock'n'Roll** Old Port ☎ 24270 22944. The busiest of four neighbouring, essentially identical bars on the steps leading up to Platía Trión Ierarhón, *Rock'n'Roll* has outdoor seating with sofas and scatter cushions; inside a DJ serves up mainstream rock, Latin and dance music. Nightly 7pm–4am.

# Skópelos

**SKÓPELOS** is bigger and more rugged than Skiáthos and its concessions to tourism are lower-key and in better taste, despite a boom in recent years fuelled by the filming here of the *Mamma Mia!* film. Much of the countryside, especially the southwest coast, really is as spectacular as it appears in the film, with a series of pretty cove beaches backed by extensive pine forests as well as olive groves and orchards of plums (**prunes** are a local speciality), apricots, pears and almonds. **Skópelos Town (Hóra)** and **Glóssa**, the two main towns, are among the prettiest in the Sporades, their hillside houses distinguished by painted wooden trim and grey slate roofs.

## ARRIVAL AND DEPARTURE

**By ferry** Hellenic Seaways (w hsw.gr) flying dolphins and ferries run three times daily for most of the year – more in midsummer – to and from Alónissos (20–35min), and to Skiáthos (50min–1hr) and either Vólos (2hr 45min–3hr 45min) or Áyios Konstandínos (2hr 15min–4hr); some of these call at Loutráki, the port for Glóssa (and known as Glóssa on ferry and hydrofoil schedules), as well as Skópelos Town. In summer NEL Lines (w nel.gr) also have a ferry with daily connection to Alónissos, Skiáthos and Áyios Konstandínos, and Skyros Shipping (w sne.gr) go twice a week to Alónissos and Kými on Évvia (3hr 20min). Connections to flights in Skiáthos can be very busy: try to book in advance.

**Tickets and agencies** There are ticket booths on the dock in Skópelos Town at busy times; otherwise the Hellenic Seaways agent (☎ 24270 22767) is directly opposite the harbour gate, and NEL and Skyros Shipping are handled by Lemonis Travel (☎ 24270 22363), by the National Bank, on the far side of the harbour close to the old port. The harbour agent in Loutráki is Triandafyllou (☎ 24240 33435).

## INFORMATION

**Services** Several banks with ATMs are on the quayside in Skópelos Town; the post office is on Dhoulídhi, just off Platía Plátanos ("Souvláki Square"), which lies directly up from the ferry harbour. Cafés all along the front have wi-fi; Blue Sea, the very last place at the northern (old port) end of the harbour, is a large internet café.

**Useful websites** w skopelos.net, w skopelosweb.gr and w skopelos.com. There's no tourist office on the island.

**Newspapers** English-language newspapers are sold at a shop just off Souvláki Square.

## GETTING AROUND

**By bus** Services run from Skópelos Town, across to the island's south coast, and then along the south and west coast past all the major beaches; in summer at least a dozen buses a day ply to Miliá – just over half of them continue as far as Glóssa. The bus stop is immediately to the left as you leave the ferry dock in Hóra.

**By car and scooter** There are numerous car and scooter rental outlets near the ferry dock in Hóra, around the corner of the coast road and the main road heading inland, and along this inland road; they include Magic (☎ 22420 23250, w skopeloscars.com) and Discovery (☎ 24240 23033, w skopelosweb.gr/discovery).

**By taxi** The central taxi stand is to the left as you leave the ferry dock in Hóra.

**By bicycle** Skópelos Cycling (☎ 22420 22398), based at Stáfylos beach, rents out mountain bikes.

**Boat trips** A huge variety of boat trips is on offer around the harbour, at prices ranging from around €10, for a return shuttle to Glystéri beach, to €30 for a trip to Alónissos; island circuits, many of them *Mamma Mia!* themed, go for around €20.

# Skópelos Town

**SKÓPELOS TOWN** (Hóra) pours off a hill on the west flank of a wide, oval bay: a cascade of handsome mansions and slate-domed churches below the ruined Venetian **kástro**.

Away from the waterside commercial strip, the hóra is endearingly time-warped – indeed among the most unspoilt in the islands – with wonderfully idiosyncratic shops of a sort long vanished elsewhere, and vernacular domestic architecture unadulterated with tasteless monstrosities.

## The folklore museum

June–Sept Mon–Sat 10am–2pm & 7–10pm • €3

The disorganized **folklore museum** musters a motley collection of weaving, embroidery and costumes; detailed panels explaining local customs and the religious calendar redeem it.

## Old Skopelitian Mansion Museum

Tues–Sun 10am–2pm & 6–9pm • €3

The **Old Skopelitian Mansion Museum**, former home of the island's doctor – subsequently occupied by his three daughters, all spinsters and all doctors – was left to the town by the last surviving daughter and is displayed much as it was when they lived here. It's a comfortable, bourgeois home full of everyday items: furniture, clothing, books and ephemera.

## ACCOMMODATION SKÓPELOS TOWN 10

There are numerous rooms for rent in the backstreets, as well as entire houses, but in high season everything is very booked up. In mid-summer a Rooms Association office (☎ 24240 24567) opens in the lane leading up to Souvláki Square; a wider choice, including apartments and hotels across the island, can be arranged through helpful Madro Travel, by the old port (☎ 24240 22145, ⓦ madrotravel.com). August prices are roughly halved the rest of the year.

**Adonis** ☎ 24240 22231. Old-fashioned establishment above a taverna, whose central waterfront position (above the the ferry quay, reached via Souvláki Square) means noise can be a problem. A couple of the simple wooden-floored, a/c rooms at the front have huge terraces. **€80**

**Georgios L** ☎ 24240 24625, ⓦ www.skopelos-hotels .gr. The last building at the northern end of the harbour, above the *Blue Sea* café, houses this small hotel with basic, old-fashioned, stone-floored rooms with a/c and TV; those at the front have great views. **€80**

**Kir Sotos** ☎ 24240 22549, ⓦ skopelos.net/sotos. Rambling old-house *pension*, set back from the middle of the harbour, behind the giant plane trees, whose wood-floored, a/c, en-suite rooms are justifiably a favourite budget option, though perhaps due for a revamp. Go for the quieter rear units, especially no. 4, with its fireplace; there's a communal kitchen and sunny courtyards. **€45**

**Mylos** ☎ 24240 24034, ⓦ skopelosweb.gr/milos. White-painted studios and apartments behind the kástro (all the way round the ring road, or a steep climb up from the harbour) with flagstone floors and mini kitchens. They enjoy great views towards Alónissos. **€45**

**Skopelos Village** ☎ 24240 22517, ⓦ skopelosvillage .gr. Pricey, self-catering complex, 600m east around the bay, with luxurious studios and suites set among landscaped grounds with two pools and a restaurant. The Seabreeze studios are worth the extra for their modern design and sleek bathrooms, though it's only good value if you get a good off-season deal. **€125**

★ **Thea Home** Ring road ☎ 24240 22859, ⓦ skopelosweb.gr/theahome. Lovely rooms and a family apartment with sweeping views from the top of the town; accommodation is cosy but very comfortable, with fridge and a/c. Bikes are available (free) and there's an excellent home-made breakfast (extra); new studios and a pool are being added. **€55**

## EATING AND DRINKING

The seafront is lined with cafés and tavernas, the best of which are up at the old port end; for something rather more modest, aptly nick-named Souvláki Square is packed with decent fast-food outfits.

**Englezos** Harbour ☎ 24240 22230. Greek food with a slight edge, served with a view towards the old port end of the harbour. There are plenty of straightforward dishes and great, spit-roasted lamb, pork and chicken (around €10 a portion), but also some more inventive recipes such as aubergine (eggplant) millefeuille, feta with chili and tomato, or beetroot salad. Daily lunch & dinner.

**Gorgones** ☎ 24240 24709. Popular ouzerí in town (beside the well-signed *Oionos Blue Bar*), with tables in a stepped alley, garden courtyard and indoors. The usual meat and seafood at fair prices (prawn pasta €15, *soutsoukákia* €7), though occasionally erratic service. Daily lunch & dinner.

**Klimataria** Harbour ☎ 24240 22273. Good standard taverna, just a couple of doors from *Englezos*, with plenty of

local customers. Menu includes a good selection of fish by the kilo and local specialities like pork with plums; best to stick to the simpler dishes. Daily lunch & dinner.

**Perivoli** ☎ 24240 23758. A beautiful spot in the garden courtyard of an old house, up an alley just above Souvláki Square. The upmarket Greek/Mediterranean menu includes pasta and risotto as well as inventive Greek dishes like rolled pork with apple and plum in wine sauce (€11) or stuffed zucchini (€7.50) – plus a selection of wines by the glass. Evenings only, from 7.30pm.

★ **Ta Kymata (Angelos)** Old port ☎ 24240 22381. About the oldest taverna on Skópelos, a shrine of quality *mayireftá* such as *exohikó* (a local speciality of lamb and vegetables in a filo triangle) and *mezédhes* like fresh beets with their own greens. Daily lunch & dinner.

## NIGHTLIFE

**Anatoli** Kástro ☎ 24240 22851. Veteran rembétika musician Yiorgos Xintaris performs at this tumbledown place on top of the kástro; music from late June to early Sept, when his sons (who accompany him) return from university in Athens. By day there's a café with incomparable views. Daily 10am–late.

**Bardon** Old Olive Factory ☎ 24240 24494. Vast lounge bar in this food-and-nightlife complex, occupying a restored industrial area directly opposite the harbour car park. Cocktails, dance music and occasional live bands. Daily 6pm–3am.

**Merkourio (Mercurius)** ☎ 24240 24593. Cool bar, just up from the ferry jetty between Souvláki Square and the Folklore Museum, with views over the harbour action. Cocktails are served on candle-lit terraces, to a soft-rock and Latin soundtrack; also open during the day for breakfast and coffee. Daily 10am–2am.

**Oionos Blue Bar** ☎ 694 24 06 136. Old-house bar, well signed inland from the centre of the harbour, with a jazz, blues and world-music playlist, plus a staggering variety of imported beers and whiskies. Daily 10am–2am.

**Platanos** Harbour ☎ 24240 23661. Evergreen bar on the northwest quay, just past *Englezos* restaurant, with jazz and world-music soundtrack. Great too for a morning coffee or breakfast and people-watching under the namesake plane tree outside. Daily 9am–3am.

## South and west coast

Many of the island's best, and certainly the most accessible, **beaches** lie just off the main road and bus route, which heads south across the island from Hóra and then up the west coast.

### Stáfylos

Barely 4km from Hóra, **Stáfylos** is the closest decent beach, though it gets very crowded in season. There's a noisy beach bar, so if it's peace you're after walk to the end of the beach and climb over the headland to larger, more scenic, sand-and-fine-gravel **Velanió**, with a summer-only *kantína* and a bit of a nudist scene.

### Agnóndas and Limnonári

The beautiful bay of **AGNÓNDAS** has very much the feel of traditional old Greece, with yachts moored and a pretty fishing harbour where the water laps right up to the tables of several tavernas. There's not much of a beach, though, so for that follow the side road to **LIMNONÁRI**, about 1km west, 300m of white sand in a steep-sided bay.

### Pánormos and around

**PÁNORMOS** is the biggest resort outside Skópelos Town, though still very understated and low-key. An extensive pebble beach lines the expansive bay, with plenty of tavernas (most offering free loungers for customers), shops and rooms. Adjoining **Blo** inlet is a beautiful, quiet anchorage, though there's no beach here.

The wide-open spaces of **Miliá**, immediately beyond Pánormos, comprise two 400m sweeps of grey sand and pebbles opposite Dhassiá islet, divided by a headland with a sometimes obtrusively noisy beach bar at the south cove. Having found fame as the *Mamma Mia!* beach, **Kastáni**, almost adjacent to Miliá, has become very crowded, with a big beach bar pumping out dance music. Nonetheless it's a beautiful place, with fine sand and crystal-clear water. Beyond unattractive **Élios (Néo Klíma)**, isolated **Armenópetra** boasts two spectacular beaches either side of a point. There's no shade and no facilities, but great views of Glossá on the hillside above.

## ACTIVITIES

### SOUTH AND WEST COAST

**Watersports** In Pánormos you can rent motorboats (☎ 24240 24788, ⊛ holidayislands.com/boathire) or kayaks (☎ 694 70 44 870) to explore the surrounding bays.

## ACCOMMODATION AND EATING

**Adrina Beach** 1km north of Pánormos ☎ 24240 23371, ⊛ adrina.gr. Beautiful, ivy-clad, four-star bungalow complex tumbling down a hillside to its own private beach. Wonderful sea views from the rooms and duplex

> ## WALKING ON SKÓPELOS
>
> Away from the main roads there's plenty of **walking** on Skópelos. Long-time resident Heather Parsons battles to maintain paths and leads spring/autumn walks along what remains (☎694 52 49 328, ⓦskopelos-walks.com), as well as publishing a hiking guide, *Skopelos Trails*. Among the better walks are those east of Skópelos Town, where three historic **monasteries**, Metamórfosis, Evangelistrías and Prodhrómou (all open approx 8am–1pm & 5–8pm daily), stand on the slopes of Mount Paloúki. Near Glóssa there's a beautiful 45-minute trail to the renovated village of **Palió Klíma**, via the island's oldest settlement, **Athéato** (Mahalás), slowly being restored by outsiders, and the foreigner-owned hamlet of **Áyii Anáryiri**.

**10**

maisonettes, plus seawater pool and taverna. **€175**

**Limnonari Beach Restaurant** Limnonári ☎ 24240 23046, ⓦskopelos.net/limnonarirooms. An excellent taverna serving simple but delicious food, such as a rich goat *kokkinísto* and delicious local spiral *tyrópittes*. Above there are pleasant rooms, also simple and mostly with inland views. Open all day, breakfast to dinner. Rooms **€55**

★ **Mando** Stáfylos ☎ 24240 23917, ⓦwww.mando-skopelos.gr. Some of the best accommodation on the island, very friendly and quiet with stone-floored, a/c rooms (and a family suite) set among manicured lawns, with steps leading down to a private swimming platform. There are fridges and tea- and coffee-making equipment in the rooms, plus an outdoor communal kitchen area. **€80**

**Milia Studios** Miliá ☎ 24242 23998, ⓦskopelosweb .gr/milia. Studio complex with doubles and galleried quads; breakfast can be supplied to the rooms and there's a decent taverna nearby. Before the crowds arrive, you have your own private beach. **€70**

**Panormos Beach Hotel** Pánormos ☎24240 22711, ⓦpanormos-beach.com. Looking down over Pánormos from its hillside setting, *Panormos Beach Hotel* offers comfortable stone-floored, a/c rooms with fine views set amid a huge lawn studded with fruit trees. Breakfast included. **€80**

★ **Pavlos** Agnóndas ☎24240 22409. The most popular of the simple harbourside tavernas here, *Pavlos* is an unpretentious place with fair prices for fish and plenty of well-prepared Greek dishes (mains €7.50–9), plus decent house wine. They also have simple rooms (**€60**). Daily lunch & dinner.

## Glóssa and around

Skópelos's second town, **GLÓSSA**, 26km from Hóra near the northwest tip of the island, is spectacularly arrayed in stepped, hillside tiers, high above the coast. A traditional, rural place where many of the vernacular houses have overhanging balconies and lush gardens, it is explored along narrow, steep, mostly car-free lanes (there's an unsigned car park behind the church on the main road), with breathtaking views around almost every corner. Apart from wandering the photogenic alleys and visiting the excellent tavernas, there's not a great deal to do here, and the only official accommodation in town is in rented houses (rarely available locally); there is a small **Folklore Museum** just above the main square, though (Tues, Wed & Fri–Sun 10am–2.30pm & 5.30–9pm, Thurs 10am–2.30pm; free).

**LOUTRÁKI**, some 3km steeply down a serpentine road from Glóssa (or on foot by a shorter, well-signed *kalderími*), is a pretty little place with views of Skiáthos. The port of the larger town, it has a line of cafés and tavernas around the dock, an archeological kiosk with information on local sites and island history, lots of **yachts** at anchor and a narrow pebble beach.

### ACCOMMODATION AND EATING
### GLÓSSA AND AROUND

★ **Agnanti** ☎24240 33606. Traditional taverna, well signposted in the centre of Glóssa, with upmarket takes on traditional recipes – pork with prunes or *hortokeftédhes* (vegetable croquettes) – served indoors and on a terrace with spectacular views. Only marginally pricier than average, and well worth it. Daily lunch & dinner.

**Selenunda Hotel** ☎24240 34073, ⓦhotelselenunda .com. High above the harbour at Loutráki, the peaceful *Selenunda* has stunning views from every room. All the tile-floor rooms come with a/c, TV and kitchenette; also bigger family apartments. Steps lead down to the waterfront, but with luggage you may want to call to be picked up. **€80**

**To Steki tou Mastora** ☎24240 33563. Café-restaurant by the church on the main road in Glóssa, with wonderful views of Loutráki, Skiáthos and the mainland. It does a brisk trade in coffee and sandwiches as well as fabulous charcoal-grilled meats, including whole roast lamb or goat on the spit (daily in midsummer, weekends only off-season). Daily all day.

## Northeast coast

The island's northeast coast is tricky to reach; just a few paved roads go there, from Skópelos to Glystéri, and from Glóssa to Perivolioú or Áyios Ioánnis Kastrí.

### Perivolioú

A narrow, winding road through mature pine forest leads to beautiful little **Perivolioú** beach, some 7km from Glóssa close to the island's northern tip. There's ice-clear water and no development at all at this sandy cove, nor at nearby **Hondroyiórgis** beach, reached along a driveable track. Continue on this track, and you'll join the road down to Áyios Ioánnis Kastrí.

### Áyios Ioánnis Kastrí

The tiny sand cove at **Áyios Ioánnis Kastrí** is one of the busiest on the island, thanks to its position at the base of the *Mamma Mia!* wedding chapel. Perched on a rock monolith (steps lead up), the chapel is almost ridiculously photogenic, and attracts tour boats from Skiáthos as well as being an essential halt on the round-island trip. Late afternoon, when they've all left, is generally the quietest time; there's an excellent snack bar here, serving a mean Greek salad.

### Glystéri

Less than 4km northwest of Skópelos Town, **Glystéri** is a small sand-and-pebble beach at the base of an almost completely enclosed bay. Plenty of people brave the narrow, steep road and many more arrive by boat – there's a regular shuttle from town – so it can get busy, especially at weekends when locals pack out the taverna here.

### EATING AND DRINKING
NORTHEAST COAST

**Palio Karnayio** Glystéri ☎694 43 54 705. Locals rate the taverna at Glystéri beach one of the island's best, while *Mamma Mia!* fans are drawn by the reconstructed arch from the film's *Villa Donna*, so on summer weekends it's extremely busy. Their speciality is blackfish or Alónissos tuna stifádo. Daily lunch & dinner.

# Alónissos

**ALÓNISSOS** is the largest and only permanently inhabited member of a mini-archipelago at the east end of the Sporades. It's more rugged and wild than its neighbours, but no less green; pine forest, olive groves and fruit orchards cover the southern half, while a dense maquis of arbutus, heather, kermes oak and lentisc cloaks the north. In part thanks to its marine park status (see p.687), some of Greece's cleanest sea surrounds Alónissos – the **beaches** rarely match those of Skópelos or Skiáthos for sand or scenery, but the white pebbles on most of them further enhance the impression of gin-clear water. Remoteness and limited ferry connections mean that **Alónissos** attracts fewer visitors than its neighbours. There is, however, a significant British and Italian presence (the latter mostly in all-inclusive hotels), while Greeks descend in force all summer.

### ARRIVAL AND DEPARTURE
ALÓNISSOS

**By ferry** Hellenic Seaways (ⓦhsw.gr) flying dolphins and ferries run three times daily for most of the year – more in midsummer – to and from Skópelos (20–30min), Skiáthos (1hr 25min–1hr 45min) and either Vólos (3hr 15min–4hr 30min) or Áyios Konstandínos (3hr–5hr). In summer NEL Lines (ⓦnel.gr) also have a ferry with daily connection to Skópelos, Skiáthos and Áyios Konstandínos, and Skyros Shipping (ⓦsne.gr) go twice a week to Skópelos and to Kými on Évvia (2hr 30min). Connections to flights in Skiáthos can be very busy: try to book in advance.

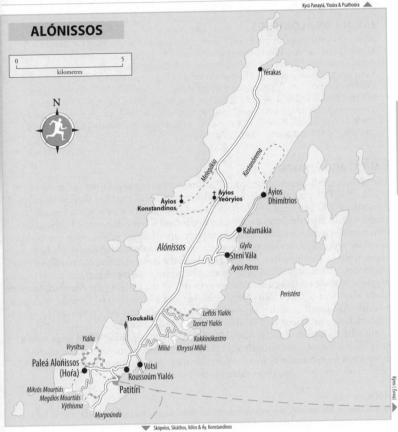

Kyrá Panayiá, Yioúra & Psathoúra ▲

**ALÓNISSOS**

0    5
kilometres

N

Yérakas

Megálokia

Kastanórema

Áyios
Konstandínos †

† Áyios
Yeóryios

Áyios
Dhimítrios

Kalamákia

Alónissos

Glyfa
Stení Vála

Áyios Petros

Peristéra

Leftós Yialós
Tzortzí Yialós

Tsoukaliá

Yiália
Vrysítsa

Kokkinókastro

Miliá   Khryssí Miliá

Paleá Alónissos
(Hóra)

Vótsi
Roussoúm Yialós

Patitíri

Mikrós Mourtiás
Megálos Mourtiás
Výthisma

Marpoúnda

Kými (Évvia) ▶

▼ Skópelos, Skiáthos, Vólos & Áy. Konstandínos

**Operators and tickets** The Hellenic Seaways agent is Alkyon Travel (☎24240 65220, ⓦalkyon-travel.gr), under the *Alkyon Hotel* on the harbourfront at the bottom of the first (eastern) inland street; NEL is handled by Albedo Travel (☎24240 65804, ⓦalbedotravel.com), at the bottom of the second (western) inland street, and Skyros Shipping by Alonnisos Travel (☎24240 66000, ⓦalonnisostravel.gr), between the two.

### INFORMATION

**Services** There's a bank with an ATM on the eastern shopping street leading up from the harbour in Patitíri. The post office is also up here, while Play internet café is close to the post office.

**Newspapers** English-language newspapers are sold near the bottom of the western shopping street in Patitíri.

### GETTING AROUND

**By bus** There are just two bus routes on Alónissos: from Patitíri up to Hóra (11 daily, including hourly from 7pm–midnight; €1.60) and to Stení Vála (3 daily; €1.70). In Patitíri the bus stop is on the harbour at the bottom of the eastern inland street.
**By taxi** The taxi stand in Patitíri is on the harbour opposite the bus stand.
**By car and scooter** There are numerous car and scooter rental outlets near the harbour, including Albedo Travel (see above) and others in the inland street immediately beyond it.
**Boat trips and excursions** Various boat trips are on offer around the harbour; the best marine park tours cost around €30 a head (including lunch and drinks), but check their itineraries as some don't go far in; walking (see p.684) and sea kayak excursions can be arranged through Albedo Travel.

**10**

## HIKING ON ALÓNISSOS

Although its often harsh, rugged landscape might suggest otherwise, of all the Sporades Alónissos caters best to **hikers**. Fifteen routes have been surveyed, numbered and admirably signposted: many provide just short walks from a beach to a village or the main road, but some can be combined to make meaty circular treks. The best of these are trail #11 from Áyios Dhimítrios, up the Kastanórema and then back along the coast on #15 (2hr 30min), or trails #13 plus #12, Melegákia to Áyios Konstandínos and Áyios Yeóryios (just over 2hr, including some road-walking to return to start). Island resident Chris Browne's comprehensive walking guide, *Alonnisos Through the Souls of Your Feet*, is available locally; he also leads guided treks (☎697 91 62 443, ⓦalonnisoswalks.co.uk).

## Patitíri and around

The island's southeastern corner contains almost its entire population and most of its visitors. **PATITÍRI**, port and de facto capital, occupies a sheltered bay flanked by steep, pine-tufted cliffs and ringed by bars, cafés and tavernas. It's a bit soulless – much is modern, built after the 1965 earthquake (see below) – but it has tried to compensate with a stone-paved waterfront and general tidy-up, while the unassuming streets shelter some unexpectedly fancy shops. The waterfront **MOM Information Centre** (daily 10am–4pm & 6–10pm; free; ⓦmom.gr), above the *Avra* café, next to the *Alkyon Hotel*, has models and multimedia displays about the endangered **monk seal** (see p.687). In an unmissable stone building above the western side of the harbour, the **Alonissos Museum** (daily May, Sept & Oct 11am–7pm, June–Aug 11am–9pm; €4) is crammed with local artwork, traditional costumes, reconstructed island interiors, war memorabilia, wine-making equipment, and exhibits on piracy and seafaring.

Immediately outside Patitíri, **ROUSSOÚM YIALÓS** and adjoining **VÓTSI**, each with a little fishing harbour, are virtually suburbs. You can walk to the beach at Roussoúm, down steps from town, which is considerably more pleasant than swimming in Patitíri itself. Both offer pleasant, good-value rooms and tavernas.

### Hóra

**HÓRA (Paleá Alónissos)**, the island's original settlement, was severely damaged by a Sporades-wide earthquake in March 1965, after which most of the reluctant population was compulsorily moved to Patitíri (see above); the issue was essentially forced in 1977 by the school's closure and cutting off of electricity. Outsiders later acquired the abandoned houses for a song and restored them in variable taste; only a few locals still live here, which gives the village a very twee, un-Greek atmosphere, abetted by multiple knick-knack and crafts shops. But it's stunningly picturesque, with great views as far as Mount Áthos in clear conditions. For much of the year, and indeed for much of most days, there are more hedgehogs than people about; the place only really comes to life – noisily so – on midsummer evenings. As an alternative to the bus ride, you can walk up on a well-preserved *kalderími* (45min uphill, 30min down), signposted off Patitíri's western inland street, almost at the edge of town.

### Southern beaches

Numerous small cove beaches surround Alónissos's southern tip. Closest to Patitíri is **Výthisma** – less than 1km down a track off the road to **Marpoúnda** beach (monopolized by an all-inclusive Italian complex) and then a scramble down into the cove. Look out for the latest signs, as the paths down are regularly washed out. The grey sand-and-pebble beach is pretty, and part nudist, but without facilities or shade. **Megálos Mourtiás** is just a short swim further round, and there is a path which continues that way, but most people get here on the steep paved road from Hóra. With bright white pebbles and two tavernas, it's a complete contrast; crowded and noisy. **Mikrós Mourtiás**, just west, is served by a well-maintained footpath from Hóra (#1), or you can get most of the way down on a driveable dirt track. Another enclosed cove, it has graffiti proclaiming it a nudist beach – though in practice it doesn't seem to be. Immediately north of Hóra, visible tucked into their respective finger-like inlets, compact **Vrysítsa** and **Yiália** (with a picturesque windmill) both have more sand than pebbles, but no facilities.

## ACCOMMODATION PATITÍRI AND AROUND

Most Alónissos accommodation is in Patitíri or immediately around; you may be approached with offers as you disembark at the port. Albedo Travel (☎ 24240 65804, ⓦ albedotravel.com) handles hotels, studios and villas across the island, while the local room-owners' association booth (☎ 24240 66188, ⓦ alonissos-rooms.gr), on the waterfront, can also find you a room.

### PATITÍRI

**Nereides Hotel** Paliohoráfina ☎ 24240 65643, ⓦ nereides.gr. Classy place high above the western edge of town, with stunning views, small pool and recently refurbished rooms, studios and family apartments, all with free wi-fi, flat-screen TVs, modern wooden furniture, and quality bathrooms. Very good deals out of season. Breakfast included. **€100**

**Paradise Hotel** ☎ 24240 65213, ⓦ paradise-hotel .gr. Two-star hotel above the eastern side of the harbour, overlooking Roussoúm, with pool, bar, and an exceptionally friendly welcome. Plain rooms have a/c and balcony but no TV; many have views over the bay. Breakfast included. **€70**

**Pension Pleiades** ☎ 24240 65235, ⓦ pleiadeshotel .gr. Fairly simple studio rooms, plus a couple of apartments available year-round (with a/c and heating), above the harbour in a backstreet behind Albedo Travel. Few have unobstructed views from their balconies, but you can enjoy those from the restaurant downstairs – there's also a washing machine and free wi-fi for guest use. **€50**

### HÓRA

**Elma's Houses** ☎ 24240 66108, ⓦ elmashouses.com. Two exquisitely restored studios (a one-bed and a two-bed) and two houses in the upper part of the village. They accommodate up to four people, and are beautifully furnished from the owner's Gorgona antique shop; upmarket, but worth it. **€75**

**Fantasia House** ☎ 24240 65186. Beamed ceilings and a terrace with amazing views to the south and east are the big attractions of these simple, a/c rooms, off the main square at the bottom of the village. **€60**

**Konstantina's Studios** ☎ 24240 66165, ⓦ konstantina studios.gr. A renovated building in the lower part of the village, past *Fantasia*, with eight fully equipped studios and one apartment, all enjoying exceptional views. There's a lovely garden, and Konstantina will collect you from the port on request. **€80**

### VÓTSI

**Hippocampus** ☎ 24240 65886, ⓦ hippocampus.com .gr. Modern block of studios and apartments on the road down to the bay whose balconies have fine views down over Vótsi and out to sea. Comfortable tiled-floor rooms have a/c, TV and functional kitchenettes. **€70**

## EATING AND DRINKING

Though there's no shortage of places to eat in Patitíri, only a couple stand out from the crowd; nightlife here consists of a few music bars over on the western side of the harbour, below the museum. There's generally better, if pricier, food, and more night-time activity, up in Hóra. Hóra's main street is lined with restaurants, mostly with wonderful views, but few that are good value or particularly high quality. Locals and those in the know tend to eat further down, or in the backstreets.

### PATITÍRI

**Archipelagos** Harbour ☎ 24240 65031. The waterfront restaurants are generally nothing special; an exception, popular with locals, is *Archipelagos*, at the bottom of the western street, with good mezédhes, fish and traditional Greek cooking – plus excellent home-made chips. Daily lunch & dinner.

**Pleiades** ☎ 24240 65235. On a terrace overlooking the harbour (signed uphill behind Albedo Travel), *Pleiades* makes a conscious attempt to offer something different, with more elegant than usual tableware and dishes such as seafood chowder, chicken in lemon and ginger, and a choice of puddings; there's a daily special for €10. Regular events including live music, barbecues and quizzes make it

popular with expats. Daily from 7.30pm.

**To Kamaki** ☎ 24240 65245. Authentic, welcoming ouzerí on the eastern street, 150m from the waterfront. Portions are not huge but the seafood-heavy menu encompasses unusual dishes like crab croquettes, skate and *tsitsíravo* shoots. Meze €4–5, mains €7.50–9. Dinner daily, plus lunch at weekends.

### HÓRA

**Acquasanta** ☎ 693 28 32 748. An elegant hideaway (signed off the main street, just above the square) with a predominantly Italian menu, not badly priced considering the sophisticated food, swish surroundings and sparkling vistas from the terrace; pasta and fish are the specialities

**10**

10

but not all they serve, and there's also a children's menu. Daily, evenings only.

**Astrofeyia** ☎ 24240 65182. Unusual (for Greece) dishes like chicken curry or chile con carne (each €10) as well as vegetarian options and more ambitious offerings such as calamari with a cream, garlic and saffron wine sauce, all served on a terrace with a friendly welcome and great view, not far from the lower square. Daily, evenings only.

⭐ **Hayiati** Right at the end of the main street, *Hayiati* has probably the best view in Hóra (which is saying something); an unbeatable setting for coffees and traditional sweets like *kazandibí*. In the evening it's a piano bar with occasional live music. Cocktail prices are steep, but otherwise not too bad considering the location, though it can be very busy. Daily all day.

**Peri Orexeos** ☎ 24240 65186. Not a very glamorous setting, on the lower square, by the bus stop, but the food is a great deal better than you might guess from the fast-food style menu. Snacks, sandwiches and burgers as well as Greek standards, but also delicious, innovative salads and dishes like honey-and-lemon pork belly, or paella-like fried rice with tuna. Daily lunch & dinner.

### ROUSSOÚM

**Remezzo** ☎ 24240 65123. Tranquil spot by the little fishing harbour and beach serving coffee and breakfast early, taverna standards and spit-roast meat at lunch and dinner. Good value, and frequent live music in the evenings. Daily all day.

## Northern Alónissos

A single road runs northeast from Patitíri up the spine of the island, giving access to beaches, almost exclusively on the east coast. The first turning, though, heads westwards to **Tsoukaliá**, a scruffy cove signed as an archeological site; there was an ancient kiln here, and pottery continued to be made until recently, so thousands upon thousands of potsherds strew the closed, fenced site and beach.

First of the east-coast beaches are **Miliá** and **Khryssí Miliá**: the former is busy, with white pebbles, piney cliffs, a *kantína* and watersports in summer; the latter sandy and beautiful, and hence very busy, with loungers and beach bars. Next up is scenic **Kokkinókastro**, named for the red-rock cliffs which overlook it. Pebbles on a red-sand base extend both sides of a promontory, and there's a seasonal bar,. Another road leads to **Leftós Yialós** and **Tzórtzi Yialós**: the pretty white-pebble beach at Leftós, with its tavernas and loud beach bars, attracts plenty of day-trip boats; Tzórtzi is smaller and less attractive, but much quieter.

**STENÍ VÁLA**, about halfway up the east coast, is the biggest settlement away from the island's southern corner, though still barely a village. There are plenty of rooms, while the harbourfront shops and tavernas attract yachts and day-trip boats. A long pebble beach – **Glýfa** – lies immediately north, and a better, partly sandy one, **Áyios Pétros**, is a ten-minute walk south. **KALAMÁKIA**, the next hamlet north, has no beach but does have a timeless fishing-port feel and some great waterfront **tavernas**. At **Áyios Dhimítrios**, the final beach easily accessible by road, brilliantly white pebbles stretch around both sides of a narrow point; the south-facing side has loungers and a couple of café/bars, the other is quite undeveloped. **Yérakas**, almost at the island's northern tip, is the end of the road and feels like it; there's a tiny fishing harbour in the deep bay and a dirty-white pebble beach where a snack truck parks in summer – the water, however, is spectacularly clean and clear.

### ACTIVITIES

**Scuba diving** There's a good diving outfit, Ikion Diving (☎ 24240 65158, ⊛ ikiondiving.gr), at Steni Vála.

### ACCOMMODATION AND EATING

**Eleonas** Leftós Yialós ☎ 24240 66066. Set in an olive grove immediately behind the beach, this is the better of the popular tavernas at Leftós Yialós. Alónissos pies (from €8) are their speciality, from excellent plain cheese to more exotic octopus and goat varieties. Prices are relatively high but portions big – a single pie and a salad makes a substantial lunch for two. Daily lunch & dinner.

**Margarita** Kalamákia ☎ 24240 65738. The best of four tavernas lined up along the quayside, each with its own fishing boat, *Margarita* serves excellent fish and mezédhes. They also have simple a/c rooms out back. Daily lunch & dinner. Rooms €50

**Milia Bay Hotel Apartments** Miliá ☎ 24240 66032, ⊛ milia-bay.gr. Great position above Miliá beach, where

## THE MEDITERRANEAN MONK SEAL

The **Mediterranean monk seal** (*Monachus monachus*) has the dubious distinction of being the most endangered European mammal – fewer than 600 survive, almost half or them here, the rest elsewhere in the Aegean or around islands off the coast of West Africa.

Females have one **pup** about every two years, which can live for 45 years, attaining 2m in length and over 200kg as **adults**. Formerly pups were reared in the open, but disturbance by man led to whelping seals retreating to isolated sea caves with partly submerged entrances. Without spending weeks on a local boat, your chances of seeing a seal are slim (marine-park cruises are far more likely to spot dolphins; if seals are spotted (usually dozing on the shore or swimming in the open sea), keep a deferential distance.

Monk seals can swim 200km a day in search of food – and compete with fishermen in the overfished Aegean, often destroying nets. Until recently fishermen routinely killed seals; this occasionally still happens, but the establishment of the **National Marine Park of Alónissos-Northern Sporades** has helped by banning September–November fishing northeast of Alónissos and prohibiting it altogether within 1.5 nautical miles of Pipéri. These measures have won local support through the efforts of the **Hellenic Society for the Protection of the Monk Seal** (ⓦmom.gr; see p.684), even among Sporadean fishermen, who realize that the restrictions should help restore local fish stocks. The society has reared several abandoned seal pups (bad weather often separates them from their mothers), subsequently released in the sea around Alónissos.

the modern studios and apartments have views out to sea over the landscaped grounds as well as being handy for town. There's a pool and pool-bar. **€110**

**Sossinola** Stêni Vála ☎24240 65776, ⓦsossinola.gr. Harbourfront taverna that also has modern, a/c studios and two-room apartments, with balconies looking out over the harbour or out to sea. Plenty of fish on the menu, plus Alónissos pies and a meaty goat in tomato sauce. Daily lunch & dinner. Studios & apartments **€80**

## The National Marine Park of Alónissos-Northern Sporades

ⓦalonissos-park.gr

Founded in 1992, the **National Marine Park** protects monk seals, dolphins, wild goats and rare seabirds in an area encompassing Alónissos plus a dozen **islets** speckling the Aegean to the east. None of these (save one) has any permanent population, but a few can be visited by excursion boats, weather permitting. **Pipéri** islet forms the core zone of the park – an off-limits seabird and monk-seal refuge, approachable only by government-authorized scientists. **Peristéra**, opposite Alónissos, is uninhabited, though some Alonissans cross to tend olive groves in the south; it's little visited by excursion craft except for a brief swim-stop at the end of a cruise. Well-watered **Kyrá Panayiá**, the next islet out, has a tenth-century monastery whose old bakery and wine/olive presses, restored in the 1990s, are maintained by one farmer-monk. Nearby **Yioúra** has a stalactite cave which mythically sheltered Homer's Cyclops, plus the main wild-goat population, but you won't see either as *kaïkia* must keep 400m clear of the shore. Tiny, northernmost **Psathoúra** is dominated by its powerful lighthouse, the tallest in the Aegean; some excursions stop for a swim at a pristine, white-sand beach.

# Skýros

Despite its natural beauty, **SKÝROS** has a relatively low profile. There are few major sites or resorts, and access, wherever you're coming from, is awkward. Those in the know, however, realise it's worth the effort, and there are increasing numbers of trendy Athenians and Thessalonians taking advantage of domestic flights – and making Skýros Town a much more cosmopolitan place than you might expect – plus steadily growing international tourism. The New Age Skyros Centre, pitched mostly at Brits, has also effectively publicized the place. There are plenty of **beaches**, but few that can rival the sand of

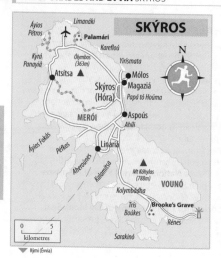

Skiáthos or film-set scenery of Skópelos. There's also a substantial air-force presence around the airport in the north, and a big naval base in the south; almost all the accommodation and tourist facilities cluster around Skýros Town in the centre of the island.

A position bang in the centre of the Aegean has guaranteed the island a busy **history**: it was occupied from prehistory, with a truly impressive Bronze Age settlement currently being excavated, was a vital Athenian outpost in the Classical era, and an equally important naval base for the Byzantines and under Venetian and Turkish rule, when it was an important staging post on the sea-lanes to Constantinople.

## ARRIVAL AND DEPARTURE

SKÝROS

**By plane** Sky Express (w skyexpress.gr) operate three flights a week (2 only Oct–April) from Athens (40min) to Skýros to Thessaloníki (40min) and back. The airport is about 10km from town; there's no public transport, so you'll have to take a taxi or rent a car – a Pegasus car rental booth opens at flight times (see p.690).

**By ferry** Skyros Shipping (w sne.gr) sail daily from Kými, on Évvia (see p.696), to Linariá, Skýros's port. The crossing takes around 1hr 45min and leaves Kými every evening, returning from Skýros early in the morning. In July and August there are additional daytime crossings several times a week (especially at weekends), and a twice-weekly connection via Kými to

Alónissos and Skópelos. To get to Kými there are direct KTEL buses from Athens' Liossion bus station, with early afternoon departures connecting with the ferry, or Skyros Travel (t 22220 91600, w skyrostravel.com) organizes two transfers a week direct from Athens airport (Mon & Fri early afternoon, €58 per person including ferry ticket).

**Agents and tickets** Skyros Travel, about 100m above the platía on the main street in Skýros Town, is the local agent for both plane and ferry tickets (Mon–Sat 9.15am–1.30pm & 6.45–10pm, Sun 9.45am–1.45pm & 7–10pm; timetables and other useful info displayed outside); they also have a ticket office in Linariá that opens an hour before departures.

## INFORMATION

**Services** The post office and National Bank (with ATM) are on the platía in Skýros Town, and there's a further ATM higher up the main street; the most reliable internet café is Xanthoulis (w Mano.com), also on the main street.

**Useful website** w skyros.gr.
**Newspapers** English-language newspapers are sold from a hut opposite the platía in Skýros Town.

## CARNIVAL ON SKÝROS

Skýros has a particularly outrageous *apokriátika* (pre-Lenten) **carnival**, featuring its famous **goat dance**, performed by groups of masked revellers in the streets of Hóra. The leaders of each troupe are the **yéri**, menacing figures (usually men but sometimes sturdy women) dressed in goat-pelt capes, weighed down by huge garlands of sheep bells, their faces concealed by kid-skin masks, and brandishing shepherds' crooks. Accompanying them are their "brides", men in drag known as **korélles** (maidens), and **frángi** (maskers in assorted "Western" garb). When two such groups meet, the *yéri* compete to see who can ring their bells longest and loudest with arduous body movements, or even get into brawls using their crooks as cudgels.

These rites take place on each of the four weekends before Clean Monday (see p.45), but the final one is more for the benefit of tourists, both Greek and foreign. The Skyrians are less exhausted and really let their (goat) hair down for each other during the preceding three weeks. Most local hotels open for the duration, and you have to book rooms well in advance.

KASTÁNI AND MILIÁ BEACHES (P.686) >

**10**

## GETTING AROUND

**By bus** Buses run five times daily between Skýros Town and Linariá (€1.60), connecting with the ferries; in town the bus stop is near the bottom of the main street, by the school. In summer there are also four buses daily from Linariá to Magaziá and Mólos via town, and two daily from Skýros Town to Kalamítsa.

**By taxi** There are plenty of taxis (☎ 22220 91666) to meet the ferries, with taxi stands by the main square in town, and close to the bus stop.

**By car and scooter** Skyros Travel (see p.688) rent cars (trading as Pegasus; ☎ 22220 91600, ⬥ skyrosrentacar .com), or you can get scooters from several places including Vagios (☎ 22220 92957), in a side street just below the main square in town.

# Skýros Town and around

Once through the rather scruffy outskirts, **SKÝROS TOWN (Hóra)** is a beautiful place, its Cycladic-style white, flat-roofed, red-tiled houses clinging to the inland slope of a pinnacle rising precipitously from the coast. In legend, King Lykomedes raised the young Achilles in his palace here, and also pushed Theseus to his death from the summit. A single main street leads up to a central platía; beyond that, cobbled and increasingly narrow and traffic-free, lies a 150m stretch lined with almost everything you'll need – shops, many of them selling classy jewellery, crafts and antiques, restaurants, banks and sophisticated bars. Wander off the main street and the place is suddenly bigger than it first seemed. There are always fascinating glimpses – covered passageways, churches and front doors open to reveal traditional house interiors with gleaming copperware, antique embroideries and the proud local crafts of painted ceramics and elaborately carved wooden furniture.

### Kástro

The Byzantine-Venetian **kástro** atop the ancient **acropolis** above town is a very steep climb, so unless you're interested in seeing the picturesque old quarter along the way, you may want to check that it is open following reconstruction – it was badly damaged by an earthquake in 2001. Even from outside there are great views; inside is the Byzantine **monastery of Áyios Yeóryios**.

### Rupert Brooke memorial

The British poet Rupert Brooke is always associated with Skýros, though in fact he spent only a few days here, arriving as a naval officer off the south of the island on April 17, 1915, and dying six days later of blood poisoning on a French hospital ship. He lies buried in an olive grove above the bay of Trís Boúkes (see p.693). The **Rupert Brooke memorial** comprises a nude bronze statue of "Immortal Poetry", in a quiet square overlooking the coast; it's right on the edge of town, reached by following the main street uphill and taking the signed left fork, or by steps up from Magaziá.

### The archeological museum

Below the Rupert Brooke memorial • Tues–Sun 8.30am–3pm • €2

Skýros's two-room **archeological museum** is far better than you might expect, with the added bonus of a lovely setting above the sea. The highlights are Early Bronze Age pottery, obsidian axe-heads and stone blades and tools from Palamári (see p.692); later artefacts include a Geometric-era ceramic rhyton in the form of a Skyrian pony and a vase with eight ducks being beset by snakes. There's also a side room in the form of a traditional Skyrian house, with carved wooden screen and furniture.

### Manos Faltaïts Museum

Below the Rupert Brooke memorial • Daily 10am–2pm & 6–9pm • €2 • ⬥ faltaits.gr

An early nineteenth-century mansion built over a bastion in the ancient walls houses the eccentric **Manos Faltaïts Museum**, in the family home of a prolific local painter. Along with his own works it's an Aladdin's cave of local history and folklore, with traditional furnishings and costumes, curios and books.

## Magaziá and Mólos

Immediately below Skýros Town, reached by a direct stairway or more roundabout roads, is the beach hamlet of **MAGAZIÁ**. From here a long sandy beach extends to **MÓLOS**; these days the two are pretty much joined by low-key, low-rise development – much of the island's accommodation is down here, along with plenty of restaurants and a couple of lively beach bars. Around the point beyond Mólos, a much more exposed beach is punctuated by rock outcrops, whose weird, squared-off shapes are the result of Roman (and later) quarrying rather than natural erosion; one monolith, by the cape with its snack-bar/windmill, has a rock-hewn chapel inside.

**10**

## Linariá

**LINARIÁ**, where the ferries dock, is a pleasant enough place, with plenty of options for eating and drinking if you're waiting for a boat, but little reason to stay. In high season, **excursion boats** (€30 including lunch) offer trips to the islet of **Sarakinó**, with its white-sand beach, stopping at various sea-caves en route. Should you want to stay around here, the next little bay, **Aheroúnes**, is a peaceful spot with a much better beach, only about fifteen minutes' walk away.

### ACCOMMODATION | SKÝROS TOWN AND AROUND

#### SKÝROS TOWN

★ **Nefeli** ☎ 22220 91964, ⓦ skyros-nefeli.gr. The island's plushest hotel, on the main road as you enter town, has a range of lovely designer rooms, studios and apartments, arrayed around a large salt-water pool. Breakfast (included) on an outdoor terrace and free wi-fi in the lobby. **€120**

**Pension Nikolas** ☎ 22220 91778, ⓔ pension_nicholas @hotmail.com. Located on the edge of town, this friendly rooms establishment offers doubles and quads; many have traditional wooden sleeping platforms, and all have a/c and TVs. **€60**

#### MAGAZIÁ/MÓLOS

**Angela** Mólos ☎ 22220 91764, ⓦ angelahotelskyros .com. Large complex of two-storey rooms and studios, close to the beach at the northern end of Mólos, beyond the harbour, in extensive gardens around a pool. All with a/c, TV and fridge, some with kitchenette. **€90**

★ **Perigiali** Magaziá ☎ 22220 92075, ⓦ perigiali .com. Sparkling new rooms, studios and family apartments

around a good-sized pool, in a narrow lane behind the beach at the southern end of Magaziá. A few have sea views, though most look over the gardens, and there are a few simpler, cheaper rooms in the original wing; all have a/c, wi-fi and cooking facilities. **€100**

**Yeoryia Tsakami** Magaziá ☎ 22220 91357, ⓔ gtsakamis@yahoo.gr. Simple, old-fashioned rooms with fridge and electric ring, in a great position directly behind the beach. Most have private balcony at the back, with communal terrace at the front. **€50**

#### LINARIÁ/AHEROÚNES

**King Lykomides** Linariá ☎ 22220 93249, ⓔ soula @skyrosnet.gr. Spotless *dhomátia* with wooden-shuttered balconies overlooking the harbour; all have a/c and tv, some with cooking facilities. **€60**

**Pegasus** Aheroúnes ☎ 22220 93442, ⓦ skyrosvillas .com. A variety of studios and apartments, most with good views, in a tranquil spot behind the beach. All come with a/c, TV and a friendly welcome. **€70**

### EATING, DRINKING AND NIGHTLIFE

#### SKÝROS TOWN

**Akamatra** Main square ☎ 22220 29029. Large, fancy bar on two floors, with leather seating and terraces overlooking both platía and street. Open during the day for coffee, and regular DJ events till the early hours. Daily 10am–2am.

**Kalypso** Main street ☎ 22220 92696. The last of the places as you climb the street, *Kalypso* is a long-established café-bar with a jazz and blues soundtrack, attracting a slightly older, more touristy crowd than the places around the platía, though it can get lively later on. Daily from around 7pm.

**Maryetis** Main street ☎ 22220 91311. Much the most

popular place in town, with only a few tables on the street-side terrace, opposite Skyros Travel, so you may well have to wait. Simple Greek oven dishes and grilled meat or fish at reasonable prices are the attraction, washed down with decent house wine. Daily lunch & dinner.

#### MAGAZIÁ/MÓLOS

**Asterias** Mólos ☎ 22220 93008. Excellent restaurant on the waterfront platía with a pretty beachfront terrace and sunbeds below for customer use. There's no printed menu – usually a good sign – just half a dozen daily specials reeled off by the waiter, plus the usual salads and sides. Daily lunch & dinner.

**10**

## SKYRIAN HORSES

Skýros has a race of **native pony**, related to the breeds found on Exmoor and Dartmoor. They are thought to be the diminutive steeds depicted in the Parthenon frieze; according to legend, Achilles went off to fight at Troy mounted on a chestnut specimen. In more recent times they were used for summer threshing; communally owned, they were left to graze wild ten months of the year on Vounó, from where each family rounded up the ponies they needed. Currently only about 150 individuals survive, and the breed is **threatened** by the decline of local agriculture, indifference and cross-breeding. To be classed as a true Skyrian pony, the animal must be 98–115cm in height, and 130cm maximum from shoulder to tail. They're elusive in the wild, but you can see (and ride) them at the centre opposite *Mouries* restaurant (opposite).

★ **ly Istories tou Barba** Mólos ☎22220 91453. Lovely setting with blue chairs on a blue terrace above the Magaziá end of Mólos beach. The food is traditional and interesting – crab salad, or cuttlefish with fennel sauce and leeks – the atmosphere also, with black-and-white photos of old island life in the menu. Daily lunch & dinner.

**Juicy Beach Bar** Magaziá ☎22220 93337. Beach bar with loungers and umbrellas, plus a terrace with food (sandwiches, crêpes, pasta), free wi-fi and a bar. Quiet music by day, cranked up at night with summer events such as a full moon party. Daily all day, breakfast till the early hours.

**Stefanos** Magaziá ☎22220 91272. Attractive, traditional taverna with wooden tables on a terrace hanging out over the sand at the southern end of Magaziá beach. Standard dishes like stifádo (€9) or lamb with potatoes (€7.50) are deliciously prepared. Daily all day.

**Thalassa** Mólos beach ☎22220 92044. Beach bar by day, with wi-fi, sunbeds, bar and snacks, cocktail bar and club at night, when there's a huge dance space, though that is only really busy in August. Daily 9am–3am.

### LINARIÁ

**Kavos** All-day bar tumbling down a rocky cliff on a series of terraces, with steps down to a private swimming area below. Quiet daytime sounds which are often turned up loud to greet the evening ferry; wi-fi, drinks and light meals, plus late-night revelry in mid-season. Daily 10am–late.

**Psariotis** ☎22220 93250. Probably the best of the tavernas around Linariá's harbour, Psariotis has its own boat to catch fish, which is marginally less expensive than elsewhere. Also a good fish soup (€10) or lobster spaghetti (€20), plus plenty of standard Greek dishes at regular prices. Daily lunch & dinner.

# Merói

A single paved road loops around Skyros's northern half, **Merói**. Heading anticlockwise from Hóra the first possible stop is at secluded **Kareflóu** beach, 1.5km down a poorly signed rough track. Sandy and extensive, it's also exposed with no facilities at all.

## Palamári

Mon–Fri 7.30am–2.30pm • Free

The early Bronze Age settlement of **Palamári**, inhabited from around 2800 to 1600 BC, and then lost for 3500 years, is set on the ridge of a low cape at the northeastern edge of the island, above a beach and a river which once formed a lagoon and natural harbour. The site, still being excavated, is extraordinary: you can make out the houses, streets, drainage and walls of a well-organized city, which must have been at the heart of Aegean trading in the Minoan era. Informative signage and a small exhibition fill in the background.

## Atsítsa and around

Past the airport at the island's northern tip, the west coast is infinitely greener, heavily forested in pine. Around 2.5km of rough track leads to a couple of the island's most scenic and remote beaches: nudist **Áyios Pétros**, more respectable **Limanáki**, right by the airport almost at the end of the runway, and still more isolated **Agalípa**. **Atsítsa** itself is well-known as the home of the Skyros Centre; its attractive, pine-fringed bay is sheltered by an islet and has lovely clear water for swimming, but not much of a beach.

Beyond Atsítsa, you can head back across the centre of the island on a good dirt road through the woods, or carry on around the coast, through an area devastated by forest fire in 2007 and still characterized by charred stumps. **Áyios Fokás**, in the heart of this area, is a quiet, sandy beach that makes a great lunch spot; the descent through woods to deeply indented **Péfkos**, the best of the southwest-coast bays with a fine, long, sandy beach, offers spectacular views.

### EATING AND DRINKING                                        MERÓI

**10**

**Perasma** ☎ 22220 92911. Excellent, reasonably priced taverna at the junction of the airport road not far from Palamári; apparently in the middle of nowhere, but with plenty of custom from local air-force families. Family-style cooking based on local produce, much of it organic and produced in the taverna's own fields, served beneath a shady awning. Daily lunch & dinner.

**Taverna tis Kira Kalis** Áyios Fokás. A wonderfully out-of-the-way lunch spot, with octopus and sardines thrown on a charcoal grill on the beach and simple Greek home-style cooking. Lush vines and pot plants compensate for the burnt slopes roundabout. Daily lunch & dinner.

## Vounó

South of Skýros Town you turn off at **Aspoús**, where there's a decent, grey-sand beach, to reach **Vounó**. Much of this southern half of the island, especially as you ascend **Mount Kóhylas**, is almost eerily barren, home only to goats and a few stunted trees, but it's here also – high on the mountain – that you're most likely to see wild Skyrian horses and other wildlife, including abundant Eleonora's falcon. En route there's a narrow pebble strand at **Kalamítsa**, and a slightly better beach at **Kolymbádha**. The one sight down here is Rupert Brooke's grave at **Trís Boúkes**, a simple marble tomb inscribed with his most famous poem, *The Soldier* ("If I should die, think only this of me/That there's some corner of a foreign field/That is for ever England…"). The grave is very hard to spot: follow the turning to the naval base for just over 1km and it lies in an olive grove off to the left of the road.

### EATING AND DRINKING                                        VOUNÓ

**Mouries** Fléa ☎ 22220 93555. Big, traditional taverna in this tiny hamlet on the road between Aspoús and Kalamítsa, serving local lamb and wine under the namesake mulberries. It's very popular at weekends when they often have live Greek music, and over the road they run a Skyrian Horse Centre, with riding and pony-and-trap rides. Daily lunch & dinner.

★ **O Pappous ki Ego** ☎ 22220 93200. "My Grandfather and I", on the road approaching Kalamítsa, serves traditional Skyrian dishes such as fried bread with Skyrian cheese, and at weekends spit-roasted lamb and *kokorétsi*, plus fish, grills, pastas and risotto. Classier than your average Greek taverna, with mains around €10. Daily lunch & dinner.

# Évvia

The second largest of the Greek islands after Crete, **ÉVVIA (Euboea)** – separated only by a narrow gulf from central Greece – often feels more like an extension of the mainland than an entity in its own right. At **Halkídha**, the old drawbridge spans a mere 40m channel where Évvia was mythically split from Attica and Thessaly by a blow from Poseidon's trident. Easy access from Athens means that in summer Évvia can seem merely a beach annexe for Athens and the mainland towns across the Gulf.

Nevertheless, Évvia *is* an island, often a very beautiful one, and in many ways its problems – long distances to cover, poor communications, few concessions to tourism – are also its greatest attractions, ensuring that it has remained out of the mainstream of tourism. Exceptionally fertile, Évvia has always been a quietly prosperous place that would manage pretty well even without visitors. The classical name, Euboea, means "rich in cattle", and throughout history it has been much coveted. Today agriculture still thrives, with plenty of local goat and lamb on the menu, along with highly rated local retsina.

Évvia divides naturally into three sections, with just a single road connecting the northern and southern parts to the centre. The **south** is mountainous, barren and rocky; highlights are low-key Kárystos and hiking the nearby mountains and gorges. The **centre**, with the sprawling island capital at Halkídha, is green, wealthy and busy with both industry and agriculture, but for visitors mainly a gateway, with the bridges at Halkídha and onward transport to Skýros from the easterly port of Kými. In the **north**, grain fields, olive groves and pine forest are surrounded by the bulk of the island's resorts, most dominated by Greek holiday homes.

### ARRIVAL AND DEPARTURE ÉVVIA

**By ferry** Ferries make the short crossing from the mainland to Évvia at various points all the way up the coast: from Ráfina to Marmári, Ayía Marína to Néa Stýra, Skála Oropoú to Erétria, Arkítsa to Loutrá Edhipsoú and Glýfa to Ayiókambos. Which you choose depends on where you are heading on Évvia; most run very frequently – details are given under the individual ports.

**By car** Two bridges link Évvia to the mainland, the old drawbridge right in the heart of Halkídha and a suspension bridge on the outskirts. If you are driving you can use these or any of the ferries (more expensive, but the mainland motorway is far faster than roads on the island if you're heading to the north or south).

**By bus** KTEL buses run direct from Athens' Liossion bus station to many destinations on Évvia including Halkídha, Kárystos, Kými, Límni and Loutrá Edhipsoú. There are also buses from Athens to all of the mainland ports above.

**By train** Frequent trains connect Athens with Halkídha.

### GETTING AROUND

**By bus** Most places in Évvia can be reached by bus, but services tend to run just a couple of times a day, so if you hope to explore you'll really need a car. All the major rental companies have offices in Halkídha, and there are local operations in the resorts.

## Halkídha

Évvia's capital, **HALKÍDHA** (ancient Chalkis), has a population of around 100,000, making it one of the ten biggest cities in Greece. So it's not entirely surprising if it often has an urban feel, rather than an island one. Nonetheless the centre is compact and easy to explore, and the busy waterfront thoroughly attractive. Right at the centre, beneath the drawbridge across the narrow **Évripos channel** to the mainland, the gulf-water swirls by like a river; every few hours the current reverses. Aristotle is said to have thrown himself into the waters in despair at his inability to understand what was happening; there is still no entirely satisfactory explanation for the capricious currents.

An impressive **fortress**, floodlit at night, protects Halkídha from the mainland side. Across the bridge, Odhós Kótsou heads directly uphill towards the centre through the old **Kástro** district, where a few relics of an older city survive. Chief of these is a handsome fifteenth-century **mosque** (locked), now a warehouse of Byzantine artefacts, with an exceptionally ornate carved **Ottoman fountain** out front. Off to the right further up Kótsou you'll find the **Folklore Museum** (Wed 10am–1pm & 6–8pm, Thurs–Sun 1pm; €3). Housed in the old jail, it has a jumbled collection of costumes, furniture and local traditions in a series of reconstructed rooms. Higher up still, then left on the main street, the **archeological museum** at Venizélou 13 (Tues–Sun 8.30am–3pm; €2) offers a pleasant escape from the raucous surrounds; a tortoise roams the statuary in the shady garden, while inside there's a good display of finds from across the island.

**10**

### ARRIVAL AND DEPARTURE

HALKÍDHA

**By train** The train station is very close to the bridge on the mainland side, with at least sixteen services to and from Athens daily (6am–11pm; 1hr 25min).

**By bus** The KTEL bus station is almost 2km from the centre at Stíron 1, on the ring road at the east edge of town; local buses will take you in to the market area, but it's much easier to use a taxi (about €5). Very frequent departures to Athens (every 30min 5am–10pm; 1hr 15min), less often along all the island's main routes including to Erétria (18 daily; 30min); Kárystos (2 daily; 3hr); Kými (8 daily; 2hr); Límni (3–4 daily; 2hr); Loutrá Edhipsoú (3–4 daily; 2hr 30min).

### ACCOMMODATION

**Kentrikon** Angéli Govíou 5 ☎22210 22375, ⓦhotel-kentrikon.com. Rather forbidding nineteenth-century mansion, just up from the bridge, which conceals unexpectedly modern a/c rooms, with wi-fi and satellite TV. No real views, though. €55

**Kymata** Liáska 1 ☎22210 74724, ⓦkimata.com.gr. Simple, minimally furnished rooms above a busy main road overlooking the port; modern double glazing and a/c keep out most of the noise, and it's very good value. €45

**Lucy** Voudoúri 10 ☎22210 23831, ⓦlucy-hotel.gr. Big, high-rise Best Western hotel with luxurious rooms, many with great views across the water; all with wi-fi and cable TV. €75

### EATING AND DRINKING

A long line of cafés and restaurants extends along the waterfront to the north of the bridge; there are plenty of fancy seafood restaurants and elegant café-bars (most with wi-fi) but also a number of simpler places. Prices are lower inland towards the centre, though.

**Apanemo** Ethníkis Symfilíosis 78, Fanári ☎22210 22614. Very popular, decent-value seafood restaurant with tables on the sand; it's a good half-hour walk from the centre, just before the lighthouse at the far north end of the shoreline, so you may want to book, and/or take a taxi.

Daily lunch & dinner.

**Paralia** Voudoúri 10 ☎22210 87932. Long-established, old-fashioned, waterfront *psistariá*, serving up large portions of grilled meat at very reasonable prices; salads and oven-baked dishes too. Daily lunch & dinner.

**Tsaf** Papanastasíou 3 ☎694 81 80 857. An imposing stone building, off Platía Agorás near the top of Kótsou, houses this bustling ouzerí, with good fish and mezédhes. It's busiest late in the evening. Daily, evenings only.

## Central Évvia

The **coast road** southeast of Halkídha heads through industrial suburbs to a coastline of second homes, small hotels and beaches which make popular escapes from the city. At **Lépoura** it forks, to the right for the south of the island, left to curl around towards the east coast and **Kými**. Beyond Kými you can cut back across the mountainous heart of the island via **Metóhi** and **Stení**, a spectacular road with a short unpaved section.

**10**

## Erétria

Modern **ERÉTRIA** is a dull-looking resort on a grid plan; for most travellers its main asset is a ferry service across to Skála Oropoú. The place deserves a closer look, though. For a start it boasts some of the best **beaches** on this stretch of coast, to the east of the harbour, and more importantly it preserves the remains of **Ancient Eretria**, the most impressive on the island. Eretria was an important city from the eighth century BC to the sixth century AD, flourishing above all around 400 BC following the decline of Athens. First stop on your exploration should be the **museum** (Tues–Sun 8.30am–3pm; €2), on the edge of town by the main road, where you can pick up a leaflet with a map showing all the main sites around town. Among the museum's displays of ceramics, statues and jewellery, labelled mainly in Greek and French, the tenth-century BC Lefkandi Centaur stands out – a lovely piece and one of the earliest known examples of figurative pottery. There are also fascinating models of the ancient city.

It's worth crossing the road from the museum to see the overgrown West Gate and **theatre**, but of the other sites, many of them locked, the unarguable highlight is the **House of Mosaics**. Here, under a modern cover, four magnificent mosaic floors dating from around 370 BC have been preserved, vividly depicting animals and mythical scenes.

### ARRIVAL AND DEPARTURE
ERÉTRIA

**By ferry** Ferries shuttle the short crossing to Skála Oropoú roughly every 20min (6.30am–9.30pm; 25min; ☎ 22290 62201 or 64990).

**By bus** Erétria is linked to Halkídha (18 daily; 30min).

### ACCOMMODATION

**Eviana Beach** Oníron ☎ 22290 62113, ⊛ evianabeach .gr. Smart hotel at the start of the beach road, right behind the beach, handy for town and with great sea views; all the rooms have balcony, wi-fi and attractive modern decor. **€60**

## Kálamos

The most accessible of a number of beautiful coves on the west coast is **Kálamos**, about 7km down narrow lanes from Neohóri on the main road. This stretch of the main road is dotted with medieval remains – Byzantine chapels and watchtowers which gave warning of approaching pirates. Kálamos itself is a tiny but stunning cove enclosing a sandy beach, surrounded by half a dozen tavernas and rooms establishments. In August it's packed; the rest of the year often deserted.

### ACCOMMODATION AND EATING
KÁLAMOS

**Tota Marinou** ☎ 22230 41881. One of many simple rooms places right behind the beach, with a welcoming waterfront taverna too. Restaurant open lunch & dinner. **€50**

## Kými

**KÝMI** consists of two parts: the ferry port, properly known as Paralía Kýmis, and the upper town, 4km up a spectacularly winding road. The port offers plenty of accommodation and a long row of harbourfront restaurants and cafés should you be waiting for a ferry, but the upper town is far more attractive, with great views towards Skýros from its lush, green hillside location. There's a small **folklore museum** (daily 10am–1pm & 6–8.30pm; €2) with costumes, rural implements and old photos recording the doings of Kymians both locally and in the US, home to a huge emigrant community. Among them was Dr George Papanikolaou, deviser of the "Pap" cervical smear test, who is honoured with a statue up on the platía.

**By bus** Buses generally drop off in the upper town, except for those connecting with Skýros ferries; there are 8 daily to Halkídha (2hr) and 5 to Athens (4hr).

**By ferry** Skyros Shipping (☎ 22220 22020, ⓦ sne.gr) sail every evening to Linariá on Skýros (1hr 45min), returning from Skýros early in the morning. In July and August there are additional daytime crossings several times a week (especially at weekends), and a twice-weekly connection to Alónissos (2hr 30min) and Skópelos (3hr 20min). The ticket office is on the quayside; Athens buses connect with all the ferries.

**ACCOMMODATION AND EATING**

**Hotel Beis** Waterfront ☎ 22220 22604, ⓦ hotel-beis .gr. A straightforward, good-value four-storey hotel, very handy for the ferries, whose a/c rooms have balconies overlooking the harbour. **€60**

**Ouzeri Skyros** Waterfront ☎ 22220 22641. 150m north of the jetty, past the *Hotel Beis*, so quieter than the places right by the harbour. A terrace over the water and blue-and-white decor lend a classic island look. Good mezédhes. Daily lunch & dinner.

**10**

## Stení

At bustling Néa Artáki, 5km north of Halkídha, a side road leads east to **STENÍ**, a village-cum-hill-station at the foot of Mount Dhírfys. There are marked hiking trails up the mountain, Évvia's highest summit where traces of snow survive till early summer, and it's a beautiful place, cool in summer and full of rushing streams. It's also pretty much the halfway point of a wonderfully scenic **road link to Kými**, all paved except for 8km just before Metóhi; it's 51km or 95 minutes' drive (follow signposting for Metóhi if starting from Kými).

**Steni** ☎ 22280 51221. Cosy, welcoming hotel towards the top of the village with spectacular views from its sumptuous common areas and simple, comfortable if rather small rooms with modern bathrooms. **€60**

**Vrahos** ☎ 22280 51546. Numerous tavernas specializing in meaty fare line the road as it passes through Steni, all popular for weekend outings. *O Vrahos*, on the village-centre platía, is the most atmospheric, with seating under a mulberry tree and views of the village goings-on. Daily lunch & dinner.

# Southern Évvia

So narrow that you sometimes spot the sea on both sides, mountainous **southern Évvia** is often barren, bleak and windswept. The single road from the north is winding and tortuous – most people who come here arrive by ferry, and though Greeks have holiday homes in numerous coastal spots there's really just one attractive resort, at **Kárystos**.

Heading south by road you'll pass what maps mark as **Lake Dhýstos**; these days it has been largely reclaimed as farmland, and there's barely any water. Atop conical Kastrí hill on the east shore are sparse fifth-century BC ruins of **ancient Dystos** and a medieval citadel. At **STÝRA**, 35km from Lépoura, three **dhrakóspita** ("dragon houses") are signposted and reachable by track. So named because only dragons were thought capable of installing the enormous masonry blocks, their origins and purpose remain obscure. The shore annexe of **NÉA STÝRA**, 3.5km downhill, is a dull, Greek-frequented resort, worth knowing about only for its handy ferry connection to Ayía Marína. Much the same is true of **MARMÁRI**, 20km south, except here the link is with Rafína. Both have plenty of food and accommodation should you be stuck waiting for a bus or ferry.

**By ferry** There are at least a dozen ferries daily shuttling between Néa Stýra and Ayía Marína (45min; information ☎ 22240 41533), and five to eight a day linking Marmári and Rafína (4–6 Oct–April; 1hr; information ☎ 22240 32340). Tickets are sold on the quayside.

**By bus** Most ferries in Marmári are met by a bus to Kárystos (4 daily). In Néa Stýra buses (3 daily) stop on the main street, inland from the front. Connecting buses link Athens Mavrommatéon terminal with both Rafína (see p.118) and Ayía Marína.

10

## Kárystos

KÁRYSTOS is a delightfully old-fashioned, thoroughly Greek resort, strung out along a broad bay flanked by good (if often windy) beaches. It's a quiet place – even in August, when thousands of Greeks descend, they're a fairly staid crowd – but its attractions grow on you; graceful Neoclassical buildings in the centre, endearingly old-fashioned shops and tavernas, and a magnificent setting. On the main town **beach**, west of the centre, there are beach bars, sunbeds and kayak rental; further out this way, and around the bay to the east, there are plenty of empty patches of sand.

Though a place of some importance in antiquity, mentioned by Homer and a rival of Athens, there's very little trace now of this history: only a fenced-in **Roman heroön** or mausoleum, a block from the water at the corner of Kotsíka and Sakhtoúri, and the thirteenth-century, waterfront **Boúrtzi** (locked except for special events), all that's left of once-extensive fortifications. Just uphill from this small Venetian tower, a small but well-explained **archeological museum** (Tues–Sun 8.30am–3pm; €2) displays statues, temple carvings and votive objects from the region.

## ARRIVAL AND INFORMATION

**By bus** The bus station is on Amerikís to the east of the Town Hall, about three blocks in and one east from central, waterfront Platía Amalías. Departures to Halkídha (2 daily, 3hr), Marmári (4 daily, 30min) and Néa Stýra (3 daily, 1hr). **Taxis** There's a taxi office (☎ 22240 26500) on Platía Amalías. **Services** The post office and ATMs lie within sight of Platía Amalías.

**Travel agency** There's no tourist office, but helpful South Evia Tours at Platía Amalías 7 (☎ 22240 26200, ⓦ eviatravel.gr) sells ferry tickets, rents cars and bikes, finds lodging, arranges excursions and also has a shop selling souvenirs, maps and foreign newspapers. **Useful websites** ⓦ southevia.gr and ⓦ in-karystos.gr.

## ACCOMMODATION

★ **Galaxy** Odysséos 1 ☎ 22240 22600, ⓦ galaxy hotelkaristos.com. Big old hotel at the western end of the waterfront with a friendly, family atmosphere. The rooms are gradually being upgraded with stylish furnishings and new bathrooms; get one of the new ones with a view and it's excellent value. **€50**

**Karystion** Kriezótou 3 ☎ 22240 22391, ⓦ karystion .gr. A lovely spot on a quiet, pine-covered promontory with direct access to the adjacent beach. The rather old-fashioned rooms are not quite what the modern exterior and public areas would lead you to expect, though. **€70**

## EATING, DRINKING AND NIGHTLIFE

Seafront Kriezótou is lined with cafés and touristy tavernas, though you'll generally find better value away from the front. Theohári Kótsika, one of the lanes leading inland from here to parallel Sakhtoúri, just to the west of the platía, has several *psistariés* and takeaway kebab places, as does I. Kótsika, between Platía Amalías and the Town Hall.

**Aeriko** West beach ☎ 22240 22365. Lounge bar behind the beach and a beach bar area on it; probably the best of a selection of bar/clubs behind the beach here. Live music and club nights in summer. Daily all day till late.

★ **Cavo D'oro** Paródos Sakhtoúri ☎ 22240 22326. Despite the name, this is an absolutely traditional Greek taverna, always busy, serving the likes of cheese-stuffed peppers, home-made tzatziki and goat in tomoto sauce. There's no menu, so choose from the bubbling pots or raw ingredients in the kitchen. You'll find it in the first alley off the waterfront west of the square. Lunch & dinner; closed Tues & 4.30–7pm.

**Hovolo** Kriezótou 118. Elegant café on the waterfront

serving coffee and sweets by day, wine by the glass and beer at night; somewhat pricey, but offset by the delicious traditional snacks that come with each drink. Daily all day till late.

**Marinos** Kriezótou 106 ☎ 22240 24126. Waterfront taverna with an enticing display of fish out front, sold by the kilo at reasonable prices. Also all the usual meat and traditional dishes, including good stuffed vegetables. Daily lunch & dinner.

**To Kyma** Káto Aetós ☎ 22240 23365. Big seaside restaurant 2km east of town, with a terrace above the water and another further up; popular weekend excursion for big parties so it's safest to book. Fri–Sun lunch & dinner.

## Mount Óhi

**Mount Óhi** (1399m), inland from Kárystos, is Évvia's third-highest peak and the focus of trails of sufficient quality to attract overseas trekkers. **MÝLI**, a fair-sized village around a spring-fed oasis with a few tavernas, is a natural first stop. Medieval **Castello Rosso (Kokkinókastro)** lies a twenty-minute climb above the village; inside, the castle is ruinous, except for an Orthodox **chapel** built over the water cistern, but sweeping views make the trip worthwhile.

From Mýli, it's a three-hour-plus **hike** up the bare slopes of Óhi, mostly by a good path short-cutting the road; about forty minutes along are various finished and half-finished cipollino marble **columns**, abandoned almost two thousand years ago. The Romans loved the stuff and extensively quarried southern Évvia, shipping the marble back to Italy. The path reaches an alpine club shelter just below the summit (springwater outside; ☏ 22240 24414 to get the keys), and a **dhrakóspito**, more impressive than the Stýra trio (see p.697), seemingly sprouting from the mountainside.

**10**

## The Dhimosári Gorge

The one unmissable excursion in southern Évvia is the three-hour hike down the **Dhimosári Gorge**. The descent northeast, mostly in deep shade past various springs and watermills, follows a path (often *kalderími*) as far as the farming hamlet of Lenoséi, then a track to **Kallianós** village, with another path just before the latter down to a beach. South Evia Tours (see opposite) organize a weekly guided trek here in summer as well as other walking trips; otherwise you'll have to arrange a taxi transfer back, or hitch.

# Northern Évvia

Leaving Halkídha to the north, the main road snakes steeply over a forested ridge, with spectacular views back over the city and the narrow strait, and then down through the Dhervéni Gorge, gateway to Évvia's northwest.

### ARRIVAL AND DEPARTURE

### NORTHERN ÉVVIA

**By ferry** Ten or more ferries a day shuttle between Loutrá Edhipsoú and Arkítsa (45min; ☏ 22260 23330 or 22395, ⓦ ferriesedipsos.gr), and between Ayiókambos and Glýfa (25min; ☏ 22260 31680, ⓦ ferriesglyfa.gr). Tickets are sold on the quayside, and buses from Athens' Liossíon 260 terminal serve both mainland ports.

**By bus** Buses run from Halkídha to most points; there are three or four daily to Límni and Roviés, to Loutrá Edhipsoú and to Istiéa, the hub for north- and west-coast beaches.

## Prokópi

**PROKÓPI**, in a broad wooded upland where the road emerges from the gorge, is famous for its hideous 1960s pilgrimage **church of St John the Russian**, actually a Ukrainian soldier captured by the Ottomans early in the eighteenth century and taken to central Anatolia, where he died. His mummified body began to work miracles, leading to canonization; the saint's relics were brought here in the 1923 population exchange. A vast pilgrimage in late May sees people walking from Halkídha (and beyond) and camping all around the church.

The large manor house overlooking the village is home to Philip Noel-Baker, a descendant of English Philhellene nobleman Edward Noel, a relative of Lady Byron, who bought the estate from the Turks in 1832 in order to support the new Greek state. The house (ⓦ candili.gr) now operates as a tranquil centre for conferences and courses (yoga, art, etc).

## Límni and around

**LÍMNI**, a well-preserved Neoclassical town and sheltered port, with magnificent views west to the mainland, rivals Kárystos as the most characterful resort on Évvia. The main drawback is a lack of decent beaches, though there are plenty of pebble strands all around. Behind the waterfront is a maze of unnamed alleys; on one such is the little **museum** (Mon–Fri 9am–1pm, Sat 10am–1pm, Sun 10.30am–1pm; €2). This traces the history of the place from Mycenaean times – ancient Elymnia was an important city in Euboea – to the twentieth century, with some wonderful old photos, and it's a fun visit, where you're likely to get a personal tour from the curator, who speaks little English.

Immediately west of Límni, the hamlets of **Sipiádha** and **Khrónia** are virtually suburbs, each with good pebbly beaches and a choice of accommodation. **ROVIÉS**, 7km from Límni, is a bigger place, famous for its olives and with a picturesque, ruined medieval tower at its heart.

### Ayíou Nikoláou Galatáki

Daily: winter 9am–noon & 2–5pm; summer 9am–noon & 5–8pm; knock and wait for entry • Free • Strict clothing rules apply

Around 7km southeast of Límni, the beautiful monastery of **Ayíou Nikoláou Galatáki** perches on the wooded slopes of Mount Kandíli, overlooking the Evvian Gulf. Though much rebuilt since its original Byzantine foundation atop a temple of Poseidon, the convent retains a thirteenth-century anti-pirate tower and a crypt. One of the six nuns will show you **frescoes** dating from a sixteenth-century renovation. Especially vivid, on the right, is the *Entry of the Righteous into Paradise*: the virtuous ascend a perilous ladder to be crowned by angels and received by Christ, while the wicked miss the rungs and fall into the maw of Leviathan.

There are pebble-and-sand **beaches** scattered along the road to the monastery, and more that can only be reached on foot immediately below it.

## ARRIVAL AND DEPARTURE

### LÍMNI AND AROUND

**By bus** Buses stop on Límni's central waterfront near the bottom of the main street, Angéli Govioú. Tickets are sold at the nearby Kafenío Neon.

## ACCOMMODATION

**Dennis House** Khrónia ☎ 22270 31787, ⊕ dennishotel .gr. Apartment block in lush gardens, 500m out of the village towards Límni, with its own bar and restaurant; studios and two-room apartments with a/c, tv and great sea views. **€55**

★ **Eleonas** Roviés ☎ 22270 71619, ⊕ eleonashotel .com. Classy, peaceful place in a secluded olive grove outside town, with ground-floor a/c garden rooms or first-floor ones with balconies. Set back some way from the sea, but still with fine views. Breakfast included. **€80**

**Graegos Studios** Límni ☎ 22270 31117, ⊕ graegos .com. Just four comfortable a/c studios, with well-equipped kitchens, right at the eastern end of the waterfront. The two at the front have fabulous big balconies with views of the fishing port. **€70**

**Livaditis Beach** Sipiádha ☎ 22270 31640, ⊕ livaditis beach.com. Modern-looking beachfront apartment complex; the units are not as new as you might think, but spotless and in a great location, with a playground, taverna, kayaks and pedaloes on the beach, and a van for transfers to town. **€60**

## EATING AND DRINKING

**7 Anemous** Límni ☎ 22270 32121. Unexpectedly fancy, though not overly expensive restaurant in a restored stone building in a backstreet behind the eastern seafront. Mediterranean menu includes pizza, pasta with salmon, salads and a few grills served in a garden or (in winter) inside by a roaring fire. Dinner only; closed Tues Oct–May.

**Kalderimi** Límni. Café ouzerí in an alley above the plaza, behind the *Plaza Hotel*, serving everything from omelettes for breakfast to octopus and fish in the evenings. Great for a morning coffee, but better in the evening when there's ouzo and excellent mezédhes. Daily all day, till late.

**Lamaros** Límni ☎ 22270 31351. Immaculate setting with a waterfront terrace and steps down to the water in an absolutely tranquil spot, 500m out of town, on the road to the monastery. Food is the regular Greek taverna array, with plenty of fish, cooked with care. Daily, evenings only.

**To Pikandiko** Límni ☎ 22270 31300. Simple, inexpensive grill-and-*souvláki* place with a great seafront position. *Yíros* pita and kebabs as well as more substantial meat dishes, with seating indoors and out. Daily lunch & dinner.

## Loutrá Edhipsoú

**LOUTRÁ EDHIPSOÚ** is one of Greece's most popular **spa** towns, with a line of grand hotels gracing the front. If your wallet doesn't stretch to services at the *Thermae Sylla Spa* (see opposite), you can bathe for free at the adjacent public **beach**, where geothermal water pours into an artificial set of cascades. There are more free, open-air **hot springs** at **Ília**, 8km east, where sulphurous water boils up at 65°C on the pebble beach, then is channelled at more bearable temperatures into ad hoc pits dug by shovel-wielding locals.

**10**

### ARRIVAL AND DEPARTURE

**By ferry** Ferries arrive on the central seafront.
**By bus** The bus station is a couple of blocks south on Thermopotámou, which runs inland by the *Aegli* hotel.

**Taxis** The taxi stand (☎ 22260 23280) is directly opposite where the ferry docks.

### ACCOMMODATION

**Aegli** Waterfront ☎ 22260 22215. A rather magnificent 1930s hotel that has clearly seen better days – they claim that Greta Garbo and Winston Churchill were among former guests. If faded grandeur is your thing, look no further. It's just north of the ferry dock, and also has a good waterfront terrace restaurant. **€50**
**Avra** Waterfront ☎ 22260 22226, ⓦ avraspahotel.gr. Grand old hotel, similar in style to the next-door *Aegli* (see above) if rather less interesting. Here the rooms have been

recently refurbished, however, and there's a variety of treatments on offer. **€70**
**Thermae Sylla** Waterfront ☎ 22260 60100, ⓦ thermaesylla.gr. Five-star pentagonal complex at the northern end of the seafront promenade that's by far the grandest of the surviving hotels, with indoor and outdoor pools. Pricey treatments, available to non-guests too, include a 45min "oriental bath" for €131 or 90min mud therapy for €95. **€250**

## The north and west coasts

Northern Évvia's north and west coasts are home to most of the island's resorts – none, however, that is particularly attractive or sees many foreign visitors. On the whole they consist of long, exposed pebble beaches, backed by scrappy hamlets of second homes and small hotels. Heading clockwise from Loutrá Edhipsoú, you come first to **AYIÓKAMBOS**, with regular **ferry** connections to Glýfa on the mainland. **OREÍ** and **NÉOS PÝRGOS**, next up, pretty much merge together into a single resort; the former with good restaurants around its harbour, the latter quieter, but with only a tiny beach. **PÉFKI** is another small, pleasant resort with extensive beaches either side. At **Psaropoúli**, steeply below the town of **VASILIKÁ**, there's a vast, barely developed bay of grey sand and pebbles. **PARALÍA AYÍA ÁNNA**, by contrast, is a substantial resort on a couple of kilometres of brownish sand, with showers and loungers at the resort end, and plenty of empty space beyond. Finally, at the tiny hamlet of **KRÝA VRÝSSI**, there's a lovely brown-sand beach with the ruins of ancient Kirinthos at its southern end.

### ACCOMMODATION AND EATING

**Agali Hotel** Paralía Ayía Ánna ☎ 22260 41208, ⓦ hotelagali.gr. Modern hotel at the northern end of the beach with an attractive, designer look. Rooms are less fancy than the exterior might lead you to expect, but comfortable and well equipped. Buffet breakfast included. **€70**
**Galini Hotel** Péfki ☎ 22260 41208, ⓦ pefkigalinihotel.gr. Right in the centre of the beach area, this is the largest and, in yellow and dark red, most brightly coloured of the beachfront hotels here, with a café-bar and restaurant out

front. Standard, modern a/c rooms. **€60**
**To Pirofani** Néos Pýrgos ☎ 22260 71448. A good *psarotavérna* overlooking the fishing harbour, serving all the usuals at waterfront tables and on a substantial roof terrace across the road. Daily lunch & dinner.
**To Steki tis Yiannas** Oreí ☎ 22260 71540. Excellent taverna with a lovely seaside setting by the harbour, serving fresh fish, octopus and calamari, plus daily oven-baked specials. Daily lunch & dinner.

# The Ionian islands

**707** Corfu

**724** Paxí and Andípaxi

**727** Lefkádha

**736** Kefaloniá

**745** Itháki

**749** Zákynthos

SHIPWRECK BAY, ZÁKYNTHOS

# The Ionian islands

The six core Ionian islands, shepherding their satellites down the west coast of the mainland, float on the haze of the Ionian Sea, their lush green contours, a result of heavy winter rains, coming as a shock to those more used to the stark outlines of the Aegean. The west coasts of the larger islands also boast some of Greece's most picturesque cliff-backed beaches, whose sands are caressed by a band of milky turquoise water leading to the deeper azure sea.

**11**

Tourism is the dominant influence these days, as it has been for decades on **Corfu** (Kérkyra), which was one of the first Greek islands established on the package-holiday circuit, though the continuing downturn means it does not feel as swamped as in the past. And while parts of its coastline are among the few stretches in Greece with development to match the Spanish *costas*, the island is large enough to contain parts as beautiful as anywhere in the group. The southern half of **Zákynthos** (Zante) has also gone down the same tourist path, but elsewhere the island's pace is a lot less intense. Little **Paxí** lacks the water to support large-scale hotels and has limited facilities tucked into just three villages, meaning it gets totally packed in season. Perhaps the most rewarding trio for island-hopping are Kefaloniá, Itháki and **Lefkádha**. The latter is connected to the mainland by a causeway and iron bridge but still has quite a low-key straggle of tourist centres and only two major resorts, despite boasting some excellent beaches, strung along its stunning west coast. **Kefaloniá** offers a series of "real towns" and more stunning beaches, as well as a selection of worthwhile attractions, while **Itháki**, Odysseus's rugged capital, is protected from a tourist influx by an absence of sand. Although officially counted among the Ionians and constituting the seventh of the traditional *eptánisos* (heptanese or "seven islands"), rugged Kýthira is geographically quite separate from the six main islands. Only accessible from the southern Peloponnese, it is covered in chapter 2 (see p.150).

## Brief history

The Ionian islands were the Homeric realm of Odysseus, centred on Ithaca (modern Itháki), and here alone of all modern Greek territory the Ottomans never held sway – except on Lefkádha. After the fall of Byzantium, possession passed to the **Venetians**, and the islands became a keystone in Venice's maritime empire from 1386 until its collapse in 1797. Most of the population remained immune to the establishment of Italian as the official language and the arrival of Roman Catholicism, but Venetian influence remains evident in the architecture of the island capitals, despite damage from a series of earthquakes.

The Ionian School of painting p.711
Mount Pandokrátor p.714
Boat trips from Paleokastrítsa p.719
Walking the Corfu Trail p.723
Walks around Lákka p.726
Lefkádha's summer festivals p.730

Boat trips from Nydhrí p.732
Lover's leap p.735
Odysseus sights around Vathý p.746
Boat trips from Zákynthos Town p.749
Loggerhead turtles p.753

# Highlights

**❶ Corfu Town** Venetian fortresses, beautiful churches, fine museums and appealing Venetian architecture. **See p.707**

**❷ Longás beach, Corfu** Shaded till early afternoon and backed by sheer vertical red cliffs, this beach is an excellent hangout. **See p.725**

**❸ Andípaxi** Some of the Ionians' best swimming and snorkelling is on offer at the exquisite beaches of Paxí's little sister. **See p.724**

**❹ Lefkádha's west coast** Between Áï Nikítas and Pórto Katsíki lie some of the archipelago's finest and least crowded beaches. **See p.727**

**❺ Melissáni Cave, Kefaloniá** See dappled sunlight on the water amid rock formations on a boat trip inside this once-enclosed underwater cave. **See p.743**

**❻ Mount Énos, Kefaloniá** The highest point in the Ionians has stunning vistas of sea and distant land, plus a unique species of pine. **See p.740**

**❼ Itháki's Homeric sites** Relive the myths on Odysseus's island by visiting locations described by Homer. **See p.746**

**❽ Boat tour around Zákynthos** The best way to see the impressive coastline, including the Blue Caves and Shipwreck Bay, is to cruise from Zákynthos Town. **See p.749**

HIGHLIGHTS ARE MARKED ON THE MAP ON P.706

On Corfu, the Venetian legacy is mixed with that of the **British**, who imposed a military "protectorate" over the Ionian islands at the close of the Napoleonic Wars, before ceding the archipelago to Greece in 1864. There is, however, no question of the islanders' essential Greekness: the poet Dhionyssios Solomos, author of the national anthem, hailed from the Ionians, as did Nikos Mantzelos, who provided the music, and the first Greek president, Ioannis Kapodhistrias.

**HIGHLIGHTS**
1. Corfu Town
2. Longás beach
3. Andípaxi
4. Lefkádha's west coast
5. Melissáni Cave
6. Mount Énos
7. Itháki's Homeric sites
8. Boat tour around Zákynthos

**THE IONIAN ISLANDS**

# Corfu

Dangling between the heel of Italy and the west coast of mainland Greece, green, mountainous **CORFU (Kérkyra)** was one of the first Greek islands to attract mass tourism in the 1960s. Indiscriminate exploitation turned parts into eyesores but a surprising amount of the island still consists of olive groves, mountains or woodland. The majority of package holidays are based in the most developed resorts and unspoilt terrain is often only a few minutes' walk away.

Corfu is thought to have been the model for Prospero and Miranda's place of exile in Shakespeare's *The Tempest*, and was certainly known to writers such as Spenser, Milton and – more recently – Edward Lear and Henry Miller, as well as Gerald and Lawrence Durrell. Lawrence Durrell's *Prospero's Cell* evokes the island's "delectable landscape" still evident in some of its beaches, the best of the whole archipelago.

The staggering amount of accommodation on the island means that competition keeps prices down even in high season, at least in many resorts outside of Corfu Town. Prices at restaurants and in shops also tend to be a little lower than average for the Ionians.

**11**

## ARRIVAL AND DEPARTURE
CORFU

**By plane** Corfu receives seasonal charter flights from all over northern Europe but only has year-round scheduled services to Athens (4–6 daily; 1hr).

**By ferry** The vast majority of domestic services and all those to Italy run from Corfu Town, although there are a few boats to the mainland from Lefkímmi. Most of the ferry offices are on the main road opposite the New Port; ferries to Italy or south towards Pátra become very busy in summer and booking is advisable. The port authority (domestic ☎ 26610 32655, international ☎ 26610 30481) can advise on services. There are buses that board the ferry

from the island capital to Greece's two largest cities, Athens (3 daily; 9–10hr) and Thessaloníki (2 daily; 8–9hr); schedules are year-round. For the additional destinations below, frequencies given are for the summer season and are greatly reduced in winter.

Corfu Town to: Ancona (1–2 daily; 14hr); Bari (2–3 daily; 11hr); Brindisi (3–5 daily; 4–9hr); Eríkoussa/Mathráki/Othoní (3 weekly; 2–4hr); Igoumenítsa (every 10–45min; 1hr 15min); Pátra (6–10 daily; 6–9hr); Venice (3–4 weekly; 25hr).

**By hydrofoil** Services run from Corfu Town to Gáïos (Paxí; May–Oct 1–3 daily; 50min).

## GETTING AROUND

**By bus** Corfu's bus service radiates from the capital. Islandwide services stop operating between 6 and 9pm, suburban ones at between 9 and 10.30pm. Printed English timetables are available for both and can be picked up at the respective terminals.

**By car or motorbike** Many people rent vehicles to get around the island and there are numerous international and local companies in the capital (see p.712) and around the resorts.

## Corfu Town

The capital, **CORFU TOWN**, has been one of the most elegant island capitals in the whole of Greece since it was spruced up for the EU summit in 1994. Although many of its finest buildings were destroyed by Nazi bombers in World War II, two massive forts, the sixteenth-century church of Áyios Spyrídhon and some buildings dating from French and British administrations remain intact. As the island's major port of entry by ferry or plane, Corfu Town can get packed in summer.

Corfu Town comprises a number of distinct areas. The **Historic Centre**, the area enclosed by the Old Port and the two forts, consists of several smaller districts: **Campiello**, the oldest, sits on the hill above the harbour; **Kofinéta** stretches towards the Spianádha (Esplanade); **Áyii Apóstoli** runs west of the Mitrópolis (Orthodox cathedral); while tucked in beside the Néo Froúrio is what remains of the old **Jewish quarter**. These districts and their tall, narrow alleys conceal some of Corfu's most beautiful architecture. The **New Town** comprises all the areas that surround the Historic Centre.

11

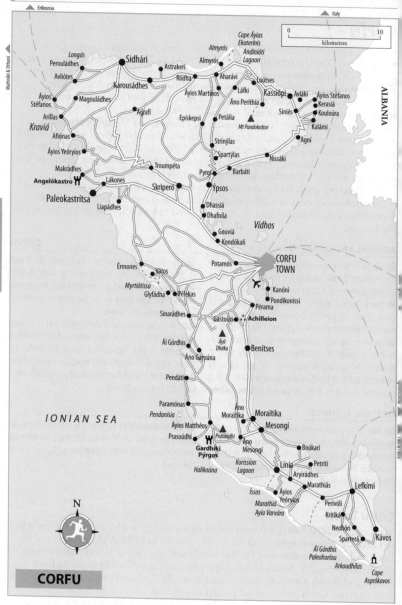

CORFU

## The Historic Centre

The most obvious sights are the forts, the **Paleó Froúrio** and **Néo Froúrio**, whose designations (*paleó* – "old", *néo* – "new") are a little misleading, since what you see of the older structure was begun by the Byzantines in the mid-twelfth century, just a hundred years before the Venetians began work on the newer citadel. They have both been damaged and modified by various occupiers and besiegers, the last contribution being the Neoclassical shrine of St George, built by the British in the middle of Paleó Froúrio during the 1840s.

## Néo Froúrio

Daily: April–Oct 9am–9pm (or sunset if earlier); Nov–March 8am–3pm • €3

Looming above the Old Port, the **Néo Froúrio** is the more architecturally interesting of the two forts. The entrance, at the back of the fort, gives onto cellars, dungeons and battlements, with excellent views over the town and bay; there's a small gallery and seasonal café at the summit.

## Paleó Froúrio

April–Oct Mon–Sat 8am–8pm, Sun 8.30am–3pm; Nov–March daily 8.30am–2.30pm • €4 • ☎ 26610 48310

The **Paleó Froúrio** is not as well preserved as the Néo Froúrio and contains some incongruous modern structures, but has an interesting **Byzantine Museum** just inside the gate, and even more stunning views from the central Land Tower. It also hosts daily son et lumière shows.

**11**

## The Listón and Spianádha

Just west of the Paleó Froúrio, the focus of town life is the **Listón**, an arcaded café-lined street built during the French occupation by the architect of the Rue de Rivoli in Paris, and the green **Spianádha** (Esplanade) it overlooks. The cricket pitch, still in use at the northern end of the Spianádha, is another British legacy, while at the southern end the **Maitland Rotunda** was built to honour the first British High Commissioner of Corfu and the Ionian islands. The neighbouring statue of Ioannis Kapodhistrias celebrates the local hero and statesman (1776–1831) who led the diplomatic efforts for independence and was made Greece's first president in 1827.

## Palace of SS Michael and George

Listón • **Asiatic Museum** Tues–Sun: May–Oct 8.30am–8pm; Nov–April 8.30am–3pm • €3 **Modern Art Gallery** Wed–Sun 9am–3pm • €4

At the far northern end of the Listón is the nineteenth-century **Palace of SS Michael and George**, a solidly British edifice built as the residence of their High Commissioner (one of whom was the future British prime minister William Gladstone) and later used as a palace by the Greek monarchy. The former state rooms house the **Asiatic Museum**, a must for aficionados of Oriental culture. Amassed by Corfiot diplomat Gregorios Manos (1850–1929) and others, it includes Noh theatre masks, woodcuts, wood and brass statuettes, samurai weapons and artworks from Thailand, Korea and Tibet. The adjoining **Modern Art Gallery** holds a small collection of contemporary Greek art.

## Solomos Museum

3rd Párodhos Arseníou • Mon–Fri 9.30am–2pm • €1 • ☎ 26610 30674

This hidden museum is dedicated to modern Greece's most famous nineteenth-century poet, **Dhionysios Solomos**. Born on Zákynthos, Solomos was author of the poem *Amnos stín Elefthería* ("*Hymn to Liberty*"), which was to become the Greek national anthem. He studied at Corfu's Ionian Academy, and lived in a house on this site for much of his life. On display are a number of his personal effects and manuscripts of some works.

---

**CORFU TOWN COMBINATION TICKET**

There is a handy **combination ticket** that covers four of Corfu Town's main attractions: the Paleó Froúrio, Byzantine Museum, Archeological Museum and Asiatic Museum. The ticket costs €8 and is available at any of the four sights.

## Byzantine Museum

Arseníou • Tues–Sun 9am–3pm • €2 • ☎ 26610 38313

Up a short flight of steps on Arseníou, the **Byzantine Museum** is housed in the restored church of the Panayía Andivouniótissa. It houses church frescoes and sculptures and sections of mosaic floors from the ancient site of Paleópolis, just south of Corfu Town. There are also some pre-Christian artefacts, and a collection of icons dating from between the fifteenth and nineteenth centuries.

## Church of Áyios Spyrídhon

Spyrídhonos • Daily 8am–9pm

A block behind the Listón is the sixteenth-century **church of Áyios Spyrídhon**, whose maroon-domed campanile dominates the town. Here you will find the silver-encrusted coffin of the island's patron saint, **Spyrídhon** – Spyros in the diminutive – after whom seemingly half the male population is named. Four times a year (Palm Sunday and the following Sat, Aug 11 and the first Sun in Nov), to the accompaniment of much celebration and feasting, the relics are paraded through the town streets. Each of the days commemorates a miraculous deliverance of the island credited to the saint – twice from plague, once from a famine and, in the eighteenth century, from the Turks.

## The Mitrópolis

Platía Mitrópoleos • Daily 8am–7pm

After Áyios Spyrídhon the next most important of the town's many churches, the **Mitrópolis** (Orthodox cathedral), is perched at the top of its own square opposite the Old Port. It also houses the remains of a saint, in this case St Theodora, the ninth-century wife of Emperor Theophilos. The building dates from 1577, and the plain exterior conceals a splendid iconostasis, as well as some fine icons, including a sixteenth-century image of *Saint George Slaying the Dragon*.

## The New Town

There are a couple of noteworthy sights in the New Town that surrounds the Historic Centre. This area also encompasses much of Corfu Town's commercial heart, centred around busy **Platía Saróko**.

### Archeological Museum

Bráïla 1 • Tues–Sun 8.30am–3pm • €3 • ☎ 26610 30680

Corfu Town's **Archeological Museum**, just round the coast from the southern end of the Spianádha, is the best in the archipelago. The most impressive exhibit is a massive (17m) Gorgon pediment excavated from the Doric temple of Artemis at Paleópolis, just south of Corfu Town; this dominates an entire room, the Gorgon flanked by panthers and mythical battle scenes. The museum also has fragments of Neolithic weapons and cookware, and coins and pots from the period when the island was a colony of ancient Corinth.

### The British cemetery

Cnr of Zafiropoúlou and Kolokotróni • Open access

Just south of Platía Saróko, the well-maintained **British cemetery** features some elaborate civic and military memorials. It's a quiet green space away from the madness of Saróko and, in spring and early summer, comes alive with dozens of species of orchids and other exotic blooms.

## The outskirts

Each of the sights on the sprawling outskirts of the city can easily be seen in a morning or afternoon, and you could conceivably cover several in one day.

### Mon Repos and around

Estate daily 8am–7.30pm • Free • ☎ 26610 41369

About 1.5km around the bay from the Rotunda and Archeological Museum, tucked behind Mon Repos beach, the area centred on the **Mon Repos** estate contains the most accessible archeological remains on the island, collectively known as **Paleópolis**. Within the estate, thick woodland conceals two **Doric temples**, dedicated to Hera and Poseidon. The Neoclassical **Mon Repos villa**, built by British High Commissioner Frederic Adam

11

---

### THE IONIAN SCHOOL OF PAINTING

The Ionian islands have a strong tradition of excellence in the fine arts, particularly iconography. Having been occupied by the Venetians and later the British, the islands spent centuries more in touch with developments in western Europe than in the Ottoman empire.

Until the late seventeenth century, religious art in the Ionians, as elsewhere, was dominated by the stylistic purity and dignified austerity of the Cretan School. The founder of the **Ionian School of painting** is considered to be **Panayiotis Dhoxaras**, who was born in the Peloponnese in 1662 but, after studying in Venice and Rome, moved to Zákynthos and later lived and worked in Lefkádha and Corfu until his death in 1729. From his travels Dhoxaras absorbed the spirit of Italian Renaissance art, and brought a greater degree of naturalism into iconography by showing his subjects, usually saints, in more human poses amid everyday surroundings. He is also credited with introducing the technique of **oil painting** into Greece in place of the older method of mixing pigments with egg yolk.

Dhoxaras's work was carried on by his son, **Nikolaos** (1710–1775), and over the next two centuries the tradition flourished through the skilled brushwork of a host of talented artists, such as Corfiot **Yioryios Khrysoloras** (1680–1762), Zakynthian **Nikolaos Kandounis** (1768–1834) and three generations of the Proselandis family, starting with **Pavlos Proselandis** (1784–1837).

in 1824 and handed over to Greece in 1864, is the birthplace of Britain's Prince Philip and has been converted into the **Paleópolis Museum** (daily 8.30am–7.30pm; €3). As well as various archeological finds from the vicinity, including some fine sculpture, it contains period furniture *in situ*, and temporary modern art exhibitions.

Other remains worth a peek outside the confines of the estate include the **Early Christian Basilica** (Tues–Sun 8.30am–3pm; free) opposite the entrance, the **Temple of Artemis**, a few hundred metres west, and the eleventh-century church of **Áyii láson and Sosípater**, back towards the seafront on Náfsikas.

### Vlahérna and Pondikoníssi

Bus #2 leaves Platía Saróko every 30min for Vlahérna convent • Boats leave the dock at Vlahérna for Pondikoníssi (€3 return)

The most famous excursion from Corfu Town is to the islets of Vlahérna and Pondikoníssi, 2km south of town below the hill of Kanóni, named after the single cannon trained out to sea atop it. Reached by a short causeway, the tiny, white convent of **Vlahérna** is one of the most photographed images on Corfu. **Pondikoníssi**, tufted by greenery from which peeks the small chapel of Panayía Vlahernón, is identified in legend with a ship from Odysseus's fleet, petrified by Poseidon in revenge for the blinding of his son Polyphemus.

### Vídhos

Hourly shuttle *kaïkia* run from the Old Port (€1.50 return, last boat back 1.30am)

**Vídhos**, the wooded island visible from the Old Port, is a quieter destination then Vlahérna or Pondikoníssi. It makes a particularly pleasant summer evening excursion, when there is live music at the municipal restaurant near the jetty.

### The Achilleion

Daily: May–Oct 8am–7pm; Nov–April 8am–4pm • €7 • ☎ 26610 56245

Some 6km south of Corfu Town, past the resort sprawl of Pérama, is the bizarre **Achilleion**, a palace built in a mercifully unique blend of Teutonic and Neoclassical styles in 1890 by Elizabeth, Empress of Austria. Henry Miller considered it "the worst piece of gimcrackery" that he'd ever laid eyes on and thought it "would make an excellent museum for surrealistic art". The house is predictably grandiose but the gardens are pleasant to walk around and afford splendid views in all directions.

## ARRIVAL AND INFORMATION
## CORFU TOWN

**By plane** The airport is 2km south of the town centre. A dedicated bus connects with central Corfu Town 8 times daily or blue city buses #5 and #6 can be flagged at the junction 500m north of the terminal. Taxis charge a rather steep €10 into town.

**By bus** There are two terminals: the islandwide green bus service is based on Avramíou (also for Athens and Thessaloníki), and the suburban blue bus system, which also serves nearby resorts such as Benítses and Dhassiá, is based in Platía Saróko.

**By ferry or hydrofoil** All vessels dock at the New Port (Néo Limáni), just west of the Néo Froúrio. The Old Port (Paleó Limáni), east of the New Port, is used only for day excursions.

**By car** For car rental, try Avis, Ethnikís Andístasis 42 (☎ 26610 24404, airport ☎ 26610 42007), behind the New Port; Budget, Venizélou 22 (☎ 26610 28590; airport ☎ 26610 44017); or Hertz, Ethnikí Lefkímis (☎ 26610 38388, airport ☎ 26610 35547). Among local companies, Sunrise, Ethnikís Andístasis 14 (☎ 26610 44325), is reliable.

**By motorbike or scooter** Motorbikes and scooters can be rented from Easy Rider, Venizélou 4 (☎ 26610 43026), or Atlantis, Xenofóndos Stratigoú 48 (☎ 26610 40580), both in the New Port.

**Services** There is no official tourist office, amazing for such a touristic island. The post office (Mon–Fri 7.30am–8pm) is on the corner of Alexándhras and Zafirópoulou. Many regular cafés have wi-fi and there are some internet cafés dotted around, such as X-plore, N. Lefteríti 4, two blocks north of Platía Saróko.

## ACCOMMODATION

Accommodation in Corfu Town is busy all year round and expensive in comparison to the rest of the island. For rooms you can try the Room Owners' Association at D. Theotóki 2A (Mon–Fri 9am–1.30pm, plus summer Tues, Thurs & Fri 6–8pm; ☎ 26610 26133, ✉ oitkcrf@otenet.gr).

**Atlantis** Xenofóndos Stratigoú 48 ☎26610 35560, ⓦ atlantis-hotel-corfu.com. Large and spacious a/c hotel in the New Port; with its functional 1960s ambience it rather lacks character but the rooms are perfectly adequate. **€68**

★ **Bella Venezia** Zambéli 4 ☎26610 46500, ⓦ bellaveneziahotel.com. Smart, yellow Neoclassical building, blending elegance with a cosy atmosphere. The elegant rooms are furnished and decorated in warm hues. Breakfast in the airy conservatory included. **€107**

**Cavalieri** Kapodhistríou 4 ☎26610 39041, ⓦ cavalieri -hotel.com. Classy and large yet still welcoming, with all mod cons in the lavishly decorated rooms, great views and a roof bar open to non-residents. Breakfast included. **€90**

**Corfu Palace Hotel** Leofóros Dhimokratías 2 ☎26610 39485, ⓦ corfupalace.com. The most luxurious hotel on the island, with sweeping staircases up from the lobby, indoor and outdoor pools, landscaped gardens and well-appointed rooms, each with a marble bath. Breakfast included. **€220**

**Konstantinoupolis** Zavitsiánou 1 ☎26610 48716, ⓦ konstantinoupolis.com.gr. Classy hotel in the Old Port with tasteful decoration and comfortable rooms, most with fine harbour views. Good discounts out of high season. **€75**

## EATING AND DRINKING

### RESTAURANTS

**Adherfi Theotoki** M. Athanassíou, Garítsa ☎26610 45910. By far the best of the several establishments tucked behind the seafront park, this popular family taverna serves excellent mezédhes, meat and good-value fish dishes. March–Oct daily noon–2am.

**Alekos Beach** Faliráki jetty ☎26610 31030. Set in the tiny harbour below the palace, with great views, this place offers simple, mostly grilled meat and fish dishes at good prices. May–Sept daily 11am–midnight.

**La Cucina** Guildford 15 ☎26610 80011. The town's most authentic Italian food, including fine antipasti and meat or seafood spaghetti dishes at around €10–15. Two separate locations on the same block. Daily noon–1am.

**Mourayia** Arseníou 15–17 ☎26610 33815. This unassuming, good-value ouzerí near the Byzantine Museum does a range of tasty mezédhes, including sausage or seafood such as mussels and shrimp in exquisite sauces. Also boasts views of passing ferries and Vídhos island. March–Nov daily noon–midnight.

**Rex** Kapodhistríou 66 ☎26610 39649. Slightly pricey, owing to its location just behind the Listón, but this place has some of the best food in town, especially the delicious oven dishes, such as pork stuffed with plum and fig (€12). Daily 11am–1am.

**To Paradosiakon** Solomoú 20 ☎26610 37578. Behind the Old Port, this friendly place serves good inexpensive fresh food, especially home-style oven dishes such as *stifádho* and *kokkinistó*. April–Oct daily 10.30am–midnight.

★ **Venetian Well Bistro** Platía Kremastí ☎26610 44761. Tucked in a tiny square a few alleys north of the cathedral, this is the place for Greek nouvelle cuisine, with exotic main courses such as Iraqi lamb and Albanian calves' livers in ouzo for around €16–22. Easter–Oct daily 7pm–midnight.

### CAFÉS

**Art Café** In a delightful garden behind the art gallery of the Palace of SS Michael and George, this is a great relaxed spot to take in some refreshment in between sightseeing. Daily 9am–midnight.

**En Plo** Faliráki jetty ☎26610 27000. This popular café boasts an unbeatably brilliant, breezy setting, with views of the Paleó Forúrio. Fine spot for a pre-prandial ouzo or late night brandy. Daily 10am–late.

## NIGHTLIFE AND ENTERTAINMENT

There are some hip youth bars in town and a few remaining clubs on the "disco strip" of Ethnikís Andistáseos, a couple of kilometres north of town, past the New Port, though much of the action has shifted to the resorts. There are two cinemas, both showing mostly English-language films.

### CLUBS

**Au Bar** Emborikó Kéndro, Ethnikís Andistáseos ☎26610 80909, ⓦ aubarcorfu.com. Happening club in a shopping centre that has regular theme nights, mixing mainstream international dance and Greek hits, plus occasional live shows. Daily 9pm–late.

**Hook** Kapodhistríou 14. Along with *Base* next door but one, this bar features cutting-edge sounds, ranging from indie to house and techno. Popular with students in term and locals plus a few tourists in summer. Daily 10pm–late.

**Sodoma** Ethnikís Andistáseos ☎26610 37227. Club with a large dancefloor, where an impressive light show accompanies techno, trance, some rock and Greek sounds. Daily 10pm–late.

### CINEMAS

**Cine Finikas** Akadhimías ☎26610 39768. Down the cul-de-sac extension of Akadhimías, the town's open-air summer cinema is a lovely place to take in a film. June–Sept, showings usually 9pm & 11pm.

**Cine Orfeus** Cnr of Akadhimías and Aspióti ☎26610 39768. Corfu's winter cinema has comfy seats and a big screen. Oct–May, times vary.

11

# The northeast

The **northeast**, at least beyond the suburban resorts near Corfu Town, is the most typically Greek part of Corfu – it's mountainous, with a rocky coastline chopped into pebbly bays and coves, above wonderfully clear seas.

## Dhassiá and Ýpsos

Six kilometres from Corfu Town the coastline begins to improve at **Dhafníla** and **DHASSIÁ**, set in adjacent wooded bays with pebbly beaches. The latter, the first worthwhile place to stop in this direction, is much larger and contains nearly all the area's facilities, including a trio of **watersports** enterprises.

**ÝPSOS**, 2km north of Dhassiá, can't really be recommended to anyone but hardened bar-hoppers, though it is home to a diving centre (see opposite). The thin pebble beach lies right beside the busy coast road, and the resort is generally pretty tacky.

## Barbáti

At **BARBÁTI**, 4km north of Ýpsos, you'll find the sandiest beach on this coast, though its charm has been somewhat diminished recently by the construction of the gargantuan *Riviera Barbati* apartment complex. The beach is a favourite with families and much accommodation is prebooked in advance.

## Agní, Kalámi and Kouloúra

The first of three unmissable pebbly coves you encounter when travelling north from largely missable Nissáki is **AGNÍ**, a favourite mooring spot for yachties, largely because of its well-established reputation as something of a gourmet's paradise.

**KALÁMI**, around 3km north of Agní, is somewhat commercialized, but the village is still small and you can imagine how it would have looked in the year Lawrence Durrell spent here on the eve of World War II. The **White House**, where Durrell wrote *Prospero's Cell*, is now split in two: the ground floor is an excellent taverna, while the upper floor houses exclusive accommodation.

The tiny harbour of **KOULOÚRA**, barely a kilometre north of Kalámi, has managed to keep its charm intact, set at the edge of an unspoilt bay with nothing to distract from the pine trees and *kaïkia* apart from its idyllically located taverna.

---

### MOUNT PANDOKRÁTOR

**Mount Pandokrátor**, Corfu's highest mountain, is crowned by the moderately interesting **Pandokrátoras monastery**, whose main sanctuary, built in the seventeenth century, is open to visitors; nothing remains of the original buildings from three centuries earlier.

The most direct route from the south is signposted via Spartýlas and then the village of **Strinýlas**, a popular base for walkers served by buses from Corfu Town. An alternative approach from the north coast goes via Loútses to the charming ghost village of **Áno Períthia**, from where you are a steep 5km from the summit and can only climb any higher on foot or in a four-wheel drive. Apart from taking a quick peek at the crumbling remains of half a dozen churches, there is good eating in the village. The main westerly route ascends via **Láfki** to **Petália**, just south of which a paved road leads the final 5km east to the summit.

Anyone interested in walking the Pandokrátor paths is advised to get the **map** of the mountain by island-based cartographer Stephan Jaskulowski or one of Hilary Whitton-Paipeti's walking books, available from the better English-language bookshops in Corfu Town.

#### RESTAURANT

⭐ **Old Perithia** Áno Períthia ☎ 26630 98055. Worth climbing any mountain for, this traditional taverna is renowned for succulent goat and home-produced feta cheese. The views are splendid too, of course. Noon–midnight: May–Sept daily; Oct–April Sat & Sun.

## Áyios Stéfanos

The most attractive resort on this stretch of coast, 3km down a lane from Siniés on the main road, is **ÁYIOS STÉFANOS** (officially Áyios Stéfanos Sinión to distinguish it from its namesake in northwestern Corfu). The delightful bay bends almost at a right angle, the northern section of which contains the beach, beyond the string of restaurants.

### ARRIVAL AND GETTING AROUND
THE NORTHEAST

**By bus** Green buses between Corfu Town and Kassiópi serve all resorts, along with some blue suburban buses as far as Dhassiá.

**By boat** In Áyios Stéfanos, Giannis Boats (☎ 26630 81322, �𝕨 giannisboats.gr) rents out vessels of varying sizes from €50 per day.

### ACTIVITIES

**Diving** Ýpsos is home to one of the island's major diving centres, Waterhoppers (☎ 26610 93867, ✉ diverclub @hotmail.com).

**Watersports** Corfu Ski Club, the most established watersports outfit in Dhassiá (☎ 694 28 52 188, ⟨w⟩ corfuskiclub.com), claims to be the world's first paragliding operator.

**11**

### ACCOMMODATION

In **Agní**, various high-quality studios and villas can be booked through Kalami Tourist Services, based in the eponymous village. Kalami Tourist Services (☎ 26630 91062, ⟨w⟩ kalamibay.com) in **Kalámi** has a range of rooms in the area on their books.

#### DHASSIÁ AND ÝPSOS

**Corfu Camping Ipsos** Ýpsos ☎ 26610 93579, ⟨w⟩ corfucampingipsos.com. The only campsite on this coast apart from the superior *Dionysus* at Dhafníla has a bar and restaurant, and offers standing tents. May–Oct. Adult plus tent €9

**Dassia Beach/Dassia Margarita** Dhassiá ☎ 26610 93224, ⟨w⟩ dassiahotels.gr. Two almost adjacent sister hotels, the best options on the beach itself, with large dining rooms and adequate balconied guest rooms. Breakfast included. April–Oct. €50

**Dassia Chandris/Corfu Chandris** Dhassiá ☎ 26610 97100, ⟨w⟩ chandris.gr. These twin luxury hotels dominate the resort imperiously from the main road, and have extensive grounds, pools and beach facilities, as well as huge stylish rooms and suites. Breakfast included. €120

★ **Dionysus Camping Village** Dhassiá ☎ 26610 91417, ⟨w⟩ dionysuscamping.gr. The best campsite on Corfu, where tents are pitched under terraced olive trees. There are also bungalow huts, a pool, shop, bar and a restaurant. Adult plus tent €9.70

#### BARBÁTI

**Paradise** ☎ 26630 91320. Up above the main road set amid a colourful tiered garden, this place offers decent-sized rooms with balconies, offering bird's-eye sea views. April–Oct. €35

#### ÁYIOS STÉFANOS

**Kochili** ☎ 26630 81522. This fine family taverna, which serves good home-style oven food and grills, also has the only independently bookable rooms in the village, simply furnished but with lovely bay views. May–Oct. €40

### EATING, DRINKING AND NIGHTLIFE

#### DHASSIÁ AND ÝPSOS

**B52** Ýpsos. One of the most enduring clubs that line the northern end of the seafront, popular for its large outdoor dancefloor, where you can shake it to pop, soul, funk and reggae. May to mid-Oct 8pm–late.

**EDEM** Dhassiá ☎ 26610 93013, ⟨w⟩ edemclub.com. Corfu's prime beach nightclub draws revellers from far and wide. International DJs play cutting-edge techno, trance and other latest genres to a lively crowd. Occasional rock and other theme nights. May–Sept daily 9pm–late.

**Karydia** Dhassiá ☎ 26630 93562. A good restaurant on the main road, with a pleasant garden, serving well-prepared versions of Corfiot specialities such as *sofríto* and *pastitsadha*, accompanied by decent barrelled wine. April–Oct 2pm–midnight.

#### AGNÍ, KALÁMI AND KOULOÚRA

★ **Nikolas** Agní ☎ 26630 91243. The oldest taverna of the excellent trio here. Superb home-style dishes such as lamb *kléftiko* are served with a smile and there are plenty of tasty *mezédhes* to choose from. April–Oct daily 9am–1am; Nov–March Fri–Sun noon–1am.

**Toula's** Agní ☎ 26630 91350. Rather upmarket restaurant with a grand terrace, where the huge menu includes a range of home-made pies and even Black Angus Argentinian steaks (upwards of €20). May–Sept 12.30–11pm.

**White House** Kálami ☎ 26630 91040. Located in the old Durrell house and recommended for its specials – mussels and swordfish with garlic – but also good for simple grills, salads and a variety of *mezédhes*. April–Oct daily, Nov–March Fri–Sun, noon–1am.

### ÁYIOS STÉFANOS
★ **Fagopotion** ☎ 26630 82020. With a deck right on the quay, this place offers finely prepared seafood, dishes such as rabbit *stifádho* and unusual items such as a *zogorítiki* soufflé with four cheeses. Most main dishes €10–13. Noon–1am: April–Oct daily; Nov–May Fri–Sun.

## The north coast

The north coast between **Kassiópi** and **Sidhári** is blessed with some of the island's best stretches of sand and, as a direct result, is also home to a few of Corfu's most crowded package tourism resorts, varying in degrees of development but still with plenty to offer the independent traveller.

### Kassiópi

At the far east end of the north coast is **KASSIÓPI**, a fishing village that's been transformed into a major party resort. The Roman emperor Tiberius had a villa here, and the village's sixteenth-century Panayía Kassópitra church is said to stand on the site of a temple of Zeus once visited by Nero. Little of Kassiópi's past survives, apart from an abandoned Angevin kástro on the headland – most visitors come for the nightlife and the five **pebbly beaches**, the largest of which is Kalamiónas, close to the coast road.

### Almyrós beach and around

Little-developed **Almyrós beach**, around 10km west along the marshy, overgrown coastline from Kassiópi, is one of the longest on the island, with only a few apartment buildings and one huge new resort dotted sporadically behind it. The **Andinióti lagoon**, a haven for birds and twitchers, backs Cape Ayías Ekaterínis to the east, which marks the northern end of the Corfu Trail (see box, p.723).

### Aharávi

At the western end of Almyrós beach, **AHARÁVI**'s old village is tucked on the inland side of the busy main road in a quiet crescent. The village serves as a base for those seeking alternative routes up onto **Mount Pandokrátor** (see box, p.714). Roads to small hamlets such as Áyios Martínos and Láfki continue onto the mountain, and even a stroll up from the back of Aharávi will find you on the upper slopes in under an hour.

### Ródha

**RÓDHA**, barely 3km west of Aharávi, has tipped over into overdevelopment, and is certainly not the place to come for a quiet time. The resort does, however, offer some handy facilities. "Old Ródha" is a small warren of alleys between the main road and the seafront, where you'll find the best restaurants and bars.

### Sidhári

At the west end of the north coast, **SIDHÁRI** is totally dominated by British package tourists; its small but pretty town square, with a bandstand set in a small garden, is lost in a welter of restaurants, bars and shops. The beach is sandy but not terribly clean, and many people tend to head just west to the curious coves, walled by wind-carved sandstone cliffs, around the vaunted Canal d'Amour. Sidhári also has its own modest water park (free entry), a good place to keep the kids happy.

### GETTING AROUND                                               THE NORTH COAST

**By car or motorbike** Vlasseros Travel (☎ 26630 95695) is Sidhári's biggest general tourist agency and handles car rental. In Ródha, Myron offers good rates for motorbike rental (☎ 26630 63477).
**By boat** Voyager in Ródha (☎ 693 29 08 173) has boat rental from €15/hr.

## ACTIVITIES

**Diving** Kassiópi is home to one of the island's most reliable diving operations, Corfu Divers (☎ 26630 81218, ⓦ corfu-divers.com), which is partly British-run.

**Horseriding** Costas in Ródha offers horseriding (☎ 694 41 60 011; €20/2hr), as does Vlasseros Travel in Sidhári (see opposite).

## ACCOMMODATION

### KASSIÓPI

★ **Kastro** ☎ 26630 81045, ⓦ kastrokassiopi.com. Overlooking the beach behind the castle, these smart a/c apartments have balconies with sweeping views, as does the attached restaurant, which does excellent fresh food. May to mid-Oct. €50

**Panayiota Apartments** ☎ 26630 81063, ⓦ panayotakassiopi.com. Bargain studios, quite small and simply furnished, one block behind Kalamiónes beach on the west side of the castle's peninsula. April–Oct. €35

### ALMYRÓS BEACH AND AROUND

**Villa Maria** ☎ 26630 64284. The ideal place for a peaceful escape, this attractively designed two-storey block sits on a grassy plot close to the quiet beach and has sea-facing balconies. May–Oct. €40

### AHARÁVI

**Dandolo** ☎ 26630 63557, ⓦ dandolo.gr. Set in lush grounds on the edge of the old village, the refurbished complex contains fair-sized studios with well-equipped kitchens and verandas. April–Oct. €45

### RÓDHA

**Roda Camping** ☎ 26630 93120, ⓦ rodacamping.gr. Around 2km east of the resort, one of the island's best campsites offers a plethora of amenities, including a pool, restaurant and minimarket. May–Sept.

**Roda Inn** ☎ 26630 63358, ⓦ rodainn.com. On the seafront at the edge of the old town, the oldest hotel in the resort (dating from 1975) is one of the few places not exclusively rented by package companies. May–Oct. €40

## EATING, DRINKING AND NIGHTLIFE

### KASSIÓPI

**Eclipse** The liveliest and most established of the cluster of bars around the only junction in the resort, which shows DVDs before assuming full-on club mode as the night wears on. April–Oct daily 11am–late.

**Janis** ☎ 26630 81082. Where Kalamiónes beach meets the coast road, this huge taverna has an equally extensive menu, or, for a splurge, you can choose a live lobster from the tank (€70/kg). April–Oct daily 9am–2am.

**Porto** ☎ 26630 81228. Fish restaurant at the harbour, which has plenty of smaller fry for €7–9 per generous portion, plus meat dishes, salads and all the standard dips. May–Oct daily 11am–1am.

### AHARÁVI

★ **Theritas** ☎ 26630 63527. This taverna in the old village is the most authentic in the area, serving good home-cooked dishes such as beef in a rich red sauce or *sofríto*, grills and various starters, as well as very palatable wine. May–Oct daily noon–1am.

**Votsalakia** ☎ 26630 63346. At the western end of the beach, this is the best seaside restaurant, serving fresh fish and seafood at reasonable prices, as well as the usual array of salads and *mezédhes*. May–Oct daily 10am–midnight.

### RÓDHA

**Crusoe's** ☎ 693 22 50 487. Cheerful British-run pub which has decent snacks and features pub games, quizzes and Sky Sports on TV, as well as a range of music. May–Oct daily 9am–2am.

**Dolphin** ☎ 26630 63431. This seafront taverna in Old Ródha is the best place for fish or seafood, which you can enjoy with some good local barrelled wine beside the waves that lap below the patio. May–Oct daily 11am–1am.

### SIDHÁRI

**Babylon** ☎ 26630 95065. Fairly typical of the resort's numerous bars in appearance and ambience but one of the most popular, getting livelier the later it gets, with a mixture of pop and disco hits. May–Oct daily noon–late.

**Kavvadias** ☎ 26630 99032. Reliable taverna on the eastern stretch of beach, which dishes up all the Greek favourites and has the odd foray into Asian cuisine. Three-course specials for €7.50. April–Oct daily 10am–midnight.

**Kohenoor** ☎ 26630 95111. One of Corfu's best curry houses, serving a wide range of subcontinental favourites from tandoori to vindaloo for as little as €7–8. May–Sept daily 6pm–midnight.

# Corfu's satellite islands

Only three of Corfu's quintet of **Dhiapóndia islands**, scattered up to 20km off the northwest coast, are inhabited: Eríkoussa, Othoní and Mathráki. Each of them supports a tiny year-round community but they only really come alive in summer and even then the islands remain a relaxed backwater.

Flattish **Eríkoussa** is the sandiest and most visited of the three. There is an excellent golden sandy beach right by the harbour and quieter **Bragíni beach**, reached by a path across the wooded island interior. **OTHONÍ** is the largest island and has a handful of places to stay and eat in its port, **Ámmos**, which has two pebbly beaches. The village of **Horió** in the island's centre and sandy but deserted **Fýki Bay** are worth visiting if you stay. Hilly, densely forested and with long, almost invariably deserted **Portéllo beach**, beautiful **MATHRÁKI** has the fewest inhabitants, though it is gradually gearing up towards visitors.

## ARRIVAL AND DEPARTURE
## CORFU'S SATELLITE ISLANDS

**Day-trips** Some travel agencies in the northern resorts offer day-trips just to Eríkoussa, while a trip taking in all three islands from Sidhári or Áyios Stéfanos is excellent value. Vlasseros Travel in Sidhári (☎ 26630 95695) offer trips, while on the west coast, day-trips run several times a week in season (€20 per person) from Áyios Stéfanos to all three islands.

**By kaïkia and ferry** You can travel independently between the islands on regular *kaïkia* from Sidhári; there are also passenger services on the Aspiotis lines *kaïki* (3–5 weekly; €10–12 return; ☎ 26630 41297, ⊚ aspiotislines.gr) from Áyios Stéfanos. The thrice-weekly ferry from Corfu Town (2–4hr) is the least efficient way to get there.

## ACCOMMODATION, EATING AND DRINKING

The only rooms are those rented by locals such as Tassos Kassimis (☎ 26630 71700; €30) and Khristos Aryiros (☎ 26630 71652; €40), both on Portéllo beach.

**Erikousa** Eríkoussa ☎ 26630 71110, ⊚ hotelerikousa .gr. Busy throughout the season by virtue of being the island's sole hotel, with simple but adequate rooms, it also boasts the only bona fide taverna. Breakfast included. May–Sept. **€60**

**Hotel Calypso** Othoní ☎ 26630 72162. Some 200m east of the jetty, Othoní's only hotel has pleasant, comfortably furnished rooms with balconies plus a small bar. May–Sept. **€40**

**La Locanda dei Sogni** Othoní ☎ 26630 71640. Quality but not unreasonably priced Italian restaurant, which does a line in authentic antipasti, pasta and pizza dishes, plus plenty of Greek items. Also has some rooms. Restaurant May–Sept daily noon–1am. **€35**

**Port Centre** Mathráki. Good restaurant on the harbour that specializes in freshly caught fish at very decent prices, plus a few simple salads and mezédhes. Late May to Sept daily noon–midnight.

# Paleokastrítsa

**PALEOKASTRÍTSA**, a sprawling village 23km west of Corfu Town, surrounded by dramatic hills and cliffs, has been identified as the Homeric city of Scheria, where Odysseus was washed ashore and escorted by Nausicaa to the palace of her father Alkinous, king of the Phaeacians. It's a stunning site, as you would expect, with a delightful centre, though it's one that's long been engulfed by tourism.

## Beaches

The focal point of the village is the largest and least attractive of three **beaches**, home to sea taxis and *kaïka* (see box opposite). The second beach, to the right, is stony with clear water, but the best of the three is a small, unspoilt strand reached along the path by the *Astakos Taverna*. Protected by cliffs, it's almost entirely undeveloped.

## Theotókou monastery

7am–1pm & 3–8pm • Free, donations welcome

On the rocky bluff above the village, the **Theotókou monastery** is believed to have been established in the thirteenth century. There's also a museum, resplendent with icons, jewelled Bibles and other impediment of Greek Orthodox ritual, though the highlight is the gardens, from which there are spectacular coastal views.

> ## BOAT TRIPS FROM PALEOKASTRÍTSA
> From Paleokastrítsa's first beach you can get a boat trip to some nearby seawater caves, known as the **"blue grottoes"** (€10 for a 30min trip), which is worth taking for the spectacular coastal views. Boats also serve as a taxi service to three neighbouring **beaches**, Áyia Triánda, Palatákia and Alípa, which all have snack bars.

### Angelókastro
June–Oct daily 8.30am–2pm • €2

Paleokastrítsa's ruined Byzantine castle, the **Angelókastro**, is around 6km up the coast; only approachable by a path from the hamlet of **Kríni**, en route to which there are a couple of outstanding spots around the village of **Makrádhes** for a snack or drink while taking in the whole vista of Paleokastrítsa's promontory. The fortress itself has been partially restored for visitor safety and is worth the steep climb for the stunning, almost circular views of the surrounding sea and land from the battlements.

### ACCOMMODATION AND EATING — PALEOKASTRÍTSA

Accommodation isn't hard to find but sprawls a long way back from central Paleokastrítsa, often leaving quite a walk to the beach. Nightlife is pretty low-key, mostly comprising similar garden bars dotted along the main road.

**Astacos Taverna** ☎ 26630 41068, ⓦ astacos.biz. Just behind the second beach, highlights at this friendly taverna include the lobster after which it's named or more pocket-friendly moussaka. There are also some well-appointed studios just behind. May–Sept. **€40**

**Dolphin Snackbar** ☎ 26630 41035. Just down some steps from the main road and above Alípa beach, the simple rooms here are adequate, with easy beach access, and the food on offer (April–Oct 8.30am–midnight) is more substantial than the name suggests. **€35**

**Odysseus** ☎ 26630 41209, ⓦ odysseushotel.gr. On the road into town, this 65-room hotel has a pool, snack bar,

a/c restaurant and balconies facing either the garden or the sea. Breakfast included. April–Oct. **€50**

**Paleo Camping** ☎ 26630 41204, ⓦ camping paleokastritsa.com. Just off the main road, almost a 30min walk from the centre, this campsite has good facilities, shady if slightly cramped tent pitches and a mini-market. May–Sept. Adult plus tent **€7.50**

**Vrahos** ☎ 26630 41128. Upmarket taverna with starched tablecloths and rather stiff service but offering pricey top-of-the-range fish and some unusual dishes like artichokes. Reckon on at least €25–30 per head. April to mid-Oct noon–1am.

## The northwest coast

The northwest conceals some of the island's most dramatic coastal scenery, the violent interior mountainscapes jutting out of the verdant countryside. North of Paleokastrítsa, the densely olive-clad hills conceal good sandy beaches, such as **Áyios Yeóryios** and **Áyios Stéfanos**. Public **transport** between west coast resorts is difficult: virtually all buses ply routes from Corfu Town to single destinations and rarely link resorts.

### Áyios Yeóryios

Like many of the west-coast resorts, **ÁYIOS YEÓRYIOS**, around 9km north of Paleokastrítsa, isn't actually based around a village, though it is sometimes referred to as Áyios Yeóryios Pagón after the inland village of Payí to avoid confusion with its southern namesake. The resort has developed in response to the popularity of the large sandy bay, and it's a major **windsurfing** centre, especially towards the northern end, where boats can also be rented.

### Afiónas

The village of **AFIÓNAS**, perched high above the north end of Áyios Yeóryios bay, has been suggested as the likely site of **King Alkinous's castle** – there are vestigial Neolithic remains outside the village – and the walk up to the lighthouse on Cape Aríllas affords excellent views over Áyios Yeóryios and Aríllas Bay to the north.

## Áyios Stéfanos

The northernmost of the west coast's resorts, **ÁYIOS STÉFANOS** is low-key, popular with families and a quiet base from which to explore the northwest and the Dhiapóndia islands (see p.717), visible on the horizon. The small harbour lies a good kilometre south of the long sandy beach.

## Avliótes and around

In the northwest corner of Corfu stands **AVLIÓTES**, a handsome hill town with the odd *kafenío* and tavernas but few concessions to tourism. The town is useful for its accessibility to the small, quiet village of **Perouládhes** in the very northwest and stunning **Longás beach** below, bordered by vertical reddish layer-cake cliffs that make for shady mornings.

### ACCOMMODATION, EATING AND DRINKING

### THE NORTHWEST COAST

#### ÁYIOS YEÓRYIOS

★ **Ostrako** ☎ 26630 96028. Gaily painted taverna with a terrace overlooking the southern end of the beach, unbeatable for seafood such as squid and octopus. The eclectic recorded folk music helps create a pleasant atmosphere. May–Oct 11am–1am.

**Pension Vrahos** ☎ 26630 96366, ⓦ pension-vrachos .com. At the far northern end of the beach, under the eponymous cliff, this pension offers bright, good-value rooms in the building behind its taverna, which serves Greek and international cuisine. May–Oct. €40

**Studio Eleana** ☎ 26630 96366. Smart modern studios with crisp white linen, nice kitchenettes and some sea-view balconies, 50m behind the central section of beach. Late May–Sept. €35

#### AFIÓNAS

**To Panorama** ☎ 26630 51846, ⓔ panorama_afionas @hotmail.com. Friendly family restaurant which serves tasty meals made from organic produce and has great views from its terrace; it has also some good-value rooms. May–Sept. €30

#### ÁYIOS STÉFANOS

**Nafsika** ☎ 26630 51051, ⓦ nafsikahotel.com. Behind the southern strip of beach, the resort's oldest hotel has comfy rooms, a popular restaurant and gardens with a pool and bar. April–Oct. €40

★ **O Manthos** ☎ 26630 52197. The oldest taverna, behind the southern beach, is still the best, and serves Corfiot specialities such as *sofrito* and *pastitsádha*. Ask the venerable owner to show you his memorabilia. Music and dance every Sat. May–Oct noon–1am.

**Restaurant Evinos** ☎ 26630 51766. Has small apartments above the northern end of the village and serves up wholesome food, a mixture of *mayireftá* and grilled meat or fish. May to mid-Oct. €35

#### AVLIÓTES AND AROUND

**Panorama** Longás beach ☎ 26630 51846. The taverna's name gives the game away – perched on the cliff above the beach, its garden terrace is a great spot for a sunset dinner or cocktail at the attached *7th Heaven Café*. May–Sept daily 11am–midnight.

# Central Corfu

Much of central Corfu is occupied by the **plain of Rópa**, whose fertile landscape backs onto some of the best beaches on the west coast, such as delightful **Myrtiótissa**, as well as the island's only mountain resort, **Pélekas** – all a quick bus ride across the island from Corfu Town. The only place of note on the central east coast is **Benítses**.

## Érmones and around

**ÉRMONES**, around 15km south of Paleokastrítsa by road, is one of the busiest resorts on the island, its lush green bay backed by the mountains above the Rópa River but rather marred by the ugly tiered *Ermones Beach Hotel* and its private funicular. Just inland is the **Corfu Golf and Country Club** (☎ 26610 94220, ⓦ corfugolfclub.com), the only golf club in the archipelago, and reputed to be one of the finest in the Mediterranean.

## Myrtiótissa

Far preferable to the gravelly sand of Érmones is the idyllic strand of **MYRTIÓTISSA**, about 3km south. In *Prospero's Cell*, Lawrence Durrell described Myrtiótissa as "perhaps the loveliest beach in the world"; it was for years a well-guarded secret but is now a firm favourite, especially with nudists, and gets so busy in summer that it supports three *kantínas*, meaning it's at its best well out of high season. Above the north end of the beach is the tiny, whitewashed **Myrtiótissa monastery**, dedicated to Our Lady of the Myrtles.

## Pélekas and around

**PÉLEKAS**, inland and 5km southeast of Érmones, has long been popular for its views – the **Kaiser's Throne** viewing tower, just above the town, was Wilhelm II's favourite spot in the area. On the small square the **Odhiyítria church**, renovated in 1884, is worth a peek. Pélekas's sandy **beach** is reached down a short path, though sadly it's been rather spoilt by the monstrous *Pelekas Beach* hotel that now looms over it.

The inland area around Pélekas holds some of Corfu's most traditional villages. This atmosphere of days gone by is best reflected in **SINARÁDHES**, around 4km away, which has the **Folk Museum of Central Corfu** (Tues–Sun 9.30am–2.30pm; €2). The museum comprises an authentic village house, complete with original furniture, fittings and decoration and full of articles and utensils that formed an intrinsic part of daily rural life.

## Áï Górdhis and around

Around 7km south of Pélekas, **ÁÏ GÓRDHIS** is one of the major party beaches on the island, largely because of the activities organized by the startling *Pink Palace* complex (see p.722), which dominates the resort.

Inland from the resort is the south's largest prominence, the humpback of **Áyii Dhéka** (576m), reached by path from the hamlet of Áno Garoúna; it is the island's second-largest mountain after Pandokrátor. The lower slopes are wooded, and it's possible to glimpse buzzards wheeling on thermals over the higher slopes. The monks at the tiny monastery just below the summit lovingly tend a bountiful orchard.

## Áyios Matthéos

The town of **ÁYIOS MATTHÉOS**, 3km inland, is still chiefly an agricultural centre, although a number of *kafenía* and tavernas offer a warm welcome to passers-by. On the other side of Mount Prasoúdhi, 2km by road, is the **Gardhíki Pýrgos**, the ruins of a thirteenth-century castle built in this unlikely lowland setting by the despots of Epirus.

## Benítses

South of Corfu Town on the east coast, there's nothing to recommend before **BENÍTSES**, a once-notorious bonking-and-boozing resort, whose old centre at the north end has long since reverted to a quiet bougainvillea-splashed Greek village. There are a couple of minor attractions, namely the modest ruins of a **Roman bathhouse** at the back of the village and the small but impressive **shell museum** (March–May & Oct daily 10am–6pm, June–Sept 9am–8pm; €4; ☎ 26610 72227, ⑩corfushellmuseum.com).

### ACCOMMODATION, EATING AND DRINKING — CENTRAL CORFU

**ÉRMONES**

**Nafsica** ☎ 26610 94911. Perched just above the southern end of the beach, with a huge terrace, *Nafsica* provides good, filling mezédhes and main courses of both meat and fish. April–Oct 11am–1am.

**Philoxenia** ☎ 26610 94091, ⑩hotelphiloxenia.gr. Far better value than the *Ermones Beach*, this spacious modern hotel on the south side of the creek has two pools, a bar and all the rooms face the sea. May to mid-Oct. **€60**

**MYRTIÓTISSA**

★ **Myrtia** ☎ 26610 94113, ✉sks_mirtia@hotmail .com. Delightful taverna with an olive-shaded garden, which serves tasty home-style cooking and offers a few simple but clean and cosy rooms. May–Oct. **€40**

**PÉLEKAS AND AROUND**

**Alexandros** Pélekas ☎ 26610 94215, ⑩alexandros pelekas.com. Lots of the usual Greek favourites, plus pizza and pasta dishes, can be sampled here and the studios above are reasonably sized and comfortably furnished. April–Oct. **€50**

**Pension Paradise** Pélekas ☎ 26610 94530, ⑩paradisepelekas.com. On the road in from Vátos, this ochre-tinted year-round *pension* run by a friendly old couple has simple homely rooms at bargain rates. **€30**

★ **Pink Panther** Pélekas ☎ 26610 94360. Serves quite a few imaginative dishes, with a refreshing array of peppery sauces, all at under €10, which can be enjoyed along with a glass or two of aromatic local wine while gazing at the splendid view from the lofty terrace. Easter–Oct.

### AÏ GÓRDHIS AND AROUND

★ **Elena's** ☎ 26610 53210, ⓦ elenasapartments.com. A variety of rooms and apartments in the village is available through the seafront taverna, which is painted marine blue and white and serves excellent home-style cuisine at low prices, like beef in mustard sauce. April–Oct. €30

**Pink Palace** ☎ 26610 53103, ⓦ thepinkpalace.com. Legendary year-round backpackers' haunt, with pools, games courts, internet access, restaurants, a shop and a disco. Apart from the dorms for up to ten a night, which include breakfast and an evening buffet, there are compact singles and doubles. Dorms from €18; doubles €50

### BENÍTSES

**Benitses Arches** ☎ 26610 72113, ⓦ hotelbenitsesarches.com. Pleasant bougainvillea-adorned hotel, just south of the centre of the resort, with quiet rooms set a couple of blocks back from the main road. April–Oct. €45

**O Paxinos** ☎ 26610 72339. Intimate taverna in the old village, specializing in Corfiot dishes such as *sofríto* and *pastitsádha*, not cheap at €12 a pop but expertly prepared and washed down with fine barrelled wine. Daily noon–1am.

**Stadium** Huge club at the southern end of the main strip. The interior opens only occasionally, hosting concerts or big dance nights, but the lively outdoor pool bar is open throughout the season. May–Sept daily noon–late.

## Southern Corfu

Corfu's southwest coast offers perhaps the island's finest stretches of sand, from the peaceful **Korissíon lagoon** on down, almost unbroken to the island's tip. On the east side, there is a mixture of resorts, ranging from peaceful enclaves like **Boúkari** to the full-on party antics of **Kávos**, by way of Corfu's second-largest settlement, traditional **Lefkími**.

### Moraïtika and Mesongí

On the east coast roughly 20km south of the capital, the first real development after Benítses is **MORAÏTIKA**, whose main street is an ugly strip of bars, restaurants and shops, but its beach is the best between Corfu Town and Kávos. The original village, **ÁNO MORAÏTIKA**, is signposted a few minutes' hike up the steep lanes inland and is virtually unspoilt, its tiny houses and alleys practically drowning in dazzling bougainvillea. The resort has become very popular with eastern Europeans.

Commencing barely a hundred metres on from the Moraïtika seafront and separated only by the Mesongí River, **MESONGÍ** continues this stretch of package-tour-oriented coast but is noticeably quieter and has a range of accommodation deals.

### Boúkari and around

**BOÚKARI**, linked to Mesongí by a quiet road that follows the seashore for about 3km, often only a few feet above it, comprises little more than a handful of tavernas, a shop and a few small, family-run hotels. Out of the way, it's an idyllic little strip of unspoilt coast for anyone looking to relax. It is also handily placed for the unspoilt wooded region inland around **Aryirádhes**, rarely visited by tourists and perfect for quiet walks.

### Petrití and around

Four kilometres south of Boúkari, the village of **PETRITÍ**, only created in the 1970s when geologists discovered the hill village of Korakádhes was sliding downhill, fronts onto a small but busy harbour. It is mercifully free of noise and commerce, with a beach of rock, mud and sand set among low olive-covered hills. Barely 2km south of Petrití, the picturesque rocky coves of **Nótos beach** are little visited.

### Korissíon lagoon and around

Over on the southwest coast, one of the island's most distinctive geographical features is the **Korissíon lagoon**, home to turtles, tortoises, lizards and numerous indigenous and

## WALKING THE CORFU TRAIL

The **Corfu Trail**, 200km in length and open since 2001, covers the whole island from **Cape Asprókavos** in the south to Áyios Spyrídhon beach, next to **Cape Ayías Ekaterínis** in the far north. The route avoids roads as much as possible and takes walkers across a variety of terrain – from beaches to the highest peaks – passing by Lefkími, Korissíon lagoon, Áyii Dhéka, Pélekas, Myrtiótissa, Paleokastrítsa, Áyios Yeóryios Pagón, Spartýlas and Mount Pandokrátor.

Paths along the entire route are **waymarked** with yellow aluminium signs. As usual, ramblers are advised to wear headgear and stout footwear and carry ample water and provisions, as well as all-weather kit in all but the high summer months. It is reckoned that strong walkers can cover the route in ten days.

Those interested in attempting all or part of the trail should pick up Hilary Whitton Paipeti's excellent *Companion Guide to the Corfu Trail* (W corfutrailguide.com; €10), which contains detailed **maps** and descriptions of the route, divided into ten daily sections. A proportion of the profits goes towards maintenance of the trail, and anyone using the trail is asked to contribute €3 for the same reason. You can also log on to W travelling.gr/corfutrail for information on organized walking packages, including accommodation.

**11**

migratory birds. Its northern section, which is over 5km long and 1km wide at its centre, is separated from the sea by the dunes of **Halikoúna beach**, an idyllic spot for swimming and rough camping, while more touristic **Íssos beach** borders the southern end.

## Áyios Yeóryios, Marathiá and Ayía Varvára

Far pleasanter than **Áyios Yeóryios**, the main Brit-dominated but rather brash resort on the coast south of the Korissíon lagoon, are **MARATHIÁ** and **AYÍA VARVÁRA**, both essentially forming a single resort further southeast along the same continuous strand. They are separated only by a stream that you can easily cross on the beach but each settlement must be approached by different roads. The most direct route to Marathiá beach is signposted from the tiny village of **Marathiás**, a couple of kilometres southeast of Aryirádhes on the main road, while **AYÍA VARVÁRA** is signposted from the village of Perivóli further south.

## Lefkími

Anyone interested in how a Greek town works away from the bustle of tourism shouldn't miss **LEFKÍMI**, towards the island's southern tip. The second-largest settlement after Corfu Town, it's the administrative centre for the south of the island as well as the alternative ferry port for Igoumenítsa. The town has some fine architecture, including several striking churches: **Áyii Anáryiri** with a huge double belfry, **Áyios Theódhoros**, on a mound above a small square, and **Áyios Arsénios**, with a vast orange dome that can be seen for miles.

## Kávos

There are no ambiguities in **KÁVOS**, 6km south of Lefkími: either you like 24-hour drinking, clubbing, bungee-jumping, go-karts and chips with almost everything, or you should avoid the resort altogether. Kávos stretches over 2km of decent sandy beach, with watersports galore. As numbers have dropped in recent years, unbelievable accommodation bargains can be had, should you choose to stay.

## South of Kávos

Beyond the limits of Kávos, where few visitors stray, a path leaving the road south to the hamlet of Sparterá heads through unspoilt countryside; after around thirty minutes of walking it reaches the cliffs of **Cape Asprókavos** and the crumbling **monastery of Arkoudhílas**. The cape looks out over the straits to Paxí, and down over deserted **Arkoudhílas beach**, which can be reached from Sparterá, a pleasant village 5km by road but only 3km by the signed path from Kávos. Even wilder is **Áï Górdhis Paleohoríou beach**, 3km further on from Sparterá, one of the least visited on the island and not to be confused with the eponymous beach further north; a municipal café provides the only refreshment. The Cape is also the southern starting point for the **Corfu Trail** (see box, p.723).

## ARRIVAL AND DEPARTURE
### SOUTHERN CORFU

**By ferry** Lefkími has a year-round ferry connection to Igoumenítsa (6 daily; 40min).

**By bus** Lefkími is on the frequent bus route from Corfu Town to Kávos (11 Mon–Fri, 8 Sat, 4 Sun; 1hr 20min).

## ACCOMMODATION, EATING AND DRINKING

### MORAÏTIKA AND MESONGÍ

**Bella Vista** Áno Moraïtika ☎ 26610 75460. The menu is fairly basic but wholesome, with grills and fresh salads, but the place justifies its name with a lovely garden, sea views and breezes. March–Nov daily noon–midnight.

**Charlie's** Moraïtika. The village's oldest bar, which opened in 1939, is a meeting place for locals and tourists alike, with a central location on the main road. Light snacks are available and the music consists of old pop favourites. Daily noon–late.

**Firefly** Moraïtika ☎ 26610 75850. On one of the northernmost lanes down to the beach, this taverna has a good range of meat, fish, salads and dips, plus it rents those rooms not booked by Romanian tour operators. May–Sept. **€30**

**Hotel Gemini** Mesongí ☎ 26610 75221, ⓦ geminihotel .gr. This rather elegant hotel boasts a large pool and manicured gardens, plus sizeable en-suite rooms with balconies. Breakfast included. May–Sept. **€65**

**Spiros on the Beach** Mesongí ☎ 26610 75285. Beachfront restaurant with two premises 20m apart, good for tasty €8 fish soup plus other offerings from the deep, plus various carnivorous or vegetarian options. May to mid-Oct daily 11am–2am.

### BOÚKARI AND AROUND

★ **Boukari Beach** Boúkari ☎ 26620 51791, ⓦ boukaribeach.gr. Right on the sea 1km north of Boúkari's harbour, one of Corfu's best tavernas offers delicious home cooking, and fresh fish and live lobster. The friendly family also run the smart and comfortable *Penelopi* and *Villa Alexandra*, with huge self-catering suites. Breakfast included. April–Nov. **€40**

### PETRITÍ AND AROUND

★ **Panorama Villas** Nótos beach ☎ 26620 51707, ⓦ panoramacorfu.gr. A wonderfully friendly haven worth making the detour to, whether to stay or for its fine shady restaurant, renowned for its excellent home cooking. Breakfast included. April–Oct. **€40**

**Pension Egrypos** Petrití ☎ 26620 51949, ⓦ egrypos .gr. Pleasantly landscaped complex with a pool, bar and a restaurant. The rooms are smart, modern and fully equipped. Breakfast included. May to mid-Oct. **€50**

**Stamatis** Petrití ☎ 26620 51920. The best of the bunch clustered around the harbour, this year-round local taverna rustles up goodies like mussels and small fish for around €7–8. Daily noon–1am.

### ÁYIOS YEÓRYIOS, MARATHIÁ AND AYÍA VARVÁRA

**Akroama** Marathiá ☎ 26620 52736. Good family-run taverna with treats like swordfish and local sausage, which can be enjoyed from the low-lying cliff terrace. They also rent some comfortable rooms. May–Sept. **€30**

### LEFKÍMI

**Cheeky Face** ☎ 26620 22627. The old couple who run this simple year-round *estiatório*, by the bridge over the canal in the lower part of town, provide inexpensive staples and a few equally basic rooms upstairs. **€40**

### KÁVOS

**Future** The most lively club of the dozens that line the main drag, with imported north European DJs, state-of-the-art sound-and-light systems, shots galore and a constant parade of the scantily clad. May–Oct daily 10pm–late.

# Paxí and Andípaxi

Unusually verdant and still largely unspoilt, **PAXÍ (Paxos)** has established a firm niche in Greece's tourist hierarchy, despite being the smallest of the main Ionian islands at barely 12km by 4km, with only mediocre beaches and no historical sites. Yet it has become so popular it is best avoided in high season. It's a particular favourite of yachting flotillas, whose spending habits have brought the island an upmarket reputation, making it just about the most expensive place to visit in the Ionian islands. The capital, **Gáïos**, is quite cosmopolitan, with delis and boutiques, but northerly **Lákka** and tiny **Longós** are where hardcore Paxophiles head, while by far the best swimming is at Paxí's little sister island, **Andípaxi**.

# Gáïos

The island's capital, **GÁÏOS**, is a pleasant town built around a small square in the middle of an elongated seafront overlooking two islands, Áyios Nikólaos and Panayía. Nearly all the town's facilities are to be found on the seafront or within little over 100m of it.

## Folk Museum

June to mid-Sept daily 10am–2pm & 7–11pm • €2

The island's only museum, the **Folk Museum**, is housed in an old school building on the seafront about 200m south of the main square. One room is set up as an eighteenth-century bedroom with some period furniture and costumes. Other items on display from different epochs include kitchen implements, musical instruments, china, stationery and guns.

# Around Gáïos

**Inland** are some of the island's oldest settlements, such as Oziás and Vellianitátika, in prime walking country but with scarcely any facilities. The **coast south** of Gáïos is punctuated by the odd shingly cove, none ideal for swimming, until matters improve towards the tip at **Mogoníssi beach**, which shares some of Andípaxi's sandier geology.

# Longós and around

**LONGÓS** is the prettiest village on the island, though it's dominated by the upmarket villa crowd. Its scruffy beach is favoured by local grannies for the sulphur springs, so most people swim off **Levrehió beach** in the next bay south. Longós is at the bottom of a steep winding hill, making **walking** a bit of a chore, but the short circuit around neighbouring **Dhendhriátika** provides spectacular views and allows access to the small

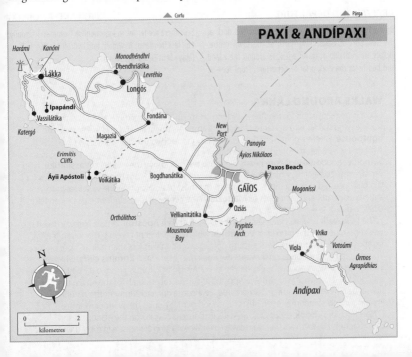

but excellent **Monodhéndhri beach**. You can also walk to **Fondána** and the former capital of **Magaziá**, back on the main road.

## Lákka and around

Buses run 3–4 times Mon–Sat between Gáïos and Lákka, most diverting through Longós; taxis between Gáïos and Lákka cost around €10

Approached from the south, **LÁKKA** is an unprepossessing jumble of buildings, but once in its maze of alleys and neo-Venetian buildings or on the quay with views of distant Corfu, you do get a sense of its charm. Lákka's two **beaches**, Harámi and Kanóni, are none too brilliant for swimming or sunbathing, but there's a sense of community about the place and overall it's the best place to hang out on the island, with plenty of great dining and local walking.

## Andípaxi

Frequent seasonal *kaïkia* shuttle between Gáïos and Andípaxi (€10 return); the glass-bottomed boat from Gáïos to Andípaxi (€15 return) also takes you to its sea stacks and caves

Less than 2km south, Paxí's tiny sibling **ANDÍPAXI** has scarcely any accommodation and no facilities beyond several beach tavernas open during the daytime in season. Andípaxi's sandy, blue-water coves have been compared with the Caribbean, but you'll have to share them with *kaïkia* and sea taxis from all three villages on Paxí, plus larger craft from Corfu and the mainland resorts.

Boats basically deposit you either at the sandy **Vríka beach** or the longer pebble beach of **Vatoúmi**, although quieter bays are accessible to the south. Paths also lead inland to connect the handful of homes and the southerly lighthouse, but there are no beaches of any size on Andípaxi's western coastline and thick thorny scrub makes access difficult.

### ARRIVAL AND DEPARTURE                    PAXÍ AND ANDÍPAXI

**By ferry/hydrofoil** Both ferries and hydrofoils dock at the new port of Gáïos, 1km north of the town centre. Tickets are available at travel agencies around the island and booths at the dock prior to departure. From June to Sept there are ferries to Igoumenítsa (summer 1–2 daily; 1hr; less frequently in winter) and hydrofoils to Corfu Town (May–Sept 1–3 daily; 50min).

---

### WALKS AROUND LÁKKA

Lákka is perfectly sited for the finest walking on the island. For a simple, short hike, take the track leaving the far end of Harámi beach. This mounts the headland and leads on to the **lighthouse**, where a goat track descends through tough scrub to a sandy open-sea beach with rollers best left to confident swimmers.

Another good walking route heads west into the hills above the village to **Vassilátika**, high on the west-coast cliffs, which has stunning views out to sea. From here, the path to the left of the blue-painted stone archway leads on to the most dramatic cliff-edge views (vertigo sufferers beware) and continues to **Magaziá** in the centre of the island, where you can flag down a bus or taxi.

The best **walk** on Paxí, however, is to the church at **Áyii Apóstoli**, almost halfway down the west coast, next to the hamlet of **Voïkátika**, which has a decent taverna. The rough track is signposted a few hundred metres south of Magaziá, and takes less than half an hour on foot. The church and surrounding vineyards overlook the sheer 150m **Erimítis cliffs**, which at sunset are transformed into a seaside version of Ayers Rock, turning from dirty white to pink and gold and brown. If you visit Áyii Apóstoli at sunset, take a torch for the return trip. The *Sunset* **bar**, next to the church, can provide a welcome drink to augment the natural splendour and sometimes even hosts full-moon parties during the warmer months.

Noel Rochford's **book**, *Landscapes of Paxos*, lists dozens of walks on the island; this and cartographers Elizabeth and Ian Bleasdale's *Paxos Walking Map* are on sale in most travel agencies.

## ACCOMMODATION, EATING, DRINKING AND NIGHTLIFE

As there are only three hotels and most accommodation on Paxí is booked by foreign tour companies, rooms and villas are best arranged in advance through one of the island's travel agencies: Gaïos Travel (☎ 26620 32033, ⊛ gaiostravel.co.uk) and Bouas Tours (☎ 26620 32401, ⊛ bouastours.gr), both on the capital's seafront; or Routsis (☎ 26620 31807, ⊛ routsis-holidays.com) and British-owned Planos Holidays (☎ 26620 31744 or UK +44 1373 814200, ⊛ planos.co.uk), both based in Lákka, for northern Paxí.

### GAÏOS

**Dodos** ☎ 26620 32265. Set in a garden inland from the Anemoyiannis statue towards the southern end of the seafront, this old favourite has a full range of mezédhes and main courses, mostly under €10. May to early Oct daily noon–midnight.

★ **Genesis** ☎ 26620 32495. Convivial, brightly decorated taverna-cum-café, by far the best of the seafront establishments, right opposite the Anemoyiannis statue, serving great wine and home-cooked dishes such as several types of *stifádho*, including octopus. May–Oct daily 10am–1am.

★ **Paxos Beach Hotel** ☎ 26620 32211, ⊛ paxosbeachhotel.gr. Attractive en-suite bungalows with balconies on a hillside above a pebbly beach 2km south of town; amenities include a saltwater pool, yoga sessions, tennis court and mini-golf. Free shuttle bus. Breakfast included. May–Oct. **€120**

**Paxos Club** ☎ 26620 32450, ⊛ paxosclub.gr. Nearly 2km inland from Gaïos, this luxury resort set in lavish gardens offers large, well-furnished rooms and suites with kitchens, as well as a classy restaurant, pool and bar. Breakfast included. May–Sept. **€110**

**PhoenixDisco** ☎ 26620 32210. On a hill overlooking the bay, with a large outdoor dancefloor and the usual mix of foreign and Greek disco hits, this is the island's premier nightclub. June–Sept daily 10pm–late.

### LONGÓS AND AROUND

**O Gios** ☎ 26620 31735. A simple and cheap taverna in the middle of the harbour, where you can get great grills, the odd oven dish and some basic salads and dips. June–Sept daily noon–midnight.

★ **Vassilis** ☎ 26620 30062. Friendly portside restaurant, where the bus has to squeeze past the pavement tables. Terrific fish dishes and tasty starters, outlined on a memorable newspaper-style menu. May–Oct daily 11am–1am.

### LÁKKA AND AROUND

★ **Alexandros** Platía Edward Kennedy ☎ 26620 30045. Very friendly taverna tucked in the southwest corner of the village, great for fresh fish, *gourounópoulo* (roast suckling pig), creamed mushrooms and pork roll for €10. May–Oct daily 1pm–1am.

**Amfitriti Hotel** ☎ 26620 30011, ⊛ amfitritihotel.gr. Hidden among olive groves behind Harámi beach, the least expensive of Paxí's three hotels offers comfortable rooms with private balconies and kitchenettes. May–Oct. **€65**

**Harbour Lights** ☎ 26620 31412. Perennial favourite bar in the middle of the harbour, most likely to stay open the longest hours. Good range of drinks and mostly well-known pop and rock sounds. May–Oct daily noon–late.

**La Rosa di Paxos** ☎ 26620 31471. Slightly upmarket seafront restaurant, which does good risottos and ravioli, a variety of salads and some more standard Greek favourites. Mid-May to mid-Oct daily noon–1am.

**Nionios** ☎ 26620 31315. Serving a fine range of Hellenic favourites on the main square, from fish and meat grills to some tasty oven-baked veggie options, as well as fine barrelled wine. May–Oct daily noon–midnight.

### ANDÍPAXI

**Bella Vista** Vatoúmi beach ☎ 26620 31766. Perched on a cliff overlooking the cove, this taverna justifies its name and also dishes up fresh fish and meat grills, plus a suitable range of salads and mezédhes. June–Sept noon–6pm.

**Spiros** Vríka beach ☎ 26620 31172. The oldest taverna on the island has great grilled and oven food. They can also arrange self-catering accommodation up in Vígla, the island's hilltop settlement, on a weekly basis. Late May to mid-Sept 11am–7pm.

# Lefkádha

**LEFKÁDHA** (Lefkás) is an oddity, which is exactly why it is some people's favourite Ionian island. Connected to the mainland by a long causeway through lagoons and a 30m pontoon swivel bridge, it barely feels like an island, at least on the busier eastern side. Lefkádha was long an important strategic base and approaching the causeway you pass a series of fortresses, climaxing in the fourteenth-century castle of **Santa Maura** – the Venetian name for the island. These defences were too close to the mainland to avoid an Ottoman tenure, which began in 1479, but the Venetians wrested back control a couple of centuries later. They were in turn overthrown by Napoleon in 1797 and then the British took over as Ionian protectors in 1810 until reunification with Greece in 1864.

The whiteness of its rock strata – *lefkás* has the same root as *lefkós*, "white" – is apparent on its partly bare ridges. While the marshes and boggy inlets on the east coast can lead to a mosquito problem, the island is a fertile place, supporting cypresses, olive groves and vineyards, particularly on the western slopes. The rugged west coast, however, is the star attraction, boasting some of the finest beaches in the archipelago.

Lefkádha remains relatively undeveloped, with just two major resorts: **Vassilikí**, in its vast bay in the south, claims to be Europe's biggest windsurfing centre; **Nydhrí**, on the east coast, overlooks the island's picturesque set of satellite islets, including laidback **Meganíssi**. The capital's superb **marina** also appeals to yachties in large numbers.

## ARRIVAL AND INFORMATION                                          LEFKÁDHA

**By plane** Lefkádha itself does not have an airport but is less than 20km from the one at Préveza, served by charter flights from northern and eastern Europe, as well as domestic connections to Athens (1–2 daily; 50min). There is no airport bus but KTEL services from Préveza stop at the terminal entrance and taxis are readily available.

**By bus** The new bus station is out past the marina, around 1km from the centre of Lefkádha Town.
Destinations Athens (4 daily; 5hr 30min); Igoumenítsa (5 weekly; 3hr); Pátra (2 weekly; 3hr); Préveza (4 Mon–Sat, 3

Sun; 30min); Thessaloníki (2 weekly; 8–9hr).
**By ferry** Apart from the shuttle ferry from Nydhrí to Meganíssi (see p.734), the only ferries departing from Lefkádha now leave from Vassilikí; the summer schedules below are reduced drastically in the low season.
Destinations Fiskárdho (Kefaloniá; 1–2 daily; 1hr); Fríkes (Itháki; 1 daily; 1hr 30min).
**Information** There is no tourist office on Lefkádha but for further information you can check out Ⓦ lefkasgreece.com, the most comprehensive site on the island.

## GETTING AROUND

**By bus** There are services from Lefkádha Town to almost every village on the island, with frequent daily schedules to Nydhrí, Vassilikí and Áyios Nikítas/Káthisma, especially in summer.

**By car or motorbike** Two outlets for car and motorbike rental in the capital are EuroHire, Golémi 5 (ⓣ 26450

26776, Ⓦ eurohire.gr), near the bus station, and Santas (ⓣ 26450 25250, Ⓦ ilovesantas.gr), next to the *Ionian Star* hotel. There are numerous other rental agencies throughout the island, especially Nydhrí, Vassilikí and Áyios Nikítas.

# Lefkádha Town

**LEFKÁDHA TOWN** sits at the island's northernmost tip, right where the causeway joins it to the mainland. Like other capitals in the southern Ionian, it was hit by the earthquakes of 1948 and 1953 and the town was devastated, with the exception of a few Italianate churches. It's a small town – you can cross it on foot in little over ten minutes – and still very attractive, especially around the main square, **Platía Ayíou Spyridhónos**, and the arcaded high street of Ioánnou Méla. The largely pedestrian-only centre boasts over half a dozen richly decorated private family **churches**, best visited around services as they are usually locked at other times. Many contain rare works from the Ionian School of painting, including work by its founder, Zakynthian Panayiotis Doxaras.

## Phonograph, Radio and Tradition Museum

Panayióti Políti 1–3 • May–Oct daily 10am–2pm & 7pm–midnight • Free • ⓣ 26450 21088
You can catch a glimpse of the old way of life at the quaint little **Phonograph, Radio and Tradition Museum**, which is dedicated to antique phonographs, radios and an astounding array of bric-a-brac. It also sells recordings of rare traditional music and a few assorted souvenirs.

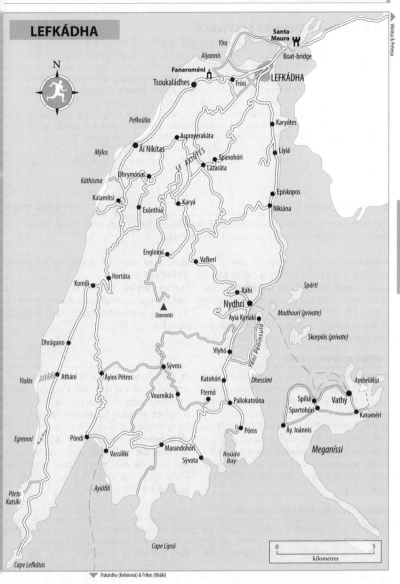

Vónitsa & Préveza

# LEFKÁDHA

Santa Maura

Boat-bridge

Yíra

Aïyannis

Faneroméni

Tsoukaládhes · Fríni · **LEFKÁDHA**

Pefkoúlia

Asproyerakáta

Karyótes

Mýlos · Aï Nikítas

Liyiá

Spanohóri

Dhrymónas · SF. AKTÓTES · Lazaráta

Káthisma

Episkopos

Kalamítsi · Exánthia · Karyá

Nikiána

Englouví · Vafkerí

Hortáta

Spárti

Komíli · Ráhi

▲ · **Nydhrí** · Madhoúri (private)

Stavrotás · Ayía Kyriakí

Skorpiós (private)

Dhrágano · Vlyhó

Teni Peninsula

Athání · Sývros · Ambelákia

Yialós · Áyios Pétros

Katohóri · Dhessími · Vathý

Vournikás · Fterno · Spiliá

Paliokatoúna · Spartohóri · Katoméri

Póndi · Póros

Marandohóri · Ay. Ioánnis

Vassilikí · Roúda Bay · **Meganíssi**

Egremní · Sývota

Ayiófili

Pórto Katsíki

0 — kilometres — 5

Cape Lipsó

Cape Lefkátas

Fiskárdho (Kefaloniá) & Fríkes (Itháki)

**11**

## Archeological museum

Cnr of Sikelianoú & Svorónou · Tues–Sun 8.30am–3pm · €2 · ☎ 26450 21635

On the northwestern seafront the modern cultural centre houses the newly
expanded **archeological museum**, which contains interesting, well-labelled displays
on aspects of daily life, religious worship and funerary customs in ancient times, as
well as a room on prehistory dedicated to the work of eminent German archeologist
Wilhelm Dörpfeld.

## LEFKÁDHA'S SUMMER FESTIVALS

Lefkádha has been home to various literati, including two prominent Greek poets, Angelos Sikelianos and Aristotelis Valaoritis, and the American writer Lafcadio Hearn. Fittingly then, each summer for over fifty years, Lefkádha has hosted two parallel and wide-ranging cultural festivals, which these days attract performers and visitors from around the world. These are the **International Folklore Festival** and **Speech & Arts Events**. Originally only lasting for two to three weeks in August, they now extend from June to September, and troupes come from eastern and western Europe, South America and elsewhere, performing mainly at Santa Maura castle near Lefkádha Town, but also in villages around the island. The island and mainland Greece respond with troupes of their own musicians, dancers and theatrical companies. You can usually enjoy occasional performances of world music and jazz too, as well as art exhibitions and special cinema showings. For details, contact ☎ 26450 26711 or see ⓦ lefkasculturalcenter.gr.

**11**

### ACCOMMODATION                                LEFKÁDHA TOWN

The Lefkádha Room Owners Association (☎ 26450 21266; from €30) can help find rooms in Lefkádha Town, mostly in the dormitory area northwest of Dörpfeld, and around the rest of the island.

**Ionian Star** Panágou 2 ☎ 26450 24672, ⓦ ionian-star .com. With its own pool, a games room and free internet access for guests, the island's top hotel has comfortable spacious rooms, many with sea-view balconies. Breakfast included. €85

**Nirikos** Ayías Mávras ☎ 26450 24132, ⓦ nirikos.gr. This fairly standard four-storey block contains fairly spacious rooms that are stylish in a minimalist sort of way. Breakfast included. April–Oct. €65

**Pension Pyrofani** Dörpfeld ☎ 26450 25844. This smallish deep ochre-coloured *pension*, just on the sea side of the main square, offers warmly decorated, comfortable rooms. May–Oct. €60

### EATING AND DRINKING

**Burano Golémi** ☎ 26450 26025. Smart *mezedhopolío* on the seafront almost opposite the marina, which has candlelit tables within, as well as pavement seating to enjoy the wide range of items available. May–Oct daily noon–1am.

**Eftyhia** Alley just off Dörpfeld ☎ 26450 24811. A fine little old-fashioned *estiatório* where you can make your choice from the mostly baked delights such as stuffed marrow once you've perused the glass window in the kitchen. April–Oct daily, plus occasional winter days 11am–11pm.

**Ev Zin** Filarmonikís 8 ☎ 697 46 41 160. Self-proclaimed "soul food place" with a slightly bohemian atmosphere, imaginative decor and unusual dishes such as Tex-Mex, risotto and Roquefort steak for €14. April–Oct daily noon–1am.

**★ Regantos** Dhimárhou Venióti ☎ 26450 22855. Well-established local favourite, serving a delicious array of meat like stuffed pork, fish and starters such as baked octopus, all around €6–8. Often has live Lefkadan *kantádhes*. Feb–Nov daily 7pm–2am.

### NIGHTLIFE AND ENTERTAINMENT

**Cäsbäh** Platía Ayíou Spyridhónos ☎ 26450 25486. One of the most enduring café-bars in town, which echoes its name by playing some ethnic sounds and having touches of eastern decor. Daily 11am–late.

**Coconut** Sikelianoú ☎ 26450 23341. Airy and relaxed café on the seafront west of the bridge, which turns into a lively club as the night wears on. Sip a cocktail or down shots to the latest dance tunes. May–Oct noon–late.

**Eleni** Faneroménis 51 ☎ 26450 24550. The town's outdoor cinema has two showings of mostly English films, with programmes changing daily. May to mid-Oct daily from 9pm.

## Around Lefkádha Town

Lefkádha has the best swimming close to town of any Ionian capital, thanks to the sandy borders to the lagoon at **Yíra** and **Aïyánnis**. Inland, there is also the attractive **Faneroméni monastery** and some traditional mountain villages centred around **Karyá**.

## Yíra and Aïyánnis

There is a decent and lengthy shingle-and-sand beach west of the lagoon at **YÍRA**, a thirty-minute walk from the centre of Lefkádha Town. Roughly 4km long, the beach is often virtually deserted even in high season. Its western extension, **AÏYÁNNIS**, is a popular yet relaxed spot with several restaurants.

## Faneroméni monastery

Daily 8am–2pm & 4–8pm • Free

The uninhabited **Faneroméni monastery** is reached by any of the west-coast buses or by a steep 45-minute hike on foot from town through the hamlet of Fríni. There's a small museum and chapel, and an ox's yoke and hammer, used when Nazi occupiers forbade the use of bells.

## Karyá and the interior

The island's **interior** offers imposing mountainscapes and excellent walking between villages only a few kilometres apart. **KARYÁ** is at the centre of the interior, and offers some rooms. This is the centre of the island's lace and weaving industry, with a small but fascinating **folklore museum** set in a lacemaker's home (April–Oct daily 9am–9pm; €2.50). The historic and scenic villages of **Vafkerí** and **Englouví** are within striking distance, with the west-coast hamlets of **Dhrymónas** and **Exánthia** a hike over the hills.

### ACCOMMODATION, EATING AND NIGHTLIFE — AROUND LEFKÁDHA TOWN

For rooms in Karyá, contact the Kakiousis family (☎ 26450 61136; €30) or Haritini Vlahou (☎ 26450 41634; €25).

**Club Milos** Yíra ☎ 26450 21332. This lively club in a disused windmill is so far from any other buildings that it can pump out the hottest disco sounds at full volume far into the night. May–Sept daily 10pm–late.

**Ta Platania** Karyá ☎ 26450 41247. The best of the trio of tavernas that fringe the beautiful plane-shaded square dishes up ample portions of mostly meat dishes such as *frigadhéli*, for around €5–7. Daily 11am–1am.

**Tilegraphos** Aïyánnis ☎ 26450 24881. Good restaurant with a shady elongated garden, serving a decent range of mezédhes and seafood, and also has some simple rooms. May–Oct. **€40**

# The east coast

Anchored by the island's busiest resort of **Nydhrí**, Lefkádha's east coast is the most accessible and the most developed part of the island, much more so, in fact, than the nearby mainland coast. The beaches are mostly shingly and unspectacular, with the exception of **Dhessími** and **Rouda** bays, until you reach the long strand on the bay of **Vassilikí**.

## Northeast coast

The stretch of the **northeast coast** between the capital and Nydhrí is a rather unprepossessing sprawl of seaside villages linked by almost unbroken development. Unless you choose to camp at **Karyótes**, there's little point stopping before the small fishing port of **Liyiá**. Further on lies **Nikiána**, another reasonably picturesque fishing village. Beaches all along this part of the coast tend to be pebbly and small.

## Nydhrí

Most package travellers will find themselves in **NYDHRÍ**, the island's biggest resort by far and also the jumping-off point for Meganíssi (see p.734). It's an average resort but has a lovely setting and a reasonable pebble beach offering watersports. The town's focus is the Aktí Aristotéli Onássi **quay**, where most of the restaurants and bars are found. The German archeologist **Wilhelm Dörpfeld** is honoured with a statue here for promoting the theory that Nydhrí, rather than Itháki, was the site of Odysseus's capital, while his tomb is tucked away at Ayía Kyriakí on the opposite side of the bay. The turning signposted Ráhi leads to Nydhrí's modest **waterfall**, a 45-minute walk inland.

## BOAT TRIPS FROM NYDHRÍ

Nydhrí is the base for myriad **boat trips** around the nearby satellite islands and further afield to Itháki and Kefalloniá. The boats line up along the quay each morning, ready for departure between 9 and 10am, returning late afternoon. Tickets are around €12 per person for the local trips, €20–25 for the longer distances. Most craft to the nearby islets are interchangeable: small fibreglass *kaïkia*, with bars and toilets, and open seating areas on the top deck or aft. Where they do differ, however, is in their itinerary – some will take in the sea caves of Meganíssi, others not, so it's advisable to check.

### Dhessími Bay, Roúda Bay and around

Just south of Nydhrí, beyond somnolent **Vlyhó**, the neck of the Yéni peninsula to the east joins the main body of the island. Across this thin but steep strip of land, sizeable **Dhessími Bay** is perhaps the prettiest spot on the whole east coast, carved out by deep pine-ridged promontories.

South of Vlyhó, the coast road turns inland and climbs the foothills of Mount Stavrotás, through the hamlets of Katohóri and Paliokatoúna to the quiet village of **Póros**. Just south of here is the increasingly busy beach resort of **Roúda Bay**, officially Mikrós Yialós, some 10km from Nydhrí.

### Sývota

Around 14km south of Nydhrí, the fjord-like inlet of **SÝVOTA**, 2km down a steep hill from the main road, cuts a deep gash into the coastline. This is one of the most popular stops for yachting flotillas. There's no beach except for a remote cove, but some fine tavernas, mostly specializing in fish.

### Vassilikí, Póndi and around

Around 5km due west of Sývota but longer by the winding road, **VASSILIKÍ**, the island's premier watersports resort, lies at the east end of a huge bay, cut off from the rest of the east coast by the barren peninsula of Cape Lipsó. Winds in the huge bay draw vast numbers of windsurfers, with light morning breezes for learners and tough afternoon blasts for advanced surfers.

The beach at Vassilikí is stony and poor but improves 1km west at tiny **Póndi**. Most non-windsurfers, however, use the daily *kaïki* trips to superior beaches on the sandy west coast (see p.735).

### ACTIVITIES

### THE EAST COAST

**Windsurfing** In Vassilikí, the largest of the three beach windsurf centres, British-run Club Vassiliki (☎26450 31588, ⓦclubvass.com) offers all-in windsurfing tuition and accommodation deals; Wildwind is another UK-based operation (☎697 91 10 665, ⓦwildwind.co.uk).

### ACCOMMODATION, EATING AND DRINKING

#### NORTHEAST COAST

**Camping Kariotes Beach** Karyótes ☎26450 71103, ⓦcampingkariotes.com. The nearest campsite to Lefkádha Town has shady pitches, a small shop and a nice pool, handy as the local beach is poor. May–Oct.

★ **Limni** Liyiá ☎26450 72013. Excellent and friendly taverna with a newly landscaped terrace garden and a range of tasty dishes such as *spartiátiko* (pork, peppers, mushroom and cheese in a wine and cognac sauce) and lamb *ladhókolla*. May–Sept daily noon–midnight.

**Pantazis** Nikiána ☎26450 71211. A good fish restaurant

at the south end of the small curved beach, which also has simple rooms to let in a row of adjoining bungalows at the back. May–Sept. **€35**

#### NYDHRÍ

★ **Ionian Paradise** ☎26450 92268, ⓦionianparadise .gr. Set in a lush garden only a minute along the Ráhi turning from the main road. The rooms have been recently refurbished with smart furniture and kitchenettes. May–Oct. **€50**

**Mamma Mia** ☎26450 93102. Towards the south end of the resort, this restaurant has a huge patio, where you can

enjoy a wide range of mezédhes and some unusual main courses such as swordfish in sweet lemon sauce. Noon–1am: Easter–Nov daily, Dec–Easter Fri–Sun.

### DHESSÍMI BAY, ROÚDA BAY AND AROUND
**Camping Santa Maura** Dhessími Bay ☎ 26450 95007, Ⓦ campingsantamaura.nl. This is marginally the better of the two huge campsites that dominate the olive groves behind Dhessími Bay. May–Oct.

**Pirofani** Dhessími Bay. This beach taverna in between the two Dhessími Bay campsites is very good, dishing up exquisite mezédhes such as octopus in wine sauce and *koloukythopittákia* (little courgette pies). May to mid-Oct daily 11am–midnight.

**Póros Beach Camping** Roúda Bay ☎ 26450 95452, Ⓦ porosbeach.com.gr. One of the smartest campsites in the archipelago, with a bar, post office, shop, pool, vehicle rental and forty spanking new studios. May–Oct. Studios **€40**

★ **Rouda Bay** Roúda Bay ☎ 26450 95634, Ⓦ roudabay.gr. Taverna-cum-studios venture right opposite the beach. The food includes excellent home-cooked dishes and the accommodation is in luxurious and spacious suites. Breakfast included. May–Oct. **€80**

### SÝVOTA
★ **Palia Apothiki** ☎ 26450 31895. By far the most attractive of Sývota's tavernas, located in an old storehouse as the name indicates, and serving unique dishes such as giant shrimps wrapped in bacon. May–Oct 11am–midnight.

**Sivota Apartments** ☎ 26450 31347. Just above the middle of the harbour, these pleasant rooms are of varying sizes and most have balconies overlooking the bay. May–Sept. **€40**

### VASSILIKÍ, PÓNDI AND AROUND
**Akroyiali** Póndi ☎ 26450 31569. A welcoming old couple run this taverna, which has a beachside seating and offers delights such as garlic prawns and steak Diane, as well as fine barrelled wine. May–Oct daily 11am–1am.

**Alexander** Vassilikí ☎ 26450 31355. Well-established taverna on the western quay, which dishes up pizza and pasta and has a massive menu of Greek cuisine and a variety of wines. April–Oct daily 10am–1am.

**Grand Nefeli** Póndi ☎ 26450 31378, Ⓦ grandnefeli .com. Right on the beach, this smart block has comfortably furnished rooms, many with sea-view balconies, and some luxury suites. Arranges windsurfing lessons. Breakfast included. May to mid-Oct. **€60**

**Pension Holiday** Vassilikí ☎ 26450 31011, Ⓔ pensionholidays@hotmail.com. Round the corner from the ferry dock, this remains the best value option, with a/c and TV in all the cosy rooms. May–Oct. **€35**

**Volero Club** Vassilikí ☎ 26450 31859. The resort's liveliest club, a short way back from the seafront, provides post-windsurfing dancefloor frolics to the predominantly young crowd that spend the summer here. May–Sept daily 7pm–late.

## Lefkádha's satellites
Lefkádha has four satellite islands clustered off its east coast, although only one, **Meganíssi**, the largest and most interesting, is accessible. **Skorpiós**, owned by the Onassis family, fields armed guards to deter visitors. **Madhourí**, owned by the family of poet Nanos Valaoritis, is private and similarly off-limits, while tiny **Spárti** is a large scrub-covered rock. Day-trips from Nydhrí skirt all three islands (see box, p.732), and some stop to allow swimming in coves. Though officially a dependency of Lefkádha, the more remote island of **Kálamos** is only accessible from the mainland.

### Meganíssi
Ferries run from Nydhrí (7 daily; 20min)

**Meganíssi** is a sizeable island with a growing number of facilities and a magical, if somewhat bleak and scrubby, landscape. The locals – many returned émigrés from Australia – live from farming and fishing and are genuinely welcoming. There are actually two ports, the main one of **Vathý** in the north, and **Spiliá** on the west coast, ten minutes' steep walk below **Spartohóri**, an immaculate village with whitewashed buildings and an abundance of bougainvillea. The walk between the two docks takes little over an hour, by way of the attractive inland village of **Katoméri**. From here, paths lead from Katoméri to remote beaches, including popular **Ambelákia**.

### ACCOMMODATION, EATING AND DRINKING
MEGANÍSSI

**Different Studios** Vathý ☎ 26450 22170, Ⓦ different-studios.com. This small complex of six studios and two 2-bedroom apartments stands right on the harbour. All units are nicely furnished and well

## LOVER'S LEAP

Fourteen kilometres south along the main road from Atháni, barren **Cape Lefkátas** drops abruptly 75m into the sea. Byron's Childe Harold sailed past this point, and "saw the evening star above, Leucadia's far projecting rock of woe: And hail'd the last resort of fruitless love". The fruitless love is a reference to Sappho, who in accordance with the ancient legend that you could cure yourself of unrequited love by leaping into these waters, leapt – and died. In her honour the locals termed the place Kávos tis Kyrás ("lady's cape"), and her act was imitated by the lovelorn youths of Lefkádha for centuries afterwards. And not just by the lovelorn, for the act (known as *katapondismós*) was performed annually by scapegoats – always a criminal or a lunatic – selected by priests from the Apollo temple whose sparse ruins lie close by. This purification rite continued into the Roman era, when it degenerated into little more than a fashionable stunt by decadent youth. These days, in a more controlled modern re-enactment, Greek hang-gliders hold a tournament from the cliffs every July.

equipped. May–Sept. €40

**Meganissi** Katoméri ☎26450 51240. The island's longest-established hotel is a comfortable place with decent-sized, comfortable rooms, a restaurant and pool, and is handily located for exploring. May–Sept. €45

**Rose Garden** Vathý ☎26450 51216. Popular place tucked into the corner of the square and seafront, where

you can get good fresh fish or a few meat or veg options from the oven. May–Sept daily noon–midnight.

**Tropicana** Spartohóri ☎26450 51486. This simple summertime restaurant (daily noon–11pm) offers a variety of pizzas and some other basic snacks and meals, plus they are the point of contact for good-value rooms in the village. May–Sept. €30

# The west coast

Lefkádha's **west coast** vies with anywhere in Greece in displaying coastal scenery at its most dramatic. On both sides of **Áï Nikítas**, the only real resort, mountainous roads rise and descend from the sea, offering tantalizing glimpses of the stunning sandy beaches that are sandwiched between imposing cliffs and lapping waves of turquoise.

## Áï Nikítas and around

Jammed into a picturesque gorge 12km southwest of Lefkádha Town is **ÁÏ NIKÍTAS**, the prettiest resort on Lefkádha, a jumble of lanes and small wooden buildings. To add to its appeal, the village itself is now a pedestrian zone, at least in theory. Sea taxis (€3 one-way) ply between Áï Nikítas and **Mýlos beach**, the delightful cove just round the southern promontory. A couple of kilometres back north, sand-and-pebble **Pefkoúlia beach** is one of the longest on the island.

## Káthisma beach

It's a 45-minute walk (or a short bus ride) from Áï Nikítas to the most popular beach on the coast, **Káthisma**, a shadeless kilometre of fine sand, which becomes nudist and a lot less crowded beyond the large jutting rocks halfway along – freelance camping still goes on at this end too.

## Atháni and around

South of Kalamítsi, past the hamlets of Hortáta and Komíli, the landscape becomes almost primeval. At 38km from Lefkádha Town, **ATHÁNI** is the island's most remote spot to stay. Three of the Ionian's choicest **beaches**, where azure and milky turquoise waves buffet strands enclosed by dramatic cliffs, are accessible from Atháni: the nearest, reached by a 4km paved road, is **Yialós**, followed by **Egremní**, down a steep incline unpaved for the last 2km. Further south, an asphalted road leads to the dramatic and popular twin beach of **Pórto Katsíki**.

## ACCOMMODATION, EATING AND DRINKING

**THE WEST COAST**

### ÁÏ NIKÍTAS AND AROUND

**Captain's Corner ☎** 26450 97493. Near the beach, this is the liveliest drinking venue in the village, with a pub-style atmosphere, a decent selection of drinks, snacks and mostly rock tunes. May to mid-Oct daily 10am–late.

**Deck** Pefkoúlia beach **☎** 26450 97070, **⊛** mydeck.gr. Buzzing café-restaurant halfway along the huge beach, with a selection of coffees, cocktails and full meals to choose from, plus some well-equipped studios. May–Sept. **€50**

**O Lefteris ☎** 26450 97495. Simple grilled fish and meat dishes for €7–8, accompanied by the expected choice of salads, dips and starters, and washed down with quaffable local wine. May to mid-Oct daily 11am–midnight.

★ **Pension Ostria ☎** 26450 97483. A beautiful blue-and-white building above the village, decorated in a mix of beachcomber and ecclesiastical styles, with compact but comfortable rooms and a snack bar with terrace. Breakfast included. May–Oct. **€85**

**T'Agnantio ☎** 26450 97383. Just above and south of the main street, this place serves excellent traditional cuisine, much of it oven baked such as *pastítsio* or *hirinó krasáto* (pork in wine sauce) and nearly all under €10. May–Sept daily noon–1am.

### KÁTHISMA BEACH

**Club Copla ☎** 26450 29411. This beach bar-cum-club has long established itself as a favourite with the night-time crowd, holding regular parties and raves to a techno soundtrack. May–Sept daily 11am–late.

**Kathisma ☎** 26450 97050, **⊛** kathisma.com. Vast taverna at the north end of the beach, with an equally extensive menu of Greek staples and some smart apartments. May–Oct. **€50**

### ATHÁNI AND AROUND

★ **Lygos** Hortáta **☎** 694 85 91 543, **⊛** amadryades-villas.gr. Good local taverna, serving up simple home recipes such as moussaka or *briám*, expertly cooked and accompanied by inexpensive barrelled wine. Nicely designed stone villas available too. May–Sept. **€70**

★ **Panorama** Atháni **☎** 26450 33291. One of the most welcoming tavernas on the island (daily 10am–midnight), where you can enjoy excellent fresh local dishes while gazing towards the distant sea from the terrace. Great-value rooms also available. May–Oct. **€30**

★ **Serenity** Atháni **☎** 698 18 53 064, **⊛** serenity-th.com. Wonderful new retreat and health spa run by two Israeli women, beautifully constructed in stone on the hillside 500m south of the village. The five rooms are decorated in ethnic style, and there are chill-out tents and an infinity pool. May–Oct. **€100**

# Kefaloniá

**KEFALONIÁ** (also known in English as Cephalonia) is the largest of the Ionian islands, a place that has real towns as well as resorts. Like its neighbours, Kefaloniá was overrun by Italians and Germans in World War II; the "handover" after Italy's capitulation in 1943 led to the massacre of over five thousand Italian troops on the island by invading German forces, as chronicled by Louis de Bernières in his novel, *Captain Corelli's Mandolin*. Virtually all of its towns and villages were levelled in the 1953 earthquake and these masterpieces of Venetian architecture had been the one touch of elegance in a severe, mountainous landscape.

Until the late 1980s, the island paid scant regard to tourism; perhaps this was partly due to a feeling that Kefaloniá could not be easily marketed. A more likely explanation, however, for the island's late emergence on the Greek tourist scene is the Kefalonians' legendary reputation for insular pride and stubbornness, plus a good measure of eccentricity. There are, however, definite attractions here, with some **beaches** as good as any in Greece and the fine local wines of Robola. Moreover, the island seems able to soak up a lot of people without feeling at all crowded and the magnificent scenery speaks for itself.

## ARRIVAL AND DEPARTURE

**KEFALONIÁ**

**By plane** Kefaloniá airport lies 7km south of Argostóli. Apart from international charters, the only domestic scheduled flights are to Athens (2 daily; 1hr).

**By ferry** Kefaloniá has no fewer than four ports that provide ferry connections with neighbouring islands and the mainland. The following are summer schedules, which are reduced drastically in winter; any services that stop altogether are indicated by months of operation.

Argostóli to: Kyllíni (1 daily; 2hr 15min).

Pessádha to: Áyios Nikólaos (Zákynthos; 2 daily May–Sept; 1hr 30min). Be warned that the pathetic bus service from Argostóli to Pessádha is no good for connecting with the boats. You'll have to hitch or take an expensive taxi in most cases.

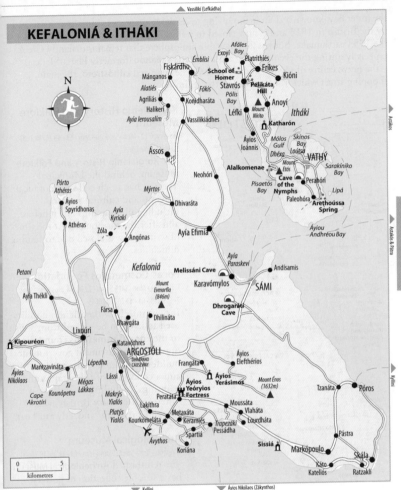

**KEFALONIÁ & ITHÁKI**

Póros to: Kyllíni (3–5 daily; 1hr 15min).
Sámi to: Astakós (1 daily; 2hr 30min); Pátra (1–2 daily; 3hr 30min); Pisaetós (Itháki; 2–3 daily; 40min); Vathý (Itháki; 1–2 daily; 1hr).

**By bus** There are buses from Argostóli via Sámi to Athens (2–3 daily; 7hr); and from Póros to Athens (1 daily; 6hr 30min) and to Pátra (1 daily; 4hr).

### GETTING AROUND

**By bus** Kefaloniá's basic KTEL bus network radiates out from Argostóli (see p.739). There are 2–3 services to all the main island destinations on Mon–Fri, 1–2 on Sat but no buses on Sun. KTEL also runs a seasonal tour of the island

from Argostóli every Thurs and Sat (9am–6pm; €18).
**By car or motorbike** The island-wide Sunbird agency (☎26710 23723, ⌨sunbird.gr) is a reliable rental agency.

# Argostóli

**ARGOSTÓLI**, Kefaloniá's capital, is a large and thriving town – virtually a city – with a marvellous position on a bay within a bay. The causeway connecting the two sides of

**11**

the inner bay, known as Dhrápano owing to its sickle shape, was initially constructed by the British in 1813 and is now closed to traffic. The town was totally rebuilt after the 1953 earthquake, but has an enjoyable atmosphere that remains defiantly Greek, especially during the evening *vólta* around **Platía Valianou** (formerly Platía Metaxá) – the nerve centre of town – and along the pedestrianized **Lithóstroto**, the main shopping street which runs parallel to the seafront.

ARGOSTÓLI

**ACCOMMODATION**
| Camping Argostoli | 1 |
| Chara | 5 |
| Ionian Plaza | 3 |
| King Agamemnon Studios | 2 |
| Olga | 4 |

**CAFÉS, BARS & CLUBS**
| Aristofanis | 4 |
| Bass | 3 |
| Notes | 1 |
| Pub Old House | 2 |

**RESTAURANTS**
| Arhondiko | 3 |
| Karamosal | 1 |
| Kiani Akti | 2 |
| Kohenoor | 4 |
| Tzivras | 5 |

### Korgialenio History and Folklore Museum

Ilía Zervoú 12 • Mon–Sat 9am–2pm • €3 • ☎ 26710 28835, ⓦ corgialenios.gr

The **Korgialenio History and Folklore Museum**, behind the Municipal Theatre, has a rich collection of local religious and cultural artefacts, including photographs taken before and after the earthquake. At the time of writing it was closed due to staffing difficulties.

### Focas-Cosmetatos Foundation

Valiánou 1 • Mon–Sat 9.30am–12.30pm, plus June–Sept 7–9.30pm • €3 • ☎ 26710 26595

Insight into how the island's nobility used to live can be gained from a visit to the **Focas-Cosmetatos Foundation**, opposite the provincial government building. It contains elegant furniture and a collection of lithographs and paintings, including works by nineteenth-century British artists Joseph Cartwright and Edward Lear.

### Archeological Museum

Y. Vergóti • Tues–Sun 8.30am–3pm • €3 • ☎ 26710 28300

The refurbished **Archeological Museum** has a sizeable collection of pottery, jewellery, funerary relics and statuary from prehistoric, through Mycenaean to late Classical times. It is well laid out and labelled, rivalling Corfu Town's (see p.711) as the best such museum in the Ionians.

### Botanical Gardens

Tues–Sat 9am–2.30pm • Free • ☎ 26710 26595

Around 2km south of the town centre, the pleasantly relaxing **Botanical Gardens** have been transformed under the stewardship of the Focas-Cosmetatos Foundation into a diverse collection of the island's flora, arranged in a natural fashion with a stream running through the middle.

## ARRIVAL AND INFORMATION
ARGOSTÓLI

**By plane** There are no airport buses, so taxis (at least €10) are the only way into town.

**By bus** The KTEL bus station is 100m south of the Dhrápano causeway in the south of town. A city bus links the centre of town with Lássi at least hourly in season (30min).

**By ferry** There are frequent flat-bottomed boats to Lixoúri (Mon–Sat every 30min, Sun hourly; 20min).

**Tourist office** Andoníou Trítsi, at the north end of the seafront next to the port authority (Mon–Fri 7.30am–2.30pm; ☎ 26710 22248).

## ACCOMMODATION

The Kefalonia & Ithaca Federation of Lodgings (☎ 26710 29109, �ⓦ kefalonia-ithaca.gr) can arrange rooms in Argostóli and around the island, as can travel agencies such as Ainos Travel (☎ 26710 22333, ⓦ ainostravel.gr).

**Camping Argostoli** ☎ 26710 23487, ⓦ camping argostoli.gr. Although it's an inconvenient 2km north of the centre, just beyond the Katavóthres sea mills, this campsite has decent facilities, including a minimarket. May–Sept. One person plus tent. **€11.50**

**Chara** Cnr Dhevossétou/Y. Vergóti ☎ 26710 22427. Small house very close to the bus station with extremely simple rooms with shared bathrooms, whose friendly owner offers coffee in the leafy courtyard. The only budget hotel left in town. **€23**

⭐ **Ionian Plaza** Platía Valiánou ☎ 26710 25581, ⓦ ionianplaza.com. One of the ritziest hotels on the island and surprisingly reasonable for what it is – designer decor from the lobby up to the chic bathroom fixtures. Breakfast included. **€85**

**King Agamemnon Studios** A. Trítsi ☎ 26710 24260, ⓔ kathya@europe.com. Good-value modern studios with kitchenettes in a brightly painted block north of the Lixoúri ferry dock, all with a/c and TV, some with sea-facing balconies. **€35**

**Olga** A. Trítsi 82 ☎ 026710 24981, ⓦ olgahotel.gr. Imposing seafront hotel with a/c and TV in all rooms, which are fairly compact and do not match the grandeur of the lobby. Sizeable off-season discounts. **€45**

## EATING, DRINKING AND NIGHTLIFE

### RESTAURANTS

⭐ **Arhondiko** Rizospastón 5 ☎ 26710 27213. Classy stone building with a small patio out front, where the *kandádhes* from pricey *The Captain's Table* next door can often be heard. The friendly proprietress serves tasty dishes such as *exohikó*, *strapatsádha* and *biftéki* in Roquefort sauce. Daily noon–1am.

**Karamosal** A. Trítsi ☎ 26710 28590. Good ouzerí, with an artistic touch in the bright decor and a fair bit of imagination in the preperation of the *mezédhes*, which include cheese croquettes, pickled anchovies, meatballs and various veg options. Daily noon–1am.

⭐ **Kiani Akti** A. Trítsi ☎ 26710 26680. Unmissable dining experience on a large wooden deck jutting out over the water by the new cruise-ship dock, about 400m north of Platía Valianou. Specializes in seafood such as razor clams in mustard sauce and shrimps in ouzo. Friendly service and reasonable prices. Daily 1pm–2am.

**Kohenoor** Lavrága ☎ 26710 26789. Just southeast of Platía Valiánou, this British-run curry house has an Indian chef and is one of the most authentic in the Ionians. Daily 6pm–midnight; closed Mon Nov–April.

**Tzivras** V. Vandhórou 1. A classic daytime-only *estiatório* with an impressive range of staples from the oven,

including a lot of vegetarian options such as *briám*, helpings of which tend to be large. Daily 10am–5pm.

### CAFÉS, BARS AND CLUBS

**Aristofanis** A. Trítsi ☎ 26710 28012. Right by the Dhrápano bridge, this simple old-style *kafenío* might have a limited repertoire of coffee and basic booze but it enjoys one of the best locations in town, ideal for some gentle people-watching. Daily 8am–midnight.

**Bass** P. Valiánou ☎ 26710 25020, ⓦ bassclub.gr. Opposite the archeological museum, this is the town's main late-night indoor disco, whose hi-tech interior shakes to the latest vibes of various dance genres and hosts occasional live acts. Daily 10pm–late.

**Notes** ☎ 26710 23597. Argostóli's big summer *bouzoúki* club, nearly 2km north of town before the Katavóthres sea mills, is the place to head if you want to join the Greeks in rose-throwing and whiskey-drinking escapades. June–Sept daily 10pm–late.

⭐ **Pub Old House** Harboúri 13–15 ☎ 26710 23532. Tucked behind the kids' playground, the most relaxed and welcoming hangout on the island is a great place to have a drink in the magical garden and unwind to an eclectic range of mostly rock sounds. Daily 7pm–late.

# The Livathó peninsula

The bulge of land southeast of Argostóli known as the **Livathó peninsula** is a patchwork of small villages and agricultural land bordered by some attractive coastline. Many package travellers will find themselves staying in **Lássi**, a short bus ride or half-hour walk from town. The only other reason you might come to this corner of the island is for the summer ferry link with Zákynthos from **Pessádha** (see.p.736).

## Áyios Yeóryios

The best inland excursion from Argostóli is to **ÁYIOS YEÓRYIOS**, the medieval Venetian capital of the island, 7km southeast of Argostóli but not connected by public transport. The old town here supported a population of fifteen thousand until its destruction by an earthquake in the seventeenth century: substantial ruins of its **castle** (Tues–Sun 8.30am–3pm; free) can be visited on the hill above the modern village of Peratáta, a steep 1km walk below on the main southeast bus routes.

## Mount Énos and around

At 15km from a point halfway along the Argostóli–Sámi road, **Mount Énos** isn't really a walking option but roads nearly reach the official 1632m summit. The mountain has been declared a national park, to protect the *Abies cephalonica* firs named after the island, which clothe the slopes. There are absolutely no facilities on or up to the mountain but the views from the highest point in the Ionian islands out over Kefaloniá's neighbours and the mainland are wonderful. Out of summer, watch the weather, which can deteriorate with terrifying speed.

## Áyios Yerásimos monastery and around

**Áyios Yerásimos monastery** Daily 9am–1pm & 4–8pm **Robola winery** April–Oct daily 7am–8.30pm, Nov–March Mon–Fri 7am–3pm • Ⓦ robola.gr

Not far west of the mountain turning, taking a detour towards Frangáta is doubly rewarded, firstly by the huge and lively **Áyios Yerásimos monastery**, which hosts two of the island's most important festivals (Aug 15 and Oct 20); the most interesting feature is the double cave beneath the back of the sanctuary, where the eponymous saint meditated for lengthy periods. Right behind the monastery, the **Robola winery** offers a free self-guided tour and generous wine tasting.

## Lixoúri and its peninsula

Ferries run to Lixoúri from Argostóli till well after midnight (summer Mon–Sat every 30min, Sun hourly; winter hourly; 20min)

Across the water from Argostóli, the town of **LIXOÚRI** was flattened by successive earthquakes and hasn't risen much above two storeys since. It's a little drab but has good restaurants, quiet hotels and is favoured by those who want to explore the eerie quake-scapes left in the south and the barren north of the peninsula.

### Beaches around Lixoúri

Xi and Mégas Lákkos are served by bus from Lixoúri

Lixoúri's nearest beach, a 2km walk south, is **Lépedha**, composed of rich-red sand and backed by low cliffs, as are **Xi** and **Mégas Lákkos** (the name means "big hole") beaches, both of which have good facilities. Around 4km southwest lies the quieter beach at **Kounópetra**, site of a curious rock formation. Until the 1953 earthquake, this "rocking stone" (as the name signifies in Greek) had a strange rhythmic movement that could be measured by placing a knife into a gap between the rock and its base. However, after the quake the rock became motionless. Some 2km further west, in an area known as Vátsa, the last beach of any size on the southern tip of the peninsula is sandy **Áyios Nikólaos**, a very quiet and scenic strand.

## The western coast

Those with transport can also strike out for the rugged western coast of the peninsula, first visiting the monastery at **Kipouréon** (daily 8am–6pm; free), now home to just a single monk, then heading north to the spectacular beach at **Petaní**, one of the best in the Ionians. Tucked in the fold of the **Áyios Spyrídhonas** inlet further north, the beach of **Pórto Athéras**, which serves the traditional village of Athéras, a short way inland, is another fine strip of sand with shallow water.

### ACCOMMODATION AND EATING — LIXOÚRI AND ITS PENINSULA

★ **Akrogiali** Lixoúri ☎ 26710 92613. Wonderful unpretentious taverna on the seafront, which draws admirers from all over the island for its excellent and inexpensive grilled and baked meat, fish and seafood. Daily noon–1am.

★ **La Cité** Lixoúri ☎ 26710 92701, ⓦ lacitehotellixouri .gr. Four blocks back from the front, this great-value hotel has a uniquely shaped pool in its exotic garden, while the rooms are spacious and colourfully furnished. April–Oct. €45

★ **Spiaggia** Áyios Nikólaos ☎ 697 76 31 053, ⓦ vatsa .gr. Atmospheric restaurant with an attractive wood and bamboo deck, where you can tuck into excellent pasta, seaweed salad and seafood. There are four well-equipped

luxury chalets behind. May–Oct; restaurant daily 11am–late. €80

**Xouras** Petaní ☎ 26710 97128, ⓔ petanoi@gmail.com. By far the better of the two tavernas here, whose friendly Greek-American owner Dina serves a fine selection of grills, salads and some oven-cooked dishes. There are comfortable studios attached too. May–Oct; restaurant daily 11am–midnight. €50

**Yialós** Pórto Athéras. Good all-round taverna at the back of the beach, which serves mostly grills and whose garden acts as home for families with camper vans and could be used for camping. May–Sept daily noon–1am.

# Southeast Kefaloniá

**Southeast Kefaloniá** contains some fine beaches and much of the island's package tourism, from smaller resorts such as **Lourdháta** and **Káto Kateliós** east via the busiest foreign enclave of **Skála** to the port resort of **Póros**. One or two of the villages strung along the main Argostóli–Póros road, which follows the southern contours of Mt Énos, are also worth a brief halt, especially **Markópoulo**.

## Lourdháta and around

From the pleasant village of Vlaháta, around 15km east of Argostóli, a couple of turnings bear 2km down the mountainside to **LOURDHÁTA**, which has a kilometre-long shingle beach, mixed with imported sand. Another fine beach, reached by a turning from Moussáta, 2km west of Vlaháta, is **Trapezáki**, a relatively slim but appealing strand with just one restaurant by the small jetty.

## Markópoulo

The inland village of **MARKÓPOULO** witnesses a bizarre snake-handling ritual every year on August 15, on the occasion of the **Assumption of the Virgin festival**, when a swarm of harmless snakes "appears" in commemoration of a legend that the nuns of the former convent here prayed to be turned into snakes to avoid an attack by pirates. The church at which the ritual is enacted is well worth visiting at any time of year.

## Káto Kateliós and around

Some of the finest sandy beaches on the island are to be found around the growing micro-resort of **KÁTO KATELIÓS**, which already has a couple of hotels, and below the village of **Ratzaklí** just before the resort of Skála. The coast around Káto Kateliós is also Kefaloniá's key breeding ground for the loggerhead **turtle** (see p.753); camping on the nearby beaches is therefore prohibited.

## Skála

**SKÁLA** is a low-rise resort set among handsome pines above a few kilometres of good sandy beach. A **Roman villa** (daily 10am–2pm & 5–8pm, longer hours in summer;

free) and some mosaics were excavated here in the 1950s, near the site of the *Golden Beach Palace* rooms, and are open to the public.

## Póros

Connected to Skála by a lovely 12km coastal route that at times seems to skim across the shallow sea, **PÓROS** was one of the island's earliest developed resorts, though it definitely gives the impression of having seen better days. The town's small huddle of hotels and apartment blocks is almost unique on Kefaloniá, and not enhanced by a scruffy seafront and thin pebbly beach. Póros is actually made up of two bays: the northern one, where most tourists are based, and the harbour bay, a few minutes over the headland, with connections to Kyllíni on the Peloponnesian coast.

## ACCOMMODATION, EATING AND DRINKING
SOUTHEAST KEFALONIÁ

### LOURDHÁTA AND AROUND
**Christina Studios** Lourdháta ☎ 26710 31130, ⓦ christinastudio.gr. Fully equipped kitchen-studios with side views to the sea are available at this lovely building set into the lush vegetation behind the beach. May–Oct. €40

★ **Denis** Trapezáki ☎ 26710 31454. This friendly taverna does not abuse its monopoly, instead maintaining a fine level of quality in the typical Greek menu of grills with salads and dips, plus good service when especially busy around lunchtime. May–Oct daily 11am–11pm.

★ **Lorraine's Magic Hill** Lourdháta ☎ 26710 31605. With a lovely airy terrace on the hill just behind the beach, this relaxed joint serves a wide range of home produce, including tender calves' liver. Also does cocktails in its alter ego as a bar. May–Oct daily noon–late.

**Trapezaki Bay Hotel** Trapezáki ☎ 26710 31503, ⓦ trapezakibayhotel.com. Luxury hotel 500m uphill from the beach, offering all mod cons, including spa and beauty treatments. The fixed price all summer means good value in peak season and the rate includes airport transfer and breakfast. May–Oct. €115

### KÁTO KATELIÓS
**Blue Sea** ☎ 26710 81122. Seafront taverna renowned for the freshness and quality of its fish, though much of it is pricey. Also does the usual accompanying dishes, plus pizza and pasta. April–Oct daily 11am–1am.

**Cozy** ☎ 26710 81031. This little bar with a fitting name is the prime drinking location, where you can enjoy a beer or cocktail to the accompaniment of some laidback summer sounds. May–Oct daily 10am–late.

**Galini Resort** ☎ 26710 81582, ⓦ galini.de. This spacious complex with a pool and manicured grounds, around 500m back from the beach, has good deals on fully equipped rooms and larger apartments. May–Sept. €50

**Ostria** ☎ 26710 81765. At the western end of the front, this ouzerí-cum-taverna offers a wide selection of dishes such as stuffed pork or baked swordfish for around €8. May–Oct daily noon–1am.

### SKÁLA
**Captain's House** ☎ 26710 83389, ⓦ captainshouse .net. On the road parallel to the main street to the east, the good Captain can steer you towards a warmly decorated room or studio. April–Oct. €40

**The Old Village** ☎ 26710 83513. A standard range of Greek and continental cuisine, including large steaks for around €10–12, and very palatable local wine from the barrel. May–Oct daily 10am–1am.

**Paspalis** ☎ 26710 83140. The well-established beachside frontrunner serves fish and home-cooked meat and vegetable dishes. Especially popular during the day, as it has a pool for patrons. May–Oct daily 11am–midnight.

**Tara Beach Hotel** ☎ 26710 83250, ⓦ tarabeach.gr. The best of the large seafront hotels has smart rooms and individual bungalows in lush gardens on the edge of the beach. Breakfast included. April–Oct. €60

### PÓROS
**Fotis Family** ☎ 26710 72972. Tucked into the rocky corner of the northern bay, this taverna serves an array of grilled meat and fish, plus plenty of salads and mezédhes. April–Oct daily 11am–midnight.

**Santa Irina** ☎ 26740 72017, ⓔ maki@otenet.gr. By the crossroads inland, this medium-sized *pension* has basic but clean rooms that offer superb value. Breakfast included. Mid-May to Sept. €40

# Sámi and around

Most boats to the island dock at the large and functional port town of **SÁMI**, near the south end of the Itháki straits, more or less on the site of ancient Sami. This was the capital of the island in Homeric times, when Kefaloniá was part of Ithaca's maritime kingdom. Ironically, today the administrative hierarchy is reversed, with Itháki being considered the backwater. In more recent times, Sámi was used as the set for much of the filming of *Captain Corelli's Mandolin*. The long sandy beach that stretches round the bay to the village of **Karavómylos** is perfectly adequate, but 2km further east, beyond ancient Sami, lies a more dramatic pebble beach, **Andísamis**, set in a stunning curved bay.

## Dhrogaráti cave

April–Oct daily 9am–8pm • €4

Five kilometres from Sámi, signposted just off the Argostóli road, lies a very impressive stalagmite-bedecked chamber, known as **Dhrogaráti**. The cave, which reaches a depth of 60m and was discovered over 300 years ago, is occasionally used for concerts thanks to its marvellous acoustics.

## Melissáni cave

Daily 8am–7pm • €7

Three kilometres north of Sámi towards Ayía Efimía, **Melissáni** is partly submerged in brackish water, which, amazingly, emerges from an underground fault extending the whole way underneath the island to a point near Argostóli. At that point, known as Katavóthres, the sea gushes endlessly into a subterranean channel – the fact that the water ends up in the cave has been shown with fluorescent tracer dye. The beautiful textures and shades created by the light pouring through the collapsed roof of the cave make the short boat excursion into it a must.

## Ayía Efimía

**AYÍA EFIMÍA**, 9km north of Sámi along a scenic coastal drive that includes coves such as **Ayía Paraskeví**, is a small fishing harbour popular with package operators, yet with no major developments. Its main drawback is its beaches, or lack thereof – the largest, risibly named Paradise beach, is a pathetic 20m of shingle. It is, however, home to one of the island's few **scuba diving** enterprises.

## ARRIVAL AND GETTING AROUND

**By ferry** The dock is towards the southern end of the long seafront.

**By bus** Island buses congregate outside the KTEL office about 100m from the dock.

### SÁMI AND AROUND

**By car and motorbike** The seafront Sami Center (☏ 26740 22254) rents out motorbikes at fair rates, and Island (☏ 26740 23084, ✉ islecars@otenet.gr) is a reliable local car rental company.

## ACTIVITIES

**Diving** The Aquatic Scuba Diving Club in Ayía Efimía (☏ 26740 62006, 🌐 aquatic.gr) is the island's premier scuba diving outfit. It runs courses, does wreck diving and offers introductory dives.

## ACCOMMODATION, EATING AND DRINKING

### SÁMI AND AROUND

**Akrogiali** Sámi ☏ 26740 22494. At the far northern end of the seafront, this family taverna with seating right above the beach offers a range of fish and meat dishes for around €7. May–Sept daily noon–midnight.

**Camping Karavomilos Beach** Karavómylos ☏ 26740 22480, 🌐 camping-karavomilos.gr. Just 1km along the beach from Sámi, the better of the island's two campsites has over three hundred well-shaded spaces, a taverna, shop and bar. May–Oct. One person plus tent **€12.50**

**Kastro** Sámi ☏ 26740 22282. Smart two-storey hotel in the middle of the seafront, with compact but comfy rooms and a small café on the ground floor. June–Sept. **€50**

**Melissani** Sámi ☏ 26740 22464. Up a couple of blocks behind the main dock, this slightly old-fashioned but welcoming hotel has cosy, good-value rooms, many with good views from their balconies. May–Sept. **€35**

**Mermaid** Sámi ☏ 26740 22202. With a decent selection of vegetable and meat dishes, including the famous local meat pie, this is the best of the central bunch of portside tavernas. April–Oct daily 11am–2am.

### AYÍA EFIMÍA

**Amalia** Ayía Efimía ☏ 26740 61088. Round the headland past the harbour, this is the place for moderately priced island cuisine such as small fried fish and local sausage. May–Sept daily noon–1am.

**★ Ayía Paraskeví** Ayía Paraskeví ☏ 26740 23061.

Named after the tiny cove it sits above, this taverna with a huge sunken terrace is famous for its delicious spaghetti with mussels. There is a separate chill-out beach bar on the premises too. May–Sept daily 10am–midnight.

**Captain Corelli's** Ayía Efimía ☎ 26740 61955. Predictably renamed after the film crew and cast who spent hours unwinding here, this café-restaurant is nonetheless a good spot right on the harbour for a refreshing drink or light snack. April–Oct daily 8am–2am.

**Moustakis** Ayía Efimía ☎ 26740 61030, ⓦ moustakishotel.com. Around 100m along the main road inland, the resort's only bona fide hotel has old-fashioned yet comfortable rooms, all with small balconies. April–Oct. €50

**To Steki** Ayía Efimía ☎ 26740 61025. A wide range of island specialities such as meat pie and standard Greek dishes from pork chops to beef in red sauce, all under €10 at this mid-harbour taverna. May–Sept daily noon–1am.

# Northern Kefaloniá

Northern Kefaloniá offers some splendid beaches, an architecturally attractive village in **Fiskárdho**, and some amazing coastal scenery. Indeed, the northern half of the road between Argostóli and Fiskárdho, starting at the point where a side road peels off to the long sandy beach of **Ayía Kyriakí**, is the most spectacular ride in the Ionian archipelago.

## Mýrtos beach and around

Four kilometres by paved road below the main north–south artery, stunningly photogenic **Mýrtos** is regarded by many as the most dramatic beach in the Ionian islands – a splendid strip of pure-white sand and pebbles. Sadly, it has no natural shade for most of the day and gets mighty crowded in high season, with just a couple of seasonal snack-shacks for refreshment.

Back at the crossroads, the small settlement of **Dhivaráta** has the nearest amenities to Mýrtos.

## Ássos

Six kilometres beyond Dhivaráta is the turning for the atmospheric village of **ÁSSOS**, clinging to a small isthmus between the island and a huge hill crowned by a ruined fort. It can get a little claustrophobic, but there's nowhere else quite like it in the Ionians. Ássos has a small pebble beach, and three tavernas on a plane-shaded village square backed by mansions, mostly now restored after being ruined in the 1953 quake.

## Fiskárdho

Boats from Itháki and Lefkádha dock on the far side of the small bay; island buses terminate in the car park up at the back of the village

**FISKÁRDHO**, on the northernmost tip of the island, sits on a bed of limestone that buffered it against the worst of the quakes. Two **lighthouses**, Venetian and Victorian, guard the bay, and the ruins on the headland are believed to be from a twelfth-century chapel begun by Norman invader Robert Guiscard, who gave the place its name. The nineteenth-century harbour frontage is intact, and is nowadays occupied by smart restaurants and chic boutiques. There is an **Environmental and Nautical Museum** (summer Mon–Fri 10am–6pm, Sun 10am–2pm; donation; ☎ 26740 41182), housed in a renovated Neoclassical mansion on the hill behind the village. The volunteers who curate it conduct valuable ecological research and can also arrange **scuba diving**.

## Around Fiskárdho

There are two good pebble beaches close to Fiskárdho – **Émblisi** 1km back out of town and **Fókis** just to the south – and a nature trail on the northern headland. It is worth making the effort to explore the coastal region west of **Mánganos: Alatiés** has a tiny beach tucked in between folds of impressive white volcanic rock, but the real gem is the small bay of **Ayía Ierousalím**, whose gravel-and-sand beach remains quiet even in August.

## ACCOMMODATION, EATING AND DRINKING

## MÝRTOS BEACH AND AROUND

**Mina Studios** Dhivaráta ☎26740 61716, ✉markela1
@hol.gr. Just above the main junction, these large and
well-appointed studios with kitchenettes are the best
accommodation close to Mýrtos beach. April–Oct. **€50**

## ÁSSOS

**Cosi's Inn** ☎26740 51420, ⓦcosisinn.gr. Brightly
decorated and well-furnished, good-value rooms are the
attraction at this pleasant hill on the approach road to the
centre. Breakfast included. April–Oct. **€50**

**Kanakis Apartments** ☎26740 51631, ⓦkanakis
apartments.gr. Very smart studios and spacious maisonettes,
all equipped with all mod cons and sharing a pool. Only 100m
from the heart of the village. April–Oct. **€65**

**Nefeli** ☎26740 51251. With its prime location on the
quay beside the beach, this taverna does a nice line in
seafood, mezédhes and salads. Most main courses around
€9–10. April–Oct daily 10am–1am.

**Platanos Grill** Set just back from the seafront, as the
name suggests, this place is good for grilled meat and fish.
There's also a wide selection of salads and starters, plus
aromatic local wine. April–Oct daily 11am– midnight.

## FISKÁRDHO

**Archontiko** ☎26740 41342. Beautiful traditional stone
mansion that has been converted into luxurious rooms
above and behind a harbourfront minimarket. The furniture
is period style but all the equipment, such as TVs, is cutting
edge. April–Oct. **€100**

**Kastro Club** ☎26740 41010. Up behind the main bypass
road, the oldest club in northern Kefaloniá has tiered

## NORTHERN KEFALONIÁ

terraces and a big outdoor dancefloor. The isolated location
allows the volume to be jacked up on the usual mix of
international and Greek hits. July–Sept daily
10pm–late.

**Lagoudera** ☎26740 41275. With two premises, one
on the harbour, the other just off the small square,
*Lagoudera* specializes in tasty oven food for €7–9 but
also does grills and all the usual side dishes. April–Oct
daily noon–2am.

**Lord Falcon** ☎26740 41072. One block back from the
harbour, the Ionians' first Thai restaurant does a fine array
of soups, stir-fries and red, green and Penang curries for
around €10–12. May–Oct Mon–Sat 6.30pm–midnight,
Sun 1–4.30pm.

**Panormos** ☎26740 41203. Just round the headland
with a great location, offering sweeping bay views from its
outdoor terrace, this taverna does simple grills, salads and
starters at very reasonable prices. April–Oct daily
noon–1am.

★ **Regina's** ☎26740 41125. Up by the car park, these
friendly family-run studios are compact but great value.
Some have balconies looking over the village to the bay
and there's a lovely courtyard. Can arrange motorboat
rental too. April–Oct. **€30**

## AROUND FISKÁRDHO

★ **Odisseas** Ayía Ierousalím ☎26740 41133.
Extremely friendly brother-sister-mum trio serve up
exquisite traditional dishes from free-range meat and do a
line in olive bread and other baked goodies, plus jams and
preserves. They also allow camping on their grounds.
April–Oct daily noon–midnight.

**11**

# Itháki

Rugged **ITHÁKI**, Odysseus's legendary homeland, has yielded no substantial archeological
discoveries but it fits Homer's description to perfection: "There are no tracks, nor
grasslands … it is a rocky severe island, unsuited for horses, but not so wretched, despite
its small size. It is good for goats." Despite its proximity to Kefaloniá, relatively little
tourist development has arrived to spoil the place. This is doubtless accounted for in part
by a dearth of beaches beyond a few pebbly coves, though the island is good walking
country, and indeed the interior with its sites from **The Odyssey** is the real attraction. In
the scheme of modern Greek affairs, the island is a real backwater and its inhabitants
rather resentful that it is officially a subsection of Kefaloniá prefecture.

## ARRIVAL AND DEPARTURE

**ITHÁKI**

**By ferry** For such a small island, Itháki perhaps surprisingly
has three active ports. The following are summer schedules,
which are often reduced drastically in winter; any services
that stop altogether are denoted by months of operation.
Fríkes to: Fiskárdho (Kefaloniá; May–Oct 4 weekly; 1hr);
Vassilikí (Lefkádha; May–Oct 1 daily; 1hr 30min).

Pisaetós to: Astakós (1–2 daily; 2hr 30min); Pátra (1–3
daily; 3hr 45min); Sámi (Kefaloniá; 4 daily; 45min); Vathý
(1–2 daily; 1hr).
Vathý to: Astakós (1–2 daily; 1hr 30min); Pátra (1–3 daily;
2hr); Pisaetós (1–2 daily; 1hr); Sámi (Kefaloniá; 1–3 daily;
1hr 45min).

### GETTING AROUND

**By bus** There is effectively no public transport on the island, though you might be able to flag down the school bus during term.

**By taxi** Taxis are available, especially at Vathý's square.

**By car and motorbike** Cars and motorbikes can be rented through the two main travel agencies, based in Vathý, Polyctor Tours (☎ 26740 33120, ⬤ ithakiholidays .com) and Delas Tours (☎ 26740 32104, ⬤ ithaca.com.gr).

## Vathý and around

Itháki's main port and capital is **VATHÝ**, enclosed by a bay within a bay so deep that few realize the mountains out "at sea" are actually the north of the island. This snug town is compact, relatively traffic-free and boasts the most idyllic seafront setting of all the Ionian capitals. Like its southerly neighbours, it was heavily damaged by the 1953 earthquake but some fine examples of pre-quake architecture remain. Vathý has a small **archeological museum** on Kalliníkou (Tues–Sun 8.30am–3pm; free), a short block back from the quay. Near the corner of the quay behind the Agricultural Bank, there is also the moderately interesting **Folklore & Cultural Museum** (April–Oct Mon–Fri 10am–2pm & 7.30–9.30pm; €1).

### Beaches around Vathý

There are two reasonable pebble **beaches** within fifteen minutes' walk of Vathý: **Dhéxa**, over the hill above the ferry quay, and tiny **Loútsa**, opposite it around the bay. The better beaches at **Sarakíniko** and **Skínos** are an hour's trek along paved roads leaving the opposite side of the bay. In season, daily *kaïkia* ply between the quay and remote coves.

---

#### ODYSSEUS SIGHTS AROUND VATHÝ

Three of the main **Odysseus** sights are just within walking distance of Vathý: the Arethoússa Spring, the Cave of the Nymphs and ancient Alalkomenae, although the last is best approached by **moped** or **taxi**.

##### THE ARETHOÚSSA SPRING

The walk to the **Arethoússa Spring** – allegedly the place where Eumaeus, Odysseus's faithful swineherd, brought his pigs to drink – is a three-hour round trip along a track signposted next to the seafront telecoms office. The unspoilt but shadeless landscape and sea views are magnificent but some of the inclines can be slippery.

Near the top of the lane leading to the spring path, a signpost points up to what is said to have been the **Cave of Eumaeus**. The route to the spring continues for a few hundred metres, and then branches off onto a narrow footpath through steep gorse-covered cliffs. Parts of the final downhill track involve scrambling across rock fields (follow the splashes of green paint), and care should be taken around the small but vertiginous ravine that houses the **spring**. The ravine sits below a crag known as **Kórax** (the raven), which matches Homer's description of the meeting between Odysseus and Eumaeus. In summer it's just a dribble of water.

##### THE CAVE OF THE NYMPHS

The **Cave of the Nymphs** (Marmarospíli) is about 2.5km up a rough but navigable road signposted on the brow of the hill above Dhéxa beach. The cave is atmospheric, but it's underwhelming compared to the caverns of neighbouring Kefaloniá and, these days, is illuminated by coloured lights. The claim that this is *The Odyssey*'s Cave of the Nymphs, where the returning Odysseus concealed the gifts given to him by King Alkinous, is enhanced by the proximity of Dhéxa beach.

##### ALALKOMENAE

**Alalkomenae**, Heinrich Schliemann's much-vaunted "Castle of Odysseus", is signposted on the Vathý–Pisaetós road, on the saddle between Dhéxa and Pisaetós, with views over both sides of the island. The actual site, however, some 300m uphill, is little more than foundations spread about in the gorse, and in fact the most likely contender for the site of Odysseus's castle is above the village of Stavrós (see opposite).

---

## Pisaetós

The harbour of **PISAETÓS**, around 5km west of Vathý via a steep route across the island's neck, has a fair-sized rocky beach that's all right for a pre-ferry swim and popular with local rod-and-line fishermen. Little goes on here except during the busy period around ferry arrivals, when a small canteen on the quay is the focus of activity.

### INFORMATION

**Services** There is no tourist office but a smattering of banks, a post office, police and a medical centre. An excellent website on the island is ⓦithacagreece.com.

### ACCOMMODATION

The best source of rooms, studios or villas around the capital or all over the island are the two main quayside travel agencies (see opposite).

★ **Captain Yiannis** ☎26740 33311, ⓦcaptainyiannis.com. Complete with tennis court and pool with bar, this great-value resort round the east side of the bay is spread over several blocks of modern rooms and apartments. Breakfast included. Mid-May to Sept. **€55**

**Mentor** ☎26740 32433, ⓦhotelmentor.gr. In the southeast corner of the harbour, the town's oldest hotel was refurbished a few years ago and its comfortable rooms have balconies either with direct or side views of the water. **€45**

**Omirikon** ☎26740 33596, ⓦomirikonhotel.com. Stylish boutique hotel, yet with a personal, family-run touch. All its rooms are classed as suites, and are spacious and well furnished with sea-view balconies. Breakfast included. May–Oct. **€70**

**11**

### EATING AND DRINKING

**O Nikos** ☎26740 33039. Just off the square, this is a good old-fashioned *estiatório*, where you can feast on heaps of oven-baked goodies, on show behind the glass panel within. Pavement seating in summer. Daily 11am–midnight.

**Paliocaravo (aka Gregory's)** ☎26740 32573. Popular for its lamb and fish, with a good range of accompanying dishes and beverages, plus the occasional impromptu music session. April–Oct daily noon–1am.

★ **To Kohili** ☎26740 33565. By far the best of the half-dozen harbourside tavernas, serving a good range of mezédhes as well as tasty meat dishes such as lamb *kléftiko*, *yiouvétsi* and *soutsoukákia*, plus grills and pasta. Daily 11am–1am.

# Northern Itháki

The main road out of Vathý continues across the isthmus and takes a spectacular route to the northern half of Itháki, based around **Stavrós**. This is excellent scooter country, and the close proximity of the settlements, small coves and Homeric interest also make it good rambling terrain. As with the rest of Itháki there are only limited tourist facilities, concentrated mostly in **Fríkes** and **Kióni**.

## Stavrós

**STAVRÓS**, the second-largest town on the island, is a steep 2km above the nearest beach at Pólis Bay. It's a pleasant enough town, with *kafenía* edging a small square dominated by a rather fierce statue of Odysseus. There is even a tiny **museum** (Tues–Sun 8.30am–3pm; free) off the road to Platrithriés, displaying local archeological finds. Most of these come from the early Helladic site on the side of **Pelikáta Hill**, where remains of roads, walls and other structures have been suggested as the possible site of Odysseus's palace.

## Anoyí

Some 5km southeast of Stavrós along a scenic mountain road is **ANOYÍ**, which translates roughly as "upper ground". Once the second-most important settlement on the island, it is almost deserted today. The centre of the village is dominated by a freestanding Venetian campanile, built to serve the church of the **Panayía**, which features heavily restored Byzantine frescoes. The church comes alive for the annual *paniyíri* on August 14, the eve of the Virgin's Assumption; at other times enquire at the *kafenío* about access. In the surrounding countryside are some extremely strange rock formations, the biggest being the 8m-high Iraklis (Hercules) rock, just east of the village.

## Monastery of Katharón

The **monastery of Katharón**, 3km south of Anoyí, boasts stunning views down over Vathý and the south of the island. It houses an icon of the *Panayía* discovered by peasants clearing scrubland in the area. The monastery celebrates its festival on September 8 with services, processions and music.

## Afáles Bay area

Local British expat Katrina (☎ 697 59 28 240) offers expert guided rambles in the area

**Afáles**, the largest bay on the entire island, with an unspoilt and little-visited pebble-and-sand beach, can be accessed by a track down from the outskirts of **Platrithriés**. This quiet yet rather spread-out village lies on the less direct westerly route from Stavrós to Fríkes, which first loops below the hill village of Exoyí. Just off the start of the road up to Exoyí a signpost points about 1km along a rough track to the supposed **School of Homer**, where excavations still in progress have revealed extensive foundations, a well and ancient steps. The site is unfenced and well worth a detour for its views of Afáles Bay as much as the remains.

## Fríkes

Wedged in a valley between two steep hills, **FRÍKES** was only settled in the sixteenth century and emigration in the nineteenth century almost emptied the place – as few as two hundred people live here today – but the protected harbour is a natural port. There are no beaches in the village, but plenty of good, if small, pebble coves a short walk away towards Kióni; it also offers superior dining options to its neighbour. When the ferries and their cargoes have departed, Fríkes falls quiet and this is its real charm.

## Kióni

**KIÓNI** sits at a dead end 5km southeast of Fríkes. On the same geological base as the northern tip of Kefaloniá, it avoided the very worst of the 1953 earthquake and so retains some fine examples of pre-twentieth-century architecture. It's an extremely pretty village, wrapped around a tiny harbour, and tourism here is dominated by British blue-chip travel companies and visiting yachts. The bay has a small **beach**, 1km along its south side, a sand-and-pebble strand below a summer-only snack-bar.

## ACCOMMODATION AND EATING                                NORTHERN ITHÁKI

### STAVRÓS

**Margarita** ☎ 26740 31229. This large, friendly *zaharoplastío* is a good place for a coffee, a refreshing drink or to sample the local sweet *rovaní* (syrupy rice cakes). Daily 8am–11pm.

**Petra** ☎ 26740 31596. Popular village taverna that serves grilled and oven dishes, plus some pizza and pasta. It also offers basic but clean and good-value rooms above the restaurant. March–Nov noon–midnight. **€35**

### FRÍKES

**Aristotelis Apartments** ☎ 26740 31079, ⓦ aristotelis-ithaca.gr. Smart apartments only 100m or so back from the harbour, with attractive wooden eaves in the upper rooms and colourful rustic decoration throughout. May–Oct. **€50**

**Nostos** ☎ 26740 31644, ⓦ hotelnostos-ithaki.gr. Around 100m from the seafront, the only conventional

hotel in northern Itháki has a pool in its relaxing grounds and smart, spacious rooms. Buffet breakfast included. May to mid-Oct. **€80**

★ **Rementzo** ☎ 26740 31719. Friendly taverna in the corner of the quay, offering a selection of fresh fish, baked meat and vegetable dishes, salads and pizza, plus good wine and ouzo. April–Oct daily 10am–1am.

**Ulysses** ☎ 26740 31733. Specializing in succulent home-style cuisine, this popular restaurant in the middle of the seafront also provides plenty of snacks, sweets and beverages. May–Oct daily 11am–midnight.

### KIÓNI

**Calypso** ☎ 26740 31066. Pleasant taverna in the middle of the tiny bay, which has imaginative dishes like pork with artichokes and some very drinkable aromatic wine. May–Oct daily noon–midnight.

**Captain's Apartments** ☎26740 31481, ⓦcaptains -apartments.gr. Set up above the village with sweeping views of the bay, these roomy apartments are decorated in warm rustic colours. May–Sept. **€50**

**Maroudas Apartments** ☎26740 31691, ⓔmaroudas @greek-tourism.gr. Just a couple of blocks from the harbour, these compact, convenient and comfortable apartments offer modern amenities and a warm welcome. May–Sept. **€40**

**Oasis** ☎26740 31317. Harbourside taverna that offers the usual selection of fresh salads, some dips and a good choice of mainly grilled meat and fish courses. May–Sept daily noon–1am.

# Zákynthos

**ZÁKYNTHOS**, (Zante) southernmost of the six core Ionian islands, is somewhat schizophrenically divided between relative wilderness and indiscriminate commercialization. Much of the island is still green and unspoilt, with only token pockets of tourism, however, and the main resorts seem to be reaching maximum growth without encroaching too much on the quieter parts. The island has three distinct zones: the barren, mountainous northwest; the fertile central plain; and the eastern and southern resort-filled coasts. The biggest resort is **Laganás**, on Laganás Bay in the south, a 24-hour party venue that doesn't give up from Easter until the last flight home in October. There are smaller, quieter resorts north and south of the capital, and the southerly Vassilikós peninsula has some of the best countryside and beaches, including exquisite **Yérakas**.

The island still produces fine wines, such as the white Popolaro, as well as sugar-shock-inducing *mandoláto* nougat, whose honey-sweetened form is best. Zákynthos is also the birthplace of *kantádhes*, the Italianate folk ballads which can be heard in tavernas in Zákynthos Town and elsewhere. In addition, the island harbours one of the key breeding sites of the endangered **loggerhead sea turtle** at Laganás Bay (see box, p.753).

## ARRIVAL AND DEPARTURE                                                            ZÁKYNTHOS

**By plane** Zákynthos' airport is 4km southwest of the capital. It receives mostly European charters, plus a seasonal daily easyJet flight from London and year-round domestic flights from Athens (1–2 daily; 55min).

**By bus** Buses from Zákynthos Town to the following mainland destinations are timed to connect with ferry sailings:

Destinations Athens (4–6 daily; 5hr 30min); Pátra (3–4 daily; 3hr); Thessaloníki (2 weekly; 11–12hr).

**By ferry** The island is well connected year-round with Kyllíni on the Peloponnesian coast and has a seasonal ferry link with Kefaloniá from the northern Áyios Nikólaos (aka Skinári).

Áyios Nikólaos to: Pessádha (Kefaloniá; 2 daily May–Sept; 1hr 30min).

Zákynthos Town to: Kyllíni (5–7 daily; 1hr 30min).

## GETTING AROUND

**By bus** The local KTEL network radiates out from Zákynthos Town with frequent summer services to the busiest tourist resorts, especially Argási, Kalamáki and Laganás, but few or no buses to the far north or the west coast.

**By cars and motorbike** There are many rental outlets around the island, such as Eurosky (☎26950 26278, ⓦeurosky.gr), whose head Zákynthos Town office is at Makrí 6, two blocks south of the main square.

**By taxi** Taxis are widely available and can be called on ☎26950 48400.

---

### BOAT TRIPS FROM ZÁKYNTHOS TOWN

At least ten pleasure craft offer **day-trips** around the island from the quay in Zákynthos Town (around €20). All take in sights such as the **Blue Caves** at Cape Skinári, and moor in **Tó Naváyio (Shipwreck Bay)** and at the Marathiá caves at **Cape Kerí** in the southwest. You might want to shop around for the trip with the most stops, as eight hours bobbing round the coast can become a bore. Check also that the operators actually take you into the caves. There are also shorter trips to Kerí and turtle-spotting in Laganás Bay for €15, including on one vessel with underwater seating. **Cavo Grosso** at Lombárdhou 22 (☎26950 48308, ⓦcavogrosso.gr) offers a range of excursions.

**ZÁKYNTHOS**

Cape Skinári
Blue Caves
Shipwreck Bay
Volímes
Anafonítria
Mt Astéri (583m)
Anafonítria
Áyios Nikólaos
Vnómi Bay
Skinári
Makrýs Yialós
Xygiá
Stenítis Bay
Mariés
Mt Vrahiónas (756m)
Alykés
Kambí
Éxo Hóra
Katastári
Pigadhákia
Alikanás
Dhrossiá
Ayía Marína
Yerakári
Pahiá Ámmos
Áyios Léon
Tragáki
Mt Athéras
Kiliómeno
Tsiliví
Limniónas
Maherádho
Plános
Vanáto
Megálo Vounó
ZÁKYNTHOS TOWN
Bóhali
Argási
Laganás
Límni Kerioú
Kalamáki
Mount Skopós (492m)
Kerí
Mt Kakavakía (413m)
Marathiá Caves
Marathoníssi
Kamínia
Dháfni
Pórto Zóro
Áno Vassilikós
Banána
Áyios Nikólaos
Pórto Róma
Peloúzo
Yérakas

0    25
kilometres

Psettálsa (Kefaloniá)
Alykés Bay
Kyllíni

# Zákynthos Town

The town, like the island, is known as both **ZÁKYNTHOS** and Zante. This former "Venice of the East" (*Zante, Fior di Levante*, "Flower of the Levant", in an Italian jingle), rebuilt on the old plan after the 1953 earthquake, has bravely tried to re-create some of its style, though reinforced concrete can only do so much.

The town stretches beyond the length of the wide and busy harbour, its main section bookended by the grand **Platía Solomoú** at the north, and the church of **Áyios Dhionýsios**, patron saint of the island, at the south. Zákynthos is a working town with limited concessions to tourism, although there are sufficient facilities and it's the only place to stay if you want to see the island by public transport.

## Áyios Dhionýsios

**Church** Daily 8am–1pm & 5–10pm **Museum** Daily May–Sept 8am–11pm, Oct–April 9am–noon & 5–8pm • €2

The church of **Áyios Dhionýsios** is well worth a visit for the dazzling giltwork and fine modern murals inside, which were completely repainted at the turn of the millennium. Behind the church there is also a **museum**, which has some fine paintings and icons.

## Platía Solomoú

**Platía Solomoú** is named after the island's most famous son, the poet Dhionysios Solomos, the father of modernism in Greek literature, who was responsible for establishing demotic Greek (as opposed to the elitist *katharévousa* form) as a literary idiom. He is also the author of the lyrics to the national anthem, an excerpt from which adorns the statue of Liberty in the square.

Platía Solomoú is home to the town's **library**, which has a small collection of pre- and post-quake photography, and the massive **Byzantine Museum**, sometimes referred to as the Zákynthos Museum. On the seaward corner of the square stands the squat restored church of **Áyios Nikólaos tou Mólou**, where the vestments of St Dhionysios are kept.

### Byzantine Museum

Platía Solomoú • Tues–Sun 8.30am–3pm • €3 • ☏ 26950 42714

The **Byzantine Museum** is most notable for its collection of artworks from the Ionian School (see box, p.711), the region's post-Renaissance art movement, spearheaded by Zakynthian painter Panayiotis Doxaras. The movement was given impetus by Cretan refugees, unable to practise their art under Turkish rule. It also houses some secular painting and a fine model of the town before the earthquake.

## Solomos museum

Platía Ayíou Márkou • Daily 9am–2pm • €3

This impressive **museum** is devoted to the life and work of **Solomos** and other Zakynthian luminaries. It shares its collection of manuscripts and personal effects with an eponymous museum on Corfu (see p.709), where Solomos spent most of his life. There are also plenty of photographs and paintings of notable islanders.

## The kástro

Daily: June–Sept 8am–8pm; Oct–May 8.30am–3pm • €1.50

Zákynthos's massive **kástro** broods over the hamlet of Bóhali on its bluff above the town. The ruined Venetian fort has vestiges of dungeons, armouries and fortifications, plus stunning views in all directions. Its shady carpet of fallen pine needles makes it a great spot to relax or picnic.

### ARRIVAL AND INFORMATION

ZÁKYNTHOS TOWN

**By bus** The bus station is inconveniently located nearly 2km up from the seafront, near the hospital.
Destinations Athens (5–6 daily; 5hr 30min); Pátra (4 daily; 3hr); Thessaloníki (3 weekly; 12–13hr).
**By ferry** The ferry quay is at the southern end of the town's seafront.
**Services** The tourist police is in the main police station, halfway along the seafront. They can supply basic information and keep a list of accommodation (May–Oct daily 8am–10pm; ☏ 26950 24482).

### ACCOMMODATION

The Room Owners Association (☏ 26950 49498) can be contacted for accommodation around town and all over the island. Some of the best hotels are in the quiet Repára district, just north of the centre.

**Egli** Loútzi ☏ 26950 28317. Smallish hotel whose entrance is just off the seafront, tucked in beside the gargantuan *Strada Marina*, though some of its clean, compact rooms face the harbour. €40

★ **Palatino** Kolokotróni 10, Repára ☏ 26950 27780, ⓦ palatinohotel.gr. Classy and surprisingly good-value place, which has beautifully furnished rooms with all mod cons and ritzy common areas. Ample buffet breakfast included. €70

**Plaza** Kolokotróni 2, Repára ☏ 26950 45733, ⓦ plazazante.gr. Barely 50m from the town beach, this pleasant four-storey hotel has comfortable, modern rooms, some with sea-facing balconies, and a relaxing lobby café. Breakfast included. €60

### EATING AND DRINKING

★ **Arekia** Dhionyssíou Romá ☏ 26950 26346. Beyond the town beach, this cosy, welcoming taverna offers a succulent range of fresh grilled meat and fish, but the real reason to come is for the best nightly *kantádhes* to be heard anywhere. Daily 8pm–2am.

**Iy Padella** Dhessylá 15 ☏ 26950 23356. Just a couple of blocks inland south of the main square, this simple *estiatório* offers wholesome home cooking at the best prices in town. Daily 11am–midnight.

**Iy Thymalos** Lombárdhou 78 ☏ 26950 26732. Huge seafront taverna with a nautical theme and pavement seating, where you can feast on imaginative prawn and crab salad, plenty of quality fish and some Cypriot dishes such as *seftaliá*. March–Nov daily noon–2am.

**Komis** Bastoúni tou Ayíou ☏ 26950 26915. Across the quay from Áyios Dhionýsios, this upmarket favourite serves unusual seafood dishes like clams and urchins, along with multiple mezédhes and good barrelled wine. Daily noon–2am.

### NIGHTLIFE

**Base** Platía Ayíou Márkou ☏ 26950 42409. Perennially busy favourite, in a prime location, which plays an eclectic dance mix at night, while its daytime café mode is more prone to rock and ethnic sounds. Daily 11am–late.

**Iy Proza** 21 Maïou 23. Lively upstairs rock bar where black is the colour apart from the startling metallic pipework, the drinks are fairly cheap and the soundtrack is mostly punkish and indie. Daily 10pm–late.

## The Vassilikós peninsula

The busy southern end of the island's most noticeable feature is the **Vassilikós peninsula**, which points in somewhat phallic mimicry of Florida towards the

Peloponnese. It is headed by the package resort of **Argási** but its treasures really lie in the succession of sandy beaches, mostly on the eastern side, which culminate in the stunning strand of **Yérakas**.

## Argási

Barely 4km south of Zákynthos Town, **ARGÁSI** is the busiest resort on this coast, sprawling for over a kilometre behind a beach that is scarcely a few feet wide in parts. Although the rest of the peninsula is far more appealing, it does offer a wide choice of facilities, including a popular concentration of clubs, and is a closer base for exploring the rest of the island.

## The east coast

The first two coves south of Argási are **Kamínia** and the more scenic **Pórto Zóro**. The main road dips and dives along the east coast of the peninsula, with short access roads descending to these and other longer beaches further south, such as **Iónio** and **Banana**. Above these contiguous strands, the only real facilities away from the coast are to be found at the rather formless village of **Áno Vassilkós**.

The coast ends up at **ÁYIOS NIKÓLAOS**, which has a good beach and lures day-trippers from Argási, Kalamáki and Laganás with a free bus service in season. It's a fast-emerging hamlet with a fair range of amenities.

## The west coast

At the very southwestern tip of the peninsula, **Yérakas** is the star attraction: a sublime crescent of golden sand. It's also a key loggerhead turtle breeding ground, and is therefore off-limits between dusk and dawn, as well as being subject to strict rules on the number and placement of umbrellas. The excellent open-air **Turtle Information Centre** (ⓦearthseasky.org) provides interesting background on these and other sea creatures, some of which are on display in its recently acquired aquarium.

Further north along the rugged west coast of the peninsula, accessed by the only (partly unpaved) road which crosses it, is **Dháfni**, home to a couple of tavernas.

| ACTIVITIES | THE VASSILIKÓS PENINSULA |
|---|---|

**Watersports** St Nicholas Beach Watersports in Áyios Nikólaos (ⓣ693 71 07 652) rents equipment for a range of activities, including windsurfing, parasailing and scuba diving.

## ACCOMMODATION, EATING AND NIGHTLIFE

### ARGÁSI

**Barrage** ⓣ693 24 52 020. One of the big outdoor clubs that line the road from Zákynthos Town into Argási, where well-known DJs play house, techno and other dance vibes to a crowd of gyrating bodies. May to mid-Oct daily 10pm–late.

**Locanda** ⓣ26950 45386, ⓦlocanda.gr. Smart seafront hotel with a choice of standard doubles or larger studios, all with kitchenettes and balconies facing the sea or mountain. Also pool and bar. Breakfast included. April–Oct. €60

**Pension Vaso** ⓣ26950 44599. Just off the main road entering the village from Zákynthos Town, this simple guesthouse has basic but clean rooms and you can be sure of a warm welcome from the owner whose name it bears. May–Oct. €30

**Three Brothers** ⓣ26950 44479. One of the oldest tavernas in the resort, with a wide but familiar menu and the cute claim that the fish is "caught by two brothers and cooked by the third". May–Oct daily 10am–1am.

### THE EAST COAST

**Christina's** Áyios Nikólaos ⓣ26950 39474, ⓔchristina _law8@hotmail.com. One of the best deals on the island: The neat, brilliant-white studios with cooking facilities are comfortably furnished and the welcome adds to an all-round cosy atmosphere. May–Oct. €30

★ **Levantino Studios & Apartments** Kamínia ⓣ26950 35366, ⓦlevantino.gr. Well-equipped units of varying size, set in carefully manicured grounds at the back of the beach. Also a snack bar and free sunbeds with umbrellas. May–Oct. €30

**Logos** Áno Vassilkós ⓦlogosbar.com. Legendary rustic club which occupies a large space in the pine woods, where night owls dance to a mixture of rock and disco sounds and sip exotic cocktails. June–Sept Mon, Wed, Fri & Sat 9pm–late.

**Porto Zorro** Pórto Zóro ⓣ26950 35304, ⓦportozorro .gr. This good-value hotel, right on the eponymous beach, has decent-sized rooms whose stark white linen is tempered by the brown wood-panelling. The attached taverna offers a full menu. €40

**Vasilikos Beach** Áyios Nikólaos ☎ 26950 35325, ⊛ hotelvasilikosbeach.gr. Huge beach-resort complex that has a variety of rooms but also offers a pool, jacuzzi and watersports among its many amenities. Buffet breakfast included. May–Oct. €65

**THE WEST COAST**

**Antonis** Dháfni ☎ 26950 26989. Fine taverna-cum-bar, where you can have a full meal of fresh fish or home-cooked meat, a lighter snack or just sip a sunset cocktail. June–Sept daily 10am–10pm.

★ **To Triodi** Yérakas ☎ 26950 35215. Excellent taverna with a leafy garden, where you can sample fresh fish or well-prepared meat dishes, plus all the usual salads, dips and good local wine. May–Oct daily 11am–1am.

## Laganás Bay

The large sweep of **Laganás Bay**, anchored on the major party resort of **Laganás** itself, dominates southern Zákynthos. **Kalamáki** is another busy resort at the eastern end, while delightful **Límni Kærioú** in the southwest completes the picture. As the bay is also a prime home to the loggerhead turtle, there has long been an uneasy coexistence between mass tourism and conservation (see box below).

**11**

### Laganás

The majority of the hundreds of thousands of people who visit Zákynthos each year find themselves in **LAGANÁS**. Set amid the fine 9km beach that runs almost the entire length of the bay, it offers entertainments from watersports to ballooning, and even an occasional funfair. Beachfront bars and restaurants stretch for well over 1km, the bars and restaurants on the main drag another kilometre inland. Some stay open around the clock; others just play music at deafening volume until dawn. The competing video and music bars can make Laganás at night resemble the set of *Blade Runner* but that's how its predominantly English visitors like it.

---

#### LOGGERHEAD TURTLES

The Ionian islands harbour the Mediterranean's main concentration of **loggerhead sea turtles**, a sensitive species which is, unfortunately, under direct threat from the tourist industry. These creatures lay their eggs at night on sandy coves and, easily frightened by noise and lights, are therefore uneasy cohabitants with rough campers and late-night discos. Each year, many turtles fall prey to motorboat injuries, nests are destroyed by bikes and the newly hatched young die entangled in deckchairs and umbrellas left out at night.

The Greek government has passed laws designed to protect the loggerheads, including restrictions on camping at some beaches, but local economic interests tend to prefer a beach full of bodies to a sea full of turtles. On **Laganás**, nesting grounds are concentrated around the 14km bay, and Greek marine zoologists are in angry dispute with those involved in the tourist industry. The turtles' nesting ground just west of **Skála** on Kefaloniá is another important location, although numbers have dwindled to half their former strength and now only about eight hundred remain. Ultimately, the turtles' best hope for survival may rest in their potential draw as a unique tourist attraction in their own right.

While capitalists and environmentalists are still at, well, loggerheads, the **World Wildlife Fund** has issued guidelines for visitors:

· Don't use the beaches of Laganás and Yérakas between sunset and sunrise.
· Don't stick umbrellas in the sand in the marked nesting zones.
· Take your rubbish away with you – it can obstruct the turtles.
· Don't use lights near the beach at night – they can disturb the turtles, sometimes with fatal consequences.
· Don't take any vehicle onto the protected beaches.
· Don't dig up turtle nests – it's illegal.
· Don't pick up the hatchlings or carry them to the water.
· Don't use speedboats in Laganás Bay – a 9kph speed limit is in force.

## Kalamáki

Neighbouring Laganás to the east, **Kalamáki** has a better, much wider beach than its westerly neighbour and is altogether quieter, with a slightly more family-oriented feel. Even the bars are more laidback, although it does suffer from some airport noise.

## Límni Kerioú

**Límni Kerioú**, at the southwestern end of Laganás Bay, has gradually evolved into a relaxing and picturesque resort, and has a couple of diving operations. It's reached by a turning that branches off the main road before it climbs up towards the west coast, after the hill village of **Lithákia**.

### ACTIVITIES

LAGANÁS BAY

**Diving** Límni Kerioú is home to the Turtle Beach Diving Centre (☎ 26950 49424, ⓦ diving-center-turtle-beach .com).

**Horseriding** Nana's Horses (☎ 26950 23195), just outside Kalamáki, can arrange riding trips.

### ACCOMMODATION, EATING, DRINKING AND NIGHTLIFE

#### LAGANÁS

**Ionis** ☎ 26950 51141, ⓦ zante-ionis-hotel.com. On the main drag towards the beach, one of the few places not block-booked is this surprisingly classy boutique hotel with tastefully designed rooms and a huge pool. Breakfast included; open May–Oct. If they're full try the local Union of Room Owners (daily 8.30am–2pm & 5–8pm; ☎ 26950 51590), which has a range of accommodation. **€80**

**Rescue Club** ☎ 26950 51612. Proclaiming itself to be the biggest club on the island, this place has an outdoor bar area and huge indoor dancefloor with top sound and lighting equipment to enhance the nonstop dance favourites. May–Oct daily 10pm–late.

★ **Sarakina** ☎ 26950 51606. Best taverna in the area, serving tasty dishes such as pork in wine sauce and featuring nightly *kantádhes*. There's a free minibus to convey diners to its leafy location nearly 2km inland. May–Oct 6pm–2am.

**Zeros** ⓦ zerosclubzante.com. Massive club with state-of-the-art sound systems and top DJs, which hosts various big events through the summer and regular foam parties and other themes. May–Oct daily 9pm–late.

#### KALAMÁKI

**Cave Club** ☎ 26950 48278. Set into a real cave on the hillside above the village, with a pleasantly leafy patio garden where you can enjoy a cocktail to the mostly laid-back rock sounds. May–Oct daily 9pm–3am.

**Crystal Beach** ☎ 26950 42788, ⓦ crystalbeach.gr. Large resort hotel, which has smart rooms for independent

as well as package holiday-makers, plus restaurant, bar, pool and watersports on the beach. Breakfast included. May–Oct. **€70**

**Stanis** ☎ 26950 26374. Both branches of this well-established taverna have extensive menus of Greek and international dishes, although the one by the beach is predictably busier during the day. May–Oct daily 11am–1am.

#### LÍMNI KERIOÚ

**Camping Tartaruga** ☎ 26950 51967, ⓦ tartaruga -camping.com. Easily the best campsite on the island, though reaching it requires a vehicle as it's on a remote stretch of Laganás Bay below Lithákia. Shady pitches, a pebble beach and minimarket all to hand. May–Oct. Adult plus tent **€7.40**

★ **Pansion Limni** ☎ 26950 48716, ⓦ pansionlimni .com. Disarmingly friendly family guesthouse, with comfortable self-catering rooms and a shared wraparound balcony with sea views. Their wonderful stone *Porto Tsi Ostrias pension* nearby has huge, beautifully designed apartments. May–Oct. **€40**

**Poseidon** ☎ 26950 48708. Overlooking the bay from the hill at the east end, and serving a variety of grilled meat and fish, plus good daily specials. May–Oct daily noon–1am.

**Rock Café** ☎ 26950 23401. Chilled-out joint with an airy wooden balcony overlooking the beach, a well-stocked bar and, as the name suggests, a decent line in rock sounds. May–Oct daily noon–2am.

# Western Zákynthos

At the far southwest end of Laganás Bay, the landscape ascends into the mountains around **Kerí**, the first of a series of pretty villages along the sparsely inhabited **west coast**. The bus system does not reach the wild western side of the island, so a rental car or sturdy motorbike is required to get there.

## Kerí

Hidden in a fold above the cliffs at the island's southernmost tip, the village of **KERÍ** retains several pre-quake Venetian buildings, including the **Panayía Kerioú** church; the Virgin is said to have saved the island from marauding pirates by hiding it in a sea mist. A road leads 1km on to the lighthouse, with spectacular views of the sea, rock arches and stacks.

## Maherádho

**MAHERÁDHO** boasts impressive pre-earthquake architecture set in beautiful arable uplands, surrounded by olive and fruit groves. The church of **Ayía Mávra** has an impressive freestanding campanile and, inside, a splendid carved iconostasis and icons. The town's major **festival** – one of the biggest on the island – is the saint's day, which falls on the first Sunday in June. The other notable church in town, that of the **Panayía**, commands breathtaking views over the central plain.

## Kiliómeno and around

**KILIÓMENO** is the best place to see surviving pre-earthquake domestic architecture, in the form of the island's traditional two-storey houses. The town was originally named after its church, **Áyios Nikólaos**, whose impressive campanile, begun over a hundred years ago, still lacks a capped roof. The road from Kiliómeno passes through the nondescript village of Áyios Léon, from where two turnings lead through fertile land and down a paved loop road to the impressive rocky coast at **Limniónas**, where there is a tiny bay.

## Kambí

The tiny clifftop hamlet of **KAMBÍ** is popular with day-trippers, who come to catch the sunset over the sea; there are extraordinary views to be had of the 300m-high cliffs and western horizon from Kambí's three clifftop tavernas.

## Mariés and around

Set in a wooded green valley 5km north of Kambí, the tiny village of **MARIÉS** is the only other place with coastal access on this side of Zákynthos: a 7km track leading down to the rocky inlet of **Stenítis Bay**, where there's a taverna and yacht dock. Another steep road leads to the uninspiring **Vrómi Bay**, from where speedboats run trips to Shipwreck Bay (see p.757), while the main road continues north towards Volímes (see p.757).

---

**ACCOMMODATION AND EATING**                                    **THE WEST COAST**

**KERÍ**

**Apelati** ☎ 26950 43324. Just off the main road before the incline east of the village, this farm-like taverna serves home-style dishes from fresh ingredients and has a few simple rustic rooms. May–Oct 11am–midnight. **€30**

**Keri Lighthouse** ☎ 26950 43384. Scenically situated taverna, 1km west of the village, where people flock for sunset dinners in the large and lush patio garden. The food is standard fare but the view unsurpassed. May–Sept daily noon–midnight.

**KILIÓMENO AND AROUND**

★ **Alitzerini** Kiliómeno ☎ 26950 48552. At this beautifully restored eighteenth-century stone house with a terrace the friendly owner serves up traditional cuisine with a twist, such as *sfigadoúra* – beef in tomato sauce with cheese and red pepper. 7pm–1am: May–Sept daily, Oct–April Sat & Sun; also some Sun lunches.

**Porto Limnionas** Limniónas. Perched on a rocky outcrop just above the tiny harbour, this *psarotavérna* is known for its high-quality if rather pricey fish and also has a huge selection of tasty mezédhes. May–Oct daily noon–11pm.

# The northeast

A few kilometres north of the capital the amalgamated resorts of **Tsiliví** and **Plános** are the touristic epicentre of this part of the island. Further north they give way to a series of tiny beaches, while picturesque villages punctuate the lush landscape inland. Beyond **Alykés**, as you approach the island's tip at **Cape Skinári**, the coast becomes more rugged, while the mountains inland hide the weaving centre of **Volímes**.

## Tsiliví, Plános and around

North and inland from Zákynthos Town, the roads thread their way through luxuriantly fertile farmland, punctuated with tumulus-like hills. **TSILIVÍ**, 5km north of the capital, is the first beach resort here and is in effect one with the hamlet of **PLÁNOS**, the resultant conglomeration rivalling Argási for development.

The beaches further along this stretch of coast become progressively quieter and more pleasant, and all have at least some accommodation and restaurants to choose from. Good choices include **Pahiá Ámmos** and **Dhrossiá**.

## Alykés Bay

**Alykés Bay**, 12km north of Tsiliví, is a large sandy bay with lively surf and the northeast's two largest resorts. The first, **ALIKANÁS**, is a small but expanding village, much of its accommodation being foreign-owned villa rentals. The second, **ALYKÉS**, named after the spooky saltpans behind the village, has the best beach north of the capital.

## Makrýs Yialós and around

Tiny **Xygiá beach**, cut into a deep cove 4km north of Alykés, has sulphur springs flowing into the sea – follow the smell – which provide the odd sensation of swimming in a mix of cool and warm water. The next, somewhat longer, beach of **Makrýs Yialós** also makes for an extremely pleasant break on a tour of the north. Just to the north of Makrýs Yialós you come to a pretty promontory with a small harbour, called **Mikró Nissáki**.

## Áyios Nikólaos and around

Just over 20km from Zákynthos Town, **ÁYIOS NIKÓLAOS**, known to locals as **Skinári** (after the nearby inland village) to avoid confusion with its namesake on the Vassilikós peninsula, is a small working port with a daily summer ferry connection to Pessádha on Kefaloniá but unfortunately there is no bus service, so travellers using the crossing without their own transport are forced to fork out for a taxi or hitch a ride south.

### The Blue Caves

Boat trips €7.50; €15 combined with Shipwreck Bay

The **Blue Caves** are some of the more realistically named of the many contenders in Greece; ignore scams claiming that Áyios Nikólaos is the last place from which you can catch a boat. They're terrific for snorkelling and when you go for a dip here your skin will appear bright blue. To reach them, follow the road as it snakes onwards from Áyios Nikólaos through a landscape of gorse bushes and dry-stone walls until it ends at the lighthouse of **Cape Skinári**, from below which the cheapest **boat trips** operate.

## Katastári

Two kilometres inland from Alykés, **KATASTÁRI** is the largest settlement after the capital. Precisely because it's not geared towards tourism, it's the best place to see Zakynthian life as it's lived away from the usual racket. Its most impressive edifice is the huge rectangular church of Iperáyia Theotókos, with a twin belfry and small new amphitheatre for festival performances.

## Pighadhákia

A couple of kilometres south of Katastári, the tiny hamlet of **PIGHADHÁKIA** is the unlikely setting for the **Vertzagio Cultural Museum** (March to early Nov Mon–Fri & Sun 9am–2pm & 6–8pm, Sat 9am–2pm; €3), which houses an interesting array of agricultural and folk artefacts. There is also the diminutive **Áyios Pandeléïmon** chapel, which has the unusual feature of a well, hidden beneath the altar.

## Ayía Marína

**AYÍA MARÍNA**, a few kilometres southwest of Katastári, has a church with an impressive Baroque altar screen, and a belfry that's being rebuilt from the remnants left after the 1953 earthquake. As in most Zákynthos churches, the bell tower stands detached, in Venetian fashion. In the upper part of the village is the new **Helmi's Natural History Museum** (May–Oct 9am–6pm, Nov–April 9am–2pm; €2; ⊕museumhelmis.gr), which displays plenty of stuffed birds and mammals, seashells and the largest ammonite found in Greece, as well as showing an informative film about turtles.

## Volímes and around

Divided into three contiguous parts, **VOLÍMES** is the centre of the island's embroidery industry and numerous shops sell artefacts produced here. With your own transport, you could make it to the **Anafonítria monastery**, 3km south, thought to have been the cell of the island's patron saint, Dhionysios, whose festivals are celebrated on August 24 and December 17.

### Shipwreck Bay

A paved road leads on from Volímes to the cliffs overlooking **Shipwreck Bay** (Tó Naváyio), with hair-raising views down to the shipwreck, a cargo ship which was mistaken for a drug-running vessel and run aground by the coastguard in the 1960s.

**11**

---

| ACCOMMODATION AND EATING | THE NORTHEAST |
|---|---|

### TSILIVÍ, PLÁNOS AND AROUND

**Anetis Hotel** ☎ 26950 44590, ⊕anetishotel.gr. Comfortable, good-value hotel with sizeable a/c rooms, many with sea-facing balconies overlooking the lively beach bar. April–Oct. **€35**

**The Olive Tree** ☎ 26950 62834. The best of the predictably touristy bunch, with a huge menu, including grilled meat and fish, a host of starters and perfectly acceptable wine by the kilo. May–Oct daily noon–1am.

**Passage to Asia** ☎ 26950 43788. One of the best oriental restaurants on the island, serving authentic enough versions of both Indian and Chinese cuisine. Has meal deals for two people at around €20. May–Oct daily noon–midnight.

### ALYKÉS BAY

**Eros Piccadilly** ☎ 26950 83606, ⊕piccadilly.com.gr. Near the beginning of the road to Katastári, this hotel often has super deals going on its studios and compact but comfortable rooms. April–Oct. **€25**

**Fantasia** ☎ 26950 83249. Fairly standard tourist fare with a dash of flair makes this one of the better options in the resort. Also does full English breakfasts for €3.50. May–Oct daily 9am–1am.

### MAKRÝS YIALÓS AND AROUND

**Pilarinos** ☎ 26950 31396. This good taverna on the flattish hillock behind the beach does a decent line in grills, fish and the usual accoutrements, plus there's a makeshift campsite on the grounds. May–Oct daily 11am–midnight.

### ÁYIOS NIKÓLAOS AND AROUND

★ **Anemomilos** Cape Skinári ☎ 26950 31241, ⊕potamitisbros.gr. Two expertly converted windmills make for a unique place to stay. There are also some more conventional rooms, a snack bar, and the same family run the excellent *To Faros* taverna nearby. May–Oct. **€50**

**Panorama** Áyios Nikólaos ☎ 26950 31013, ⊖panorama -apts@ath.forthnet.gr. Great if you are leaving on the morning ferry to Kefaloniá or want a northern base, these friendly studios are a good-value option. Breakfast included. April–Oct. **€35**

### PIGHADHÁKIA

★ **Kaki Rahi** ☎ 26950 83670. Traditional family-run taverna, which serves tasty local cuisine from home-grown ingredients, its own barrelled wine and provides transportation on its little train twice daily from Alykés. €12.50 including set mixed plate. Live music Sat evenings. May–Oct daily 11am–midnight.

ERECHTHEION TEMPLE, ATHENS

# Contexts

**759** History

**785** Archeology

**790** Wildlife

**795** Music

**801** Books

**807** Greek

# History

Greece's position at the heart of the eastern Mediterranean and at the crossroads of Europe, Asia and Africa, has long presented it with unique opportunities and dangers. The Greeks are a people who have suffered calamities, yet they have also achieved the highest reaches of human accomplishment. In the areas of politics, philosophy, literature, science and art, Greece has influenced Western society more than any other nation in history; in the twenty-first century, it seems their economic policy may have to be added to that list.

## Prehistoric Greece: to 2100 BC

Evidence of human habitation in Greece goes back half a million years, as demonstrated by the skeleton of a **Neanderthal** youth in the **Petralóna Cave**, 50km east of the northern city of Thessaloníki, along with the earliest known site of a man-made fire in Europe.

Only very much later, about **40,000 years ago**, did **Homo sapiens** make his first appearance in Greece after migrating out of Africa. At several sites in **Epirus** in northwest Greece, Homo sapiens used tools and weapons of bone, wood and stone to gather wild plants and hunt. Even between **20,000 and 16,000 years ago**, when the Ice Age was at its peak, **Stone Age man** continued to make a home in Greece, though only when the glaciers finally receded about **10,000 BC** did a considerably warmer climate set in, altering the Greek environment to something more like that of present times.

### The Neolithic period

**Agricultural communities** first appeared in northern Greece around **6500 BC**. Whether agriculture developed indigenously or was introduced by migrants from Asia Minor is much debated: what is certain, however, is its revolutionary effect.

An assured supply of food enabled the Stone Age inhabitants of Greece to settle in fixed spots, building mud-brick houses on stone foundations. Though still reliant on stone implements, this new farming culture marked a significant break with the past, so a "new stone age" or **Neolithic period** is said to have begun. As the flint needed for weapons and tools was rare in Greece, mainlanders imported obsidian from the island of **Melos** (Mílos) in the southern Cyclades. The earliest **seaborne trade** known anywhere in the world, this clearly involved a mastery of building and handling boats.

### Cycladic culture and the beginnings of the Greek Bronze Age

Around **3000 BC** a new people settled in the **Cyclades**, probably from Asia Minor, bringing with them the latest metallurgical techniques. While continuing the old trade in obsidian, they also developed a **trade in tin** and were making prodigious voyages westwards as far as Spain by 2500 BC. The mining of **gold and silver** in the Cyclades

| c.40,000 BC | c.6500 BC | c.3000 BC | c.2100 BC |
|---|---|---|---|
| Stone Age Homo sapiens arrives in Greece. | Permanent communities and the world's earliest sea-borne trade herald the Neolithic era. | In the Cycladic islands, a new people introduce striking new art forms. The dawn of the Bronze Age. | The Greek language is heard in Greece for the first time. |

may have dated from this period, too. Long before Crete or the Greek mainland, these new islanders became specialists in **jewellery-making**, **metalwork** and **stone-cutting**. From the abundant marble of the Cyclades, they sculpted statuettes, mostly of female figures. Slender, spare and geometric, these **Cycladic sculptures** are startlingly modern in appearance, and were exported widely, to Crete and mainland Greece, along with other ritual objects.

In about 3000 BC, the introduction of bronze technology to the mainland, also from the Cyclades, marked the start of the **Bronze Age** in Greece. By **2500 BC** the widespread use of bronze had transformed farming and fighting throughout the Eastern Mediterranean and the Middle East. Because **tin** (which when alloyed with copper creates bronze) came from so far afield – in the east from the Caucasus, Persia and Afghanistan, in the west from Cornwall, Brittany, northwest Spain and northern Italy – the Aegean became an important trade route. Hence the burst of development that now took place along the eastern coast of **central Greece** and the **Peloponnese**, and on the **Aegean islands** which linked the Greek mainland to Asia Minor and the Middle East.

It is uncertain what **language** was spoken at this time but one thing is clear: it was not yet Greek. Indeed, when **Greek-speaking people** did arrive on the mainland in about 2100 BC, their destructive impact paralyzed its development for five hundred years.

### The coming of the Greeks

The destruction of numerous mainland sites in about **2100 BC**, followed by the appearance of a new style of pottery, has suggested to archeologists the violent arrival of a **new people**. They domesticated the horse, introduced the potter's wheel and possessed considerable metallurgical skills. These newcomers replaced the old religion centred on female fertility figures with **hilltop shrines**, thought to have been dedicated to the worship of male sky gods like Zeus. And with them came a new language, an early form of **Greek**, though they were obliged to adopt existing native words for such things as olives, figs, vines, wheat and the sea, suggesting that these new migrants or invaders may have come from distant inland steppes where they had been pastoral highlanders, not farmers, fishermen or sailors.

## Minoan and Mycenaean civilizations: 2100–1100 BC

The history of the Aegean during the second millennium BC can be seen as a struggle between the **Mycenaean culture** of the Greek mainland and the **Minoan culture** of Crete. Situated halfway between mainland Greece and Egypt, Crete exploited the Bronze Age boom in trade, to become the dominant power in the Aegean by the start of the second millennium BC. Its influence was felt throughout the islands and also on the mainland, where the Greek-speaking invaders were "Minoanized", gradually developing a culture known as Mycenaean (after Mycenae, a principal mainland Bronze Age site) that owed a lot to Crete.

### Minoan Crete

Living on a large and fertile island with good natural harbours, the people of **Crete** raised sufficient crops and livestock to export surplus quantities of oil and wool.

| c.2000 BC | c.1700 BC | c.1500 BC | c.1220 BC |
|---|---|---|---|
| On Crete, the great Minoan palaces are built. | Knossos and the other palaces are destroyed by earthquake, but rebuilt even more grandly. | Mainland Mycenaeans gain control of Crete. | Trojan War, whose events are immortalized by Homer and enter the realm of myth. |

## THE TROJAN WAR

For the Greeks, the story of the **Trojan War** was the central event in their early history, and in their minds Homer's **Iliad** was not just a poem of heroic deeds sung at noble courts, but the epic of their first national adventure.

Excavations in the late nineteenth century by Heinrich Schliemann (see p.786) uncovered many Troys of several periods, but the layer known as **Troy VIIa** clearly suffered violent destruction in about 1220 BC. The Mycenaeans are the likeliest perpetrators, though the abduction of a Greek beauty called **Helen** would not have been the only reason they launched a thousand ships against the Trojans. Mycenaean prosperity greatly depended on trade with the Eastern Mediterranean, where increasingly unsettled conditions made it imperative that they secure their lines of **trade and supply**. Troy commanded a strategic position overlooking the Hellespont, the narrow waterway (today called the Dardanelles) dividing Europe and Asia and linking the Aegean to the Black Sea, where it controlled important trade routes.

The capture of Troy was the last great success of the Mycenaeans, and perhaps for that reason it was long remembered in poetry and song. It inspired later generations of Greeks to dream of overseas expansion, culminating in the fourth century BC when Alexander the Great carried a copy of the Iliad as he marched across Asia, founding Greek cities as he went, and stood with his army on the banks of the Indus River.

Among their most impressive tools, literally at the cutting edge of new technology, was a meter-long bronze saw that readily converted the forest-clad mountains into an ample source of **timber for ships**. Some timber was probably also exported, most likely to treeless Egypt, while metalwork, jewellery and pottery of superb Cretan craftsmanship were shipped to the mainland and beyond. **Kamares ware**, as Cretan pottery of this period is known, was especially valued; it has been found all along the Cretans' 875km-long maritime trade route to the East – on the Aegean islands of Rhodes and Sámos, on the coast of Asia Minor at Miletus, and in Syria and Egypt.

On Crete itself, Minoan power was concentrated on three vast **palace complexes** – at **Knossos**, **Phaestos** and **Malia**, all in the centre of the island. First built around 2000 BC, their similarity of plan and lack of defences suggest that some form of confederacy had replaced any regional rivalries on the island, while Minoan sea power induced a sense of security against foreign invasion. Not that prosperity was confined to the palace centres; the numerous remains of villas of the Minoan gentry, and of well-constructed villages, show that the wealth generated by the palaces was redistributed among the island's population. Following an **earthquake** around 1700 BC, the palaces at Knossos and Phaestos were rebuilt, and a more modest palace constructed at **Zakros** on the east coast. This activity coincided with an apparent centralization of power at Knossos, giving rise to a **Minoan golden age**.

### Mycenaean dominance

Suddenly, however, around **1500 BC**, the Mycenaeans gained control of the palace of Knossos and were soon in full possession of Crete. How this happened is unknown, but it probably marked the culmination of a growing rivalry between the Mycenaeans and the Minoans for control of the Aegean trade, which perhaps coincided with a **volcanic explosion** on the island of Thera (Thíra/Santoríni) and its consequent **tsunami**.

| **c.1150 BC** | **c.1100 BC** | **c.620–570 BC** |
|---|---|---|
| The so-called Sea Peoples sweep across Greece, ushering in a new Dark Age. | The first iron tools and weapons begin to transform agriculture and warfare. | Sappho, from whom we get the words sapphic and lesbian (after her birthplace, Lésvos), was regarded as one of the greatest poets of the ancient world. |

**Greek** now became the language of administration at Knossos and the other former Minoan palaces, as well as on the mainland – indeed this is the earliest moment that Greek language can definitely be identified, as the palace records on Crete are from now on written in a script known as **Linear B**, which when deciphered in 1953 was shown to be a form of Greek. Having wrested control of the Aegean trade from the Minoans, the **Mycenaeans** were dominant for another three hundred years. At the end of that period, in about 1220 BC, they famously laid siege to, and destroyed, yet another rival, the city of **Troy**.

Yet within a generation the Mycenaean world was overwhelmed by a vast **migration** of northerners from somewhere beyond the Black Sea. Probably victims of a catastrophic change in climate that brought drought and famine to their homelands, these **Sea Peoples**, as the ancients called them, swept down through Asia Minor and the Middle East and also crossed the Mediterranean to Libya and Egypt, disrupting trade routes and destroying empires as they went. With the palace-based Bronze Age economies destroyed, the humbler **village-based economies** that replaced them lacked the wealth and the technological means to make a mark in the world. Greece was plunged into a Dark Age, and knowledge of the Minoan and Mycenaean civilizations slipped into dim memory.

## The Dark Age and the rise of the city-state: 1150–491 BC

The poverty and isolation that characterized Greece for the next five hundred years did have one lasting effect, **emigration**. Greeks spread to the Dodecanese islands, to Cilicia along the south coast of **Asia Minor**, and to **Cyprus**, which now became Greek-speaking. Later, around 1000 BC, they also settled in large numbers along the western coast of Asia Minor. Even in the Dark Age there were a few glimmers of light: **Athens**, for example, escaped the destruction that accompanied the fall of Mycenaean civilization and maintained trading links abroad. It became the route through which the **Iron Age** was introduced to mainland Greece with the importation of iron weapons, implements and technological know-how around 1100 BC. A new cultural beginning was also made in the form of pottery painted in the **Geometric style**, a highly intricate and controlled design that would lie at the heart of later Greek architecture, sculpture and painting. But it was the **Phoenicians**, sailing from Sidon and Tyre in present-day Lebanon, who really re-established trading links between the Middle East and the Aegean world in the eighth century BC, and Greeks followed swiftly in their wake.

With wealth flowing in again, Greek civilization developed with remarkable rapidity; no other people achieved so much over the next few centuries. The institution most responsible for this extraordinary achievement, the **city-state** or **polis**, came into being at a time of rapidly growing populations, greater competition for land and resources, increasing productivity and wealth, expanding trade and more complex relationships with neighbouring states. The birthplace of **democracy** and of equality before the law, the city-state became the Greek ideal, and by the early seventh century BC it had spread throughout Greece and wherever Greeks established colonies overseas.

Trade also acted as a cultural stimulus; contact with other peoples made the Greeks aware of what they shared among themselves, and led to the development of a **national sentiment**, notably expressed and fostered by the **panhellenic sanctuaries** that arose

| 900–700 BC | c.800 BC | 776 BC | 750–650 BC |
|---|---|---|---|
| Geometric Period. | Revival of trade between Greece and the Middle East kick-starts an economic revival. | The first Olympic Games staged at Olympia. | Greeks colonize the Eastern Mediterranean, from Italy to Asia Minor. |

## THE ILIAD AND THE ODYSSEY

The **Iliad** and the **Odyssey**, the oldest and greatest works in Greek literature, were the brilliant summation of five centuries of poetic tradition, first developed by nameless bards whose recitations were accompanied by music. Completed by 725 BC, they are far older than the *Pentateuch*, the first five books of the Old Testament, which achieved their finished form only around 400 BC. The whole Greek world knew the Homeric epics, and their influence upon the subsequent development of Greek literature, art and culture in general cannot be overstated. Few works, and probably none not used in worship, have had such a hold on a nation for so long.

The Iliad is the story of a few days' action in the tenth and final year of the Trojan War, which in its tales of heroic exploits recalls the golden age of the Mycenaeans. The Odyssey begins after the war and follows the adventures of Odysseus, who takes ten years to return to his island home of Ithaca on the western side of Greece. The story of his voyages demonstrates the new Greek interest in the area around the Black Sea and in Italy and Sicily to the west. They are also a celebration of an emerging hellenic identity, of a national adventure encompassing both shores of the Aegean and beyond.

during the eighth century BC, of Hera and Zeus at **Olympia** and of Apollo and Artemis at **Delos**, as well as the **oracles** of Zeus at **Dodona** and of Apollo at **Delphi**.

### Expansion and colonization

Around 750 BC, Greeks began to found **colonies** in the Western Mediterranean – in **Sicily** and **southern Italy** especially – while a century later, around 650 BC, further colonies were established round the shores of the **Black Sea**. By the fifth century BC Greeks seemed to sit upon the shores of the entire world, in Plato's words like "frogs around a pond".

One impetus for expansion was competition between the Greeks and the Phoenicians over trade routes; but there was also rivalry between the Greek city-states themselves. **Chalkis**, **Eretria** and **Corinth** were the major colonizers in the West, while the **Ionian Greeks** were the chief colonizers around the Black Sea. When the Spartans needed more land, they conquered neighbouring Messenia in 710 BC, but generally land shortage drove Greeks overseas. Thus colonists were sent from Thera (Thíra) to found Cyrene in North Africa, and were forbidden to return on pain of death. Whatever the reason for their foundation, however, most colonies kept up close relations with their mother cities.

### Democracy, tyranny and slavery

Meanwhile, at home in the city-states, political tensions were building between the **aristocratic rulers** and the **people**. A large class of farmers, merchants and the like was excluded from political life but forced to pay heavy taxes. The pressure led to numerous reforms and a gradual move towards **democracy**. Ironically, the transition was often hastened by **tyrants**. Despite the name – which simply means they seized power by force – many tyrants were in fact champions of the people, creating work, redistributing wealth and patronizing the arts. **Peisistratos**, tyrant of Athens during the sixth century BC, is perhaps the archetype. Successful and well-liked by his people, his populist rule ensured Athenian prosperity by gaining control of the route into the Black Sea. He also ordered that Homer's works be set down in their definitive

| c.725 BC | 700–480 BC | 621 BC | 546 BC |
|---|---|---|---|
| The Iliad and Odyssey, hitherto retold as oral sagas, are set down in writing. | Archaic period. | Draco's reforming "draconian" law code is published in Athens. | Peisistratos seizes power in Athens. |

form and performed regularly, and encouraged the theatrical festivals where Greek drama would be born.

## Athens and the Golden Age: 490–431 BC

**Democracy** was a very long way from universal. The population of **Athens** and surrounding Attica amounted to some 400,000 people, of whom about 80,000 were slaves, 160,000 foreigners, and another 160,000 free-born Athenians. Out of this last category came the **citizens**, those who could vote and be elected to office, and their number amounted to no more than 45,000 adult men.

Yet if the powers of democracy were in the hands of the few, the energy, boldness and creative spirit that it released raised Athens to greatness. Throughout the **fifth century BC** the political, intellectual and artistic activity of the Greek world was centred on the city. In particular Athens was the patron of **drama**, both tragedy and comedy. Athenian tragedy always addressed the great issues of life and death and the relationship of man to the gods. And the Athenians themselves seemed to be conscious of living out a high drama as they fought battles, argued policy, raised temples and wrote plays that have decided the course and sensibility of Western civilization.

### The Persian Wars

The wars between Greece and Persia began with a revolt by Ionian Greeks in Asia Minor. Athens and Eretria gave them support, burning the city of Sardis in 498 BC. Provoked by their insolence, **Darius**, the Persian king, launched a punitive expedition. The **Persians'** unexpected repulse at **Marathon** in 490 BC persuaded Darius to hurl his full military might against Greece, to ensure its subjection once and for all to the Persian Empire.

After Darius died in 486 BC, his son **Xerxes** took over. In 483 BC, he began preparations that lasted two years and were on a fabulous scale. Bridges of boats were built across the Hellespont for Persia's vast imperial army to parade into Europe, and a canal was cut for the fleet through the Athos peninsula. Though the Greek historian **Herodotus** claimed that Xerxes' army held one million eight hundred thousand soldiers, his figure is probably a tenfold exaggeration. Even so, it was a massive force, an army of 46 nations, combined with a fleet of eight hundred triremes carrying almost as many sailors as there were soldiers in the army.

Despite their numerical superiority, the might of Asia was routed both at sea off **Salamis** in 480 BC and on land at **Plataea** the following year. Within a few days of that second battle came another naval victory at **Mycale**, off Sámos, where the battle was won when Xerxes' subject Ionians went over to their fellow Hellenes. Xerxes could do no more than return to Susa, his capital deep in Persia, leaving the entire Aegean free.

Despite occasional reversals, this sudden shift in the balance of power between East and West endured for the next 1500 years. Within 150 years, Alexander the Great achieved in Asia what Xerxes had failed to achieve in Europe, and the Persian Empire succumbed to a Greek conqueror.

### Themistocles and the rise of sea power

The greatest Athenian statesman, and architect of the victory over Persia, was **Themistocles**. Following the Ionian revolt he understood that a clash between Persia

| **498 BC** | **490 BC** | **480 BC** |
|---|---|---|
| Rebellious Ionian Greeks burn the city of Sardis, provoking a Persian invasion of Greece. | Victory by the Athenians and Plataeans at the Battle of Marathon ends the first Persian campaign. Pheidippides runs to Athens to convey the good news. | Greek defeat at the Battle of Thermopylae, scene of heroic Spartan defiance. |

## THE BATTLE OF MARATHON

For the Athenians, victory in the **Battle of Marathon** set the seal on their democracy and marked the start of a new self-confident era. And indeed, it was the most remarkable of victories.

The Athenian army, with their allies the Plataeans, fearful of the Persians' superior numbers and of their cavalry and archers, held a defensive position astride the mountain pass leading into the plain of Marathon for five days, waiting for Spartan reinforcements. On the fifth day the Persians gave up hope of joining battle at Marathon and embarked their cavalry to advance on Athens by sea, sending their infantry forwards to cover the operation. With the Persian forces divided, Athenian general **Miltiades** saw his opportunity, Spartan help or no, and sent his hoplites racing downhill to get quickly under the hail of Persian arrows and engage their infantry in close combat. The Athenian centre was kept weak while the wings were reinforced, so that when the Persians broke through the centre of the charging line, the momentum of the Greek wings soon engulfed them on either side and to the rear. The Persians panicked, fell into disorder, and were beaten into the marshes and the sea. Seven ships were lost and 6400 Persians killed. The 192 Athenian dead were buried on the spot, and covered by a mound that can still be seen today.

The remainder of the Persian force sailed round Cape Sounio to land within sight of the Acropolis, but Miltiades had brought the army back to Athens by forced march and stood ready to meet the enemy again. That astonishing burst of energy – 10,000 men marching 26 miles in full armour after fighting one battle to fight, if need be, another – overwhelmed the Persians' morale, and their expedition returned to Asia.

and Greece was inevitable, and he had the genius to recognize that Athens' security and potential lay in its command of the sea. Thus he began in 493–492 BC to develop **Piraeus** (Pireás) as the harbour of Athens. Though his initial pretext was the hostility of the island of Aegina (Égina), his eyes were always on the more distant but far greater Persian danger.

When the Persians marched into Attica in the late summer of 480 BC, the oracle at Delphi told the Athenians to trust in their wooden wall. Many took that to mean the wooden wall around the citadel of the Athenian Acropolis, but Themistocles argued that it referred to the Athenian fleet. Determined to fight at sea, Themistocles warned his Peloponnesian allies against retreating to the Isthmus where they too had built a wall, threatening that if they did the entire citizenry of Athens would sail to new homes in southern Italy, leaving the rest of Greece to its fate. On the eve of the Battle of Salamis, as the Persians stormed the Acropolis, slaughtering its defenders and burning down its temples, the taunt came back from the Peloponnesians that Athens had no city anyway. Themistocles replied that so long as the Athenians had 200 ships they had a city and a country.

The naval victory at Salamis that he masterminded cut the Persians' maritime lines of supply and contributed to their defeat at Plataea the following year. It gave Athens and its allies command of the sea, ensuring their eventual victory throughout the Aegean. For his pains the Athenians later drove Themistocles into exile.

### The rise of the Athenian Empire: 478–431 BC

The first consequence of the Greek victory against the Persians was not, as might have been expected, the rise of **Sparta**, the pre-eminent Greek military power, whose soldiers

| 480 BC | 480 BC | 480–323 BC | 479 BC |
|---|---|---|---|
| Persians sack and burn Athens. | Battle of Salamis; the Persian fleet is destroyed and supply lines cut. | Classical Period. | Persians defeated at the Battle of Plataea and are forced out of Greece. |

## GREEK TRAGEDY

**Greek tragedy** has its roots in a fertility ritual celebrating the life and death of Dionysus, the god of the vine. Because goats were sacrificed in his honour, this ritual, in which a chorus danced and sang, was called *trag-odia*, a goat-song. Around 520 BC an actor was introduced who came and went, changing costumes and playing different roles in successive episodes.

**Aeschylus** transformed matters by introducing a second actor and increasing the amount of dialogue, while correspondingly reducing the size and role of the chorus. Thus tragedy became drama, driven by exchanges of words and actions. That Aeschylus had fought at Marathon and, probably, Salamis, may explain the urgency of his play, *The Persians*, the oldest surviving Greek tragedy. Although a religious man who believed in the overwhelming power of the gods, Aeschylus makes clear that it is man himself, through the free choices he makes, who steps into the appalling conflicts of the tragic situation. His later work the *Oresteia*, a great drama of revenge, focused on Agamemnon's return home from the Trojan War and his murder. By now Aeschylus was using a third actor and also painted scenery, ideas taken from **Sophocles**, his younger rival.

Sophocles' innovation made it possible to present plots of considerable complexity. His was a world of inescapable consequences – in his *Oedipus Rex*, for example, to be unseeing is not enough, while *Antigone* presents the ultimate tragic conflict, between right and right.

The effect of the tragedies of Aeschylus and Sophocles was to leave their audiences with an enhanced sense of pity or of terror. The unspoken moral was "You are in this too", the cathartic experience leaving everyone stronger – as though Athens, democratic, confident and imperial, was preparing itself to meet the blows of destiny.

had obediently sacrificed themselves at Thermopylae and won the final mainland battle at Plataea. Instead, many Greek city-states voluntarily placed themselves under the leadership of Athens.

This Aegean confederation was named the **Delian League**, after the island of Delos where the allies kept their treasury. Its first task was to protect the Greeks of Asia Minor against a vengeful Xerxes. This was the opposite of the policy proposed by Sparta and its Peloponnesian allies, which called for the abandonment of Greek homes across the Aegean and the resettlement of Asian Greeks in northern Greece.

That typified the Spartan attitude throughout the Persian crisis, in which Sparta had shown no initiative and acted only at the last minute. Its policy was provincial, protecting its position in the Peloponnese rather than pursuing the wider interests of Greece. Sparta persistently lacked vision, adventure and experience of the sea, believing that what could not be achieved by land was impossible. Thus over the coming decades Sparta lost prestige to Athens, which Themistocles had established as a maritime power and whose imperial potential was realized under Pericles.

This was the **Athenian golden age** (see p.764), and indeed a golden age for all Greece. The fifty years following Salamis and Plataea witnessed an extraordinary flowering in architecture, sculpture, literature and philosophy whose influence is felt to this day. Greeks of the time recognized the historical importance of their experience and gave it realization through the creative impulse. Just as **Herodotus**, the "father of history", made the contest between Europe and Asia the theme of his great work, so **Aeschylus**, who fought at Marathon, made Xerxes the tragic subject of *The Persians* and thereby brought the art of drama to life. Indeed in the intoxicating Athenian atmosphere, the

| 458 BC | 447–438 BC | 431–415 BC | 429 BC |
|---|---|---|---|
| Aeschylus produces the Oresteia trilogy in Athens. | Parthenon constructed, the symbol of Athens' Golden Age. | Peloponnesian War marks the end of Athens' ascendancy. | Death of Pericles brings uncertainty to Athens. |

warriors who turned back the Persian tide seemed to have fought in the same cause as Homer's heroes at Troy. In thanksgiving and celebration the temples upon the Acropolis that the Persians had destroyed were rebuilt – most notably with the building of the **Parthenon**.

Yet Athens was still just one among numerous city-states, each ready to come together during a common danger but reasserting its sovereignty as the foreign threat receded. This was illustrated by the ten-year struggle from 461 BC onwards between Athens and various **Peloponnesian states**, itself a warning of a yet greater war to come between Athens and Sparta.

## Pericles

In 461 BC, **Pericles** (c.495 – 429 BC) was first elected to Athens' most important elected position, of *strategos* (general). The ten *strategoi* proposed the legislation that was then voted on in the Assembly. Pericles was so brilliant at winning over audiences in a society where the people were sovereign, that in practice he governed the state for around thirty years; with only two exceptions, he was annually re-elected until his death in 429 BC.

Among his early triumphs – in the face of conservative opposition – was to make **peace with Persia** in 449 BC, the better to turn his attention to **Sparta**. Pericles believed that Athenian power was not only Greece's best defence against Persia but also the best hope for the unification of Greece under enlightened rule.

Ultimately the jury remains out as to whether Pericles preserved Athens' greatness for as long as possible, or hurried its demise. On the one hand many believe that it was thanks to Pericles that Athens was able to avoid **war with Sparta** for as long as it did. Thucydides, the historian of the Peloponnesian War, greatly admired Pericles for his integrity and for the restraint he exercised over Athenian democracy. Others hold him responsible for passing up the opportunity to create an institution more generous, and more inclusive, than the city-state. Pericles supported the parochial and populist demand that **Athenian citizenship** should not be extended to its allies, thereby stoking up the flames of envy and foregoing the chance of creating a genuine and enduring Greek confederacy.

## The decline of the city-state: 431–338 BC

The **Peloponnesian War** that began in **431 BC** was really a continuation of earlier conflicts between Athens and its principal commercial rivals, Corinth and Aegina and their various allies in the Peloponnese. Sparta had earlier stood aside, but by 432 BC when Corinth again agitated for war, the **Spartans** had become fearful of growing Athenian power.

The Athenian empire was built on trade, and the city was a great sea power, with 300 triremes. The members of Sparta's **Peloponnesian League**, meanwhile, had powerful armies but no significant navy. Just as Themistocles had sought to fight the Persians by sea, so Pericles followed the same strategy against Sparta and its allies, avoiding major battles against superior land forces. Athens and Piraeus were protected by their walls, but the Peloponnesians and their allies were allowed to invade Attica with impunity nearly every year, and Thrace saw constant warfare. On the other hand the

| 399 BC | 380 BC | 371 BC | 362 BC |
|---|---|---|---|
| Socrates condemned to death for corrupting the minds of the youth of Athens. | Plato establishes his Academy in Athens. | Sparta defeated by Thebes at the Battle of Leuctra. | Epaminondas of Thebes killed at the Battle of Mantinea. |

## THUCYDIDES: THE FIRST MODERN HISTORIAN

The writing of history began among the Greeks, first with **Herodotus**, then with Thucydides. Whereas Herodotus gives the feeling that he prefers telling a good story, that he still inhabits Homer's world of epic poetry, with **Thucydides** the paramount concern is to analyze events. In that sense Thucydides is the first modern historian; wherever possible he seeks out primary sources, and his concern is always with objectivity, detail and chronology. Not that there is anything dry about his writing; its vividness and insight make reading him as powerful an experience as watching a Greek drama.

Thucydides began writing his history at the outset of the **Peloponnesian War**, intending to give an account of its whole duration, For reasons unknown, however, he abruptly stopped writing in the twentieth year, though he is thought to have survived the war by a few years, living until about 400 BC. Born into a wealthy, conservative Athenian family around 455 BC, he was a democrat and an admirer of Pericles; his reconstruction of Pericles' speeches presents the most eloquent expression of the Athenian cause. But when Thucydides was exiled from his city seven years into the war, this was the making of him as a historian. As he put it, "Associating with both sides, with the Peloponnesians quite as much as with the Athenians, because of my exile, I was thus enabled to watch quietly the course of events".

Thucydides was himself a military man, who understood war at first hand. Hence his concern for method in his research and analysis in his writing, for he intended his book to be useful to future generals and statesmen. For these reasons we have a better understanding of the Peloponnesian War than of any ancient conflict until Julius Caesar wrote his own first-hand accounts of his campaigns. And for these reasons too, Thucydides' history stands on a par with the greatest literature of ancient Greece.

Peloponnesians lacked the sea power to carry the fighting into Asia Minor and the Aegean islands or to interfere with Athens' trade, while the Athenians used their maritime superiority to launch attacks against the coasts of the Peloponnese, the Ionian islands and the mouth of the Gulf of Corinth, hoping to detach members from the Peloponnesian League. So long as Athens remained in command of the sea, it had every reason to expect that it could wear down its enemies' resolve.

**Pericles' death** in 429 BC was an early blow to the Athenian cause. Although **Kleon**, his successor, is widely blamed for Athens' eventual defeat, after Pericles the city was in fact always divided into a peace party and a military one, unable to pursue a consistent policy. The final straw came in 415 BC, when a bold operation designed to win Sicily to the Athenian cause turned into a catastrophic debacle. Though not entirely defeated, Athens was never to be a major power again.

### City-state rivalries

The Peloponnesian War left **Sparta** the supreme power in Greece, but those whom the Spartans had "liberated" swiftly realized that they had simply acquired a new and inferior master, one that entirely lacked the style, the ability and the intelligence of Athens. Meanwhile Athens had lost its empire but not its trade, and as it rapidly rebuilt its navy its mercantile rivals faced no less competition than before.

Adding to the intrigues between Persia, Athens and Sparta was a bewildering and unstable variety of alliances involving other Greek states. The most important of these was **Thebes**, which had been an ally of Sparta during the Peloponnesian War but came

| 359 BC | 338 BC | 336 BC | 335 BC |
|---|---|---|---|
| Philip II becomes king of Macedonia. | Philip II's victory at Chaeronia unites Greece under Macedonian rule. | Alexander the Great succeeds his father, and within six years has conquered all of Persia. | Aristotle founds the Lyceum in Athens. |

round to the Athenian side, and then for a spectacular moment under its brilliant general **Epaminondas** became the greatest power in Greece, in the process dealing Sparta a blow from which it never recovered. Theban supremacy did not survive the death of Epaminondas, however, and Greece subsequently found itself free for the first time in centuries from the dictates of Persia or any over-powerful Greek city-state. Exhausted and impoverished by almost continuous war, it was an opportunity for Greece to peacefully unite. But the political and moral significance of the city-state had by now eroded, and with the **rise of Macedonia** came the concept of an all-embracing kingship.

## The Macedonian Empire

Despite its large size and population, **Macedonia** played little role in early Greek affairs. Many in Greece did not consider the Macedonians to be properly Greek; not in speech, culture or political system. They did not live in city-states, which Aristotle said was the mark of a civilized human being, but as a tribal people, led by a king, and were closer to the barbarians (such attitudes still rankle today, and inform some of the bitter debate over the name and status of FYROM, the Former Yugoslav Republic of Macedonia).

Towards the middle of the fourth century, however, the power of Macedonia grew under the leadership of **Philip II**. Philip was determined to Hellenize his country; borrowing from Greek ways and institutions, he founded the city of **Pella** as his capital and lured teachers, artists and intellectuals to his court, among them **Aristotle** and **Euripides**. An admirer of Athens, Philip sought an alliance that would make them joint-masters of the Greek world. But the Athenians opposed him, and he took matters into his own hands.

In **338 BC** Philip brought about the unity of the mainland Greeks by force, defeating the Theban and Athenian forces at **Chaeronia** with one of the most formidable fighting units the world has ever seen, the **Macedonian phalanx**. Armed with the *sarissa*, a eighteen-foot pike tapering from butt to tip, its infantrymen were trained to move across a battlefield with all the discipline of a parade ground drill. Instead of relying on a headlong charge, its effectiveness lay in manipulating the enemy line – seeking to open a gap through which the cavalry could make its decisive strike.

### Alexander the Great

After Chaeronia, Philip summoned the Greek states to Corinth, and announced his plans for a panhellenic conquest of the Persian Empire. But Philip was murdered two years later and to his son **Alexander** fell his father's plans for an **Asian campaign** – throughout which, it is said, he slept with the *Iliad* under his pillow.

In the East too there was an assassination, and in 335 BC the Persian throne passed to **Darius III**, namesake of the first and doomed to be the last king of his line. Using essentially his father's tactics, Alexander led his army through a series of astonishing victories, usually against greater numbers, until he reached the heart of the Persian Empire. Alexander crossed the Hellespont in May of **334 BC**, with thirty thousand foot soldiers and five thousand horses. By autumn all the Aegean coast of **Asia Minor** was his; twelve months later he stood on the banks of the Orontes River in **Syria**; in the winter of 332 BC **Egypt** hailed him as pharaoh; and by the spring of 330 BC the great Persian cities of **Babylon**, **Susa**, **Persepolis** and **Pasargadae** had fallen to him in rapid succession until, at **Ecbatana**,

| 326 BC | 323 BC | 323–146 BC | c.300 BC |
|---|---|---|---|
| Alexander's army reaches India. | Death of Alexander. | Hellenistic Period. | Euclid's Elements published, its 13 volumes creating the basis or much of modern maths and science. |

## BIG IDEAS: SOCRATES, PLATO AND ARISTOTLE

The Golden Age of Athens under Pericles, and the city-state rivalry after the Peloponnesian War, saw the **birth of Western philosophy** under the towering figures of Socrates, Plato and Aristotle.

### SOCRATES (c.470–399 BC)

The son of an Athenian sculptor, Socrates was for a time a sculptor himself. Though he fought bravely for Athens as a hoplite in the Peloponnesian War, much earlier, in his twenties, he had turned to philosophy, which he practised in his own peculiar style. Promoting no philosophical position of his own, he asserted, ceaselessly, the supremacy of reason. Often this was done in the streets of Athens, buttonholing some self-regarding Athenian of the older generation, asking him questions, picking his answers to pieces, until he came up with a definition that held water or, more likely, the spluttering victim was reduced to confess his own ignorance before crowds of Socrates' mirthful young supporters.

By this "Socratic method" he asked for definitions of familiar concepts such as piety and justice; his technique was to expose the ignorance that hid behind people's use of such terms, while acknowledging his own similar ignorance. Indeed when the Delphic oracle proclaimed that no man was wiser than Socrates, he explained this by saying wisdom lies in knowing how little one really knows. Because he valued this question-and-answer process over settling on fixed conclusions, Socrates never wrote anything down. Yet his influence was pivotal; before his time philosophical inquiry concerned itself with speculations on how the natural world was formed and how it operates; afterwards it looked to the analysis of concepts and to ethics.

Socrates' method could be irritating, especially when he questioned conventional morality, and this, coupled with powerful friendships with unpopular oligarchs, led to a backlash. Having tried him for impiety and corrupting the young, and sentenced him to death, the city gave him the option of naming another penalty, probably expecting him to choose exile. Instead Socrates answered that if he was to get what he deserved, he should be maintained for life at public expense. At this the death penalty was confirmed, but even then it was not to be imposed for two months, with the tacit understanding that Socrates would escape. Instead Socrates argued that it was wrong for a citizen to disobey even an unjust law, and in the company of his friends he drank the cup of hemlock. "Such was the end," wrote Plato, "of our friend; of all the men of his time whom I have known, he was the wisest and justest and best."

### PLATO (c.427–c.347 BC)

As a young man, Plato painted, composed music and wrote a tragedy, as well as being a student of Socrates. He intended a career in politics, where his connections would have ensured success, but Socrates' death made Plato decide that he could not serve a government that had committed such a crime, and instead his mission became to exalt the memory of his teacher. In Plato's writings, many of them dialogues, Socrates is frequently the leading participant, while at the Academy in Athens, which Plato founded, the Socratic question-and-answer method was the means of instruction.

---

he found Darius in the dust, murdered by his own supporters. Alexander wrapped the corpse in his Macedonian cloak, and assumed the lordship of Asia.

## Hellenistic Greece

No sooner had **Alexander** died, at Babylon in 323 BC, aged thirty-three, than Athens led an alliance of Greeks in a **war of liberation** against Macedonian rule. But the

| c.287 BC | 215–213 BC | 200–197 BC | 146 BC |
|---|---|---|---|
| Mathematician, inventor and scientist Archimedes is born on the Greek colony of Sicily. | First Macedonian War extends Roman influence in Greece. | Second Macedonian War, culminating in the Roman victory at Cynoscephalae. | Greece divided into Roman provinces. |

Plato's philosophy is elusive; he never sets out a system of doctrines, nor does he tell us which of his ideas are most basic, nor rank them in hierarchical order, nor show how they interrelate. Nevertheless, certain themes recur. He believed that men possess immortal souls separate from their mortal bodies. Knowledge, he believed, was the recollection of what our souls already know; we do not gain knowledge from experience, rather by using our reasoning capacity to draw more closely to the realm of our souls. The true objects of knowledge are not the transient, material things of this world, which are only reflections of a higher essence that Plato called Forms or Ideas. Forms are objects of pure thinking, cut off from our experience; but also Forms motivate us to grasp them, so that the reasoning part of us is drawn to Forms as a kind of mystic communion.

Plato's notion of a mystic union with a higher essence would play an important role in later religious thought. But more immediately his teachings at the Academy concerned themselves with logic, mathematics, astronomy and above all political science, for its purpose was to train a new ruling class. Prominent families sent him their sons to learn the arts of government. Plato taught that the best form of government was a constitutional monarchy, at its head a wise and just philosopher-king. Though it was a utopian vision, Plato's political philosophy helped prepare the intellectual ground for the acceptance of an absolutist solution to the increasing uncertainties of fourth-century BC Greece.

### ARISTOTLE (384–322 BC)

Aristotle grew up in Pella, the capital of an increasingly powerful Macedonia, where his father had been appointed doctor to King Amyntas II; it is therefore not unlikely that Amyntas' son, the future Philip II, and Aristotle were boyhood friends. Aged seventeen, Aristotle was sent to Plato's Academy at Athens to continue his education, and he remained there, first as a student, then as a teacher, a faithful follower of Plato's ideas. His independent philosophy matured later, during the years he spent, again at Pella, as tutor to Alexander the Great, and later still, after 335 BC, when he founded his own school, the Lyceum, in Athens.

Aristotle came to reject Plato's dualism. He did not believe that the soul was of a substance separate from the body, rather that it was an aspect of the body. Instead of Plato's inward-looking view, Aristotle sought to explain the physical world and human society from the viewpoint of an outside observer. Essentially a scientist and a realist, he was bent on discovering the true rather than establishing the good, and he believed sense perception was the only means of human knowledge. His vast output covered many fields of knowledge – logic, metaphysics, ethics, politics, rhetoric, art, poetry, physiology, anatomy, biology, zoology, physics, astronomy and psychology. Everything could be measured, analyzed and described, and he was the first to classify organisms into genera and species.

The exactitude of Aristotle's writings does not make them easy reading, and Plato has always enjoyed a wider appeal owing to his literary skill. All the same, Aristotle's influence on Western intellectual and scientific tradition has been enormous.

Macedonians had built up a formidable navy which inflicted heavy losses on the Athenian fleet. Unable to lift the Macedonian blockade of Piraeus, Athens surrendered and a pro-Macedonian government was installed. The episode marked the end of Athens as a sea power and left it permanently weakened.

Greece was now irrevocably part of a new dominion, one that entirely altered the scale and orientation of the Greek world. Alexander's strategic vision had been to see the Mediterranean and the East as two halves of a greater whole. Opened to Greek

| **86 BC** | **31 BC** | **49–52 AD** |
|---|---|---|
| Romans, led by Sulla, sack Athens. | Defeat of Antony and Cleopatra at the Battle of Actium brings all of Greece and the Middle East under Roman sway. | St Paul lives and preaches in Corinth and Athens, first introducing Christianity to Greece. |

settlement and enterprise, and united by Greek learning, language and culture, if not always by a single power, this **Hellenistic Empire** enormously increased international trade and created unprecedented prosperity.

Asked on his deathbed to whom he bequeathed his empire, Alexander replied "To the strongest". Forty years of warfare between his leading generals gave rise to three dynasties, the **Antigonid** in Macedonia, which ruled over mainland Greece, the **Seleucid** which ultimately centred on Syria and Asia Minor, and the **Ptolemaic** in Egypt, ruled from Alexandria, founded by Alexander himself, which in wealth and population, not to mention literature and science, soon outshone anything in Greece.

Meanwhile, in the Western Mediterranean, **Rome** was a rising power. **Philip V** of Macedonia had agreed a treaty of mutual assistance against Rome with Hannibal. After Hannibal's defeat, Rome's legions marched eastwards, and routed Philip's army at **Cynoscephalae** in Thessaly in 197 BC.

## Roman Greece: 146 BC–330 AD

Rome was initially well disposed towards Greece, which they regarded as the originator of much of their culture, and granted autonomy to the existing city-states. However, after a number of uprisings, the country was divided into **Roman provinces** from 146 BC.

During the first century BC Rome was riven by civil wars, many of whose climactic battlefields were in Greece: in 49 BC **Julius Caesar** defeated his rival Pompey at **Pharsalus** in Thessaly; in 42 BC Caesar's assassins were beaten by **Mark Antony** and **Octavian** at **Philippi** in Macedonia; and in 31 BC **Antony** and his Ptolemaic ally **Cleopatra** were routed by **Octavian** in a sea battle off **Actium** in western Greece. The latter effectively marked the birth of the **Roman Empire** – an empire that in its eastern half continued to speak Greek.

By the first century AD Greece had become a **tourist destination** for well-to-do Romans; they went to Athens and Rhodes to study literature and philosophy, and toured the country to see the temples with their paintings and sculpture. They also visited the by now thoroughly professional **Olympic Games**. When the emperor **Nero** came to Greece in AD 67, he entered the Games as a contestant; the judges prudently declared him the victor in every competition, even the chariot race, in which he was thrown and failed to finish.

### Barbarian incursions

During the mid-third century the **Heruli**, a tribe from southern Russia, succeeded in passing through the Bosphorus and into the Aegean. Ravaging far and wide, they plundered and burned **Athens** in 267. New city walls were built with the marble rubble from the wreckage, but their circumference was now so small that the ancient Agora, littered with ruins, was left outside, while what remained of the city huddled round the base of the Acropolis. It was a familiar scene throughout Greece, as prosperity declined and population fell. Only in the north along the **Via Egnatia**, the Roman road linking ports on the Adriatic with Thessaloníki on the Aegean, did Greece continue to thrive.

| 117–138 | 267 | 395 |
|---|---|---|
| The reign of Emperor Hadrian, a hellenophile who left many monuments, above all his great library and monumental arch in Athens. | Barbarians pillage Athens. | Roman empire splits; Greece becomes part of the eastern, or Byzantine, empire; Olympic Games suppressed. |

# Byzantine and medieval Greece: 330–1460 AD

The **Byzantine Empire** was founded in May 330 when the **emperor Constantine** declared Nova Roma (as he called the city of Byzantium – known today as Istanbul) the new capital of the Roman Empire. Founded on the banks of the Bosphorus by Greek colonists in the seventh century BC, Byzantium occupied a commanding point from where the entire trade between the Black Sea and the Mediterranean could be controlled. **Constantinople**, the city of Constantine, as it became popularly known, was perfectly positioned for the supreme strategic task confronting the empire: the defence of the Danube and the Euphrates frontiers. Moreover, the new capital stood astride the flow of goods and culture from the East, that part of the empire richest in economic resources, most densely populated and rife with intellectual and religious activity.

## The Christian empire

Constantine's other act with decisive consequences was to **legalize** and patronize the **Christian Church**. Here again Constantinople was important, for while Rome's pagan traditions could not yet be disturbed, the new capital was conceived as a Christian city. Within the century Christianity was established as the religion of state, with its liturgies (still in use in the Greek Orthodox Church), the Creed and the New Testament all in Greek.

In 391 emperor **Theodosius I** issued an edict banning all expressions of **paganism** throughout the empire. In Greece the mysteries at Eleusis ceased to be celebrated the following year, and in 395 the Olympic Games were suppressed, their athletic nudity an offence to Christianity. Around this time too the Delphic oracle fell silent. The conversion of pagan buildings to Christian use began in the fifth century. Under an imperial law of 435 the Parthenon and the Erechtheion on the Acropolis, the mausoleum of Galerius (the Rotunda) in Thessaloníki and other temples elsewhere became churches. Even this did not eradicate pagan teaching: philosophy and law continued to be taught at the Academy in Athens, founded by Plato in 385 BC, until prohibited by the emperor Justinian in 529.

In 395 the Roman Empire split into **Western and Eastern empires**, and in 476 **Rome fell** to the barbarians. As the Dark Ages settled on Western Europe, Byzantium inherited the sole mantle of the empire. Latin remained its official language, though after the reign of Justinian (527–565) the emperors joined the people in speaking and writing Greek.

**Thessaloníki**, the second city of the Byzantine Empire, was relatively close to Constantinople, yet even so the journey by land or sea took five or six days. The rest of Greece was that much farther and Attica and the Peloponnese grew decidedly provincial. Conditions worsened sharply in the late sixth century when Greece was devastated by **plague**. In Athens after 580 life came almost to an end, as the remaining inhabitants withdrew to the Acropolis, while at Corinth the population removed itself entirely to the island of Égina. Only Thessaloníki fully recovered.

## The rise of Islam and the Crusades

The advent of **Islam** in the mid-seventh century had its effect on Greece. The loss to the Arabs of the Christian provinces of Syria in 636, and Egypt in 642, was followed by an attack by an Arab fleet in 677 on Constantinople itself. In 717–718 a combined Arab

| 435 | 600–700 | 730 |
| --- | --- | --- |
| The Parthenon and other Greek temples converted to churches. | For historians and classicists, the Christianization of Greece in the sixth century marks the end of the Ancient Greek era. | Icons and other images banned in the Orthodox Church for being idolatrous; the height of the iconoclastic controversy. |

## THE ORIGINS OF THE ORTHODOX CHURCH

The split between the Orthodox and Catholic Churches is traditionally dated to the "**Great Schism**" of 1054. But in practice the Churches had been diverging for centuries, and arguably the final break came much later. The causes of the split were as much linguistic – following the division of the Roman Empire, the language of the Church in Rome was Latin, while in the East it was Greek – and political as they were doctrinal, though there were certainly significant theological differences. Chief among these were the **iconoclastic controversy** – over the use of images in worship – the use of leavened (in the East) or unleavened bread (in the West) in the liturgy, and the Roman adjustment of the Creed, in 1014, to include the word "filioque" (and the Son).

The final schism was precipitated by the pope's claim to **supremacy over the Church**. While the patriarch in Constantinople and other Orthodox leaders accepted the bishop of Rome as "first among equals", they were not prepared to accept his ultimate authority over all the Church – or his subsequent claims to infallibility. In 1054, papal legates went to Constantinople to press the patriarch, Michael Celaurius, to accept Rome's claims. When he refused, Cardinal Humbert, leader of the Latin contingent, excommunicated Celaurius, who responded by in turn excommunicating Humbert and his colleagues.

Any hope of reconciliation disappeared with the sacking of Constantinople during the Fourth Crusade, when Orthodox churches were looted by Catholic crusaders, and forcibly converted to Catholic worship, and by the centuries of separation which followed the fall of Constantinople, when much of the Orthodox East came under Ottoman rule.

naval and land force beleaguered the city again, while in 823 the Arabs occupied Crete.

In 1071 the **Byzantine army** was destroyed at **Manzikert**, a fortress town on the eastern frontier, by the **Seljuk Turks** who went on to occupy almost all Asia Minor. After the Byzantine emperor turned to the West for help, the Roman Catholic pope replied by launching the **First Crusade** in 1095. Together, the Crusaders and the Byzantines won a series of victories over the Seljuks in Asia Minor, but the Byzantines, wary of possible Crusader designs on the empire itself, were content to see their Latin allies from the West advance alone on Jerusalem, which they captured in 1099.

The worst fears of the Byzantines were borne out in 1204 when the **Fourth Crusade** attacked and sacked **Constantinople** itself. Greece was shared out between Franks, Venetians and many others in a bewildering patchwork of feudal holdings. Amid endless infighting in the West, a new Turkish dynasty, the **Ottomans**, emerged in the late thirteenth century. By 1400 they had conquered all of Byzantine Greece except Thessaloníki and the Peloponnese. In 1452 they invaded the Peloponnese as a diversion to the main attack on **Constantinople**, which fell on May 23, 1453. In 1456 the Ottomans captured **Athens** from the Venetians and turned the Parthenon church into a mosque, and in 1460 they conquered the **Peloponnese**. **Trebizond** fell the following year, and the Byzantine empire was no more.

## Greece under Turkish occupation: 1460–1821

Western possessions in Greece after 1460 amounted to **Rhodes** – held by the Knights of St John – and, under **Venetian rule**, the Peloponnesian ports of **Koróni**, **Methóni** and **Monemvasiá**, and the islands of **Évvia**, **Crete**, **Corfu** and **Égina**. In 1522 the Ottomans

| 824 –961 | 1071 | 1095 | 1204 |
|---|---|---|---|
| Arab occupation of Crete; a warning of things to come. | Byzantine army defeated by the Turks. | First Crusade drives back the Turks. | Fourth Crusade sacks Constantinople; much of Greece taken over by western European powers. |

drove the Knights of St John from Rhodes, and within two more decades they had captured all the Venetian mainland colonies in Greece, leaving them only Crete.

Although the Greeks refer to the Turkish occupation as *sklavía* – "slavery" – in practice, in exchange for submitting to Muslim rule and paying tribute, the Greeks were free to pursue their religion and were left very much in charge of their own religious and civil affairs. The essence of the Turkish administration was **taxation**. Tax collection was often farmed out to the leaders of the Greek communities, and some local magistrates profited sufficiently to exercise a dominant role not only within their own region but also in the Ottoman Empire at large.

The other important institution within Greece was the **Orthodox Church**. The Church was wealthy and powerful; Greeks preferred to give their lands to the monasteries than have them occupied by the Turks, while the Muslims found it easier to work with the Church than to invent a new administration. Though often corrupt and venal, the Church did at least preserve the traditional faith and keep alive the written form of the Greek language, and it became the focus of Greek nationalism.

## Western resistance

In 1570 Ottoman troops landed on **Cyprus**. Nicosia was swiftly captured, and 30,000 of its inhabitants slaughtered. Turkish brutality in Cyprus horrified Europe, and the **Holy League** was formed under the aegis of the pope. Spain and Genoa joined Venice in assembling a fleet led by Don John of Austria, the bastard son of the Spanish king, its lofty aim not only to retake the island but to recapture all Christian lands taken by the Ottomans. In the event, it was utterly ineffectual, yet out of it something new arose – the first stirrings of **Philhellenism**, a desire to liberate the Greeks whose ancient culture stood at the heart of Renaissance thought and education.

There was, too, the encouragement of a naval victory, when in 1571 Don John's fleet surprised and overwhelmingly defeated the much larger Ottoman fleet, at its winter quarters at **Lepanto** on the Gulf of Corinth in western Greece. Two hundred and sixty-six Ottoman vessels were sunk or captured, fifty thousand sailors died, and fifteen thousand Christian galley slaves were freed. Throughout Europe the news of Lepanto was received with extraordinary rejoicing; this was the first battle in which Europe had triumphed against the Ottomans, and its symbolic importance was profound. Militarily and politically, however, the Ottomans remained dominant. They finally took **Crete** in 1669, marking the end of the last bastion of Byzantine culture.

## Greek nationalist stirrings

During the eighteenth century the islanders of **Ýdhra** (Hydra), **Spétses** and **Psará** built up a merchant fleet that traded throughout the Mediterranean, where thriving colonies of Greeks were established in many ports. Greek merchant families were also well established, often in important administrative positions, throughout the Ottoman Empire.

These wealthier and more educated Greeks enjoyed greater than ever opportunities for advancement within the Ottoman system, while the Greek peasantry, unlike the empire's Muslim inhabitants, did not have to bear the burden of military service. Nevertheless the Greeks had their grievances against the Ottoman government, which mostly concerned the arbitrary, unjust and oppressive system of taxation. But among

| **1453** | **1522** | **1571** | **1669** |
|---|---|---|---|
| Constantinople falls to the Ottoman Turks, followed by much of Greece. | Knights of St John driven from Rhodes. | Battle of Lepanto – the first significant military defeat for the Ottoman Empire. | Iráklion falls to the Ottomans – the end of a brutal 25-year conquest of Crete. |

the Greek peasantry it was primarily their religion that opposed them to their Muslim neighbours – as much as one-fifth of the population – and to their Ottoman overlords. Muslim leaders had long preached hatred of the infidel, a view reciprocated by the priests and bishops of the Orthodox Church.

## The War of Independence: 1821–32

The **ideology** behind the **War of Independence** came from the Greeks of the diaspora, particularly those merchant colonies in France, Italy, Austria and Russia who had absorbed new European ideas of nationalism and revolution. Around 1814, assorted such Greeks formed a secret society, the **Filikí Etería** (Friendly Society). Their sophisticated political concepts went uncomprehended by the peasantry, who assumed the point of an uprising was to exterminate their religious adversaries. And so when war finally broke out in **spring 1821**, almost the entire settled **Muslim population of Greece** – farmers, merchants and officials – was **slaughtered** within weeks by roaming bands of Greek peasants armed with swords, guns, scythes and clubs. They were often led by Orthodox priests, and some of the earliest Greek revolutionary flags portrayed a cross over a severed Turkish head.

### The war

While the Greeks fought to rid themselves of the Ottomans, their further aims differed widely. Landowners sought to reinforce their traditional privileges; the peasantry saw the struggle as a means towards land redistribution; and westernized Greeks were fighting for a modern nation-state. Remarkably, by the end of **1823** the Greeks appeared to have won their independence. Twice the sultan had sent armies into Greece; twice they had met with defeat. Greek guerrilla leaders, above all **Theodoros Kolokotronis** from the Peloponnese, had gained significant military victories early in the rebellion, which was joined by a thousand or so **European Philhellenes**, almost half of them German, though the most important was the English poet, **Lord Byron**.

But the situation was reversed in 1825, when the Peloponnese was invaded by formidable Egyptian forces loyal to the sultan. Thus far, aid for the Greek struggle had come neither from Orthodox Russia, nor from the Western powers of France and Britain, both wearied by the Napoleonic Wars and suspicious of a potentially anarchic new state. But the death of Lord Byron from a fever while training Greek forces at **Mesolóngi** in 1824 galvanized European public opinion. When Mesolóngi fell to the Ottomans in 1826, Britain, France and Russia finally agreed to seek autonomy for certain parts of Greece, and sent a combined fleet to put pressure on the sultan's army in the Peloponnese and the Turkish-Egyptian fleet harboured in Navaríno Bay. Events took over, and an accidental naval battle at **Navaríno** in October 1827 resulted in the destruction of almost the entire Ottoman fleet. The following spring, Russia itself declared war on the Ottomans, and Sultan Mahmud II was forced to accept the existence of an autonomous Greece.

At a series of conferences from 1830 to 1832, **Greek independence** was confirmed by the Western powers, and borders were drawn in 1832. These included just 800,000 of the six million Greeks living within the Ottoman Empire, and territories that were largely the poorest of the classical and Byzantine lands: **Attica**, the **Peloponnese** and the

| 1821 | 1824 | 1827 |
|---|---|---|
| Rebellion breaks out in various parts of the Empire; much of Greece liberated. | Lord Byron dies, becoming a Greek national hero in the process. | Ottoman fleet destroyed at the Battle of Navaríno, encouraging Great Power intervention. |

islands of the **Argo-Saronic**, the **Sporades** and the **Cyclades**. The rich agricultural belt of **Thessaly**, **Epirus** in the west and **Macedonia** in the north remained in Ottoman hands, as did the Dodecanese and Crete.

## The emerging state: 1832–1939

Modern Greece began as a **republic**. Ioannis Kapodistrias, its first president, concentrated his efforts on building a viable central authority. Almost inevitably he was assassinated, and perhaps equally inevitably the "Great Powers" – Britain, France and Germany – stepped in. They created a **monarchy**, setting a Bavarian prince, Otto (Otho), on the throne, with a new capital at Athens. By 1834, Greece also had its own national, state-controlled **Orthodox Church**, independent from the Patriarchate in Constantinople; at the same time, two-thirds of the monasteries and convents were closed down.

Despite the granting of a constitution in 1844, **King Otto** proved autocratic and insensitive, filling official posts with fellow Germans and ignoring all claims by the landless peasantry for redistribution of the old estates. When he was forced from the country by a popular revolt in 1862, the Europeans produced a new prince, this time from Denmark. The accession of **George I** (1863–1913) was marked by Britain's decision to hand over the **Ionian islands** to Greece. During his reign, Greece's first roads and railways were built, its borders were extended, and land reform began in the Peloponnese.

### The Great Idea and expansionist wars

From the start, Greek foreign policy was motivated by the **Megáli Idhéa** (Great Idea) of redeeming ethnically Greek populations outside the country and incorporating the old territories of Byzantium into the new kingdom. There was encouragement all around, as Ottoman control was under pressure across the Balkans.

In 1881, revolts broke out among the Greeks of **Crete**, **Thessaly** and **Epirus**, aided by guerrillas from Greece. Britain forced the Ottoman Empire to cede Thessaly and Arta to Greece, but Crete remained Ottoman. When Cretan Greeks set up an independent government in 1897, declaring *énosis* (union) with Greece, the Ottomans responded by invading the mainland and came within days of reaching Athens. The Great Powers came to the rescue by warning off the Turks and placing Crete under an international protectorate. Only in 1913 did **Crete** unite with Greece.

It was from Crete, nonetheless, that the most distinguished modern Greek statesman emerged: **Elefthérios Venizélos**, having led a civilian campaign for his island's liberation, was elected as Greek prime minister in 1910. Two years later he organized an alliance of Balkan powers to fight the **Balkan Wars** (1912–13), campaigns that saw the Ottomans virtually driven from Europe, and the Bulgarian competition bested in the culmination of a bitter, four-decade campaign for the hearts and minds of the **Macedonian** population. With Greek borders extended to include the **northeast Aegean islands**, **northern Thessaly**, **central Epirus** and parts of **Macedonia**, the Megáli Idhéa was approaching reality.

### World War I

Divisions appeared with the outbreak of **World War I**. Although Venizélos urged Greek entry on the Allied side, hoping to liberate Greeks in Thrace and Asia Minor, the new

| 1832 | 1834 | 1881 | 1896 |
|---|---|---|---|
| Independent Greek state established, with its capital in Náfplio. | Capital transferred to Athens. | Following revolts, much of northern Greece added to the new nation. | Inspired by Baron Pierre de Coubertin, the first modern Olympics are held in Athens. |

king, **Constantine I**, who was married to the German Kaiser's sister, imposed neutrality. Eventually Venizélos set up a revolutionary government in Thessaloníki, polarizing the country into a state of **civil war**. In 1917 Greek troops entered the war to join the French, British and Serbians in the Macedonian campaign against Bulgaria and Germany. Upon the capitulation of Bulgaria and the Ottoman Empire, the Greeks occupied **Thrace**, and Venizélos presented demands at Versailles for predominantly Greek **Smyrna** (modern Izmir), on the Asia Minor coast, to become part of the Greek state.

## The Catastrophe and its aftermath

The demand for Smyrna triggered one of the most disastrous episodes in modern Greek history, the so-called **Katastrofí** (Catastrophe). Venizélos was authorized to move forces into Smyrna in 1919, but a new Turkish nationalist movement was taking power under Mustafa Kemal, or **Atatürk**. After monarchist factions took over when Venizélos lost elections in 1920, the Allies withdrew support for the venture. Nevertheless the monarchists ordered Greek forces to advance upon Ankara, seeking to bring Atatürk to terms. The Greeks' **Anatolian campaign** ignominiously collapsed in summer 1922 when Turkish troops forced the Greeks back to the coast. As the Greek army hurriedly evacuated from **Smyrna**, the Turks moved in and **massacred** much of the **Armenian and Greek** population before burning most of the city to the ground.

For the Turks, this was the successful conclusion of what they call their War of Independence. The borders of modern Turkey, as they remain today, were established by the **1923 Treaty of Lausanne**, which also provided for the **exchange of religious minorities** in each country – in effect, the first large-scale regulated ethnic cleansing. Turkey was to accept 390,000 Muslims resident on Greek soil. Greece, with a population of under five million, was faced with the resettlement of over **1.3 million Christian refugees** from **Asia Minor**.

The Katastrofí had intense and far-reaching consequences. The bulk of the agricultural estates of **Thessaly** were finally redistributed, to Greek tenants and refugee farmers, and huge shanty towns grew into new quarters around **Athens**, **Pireás** and **Thessaloníki**, spurring the country's then almost non-existent industry. Politically, reaction was even swifter. By September 1922, a group of Venizelist army officers "invited" King Constantine to abdicate and executed six of his ministers held most responsible for the debacle. Democracy was nominally restored with the proclamation of a **republic**, but for much of the next decade changes in government were brought about by factions within the armed forces. Meanwhile, among the urban refugee population, unions were being formed and the **Greek Communist Party** (**KKE**) was established.

## The rise of Metaxás

In 1935 a plebiscite restored the king, **George II**, to the throne, and the next year he appointed **General John Metaxás** as prime minister. Metaxás had opposed the Anatolian campaign, but had little support in parliament, and when KKE-organized strikes broke out, the king dissolved parliament without setting a date for new elections. This blatantly unconstitutional move opened the way for five years of ruthless and at times absurd **dictatorship**. Metaxás proceeded to set up a state based on the fascist models of the era. Left-wing and trade-union opponents were imprisoned or forced into exile, a state youth movement and secret police were set up, and rigid censorship, extending

| 1912–13 | 1923 | 1924 | 1935 |
| --- | --- | --- | --- |
| Balkan Wars extend Greece's borders close to its modern extent; Crete also becomes part of the new nation. | Following a disastrous campaign against Turkey, over one million Christian refugees are resettled in Greece. | Plebiscite abolishes the monarchy and establishes a republic. | Monarchy restored. |

even to passages of Thucydides, was imposed. But it was at least a Greek dictatorship, and while Metaxás was sympathetic to fascist organizational methods and economics, he utterly opposed German or Italian domination.

## World War II and civil war: 1939–1950

When World War II broke out, the most immediate threat to Greece was **Italy**, which had invaded Albania in April. Even so, Metaxás hoped Greece could remain neutral, and when the Italians torpedoed the Greek cruiser *Elli* in Tinos harbour on August 15, 1940, they failed to provoke a response. **Mussolini**, however, was determined to have a war with Greece, and after accusing the Greeks of violating the Albanian frontier, he delivered an ultimatum on October 28, 1940, to which Metaxás famously if apocryphally answered "**ohi**" (no). Galvanized by the crisis, the Greeks not only drove the invading Italians out of Greece but managed to gain control over the long-coveted and predominantly Greek-populated area of northern Epirus in southern Albania. ("Ohi Day" is still celebrated as a national holiday.)

Mussolini's failure, however, only provoked Hitler into sending his own troops into Greece, while the British rushed an expeditionary force across the Mediterranean from Egypt. Within days of the **German invasion**, on April 6, 1941, the German army was pouring into central Greece. Outmanoeuvred by the enemy's highly mechanized forces and at the mercy of the Luftwaffe, resistance was soon broken. When the Germans occupied Crete in May, King George and his ministers fled to Egypt and set up a government-in-exile. Metaxás himself had died before the German invasion.

### Occupation and resistance

The joint Italian-German-Bulgarian **occupation of Greece** was among the most bitter experiences of the European war. Nearly half a million Greek civilians starved to death over the winter of 1941–42, as all food was requisitioned to feed the occupying armies. In addition, entire villages throughout the mainland, but especially on Crete, were burned at the least hint of resistance and nearly 130,000 civilians were slaughtered up to autumn 1944. In their northern sector, which included Thássos and Samothráki, the Bulgarians demolished ancient sites and churches to support any future bid to annex "Slavic" Macedonia.

No sooner had the Axis powers occupied Greece than a spontaneous resistance movement sprang up in the mountains. The National Popular Liberation Army, known by its initials **ELAS**, founded in September 1941, quickly grew to become the most effective resistance organization, working in tandem with **EAM**, the National Liberation Front. Communists formed the leadership of both organizations, but opposition to the occupation and disenchantment with the prewar political order ensured they won the support of many non-communists. By 1943 ELAS/EAM controlled most areas of the country, working with the British SOE, Special Operations Executive, against the occupiers.

But the Allies were already eyeing the shape of postwar Europe, and British prime minister **Winston Churchill** was determined that Greece should not fall into the communist sphere. Ignoring advice from British agents in Greece that ELAS/EAM were the only effective resistance group, and that the king and his government-in-exile

| 1936–41 | 1940 | 1941 | 1944–49 |
|---|---|---|---|
| Fascist-style dictatorship of Ioánnis Metaxás. | Italian invasion of Greece is successfully repelled. | German invasion rapidly overruns the country; mass starvation in the Greek cities in the winter. | German withdrawal is promptly followed by the outbreak of bitter Civil War. |

## GREEK JEWS AND WORLD WAR II

Following the German invasion of Greece, Jews who lived in the Italian zone of occupation were initially no worse off than their fellow Greeks. But after Italy capitulated to the Allies in September 1943 and German troops took over from the Italians, the Jewish communities in Rhodes and Kos in the Dodecanese, as well as in Crete, Corfu, Vólos, Évvia and Zákynthos, were exposed to the full force of Nazi racial doctrine. The Germans applied their "final solution" in Greece during the spring and summer of 1944 with the deportation of virtually the entire Jewish population, about 80,000 in all, to extermination camps in Poland. Thessaloníki alone contained 57,000, the largest Jewish population of any Balkan city.

Greek Christians often went to extraordinary lengths to protect their persecuted countrymen. Thus when the Germans demanded the names of the Jews of Zákynthos prior to a roundup, Archbishop Khrysostomos and Mayor Loukas Karrer presented them with a roster of just two names – their own – and secretly oversaw the smuggling of all the island's 275 Jews to remote farms. Their audacious behaviour paid off, as every Zakynthian Jew survived the war. In Athens, the police chief and the archbishop arranged for false identity cards and baptismal certificates to be issued. Elsewhere, others were warned in good time of what fate the Germans had in store for them, and often took to the hills to join the partisans.

had little support within the country, Churchill ordered that only right-wing groups like **EDES**, the National Republican Greek Army, should receive British money, intelligence and arms. In August 1943 a resistance delegation asked the Greek king, George, in Cairo, for a postwar coalition government in which EAM would hold the ministries of the interior, justice and war, and requested that the king himself not return to Greece without popular consent expressed through a plebiscite. Backed by Churchill, King George flatly rejected their demands.

### Liberation and civil war

As the Germans began to withdraw from Greece in September 1944, most of the ELAS/EAM leadership agreed to join an interim government headed by the liberal anti-communist politician **George Papandréou**, and to place its forces under that government's control, which effectively meant under command of the British troops who landed in Greece that October. But many partisans felt they were losing their chance to impose a communist government and refused to lay down their arms. On December 3, 1944 the police fired on an EAM demonstration in Athens, killing at least sixteen. The following day, vicious **street fighting** broke out between members of the Greek Communist Party (KKE) and British troops which lasted throughout the month, until eleven thousand people were killed and large parts of Athens destroyed. In other large towns, ELAS rounded up its most influential and wealthy opponents and marched them out to rural areas in conditions that guaranteed their deaths.

After Papandréou resigned and the king agreed not to return without a plebiscite, a **ceasefire** was signed on February 12, 1945, and a new British-backed government agreed to institute democratic reforms. Many of these were not implemented, however. The army, police and civil service remained in right-wing hands, and while collaborators were often allowed to retain their positions, left-wing sympathizers were excluded. A KKE boycott of elections in March 1946 handed victory to the parties of the right, and a **rigged plebiscite** followed that brought the king back to Greece.

| 1952 | 1952 | 1955 | 1959 |
|---|---|---|---|
| Greece, now firmly part of the Western bloc, joins NATO. | New constitution establishes a parliamentary democracy, with king as Head of State. | Karamanlís becomes prime minister. | Cyprus gains independence. |

Right-wing gangs now roamed the towns and countryside with impunity, and by the summer of 1946 eighty thousand leftists who had been associated with ELAS had taken to the mountains.

By 1947 guerrilla activity had again reached the scale of a **full civil war**, with ELAS reorganized into the Democratic Army of Greece (DSE). In the interim, King George had died and been succeeded by his brother Paul, while the Americans had taken over the British role and began implementing the Cold War **Truman Doctrine**, in which massive economic and military aid was given to an amenable Greek government. In the mountains American military advisors trained the initially woeful Greek army for campaigns against the DSE, while the cities saw mass arrests, courts martial and imprisonments. From their stronghold on the slopes of Mount Grámmos on the border of Greece and Albania, the partisans waged a losing guerrilla struggle. At the start of 1948 Stalin withdrew Soviet support, and in the autumn of 1949, after Tito closed the Yugoslav border, denying the partisans the last means of outside supplies, the remnants of the DSE retreated into Albania and the KKE admitted defeat by proclaiming a supposedly temporary suspension of the civil war.

## Reconstruction and dictatorship: 1950–74

After a decade of war that had shattered much of Greece's infrastructure (it is said that not one bridge was left standing by 1948), and had killed twelve percent of the 1940 population, it was a demoralized, shattered country that emerged into the Western political orbit of the 1950s. Greece was **American-dominated**, enlisted into the **Korean War** in 1950 and **NATO** not long after. The US embassy – still giving the orders – foisted an electoral system on the Greeks that ensured victory for the Right for the next twelve years. Overt leftist activity was banned (though a "cover" party for communists was soon founded), and many of those who were not herded into political "re-education" camps or dispatched by firing squads, legal or vigilante, went into exile throughout Eastern Europe, to return only after 1974. The 1950s also saw the wholesale **depopulation of remote villages** as migrants sought work in Australia, America and Western Europe, or the larger Greek cities.

### Constantine Karamanlís and Cyprus

The American-backed right-wing **Greek Rally** party, led by **General Papágos**, won the first decisive post-civil-war elections in 1952. After the general's death, the party's leadership was taken over – and to an extent liberalized – by **Constantine Karamanlís**. Under his rule, stability of a kind was established and some economic advances registered, particularly after the revival of Greece's traditional German markets.

The main ongoing crisis in foreign policy was **Cyprus**, where Greek Cypriots demanding *énosis* (union) with Greece waged a long terrorist campaign against the British. Turkey adamantly opposed *énosis* and said that if Britain left Cyprus it should revert to Turkish rule. A 1959 compromise granted independence to the island and protection for its Turkish Cypriot minority but ruled out any union with Greece.

By 1961, unemployment, the Cyprus issue and the presence of US nuclear bases on Greek soil were changing the political climate, and when Karamanlís was again elected there was strong suspicion of intimidation and fraud carried out by right-wing

| 1964 | 1964 | 1967 | 1973 |
| --- | --- | --- | --- |
| King Constantine II succeeds his father, Paul. | The film of *Zorba the Greek* released, its soundtrack going on to grace (or blight) every Greek restaurant ever since. | Colonels' coup marks the start of seven years of repressive military rule. | Monarchy abolished and a republic declared. |

elements and the army. After eighteen months of strikes and protest demonstrations, Karamanlís resigned and went into voluntary exile in Paris.

## George Papandréou and the colonels

New elections in 1964 gave the **Centre Union Party**, headed by **George Papandréou**, an outright majority and a mandate for social and economic reform. The new government was the first to be controlled from outside the right since 1935, and in his first act as prime minister, Papandréou sought to heal the wounds of the civil war by **releasing political prisoners** and allowing exiles to return. When King Paul died in March and his son came to the throne as **Constantine II**, it seemed a new era had begun.

But soon **Cyprus** again took centre stage. Fighting between Turkish and Greek Cypriots broke out in 1963, and only the intervention of the United States in 1964 dissuaded Turkey from invading the island. In the mood of military confrontation between Greece and Turkey – both NATO members – Papandréou questioned Greece's role in the Western alliance, to the alarm of the Americans and the Greek right. When he moved to purge the army of disloyal officers, the army, with the support of the king, resisted.

Amid growing tension, elections were set for May 1967. It was a foregone conclusion that Papandréou's Centre Union Party would win, but **King Constantine**, disturbed by the party's leftward shift, was said to have briefed senior generals for a coup. True or not, the king, like almost everyone else in Greece, was caught by surprise when a group of unknown **colonels** staged their own **coup** on April 21, 1967. In December the king staged a counter-coup against the colonels, and when it failed he went into exile.

The junta announced itself as the "**Revival of Greek Orthodoxy**" against corrupting Western influences, not least long hair and miniskirts. Political activity was banned, independent trade unions were forbidden to recruit or meet, the press was so heavily censored that many papers stopped printing, and thousands of communists and others on the left were arrested, imprisoned and often tortured. Culturally, the colonels put an end to popular music and inflicted ludicrous censorship on literature and the theatre, including a ban on the production of classical tragedies. In 1973, chief colonel **Papadópoulos** abolished the monarchy and declared Greece a republic with himself as president.

## Restoration of democracy

The colonels lasted for seven years. Opposition was voiced from the start by exiled Greeks in London, the US and Western Europe, but only in 1973 did demonstrations break out openly in Greece – the colonels' secret police had done too thorough a job of infiltrating domestic resistance groups and terrifying everyone else into docility. After students occupied the **Athens Polytechnic** on **November 17**, the ruling clique sent armoured vehicles to storm the gates. A still-undetermined number of students (estimates range from 20 to 300) were killed. Martial law was tightened and Colonel Papadópoulos was replaced by the even more noxious and reactionary **General Ioannídes**, head of the secret police.

The end came within a year when the dictatorship embarked on a disastrous adventure in **Cyprus**. By attempting to topple the Makários government, the junta provoked a **Turkish invasion** and occupation of forty percent of Cypriot territory. The army finally mutinied and **Constantine Karamanlís** was invited to return from Paris to resume office.

| 1974 | 1975 | 1981 | 1982 |
| --- | --- | --- | --- |
| Greek-backed attempted coup in Cyprus leads to Turkish invasion and the division of the island; and to the end of the colonels' regime. | New constitution provides for parliamentary government with president as Head of State. | Greece joins the EU. | The *Rough Guide to Greece*, the first ever Rough Guide, published. |

Karamanlís swiftly negotiated a ceasefire in Cyprus, and in November 1974 he and his **Néa Dhimokratía** (New Democracy) party were rewarded by a sizeable majority in elections. The chief opposition was the new Panhellenic Socialist Movement (PASOK), led by **Andreas Papandréou**, son of George.

## Europe and a new Greece: 1974–2000

To Karamanlís's enduring credit, his New Democracy party oversaw an effective return to **democratic stability**, even legalizing the KKE (the Greek Communist Party) for the first time. Karamanlís also held a **referendum on the monarchy**, in which seventy percent of Greeks rejected the return of Constantine II. So a largely symbolic presidency was instituted instead, occupied by Karamanlís from 1980 to 1985, and again from 1990 to 1995. In 1981, Greece joined the **European Community**.

In the same year the socialist party, **PASOK**, and its leader **Andréas Papandréou** swept to power. The new era started with a bang as long-overdue **social reforms** were enacted; peasant women were granted pensions; wages were indexed to the cost of living; civil marriage was introduced; family and property law was reformed in favour of wives and mothers; and equal rights legislation was passed. By the time PASOK was returned to power in 1985, it was apparent the promised economic bonanza was not happening: hit by low productivity, lack of investment (not helped by anti-capitalist rhetoric from the government) and world recession, unemployment rose, inflation hit 25 percent and the national debt soared.

In the event it was the European Community, once Papandréou's *bête noire*, which rescued him, with a huge loan on condition that an austerity programme was maintained. Forced to drop many of his populist policies, the increasingly autocratic Papandréou turned on his former left-wing allies. Combined with the collapse of Soviet rule in Eastern Europe, his own very public affair with an Olympic Airways hostess half his age, and a raft of economic scandals, PASOK's hold on power was not surprisingly weakened. Since 1989, when New Democracy was elected once more, the two parties have exchanged power on a regular basis.

The 1990s were not easy, with an economy riven by unrest and division, and huge foreign policy headaches caused by the break-up of the former Yugoslavia and the ensuing wars on Greece's borders. Alone among NATO members, Greece was conspicuous for its open support of **Serbia**, ostentatiously supplying trucks to Belgrade via Bulgaria.

By the end of the 1990s, the economy was apparently stabilizing, with inflation consistently in single figures, and in 1997 national morale was further boosted with the award of the 2004 Olympic Games to Athens. Abroad, a dramatic and unexpected change in Greece's always distrustful **relations with Turkey** came when a severe **earthquake** struck northern Athens on September 7, 1999, killing scores and rendering almost 100,000 homeless. Coming less than a month after a devastating earthquake in northwest Turkey, it spurred a thaw between the two historical rivals. Greeks donated massive amounts of blood and foodstuffs to the Turkish victims, and were the earliest foreign rescue teams to reach Turkey; in turn they saw Turkish disaster-relief squads among the first on the scene in Athens. Soon afterwards, foreign minister George Papandréou (son of Andreas, later Prime Minister) announced that Greece had dropped its opposition to EU financial aid to Turkey and that Greece would no longer oppose Turkish candidacy for the EU.

| 1991 | 1999 | 2001 |
|---|---|---|
| Yugoslav Republic of Macedonia declares independence; Greece objects to use of the name Macedonia. | Athens earthquake; rapprochement between Greece and Turkey. | Greece adopts the euro, consigning Europe's oldest currency, the drachma, to history after some 3000 years. |

## IMMIGRATION – AND THE ALBANIAN INFLUX

Greece may continue to occupy the EU's economic cellar, but it's still far wealthier than many of its neighbours. This has acted as a magnet for a permanent underclass of immigrants. Since 1990 they have arrived in numbers estimated at over a million, a huge burden for a country of just over ten million citizens. These days your waiter, hotel desk clerk or cleaning lady is most likely to be Albanian, Bulgarian or Romanian, to cite the three largest groups. There are also significant communities of Pakistanis, Egyptians, Poles, Bangladeshis, Syrians, Filipinos, Ukrainians, Russians, Equatorial Africans, Kurds and Georgians, not to mention ethnic Greeks from the Caucasus – a striking change in what had hitherto been a homogeneous and parochial culture.

The Greek response has been decidedly mixed. Albanians, who make up roughly half the influx, are almost universally detested, and blamed for all manner of social ills. For the first time, crime – especially burglaries – is a significant issue. The newcomers have also prompted the first significant anti-immigration measures in a country whose population is more used to being on the other side of such laws. A member of the Schengen visa scheme, Greece sees itself, as in past ages, as the first line of defence against the barbarian hordes from the East. The Aegean islands regularly receive boatloads of people from every country in Asia.

### The twenty-first century: boom … and bust?

Greece entered the twenty-first century on a high; entry to the **eurozone** in 2001 was seen as hugely prestigious, while the **2004 Olympic Games** were considered a triumph – which, in sporting and public relations terms, they probably were. EU funds and Olympic investment kick-started widespread infrastructure improvements, and the future seemed rosy. Both these events, however, turned out to be symptomatic of Greece's **problems**. Even at the time of entry to the euro, it was an open secret that the figures had been massaged to ensure Greece met the strict criteria – the extent of that fix only became apparent later. And behind the successful facade of the Olympics were vast cost overruns in the desperate rush to complete the facilities, and a complete lack of legacy planning that has left many venues to rot.

In December 2008, **rioting** broke out in Athens, provoked by the police shooting of a 15-year-old student. The weeks of unrest that followed – as young people, in particular, protested their lack of opportunities – were the first sign that the wider world had of Greece's deep-rooted troubles and impending **crisis**. When PASOK was returned to power in 2009, now led by **George Papandréou**, the extent of the economic problems began to be fully revealed, with a **national debt** of €262 billion and a deficit running at 12.7 percent of GDP (against a euro limit of 3 percent). As Greece's huge public sector, lax tax collection and allegedly widespread corruption came increasingly into the spotlight, government attempts to cut spending and increase revenue ran into the double whammy of popular opposition and economic downturn. As we went to press at the end of 2011, Papandréou had stood down in favour of a government of "national unity", while the latest of a series of **EU bailouts** again failed to make much impact on the financial markets, or on Greece's ever-growing debt. Default or a humiliating departure from the eurozone looks inevitable. Whatever the outcome, Greece's short-term economic future looks bleak.

| 2004 | 2004 | 2008 | 2011 |
|------|------|------|------|
| Athens Olympics pass off triumphantly, though their legacy is less happy. | No-hopers Greece triumph at the European Football Championships in Portugal. | Rioting breaks out in Athens, bringing the country's economic crisis to world attention. | Greek debt crisis threatens to engulf the whole of Europe. |

# Archeology

Until the second half of the nineteenth century, archeology was a very
hit-and-miss, treasure-hunting affair. The early students of antiquity went to
Greece to draw and make plaster casts of the great masterpieces of Classical
sculpture. Unfortunately, a number soon found it more convenient or more
profitable to remove objects wholesale and might be better described as
looters than scholars or archeologists.

## Early excavations

The **British Society of Dilettanti** was one of the earliest promoters of Greek culture,
financing expeditions to draw and publish antiquities. Founded in the 1730s as a
reputedly drunken club for young aristocrats who had completed the Grand Tour
(among them Sir Francis Dashwood, founder of the Hellfire Club), the society was the
first body organized to sponsor systematic research into Greek antiquities, though it
was initially most interested in Italy, as Greece was then still a backwater of the
Ottoman Empire.

One of the first expeditions sponsored by the society was that of two young artists,
**James Stuart** and **Nicholas Revett**, who spent three years in Greece, principally in
and around Athens, drawing and measuring the antiquities. The publication of their
exquisite illustrations and the 1764 publication of **Johann Winckelmann**'s *History of
Art*, in which the **Parthenon** and its sculptures were exalted as the standard for
architectural beauty, gave an enormous boost to the study (and popularity) of all
things Greek; many European Neoclassical town and country houses date from
this period.

The Dilettanti financed a number of further expeditions to study Greek antiquities,
including one to Asia Minor in 1812. While waiting in Athens for a ship to Turkey, the
party employed themselves in excavations at **Eleusis**, where they uncovered the **Temple
of Demeter**. After extensive explorations in Asia Minor, the participants returned via
Attica, where they excavated the **Temple of Nemesis** at **Rhamnous** and examined the
**Temple of Poseidon** at **Soúnio**.

## Pilfering and preservation

Several other antiquarians of the age were less interested in discoveries for their own
sake. A French count, **Choiseul-Gouffier**, removed part of the **Parthenon frieze** in 1787
and his example prompted **Lord Elgin** to detach much of the rest in 1801. These were
essentially acts of looting – "Bonaparte has not got such things from all his thefts in
Italy", boasted Elgin – and their legality was suspect even at the time.

Other discoveries of the period were more ambiguous. In 1811, a party of English
and German travellers, including the architect **C. R. Cockerell**, uncovered the **Temple of
Aphaea** on **Égina** and shipped away the pediments. They auctioned off the marbles for
£6000 to Prince Ludwig of Bavaria, and, inspired by this success, returned to Greece
for further finds. This time they struck it lucky with 23 slabs from the **Temple of Apollo
Epikourios** at **Bassae**, for which the British Museum laid out a further £15,000. These
were huge sums for the time and highly profitable exercises, but they were also
pioneering archeology for the period. Besides, removing the finds was hardly
surprising: Greece, after all, was not yet a state and had no public museum, so
antiquities discovered were invariably sold by their finders.

## The new nation

The Greek War of Independence (1821–28) and the establishment of a modern Greek nation changed all this. As a result of the selection of Prince Otto of Bavaria as the first king of modern Greece in 1832, the **Germans**, whose education system stressed Classical learning, were in the forefront of archeological activity. One such figure was **Ludwig Ross**, who in 1834 began supervising the excavation and restoration of the **Acropolis**, later dismantling its accretion of Byzantine, Frankish and Turkish embellishments that obscured its Classical structure.

The Greeks themselves had begun to focus on their ancient past when the first stirrings of the independence movement were felt. In 1813 the **Philomuse Society** was formed, aiming to uncover and collect antiquities, publish books and assist students and foreign philhellenes. In 1829 an orphanage on the island of Égina became the first **Greek archeological museum**.

In 1837 the **Greek Archeological Society** was founded by **Kyriakos Pittakis**, a remarkable figure who during the War of Independence had used his knowledge of ancient literature to discover the Klepsydra spring on the Acropolis – solving the problem of lack of water during the Turkish siege. In the first four years of its existence, the Archeological Society sponsored excavations in Athens at the **Theatre of Dionysos**, the **Tower of the Winds**, the **Propylaia** and the **Erechtheion**.

## The great Germans

Although King Otto was deposed in 1862 in favour of a Danish prince, Germans remained in the forefront of Greek archeology in the 1870s. Two men dominated the scene: Heinrich Schliemann and Ernst Curtius.

**Ernst Curtius** was a traditional Classical scholar. He had come to Athens originally as tutor to King Otto's family and in 1874 returned to Greece to secure permission to conduct excavations at **Olympia**. He set up a **German Archeological Institute** in Athens and negotiated the **Olympia Convention**, under the terms of which the Germans were to pay for and have total control of the dig; all finds were to remain in Greece, though the excavators could make copies and casts; and all finds were to be published simultaneously in Greek and German.

This was an enormously important agreement, which almost certainly prevented the treasures of Olympia and Mycenae following that of Troy to a German museum. But other Europeans were still in acquisitive mode: **French consuls**, for example, had been instructed to buy any "available" local antiquities in Greece and Asia Minor, and had picked up the Louvre's great treasures, the **Venus de Milo** and **Winged Victory of Samothrace**, in 1820 and 1863 respectively.

At **Olympia**, digging began in 1875 on a site buried beneath river mud, silt and sand. Only one corner of the **Temple of Zeus** was initially visible, but within months the excavators had turned up statues from the east pediment. Over forty magnificent sculptures, as well as terracottas, statue bases and a rich collection of bronzes, were uncovered, together with more than four hundred inscriptions. The laying bare of this huge complex was a triumph for official German archeology.

While Curtius was digging at Olympia, another German was standing archeology on its head. **Heinrich Schliemann** had amassed a private fortune through various Midas-like enterprises and had embarked on the **search for Troy** and the vindication of his lifelong belief in the truth of Homer's tales of prehistoric cities and heroes. Although most of the archeological establishment, led by Curtius, was unremittingly hostile, Schliemann achieved spectacular success in 1873 by unearthing the so-called **Treasure of Priam**, a stash of gold and precious jewellery and vessels. To his mind this vindicated his search for Homer's city of Priam and Hector.

Three years later Schliemann turned his attentions to **Mycenae**, again inspired by Homer, and once more following a hunch. Alone among contemporary scholars, he sought and found the legendary graves of Mycenaean kings inside the existing Cyclopean wall of the citadel rather than outside it, unearthing in the process the magnificent treasures that today form the basis of the **Bronze Age collection** in the National Archeological Museum in Athens. In 1884 Schliemann returned to Greece to excavate another famous prehistoric citadel, this time at **Tiryns**.

Almost single-handedly, and in the face of continuing academic obstruction, Schliemann had revolutionized archeology and the study of Greek history and civilization. Although some of his results have been shown to have been deliberately falsified in the sacrifice of truth to beauty, his achievement remains enormous.

The last two decades of the nineteenth century saw the discovery of other important Classical sites. Excavation began at **Epidaurus** in 1881 under the Greek archeologist **Panayotis Kavvadias**, who made it his life's work. Meanwhile at **Delphi**, the **French** began digging at the **sanctuary of Apollo**. Their excavations continued nonstop from 1892 to 1903, revealing the extensive site visible today; work on the site has continued sporadically ever since.

## Evans and Knossos

The early twentieth century saw the domination of Greek archeology by an Englishman, **Sir Arthur Evans**. An egotistical maverick like Schliemann, he too was independently wealthy, with a brilliantly successful career behind him when he started his great work at **Knossos** on **Crete**, discovering one of the oldest and most sophisticated of Mediterranean societies, which he christened Minoan.

Evans first visited Crete in 1894 and headed for the legendary site of Knossos, which had earlier attracted the attention of Schliemann. Evans succeeded in buying the site and in March 1900 began excavations. Within a few days, evidence of a great complex building was revealed, along with artefacts that indicated an astonishing cultural sophistication: elegant courtyards and verandas, colourful wall-paintings, pottery, jewellery and sealstones – the wealth of a civilization which dominated the eastern Mediterranean 3500 years ago.

### TOP ARCHEOLOGICAL SITES

In a country with such a wealth of ancient remains as Greece, it's hard to pick out a definitive list of highlights, but here are some of the most famous and unmissable sites.

#### THE CLASSICS

**The Acropolis, Athens** Can rightfully claim to be one of the most iconic images of Western civilization. See p.65

**Mycenae** The citadel of King Agamemnon and cavernous tholos tombs never fail to impress. See p.133

**Knossos** The lava-preserved Minoan palace contains some beautiful ancient frescoes. See p.457

**Delphi** Known as the earth's navel, this extensive mountainside site still enchants visitors. See p.204

**Delos** Guarded by majestic lions, the treasury of the Athenian Empire occupied the entire island. See p.394

**Vergina** The dazzling wealth of the Macedonian dynasty is on display beneath an apparently mundane earth mound. See p.287

#### THE BEST OF THE REST

**Sanctuary of the Great Gods, Samothráki** Idyllically located site that was a major centre of an ancient mystery cult. See p.657

**Olynthos** One of the best examples of an ancient town, all laid out in neat grids. See p.299

**Bassae** This superbly well-preserved temple is enhanced by its stunning location in the Arcadian mountains. See p.176

**Philippi** Extensive site that was equally important in Roman and early Christian history. See p.311

**Paleopolis, Corfu** Relatively few people visit the scattering of temples and basilicas in the suburbs of Corfu Town. See p.711

**Tiryns** Squat Mycenaean period citadel that boasts some of the most impressive Cyclopean walls ever built. See p.137

Evans continued to excavate at Knossos for the next thirty years, during which time he established, on the basis of changes in the pottery styles, the **system of dating** that remains in use today for classifying **Greek prehistory**: Early, Middle and Late Minoan (Mycenaean on the mainland). Like Schliemann, Evans attracted criticism and controversy for his methods – most notably his decision speculatively to reconstruct parts of the palace in concrete – and for many of his interpretations. Nevertheless, his discoveries and his dedication put him near the pinnacle of Greek archeology.

## Into the twentieth century: the foreign institutes

In 1924 Evans gave to the **British School at Athens** the site of **Knossos** and all other lands within his possession on Crete (it was only in 1952 that Knossos became the property of the Greek State). At the time the British School was one of several foreign archeological institutes in Greece; founded in 1886, it had been preceded by the **French School**, the **German Institute** and the **American School**.

Greek archeology owes much to the work and relative wealth of these foreign schools and others that would follow. They have been responsible for the excavation of many of the most famous sites in Greece: the **Heraion** on **Sámos** (German); the sacred island of **Delos** (French); sites on **Kos** and in southern **Crete** (Italian); **Corinth**, **Samothráki** and the **Athenian Agora** (American), to name but a few.

One of the giants of this era was **Alan Wace** who, while director of the British School at Athens from 1913 to 1923, conducted excavations at **Mycenae** and proposed a new chronology for prehistoric Greece, which put him in direct conflict with Arthur Evans. Evans believed that the mainland citadels had been ruled by Cretan overlords, whereas Wace was convinced of an independent Mycenaean cultural and political development. Wace was finally vindicated after Evans's death, when in the 1950s it emerged that Mycenaean Greeks had conquered the Minoans in approximately 1450 BC.

The period between the wars saw many new discoveries, among them the sanctuary of **Asklepios** and its elegant Roman buildings on **Kos**, excavated by the Italians from 1935 to 1943, and the Classical Greek city of **Olynthos**, in northern Greece, which was dug by the American School from 1928 to 1934. After the wholesale removal of houses and apartment blocks that had occupied the site, the American School also began excavations in the **Athenian Agora**, the ancient marketplace, in 1931, culminating in the complete restoration of the **Stoa of Attalos**.

## More recent excavations

Interrupted by World War II and the Greek civil war, it was not until 1948 that excavations were resumed with a Greek clearance of the **Sanctuary of Artemis** at **Brauron** in Attica, and in 1952 **Carl Blegen** cleared **Nestor's Palace** at **Pylos** in Messenia. Greek archeologists began work at the Macedonian site of **Pella**, the capital of ancient Macedonia, and at the **Nekromanteion of Ephyra** in Epirus.

In comparison to earlier digs, these were minor operations, reflecting a modified approach to archeology, which laid less stress on discoveries and more on **documentation**. Which is not to say that there were no spectacular finds. At **Mycenae**, in 1951, a second circle of graves was unearthed, and at Pireás, a burst sewer in 1959 revealed four superb Classical bronzes. In 1961 the fourth great **Minoan palace** of **Káto Zákros** (following the unearthing of Knossos, Phaestos and Malia) was revealed by torrential rains at the extreme eastern tip of Crete.

At **Akrotíri** on the island of **Thíra** (Santoríni), **Spyros Marinatos** revealed, in 1967, a Minoan-era site that had been buried by volcanic explosion in either 1650 or 1550 BC – the jury is still deliberating that one. Its buildings were two or three storeys high, and superbly frescoed. Marinatos was later tragically killed while at work on the site when he fell off a wall, and is now buried there.

A decade later came an even more dramatic find at **Vergina** – **ancient Aegae** – in northern Greece, the early capital of the Macedonian kingdom, which later became its necropolis. Here, **Manolis Andronikos** found a series of royal tombs dating from the fourth century BC, containing an astonishing hoard of exquisite gold treasures. Andronikos showed this to have been the **tomb of Philip II** of Macedon, father of Alexander the Great.

At the beginning of this century archeologists are still at work in the field, although the emphasis today is as concerned with **conservation**. All too often newly discovered sites have been inadequately fenced off or protected, and a combination of the elements, greedy developers and malicious trespassers – sometimes all three – has caused much damage and deterioration. On a happier note, many of the finds unearthed during the **Athens metro** expansion were saved and have been tastefully incorporated into displays at the respective stations, such as Panepistímio, Sýndagma and Akrópoli.

# Wildlife

For anyone who has seen Greece at the height of summer with its brown parched hillsides and desert-like ambience, the richness of the wildlife – in particular the flora – may come as a surprise. As winter warms into spring, the countryside transforms itself into a mosaic of coloured flowers, which attract a plethora of insect life, followed by birds. Isolated areas, whether islands or remote mountains such as Olympus, have had many thousands of years to develop their own individual species. Overall, Greece has around six thousand species of native flowering plants, nearly four times that of Britain but in the same land area. Many are unique to Greece, and make up about one-third of Europe's endemic plants.

## Plants

Whereas in temperate northern Europe plants flower from spring until autumn, the arid summers of Greece confine the main **flowering period** to the spring, a narrow window when the days are bright, the temperatures not too high and the groundwater supply still adequate. In Rhodes and eastern Crete this begins in early March, western Crete in early April, the Peloponnese and eastern Aegean mid- to late April, and the Ionian islands in early May, though a cold dry winter can cause several weeks' delay. In the high mountains the floral "spring" arrives in summer, with the alpine zones of central and western Crete in full flower in June, and mainland mountain blooms emerging in July.

The delicate flowers of early spring – orchids, fritillaries, anemones, cyclamen, tulips and small bulbs – are replaced as the season progresses by more robust shrubs, tall perennials and abundant annuals, but many of these close down completely for the fierce **summer**. A few tough plants, like shrubby thyme and savory, continue to flower through the heat and act as magnets for butterflies.

Once the worst heat is over, and the first showers of **autumn** arrive, so does a second "spring", on a much smaller scale but no less welcome after the brown drabness of summer. Squills, autumn cyclamen, crocus in varying shades, pink or lilac colchicum, yellow sternbergia and other small bulbs all come into bloom, while the seeds start to germinate for the following year's crop of annuals. By the new year, early spring bulbs and orchids are flowering in the south.

### Coastal species

Plants on the **beach** grow in a difficult environment: fresh water is scarce, salt is in excess, and dehydrating winds are often very strong. Feathery **tamarisk** trees are adept at surviving this habitat, and consequently are often planted to provide shade. On hot

---

### THE FIRST NATURALISTS

Despite an often negative attitude to wildlife, Greece was probably the first place in the world where it was an object of study. **Theophrastos** (372 – 287 BC) from Lésvos was the first recorded botanist and a systematic collector of general information on plants, while his contemporary, **Aristotle**, studied the animal world. During the first century AD the distinguished physician **Dioscorides** compiled a herbal study that remained a standard work for over a thousand years.

days or nights you may see or feel them sweating away surplus saltwater from their foliage. Sand dunes also provide shelter for a variety of colourful small plants as well as giant reed or **calamus**, a bamboo-like grass reaching up to 6m in height and often cut for use as canes. It frequently grows in company with the shrubby, pink- or white-flowered and highly poisonous **oleander**.

## Meadow and hill plants

**Arable fields** can be rich with colourful weeds: scarlet poppies, blue bugloss, yellow or white daisies, wild peas, gladioli, tulips and grape hyacinths. Small, unploughed **meadows** may be equally colourful, with slower-growing plants such as orchids in extraordinary quantities.

The rocky earth makes cultivation on some **hillsides** difficult and impractical. Agriculture is often abandoned and areas regenerate to a rich mixture of shrubs and perennials – known as **garigue**. With time, a few good wet winters, and in the absence of grazing, some shrubs will develop into small trees, intermixed with tough climbers – the much denser **maquis** vegetation. The colour yellow often predominates in early spring, with brooms, gorse, Jerusalem sage and giant fennel followed by the blues, pinks and purples of bee-pollinated plants. An abundance of the pink and white of Cistus rockroses is usually indicative of an earlier fire, since they are primary recolonizers. A third vegetation type is **phrygana** – smaller, frequently aromatic or spiny shrubs, often with a narrow strip of bare ground between each hedgehog-like bush. Many aromatic herbs such as lavender, rosemary, savory, sage and thyme are native to these areas.

## Orchids

Nearly 190 species of **orchid** are believed to occur in Greece; their complexity blurs species' boundaries and keeps botanists in a state of taxonomic flux. In particular, the Ophrys bee and spider orchids have adapted themselves, through subtleties of lip colour and false scents, to seduce small male wasps. These insects mistake the flowers for a potential mate, and unintentionally assist the plant's pollination. Though all species are officially protected, many are still picked.

## High-altitude plants

The **higher mountains** of Greece have winter snow cover, and cooler weather for much of the year, so flowering is consequently later than at lower altitudes. The **limestone peaks** of the mainland, and of islands such as Corfu, Kefaloniá, Crete, Rhodes, Sámos and Samothráki, hold rich collections of attractive **rock plants**, flowers whose nearest relatives may be from the Balkan Alps or from the Turkish mountains. **Gorges** are another spectacular habitat, particularly rich in Crete. Their inaccessible cliffs act as refuges for plants that cannot survive the grazing, competition or more extreme climates of open areas. Many of Greece's endemic plants are confined to cliffs, gorges or mountains.

Much of the surviving **original woodland** is in mountain areas. In the south it includes cypress: native to the south and east Aegean. The cooler shade of woodland provides a haven for plants that cannot survive full exposure to the Greek summer, including peonies and numerous ferns.

With altitude, the forest thins out to scattered individual conifers and kermes oak, before finally reaching a limit at around 1500 – 2000m on the mainland – much lower on the islands. Above this tree line are **summer meadows**, and then bare rock. If not severely grazed, these habitats are home to many low-growing, gnarled, but often splendidly floriferous plants.

# Birds

**Migratory species** that have wintered in East Africa move north, through the eastern Mediterranean, from around **mid-March to mid-May**. Some stop in Greece to breed;

## GREECE'S BEST WILDLIFE SPOTS

**Samariá Gorge** Crete's most famous ravine is not only one of Europe's longest but hides some of Greece's rarest plants. See p.499

**Préspa Lakes** Straddling the Albanian border, these serene bodies of water provide refuge for a host of waterfowl. See p.290

**Laganás Bay** Though much of it is touristic, the bay is still a prime breeding ground for the loggerhead turtle. See p.753

**Mount Olympus** The mountain of the Gods is also home to over 1600 species of plants. See p.280

**Dhadhiá Forest Reserve** This haven contains some of Greece's last virgin forest, which hosts 36 species of birds of prey. See p.322

**North Pindhos** The wooded valleys of this natural wilderness are the place to spot Greece's largest mammals. See p.242

others move on into the rest of Europe. The southern islands are the first landfall after a long sea crossing, and smaller birds recuperate for a few days before moving on. Larger birds such as storks and ibis often fly very high, and binoculars are needed to spot them as they pass over. In autumn birds return, but usually in more scattered numbers. Although some are shot, there is not the wholesale slaughter that takes place in some other Mediterranean countries.

At **night**, the tiny scops owl has a very distinct, repeated single-note call, very like the sonar beep of a submarine; the equally diminutive little owl, with a weird repertoire of cries, may be visible by day in ruined buildings. Near wooded streams, the most evocative nocturnal bird is the nightingale, most audible in the May mating season.

**Larger raptors** occur in remoter areas, preferring mountain gorges and cliffs. Buzzards are the most abundant, and often mistaken by optimistic birdwatchers for the rarer, shyer eagles. Griffon vultures, however, are unmistakable, soaring on broad, straight-edged wings, whereas the lammergeier is a state-of-the-art flying machine with narrow, swept wings, seen over mountain tops by the lucky few; the remaining ten or so pairs in Crete are now the Balkans' largest breeding population.

In **lowland areas**, hoopoes are a startling combination of pink, black and white, obvious when they fly and the only natural predator of the processionary caterpillar, a major pest of pine forests. The shy golden oriole has an attractive song but is adept at hiding its brilliant colours among the olive trees. Multicoloured flocks of elegant bee-eaters fill the air with their soft calls as they hunt insects. Brightest of all is the kingfisher, more commonly seen sea-fishing here than in northern Europe.

In areas of **wetland** that remain undrained and undisturbed, such as saltmarshes, coastal lagoons, estuaries and freshwater ponds, ospreys, egrets, ibis, spoonbills, storks, pelicans and many waders can be seen feeding. Flamingoes sometimes occur, as lone individuals or small flocks, particularly in the eastern Aegean saltpans between December and May.

## Mammals

Greece's small **mammal** population ranges from rodents and shrews to hedgehogs, hares and squirrels (including the dark-red Persian squirrel on Lésvos). Medium-sized mammals include badgers and foxes and the persecuted golden jackal, but the commonest is the ferret-like stone (or beech) marten, named for its habit of decorating stones with its droppings to mark territory.

In the mainland mountains, mostly in the north, are found the shy chamois and wild boar, with even shyer predators like lynx, wolves and brown bear. Occasionally seen running wild in Crete's White Mountains, but more often as a zoo attraction, is an endemic ibex. Formerly in danger of extinction, a colony of them was established on the offshore islet of Dhía, where they thrived, exterminating the rare local flora.

# Reptiles and amphibians

Reptiles flourish in the hot dry summers of Greece, the commonest being **lizards**. Most of these are small, agile and wary, rarely staying around for closer inspection. They're usually brown to grey, subtly spotted, striped or tessellated, though in adult males the undersides are sometimes brilliant orange, green or blue. The more robust green lizards, with long whip-like tails, can be 50cm or more in length, but are equally shy and fast-moving unless distracted by territorial disputes with each other.

Nocturnal **geckos** are large-eyed, short-tailed lizards. Their spreading toes have claws and ingenious adhesive pads, allowing them to cross house walls and ceilings in their search for insects, including mosquitoes. The rare **chameleon** is a slow-moving, swivel-eyed inhabitant of eastern Crete, Yiálova and some eastern Aegean islands such as Sámos. Essentially green, it has the ability to adjust its coloration to match the surroundings.

Once collected for the pet trade, **tortoises** can be found on much of the mainland, and some islands, though not Crete. Usually their noisy progress through hillside scrub vegetation is the first signal of their presence, as they spend their often long lives grazing the vegetation. Closely related **terrapins** are more streamlined, freshwater tortoises that love to bask on waterside mud by streams or ponds. Usually only seen as they disappear under water, their numbers have recently declined steeply on many islands.

**Sea turtles** occur mostly in the Ionian Sea, but also in the Aegean. The least rare are the loggerhead turtles (*Caretta caretta*), which nest on Zákynthos and Kefaloniá, the Peloponnese, and occasionally in Crete. Their nesting grounds are disappearing under tourist resorts, although they are a protected endangered species (see p.753).

**Snakes** are abundant in Greece and many islands; most are shy and non-venomous. Several species, including the Ottoman and nose-horned vipers, do have a venomous bite, though they are not usually aggressive; they are adder-like and often have a very distinct, dark zigzag stripe down the back. Snakes are only likely to bite if a hand is put in the crevice of a wall or a rock-face where one of them is resting. Leave them alone, and they will do the same for you, but if bitten, seek immediate treatment (see p.43). Most snakes are not only completely harmless to humans but beneficial since they keep down populations of pests such as rats and mice.

**Frogs and toads** are the commonest and most obvious amphibians throughout much of Greece, particularly during the spring breeding season. Frogs prefer the wettest places, and the robust marsh frog revels in artificial water-storage ponds, whose concrete sides magnify their croaking impressively. Tree frogs are tiny emerald-green jewels, with huge and strident voices at night, sometimes found in quantity on the leaves of waterside oleanders.

## TOURISM AND THREATS TO WILDLIFE

Since the 1970s, tourist developments have ribboned along **coastlines**, sweeping away both agricultural plots and wildlife havens as they do so. These expanding resorts increase local employment, often attracting inland workers to the coast; the generation that would once have herded sheep on remote hillsides now works in tourist bars and tavernas. Consequently, the pressure of domestic animal grazing, particularly in the larger islands, has been significantly reduced, allowing the regeneration of tree seedlings; Crete, for example, has more woodland now than at any time in the last five centuries. However, **forest fires** remain a threat everywhere. Since 1980 blazes have destroyed much of the tree cover in Thássos, southern Rhodes, Kárpathos, Híos, Sámos and parts of the Peloponnese; the trees may well regenerate eventually, but by then the complex shade-dependent ecology is irrecoverably lost.

In the mainland interior, increasing demand for power brings huge **hydroelectric schemes** to remote rivers and gorges with little chance for opposition to be heard. Even the **Orthodox Church**, whose lands once often provided wildlife with a refuge from hunters, now looks to capitalize on their value for major tourist developments. In the north, the forests of sacred **Mount Áthos** are being surrendered to commercial logging. On the bright side, the **Kárla marsh-lake** near Vólos is being allowed to partially refill again, to the delight of migratory birds.

## FLORA AND FAUNA FIELD GUIDES

### FLOWERS

**Marjorie Blamey and Christopher Grey-Wilson** *Mediterranean Wild Flowers*. Comprehensive field guide, with coloured drawings; recent and taxonomically reasonably up to date.

**Lance Chilton** *Plant Check-Lists*. Small booklets that also include birds, reptiles and butterflies, for a number of Greek islands and resorts. Available direct at ☎ 01485/532710, ⒲ www.marengowalks.com.

**Pierre Delforge** *Orchids of Britain and Europe*. A comprehensive guide, with recent taxonomy.

**John Fielding & Nicholas Turland** *Flowers of Crete*. Large volume with 1900 coloured photos of the Cretan flora, much of which is also widespread in Greece.

### BIRDS

**George Handrinos and T. Akriotis** *Birds of Greece*. A comprehensive guide that includes island birdlife.

**Lars Jonsson** *Birds of Europe with North Africa and the Middle East*. The ornithologist's choice for the best coverage of Greek birds, with excellent descriptions and illustrations.

### MAMMALS

**Corbet and Ovenden** *Collins Guide to the Mammals of Europe*. The best field guide on its subject.

### REPTILES

**Arnold, Burton and Ovenden** *Collins Guide to the Reptiles and Amphibians of Britain and Europe*. A useful guide, though it excludes the Dodecanese and east Aegean islands.

### INSECTS

**Michael Chinery** *Collins Guide to the Insects of Britain and Western Europe*. Although Greece is outside the geographical scope of the guide, it will provide generic identifications for many insects seen.

**Lionel Higgins and Norman Riley** *A Field Guide to the Butterflies of Britain and Europe*. A thorough and detailed field guide that illustrates nearly all species seen in Greece.

### MARINE LIFE

**B. Luther and K. Fiedler** *A Field Guide to the Mediterranean (o/p)*. Very thorough; includes most Greek shallow-water species.

## Insects

Greece teems with insects: some pester, like flies and mosquitoes, but most are harmless to humans. **Grasshoppers** and **crickets** swarm through open areas of vegetation in summer, with larger species that are carnivorous and can bite if handled. Larger still are grey-brown locusts, flying noisily before crash-landing into trees and shrubs. The high-pitched, endlessly repeated chirp of house crickets can drive one to distraction, as can the summer whirring of cicadas on the trunks of trees.

From spring through to autumn, Greece is full of **butterflies**. Swallowtail species are named for the drawn-out corners of the hindwings, in shades of cream and yellow, with black and blue markings. The unrelated, robust brown-and-orange pasha is Europe's largest butterfly. In autumn, black-and-orange African monarchs may appear, sometimes in large quantities. However, the "butterflies" occurring in huge quantity in sheltered sites on islands such as Rhodes, Níssyros and Páros are in fact tiger moths, with their black-and-white forewings and startling bright orange hindwings.

Other insects include the camouflaged **praying mantis**, holding their powerful forelegs in a position of supplication until another insect comes within reach. The females are notorious for eating the males during mating. Hemispherical **scarab beetles** collect balls of dung and push them around with their back legs.

Corfu and the Epirot mainland opposite are famous for extraordinary **fireflies**, which flutter in quantities across meadows and marshes on May nights, speckling the darkness with bursts of cold light to attract partners; look carefully in nearby hedges, and you may spot the less flashy, more sedentary glow-worm.

Other non-vertebrates of interest include the **land crabs**, which are found in the south and east of Greece. They need water to breed, but can surprise when seen crawling across remote hillsides.

# Music

Music is ubiquitous in modern Greek culture; even the most indifferent visitor will notice it in tavernas and other public spaces. Like so many aspects of the country, it amalgamates "native" and eastern styles, with occasional contributions from points west, and flourishes alongside and often in preference to Western pop. Many traditional songs can trace their routes back to Byzantine **religious chants** or to the popular music of the **Ottoman Empire**, though more nationalist-minded musicologists claim their original descent from the now-lost melodies of ancient Greece.

## Folk music and instruments

The best opportunities to hear live Greek folk music are the numerous summer **paniyíria** (saints' day festivals) or more tourist-oriented **cultural programmes**, when musicians based in Athens clubs during winter tour the islands and villages. Various high-quality revival groups are attempting to recapture the musicianship of the old-timers, fortunately well archived on CD.

### Island music

The arc of southern Aegean islands comprising **Crete, Kássos, Kárpathos** and **Hálki** is one of the most promising areas to hear live music. The dominant instrument here is the **lýra**, a lap-fiddle related to the Turkish *kemençe*. It is played not on the shoulder but balanced on the thigh, with a loose bow that can touch all three strings simultaneously, making double chords possible. The contemporary **Cretan lýra** is larger, tuned lower (like a Western violin), and played with a much tauter bow. Usually, the *lýra* is backed up by a **laoúto**, closely resembling a mandolin, with a long fretted neck and four sets of double strings.

In parts of the southeastern Aegean, most notably **Kálymnos** and northern **Kárpathos**, you also find a simple, **droneless bagpipe** – the **askomandoúra** or *tsamboúna*, though few people now know how to play it. Much the same goes for the **sandoúri** (hammer dulcimer) – which in Kazantzakis's classic novel, or its film, *Zorba the Greek*, was played by his Cretan hero.

On most Aegean islands, particularly the **Cyclades**, the *lýra* is replaced by a more familiar-looking **violí**, essentially a Western violin. Accompaniment was provided until recently by *laoúto* or *sandoúri*, though these days you're most likely to be confronted by a bass guitar and rock drums.

**Island folk songs** – **nisiótika** – feature melodies which, like much folk music the world over, rely heavily on the pentatonic scale. Lyrics, especially on smaller islands, touch on the perils of the sea, exile and thwarted love.

**Lésvos** occupies a special place in terms of island music, having absorbed melodies and instrumentation from various nationalities of neighbouring Anatolia; it is the only island with a vital **brass band** tradition, and nearly every Greek dance rhythm is represented in local music.

By way of contrast, the **Ionian islands** (except Lefkádha) alone of all modern Greek territory never saw Turkish occupation and have a predominantly Western musical tradition. Their indigenous song-form is Italian both in name – **kantádhes** – and in instrumentation (guitar and mandolin) and vocalization (major scales, choral delivery); it's most often heard now on Lefkádha, Kefaloniá and Zákynthos.

## Mainland music

In the **Peloponnese** and **central/western Greece**, many folk songs – known as **paliá dhimotiká** – hark back to the Ottoman occupation and the War of Independence; others, in a lighter tone, refer to aspects of pastoral life. Their essential instrument is the **klaríno** (clarinet), which reached Greece during the 1830s, introduced either by Gypsies or King Otto's Bavarian entourage. Backing was traditionally provided by a *koumpanía* consisting of *kythára* (guitar), *laoúto*, *laoutokythára* (a hybrid instrument) and *violí*, with *toumberléki* (lap drum) or *défi* (tambourine) for rhythm.

Many mainland melodies are **dances**, divided by rhythm into such categories as *kalamatianó* (a line dance), *tsámiko*, *hasaposérviko* or *syrtó*, the quintessential circle dance of Greece. Those that aren't danceable include the slow, stately *kléftiko*, which relate, baldly or in metaphor, incidents or attitudes from the Ottoman era and the fight for freedom.

The folk music of **Epirus (Ípiros)** shows strong resemblances to that of neighbouring Albania and the Republic of Macedonia, particularly in the **polyphonic pieces** sung by both men and women. The repertoire divides into three categories, also found further south: *mirolóyia* or laments; drinking songs or *tís távlas*; and various danceable melodies as noted above, common to the entire mainland and many islands also.

**Macedonia and Thrace** in the north remained Ottoman territory until the early 1900s, with a bewilderingly mixed population, so music here still sounds more generically Balkan. Worth special mention are the **brass bands** peculiar to western Macedonia, introduced during the nineteenth century by Ottoman military musicians. Owing to the huge, post-1923 influx of Anatolian refugees, these regions have been a treasure-trove for collectors and ethnomusicologists seeking to document the old music of Asia Minor.

Among Thracian instruments, the **kaváli** (end-blown pastoral flute) is identical to the Turkish and Bulgarian article, as is the local drone bagpipe or **gáïda**, made like its island counterpart from a goat-skin. The **zournás**, a screechy, double-reed oboe similar to the Islamic world's *shenai*, is an integral part of weddings or festivals, along with the deep-toned *daoúli* drum, as a typically Gypsy ensemble. Other percussion instruments like the *daïrés* or tambourine and the *darboúka* provide sharply demarcated dance rhythms such as the *zonarádhikos*. The *klaríno* is present here as well, as are two types of *lýra*, but the most characteristic melodic instrument of Thrace is the **oúti** (*oud*), whose popularity received a boost after refugee players arrived.

## Rembétika

Often known as the Greek "blues", **rembétika** began as the music of the urban dispossessed. It existed in some form in **Greece**, **Smyrna** and **Constantinople** since at least the very early 1900s – probably a few decades earlier. But its evolution is as hard to define as American blues, with which half-useful comparisons are often made. Although rembétika shares marked similarities in spirit with that genre, there's little or none in its musical form.

The 1919–22 Greco-Turkish war and the subsequent **1923 exchange of populations** were key events for rembétika, resulting in the influx to Greece of over a million Asia Minor Greeks, many of whom settled in shanty towns around Athens, Pireás and Thessaloníki. Here a few men would sit around a charcoal brazier, toking from a *nargilés* (hookah) filled with hashish. One might improvise a tune on the *baglamás* or the **bouzoúki** (a long-necked, fretted, three-stringed lute) and begin to sing songs of illicit or frustrated love, disease and death; their tone – resignation to the singer's lot, coupled with defiance of authority – will be familiar to old-time blues fans.

By the early 1930s, key (male) musicians had emerged from the *tekés* culture. Foremost among them was a Pireás-based quartet: the beguiling-voiced **Stratos Payioumtzis**; composer and lyricist **Anestis Delias** (aka **Artemis**), who died in the street of a drug

## THE SOUND OF THE UNDERGROUND

This "Golden Age" of rembétika was short-lived, as the music's association with a drug-laced underworld would prove its undoing. During the strait-laced **Metaxás dictatorship** tangos and frothy Italianate love songs were encouraged instead and musicians with uncompromising lyrics and lifestyles were blackballed. In Athens, even possession of a *bouzoúki* or *baglamás* became a criminal offence and several performers did jail time. Others went to Thessaloníki, where the local police chief was a big fan of the music and allowed its practitioners to smoke in private.

The unfortunate rembétes incurred disapproval from the puritanical Left as well as the puritanical Right; the growing **Communist Party** of the 1930s considered the music and its habitués hopelessly decadent and politically unevolved. Despite this, rembétika was strangely popular among the rank-and-file on both sides of the 1946–49 civil war – perhaps the only taste uniting a fatally polarized country.

Ironically, the original rembétika material was rescued from oblivion by the 1967–74 **colonels' junta**. Along with various other features of Greek culture, most rembétika verses were banned. The generation coming of age under the dictatorship took a closer look at the forbidden fruit and derived solace, and deeper meanings, from the nominally apolitical lyrics. When the junta fell in 1974 – even a little before – there was an outpouring of reissued recordings of the old masters.

overdose in 1943; *baglamá*-player Yiorgos Tsoros, better known as **Batis**, an indifferent musician but another excellent composer; and **Markos Vamvakaris**, who became the linchpin of the group. Though a master instrumentalist, he initially considered that his voice, ruined perhaps from too much hash-smoking, wasn't fit for singing. But he soon bowed to the encouragement of record label Columbia, and his gravelly, unmistakable delivery set the standard for male rembétic vocals until the 1940s.

In the late 1940s, several *rembétisses* (female rembétika vocalists) sang with **Vassilis Tsitsanis**, the most significant composer and *bouzoúki* player after Vamvakaris. Tsitsanis performed almost up to his death in 1984 – his funeral in Athens was attended by nearly a quarter of a million people.

### The éntekhno revolution

The "Westernization" of rembétika that began with Tsitsanis preceded the rise of the **éntekhno music** that emerged during the late 1950s. *Éntekhno*, literally "artistic" or "sophisticated", was an orchestral genre where folk or rembétika instrumentation and melodies became part of a much larger symphonic fabric, but with a still recognizably Greek sound.

Its first and most famous exponents were **Manos Hatzidhakis** and **Mikis Theodhorakis**, both classically trained musicians. They combined not only rembétic and Byzantine influences with orchestral arrangements, but also successfully used the country's rich **poetic tradition**.

The downside of increased sophistication was an inevitable distancing from indigenous roots, in particular the modal scale which had served since antiquity. And with its catchy tunes, *éntekhno* fell prey to the demands of the local film industry – writing a soundtrack became a composer's obligatory rite of passage – and at its worst degenerated to muzak cover versions.

### Laïká: son of rembétika

Diametrically opposed to *éntekhno* was the **laïká** ("popular") music of the 1950s and 1960s, its gritty, tough style directly linked to rembétika, undiluted by Western influences. *Laïká* used time signatures common in Turkey and was mistakenly known overseas as belly-dance music. Once again, these "debased" oriental influences were much to the chagrin of those who also objected to the apolitical, decadent, escapist song content.

The most notable *laïká* performer was **Stelios Kazantzidhis** (1931–2001), whose volcanic, mournful style was never equalled. His work, often in duets with **Marinella** and **Yiota Lidhia**, immortalized the experiences of the Greek working class that emerged from the 1940s faced with a choice of life under restrictive regimes or emigration. "Stellaras" inspired fanatical devotion in his fans over a fifty-year career: truck-drivers emblazoned their cabs with a single word, "Yparho" (the name of his biggest hit). On the day he died nearly every CD player in the land played Kazantzidhis songs in tribute, and his funeral in industrial Elefsína was thronged by thousands.

## Singer-songwriters and folk-rock

The first significant musician to break the *bouzoúki* mould was Thessalonian **Dhionysis Savvopoulos**, who emerged in 1966 with a maniacal, rasping voice and angst-ridden lyrics, his persona rounded out by shoulder-length hair and outsized glasses. Savvopoulos's work soon became impossible to pigeonhole: perhaps equal parts twisted northern Greek folk, Bob Dylan and Frank Zappa at his jazziest. Though briefly detained and tortured, he resumed performing, and became something of a touchstone for late 1960s Greek youth.

Despite a modest discography, Savvopoulos had a considerable effect on younger artists, and during his brief tenure as a record producer, Savvopoulos gave breaks to numerous younger artists, many of them also from northern Greece. Among his protégés were **Nikos Xydhakis** and **Manolis Rasoulis**, whose landmark 1978 album, *Iy Ekdhikisi tis Yiftias* (The Revenge of Gypsydom), railed against the pretentiousness of 1960s and 1970s *éntekhno* and other "politically correct" music.

## Contemporary music

**Eleftheria Arvanitaki**, who began her career on a Savvopoulos album, and continued with rembétika revival group Opisthodhromiki Kompania, went on to dabble in various genres, and around the millennium was Greece's hottest vocalist. Look out also for **Ross Daly** who frequently appears live in Greece or tours abroad, offering fusion interpretations of traditional pieces plus his own improvisations. He plays numerous traditional Greek instruments and has absorbed influences not just from Crete, where he was long resident, but from throughout the Near East. Two other exports from Crete are mandolinist **Loudhovikos ton Anoyeion**, originally one of Hatzidhakis's late-1980s Seirios artists, and the all-acoustic group **Haïnidhes**, last heard accompanying acrobats and shadow-puppet players in a major Athens club.

Various other, less durable groups have attempted to explore foreign influences on Greek music with mixed success. Often this eclecticism has gone too far, with bells, sitar, ney and synthesizer resulting in a bland, New Age-y sound not identifiably Greek. Individuals who have managed to avoid this trap include innovative young clarinettist **Manos Achalinotopoulos**; *oud* player **Haig Yagdjian**; the group **Notios Ihos**, led by Ahilleas Persidhis; singer **Savina Yiannatou**; and the **Greeks-and-Indians** fusion concerts and recordings coordinated by visionary Alexandhros Karsiotis of Saraswati Records. Meanwhile, many of the younger generation of listeners, growing up on Hellenic versions of shows like the X-Factor, have catapulted performers of maximum looks but dubious talent such as **Anna Vissi**, **Sakis Rouvas** and 2005 Eurovison Song Contest winner **Elena Paparizou** into the limelight.

## Discography

The following CDs are among the best available for each of the genres detailed above: ★ denotes a particularly strong recommendation. Unless otherwise specified, all are Greek pressings. Athens has numerous good Greek CD stores (see p.113). Online, you'll find some of our choices at Amazon, but rather more at Thessaloníki-based Studio 52 (ⓦ www.studio52.gr), which operates a worldwide online order service.

## FOLK

### COMPILATIONS

★ **Lesvos Aiolis** *Tragoudhia ke Hori tis Lesvou/Songs & Dances of Lesvos* (2 CDs). Field recordings (1974–96) of this island's last traditional music, supervised by musicologist Nikos Dhionysopoulos. The quality and uniqueness of the pieces, and lavishly illustrated booklet, merit the expense.

**Seryiani sta Nisia Mas, vol 1**. Excellent retrospective of mostly 1950s *nisiótika* hits and artists; the easiest way to hear the vintage stars cited on p.938. A highlight is Emilia Hatzidhaki's rendering of "Bratsera".

**Thalassa Thymisou: Tragoudhia ke Skopi apo tis Inousses**. Superb result of Thessaloníki music school En Khordais' "field trip" to Inoússes, a small islet near Híos; live sessions in Inoussan tavernas plus studio recordings.

### ARTISTS

★ **Khronis Aïdhonidhis** *T'Aïdhonia tis Anatolis: Songs of Thrace and Asia Minor*. Flawlessly produced 1990 session featuring the top singer of material from Thrace and western Asia Minor, plus an orchestra directed by Ross Daly, and guest Yiorgos Dalaras.

★ **Petro-Loukas Halkias** *Petro-Loukas Chalkias and Kompania* (World Network, Germany). Halkias and his *kompanía* (group) of *laoúto*, *violí*, guitar and percussion realize the true sense of the *kompanía*: tight coordination, yet clearly articulated instrumental voices.

**Xanthippi Karathanasi** *Tragoudhia ke Skopi tis Makedhonias/Songs and Tunes of Macedonia*. A native of Halkidhikí, Karathanasi is a foremost interpreter of north-mainland material – and her sidemen are so good they almost steal the show.

**Andonis Xylouris (Psarandonis)** *Palio Krasi In'iy Skepsi Mou* and *Idheon Antron*. Psarandonis – shunned by other Cretan musicians – has an idiosyncratically spare and percussive *lýra* style, but here unusual instruments are well integrated into a densely textured whole. Daughter Niki executes a gorgeous rendition of "Meraklidhiko Pouli" on *Idheon Antron*.

## REMBÉTIKA

### COMPILATIONS

**Greek Archives**. This 1990s series has skeletal English notes but well-chosen track selections. From the 28 discs still in print, go for *Rembetiko Song in America vol 1, 1920–1940*; *Women of the Rembetiko Song*; *Anthology of Rebetiko Songs 1933–1940* and *Anthology of Smyrnean Songs 1920–1938 vol 1*.

★ **Greek Orientale: Smyrneic-Rembetic Songs and Dances** (Arhoolie-Polylyric, US). Superb collection spanning 1911 to 1937, with Roza, Rita, Marika Papagika and Dhimitris Semsis.

**Lost Homelands: The Smyrneic Song in Greece 1928–35** (Interstate/Heritage, UK). Exceptional sound quality and literate liner notes give this collection the edge over rivals.

★ **Rembetika: Songs of the Greek Underground 1925–1947** (Trikont, Germany). This crammed-full, 2-CD set makes an excellent starter collection, with classics such as Papaïoannou's "Pende Ellines ston Adhi" and Kaldaras' "Nykhtose Horis Fengari".

★ **Rough Guide to Rebetika** (World Music Network, UK). The best single introduction to the genre, with performers from its earliest recorded days to current revivalists.

### ARTISTS

**Dhimitris Moustakydhis** *16 Rebetika Paigmena se Kithara*. Thessalonian revivalist gem: 16 classics, mostly from the 1920s and 1930s, accompanied by guitar instead of *bouzoúki*.

**Roza Eskenazi: Rembettissa** (Rounder, US). Ace renditions of standards and rare gems with her usual sidemen Semsis, Tomboulis, and Lambros on *kanonáki*.

★ **Marika Ninou** *Stou Tzimi tou Hondrou/At Jimmy the Fat's*. Poor sound quality – it was a clandestine recording – but still a classic: one of the few documents of a live rembétic evening, with Ninou and Tsitsanis performing at their habitual club in 1955.

**Rebetiki Kompania** *Pos Tha Perasi Iy Vradhia* The easiest-found offering from a group that spearheaded the late-1970s rembétika revival.

★ **Tetras Iy Xakousti tou Pireos** The gang of four – Vamvakaris, Batis, Anestis and Stratos – at the height of their form.

**Vangelis Papazoglou 1897–1943** 1920s/30s compositions sung by the era's top stars, including Stellakis Perpiniadhis, Roza Eskenazi, Kostas Roukounas and Rita Abatzi. Poor sound quality, but several versions of his classic "Iy Lahanadhes".

**Vassilis Tsitsanis** *Vassilis Tsitsanis 1936–1946* (Rounder, US). Mostly male singers, but includes several rare (for him) *mastoúriaka*. The 20 hits of *Ta Klidhia* – look for the ring of three keys (*klidhiá*) on the cover – pair him with such mid-1960s stars as Grigoris Bithikotsis, Kaity Grey and Poly Panou.

**Markos Vamvakaris** *Bouzoúki Pioneer 1932–1940* (Rounder, US). Excellent sound quality, good notes and unusual material.

★ **Stavros Xarhakos** *Rembetiko*. Soundtrack to the eponymous film, and virtually the only "original" rembétika composed in the last fifty years; lyrics by Nikos Gatsos.

## ÉNTEKHNO

**Manos Hatzidhakis** *Matomenos Gamos: Paramythi horis Onoma* (Columbia). Nikos Gatsos lyrics, with Lakis Pappas singing.

⭐ **Yannis Markopoulos** *Rizitika*. "La Chante Profunde de Crète" – the French subtitle – says it all: stirring anthems like "Pote Tha Kamei Xasteria", which launched Xylouris' *éntekhno* career. *Thiteia*, with lyrics by Manos Eleftheriou, is also a sentimental favourite.

⭐ **Mikis Theodhorakis** *Epitafios/Epifaneia* with Bithikotsis and Hiotis, and *To Axion Esti* with Manos Katrakis, are among his most influential, reputation-justifying works,

in white-boxed remasters of the original sessions.

**Stavros Xarhakos** *Syllogi*. More lyrics by Nikos Gatsos, Nikos Xylouris's crystalline voice and orchestra (including funky electric guitar licks) conducted by Khristodhoulos Halaris make this a 1973 landmark.

⭐ **Nikos Xylouris** *Itane mia Fora* (2 CDs). A thorough selection of Xylouris' best 1970s work, with Yiannis Markopoulos and others, making clear why he is still worshipped nearly three decades after his tragically early death. The title track is particularly loved and still frequently heard.

## LAÏKÁ

⭐ **Haris Alexiou** Start with *Ta Tragoudhia tis Haroulas*, with lyrics by Manolis Rasoulis and Manos Loïzos, which established her as alto queen of 1980s *laïká*. *Ta Tsilika* has her rembétika interpretations; *Yirizondas ton Kosmo* is a more recent live *éntekhno*/pop disc.

⭐ **Eleftheria Arvanitaki** *Tragoudhia yia tous Mines* is upbeat and *laïká*-based; in *Ektos Programmatos* Eleftheria gets rootsily down in lively sessions at Athens and Thessaloníki clubs.

**Yiorgos Dalaras** *Latin*. A 1987 team-up with Al Di Meola, Glykeria, Alkistis Protopsalti and others, plus Latin rhythms and instrumentalists, resulted in nearly half a million copies sold.

**Glykeria (Kotsoula)** *Me ti Glykeria stin Omorfi Nhykhta*. Live recording showcases this versatile *laïká* singer and rembétika/*nisiótika* revivalist active since the 1980s.

**Stelios Kazantzidhis** *Iy Zoi Mou Oli* (2 CD). Retrospective of all the classic hits that made him a national institution.

⭐ **Sokratis Malamas** *Ena*. A 2000 release that embodies his mature, confident style, with just voice and guitar; 1992's *Tis Meras ke tis Nykhtas*, with Melina Kana, was the big breakthrough for both.

**Thanassis Papakonstandinou** He's not for everyone, but arguably among the most original musicians working in Greece. If you like his trend-setting *Vrahnos Profitis* (2000), carry on to *Agrypnia* (2002), where he reprises "Ayia Nostalgia", title track of his utterly different 1993 debut.

**Nikos Papazoglou** *Synerga*. A gentle, mystical album; 2005's *Ma'issa Selini* is rootsier and broke a long recording silence.

**Dhionysis Savvopoulos** *Trapezakia Exo* (Lyra MBI). The catchiest outing from the man who set off the folk-rock movement.

⭐ **Nena Venetsanou** This female singer has a deep, earthy voice lending itself to a number of genres. *Ikones* reworks everything from Hatzidhakis (including some premieres) to *nisiótika* to chanson; *Zeïbekika* is a surprisingly successful recasting of rembétika as "profane prayers", performed in French chapels.

## SINGER-SONGWRITERS

⭐ **Himerini Kolymvites** Eponymous first and still best of their CDs, with often surreal lyrics plus richly textured, drunken melodies.

## FOLK REVIVAL AND FUSION

⭐ **Bosphorus** (Fanari tis Anatolis) *Beyond the Bosphorus*. This tour de force, with guests Mode Plagal, revisits Constantinopolitan and Anataloian melodies, with Vassiliki Papayeoryiou on vocals.

**Haïnidhes** *Haïnidhes* (MBI) and *Kosmos ki Oneiro ine Ena* (MBI) are their first two, and arguably best, albums, with folk-influenced original compositions taking precedence over old standards.

⭐ **Loudhovikos Ton Anoyion** *O Erotas stin Kriti ine Melangolikos* helped rescue the Cretan mandolin from its rhythm-backing ghetto; *Pyli tis Ammou* exemplifies his evolution in a larger group, with guests Malamas, Papazoglou and Venetsanou.

**Mode Plagal** *Mode Plagal II*. The best of several solo

albums; folk tunes meet funky guitar and saxophone licks à la Coltrane and Miles Davis improvisations/compositions.

**Savina Yiannatou** *Anixi sti Saloniki/Spring in Salonika*. Ladino Sephardic songs, with crisp backing from Kostas Vomvolos' orchestra; Savina's voice (and trademark vibrato) can take some getting used to, though.

**Greeks & Indians** (9 vols to date): This series (vol 3, *Ta Ipirotika*; vol 4, *Ta Pondiaka*; and vol 8, *Ta Laïka* ⭐ ) sees top performers of Greek regional music – including Petro-Loukas Halkias, Ross Daly, Nikos Saragoudhas, Sofia Papazogou, Yiorgos Amarantidis and Yiorgos Koros – joining forces with some of the best North Indian musicians around.

# Books

The best books in this selection are marked by a ★ symbol; titles currently out of print are indicated as "o/p". Recommended specialist Greek booksellers include, in the UK, the Hellenic Bookservice (ⓦhellenicbookservice.com) and, in Canada, Kalamos Books (ⓦkalamosbooks.com).

## TRAVEL/IMPRESSIONS

★ **Kevin Andrews** *The Flight of Ikaros* (o/p). Intense, compelling account by a sensitive young archeologist wandering the backcountry during the civil war. Five decades on, still one of the best books on Greece as it was before "development".

★ **Gerald Durrell** *My Family and Other Animals*. Delightful evocation of Durrell's 1930s childhood on Corfu, where his family settled, and where he developed a passion for the island's fauna while elder brother Lawrence entertained Henry Miller and others.

**Lawrence Durrell** *Prospero's Cell* and *Reflections on a Marine Venus*. The former constitutes Durrell's Corfu memoirs, from his time there as World War II loomed. *Marine Venus* recounts his 1945–47 colonial-administrator experiences of Rhodes and other Dodecanese islands.

★ **Patrick Leigh Fermor** *Roumeli* and *Mani*. Sir Patrick – knighted in 2004 for his writing and contribution to British-Greek relations – is an aficionado of rural Greece's vanishing minorities and customs. These two volumes, written in the late 1950s and early 1960s respectively, are scholarly travelogues interspersed with strange yarns. Despite self-indulgent passages, they remain among the best books on modern Greece.

**Eleni Gage** *North of Ithaka*. Eleni is the namesake and granddaughter of the Eleni whose murder her son Nicholas famously set out to avenge (see p.804). A New York journalist, she decided to spend most of 2002 in her grandmother's old Epirot village in Epirus, rebuilding the family house – and more. Her open-hearted account takes in village life and travels from Albania to Árta.

**Roy Hounsell** *The Papas and the Englishman: From Corfu to Zagoria*. Roy and wife Effie forsake the usual expat arenas and settle in Koukoúli under Mount Gamíla, renovating an ancient, crumbled mansion.

**John Humphrys and Christopher Humphrys** *Blue Skies and Black Olives: A Survivor's Tale of Housebuilding and Peacock Chasing in Greece*. The irascible BBC presenter and his son, a cellist with a Greek orchestra, give their contrasting versions of the frustrations involved in building a holiday home in the Peloponnese. Enjoyable, if all a bit familiar.

**Yorgos Ioannou** *Refugee Capital* (o/p). Brilliant, wide-ranging essays on Thessaloníki by a native, touching on its

political powerlessness, its vanished Jews, the grip of the Orthodox Church, flowering shade trees, and gay cruising at its old cinemas.

**Edward Lear** *The Corfu Years*, *The Cretan Journal* and *Journals of a Landscape Painter in Greece and Albania* (latter o/p). Highly entertaining journals – the first two beautifully illustrated – from the 1840s and 1850s.

**Peter Levi** *The Hill of Kronos*. Finely observed landscapes, monuments, personalities and politics, as poet and classical scholar Levi describes his first journeys to Greece in the 1960s, before being drawn into resistance against the colonels' junta.

**Sydney Loch** *Athos: The Holy Mountain* (o/p). Resident in Ouranópoli tower on Mount Áthos from 1924 to 1954, Loch recounts the legends surrounding the various monasteries, gleaned from years of visiting the monastic republic.

**John Lucas** *92 Acharnon Street*. Fond memories of Athens in the 1980s, beautifully told by a poet with a poetic turn of phrase.

★ **Willard Manus** *This Way to Paradise: Dancing on the Tables*. American expat's memoir of nearly four decades in Líndhos, Rhodes, beginning long before its submersion in tourism. Wonderful period detail, including bohemian excesses and cameos from such as S.J. Perelman, Germaine Greer and Martha Gellhorn.

**Christopher Merrill** *Things of the Hidden God: Journey to the Holy Mountain*. Merrill, an accomplished poet and journalist, first came to Áthos in the wake of a traumatic time reporting on the breakup of Yugoslavia. With fine black-and-white photographs, this is probably the best contemporary take on Áthos, and Orthodoxy.

**Henry Miller** *The Colossus of Maroussi*. Corfu, Crete, Athens and the soul of Greece in 1939, with Miller completely in his element; funny, sensual and transporting.

**Dilys Powell** *An Affair of the Heart* and *The Villa Ariadne*. Powell accompanied archeologist husband Humfry Payne on excavations at the Hereon of Perahóra, and after his sudden death in 1936 maintained strong links with the local villagers, described in *An Affair....* The clearer-eyed, less sentimental *The Villa Ariadne* chronicles her 1950s travels to Crete.

**Leon Sciaky** *Farewell to Salonica*. Memoir of a Belle Époque boyhood in a middle-class Sephardic Jewish family, before their 1915 emigration to the US. The Sciakys had close ties with Bulgarian peasants in Kukush (now Kilkís) – and Leon is far more sympathetic to Bulgaria than to the Greek regime which assumed control of cosmopolitan Salonica in 1912.

**Tom Stone** *The Summer of My Greek Taverna*. Enjoyable cautionary tale for those fantasizing about a new life in the Aegean sun. Moving to Pátmos in the early 1980s, Stone tries to mix friendship and business at a beach taverna, with predictable (for onlookers anyway) results.

**Richard Stoneman, ed** *A Literary Companion to Travel in Greece*. Ancient and medieval authors, plus Grand Tourists – an excellent selection.

★ **Patricia Storace** *Dinner with Persephone*. A New York poet, resident for a year in Athens (with forays to the provinces), puts the country's 1990s psyche on the couch. Storace has a sly humour and an interesting take on Greece's "imprisonment" in its imagined past.

**John L. Tomkinson, ed** *Travellers' Greece: Memories of an Enchanted Land*. Seventeenth- to nineteenth-century (mostly English) travellers' impressions of islands and mainland, ranging from the enraptured to the appalled; ideal for dipping into.

★ **Sofka Zinovieff** *Eurydice Street*. An anthropologist and journalist by training, Zinovieff first came to Greece in the early 1980s, then returned in 2001 with her diplomat husband and two daughters to live in Athens. With sharp observations on nationalism, Orthodoxy, politics, November 17 and leisure (to cite just a few topics), this is the best single account of life in today's urban Greece.

## FICTION

### FOREIGN FICTION

★ **Louis de Bernières** *Captain Corelli's Mandolin*. Set on Kefaloniá during the World War II occupation and aftermath, this accomplished 1994 tragi-comedy quickly acquired cult, then bestseller, status in the UK and US. But in Greece it provoked a scandal, once islanders, Greek Left intellectuals and surviving Italian partisans woke up to its virulent disparaging of ELAS. It seems the novel was based on the experiences of Amos Pampaloni, an artillery captain on Kefaloniá in 1942–44 who later joined ELAS, and who accused De Bernières of distorting the roles of both Italians and ELAS on the island. The Greek translation was abridged to avoid causing offence.

**Meaghan Delahunt** *To The Island* Novel of an Australian woman travelling with her young son to Náxos, to meet the father she has never met, and encountering also his past, as a political activist tortured by the junta. Not your usual travelogue.

**Oriana Fallaci** *A Man* (o/p). Gripping tale of the junta years, based on the author's involvement with Alekos Panagoulis, the army officer who attempted to assassinate Colonel Papadopoulos in 1968 – and who himself died in mysterious circumstances in 1975.

★ **John Fowles** *The Magus*. Fowles' biggest and best tale of mystery and manipulation – plus Greek island life – based on his stay on Spétses as a teacher during the 1950s. A period piece that repays revisiting.

**Victoria Hislop** *The Island; The Thread*. The former leper colony of Spinalonga forms the backdrop to *The Island*, a huge-selling novel about a young woman discovering her Cretan roots. A potentially good story is marred by the cloying, derivative nature of its telling. *The Thread* attempts a similar uncovering of little-known history interwoven with family secrets, set in Thessaloníki.

**Olivia Manning** *The Balkan Trilogy, Volume 3: Friends and Heroes*. Wonderfully observed tale, in which Guy and Harriet Pringle escape from Bucharest to Athens, in the last months before the 1941 invasion.

**Steven Pressfield** *Gates of Fire; Alexander: The Virtues of War*. Two of several Greek-set historical novels by Pressfield. *Gates of Fire*, his bestselling first, is a stirring tale of the Spartans at Thermopylae; later books, including *The Virtues of War* – in which Alexander the Great recounts his warrior's life to brother-in-law Itanes in a first-person narrative – are rather more measured.

**Evelyn Waugh** *Officers and Gentlemen*. This second volume of Waugh's brilliant, acerbic wartime trilogy includes an account of the Battle of Crete and subsequent evacuation.

### GREEK FICTION

★ **Apostolos Doxiadis** *Uncle Petros and Goldbach's Conjecture*. Uncle Petros is the disgraced family black sheep, living reclusively in outer Athens; his nephew discovers that Petros had staked everything to solve a theorem unsolved for centuries. Math-phobes take heart; it's more a meditation on how best to spend life, and what really constitutes success.

**Vangelis Hatziyannidis** Hatziyannidis' abiding obsessions – confinement, blackmail, abrupt disappearances – get a workout in his creepy debut novel *Four Walls*, set on an unspecified east Aegean isle, where a reclusive landowner takes in a fugitive woman who convinces him to revive his father's honey trade – with unexpected consequences. His next novel, *Stolen Time*, revisits the same themes as an impoverished student gets a tidy fee from a mysterious tribunal for agreeing to spend two weeks in the Hotel from Hell.

★ **Panos Karnezis** Karnezis has become the most accessible, and feted, Greek writer since the millennium. He grew up in Greece but now lives in London, writing in English; however, his concerns remain utterly Greek. *Little Infamies* is a collection of short stories set in his native Peloponnese during the late 1950s and early 1960s; the

*Maze* is a darker-shaded, more successful novel concerning the Asia Minor Catastrophe. More recent works include *The Birthday Party*, based on events in the life of Aristotle Onassis and daughter Christina, and *The Convent*, a gentle whodunnit with nuns.

**Nikos Kazantzakis** *Zorba the Greek; The Last Temptation of Christ; Christ Recrucified/The Greek Passion; Freedom and Death; The Fratricides; Report to Greco.* Kazantzakis can be hard going, yet the power of his writing shines through. *Zorba the Greek* is a dark, nihilistic work, worlds away from the two-dimensional film. By contrast, the movie version of *The Last Temptation of Christ* – specifically Jesus's vision, once crucified, of a normal life with Mary Magdalene – provoked riots among Orthodox fanatics in Athens in 1989. *Christ Recrucified (The Greek Passion)* resets the Easter drama against the backdrop of Christian/Muslim relations, while *Freedom and Death,* perhaps his most approachable,

chronicles the rebellions of nineteenth-century Crete. *The Fratricides* portrays a family riven by the civil war. *Report to Greco* is an autobiographical exploration of his Cretan-ness.

**Artemis Leontis (ed)** *Greece: A Traveler's Literary Companion.* A nice idea, brilliantly executed: various regions of the country as portrayed in (very) short fiction or essays by modern Greek writers.

**Alexandros Papadiamantis** *Tales from a Greek Island; The Murderess.* The island is Skiáthos, Papadiamantis' birthplace. These quasi-mythic tales of grim fate come from a nineteenth-century writer ("the inventor of modern Greek fiction") comparable to Hardy and Maupassant.

★ **Dido Sotiriou** *Farewell Anatolia.* A perennial favourite since publication in 1962, this chronicles the traumatic end of Greek life in Asia Minor, from World War I to the 1922 catastrophe, as narrated by a fictionalized version of Sotiriou's father.

## ANCIENT GREECE

**A.R. Burn** *Penguin History of Greece.* A classic account; packed and informative on everything from philosophy to military history.

★ **Walter Burkert** *Greek Religion: Archaic and Classical.* Superb overview of deities and their attributes and antecedents, the protocol of sacrifice and the symbolism of festivals. Especially good on relating Greek worship to its predecessors in the Middle East.

**Paul Cartledge** *Cambridge Illustrated History of Ancient*

*Greece* or *Ancient Greece: A Very Short Introduction.* Two excellent general introductions to ancient Greece; choose between brief paperback or large illustrated tome.

**Paul Cartledge** *Alexander the Great: The Hunt for a New Past.* An evocative, meticulous and accessible biography, stinting neither on the man's brutality nor his achievements.

**James Davidson** *Courtesans and Fishcakes.* Absorbing book on the politics, class characteristics and etiquette of

## THE CLASSICS

Many of the classics make excellent companions for a trip around Greece; reading Homer's Odyssey when battling the vagaries of island ferries puts your own plight into perspective. Most of these good beginners' choices are published in a range of paperback editions. Particularly outstanding translations are noted.

★ **Mary Beard and John Henderson** *The Classics: A Very Short Introduction.* Exactly as it promises: an excellent overview.

**Herodotus** *The Histories.* Revered as the father of narrative history – and anthropology – this fifth-century BC Anatolian writer chronicled both the causes and campaigns of the Persian Wars, as well as the assorted tribes and nations inhabiting Asia Minor.

★ **Homer** *The Iliad* and *The Odyssey.* The first concerns itself, semi-factually, with the late Bronze Age war of the Achaeans against Troy in Asia Minor; the second recounts the hero Odysseus's long journey home, via seemingly every corner of the Mediterranean. The best prose translations are by Martin Hammond, and in verse Richmond Lattimore. For a stirring if very loose verse *Iliad,* try also Christopher Logue's recent version, *War Music.*

**Ovid** *The Metamorphoses.* Ovid was a first-century AD

Roman poet, but his masterpiece includes accessible renditions of the more piquant Greek myths, involving transformations as divine blessing or curse. Excellent verse translation by David Raeburn; prose version A.D. Melville.

**Pausanias** *The Guide to Greece.* Effectively the first-ever guidebook, intended for Roman pilgrims to central mainland and Peloponnesian sanctuaries. Invaluable for later archeologists in assessing damage or change to temples over time, or (in some cases) locating them at all. The two-volume Penguin edition is usefully annotated with the later history and nomenclature of the sites.

★ **Thucydides** *History of the Peloponnesian War.* Bleak month-by-month account of the conflict, by a cashiered Athenian officer whose affiliation and dim view of human nature didn't usually obscure his objectivity.

**Xenophon** *The History of My Times.* Thucydides' account of the Peloponnesian War stops in 411 BC; this eyewitness account continues events until 362 BC.

consumption and consummation – with wine, women, boys and seafood – in Classical Athens.

⭐ **Paul Cartledge** *The Spartans: The World of the Warrior-Heroes of Ancient Greece*. Reassessment of this much-maligned city-state, secretive and a source of outsider speculation even in its own time.

⭐ **M.I. Finley** *The World of Odysseus*. Reprint of a 1954 warhorse, pioneering in its investigation of the historicity (or not) of the events and society related by Homer. Breezily readable and stimulating.

**Simon Hornblower** *The Greek World 479–323 BC*. An erudite, up-to-date survey of ancient Greece at its zenith, from the end of the Persian Wars to the death of Alexander.

**Mary Lefkowitz** *Greek Gods, Human Lives: What We Can Learn from Myths*. Rather than being frivolous, immoral or irrelevant, ancient religion and its myths, in their bleak indifference of the gods to human suffering, are shown as being more "grown up" than the later creeds of salvation and comfort.

**Oswyn Murray** *Early Greece*. The story of Greece from the Minoans and Mycenaeans through to the beginning of the Classical period.

**Robin Osborne** *Greece in the Making 1200–479 BC*. Well-illustrated paperback on the rise of the city-state.

**Robin Lane Fox** *Alexander the Great*. Another absorbing study, mixing historical scholarship with imaginative psychological detail.

**F.W. Walbank** *The Hellenistic World*. Greece under the sway of the Macedonian and Roman empires.

## MEDIEVAL AND MODERN HISTORY

**Timothy Boatswain and Colin Nicolson** *A Traveller's History of Greece*. Well-written overview of crucial Greek periods and personalities, from earliest times to the end of the twentieth century.

⭐ **Richard Clogg** *A Concise History of Greece*. If you read only one title on "modern" Greek history, this should be it: a remarkably clear account, from the decline of Byzantium to 2000, with numerous maps and feature captions to the well-chosen artwork.

**C.M. Woodhouse** *Modern Greece: A Short History*. Woodhouse was a key liaison officer with the Greek Resistance during World War II, and later a Conservative MP. Writing from a more right-wing perspective than Clogg, his account – from the foundation of Constantinople to 1990 – is briefer and drier, but scrupulous with facts.

### BYZANTINE, MEDIEVAL AND OTTOMAN GREECE

**David Brewer** *Greece, the Hidden Centuries: Turkish Rule from the Fall of Constantinople to Greek Independence*. Readable yet authoritative history of this little-explored era of Greek history.

**Nicholas Cheetham** *Medieval Greece* (o/p). A general survey of the period's infinite convolutions in Greece, with Frankish, Catalan, Venetian, Byzantine and Ottoman struggles for power.

⭐ **John Julius Norwich** *Byzantium: The Early Centuries*; *Byzantium: the Apogee* and *Byzantium: The Decline*. Perhaps the main surprise for first-time travellers to Greece is the fascination of its Byzantine monuments. This is an astonishingly detailed yet readable – often witty – trilogy of the empire that produced them. There's also an excellent, one-volume abridged version, *A Short History of Byzantium*.

⭐ **Roger Crowley** *Constantinople: The Last Great Siege, 1453*. Thrillingly readable narrative of perhaps the key event of the Middle Ages, and its repercussions throughout Europe and the Islamic world.

### INDEPENDENT GREECE

⭐ **John S. Koliopoulos and Thanos M. Veremis** *Greece: The Modern Sequel, from 1831 to the Present*. Thematic rather than chronological study that pokes into corners rarely illuminated by conventional histories; especially good on Macedonian issues, brigandage and the Communists.

**David Brewer** *The Flame of Freedom: The Greek War of Independence 1821–1833* (o/p). The finest narrative of revolutionary events (with some black-and-white illustrations), strong on the background of Ottoman Greece as well as the progress of the war.

⭐ **Michael Llewellyn Smith** *Ionian Vision: Greece in Asia Minor, 1919–22*. Still the best work on the disastrous Anatolian campaign, which led to the population exchanges between Greece and Turkey.

### WORLD WAR II AND THE CIVIL WAR

⭐ **David H. Close** *The Origins of the Greek Civil War*. Excellent, even-handed study that focuses on the social conditions in 1920s and 1930s Greece that made the country so ripe for conflict; draws on primary sources to overturn various received wisdoms.

**Nicholas Gage** *Eleni*. Controversial account by a Greek-born *New York Times* correspondent who returns to Epirus to avenge the death of his mother, condemned by an ELAS tribunal in 1948. Good descriptions of village life, but the book has its agenda and its political "history" is at best selective.

**Iakovos Kambanellis, translated by Gail Holst-Warhaft** *Mauthausen*. Kambanellis was active in the Resistance, caught, and sent to Mauthausen, a concentration camp for politicians or partisans who opposed the Nazis' rise to power. Harrowing atrocities in flashback there are aplenty, but the book dwells equally on post-liberation, as the initially idealist inmates realize that the "New World Order" will be scarcely different from the

## BOOKS FOR KIDS

The Greek myths and legends are perfect holiday reading for kids; they're available in a huge number of versions aimed at all ages, often lavishly illustrated.

**Terry Deary** *Groovy Greeks; Greek Tales* and the *Fire Thief* trilogy. The first of these is from Deary's familiar Horrible Histories series; the three books of *Greek Tales* take a sideways look at famous myths; the *Fire Thief* is a comedy-fantasy series based on Prometheus, who stole fire from the gods.

**Caroline Lawrence** *The Roman Mysteries*. The final two volumes of this authentically detailed series of Roman-era mystery books for 8- to 11-year-olds, *The Colossus of Rhodes* and *Fugitive from Corinth*, are set in Greece.

**Mary Renault** *The King Must Die; The Last of the Wine; The Masks of Apollo; The Praise Singer; The Alexander*

*Trilogy*. The style may be a tad dense and dated, but these retellings of great Greek stories remain classics of historical fiction.

**Rick Riordan** *Percy Jackson* series. A modern setting infused with Greek mythology as Percy Jackson, twelve years old and dyslexic, discovers he is the modern-day son of a Greek god. Gripping, best-selling tales.

**Franzcesca Simon** *Helping Hercules*. Fans of *Horrid Henry* will enjoy this clever retelling of Greek myths by the same author, where young heroine Susan sorts out the not-so-heroic heroes.

---

old. The basis of a play, and the eponymous Theodhorakis oratorio.

★ **Mark Mazower** *Inside Hitler's Greece: The Experience of Occupation 1941–44*. Eccentrically organized, but the scholarship is top-drawer and the photos magnificent. Demonstrates how the utter demoralization of the country and incompetence of conventional politicians led to the rise of ELAS and the onset of civil war.

★ **Eddie Myers** *Greek Entanglement* (o/p). The inside

story of sabotaging the Gorgopotamos viaduct by the British brigadier who led it, and lots else about co-ordinating the resistance from 1942 to 1944. Myers comes across as being under no illusions about the various Greek guerrillas he dealt with.

★ **C.M. Woodhouse** *The Struggle for Greece, 1941–49*. Masterly, well-illustrated account of the so-called "three rounds" of resistance and rebellion, and how Greece emerged without a communist government.

## ART AND ARCHEOLOGY

**A.R. and Mary Burn** *The Living Past of Greece: A Time Traveller's Tour of Historic and Prehistoric Places* (o/p). This wide-ranging guide covers sites from Minoan through to Byzantine and Frankish, with good clear plans and lively text.

**Mary Beard** *The Parthenon*. Compelling, readable reassessment of the building, both in terms of its real purpose and the possible meaning of its relief sculptures, in light of the discoveries made during its ongoing reconstruction.

**John Boardman** *Greek Art*. An evergreen study in the *World of Art* series, first published in 1964. For more detailed treatment, there are three period volumes entitled *Greek Sculpture: Archaic Period, Classical Period* and *The Late Classical Period*.

**Paul Hetherington** *Byzantine and Medieval Greece:*

*Churches, Castles and Art of the Mainland and Peloponnese* (o/p). A gazetteer of all major mainland sites – readable, authoritative and with useful plans. His more recent *The Greek Islands: Guide to Byzantine and Medieval Buildings and their Art*, is equally good, with more illustrations, though there are some peculiar omissions.

**Reynold Higgins** *Minoan and Mycenaean Art*. Concise, well-illustrated round-up of the culture of Mycenae, Crete and the Cyclades, again part of the *World of Art* series.

**R.R.R. Smith** *Hellenistic Sculpture*. Appraisal of the art of Greece under Alexander and his successors; yet another *World of Art* title.

**James Witley** *The Archaeology of Ancient Greece*. An excellent overview of current scholarship, not overly academic.

## PEOPLE AND CULTURE

★ **Bruce Clark** *Twice a Stranger: How Mass Expulsion Forged Modern Greece and Turkey*. The build-up to and execution of the 1923 population exchanges, and how both countries are still digesting the experience eight-plus decades on. Compassionate and readable, especially the encounters with elderly refugees and oral histories.

**Rae Dalven** *The Jews of Ioannina*. History and culture of the thriving pre-Holocaust community, related by the poet-translator of Cavafy, herself an Epirot Jew.

**Renée Hirschon** *Heirs of the Greek Catastrophe: the Social Life of Asia Minor Refugees in Piraeus*. Wherein a district in Kokkinia maintained a separate identity for three generations after 1923. It's inevitably nostalgic, as increasing wealth has largely dissolved the community, but helps explain why Athens is so higgledy-piggledy.

★ **Gail Holst** *Road to Rembetika: Music of a Greek Subculture*. The most intriguing Greek urban musical style of the past century, evocatively traced by a Cornell

## GREEK POETRY

Modern Greece has an intense and dynamic poetic tradition. Two Greek poets – George Seféris and Odysseus Elýtis – have won the Nobel prize for literature; along with C.P. Caváfy, from an earlier generation, and Yiánnis Rítsos they are the great names of modern Greek poetry. Good English translations of pretty much all of their work are widely available, or try these anthologies:

**Peter Bien, Peter Constantine, Edmund Keeley, Karen Van Dyck, eds** *A Century of Greek Poetry, 1900–2000* (o/p). Superb bilingual anthology, with some lesser-known surprises alongside the big names.

**Nanos Valaoritis and Thanasis Maskaleris, eds** *An Anthology of Modern Greek Poetry*. English-only text, but excellent biographical info on the poets and good translations by two native Greek-speakers.

University professor and long-term observer of the Greek music scene.

**Anastasia Karakasidou** *Fields of Wheat, Hills of Blood*. Controversial work establishing how Macedonia only became "Greek" politically and ethnically in the early twentieth century, through an official Hellenization process. Initially declined for publication by Cambridge University Press after ultra-nationalists' threats both in Greece and the diaspora.

**John Cuthbert Lawson** *Modern Greek Folklore and Ancient Greek Religion: A Study in Survivals*. Exactly as it says: a fascinating, thorough study still applicable a century after first publication.

**Mark Mazower** *Salonica, City of Ghosts: Christians, Muslims and Jews 1450–1950*. Beautifully written book that masterfully records how this multi-ethnic port, the most cosmopolitan European city under Ottoman rule, became homogeneously Greek Orthodox.

★ **John L. Tomkinson** *Festive Greece: A Calendar of Tradition*. Copiously photographed gazetteer by date of festivals and events; Christian, pagan, political or plain bizarre.

### FOOD AND WINE

★ **Rosemary Barron** *Flavours of Greece*. The leading Greek cookbook – among many contenders – by an internationally recognized authority. Constantly reprinted, with over 250 recipes and background info.

**Andrew Dalby** *Siren Feasts: A History of Food and Gastronomy in Greece*; *Tastes of Byzantium: The Cuisine of a Legendary Empire*. *Siren Feasts* demonstrates just how little

Greek cuisine has changed in three millennia; also excellent on the introduction and etymology of common vegetables and herbs. *Tastes of Byzantium* adds the influences of Rome, Turkey and the Middle East.

**Konstantinos Lazarakis** *The Wines of Greece*. An excellent, up-to-2005 overview of what's happening in Greece's eleven recognized wine-producing regions.

### ACTIVITIES

**Lance Chilton** Various walking pamphlets (⊕ marengowalks.com). Small but thorough guides to the best walks at various mainland and island resorts, accompanied by three-colour maps.

**Tim Salmon, with Michael Cullen** *The Mountains of Greece: A Walker's Guide*. Updated in 2006, this volume sticks strictly to the mainland, covering mounts Pílio, Ólymbos, Áthos, the Peloponnese and the best of the Píndhos, from Delphi to Albania.

**Loraine Wilson** *The High Mountains of Crete: A Walking and Trekking Guide*. Over eighty walks and treks, from easy to gruelling, by the doyenne of foreign trekking guides in Crete; trustworthy directions and prudent warnings.

**Rod Heikell** *Greek Waters Pilot*. An indispensible reference for yachting in the Aegean or Ionian seas, updated in 2011; various regional sub-guides are available.

# Greek

So many Greeks have lived or worked abroad that you will find English-speakers in the tiniest island village. Add the thousands attending language schools or working in the tourist industry – English is the lingua franca of most resorts – and it's easy to see how so many visitors return home having learned only minimal restaurant vocabulary. You can certainly get by this way but it isn't very satisfying, and the willingness and ability to say even a few words will transform your status from that of dumb "tourístas" to the more honourable one of "xénos/xéni", which can mean foreigner, traveller and guest all combined.

## Learning basic Greek

**Greek** is not an easy language for English-speakers but it is a very beautiful one, and even a brief acquaintance will give you an idea of the debt owed to it by Western European languages. Greek **grammar** is predictably complicated; **nouns** are divided into three genders, all with different case endings in the singular and in the plural, and all adjectives and articles have to agree with these in gender, number and case. To simplify things, all adjectives are cited in the neuter form in the lists on the following pages. **Verbs** are even more complex; they're in two conjugations, in both active and passive voices, with passively constructed verbs often having transitive sense. As a novice, it's best to simply say what you want the way you know it, and dispense with the niceties.

### TEACH-YOURSELF GREEK COURSES

**Alison Kakoura and Karen Rich** *Talk Greek* (book and 2 CDs). Probably the best in-print product for beginners' essentials, and for developing the confidence to try them.

**Anne Farmakides** *A Manual of Modern Greek, 1, for University Students*. If you have the discipline and motivation, this is among the best for learning proper, grammatical Greek.

**Hara Garoufalia et al** *Read & Speak Greek for Beginners* (book & CD). Unlike many quickie courses, this provides a good grammatical foundation; new in 2008.

**David Holton et al** *Greek: A Comprehensive Grammar of the Modern Language*. A bit technical, so not for rank beginners, but it covers almost every conceivable construction.

**Aristarhos Matsukas** *Teach Yourself Greek* (book and optional cassettes or CDs). Another complete course, touching on idiomatic expressions too.

### PHRASEBOOKS AND DICTIONARIES

**Rough Guide Greek Phrasebook** Current, accurate and pocket-sized, with phrases that you'll actually need. The English–Greek section is transliterated, though the Greek–English part requires mastery of the Greek alphabet.

**The Pocket Oxford Greek Dictionary** J. T. Pring. A bit bulky for travel, but generally considered the best Greek–

English, English–Greek paperback dictionary.

**Collins Pocket Greek Dictionary** Harry T. Hionides. Very nearly as complete as the *Pocket Oxford* and probably better value for money. The inexpensive *Collins Gem Greek Dictionary* (UK only) is palm-sized but identical in contents – the best day-pack choice.

## The Greek alphabet: transliteration and accents

Besides the usual difficulties of learning a new language, Greek has an entirely separate **alphabet**. Despite initial appearances, this is in practice fairly easily mastered – a skill that will help enormously in getting around independently. In addition, certain combinations of letters have unexpected results. This book's **transliteration system** (see below) should help you make intelligible noises, but remember that the correct **stress** (marked throughout the book with an acute accent or sometimes dieresis) is crucial. With the right sounds but the wrong stress people will either fail to understand you, or else understand something quite different.

The **dieresis** (¨) is used in Greek over the second of two adjacent vowels to change the pronunciation; often in this book it can function as the primary stress. In the word *kaïki* (caique), the use of a dieresis changes the pronunciation from "keh-key" to "ka-ee-key". In the word *païdhákia* (lamb chops), the dieresis changes the sound of the first syllable from "peh" to "pah-ee", but in this case the primary stress is on the third syllable. It is also, uniquely among Greek accents, used on capital letters in signs and personal-name spellings in Greece, and we have followed this practice on our maps.

| GREEK | TRANSLITERATION | PRONOUNCED |
|---|---|---|
| A, α | a | a as in father |
| B, β | v | v as in vet |
| Γ, γ | y/g | y as in yes except before consonants or a, o or ou when it's a breathy g, approximately as in gap |
| Δ, δ | dh | th as in then |
| E, ε | e | e as in get |
| Z, ζ | z | z sound |
| H, η | i | i as in ski |
| Θ, θ | th | th as in theme |
| I, ι | i | i as in ski |
| K, κ | k | k sound |
| Λ, λ | l | l sound |
| M, μ | m | m sound |
| N, ν | n | n sound |
| Ξ, ξ | x | ks sound, never z |
| O, o | o | o as in box |
| Π, π | p | p sound |
| P, ρ | r | r sound, lightly rolled as in Scottish |
| Σ, σ, ς | s | ss sound, except z before m or g |
| T, τ | t | t sound |
| Y, υ | y | i as in ski |
| Φ, φ | f | f sound |
| X, χ | h before vowels, denoted kh before consonants but pronounced the same | harsh h sound, like ch in loch |
| Ψ, ψ | ps | ps as in lips |
| Ω, ω | o | o as in box, indistinguishable from o |

## COMBINATIONS AND DIPHTHONGS

| | | |
|---|---|---|
| AI, αι | e | e as in get |
| AY, αυ | av/af | av before voiced consonants and vowels af before voiceless consonents |
| EI, ει | i | i as in ski |
| EY, ευ | ev/ef | ev before voiced consonants and vowels ef before voiceless consonents |
| OI, οι | i | i as in ski |
| OY, ου | ou | ou as in tourist |
| ΓΓ, γγ | ng | ng as in angle; always medial |
| ΜΠ, μπ | b/mb | b at start of a word, mb if medial |
| NT, ντ | d/nd | d at start of a word, nd if medial |

## THE QUEST FOR "PURE" GREEK

When Greece achieved independence in 1832, its people were mostly illiterate, and the spoken language – **dhimotikí**, "demotic" or "popular" Greek – had undergone enormous change since the Byzantine and Classical eras. The vocabulary had numerous loan-words from the languages of the various invaders and conquerors – especially Turks, Venetians and Slavs – and the grammar had been considerably streamlined since ancient times.

The leaders of the new Greek state, filled with romantic notions of Greece's past glories, set about purging the language of foreign words and reviving its Classical purity. They accordingly created what was in effect an artificial language, **katharévoussa** (literally "cleansed" Greek). Long-forgotten words and phrases were reintroduced and complex Classical grammar reinstated. *Katharévoussa* became the language of the schools, government, business, the law, newspapers and academia. Everyone aspiring to membership in the elite strove to master it.

The split between *katharévoussa* and *dhimotikí* quickly took on a **political** dimension with intellectuals and left-wing politicians championing the demotic form, while the right, notably the colonel's junta of 1967–74, insisted on the "purer" *katharévoussa*. *Dhimotikí* returned permanently after the fall of the colonels, though the Church and the legal profession still persist with *katharévoussa*.

All this has reduced, but not eliminated, confusion. The Metaxás dictatorship of the 1930s changed scores of village names from Slavic, Turkish or Albanian words to Greek ones – often reviving the name of the nearest ancient site. These official **place names** still hold sway on most road signs and maps – even though the local people may use the *dhimotikí* or non-Greek form. Thus for example you will see "Plomárion" or "Spétsai" written, while everyone actually says "Plomári" or "Spétses".

## Polite forms and questions

Greek makes the distinction between the **informal** (*essý*) and **formal** (*essís*) second person, like the French "tu" and "vous". Young people and country people often use *essý* even with total strangers, though it's best to address everyone formally until/unless they start using the familiar with you, to avoid offence. By far the most common greeting, on meeting and parting, is *yiásou/yiásas* (literally "health to you").

To ask a **question**, it's simplest, though hardly elegant, to start with *parakaló* (please), then name the thing you want in an interrogative tone.

### GREEK WORDS AND PHRASES

**ESSENTIALS**

| | | | |
|---|---|---|---|
| Hérete/Yiássas | Hello | Pós se léne? | What's your name? |
| Kalíméra | Good morning | Mé léne … | My name is … |
| Kalíspéra | Good evening | Kýrios/Kyría | Mr/Mrs |
| Kalíníkhta | Goodnight | Dhespinís | Miss |
| Adío | Goodbye | Parakaló, o …? | Where is the …? |
| Tí kánis/Tí kánete? | How are you? | Dhén xéro | I don't know |
| Kalá íme | I'm fine | Thá sé dhó ávrio | See you tomorrow |
| Ké essís? | And you? | Kalí andhámosi | See you soon |
| Né | Yes | Páme | Let's go |
| Óhi | No | Parakaló, ná mé voithíste | Please help me |
| Parakaló | Please | (Dhen) Trógo/píno | I (don't) eat/drink |
| Efharistó (polý) | Thank you (very much) | (Dhen) Mou aréssi | I (don't) like |
| Sygnómi | Sorry/excuse me | Málista | Certainly |
| Miláte angliká? | Do you speak English? | Endáxi | OK, agreed |
| (Dhén) Katalavéno | I (don't) understand | Anikhtó | Open |
| Parakaló, na milísate pió sigá | Speak slower, please | Klistó | Closed |
| | | Méra | Day |
| Pós léyete avtó stá Elliniká? | How do you say it in Greek? | Nýkhta | Night |
| | | Edhó | Here |

| | |
|---|---|
| **Ekí** | There |
| **Grígora** | Quickly |
| **Sigá** | Slowly |
| **Poú?** | Where? |
| **Pós?** | How? |
| **Póte?** | When? |
| **Yiatí?** | Why? |
| **Tí óra … ?** | At what time … ? |
| **Tí íne/Pió íne … ?** | What is/Which is … ? |

## ACCOMMODATION

| | |
|---|---|
| **Parakaló, éna dhomátio** | We'd like a room |
| **yiá éna/dhýo/tría átoma** | for one/two/three people |
| **yiá mía/dhýo/trís vradhiés** | for one/two/three nights |
| **mé dhipló kreváti** | with a double bed |
| **mé doús** | with a shower |
| **Xenodhohío** | Hotel |
| **Xenón(as)** | Inn |
| **Xenónas neótitas** | Youth hostel |
| **Zestó neró** | Hot water |
| **Krýo neró** | Cold water |
| **Klimatismós** | Air conditioning |
| **Anamistíra** | Fan |
| **Boró ná tó dhó?** | Can I see it? |
| **Boroúme na váloume ti skiní edhó?** | Can we camp here? |
| **Kámping/Kataskínosi** | Campsite |

## SHOPPING AND SERVICES

| | |
|---|---|
| **Póso (káni)?** | How much (does it cost)? |
| **Tí óra aníyi/ klíni?** | What time does it open/ close? |
| **Parakaló, éna kiló portokália?** | May I have a kilo of oranges? |
| **Póssi, pósses or póssa?** | How many? |
| **Aftó** | This one |
| **Ekíno** | That one |
| **Kaló** | Good |
| **Kakó** | Bad |
| **Megálo** | Big |
| **Mikró** | Small |
| **Perisótero** | More |
| **Ligótero** | Less |
| **Lígo** | A little |
| **Polý** | A lot |
| **Ftinó** | Cheap |
| **Akrivó** | Expensive |
| **Mazí (mé)** | With (together) |
| **Horís** | Without |
| **Foúrnos** | Bakery |
| **Farmakío** | Pharmacy |
| **Tahydhromío** | Post office |

| | |
|---|---|
| **Gramatósima** | Stamps |
| **Venzinádhiko** | Petrol station |
| **Trápeza** | Bank |
| **Leftá/Khrímata** | Money |
| **Toualéta** | Toilet |
| **Astynomía** | Police |
| **Yiatrós** | Doctor |
| **Nosokomío** | Hospital |

## ON THE MOVE

| | |
|---|---|
| **Parakaló, ó dhrómos yiá … ?** | Can you show me the road to … ? |
| **Aeropláno** | Aeroplane |
| **Leoforío, púlman** | Bus, coach |
| **Aftokínito, amáxi** | Car |
| **Mihanáki, papáki** | Motorbike, scooter |
| **Taxí** | Taxi |
| **Plío/vapóri/karávi** | Ship |
| **Tahyplóö, katamarán** | High-speed boat, catamaran |
| **Dhelfíni** | Hydrofoil |
| **Tréno** | Train |
| **Sidhirodhromikós stathmós** | Train station |
| **Podhílato** | Bicycle |
| **Otostóp** | Hitching |
| **Mé tá pódhia** | On foot |
| **Monopáti** | Trail |
| **Praktorío leoforíon KTEL** | Bus station |
| **Stási** | Bus stop |
| **Limáni** | Harbour |
| **Ti óra févyi?** | What time does it leave? |
| **Ti óra ftháni?** | What time does it arrive? |
| **Póssa hiliómetra?** | How many kilometres? |
| **Pósses óres?** | How many hours? |
| **Poú páte/pás?** | Where are you going? |
| **Páo stó …** | I'm going to … |
| **Thélo ná katévo stó …** | I want to get off at … |
| **O dhrómos yiá …** | The road to … |
| **Kondá** | Near |
| **Makriá** | Far |
| **Aristerá** | Left |
| **Dhexiá** | Right |
| **Katefthía/ísia** | Straight ahead |
| **Éna isitírio yiá …** | A ticket to … |
| **Éna isitírio aplí/mé epistrofí** | A ticket one-way/ return |
| **Paralía** | Beach |
| **Spiliá** | Cave |
| **Kéndro** | Centre (of town) |
| **Eklissía** | Church |
| **Thálassa** | Sea |
| **Horió** | Village |

## NUMBERS

| | |
|---|---|
| énas/éna/mía | 1 |
| dhýo | 2 |
| trís/tría | 3 |
| tésseris/tésseres/téssera | 4 |
| pénde | 5 |
| éxi | 6 |
| eftá | 7 |
| okhtó | 8 |
| ennéa (or, in slang, enyá) | 9 |
| dhéka | 10 |
| éndheka | 11 |
| dhódheka | 12 |
| dhekatrís | 13 |
| dhekatésseres | 14 |
| íkossi | 20 |
| íkossi éna | 21 |
| triánda | 30 |
| saránda | 40 |
| penínda | 50 |
| exínda | 60 |
| evdhomínda | 70 |
| ogdhónda | 80 |
| enenínda | 90 |
| ekató | 100 |
| ekatón penínda | 150 |
| dhiakóssies/ dhiakóssia | 200 |
| pendakóssies/ pendakóssia | 500 |
| hílies/hília | 1000 |
| dhlo hiliádhes | 2000 |
| próto | first |
| dhéftero | second |
| tríto | third |

## TIME AND DAYS OF THE WEEK

| | |
|---|---|
| Tóra | Now |
| Argótera | Later |
| Símera | Today |
| Ávrio | Tomorrow |
| Khthés | Yesterday |
| Tó proï | In the morning |
| Tó apóyevma | In the afternoon |
| Tó vrádhi | In the evening |
| Kyriakí | Sunday |
| Dheftéra | Monday |
| Tríti | Tuesday |
| Tetárti | Wednesday |
| Pémpti | Thursday |
| Paraskeví | Friday |
| Sávato | Saturday |
| Tí óra íne? | What time is it? |
| Mía íy óra/dhýo iy óra/trís íy óra | One/two/three o'clock |
| Tésseres pará íkossi | Twenty minutes to four |
| Eftá ké pénde | Five minutes past seven |
| Éndheka ké misí | Half past eleven |
| Sé misí óra | In half an hour |
| S'éna tétarto | In a quarter-hour |
| Sé dhýo óres | In two hours |

## MONTHS AND SEASONS

| | |
|---|---|
| Yennáris | January |
| Fleváris | February |
| Mártis | March |
| Aprílis | April |
| Maïos | May |
| Ioúnios | June |
| Ioúlios | July |
| Ávgoustos | August |
| Septémvris | September |
| Októvris | October |
| Noémvris | November |
| Dhekémvris | December |
| Therinó dhromolóyio | Summer schedule |
| Himerinó dhromolóyio | Winter schedule |

# A food and drink glossary

## BASICS

| | |
|---|---|
| Katálogos, menoú | Menu |
| O logariasmós | The bill |
| Zestó | Hot |
| Krýo | Cold |
| (Horís) ládhi | (Without) oil |
| Hortofágos | Vegetarian |
| Kréas | Meat |
| Lahaniká | Vegetables |
| Neró | Water |
| Psári(a) | Fish |
| Thalassiná | Seafood |
| Aláti | Salt |
| Avgá | Eggs |
| Méli | Honey |
| Psomí.... | Bread... |
|   Olikís | Wholemeal |
|   Sikalísio | Rye |
|   Kalambokísio | Corn |
| Tyrí | Cheese |
| Yiaoúrti | Yoghurt |
| Záhari | Sugar |

## GREEK'S GREEK

There are numerous words and phrases which you will hear constantly, even if you don't have the chance to use them. These are a few of the most common.

| | | | |
|---|---|---|---|
| **Éla!** | Come (literally) but also Speak to me! You don't say! etc. | **Po-po-po!** | Expression of dismay or concern, like French "O là là!" |
| **Oríste!** | Literally, Define!; in effect, What can I do for you? | **Pedhí moú** | My boy/girl, sonny, friend, etc. |
| **Embrós!/Léyete!** | Standard phone responses | **Maláka(s)** | Literally "wanker", but often used (don't try it!) as an informal term of address |
| **Tí néa?** | What's new? | | |
| **Tí yínete?** | What's going on? | | |
| **Étsi k'étsi** | So-so | **Sigá sigá** | Take your time, slow down |
| **Ópa!** | Whoops! Watch it! | **Kaló taxídhi** | Bon voyage |

## COOKING TERMS

| | |
|---|---|
| **Akhnistó** | Steamed |
| **Frikasé** | Stew, either lamb, goat or pork, with celery |
| **Iliókafto** | Sun-dried |
| **Kokkinistó** | Cooked in tomato sauce |
| **Kourkoúti** | Egg-and-flour batter |
| **Krasáto** | Cooked in wine sauce |
| **Makaronádha** | Any spaghetti/ pasta-based dish |
| **Pastó** | Fish marinated in salt |
| **Petáli** | Butterflied fish, eel, shrimp |
| **Psitó** | Roasted |
| **Saganáki** | Cheese-based red sauce; also fried cheese |
| **Skáras** | Grilled |
| **Sti soúvla** | Spit-roasted |
| **Stó foúrno** | Baked |
| **Tiganitó** | Pan-fried |
| **Tís óras** | Grilled/fried to order |
| **Yakhní** | Stewed in oil and tomato sauce |
| **Yemistá** | Stuffed (squid, vegetables, etc) |

## SOUPS AND STARTERS

| | |
|---|---|
| **Avgolémono** | Egg and lemon soup |
| **Bouréki, bourekákia** | Courgette/zucchini, potato and cheese pie |
| **Dolmádhes, yaprákia yalantzí** | Vine leaves stuffed with rice and mince; with vegetables |
| **Fasoládha** | Bean soup |
| **Fáva** | Purée of yellow peas |
| **Féta psití** | Baked feta cheese slabs with chilli |
| **Galotýri** | Curdled creamy dip |
| **Hortópitta** | Pastry stuffed with greens |
| **Kápari** | Pickled caper leaves |
| **Kopanistí, khtypití** | Pungent, fermented cheese purée |
| **Lahanodolmádhes** | Stuffed cabbage leaves |
| **Mavromátika** | Black-eyed peas |
| **Melitzanosaláta** | Aubergine/eggplant dip |
| **Piperiés florínes** | Marinated sweet peppers |
| **Rengosaláta** | Herring salad |
| **Revythokeftédhes** | Chickpea/garbanzo patties |
| **Skordhaliá** | Garlic dip |
| **Soúpa** | Soup |
| **Strapatsádha** | Eggs scrambled with tomato and onions |
| **Taramosaláta** | Cod roe pâté |
| **Tiganópsomo** | Toasted oiled bread |
| **Trahanádhes** | Crushed wheat and milk soup, sweet or savoury |
| **Tyrokafterí** | Cheese dip with chilli |
| **Tzatzíki** | Yoghurt and cucumber dip |
| **Tzirosaláta** | Cured mackerel dip |

## VEGETABLES

| | |
|---|---|
| **Ambelofásola** | Runner beans |
| **Angináres** | Artichokes |
| **Angoúri** | Cucumber |
| **Ánitho** | Dill |
| **Bámies** | Okra/ladies' fingers |
| **Briám, tourloú** | Ratatouille |
| **Domátes** | Tomatoes |
| **Fakés** | Lentils |
| **Fasolákia** | French (green) beans |
| **Fasóles** | Small white beans |
| **Horiátiki (saláta)** | Greek salad (with olives, feta, etc) |
| **Hórta** | Steamed greens |

| | |
|---|---|
| **Kolokythákia** | Courgette/zucchini |
| **Koukiá** | Broad fava beans |
| **Maroúli** | Lettuce |
| **Melitzánes imám/ Imám baïldí** | Aubergine/eggplant slices baked with onion, garlic and copious olive oil |
| **Patátes** | Potatoes |
| **Piperiés** | Peppers |
| **Pligoúri, pinigoúri** | Bulgur wheat |
| **Radhíkia** | Wild chicory |
| **Rókka** | Rocket, arugula |
| **Rýzi/Piláfi sáltsa** | Rice (usually with sauce) |
| **Saláta** | Salad |
| **Spanáki** | Spinach |
| **Yígandes** | White haricot beans |

## FISH AND SEAFOOD

| | |
|---|---|
| **Ahini, foúskes** | Sea urchins |
| **Astakós** | Lobster |
| **Bakaliáros** | Cod or hake, usually latter |
| **Barbóuni** | Red mullet |
| **Fangrí** | Common bream |
| **Galéos** | Dogfish |
| **Garídhes** | Shrimp, prawns |
| **Gávros** | Mild anchovy |
| **Glóssa** | Sole |
| **Gónos, gonákia** | Any hatchling fish |
| **Gópa** | Bogue |
| **Hokhlí** | Sea snails |
| **Kalamarákia** | Baby squid |
| **Kalamária** | Squid |
| **Karavídhes** | Crayfish |
| **Koliós** | Chub mackerel |
| **Koutsomoúra** | Goatfish (small red mullet) |
| **Lakérdha** | Light-fleshed bonito, marinated |
| **Lithríni** | Red bream, pandora |
| **Melanoúri** | Saddled bream |
| **Ménoula** | Sprat |
| **Mýdhia** | Mussels |
| **Okhtapódhi** | Octopus |
| **Petalídhes** | Limpets |
| **Platý** | Skate, ray |
| **Sardhélles** | Sardines |
| **Sargós** | White bream |
| **Seláhi** | Skate, ray |
| **Sfyrídha** | White grouper |
| **Skáros** | Parrotfish |
| **Skathári** | Black bream |
| **Skoumbrí** | Atlantic mackerel |
| **Soupiá** | Cuttlefish |
| **Strídhia** | Oysters |
| **Thrápsalo** | Large, deep-water squid |
| **Tónos** | Tuna |

| | |
|---|---|
| **Tsipoúra** | Gilt-head bream |
| **Xifías** | Swordfish |
| **Yermanós** | Leatherback |
| **Yialisterés** | Smooth Venus; common ouzeri shellfish |

## MEAT AND POULTRY

| | |
|---|---|
| **Arní** | Lamb |
| **Bekrí mezé** | Pork chunks in spicy pepper sauce |
| **Biftéki** | Hamburger |
| **Brizóla hiriní** | Pork chop |
| **Brizóla moskharísia** | Beef chop |
| **Exohikó** | Lamb baked in tin foil or in pastry |
| **Hirinó** | Pork |
| **Keftédhes** | Meatballs |
| **Kókoras krasáto** | Coq au vin |
| **Kokorétsi** | Liver/offal roulade, spit-roasted |
| **Kondosoúvli** | Spit-roasted pork |
| **Kopsídha** | (Lamb) shoulder chops |
| **Kotópoulo** | Chicken |
| **Kounéli** | Rabbit |
| **Loukánika** | Spicy course-ground sausages |
| **Manári** | Spring lamb |
| **Moskhári** | Veal |
| **Moussakás** | Aubergine/eggplant, potato and lamb-mince casserole with béchamel topping |
| **Païdhákia** | Rib chops, lamb or goat |
| **Papoutsákia** | Stuffed aubergine/eggplant "shoes" |
| **Pastítsio** | Macaroni "pie" baked with minced meat |
| **Pastourmás** | Cured, highly spiced meat; traditionally camel, nowadays beef |
| **Patsás** | Tripe soup |
| **Patsitsádha** | beef with pasta in wine sauce |
| **Provatína** | Female mutton |
| **Psaronéfri** | Pork tenderloin medallions |
| **Salingária** | Garden snails |
| **Sofríto** | beef fried in garlic sauce |
| **Soutzoukákia** | Minced meat rissoles/ beef patties |
| **Spetzofáï** | Sausage and pepper stew |
| **Stifádho** | Meat stew with tomato and boiling onions |
| **Sykóti** | Liver |
| **Tiganiá** | Pork chunks fried with onions |

| | |
|---|---|
| Tziyéro sarmás | Lamb's liver in cabbage leaves |
| Yiouvétsi | Baked clay casserole of meat and pasta |
| Zygoúri | 1-to-2-year-old lamb |

## SWEETS AND DESSERT

| | |
|---|---|
| Baklavás | Honey and nut pastry |
| Bergamóndo | Bergamot |
| Bougátsa | Salt or sweet cream pie served warm with sugar and cinnamon |
| Galaktoboúriko | Custard pie |
| Glykó koutalioú | Spoon sweet (syrupy fruit preserve) |
| Halvás | Semolina- or sesame-based sweet meat |
| Karydhópita | Walnut cake |
| Kréma | Custard |
| Loukoumádhes | Dough fritters in honey syrup and sesame seeds |
| Pagotó | Ice cream |
| Pastélli | Sesame and honey bar |
| Ravaní | Sponge cake, lightly syruped |
| Ryzógalo | Rice pudding |

## FRUITS

| | |
|---|---|
| Akhládhia | Big pears |
| Aktinídha | Kiwis |
| Fistíkia | Pistachio nuts |
| Fráoules | Strawberries |
| Himoniátiko | Autumn (cassava) melon |
| Karpoúzi | Watermelon |
| Kerásia | Cherries |
| Krystália | Miniature pears |
| Kydhóni | Quince |
| Lemóni | Lemon |

| | |
|---|---|
| Míla | Apples |
| Pepóni | Melon |
| Portokáli | Orange |
| Rodhákino | Peach |
| Sýka | Figs |
| Stafýlia | Grapes |
| Yiarmádhes | Autumn peaches |

## CHEESE

| | |
|---|---|
| Ayeladhinó | Cow's-milk cheese |
| Féta | Salty, creamy white cheese |
| (Kefalo)graviéra | (Extra-hard) Gruyère-type cheese |
| Katsikísio | Goat cheese |
| Kasséri | Medium-sharp cheese |
| Myzíthra | Sweet cream cheese |
| Próvio | Sheep cheese |

## DRINKS

| | |
|---|---|
| Alisfakiá | Island sage tea |
| Boukáli | Bottle |
| Býra | Beer |
| Gála | Milk |
| Galakakáo | Chocolate milk |
| Kafés | Coffee |
| Krasí | Wine |
| áspro/lefkó | white |
| kokkinélli/rozé | rosé |
| kókkino | red |
| Limonádha | Lemonade |
| Metalikó neró | Mineral water |
| Portokaládha | Orangeade |
| Potíri | Glass |
| Stinyásas! | Cheers! |
| Tsáï | Tea |
| Tsáï vounoú | "Mountain" (mainland sage) tea |

## Glossary

**Acropolis** Ancient, fortified hilltop.

**Agora** Market and meeting place of an ancient Greek city; also the "high street" of a modern village (**agorá** in modern Greek).

**Amphora** Tall, narrow-necked jar for oil or wine.

**Áno** Upper; common prefix of village names.

**Apse** Curved recess at the east end of a church nave.

**Archaic period** Late Iron Age period, from around 750 BC to the start of the Classical period in the fifth century BC.

**Arhondikó** A lordly stone mansion, often restored as boutique accommodation.

**Astikó** (Intra) city, municipal, local; adjective applied to phone calls and bus services.

**Ayíasma** A sacred spring, usually flowing out of church foundations.

**Áyios/Ayía/Áyii** (m/f/plural). Saint or holy. Common place-name prefix (abbreviated Ag or Ay), often spelled **Agios** or **Aghios**.

**Basilica** Colonnaded, "hall-" or "barn-" type church adapted from Roman models, most common in northern Greece.

**Bema** Rostrum for a church oratory.

**Bouleuterion** Auditorium for meetings of an ancient town's deliberative council.

## DIALECTS AND MINORITY LANGUAGES

Ancient **dialects** survive in many remote areas of Greece, some quite incomprehensible to outsiders. The dialect of Sfákia in Crete is one such; Tsakónika of the east-central Peloponnese is another, while the dialect of the Sarakatsáni shepherds is apparently the oldest, related to the language of the Dorian settlers.

The language of the Sarakatsáni's traditional rivals, the **Vlachs**, is not Greek at all, but derived from early Latin, with strong affinities to Romanian. In the regions bordering the Republic of Macedonia and southwestern Bulgaria, you can still hear **Slavic Macedonian** spoken, while small numbers of Sephardic Jews in the north speak **Ladino**, a medieval form of Spanish. Until a few decades ago **Arvanítika** – a dialect of medieval Albanian – was the first language of many villages of inland Attica, southern Évvia, northern Ándhros, and much of the Argo-Saronic; lately the clock has been turned back, so to speak, as throngs of Albanian immigrants circulate in Athens and other parts of the country. In Thrace there is a substantial **Turkish-speaking** population, as well as some speakers of **Pomak** (a derivative of Bulgarian with a large Greco-Turkish vocabulary), while Gypsies countrywide speak Romany.

**Capital** The flared top, often ornamented, of a column.

**Cavea** Seating curve of an ancient theatre.

**Cella** Sacred room of a temple, housing the cult image.

**Classical period** From the end of the Persian Wars in 480 BC until the unification of Greece under Philip II of Macedon (338 BC).

**Conch** Concave semi-dome surmounting a church apse, often frescoed.

**Corinthian** Decorative columns, festooned with acanthus florettes; any temple built in this order.

**Dhimarhío** Town hall.

**Dhomátia** Rooms for rent in purpose-built block, without staffed reception.

**Dorian** Northern civilization that displaced and succeeded the Mycenaeans and Minoans through most of Greece around 1100 BC.

**Doric** Minimalist, unadorned columns, dating from the Dorian period; any temple built in this order.

**Drum** Cylindrical or faceted vertical section, usually pierced by an even number of narrow windows, upholding a church cupola.

**Entablature** The horizontal linking structure atop the columns of an ancient temple; same as **architrave**.

**Eparhía** Subdivision of a modern province, analogous to a county.

**Exedra** Display niche for statuary.

**Exonarthex** The outer vestibule or entrance hall of a church, when a true **narthex** is present.

**Forum** Market and meeting place of a Roman-era city.

**Frieze** Band of sculptures around a temple. Doric friezes consist of various tableaux of figures (**metopes**) interspersed with grooved panels (**triglyphs**); Ionic ones have continuous bands of figures.

**Froúrio** Medieval citadel; nowadays, can mean a modern military headquarters.

**Garsoniéra/es** Studio villa/s, self-catering apartment/s.

**Geometric period** Post-Mycenaean Iron Age era named for its pottery style; starts in the early eleventh century BC with the arrival of Dorian peoples. By the eighth century BC, with development of representational styles, the **Archaic period** begins.

**Hammam** Domed "Turkish" bath, found on Rhodes and certain northeast Aegean islands.

**Hellenistic period** The last and most unified "Greek empire", created in the wake of Alexander the Great's Macedonian empire and finally collapsing with the fall of Corinth to the Romans in 146 BC.

**Heroön** Shrine or sanctuary-tomb, usually of a demigod or mortal; war memorials in modern Greece.

**Hóra** Main town of an island or region; literally it means "the place". A hóra is often known by the same name as the island.

**Ierón** The sanctuary between the altar screen and the apse of a church, reserved for priestly activities.

**Ikonostási** Wood or masonry screen between the nave of a church and the altar, supporting at least three icons.

**Ionic** Elaborate, decorative development of the older **Doric** order; Ionic temple columns are slimmer, with deeper "fluted" edges, spiral-shaped capitals and ornamental bases.

**Kafenío** Coffee house or café.

**Kaïki** (plural **kaïkia**) Caique, or medium-sized boat, traditionally wooden and used for transporting cargo and passengers; now refers mainly to island excursion boats.

**Kalderími** A cobbled mule-track or footpath.

**Kámbos** Fertile agricultural plain, usually near a river mouth.

**Kantína** Shack, caravan or even a disused bus on the beach, serving drinks and perhaps sandwiches or quick snacks.

**Kástro** Any fortified hill, but most often the oldest, highest, walled-in part of an island hóra, intended to protect civilians.

**Katholikón** Central church of a monastery.

**Káto** Lower; common prefix of village names.

**Kendrikí platía** Central square.

**Kouros** Nude Archaic statue of an idealized young man, usually portrayed with one foot slightly in front of the other.

**Megaron** Principal hall or throne room of a Mycenaean palace.

**Meltémi** North wind that blows across the Aegean in summer, starting softly from near the mainland and hitting the Cyclades, the Dodecanese and Crete full on.

**Metope** see **Frieze**.

**Minoan** Crete's great Bronze Age civilization, which dominated the Aegean from about 2500 to 1400 BC.

**Moní** Formal term for a monastery or convent.

**Moreas** Medieval term for the Peloponnese; the peninsula's outline was likened to the leaf of a mulberry tree, *mourid* in Greek.

**Mycenaean** Mainland civilization centred on Mycenae and the Argolid from about 1700 to 1100 BC.

**Naos** The inner sanctum of an ancient temple; also, the central area of an Orthodox Christian church.

**Narthex** Western vestibule of a church, reserved for catechumens and the unbaptized; typically frescoed with scenes of the Last Judgement.

**Neolithic** Earliest era of settlement in Greece; characterized by use of stone tools and weapons together with basic agriculture. Divided arbitrarily into Early (c.6000 BC), Middle (c.5000 BC) and Late (c.3000 BC).

**Néos, Néa, Néo** "New" – a common prefix to a town or village name.

**Nomós** Modern Greek province – there are more than fifty of them. Village bus services are organized according to their borders.

**Odeion** Small theatre, used for musical performances, minor dramatic productions or councils.

**Orchestra** Circular area in a theatre where the chorus would sing and dance.

**Palaestra** Gymnasium for athletics and wrestling practice.

**Paleós, Paleá, Paleó** "Old" – again a common prefix in town and village names.

**Panayía** Virgin Mary.

**Pandokrátor** Literally "The Almighty"; generally refers to the stern portrayal of Christ in Majesty frescoed or in mosaic in the dome of many Byzantine churches.

**Paniyíri** Festival or feast – the local celebration of a holy day.

**Paralía** Beach, or seafront promenade.

**Pediment** Triangular, sculpted gable below the roof of a temple.

**Pendentive** Triangular sections of vaulting with concave sides, positioned at a corner of a rectangular space to support a circular or polygonal dome; in churches, often adorned with frescoes of the four Evangelists.

**Períptero** Street kiosk.

**Peristereónes** Pigeon towers, in the Cyclades.

**Peristyle** Gallery of columns around a temple or other building.

**Pinakothíki** Picture gallery, ancient or modern.

**Pithos** (plural **pithoi**) Large ceramic jar for storing oil, grain, etc. Very common in Minoan palaces and used in almost identical form in modern Greek homes.

**Platía** Square, plaza.

**Polygonal masonry** Wall-building technique of Classical and Hellenistic periods, using unmortared, closely joined stones; often called "Lesvian polygonal" after the island where the method supposedly originated. The much-(ab)used term **Cyclopean** refers only to Bronze Age mainland sites such as Tiryns and Mycenae.

**Propylaion** Monumental columned gateway of an ancient building; often used in the plural, **propylaia**.

**Pýrgos** Tower or bastion; also tower-mansions found in the Máni or on Lésvos.

**Skála** The port of an inland island settlement, nowadays often larger and more important than its namesake, but always younger since built after the disappearance of piracy.

**Squinch** Small concavity across a corner of a column-less interior space, which supports a superstructure such as a dome.

**Stele** Upright stone slab or column, usually inscribed with an edict; also an ancient tombstone, with a relief scene.

**Stoa** Colonnaded walkway in Classical-to-Roman-era marketplaces.

**Távli** Backgammon; a favourite café pastime, especially among the young. There are two more difficult local variations (*févga* and *plakotó*) in addition to the standard international game (*pórtes*).

**Témblon** Wooden altar screen of an Orthodox church, usually ornately carved and painted and studded with icons; more or less interchangeable with **ikonostási**.

**Temenos** Sacred precinct of ancient temple, often used to refer to the sanctuary itself.

**Theatral area** Open area found in most of the Minoan palaces with seat-like steps around. Probably a type of theatre or ritual area.

**Tholos** Conical or beehive-shaped building, eg a Mycenaean tomb.

**Triglyph** see **Frieze**.

**Tympanum** The recessed space, flat or carved in relief, inside a pediment.

**Votsalotó** Mosaic of coloured pebbles, found in church or house courtyards of the Dodecanese and Spétses.

**Yperastikó** Long-distance – as in bus services.

## ACRONYMS

**ANEK** Anónymi Navtiliakí Etería Krítis (Shipping Co of Crete, Ltd), which runs most ferries between Pireás and Crete, plus many to Italy.

**EAM** National Liberation Front, the political force behind ELAS.

**ELAS** Popular Liberation Army, the main Resistance group during World War II and predecessor of the Communist army during the civil war.

**ELTA** Postal service.

**EOS** Greek Mountaineering Federation, based in Athens.

**EOT** Ellinikós Organismós Tourismoú, National Tourist Organization.

**KKE** Communist Party, unreconstructed.

**KTEL** National syndicate of bus companies; also refers to individual bus stations.

**LANE** Lasithiakí Anónymi Navtiliakí Etería (Lasithian Shipping Company Ltd), based in eastern Crete.

**ND** Conservative (Néa Dhimokratía) party.

**NEL** Navtiliakí Etería Lésvou (Lesvian Shipping Co).

**OSE** Railway corporation.

**OTE** Telecommunications company.

**PASOK** Socialist party (Pan-Hellenic Socialist Movement).

**SEO** Greek Mountaineering Club, based in Thessaloníki.

**SYRIZA** Synaspismós tis Rizospastikís Aristerás (Coalition of the Radical Left) – alternative, "Euro"-Socialist party.

# Small print and index

**819** Small print

**822** Index

**835** Map symbols

## A ROUGH GUIDE TO ROUGH GUIDES

Published in 1982, the first Rough Guide – to Greece – was a student scheme that became a publishing phenomenon. Mark Ellingham, a recent graduate in English from Bristol University, had been travelling in Greece the previous summer and couldn't find the right guidebook. With a small group of friends he wrote his own guide, combining a highly contemporary, journalistic style with a thoroughly practical approach to travellers' needs.

The immediate success of the book spawned a series that rapidly covered dozens of destinations. And, in addition to impecunious backpackers, Rough Guides soon acquired a much broader readership that relished the guides' wit and inquisitiveness as much as their enthusiastic, critical approach and value-for-money ethos.

These days, Rough Guides include recommendations from budget to luxury and cover more than 200 destinations around the globe, as well as producing an ever-growing range of eBooks and apps.

Visit **roughguides.com** to see our latest publications.

# Rough Guide credits

**Editors**: Andy Turner, Lucy White and Edward Aves
**Layout**: Umesh Aggarwal, Pradeep Thapliyal
**Cartography**: Deshpal Dabas and Lokamata Sahu
**Picture editor**: Rhiannon Furbear
**Proofreader**: Jan McCann
**Managing editor**: Monica Woods
**Assistant editor**: Dipika Dasgupta
**Production**: Rebecca Short
**Cover design**: Nicole Newman, Michelle Bhatia and
Umesh Aggarwal
**Photographers**: Chris Christoforou and Michelle Grant
**Editorial assistant**: Eleanor Aldridge

**Senior pre-press designer**: Dan May
**Marketing, Publicity & roughguides.com**: Liz Statham
**Design director**: Scott Stickland
**Travel publisher**: Joanna Kirby
**Digital travel publisher**: Peter Buckley
**Reference director**: Andrew Lockett
**Operations coordinator**: Becky Doyle
**Operations assistant**: Johanna Wurm
**Publishing director (Travel)**: Clare Currie
**Commercial manager**: Gino Magnotta
**Managing director**: John Duhigg

# Publishing information

This thirteenth edition published May 2012 by
**Rough Guides Ltd**,
80 Strand, London WC2R 0RL
11, Community Centre, Panchsheel Park,
New Delhi 110017, India
**Distributed by the Penguin Group**
Penguin Books Ltd,
80 Strand, London WC2R 0RL
Penguin Group (USA)
375 Hudson Street, NY 10014, USA
Penguin Group (Australia)
250 Camberwell Road, Camberwell,
Victoria 3124, Australia
Penguin Group (NZ)
67 Apollo Drive, Mairangi Bay, Auckland 1310,
New Zealand
Rough Guides is represented in Canada by Tourmaline
Editions Inc. 662 King Street West, Suite 304, Toronto,
Ontario M5V 1M7
Printed in Singapore by Toppan Security Printing Pte. Ltd.
© Rough Guides 2012

MIX
Paper from
responsible sources
FSC™ C018179

# Help us update

We've gone to a lot of effort to ensure that the thirteenth
edition of **The Rough Guide to Greece** is accurate and up-
to-date. However, things change – places get "discovered",
opening hours are notoriously fickle, restaurants and
rooms raise prices or lower standards. If you feel we've got
it wrong or left something out, we'd like to know, and if
you can remember the address, the price, the hours, the
phone number, so much the better.

Please send your comments with the subject line
"**Rough Guide Greece Update**" to @ mail@uk.roughguides
.com. We'll credit all contributions and send a copy of the
next edition (or any other Rough Guide if you prefer) for
the very best emails.
Find more travel information, connect with fellow
travellers and book your trip on ⓦ roughguides.com

# Readers' letters

Thanks to all the readers who have taken the time to write in with comments and suggestions (and apologies if we've
inadvertently omitted or misspelt anyone's name):

Douglas Adler; Gabriela Barbosa de Oliveira; Dinah Bear;
Gillian Billington; John Bishop; David Black; Kathy Blandin;
Pete Chambers; Ian Chandler; Gerald Chapman; Adrian
Clement; Alison Culshaw; Laura Czebotar; Bob Dent;
Chris Deviaene; Katerina Dikaiou; Igor Fabjan; Annabell
Go; Pauline and Gordon Hinson; Xenia Kataki; Kirsty

Mackenzie; Ann, Ian and James Mason; Wendy and Diran
Meghreblian; Rhiannon Monks; John Newstead; M. Ostler;
Marianna Patané; Linda J. Reynolds; M. Rosenthal; Carola
Schupham; Brian Shepherd; Neville Spencer-Lewis; James
A. Stefan; Danielle Stewart; Will Straw; Rachel Taylor;
Donna Thornton; Michaela Urben; Alexander Zawadzki.

## ABOUT THE AUTHORS

**Nick Edwards** Since graduating in Classics & Modern Greek from Oxford, Nick spent many years living in Athens and travelling widely, especially in India. He later settled in Pittsburgh with spouse Maria, until they returned to his native south London in 2008. He's a lifelong Spurs fan, psych music aficionado and believer in universal Oneness.

**John Fisher** co-wrote the first edition of this book – the first ever Rough Guide – and has been inextricably linked with Rough Guides ever since, much of the time stuck in the office. Now living in London with his wife, Adrienne, and two boys, he is a freelance writer and editor.

**Jeffrey Kennedy** is a graduate of Stanford University and also has a Masters in interdisciplinary art education. He has been a European resident for most of his life and has been updating Rough Guides for some fifteen years.

**John Malathronas** was born in Athens but has spent most of his life in London where he has written three travelogues and contributed to nine guidebooks. He is a member of the Guild of Travel Writers and the Society of Authors as well as a social media addict and a compulsive blogger.

**Carol Palioudakis** has lived in Greece since 1986; she runs a tourism agency in western Crete, publishes a website about living in Crete and is a freelance writer and author. She lives near Haniá with her Greek husband and two children.

**Greg Ward**, who covered the Dodecanese islands for this book – and chose Sými for his honeymoon – is a London-based author and photographer specializing in history, music and travel. He has written more than a dozen travel guides to different parts of Europe and the US. His latest book is the *Rough Guide to the Titanic*; for more details, visit ⊛gregward.info

## Acknowledgements

**Nick Edwards** would like to thank all the people who offered help, hospitality and harmony along the way, including too many to mention in Macedonia and Thrace. On the islands, thanks especially to Kostas Vlachopulos at Boúkari Beach; Mariana in Horepiskopi/Gosport; Vasso and Yiorgos in Agrinio; Maria at Ionian Paradise in Nydhrí; Odisseas, Memi, Panayiotis, Andronikos and Lefteris on Kefaloniá; the *Villa Afrodite/Aphrodite Beach* hotel families of Límnos and Lésvos; Theo of To Kyma in Híos Town; Stella in Volissós and the Archipelagos Hotel on Foúrni. Many thanks for useful tips to Matt Barrett, but the greatest bundle of thanks for eastern Aegean help, advice, contacts, company, chauffeuring and accommodation on Samos goes to Marc Dubin. Finally cheers to old friends Kate for the overnight in Athens, Yiannis and Eleftheria, Makarios and Robert and Roudi for *parea* on Híos and Ikaría, plus bravo to Robert for steering the rent-a-wreck across the mountain. As ever, thanks to Maria for love and support from afar and bearing long absences in difficult circumstances.

**John Fisher** would like to thank all those who helped in Athens, the Argo-Saronic Islands and Sporades, especially Eleni Vardaki; Makis Bitzios; Kostas and Bessie Efstathiou on Alónissos; Rosy Agianozoglou and Kostas Antoniou on Angistri; Iannis Goumas, Bruce and Vassos on Égina; Kostas, Andrew and Marion on Skiáthos; Mathi and Vangelis on Skópelos; Lefteris Trakos and Maria Hadjipaniyiri on Skýros; Anastasios Naoum on Spetses; Irini Tavladoraki on Ýdhra; and Vangelis Lagoutaris, Dorina Stathopoulou, James Monteith and Kate Donnelly in Athens; not forgetting the team at Rough Guides and, as ever, A & the two Js for love, support and disrupting the research.

**Jeffrey Kennedy** would like to thank Joy Anderson Weston, Jan and Dan Andersson, Delores Beatty Lane, Panagiotis Brendas, Dimitri Mavrikios, Nicola Minnelli, Deborah Capers Starr, Dennis Sweet and Nancy Yeilding.

**John Malathronas** would like to thank NEL Lines, Kyklades Fast Ferries, Efthimios Athanasias and Makis Bitzios from

MTC Group Greece, Kostas Skayas on Mýkonos, Alexandros Konstantinou and the staff of GNTO London, as well as what seems in retrospect the whole population of the Cyclades for their help.

**Carol Palioudakis** Thanks to Kostas, Lia, Tolis and my friends and colleagues for their help and support, especially Lyn Protopsaltis and Lynn Malleli, and to all who offered their time and hospitality during my travels around Crete.

**Greg Ward** Thanks to Sam for all her love and support, in the hope we'll be back on Sými soon; aloha to Donna

Young and Chef Mavro, for a serendipitous meeting; and thanks to everyone who helped to make my Dodecanese trip so memorable, including Antonios Antonoglu; Yiorgos Berdos and Maria Martzoukou; Maria Christofí; Ian Hogg on Tilos; Annie Kalogianni and Christine at *Archontoriki*; George Koulouris; Alex Marshall and all the family at the *Spirit of the Knights*; Tom Panagos and Chloe Buchanan; Stella Sandaltzopoulou, Liz, and everyone at the *Hotel des Couleurs*; Dimitris Vlachos; Kayleen Vourtsis; Wendy Wilcox and Adriana Shum on Sými; Marina F. Zawaher; and Alexis Zikas. At Rough Guides, thanks to Andy Turner for setting it all up, and to Lucy White for another enjoyable collaboration.

## Photo credits

All photos © Rough Guides except the following:
(Key: t-top; c-centre; b-bottom; l-left; r-right)

**p.1** 4Corners/Giovanni Simeone
**p.4** Alamy/World Pictures
**p.5** Superstock/Peter Schickert
**p.10** Corbis/Louie Psihoyos/Science Faction
**p.11** Corbis/Rainer Hackenberg (t); Getty Images/Luca Trovato (b)
**p.12** 4Corners/Günter Gräfenhain/Huber
**p.13** Corbis/Michele Falzone (b)
**p.14** Corbis/Jose Fuste Raga (t); Superstock/HapsisIML (b)
**p.15** Alamy/LOOK Die Bildagentur der Fotografen GmbH (b); Alamy/ollirg (t)
**p.16** Corbis/Rene Mattes/Hemis (t); Getty Images/Juergen Richter (bl); Jean-Francois Riviere (br)
**p.17** Corbis/Paul Panayiotou (c); Roger Wilmshurst/Frank Lane Picture Agency (t)
**p.18** Corbis/Ocean (b); Getty Images/Ellen Rooney (t)
**p.19** Alamy/IML Image Group Ltd (t); Getty Images/Gallo Images (br)
**p.20** Alamy/IML Image Group Ltd (tl); Corbis/Walter Bibikow (tr); Johanna Huber/SOPA (b)
**p.21** Alamy/Hemis (c); Corbis/Paul Panayiotou (b); Superstock/KokkasIML (t)
**p.73** Corbis/Atlantide Phototravel (b)
**p.122** Getty Images/Manuel Cohen
**p.125** Corbis/Jean-Pierre Lescourret
**p.145** Corbis/Aristidis Vafeiadakis/Zuma Press (b); Superstock/Konrad Wothe (t)
**p.171** Alamy/Peter Eastland
**p.187** Alamy/Ace Stock Ltd (t)
**p.198** Corbis/Michele Falzone
**p.201** Corbis/René Mattes/Hemis
**p.219** Alamy/Terry Harris (b); Getty Images/Alvis Upitis/Brand X (t)
**p.241** Alamy/World Pictures (b); Corbis/Michele Falzone (t)
**p.262** Superstock/Peter Schickert
**p.265** Getty Images/Mark Daffey

**p.285** Alamy/Aliki Sapountzi/aliki image library (b); Superstock/Werner Bollmann (t)
**p.307** Alamy/Peter Eastland (b); Getty Images/Sakis Mitrolidis/AFP (t)
**p.324** Superstock/MeazzalML
**p.352** Getty Images/Sakis Papadopoulos/Robert Harding World Imagery
**p.355** 4Corners/Anna Serrano/SIME
**p.379** Corbis/Richard T Nowitz
**p.401** Corbis/Ted Horowitz (t)
**p.433** Getty Images/Cornelia Doerr (b); Superstock/Jean-Pierre Lescourre (t)
**p.447** Alamy/Gareth McCormack
**p.508** Corbis/Sakis Papadopoulos/Robert Harding
**p.525** Corbis/Atlantide Phototravel
**p.579** Getty Images/Jorg Greuel
**p.594** Corbis/Sakis Papadopoulos/Robert Harding World Imagery
**p.597** Getty Images/Danita Delimont/Gallo Images
**p.619** Corbis/Walter Bibikow (b); Corbis/Georg Ismar/dpa (t)
**p.645** 4Corners/Guido Cozzi (b); Getty Images/Danita Delimont/Gallo Images (t)
**p.668** Getty Images/Barry Marsden
**p.671** 4Corners/Johanna Huber/SIME
**p.675** Alamy/Nick Hanna
**p.689** Superstock/Robert Harding
**p.733** 4Corners/Gabriele Croppi/SIME (tr); Corbis/Franck Guiziou/Hemis (b)

**Front Cover** Zákynthos © Giovanni Simeone/SIME/4Corners Images
**Back Cover** Santoríni © Michele Falzone/AWL Images Ltd (t); Parthenon, Acropolis © Michelle Grant/Rough Guides (l); The evil eye © Chris Christoforou/Rough Guides (r)

# Index

Maps are marked in grey

## A

Abdera, ancient................318
**accommodation .............35–38**
Acheron, Nekromanteion of
..............................................257
Achilleion............................712
Actium, Battle of................259
Adhámas.............................373
Aegae..........................see Vergina
**AEGEAN ISLANDS .......594–667**
Aegina .........................see Égina
Aeschylus............................766
Afáles Bay...........................748
Afándou Bay.......................523
Áfyssos................................230
Áfytos.................................297
Agathoníssi.........................592
**Agathoníssi .......................593**
Agathopés...........................400
Agístri........................see Angístri
Agní....................................714
Agnóndas............................680
Agriolívadho........................589
Agriosykiá...........................553
**Aháïa ..................... 191–197**
Aharávi...............................716
Áï Górdhis (Corfu)..............721
Áï Górdhis Paleohoríou (Corfu)
..............................................723
Aï Nikítas...........................735
Aï Strátis........see Áyios Efstrátios
air conditioning....................37
airlines, international ............25
Aïyannis (Lefkádha)............731
Akronafplía.........................140
Akrotíri (Santoríni)..............441
Akrotíri peninsula................498
Alalkomenae.......................746
alcoholic drinks ....................40
Alexander the Great............769
Alexandhroúpoli.................320
Ali Pasha............................246
Alikanás.............................756
Álinda.................................584
Alistráti, village/caves.........310
Almyrós (Corfu)..................716
**Alónissos................ 683–687**
**Alónissos .......................... 683**
Alonítsi...............................650
Aloprónia...........................429
Alykés (Ammoulianí)...........303
Alykés (Zákynthos).............756
Alykí (Kímolos)...................378

Alykí (Kos)..........................566
Alykí (Thássos)...................665
Amári valley (Crete)............490
Ambelás (Páros)..................407
Ambéli (Folégandhros)........432
Ammopí...............................540
Ammouá..............................536
Ammoúdhi (Santoríni)........439
Ammoulianí.........................302
**Amorgós ................ 421–425**
**Amorgós ........................... 422**
amphibians.........................793
Anáfi..................................442
**Anáfi ................................ 442**
Anafonítria monastery .........757
Anakassiá...........................225
Análipsi..............................573
Anáryiros, Sotírios..............348
Anastenariá........................279
Ánaxos...............................648
Andhrítsena........................175
**Ándhros .................. 380–384**
**Ándhros .......................... 381**
Andikýthira.........................155
Andinióti lagoon.................716
Andíparos...........................409
**Andíparos ........................ 403**
Andípaxi.............................726
**Andípaxi .......................... 725**
Andísamis...........................743
Ándissa..............................643
Andronikos, Manolis...........789
Angáli (Folégandhros) ........432
Angelókastro......................719
**Angístri .................... 335–337**
**Angístri ........................... 336**
Áno Méra (Mýkonos)...........394
Áno Meriá (Folégandhros)....432
Áno Moraïtika....................722
Áno Pedhiná.......................253
Áno Sýros...........................398
Áno Vathý (Sámos).............601
Anoyí.................................747
Anóyia................................466
Antipaxos ............... see Andípaxi
Apalírou.............................416
Ápella.................................542
Aperáthou...........................417
Aphaea, Temple of (Égina) ....333
Apokálypsis monastery (Pátmos)
..............................................587
Apollo Coast.......................114
Apollo Epikourios Temple ....176
Apóllonas (Náxos) ..............418
Apollonía (Sífnos)...............368

Apónissos...........................337
Aráhova..............................212
**Arcadia (Arkadhía) ..... 172–177**
archeological schools, foreign
..............................................788
**archeology in Greece**
..........................................785–789
Areópoli ............................159
Aréta..................................535
Arethoússa spring...............746
Argalastí.............................231
Argási................................752
Argolid, The .......................133
Árgos.................................136
**ARGO-SARONIC ISLANDS**
..........................................324–351
**Argo-Saronic ................. 328**
Argostóli.............................737
**Argostóli ......................... 737**
Arhangélou Mihaïl convent
(Thássos)...........................665
Arhéa Kórinthos (village)......130
Aristotle.............................771
Arkádhi monastery .............486
Arkássa..............................540
Arkhoudhílas, beach/monastery
..............................................723
Arkí...................................592
Arkoúdhi.............................190
Armathiá............................536
Arméni...............................439
Armenistís...........................617
Armeós (Kálymnos).............578
Armeós (Sýros) ...................400
Artemis Tavropoleio temple
(Ikaría).............................617
Artemónas.........................368
Aryinónda...........................577
Asfendhioú villages.............566
Askéli.................................340
Asklepion (Kos)..................565
Asklipió (Rhodes)...............527
Aspoús...............................693
Ássos.................................744
Astakós..............................259
**Astypálea.................. 569–573**
**Astypálea ....................... 570**
Astypalia, ancient (Kos)......568
Atávyros, Mount.................530
Atháni...............................735
Athéato..............................681
Athenian empire..................765
Athenian golden age ...........764
**ATHENS .....................56–114**
**Athens ....................... 60–61**

**central Athens** ............... **66–67**
**metro and rail** ..................... **97**
**Athens, around** ........... **115**
Academy of Science.................... 82
accommodation .......................... 98
Acropolis ................................... 65
Acropolis Museum ..................... 71
Agora, ancient ........................... 72
airport ...................................... 94
Akadhimía (University) ............... 82
Anafiótika ................................. 75
Archeological Museum, Pireás ..... 93
Areopagus .................................. 72
arrival ....................................... 94
Athens University Museum ......... 75
Athinaïs complex ....................... 89
Ayía Ekateríni ........................... 75
Áyios Dhimítrios ....................... 87
bars ........................................ 108
bazaar ....................................... 82
beaches ..................................... 92
Benáki Museum ......................... 90
Benáki Museum of Islamic Art ..... 87
Benáki Museum Piraeus St Annexe
............................................... 88
buses, urban .............................. 97
Byzantine and Christian Museum
............................................... 90
cinemas ................................... 111
City of Athens Museum ............... 81
city transport ............................ 96
clubs ....................................... 108
dance ...................................... 110
Dionysos theatre ....................... 70
directory .................................. 113
eating and drinking .................. 101
Elgin marbles ............................ 70
Erechtheion ............................... 69
Exárhia ..................................... 83
Festival, Athens and Epidaurus ... 110
Fethiye Tzami ............................ 76
Filopáppou Hill .......................... 86
flea market ................................ 78
flower market ............................ 83
Frissiras Museum ....................... 75
gay/lesbian venues ................... 109
Gázi .......................................... 88
Hadrian's Arch ........................... 81
Hadrian's Library ....................... 78
Hephaisteion ............................. 72
Herodes Atticus theatre .............. 70
history ...................................... 62
Hotel Grande Bretagne ............... 80
Iridhanós River .......................... 78
Jewish Museum of Greece ........... 74
Kanellopoulou Museum ............... 76
Kapnikaréa ................................ 79
Kerameikos ................................ 88
Kolonáki .................................... 89
Lycabettus ............. see Lykavitós
Lykavitós Hill ............................ 89
markets ................................... 112
meat/seafood market .................. 82
Medresse .................................. 77
metro ........................................ 96
Mets ......................................... 91
Mitrópolis cathedral ................... 79
Monastiráki ............................... 77

Monument of Lysikratos .............. 75
Museum of Cycladic Art .............. 90
Museum of Greek Folk Art ........... 74
Museum of Greek Popular Musical
Instruments .............................. 77
music venues ........................... 109
National Archaeological Museum
............................................... 84
National Gallery of Art ............... 91
National Gardens ....................... 80
National Historical Museum ......... 81
National Library ......................... 82
Naval Museum ........................... 94
nightlife .................................. 108
Numismatic Museum .................. 81
Nymphs, Hill of ......................... 87
Omónia ........... see Platía Omonías
Panathenaic Stadium .................. 92
Pangráti .................................... 91
Parthenon .................................. 69
Pireás ....................................... 92
Pireás transport ......................... 95
Pláka ........................................ 74
Platía Monastirakíou .................. 77
Platía Omonías ........................... 82
Polytехnío ................................ 83
Presidential Palace ..................... 80
Propylaia .................................. 68
Psyrrí ....................................... 77
Pynx, fountain ........................... 86
Pynx, Hill of .............................. 87
Roman baths ............................. 81
Roman forum ............................. 76
Sanctuary of Pan ....................... 86
shopping .................................. 111
Socrates' prison ......................... 87
Stoa of Attalos ........................... 72
street markets .......................... 112
Sýndagma square ....................... 79
taxis ......................................... 98
Tekhnópolis .............................. 88
Temple of Athena Nike ............... 68
Temple of Olympian Zeus ............ 81
Thissío ..................................... 86
Tomb of the Unknown Soldier ...... 80
tourist information ..................... 96
tours ........................................ 96
Tower of the Winds .................... 76
trams ........................................ 97
Turkish baths ............................ 77
Voulí (Parliament) ...................... 79
War Museum .............................. 91
Záppio ...................................... 80
Athos, history .......................... 305
Athos, monasteries ................... 308
**Athos, Mount** ............ **304–309**
**Athos, Mount** ..................... **304**
Athos, permits .......................... 306
ATMs ........................................ 53
Atreus, House of ...................... 134
Atsítsa .................................... 692
**Attica** ........................... **114–121**
Ávdhira, modern ....................... 318
Avgónyma ................................ 628
Avlákia (Psérimos) .................... 569
Avlémonas ............................... 154
Avliótes .................................. 720

Avlóna .................................... 543
Axis Occupation ....................... 779
Ayía Anastasía Roméá ............... 527
Ayía Ánna (Amorgós) ................ 423
Ayía Ánna (Évvia) ..................... 701
Ayía Ánna (Náxos) .................... 415
Ayiá castle .............................. 256
Ayía Efimía ............................. 743
Ayía Eléni (Skiáthos) ................ 675
Ayía Ermióni ........................... 625
Ayía Fotiní .............................. 625
Ayía Galíni .............................. 490
Ayía Iríni (Híos) ....................... 627
Ayía Iríni gorge ....................... 503
Ayía Kyriakí (Pelion) ................ 231
Ayía Marína (Crete) .................. 499
Ayía Marína (Égina) .................. 334
Ayía Marína (Kássos) ................ 537
Ayía Marína (Léros) .................. 582
Ayía Marína (Spétses) ............... 351
Ayía Marína (Sými) ................... 548
Ayía Markélla ........................... 630
Ayía Paraskeví (Kassándra) .. 298
Ayía Paraskeví (Lésvos) ............ 641
Ayía Paraskeví (Spétses) ........... 350
Ayía Pelayía ............................ 465
Ayía Pelayía (Kýthira) ............... 152
Ayía Rouméli ........................... 502
Ayía Sofía (Kárpathos) .............. 540
Ayía Triádha (Crete) ................. 462
Ayía Triádha (Límnos) .............. 655
Ayía Triádha (Sámos) ............... 611
Ayía Triádha (Télendhos) .......... 578
Ayía Triádha monastery ............ 498
Ayías Lávras monastery ............ 197
Ayiás Triádhos (Metéora) .......... 240
Ayiássos (Lésvos) ..................... 639
Áyii Anáryiri ........................... 648
Áyii Anáryiri (Páros) ................ 404
Áyii Anáryiri (Skópelos) ........... 681
Áyii Anáryiri (Spétses) ............. 350
Áyii Dhéka (Corfu) ................... 721
Áyii Dhéka (Crete) ................... 460
Ayiókambos ............................. 701
Áyios Ahíllios ......................... 291
Áyios Andónios (Tílos) ............. 553
Áyios Dhimítrios (Aï Strátis) ... 650
Áyios Dhimítrios (Alónissos)
............................................. 686
Áyios Efstrátios (Aï Strátis) ...... 649
Áyios Emilianós (Sými) ............. 549
Áyios Fokás (Lésvos) ................ 641
Áyios Fokás (Skýros) ................ 693
Áyios Fokás (Tínos) .................. 386
Áyios Harálambos (Thrace) .... 319
Áyios Ioánnis (Límnos) ............. 653
Áyios Ioánnis (Mýkonos) .......... 393
Áyios Ioánnis (Pelion) .............. 226
Áyios Ioánnis (Sérifos) ............. 365
Áyios Ioánnis Kastrí ................. 682

Áyios Ioánnis Theológos
(Níssyros) .............................559
Áyios Kírykos .............................615
Áyios Konstandínos (Astypálea)
..............................................572
Áyios Konstandínos (Sámos)
..............................................607
Áyios Konstandínos (Stereá
Elládha) ...............................217
Áyios Matthéos (Corfu)...........721
Áyios Nektários (Égina) ...........333
Áyios Nikólaos (Anáfi) .............442
**Áyios Nikólaos (Crete)**
................................... **468–470**
**Áyios Nikólaos (Crete) ....... 468**
Áyios Nikólaos (Kálymnos).....577
Áyios Nikólaos (Kárpathos) ....540
Áyios Nikólaos (N Zákynthos)
..............................................756
Áyios Nikólaos (S Zákynthos)
..............................................752
Áyios Nikólaos (Sámos) ..........607
Áyios Nikólaos (Sými)..............549
Áyios Nikólaos (Ýdhra)............346
Áyios Nikólaos Foundouklí ....530
Áyios Pandelímonas (Attica)
..............................................118
Áyios Pétros (Ándhros)............380
Áyios Pétros (Alónissos)..........686
Áyios Pétros (Skýros) ...............692
Áyios Prokópios..........................415
Áyios Sóstis (Mýkonos)............394
Áyios Stéfanos (Mýkonos)......392
Áyios Stéfanos (NE Corfu).......715
Áyios Stéfanos (NW Corfu).....720
Áyios Theológos (Kos).............568
Áyios Vassílios (Sými) ..............549
Áyios Vassílios (Télendhos) ....578
Áyios Yeóryios (Agathoníssi)
..............................................593
Áyios Yeóryios (Ammoulianí)
..............................................303
Áyios Yeóryios (Andíparos) ....410
Áyios Yeóryios (Crete) .............473
Áyios Yeóryios (Folégandhros)
..............................................432
Áyios Yeóryios (Irakliá)............419
Áyios Yeóryios (Náxos)............414
Áyios Yeóryios (NW Corfu) .....719
Áyios Yeóryios (S Corfu) .........723
Áyios Yeóryios castle (Kefalloniá)
..............................................740
Áyios Yeóryios Dhyssálona.....549
Áyios Yeóryios Mandhilás......239
Áyios Yerásimos........................740
Áyios Yermanós........................291
Ayíou Dhionysíou monastery
(Mount Olympus)................283
Ayíou Haralámbou (Skiáthos)
..............................................676

Ayíou Ioánnou Prodhrómou
(Hálki)...................................535
Ayíou Ioánnou Theológou
monastery (Pátmos) .............588
Ayíou Nikoláou Anápafsa.......238
Ayíou Nikoláou Galatáki ........700
Ayíou Pandelímona monastery
(Tílos)...................................554
Ayíou Stefánou (Metéora)......240
Ayíou Yeoryíou Hadhión........537

# B

backpackers................................. 37
Balí..............................................466
Balkan Wars ...............................777
Bállos..........................................606
Banana Beach (Skiáthos) ........675
Banana Beach (Zákynthos) ....752
banks............................................. 53
Barbáti ........................................714
bars ............................................... 42
basketball..................................... 48
Bassae..........................................176
Batsí.............................................380
Battle of Marathon....................765
beer .............................................. 42
Benítses.......................................721
*Big Blue, The*............................421
Biláli............................................631
birds.............................................791
Bísti .............................................346
Blegen, Carl...............................788
Blue Caves .................................756
Bonátsa.......................................378
**books ............................. 801–806**
Boúka...........................................536
Boúkari.........................................722
Boúrtzi.........................................140
*bouzoúki*...................................796
breakfast..................................... 38
Brooke, Rupert..........................690
Brós Thermá ..............................566
buses ........................................... 29
Byron, Lord.................................260
Byzantine Greece......................773

# C

cafés ............................................ 41
camping........................................ 38
Cape Sounion...see Soúnio, Cape
Cape Ténaro...............................161
Cape Tripití.................................190
*Captain Corelli's Mandolin*......736,
743, 802
car rental..................................... 34

cash dispensers............. see ATMs
Castello Rosso............................699
catamarans ................................ 32
Cave of the Nymphs (Itháki)
..............................................746
cellphones................................... 54
cemetery, Allied (Límnos).......655
Cephallonia..............see Kefaloniá
Chaeronea..................................213
chemists....................................... 42
children, travelling with........... 55
children's books .......................805
Chios ............................... see Híos
Chlemoutsi.......... see Khlemoútsi
Christianity, early......................773
City-states, decline of .............767
City-states, rise of .....................762
Civil War.....................................780
classics, Greek literature..........803
climate.................................8, 52
climbing.......... 172, 227, 237, 283
Cockerell, C R.............................785
coffee .......................................... 41
colonels' junta............................782
Constantine II, King ..................782
contraception ............................ 43
**Corfu (Kérkyra)............ 707–724**
**Corfu ................................... 708**
**Corfu Town................... 707–713**
**Corfu Town ....................... 710**
Corfu Trail..................................723
Corinth, ancient ........................130
Corinth, modern .......................129
Corinth Canal.............................130
costs ........................................... 49
credit cards ................................ 53
**CRETE........................... 444–507**
**Crete ......................... 448–449**
Creteaquarium ..........................464
crime ........................................... 49
crisis, economic.........................784
Crusades....................................773
**CYCLADES, THE .......... 352–443**
**Cyclades, The.................... 356**
**Cyclades, Lesser .......... 418–420**
cycling..............................35, 48
Cyprus crises ..............................781

# D

Damoúhari..................................226
Dark Age....................................762
debt crisis...................................784
Delian League............................766
**Delos ........................... 394–396**
**Delos .................................. 395**
**Delphi ......................... 204–210**
**Delphi sites.......................... 205**
**Delphi: sacred precinct ..... 207**

Delphic oracle..........................205
democracy, ancient.................763
Dhadhiá Forest Reserve.........322
Dháfni.......................................752
Dhafníla....................................714
Dhassiá.....................................714
Dhelfí, modern.........................209
Dhervéni gorge........................699
Dhessími Bay...........................732
Dhéxa.......................................746
Dhiafáni....................................542
Dhiakoftó (Peloponnese).......195
Dhiapóndia islands..................717
Dhídhyma.................................627
Dhidhymótiho..........................323
Dhíkeos, Mount.......................566
Dhíkorfo...................................252
Dhiktean Cave.........................473
Dhílofo.....................................252
Dhílos...........................see Delos
Dhimitsána...............................175
Dhimosári Gorge......................699
dhimotikí..................................809
Dhión, modern.........................284
Dhodhekánisos.................... see
    Dodecanese
dhomátia....................................36
Dhonoússa...............................421
Dhragonéra..............................337
Dhrákano, Cape.......................615
Dhrakéï.....................................611
dhrakóspita...............................697
Dhrogaráti cave.......................743
Dhrossiá...................................756
Dhrymónas (Pátmos)...............585
Dhrymónas (Lefkádha)............731
Dhryopídha...............................363
Dhýo Liskária...........................584
Dhýstos, Lake..........................697
dialects.....................................815
Dion, ancient............................283
disabilities, travellers with........55
discounts....................................50
diving...............................47, 576
doctors.......................................42
DODECANESE, THE......508–593
Dodecanese, The.................. 512
Dodona, ancient......................249
Dovecote Trail (Tínos).............387
dress codes................................48
driving in Greece.......................33
driving to Greece.......................27
drug laws....................................50
Dystos, ancient........................697

East and North Aegean
.................................... 594–667
East and North Aegean ..... 598
Easter..........................................44
ecotourism (Crete)..................504
Édhessa....................................288
Efpalínio Órygma.....................603
Égina (Aegina)............. 329–355
Égina............................................ 330
Égina Town..............................331
Egremní....................................735
Ekatondapyliani, church of
    (Páros)..................................404
Elafonísi...................................506
Elafónissos (Peloponnese).....150
ELAS (Popular Liberation Army)
....................................................779
Eláti (Zagóri)............................252
electricity....................................50
Elefsína.......................see Eleusis
Eleoússa (Rhodes)...................530
Eleusis, ancient........................121
Elgin, Lord................................785
Eliá (Mýkonos).........................393
Élios..........................................680
Eloúnda....................................470
embassies, Greek.......................50
Émblisi......................................744
Émbona.....................................530
Emborió (Hálki)........................534
Emborió (Sými).........................549
Emboriós (Híos)........................627
Emboriós (Kálymnos)...............577
Emboriós (Kássos)....................536
Emboriós (Níssyros).................558
emergency numbers..................54
Englouví...................................731
Énos, Mount.............................740
éntekhno music........................796
entrance fees.............................50
entry requirements....................50
Epidaurus, ancient...................142
Epídhavros...........see Epidaurus
EPIRUS...................200, 242–258
Epirus....................................... 202
Eptá Piyés................................530
Eressós..............see Skála Eressoú
Eressos, ancient.......................644
Erétria......................................696
Eríkoussa.................................718
Erimítis cliffs............................726
Éristos......................................553
Ermióni.....................................144
Érmones...................................720
Ermoúpolis..............................398
Ermoúpolis........................... 399
estiatória....................................39
etiquette.....................................48
Euboea......................... see Évvia
Eumaeus, Cave of....................746

eurozone..................................784
Evangelistrías monastery
    (Skiáthos)............................674
Evans, Sir Arthur......................787
Évdhilos....................................616
Évros Delta...............................321
Évvia............................... 693–701
Évvia......................................... 694
Exánthia...................................731
Éxo Máni...................................163
Exóbourgo................................388
Eyeopelayítiko.........................298
Eyiáli........................................424
Éyio...........................................195

F

Falásarna..................................505
Faliráki.....................................523
Fanaráki...................................655
Faneroméni monastery
    (Lefkádha)............................731
Fáros (Ikaría)............................615
Fáros (Sífnos)...........................370
fast food.....................................39
Fengári, Mount.........................659
ferries...............................27, 32
festivals...............................44–47
Festós......................... see Phaestos
field guides, flora/fauna..........794
Filérimos...................................529
Fínikas (Koufoníssi)..................420
Fínikas (Sýros)..........................400
Finíki (Kárpathos)....................540
Finikoúnda...............................180
Firá (Thíra)...............................436
firewalking festivals.................279
Firipláka...................................376
Firostefáni................................436
fish.............................................40
Fiskárdho..................................744
Fléa..........................................693
Flério........................................417
flights, domestic.........................33
flights, international....................25
Flomohóri.................................162
Flórina......................................290
flying dolphins ...... see hydrofoils
Fódheli......................................465
Fóki...........................................627
Fókis.........................................744
Folégandhros................. 430–434
Folégandhros...................... 429
folk music.................................795
food and drink.................. 38–42
food and drink glossary
.................................... 811–814
football......................................48
Fourkeró...................................631

E

EAM (National Liberation Front)
....................................................779

Fournáki (Sámos)......................610
Foúrni (Rhodes)......................529
Foúrni......................................612
**Foúrni**................................. **613**
Frangokástello........................502
Fríkes......................................748
Frý..........................................536
Fylakopí..................................376
Fýsses.....................................543
Fýtema....................................616

# G

Gaïdhourávlakos.....................593
Gaidhouronísi.........................481
Gáïos......................................725
*galaktopolía*............................ 41
Galaxídhi................................213
Galissás..................................400
Gardhíki Pýrgos......................721
Gavathás.................................643
Gávdhos..................................507
Gávrio....................................380
gay travellers.............................51
George II, King........................778
Glóssa....................................681
**glossary** ...................... **814–817**
Glýfa (Alónissos).....................686
Glýfa (Andíparos)....................410
Glyfádha.................................115
Glystéri...................................682
goat dance, Skyrian................688
gods, Greek.......... see mythology
Gomáti...................................653
Górtys....................................460
Gortys, ancient (Arcadia)........175
Goúrna (Léros)........................585
Goúrnes.................................464
Gourniá, ancient.....................475
Gouvernétou monastery.........499
Grafiótissa..............................569
Gramvoússa (Amorgós)...........424
Grazia-Barozzi Tower..............417
Greek alphabet.......................808
Greek colonization.................763
**Greek language** ............ **807–817**
green tourism (Crete)..............504
Gría Váthra.............................658
Oríkou....................................589
Grótta.....................................414
Gythion...................... see Yíthio

# H

Hadzimihaïl, Theophilos.........638
Halikoúna beach.....................723
**Hálki**................................ **533–535**

**Hálki**................................... **534**
Halkí (Náxos)..........................417
Halkídha.................................694
**Halkidhikí**...................... **296–305**
**Halkidhikí**........................... **297**
**Haniá**............................. **492–498**
**Hanía**.................................. **493**
Haráki....................................524
Harkadhió cave.......................553
Harmýlio................................567
Hasa Baba Tekkés...................233
health.......................................42
Hellenistic Greece..................770
Hephaestia, ancient................656
Heraion, ancient.....................605
Herónia.................. see Chaeronea
Hersónissos............................464
Hídhira..................................642
**Híos**.............................. **620–630**
**Híos**.................................... **621**
**Híos Town**........................... **622**
**Híos Town**........................... **623**
Hippocrates............................566
**history**........................ **759–784**
Hivadholímni..........................376
Hlemoútsi............ see Khlemoútsi
Hokhlakás (Télendhos)...........578
Hokhlakás Bay (Pátmos)..........586
Hokhláki (Níssyros).................555
Hokhlakoúra (Lipsí).................591
holidays, public.........................58
Homeric epics.........................763
Hondroyiórgis.........................682
Hóra (Alónissos).....................684
Hóra (Amorgós).......................423
Hóra (Anáfi)............................442
Hóra (Ándhros).......................382
Hóra (Astypálea).....................571
Hóra (Folégandhros)...............431
Hóra (Íos)...............................426
Hóra (Kálymnos).....................575
Hóra (Kímolos)........................377
Hóra (Koufoníssi)....................420
Hóra (Kýthira).........................153
Hóra (Kýthnos).......................362
Hóra (Messinía).......................185
Hóra (Pátmos).........................588
Hóra (Samothráki)..................656
Hóra (Sérifos).........................366
Hóra (Síkinos).........................429
Hóra (Skhinoússa)..................420
Hóra (Skýros)..........................690
Hóra Sfakíon...........................501
Horeftó..................................226
Horió (Hálki)...........................535
Horió (Sými)...........................546
horses, Skyrian.......................692
Hórto......................................231
hospitals...................................42
hotels.......................................36

hostels......................................37
Hotzoviótissas monastery.......424
Hydra............................. see Ýdhra
hydrofoils..................................32

# I

Ía............................................438
Ialyssos, ancient.....................529
ice cream..................................42
Idean cave (Crete)...................467
Idhéon Ándhron...see Idean cave
Ierápetra.................................480
Ierissós...................................302
Igoumenítsa............................254
**Ikaría**............................ **614–620**
**Ikaría**.................................. **613**
**Ilía (Peloponnese)**........ **185–191**
Ília (Évvia)..............................701
Imerovígli................................436
immigration............................784
Inoússes..................................630
insects...............................43, 794
insurance..................................51
internet cafés............................51
**Ioánnina** ...................... **244–248**
**Ioánnina** ............................ **245**
**IONIAN ISLANDS, THE ...702–757**
**Ionian Islands, The............. 706**
Iónio.......................................752
**Íos** ................................ **425–428**
**Íos**...................................... **426**
Ioulídha.................................359
Irakliá.....................................419
**Iráklion** ........................ **449–456**
**Iráklion** .............................. **451**
Iréon......................................605
Íssos......................................723
Ítanos.....................................478
**Itháki (Ithaca)** ............. **745–749**
**Itháki** .................................. **737**
Íti, Mount...............................218
itineraries.................................22
Ítylo.......................................163

# J

jellyfish....................................43
Jews.......................................780
Jews, Thessaloníki..................274
junta, colonels'.......................782

# K

Kabirion, ancient....................656
*kafenía*.................................... 41

Kaïki beach ...................................350
*kaïkia* ............................................. 33
Kalafáti .........................................394
Kalamáki (Zákynthos) .............754
Kalamákia (Alónissos) .............686
**Kalamáta** ...................... **177–179**
Kalambáka ...................................236
Kalámi (Corfu) ............................714
Kalamiés (Kálymnos) ...............577
Kalamiótissa ................................443
Kalamítsi (Kímolos) ..................378
Kalamítsi (Sithonía) ..................300
Kálamos (Évvia) ..........................696
Kalandó .........................................417
Kalávria .........................................340
Kalávryta .......................................196
Kaliakoúdha, Mount ................221
Kallianós ......................................699
Kallithéa (Kassándhra) .............298
Kallithéa (Sámos) .....................611
Kalloní ..........................................642
Kalogriá ........................................195
Kalotarítissas ..............................423
Kaloutás bridge ..........................252
**Kálymnos**...................... **574–580**
**Kálymnos** ....................................... **574**
Kamáres (Sífnos) .......................368
Kamári (Kos) ...............................568
Kamári (Santoríni) .....................439
Kamariótissa ...............................656
Kambí (Foúrni) ...........................612
Kambí (Zákynthos) .....................755
Kámbos (Crete) ..........................505
Kámbos (Híos) ............................627
Kámbos (Ikaría) ..........................616
Kámbos (Lipsí) ............................590
Kámbos (Pátmos) ......................589
Kameiros, ancient ......................528
Kaméni islets (Santoríni) ........441
Kaminákia ....................................572
Kamíni (Ýdhra) ...........................345
Kamínia (Zákynthos) ................752
Kanála ...........................................363
Kanáli .............................................340
Kapodistrias, Ioannis ...............777
Kapsáli ..........................................153
Karamanlis, Constantine .........781
Karathónas ..................................141
Karávi (Sérifos) ...........................365
Karavóstamo .................................616
Karavostási (Folégandhros) ...431
Kardhámena .................................568
Kardhamýli ...................................164
Karfás ............................................625
Karítena .........................................174
Karlóvassi.......................................609
**Kárpathos** .................... **537–543**
**Kárpathos** ...................................... **538**
Kárpathos Town ..........................539
Karpeníssi .....................................220

Karterádhos ..................................436
Karthaia, ancient ........................359
Karyá (Lefkádha) ........................731
Kárystos .........................................698
Káspakas ........................................653
**Kassándhra** ................. **296–299**
Kassiópi .........................................716
**Kássos** ........................... **535–537**
**Kássos** .............................................. **536**
Kastáni (Skópelos) .....................680
Kastélli (Kíssamos) .....................505
Kastélli (Pátmos) ........................586
Kastéllo (Ýdhra) ..........................345
**Kastellórizo (Meyísti)**
.......................................... **530–533**
**Kastellórizo** ............................. **531**
Kastellórizo Town ......................531
**Kastoriá** ........................ **292–296**
**Kastoriá** ......................................... **293**
Kastráki (Metéora) .....................238
Kastrí (Kos) ..................................568
Kástro (Inoússes) ........................631
Kástro (Léros) .............................583
Kástro (Sífnos) ...........................369
Kástro (Skíathos) ........................676
Kástro (Thássos) ........................667
Kástro Kritiniás...........................529
Kástro tís Oreás (Thessaly) .....233
Kástro tís Oriás (Kýthnos) .......363
Katápola ........................................423
Katára pass ...................................242
Katarráktis ....................................625
Katastári ........................................756
*Katastrofí* (Asia Minor
Catastrophe) ...........................778
Kateloumátsa ...............................442
Katergó (Folégandhros) ............431
*katharévoussa* ............................809
Káthisma beach ...........................735
Katholikó monastery..................499
Káto Kateliós ...............................741
Káto Lákki .....................................559
Katoméri .......................................734
Katsadhiá ......................................590
**Kavála** ........................... **312–315**
**Kavála** ............................................. **313**
Kávos .............................................723
Kavvadias, Panayiotis ...............787
Kazavíti, Mikró/Megálo ...........667
**Kéa (Tzía)** ..................... **357–360**
**Kéa** .................................................. **358**
Kéa, lion of ..................................360
**Kefaloniá** ...................... **736–745**
**Kefaloniá** ...................................... **737**
Kéfalos (Kos) ...............................568
Kekés .............................................665
Kéndros (Dhonoússa) ...............421
Keramotí ........................................315
Kerí .................................................755
Kerkíni village/wetlands ..........310

Kérkis, Mount.............................611
Kérkyra ................................see Corfu
Kéros beach (Límnos) ..............655
Kérveli Bay...................................603
Khíos ..................................see Híos
Khlemoútsi castle ......................191
Khrónia .........................................700
Khroussoú (Kassándhra) .........298
Khryssí Aktí (Páros)....................409
Khryssí Ammoudhiá .................664
Khryssí Miliá (Alónissos)..........686
Khryssomiliá (Foúrni) ..............612
Khryssoskalítissa ........................506
Kiliómeno ....................................755
Kímisis monastery (Psará) ......632
Kímisis Theotókou (Rhodes)
...........................................527
Kímisis Theotókou (Sámos)....608
**Kímolos** ......................... **377–380**
**Kímolos** ......................................... **372**
Kínyra ............................................664
Kióni (Itháki) ...............................748
Kiónia (Tínos) .............................386
Kípos (Samothráki) ...................659
Kipouréon monastery................741
Kíssamos ...................see Kastélli
Kíthnos .....................see Kýthnos
Kléftiko (Mílos) ...........................376
Klió ................................................648
Klisídhi .........................................442
Klísova lagoon .............................261
**Knossos** ......................... **457–459**
**Knossos** ......................................... **458**
Kokkári ..........................................606
Kokkimídhis ................................549
Kókkines Pétres cave................296
Kókkini Ámmos ..........................442
Kókkino .........................................553
Kokkinókastro .............................686
Kolofána ........................................423
Kolymbíthra (Tínos) .................388
Kómi ..............................................627
Komotiní .......................................318
Kondiás .........................................654
Kórfos (Thirassía) .......................441
Kórinthos ......................................129
Korissía (Kéa) ..............................359
Korissíon lagoon .........................722
Koróni (Peloponnese) ..............179
Koronídha......................................418
**Kos** .................................. **560–569**
**Kos** .................................................. **561**
**Kos Town** ...................... **562–565**
**Kos Town** ....................................... **563**
Kótronas ........................................162
Kótsinas .........................................655
Koufoníssi .....................................420
Koukounariés ..............................675
Koúla ..............................................291
Kouloúra .......................................714

Koumaradhéï ....................606
Kouméïka ..........................606
Kournás lake ....................487
Kremastá Nerá ..................659
Kremastí (Lésvos) ..............641
Kríkello, Cape ..................568
Krithóni ............................584
Kríti ....................see Crete
Kritsá ................................474
Krýa Vrýssi ......................701
Kryopiyí ............................298
Kykládhes ..........see Cyclades
Kyllíni ..............................191
Kými ................................696
Kypárissos (Máni) ............161
Kyrá Panayiá (Sporades) ........687
**Kýthira** ........................ **150–155**
**Kýthira** ............................ **151**
**Kýthnos** ........................ **360–363**
**Kýthnos** ............................ **361**

# L

Ladhikó ............................523
Laganás ............................753
Lahaniá ............................527
laïká ................................797
Lákka (Paxí) ....................726
Lákka (Psará) ..................632
Lakkí (Léros) ....................581
Lalária ..............................675
Lamía ..............................218
Langádha (Híos) ..............629
Langádha, pass/gorge
   (Peloponnese) ..............172
Langadhás (Macedonia) ........279
Langádhes (Kos) ..............568
Langéri ............................407
Lápathos ..........................549
Lárdhos ............................527
**Lárissa** ........................ **232–234**
Lasíthi plateau (Crete) ......473
Lássi ................................740
Lato, ancient ....................474
laundries ..........................51
Lávrio ..............................96
Láyia ................................162
**Lefkádha (Lefkas)** ........ **727–736**
Lefkádha ............................ **729**
**Lefkádha Town** ............ **728–731**
Lefkátas, Cape ................735
Lefkáthia ..........................630
Lefkími ............................723
Lefkós ..............................541
Leftós Yialós ....................686
Lemonákia ........................607
Léndas ............................463
Leonidas of Sparta ..........217

Leonídhio ........................146
Lepanto, Battle of ............215
Lépedha ..........................740
Lepídha ............................582
**Léros** ............................ **580–585**
**Léros** ................................ **581**
**Lesser Cyclades** .......... **418–421**
**Lesser Cyclades** ................ **419**
**Lésvos** .......................... **632–649**
**Lésvos** ............................ **633**
Lethrá ..............................552
Levrehió ..........................725
Lidharío ............................650
Liendoú ............................590
Liés (Níssyros) ..................558
Limenária (Angístri) ..........337
Limenária (Thássos) ..........666
**Liménas (Thássos)** ...... **661–663**
**Liménas** ............................ **662**
Liméni (Máni) ....................163
Limnári (Arkí) ....................592
Límni (Évvia) ....................699
Límni Dhrakónda ..............321
Límni Kerioú ....................754
Limniá (Híos) ....................629
Limniónas (Pelion) ............227
Limniónas (Sámos) ..........610
Limniónas (Zákynthos) ......755
Limnonári ........................680
**Límnos** ........................ **650–656**
**Límnos** ............................ **651**
Límnos (Híos) ..................630
Límnos (Psará) ................632
Limónos monastery ..........642
Linariá (Skýros) ................691
Líndhos ............................524
Lindos, ancient ................526
Lingínou ..........................590
lion of Kéa ......................360
**Lipsí** ............................ **590–592**
**Lipsí** ................................ **591**
Lissos, ancient ................503
Lithí ................................629
Litóhoro ..........................282
Livadhákia (Sérifos) ..........365
Livádhi (Folégandhros) ......431
Livádhi (Ikaría) ................617
Livádhi (Irakliá) ................419
Livádhi (Sérifos) ..............364
Livádhi Yeranoú ..............590
Livádhia (Astypálea) ........571
Livádhia (Tílos) ................551
living in Greece ................51
Lixoúri ............................740
Liyiá ................................731
Longás beach (Corfu) ......720
Longós (Paxí) ..................725
Lourdháta ........................741
Loúsios gorge ..................175
Loutrá (Kýthnos) ..............362

Loutrá (Samothráki) ..........658
Loutrá (Tínos) ..................388
Loutrá Ayías Paraskevís
   (Kassándhra) ................298
Loutrá Eftaloú ..................648
Loutrá Ehipsoú ................700
Loutrá Thermopylíon ........217
Loutrá Yéras ....................637
Loutráki (Skópelos) ..........681
Loutró ............................502
Loútsa (Itháki) ..................746
Love Bay (Póros) ..............340

# M

**MACEDONIA** ................ **264–315**
**Macedonia** .................. **266–267**
Macedonian empire ..........769
Magaziá ..........................691
magazines ........................44
Maherádho ......................755
mail ................................52
Makrá ..............................536
Makriá Ámmos (Híos) ........628
Makryialós ......................481
Makrynítsa ......................225
Makrýs Yialós (Zákynthos) ......756
Malathiriá ............see Dhíon
Mália, palace ..................465
Mália, resort ....................464
Maltezána ........................573
*Mamma Mia!* .............. **677, 680**
mammals ........................792
Managrós ........................629
Mandhráki (Níssyros) ........554
Mandhráki (Skiáthos) ........675
Mandhráki (Ýdhra) ............345
Manganári ......................428
**Máni, the** ...................... **155–165**
**Máni, the** ............................ **156**
Maniot blood feuds ..........157
Maniot history ..................157
Manolás (Thirassía) ..........441
Manolátes ........................608
maps ................................52
Maráthi ............................592
Marathon ........................118
Marathónas ..........see Marathon
Marathónas (Égina) ..........334
Marathoúnda (Psérimos) ........569
Marathoúnda (Sými) ..........549
Mariés (Zákynthos) ..........755
Marinatos, Spyros ............788
Markópoulo ......................741
Marmári (Évvia) ................697
Marmári (Kos) ..................566
Marmári (Máni) ................161
Mármaro (Híos) ................629

Maroneia, ancient ......................319
Marónia, modern.......................319
Massoúri ....................................577
Mastihári ...................................567
Mastihohoriá (mastic villages)
.....................................................625
Mátala........................................462
Mathráki.....................................718
Mávros Yialós.............................627
*mayireftá* ...................................39
meat .............................................39
media ...........................................44
medieval Greece.......................773
Méga Spiléou.............................195
Megáli Ámmos (Ammoulianí)
.....................................................303
Megáli Ámmos (Mýkonos).....393
*Megáli Idhéa* (Great Idea)........777
Megális Panayías.......................606
Megálo Horió (Agathoníssi)....593
Megálo Horió (Tílos)................553
Megálo Neório...........................340
Megálo Pápingo........................252
Megalópoli.................................173
Megálos Asélinos......................675
Megálou Meteórou....................239
Meganíssi...................................734
Mégas Lákkos............................740
Mégas Limniónas .....................625
Melínda......................................639
Melissáni cave (Kefaloniá)......743
Melitsahás..................................577
Meloï..........................................589
Melos, ancient ..........................375
*meltemi* wind ...................354, 528
**menu guide (food and drink)**
.................................... **811–814**
Mérihas......................................362
Merikiá.......................................581
Merói..........................................692
Mersíni (Dhonoússa) ...............421
Mésa Vathý................................573
Mesaktí......................................617
Mesembria, ancient .................320
Mesimvría, modern..................320
Mesohóri....................................541
Mesolóngi..................................260
Mesongí.....................................722
Messene, ancient ......................178
**Messinía.................... 177–185**
Mestá .........................................626
Metamórfosis church (Sámos)
.....................................................609
Metaxas dictatorship ..............778
**Metéora .................... 235–242**
**Metéora, The ..................... 235**
Methóni......................................181
Metóhi (Angístri)......................336
Métsovo......................................242
Meyísti ..................see Kastellórizo

*mezédhes* .....................................39
Míkonos ....................see Mýkonos
Mikró (Pelion)...........................231
Mikró Horió (Tílos) ..................553
Mikró Pápingo..........................252
Mikrolímni.................................291
Miliá (Alónissos) ......................686
Miliá (Skópelos)........................680
Miliés (Pelionn)........................229
Milína.........................................231
military areas.............................54
**Mílos .......................... 372–377**
**Mílos ................................. 372**
mineral water.............................42
Minoan era.................................760
Minotaur, the ...........................457
Míres..........................................462
Missolóngi............see Mesolóngi
Míthymna ...............see Mólyvos
mobile phones ...........................54
Mogoníssi..................................725
Mókhlos.....................................475
Mólos (Skýros)..........................691
Mólyvos......................................646
Mon Repos.................................711
monasteries, staying in ............37
Monastiráki (Gulf of Corinth)
.....................................................215
Monastíri (Anáfi) ......................443
Monastiríou (Póros) .................341
**Monemvasía ............... 147–149**
money.........................................53
Moní (Égina) .............................335
Monodhéndhri (Zagóri).........250
Monólithos (Rhodes)...............529
Moraïtika....................................722
mosquitoes .................................43
motorbike rental.......................34
Moúdhros..................................654
Moundhón monastery .............630
Mount Athos................ 304–309
Mount Olympus .......... 280–283
Mount Zás.................................417
Moúressi ....................................227
Mourtiás, Megálos/Mikrós
.....................................................684
**music............................ 795–800**
music, contemporary ..............798
**Mycenae ................... 133–136**
**Mycenae .......................... 133**
Mycenaean era..........................761
Mycenaean history ..................133
Mykáli........................................603
Mykínes ................see Mycenae
**Mýkonos.................... 388–394**
**Mýkonos .......................... 389**
**Mýkonos Town ............ 390–393**
**Mýkonos Town .................. 391**
Mylélia.......................................640
Mýli (Évvia)...............................699

Mylopótamos......... see Mylópotas
(Íos)
Mylopótamos (Kýthira)...........152
Mylopótamos (Pelion) ............227
Mylopótas (Íos)........................426
Mýlos (Angístri) .......................337
Mýlos beach (Lefkádha)..........735
**Mýrina .......................... 651–653**
Mýrthios....................................488
Myrtiés......................................578
Myrtiótissa ...............................720
Mýrtos.......................................481
Mýrtos beach (Kefalloniá) ......744
mythology....10, 69, 120, 134,
   143, 184, 187, 204, 205, 226,
   249, 258, 280, 396, 457, 657,
   761, 763, 803
Mysteries of Eleusis.................120
mysteries of Samothráki.........658
**Mystra ........................ 167–172**
**Mystra .............................. 168**
Mystrás ........................see Mystra
**Mytilíni Town .............. 634–637**
**Mytilíni Town .................. 635**

# N

Náfpaktos ..................................215
**Náfplio ......................... 138–142**
**Náfplio .............................. 139**
Nagós.........................................629
name days...................................45
Nanoú........................................549
Náoussa (Páros)........................407
Nás.............................................617
National Marine Park of
   Alónissos-Sporades..............687
Nauplia/Navplion .......see Náfplio
Navaríno Bay.............................182
Návlakas.....................................533
**Náxos ........................... 410–418**
**Náxos ................................ 411**
**Náxos Town................. 412–415**
**Náxos Town .................... 413**
Néa Dhimokratía (New
   Democracy) ...........................783
Néa Fókea..................................297
Néa Moní ..................................628
Néa Skióni..................................298
Néa Stýra...................................697
Neápoli (Peloponnese)............149
Nekromanteion of Acheron
.....................................................257
Nemea.......................................132
Néo Klíma..................................680
Néos Marmarás.........................301
Néos Mystrás.............................170
Néos Pýrgos...............................701

Nestor's Palace................................184
newspapers.........................................44
Nídha plateau (Crete)..............467
Nikiá .......................................................559
Nikiána ...............................................731
Nikíti.......................................................301
Nikopolis, ancient.....................259
Nissí (Ioánnina)...........................246
**Níssyros** .......................... **554–560**
**Níssyros** .......................... **555**
Northeastern Macedonia .......310
Nótos beach ...................................722
Nydhrí....................................................731
Nymféo................................................289

# O

Odysseus sights, Itháki............746
Odyssey, The............745, 763, 803
Oedipus junction......................204
Óhi, Mount........................................699
Oía.........................................see Ía
olives, Kalamáta ..........................177
olives, Lésvos.................................642
Olýmbi ................................................626
Olymbía ..............................................189
Ólymbos (Kárpathos)...........542
Ólymbos (Macedonia) ........... see
   Olympus, Mount
**Olympia** ........................ **185–190**
**Olympia** ................................ **186**
Olympia, wreck of.....................424
Olympic games .............................187
Olympic Games, 2004..............784
**Olympus, Mount .... 280–283**
**Olympus, Mount ................ 281**
Ólynthos .............................................299
Olynthos, ancient .....................299
Omalós .................................................501
opening hours .................................53
Oracle of Dodona ......................249
Oreí .........................................................701
orektiká ................................................39
Oréo........................................................317
Órmos Marathokámbou..........610
Órmos Panayías.............................299
Órmos Ysterníon .......................387
Ornós .....................................................393
Orthodox Church .......................774
Ósios Loukás monastery........211
Otho, King ........................................777
Othoní ..................................................718
Óthos .....................................................542
Otto .......................... see Otho, King
Ottoman rule ..................................774
Otziás ....................................................360
Ouranoúpoli ...................................303
outdoor pursuits..........................47

ouzerís....................................................41
oúzo...........................................................42

# P

Pagóndas...........................................606
Pahiá Ámmos (Níssyros)..........558
Pahiá Ámmos (Samothráki)
   ................................................................659
Pahiá Ámmos (Zákynthos).....756
Palamári .............................................692
Palamedes........................................138
Palamídhi..........................................138
Paleá Alónissos ...........................684
Palékastro ........................................478
Paleó Klíma ......................................681
Paleó Pylí (Kos) ...........................567
Paleohóra (Crete)......................502
Paleohóra (Égina) .....................333
Paleohóra (Kýthira) .................152
Paleohóri (Mílos).......................375
Paleokastrítsa (Corfu)............718
Paleókastro (Ándhros) ..........384
Paleókastro (Kímolos)............378
Paleókastro (Níssyros)...........556
Paleópolis .........................................711
Paleópolis (Ándhros)..............382
Palioúri ...............................................298
Pálli (Agathoníssi)......................593
Pálli (Níssyros)..............................558
Palm Beach (Crete)...................488
Pamvótidha, Lake.....................246
Panayía (Iraklía)............................419
Panayía (Thássos) .....................664
Panayía Dombón........................676
Panayía Episkopí (Santoríni)
   ................................................................441
Panayía Kardhási.........................676
Panayía Katholikí .......................523
Panayía Kyrá (Crete)...............474
Panayía Kyrá (Níssyros)..........558
Panayía Makriní............................611
Panayía Palatianí........................568
Panayía Panakhrándou...........383
Panayía Protóthronis..............417
Panayía Spilianí (Níssyros).....555
Panayía Spilianí (Sámos)......604
Panayía Thermianí....................558
Pandavréhi.......................................221
Pandélli...............................................583
Pandokrátor, Mount ...............714
Panormítis.........................................550
Pánormos (Mýkonos)..............394
Pánormos (Skópelos) ............680
Papá Miná.........................................542
Papafránga........................................376
Papandhriá.......................................591
Papandreou, Andréas ..............783

Papandreou, George (elder)
   ................................................................782
Pápingo ..........see Megálo/Mikró
   Pápingo
Paradise beach (Mýkonos).....393
Paralía Kaláthou ........................524
Paralía Kopriá................................529
Paralía Kýmis .................................696
Paralía Lefkoú ...............................541
Paralía Lithíou ..............................629
Paralía Marathónas ..................118
Paralía Sykiás..................................300
Paralía Thánous............................653
Paralía Thermís ............................637
Paránga ..............................................393
**Párga** .............................. **255–257**
Parikía ...................................................403
**Parikía** ................................ **405**
Parnassós, Mount ......................212
Parnassós ski centre ...............212
**Páros** .............................. **402–410**
**Páros** ................................ **403**
Parthenónas ...................................301
PASOK ...................................................783
pastries ................................................41
Pateliá .................................................592
Patitíri ...................................................684
**Pátmos**.......................... **585–590**
**Pátmos** ................................ **586**
**Pátra (Patras)** .......... **191–197**
**Pátra** ..................................... **192**
**Paxí (Paxos)**................. **724–727**
**Paxí** ....................................... **725**
Paxos ....................................see Paxí
Pédhi.....................................................548
Péfki (Évvia) ....................................701
Péfki (Rhodes) ..............................527
Péfkos (Skýos)...............................693
Pefkoúlia ..........................................735
Pélekas................................................721
Pelikáta hill.......................................747
**Pelion peninsula ......... 221–232**
**Pelion, The....................... 222**
Pella, ancient..................................279
**PELOPONNESE, THE .... 122–197**
**Peloponnese, The ...... 126–127**
Peloponnesian War..................767
Péra Kástro (Kálymnos) ..........575
Péra Yialós .......................................571
Pérama (Lésvos) .........................639
Pérama caves .................................249
Perastá .................................................533
Pérdhika (Égina) ........................334
Pericles ................................................767
Veríssa.....................................................439
Peristéra (Sporades)..................687
Perivolioú (Skópelos) .............682
Perivolís monastery .................643
Perouládhes.....................................720
Persian Wars....................................764

personal safety ............................ 49
Pessádha ..................................... 740
Petaloúdhes (Páros) ................... 404
Petaloúdhes (Rhodes) ............... 529
Petaní beach ............................... 741
Pétra (Lésvos) ............................. 648
Pétra (Pátmos) ........................... 589
petrified forest, Lésvos ............. 644
Petrití ......................................... 722
Petrokopió .................................. 612
Phaestos ..................................... 461
**Phaestos ........................... 461**
pharmacies ................................... 42
Philip II of Macedon .................. 769
Philippi ....................................... 311
philosophy .................................. 770
phone codes ................................. 54
phones .......................................... 54
photography ................................. 54
Phylakope ........... see Fylakopí
Pigadhákia .................................. 756
Pigádhia (Kárpathos) ................. 539
Pílio, Mount ............................... 221
Pílos ...........................see Pýlos
Pinakátes .................................... 229
**Píndhos Mountains ..... 242–254**
Pipéri (Páros) ............................. 407
Pipéri (Sporades) ....................... 687
Piraeus .................... see Pireás
Pireás ............................................ 92
**Pireás ................................. 93**
Pisaetós ...................................... 747
Píso Livádhi ................................ 408
Pisses .......................................... 360
Pittakis, Kyriakos ....................... 786
Pityós .......................................... 629
Piyés Kallithéas .......................... 523
Pláka (Arcadia) ........................... 146
Pláka (Crete) .............................. 472
Pláka (Mílos) .............................. 374
Pláka (Náxos) ............................. 415
Pláka (Tílos) ............................... 553
Plákes (Astypálea) ...................... 573
Plákes (Ýdhra) ........................... 345
Plakiás (Crete) ............................ 488
Plános (Zákynthos) .................... 756
plants .......................................... 790
plants, toxic .................................. 43
Plataniá .............. see Plataniás
Plataniás ..................................... 231
Plátanos (Léros) ......................... 583
Platiá Poúnda ............................. 420
Plato ........................................... 770
Platrithiés ................................... 748
Platý (Límnos) ............................ 653
Platýs Yialós (Lipsí) .................... 591
Platýs Yialós (Sífnos) ................. 371
Plomári ....................................... 639
poetry, Greek ............................. 806
police ............................................ 49

Polikhnítos spa ........................... 640
Pollónia (Mílos) .......................... 376
Polyochni .................................... 655
Polytechnic occupation ........... 782
Póndamos ................................... 534
Póndi .......................................... 732
Pondikoníssi ............................... 712
Porí ............................................. 420
Póros (Kefaloniá) ....................... 742
Póros Town ................................ 339
**Póros ........................... 338–341**
**Póros ................................ 338**
Pórta Panayía ............................. 234
Pórtes (Égina) ............................ 334
Pórto Carrás .............................. 301
Pórto Héli ................................... 144
Pórto Katsíki .............................. 735
Pórto Káyio ............................... 161
Pórto Koufó ............................... 300
Pórto Zóro ................................. 752
Poseidon, temple of (Póros)
................................................. 341
Poseidon, temple of (Soúnio)
................................................. 117
Posídhi ........................................ 298
Posidhonía (Sýros) .................... 400
postal services ............................. 52
Potámi (Híos) ............................. 627
Potámi (Sámos) ......................... 609
Potamiá (Thássos) ..................... 664
Potamós (Kýthira) ..................... 152
Póthia .......................................... 575
Potokáki ...................................... 604
Potós ........................................... 665
Poúlithra ..................................... 146
Poúnda ........................................ 409
Pouthená ..................................... 536
Prassoníssi .................................. 527
prehistoric Greece ..................... 759
Préspa Lakes .............................. 290
Préveli ......................................... 488
Préveza ....................................... 258
Priónia ........................................ 283
Profítis Ilías (Rhodes) ............... 530
Profítis Ilías (Samothráki) ........ 659
Profítis Ilías (Ýdhra) ................. 346
Prokópi ....................................... 699
Provatás ...................................... 376
Psará ........................................... 631
Psarádhes ................................... 291
Psaralíki ...................................... 410
Psaroú ........................................ 393
Psathoúra ................................... 687
Psérimos ..................................... 569
**Psérimos ........................... 561**
Psilí Ámmos (E Sámos) ............. 603
Psilí Ámmos (Sérifos) ................ 365
Psilí Ámmos (W Sámos) ........... 610
Psilorítis, Mount ....................... 467
psistariés ....................................... 39

Psykhró ...................................... 473
Pylés (Kárpathos) ...................... 542
Pylí (Kos) ................................... 567
Pýli (Thessaly) ........................... 234
Pýlos ........................................... 181
Pyrgí ........................................... 626
Pýrgos (Peloponnese) ............... 190
Pýrgos (Sámos) .......................... 606
Pýrgos (Tínos) ........................... 387
Pýrgos Dhiroú caves .................. 160
Pýrgos Himárrou ....................... 417
Pythagório .................................. 603

# R

radio ............................................. 44
Rafína .......................................... 118
Ráhes .......................................... 618
railway, Pelion ........................... 229
railway, Peloponnese ............... 196
Ramnous ..................................... 119
rembétika ........................... 397, 796
reptiles ........................................ 793
Resistance, wartime .................. 779
restaurants ................................... 39
**Réthymnon .................. 482–486**
**Réthymnon ....................... 483**
**Rhodes (Ródhos) ........ 512–529**
**Rhodes ............................. 515**
**Rhodes Town .............. 514–522**
**Rhodes Town ..................... 516**
Rína ............................................. 580
Río (Rion) ................................... 195
Ríva ............................................. 609
Ródha .......................................... 716
Roman Greece ........................... 772
rooms, private .............................. 36
Ross, Ludwig .............................. 786
Rossikós Nafstathmós ............... 340
Roúda Bay ................................... 732
Roúkounas .................................. 442
Roussánou .................................. 240
Roussoúm Yialós ....................... 684
Roviés ......................................... 700

# S

sailing ........................................... 47
St John the Evangelist ............. 588
St John monastery, Pátmos .........
see Ayíou Ioánnou Theológou
monastery (Pátmos)
St Paul ......................................... 131
St Paul's harbour ...................... 526
Salamína ..................................... 328
Salamis .................. see Salamína

Salamis, battle of ...................329
Salonica................see Thessaloníki
**Samariá Gorge ............ 499–501**
**Samariá Gorge .................. 500**
Sámi.......................................742
**Sámos ....................... 599–611**
**Sámos ................................. 600**
Samothrace .........see Samothráki
**Samothráki ................ 656–660**
**Samothráki......................... 657**
Sanctuary of the Great Gods
............................................657
Sáni.......................................297
Sánta María (Páros).................407
**Santoríni ................... 434–442**
**Santoríni ............................ 435**
Sarakíniko (Itháki).................746
Sarakíniko (Mílos).................376
Sarakinó (Skýros)...................691
Sardhés..................................653
Sárti......................................300
Schliemann, Heinrich .............786
scooter rental......................... 34
scuba diving........................... 47
sea urchins............................. 43
seafood.................................. 40
seals, Mediterranean monk
............................................687
Seïtáni, Mikró/Megálo ...........609
**Sérifos .................... 363–366**
**Sérifos ............................. 364**
Seyhélles...............................620
Sfaktiría island ......................182
Sfinári...................................505
Shipwreck Bay (Zákynthos) ...757
Sidhári...................................716
siesta..................................... 49
**Sífnos .................... 366–372**
**Sífnos ............................. 367**
Sígri......................................644
**Síkinos ................... 428–430**
**Síkinos ............................ 429**
Síros..........................see Sýros
**Sithonía ................... 299–301**
**Sitía.......................... 475–477**
**Sitía ................................. 476**
Skála (Angístri).....................336
Skála (Astypálea) ...........see Péra
   Yialós
Skála (Kefaloniá) ...................741
Skála (Pátmos)......................586
Skála Eressoú ........................644
Skála Kallonís ........................642
Skála Kamírou ........................529
Skála Marión..........................666
Skála Potamiás ......................664
Skála Prínou...........................666
Skála Sykaminiás ...................648
Skála Vítsas............................252
Skhiniás.................................119

Skhinoússa...........................420
**Skiáthos ................... 670–677**
**Skiáthos ............................ 674**
Skiáthos Town.........................673
skiing..............................47, 212
Skinári, Cape..........................756
Skinós...................................746
Skíros ..................... see Skýros
**Skópelos ................... 677–682**
**Skópelos ............................ 678**
**Skópelos Town ............ 678–680**
**Skýros ...................... 687–693**
**Skýros ............................ 688**
Skýros Town...........................690
Smínthi...................................317
smoking................................. 49
snacks.................................... 38
soccer.................................... 48
Socrates.................................770
Sophocles...............................766
Sorós.....................................410
Sotíras (Thássos)...................667
Soudhená................................253
Souflí.....................................322
Soúnio, Cape...........................117
Sourviás monastery.................225
Soúyia...................................502
Sparta, ancient ......................166
**Spárti ...................... 165–172**
Spartohóri..............................734
**Spétses ................... 347–351**
**Spétses ............................ 347**
Spétses Town .........................348
Spiádha.................................700
Spíli......................................490
Spiliás...................................593
Spinalónga..............................472
Spóa.....................................542
sponge diving.........................576
**SPORADES, THE........... 668–693**
**Sporades, The ................... 672**
sports.................................... 47
Stáfylos.................................680
stamps................................... 52
Stavrós (Crete).......................499
Stavrós (Dhonoússa) ..............421
Stavrós (Hálki)......................535
Stavrós (Itháki)......................747
Stavrós (Tílos)......................552
Stavroúpoli.............................317
Stéfanos crater (Níssyros).......560
Stegná...................................524
Stemnítsa...............................174
Stení (Évvia)..........................697
Stení Vála...............................686
Stenó.....................................573
**STEREÁ ELLÁDHA ....... 200–220**
**Stereá Elládha ................... 202**
Stoúpa...................................163
Strinýlas................................714

Stýra......................................697
Super Paradise beach
   (Mýkonos)............................393
Sykamiá.............see Sykaminiá
   (Lésvos)
Sykaminiá (Lésvos)..................648
Sykiá (Sithonía)......................300
Sykiás Olýmbon cave...............626
Sými Town...............................545
**Sými ........................ 543–548**
**Sými ................................. 544**
**Sýros........................ 397–402**
**Sýros ................................. 397**
Sývota (Lefkádha)....................732

# T

Taïyetos (Taygettus), Mount
............................................172
tavernas ................................. 39
taxi boats ............................... 33
Taxiárhis Mihaïl Panormítis ....550
taxis ...................................... 35
Taygettus ............see Taïyetos
Télendhos................................578
**Télendhos .......................... 574**
telephones .............................. 54
television ............................... 44
Témbi, Vale of........................233
Ténaro, Cape...........................161
Thános (Koufoníssi) .................420
Thános (Límnos) .....................653
Thárri monastery .....................530
**Thássos ......................... 660–667**
**Thássos ............................. 661**
Thássos Town...........see Liménas
Thebes ...................see Thíva
theft.......................................49
Themistocles...........................764
Theóktisti monastery ...............616
Theológos................................667
Theophilos Museum
   (Lésvos)..................................638
Theotókou monastery (Corfu)
............................................718
Thériade Museum (Lésvos)....638
Thérma (Ikaría) ......................615
Thermá (Límnos).....................653
Thermá (Samothráki)...............658
Thérma Lefkádhos...................615
Thermiá ................see Kýthnos
Thérmo (Stereá Elládha) .........216
Thermon, ancient .....................216
Thermopylae, Pass of..............217
**THESSALONÍKI .......... 266–279**
**Thessaloníki .............. 270–271**
   accommodation....................276
   airport................................275
   Áno Póli..............................273

Archeological Museum..................268
arrival.........................................275
Atatürk's house...........................271
Ayía Sofía....................................272
Áyios Dhimítrios..........................272
Áyios Nikólaos Orfanós................273
bars............................................277
Byzantine churches......................273
cinema........................................278
city transport...............................277
clubs...........................................277
Dhódheka Apóstoli.......................273
directory.....................................278
eating.........................................276
entertainment.............................278
Eptapýrgio..................................274
Folk & Ethnological Museum.......275
Galerius, arch/palace...................269
history........................................267
Jewish Museum...........................274
Jewish Thessaloníki.....................274
Museum of Byzantine Culture ....269
nightlife......................................277
Ósios Dhavíd...............................273
Ottoman monuments...................272
Panayía Ahiropíitos......................273
Panayía Halkéon..........................273
Roman Forum..............................270
Rotónda (Áyios Yeóryios)............269
shopping.....................................278
theatre........................................278
tourist information.......................275
White Tower (Lefkós Pýrgos).......269
THESSALY .............200, 222–234
Thessaly......................202–203
Thíra ..................... see Santórini
Thira, ancient .............................439
Thirassía.....................................441
Thóli (Agathoníssi)......................593
Thólos (Tílos)..............................553
THRACE....................... 315–323
Thrace......................... 266–267
Thucydides..................................768
Thymianá.....................................625
Tiganákia (Arkí)...........................592
Tigáni (Híos)................................628
Tílos..............................550–554
Tílos .............................. 551
time.............................................54
Tingáki.........................................566
Tínos.............................384–388
Tínos ............................. 385
Tínos Town..................................385
tipping.........................................48
Tiryns..........................................137
Tírynthos..........................see Tiryns
toilets, public ..............................55
Toploú monastery.......................477
Toróni..........................................300
tour operators.............................28
tourist information.......................55
tourist police...............................50
Tourkopígadho.............................583
Tourlídha.....................................261

Tragéa, the .................................416
Trahiá .........................................535
trains ....................................27, 29
transliteration, Greek .................808
Trapezáki....................................741
travel agencies ...........................28
travellers' cheques......................53
Treaty of Lausanne.....................315
trekking ..................... see walking
Trenáki, Pelion............................229
Tríkala.........................................233
Trípoli.........................................172
Trís Boúkes.................................693
Tristiníka.....................................300
Trojan War...................................761
Truman Doctrine .........................781
Trypití (Mílos).............................374
Tsambíka.....................................523
Tsangarádha................................226
Tsigoúri......................................420
Tsigrádho....................................376
Tsiliví..........................................756
tsípouro ......................................41
Tsónia.........................................648
Tsougriá......................................675
Turkey, relations with.................783
Turkómnima................................591
turtles, loggerhead.....................753
Týlissos.......................................466
Tzaboú........................................607
Tzamadhoú..................................607
Tzanáki.......................................571
Tzermiádho..................................473
Tziá ...................................see Kéa
Tzórtzi Yialós..............................686


# V

Vafkerí........................................731
Váï beach (Crete)........................478
Vanánda......................................543
Vardhiá.......................................431
Vári.............................................400
Variá...........................................637
Várkiza........................................116
Varlaám (Barlaam).......................239
Vásses..............................see Bassae
Vassiliki (Lefkádha).....................732
Vassilikós peninsula (Zákynthos)
......................................751
Vaterá.........................................640
Váthia.........................................161
Vathý (Itháki).............................746
Vathý (Meganíssi)........................734
Vathý (Psérimos).........................569
Vathý (Sámos).............................601
Vathý (Sámos) ................... 602
Vathý (Sífnos).............................371
Vathý Bay (Máni).........................159

Vathýs (Kálymnos)......................576
Vátika.........................................147
Vátos (Samothráki)......................659
Vatoúmi......................................726
Vátses.........................................572
Vayiá...........................................590
Vayioniá......................................341
vegetarians .................................40
Velanió........................................680
Venetian rule...............................774
Venizelos, Eleftherios .................777
Vergina, ancient..........................287
Véria ........................... 284–287
Véssa...........................................629
Via Egnatia project......................242
Vídhos.........................................712
Víkos gorge.................................251
villa rental ...................................37
visas............................................50
Vítsa............................................252
Vlachs..........................................243
Vlahérna......................................712
Vlyhó (Lefkádha).........................732
Vlyhós (Ýdhra)............................345
Voïdhokiliá..................................183
Voládha.......................................542
Vólakas...............................see Vólax
Vólax...........................................388
Volímes.......................................757
Volissós.......................................629
Vólos...........................................223
Votsalákia...................................610
Vótsi............................................684
Voúla...........................................116
Vouliagméni................................116
Vounó (Skýros) ...........................693
Vourkári......................................360
Vourliótes...................................608
Vourvouroú.................................300
Vréllos........................................350
Vríka...........................................726
Vromólimnos (Skiáthos)..............675
Vromólithos (Léros)....................583
Vrondádhos.................................625
Vróndi Bay..................................539
Vrykoúnda..................................543
Vrysítsa......................................685
Výssa..........................................640
Výros gorge.................................165
Výthisma.....................................684
Vyzítsa........................................229


# W

Wace, Alan...................................788
walking............. 48, 165, 175, 208,
221, 237, 251, 283, 351, 450,
490, 499, 543, 549, 559, 681,
684, 806

War of Independence ............776
water, drinking ............................42
watersports.................................47
weather......................................8, 52
wildlife ........................ 790–794
windsurfing ................................47
wine...........................................40
wine tasting, Crete...................462
wine tasting, Santoríni ..........440
women travellers......................49
words and phrases, Greek
..................................809
working in Greece.....................51
World War I ................................777
World War II ...............................779

# X

Xánthi .......................................315
Xi..............................................740
Xinára.......................................388
Xirókambos ..............................582
Xygiá beach ..............................756
Xylokériza.................................351

# Y

Ýdhra (Hydra) .............. 341–347
Ýdhra................................. 342
Ýdhra Town ...............................343
Ýdhra Town ........................ 343
Yéfira (Monemvasía)............148
Yennádhi...................................527
Yeoryoúpoli ............................487
Yérakas (Zákynthos) ...............752
Yeroliménas ............................161
Yiália........................................685
Yialiskári (Ikaría) .....................617
Yialiskári (Kéa).........................359
Yialós (Íos) ..............................426
Yialós (Lefkádha)....................735
Yialós (Sými) ...........................545
Yiálova.....................................182
Yiánnena...................see Ioánnina
Yióssonas..................................629
Yioúra.......................................687
Yíra...........................................731
Yíthio (Gythion) .......................158
youth hostels ............................37
Ypsárion, Mount ......................664

Ypsiloú monastery ..................643
Ypsoúnda ............... see Stemnítsa

# Z

Zagorá ......................................225
Zagóri............................ 250–254
Zagóri ............................... 250
zaharoplastía.............................41
Zakhloroú.................................195
Zákros, Áno..............................478
Zákros, Káto.............................478
Zákros, Palace of (Crete).........479
Zákynthos .................... 749–757
Zákynthos ........................ 750
Zákynthos Town......................750
Zante..................... see Zákynthos
Zepága .....................................631
Ziá.............................................567
Zoödhóhou Piyís (Anáfi) ........443
Zoödhóhou Piyís (Límnos)
..................................655
Zoödhóhou Piyís (Síkinos)
..................................430
Zoyeriá.....................................350

# Map symbols

The symbols below are used on maps throughout the book

| | | | |
|---|---|---|---|
| ✈ International airport | ⊙ Statue | ⊠ Gate | 🦋 Shipwreck |
| ✗ Domestic airport | ⛾ Border crossing post | ⚐ Viewpoint | ⟩⟨ Bridge |
| ★ Transport stop | 🕌 Mosque | 🗻 Mountain range | Building |
| Ⓜ Metro/Subway | ⛪ Monastery | ▲ Mountain peak | Market |
| Ⓣ Tram stop | ⚱ Church (regional) | ⌒ Cave | Church |
| 🚢 Boat | ✡ Synagogue | ⚐ Swamp | Stadium |
| ⊠ Post office | ◆ Place of interest | ⚐ Hot spring | Park |
| @ Internet access | ⊤ Garden | 🌊 Waterfall | Christian cemetery |
| ✚ Hospital | ⛺ Mountain refuge/lodge | 🗼 Lighthouse | Beach |
| ⓘ Information centre | ∴ Ruin | 🏮 Windmill | Wall |
| Ⓣ Toilet | ♙ Castle | 🍇 Vineyards | Ferry |
| Ⓟ Parking | ⚡ Skiing | ⚐ Gorge | Cable car |
| Ⓧ Campsite | ⌒ Arch | Steep slope | Tram line |

## Listings key

- ■ Accommodation
- ● Eating & Drinking
- ■ Nightlife
- ● Shop